# A HISTORICAL ATLAS OF
# THE JEWISH PEOPLE

## TEXT BY

Michel Abitbol, Haim Avni, Ron Barkai, Eli Barnavi, Israel Bartal, Malachi Beit-Arié, Mireille Bélis, Dov Ben-Eliezer, Menachem Ben-Sasson, Alain Boureau, Richard I. Cohen, Michael Confino, Dan Daor, Sergio DellaPergola, Dan Diner, Yigal Elam, David Engel, Haggai Erlich, Saul Friedländer, Isaiah Gafni, Allon Gal, Yair Hoffman, Moshe Idel, David Jacoby, David S. Katz, Annie Kriegel, Maurice Kriegel, Marcin Kula, Yeshaiahu Leibowitz, Bernard Lewis, Daniel S. Milo, Amnon Netzer, Yehuda Nini, Elchanan I. Reiner, Minna Rozen, Angel Sáenz-Baddillos, Yaacov Shavit, Amnon Shiloah, Avigdor Shinan, Jean Soler, Gedaliahu G. Stroumsa, Ariel Toaff, Chava Turniansky, Raphael Vago, Pierre Vidal-Naquet, David Vital, Jehuda Wallach, R.J. Zwi Werblowsky, Idith Zertal

## EDITORIAL COMMITTEE

Michel Abitbol *(Mediterranean Contemporary History)*, Israel Bartal *(Modern Europe)*, Menachem Ben-Sasson *(Medieval Muslim World)*, Sergio DellaPergola *(Demographic History)*, Isaiah Gafni *(Second Temple and Talmudic Periods)*, Yair Hoffman *(Biblical Period)*, Maurice Kriegel *(Medieval Europe)*, Yaacov Shavit *(Modern Palestine)*, Idith Zertal *(Holocaust)*

Cartography and design: Michel Opatowski
Computerized maps: Sharon Barchil,
Yoav Goren, Avshalom Polac, Yaron Tracz
Picture research: Naama Sifrony, Dvora Gruda
Historical research: Oren Kenner
Style editors: Sonja Laden, Marcy Shain
Secretaries: Karena Gold, Ordit Kotler

Project Director: Dani Tracz
Executive Editor: Mulli Melzer
Editorial Advisor: Françoise Cibiel-Lavalle

Conceived, edited and designed by Tel Aviv Books
Editorial responsibility: Hachette

Library of Congress Cataloging-in-Publication Data

Juifs, une histoire universelle. English
    A historical atlas of the Jewish people / edited by Eli Barnavi.
        p.    cm.
    Includes bibliographical references and index.
    ISBN 0-679-40332-9
    1. Jews—History.    2. Jews—History—Maps.    I. Barnavi, Eli.
II. Title.
DS117.J8513    1992
909'.04924–dc20

92-53169
CIP

9 8 7 6 5 4 3 2

# A
# HISTORICAL ATLAS
# of the
# JEWISH PEOPLE

From the Time of the Patriarchs
to the Present

General  Editor
## ELI BARNAVI

English Edition Editor
## MIRIAM ELIAV-FELDON

Cartography
## MICHEL OPATOWSKI

Schocken Books, New York

# Introduction I

1. Larry Rivers, History of the Mazzah (unleavened bread), 2nd part of his History of the Jews, 1984.

Stereotypes are sometimes grounded in reality. The word "Jew," whether it is used pejoratively or not, immediately evokes the association of *mobility*, a propensity to wander, to move from one place to another. This association is conveyed by the basic legend concerning the birth of the Jewish nation – the peregrinations of the Patriarchs. "Jews" also implies *dispersion*: they are thought to be everywhere even when absent – how else can one explain anti-Jewish campaigns in "Jewish-free" places such as Paris in 1652 or Poland in the 1960s? Obviously, all human communities have been subject to mobility and dispersion; but it seems that none but the Jews has known movement and dispersion so expanded in space and so extended in time.

The Jewish perception of space is marked by two unique characteristics: it comprises a notion of multiple spaces, rather than one of a single space; and between these spaces – a void. In other words, the Jewish spatial experience is *differential* and *discontinuous*. Although this applies to some extent to mankind in general (a one-spatial man does not exist and has never existed), Jewish history has extended this existential condition to stereotypical dimensions.

"My heart is in the East [Jerusalem], my body in the extreme-West [Spain]" – in this famous verse, Judah Halevi, the greatest poet of the Jewish Golden Age in Spain, epitomizes the perception of multiple spaces and their discontinuity. A space of the heart, a space of the body, and in between them a void (albeit traversed by the poet himself on his journey to the Holy Land). Yet Jewish spatial experience goes beyond the polarity of Land of Israel–Diaspora: it is not necessarily rent between two poles, for besides the experience of two places separated by a gulf, it also incorporates other spaces for which the Jew has a variety of mental stances, including indifference. This uniqueness of Jewish spatial experience has been a constant factor in Jewish history, both when dominated by religion and when molded by Zionism or modern secular ideologies. Jewish consciousness constantly shifts between awareness of physical spaces (the birth-place, for example) to spaces of reference (the ancestral homeland, Hebrew, etc.), a shift which actually *constitutes* the Jewish spatial experience.

How can one understand such an experience in a tangible manner? We shall try to explain it through two examples of "spatial biographies," one of Chaim Weizmann, scientist and statesman (b. Motol, Belorussia, 1874 – d. Rehovot, Israel, 1952), the other of Glueckel of Hameln, a wealthy woman merchant who lived in Ger-

many three centuries earlier (b. Hamburg, 1646 – d. Metz, 1724). Both lived, on the whole, successful lives, well-documented thanks to their memoirs; and while these are not necessarily "representative" of Jewish biographies, they are at least suggestive.

In order to understand the "management of space" in Weizmann's case, let us turn to the first chapters of his autobiography *Trial and Error* (1949), describing the years prior to his becoming the incontestable leader of the Zionist movement. The very first paragraph highlights precisely the point we are trying to make: "The townlet of my birth, Motol, stood – and perhaps still stands – on the banks of the little river in the great marsh area which occupies much of the province of Minsk and adjacent provinces in White Russia; flat, open country, mournful and monotonous but, with its rivers, forests and lakes, not wholly unpicturesque... All about, in hundreds of towns and villages, Jews lived, as they had lived for many generations, *scattered islands in a gentile ocean*; and among them my own people, on my father's and mother's side, made up a not inconsiderable proportion." Thus, within a natural continuous environment (the "territory"), the experience of the Jew is one of discontinuity.

# The Perception of Space

The following passages describe the comings and goings between the isolated *shtetl* (the Jewish townlet) and the world beyond. For the Jews of Motol, space did not extend to the very limits of the village itself because of the rupture between "them" (gentiles) and "us" (Jews): "Even in that townlet we lived mainly apart. And much more striking than the physical separation was the spiritual. We were strangers to each other's ways of thought, to each other's dreams, religions, festivals, and even languages." In order to overcome the isolation of the *shtetl*, the Weizmann family, like many of their co-religionists, used four "techniques": the economy, the Pale of Settlement, culture, and emigration (provisional or definitive).

Thanks to his father's occupation – Oser Weizmann was a "transportierer" of timber who travelled down the Pina, the Bug, and the Vistula rivers as far as Danzig – young Chaim's "cosmology" was much broader than that of the peasants' children. The widening of the horizons through commerce was a well-known phenomenon in Jewish history, and requires no further elaboration.

"From Motol to Pinsk" – the capital, where Chaim Weizmann studied in 1885, at the age of eleven – "was a matter of six Russian miles, or twenty-five English miles; but in terms of intellectual displacement the distance was astronomical." Pinsk was omnipresent in Motol, as an economic and cultural term of reference, as well as a major Jewish center. For not only was Pinsk the provincial capital, it was also (after Berdichev) the second largest Jewish city within the Pale of Settlement.

"The language of the peasants in our part was an obscure dialect of Russian. Unlike the Ukrainian, it had no literature, and was not even written." The peasants were illiterate, Weizmann tells us, while the Jews "by contrast... had a high degree of literacy" but solely in Hebrew or Yiddish: "I myself knew hardly a word of Russian till I was eleven years old." Nevertheless, this did not mean cultural exclusion: his father's bookshelves held copies of the Talmud, Maimonides, Gorki and Tolstoy, and "on the walls were pictures of Maimonides and Baron de Hirsch, of the Wailing Wall in Jerusalem and of Anton Chekhov." An impressive eucumenical collection.

Could the Jews in this forsaken townlet in the marshes of Belorussia maintain contact, if not real at least symbolic, with the great Russian culture? Five years later, when in Pinsk, "I think I may say that we spoke and wrote the [Russian] language better, were more intimately acquainted with its literature than most Russians. But we were rooted heart and soul in our own culture," that is, in Yiddish, and even more, in Hebrew. "I, for instance, never corresponded with my father in any other language, though to my mother I wrote in Yiddish. I sent my father only one Yiddish letter; he returned it without an answer."

Languages played an important role in Weizmann's life: born to Yiddish (Motol), educated first in Hebrew then in Russian (Pinsk), he wrote a thesis in German (Darmstadt, Berlin, Fribourg), and taught in French (Geneva), and, after 1904, spent most of his life in an English-speaking environment (Manchester, London, then in Rehovot). It was in the latter language, chronologically his sixth, that he wrote his memoirs – an unprecedented case in the history of autobiographies. During the first thirty years of his life, each change of address entailed the acquisition of another language. Unlike Nikolai Gogol who abandoned Ukrainian in favor of Russian, or Joseph Conrad who exchanged Polish for English, Chaim Weizmann accumulated languages, and with each language he accumulated in turn additional spaces of reference, as attested by his immense correspondence (over 30,000 surviving letters). Yet in all his writings there is one striking fact: this man who traversed the world, first as an emigrant, then as a diplomat, describes a landscape only on one single occasion: the landscape of Motol.

His first country of "immigration" was Germany. Arriving at the age of eighteen at Pfungstadt near Darmstadt, he made two perplexing discoveries. The space of "them," which he thought was homogenous, turned out to be quite different: "It was a marvelous new world

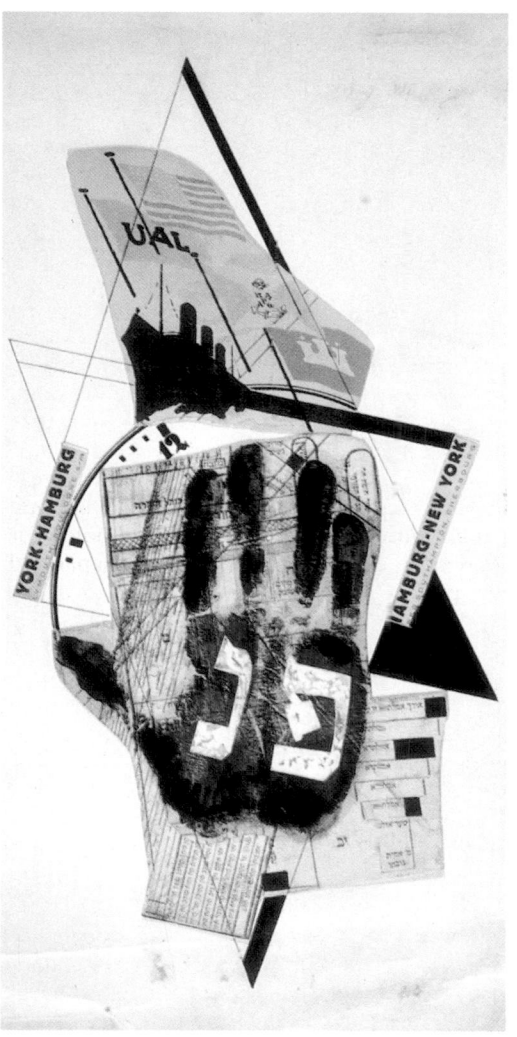

2. Collage by El Lissitzky; illustration for the novel Boat Ticket by Ilya Ehrenburg, published in 1922. The two Hebrew letters inscribed on the hand (the hand itself being an ancient Hebrew symbol) are the initials for the words "Here Lies" inscribed on tombstones.

that I entered with a beating heart, a clean, neat, orderly world... so different from the gentile world I had been accustomed to." The world of "us" was even more surprising: "Pfungstadt was my introduction to one of the queerest chapters in Jewish history: the assimilated Jewry of Germany." Even their religiosity was different: "It was not the orthodoxy I had known and loved at home. It was stuffy, it was unreal, it had no folk background. It lacked warmth and gaiety and color and intimacy. It did not interpenetrate the life of the teachers and the pupils; it was a cold discipline imposed from the outside." Weizmann fled back home, to Pinsk. On his next adventure abroad, however, in Berlin, he once more encountered a "ghetto," the colony of Russian Jewish students: "It was a curious world, existing, for us Jewish students, *outside of space and time.*" And even though "toward the end of my Berlin period we had managed to establish a certain relationship with part of the Jewish community of the city... The gap between the two worlds was almost unbridgeable." The only exception, then as always, was the language. As in Pinsk, the Jewish students plunged head down into the study of the local language. Thus emerged those circles of young people who lived their family lives in Yiddish, their friendship and ideology in Russian, their utopian dreams in Hebrew, and their cultural lives in German. And yet it was they who rose to the historical challenge of leading a single mythical Jewish Destiny and "squeezing" it into a single mythical space: Zion.

Glueckel of Hameln, a contemporary of Louis XIV, would have liked, no doubt, to adopt, like Weizmann, the same radical solution to what would later be called the "Jewish question." She shared, at least, similar spatial experiences. A simple trader according to some, a proto-capitalist according to others, she neither travelled the five continents nor crossed the seven seas. Nevertheless, she travelled far and wide. And when on rare occasions she stayed at home, spaces were clearly delineated for her (and for us through her descriptions). Her spatial experience, far more fragmented in certain respects than Weizmann's, was organized in three distinct categories: economy, family, nation.

On the economic level, Glueckel knew one space only: northern and central Europe, "Ashkenaz" in her terminology. She and her husband Chaim regularly frequented the great fairs in Frankfort-on-Main, Leipzig, and Brunswick. But their network extended as far north as Copenhagen, to the northeast as far as Danzig and Stettin ("We sent our son Nathan Segal, who was then about fifteen years old, to Stettin to see how things were, and began to send big parcels of silver. This was soon made up into coin and we were sent Stettiner *drittels*, which we could sell immediately on the Bourse. There was a fine profit in this – about two in the hundred"), to the east, as far as Prague ("We had lost 1500 *reichstaler* through a bankruptcy in Prague"), to the southeast, as far as Vienna,

# Introduction I

to the west as far as Amsterdam, and they even had plans for business in England.

We do not know the complete genealogy of the Weizmann family, yet there is no doubt that matrimonial alliances were concluded within the same town, or at most with families in nearby towns and villages. Glueckel's family, however, followed a totally different pattern. For obvious demographic reasons (the German Jewish communities were much smaller than the communities in the Russian Pale of Settlement), as well as for socio-economic reasons (compared with the status of Glueckel's merchant family, Weizmann's kin were "little people"), the seventeenth-century Jewish lady concluded matrimonial alliances for her family in a manner more reminiscent of the high nobility of the Ancien Régime than of Weizmann's family. Her memoirs elaborate on the negotiations which preceded the signing of each marriage contract. Glueckel herself married at Hameln, one of her brothers married the daughter of a rich dignitary of the Prague community, one of her sisters was matched to a Jew from Emmerich, another to a Jew from Bonn, a son and a daughter in Berlin, another son almost married a daughter of the Oppenheimers of Vienna but finally remained in Hamburg, a third son married in Copenhagen, a fourth in Bamberg, a fifth in Baiersdorf, a third daughter in Altona, and a fourth in Metz. And when Glueckel herself was ready for re-marriage: "Matches with the most distinguished men in the whole of Germany had been broached to me." Economic space and matrimonial space were thus, as we can see, congruent. Within the territory that was destined to become Germany, however, she did not cross a southern line which excluded Stuttgart, Nuremberg, and Munich. It seems as if she could operate only within Lutheran territory.

But the notion of "space" is misleading, for it suggests a continuity that is absent in the picture evoked by Glueckel's memoirs. What was "Home" to Glueckel? In order to answer this question, let us follow the family to Cleves, where the eldest daughter was to be married. They took the boat from Altona to Amsterdam, where they lodged with a Jewish associate and conducted business. After the ceremony, Glueckel went to pay her respects to her sister's grave in Emmerich, and then the whole family began the voyage back. They spent fifteen days in Amsterdam, again on business. Arriving at Delftzil on the eve of *Rosh ha-Shanah* (the Jewish New Year), they stayed with a Jew from Hamburg. In Emden, they lodged with Chaim's cousin. In Wangerooge, they spent *Yom Kippur* with another of Chaim's cousins. From there to Hanover, where Chaim's parents lived; but there they were seized by anguish, for there were no more relatives to visit nor business to conduct. Clearly, then, it was not a matter of proper "space," but rather scattered *points* here and there, and between these points were blank spaces in which there was nothing to do. In other words, Glueckel did not know Germany, nor did she actually "see" it. The only places that really existed for her were those where she could find business, relatives, or coreligionists.

Three places, however, held special significance for Glueckel: Metz, Poland, and the Land of Israel. Each of these places was an "elsewhere" which defined her spaces – matrimonial, economic, cultural, or emotional. In Metz she conducted negotiations for the marriage of one of her daughters, revealing even then a profound lack of cultural comprehension. When she herself remarried, she settled in Metz and spent the remaining years of her life there. The two last chapters of her *Life*, full of bitterness, convey a feeling of displacement: in Metz men wore wigs in a style imported from Paris; stranger still, the Jews there brought their commercial disputes before a non-Jewish tribunal! The French-German frontier was thus also the edge of her universe.

The same applied in the east. Glueckel's space was defined by geopolitical conditions, but her borders were also Judaized and flexible. With the Jews of Poland one concluded neither marriages nor business. Poland was a land of disaster: two of Glueckel's brothers-in-law were ruined by the pogroms of 1648. But above all, it was a land of knowledge: more than once Glueckel mentions members of her family who either travelled to a *yeshivah* in Poland or were instructed in Germany by a Polish Jewish teacher. Yet the sages of Poland shared the norms of their country. One of Glueckel's sons became a hostage of his rabbi in Lissa (Leszno), and in his letter to his mother he writes: "It is Poland and if this befalls me, it will cost ten times as much. So, dear, beloved mother, do not forsake your child because of a little money and see that I am not delivered into their hands, for from them it will be hard to be freed."

Let us summarize: while Glueckel's "cartography" has all the apparent features of German cartography, it is in fact Jewish. On the other hand, at that time (paradoxically perhaps) only the Jews could really experience a "Germany." Two centuries before Bismarck, Glueckel lived in a land united around the core of Prussia, a Germany where borders between principalities, duchies, and free cities, simply did not exist, as she was totally oblivious to them. As a Zionist leader was to say centuries later to Thomas Masaryk: "Among you there are either Czechs or Slovaks; only we, the Jews, are Czechoslovaks."

For Glueckel, while Poland represented disaster and knowledge, Palestine was the incarnation of the past and of hope: "I should

3. *The labors of Egypt, by the Jewish painter Joseph Leipnik. Passover Haggadah, Hamburg, 1740.*

# The Perception of Space

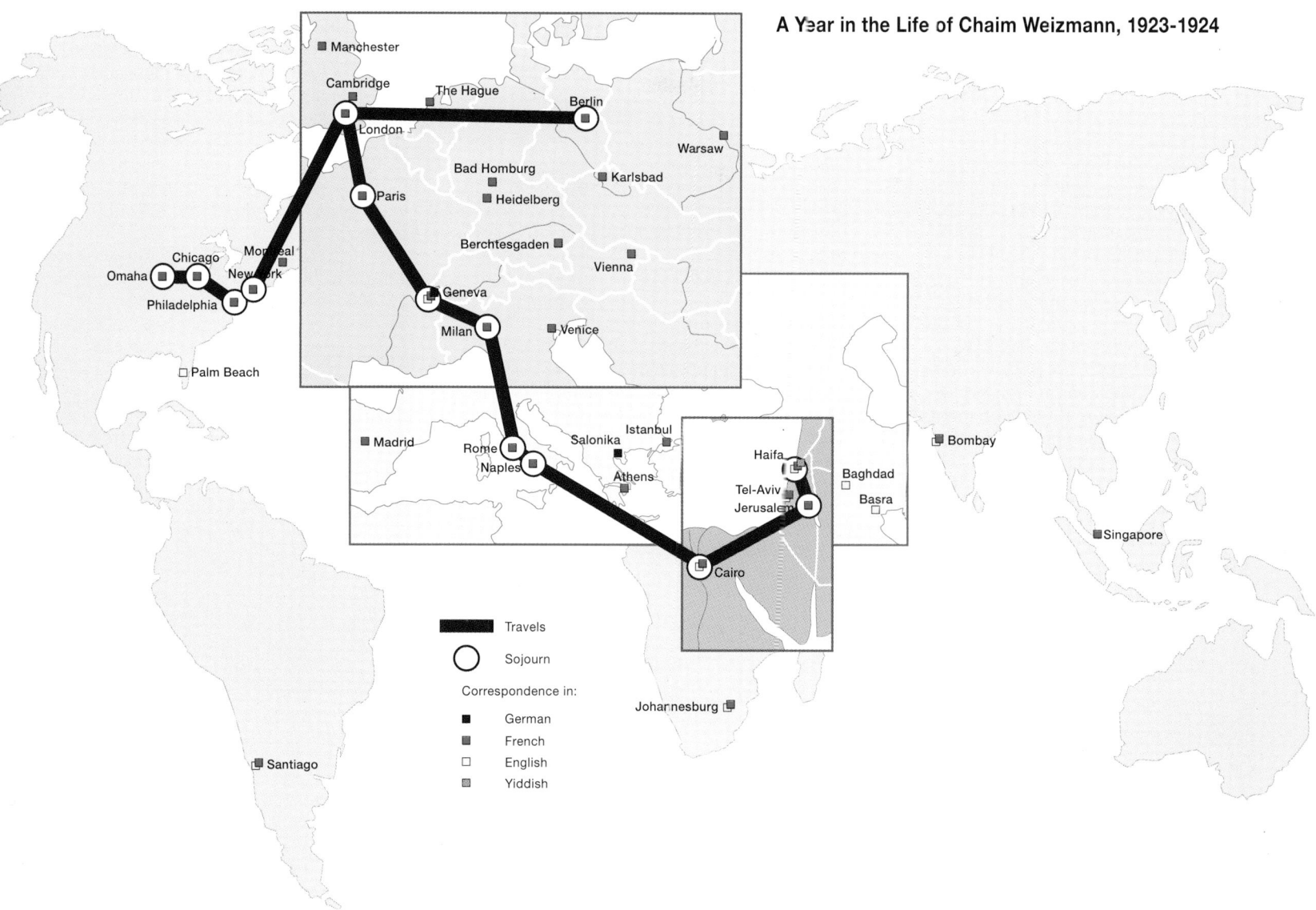

A Year in the Life of Chaim Weizmann, 1923-1924

Travels

Sojourn

Correspondence in:

■ German

■ French

□ English

■ Yiddish

have forsaken the vanity of this world and with the little left, gone to the Holy Land and lived there, a true daughter of Israel." But she took no steps towards realizing this pious wish. In her memoirs, as in the mental universe of the Jews in general, the status of the Land of Israel was far from evident. By turning such pious wishes into action, political Zionism, and before that militant messianism, interpreted this longing more literally than most Jews had intended. Glueckel, for example, remained quite detached from the tumults of the Shabbatean adventure; Weizmann recounts the fate of a popular preacher from Pinsk who settled in America: "He died a few years ago, an octogenarian, one of the last remaining links with the heroic early days of Zionism," as if Palestine and America were perfectly interchangeable and equally relevant to Zionism.

In conclusion, let us pose two fundamental questions: one concerning "roots," the other in regard to the present. Weizmann and Glueckel – were they uprooted, rootless, or persons with multiple roots? Or, in other words, did their multiple spaces render them over-sensitive to the problem of space, or,

on the contrary, totally indifferent to the problem? One possible hypothesis is that in order to be able to bear such extreme fragmentation, Jews have had to neutralize space in the physical sense and to live in metaphorical spaces: the past, the language, Scriptures, the destiny of the Chosen People, the Promised Land, as well as in socialism, physics, music, etc. It was precisely this existence in intangible "spaces" which enabled them to survive. It would be wrong to attribute such a "mentality" only to life in Exile. The deconcretization of space in Jewish history undoubtedly originated in the formative role of the written word: if Weizmann never bothered to describe a landscape, if Glueckel never "saw" Germany, it was because their mental universe was formed by a text which was divorced from actual reality; the Bible and the Talmud, so vividly evoking the Holy Land on the one hand, and the country where men and women lived here and now, on the other hand. From earliest infancy they were imbued with images of a landscape, of fauna and flora, of a reality which completely escaped them – who had ever seen a camel or a fig in Motol? A formation of this kind was hardly the best way to forge an awareness of material space.

To this "anomaly," the modern age offered two solutions: secularization silenced the source of the divorce between image and reality, i.e., the Scriptures; Zionism, on the other hand, offered the possibility of rejoining "heart" and body. Nevertheless, the Jewish perception of space has not been normalized; the "anomaly" has simply shifted. In the contemporary Jewish world, the model of the isolated *shtetl* applies above all to the State of Israel. As an island of democracy in an ocean of despotism, as a western oasis in an oriental desert, or as a besieged fortress whose hinterland lies elsewhere, Israel seeks legitimacy in metaphorical images rather than in a physical space.

"My body is in the East, my heart in the extreme-West" – an inversion of Halevi's verse seems most appropriate to the inhabitants of Israel. And they are not simply suffering from the syndrome of someone provincial dreaming of life in the metropolis: for even when he follows his "heart" to Paris, London or New York, the Israeli feels that he has left some of it behind, in Tel Aviv. The present protagonist in the mental drama created by a differential and discontinuous space is no longer the Diaspora Jew but the Israeli.

# Introduction II

Is there such a thing as a "Jewish" perception of time? Judging by Jewish attitudes to history from the Middle Ages on, apparently there is. Jews have never perceived time as progressive, but rather as a fragmented line. Its parts – past, present, and future – were not perceived as a continuous process in which one stage is a sequel of its antecedents; Jewish history was not an evolutionary flow but a three-part drama in which each act was viewed as independent of the others.

The Past was the era of glory during which Jews had experienced a collective existence and had been able to express fully their national identity. Philosophically-inclined Jews in the Middle Ages perceived themselves as inferior in virtue (though not necessarily in knowledge) to preceding generations. This inferiority complex was not simply a reflection of the general medieval view of history as an ongoing process of degeneration, but rather a specific "Jewish" belief that the ancient Hebrews had the advan-

1. Elijah's cup. In exile, the prophet became identified with the harbinger of the Messiah. Bohemia, crystal, 19th century.

tage of political independence in their own land, while the spiritual resources of "modern" Jews were depleted by exile and dispersion.

The Present was the long era of Exile. Its beginning was a well-defined point in time (the destruction of the Second Temple); but its end was shrouded in mist (as rabbinical Judaism rejected all eschatological calculations or detailed descriptions of the End of Days). Whether the trials and tribulations of exile were repre-

sented as part of a divine plan, or, on the contrary, as evidence of God's abdication, the "present" was in any event just an insignificant interlude.

The Jewish perception of the Future was most revealing of all; it was at once the most enduring element in this unique collective mentality, and the most contradictory. An impatient expectation for imminent cosmic upheavals which would transform the nature of Jewish existence was combined with resignation – acceptance that these events might be postponed until the end of time. It is irrelevant whether this near-distant future was perceived as a return to the past (a restoration of political sovereignty), or as an era which would transcend all that has ever been; whether it would be attained by an apocalyptic leap to an a-historical time through divine intervention, or rather – as stipulated by "realistic" messianism – accomplished by human efforts alone and not very different from present reality.

The thrust of the matter is that rabbinical Judaism adopted a view of the future which was based on a compromise between two seemingly incompatible attitudes: on the one hand, an eschatology which promised deliverance in the foreseeable future, and a strategy designed to ensure the evasion of a history of suffering by posing (as an American historian put it) the question of "how" rather than "when," on the other. This compromise formula was apparently powerful enough to become a fixed element in Jewish culture: a frantic search for signs of imminent redemption combined with caution and circumspection which prevented bitter disillusionment in the face of delay.

Jewish culture from the Second Temple period to the nineteenth century produced relatively few historiographical works. Was this apparent lack of interest in history the outcome of a perception of time as discontinuous, of regarding past, present and future as nonsequential? A passage from Maimonides' commentary on the talmudic tractate *Sanhedrin* is often quoted in this context: "It is sheer waste of time; as in the case of books found among the Arabs describing historical events, the government of kings and Arab genealogy, or books of songs and similar works which neither possess wisdom nor yield profit for the body, but are merely a waste of time." This paragraph has at times been interpreted by some modern scholars as indicative of the influence of Greek rationalist philosophy which considered the single individual to be unworthy of scientific inquiry. Others claimed that these words attest to the fact that Maimonides, one of the greatest representatives of Judaism of all times, was totally indifferent to history.

Yet the significance of this passage for the understanding of the Jewish attitude to history is, in fact, rather limited. First, because Maimonides, like many Muslim philosophers, was afraid that the historical narrative might sanction admiration for bloodshed and glorification of futile battles and would thus be injurious to

ethical education. Second, because Maimonides shared the philosophers' repudiation of the kind of humanistic culture which assigned an important place to poetry and history – these anecdotal writings, they said, were mere spiritual vanities which made no contribution to true knowledge.

In Christian Europe during the twelfth and thirteenth centuries there were indeed many learned Jews who expressed a similar view: they equated historical works, which they considered no better than adventure novels, with light fiction which had no intellectual or moral merit. At best, some held, history books could

2. "Remember the sacrifice of Isaac, and have mercy on his descendants today." A prayer for Rosh Ha-Shannah (New Year) illustrated by Moses Mizrahi Shah (Teheran c.1870 – Jerusalem c.1930).

provide a refreshing diversion for the man who had exhausted (as one should) his intellectual energies in arduous religious studies. However, this scorn for historical writings should not be interpreted as indifference to the past.

In the sixteenth century the influence of the Renaissance brought about a significant change: curiosity and an interest in novelties was now no longer necessarily regarded as frivolous. In 1525, for example, Abraham Farissol in *Orhot Olam* – a book on geography, cosmology and history – explicitly expressed his intention to amuse the melancholic reader with "true stories, old and new" (denouncing, however, at the same time, licentious poetry and tales recounting ancient battles which had never taken place). David Gans of Prague wrote in 1592 a Hebrew chronicle entitled *Zemah David* which addressed "many, old and new" topics. A desire to amuse and entertain was clearly one of his intentions: in his introduction, Gans notes that the second part of his book, devoted to universal history, was written in order to provide "householders like myself," overburdened with everyday worries, with a tale to lighten their load. In other words, history was acknowledged as a form of literature which could alleviate the fatigue of individuals encumbered by the hardship of earning a living and supporting a family, just as it could relieve the anguish of a nation exhausted by the tribulations of exile. History, suggests the Renaissance historian, is not only a legitimate form of entertainment, but also a source of consolation: the historian or chronicler would choose for his subject a particular period of history in which the cycle of persecution and deliverance evidenced the constant presence of Divine Providence.

Yet in many cases curiosity drove the historian to overstep the boundaries outlined in his introduction. In their address to the reader, sixteenth-century Jewish historians listed several reasons for the study of history, similar to the justifications advanced by non-Jewish Renaissance humanists. They were also quick to adopt the new methods of research and exposition.

Elijah Capsali wrote *Seder Eliyahu Zuta* as a form of distraction during the plague of 1523 in Crete. This work is a survey of the history of the Ottoman Empire down to Capsali's day, with special reference to the Jews. Capsali's presentation is lucid, methodical and well structured, and he even acknowledges his sources, many of which were oral. David Gans, while faithful to the style of medieval chronicles, cites his written sources precisely, and is meticulous where chronological accuracy is concerned. Gedaliah ibn Yahya, born in the papal city of Imola to a distinguished family of Portuguese exiles, published in 1586 an erudite compendium of information about the history of the Jews, and many other topics as well: the plan of the Temple in Jerusalem, weights and coins, the origins of languages, a history of the sciences, heaven and hell, magic and angels. Finally, Azariah de Rossi, one of the most eminent Jewish scholars in the Renaissance, employed in his work entitled *Me'or Einayim* (1573) a technique of digression and embellishment, including in it a broad range of vignettes in order to facilitate the reading and comprehension of complex historical questions.

De Rossi made extensive use of contemporary methods of critical philology. He compared, for example, the various talmudic traditions pertaining to the death of Titus with versions recounted by Roman historians and with ancient legends relating the fate of evil kings. Anxious to prove that there existed an intermediary Aramaic version of the Old Testament, between the original Hebrew and the Greek Septuagint, De Rossi relied on both Jewish and non-Jewish literary sources, as well as on coin inscriptions. It seemed quite natural for him to employ the methods developed by Renaissance philologists, for in doing so he was simply transferring to a new field of knowledge an approach that had been prevalent among "enlightened" circles of medieval Jewish scholars. An attitude repeatedly expressed during the course of the Maimonidean controversy was that "one should listen only to the truth"; in other words, so long as a philosophical proposition was valid, its author's identity was irrelevant. Jewish thinkers in the Middle Ages shared the prevalent notion that knowledge was accumulated progressively, that it could be examined and improved indefinitely – a conception implying

3. "In every single generation, a man must consider himself as if he himself went out of Egypt." Here, a symbolic interpretation of this verse in the Passover Haggadah. A Seder meal at a home of a Jewish family from Bukhara. Jerusalem, 1930s.

the relative superiority of the "moderns." Hence medieval Jewish thinkers did not hesitate to regard talmudic information on sciences such as astronomy and mathematics as obsolete. Similarly, De Rossi was prepared to reject chronological data provided by talmudic texts as mere ignorant speculation. The rigid demarcation drawn by Renaissance humanists between fable and historical fact enabled De Rossi to acknowledge the fictional nature of tales such as "Titus' punishment." Defining such legends as figments of the imagination did not, however, preclude the possibility of exploiting them for moral and didactic purposes.

Historiography as we know it today came into being in the early nineteenth century. The pioneers of modern Jewish studies, whose earliest works appeared between 1820 and 1840, were as closely affiliated to the general renaissance of historical research as their sixteenth-century predecessors. Accusations were leveled in recent decades against the early representatives of nineteenth-century *Wissenschaft des Judentums* ("Science of Judaism") – to the effect that their aptitude lay in collecting and listing sources rather than in critically analyzing them, or that they were overly-concerned with individual historical figures, and further that they failed to integrate the methods of the new science of history. Such accusations were in

fact too harsh and too hasty. The private correspondence of some of these nineteenth-century Jewish historians – Leopold Zunz, Heinrich Graetz, Moritz Steinschneider – evokes a great deal of admiration for their notable enterprise. Laboring in social isolation and always in dire financial straits, they invested tremendous efforts in editing and publishing ancient Hebrew texts which they regarded as monuments of Jewish culture. But the universities rejected their works, and they were ignored by contemporary German Jewry. Nevertheless, the role of this scientific historiography was, all in all, more significant than is generally assumed, for it provided, to say the least, important new tools which were vital for the development of Jewish collective memory.

Today, it would appear, Jewish collective memory (or attitude to history) resembles an enclosed field in which three rival schools are engaged in battle: the traditional "orthodox" model; pure amnesia, or an elimination of the past; and the exploitation of the past by nationalist or revolutionary ideologies. In a way, the present volume is an attempt to comprehend and place in perspective this unprecedented configuration of historical approaches. Hopefully this volume will not only enhance our knowledge of Jewish history, but will also open new ways of defining the ambiguous relations between memory and the task of the historian.

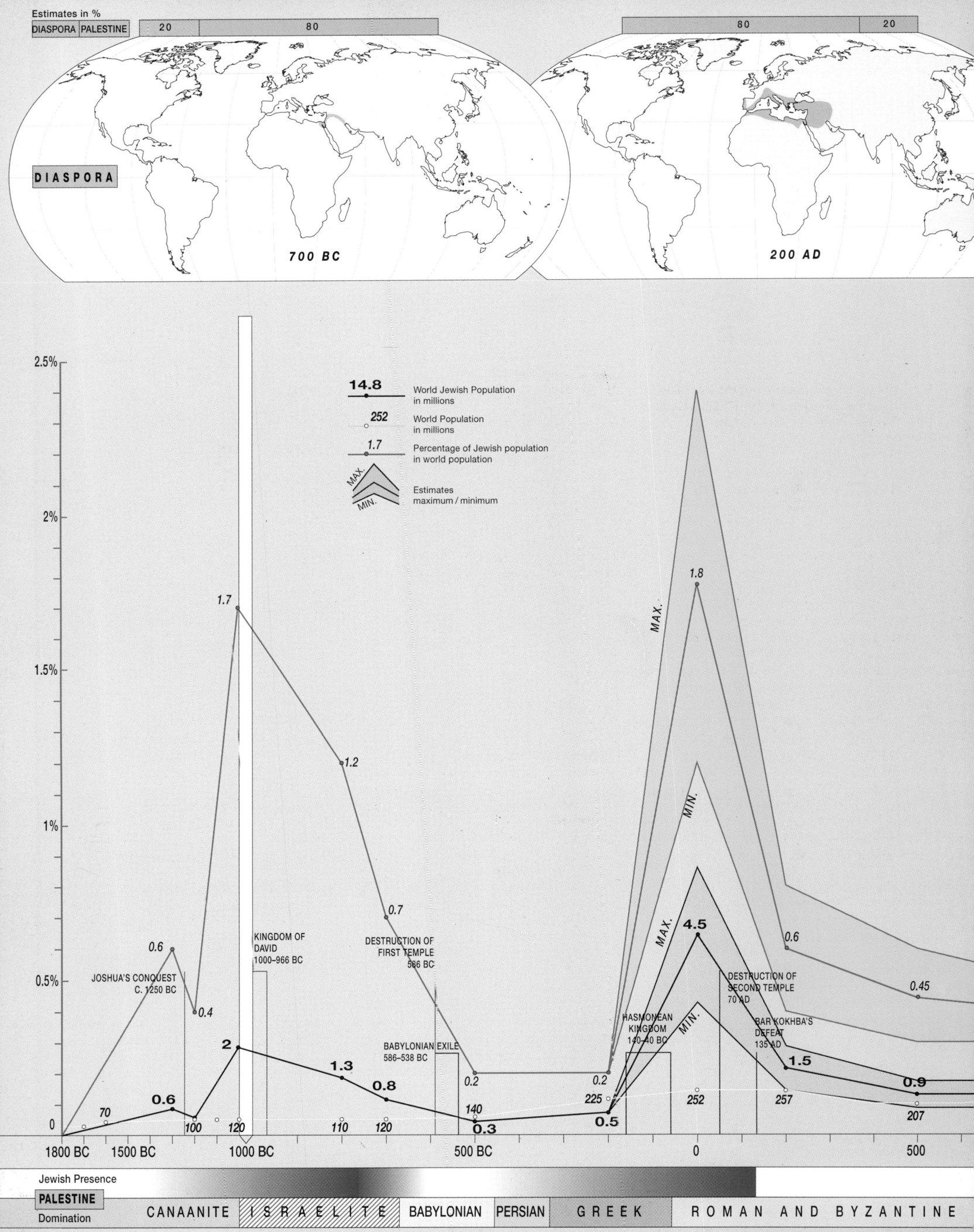

Estimates in %

DIASPORA PALESTINE

| 20 | 80 |
| --- | --- |

| 80 | 20 |
| --- | --- |

DIASPORA

**700 BC**

**200 AD**

14.8 — World Jewish Population in millions

252 — World Population in millions

1.7 — Percentage of Jewish population in world population

MAX. / MIN. — Estimates maximum / minimum

2.5%

2%

1.5%

1%

0.5%

0

1.7

1.2

0.6

0.4

0.7

0.2

0.2

MAX.

MIN.

1.8

MAX.

MIN.

0.6

0.45

JOSHUA'S CONQUEST
C. 1250 BC

KINGDOM OF
DAVID
1000–966 BC

DESTRUCTION OF
FIRST TEMPLE
586 BC

BABYLONIAN EXILE
586–538 BC

HASMONEAN
KINGDOM
140–40 BC

DESTRUCTION OF
SECOND TEMPLE
70 AD

BAR KOKHBA'S
DEFEAT
135 AD

MAX.

MIN.

4.5

1.5

0.9

**2**

**1.3**

**0.8**

**0.6**

**0.3**

**0.5**

70

100

120

110

120

140

225

252

257

207

1800 BC   1500 BC   1000 BC   500 BC   0   500

Jewish Presence

**PALESTINE**
Domination

CANAANITE   ISRAELITE   BABYLONIAN   PERSIAN   GREEK   ROMAN AND BYZANTINE

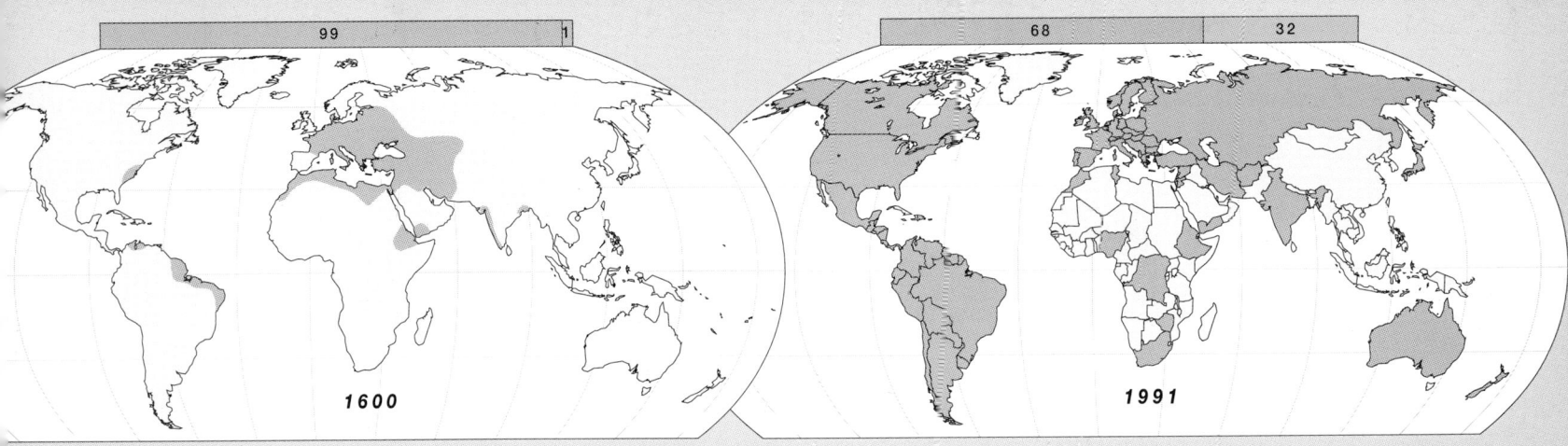

99 | 1

68 | 32

1600

1991

# Introduction III: Demography

Jewish history is largely the story of the fluctuations in the size and geographical distribution of the Jewish population. The demographic figures represent the basic patterns of the Jewish people: resilience and continuity through several millennia; cycles of expansion and decline; and, the historical experience of dispersion and constant tension between center and diaspora. The three major phases of great numerical expansion correspond to three well-defined historical periods: the consolidation of a Hebrew Kingdom in the Land of Israel (10th century BC); the time between the accession of the Hasmoneans and the destruction of the Second Temple (2nd century BC–1st century AD); and finally, the modern period during which Jewish society broke away from the legal constraints and demographic stagnation of the Middle Ages (17th–20th centuries). Yet, on the whole, there seems to be no direct overlapping between the centuries-long evolution of a unique Jewish civilization and periods of numerical growth or decline.

Another exceptional trait of Jewish demographic history is the astounding mobility of the population. The Jews are undoubtedly one of the most migratory peoples in the history of mankind. Their principal intellectual, economic and political center has shifted many times from one geographical region to another: Palestine, Egypt, Mesopotamia, Spain, the Ottoman Empire, Eastern Europe, German lands; and in recent centuries, the West, above all the United States, and finally Israel, have harbored the main concentrations of Jewish population and thus, *ipso facto*, its predominant centers. The Holocaust which destroyed European Jewry, and the creation of an independent State of Israel, where the Jews constitute the majority of the population, are the two events which mark the great divide in the recent demographic history of the Jewish people.

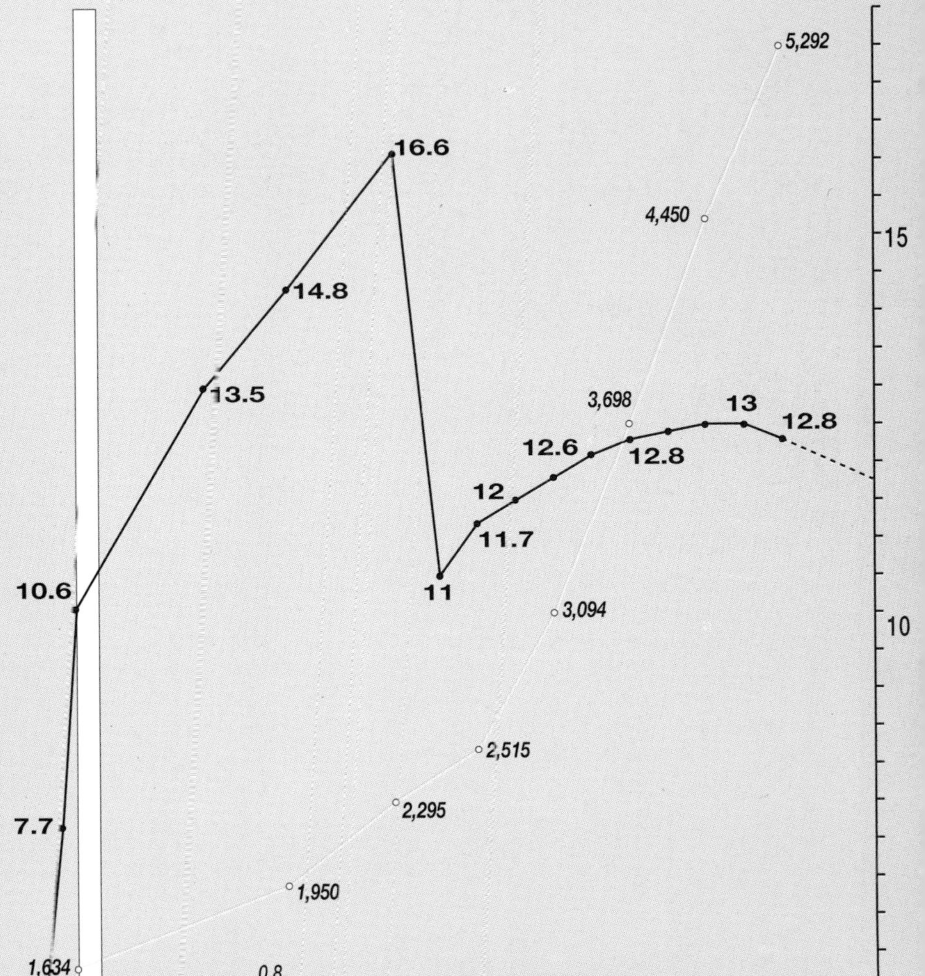

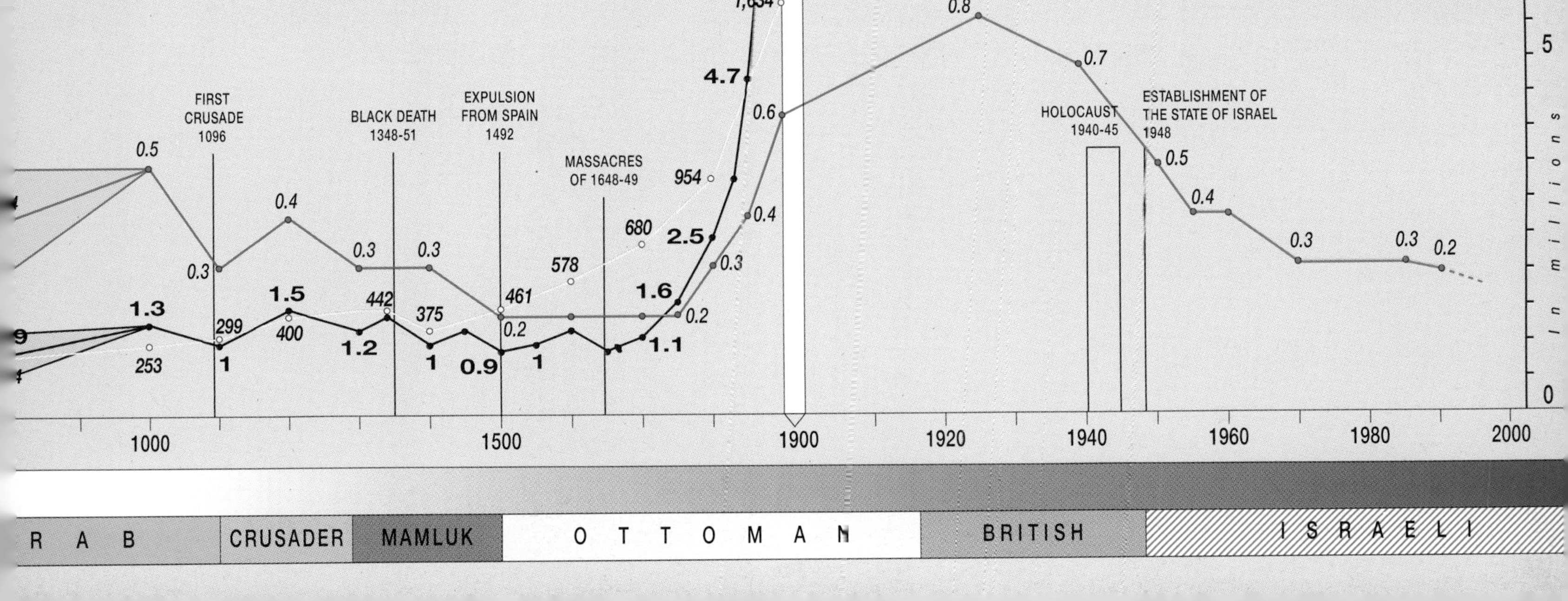

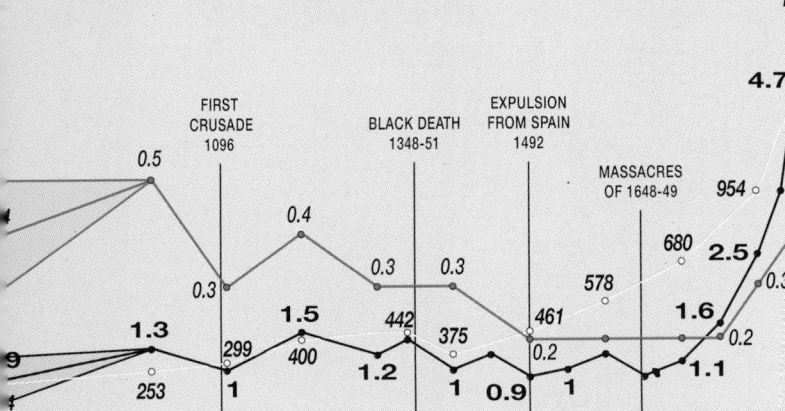

5,292

16.6

14.8

13.5

4,450

10.6

3,698

13

12.8

12.6

12.8

12

11.7

11

3,094

7.7

2,515

2,295

1,950

1,634

0.8

0.7

FIRST CRUSADE 1096

BLACK DEATH 1348-51

EXPULSION FROM SPAIN 1492

MASSACRES OF 1648-49

HOLOCAUST 1940-45

ESTABLISHMENT OF THE STATE OF ISRAEL 1948

0.5

0.5

0.4

954

0.6

0.4

0.4

0.3

0.4

680

2.5

0.3

0.3

0.3

0.3

578

0.3

442

375

461

1.6

1.3

1.5

0.2

0.2

0.2

1.1

299

400

1.2

1

0.9

1

253

1

In millions

1000 | 1500 | 1900 | 1920 | 1940 | 1960 | 1980 | 2000

5

10

15

0

RAB | CRUSADER | MAMLUK | OTTOMAN | BRITISH | ISRAELI

# The Migrations of the Patriarchs

1. Abraham, by the Jewish Austrian painter Ephraim Moses Lilien (1874–1925). Lithograph, 1908.

T he beginnings of ancient nations are always shrouded in mist. The social structures which gradually evolve into a "nation" do so in a slow, lengthy, and mainly unconscious process. The agonizing question "How did we become a nation?" usually finds its initial answer within the realm of myth; and it is the historian who needs to grapple with the difficult and uncertain demarcation between myth and historical truth.

The Book of Genesis offers some answers to the questions which the nascent Hebrew nation had to contend with at the time: How was the world created? Why does a woman bear children in pain? What is the significance of the rainbow? And first and foremost: Where did we come from? How did the Hebrew nation come into being?

The answers provided for the last question are all of a historical nature: "our father" Abraham, whom God promised to multiply into a great nation, begot Isaac; Isaac begot Jacob; and Jacob's twelve sons became in Egypt the twelve tribes of Israel. How much of this story is historical fact and what part is myth? Who was Abraham? When did he live? Was he a real-life historical figure or a mere mythological fiction?

As long as the Torah was believed to be the living word of God, queries of this kind were unthinkable; once it began to be regarded as a human document and scrutinized with modern exegetical tools, scholars needed to seek scientific corroboration. Yet even the least historically authentic biblical traditions clearly represent real events, social processes, and flesh-and-blood figures. More emphatically, it is precisely these traditions which convey the archaic culture of the people and contain the seeds of its future civilization.

Biblical narrative describes the wanderings of the patriarchs through the Fertile Crescent. Abraham and his clan left Ur, near the Euphrates delta (today Tell al-Muqayyar) and, after passing through the major centers of civilization of the time – Babylon and Mari – arrived in Haran, approximately 2000 miles from their point of departure. Their destination was the land of Canaan: "Leave your own country, your kinsmen, and your father's house, and go to a country that I will show you" (Genesis 12:1). After arriving there, however, they continued their nomadic existence. Isaac made Beersheba his home, and seldom left it. However, his son Jacob resumed peregrinating. He returned to Haran, sojourning for many years with his uncle Laban; then, returning to Canaan with a wealth of children and property, he continued to wander. Finally he took his family down to Egypt, where he died.

In the Bible the patriarchs are located in space but not in time. The background seems to be the first half of the second millennium BC. Mesopotamian sources support this assumption as they establish the existence of cultural links between Ur and Haran at the time. Both towns worshipped the same deity – the moon god, Sin. These sources also refer to western Semitic tribes who invaded the valleys of the Euphrates and Tigris and recount the ensuing decline of Ur – a possible cause for the migration of local populations to calmer regions in the north. This is where one should seek explanations for the Mesopotamian influence discernible in the Pentateuch, particularly in its legislative portions.

The stories of the patriarchs' migrations are therefore true in the sense of containing certain accepted historical facts: the ethnic basis and the social structures of the tribes about to merge into a new nation – the people of Israel.

| Ebla | Akkadian Empire | Invasion of the Gutians and destruction of Ur | Mari |
|---|---|---|---|
| 2500–2350 BC | 2350–2200 BC | 2000 BC | 1800–1760 BC |

**25th–24th centuries BC:** A period of grandeur for the city-state of Ebla, mentioned in the documents found in Mari. In 1974 the archeological site in Ebla, south of Aleppo, revealed abundant archives from the royal palace, including an important collection of tablets inscribed in a Canaanite-like language. These texts indicate the existence of close cultural and linguistic ties between Mesopotamia and the western Fertile Crescent, thus confirming the historical basis of the stories in Genesis.
**24th–23rd centuries BC:** The Akkadian Empire at its peak.
**2150–2000 BC:** Brief renaissance for the Sumerian civilization in the city-state of Lagash. Founding of the Kingdom of Ur.
**c. 2000 BC:** The Gutians destroy Ur. The kingdoms of Isin and Larsa arise in its place; their important kings are Ashm-Dagan and Iaft-Ashtar. The Amorites – western Semitic tribes – infiltrate into Mesopotamia.
**c. 1850 BC:** Sumu-Abum, of Amorite origins, makes Babylon his capital. The city-

2. A sanctuary of basalt stelae. Hazor, 15th–13th centuries BC.

states of Isin and Larsa, and later Assur, come under Amorite influence.
**c. 1800 BC:** Yahdun-Lim, the first Amorite king of Mari, creates a kingdom stretching as far as Haran and beyond. The town of Mari, under excavation since 1933 (Tell Harriri in eastern Syria), serves as capital of the kingdom from the 27th century BC.
**1800 BC–1700 BC:** Presumably when Abraham lived. Post-biblical Jewish literature ascribes the Patriarch's conversion to an intuition which preceded the Revelation: "When he was three years old, Abraham came out of the cave. He reflected: Who created heaven and earth and myself? And all through the day he prayed to the Sun. But in the evening the Sun set in the West and the Moon rose in the East. When he saw the Moon surrounded by stars, he said to himself: Here is the creator of heaven and earth and myself, and these stars are his ministers and servants. And all through the night he prayed to the Moon. In the morning, the Moon set in the West and the Sun rose

# 20th–16th Centuries BC

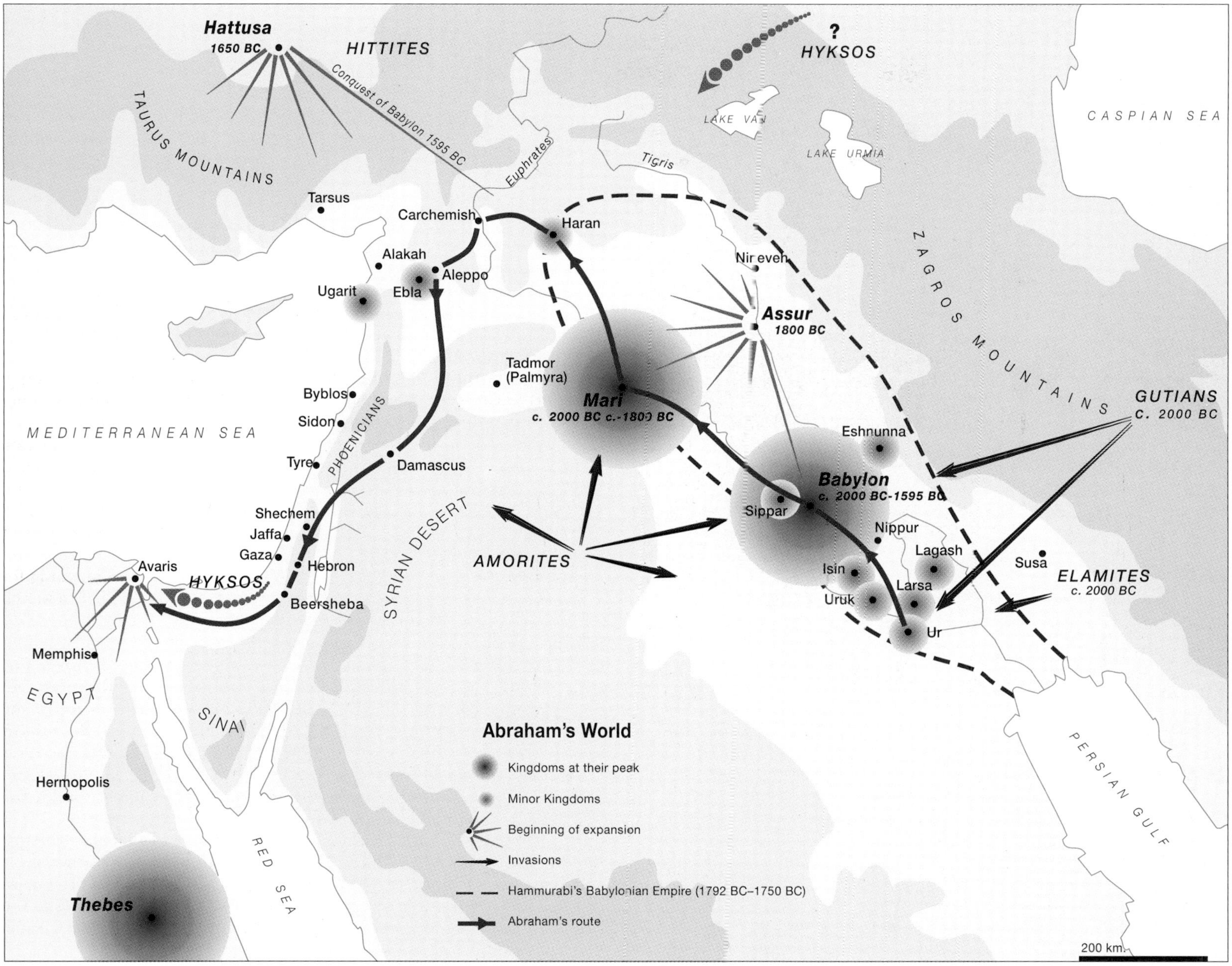

## Map: Abraham's World

**Hattusa** 1650 BC — HITTITES — Conquest of Babylon 1595 BC

TAURUS MOUNTAINS

? HYKSOS

LAKE VAN

LAKE URMIA

CASPIAN SEA

Tarsus

Carchemish — Haran

Alakah

Ugarit — Aleppo

Ebla

Tadmor (Palmyra)

Nineveh

**Assur** 1800 BC

ZAGROS MOUNTAINS

Byblos

Sidon

**Mari** c. 2000 BC c.–1800 BC

Eshnunna

GUTIANS C. 2000 BC

Tyre — PHOENICIANS

Damascus

MEDITERRANEAN SEA

**Babylon** c. 2000 BC–1595 BC

Sippar

Nippur

Lagash

Shechem

Jaffa

Gaza — Hebron

Isin — Larsa

Susa

ELAMITES c. 2000 BC

Avaris — HYKSOS

Beersheba

SYRIAN DESERT

AMORITES

Uruk

Ur

Memphis

SINAI

EGYPT

Hermopolis

RED SEA

**Thebes**

PERSIAN GULF

### Abraham's World

- Kingdoms at their peak
- Minor Kingdoms
- Beginning of expansion
- Invasions
- Hammurabi's Babylonian Empire (1792 BC–1750 BC)
- Abraham's route

200 km

## Timeline

| Hammurabi, King of Babylon | The Hyksos in Egypt | Mari conquered by Hammurabi | The Hittites in Babylon |
|---|---|---|---|
| 1792 BC | 1790 BC | 1760 BC | 1595 BC |

in the East. He said: These two are powerless. They have one master, it is to him that I shall pray, before him that I shall prostrate myself."

**1792 BC–1749 BC:** Reign of Hammurabi, son of Sin-Mubalit, in Babylon. The inscriptions glorifying his reign note the building of new temples and the restoration of old towers and temples in Babylon. Babylon – granted complete remission of debts with his accession – becomes the most important town and religious-cultural center of the entire region. As is well known, Hammurabi's famous codex of laws was to have a major influence on the laws of the Torah. In his last years Hammurabi renews his conquests; he battles amongst others with the King of Mari, Zimri-Lim (1775–1761 BC) and liquidates his kingdom. Hammurabi's dynasty rules Babylon for 150 years after his death.

**1790 BC:** The Hyksos, an Asian people, invade Egypt and gain control of the Nile Delta; as a result, many Egyptians migrate

southward to escape them. The Hyksos adopt Egyptian customs and contribute to their diffusion outside Egypt. This could be the background to the story of Joseph, his arrival in Egypt, and his sojourn there.

**1595 BC:** Mursili I, King of the Hittites, invades Babylon and puts an end to the Hammurabi dynasty. The Hittites adopt the Babylonian cuneiform script and Mesopotamian culture.

*3. Head of a Semitic slave. Bas-relief from the period of Ramses II (1304–1237 BC).*

*4. The "Seal of Temptation," A cylindrical Akkadian seal from Mesopotamia, 23rd century BC.*

# From Slavery to Liberty

1. Slaves in Egypt. Mural painting, Beni Hassan, Egypt, 19th century BC.

The Book of Genesis ends with the story of Jacob going down to Egypt with his family. The first chapter of Exodus tells how the seventy members of Jacob's clan evolved into a large people, cruelly enslaved by the kings of Egypt. The enslavement is presented in the Bible as a crucible which forged the nation of Israel. Oppressed for several centuries, the Hebrews suffered until Moses, of the tribe of Levi, brought up in Pharaoh's household, led them to freedom in the name of God, an omnipotent deity unknown to the Hebrews prior to their liberation.

The story of the Exodus is related in a few dramatic chapters: 600,000 men left Egypt on a long trek to freedom. God punished their enemies (the ten plagues of Egypt), drowned Pharaoh's army with its chariots and cavalry in the Red Sea, and brought them to Mount Sinai where they witnessed the revelation and received the Decalogue – God's commandments to his people. The First Commandment is the essence of Jewish monotheism: "I am the Lord thy God, which have brought thee out of the land of Egypt, out of the house of bondage. Thou shalt have no other gods before me" (Exodus, 20:2-3). By the time they reached the frontiers of Canaan after forty years in the desert, the Israelites had become a strong, united nation, and were ready to conquer the Promised Land.

The historical validity of this narrative is controversial. Some scholars stress the lack of Egyptian evidence testifying to the enslavement of the Israelites, pointing out that very little Egyptian influence is discernible in biblical literature and in ancient Hebrew culture. Other scholars, however, claim that it is highly improbable that a nation would choose to invent for itself a history of slavery as an explanation of its origins. If such a tradition exists, it must reflect an historical truth.

There is no doubt that slavery played a major role in the structure of the Egyptian state. It is also true that some form of single-god worship was introduced into Egypt by Akhenaton in the middle of the fourteenth century BC, and this may have been a source for Jewish monotheism. Finally, the reign of Ramses II (1279–1212 BC), known for its costly wars and vast building enterprises, may well have been the era of cruel oppression described in Exodus. But the only contemporary Egyptian source which actually mentions Israel is the stela (pillar with inscription) of King Merneptah from the fifth year of his reign (1207 BC), recording among his many victories: "Carved off is Ashkelon, seized upon is Gezer . . . Israel is laid waste, his seed is no more." This inscription implies that an entity named Israel indeed existed in Canaan at the time, yet it is difficult to determine precisely what it was. One thing, however, may be regarded as certain: if the Israelites indeed emerged out of Egypt, their migration took place before the end of the thirteenth century BC.

This single fact, however, does not resolve the enigma. Obviously, the orthodox tradition accepts the biblical account literally, despite all the miracles it describes. There are scholars who seek to explain the miraculous events in rational and natural terms. They refer to an ancient Egyptian text containing the stories of Ipu-wer, recounting a series of disasters which befell Egypt – floods, drought, slave rebellions, and invasions. Could these not be the ten plagues of Egypt? And the drowning of Pharaoh's army in the Red Sea – can it not be explained by the ebb and flow of the marshes between the Nile and the Sinai Desert? Other scholars, however, totally reject the historical validity of Exodus. The story of Ipu-wer, they say, describes the anarchy in Egypt at the end of the third millennium BC and has no bearing on the biblical story; and 600,000 men ("not counting dependents") means that approximately two million Hebrews left Egypt – is it possible that such a vast emigration left no trace in Egyptian sources? The biblical narrative, they point out, is full of contradictions concerning the topography and the sequence of events – a feature typical of folktales, not of historical texts.

Between the two opposing views there are several intermediary theories. One hypothesis is that the Israelites left Egypt in two waves, and that by the time the second wave departed – in the middle of the thirteenth century – the first group had already settled in the land of Canaan, mostly around the town of Shechem in Samaria. Another possibility is that there was no organized mass emigration, but rather a constant flow of thousands of people from different Semitic tribes who left Egypt, roamed the desert, slowly infiltrating the land of Canaan where they eventually formed a single nation.

| Accession of Ashur-uballit | Accession of Akhenaton | |
| --- | --- | --- |
| 1364 BC | 1350 BC | |

**1578–1546 BC:** Reign of Ahmose I, founder of the 18th dynasty.
**1524–1518 BC:** Reign of Thutmose I who conducts military expeditions in Asia and Mesopotamia and reaches the Euphrates.
**1504–1450 BC:** Reign of Thutmose III who fights several wars in Canaan and Syria. A detailed inscription on a wall of the temple of Amon at Karnak includes many names of settlements in Canaan.
**1498–1483 BC:** Joint reign of Queen Hatshepsut and Thutmose III. With the help of her favorite architect, Senmut, Hatshepsut erects the splendid burial temple in Deir el-Bahri near the Valley of the Kings.
**1364–1329 BC:** Reign of Ashur-uballit I in Assyria who transforms his kingdom into a power of the same order as Babylon, Hatti, Egypt, and Mitanni.
**1350–1334 BC:** Reign of Akhenaton (Amenophis IV) who suppresses the cult of Amon-Re and elevates Aton, a manifestation of the sun-god, to the status of supreme deity. His religious revolution has political

implications as he removes the priests of Amon-Re and replaces them with loyal servants. Akhenaton, with the active support of his wife Nefertiti, succeeds in strengthening his absolute rule, but after his death the priests of Amon-Re return and declare that the previous king and his followers are heretics. Some scholars believe this to be the background for the biblical drama: Joseph's rise to power in the royal court is a result of the impotence of the Egyptian magicians; the origins of Jewish monotheism in the single-god worship established by Akhenaton; and the rise of a new king "who knew nothing of Joseph" (Exodus 1:8) and reversed the attitude towards the Hebrews. Rich archives found at El-Amarna where Akhenaton had built his capital in order to escape the influence of the priests of Amon, contain, among other documents, letters by Canaanite and Babylonian kings such as the King of Shechem, the King of Akhshaf, the King of Jerusalem, the King of Hazor, and others, all

complaining of the Habiru tribes who were invading the land and undermining Egyptian rule in the region. Certain scholars identify the Habiru with the Hebrews and conclude that Israelite tribes were already occupying the land of Canaan and fighting with local kings in the 14th century BC.
**1290–1279 BC:** Seti I, King of Egypt, conducts military campaigns in Canaan. Reliefs on a wall of the Amon temple at Karnak indicate the existence of fortified towns in Canaan and of Egyptian guard-posts in the Sinai Desert.
**1279–1212 BC:** Reign of Ramses II, known for conducting many wars and great building enterprises. It is possibly the memory of his reign which is reflected in the biblical description of cruel slavery: "Therefore they did set over them taskmasters to afflict them with their burdens, and they built for Pharaoh treasure cities, Pithom and Raamses . . . and

2. Egyptian sarcophaguses. Deir el-Balah near Gaza, 14th–13th centuries BC.

# 16th–13th Centuries BC

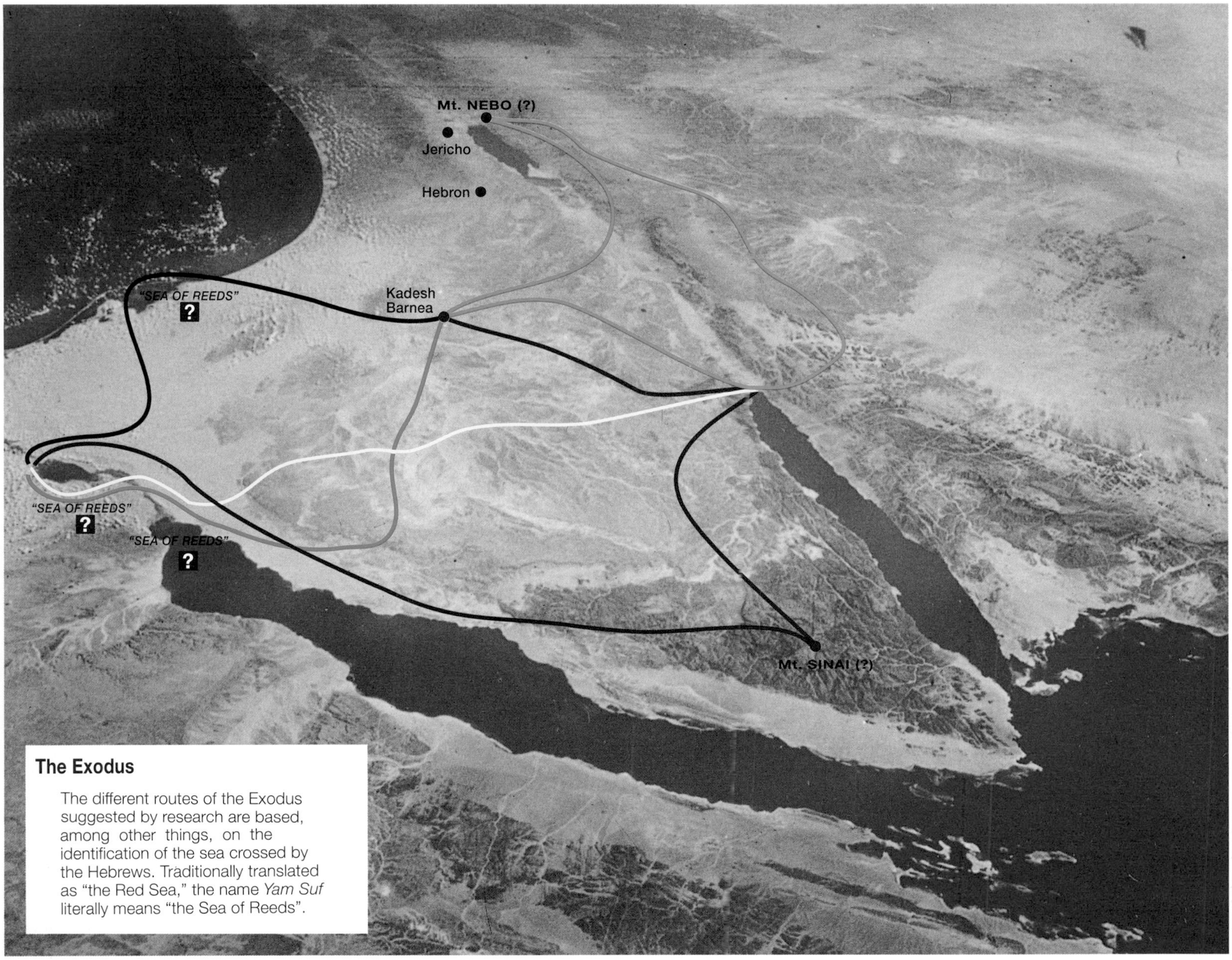

Mt. NEBO (?)

Jericho

Hebron

"SEA OF REEDS"
?

Kadesh
Barnea

"SEA OF REEDS"
?

"SEA OF REEDS"
?

Mt. SINAI (?)

## The Exodus

The different routes of the Exodus suggested by research are based, among other things, on the identification of the sea crossed by the Hebrews. Traditionally translated as "the Red Sea," the name *Yam Suf* literally means "the Sea of Reeds".

| Moses | Battle of Kadesh | The Sea Peoples |
|---|---|---|
| c. 1300 BC | 1275 BC | c. 1200 BC |

they made their lives bitter with hard bondage, in mortar, and in brick, and in all manner of service in the field" (Exodus, 1:11, 14).

**1275:** Ramses' battle with the Hittites in Kadesh on the Orontes River in western Syria. Despite Ramses' victory, the peace treaty signed between the two empires (the text of which was found both in Hattusa, the Hittite capital, and in Thebes) leaves Kadesh in the hands of the Hittites. Ramses II builds throughout Egypt and Cush on an unprecedented scale. He erects the magnificent temples in Abu Simbel and enlarges the temples of Amon in Karnak and Luxor. A document dating from that time, describing the towns in Canaan, mentions "the head of the tribe of Asher" – perhaps an indication of an Israelite presence in Canaan at this early date.

**1243–1205 BC:** Thukulti-Nunurta I, King of Assyria, vanquishes Babylon. The statue of Marduk is brought from Babylon to Assyria; the "Epic of Creation" is written in

*3. Pharaoh and his army drowned in the sea. Oil on papier-mâché, Ispahan, end of 17th century.*

celebration of this victory.

**c. 1200 BC:** Assyrian pressure from the east and the invasion of the Sea Peoples – tribes from western Anatolia and the Aegean islands – put an end to the kingdom of the Hittites and to the Ugaritic kingdom. Ugarit, a port town in northern Syria (Tell Ras Shamra, under excavation since 1929), prospered and expanded between the 16th and 13th centuries BC; it left to posterity many documents in Akkadian, as well as epics written in a unique cuneiform alphabetic script closely related to Hebrew. Though it is not mentioned in the Bible, the discovery of Ugarit and the Ugaritic texts had a profound effect on biblical studies, especially in the fields of religion, literature, and language; many lyrical forms in the Bible can be explained by the Ugaritic texts: the epics of Eghat, of Baal and his consort Anath, and of Kereth; names of gods also reveal the similarity of the Ugaritic language to Hebrew: *el* (god), *baal* (master), *mott* (death), *yam* (sea), *dagan* (grain).

# "These are the beasts which ye shall eat"

1. "Whatsoever parteth the hoof, and is clovenfooted, and cheweth the cud, among the beasts, that shall ye eat" (Leviticus, 11:3). Mosaic, church in Kissufim (northern Negev), 5th century.

An orthodox Jew, in the eyes of non-Jews and of Jews who do not belong to his world, is first and foremost one who observes strict dietary laws and eats only "kosher" food. The laws of *kashrut* (from the Hebrew root meaning "fit" or "proper") are exceedingly complex and for centuries have bewildered sages and scholars who wished to find a rationale or an historical justification for this system of alimentary taboos.

The Bible only says: you shall eat this, you shall not eat that. It does not provide an explanation. Thus there were many people throughout the ages who dismissed these rules as archaic superstitions (modern Reform Judaism in America, for example, does not insist on the observance of the dietary laws since they "originated in ages and under the influence of ideas entirely foreign to our present mental and spiritual state" – the Pittsburgh Platform, 1885). The most frequently advanced theory was the hygienic explanation. In the twelfth century Maimonides claimed that all forbidden foods were unwholesome.

Today, however, sociologists and anthropologists view such "purity" laws as an expression of the need to give a coherent structure to the universe by ordering it in a series of distinctions: God/man, Hebrews/other peoples; man/animals; animals/vegetables; herbivores/carnivores; earth/water/sky, etc. According to Genesis, the world was created by the separation of the elements. To respect the order introduced by God, this separation had to be maintained or the world would return to chaos.

The dietary system of the ancient Hebrews derives, first of all, from the fundamental separation of man from God (in contrast to other religions which propose the fusion of man and divinity). The God of the Hebrews is a "living" God. His domain is Life, and to prevent man from encroaching upon it, the foremost commandment was: "Thou shall not kill" – a law applying also to animals, for they too are endowed with the "spirit of life." Accordingly, the initial nourishment for man was plants ("Of every tree of the garden thou mayest freely eat," Genesis, 2:16). Adam was a vegetarian. It was only after the Deluge that God, as a concession to man's evil inclinations, permitted the consumption of meat. "But flesh with the life thereof, which is the blood thereof, shall ye not eat" (Genesis, 9:4). Since blood was life, and as such the part belonging to God, it should never be consumed. This remains to this day one of the strongest of all Jewish dietary taboos, and the draining of blood is the basis for the process of koshering the meat. Thus the separation between man and God is maintained.

The third stage in the evolution of the dietary laws in the Bible was the distinction between clean and unclean animals. Even drained of blood, not all animals are fit for consumption. The forbidden creatures belong to two basic categories. First, all flesh-eating animals: an animal which kills its food is unclean (in the process of Creation, the animals were given "every green herb" for their nourishment). The swine, an omnivorous animal, was at first perceived as a carnivore (perhaps because the ancient Hebrews knew only the wild boar). And why are "clean" beasts only those mammals which chew the cud and have cloven hooves?

## Meat and Milk

"Thou shalt not seethe a kid in his mother's milk" (Exodus, 23:19) is perhaps the most mysterious dietary law in the Bible. The prohibition may have stemmed from ethical principles: cooking a kid in his mother's milk could be seen as an act of the utmost cruelty; or it might have been connected with idolatrous practices. It could also be interpreted as a kind of "culinary incest." And as incest is the most terrible manifestation of confusion in the divinely ordered universe, it is always one of the strictest taboos. Many Jewish religious proscriptions were greatly extended

3. A seal confirming a bar of soap as "kosher." Jerusalem, beginning of 20th century.

2. A Jewish butcher and the emblem of his guild. Prague, 1741.

throughout the ages by a process of creating a "fence around the Torah," and this prohibition was no exception. To guard against committing a transgression, even inadvertently, the interpretation of the biblical rule was stretched to include practices which were far removed from the original intention. Hence, it was no longer only a "kid" but all flesh; no longer only goat's milk, but all milk and all dairy products; not just the process of cooking them together, but even consuming the two during the same meal. All this led to detailed regulations concerning separate sinks, cooking utensils, plates, and cutlery for meat and milk products. These must be stored and washed separately, and if "contaminated," they need to be thoroughly "purified" by a very elaborate process.

4. A "clean fowl" (Deuteronomy, 14:20) par excellence. Ashkenazi Passover Haggadah, 15th century.

Because ruminants are herbivores, and split hooves indicate that they have no means for seizing prey.

The second category is that of mixed species. In God's plan of creation, each animal was connected to one single element (earth, sea, or air). An animal which partakes of two elements is impure because it represents confusion in the order of the universe. Not only birds of prey are considered impure, but fowls which walk on land rather than fly (ostriches) or those that wade in water (pelicans) too. A creature that lives in the sea and does not have marks distinctive of fish (fins and scales) is taboo: hence the prohibition on snails, shrimps, and lobsters. All amphibians are forbidden as they are obviously creatures of two media.

In support of the theory that fear of the hybrid as representing disorder lay at the basis of some dietary laws, one could cite the biblical prohibition on other mixed species (in Hebrew, *kilayim*): Jews were forbidden to sow together two kinds of grain, to graft two plant species, to crossbreed two kinds of animals, to plow with an ox and an ass together, and to mix wool and linen in the same cloth. This was also perhaps one of the reasons why the Jews rejected Jesus: Christ, the man-God, was the absolute hybrid creature, and therefore unthinkable.

Observance of the dietary laws has always been the highest partition between Jews and non-Jews. By remaining faithful to *kashrut* and unable to dine at the table of a non-Jew, the Jews have maintained for twenty centuries the alliance between a unique God and a people that "shall dwell alone" (Numbers, 23:9).

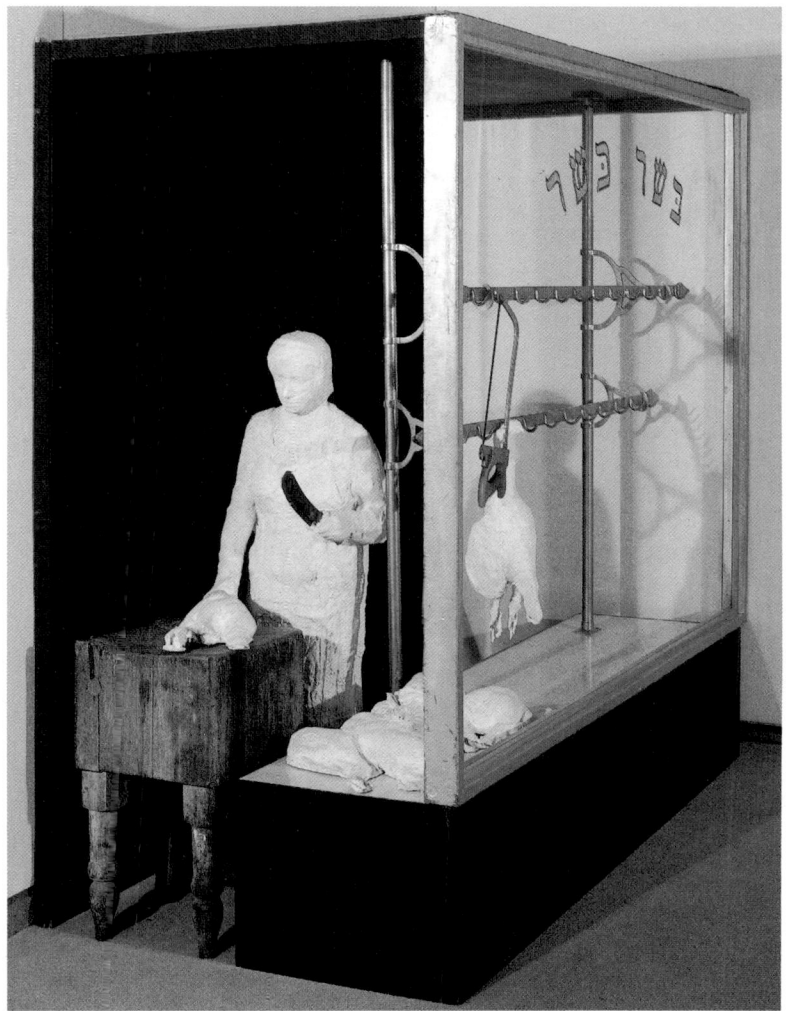

5. The butcher's shop. Sculpture by the American artist George Segal, 1965. On the window, in Hebrew: "Kosher Meat."

# The Conquest of Canaan

*1. Shalom Moskovitz (1881–1981),* The Walls of Jericho.

The Books of Numbers and Deuteronomy recount how the Israelites captured territories east of the Jordan River which were later settled by the tribes of Reuben, Gad, and half of Manasseh. The Book of Joshua then presents the "official" biblical version of the conquest and settlement of the Promised Land. The people of Israel, assembled on the eastern banks of the Jordan, were ready to cross the river and conquer the land of Canaan.

Joshua son of Nun, Moses's successor, first sent spies and, encouraged by their report about the fear of the Canaanites, immediately decided to attack Jericho, the strongest town in the area. The miraculous fall of Jericho opened the road inland. Joshua led his people southward, then towards the hills of Judea, and later to the north, in a series of successful campaigns crowned by the conquest of Hazor – the strongest town in the north. The capture of Shechem is not mentioned, but the Bible states that once the conquest was completed, the people of Israel gathered there for a national assembly, an indication that Shechem was already in the hands of the tribes of Israel.

The historical validity of this account of the conquest is highly dubious. Analysis of other biblical texts reveals many discrepancies. The Book of Judges recounts separate campaigns by individual tribes; and, although it places the events after Joshua's death, they constitute in fact a different version of the story of the conquest. The Book of Joshua describes a well-organized campaign of a people united by a common national goal, while the Book of Judges reports many separate battles against Canaanite peoples waged by individual tribes or by temporary alliances of several tribes, enlarging their territories at the expense of their neighbors.

Furthermore, according to the Book of Joshua, the entire country was taken by the Israelites, while the Book of Judges reveals that one of the severe problems of the tribes was the constant struggle with Canaanite enclaves which successfully retained their independence. Finally, in the period covered by the Book of Judges, the tribes were headed by local commanders (the "judges"), and there was no single national leader. The editor of the Book of Judges regarded this as a sign of social disintegration following the death of Joshua – divine punishment for lapses of idolatry. Modern scholars, however, believe that the state of anarchy reflected in the Book of Judges is closer to the true historical process of the colonization of Canaan.

Finally, archeological research has found no traces of any sudden violent destruction of the major Canaanite towns. Jericho, for example, was clearly not destroyed in the time of Joshua. On the other hand, excavations reveal that many small settlements began emerging on the outskirts of the existing Canaanite towns, not in place of them. Dwelling structures and pottery typical of semi-nomadic people indicate a long process of colonization rather than a short war of total conquest.

**13th–12th centuries BC:** The conquest of Canaan, accomplished – according to the Book of Joshua – in a single campaign: "So Joshua smote all the country of the hills, and of the south, and of the vale, and of the springs, and all their Kings: he left none remaining, but utterly destroyed all that breathed, as the Lord God of Israel commanded. And Joshua smote them from Kadesh-Barnea even unto Gaza, and all the country of Goshen, even unto Gibeon. And all these kings and their land did Joshua take at one time, because the Lord God of Israel fought for Israel" (10:40-42). But, although seemingly a continuation of the Book of Joshua – "Now after the death of Joshua it came to pass . . ." – the Book of Judges provides a different version altogether, making it quite clear that the Canaanite peoples had not been destroyed by Joshua's hand: "And the anger of the Lord was hot against Israel, and he delivered them into the hands of spoilers that spoiled them, and he sold them into the hands of

*3. Canaanite pottery from the period of the Patriarchs. End of the middle Canaanite period.*

# 13th–12th Centuries BC

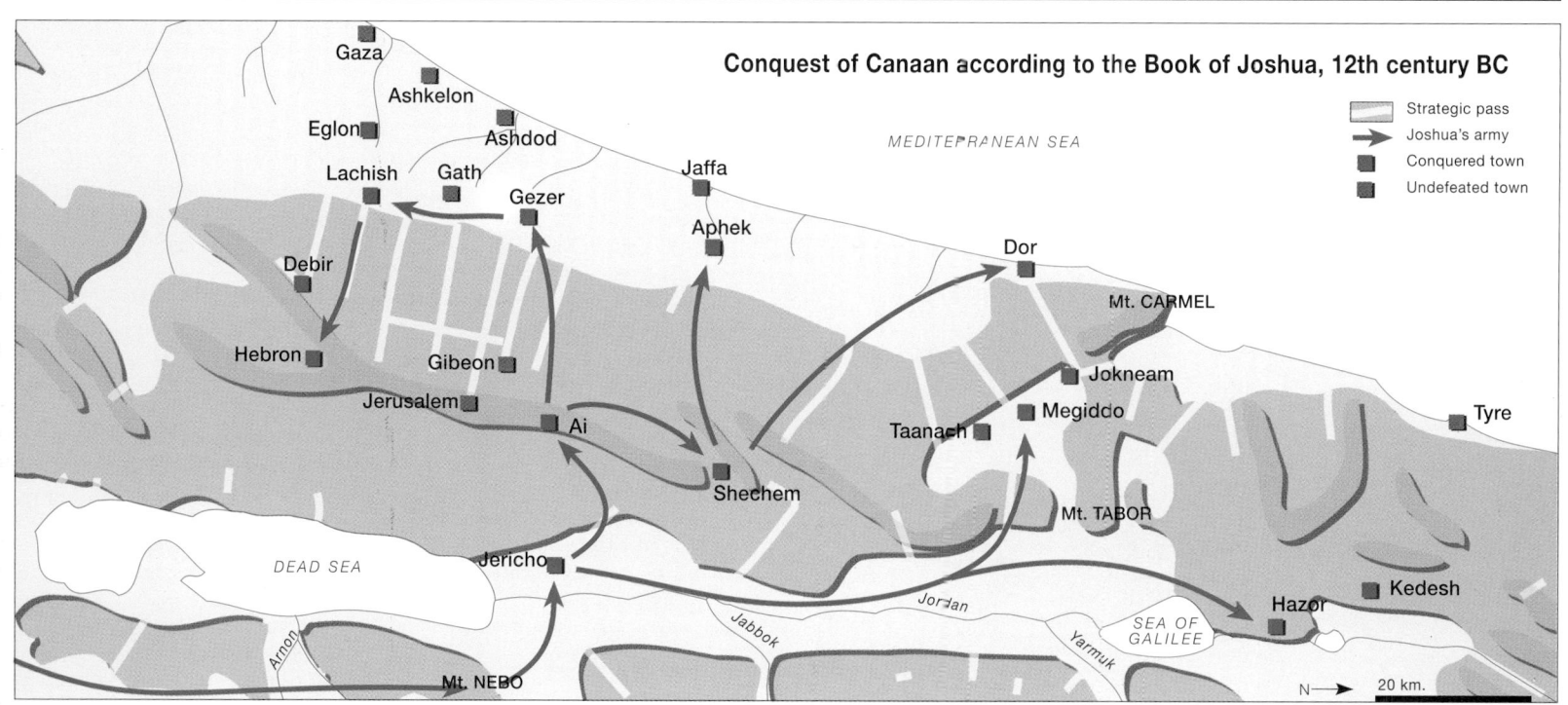

Conquest of Canaan according to the Book of Joshua, 12th century BC

Strategic pass
Joshua's army
Conquered town
Undefeated town

MEDITERRANEAN SEA

Gaza · Ashkelon · Eglon · Ashdod · Lachish · Gath · Gezer · Debir · Jaffa · Aphek · Dor · Mt. CARMEL · Hebron · Gibeon · Jerusalem · Ai · Joberan · Joberan · Jokneam · Taanach · Megiddo · Tyre · Shechem · Mt. TABOR · Jericho · DEAD SEA · Hazor · Kedesh · Mt. NEBO · Arnon · Jabbok · Jordan · Yarmuk · SEA OF GALILEE · 20 km. · N

On the basis of such evidence, modern scholarship offers three basic theories concerning the conquest and settlement of the land. The first two accept in essence the historical truth of the Exodus story: one suggests two major waves of emigration from Egypt, reaching Canaan separately within several decades and occupying the land; the second theory proposes a continuous flow of migration of nomadic tribes from Egypt through Sinai, and also from Mesopotamia, which gathered around common religious centers, forged alliances in times of crisis, and eventually consolidated into one nation.

The third model is far more "Canaanite" and underplays the importance of foreign ethnic elements. According to this view, the nucleus of the nation of Israel was comprised of slaves and oppressed people in Canaan who abandoned their masters and settled outside the towns. They were perhaps joined over the years by nomadic tribes from the Sinai desert, but these could not have been many. In any event, all the oppressed elements combined to rise against their former lords and took over the land. In the process they evolved into a national society which invented for itself the tradition of a common past.

*2. The Ark of the Covenant about to cross the Jordan River. Wall-mosaic, Santa Maria Maggiore, Rome.*

their enemies round about, so that they could not any longer stand before their enemies . . . Therefore the Lord left those nations, without driving them out hastily; neither delivered he them into the hand of Joshua" (Judges 2:14, 23). In fact, the conquest campaigns of Joshua are not mentioned anywhere in the Bible except in the book which bears his name. Only in the 2nd century BC (c. 180 BC) would Joshua's battles be glorified again by a poet. Ben Sira, writing on the eve of the Hasmonean insurrection, numbers him among the great heroes of the people of Israel: "Joshua son of Nun was a mighty warrior, who succeeded Moses in the prophetic office. He lived up to his name as great liberator of the Lord's chosen people, able to take reprisals on the enemies who attacked them, and to put Israel in possession of their territory. How glorious he was when he raised his hand and brandished his sword against cities! Never before had a man made such a stand, for he was fighting the Lord's battles. Was it

*4. Woman's head. Ivory, end of 13th–early 12th century BC.*

not through him that the sun stood still and made one day as long as two? . . . for he followed the lead of the Mighty One" (Ecclesiasticus or the Wisdom of Jesus Son of Sirach 46:1–6).
**c. 1200 BC:** The Trojan war. Troy, a strong and prosperous center in Asia Minor, is captured and destroyed by the Greek Achaeans after a long siege. The town was identified with the ruins found at Tel Hissarlik, about four miles from the southern entrance of the Hellespont, by Heinrich Schliemann, who excavated the site in 1870–1890. The Homeric epics, and particularly the stories of the wanderings after the fall of Troy, concur with what is known about the activities of the Sea Peoples during that period.
**1182–1151 BC:** The reign of Ramses III in Egypt. After a period of chaos – civil war, anarchy, struggles among factions in the court – which put an end to the 19th dynasty (Tausreth, 1193–1184 BC) and open the period of the 20th dynasty (Seth Nakt, 1184–1182 BC), Ramses III ensures

stability. He repels the Sea Peoples who disrupted navigation in the Mediterranean and strengthens his hold in Canaan, although he cannot prevent the Philistines from gaining a foothold in the coastal area.
**1126–1103 BC:** The reign of Nebuchadnezzar I in Babylon. He conquers Shushan from the Elamites and recovers the statue of the god Marduk which was taken from Babylon by the King of Elam, Kudur Nehunde III, in the 14th century BC. Elam, once an important power, declines and will not play a major role in Mesopotamia for the next 300 years.
**1115 BC:** Tiglath Pileser I ascends the throne in Assyria. The first chronicles in Assyrian history record the major events of his reign. Tiglath Pileser wages war against the peoples who threaten his kingdom, particularly the Arameans; according to these chronicles he crossed the Euphrates River twenty-eight times to fight against this people who were becoming a major force northwest of the Fertile Crescent.

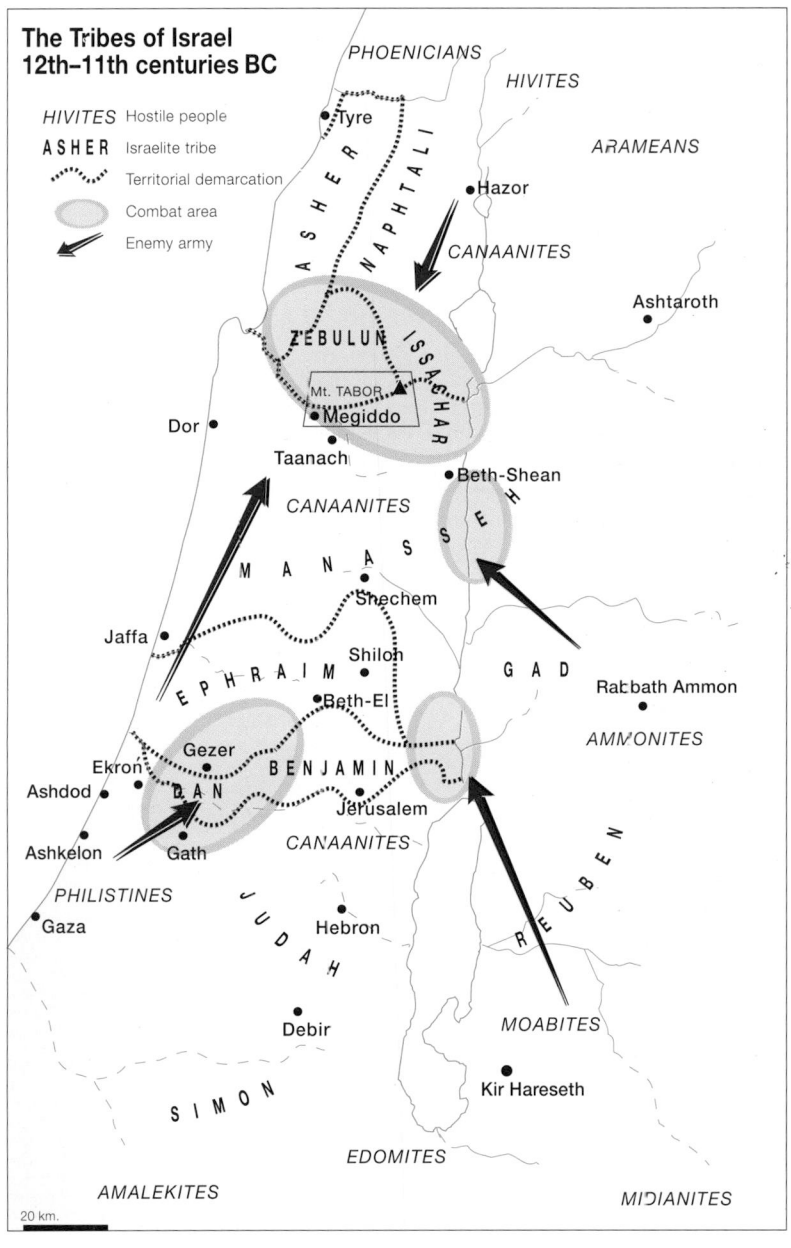

### The Tribes of Israel
### 12th–11th centuries BC

| | |
|---|---|
| HIVITES | Hostile people |
| ASHER | Israelite tribe |
| ∙∙∙∙∙∙∙ | Territorial demarcation |
| ⬭ | Combat area |
| ⬅ | Enemy army |

PHOENICIANS

HIVITES

ARAMEANS

Tyre

ASHER

NAPHTALI

Hazor

CANAANITES

Ashtaroth

ZEBULUN

ISSACHAR

Mt. TABOR

Dor

Megiddo

Taanach

Beth-Shean

CANAANITES

MANASSEH

Shechem

Jaffa

Shiloh

EPHRAIM

Beth-El

GAD

Rabbath Ammon

AMMONITES

Gezer

Ekron

BENJAMIN

DAN

Ashdod

Jerusalem

Ashkelon

Gath

CANAANITES

PHILISTINES

JUDAH

REUBEN

Gaza

Hebron

SIMON

Debir

MOABITES

Kir Hareseth

EDOMITES

AMALEKITES

MIDIANITES

20 km.

**B**efore becoming a fully consolidated national entity with the establishment of the dynasty of the House of David at the end of the eleventh century BC, the Israelites had a long history as a tribal territorial society. The twelve tribes of Israel, governed in times of peace by councils of elders, were led in times of war by charismatic commanders – the judges. The Bible presents the judges as leaders of the entire nation, and the formula "he was judge over Israel for [a given number of] years" is repeated time and again. As the stories themselves reveal, these were actually tribal chieftains, several of them active at the same time, each leading his own tribe against a different enemy.

The enemies were many: "the five lords of the Philistines, the Canaanites, the Sidonians, and the Hivites who lived in mount Lebanon" (Judges, 3:3), as well as peoples east of the Jordan. The strongest of all were the Philistines of the Sea Peoples, who landed on the shores of Canaan at the end of the thirteenth century BC. By the end of the eleventh century BC they were already firmly established in the southern coastal plain, organized in a confederation of small city-kingdoms (Gaza, Ashdod, Ashkelon, Ekron, and Gath). Led by their kings, the Philistines frequently attacked the tribes of Israel, attempting to drive them inland.

City-kingdoms were also the political units of the Canaanites who for a long time continued to hold several enclaves, including Jerusalem, within the land. The story about Jabin, King of Hazor, reveals that he

1. Jael and Sisera. An English miniature from Queen Mary's Psalter, 14th century.

2. Galilean landscape.

**12th century BC:** The prophetess Deborah, whose army is commanded by Barak, son of Abinoam, achieves a remarkable victory over Jabin, the Canaanite king of Hazor. In celebration, Deborah and Barak compose their famous song, one of the earliest of Hebrew heroic poems:
"Praise ye the Lord for the avenging of Israel, when the people willingly offered themselves.
Hear, O ye kings; give ear, O ye princes;
I, even I, will sing unto the Lord;
I will sing praise to the Lord God of Israel
Lord, when thou wentest out of Seir
when thou marchedst out of the field of Edom,
the earth trembled,
and the heavens dropped,
the clouds also dropped water.
The mountains melted from before the Lord,
even that Sinai from before the Lord, God of Israel.
In the days of Shamgar the son of Anath,
in the days of Jael,
the highways were unoccupied,

3. An Edomite goddess. The northern Negev, 8th century BC.

possessed an organized army and "nine hundred chariots of iron" with which he "oppressed Israel harshly for twenty years" (4:3). And there were also the Transjordanian enemies: nomadic or semi-nomadic tribes such as Amalek, Aram, and Midian, as well as regular kingdoms such as Ammon and Moab that periodically attacked the Israelites.

The lengthy wars, described in the Book of Judges as the realization of a predestined divine plan, forged the Israelites into hardy soldiers. "These are the nations which the Lord left as a means of testing all the Israelites, . . . his purpose being to teach succeeding generations of Israel . . . how to make war" (3:1-2). The continuous state of war also explains the inter-tribal cooperation and the formation of alliances. For example, in the war conducted by the prophetess Deborah and Barak son of Abinoam against Jabin, King of Hazor (chs. 4-5), the tribes of Zebulun, Naphtali, Ephraim, Benjamin, and Issachar all took part; the tribes of Reuben, Dan and Asher, on the other hand, were castigated by Deborah for not coming to the battlefield, although apparently committed to the alliance. The southern tribes of Simon, Judah, and Levi are not mentioned at all in connection with this war.

The basic weakness of the tribal organization was the lack of continuity in government. A strong centralized regime, maintaining a permanent army and following strict rules of hereditary succession, was by definition contrary to the nature of a tribal society. Consequently, although free of the autocratic corruption which afflicted its neighboring kingdoms, Israelite society was weak because it could not mobilize all its resources and manpower in times of need.

The Israelites were well aware of the conflict between necessity (a strong, stable, and unifying ruling power) and their tribal tradition. It is best illustrated in the story of Gideon and his son Abimelech. After Gideon had rescued the central tribes from Transjordanian invaders, the tribes offered him the kingship – "You have saved us from the Midianites; now you be our ruler, you and your son and your grandson" (8:22). Gideon, however imbued with tribal tradition, refused outright: "I will not rule over you, nor shall my son; the Lord will rule over you" (8:23). His son Abimelech could not resist the temptation. His mother, after all, had been a Canaanite woman from Shechem – an ancient city-kingdom with a deeply-rooted monarchical tradition. When his father died, Abimelech murdered his brothers – "seventy brothers . . . on a single stone block" [9:5] – and established a monarchy.

It was, however, premature. The wonderful parable told by Jotham, Gideon's only son who survived the massacre (a parable in which all the fruit trees refuse the kingship and only the thorn-bush agrees to reign, Judges 9:7-15) and the revolt provoked by Abimelech's tyranny prove that the tribal society was not yet ready for a monarchy. Before long, however, necessity would prevail.

*4. The concubine. Stone statuette. Deir al-Balah, near Gaza, 13th century BC.*

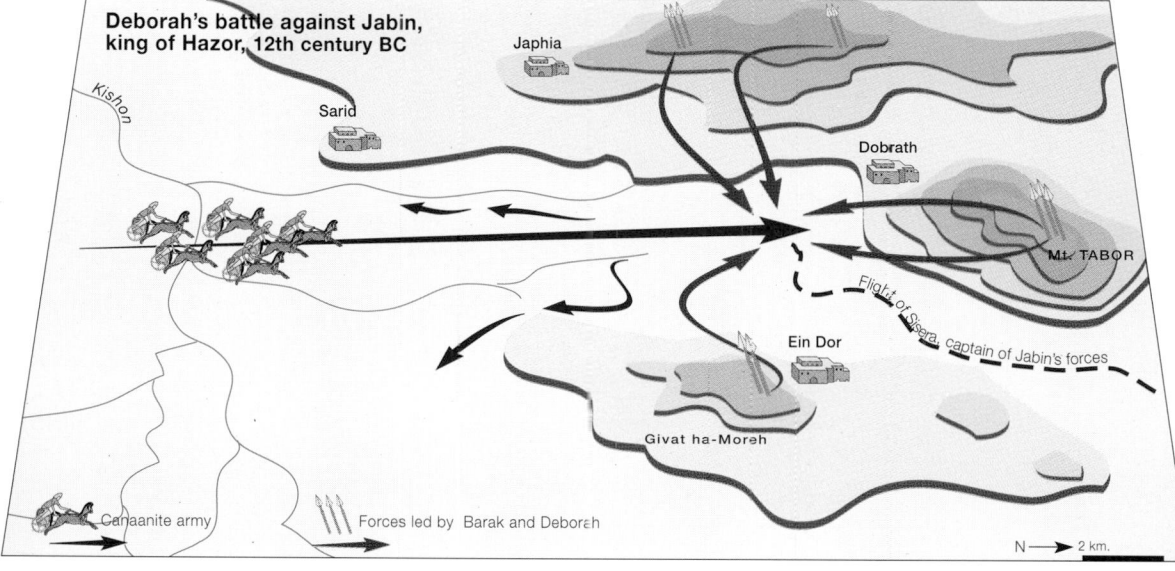

Deborah's battle against Jabin, king of Hazor, 12th century BC

Japhia
Sarid
Kishon
Dobrath
Mt. TABOR
Flight of Sisera, captain of Jabin's forces
Ein Dor
Givat ha-Moreh

Canaanite army          Forces led by Barak and Deborah

N → 2 km.

and the travellers walked through byways.
The inhabitants of the villages ceased,
they ceased in Israel,
until that I Deborah arose,
that I arose a mother of Israel.
They chose new gods;
then was war in the gates: . . .
Awake, awake, Deborah:
awake, awake, utter a song:
arise Barak, and lead thy captivity captive,
thou son of Abinoam.
Then he made him that remaineth
have dominion over the nobles among the people:
the Lord made me have dominion over the mighty . . . .
So let all thine enemies perish, O Lord:
but let them that love him be as the sun
when he goeth forth in his might" (Judges, 5:2-31).
Deborah appears in the narration of events as a national leader, as a "mother in Israel," but it is clear from her song that she had the allegiance only of some of the Israelite tribes

that came together for the purpose of defeating a common enemy. She is the only "judge" whose activities included some judicial functions. Some regard Deborah as the figure of magician or fortune-teller, inciting nomadic warriors to battle by her singing.

**12th–11th centuries BC:** A period of major changes in Israelite society. Archeological excavations and surveys show that agriculture – particularly vine and olive growing – was gradually replacing sheep and cattle raising; small settlements were being deserted while larger communities developed in sites near major routes and water sources. These settlements evolved into fortified towns where inhabitants no longer dwelt in shacks but in spacious private houses. The story of the tribe of Dan, forced to search for a new area of settlement (Judges, 18:1), is perhaps a paradigm for the mobility and migration of the tribes of Israel during the period of the judges.
**1098–1070:** Reign of Ramses XI in Egypt.

For the past two centuries, since Ramses II (1279–1212 BC), the power of the Pharaohs had been declining, while the priests of Amon were gaining strength. Egypt, deteriorating through anarchy, was falling apart: Pa-Nechsi, son of the King of Cush (Nubia), invades No-Amon (Thebes) and rules over southern Egypt for six years. The High Priest Herihor usurps royal titles and imposes a theocracy in No-Amon which is practically independent of Ramses XI's kingdom. The death of Ramses XI ends the days of the twentieth dynasty. Egypt's international position declines; when Herihor sends the priest Wen-Amon to bring cedar wood from Phoenicia, he is treated with contempt by Zacharbaal, King of Byblos.
**1079–1058:** Reign of Adadpladan in Babylon – the first king of Aramean origin. Assyria, at war with Babylon, is also fighting the Aramean kingdoms rising in the northwest; the Bible mentions Aram Beit-Rechob, Aram-Zobah, Aram Beit Maacha, and particularly Aram-Damascus.

# Monotheism

**The Expansion
of Monotheistic
Religions**

### 1000 BC

### 700 AD

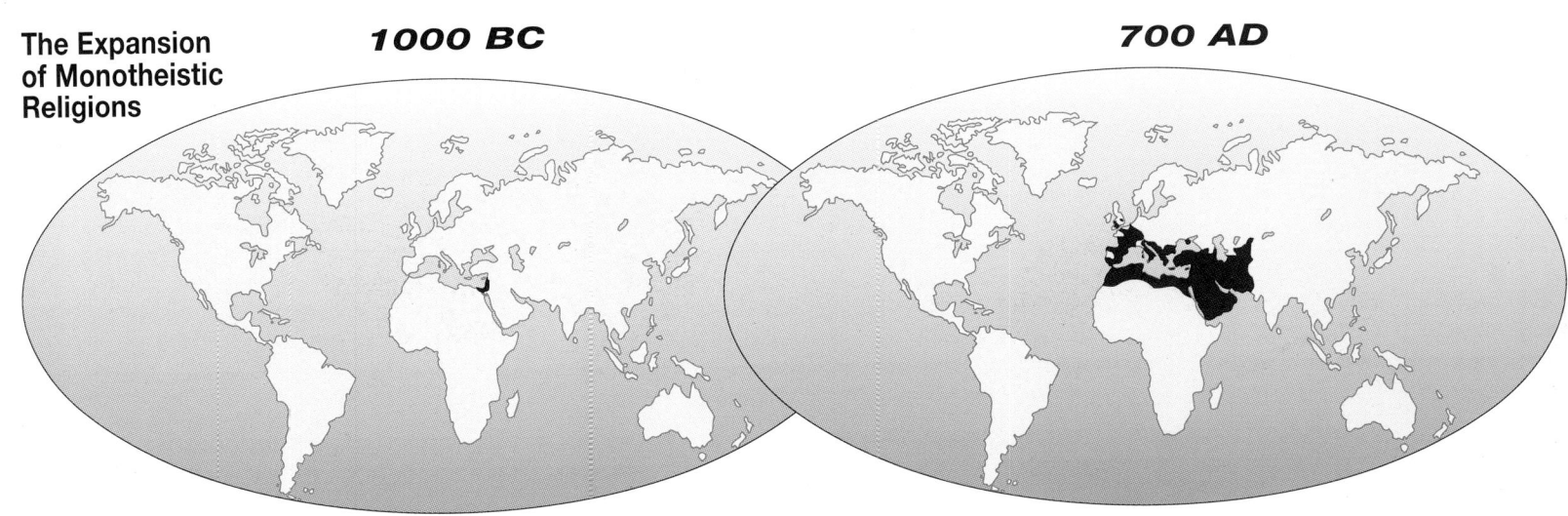

Why, when, and how did the belief in one God emerge? Traditional orthodoxy assumes monotheism to have existed since the beginning of creation, as the religion of Adam and Eve. Polytheism, according to this view, was a later development, a consequence of human corruption or original sin. Abraham had to rediscover monotheistic belief, and Moses was to institutionalize it. This view was still held by the twelfth-century philosopher Maimonides, and was revived in scientific terms by the anthropological school of Wilhelm Schmidt (the Vienna School) which claimed to have found traces of *Urmonotheismus* (original archaic monotheism) among the most primitive of tribes. According to prevalent modern evolutionary theories, however, monotheism is the highest form of religion which developed from primitive beginnings, through demonism and spirit-beliefs, into polytheism (as in the great classical civilizations of Greece and Rome), finally reaching maturity in its monotheistic form. (Some prefer to believe that it was subsequently superseded by a still higher stage, scientific atheism.)

Although undoubtedly a late development, monotheism cannot be seen simply as an inevitable evolutionary stage. Firstly, wherever it appeared, monotheism came as a radical revolution and a violent break with earlier traditions; secondly, this revolution was by no means universal. Furthermore, the transition to believing in one God is not merely a quantitative change (one deity instead of many) but qualitative as well – the single God is *unique* in every respect. The idea of uniqueness led, philosophically, to the notion of transcendence, and on the practical

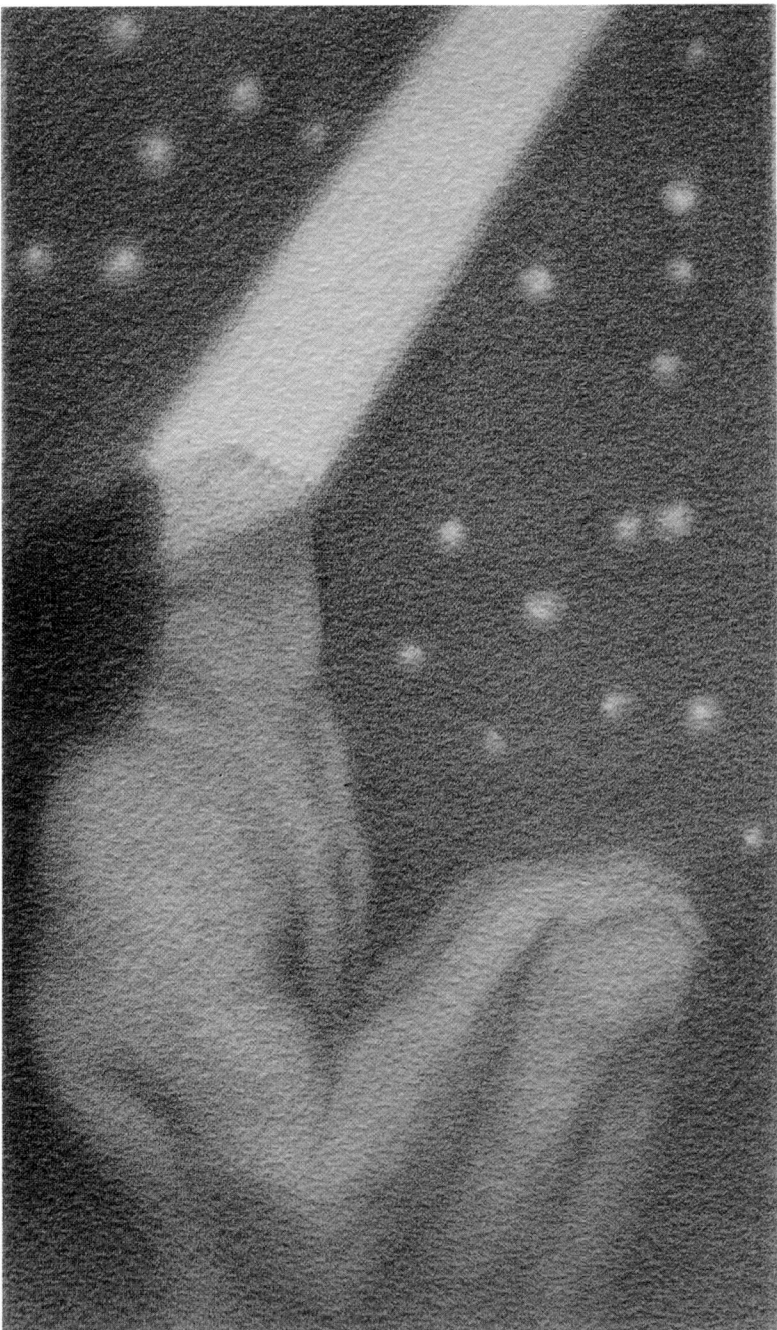

1. Abel Pann (1883–1963), He breathed into his nostrils the breath of life (Genesis, 2:7).

**Abraham**

**Moses**

1800 BC

1300 BC

2. Abraham destroys the idols, from a Passover Haggadah, Amsterdam, 1712.

# 2000 BC–2000 AD

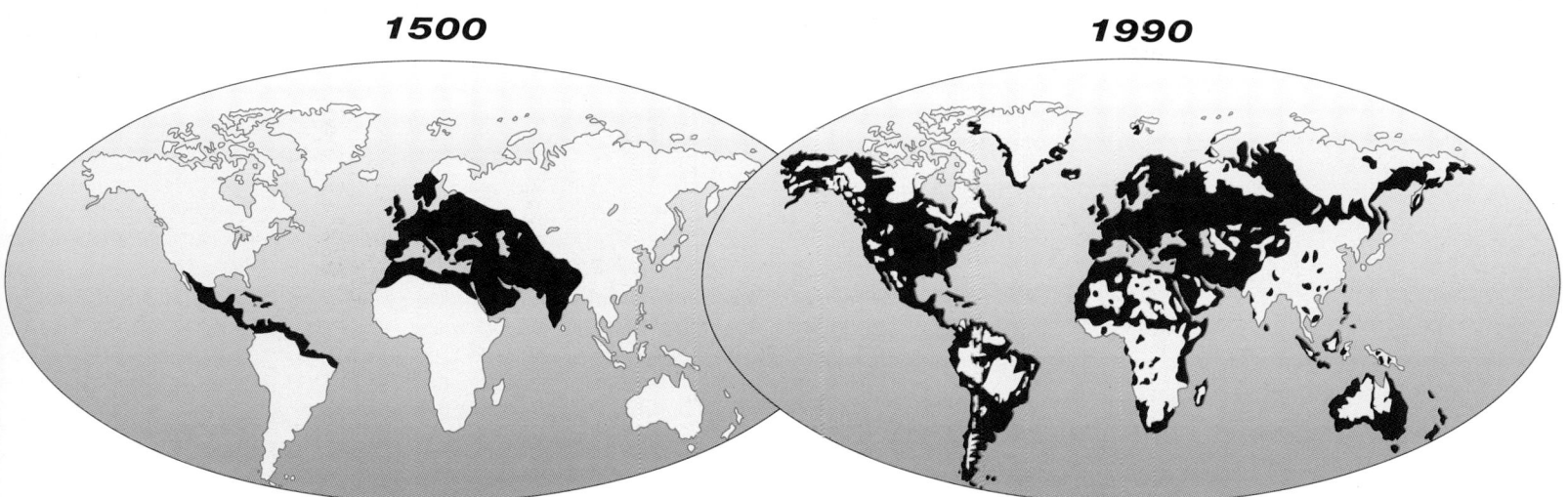

**1500**

**1990**

level, to prohibiting not only the worship of "idols" but also the making of images, as for example in the Third Commandment: "Thou shalt not make thee any graven image, or any likeness of any thing that is in heaven above, or that is in the earth beneath, or that is in the waters beneath the earth" (Deuteronomy 5: 7-8).

This single non-anthropomorphic God is nonetheless conceived of in a "personal" manner, enabling believers to relate to him in love, trust, and devotion, and to pray to him expecting forgiveness, mercy, and other "human" qualities. Indeed, the Scriptures abound with anthropomorphic metaphors for God such as King, Father, Shepherd, Judge, etc. Non-believers regard this personal God as the residue of primitive forms of human projection, while certain radical mystics try to reach out beyond the all-too-human God to a more absolute sphere of being which they call, for lack of a better term, the Divine Non-Being or Nothingness.

Was the religion introduced by the Egyptian pharaoh Akhenaton (Amenhotep IV, fourteenth century BC) monotheism in the strict sense of the word? This question is still being disputed. There are certainly some striking resemblances between his Hymn to Aton and, for instance, Psalm 104, but although Aton was declared the paramount deity of Egypt, other manifestations of the sun were worshiped in their own right.

Biblical monotheism has a long evolutionary history of its own: from "henotheism" (*hen* – Greek for one), that is, the worship of one God without denying the existence of other deities ("Who is like unto thee, O Lord, among the gods?" sang Moses, Exodus, 15:11), to the fully mature "theoretical" monotheism to be found in Psalms and the Prophets. While

some cultures developed an inclusive monotheism which regards the plurality of gods as manifold manifestations of the Ultimate, the biblical God is exclusive, tolerating no rival deity.

The monotheistic revolution of the Bible proved to be of momentous significance for it was destined to conquer, through Christianity and Islam, the greater part of the globe. In the Middle Ages, however, Jewish and Muslim theologians tended to disqualify Christianity from the family of monotheistic religions because it adhered to "idolatrous" beliefs and rituals such as the Trinity, the divinity of Jesus, the sacrament of the Eucharist, and the adoration of saints and relics.

All monotheistic religions contend with certain perennial philosophical and theological problems. Some of the most difficult dilemmas are anthropomorphism (how to avoid an overly human conception of a transcendental God), free will (how to reconcile an omnipotent and all-knowing God with man's responsibility for his actions), and theodicy (how to reconcile the existence of evil in the world with the God of mercy and justice). The last question became painfully acute for contemporary Judaism with the experience of the Holocaust.

Jewish monotheism is not only an intellectual doctrine but, above all, a daily practice. God the Creator and Lord of the universe is first and foremost He who made an eternal covenant with his chosen people and gave them the *Torah* – precepts for behavior in this world in obedience to the Lord. This dimension is best expressed in the verse (Deuteronomy, 6:4) which became the symbol of the Jewish faith: "Hear O Israel! the Lord is our God, the Lord is one."

| Isaiah | | Jesus | Muhammad |
|---|---|---|---|
| **700 BC** | | **30** | **622** |

### AKHENATON'S HYMN TO ATON

You appear in splendor on the horizon,
you, living Aton, glorified by life.
You rise in the Orient,
and all the land fills with brilliance.
You are beautiful and great
shining high above the earth.
Your rays embrace all lands,
to the ends of the universe.
You Re, you have vanquished them, and
conquered them for your beloved son
[Akhenaton].
You go down in the West,
the earth dies in darkness.
Lying down in their beds,
their heads covered,
no eye beholding another.
All their goods taken from under them,
and they are ignorant.
The lions emerge from their dens,
all reptiles will bite.
Night, and the earth is silent,
for its creator died in his horizon.

### PSALM 104

Who coverest thyself with light as with a garment; who stretchest out the heavens like a curtain . . . .
He appointed the moon for seasons,
the sun knoweth his going down.
Thou makest darkness, and it is night;
wherein all the beasts of the forest do creep forth.
The young lions roar after their prey,
and seek their meat from God.
The sun ariseth,
they . . . lay them down in their dens.
Man goeth forth unto his work
and to his labor until the evening. . . .
These wait all upon thee; that thou mayest give them their meat in due season.
That thou givest them they gather; thou openest thine hand, they are filled with good.
Thou hidest thy face, they are troubled; thou takest away their breath, they die . . . .
Thou sendest forth thy spirit, they are created . . . .

3. "Aaron cast down his rod before Pharaoh . . . and it became a serpent" (Exodus, 7:10). Ispahan, late 18th century.

# The Beginnings of the Monarchy: Saul and David

*1. The Ark of the Covenant destroyed the god Dagon; frightened, the Philistines send it back to the Israelites. A mural painting, Dura-Europos, c. 245.*

"In those days there was no king in Israel and every man did what was right in his own eyes" – this concluding verse of the Book of Judges laments the anarchy and the moral disintegration of the tribes of Israel, torn by fratricidal wars. The editor was expressing a clear political message: despite the obvious inadequacies of a monarchy, the people of Israel needed a king. Then the Book of Samuel follows as a veritable essay on monarchy, discussing at length the virtues and evils of kingship.

Samuel was apparently the last of the Judges. Like Deborah before him, he figures as a prophet, a man of God, fulfilling the role of judge in addition to his spiritual and sacramental functions. But while Deborah had been active within a tribal society, Samuel attained the position of head of all the tribes, a kind of national leader. Thus, it was to him that the people appealed: "Appoint us a king to govern us, like other nations" (1 Samuel, 8:5). The need for a centralized monarchy had plainly become acute: not only were the tribes worn out by the constant wars with neighboring peoples, but they had also suffered a major defeat at the hand of the Philistines who were relentlessly penetrating inland.

The first king, Saul, came from the tribe of Benjamin, which was known for its excellent warriors and was conveniently situated between the southern tribes led by Judah, and the northern tribes headed by Ephraim. Saul's achievements as king fulfilled all expectations. He de-feated the Ammonites in the Gilead, the Moabites, the Amalekites, the Arameans, the Edomites, and, above all, he checked the advance of the Philistines. However, the place where he was killed in battle with the Philistines, on Mount Gilboa in the Jezreel Valley, indicates that despite his victories he did not entirely succeed in driving them back to the coastal plain. And his relations with Samuel remained tense, reflecting the difficult transition from the old regime of the charismatic Judges to the new monarchical rule. Having failed several times to comply with God's orders, delivered by Samuel, the rift between Saul and the prophet became irreconcilable. Finally, the prophet informed the king that God had rejected him. Someone else was thus destined to establish the first royal dynasty in Israel – David of Bethlehem, of the tribe of Judah.

The Bible offers several accounts of David's ascent to the throne. The David of the Book of Samuel – a brave handsome youth, Goliath's slayer, captain in the king's army, skillful at playing sweet music to the old king, who maintained a deep friendship with Jonathan, and married the king's daughter, Michal – fed the imagination of future generations and is typical of popular epics. The long centuries during which the people of Israel were ruled by the House of David most likely embellished these stories with heroic touches. Nonetheless, the general outlines of David's career as King of Israel can be drawn quite accurately.

Civil war broke out after the death of Saul. David ruled over the powerful tribe of Judah, while Saul's son, Ish-Bosheth, headed the other tribes. Seven years of struggle ended when Ish-Bosheth was murdered, and David was called upon by the people to save them from the Philistines.

The new king completed the work of his predecessor. In the northeast, he defeated the Arameans and annexed Aram-Damascus; in the east he routed the Moabites, subjugated the state of Edom, and inflicted defeat upon the Ammonites. Some of these lands (Edom and Damascus, for example) were reduced to provinces governed by his commissioners; others were left as vassal states. Finally, in order to secure his northern border, he made a pact with Hiram, King of Tyre. His successes were achieved by military power as well as by diplomatic prowess. Exploiting the vacuum created by the weakness of Egypt and Assyria, and the fact that the Aramean kingdoms were only beginning to consolidate, he established a well-organized Israelite kingdom which became the strongest empire in the western region of the Fertile Crescent.

His most enduring and significant achievements, however, took place within the borders of Canaan: he struck hard at the Philistines and systematically abolished all Canaanite enclaves. With the conquest of Jerusalem from the Jebusites, on the border between the tribes of the south and those of the center and the north, David created a capital for his kingdom and a spiritual center for the entire nation of Israel – a revolution which would influence thousands of years of Jewish history.

| Saul, first king of Israel | David rules over the tribe of Judah | The Conquest of Jerusalem |
|---|---|---|
| c. 1029 BC | c. 1007 BC | c. 1000 BC |

**Second half of 11th century BC:** Philistine expansion from the coastal plain into the interior. Following their victory in Eben Ezzer, when they captured the Ark of the Covenant and destroyed the temple in the capital Shiloh, the Philistines appoint commissioners to govern over Israel in the hills of Ephraim, forbidding metal-forging in order to prevent the production of weapons by the Israelites.

**c. 1029–1007 BC:** Saul, first king of Israel, conducts many wars against the Philistines, exhausting their power and slowing down their advance. His victories over the Ammonites in Gilead, the Moabites, Amalekites, Arameans, and Edomites, determine the boundaries of the kingdom of Israel. But, victorious abroad, the king faces serious problems within the land: his relations with the Prophet Samuel deteriorate, a fact which tarnishes his image among the people; furthermore, in a single combat against Goliath, a Philistine giant, young David wins glory and popularity, as well as the friendship of Saul's son,

Jonathan; these personal rivalries seriously endanger the young monarchy of King Saul.

**c. 1007 BC:** King Saul and three of his sons, including Jonathan, are killed in battle against the Philistines. David, son of Jesse from Bethlehem, rules in Hebron over the tribe of Judah, while Saul's son, Ish-Bosheth, leads the tribes of Benjamin and Ephraim. David's lamentation: "The beauty of Israel is slain upon thy high places: how are the mighty fallen! . . . Saul and Jonathan were lovely and pleasant in their lives, and in their death they were not divided: they were swifter than eagles, they were stronger than lions. Ye daughters of Israel, weep over Saul, who clothed you in scarlet, with other delights, who put on ornaments of gold upon your apparel. How are the mighty fallen in the midst of the battle! O Jonathan, thou wast slain in thine high places. I am distressed for thee, my brother Jonathan: very pleasant hast thou been unto me:

*2. Excavations in David's City in Jerusalem.*

# 1050–970 BC

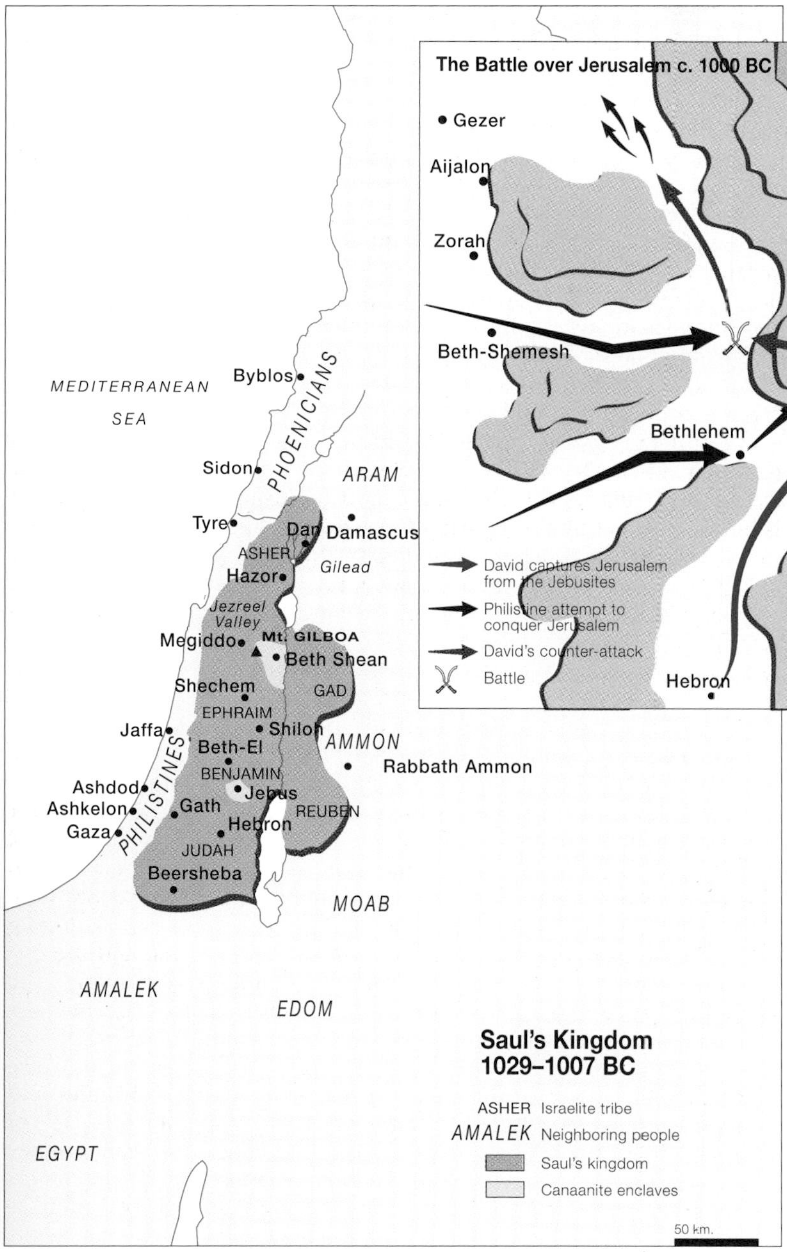

### The Battle over Jerusalem c. 1000 BC

• Gezer

Aijalon

Zorah

Beth-Shemesh

Bethlehem

Jebus (Jerusalem)

Hebron

→ David captures Jerusalem from the Jebusites
→ Philistine attempt to conquer Jerusalem
→ David's counter-attack
⚔ Battle

5 km.

N

---

**Saul's Kingdom map (left):**

MEDITERRANEAN SEA

Byblos
PHOENICIANS
ARAM
Sidon
Tyre
Dan  Damascus
ASHER
Hazor
Gilead
Jezreel Valley
Megiddo  Mt. GILBOA
Beth Shean
Shechem  GAD
EPHRAIM
Jaffa  Shiloh
Beth-El  AMMON
BENJAMIN  Rabbath Ammon
Ashdod  Jebus
Ashkelon  Gath  Hebron  REUBEN
Gaza  JUDAH
Beersheba
PHILISTINES
AMALEK  EDOM
MOAB
EGYPT

**Saul's Kingdom 1029–1007 BC**

ASHER Israelite tribe
AMALEK Neighboring people
▨ Saul's kingdom
▨ Canaanite enclaves

50 km.

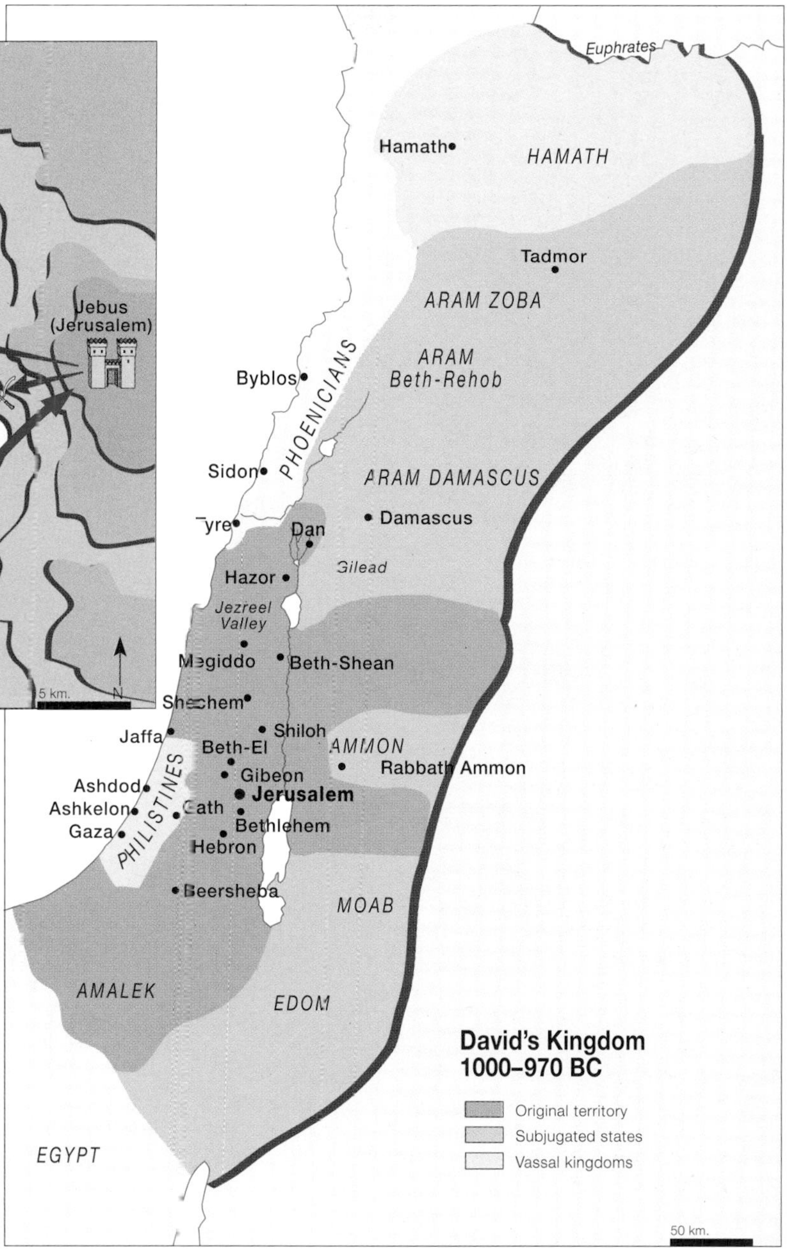

---

**David's Kingdom map (right):**

Euphrates
Hamath  HAMATH
Tadmor
ARAM ZOBA
ARAM Beth-Rehob
Byblos
PHOENICIANS
Sidon
ARAM DAMASCUS
Tyre  Dan  • Damascus
Hazor
Gilead
Jezreel Valley
Megiddo  Beth-Shean
Shechem
Jaffa  Shiloh
Beth-El  AMMON
Ashdod  Gibeon  Rabbath Ammon
Ashkelon  Gath  **Jerusalem**
Gaza  Bethlehem
Hebron
Beersheba
PHILISTINES
AMALEK  MOAB
EDOM
EGYPT

**David's Kingdom 1000–970 BC**

▨ Original territory
▨ Subjugated states
▨ Vassal kingdoms

50 km.

---

| Beginning of Solomon's reign | Death of David |
|---|---|
| c. 970 BC | c. 967 BC |

---

thy love to me was wonderful,
passing the love of women.
How are the mighty fallen, and the
weapons of war perished!"
(2 Samuel 1:19-27).
**c. 1000 BC:** David is elected king of all the tribes of Israel. During his 40-year reign he extends the borders of his kingdom and consolidates the nation around Jerusalem as the capital and religious center.
1000 BC is also the estimated date of the inscription of Ethbaal, King of Byblos, found and published in 1924: "This sarcophagus was built for Ethbaal son of Ahiram King of Gval for Ahiram his father, for he had left this world. And if a king among kings, or a leader among leaders, were to besiege Gval and take away this sarcophagus, may the scepter of his dynasty be broken, and the throne of his kingdom overthrown . . . ." The scores of inscriptions from Tyre and Sidon, discovered by 20th-century archeologists, are all written in the alphabet common to all Canaanite peoples, including Israel. (It was

from the Phoenicians that the Greeks inherited the alphabet and later spread it throughout the Mediterranean world.) Most of these inscriptions, including the one of Ethbaal, appear on sarcophaguses (stone burial-coffins); they contain a wealth of information about the kings of Tyre and Sidon and about the social and cultural customs of the Phoenicians and their relations with neighboring peoples.
**c. 967 BC:** King David dies. The last years of his reign are troubled by several rebellions. Absalom, David's favorite son, revolts and appoints himself king, but the story ends with the total defeat of the rebels and the tragic death of Absalom. Sheba ben Bichri, from the tribe of Benjamin, incites the northern tribes to rebel against David and to secede from his kingdom, but the rebels are crushed and Sheba ben Bichri is killed.

*3. "King Saul with his men of war and David with Goliath the Philistine." Naïve painting, oil on glass, Jerusalem, 20th century.*

# The Kingdom of Solomon

*1. Solomon and Hiram, by the American painter, Jack Levine. Oil, 1940.*

Now the principal claimants were David's two other sons: Adonijah, son of Haggith, and Solomon, son of Bath-Sheba. Adonijah, supported by the old establishment – the army commander, Joab son of Zeruiah, and the priest Abiathar – tried to have himself anointed in his father's lifetime. However, Bath-Sheba frustrated the attempt with the aid of the prophet Nathan and several army officers headed by Benaiah son of Jehoiadah, and she persuaded David to proclaim Solomon his rightful heir.

After David's death (c. 967 BC), Solomon began to strike out at his opponents. Some were executed (Adonijah, Joab); others were banished from Jerusalem (Abiathar). The key positions in the kingdom were handed to his loyal servants – Benaiah was made commander of the army, and Zadok was installed as high priest to the Lord (and destined to become the forefather of an illustrious line of high priests).

Solomon's iron hand soon convinced potential rebels that there was no hope of undermining his absolute rule over all the tribes. Indeed, the internal stability attained by Solomon ensured his dynasty four centuries of rule in Jerusalem. The brilliance of his reign gave birth to the mythic tradition that the House of David ruled by divine will, a tradition which became an integral part of Jewish messianic expectations (and of Christianity as well, since Jesus was accorded a Davidic pedigree). The transition from the portable Tabernacle, associated with the wanderings of Israel in the desert, to the splendid Temple built by Solomon in Jerusalem, enhanced the sanctity of the city and made it the undisputed capital of the monarchy.

The construction of the Temple was only one of Solomon's great building enterprises. He built fortified towns – Megiddo, Hazor, Gezer, Beth-Horon – as well as store-cities and garrison-towns for his cavalry, together with impressive water conduits which allowed the cities to withstand sieges. In fact, it was Solomon rather than David who built a kingdom which conformed with the international standards of those days – a truly centralized and organized monarchy. The realm was divided into twelve districts, each regularly paying tribute. The tribe of Judah was apparently exempted from this tax, thus allowing Solomon to strengthen his hold over his own tribe. However, this also deepened the tension between Judah and the other tribes, a tension which would erupt after Solomon's death, during the reign of his son Rehoboam.

King Solomon's reign also enjoyed the fruits of his commercial and political ties with neighboring lands. He entered into an alliance with Hiram, King of Tyre, who provided him with cedar wood for building the Temple, and with the Egyptian pharaoh (presumably Siamun of the twenty-first dynasty), who gave his daughter as wife to Solomon, and the town of Gezer as part of her dowry. Matrimonial alliances with foreign royal families, together with political treaties and commercial relations, bestowed on Jerusalem an international importance, evidenced by the

**D**avid's old age was not a happy time. As his authority declined, his sons and ministers began fighting over who his successor would be. Several revolts threatened the throne; the most dangerous, and most tragic, was the one headed by Absalom, David's favorite son. Fearing that he would not be appointed heir to the throne, Absalom killed his brother Amnon and raised the banner of revolt. His insurrection was crushed, but the struggle continued.

| Beginning of Solomon's reign | Hiram ascends to the throne in Tyre | David's Death |
|---|---|---|
| 970 BC | 969 BC | 967 BC |

**12th–11th centuries BC:** The alleged period (still disputed) of the composition of an Egyptian book of proverbs, published by the British scholar Sir Wallis Budge in 1923. Whole passages from this book appear almost verbatim in a Hebrew translation in the biblical Book of Proverbs (22:17-24:22), testimony to the close cultural ties between Israel and Egypt in the days of Solomon.
**970 BC:** Beginning of Solomon's reign (in David's lifetime).
**967 BC:** David's death. Solomon destroys all his opponents: he executes Adonijah, his rival for the throne; Joab ben Zeruiah, the army commander; and Shimei, son of Gera, one of the leaders of the tribe of Benjamin (the last two, upon David's express orders). The priest Abiathar is banished to Anathoth (Jeremiah's birthplace 300 years later).
**c. 965 BC:** Solomon begins building the Temple in Jerusalem. The early chapters of 1 Kings describe the kingdom at the height of Solomon's reign: "Judah and Israel were many, as the sand which is by the sea, in

multitude, eating and drinking, and making merry. And Solomon reigned over all kingdoms from the river [the Euphrates] unto the land of the Philistines, and unto the border of Egypt: they brought presents, and served Solomon all the days of his life. . . For he had dominion over all the region on this side of the river, from Tiphsah even to Azzah, over all kings on this side over the river: and he had peace on all sides round about him. And Judah and Israel dwelt safely, every man under his vine and under his fig-tree, from Dan even to Beer-Sheba, all the days of Solomon. . . And Solomon's wisdom excelled the wisdom of all the children of the east country, and all the wisdom of Egypt. . . and his fame was in all nations round about" (4:20-31).
**969–936 BC:** Reign of Hiram, son of Abibaal, in Tyre. Hiram enlarges the island of Tyre by uniting it with a smaller island, rebuilds the temples of the gods of Melqart and Astarte, and develops Tyrian shipping. Tyrian ships are already sailing as far as

*2. A gateway, Hazor, 10th century BC.*

Spain. Solomon's alliance with Hiram helped the growth of Israelite shipping. The Bible describes this maritime cooperation in full detail: "King Solomon built a fleet of ships at Ezion-Geber, near Eloth on the shore of the Red Sea, in Edom. Hiram sent men of his own to serve with the fleet, experienced seamen, to work with Solomon's men; and they went to Ophir [in Arabia or east Africa] and brought back four hundred and twenty talents of gold, which they delivered to King Solomon" (1 Kings, 9:26-28).
**960–945 BC:** Reign of Pharaoh Siamun in Egypt. A fragment of a stele (an engraved slab) found in the town of Zoan (Tanis) shows Siamun defeating an enemy from the Sea Peoples – probably testimony to his war against the Philistines. In this campaign Siamun conquered Gezer (near modern Ramleh), which he later presented to his daughter and Solomon on the occasion of their marriage.
**c. 950:** Date of the writing of the Gezer Calendar. In 1908 the archeologist R.A.S.

## Solomon's Kingdom, 970-928 BC

➤ International trade
▬ Major route
⬛ Fortified town
⬛ Solomonian site

HITTITES

Tiphsah

*horses*

HAMATH

Hamath

Aradus

Simirra

PHOENICIA

Byblos

Kadesh

ARAM ZOBA

Tadmor (Palmyra)

*cedar, cypress*

Sidon

**Tyre**

ARAM DAMASCUS

Dor

Megiddo

Dan

Damascus

Tell Qasila

Jaffa

Hazor

Ashkelon

Gaza

Horon

Gezer

*wine, oil, wheat*

Beth-Shemesh

**Jerusalem**

Rabbath Ammon

*chariots*

Beersheba

Arad

MOAB

Kadesh Barnea

Adar

EGYPT

EDOM

Yotvatah

*timber, exotic animals, gold, ivory, precious stones*

Ezion-Geber

ARAB TRIBES

N

### Phoenician trade routes, 10th-8th centuries BC

CELTS

IBERIANS

ETRUSCANS

ILLYRIANS

THRACIANS

LYDIANS

Gades

Tharros

Tingi

Lixus

Motya

CRETE

Kition

NUMIDIAN TRIBES

Carthage

Hadrumetum

Tyre

Leptis Magna

Pelusium

Jerusalem

EGYPT

Ezion-Geber

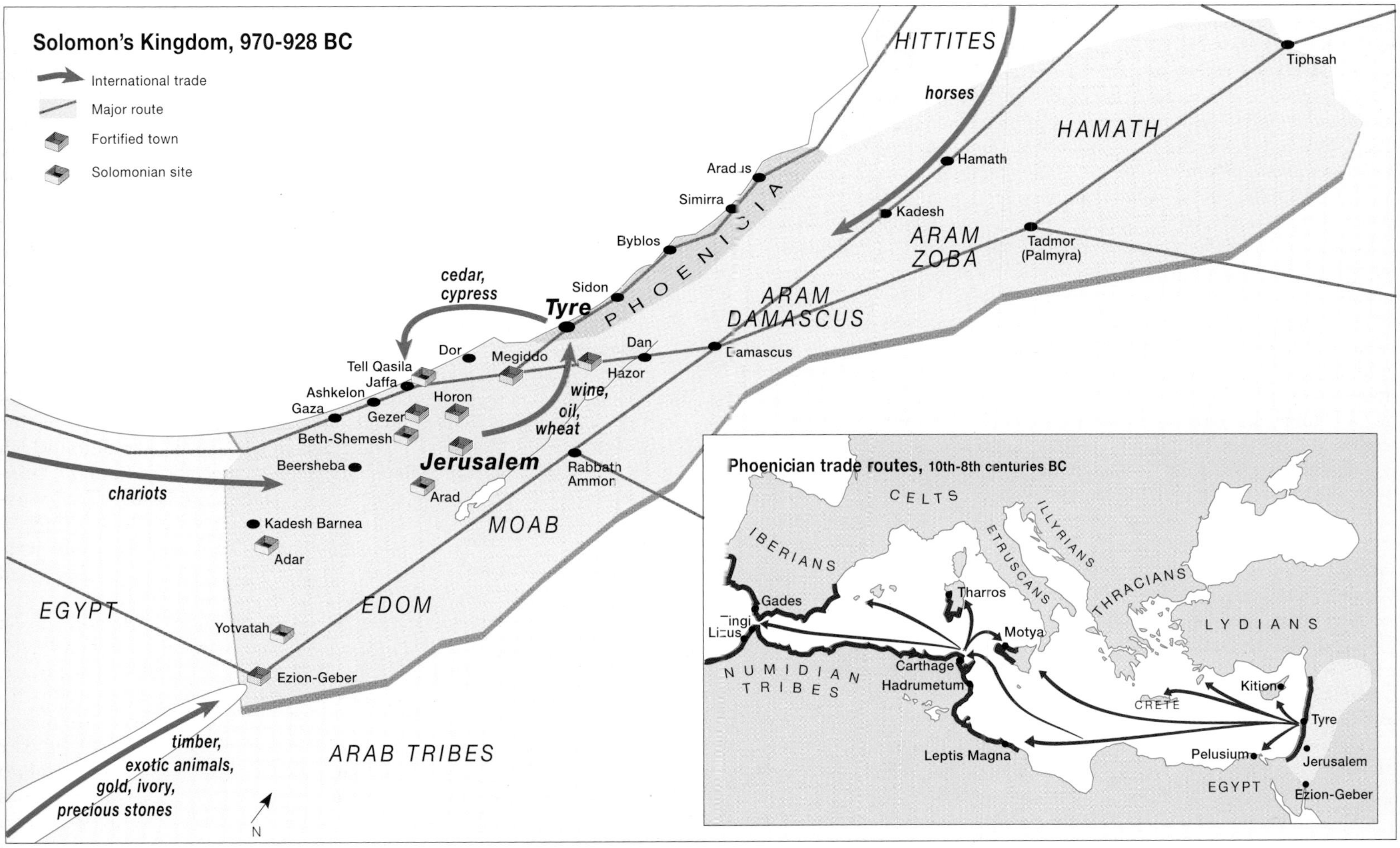

famous visit of the Queen of Sheba (1 Kings, 10). The king also acquired a reputation of sound judgement and great wisdom. It is therefore not surprising that later generations attributed the biblical wisdom books (Proverbs and Ecclesiastes) to Solomon the Wise.

After centuries of endless warring, the people of Israel finally found peace: "Judah and Israel continued at peace, every man under his own vine and fig-tree" (1 Kings, 5:7). But Israelite society paid dearly for this peace. Solomon's enormous projects imposed a heavy yoke on his sub-

jects. In addition to taxes paid in cash and in kind, tens of thousands of men were recruited into forced labor.

Towards the end of Solomon's reign, internal tensions intensified. At the same time the international standing of the kingdom began to decline. Edom tried to revolt in the east; and Egypt – Solomon's former ally – began to give shelter to his enemies. As long as the king lived, unity was maintained; but the seeds of the kingdom division were already sown in the days of Solomon – the greatest king of ancient Israel.

| Beginning of Siamun's reign in Egypt | The Gezer Calendar | Solomon's Death |
|---|---|---|
| 960 BC | c. 950 BC | 928 BC |

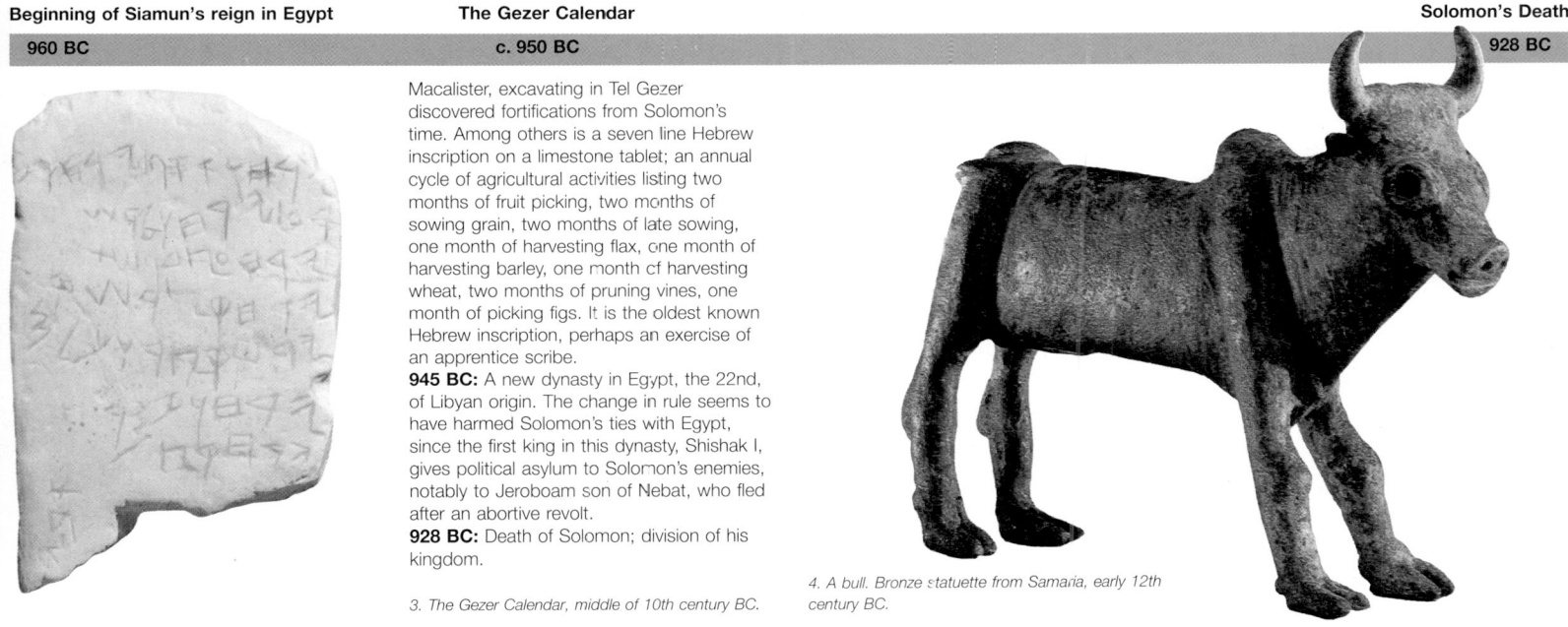

Macalister, excavating in Tel Gezer discovered fortifications from Solomon's time. Among others is a seven line Hebrew inscription on a limestone tablet; an annual cycle of agricultural activities listing two months of fruit picking, two months of sowing grain, two months of late sowing, one month of harvesting flax, one month of harvesting barley, one month of harvesting wheat, two months of pruning vines, one month of picking figs. It is the oldest known Hebrew inscription, perhaps an exercise of an apprentice scribe.

**945 BC:** A new dynasty in Egypt, the 22nd, of Libyan origin. The change in rule seems to have harmed Solomon's ties with Egypt, since the first king in this dynasty, Shishak I, gives political asylum to Solomon's enemies, notably to Jeroboam son of Nebat, who fled after an abortive revolt.

**928 BC:** Death of Solomon; division of his kingdom.

*3. The Gezer Calendar, middle of 10th century BC.*

*4. A bull. Bronze statuette from Samaria, early 12th century BC.*

# Literature of the First Temple Period

Israelite culture of the First Temple period constitutes the foundation of Jewish civilization throughout its history. Its prophetic literature – which became a source of inspiration to many other cultures – and many other major works of law, sacred and profane prose, poetry, historiography, and philosophy, were composed in those days. The extensive literary production of ancient Israel has only survived in part, mostly in the corpus of the scriptures which were canonized, that is, the Bible or the "Old Testament."

Biblical law is presented in the Pentateuch as the Word of God spoken to Moses on Mount Sinai and revealed to the people of Israel during their wanderings in the desert. The belief in the divine origin of the Torah made it the sole constitutional basis for Jewish Law (*Halakhah*) at all times. The scientific approach, of course, regards the Torah as an historical document which requires analysis of content and language as well as comparison with other contemporary sources in order to determine its origins. In his famous *Tractatus Theologico-Politicus*, Baruch Spinoza claimed as early as 1670 that it was Ezra rather than Moses who composed the Pentateuch. It was the German scholar, however, Julius Wellhausen, in his work *Prolegomena to the History of Ancient Israel* (1878), who established an entire school of Biblical criticism. Its main argument was that the Torah had not been composed all at once but was a compilation of several texts, the earliest dating from the ninth century BC and the latest from the fifth century BC, that is, from about one hundred years after the destruction of the First Temple. Although some of the arguments of this school have been refuted by modern research, its basic approach is still accepted at least on two essential points: first, that the Torah could not have been composed all at once since it contains contradictions and repetitions which indicate legislation introduced at different periods; second, that none of the legal texts in the Pentateuch could have been composed before the establishment of the monarchy. It is therefore legitimate to regard the law of the Torah as one of the greatest achievements of the First Temple period.

Many of the laws of the Torah are similar in content as well as in style to ancient Mesopotamian constitutions, yet the resemblance in details should not detract from the uniqueness of the Hebrew law. Being of divine origin, its edicts are absolute, eternal, immutable, and universal in the sense that they apply to every member of the nation of Israel, subject and king alike. Also, it is a law given unto a people, not to a state, and thus pertinent in all historical circumstances, whether political independence, occupation, or exile. Judaism is therefore a national religion. Furthermore, the Torah, more than any other ancient constitution, insists on the connection between civil and religious law, between man's duties toward his neighbor and his obligations to God. Finally, the law of the Torah attaches great importance to values such as social justice, the sanctity of human life, and equality of all people, Hebrew and gentile, before the law. All these characteristics are concisely expressed in the Ten Commandments – a unique pronouncement of the principles of monotheistic law, the fountainhead for all other laws and constitutions.

Another cultural achievement of the First Temple period was the creation of Hebrew historiography, mainly contained in the books of the former prophets: Joshua, Judges, Samuel, and Kings. Its underlying assumption is that history knows no chance – all events are part of a divine plan. The fate of Israel, according to these chroniclers, was always determined by the covenant between God and his people. As long as the Hebrews remembered their obligations, peace and prosperity were ensured; when they sinned, they were punished by destruction and exile. History is thus perceived not as a random collection of events but as a process governed by laws. Furthermore, it is a process directed towards a

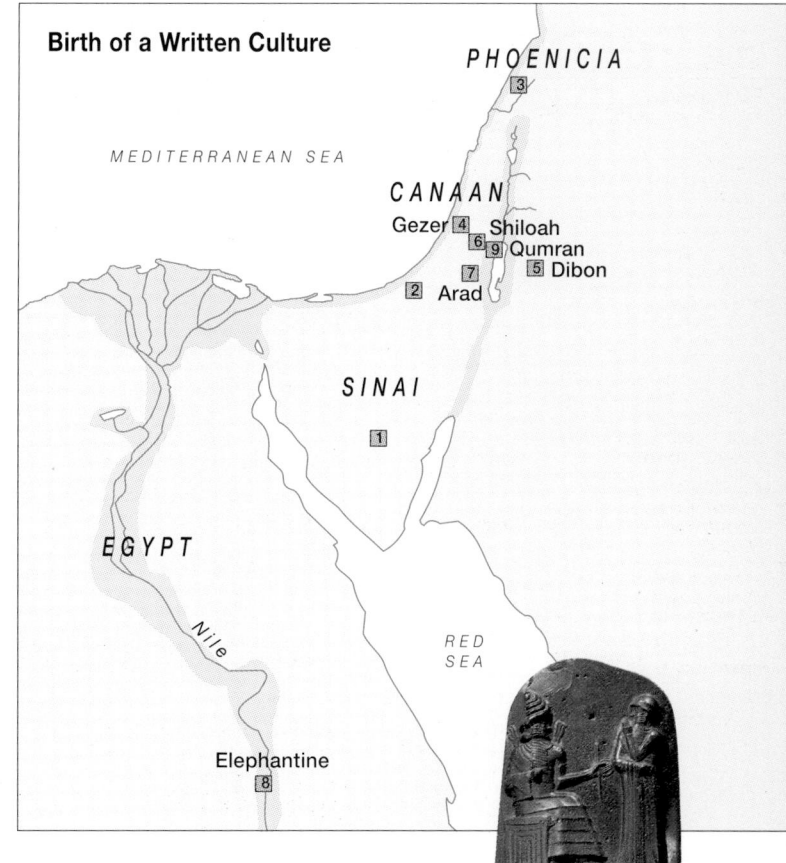

**Birth of a Written Culture**

PHOENICIA
MEDITERRANEAN SEA
CANAAN
Gezer
Shiloah
Qumran
Dibon
Arad
SINAI
EGYPT
Nile
RED SEA
Elephantine

**Hammurabi**

**18th century BC**

**Moses**

**13th century BC**

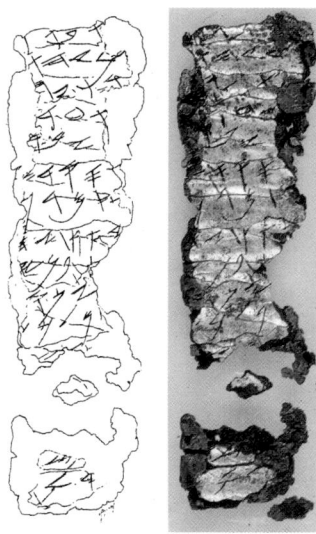

**20th century BC:** The Code of Lipit Ishtar, King of Isin – a city-state in Mesopotamia, northeast of Babylon.

**19th century BC:** The Code of the city-state of Eshnunna, southeast of Babylon.

**18th century BC:** The Code of Hammurabi, King of Babylon c. 1792–1750 BC. The laws are engraved on a pillar found at Susa in 1901. Framed in a hymnic prologue that catalogues his conquests and an epilogue that stresses his concern for justice, Hammurabi's laws are partly based on older Sumerian and Akkadian codes. They contain 282 articles classified by subjects: property, commerce, family, etc. Among them is the principle of proportional punishment, an idea later expressed in Exodus as "an eye for an eye, a tooth for a tooth." This code is thus regarded as the starting point for the

understanding of all Near Eastern legal ideals. Many of its individual formulations are paralleled by the legislation of Exodus and Deuteronomy.

**c. 900–800 BC:** First codification of the most ancient laws of the Torah; mostly concentrated in Exodus (chs.21-23), these laws concern slavery (for example, the obligation to free a Hebrew slave in the seventh year), homicide and assault, seduction, injury to property, the obligations of borrowers, as well as religious-moral admonitions and a cultic calendar.

**c. 850 BC:** The Greeks adopt the alphabetic script, a development of the Phoenician-Canaanite (=Hebrew) script, enabling them to transcribe orally transmitted traditions. This is also the assumed date for the birth of Homer, the great Greek epic writer, on the banks of the River Meles in Ionia (Turkey).

**8th century BC:** Prophecies of Amos,

*1. "The Blessing of the Priests" (Numbers 6:24-26; Psalm 67), the most ancient biblical document found to date. Plate of silver, Jerusalem, 7th century BC.*

*2. The Code of Hammurabi. Stele from the 18th century BC.*

# 13th–6th Centuries BC

goal – a period of eternal bliss at the End of Days. These two ideas – the laws of history and the eschatological vision – constitute the basis of western historical thought.

The books of the Pentateuch and the former prophets contain many short stories about the principal protagonists – patriarchs, kings, prophets, and others. Based on orally transmitted tales and transcribed in prose during the First Temple period, these stories constitute a unique genre revealing astounding literary maturity. Concise and economical, omitting descriptions of landscape and physical appearance, using sophisticated techniques for expressing psychological conflicts, the biblical tales are dramatic and gripping. The omniscient narrator often hints at the inevitable consequences of the unfolding events, for in all cases it is always God who manipulates the major developments, leaving man only with the choice between good and evil.

In addition to prose, the men and women of ancient Israel expressed themselves in other literary forms. The Bible contains several kinds of poetry: victory epics, songs of prophecy, and hymns of praise to God – the latter mostly in Psalms. The Book of Proverbs is an instance of the genre of wisdom literature – adages formulating the laws of nature, human relations, man's discourse with God. The Book of Job, on the other hand, is in a class of its own. Often described as a book of wisdom, it consists of a narrative prose framework and poetic disputation; and its message remains enigmatic to this day. Foreign influences are discernible in all these genres – usually Ugaritic on the poetry and Egyptian on the wisdom literature. On the whole, however, the literary creation of Israel during the First Temple period was richer and more mature than that of its neighbors. These singular qualities helped it survive and outlive all its sources of influence.

**Development of the alphabet** (read right to left; beginning with Aleph on the right)

|  |  |
|---|--------|
| 1 | Proto-Canaanite, Sarabit al-Khadim, Sinai 1500 BC. |
| 2 | Proto-Canaanite, 13th–12th centuries BC. |
| 3 | Phoenician, Hiram's sarcophagus, 1000 BC. |
| 4 | Hebrew, Gezer Calendar, late 10th century BC. |
| 5 | Hebrew, Mesha Stele, mid-9th century BC. |
| 6 | Hebrew, Shiloah Inscription, late 7th century BC. |
| 7 | Hebrew, ostraca, Arad (Palestine), early 6th century BC. |
| 8 | Aramean, Elephantine papyri, late 5th century BC. |
| 9 | Hebrew, square characters, Isaiah's Scroll, 2nd century BC. |
| | Hebrew, modern square characters: ת ש ר ק צ פ ע ס נ מ ל כ י ט ח ז ו ה ד ג ב א |
| | Greek, classic characters: Τ Σ Ρ Π Ο Ξ Ν Μ Λ Κ Ι Θ Η Ζ Ε Δ Γ Β Α |
| | Latin: T S R Q P O X N M L K I H Z F E D C B A |

| Homer | Isaiah | Zoroaster | Solon |
|-------|--------|-----------|-------|
| 9th century BC | 8th century BC | 7th century BC | 6th century BC |

Hosea, Isaiah, and Micah.

**7th century BC:** Prophecies of Jeremiah, Zephaniah, Habakkuk, and Nahum.

**680–669 BC:** The reign of Esarhaddon, King of Assyria. Several copies of his alliance treaties with vassal kings survived, all following the same formula: an historical introduction, followed by the conditions of the treaty, and ending with maledictions upon he who violates the agreement. Esarhaddon's treaties are very similar in structure and style to the Book of Deuteronomy.

**621 BC:** The Grand Priest Hilkiah finds the "Book of the Torah" in the Temple in Jerusalem; King Josiah bases his legal and liturgical reforms upon it. This book, written on the basis of 300-year-old traditions and laws, is generally believed to be the nucleus of Deuteronomy. In the very same year the archon Dracon institutes his harsh laws in Athens; although minor misdemeanors carry the death penalty, the Draconian code, like the biblical lawgiver, makes the distinction between murder and accidental or justifiable manslaughter.

**c. 600:** In northeastern Iran Zoroaster (Zarathustra) founds the religion named after him: the belief that life revolves around the struggle between the good deity Ahura Mazda (the Wise Lord) and his evil opponent Ahriman (the Lie). Zoroaster's laws are contained in the *Gathas*, hymns preserved in the Persian holy scriptures, the Avesta.

**6th century BC:** Prophecies of Ezekiel, Deutero Isaiah, Haggai, Zechariah, and Malachi.

**594 BC:** Solon, ruler of Athens, abolishes the penalty of slavery for debts and institutes reforms for the benefit of small landholders.

**586 BC:** Destruction of the First Temple.

**Second half of 6th century BC:** Final redaction of the Pentateuch.

3. The Epic of Gilgamesh, King of Uruk. Tablet XI, out of a series of 12, relates the adventures of Utnapishtim, the Mesopotamian Noah. Terracotta, Nineveh, 17th century BC.

4. The Sumerian Epic of Atrhasis, probably from the city-state of Sippar in Mesopotamia, 17th century BC.

# Jerusalem and Samaria

1. The Assyrian peace: Jehu, King of Israel, pays tribute to the King of Assyria. Detail from the black obelisk Calah (Namrud), c. 830 BC.

there after an aborted revolt against Solomon. Wishing to create centers of worship in his kingdom to rival Solomon's Temple in Jerusalem, Jeroboam selected two pagan temples – one in Beth-El in the south, another in Dan in the north.

The two kingdoms spent the following decades fighting a merciless war. The struggle was not only over territory but over religion and culture as well, and sought to determine the true heir to the divinely created monarchy of the people of Israel. Prolonged confrontation obviously weakened both kingdoms and encouraged their neighbors to throw off Israelite rule or to enlarge their own territories at the expense of Israel and Judah. Thus Aram became the kingdom of Ephraim's most serious enemy, Edom regained complete independence from Judah in the reign of King Jehoram (849–842 BC), and Moab was liberated after defeating Ephraim.

These military and political disasters finally forced the two kingdoms to compromise. The kings of Judah eventually accepted the existence of the kingdom of Ephraim, and the two even began to forge an alliance, as, for example, in the time of Jehoshaphat, King of Judah for twenty-five years (from c. 870 BC), and during the reign of his son Jehoram who married the daughter of the King of Israel (Athaliah, daughter of Omri, or of Ahab).

The unity of the kingdom did not outlive Solomon's death. With the accession of his son Rehoboam, Israel was divided into two kingdoms, each named after its leading tribe: in the south was the kingdom of Judah with Jerusalem as its capital, and in the north – the kingdom of Ephraim, where Shechem was initially the seat of its government. Half a century later, during the reign of King Omri, the state ruled by the tribe of Ephraim adopted the name of its new capital, Samaria; but in the Bible the northern Kingdom is generally referred to as Israel.

The Bible presents the split as the immediate result of Rehoboam's refusal to reduce the heavy taxes imposed by King Solomon. "My father hath chastised you with whips, but I will chastise you with scorpions," was his notoriously harsh reply to the people of Shechem. However, the real causes of the secession were rooted in the old tensions between the northern and southern tribes, tensions which had not been obliterated despite almost a century of kingship. The leader of the northern tribes was Jeroboam, son of Nebat, recently returned from Egypt having fled

The kingdoms of Judah and Ephraim existed side by side for over two hundred years; one may only condense their history by listing those kings who brought them to the peak of power. Ephraim was strong and prosperous in the ninth century BC, during the reigns of Omri and his son Ahab, and particularly in the early eighth century BC. Jeroboam II, son of Joash, extended the borders of the kingdom as far north as in King David's time, and consolidated his hold over the territories east of the Jordan. In Judah the most powerful kings were Jehoshaphat and Uzziah, both of whom maintained alliances with the kingdom of Samaria. Jehoshaphat (r. 870–846 BC) extended his rule in the south and built fortifications and guard posts along the trade routes in the Negev. He re-established the domination of Judah over Edom, and in collaboration with Ahaziah, son of Ahab, built a fleet in Ezion-Geber, Elath of today. He also divided his kingdom into provinces and apparently reorganized the judicial system. Uzziah (r. 785–733 BC), son of Amaziah who had defeated Edom, followed in his father's footsteps. He reorganized the army, strengthened fortifications, extended his rule in the south, and built

| The secession | Founding of Samaria | Reign of Ahab |
|---|---|---|
| **928 BC** | **877 BC** | **871–852 BC** |

**928–911 BC:** Rehoboam, son of Solomon, reigns in Judah while Jeroboam, son of Nebat, rules (928–907 BC) in the northern kingdom which seceded from the kingdom of Jerusalem.

**c. 923 BC:** Shishak, King of Egypt (946–923 BC), invades Palestine: he marches through southern Judah, the valley of Jezreel, the valley of Beth Shean, even crossing the Jordan to the east. A list of the cities he sacked is preserved in the temple of Amon at Karnak: it includes Gibeon, Jerusalem, Megiddo – where part of a stele bearing his name was found – Aijalon, Beth Shean, and many more. His campaign badly weakens Israel which has only recently split into two kingdoms.

**c. 906–883 BC:** Baasha rebels against Jeroboam and establishes a new dynasty in the northern kingdom of Israel. Border wars with the kingdom of Judah weaken his power in the north thus allowing Ben Hadad, King of Aram, to conquer territories in the Galilee and the Gilead.

**883–859 BC:** Ashurnasirpal II reigns in Assyria. He is the first of the Assyrian kings to conquer territories west of the Euphrates. The new capital which he builds in Calah (Namrud of today), a huge town by the standards of those days, is colonized by peoples he vanquished and transferred by force.

**c. 877 BC:** Omri, King of Israel (882–871 BC), contemporary of King Asa of Judah, founds a new capital for the kingdom of Ephraim – Samaria – which from then on gives its name to the kingdom. Built on a hill, about seven miles northwest of Shechem, the town today is an archeological treasure. Its most impressive stratum dates from the Roman-Herodian period; the Israelite stratum revealed a royal palace and an inner wall from the days of Omri, and an outer wall from the days of his son Ahab, repaired by several of the kings who ruled the kingdom till its fall in 722 BC; there were also ivory tablets engraved with mythological figures and geometrical designs and Hebrew

3. A winged sphinx from Samaria, ivory, 9th–8th centuries BC.

inscriptions on pieces of pottery with details about wine, oil, and other food products which were probably brought to Samaria as payment of taxes. These objects are

generally considered to date from the time of Ahab (871–852 BC) or Jeroboam II (789–748 BC).

**871–852 BC:** Reign of Ahab in Israel. An energetic sovereign, Ahab devotes himself to enlarging his capital, Samaria, and fortifies many of the towns including Jericho; he conducts several wars against the Arameans and the Assyrians. His marriage to a Phoenician princess, Jezebel, strengthens his ties with his northern neighbor, but also causes a rift between him and the fiery prophet Elijah.

**853 BC:** The battle of Karkar in northern Syria: an alliance of twelve kings from Syria and Palestine, including Ahab, stops the expansion of Shalmaneser III, King of Assyria. But in a war which breaks out several years later between Ben Hadad of Aram and Ahab, the king of Samaria is killed; the small Aramean kingdoms unite to form a local power which survives until 732 BC, when it is finally conquered by Assyria and divided into provinces.

# 10th–8th Centuries BC

*2. The fortress at Uzzah, on the southern frontier of the Kingdom of Judah, 6th century BC.*

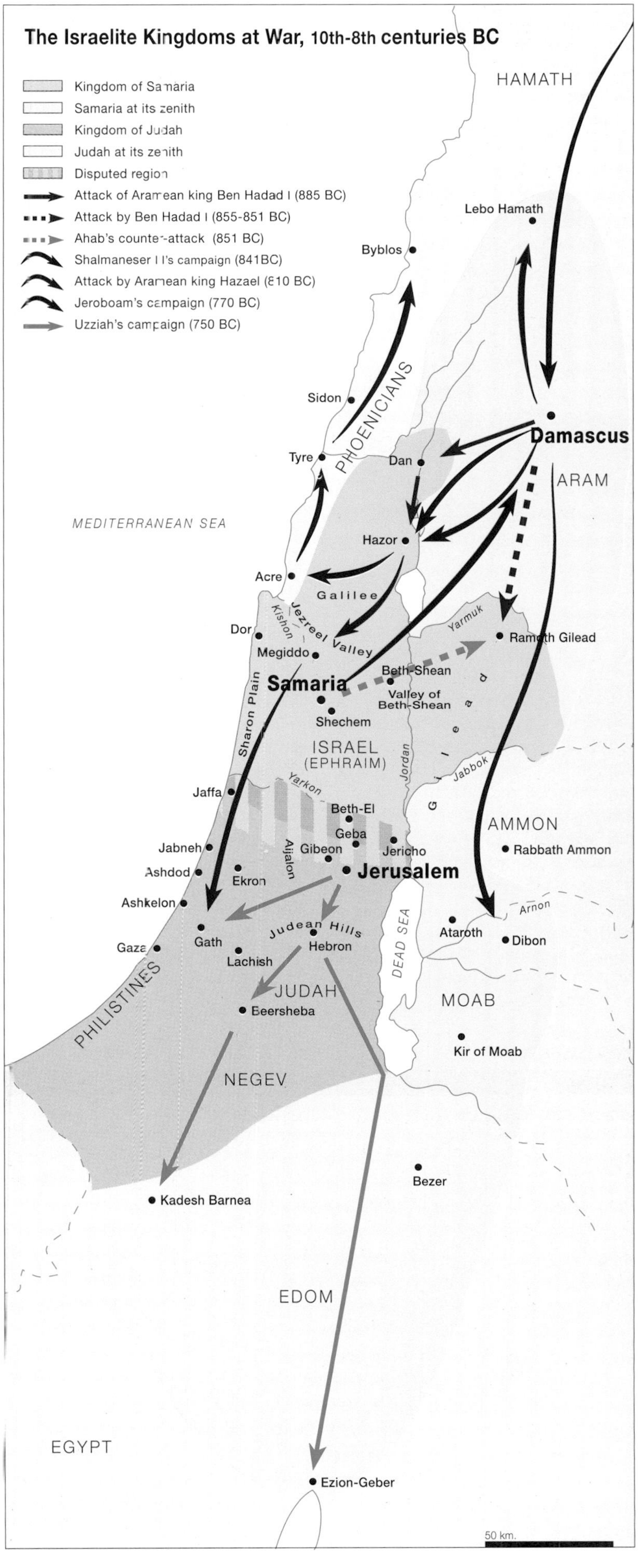

Elath; in the west he captured from the Philistines Gath, Jabneh, and Ashdod – the latter a major port which enabled him to maintain commercial ties between the Red Sea and the Mediterranean. During the reign of Uzziah, who according to the Bible "loved the soil" (2 Chronicles, 26:10), cisterns were dug and fortifications for the people's protection were built, facilitating the construction of new settlements in the Negev desert and in the Judean plain and hills.

Although similar in many respects, there was one significant difference between the two Israelite kingdoms: Judah was ruled throughout the period by a single dynasty – the House of David, while the kingdom of Ephraim witnessed within two hundred years the rise and fall of nine different dynasties as a result of a constant power struggle among its various tribes. While the kingdom of Jerusalem remained relatively united by virtue of the mighty tribe of Judah, the tribal structure of the kingdom of Samaria led to military weakness and political instability, thus preventing religious consolidation and cultural cohesion of the kind achieved by the kings of the House of David.

**The battle of Karkar**            **The Mesha stele**

**853 BC**                                        **c. 850**

*4. Canaanite altar, clay, Taanach, end of 10th century BC.*

**850 BC:** Mesha, King of Moab, erects a stele (inscribed pillar) to his deity Chemosh after the victory over Jehoram, son of Ahab, King of Israel. The large stele (over 40 inches in height), discovered in 1868 near Dibon in Jordan, is inscribed in Moabite, a dialect of the Canaanite language, very similar to Hebrew: "As for Omri, king of Israel, he humbled Moab for many days, for Chemosh was angry with his land. And his son followed him and he also said 'I will humble Moab.' In my time he spoke, but I have triumphed over him and over his house, while Israel hath perished forever." The famous Mesha stele is now located in the Louvre museum in Paris.

**734–733 BC:** Pekah ben Remaliah, King of Samaria, and Rezin, King of Aram, wage war on Jerusalem in order to replace King Ahaz and to create a triple alliance against Assyria. Ahaz, encouraged by the prophet Isaiah, refuses to join the alliance, thus saving Jerusalem from the fate of Samaria and Aram which are destroyed by the Assyrians.

## The Israelite Kingdoms at War, 10th-8th centuries BC

Kingdom of Samaria
Samaria at its zenith
Kingdom of Judah
Judah at its zenith
Disputed region
Attack of Aramean king Ben Hadad I (885 BC)
Attack by Ben Hadad I (855-851 BC)
Ahab's counter-attack (851 BC)
Shalmaneser III's campaign (841BC)
Attack by Aramean king Hazael (810 BC)
Jeroboam's campaign (770 BC)
Uzziah's campaign (750 BC)

HAMATH
Lebo Hamath
Byblos
PHOENICIANS
Sidon
MEDITERRANEAN SEA
Tyre
Dan
Damascus
ARAM
Hazor
Acre
Galilee
Dor
Jezreel Valley
Yarmuk
Ramoth Gilead
Megiddo
Beth-Shean
Samaria
Valley of Beth-Shean
Kishon
Sharon Plain
Shechem
ISRAEL (EPHRAIM)
Jordan
Jabbok
Jaffa
Yarkon
Beth-El
Geba
AMMON
Rabbath Ammon
Jabneh
Gibeon
Ajalon
Jericho
Ashdod
Ekron
Jerusalem
Ashkelon
Judean Hills
Hebron
Arnon
Gaza
Gath
Lachish
Ataroth
Dibon
DEAD SEA
PHILISTINES
JUDAH
Beersheba
MOAB
Kir of Moab
NEGEV
Bezer
Kadesh Barnea
EDOM
EGYPT
Ezion-Geber

50 km.

# The Destruction of Samaria and the Exile of Israel

1. Conquest of Lachish by the Assyrians in 701 BC. Bas-relief in Sennacherib's palace in Nineveh.

I n the year 722 BC the kingdom of Israel, after two centuries of independence, ceased to exist. Samaria, capital of the northern Israelite kingdom, was captured by the Assyrians and transformed into a province of the Assyrian Empire.

The conquest of Samaria and the deportation of its population is one of the few events in the history of the First Temple period documented in sources other than the Bible. The tragedy of a whole people recounted in 2 Kings 17 is drily noted in the annals of Sargon II, King of Assyria: "In the beginning of my royal rule, I have [besieged and conquered] the city of the Samarians . . . . I led away 27,290 of its inhabitants as captives and took some of them as soldiers for the fifty chariots of my royal regiments. I have rebuilt the city better than it had been before and settled it with people which I brought from the lands of my conquests. I have put an officer of mine as their lord, and imposed upon them a tribute as on other Assyrian subjects."

Assyria's policy of expansion in the western Fertile Crescent was begun in the mid-ninth century BC by Ashurnasirpal II, involving her in endless wars in Syria and northern Palestine. The kingdom of Israel, playing a major role in these wars (as, for example, in the days of Ahab), was considerably weakened in the process. During the reign of Tiglath-Pileser III (745–727 BC), Israel's status deteriorated to such an extent that in 738 BC it became a tax-paying vassal of Assyria.

Pekah ben Remaliah, who usurped the throne of Samaria in 737 BC, attempted to free his country from the Assyrian yoke. He allied himself with Rezin, King of Aram-Damscus, and tried to force Ahaz, King of Judah, to join them. But Ahaz refused, and the allies, contemptuously described by the prophet Isaiah as "two tails of smoking firebrands" (7:4), were easily vanquished by Tiglath-Pileser, who occupied Syria and turned it into an Assyrian province (733–734 BC). He then went on to conquer large areas of Israel, deporting the population to Assyria and imposing heavy taxes on the truncated kingdom. With the death of Tiglath-Pileser III, widespread revolt broke out in Syria and Palestine, and Hoshea ben Elah, King of Israel, encouraged by Egypt, joined the revolt. The new Assyrian king, Shalmaneser V, immediately attacked Samaria, and after three years of siege his successor Sargon II took the city and destroyed the remaining vestiges of the kingdom of Israel.

This political disaster meant national annihilation. Some of the population had already been exiled in the days of Pekah ben Remaliah; others were deported after the fall of Samaria. Those who remained in the land were soon assimilated with the peoples Sargon II brought to Palestine in accordance with the Assyrian policy which sought to obliterate national entities by way of population transfer. This mixed populace was to form the nucleus of a new people in the land of Israel – the Samaritans.

A combination of social, political, and economic factors was responsible for the decline of the kingdom of Israel prior to its destruction. Five royal dynasties rose and fell within half a century – a sure sign of social instability. Wealth was concentrated in the hands of a minority of landowners while the masses were pauperized. Long before it actually happened, the prophet Amos predicted that such social decadence would lead to national ruin and exile. Religion also influenced the fate of the people after political destruction, for in Samaria – unlike in the neighboring kingdom of Judah which had remained fast in its monotheistic faith – worship of Baal and other idolatrous cults was prevalent. The inhabitants of Samaria had no cultural shields to safeguard them from total assimilation with the pagan peoples they converged with, and they eventually disappeared altogether.

Thus, the end of Samaria was not simply a change in the political map of the Near East, but was an event of far greater historical significance: a large sector of the people of Israel was lost forever. The specter of the "ten lost tribes" has haunted Jewish memory throughout its history.

| Prophecies of Amos | Tiglath-Pileser III in Syria | The "First Isaiah" | |
|---|---|---|---|
| **750 BC** | **743–738 EC** | **740–700 BC** | |

**Middle of 8th century BC:** The prophet Amos is born in Tekoa in Judah. He prophesies in the northern kingdom of Israel. A herdsman by origin, Amos is considered to be the first of the "literary prophets." He criticizes the decadence of Jeroboam's monarchy, in particular the exploitation of the poor by rich landowners. Amos predicts the death of Jeroboam, the end of his dynasty, and the exile of Israel.
**c. 750–730 BC:** Reign of Rezin, last king of Aram-Damascus.
**c. 748 BC:** Death of Jeroboam II, King of Israel; brief reign of his son Zechariah, assassinated six months later by Shallum ben Jabesh who is deposed one month later. End of the Jehu dynasty which ruled over Israel for a century.
**c. 747–737 BC:** Reign of Menahem ben Gadi in Israel.
**745–727 BC:** Reign of Tiglath-Pileser III. It is he who builds Assyria into the strongest power in the region; in 729 BC, on becoming ruler of Babylon as well, he is given the name Pulu (Pul, in the Bible).
**743–727 BC:** Following the death of Jotham, Judah is ruled by Ahaz, first as regent and then in 733 BC as a king in his own right.
**743–738 BC:** Tiglath-Pileser's campaigns in the west; conquest of the kingdom of Hamath; Menahem, King of Israel, pays 1,000 talents of silver to retain his throne

2. Roaring lions. Ivory, Samaria, 9th–8th centuries BC.

3. An offering "to the House of the Lord" (Solomon's Temple), this pomegranate, recently discovered, was a common symbol of fertility. Ivory, Jerusalem, 8th century BC.

# 750–722 BC

## The End of the Kingdom of Israel 734–722 BC

Assyrian campaigns

➤ Tiglath-Pileser III, 734 BC
➤ Tiglath-Pileser III, 733 BC
➤ Tiglath-Pileser III, 732 BC
➤ Shalmaneser V and Sargon II, 724–722 BC

Limit of expansion under:
--- Tiglath-Pileser III
···· Sargon II

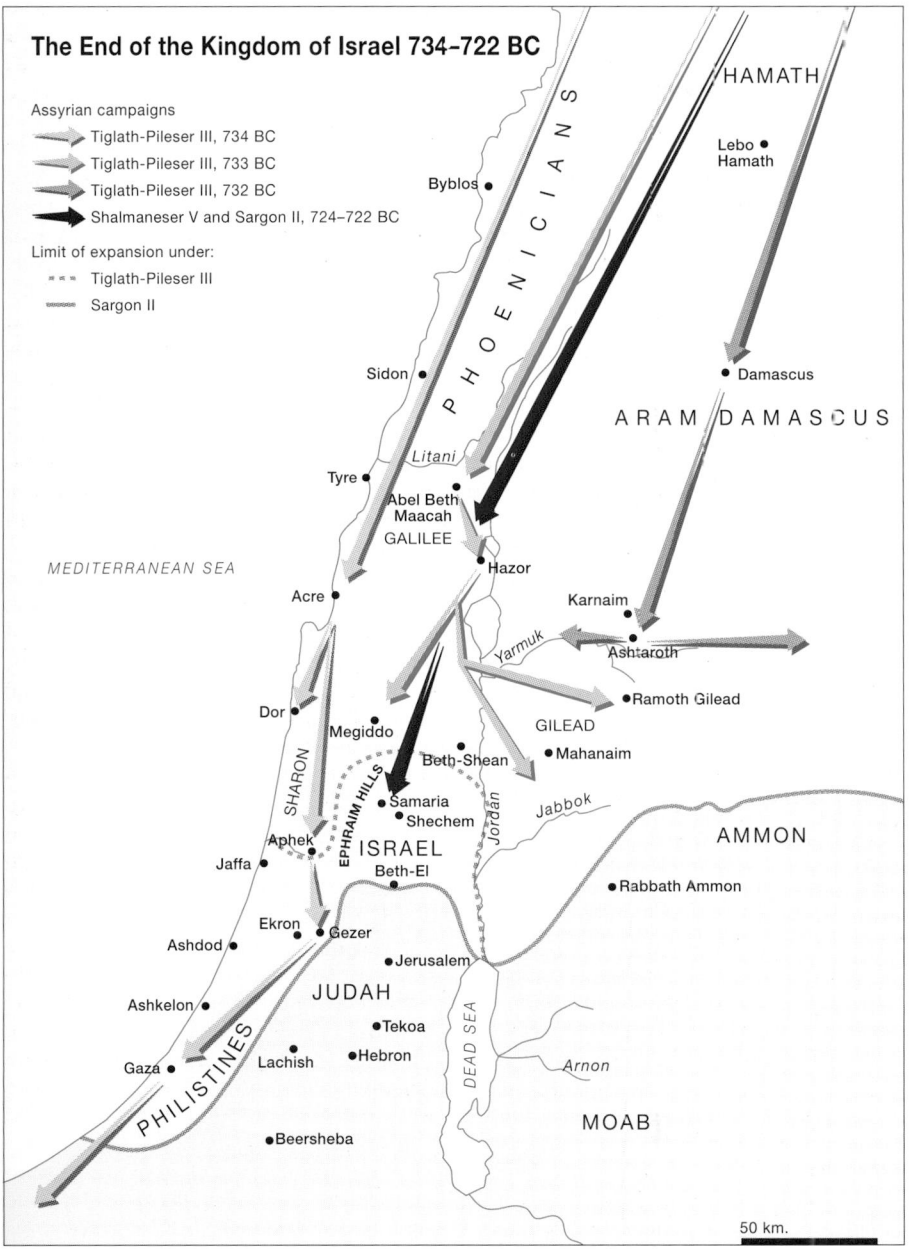

## Assyrian Expansion 9th–7th centuries BC

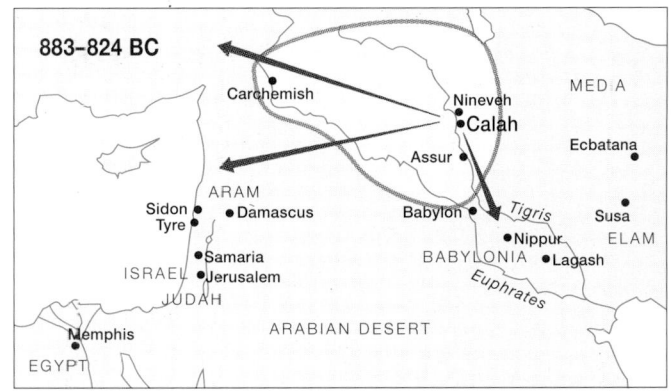

883–824 BC

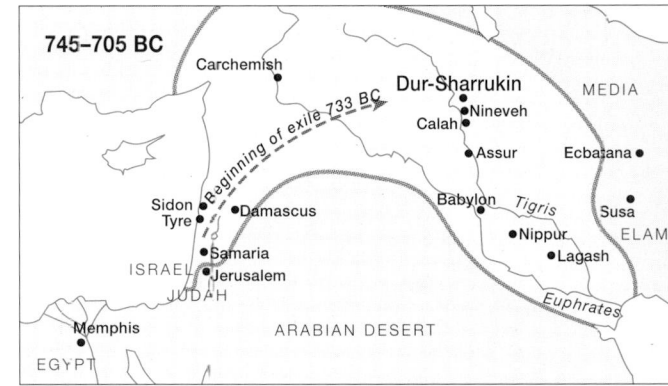

745–705 BC

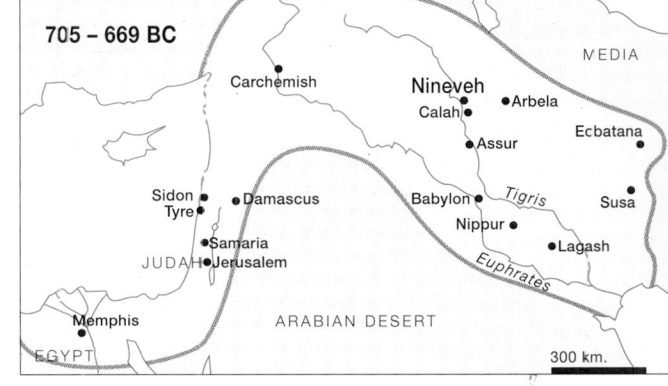

705–669 BC

---

**Tiglath-Pileser III in Palestine**

**734–733 BC**

and becomes a vassal of Assyria.

**c. 740–700:** Prophetic career of Isaiah ben Amoz (the "First Isaiah") in the kingdom of Judah. Undoubtedly a man of substance (perhaps a *cohen*, a priest in the Temple), Isaiah has influence in political circles and advises the king on matters of foreign policy.

**c. 737 BC:** Death of Menahem ben Gadi, King of Israel; he is succeeded by his son Pekahiah.

**c. 735 BC:** King Pekahiah is assassinated by one of his officers, Pekah ben Remaliah, who will reign till 733 BC.

**c. 734–733 BC:** First campaign of Tiglath-Pileser III in Palestine. Alliance of Pekah ben Remaliah, King of Israel, with Rezin, King of Aram; refusal of Ahaz, King of Judah, to join their alliance; the allies' campaign against Jerusalem in order to force Ahaz to join them; Ahaz calls for Assyrian aid. In Tiglath-Pileser's second campaign he conquers Syria, reduces it to an Assyrian province, and kills King Rezin; Assyrian conquest of large parts of Palestine – the Galilee, the

Gilead, the Jordan Valley, and the Sharon plain; deportation of the population in the regions which become Assyrian provinces.

**c. 733 BC:** Failure of the anti-Assyrian alliance leads to the assassination of Pekah ben Remaliah; accession of Hoshea ben Elah under the patronage of the Assyrians.

**733–724 BC:** Reign of Hoshea ben Elah; his rule is confined to the city of Samaria and to the hills of Ephraim, and he is impoverished by the taxes paid to Assyria.

**c. 727 BC:** Death of Ahaz, King of Judah, and accession of his son Hezekiah who will rule till 698 BC; political and religious reforms inaugurated under the influence of the prophet Isaiah.

**727–722 BC:** Reign of Shalmaneser V, son of Tiglath-Pileser III.

**725–724 BC:** Hoshea, King of Israel, turns for help to "So, King of Egypt" (most probably, Osorkon V, ruler of Egypt 735–717 BC), and with the latter's encouragement rebels against Assyria; the rebellion provokes Shalmaneser's campaign against Samaria

**Accession of Shalmaneser V**

**727 BC**

4. "The Seal of Queen Jezebel," attributed to the notorious wife of Ahab, King of Israel. Opal, 9th century BC.

**Siege and fall of Samaria**

**724–722 BC**

and leads to the final destruction of the kingdom of Israel at the hands of Shalmeneser's successor, Saragon II.

**722 BC:** The fall of Samaria. Several thousand inhabitants are deported to Assyria and are replaced by foreign colonists brought to the land of Israel from other Assyrian provinces. The Bible ascribes this calamity to Hoshea's sins: "The king of Assyria took Samaria, and carried Israel away into Assyria, and placed them in Halah and in Habor by the river of Gozan, and in the cities of the Medes . . . Until the Lord removed Israel out of his sight, as he had said by all his servants the prophets. So was Israel carried away out of their own land to Assyria unto this day. And the king of Assyria brought men from Babylon, and from Cuthah, and from Ava, and from Hamath, and from Sepharvaim, and placed them in the cities of Samaria instead of the children of Israel; and they possessed Samaria, and dwelt in the cities thereof"
(2 Kings, 17:6,23-24).

# The Fall of Jerusalem

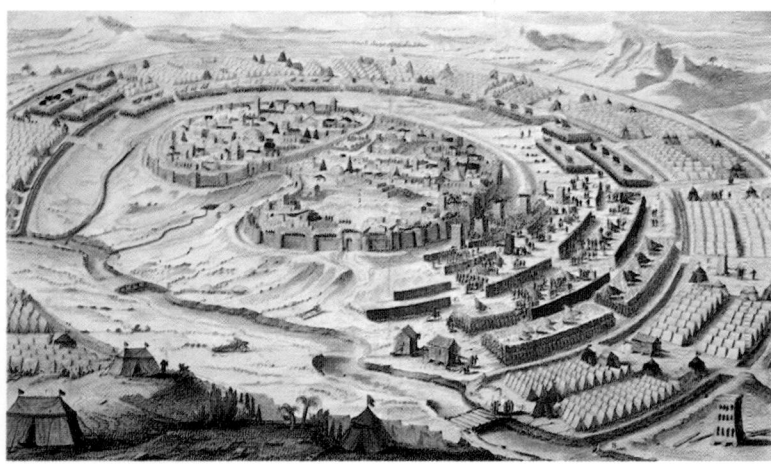

*1. Jerusalem besieged by Nebuchadnezzar, according to the Book of Kings. Card from the early 18th century.*

In 701 BC, twenty years after the fall of the kingdom of Israel, Sennacherib, King of Assyria, besieged Jerusalem. Although he devastated the countryside and imposed a heavy burden of taxation on King Hezekiah and later on his son Manasseh, he was unable to take the city. A few years later, when Assyrian power was waning, King Josiah, Manasseh's grandson, initiated a remarkable recovery for his country. He conducted an independent policy and made comprehensive reforms in religion, purifying it of all pagan cults introduced by his grandfather. When he died in 609 BC, Judah began a period of decline which was to lead to its destruction twenty-three years later.

The void left by the Assyrians was soon filled by the rising power of Babylon, which began a struggle with Egypt for territories that had been part of the Assyrian Empire. When Jehoiakim (609–597 BC) attempted a revolt in 598 BC, Nebuchadnezzar entered Palestine, and Jerusalem was besieged once again. The king was killed, and his son Jehoiachin was exiled to Babylon together with over 10,000 men from the leading families of Judah: "and Nebuchadnezzar King of Babylon . . . carried away all Jerusalem, and all the princes, and all the mighty men of valor, even ten thousand captives, and all the craftsmen and smiths: none remained, save the poorest sort of people of the land" (II Kings, 24:14). Among the exiles was Ezekiel, son of a family of priests, whose book constitutes an important source of information about the life of the exiles, their communities, hopes, and the ties they continued to maintain with their brethren in Judah.

When Zedekiah came to the throne in Jerusalem under the patronage of the King of Babylon, he faced a grave dilemma: to either submit meekly to the yoke of Babylon, or to find a way to rebel in accordance with the pro-Egyptian policy of his brother Jehoiakim, a policy that had ended so disastrously. In Jerusalem there were two opposing factions at the time: one resolutely anti-Babylonian, encouraged by dignitaries in exile (the book of Jeremiah reveals that the exiles maintained continuous correspondence with Jerusalem); and the other pro-Babylonian, represented by Jeremiah himself. The prophet regarded rebellion as suicidal and supported his position with theological arguments – God had appointed Nebuchadnezzar to rule the world for seventy years, thus any insurrection against him was an attempt to defy God's will and would inevitably lead to disaster.

Zedekiah apparently favored submission. Unable, however, to withstand the pressure of his ministers, and encouraged by Egypt, he finally decided to prove that he was not simply a pawn in the hands of the Babylonians. It was a fatal decision: "And it came to pass in the ninth year of his reign, in the tenth month, in the tenth day of the month, that Nebuchadnezzar King of Babylon came, he, and all his host, against Jerusalem, and pitched against it; and they built forts against it round about" (II Kings, 25:1). A belated Egyptian attempt to come to the rescue of the city failed. The siege lasted for two years. In the eleventh year of Zedekiah's reign (586 BC) on the ninth day of *Tammuz*, the walls of the city were breached. Zedekiah tried to escape but was caught in the lowlands of Jericho and brought to Nebuchadnezzar in Riblah. His sons were slain in his presence and then his eyes were put out. Blind and in chains, the last king of Judah was led to Babylon. Jerusalem was destroyed, its walls were pulled down, and a large part of the population of Judah was carried off into captivity. A new epoch began for the people of Israel: the Babylonian Exile.

The exact number of exiles is unknown. Recent excavations suggest that the country was not emptied of its Jewish population. According to the Bible, the King of Babylon left behind "the poor of the people, which had nothing" (Jeremiah, 39:10; II Kings 25:12) under the rule of Gedaliah ben Ahikam. When Gedaliah was assassinated, many of the Jews, fearing Babylonian retaliation, fled to Egypt. It was these refugees who created the first nucleus of a Jewish diaspora on the banks of the Nile.

The exiles who arrived in Babylon joined their brethren of the previous wave – the exiles of Jehoiachin. Together they formed an organized community, practically autonomous, structured according to places of origin, clan, and social status. In this manner they preserved their singularity as a nation – a nation believing in one God within a pagan society, a nation with sufficient inner resources to be able to send several thousand people back to their homeland after fifty years of exile to rebuild Jerusalem.

| The Assyrians besiege Jerusalem | Founding of the Neo-Babylonian Empire | Josiah's reforms |
|---|---|---|
| 701 BC | 627 BC | 621 BC |

**701 BC:** Sennacherib besieges Jerusalem. In preparation for the siege, King Hezekiah ensures the water supply to Jerusalem by closing off the outlet of the Gihon spring and diverting the waters by means of a tunnel to the pool of Siloam within the city-walls; the inscription on the wall of the tunnel was engraved by the workers when their work was nearing completion.
**698–642 BC:** Manasseh, son of Hezekiah, reigns in Jerusalem as vassal of Assyria and introduces idols into the Temple.
**689 BC:** Thirteen years after a Babylonian revolt against Assyria, Sennacherib attacks Babylon and destroys the dams around it, thus inundating the city and turning it into an immense swamp.
**633 BC:** Years of struggle against northern tribes and internal conflicts lead to the partition of the Assyrian Empire into two rival kingdoms, Haran and Nineveh.
**627 BC:** Nabopolassar seizes the throne and establishes a new dynasty known as the Neo-Babylonian, or Chaldean, dynasty; he

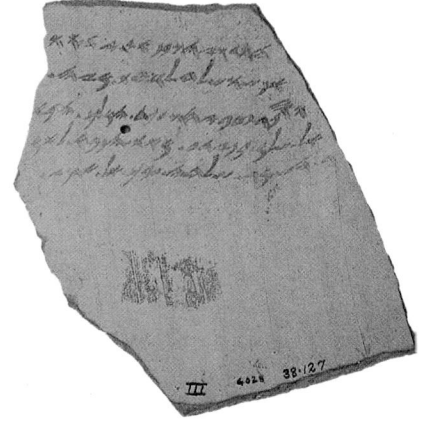

*2. One of the eighteen "Lachish Letters," sent shortly before the fall of the city to the commander of the fortress. 6th century BC.*

successfully defends Babylon's independence and finally eliminates Assyria itself.
**621 BC:** Religious reforms by King Josiah in Jerusalem – a merciless battle against idolatry: "And he did that which was right in the sight of the Lord, and walked in all the ways of David his father . . . . And the king commanded . . . to bring forth out of the temple of the Lord all the vessels that were made for Baal" (II Kings 22:2; 34:4).
**604 BC:** Campaign of Nebuchadnezzar in Palestine in the course of which he conquers Ashkelon. The prophet Jeremiah sends a collection of his prophecies to King Jehoiakim to warn him against the Babylonian peril (Jeremiah, 36). The prophet preaches submission to Babylon and predicts Nebuchadnezzar's victories throughout the region. In 594 BC he writes a scroll predicting the downfall of Babylon itself at the end of a period of universal domination assigned to it by God (51:1-58). He gives the scroll to Seraiah son of Neriah,

*3. Head of a god (?). Sculpture in Ammonite style, between the 8th and 6th centuries BC.*

# 586 BC

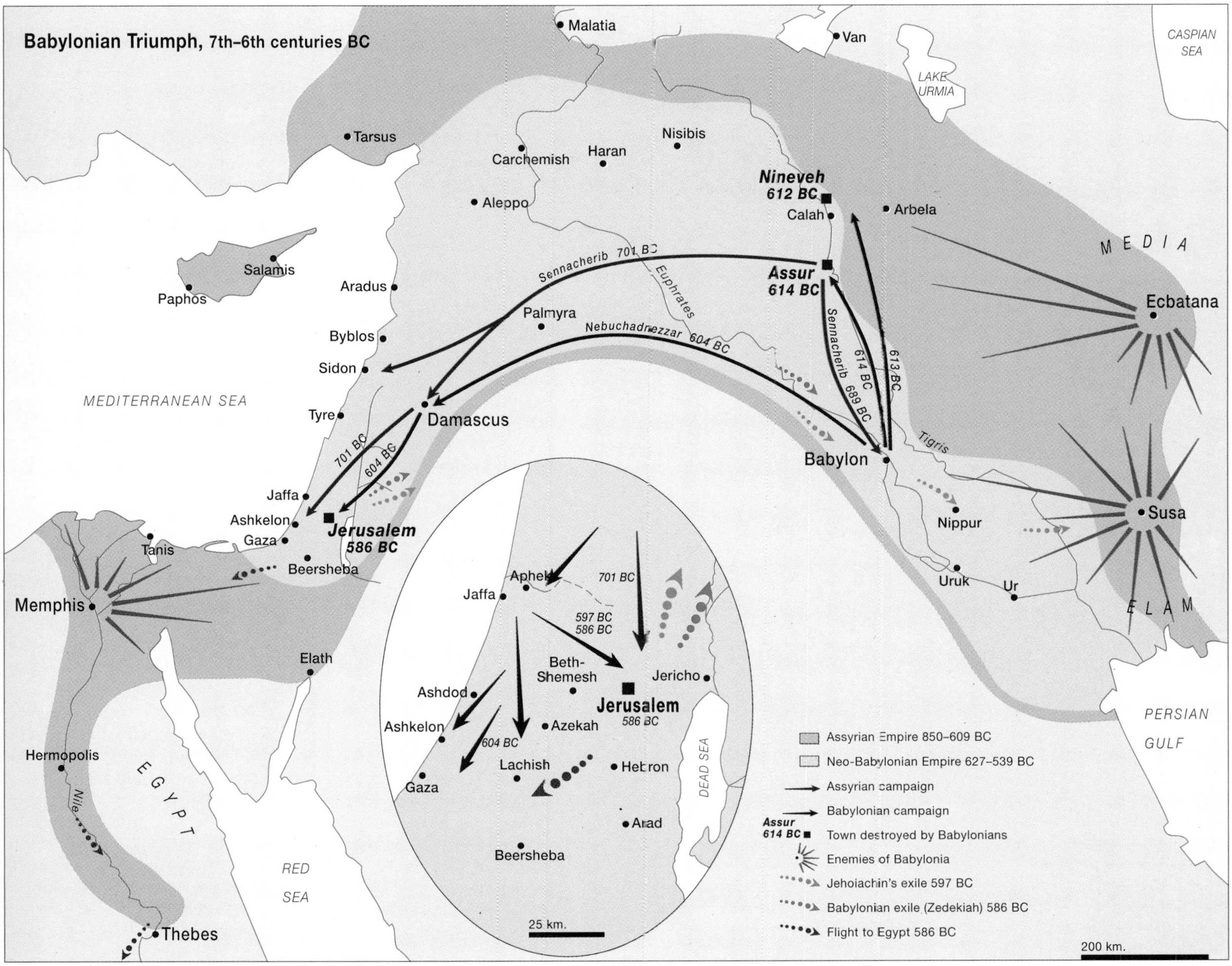

## Babylonian Triumph, 7th–6th centuries BC

Malatia

Van

CASPIAN SEA

LAKE URMIA

Tarsus

Nisibis

Carchemish

Haran

Nineveh
612 BC

Aleppo

Calah

Arbela

MEDIA

Salamis

Aradus

Sennacherib 701 BC

Euphrates

Assur
614 BC

Ecbatana

Paphos

Palmyra

Nebuchadnezzar 604 BC

Sennacherib 614 BC

689 BC

613 BC

Byblos

Sidon

MEDITERRANEAN SEA

Tyre

701 BC

604 BC

Damascus

Babylon

Tigris

Susa

Jaffa

Nippur

ELAM

Ashkelon

Jerusalem
586 BC

Gaza

Uruk

Ur

Beersheba

Memphis

Tanis

PERSIAN GULF

Elath

Jaffa

Aphek

701 BC

597 BC
586 BC

Ashdod

Beth-Shemesh

Jericho

Ashkelon

Jerusalem
586 BC

Azekah

604 BC

Hermopolis

EGYPT

Lachish

Hebron

DEAD SEA

Nile

Gaza

Arad

Beersheba

25 km.

RED SEA

Thebes

Assyrian Empire 850–609 BC

Neo-Babylonian Empire 627–539 BC

Assyrian campaign

Babylonian campaign

Assur
614 BC ■ Town destroyed by Babylonians

Enemies of Babylonia

Jehoiachin's exile 597 BC

Babylonian exile (Zedekiah) 586 BC

Flight to Egypt 586 BC

200 km.

---

**Nebuchadnezzar's campaign** — **604 BC**

**Jehoiakim's revolt** — **597 BC**

**Fall of Jerusalem and the Exile to Babylon** — **586 BC**

---

the king's emissary to Babylon, and commands him to read it aloud and then bind it with a stone and throw it in the Euphrates River: "thus shall Babylon sink" (51:63-64).

**597 BC:** Jehoiachin, King of Judah, is exiled to Babylon together with 10,000 men; accession of Zedekiah. In the words of the *Babylonian Chronicle*: "On the second day of the month of Adar he [Nebuchadnezzar] seized the city and captured the king. He appointed there a king of his own choice, received its heavy tribute and sent it to Babylon." The deported king was apparently treated in Babylon as a captive ruler rather than a prisoner. Babylonian documents indicate that he and his family lived together, he enjoyed the title "King of Judah," and received generous food-rations from the palace storerooms. After Nebuchadnezzar's death, Jehoiachin's status improved: "Evil-merodach King of Babylon in the year that he began to reign did lift up the head of Jehoiachin . . . and set his throne above the

throne of all the kings that were with him in Babylon" (II Kings, 25:28).

**587 BC:** In the midst of the siege of Jerusalem, the prophet Jeremiah buys a field as a symbol of future redemption; he puts the sealed deed of purchase in an earthenware jug, leaving it for safekeeping in the hands of the scribe Baruch ben Neriah "that they may continue many days" (32:14). Recent excavations in Jerusalem and Judah have yielded a large number of seals from the 6th century BC, including one to "Berachiah ben Neriah the scribe" and another belonging to "Jerahmeel, a royal prince" mentioned in Jeremiah 36:26. Tell al-Duwayr, identified as the site of the city of Lachish, yielded in 1935 a rich collection of Hebrew ostraca (inscribed sherds) from the period of the destruction of the kingdom. One of the letters describes the dreadful conditions in Jerusalem in the last days before it was conquered and after the cities around it had already fallen into the hands of the Babylonian army.

4. *Ephraim Moses Lilien (1874–1925)*, On the banks of the rivers of Babylon.

# Biblical Prophecy

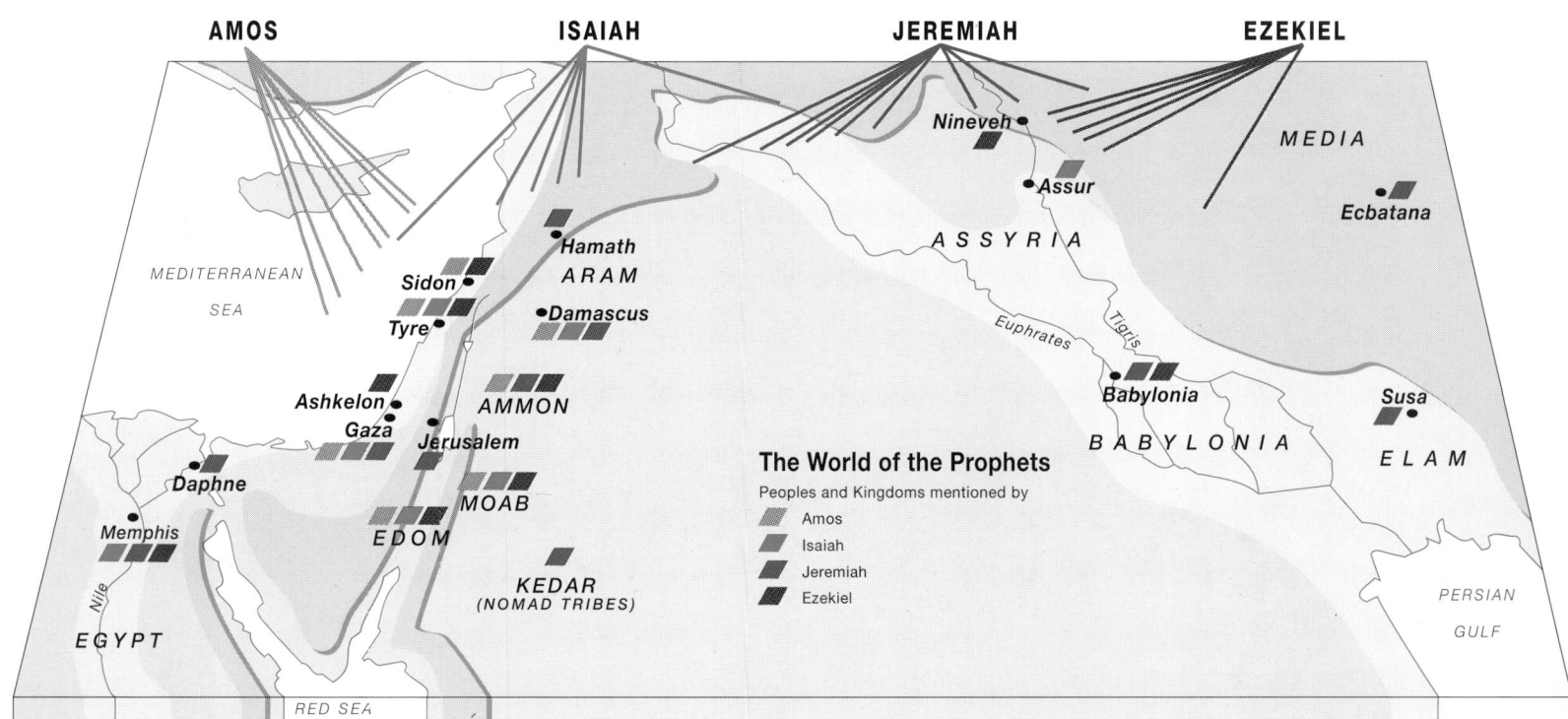

**AMOS**  **ISAIAH**  **JEREMIAH**  **EZEKIEL**

The World of the Prophets

Peoples and Kingdoms mentioned by

- Amos
- Isaiah
- Jeremiah
- Ezekiel

*(Map labels: MEDITERRANEAN SEA, Hamath, ARAM, Sidon, Damascus, Tyre, Ashkelon, AMMON, Gaza, Jerusalem, Daphne, MOAB, Memphis, EDOM, Nile, EGYPT, RED SEA, KEDAR (NOMAD TRIBES), Nineveh, Assur, ASSYRIA, Euphrates, Tigris, Babylonia, BABYLONIA, MEDIA, Ecbatana, Susa, ELAM, PERSIAN GULF)*

The importance of prophecy in the First Temple period cannot be overstated. It was a phenomenon of universal significance since it established the ethical foundation for all monotheistic religions. Judaism, Christianity, and Islam are all based on three principles defined by the prophets of Israel: God is one; God is moral in essence; God had elected certain individuals to whom he revealed his will and instructed them to impart his message to the people.

Prophecy was not exclusive to ancient Israel; the science of divination was well known throughout the ancient Near East, particularly in Mesopotamia. Excavations began in 1933 at Tell Hariri, site of the great city of Mari on the banks of the Euphrates River, have uncovered cuneiform documents from the eighteenth century BC which speak of charismatic persons who delivered a message from their deity to the king on how to conduct himself in times of war. The parallel to biblical prophecy is clear: a divine being sends messengers to transmit its will to man, and man – in this case, the king – must obey. The similarity goes no further, however, for in content and in cultural and social function the two phenomena are radically different.

The early biblical prophets (who are also referred to as "seers") were indeed called upon to transmit the Word of God to the king. They were all members of the upper stratum of Israelite society. Samuel was himself a leader of the people; Nathan, Gad, and others like them served at the king's court. Although they exhibited their independence by castigating the king for his wrongdoings, they were nonetheless part of the ruling establishment. A change in the status of the prophet occurred for the first time in the ninth century BC in the northern kingdom. Elijah, although he still addressed the king, was no longer a member of the royal entourage, but a persecuted zealot forced to flee the monarch's wrath. Elijah reproved King Ahab and his wife Jezebel for two major transgressions: immorality and idolatry.

The figure of Elijah, whose primary mission was not to predict the future but to remind the people of their moral and religious obligations, heralds the appearance of the "classical" prophets. Beginning with Amos, the "literary" prophets left books for posterity containing their admonitions, visions, and predictions. These writings, reflecting the system of beliefs which the prophets sought to impose, constitute a major source of

*2. Hannah praying under the gaze of the priest Eli (his promise was to come true: Hannah gave birth to the prophet Samuel). Yahuda Haggadah, South Germany, 1470–1500.*

**Middle of 8th century BC:** Prophecies of Amos and Hosea. A contemporary of the Greek poet Hesiod, Amos is the first of the "literary prophets." A herdsman from Tekoa in Judah but active mainly in Israel, he castigates the rich subjects of Jeroboam II for oppressing the defenseless poor. Hosea accuses the people of Israel of "prostitution" and compares the relations between God and his people to those of husband and wife, equating idolatry with adultery.

**Second half of 8th century BC:** Prophecies of Isaiah and Micah. Isaiah, probably the greatest of the "literary prophets," was active in Judah throughout the four successive reigns of Uzziah, Jotham, Ahaz, and Hezekiah. A man of God, but also the king's adviser, his considerable influence was mostly felt in the court of Ahaz and Hezekiah at the time Assyria was threatening to absorb all the small states in

*3. Samuel dedicated to the Lord by his parents. Yahuda Haggadah, South Germany, 1470–1500.*

# 10th–6th Centuries BC

1. The prophet Micah by Jan Van Eyck (detail). Ghent, Saint-Bavon Cathedral, 1432.

information about the social and cultural evolution of Israel. A new set of values was established: nation, ritual, and certainly material wealth and military strength should always be subordinated to moral imperatives.

The supremacy of morality was derived from the religious postulate of a unique God, the single creator of the universe, the sole director of history, deciding the fate of individuals, nations, and states. It was this universal claim which served Amos, Isaiah, Nahum, Jeremiah, Zephaniah, and Ezekiel as justification for addressing foreign nations, even those that were not linked to the fate of Israel. Classical prophecy was at its peak during the rise and fall of world empires (Assyria, Babylonia, Egypt, and Persia), and the prophets did not view this drama as a mere collection of random events. History was the instrument by which God expressed his will in order to inculcate mankind with the right values. A prophet was not simply an oracle but a mouthpiece for God, sent to warn men that evil doings would inevitably lead to ruin.

Yet God was not bound by his own design and nothing was preordained: the absoluteness of God did not abolish human liberty; man was inherently capable of improvement and thus of influencing divine deci-

sions. Hence the strong emphasis upon the idea of "conversion," the sinner's repentance being the cornerstone of the prophetic system: "Return ye now every one from his evil way, and make your ways and your doings good" (Jeremiah, 18:11). Hence too the optimistic conception of the ultimate fate of Israel. Following the catastrophes of destruction and exile, the time will come for Redemption and Return. And not only Israel will be redeemed, but all nations, for the God absolute of Israel is the universal God.

History, then, not only has a logical design but also has a direction. Its ultimate goal is universal salvation, which will be attained after the destruction of idolatry and the demise of arrogance. At the end of the road peace and harmony will reign for all eternity: "He shall judge among the nations, and shall rebuke many people; and they shall beat their swords into plowshares, and their spears into pruninghooks; nation shall not lift up sword against nation, neither shall they learn war any more" (Isaiah, 2:4). For it was the prophets of Israel who invented eschatology, an idea without which the entire history of the western world, from Jesus to Marx, is incomprehensible.

the region. Like other prophets, he sees a relation of cause and effect between the immoral behavior of the people and the afflictions which they suffer; ceremonies and ritual, he says, are not sufficient to appease the wrath of God. One of his great innovations is the eschatological vision of a world reconciled to God and at peace within itself. The Judean Micah is the first prophet to predict the destruction of Jerusalem as punishment for its sins, but he also describes its future of incomparable glory.

**Second half of 7th century BC:** Prophecies of Zephaniah attacking idolatrous cults and the aping of foreign customs, and those of Nahum expressing joy over the fall of Nineveh.

**End of 7th–beginning of 6th century BC:** Prophecies of Jeremiah. Native of Anathoth and active in Jerusalem, Jeremiah prophesies during a period of particularly dramatic events: the fall of Nineveh (612 BC) which heralds the downfall of Assyria, the battle of Carchemish (605 BC),

the Jehoiachin exile (597 BC), the fall of Jerusalem, and the Babylonian exile (586 BC). The assassination of Gedaliah forces Jeremiah to migrate to Egypt where he dies. A political prophet, unafraid to voice unpopular ideas which bring him much grief, Jeremiah is the first to distinguish between true and false prophets. Under the Judean kings Josiah (640–609 BC) and Jehoiakim (609–598 BC), the prophet Habakkuk elaborates a novel answer to the moral problem of theodicy: "The just shall live by his faith" (2:4).

**First half of 6th century BC:** The prophetic career of Ezekiel in Babylonia. A priest exiled with Jehoiachin in 597 BC, Ezekiel is a distinguished member of the community of deportees. His dramatic and symbolic prophecies deal harshly with Israel's enemies

*4. Moses, paragon of all prophets, descending from Mount Sinai. Illustration from the Alba Bible, a Spanish translation commissioned by Don Luis de Guzman from Moses Arragel de Guadalajara, 1422.*

who are but rods of wrath in the hands of a God punishing Israel for its long history of sin. But Ezekiel also offers prophecies of consolation, including the famous vision of resurrection: "O ye dry bones, hear the word of the Lord . . . I will cause breath to enter into you, and ye shall live. And I will lay sinews upon you, and will bring up flesh upon you, and cover you with skin, and put breath in you, and ye shall live; and ye shall know that I am the Lord . . . and the bones came together, bone to his bone . . . and they lived . . . Behold, O my people, I will open your graves, and cause you to come out of your graves, and bring you into the land of Israel" (37:4-12). The anonymous prophet known as Deutero-Isaiah, whose prophecies are contained in chs. 40-55 of the book of Isaiah, was a contemporary of Ezekiel.

**Second half of 6th century BC:** Prophecies of Haggai, Zechariah, and Malachi, active during the Return to Zion, promising a glorious future.

# The Return to Zion

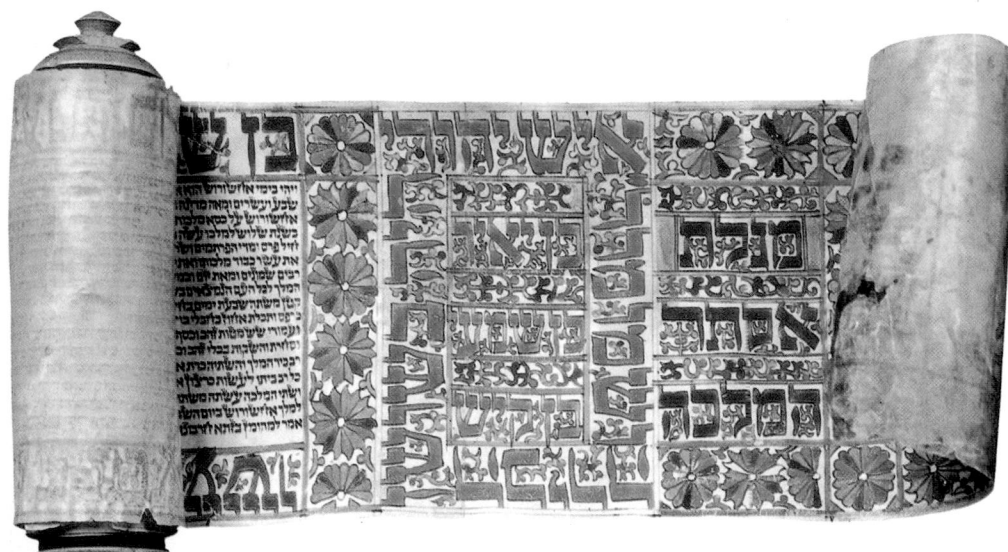

*1. A scroll containing the Book of Esther. Parchment, Iran, 1848.*

After the conquest of Babylonia in 539 BC, King Cyrus of Persia – now ruling over all of western Asia – tried to consolidate his empire by adopting a benevolent policy towards the conquered peoples. Part of this policy was the decree of 538 BC, known in Jewish history as The Cyrus Proclamation. It granted permission to the exiles of Jerusalem to return to their homeland and rebuild their temple. Cyrus even declared that he wished to obey the God of Israel (in the same manner as he conquered Babylonia in the name of Marduk, the Babylonian god), and he therefore gave the returning exiles his aid and support. Thus began the period known as the Return to Zion: repatriation from Babylon to Jerusalem.

Our main sources of information for this period, besides archeological findings, are the books of the prophets of that time: Haggai, Zechariah, and Malachi, as well as the books of Ezra and Nehemiah. These contain historiographical segments, authentic documents from the archives of the Persian governors in Jerusalem, and autobiographical sections.

Leading the caravan of the returning exiles were two men: Sheshbazzar, named "Prince of Judah" (who was perhaps the son of Jehoiachin, King of Judah, mentioned in 1 Chronicles 3:18 as Shenazzar), and Zerubbabel, son of Shealtiel, and grandson of Jehoiachin. Of the two it was Zerubbabel's personality that left the most significant imprint on the early years of the return. The religious leader at his side was Joshua, son of the high priest Jehozadak.

Approximately 50,000 people returned to Zion in the wake of the Cyrus Proclamation, apparently in several waves. Most of them, it seems, came from the poorer strata of Babylonian Jewry, which was to determine the economic and social nature of the future community in Jerusalem.

Restoration proved an arduous task. There was immediate tension between the returnees and the Israelite inhabitants who had not been exiled by the Babylonians. The severest conflict was with the Samaritans. They regarded themselves as entirely Israelite, while the repatriates saw them as a mixed race of Israelites and other ethnic elements that had been brought to the region by Assyria. The returned exiles therefore excluded the Samaritans from participating in building the Temple. Rebuffed, the Samaritans opposed its construction.

Another difficulty was the grave economic situation. Apparently the land suffered a drought during the first few years after the return, and many of the repatriates accumulated heavy debts. With the city walls in ruins, their security was also precarious. Finally, there was dissension among the leaders: Zerubbabel, of royal blood, aspired to political independence, even perhaps to re-establishing the Davidic dynasty; while Joshua, son of Jehozadak, was willing to settle for the religious autonomy granted by the Persian rulers. In brief, the harsh realities of Jerusalem did not fulfill the expectations raised by the ardent promises of Isaiah (chs. 40-55) and of Jeremiah (chs. 30-32), and demoralization set in.

All this helps to explain why the building of the Temple only began in 516 BC, and then only because prophets Haggai and Zechariah persuaded the people that it would bring them salvation. When the situation did not improve after its completion, disillusionment grew all the more acute: "But Zion says: The Lord has forsaken me; my God has forgotten me" (Isaiah, 49:14).

Nevertheless, despite all its tribulations, the return to Zion was a chapter of primary importance in the history of the Jewish people. For the first time in the history of mankind, a nation returned to its homeland and resumed life as it had been before the exile. Had they not returned, the Jewish people would have in all likelihood suffered the fate of other exiled nations: a loss of national identity and total assimilation.

| Cyrus II, King of Persia | Babylon conquered by the Persians | The Cyrus Proclamation |
|---|---|---|
| 559 BC | 539 BC | 536 BC |

**559 BC:** Cyrus II of the Achaemenian Dynasty ascends the throne as a vassal of Astyages, king of the Median Empire.

**556 BC:** Nabonidus, one of Nebuchadnezzar's officials, usurps the throne of Babylon; he restores the temple of the moon god Sin in Haran, his native town, declaring Sin the supreme deity and arousing the wrath of the priests of Marduk.

**550 BC:** Cyrus rebels against Astyages and, with the assurance of support from Nabonidus, conquers Ecbatana, the capital of Media. Freed of Median tutelage, Persia becomes a serious threat to Babylon, but Cyrus prefers to concentrate his first efforts in Asia Minor. Lydia, Armenia, Cappadocia, and Cilicia fall to the Persians.

**539 BC:** Conquest of Babylon – Cyrus now rules over the largest empire ever known. The conquest was aided by the priests of Marduk, Cyrus having declared himself an emissary of Marduk, coming to deliver Babylon from the suffering inflicted upon it by Nabonidus.

**538 BC:** The Cyrus Proclamation: "Thus saith Cyrus King of Persia, The Lord God of heaven hath given me all the Kingdoms of

*2. Glass amphoras. Palestine and Syria. 6th–4th centuries BC.*

*3. Seal engraved on a vase handle. Ramat Rachel, early 4th century BC.*

# 6th Century BC

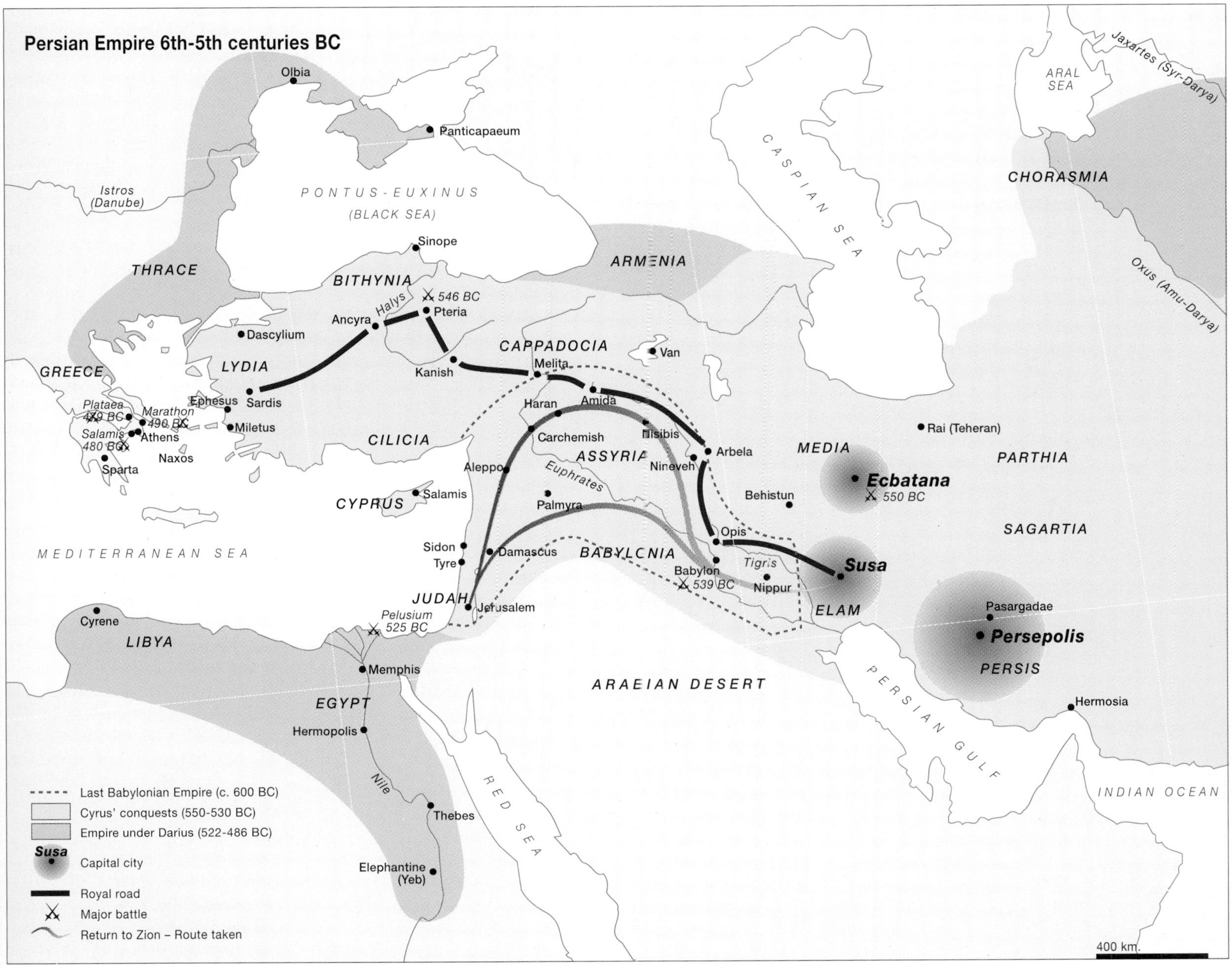

## Persian Empire 6th-5th centuries BC

[Map of the Persian Empire showing regions including THRACE, GREECE, LYDIA, CILICIA, CYPRUS, BITHYNIA, ARMENIA, CAPPADOCIA, ASSYRIA, BABYLONIA, JUDAH, LIBYA, EGYPT, MEDIA, PARTHIA, SAGARTIA, PERSIS, ELAM, CHORASMIA, and bodies of water including PONTUS-EUXINUS (BLACK SEA), CASPIAN SEA, MEDITERRANEAN SEA, ARABIAN DESERT, RED SEA, PERSIAN GULF, INDIAN OCEAN, ARAL SEA. Cities marked include Olbia, Panticapaeum, Sinope, Istros (Danube), Ancyra, Pteria, Dascylium, Ephesus, Sardis, Miletus, Kanish, Melita, Van, Rai (Teheran), Haran, Amida, Carchemish, Nisibis, Nineveh, Arbela, Ecbatana, Aleppo, Palmyra, Behistun, Salamis, Sidon, Tyre, Damascus, Babylon, Opis, Nippur, Susa, Pasargadae, Persepolis, Hermosia, Cyrene, Jerusalem, Pelusium, Memphis, Hermopolis, Thebes, Elephantine (Yeb), Plataea, Marathon, Salamis, Athens, Naxos, Sparta. Battles marked: 546 BC (Pteria), 550 BC (Ecbatana), 539 BC (Babylon), 525 BC (Pelusium), 490 BC (Marathon), 480 BC (Salamis), 479 BC (Plataea).]

Legend:
- - - - - Last Babylonian Empire (c. 600 BC)
- ☐ Cyrus' conquests (550-530 BC)
- ☐ Empire under Darius (522-486 BC)
- **Susa** Capital city
- ▬▬ Royal road
- ✕ Major battle
- ∿ Return to Zion – Route taken

400 km.

---

**Death of Cyrus II, Accession of Cambyses II**
**530 BC**

**Darius I, King of Persia**
**522 BC**

**Inauguration of the Second Temple**
**516 BC**

the earth; and he hath charged me to build him a house at Jerusalem, which is in Judah. Who is there among you of all his people? His God be with him, and let him go up to Jerusalem, which is in Judah, and build the house of the Lord God of Israel (he is the God) which is in Jerusalem. And whosoever remaineth in any place where he sojourneth, let the men of his place help him with silver, and with gold, and with goods, and with beasts, beside the freewill offering for the house of God that is in Jerusalem" (Ezra, 1:2-4). The proclamation also appears as the last verse of the Old Testament in 2 Chronicles, 36:23.

**530 BC:** Cyrus is killed in battle with the Scythian tribe of the Massagetae; he is succeeded by his son Cambyses (who reigned till 522 BC) who continues his father's liberal policy towards the Jews. When he conquers Egypt in 525 BC, he allows the Egyptian Jews to maintain their temple in Yeb (Elephantine, a city on a small island in the Nile).

**c. 530 BC:** The time of Buddha, Pythagoras, and Confucius.
**522–486 BC:** The reign of Darius I in Persia. He conquers India in the east and Thrace and Macedonia in the west, but is defeated at Marathon by the Greeks and their leader Militiades. Darius divides his empire into twenty large administrative regions

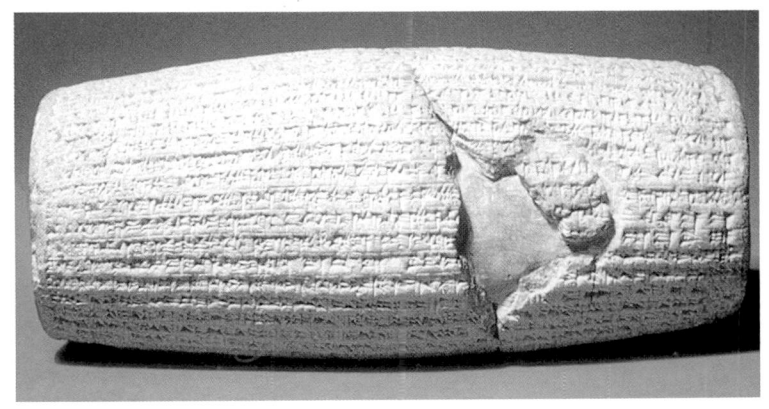

*4. Cylinder of Cyrus relating the conquest of Babylon. Terracotta, 6th century EC.*

(satrapies), constructs roads and sets up a postal system. He also introduces a standard coin, and builds a beautiful new capital city – Persepolis – on the ruins of Shushan.

**516 BC:** The inauguration of the Second Temple in Jerusalem: "And when the builders laid the foundation of the temple of the Lord, they set the priests in their apparel with trumpets, and the Levites the sons of Asaph with cymbals, to praise the Lord, after the ordinance of David King of Israel. And they sang together by course in praisings and giving thanks unto the Lord, because he is good, for his mercy endureth forever toward Israel. And all the people shouted with a great shout, when they praise the Lord, because the foundation of the house of the Lord was laid. But many of the priests and Levites and chief of the fathers, who were ancient men, that had seen the first house, when the foundation of this house was laid before their eyes, wept with a loud voice. . ." (Ezra, 3:10-13).

# Babylonian and Egyptian Jewry: The Persian Era

The exile of Jehoiachin in 597 BC, the destruction of Jerusalem and the exile of 586 BC, the return to Zion in 538 BC – this chain of dramatic events within sixty years created an unusual demographic situation. Jews came to regard it as a permanent and immutable reality: a Jewish community in the land of Israel constituting a center for a widely dispersed nation. Indeed, the concept persisted even in periods when the center in Palestine was comparatively small and incapable of imposing its authority on the diaspora.

*1. The prophet Ezekiel in the valley of the dry bones (ch. 37). Detail from a wall painting in the synagogue of Dura-Europos. Syria, c. 245.*

Following the destruction of the First Temple, two large and flourishing Jewish communities emerged in the major centers of civilization at the time: Babylon and Egypt.

Our principal sources of information about Babylonian Jewry in the sixth and fifth centuries BC are the Books of Jeremiah, Ezekiel, Ezra, and Nehemiah, as well as various Babylonian documents. All these sources portray a similar picture. The Book of Ezekiel, which relates to the early sixth century BC, describes an organized Jewish community enjoying religious freedom and considerable autonomy, well integrated into the surrounding society – to such an extent, in fact, that some of its sons refused to regard themselves as exiles. In the words of the prophet: "You say to yourselves: Let us become like the nations and tribes of other lands and worship wood and stone" (Ezekiel, 20:32). The image of a normal,

comfortable life is corroborated by other sources: Jeremiah's letter to the Jehoiachin exiles (Jeremiah 29); stories of Ezra and Nehemiah about Jews in prominent positions in the king's court (as was Nehemiah himself) or affluent enough to finance the return to Zion – though not joining it themselves (Ezra, 8). Another independent source was found in the archives of the Babylonian family Murashu from the city of Nippur, dating from the reign of Artaxerxes I and Darius II (465–404 BC). The Murashu Tablets reveal that the Jews of Babylon, only one community of foreigners among several, were engaged throughout the region of Nippur in a wide range of occupations, as soldiers, farmers, royal officials, customs officials, merchants, slaves, and one, a certain Hananiah ben Menahem, was even the king's bird-keeper.

This image was, no doubt, only partially true. At least one source, chapters 40-48 in Isaiah, attributed to an unknown prophet referred to as Deutero-Isaiah, speaks of "the wretched and the poor" (41:17), depicting the people as inmates of a prison: "Here is a people plundered and taken as prey, all of them ensnared, trapped in holes, lost to sight in dungeons, carried off as spoil without hope of rescue" (42:22). These words, however, may reflect the cultural conflict between the adherents of a monotheistic religion and their pagan neighbors, and also perhaps with nascent Zoroastrianism.

As for the Jews of Egypt, we know from Jeremiah that they mainly settled in the Delta region and maintained an organized community. However, on the whole, biblical evidence of the community in Egypt is very scant. Invaluable information is contained in the archive of documents discovered during 1893–1908, known as the Elephantine Papyri. Dating from the fifth century BC (the latest is from 399 BC) and written in Aramaic, they reveal the existence of a Jewish community in Yeb (Elephantine) – a frontier fortress defending southern Egypt, situated on a small island on the Nile opposite modern Aswan. Companies of Jewish mercenaries were garrisoned there, perhaps even prior to the destruction of the First Temple. At the center of their special quarter stood a temple to the God of Israel, probably built after the destruction of the Temple in Jerusalem. When the Persian king Cambyses conquered Egypt in 525 BC, the temple was already standing. The community observed the Sabbath, celebrated Passover, obeyed the Torah laws of marriage and divorce, inheritance, and manumission of slaves. But the fact that they built a temple of their own suggests religious practices which were not shared by the communities in the land of Israel and in Babylon.

The beginning of the fourth century BC saw the end of the community of Jewish warriors in Yeb, and the fate of its people remains unknown. Nevertheless, the notion of a temple in a place other than Jerusalem survived among Egyptian Jews, as was proved 250 years later when the Temple of Onias was built in Leontopolis.

| Cambyses conquers Egypt | Accession of Darius I | | Destruction of the temple in Elephantine | Redaction of Chronicles |
|---|---|---|---|---|
| 525 BC | 522 BC | | 410 BC | c. 400 BC |

**c. 551 BC:** Death of Zoroaster, founder of a faith resting on a dualist conception of divinity. By reducing the number of deities to two, Zoroastrianism came closer to monotheism. Its influence on Judaism is mainly discernible in eschatological elements; it is possible that the words of the prophet called "Deutero-Isaiah," living in Babylon in the mid-sixth century BC, are directed against this new religion: "I am the Lord, and there is none else. I form the light, and create darkness; I make peace, and create evil; I the Lord do all these things" (Isaiah, 45:6-7).
**522 BC:** Rebellion in Egypt against Cambyses King of Persia. Darius I ascends the throne after a period of political turmoil; two years of war threaten the integrity of the Persian Empire, but Darius finally imposes his rule and founds a dynasty which ruled Persia until the conquest of the empire by Alexander the Great in 331 BC.
**c. 484–c. 425 BC:** Life of Herodotus, the great Greek historian who documented the

wars between Greece and Persia.
**458 or 428 BC:** In the reign of Artaxerxes, Ezra "the priest and scribe" is authorized by the king to "investigate" the situation in Jerusalem and Judah. Some scholars assume that revolts in Egypt were the reason for the Persian King's decision to strengthen his hold on the territory bordering on Egypt.
**c. 420 BC:** The composition of the Aramaic "Book of Ahikar," part of which was discovered among the Elephantine Papyri. The book tells the story of Ahikar the scribe who rose to prominence in Sennacherib's court: slandered by his adopted son and expelled from the court, Ahikar was later reinstated after solving a difficult riddle for the king. The story contains many aphorisms and parables similar to those in the Book of Proverbs. The figure of Ahikar appears to represent a certain prototype of the Wise Jew who, like Daniel or Nehemiah, attains high rank in the court of a foreign monarch.
**419 BC:** King Darius II's edict to the governor Arsames that the Jewish force in

Elephantine was to celebrate Passover.
**410 BC:** Destruction of the Jewish temple in Yeb. The Greek name Elephantine, "the city of ivories," is a rendering of the original Egyptian one. Yeb was important not only as a military camp but also as a city of the god Khnub and as a commercial center. The Elephantine Papyri contain the letter written by the community leader Yedonyah ben Gemariah and his colleagues to Bigvai, governor of the *pahwa* of Yahud (Palestine). The Jews tell him in Aramaic how the Egyptians destroyed the "temple of the God Yahu": in the month of Tammuz in the 14th year of King Darius' reign, the priests of Khnub, with the help of the Persian commander Waidrang, came to Yeb and destroyed the temple; its stone pillars, its five gates with bronze hinges, the roof of cedar, were all burnt, and the vessels of gold and silver were pillaged. Earlier, they say, they appealed to Jehohanan, the high priest in Jerusalem, but he did not see fit to answer them, and they remained in mourning ever

since. They request Bigvai's permission to rebuild their temple on its ruins.
**c. 400 BC:** The approximate date of composition of Chronicles, the last historiographical book of the Old Testament dealing with the First Temple period. The book is based on earlier biblical sources (Genesis, Samuel, and Kings) and above all attempts to glorify the House of David and praise the servants of the Lord – the priests, the Levites, and the singers; the author expresses a similar attitude to the Jewish society in his own time. At the same time (and perhaps by the same pen) the Books of Ezra and Nehemiah were composed describing the return to Zion, as was the Book of Judith, one of the earliest apocryphal ("external") books.
**End of 5th century BC:** Expulsion of the Persians from Egypt. The position of the Jews there undoubtedly deteriorates: they "fear robbery because they are few." Little is known of the community until its conquest by Alexander the Great in 332.

# 6th–4th Centuries BC

2. A gift-deed for a house from a father to his daughter. Papyrus in Aramaic from Elephantine, 5th century BC.

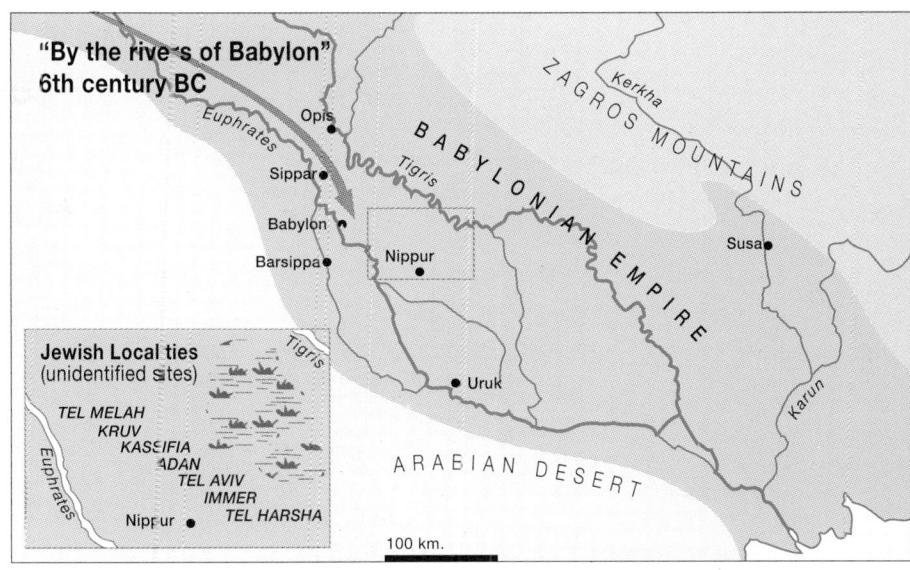

### "By the rivers of Babylon" 6th century BC

ZAGROS MOUNTAINS

Kerkha

Euphrates

Opis

Tigris

BABYLONIAN EMPIRE

Sippar

Babylon

Nippur

Susa

Barsippa

Tigris

Uruk

Karun

ARABIAN DESERT

#### Jewish Local ties (unidentified sites)

TEL MELAH
KRUV
KASEIFIA
ADAN
TEL AVIV
IMMER
TEL HARSHA

Euphrates

Nippur

100 km.

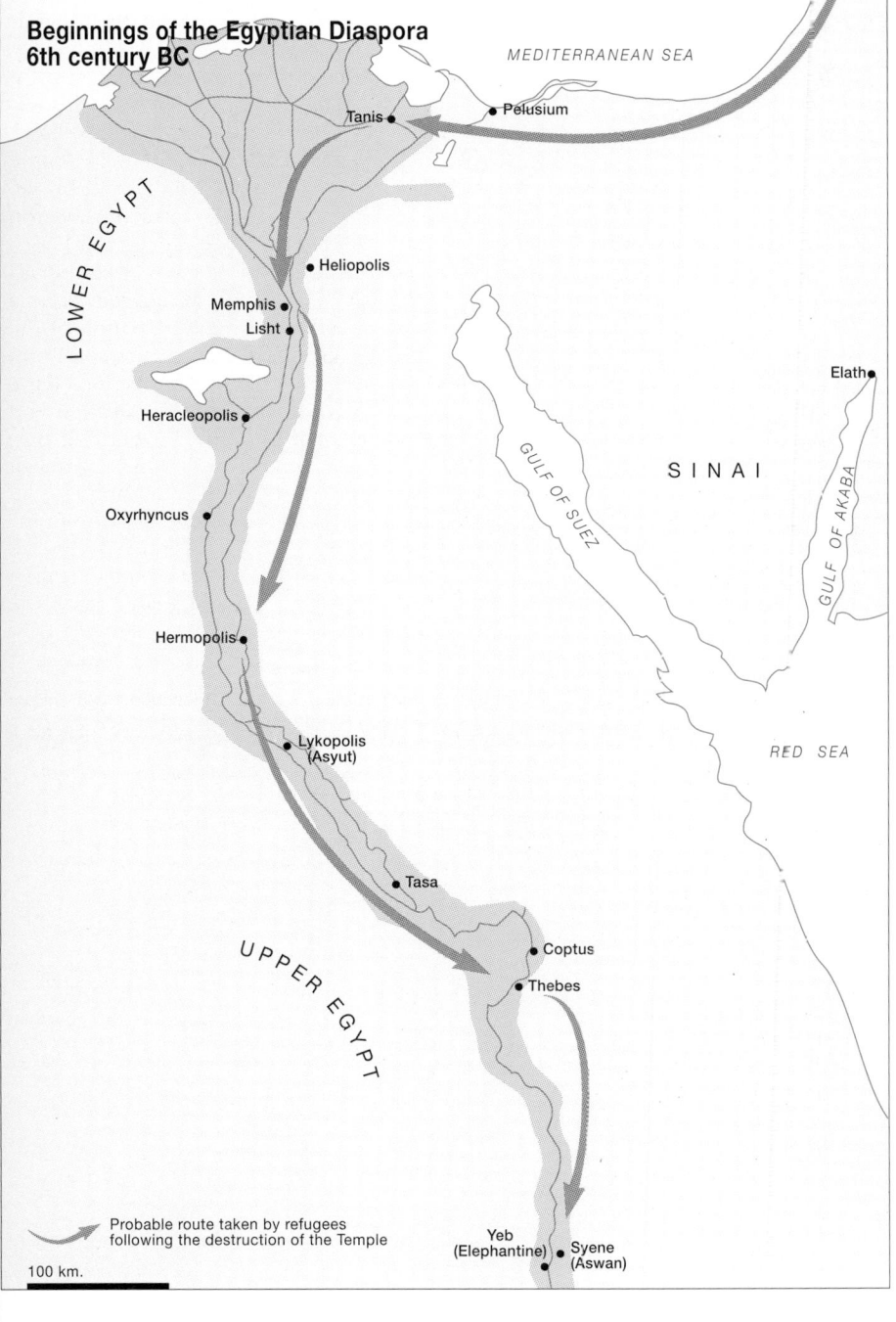

### Beginnings of the Egyptian Diaspora 6th century BC

MEDITERRANEAN SEA

Tanis

Pelusium

LOWER EGYPT

Heliopolis

Memphis

Lisht

Heracleopolis

Elath

GULF OF SUEZ

SINAI

GULF OF AKABA

Oxyrhyncus

Hermopolis

RED SEA

Lykopolis (Asyut)

Tasa

UPPER EGYPT

Coptus

Thebes

→ Probable route taken by refugees following the destruction of the Temple

Yeb (Elephantine)

Syene (Aswan)

100 km.

3. A rent-deed. A document from the Murashu archives of the Jewish commerce and banking family from the city of Nippur. Clay tablet inscribed in cuneiform and some Aramaic. Babylon, 5th century BC.

# Jerusalem and Judea under Persian Rule

1. Temple Mount
2. City of David
3. Upper city
4. Lower city
5. Valley of Kidron
6. Nehemiah's Wall
7. Siloam Pool
8. Dung Gate
9. Fountain Gate
10. Water Gate
11. Valley Gate
12. Horse Gate
13. East Gate
14. Miphkad Gate
15. Sheep Gate
16. Fish Gate
17. Old Gate
18. Solomon's Wall
19. Present-day Wall (Ottoman)

**Biblical Jerusalem** (probable locations)

# 6th–5th Centuries BC

Since the Return to Zion, Jerusalem was capital of the Persian province of "Yehud." A province was part of a larger administrative unit which Greek historians named satrapy. Each satrapy was governed by a member of the royal Persian household, while the provinces were ruled by local administrators nominated by the Persians, as in the case of Zerubbabel, son of Shealtiel, at the beginning of the repatriation.

The period between the inauguration of the Second Temple (516 BC) and the arrival of Ezra (458 BC) is one of the most obscure in Jewish history. While some details are provided by the Book of Ezra, the rest is conjecture based on comparisons with the situation in Judea before and after that period. Apparently the standing of the high priest rose at the expense of Zerubbabel whose name disappears from the sources at a certain point. One assumption is that Zerubbabel tried to organize a revolt against Persian rule and was subsequently punished, and another – that he was dismissed from office before making the attempt. It also seems that the rising priesthood began to form ties with notable and affluent families among the population which had not been exiled – the very same families that had been refused permission to participate in the building of the Temple. In this manner the differences between the Samaritans and the returnees began to blur – the first recognizing the Temple as their ritual center, and the latter absorbing Samaritan culture and some of their customs.

The economic and social gap within Judean society widened, partly as a result of the heavy taxation imposed by the governors of the province. The poor were forced to take costly loans, mortgage their property, and even sell their children into slavery. The Temple's standing suffered as well: the prophet Malachi blamed the priests and Levites for not respecting the House of the Lord, and the people for not bringing the customary tribute to the priests.

This was the situation which Ezra and Nehemiah encountered in Judea when they arrived in the middle of the fifth century BC. Ezra came in the seventh year of the reign of Artaxerxes, at the head of an organized group of exiles officially authorized by the king to impose the "law of the God of heaven" (Ezra, 7:21) in Jerusalem. And indeed, on his arrival in Jerusalem, Ezra organized a public reading of the Torah which lasted seven consecutive days – "They read from the book of the law of God clearly, made its sense plain and gave instruction in what was read" (Nehemiah, 8:8). There is reason to believe that this episode represents the culmination of the centuries-long process of the composition of the Torah; it gave us the Pentateuch as we know it today. In addition, Ezra campaigned for the expulsion of foreign women from Jerusalem and sought every other measure to prevent the assimilation of the Jews.

Nehemiah arrived in Jerusalem in 445 BC, the twentieth year of the

1. Samaritans on Mount Gerizim during the festival of Sukkot. The priest holding a bible manuscript.

reign of Artaxerxes. He had been an important member of the court ("I was the king's cupbearer," Nehemiah 1:11); and when he requested permission to return to the land of his fathers to rebuild the ruins of Jerusalem, the king made him governor of the province and authorized him to carry out extensive social reforms: remission of debts, restoration of property confiscated for debts, and abolition of the tribute to the governor. All these greatly ameliorated the economic situation of the people of Jerusalem.

Nehemiah's most ambitious project was the reconstruction of the city walls. The inhabitants had attempted to do this for years but had always failed. A permanent obstacle was the opposition of neighboring peoples who sent letters to the Persian king accusing the Jews of wanting the walls because they planned to rebel; there were also attempts to stop the building by force. Nehemiah, thanks to his high position and forceful personality, saw the work to completion, thus laying the ground for the city's development and prosperity.

Finally, in collaboration with Ezra, Nehemiah conducted a public ceremony to celebrate the renewal of the covenant between the people and their God: the leaders signed a written pledge promising "To walk in God's law, which was given by Moses ... to observe and do all the commandments of the Lord our Lord, and his judgements and his statutes" (Nehemiah, 10:29). This was the climax of the reforms begun by Ezra. From then on the Torah would be the Law, and Jerusalem the only Jewish center officially committed to obeying it as its constitution.

| Inauguration of the Second Temple | Ezra in Jerusalem | The Covenant of Jerusalem |
|---|---|---|
| **516 BC** | **458 BC** | **445 BC** |

**490 BC:** Battle of Marathon. Nine years after the revolt of the Greek cities in Asia Minor against Persia, the Greeks, led by Militiades, defeat the army of Darius I.
**486–465 BC:** Reign of Xerxes I, "the Ahasuerus who ruled from India to Ethiopia, a hundred and twenty-seven provinces" (Esther 1:1). After contending with rebellions in Egypt and Babylon, Xerxes invades Greece in 480 BC, defeats the Spartans and their commander Leonidas in Thermmopyles, but loses the naval battle of Salamis to the fleet of Themistocles. Against this background the people in Palestine write to Xerxes warning him that Jerusalem too plans to revolt and that its inhabitants are building the city walls for that purpose (Ezra 4:12).
**464–423 BC:** Reign of Artaxerxes I; under his protection Ezra and Nehemiah go to Judea and the walls of Jerusalem are rebuilt. This is the time of the Greek historian

2. Hercules. Clay, Michmash (Judean hills), Persian period.

Herodotus, whose work is an important source of information regarding the Persian Empire and the great cultural confrontation between the Greeks and the Persians.
**460 BC:** Encouraged by Athens, the leading Greek polis, Egypt rebels against Persia; this rebellion was only crushed in 454 BC.
**458 BC:** Ezra organizes a large caravan of returning exiles and is authorized by Artaxerxes to impose the law of the Torah in Jerusalem.
**445 BC:** Nehemiah in Jerusalem; the new governor initiates the rebuilding of the city walls; despite violent resistance of neighboring peoples, the work is soon completed. Signing of the covenant in Jerusalem; among its important decrees: prohibition of mixed marriages, prohibition of trade on the Sabbath, obligation to remit debts and to return confiscated land to its owner every seventh year (shemittah), and regular payment of taxes and tithes to the priests of the Temple. "And the rulers of the people dwelt at Jerusalem... And the residue of

Israel... were in all the cities of Judah" (Nehemiah 11:1,20)

3. A silver piece coined between 361 and 333 BC by the Persian governor of the province "beyond the river" (Euphrates) and of Cilicia, a province which included Syria and Palestine.

# From Alexander to Pompey

1. A Hellenistic sepulcher. Marissa, Idumea, 2nd century BC.

**D**uring the Hellenistic-Roman episode of its history, the Jewish settlement in the Land of Israel underwent considerable territorial changes, mostly as a result of frequent political upheavals. When Alexander the Great's army conquered the region (332 BC), the borders of the Jewish entity were approximately the same as they had been after the Return to Zion. During two centuries of Persian domination, most of the Jewish population was concentrated in the mountainous area of Jerusalem and its environs. To the west Jewish settlement reached the edge of the coastal plain; to the east it reached as far as the Jordan River in the Jericho valley, including a small portion of Transjordan. The Jewish territory, then, was deprived of access to the sea and surrounded by a foreign and often hostile population.

This demographic distribution remained basically unchanged during the Hellenistic period. Until the Hasmonean revolt (167 BC), there was

no significant enlargement of the Jewish settlement except for a few incursions northward towards the Galilee. But these small colonies of settlers, particularly in the western Galilee, constituted such a vulnerable minority in the midst of a non-Jewish population that when the revolt began, Mattathias and his sons had to transfer the Jews to the safety of Jerusalem. Admittedly, there were some larger Jewish enclaves inhabiting the eastern Galilee and the Jezreel valley, but the vast majority of the Jewish population of Palestine remained concentrated in the Judean hills and in Jerusalem.

It was only during the time of Jonathan and Simeon that a significant expansion of Jewish settlement began, as territories of southern Samaria and of the lowlands were annexed to the budding Hasmonean state. Simeon (r. 142–134 BC) seized both Gezer and Jaffa and in this way created a continuous strip of land between Jerusalem and the Mediterranean. Jaffa was to be the principal Jewish port for the rest of the Second Temple period since the other coastal towns remained Greek cities.

The really spectacular turning point, however, occurred during the reign of John Hyrcanus (134–104 BC). Following the Idumeans' conversion to Judaism, the border of the Jewish domain was pushed southward as far as the northern Negev, and conquests in the north added large territories of Samaria to Judea, including the city of Bet-Shean. The annexation of the Galilee was completed during the reign of John Hyrcanus' son, Aristobulus I (104–103 BC). Finally, the latter's brother, Alexander Yannai (103–76 BC), enlarged the Hasmonean state to its maximum territorial expansion. He conquered territories which were populated mostly by non-Jews – the coastal plain in the west, northern Transjordan and the Golan in the east – thus extending the Jewish kingdom to dimensions which it had not known since the unified monarchy in the days of David and Solomon nine centuries earlier.

Less than two decades after Yannai's death, the Roman conquest by Pompey's legion (63 BC) shrank the expanse of the Jewish state once again. Although it retained its autonomy in internal affairs, the country was nonetheless a vassal state, and the policy of the Roman ruler was unequivocal: only territories populated by a Jewish majority were to remain under the administration of Hyrcanus II (63–40 BC). All the territorial gains of Alexander Yannai, as well as some of the acquisitions of John Hyrcanus, were lost; and the Jewish state was reduced to the territories of Judea, the Galilee, eastern Idumea, and western Transjordan. As for the Greek towns in Palestine, they either regained their autonomy or were annexed to Syria. There was a slight improvement when Julius Caesar, in his enmity towards Pompey and in gratitude to Hyrcanus II and to the Antipater family for their loyalty, restored the port of Jaffa to Judea and a few other territories which had belonged to the Hasmonean state.

| The Hellenistic conquest | The Hasmonean revolt | John Hyrcanus |
|---|---|---|
| 332 BC | 167 BC | 134–104 BC |

2. A seal of an Epiagoranomos (an official in charge of inspection of the markets). Imprint on a jug handle, Jaffa, 130–129 BC.

**333 BC:** The Battle of Issus: Alexander defeats Darius III and then turns to the Near East in order to cut off the Persian fleet from its bases in Phoenicia.
**332 BC:** Alexander dispatches his lieutenant

Parmenio to conquer Syria and Palestine.
**323 BC:** Death of Alexander the Great.
**306–304 BC:** Alexander's generals, the Diadochi ("successors"), fight over his empire, each taking the title of king and

founding a dynasty; Asia falls to the Seleucids, Egypt to the Ptolemies.
**300 BC:** Founding of Antioch.
**247 BC:** Founding of the Parthian kingdom.
**188 BC:** Peace of Apamea; after defeating Antiochus III near Magnesia, the Romans dominate Asia Minor.
**167 BC:** Beginning of the Hasmonean revolt.
**162 BC:** Beginning of fratricidal wars among the Seleucids. Bacchides, governor of *Coele Syria* (southern Syria, part of Lebanon and northern Palestine) is sent to Palestine where he installs Alcimus, a hellenizer faithful to the Seleucids, as high priest.
**160–155 BC:** Bacchides builds a series of fortresses around Jerusalem to strengthen the Seleucid hold on the city.
**147 BC:** Jonathan attacks the forces of Appolonius, general of Demetrius II, and defeats them in a campaign between Jabneh and Ashdod – the first military action of a regular army outside Judea.
**139 BC:** The delegation sent by Simeon to Rome returns armed with the Senate's order

3. "Gezer's boundary." Over this Hebrew inscription the name Alkios – probably the name of the town's governor – is engraved in Greek letters in reverse. Western Judea, 1st century BC.

to the kings of Egypt, Syria, Cappadocia, and Phrygia not to harm the land of the Jews.

# 332 BC–63 BC

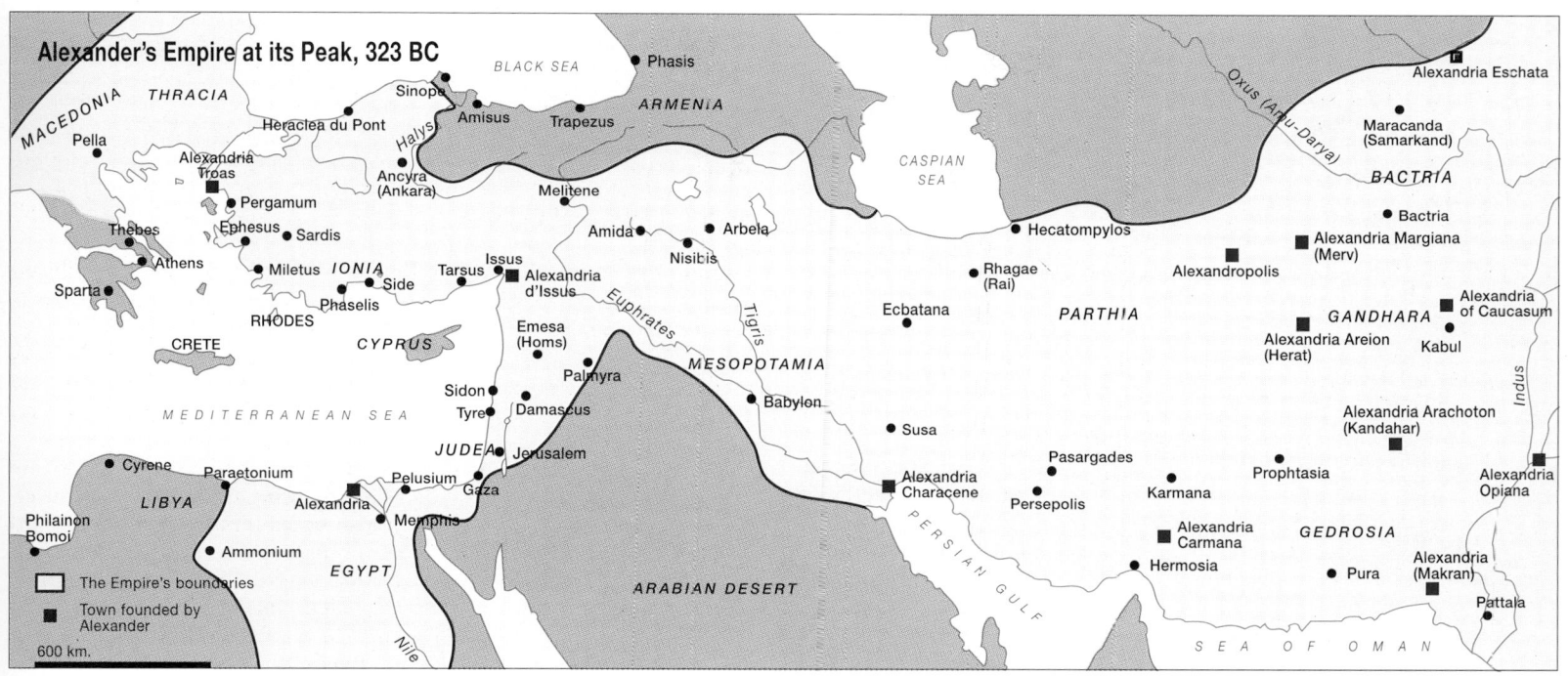

## Alexander's Empire at its Peak, 323 BC

BLACK SEA
MACEDONIA
THRACIA
Pella
Alexandria Troas
Thebes
Ephesus
Sardis
Athens
Miletus
IONIA
Sparta
Side
Phaselis
RHODES
CRETE
CYPRUS
MEDITERRANEAN SEA
Cyrene
Paraetonium
LIBYA
Alexandria
Philainon Bomoi
Memphis
Ammonium
EGYPT
Nile
Phasis
Sinope
Amisus
Trapezus
ARMENIA
Heraclea du Pont
Halys
Ancyra (Ankara)
Melitene
Amida
Arbela
Nisibis
Tarsus
Issus
Alexandria d'Issus
Emesa (Homs)
Euphrates
Tigris
Sidon
Palmyra
Tyre
Damascus
Babylon
JUDEA
Jerusalem
Pelusium
Gaza
ARABIAN DESERT
CASPIAN SEA
Oxus (Amu-Darya)
Alexandria Eschata
Maracanda (Samarkand)
BACTRIA
Bactria
Hecatompylos
Rhagae (Rai)
Alexandropolis
Alexandria Margiana (Merv)
Ecbatana
PARTHIA
GANDHARA
Alexandria of Caucasum
Alexandria Areion (Herat)
Kabul
Susa
Pasargades
Persepolis
Karmana
Prophtasia
Alexandria Arachoton (Kandahar)
Indus
Alexandria Opiana
Alexandria Characene
PERSIAN GULF
Alexandria Carmana
GEDROSIA
Hermosia
Pura
Alexandria (Makran)
Pattala
SEA OF OMAN

The Empire's boundaries
Town founded by Alexander
600 km.

## Judea before Alexander, C. 350 BC

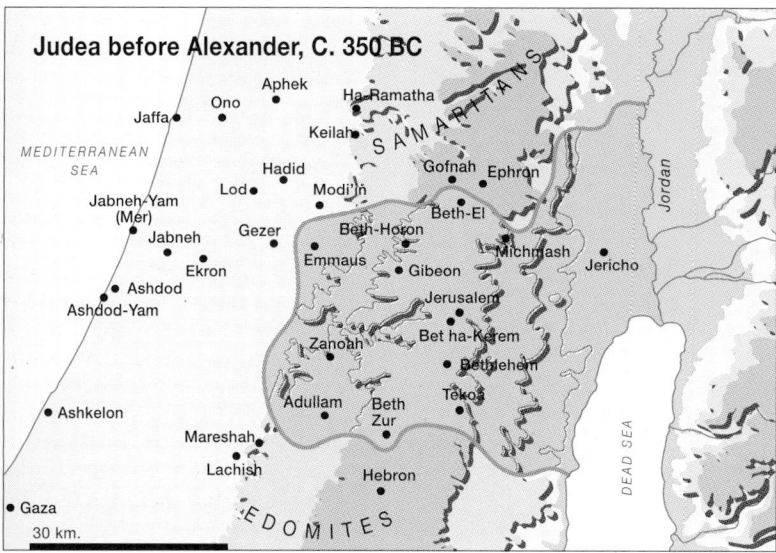

MEDITERRANEAN SEA
Jaffa
Ono
Aphek
Ha-Ramatha
Keilah
SAMARITANS
Hadid
Gofnah
Ephron
Lod
Modi'in
Jabneh-Yam (Mer)
Gezer
Beth-El
Jabneh
Beth-Horon
Michmash
Jericho
Ekron
Emmaus
Gibeon
Ashdod
Jerusalem
Ashdod-Yam
Zanoah
Bet ha-Kerem
Bethlehem
Adullam
Beth Zur
Tekoa
Mareshah
Lachish
Hebron
Gaza
EDOMITES
Jordan
DEAD SEA
30 km.

**Alexander Yannai**
**103–76 BC**

**The Roman Conquest**
**63 BC**

**129 BC:** Creation of the province of Asia. Antiochus VII is killed during a campaign against the Parthians. The Seleucid kingdom ceases to exist. The Parthian Empire swallows Babylonia.
**128 BC:** John Hyrcanus' conquests in Transjordan ensure his control over the ancient "royal road" from Damascus to Elath.
**125 BC:** John Hyrcanus conquers Idumea (Edom) and compels its people to adopt Judaism.
**108–107 BC:** John Hyrcanus attacks Greek towns outside Judea; siege and destruction of Samaria, conquest of Scythopolis (Bet-Shean).
**103–102 BC:** Alexander Yannai's campaign against Acre. Wars against Ptolemy Lathyrus.
**101 BC:** Alexander Yannai's first campaign in Transjordan.
**100 BC:** Alexander Yannai's campaign against Gaza and its colonies.
**99–95 BC:** Alexander Yannai's campaign against the Nabatean kingdom (Negev).

**95 BC:** The Parthians sign a treaty with Rome which fixes the Euphrates as their western frontier.
**94 BC:** Ptolemy Lathyros succeeds in placing Demetrius III on the throne of Syria.
**88–74 BC:** First war of Mithridates, King of Pontus in northern Anatolia, against Rome. Conquests of Tigranes I, King of Armenia.
**83–80 BC:** Second campaign of Alexander Yannai in Transjordan; conquest of most of the Greek towns and invasion of the Golan.
**76 BC:** Death of Alexander Yannai; his widow Salome Alexandra rules the country; his son Hyrcanus II is high priest.
**74 BC:** Tigranes returns home after conquering Acre and endangering the independence of the Hasmonean state.
**74–64 BC:** Second war by Mithridates of Pontus against Rome. The conquests of Lucullus and Pompey in Asia Minor.
**67 BC:** Death of Salome; beginning of an open war between her sons Hyrcanus II and Aristobulus II.
**63 BC:** Pompey conquers Palestine.

*4. The fortress Alexandrium, probably built by Alexander Yannai. Sartaba, eastern Samaria.*

# Between Jerusalem and Alexandria

The existence of a widespread and dynamic diaspora was one of the distinctive features of the Second Temple period. What had been a prophetic threat in biblical times became a permanent reality. This reality bears a remarkable similarity to the situation modern Jewry has been in from the beginning of the twentieth century: a strong center in Palestine, and a rich and powerful diaspora, comfortably integrated into its surroundings, but also most solicitous toward this center, supporting it by sending money, sympathy and pilgrims. The painful question of "dual allegiance" arose among the Jews living within the highly-attractive Greco-Roman civilization as frequently as it does today for the Jews in the western world.

The dispersal began with the great deportations at the end of the First Temple period. Inhabitants of the Israelite kingdoms had been forcibly transferred to Mesopotamia, while others fled to neighboring countries. The communities they formed were able to absorb other exiles forced to leave Palestine by new conquerors. In Egypt, with the exception of the community in Elephantine (Yeb) which had existed there since Persian times, the Jews probably arrived after the conquest of Alexander (332 BC). But there is no doubt that the great Alexandrian community was established when Ptolemy I, having conquered Palestine, deported a large number of Jews to Egypt (301 BC). Other conquests followed, notably by Pompey (63 BC), then the short-lived occupation by the Parthians (40 BC); all these had similar consequences.

Yet the dispersal was not entirely the result of forced exile. Hellenistic rule unified the Mediterranean world and enabled merchants to travel longer trade routes. Jewish merchants tempted by new opportunities abroad would later bring over more of their relatives and friends, thus encouraging emigration from Palestine. Furthermore, this diaspora experienced a phenomenon previously unknown on such a large scale: conversions to Judaism. Long before the arrival of the early Christian missionaries, the Jews, as all documentary sources confirm, were busy propagating their faith. Many aristocrats as well as simple folk, in Rome and in the East, embraced Judaism. The example of Adiabene, a small kingdom in northern Mesopotamia, is particularly striking because the entire royal household including the reigning Queen Helena converted to Judaism and established strong ties with Jerusalem.

The political status of the Jews varied from country to country. The "feudal" and heterogenous character of the Parthian kingdom ensured considerable autonomy to the various ethnic groups so long as they proved their loyalty in times of war (mostly against Rome). On the other hand, the Hellenistic kingdoms (and the Roman Empire which was to succeed them), being centralized states and bearers of a highly assimilative culture, intervened in the affairs of their subjects and affected their way of life to a much greater extent. This resulted in a new kind of Jew:

1. The synagogue in Sardis. Lydia, end of 2nd century AD.

the "Hellenizer" – Jewish by virtue of his ethnic origin, Greek by virtue of his language, dress, and daily habits. This acculturation also gave birth to a new type of Jewish thinker, best exemplified by Philo of Alexandria: perfectly at ease within the general culture, adopting Greek ideas and techniques, yet loyal to his ancestral tradition and eager to represent it to his Greek readers in the most favorable light. The hellenized Jew would faithfully send his annual donation – his *shekel* – to the priests in the Temple, occasionally "ascend" to Jerusalem to participate in person in the ritual, but would nevertheless consider Alexandria his second yet true motherland.

| First Jews in Alexandria | The Septuagint Bible | Judah Maccabee's delegation to Rome |
|---|---|---|
| **301 BC** | **c. 250 BC** | **161 BC** |

2. Ossuary with architectural decoration. Jerusalem, Mount Scopus, 1st century BC.

**332 BC:** Egypt is conquered by Alexander the Great. Jews begin to flock to Hellenistic Egypt.
**301 BC:** Ptolemy I, King of Egypt, attacks Palestine and sends Jewish prisoners to Alexandria.
**Middle of 3rd century BC:** Bible translated into Greek (the Septuagint) in Alexandria.
**Between 170 and 160 BC:** The Hellenizers' party rules Jerusalem; the high priest Onias III is deposed and his son, Onias IV, prefers to depart for Egypt where he founds a temple near the Jewish military colony at Leontopolis (the "Temple of Onias").
**161 BC:** Judah Maccabee's emissaries establish diplomatic relations with the Roman Republic.
**139 BC:** The Roman authorities forbid Jews to proselytize and to open houses of prayer in the city; Jewish missionaries are banished from Rome.
**132 BC:** Ben Sira's grandson settles in Egypt where he will translate his grandfather's book, *The Wisdom of Ben Sira*

3. A cup bottom. Rome, 4th century AD.

or *Ecclesiasticus*, from Hebrew to Greek.
**59 BC:** Flaccus, the Roman governor of Asia Minor, prevents the Jews in his province

# 4th Century BC–2nd Century AD

The Diasporas, 4th century BC – 2nd century AD

MACEDONIA
BLACK SEA
THRACIA
PONTUS
GALATIA
CAPPADOCIA
ARMENIA
ADIABENE
MESOPOTAMIA
MEDITERRANEAN SEA
CYRENE
EGYPT
ARABIA

Rome, Capua, Beneventum, Brundisium (Brindisi), Neapolis (Naples), Tarentum, Dyrrachium, Philippi, Byzantium, Heraclea, Sinope, Amisos, Trapezus (Trebizonde), Nicopolis, Beroea, Thessaloniki, Larissa, Gangra, Ancyra, Caesarae, Melitene, LESBOS, Mytilene, Pergamum, Amida, Edessa, Nisibis, Singara, Arbela, Hatra, Patras, Delphi, CHIOS, Smyrna, Sardis, Iconium, Sicyon, Corinth, Athens, Ephesus, SAMOS, Miletus, Laodicea, Tarsus, Dura-Europos, Samarra, Ecbatana, Sparta, DELOS, Halicarnassus, Perga, Sice, Phaselis, Antioch, Aradus, CYPRUS, Salamis, Palmyra, Ctesiphon, Seleucia, Babylon, Susa, CRETE, RHODES, Gortyna, Beyrouth, Damascus, Nippur, Tyre, Bozrah, Apollonia, Ptolomais, Cyrene, Berenice, Barqa, Jaffa, Jabneh, Jerusalem, Alexandria, Pelusium, Athribis, Leontopolis, Memphis, Elath, Arsinoe, Heracleopolis

Prior to conquest of Ptolemy 301 BC
During the Hellenistic period 301-63 BC
After Pompey's conquest 63 BC

300 km.

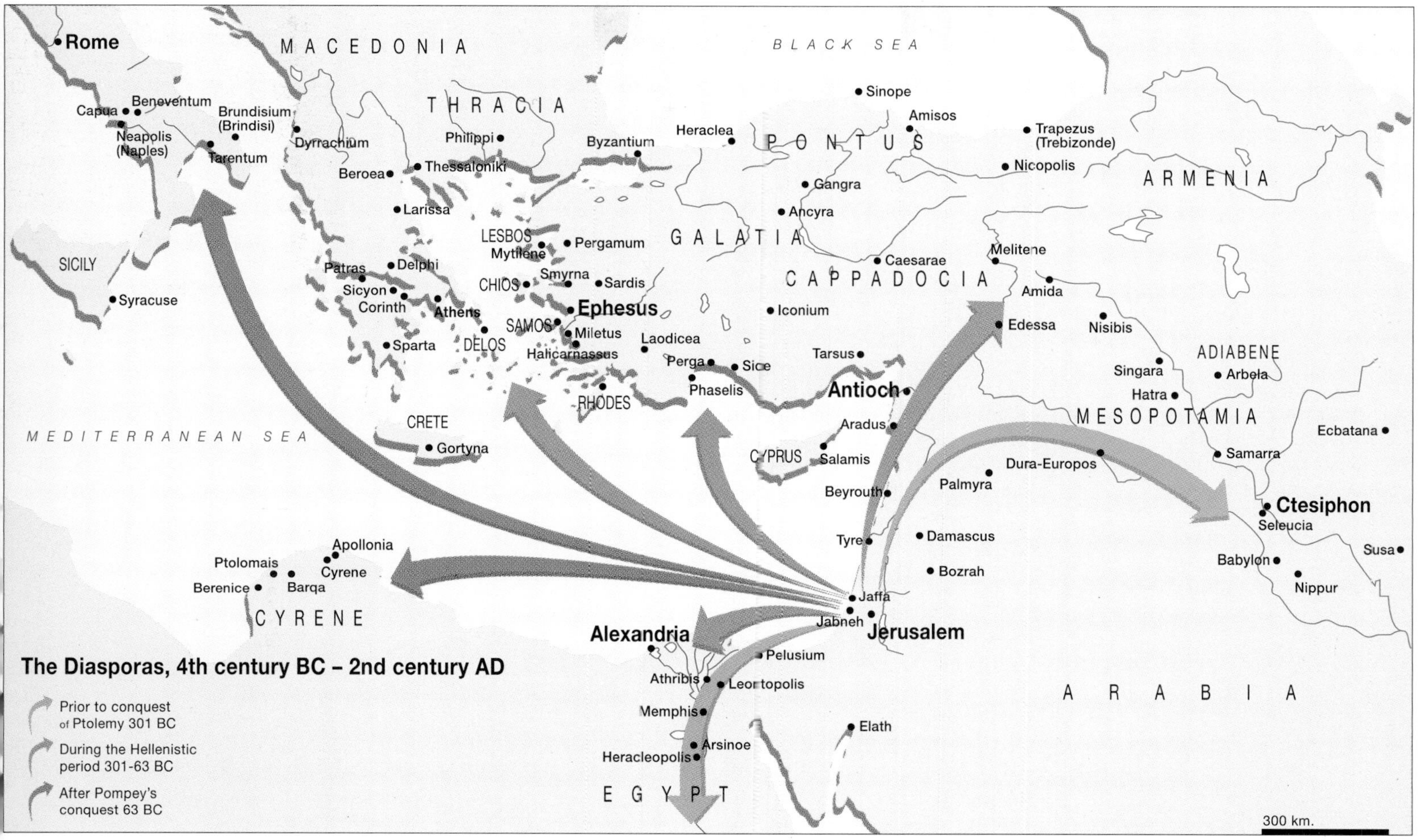

As long as the Temple was standing, its attraction was great enough to connect the Jews of the diaspora to the land of Israel. It was Jerusalem which imparted religious law, it was there that instructions concerning the Hebrew calendar were announced – at first by lighting torches on mountaintops, then by messengers. The destruction of the Temple (70 AD), and even more so, Bar Kokhbah's disastrous revolt (135 AD), inevitably weakened these ties. It is true that with the exception of Babylonia, Egypt, and North Africa (at least until the terrible blows inflicted by Emperor Trajan upon the African diaspora in 117), we know very little about other Jewish communities during the early centuries of the Christian era. Our basic information about them derives from archeological findings – synagogues throughout the Empire or catacombs in the city of Rome. Beginning with the fourth century AD, our knowledge is enriched by documents of Roman legislation. These texts, containing laws adopted mostly under the pressure of the Church, reveal that the diaspora still maintained contacts with Palestine, that the *nasi* (president) in Tiberias continued to receive donations from the communities abroad, and that he was still capable of nominating and dismissing their leaders. Rome attempted to undermine this unifying institution of the Jewish world, finally abolishing it in the fifth century.

| Riots in Alexandria | Great Revolt in Palestine | Revolts in the diaspora |
|---|---|---|
| 37–41 | 66–73 | 115–117 |

from sending their contributions to the Temple in Jerusalem; brought to justice before the Senate, he is defended by Cicero (*Pro Flacco*).

**44 BC. March:** Assassination of Julius Caesar who is mourned by the Jews of Rome as a benefactor of their people. At that time, according to Strabo, a Greek historian cited by Josephus Flavius (*Antiquities XII*), the Jews "are scattered in all the towns, and it is difficult to find a place in all the inhabited world which has not received them . . . ."

**12 BC:** An edict of Augustus confirms the right of Jews to send their *shekel* to the Temple.

**19 AD:** In Tiberius' reign, a new attempt to prohibit the spread of Judaism in Rome; 4000 Jews of military age are dispatched to Sardinia to crush a local revolt, and the rest are banished (although it is doubtful that all of them actually left).

**37–41:** Bloody anti-Jewish riots in Alexandria during the reign of Gaius Caligula; many

Jews are killed, the rest abandon their homes and congregate in one quarter of the city; 38 members of the *Gerusia* (the community's council of elders) are arrested and publicly flogged.

**41:** Emperor Claudius confirms the rights of Jews in Alexandria and throughout the Empire: "Bwecause I believe they are worthy of it for their loyalty and friendship to the Romans" (*Antiquities XIX*).

**66:** During the events preceding the revolt in Judea, scores of Jews in Damascus are driven into a gymnasium and massacred.

**73:** After the fall of Masada, some Judean zealots flee to Egypt to incite the Jews of Alexandria to rebel, but most are denounced to the authorities.

**73–74:** The "Temple of Onias" in Egypt is closed down.

**115–117:** Revolt of the diaspora Jews during the reign of Emperor Trajan.

*4. Jewish occupations in Alexandria during the Hellenistic period. Reconstruction.*

# Literature in the Second Temple Period

The great diversity of the Jewish people and its culture during the Second Temple period is well reflected in the variety of literary genres produced both in Palestine and in the diaspora. Yet, since this was when the books of the bible were being canonized and incorporated into a single corpus of Holy Scriptures, later works could not possibly attain the same level of acceptance by all strata of Jewish society. Consequently, most Jewish writings from these centuries survived, paradoxically perhaps, only if they were translated into Greek and included in the Christian canon of scriptures, in addition to the "Old" and "New" Testaments.

Jews consider almost all the literature of the Second Temple period as apocryphal ( "*Sefarim Hizonim,*" extraneous books, as they are called in Hebrew). Although this in itself did not invalidate these works, the fact that they were excluded from the biblical canon has led to their being left out of Jewish collective memory. Thus, the only texts of that period to have reached us – not through the transmission of the various churches, but in their original Hebrew or Aramaic – are those that have been discovered in the twentieth century in caves or ravines on the shores of the Dead Sea. These precious documents contain not only the writings of the Judean Desert (or the Dead Sea) sect, but also substantial fragments of the "extraneous" books.

The period saw a proliferation of apocalyptical writing. Intended to offer solace to Jews during times of great hardship, these works describe the blessings of a better future. Some of the visions predicted improvements which were to follow as a natural development of human history, but in most cases the promise is eschatological: the End of Days was to follow a world-wide catastrophe which would change the entire cosmic order. Were these texts related to the prevalence of messianic expectations? If they were, then one should inquire to what extent these visions inspired the movements of revolt against the political order. Furthermore, since it was generally believed by the Jews at the time that prophecy in the biblical sense had ceased to exist, apocalyptical visions were either pseudepigraphical, i.e. attributed to biblical figures – Enoch, Baruch son of Neriah, Ezra (Esdras), and so forth – or were written anonymously (the Book of Maccabees, for example).

Historiography, on the other hand, was quite rare. Some works of an "historical" nature were, in fact, fictitious tales of ancient heroes performing deeds of piety (Tobit), of valor (Judith), or of sagacity (the story of Susanna saved by Daniel from false accusations). The single famous Palestine-born Jewish historian in that period was the one regarded by the Jews as a defector to the Romans: Joseph ben Mattathias, known as Josephus Flavius. One of his major works, *The Jewish War*, concerns a short and well-defined period: the great revolt against the Roman occupation (66–73 AD). The other, *Jewish Antiquities*, unfolds a wide fresco of Jewish history from its beginnings. The influence of Hellenistic historiography is evident in both works. As Josephus himself admits in book XX of his *Antiquities*, historiography was not a Jewish vocation. Admittedly, others besides Josephus wrote history books, but almost all of them lived in the Hellenistic diaspora, mostly in Egypt and North Africa; and we have only fragments of their works in citations by Greek, Roman, or ecclesiastical writers. The single historiographical work of the Hellenistic diaspora to have survived in its entirety is II Maccabees. Written by a Jew devoted to his heritage and religion, it utilizes the best of Hellenistic historiographical methods in order to transmit a purely Jewish message.

In a remarkable effort of syncretism, the Jews in the Hellenistic-Roman diaspora attempted to maintain their "national" identity within the Greek intellectual mold. Thus, as Ptolemaic Egypt had produced the Greek translation of the Bible (the Septuagint), Egypt of the first century AD produced the greatest Jewish thinker of the Hellenistic world: Philo of Alexandria. Thoroughly versed in classical literature, philosophy, and science, Philo was also an allegorical commentator on the Pentateuch and a vigorous propagandist for Judaism, presenting the Jewish religion to the Greek reader in a light as attractive and as flattering as possible. Philo's works, as well as Jewish wisdom literature produced in Palestine and throughout the Hellenistic diaspora, were to have a great influence on the early Church Fathers.

1. Francesco di Giorgio Martini (1439–1502), Susanna in the bath.

| Ecclesiastes | | Daniel | Psalms of Solomon |
|---|---|---|---|
| **3rd century BC** | | **2nd century BC** | **1st century BC** |

**3rd century BC:** Writing of Ecclesiastes, to be included in the biblical canon. Written in Hebrew similar to that of the Mishnah, the book contains oriental and Greek wisdom themes. Probably about the same time, the composition of the Book of Tobit, a story about an upright young man and his pious deeds among the Jews in Persia.
**3rd–2nd centuries BC:** *Testaments of the Twelve Patriarchs,* a pseudepigraphic work, apocalyptic in part; a fragment of the Hebrew original was found in Qumran, but the entire text exists only in Greek. *The Book of Jubilees,* a work containing the words of God addressed to Moses and the laws given to the people of Israel; fragments of the original Hebrew were found in the Judean Desert, but the entire text was only preserved in the Ethiopian version. The composition of the biblical book of Daniel (chs. 7-12) and chapters from the book of Enoch – prophetic and apocalyptic literature which aroused hopes for redemption.
**c. 170 BC:** Composition of the *Wisdom of*

*Ben Sira;* this Hebrew sage and aphorist is the most eminent representative of Jewish literature in the Hellenistic period; his work, composed of maxims in the manner of the Book of Proverbs, reflects life in Jerusalem at the time it was captured by the Syrian Seleucids from the Egyptian Ptolemies; translated into Greek by Jesus Ben Sira's grandson who left for Egypt in 132 BC, the book was included in the Septuagint and then in the Christian Bible. About the same time a Judean historian, Eupolemos, wrote *On the Kings of Judah,* from which only a few passages survived in works of the Church Fathers.
**Middle of 2nd century BC:** The first Jewish philosopher appears to have been Aristobulus of Paneas. Fragments of his allegorical commentary on the Pentateuch have been preserved by Christian Church Fathers. He argues that Greek philosophers and poets derived their teachings from the wisdom of Moses.
**c. 120–110 BC:** I Maccabees is composed

in Hebrew in Palestine describing the period between the accession of Antiochus IV Epiphanes (175 BC) and the death of Simeon ben Mattathias. Only the Greek version in the Septuagint survived. Probably before the Roman conquest of the East, II Maccabees is composed anonymously in Egypt. It is, in fact, an abridgement of a five-volume history written by the Hellenistic Jew, Jason of Cyrene, elaborating the exploits of Judah Maccabee.
**1st century BC:** Composition of the *Psalms of Solomon,* patriotic and messianic hymns, written shortly after the Roman conquest of Palestine (63 BC); and *The Testament of Moses,* an apocalyptic and prophetic work, hostile to the Hasmoneans as well as to the Herodian dynasty. This is also the probable period of the texts known as the Dead Sea Scrolls: *The Thanksgiving Psalms,* composed perhaps by the founder of the sect at the end of the Hasmonean period; *Rule of the Congregation,* a text from Qumran revealing the community's way of life; and *Book of*

*Covenant of Damascus,* first discovered in the 19th century in the Cairo *Genizah.*
**c. 20 BC–c. 54 AD:** Lifespan of Philo of Alexandria, a Jewish philosopher, whose works were preserved by the Church mostly in the original Greek. In addition to his treatises in philosophy and biblical commentary, he wrote two works on contemporary events. In *Flaccus* he describes the anti-Jewish riots in Alexandria; *On the Embassy to Gaius* (Caligula) he relates his journey to Rome in 40 AD as head of a delegation of Alexandrian Jews protesting against the erection of the statue of the emperor in the Temple.
**c. 37–c. 100:** Lifespan of Joseph ben Mattathias, better known as Josephus Flavius, born in Jerusalem to a priestly family related to the Hasmonean dynasty. Commander of the Galilee during the great revolt in 66, he surrendered to the Romans and later composed four works: *The Jewish War* (75–79), constitutes the best and most detailed, albeit biased, exposition of

# 3rd Century BC–1st Century AD

*2. The Temple in Jerusalem, illustration in a Passover* Haggadah, *Germany, 18th century.*

| Philo of Alexandria | Josephus Flavius | IV Ezra |
|---|---|---|
| First half of 1st century AD | Second half of 1st century AD | End of 1st century AD |

*3. "Psalm 151" (the Hebrew Bible contains only 150 psalms). Manuscript of the Dead Sea, Qumran.*

the Great Revolt; *Jewish Antiquities* (73–79), a monumental history of the people of Israel from the beginning of the biblical period to the last generation before the revolt; *Life*, an appendix to the *Antiquities*, an apologetical

autobiography; *Against Apion*, a reply to criticisms on the *Antiquities* and to attacks on the Jewish people. Jews have preferred to ignore the writings of Josephus, and he is not mentioned in talmudic literature. His

works were translated into Latin in the early centuries of the Christian era.
**End of 1st century:** Two prophetic works composed in Hebrew in Palestine: *The Apocalypse of Baruch* – visions ascribed to

Jeremiah's scribe, promising redemption after the destruction of Jerusalem, and *The Apocalypse of Ezra* (or, IV Ezra) containing the vision of a weeping woman transformed into the heavenly Jerusalem.

# Hellenistic Judea

*1. The "hellenizers" in the town of Marissa. Wall painting, 3rd century BC.*

After the death of Alexander the Great (323 BC), Judea became part of "Syria and Phoenicia," ruled by the Ptolemies. For almost two centuries it was caught in the vortex of wars between both dynasties fighting over Alexander's inheritance – the Ptolemaic in Egypt and the Seleucid in Syria. The fate of Judea was determined by two factors: the attitude of the ruling sovereign towards the fundamentals of Judaism; and the outcome of the wars, conducted outside its borders but weighing heavily on the treasury of the vanquished kings. The latter was one of the causes of the great rebellion that ended Seleucid hegemony in the region.

During the third century BC, Judaism first encountered Hellenism within Judea itself. The Jewish diaspora had already been acquainted with Hellenistic civilization for a long time and had embraced some of its attributes. Jews outside Palestine became increasingly Greek-speaking, although many continued to make pilgrimages to Jerusalem and to bring the annual tribute to the Temple. In order to maintain the unity of this diversified Jewry, the high priests themselves were willing to hellenize; the crucial question was the extent of their Greek acculturation. The coastal plain of Palestine was more susceptible to Hellenistic influences since its population was mixed, and commercial negotiations facilitated cultural exchange. We have little information, however, on the measure of Hellenization in the country's interior where there were no major commercial thoroughfares.

Judea, considered by the Ptolemies as "the land of the Jews," was granted considerable autonomy. The high priest was its religious as well as its political leader; Ptolemaic sovereignty was manifested mostly in the levy of taxes collected by especially appointed tax-farmers. The fiscal burden was heavy, particularly on the peasants, but the Ptolemies never interfered with essential matters of religion or social organization. Although they encouraged those who climbed the social and economic ladder by adopting Hellenistic culture, they did not antagonize the more orthodox. Moreover, it was Ptolemy II Philadelphus who sponsored the Septuagint translation of the Bible into Greek. Thus, throughout the third century BC not even a single confrontation took place between the Jewish population and their overlords.

At the end of the fifth Syrian War, Judea came under the rule of the Seleucid Antiochus III. His first gesture was to grant the Jews a series of privileges intended to reconcile them to foreign rule. The burden of taxes was decreased, and the purity laws concerning Jerusalem reconfirmed – a guarantee that the "ancestral laws" would be respected. However, the terms of the peace of Apamea in 188 BC following the victory of the Romans over Antiochus III imposed enormous idemnity payments on the Seleucids. Antiochus IV, put on the throne by the Romans, committed a twofold mistake: he doubled the tax burden on Judea, and abused sacred Jewish values. The high priests he appointed were servile hellenizers, the treasury of the Temple was plundered, and the legal status of Judea was severely weakened. Acra, a fortified citadel built in the very heart of Jerusalem and occupied by a Syrian garrison, was a small Greek *polis* exempted from taxation.

All these elements fuelled the major revolt which was sparked off when Antiochus ordered the Jews, under penalty of death, to abandon their religion (though not necessarily to hellenize). As the decree applied only to Jews in Judea and adjacent regions, it should be seen as a political move rather than as an act of religious fanaticism. Yet, faced with the choice of apostasy or rebellion, the Jews chose to rebel. The results of the revolt fulfilled hopes nourished for centuries. For the first time since the destruction of the First Temple, Judea was to be ruled once again by Jewish kings.

| Death of Alexander | Judea comes under Ptolemaic domination | The Septuagint Bible |
|---|---|---|
| 323 BC | 301 BC | c. 250 BC |

**332 BC:** According to legend, Alexander the Great visits Judea.
**332–331 BC:** Founding of Alexandria in Egypt.
**323 BC:** Death of Alexander the Great.
**323–301 BC:** Struggles between the Diadochi, Alexander's heirs.
**301 BC:** Judea comes under the rule of the Ptolemies as part of the province of Syria and Phoenicia.
**c. 300:** The Samaritan religion, centered on Mount Gerizim, is finally severed from the Jewish faith centered in the Temple in Jerusalem.
**c. 255 BC:** The Greek Zeno is sent on a mission to Syria and Phoenicia by Apollonius, the finance minister of Ptolemy II; his archives, "the Zeno Papyri," discovered in 1915 at the site of the Hellenistic city Philadelphia east of Faiyum, provide important information about Jewish economic and social life in Egypt and Palestine at that time. Palestine exports a variety of agricultural products, mainly wheat,

*3. Glass vessels of the Hellenistic period. 2nd–1st centuries BC.*

wine, and olive oil; it also constitutes a thoroughfare for the perfume and slave trade between Egypt and southern Arabia.
**c. 250 BC:** Ptolemy II Philadelphus orders the translation of the Bible into Greek (the Septuagint).
**Last quarter of 3rd century BC:** A Jew, Joseph ben Tobiah, is appointed tax-collector for all Judea; he represents the typical hellenizer whose life-style is completely alien to that of most of his fellow countrymen, and belongs to the class of financial agents who arouse the anger of the peasants.
**202–201 BC:** The fifth Syrian War: the Seleucid Antiochus III conquers all of Syria and Phoenicia except Gaza.
**200 BC:** Antiochus becomes ruler of Judea after the battle of Pandion; privileges granted to the Jews.
**188 BC:** Peace of Apamea: Antiochus III is forced to relinquish Asia Minor and pay Rome enormous indemnities.
**187 BC:** Death of Antiochus III; his son

# 332 BC–167 BC

*2. Greek vase with a narrow neck (lecythe). Tell Jemmeh, c. 450 BC.*

**Greek Palestine
3rd - 2nd centuries BC**

| | |
|---|---|
| | Seleucids |
| | Ptolemies |
| | Antigonids |
| | Region with a large Jewish population |
| 🏛 | Hellenistic city |
| IAMNIA | Greek name |
| Jabneh | Traditional name |
| ✗ 312 BC | Battle between Ptolemies and Seleucids |

**BLACK SEA
(PONTUS-EUXINUS)**

THRACIA · MACEDONIA · EPIRUS · Byzantium · Sinope · Trebizonde · ARMENIA · BITHYNIA · CAPPADOCIA · Larissa · **Pergamum** · GALATIA · Thebes · Corinth · SAMOS · IONIA · Apamea · **Athens** · Ephesus · Sparta · Halicarnassus · PHRYGIA · CILICIA · Tarsus · **Antioch** · Antioch Migdonia (Nisibis) · Nineveh · NAXOS · RHODES · Euphrates · Dura-Europos · Tigris · MESOPOTAMIA · MEDITERRANEAN SEA · CRETE · **Seleucia** · Babylon · Cyrene · **Alexandria** · EGYPT

ANTIOCH 🏛 PANION ✗ 200 BC · SELEUCIA 🏛 · ANTIOCHIA Hippus · PTOLEMAIS Acre 🏛 · SELEUCIA Abila 🏛 · BUCOLONPOLIS Dor 🏛 · PHILOTERIA 🏛 · ANTIOCH SELEUCIA Gadara 🏛 · CROCODILOPOLIS 🏛 · SCYTHOPOLIS Beth-Shean 🏛 · STRATON'S TOWER 🏛 · BERENICE Pella 🏛 · APOLLONIA 🏛 · SAMARIA 🏛 · ANTIOCH Gerasa 🏛 · PEGAI Aphek 🏛 · Jaffa 🏛 · IAMNIA Jabneh 🏛 · Jericho 🏛 · PHILADELPHIA Rabbath-Ammon 🏛 · AZOTUS Ashdod 🏛 · ANTIOCHIA Jerusalem 🏛 · Ashkelon 🏛 · MARISSA Mareshah 🏛 · ANTHEDON 🏛 · DEMOS SELEUCIA Gaza ✗ 312 BC · 25 km. · Thebes · ARABIA · Elephantine · Syene · Nile · RED SEA

200 km.

---

**Judea comes under Seleucid rule**

**200 BC**

**Accession of Antiochus IV**

**175 BC**

**Revolt of the Maccabees**

**167 BC**

*5. Head of Antiochus IV Epiphanes, king 175–163 BC, on a coin. On the reverse side he is portrayed as Zeus.*

*4. Letters and orders of Antiochus III (223–187 BC). Copies of Greek texts engraved on stone, Tell el-Fir, Beth-Shean valley, c. 195 BC.*

Seleucus IV ascends the throne; the future Antiochus IV is held hostage in Rome.
**175 BC:** Assassination of Seleucus IV; Antiochus IV, supported by Rome and the kingdom of Pergamum, is made king; Jason is appointed high priest and establishes in Jerusalem a *gymnasium* and an *ephebeion* (educational institutions based on the Greek model, stressing learning and athletics).
**172 BC:** Jason is deposed and replaced by Menelaus; the tax burden is increased and the treasury of the Temple is confiscated by the Seleucid king.
**170 BC:** The sixth Syrian War.
**169 BC:** Antiochus IV Epiphanes in Jerusalem.
**168–167 BC:** Apollonius, sent to Jerusalem by the king, devastates the city; Acra, a fortified citadel within Jerusalem is built; the Temple is desecrated and turned into a pagan temple; a decree compelling the Jews to abandon their religion is proclaimed, followed by the first cases of martyrdom; Mattathias raises the banner of revolt.

*6. A tower from the Hellenistic period. Samaria, end of 4th century BC.*

# Religious and Social Agitation

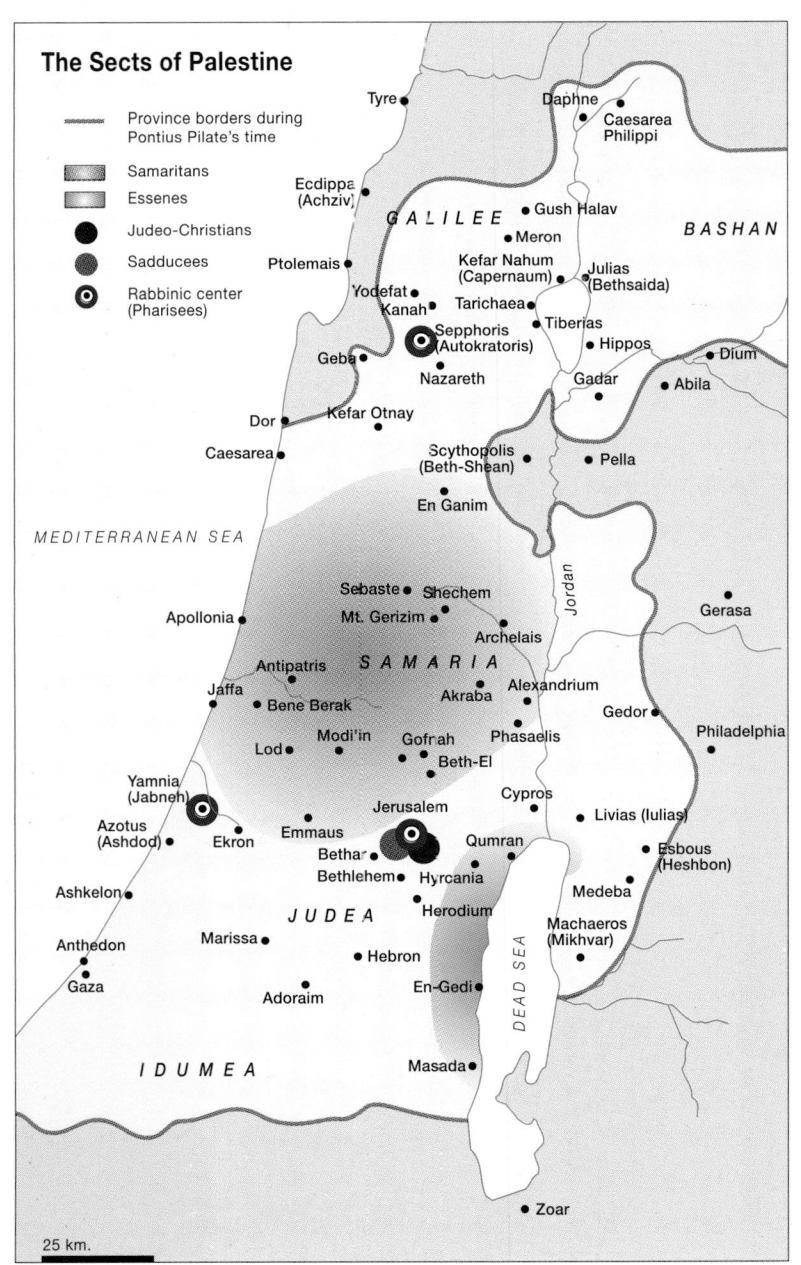

**The Sects of Palestine**

Legend:
- Province borders during Pontius Pilate's time
- Samaritans
- Essenes
- Judeo-Christians
- Sadducees
- Rabbinic center (Pharisees)

Tyre
Daphne
Caesarea Philippi
Ecdippa (Achziv)
Gush Halav
GALILEE
Meron
BASHAN
Ptolemais
Kefar Nahum (Capernaum)
Julias (Bethsaida)
Yodefat
Tarichaea
Kanah
Tiberias
Sepphoris (Autokratoris)
Hippos
Geba
Dium
Nazareth
Gadar
Abila
Dor
Kefar Otnay
Caesarea
Scythopolis (Beth-Shean)
Pella
MEDITERRANEAN SEA
En Ganim
Jordan
Sebaste
Shechem
Gerasa
Apollonia
Mt. Gerizim
SAMARIA
Archelais
Antipatris
Alexandrium
Jaffa
Akraba
Bene Berak
Gedor
Philadelphia
Lod
Modi'in
Gofrah
Phasaelis
Beth-El
Yamnia (Jabneh)
Cypros
Jerusalem
Livias (Iulias)
Azotus (Ashdod)
Emmaus
Qumran
Esbous (Heshbon)
Ekron
Betha
Ashkelon
Bethlehem
Hyrcania
Medeba
Herodium
Machaeros (Mikhvar)
Anthedon
Marissa
JUDEA
DEAD SEA
Gaza
Hebron
Adoraim
En-Gedi
IDUMEA
Masada
Zoar

25 km.

**Jesus in the Galilee**

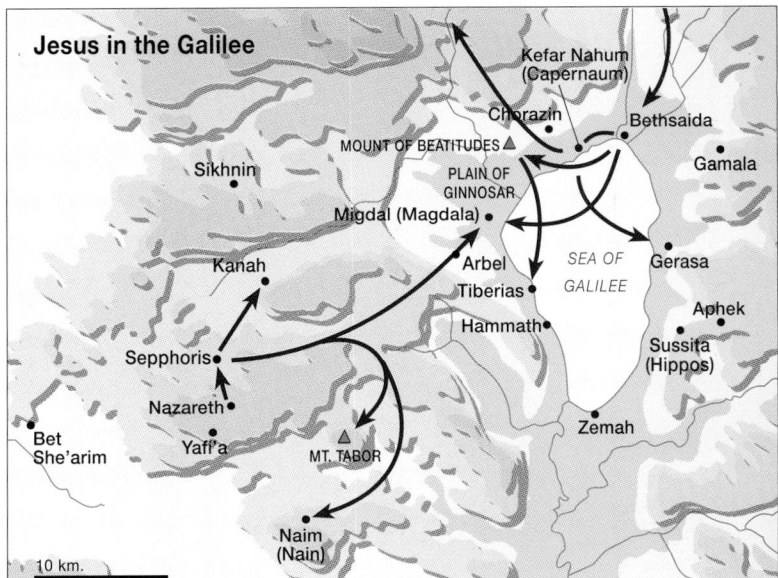

Kefar Nahum (Capernaum)
Chorazin
Bethsaida
MOUNT OF BEATITUDES
Sikhnin
Gamala
PLAIN OF GINNOSAR
Migdal (Magdala)
Kanah
Arbel
SEA OF GALILEE
Gerasa
Tiberias
Aphek
Hammath
Sussita (Hippos)
Sepphoris
Nazareth
Zemah
Bet She'arim
Yaff'a
MT. TABOR
Naim (Nain)

10 km.

J ewish society in Palestine during the Second Temple period was extremely fragmented, far beyond the natural social stratification in most human societies. On the one hand, there was confrontation between the oligarchies – both priestly and lay – which were willing to adopt Roman-Hellenistic culture; on the other hand, the masses resisted all foreign influence. This difference was to prevail throughout the period, but there were also other fiercely disputed issues. Which beliefs and ideas were to be considered as normative Judaism? What were the practical implications of these norms (implications which covered the whole range of the *mitsvoth*, all positive and negative precepts for the activities of daily life)? In other words, the crucial debate among the various groups was over the essence of Judaism.

For the Persian period we have no information about factions of this kind, but during the Hasmonean revolt we encounter a group of *Hasidim*. These "pietists" fighting alongside the Maccabees seemed to be guided by spiritual aspirations and, unlike other Jewish freedom fighters at the time, were not motivated by any "nationalist" political goals. Their objectives were the liberation of the Temple and the restoration of proper worship. Once these objectives were attained and the decrees of Antiochus IV Epiphanes revoked, they saw no reason to continue the struggle against the foreign ruler.

---

## The Opinion of an informed contemporary: Josephus Flavius

The *PHARISEES* simplify their standard of living, making no concession to luxury. They follow the guidance of that which their doctrine has selected and transmitted as good, attaching the chief importance to the observance of those commandments which it has seen fit to dictate to them. They show respect and deference to their elders, nor do they rashly presume to contradict their proposals. Though they postulate that everything is brought about by fate, still they do not deprive the human will of the pursuit of what is in man's power . . . . They believe that souls have power to survive death and that there are rewards and punishments under the earth for those who have led lives of virtue or vice: eternal imprisonment is the lot of evil souls, while the good souls receive an easy passage to a new life. Because of these views they are, as a matter of fact,

extremely influential among the townsfolk; and all prayers and sacred rites of divine worship are performed according to their exposition . . .

The *SADDUCEES* hold that the soul perishes along with the body. They own no observance of any sort apart from the laws; in fact, they reckon it a virtue to dispute with the teachers of the path of wisdom that they pursue. There are but few men to whom this doctrine has been made known, but these are men of the highest standing. They accomplish practically nothing, however. For whenever they assume some office, though they submit unwillingly and perforce, yet submit they do to the formulas of the Pharisees, since otherwise the masses would not tolerate them.

The doctrine of the *ESSENES* is wont to leave everything in the hands of God. They regard the soul as immortal and believe

that they ought to strive especially to draw near to righteousness. They send votive offerings to the temple, but perform their sacrifices employing a different ritual of purification. For this reason they are barred from those precincts of the temple that are frequented by all the people and perform their rites by themselves. Otherwise they are of the highest character, devoting themselves solely to agricultural labor . . . Moreover, they hold their possessions in common, and the wealthy man receives no more enjoyment from his property than the man who possesses nothing. The men who practise this way of life number more than four thousand. They neither bring wives into the community nor do they own slaves, since they believe that the latter practice contributes to injustice and that the former opens the way to a sort of dissension. Instead they live by themselves and

perform menial tasks for one another . . .

As for the fourth of the philosophies, Judas the Galilaean set himself up as leader of it. This school agrees in all other respects with the opinions of the Pharisees, except that they have a passion for liberty that is almost unconquerable, since they are convinced that God alone is their leader and master. They think little of submitting to death in unusual forms and permitting vengeance to fall on kinsmen and friends if only they may avoid calling any man master . . . The folly that ensued began to afflict the nation after Gessius Florus, who was governor, had by his overbearing and lawless actions provoked a desperate rebellion against the Romans. Such is the number of the schools of philosophy among the Jews.

*Jewish Antiquities*, XIII, 11–27, translated by Louis H. Feldman, The Loeb Classical Library.

1. Sandals found in one of the hiding caves of the Bar-Kokhba rebels. Judean Desert, 2nd century AD.

2. Ritual baths used by the Dead Sea sect. Qumran, Judean Desert, 1st century AD.

The creation of the Hasmonean state undoubtedly raised new questions concerning the desired character of a "Jewish" state. Political independence was a powerful catalyst which sharpened religious and social differences. Indeed, it is during this period that we first hear of parties and sects which were to become renowned through the historiographical literature of the Second Temple period (Josephus Flavius and the New Testament), and are even better known to us thanks to the discoveries made in recent decades in the Judean Desert.

The two principal factions mentioned in the literary sources, the Pharisees and the Sadducees, were divided over a whole series of basic questions of faith. The former believed in the immortality of the soul, in just retribution in the after-life, in a combination of Providence which directs human actions together with free will which enables man to choose between good and evil, and in the validity of the Oral Law in addition to the Torah as the sources of Jewish religion. The Sadducees, apparently supported only by a minority of the aristocracy and of the priesthood, maintained that only the written Law was valid, that the world was only what our senses perceived, harboring no angels or spirits, and that there was no divine intervention in human affairs. Rabbinical Judaism, which emerged after the destruction of the Temple, was undoubtedly the progeny of the Pharisees. Early Christianity, being one

of the many trends within Judaism at the end of the Second Temple period, was also influenced extensively by Pharisaic doctrines.

Besides these trends, there were many other sects, although internally divided, which tended to congregate in uninhabited secluded areas, away from the tumult of the city. Leading ascetic lives, often organized in communes, these men saw themselves as the ultimate generation before the coming of the Messiah or before a universal apocalypse which would destroy all the "Sons of Darkness." Josephus writes of the Essenes, but since the discovery of the Qumran scrolls we now know that they were not unique but one group among many which proliferated in Palestine before the destruction of the Temple.

A further division existed on the political level between those opposing Roman rule out of religious conviction and those whose opposition stemmed from social or national-messianic beliefs. It is hardly surprising then that the intellectual leaders at the time and during the following generations – the Sages – denounced the phenomenon of factionalism, describing it as a major cause for the downfall of the Jewish state. Therefore, one of the main objectives of the "Jabneh generation" – the Sages who established a new center of learning after the destruction – was to accurately define the principles of Judaism and to discredit sectarianism which constituted such a grave threat to Jewish unity.

3. Scroll of the War of the Sons of Light against the Sons of Darkness. Judean Desert, 1st century AD.

4. A decorated sarcophagus from the Second Temple period. Jerusalem, 1st century AD.

# The Revolt of the Maccabees

The revolt launched by the priest Mattathias and later led by his third son, Judah Maccabee, was both a civil war and a war against an outside enemy. The company of Greek officers who arrived at Modi'in intending to enforce the king's ordinances addressed Mattathias first, for he was held in high esteem by the villagers. They ordered him to begin the sacrificial offerings to the pagan idols, promising that in return he and his sons would be admitted to the circle of the king's "friends." Mattathias refused outright. He killed a Jew who obeyed the command and then one of the king's men. His flight to the mountains, together with his sons and his friends, marks the beginning of the uprising. Thus it appears that the revolt was directed first of all against those Jews who were willing to submit to Greek custom. Only then was it directed against the foreign occupier, the Syrian ruler who was forcibly imposing his culture upon the Jewish population and plundering the Temple and the land.

Our information about the rebellion is derived mainly from texts which eulogize Mattathias's dynasty (I Maccabees) and in particular the figure of Judah, depicted as a lion of the desert (II Maccabees). We know much less of the *Hassideans*, the "pious," who fought alongside Mattathias's sons. What is obvious, however, is that one cannot win a war armed solely with religious purity. Compromise was essential from the beginning as, for example, Mattathias's decision to fight on the Sabbath.

Moreover, the Seleucid army could not be defeated by guerrilla warfare alone. The Jewish rebels soon organized a real army modeled on the Greek military forces and capable, when fighting on its own terrain, of overcoming the Syrian troops. With great diplomatic skill they learned how to exploit the quarrels within the Seleucid dynasty, opportunely supporting some of the "usurpers" and obtaining various concessions in return. They also cultivated relations with distant nations, either for symbolic reasons, as in the case of the alliance with Sparta which was based upon the notion of affinity between the heirs of Lycurgus and the heirs of Moses, or for practical purposes, as in the alliance with Rome, the most formidable enemy of the Greeks. The negotiator with Rome was a Jewish historian of Greek culture, Eupolemus, whose father could have been the man who had negotiated with Antiochus III in 200 BC.

Maccabee diplomacy did not exclude propaganda. The Book of Daniel glorified the kingdom of the "saints" which would follow the four successive kingdoms of the beasts. Judith and Esther, heroines of the recent past, were depicted as the daughters of the bold prophetess Deborah, while Judah himself was presented as an incarnation of Joshua – judge and conqueror of the land.

The revolt achieved rapid success. At the end of the year 164 BC, the first Festival of Light (*Hanukkah*, "inauguration") was celebrated in a Temple purified of all pagan cults. (It is only through this festival that

1. Scene of the drama in the market place at Modi'in, as conceived by the monks of St. Gallen, Switzerland. Manuscript of the Book of Maccabees, 10th century.

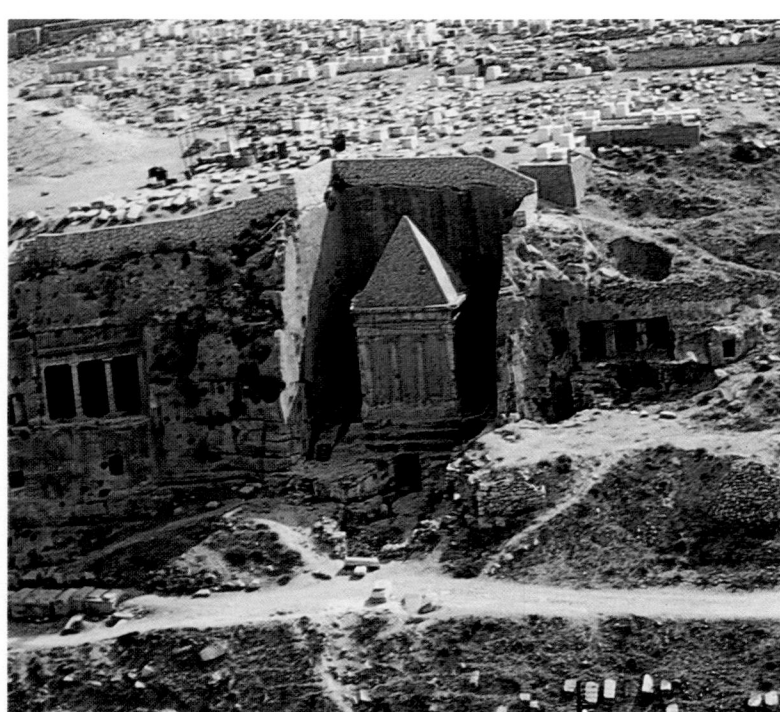

3. Hasmonean burial monuments in Nahal Kidron, Jerusalem. In the center, the one known as "Zechariah's tomb."

**Antiochus IV's edict and the beginning of the revolt** — **Hanukkah**

**167 BC** — **164 BC**

**175–174 BC:** Hellenized Jews transform Jerusalem into a Hellenistic *polis* to be known as Antioch. As an ardent "Hellenizer," high priest Jason sends delegates of the new Antioch to Tyre to represent the city at the games in honor of Hercules.
**169 BC:** Antiochus IV Epiphanes visits Jerusalem.
**168 BC:** A rumor about the death of Antiochus provokes riots in Jerusalem and in many southern towns; Jason, returning to the capital, seizes power.
**167 BC:** Antiochus IV's edict: the Jews are forced to abandon the essential practices of their religion; the Temple is consecrated to Zeus Olympius. Mattathias raises the banner of revolt.
**167–166 BC:** Apollonius, commander of the Greek forces in Samaria, is killed in a battle with Judah Maccabee's men.

4. Judah Maccabee. The Book of Jossippon, a 10th–century Jewish version of Josephus' The Jewish War, northern Italy, 1450–1470.

# 167 BC–140 BC

2. An elephant in a Seleucid battle. Painted terracotta, Myrina (western Asia Minor), 3rd century BC.

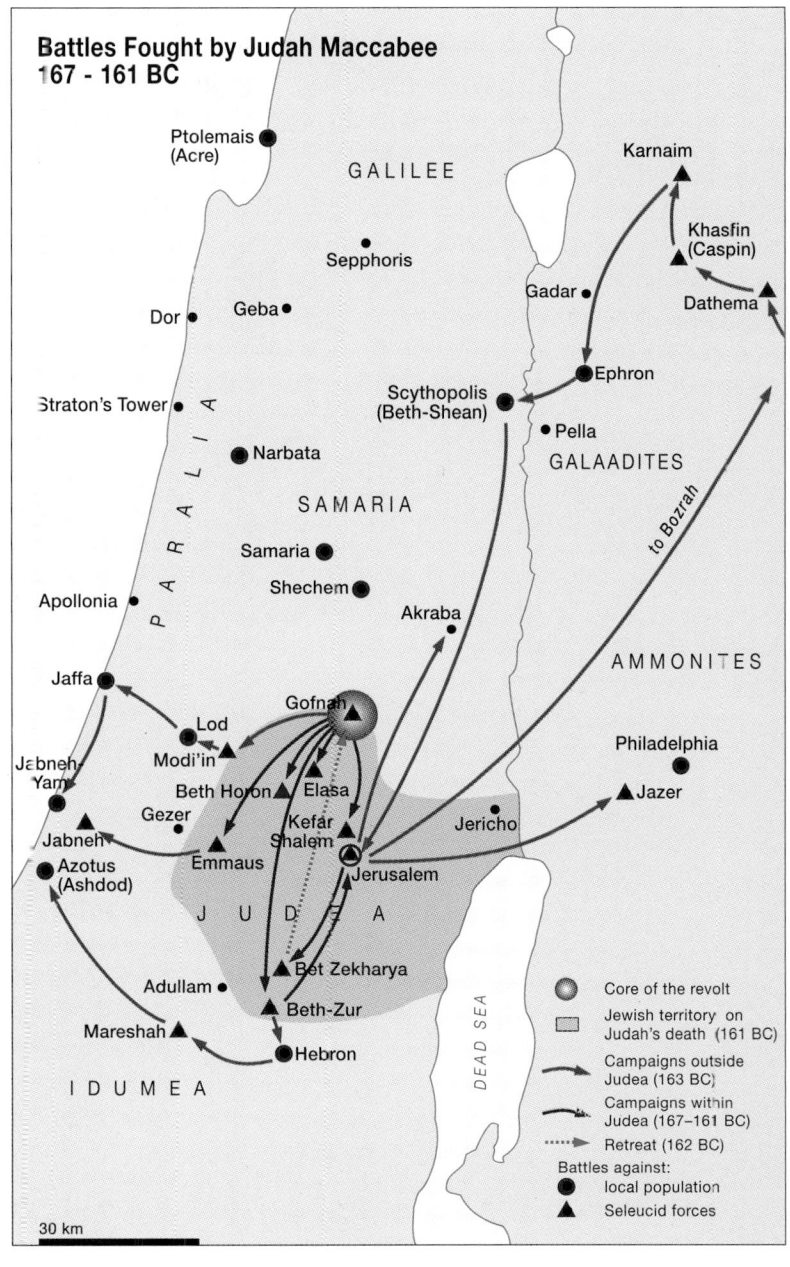

the revolt was transmitted to rabbinical posterity. The history of the revolt was retained only in Greek texts later preserved by Christian authors.) Until 141 BC, however, a Seleucid garrison remained in the citadel (*Acra*) of Jerusalem, protecting by its very presence those Jews who wished to maintain the Hellenistic way of life. Meanwhile, the Jewish state was consolidating its achievements: "purifying" the land by imposing the circumcision of all infants, eliminating "arrogant spirits," and capturing enemy cities such as Caspin on the Golan, and even tolerant Scythopolis (Beth-Shean). The frontiers of the state were enlarged to include, even before its independence, the whole of the Land of Israel. Jonathan, and later Simeon, were recognized by the Seleucids as high priests and even as governors. But the Maccabees' vision, the revival of the era of the Judges, was still but a distant dream.

**Death of Judah. Accession of Jonathan**

**161 BC**

**166 BC:** Battle of Beth Horon; Seron, commander of the Seleucid army, is defeated.
**165 BC:** Defeat of Gorgias at Emmaus. The approximate date of composition of the Book of Daniel.
**164 BC:** Death of Antiochus IV; end of the persecutions; purification and rededication of the Temple – first celebration of the Hanukkah festival (December).
**163–162 BC:** Eleazar, fourth son of Mattathias, is killed in the battle of Bet Zekharyah: thrusting his spear into a belly of an elephant on which he thought the king was riding, the beast falls on him and crushes him to death.
**162 BC:** Accession of Demetrius I in Syria; beginning of the fratricidal wars among the Seleucids. The new governor of Judea, Bacchides, brings with him the Hellenizer Alcimus to serve as high priest.
**161 BC:** Nicanor is killed in combat with Judah's forces and his army is destroyed; but in the spring Judah is also killed in battle

(near Elasa). His brother Jonathan succeeds him. Alliance with Rome.
**160–158 BC:** Hellenizers constitute the strongest party in Jerusalem; Bacchides builds fortifications around Jerusalem.
**c. 153 BC:** Onias IV, the exiled high priest, founds a temple near Leontopolis in Egypt.
**150 BC:** Death of Demetrius I.
**143 BC:** Jonathan's delegations to Rome and Sparta; his forces reach the gates of Damascus; Jaffa is captured.
**142 BC:** Tryphon, Demetrius II's rival, clashes with Jonathan at Acre and later kills him in the eastern Galilee. Accession of Simeon, Jonathan's brother and Mattathias' youngest son. Demetrius recognizes the independence of the Hasmonean state.
**141 BC:** Expulsion of the last Seleucid garrison from Jerusalem.
**140 BC:** The Great Assembly in Jerusalem proclaims Simeon as high priest, *strategus* and *ethnarch*, and makes these offices hereditary (I Maccabees 13:42). Beginning of the Hasmonean era.

**Accession of Simeon. Beginning of the Hasmonean era**

**142–140 BC**

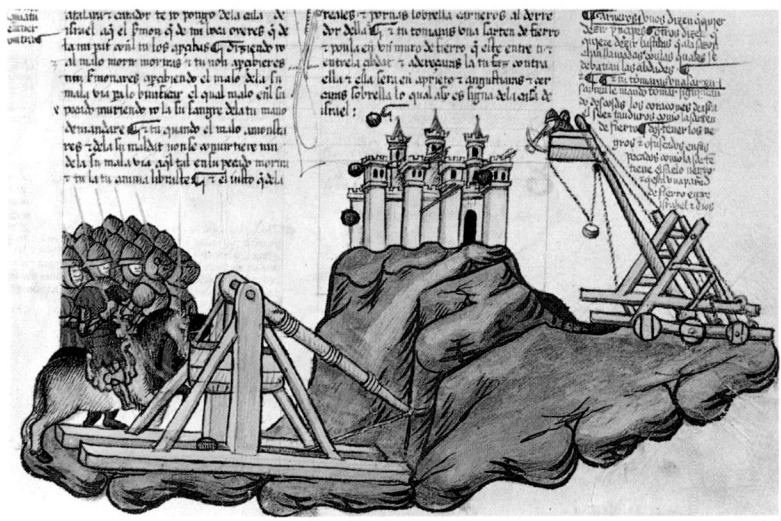

5. Judah Maccabee's assault on the Acra of Jerusalem. Alba Bible, 15th century.

# The Rise and Fall of the Hasmonean State

The political entity established by the Maccabees soon encompassed the entire territory of Judea. Skillfully manipulating the internal conflicts of the Seleucid dynasty, as well as the long-standing enmity between the northern kingdom (Syria) and the southern kingdom (Egypt), the Hasmonean rulers gradually extended their borders to include territories where Judaism was not the religion of the majority.

This "loose and multi-colored" state ruled by John Hyrcanus and his successors was not, strictly speaking, a Jewish state, but rather a Greek kingdom, closely resembling its Seleucid neighbor even in its history of family quarrels. The civil war between Alexander Yannai's sons, Hyrcanus II and Aristobulus II, was in the exact image of the fraternal rivalry which destroyed the last Seleucids. The Roman *imperator*, courted by the Hasmoneans as by the Seleucids, put an end to these struggles by establishing direct Roman domination in Syria and an indirect rule in Judea where the high priest Hyrcanus II was to enjoy a semblance of autonomy.

The Greek nature of the kingdom was evident in many aspects. Aristobulus I called himself "philhellene," and Alexander Yannai was the first to adopt the title of *basileus* (king). Even more important, these sovereigns had Greek names in addition to their Hebrew names. The "double name" phenomenon was typical of the Hellenistic period, reflected upon even in the Book of Daniel. Moreover, the rulers of the Jewish nation minted coins inscribed with their names, although not with their likeness, and the whole organization of the military and civil structures was based on Greek models, except for the imposing presence of the Temple.

Architecture too was revolutionized by Hellenism. Although nothing remains today of the Hasmonean mausoleum at Mod'in, we know from Josephus and the Book of Maccabees that it consisted of a high structure with seven towers crowned with pyramidal tops. Similar edifices have survived in the Nabatean city of Petra. In Jerusalem itself the monuments known as Jason's Tomb and the Tomb of Absalom testify to the prevalence of Hellenistic art among even non-royal circles.

It was therefore not surprising that those who were devoted to traditional Judaism could not but oppose this Greek kingdom of the Hasmoneans. At the outset the Hasmonean dynasty was borne along on a tide of religious-national enthusiasm. Yet early on, in the days of Judah Maccabee himself (165–160 BC), the first conflicts began to appear. When the Great Assembly in Jerusalem bestowed upon Simeon and his sons the functions of high priesthood, civil rule, and military command, the fears from Hasmonean power grew deeper. In the days of John Hyrcanus (134–104 BC) and his son Alexander Yannai (103–76 BC), the breach between the Pharisees and the Hellenized monarchy greatly widened. Although it is difficult to establish whether Josephus Flavius was right in dating the emergence of the Jewish sects to the period of John Hyrcanus, it seems credible that the latter "abrogated the practices imposed on the people by the Pharisees, and punished those who observed them."

Matters deteriorated even further during the reign of Alexander Yannai, who used Greek soldiers against Jewish rebels, crucifying dozens of them, and conducting a merciless war against the Pharisees. This ruthless king became a subject for admiration only after his death. Paradoxically, his widow Salome Alexandra would be remembered for her close cooperation with the Pharisees. It would seem that in rabbinical tradition no Jewish monarch could be considered good unless dead or female.

During the struggle between Hyrcanus II and Aristobulus II (67–63 BC), the "nation" (*ethnos*) was opposed to the one as much as to the other. According to Josephus, the people did not want to be governed by a king: "Tradition commands us to obey the priests of God worshipped by the Jews, but the two contenders, descendants of priests, wish to change the form of government and to reduce the Jews to the condition of an enslaved nation." Several appeals of this kind were made to the Roman authorities. Pompey's conquest and annexation brought all this strife to an end, together with the independence of the Hasmonean state.

3. Hyrcania, fortress built by John Hyrcanus. Judean Desert, c.120 BC.

| Simeon is "leader of the nation" | Accession of John Hyrcanus |
|---|---|
| 140 BC | 134 BC |

**142 BC:** Jonathan is killed by the Seleucid Tryphon, the rival of Demetrius II. Simeon, Jonathan's brother and last of the Maccabees, assumes leadership.
**140 BC:** The Great Assembly in Jerusalem proclaims Simeon high priest, *strategus* (commander), and *ethnarch* (leader), and makes these offices hereditary. The author of the First Book of Maccabees presents this year as the beginning of a new era.
**140–139 BC:** The struggle between Tryphon and Demetrius II allows Simeon to consolidate his power. Demetrius is captured by the Parthian king, Mithridates I.
**138 BC:** Accession of Antiochus VII Sidetes. Simeon's refusal to pay him taxes results in a military clash west of Gezer between a Seleucid army and a Jewish force commanded by Simeon's sons, John and Judah.
**134 BC:** Simeon is assassinated in Jericho by his son-in-law Ptolemy, governor of the region; but Simeon's son, John Hyrcanus, escapes the conspiracy which was instigated

by the Seleucids. With the army's support, John Hyrcanus assumes leadership. Antiochus VII's campaign in Palestine; siege of Jerusalem.
**131 BC:** After a siege lasting more than two years, Antiochus withdraws his troops and recognizes John Hyrcanus' rule over Judea; but at the same time, John Hyrcanus has to accept the status of vassal-king of the Seleucids.
**131–129 BC:** The first Seleucid coin inscribed with John Hyrcanus' monogram.
**129 BC:** Death of Antiochus VII during a Parthian invasion; freed of his obligations John Hyrcanus begins a vast campaign of conquests.
**128 BC:** Conquests of John Hyrcanus in Transjordan.
**126:** Beginning of the war against the Samaritans; fall of Shechem and the Samaritan temple on Mount Gerizim.
**126–125 BC:** A Jewish embassy is sent to Rome.
**125 BC:** John Hyrcanus' conquests in

## The Rise of the Hasmonean State
## 2nd - 1st centuries BC

Independent Judea at the time
of Judah Maccabee's death (161 BC)

Territorial expansion under:

Jonathan (161-142 BC)

Simeon (142-134 BC)

John Hyrcanus (134-104 BC)

Aristobulus I (104-103 BC)

Alexander Yannai (103-76 BC)

Alexander Yannai's campaigns :

⟶ 103-101 BC

⟶ 100-95 BC

⟶ 83-76 BC

□ Fortress

MEDITERRANEAN SEA

*Map labels:* Tyre, Panion (Banias), Kedesh, PHOENICIA, Seleucia, GAULANITIS, BATANAEA, Ptolemais (Acre), GALILEE, Gamala, Raphon, Asokhis (Sikhnin), Hippus, Arbel, Sepphoris, Philoteria, Abila (Avel), Dium, Dor, Gadara, Scythopolis (Beth-Shean), Dathema, Narbata, GALAADITIS, Pella, Samaria, Shechem, Regev, Gerasa, Apollonia (Arsuf), SAMARIA, Akraba, Arethusa (Pegai), Alexandrium (Sartaba), Jaffa, Ramatayim, Gedor, Modi'in, Docus, Philadelphia, Lod, Jabneh, Beth Horon, Michmash, Jericho, Gezer, Emmaus, Esbus (Heshbon), Azotus (Ashdod), Ekron, Jerusalem, Therex, Medeba, JUDEA, Hyrcania, PERAEA, Ashkelon, Hyrcania, Anthedon, Bet Zekharyah, Mareshah, Beth-Zur, Machaerus (Mikhvar), Gaza, Hebron, Adoraim, DEAD SEA, IDUMEA, MOAB, Kir of Moab, Raphia, Rhinokoroura, Zoar, NABATEANS

25 km.

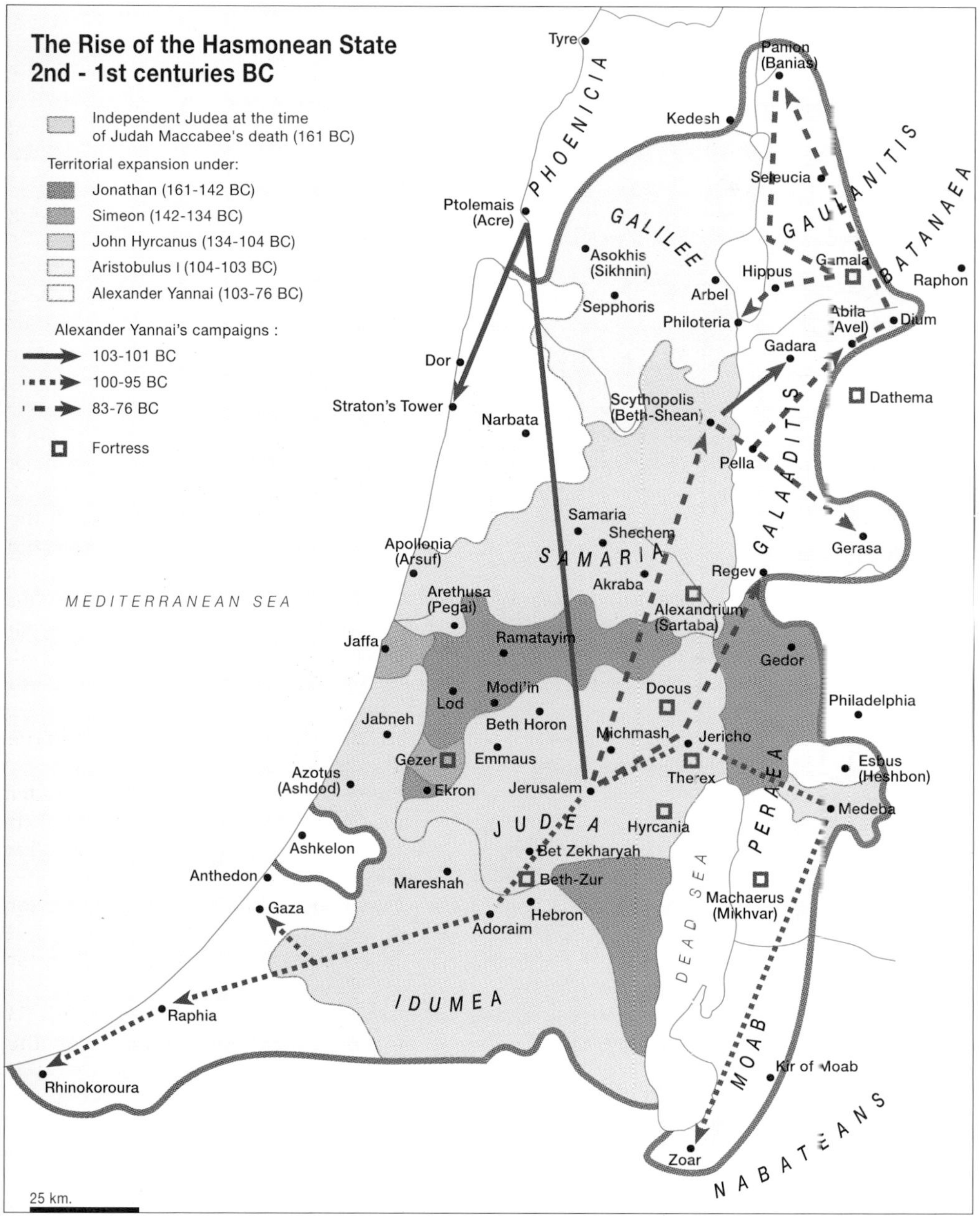

1. Nabatean art. Clay, probably from Petra in Transjordan.

2. Nabatean tomb or temple in Petra. Rock-cut architecture imitating a Hellenistic theater.

**Accession of Alexander Yannai**

103 BC

**Accession of John Hyrcanus II and Aristobulus II**

67 BC

**Pompey in Jerusalem**

63 BC

4. Bronze coin of John Hyrcanus. Obverse: double cornucopia; reverse: "John the high priest."

5. Coin of Alexander Yannai. Obverse: his Greek title ""King Alexander"); reverse: his Hebrew name, "Jonathan the king."

Idumea (northern Negev) and conversion of the Idumeans to Judaism.

**c. 120 BC:** Jason of Cyrene composes the history on which the Second Book of Maccabees will be based. Founding of the Essene settlement in Qumran.

**108–107 BC:** John Hyrcanus' war against the federation of Greek cities; siege of Samaria, capture of Beth-Shean, fall of Samaria, and the opening of the road to the Galilee.

**104 BC:** Death of John Hyrcanus.

**104–103 BC:** Reign of Aristobulus I; conquest of the Galilee and Judaization of its inhabitants.

**103–76 BC:** Reign of Alexander Yannai; as the first truly absolute Hasmonean king, he provokes strong opposition among his Jewish subjects; numerous conquests, most of them short-lived. Composition of the First Book of Maccabees.

**76–67 BC:** Reign of Salome Alexandra, Alexander Yannai's widow.

**67–63 BC:** Reign of Hyrcanus II (who will remain high priest and *ethnarch* till 30 BC); parallel reign of Aristobulus II. Since the father of these enemy brothers, Alexander Yannai, had abandoned the traditional alliance with Rome, the latter had no commitment to the land of Judea nor to the Jewish nation.

**63 BC:** Pompey creates a Roman province in Syria and thus ends the Seleucid dynasty. Then he conquers Palestine and storms Jerusalem.

# Roman Palestine

*1. The Roman aqueduct at Caesarea. 1st century BC.*

Pompey's conquest in 63 BC brought Judea into the Roman sphere of influence for the first time. From then on, except for brief intervals of invasions or internal revolts, Palestine was ruled by Rome for seven centuries, until the Arab conquest. This extended period can be divided into three stages, in which the Romans experimented with different methods of government, progressively reducing the extent of Jewish autonomy.

During the first stage, the Romans, well aware of the differences between the Judeans and their Syrian neighbors, avoided annexing Judea to the new Roman province in the north, despite potential military and administrative advantages that might have been gained. Neither did they attempt to transform Palestine into a province in itself, for this would have been too costly an operation for such a small territory. Pragmatic as always, the Romans opted for a middle course: an autonomous Jewish state, ruled, at least in theory, by a scion of the Hasmonean house, but confined to territories inhabited by a Jewish majority from which the territories conquered by the later Hasmoneans, particularly by Alexander Yannai, were severed. This partition of the land not only determined new geographical boundaries, but also underlined the old conflict between Jews and "Greeks," a conflict that would flare up each time the Romans introduced further changes in the region's administration.

Not only did the Jews suffer the loss of Hasmonean territories, they were also deprived of the Hasmonean kingship. Alexander Yannai's son, Hyrcanus II, was acknowledged by the Romans only as "ethnarch" ("leader of the people") and high priest. Ranked just beneath him was a noble Idumean family (Antipater and his sons, Herod among them) who was completely devoted to the Romans. This stage of Roman rule ended in 40 BC when the Parthians invaded Judea. They deposed Hyrcanus, exiled him to Babylonia, placing on the throne another member of the Hasmonean dynasty – Mattathias Antigonus.

The latter's reign, a brief Hasmonean renaissance, was but an interval in the mainstream of events. Herod, crowned in Rome by the Senate in 40 BC, repossessed the land in 37 BC. Thus began the second stage of Roman rule in Palestine which was to end in 6 AD with Herod's son Archelaus. This was a stage of transition, wedged between a period of autonomy under the auspices of an aristocratic Jewish family, and a time of direct Roman administration. The trend was obvious: the ruling power became less and less Jewish, and more and more Roman. Admittedly, the house of Antipater had converted to Judaism during the Hasmonean period, probably during the reign of John Hyrcanus (134–104 BC). However, despite Herod's formal "Jewishness" and his attempts to avoid offending his subjects by insisting that all non-Jewish males marrying into

| Pompey's conquest | Herod King of Judea | Herod's death | Judea becomes a Roman province |
|---|---|---|---|
| **63 BC** | **37 BC** | **4 BC** | **6 AD** |

**67 BC:** Death of Queen Salome; civil war between her two sons, Hyrcanus and Aristobulus.
**63 BC:** Pompey puts an end to the struggle when he occupies the land. Hyrcanus II, Salome's eldest son, is made high priest. In Rome this is the time of Cicero's consulate and of Catilina's rebellion.
**59 BC:** Julius Caesar's first consulate.
**55 BC:** The last Hasmonean attempt at rebellion: Alexander, Aristobulus' son, escapes to Rome, recruits an army of 30,000 men, and tries to regain the land by killing Romans and inciting the people to revolt; the proconsul Gabinius defeats him in a decisive battle at Mt. Tabor.
**53 BC:** Licinius Crassus pillages the Temple.
**47 BC:** During a civil war in Rome, Julius Caesar visits Palestine.
**47–43 BC:** After Pompey's death Caesar confirms the position of Hyrcanus II as high priest and *ethnarch*, but nominates the Idumean Antipater regent of Judea; the latter's two sons, Phasael and Herod, are

respectively governors (*tetrarchs*) of Jerusalem and the Galilee; the walls of Jerusalem are rebuilt; Jaffa and territories in the Jezreel Valley and in the Galilee are returned to the Jewish state.
**44 BC:** Caesar's assassination. Cassius occupies the eastern provinces of the empire; after the death of Antipater, Cassius nominates Herod as governor of *Coele Syria* and provides him with an army comprising non-Jewish mercenaries.
**40 BC:** The Parthians invade Palestine, capture Hyrcanus II, and exile him to Babylonia. A refugee in Rome, Herod is proclaimed King of Judea by the Senate, while Aristobulus II's son, Mattathias Antigonus, reigns in Jerusalem for three years under the protection of the Parthians.
**39 BC:** Returning from Rome, Herod begins to reconquer the country.
**37–4 BC:** Herod's reign. Liquidation of the Hasmonean dynasty.
**4 BC:** The "Varus' War": after Herod's death, uprisings in Judea are brutally put down by

the governor of Syria, Varus.
**4 BC–6 AD:** Herod's three surviving sons, Archelaus, Herod Antipas, and Philip, partition the land: the first takes Judea, Samaria, and Idumea; in 6 AD he is recalled to Rome and exiled to Gaul.
**6–66:** The Land of Israel becomes *Judaea* – a Roman province governed by a procurator, an official of equestrian rank.
**26–36:** Pontius Pilate's procuratorship; a period of tense relations between the Roman rulers and the Jews.
**30:** Death of John the Baptist. Accused of pretending to be King of the Jews, Jesus of Nazareth is condemned to death by Pontius Pilate and crucified.
**37–41:** Caligula nominates Agrippa I, Herod's grandson, as king of the territories held by Philip (37) and by Herod Antipas (39); when the emperor decides to place his statue in the Temple, the communities in the

*2. The Aphrodite of Mt. Carmel. Terracotta, 1st century AD.*

# 63 BC–3rd Century AD

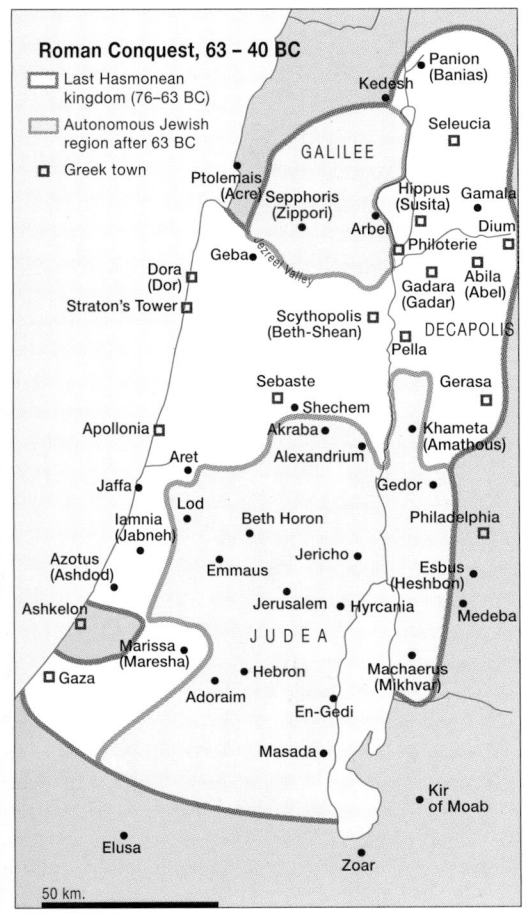

**Roman Conquest, 63 – 40 BC**

- ▭ Last Hasmonean kingdom (76–63 BC)
- ▭ Autonomous Jewish region after 63 BC
- □ Greek town

50 km.

*Map labels:* Panion (Banias), Kedesh, Seleucia, GALILEE, Ptolemais (Acre), Sepphoris (Zippori), Hippus (Susita), Gamala, Arbel, Dium, Geba, Philoterie, Dora (Dor), Gadara (Gadar), Abila (Abel), Straton's Tower, Scythopolis (Beth-Shean), DECAPOLIS, Pella, Sebaste, Gerasa, Shechem, Apollonia, Akraba, Khameta (Amathous), Aret, Alexandrium, Jaffa, Gedor, Iamnia (Jabneh), Lod, Beth Horon, Philadelphia, Jericho, Esbus (Heshbon), Azotus (Ashdod), Emmaus, Jerusalem, Hyrcania, Medeba, Ashkelon, JUDEA, Marissa (Maresha), Hebron, Machaerus (Mikhvar), Gaza, Adoraim, En-Gedi, Masada, Kir of Moab, Elusa, Zoar

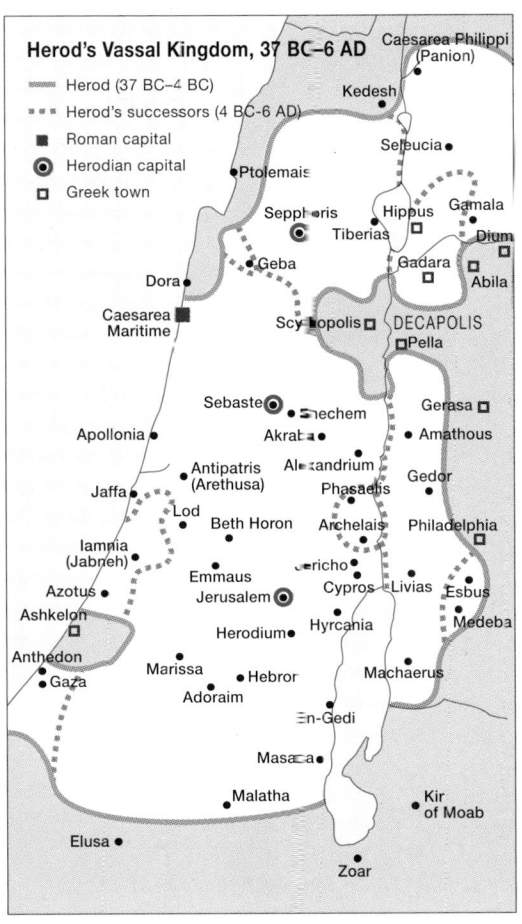

**Herod's Vassal Kingdom, 37 BC–6 AD**

- —— Herod (37 BC–4 BC)
- ••• Herod's successors (4 BC–6 AD)
- ■ Roman capital
- ◉ Herodian capital
- □ Greek town

*Map labels:* Caesarea Philippi (Panion), Kedesh, Seleucia, Ptolemais, Sepphoris, Hippus, Gamala, Tiberias, Geba, Dium, Dora, Gadara, Abila, Caesarea Maritime, Scythopolis, DECAPOLIS, Pella, Sebaste, Shechem, Gerasa, Apollonia, Akraba, Amathous, Antipatris (Arethusa), Alexandrium, Jaffa, Phasaelis, Gedor, Lod, Beth Horon, Iamnia (Jabneh), Emmaus, Archelais, Philadelphia, Azotus, Jerusalem, Jericho, Cypros, Livias, Esbus, Ashkelon, Herodium, Hyrcania, Medeba, Anthedon, Machaerus, Gaza, Marissa, Hebron, Adoraim, En-Gedi, Masada, Malatha, Kir of Moab, Elusa, Zoar

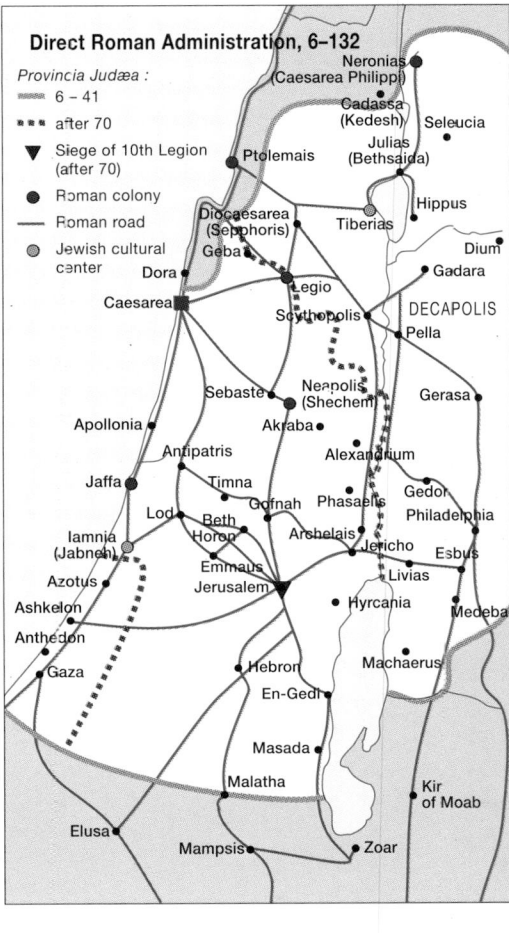

**Direct Roman Administration, 6–132**

*Provincia Judæa :*
- ▬▬ 6 – 41
- ••• after 70
- ▼ Siege of 10th Legion (after 70)
- ● Roman colony
- —— Roman road
- ◉ Jewish cultural center

*Map labels:* Neronias (Caesarea Philippi), Cadassa (Kedesh), Seleucia, Julias (Bethsaida), Ptolemais, Diocaesarea (Sepphoris), Hippus, Tiberias, Geba, Dium, Dora, Legio, Gadara, Caesarea, Scythopolis, DECAPOLIS, Pella, Sebaste, Neapolis (Shechem), Gerasa, Apollonia, Akraba, Antipatris, Timna, Alexandrium, Jaffa, Gofnah, Phasaelis, Gedor, Lod, Beth Horon, Archelais, Philadelphia, Iamnia (Jabneh), Emmaus, Jericho, Esbus, Azotus, Jerusalem, Livias, Ashkelon, Hyrcania, Medeba, Anthedon, Hebron, Machaerus, Gaza, En-Gedi, Masada, Malatha, Kir of Moab, Elusa, Mampsis, Zoar

the royal family be circumcised, his reign was never acknowledged by his people as a true Jewish monarchy of Davidic lineage. Everyone knew that Herod ruled only by virtue of his absolute loyalty to Rome and his close personal relations with Augustus, who was just then introducing the autocratic regime in Rome known as the principate.

During the third stage Palestine was under direct Roman rule. The system of governing through a vassal king had produced in Herod a unique example of a tyrannical and cruel ruler, efficient perhaps, but incapable of establishing a stable dynasty. Indeed, when Herod died riots broke out in Judea, and demands were voiced for a new regime. Ten years later, in 6 AD, Herod's son Archelaus was exiled, and the land was set up

as a Roman province named *Judaea*. At first the governors bore the title of *Praefecture*, and after the death of Agrippa I they were officially referred to as procurators. As a rule the Roman authorities granted a large measure of autonomy to the Jewish institutions in religious matters, but even the priestly class was controlled by the procurators who had the power to nominate or dismiss any of the priests.

Perhaps the most significant change at the time was of a symbolical nature. Shortly before or after the Bar Kokhba rebellion (the exact date is uncertain), Emperor Hadrian changed the name of the province from *Judaea* to *Palestina* – an obvious attempt to obliterate the connection between the land and the Jewish nation.

| Pontius Pilate is procurator | The Crucifixion | The Great Revolt | Bar Kokhba |
|---|---|---|---|
| 26 | 30 | 66–70 | 132–135 |

*3. Floor mosaic from a Roman villa. Nablus (Shechem), 3rd century AD.*

**End of 50s:** Violent Jewish-Greek confrontations in Caesarea.

**64:** Herod's ambitious project of rebuilding the Temple is completed; but Jerusalem will enjoy this glory for a few years only.

**66–70:** The Great Revolt against Rome and the fall of Jerusalem; henceforth Judea is a province ruled by a Roman official of praetorian rank. Until then the Romans had not considered it necessary to maintain a legion in the country and were content with meager *auxilia*, while in Syria they kept up to four legions. Now they send permanent troops to the province: the Xth legion is stationed in Jerusalem where it will be joined during the Bar Kokhba revolt by the Vth, *Ferrata*, legion. Johanan ben Zakai founds a rabbinical center in Jabneh.

**115–117:** Revolts throughout the diaspora.

**117:** Judea becomes a consular province. Accession of Hadrian.

**129:** Hadrian visits Judea.

**132–135:** Bar Kokhba's revolt; Hadrian founds a pagan city, Aelia Capitolina, on the

*4. The Roman theater in Scythopolis (Beth Shean).*

diaspora and in Palestine are in turmoil for a year, until the emperor's death (41).

**41:** Accession of Claudius; wishing to appease the Jews, and because of his personal friendship with Agrippa I, the new Caesar unites all the territories ruled by Herod and places them under Agrippa's rule;

for the first time in half a century a Jew rules over all of Palestine.

**41–44:** Reign of Agrippa I, a sovereign attentive to all classes and sects in his kingdom and far more concerned for the welfare of his people than his grandfather Herod "The Great".

ruins of Jerusalem. From that date, probably until the Arab conquest, Jews are not allowed to live in the city.

**212:** Emperor Caracalla grants Roman citizenship to all free residents of the empire; parity is nominally granted to the Jews for the first time.

# Herod The Great

*1. The Herodium fortress, near Bethlehem.*

I
n the process of the consolidation of Roman rule in Palestine, the ostentatious and cruel reign of Herod was in every respect a period of transition. It enabled the transformation from the rule of the Hasmonean vassal kings to the imposition (following the short reign of Archelaus, Herod's son) of direct Roman administration and the creation of the province *Judaea*.

The Herodian monarchy accomplished a political and social revolution which was no less dramatic than the great changes effected by the early Hasmoneans. A descendant of an Idumean family which had converted to Judaism only two generations earlier, Herod was forced to seek supporters among social groups which were not associated with the Hasmonean dynasty. For this reason he recalled from the diaspora several distinguished priestly families such as the Phabi, Kathros, and Boethus. These men had not taken part in the upheavals during Herod's struggle for power, and, coming from the Hellenistic diaspora, they were nurtured, like Herod himself, on Greco-Roman culture. The king was obviously attempting to replace the Hasmonean aristocracy with one of his own, relying upon the Jewish communities in the Parthian East and the Roman West. It was therefore not surprising that during his reign a great

Babylonian scholar such as Hillel the Elder rose to prominence among the Pharisees of Jerusalem.

Herod had two important attributes: absolute loyalty to Rome, and political prowess, which he exercised with extraordinary brutality by extirpating all signs of opposition, even within his own family. He did not hesitate to execute several of his own sons whom he suspected of plotting against him, as well as his favorite wife, the Hasmonean Mariamne (or Miriam). This earned him the saying attributed to Augustus: "It is better to be Herod's pig than his son."

On the other hand, Herod knew well enough how to curry favor with his masters. He worked hard at cultivating relations with Augustus and with Agrippa, the Roman governor of the eastern provinces and Augustus' designated heir. The two wings of his grand palace in Jerusalem were named *Agrippium* and *Caesarium*. In fact, Herod did everything he could to be included in the intricate struggle which led to the establishment and consolidation of the Principate. The centralization of the new regime, however, did not allow the client-king the possibility of conducting an independent and vigorous foreign policy. This limitation could partially explain the enormous energy which he poured into grandiose building projects.

The jewels in the crown of Herodian architecture were two new towns. Caesarea, on the coast, adorned with all the public edifices of a Roman city (theater, amphitheater, hippodrome), was to become the major port of the future province and the seat of the procurator. Sebaste, founded near ancient Samaria, was to provide the king with loyal soldiers.

There were also the royal citadels erected throughout the land, often on sites of former Hasmonean structures. The most famous example is Masada. This isolated rock on the edge of the Judean Desert was fortified in the Hasmonean period, and later transformed by Herod into a splendid palace and fort. Another citadel, Herodium, built on a hill near Bethlehem, was intended by Herod to serve as his burial place in imitation of such mausoleums built by Augustus. Other fortresses overlooked the Judean Desert. Indeed, the route leading up from the valley of Jericho to Jerusalem was of prime strategic importance. Yet strategy was not the sole motivation: in these splendid winter palaces, the king could relax and live as he pleased, far away from the reproving eyes of his orthodox subjects in Jerusalem.

Jerusalem, however, was not neglected. Not only did he adorn his capital in Roman style, but with the idea of immortalizing himself while demonstrating his loyalty to Judaism, Herod also rebuilt the Temple in magnificent proportions. Even the sages, who disapproved of his conduct in private and public affairs, could not but express admiration for his splendid Temple, saying that "He who has not seen Herod's building, has never seen a beautiful building."

| Caesar's assassination | Herod's accession | Founding of Sebaste |
| --- | --- | --- |
| | 37 BC | 27 BC |

*4. A staircase leading to the Huldah Gate, the pilgrims' entrance to the Temple Mount.*

**73 BC:** Herod is born in Ashkelon, which at the time was in the region of Idumea (the Greek name for ancient Edom; but Idumea was larger, extending as far as the Northern Negev and the coastal plain).

**47 BC:** Appointed governor of the Galilee by his father Antipater, Herod crushes a revolt led by Hezekiah and has the rebels put to death without trial. Arraigned before the *Sanhedrin*, the high court in Jerusalem, he flees before they pass sentence. It is Hyrcanus II himself, high priest and president of the Sanhedrin, who helps him escape.

**44 BC:** Assassination of Julius Caesar. Cassius, the Roman military commander in the East, imposes heavy taxes on Judea, with the help of Herod.

**43 BC:** The Jew Malichus kills Antipater, Herod's father; Herod and his brother Phasael persuade Cassius to have Malichus murdered without trial. Herod is appointed

governor of *Coele Syria*.

**40 BC:** A large portion of the Roman East, including Palestine, falls into the hands of the Parthians. Hyrcanus II is exiled, Phasael dies, and the Hasmonean Mattathias Antigonus seizes the throne in Jerusalem. Herod takes refuge in Rome where the Senate crowns him King of Judea.

**39–37 BC:** Herod returns to Palestine; the Romans, having defeated the Parthians, help Herod to capture the land from Mattathias Antigonus; Jerusalem surrenders to Herod after five months of siege in the summer of 37 BC.

**37–4 BC:** Herod's reign.

**31 BC:** Octavian defeats Antony at Actium; Herod hastily proclaims his loyalty to the victor, the future Augustus.

**30 BC:** Herod presents himself to Octavian in Rhodes and receives confirmation from him regarding his rule over Palestine. On his way to Egypt, Octavian goes through Palestine and Herod welcomes him in Acre; he then goes down to Egypt to congratulate

# 37 BC–4 BC

2. Fragment of of a decoration discovered near the Western ("Wailing") Wall (part of the western side of the walls surrounding the Temple Mount).

3. One of the gates in the walls built by Herod around the Temple Mount.

Herodian Palestine
Tyre
Caesarea Philippi (Banias)
Cadassa (Kedesh)
Hulatah
Ekdippa (Achziv)
GALILEE
GAULANITIS
TRACHONITIS
Julias (Bethsaida)
Seleucia
Ptolemais (Acre)
Gamala
BATANAEA
Yodefat
Migdal
MEDITERRANEAN SEA
Sepphoris
Arbel
Tiberias
Hippus
Nazareth
Dium
Kenath
Geba
Yarmuk
Abila
Edrei
Dora
Gadara
Legio
Caesarea
Scythopolis
Bozrah
Pella
Narbata
DECAPOLIS
Amathus
Sebaste
Gerasa
SAMARIA
Shechem
Apollonia
Akraba
Alexandrium
Antipatris
Gedor
Jaffa
Phasaelis
PERAEA
Jordan
Timna
Gofnah
Philadelphia
Lod
Archelais
Beth Horon
Iamnia (Jabneh)
Emmaus
WADI QILT
Jericho
Esbus
ARABIA
Cypros
Jerusalem
Livias
Azotus (Ashdod)
Bethlehem
(Beth Ramata)
JUDEA
Medeba
Ashkelon
Beth Leptepha
Herodium
Machaerus
Anthedon
Marissa
Libba
Hebron
Gaza
Adoraim
Ein Ghédi
DEAD SEA
IDUMEA
Masada
Autonomous town
Herod's military camp
Founded or renovated by Herod
Kir of Moab
Malatha
Tiberias
Founded or renovated by Herod's successors
Elusa
Strategic pass
Mampsis
Zoar
20 km.


**Founding of Caesarea** — 22 BC

**Execution of Alexander and Aristobulus** — 7 BC

**Execution of Antipater. Herod's death** — 4 BC

5. Herod's winter palace in Jericho.

Octavian on his decisive victory over Antony, and to receive from the new master of Rome the territories of Jericho, Gaza, Anthedon, Jaffa, and Stratoneos Pirgos (Straton's Tower, the future Caesarea).

**29 BC:** Cypros, Herod's mother, and his sister Salome accuse Mariamne of attempting to poison her husband; Herod orders her execution

**27 BC:** Founding of Sebaste on the site of biblical Samaria; the city, constructed within a few years, becomes the seat of Herodian power.

**23 BC:** Augustus authorizes Herod to designate his successor and gives him parts of Syria (Trachonitis and Batanaea); later he will receive the Golan (Gaulanitis), part of the upper Galilee, as well as the towns of Ulatha and Paneas in the Huleh Valley. With the exception of the coastal plain north of Caesarea and the town of Ashkelon in the south, the whole of Palestine, including Transjordan, is under Herod's domination.

**22 BC:** Founding of Caesarea. Both Sebaste and Caesarea are built for the benefit of the non-Jewish population of the kingdom, with the intent of buying their loyalty; both towns bear the name of the Roman Caesar.

**19 BC:** The Temple is rebuilt.

**17 BC:** Two of Herod's sons, Alexander and Aristobulus (Mariamne's children), return from Rome where they received their education.

**15 BC:** Marcus Vipsanius Agrippa, Augustus' closest friend, visits Jerusalem.

**14–13 BC:** Antipater, Herod's eldest son, is restored to court and sent to Rome to strengthen Herod's ties with his suzerain.

**7 BC:** Herod executes Alexander and Aristobulus whom he suspects of plotting to murder him.

**4 BC:** Herod executes Antipater, his designated heir. Five days later, Herod himself dies in his palace in Jericho. The three sons who survived him, Archelaus, Herod Antipas, and Philip, partition his kingdom among them.

# Revolts Against Rome

1. The Herodian citadel in Masada, overlooking the Dead Sea and the Judean Desert.

The people of Israel conducted three major wars against the Roman Empire during the first and second centuries of the Christian era. Two of these uprisings – the war that led to the destruction of the Temple (66–73 AD) and the Bar-Kokhba revolt (132–135) – took place in the land of Palestine. In between these two, in the years 115–117, many communities of the diaspora were embroiled in a large-scale revolt against the Roman Empire during the reign of Emperor Trajan. Each of these wars may have been provoked by different events, but underlying them all were two motivating forces: the tension between the Jews and the Romans which had commenced with the conquest of Palestine by Pompey in 63 BC, and the deteriorating relations between the Jews and large sectors of the Greco-Roman population throughout the Empire.

The Roman procurators in Palestine had long since lost the confidence of their subjects. Indifferent or impotent, often corrupt, they no longer intervened in the clashes between Jews and other ethnic groups in the province. According to Josephus Flavius, the Great Revolt of 66 broke out as a result of a violent confrontation between the Jewish and Greek inhabitants of Caesarea, capital of the province. No longer able to maintain law and order, the occupation authorities were apparently losing control of large parts of the country, which were now ruled by various bands of Jewish rebels including zealots, freedom fighters, bandits, and messianic enthusiasts.

The war lasted seven years, from 66 to the fall of Masada in 73, but the major events took place between the campaign in the Galilee (67) and the fall of Jerusalem (70). From the beginning the Romans had far greater forces: three legions reinforced with auxiliaries, approximately sixty thousand well-trained professional soldiers. Far inferior in number and military experience, the Jews were further handicapped by their internecine quarrels. Although united by their hatred for Rome, they were deeply divided over religious and social issues.

Certain Jewish fighters were motivated by messianic expectations; others saw the revolt as a prelude to a social revolution against the upper classes and the priestly oligarchy who were servile to the Roman masters. Others still, driven by religious zeal, regarded the submission to Rome as a form of idolatry. It is the latter outlook which may explain the instances of collective suicides, motivated by the aspiration for the glory of martyrdom. Masada, at the end of the war, was the most famous of these cases, but there were also others at different stages of the revolt.

Almost half a century later, the diaspora witnessed a wave of uprisings of Jewish communities, each for its own immediate causes, some of which are still obscure. Beginning in Cyrenaica (Libya) and spreading to Egypt, the revolt opened with violent clashes between Jews and Greeks. Several literary and epigraphic sources indicate that both sides suffered great destruction and loss of lives. It is possible that messianic hopes were at work here, which would explain why the revolt erupted in several different places simultaneously.

The intervention of the Roman army put an end to this strife. For the Jewish population, the results were disastrous culminating in the almost total destruction of the Alexandria community, and in the decimation of all communities in North Africa and Cyprus.

In Mesopotamia too Roman legions clashed with Jews, but with one important difference. In these areas the Jews joined the local population in a general movement of resistance against the Roman conquest. It was this same obstinate resistance which forced Emperor Trajan to abandon the project of seizing further territories from the Parthian kingdom. Finally, talmudic sources mention a certain "Polemic of Kitos" (most probably the Roman general, Lusius Quietus) which took place at that time, but it is impossible to determine whether this refers to his actions against Parthia and its Jewish population, or to an additional armed struggle which took place between the Jews and the Roman army in Palestine while he was governor of Judea.

| Beginning of the Great Revolt | Fall of Masada | | Revolt in Cyrenaica | Revolt in Mesopotamia |
|---|---|---|---|---|
| 66 | 73 | | 115 | 116–117 |

**End of 50s:** The tension between Jews and Greeks erupts into an open conflict in Caesarea.
**66. Summer:** Beginning of the Revolt. Resurgence of trouble in Caesarea; clashes with the procurator Florus in Jerusalem; Herod Agrippa II makes a public address in Jerusalem in a last attempt to prevent the insurrection; suppression of sacrifices in honor of the emperor; the Sicarii (from the Latin *sica*, "curved dagger") attack Masada, killing the Roman garrison there. Moderate leaders ask for help from Agrippa and Florus, and 2000 horsemen arrive in the capital and occupy the Upper City; the rebels, holding the Lower City and the Temple Mount, besiege the Roman garrison. During the siege, the rebels kill high priest Hanania and his brother Hezekiah. On the same day several Jews are killed in Caesarea leading to reprisals perpetrated by their brethren in other Greek cities. The Roman garrison in Jerusalem is destroyed.
**67:** War in the Galilee. Conflict between

4. *Juoaea Capta* ("subjugated Judea"). A bronze coin minted by Vespasian in 71 shortly after the fall of Jerusalem.

Joseph ben Mattathias (the future Josephus Flavius), commander of the region, and the zealot John of Giscala (Gush Halav).

Dispatched to crush the revolt, Vespasian recruits 60,000 men of the 5th and 6th legions, and his son Titus arrives from Egypt with the 15th legion.
**68:** The Romans destroy strongholds of resistance in Judea, thus isolating Jerusalem. They conquer Idumea and the Judean lowlands, but Nero's suicide and the end of Vespasian's mandate suspend the campaign for several months.
**69:** "The year of the four emperors" ends with the election of Vespasian who inaugurates the Flavian dynasty. Internal conflicts in Jerusalem: the Zealots terrorize the population; purge of the moderates.
**70:** Simeon Bar Giora becomes military commander of the rebels in Jerusalem. Siege and conquest of Jerusalem by Titus' troops who sack the town and burn down the Temple. Vespasian replaces the auxiliary troops with a permanent garrison (the 10th legion) and transforms Judea into a province administered by a governor of praetorian rank.

5. Roman parade helmet. Iron, Hebron hills, 1st–2nd centuries AD.

# 1st–2nd Centuries AD

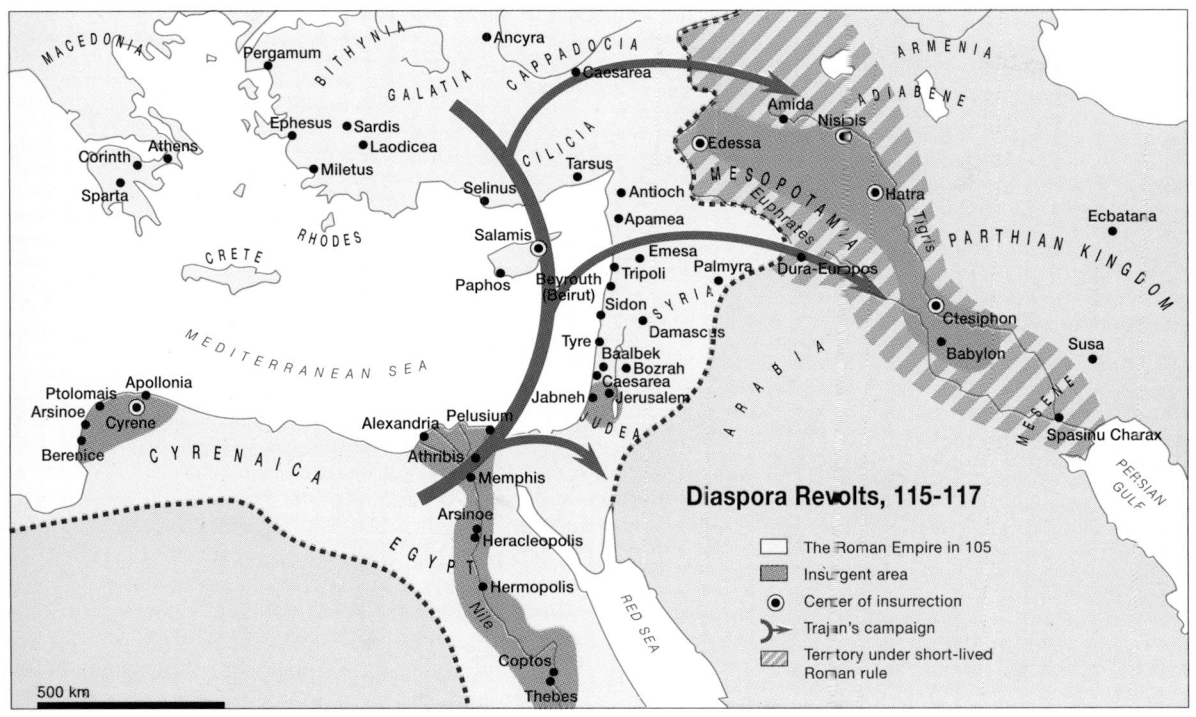

## Diaspora Revolts, 115-117

- ☐ The Roman Empire in 105
- ▨ Insurgent area
- ⊙ Center of insurrection
- ⟶ Trajan's campaign
- ▨ Territory under short-lived Roman rule

500 km

3. A Roman milestone near Cyrene. The inscription marks the reconstruction of the road after it was damaged during the Jewish revolt. Libya, 2nd century.

2. The kitchen of the Burnt House. Jerusalem, the Jewish Quarter in the Old City, 1st century AD.

## Hadrian in Judea

### 129

**71–72:** Liquidation of the last strongholds of resistance; fall of Herodium and Mikhvar.
**73:** Siege and fall of Masada. Nine hundred and sixty men, women, and children, according to Josephus Flavius, commit suicide in order not to fall into Roman hands. The Masada episode, disregarded by the rabbinical tradition, was to become one of the fundamental myths of the Israeli nation. Excavations of the site have unearthed archeological treasures.
**114:** Trajan in Antioch. Roman war against the Parthians and the annexation of Armenia.
**c. 115:** Beginning of the Jewish revolt in Cyrenaica. According to Greek sources (Eusebius and Dio Cassius), the Jews of Cyrene, led by their "king" Lukuas, enter Egypt. The Greeks, finding refuge in Alexandria, retaliate by massacring the Jews in that city. Lukuas' rebels overrun the country until a Roman army defeats them. The community in Alexandria is almost annihilated. The troubles extend as far as Cyprus where, if one believes Dio's version,

## Bar Kokhba's Revolt

### 132–135

a Jewish revolt, led by a certain Artemion, kills 240,000 persons. When the revolt is crushed, the Jews are forbidden to set foot on the island.
**116–117:** Revolt in Mesopotamia: Trajan orders Lusius Quietus to expel or exterminate all Jews in the region; Quietus kills tens of thousands, a deed which earns him the rank of praetor, then of consul, and the position of governor of Judea which becomes a consular province in 117. A second legion, probably the *Secunda Trajana*, is positioned in the northern part of the country. Death of Trajan; the new emperor, Hadrian, evacuates the lands in the East conquered by his predecessor, dismisses Lusius Quietus, and severely punishes the Greeks who had persecuted the Jews in Alexandria.
**129:** Hadrian visits Judea; the Jews are forbidden to practice circumcision; the honeymoon between the emperor and the Jews is over.
**132–135:** Bar Kokhba's revolt.

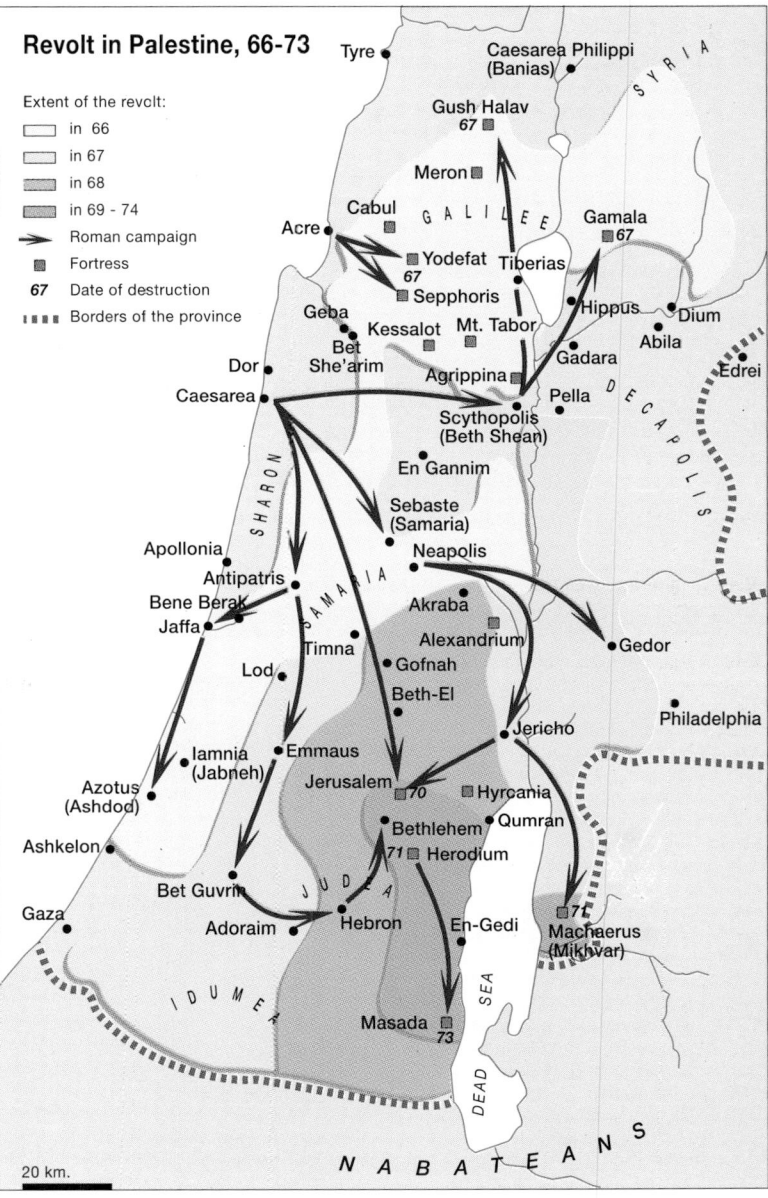

## Revolt in Palestine, 66-73

Extent of the revolt:
- ☐ in 66
- ▨ in 67
- ▨ in 68
- ▨ in 69 - 74
- ⟶ Roman campaign
- ◼ Fortress
- **67** Date of destruction
- ▪▪▪▪ Borders of the province

20 km.

# A Jewish Sect: Early Christianity

There is no doubt that as a subject, the birth of Christianity rightfully belongs to Jewish history. Although eventually denationalized, adapted to a pagan world, and spread throughout the Mediterranean, Christianity was nonetheless a transfiguration of Judaism. It was the religious and political agitation amongst the Jews of Palestine during the decades preceding the war against the Romans which gave rise to a new religion.

A comparative analysis of available Jewish and Christian sources makes it possible to conjecture an image of Palestinian Jewry at the time – a tableau of great complexity due to the diversity of prevailing ideologies and their sectarian expression. Modern research has taught us not to accept as literal the trisection, or quadrisection, offered by Josephus Flavius in his discussion of the Pharisees, Sadducees, Essenes, and the Zealots; yet it is quite clear that the sect of the Essenes comprised the social and spiritual environment for John who baptized repentant sinners in the Jordan River. Generally associated with the manuscripts and ruins found in the caves of Qumran, this sect or brotherhood would today have been labeled "fundamentalist."

Jesus, however, though baptized by John the Baptist, was also in contact with wider and less sectarian circles, particularly with the Pharisees. He came from the Galilee where he lived most of his life, and most of his ministry was amongst the Galilean Jews. Even the dissension between him and the Pharisees, vehement though it was, should be viewed against this background. One could therefore say that two streams converge in Jesus of Nazareth at once. In some respects he was influenced by the Essenes

2. Oil lamp. Bronze, Bet-Shean, 4th century AD.

(manifested, for example, by his deep sensitivity to social injustice), and in other respects – particularly in the fundaments of his theology – by the mainstream and more popular position of the Pharisees. In fact, his ardent eschatology was probably shared at the time by the vast majority of Jews in Palestine.

However, it was Paul rather than Jesus who determined the true nucleus and principles of Christianity, the "Theology of the Cross." Paul of Tarsus did not know Jesus, but he recognized in him the Messiah awaited by the people of Israel, and thus transformed the meaning of the messianic idea. The Son of God, who died on the cross to save mankind from the consequences of original sin, was a totally different concept from the Son of David who was to redeem the nation of Israel. As a young man Paul had studied in Jerusalem, and the revolutionary interpretation which he gave to Judaism, allowing the inclusion of all non-Jews who accepted Jesus into the nation of Israel, cannot be understood unless viewed from within the Jewish traditions of his time.

Thus, from its very beginnings the new religion defined itself by way of a struggle on two fronts: since it claimed to be the "true" Israel (*verus Israel*), Christianity conducted, on the one hand, a fierce disputation with rabbinical Judaism about the correct interpretation of the Scriptures, above all about the prophecies concerning the coming of the messiah. On the other hand, the Fathers of the Church fought mightily against the heterodox tendencies which inevitably accompanied the incorporation

1. Oil lamp. Bronze, Bet-Shean, 4th century AD.

| Herod in Jerusalem | Birth of Jesus | Judea becomes a Roman province | The Crucifixion | Paul in Rome | Destruction of the Temple |
|---|---|---|---|---|---|
| 37 BC | c. 6 BC | 6 AD | c. 30 | 60–62 | 70 |

**37 BC:** Herod, King of Judea, conquers Jerusalem.
**31 BC:** Qumran deserted for the first time, apparently because of an earthquake.
**c. 6 BC:** Birth of Jesus.
**4 BC:** Death of King Herod. Beginning of resettlement in Qumran.
**4 BC–39 AD:** Herod Antipas, Tetrach of the Galilee.
**6:** Judea becomes a Roman province; population census; rise of the Zealots.
**18–37:** Caiaphas is High Priest.
**26:** Pontius Pilate becomes governor of Judea.
**c. 26:** John the Baptist's preaching and baptizing.
**27–30:** Jesus' public ministry, baptized by John "in the fifteenth year of the reign of Tiberius Caesar" (Luke, 3:1), that is in 28–29.
**c. 30:** The Crucifixion.
**c. 35:** Martyrdom of Stephen, a hellenized Jew stoned to death in Jerusalem for his faith in Jesus.
**42:** Martyrdom of James, Jesus' brother and

leader of the congregation in Jerusalem.
**46–48:** The First Missionary journey of St. Paul and St. Barnabas.
**48:** The Council of Jerusalem.
**49–62:** St. Paul's Mission to the Gentiles: in Ephesus (53–56) and in Rome (60–62).
**64:** Persecution of Christians by Emperor Nero who accuses them of burning Rome.
**66–74:** The first war of the Jews.
**68:** Destruction of Qumran.
**70:** Titus conquers Jerusalem; destruction of the Temple.
**75–80:** The final composition of the Synoptic Gospels: Matthew, Mark, and Luke.
**c. 90:** The final composition of the Gospel According to John.
**c. 95:** The Apocalypse.
**c. 130:** The conversion of Justin Martyr, author of *Dialogue with Trypho*, a model for anti-Jewish disputations in the following centuries.
**130–180:** Gnostic schools in Alexandria;

3. Qumran, refuge of the "Dead Sea sect."

# 1st–4th Centuries

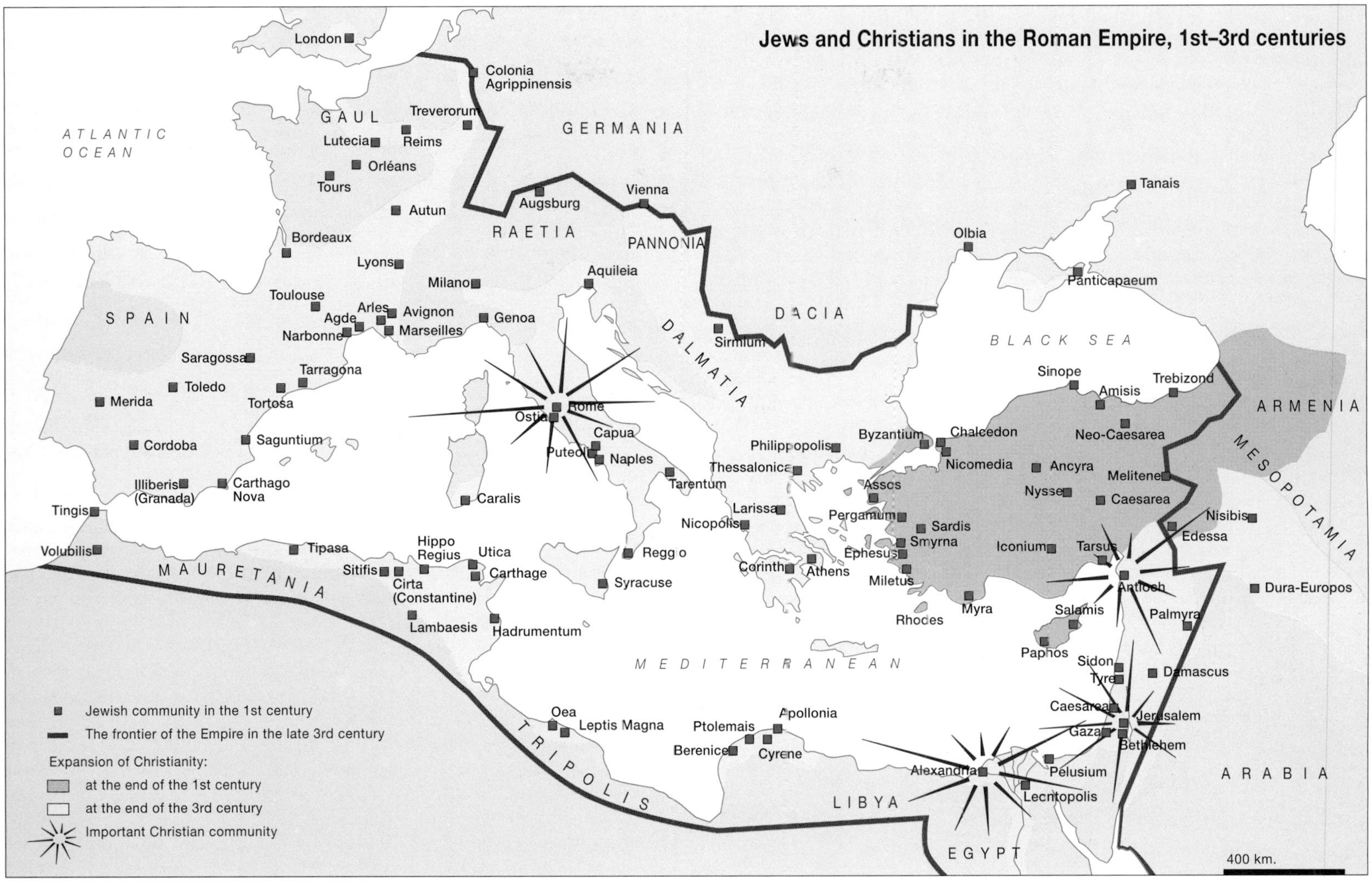

## Jews and Christians in the Roman Empire, 1st–3rd centuries

ATLANTIC OCEAN

London

Colonia Agrippinensis

GAUL
GERMANIA

Treverorum
Lutecia Reims
Orléans
Tours
Autun
Augsburg
Vienna
RAETIA
PANNONIA

Bordeaux
Lyons
Aquileia
Milano
Toulouse
Arles Avignon Genoa
Agde
Narbonne Marseilles
SPAIN
Saragossa
Tarragona
Toledo
Tortosa
Merida
Cordoba
Saguntium
Illiberis Carthago
(Granada) Nova
Tingis
Volubilis
Caralis
MAURETANIA
Tipasa
Hippo Utica
Sitifis Regius
Cirta Carthage
(Constantine)
Lambaesis Hadrumentum

DALMATIA
Sirmium
DACIA
BLACK SEA

Tanais

Olbia
Panticapaeum

Sinope
Amisis
Trebizond
ARMENIA
MESOPOTAMIA

Philippopolis
Byzantium Chalcedon Neo-Caesarea
Nicomedia
Thessalonica Nicaea Ancyra Melitene
Assos Nyssse Caesarea
Larissa Pergamum Iconium Nisibis
Nicopolis Sardis Tarsus Edessa
Smyrna
Corinth Ephesus Antioch
Athens Miletus Dura-Europos
Rome Rhodes Myra Salamis Palmyra
Ostia Paphos
Capua
Puteoli Naples Sidon Damascus
Tarentum Tyre
Regg o Caesarea Jerusalem
Syracuse Gaza
Bethlehem
ARABIA

MEDITERRANEAN

Oea
Leptis Magna Apollonia
Ptolemais
Berenice Cyrene
Alexandria Pelusium
Lecntopolis
TRIPOLIS
LIBYA
EGYPT

400 km.

■ Jewish community in the 1st century
━ The frontier of the Empire in the late 3rd century
Expansion of Christianity:
▢ at the end of the 1st century
▢ at the end of the 3rd century
✷ Important Christian community

---

of non-Jews into the new faith; for example, the dualist and gnostic beliefs which refused to identify the Father of Christ with the Lord of Israel, and viewed the latter as the creator of the material world, a lower deity who was, at best, a god of justice, but not the God of mercy.

It is within this dual and complex polemic that one should regard the phenomenon of the Christian-Jews, direct heirs to the mother-church in Jerusalem, who were rejected quite early by the dominant forces of

Christianity. Despite their marginality and the scarcity of sources referring to them (the Talmud refers to all Jewish sects and factions by the generic name *Minnim*, meaning "heretics"), modern scholarship tends to place greater emphasis on their role in the molding of early Christianity, as well as in the appearance of gnostic sects. It seems that the latter, notwithstanding their fiercely anti-Jewish theologies, were nourished on marginal Jewish traditions, transmitted through the Christian-Jews.

---

| The Synoptic Gospels | The Gospel of John | | The Edict of Milan | The Council of Nicaea |
|---|---|---|---|---|
| 75–80 | c. 90 | | 313 | 325 |

Valentinus – one of their prominent theologians.
**140–160:** Marcion, another Gnostic leader, excommunicated by the Church in Rome, begins propagating his views over a large part of the Empire.
**c. 195:** The controversy concerning the date for celebrating Easter (whether on the same day as the Jewish Passover or on a Sunday); St. Irenaeus mediates.
**202:** Emperor Severus forbids conversion to both Judaism and Christianity.
**229–230:** Origen leaves Alexandria and moves to Caesarea in Palestine where he completes his work *Hexapla*, as well as homilies and Biblical commentaries which make lavish use of *Midrashim* – Jewish works of exegesis.
**c. 270:** St. Antony's retirement to the Egyptian desert marks the beginning of monasticism.
**311:** Galerius' edict of toleration.
**312:** Constantine defeats Maxentius at the Milvian Bridge near Rome and opts for

Christianity.
**313:** The so-called Edict of Milan recognizes Christianity and proclaims toleration for all religions.
**325:** The Council of Nicaea. Constantine celebrates the Tricennalia in Jerusalem. Construction of the Basilica of the Anastasis (Resurrection), known as the Church of the Holy Sepulcher, in Jerusalem.
**354:** Birth of St. Augustine.
**356:** Pagan cults are decreed punishable by death.
**361–363:** Reign of Julian the Apostate; an attempt to rebuild the Temple in Jerusalem.
**383:** St. Jerome leaves Rome for Palestine and begins translation of the Bible into Latin (the Vulgate). From 385 to 420 he lives in Bethlehem and takes an active part in religious controversies and in the development of monasticism in Palestine, mainly in the Judean desert.

*4. Ship. Detail of a mosaic, Migdal (Magdala), 1st century AD.*

# From Jerusalem to Jabneh

In the year 70 of the Christian Era, Titus' legionnaires burned down the Temple in Jerusalem, and the history of the people of Israel took a new direction. The crisis produced by the destruction and the enormous toll in human lives shook Jewish consciousness to the core. It called into question traditional beliefs and conceptions, and created a power void which threatened the integrity and even the very existence of the Jews as a nation. The literature of the sages in that period was produced by new scholarly circles which were established in the small town of Jabneh, at first under the leadership of Johanan ben Zakkai, and later, of Rabban Gamliel. The first devoted himself to convincing his compatriots that the end of the Temple did not signify the end of the Jewish people, and that the cessation of the Temple service did not completely deprive the Jews of the power of atonement. By a series of regulations, Ben Zakkai endowed the new center with all the necessary attributes of authority and gathered an impressive group of scholars in Jabneh. Yet at the same time he made every effort to keep alive the hope for the imminent reconstruction of the Temple in Jerusalem.

This new leadership, however, encountered considerable opposition at first. Some sages would not consent to assign the unique status of Jerusalem to another place; others, from nationalist circles, accused Ben Zakkai of submission to the Roman yoke. A famous talmudic legend relates how the eminent Sage escaped from Jerusalem in a coffin carried by his disciples, thus outwitting the vigilant zealots who forbade everyone from leaving the besieged city (the Jews used to bury their dead outside the city walls so as not to defile the town). On reaching the Roman camp, according to one version, Ben Zakkai told Vespasian, commander of the siege, that he would become emperor. Since the prophecy was immediately fulfilled, the newly elected Roman ruler was willing to grant the prophet his every wish. "Give me Jabneh and its scholars," was the Jew's request. This legend is obviously chronologically impossible, for Vespasian had already become emperor in 69, and the siege of Jerusalem was commanded by his son Titus; and "Jabneh and its scholars" were only to emerge after the Temple was in ruins.

Another version modified the story of Ben Zakkai's request: "I ask only for Jabneh, where I will teach my disciples, determine the prayer and observe all the *mitsvoth* [commandments]." Although this version was also invented after the events, it nonetheless accurately describes the central role played by Johanan ben Zakkai in the establishment of Jabneh as a literary circle and the elements which were to become the basis for Jewish spiritual and social life. The priestly class lost its place at the top of the social hierarchy and was replaced by a new elite: "the Sages of the Torah," heirs of the Pharisees. This change was hardly surprising since the priests had derived their authority from the Temple, which no longer existed. The Sages, on the other hand, gained respect by virtue of their personalities, their conduct, and their knowledge – qualities not dependent on time and place but on personal charisma and intellectual ability. Such authority was far more "mobile," which explains how Ben Zakkai's successors could wonder whether their master specifically intended Jabneh to be the center or whether he meant "any place where there is a *bet din* [rabbinical court]."

Indeed, only one generation after the destruction of the Temple new schools began to appear anywhere a great rabbinical scholar could be found. Authority was scattered throughout the land, the study of the Torah became the norm for large strata of Jewish society, the

*1. The Sages of Bene-Berak. Passover* Haggadah *illuminated by Joseph of Leipnik (Moravia). Darmstadt, 1712.*

*2. Oil-lamp decorated with Jewish motifs. Roman art, 1st century AD.*

| Vespasian | Titus |
|---|---|
| 69–79 | 79–81 |

**Between 68 and 70:** Johanan ben Zakkai moves to Jabneh, a small town on the coastal plain, where he establishes an alternative center to the lost capital, but it consists only of the spiritual heirs of the Pharisees. A generation later the boundaries of Judaism are redefined by the exclusion of the various "sects": *Birkat ha-Minim* ("benediction concerning heretics"), composed in Jabneh, invokes wrath on Judeo-Christian and Gnostic sects.
**69–79:** Vespasian, commander of the Roman legions in Judea until the last stages of the revolt, is emperor.
**70. Summer:** Titus conquers Jerusalem; destruction of the Temple; suppression of traditional national institutions such as the High Priest and the *Sanhedrin*.
**c. 70–c. 85 (90?):** Johanan ben Zakkai is active in Jabneh, proclaiming a series of legal and religious regulations. The community apparently has no official contact with the Roman authorities.
**73. Passover:** Collective suicide of the defenders of Masada; the fall of this fortress, held by Eleazar ben Yair's Sicarians, ends the active phase of the battle against Rome.
**79–81:** Reign of Titus, Vespasian's son.
**81–96:** Reign of Domitian who persecutes Jews and those who converted to Judaism. "The tax on the Jews was exacted with particular rigor; it was also imposed on the proselytes who lived in the fashion of the Jews without declaring themselves Jewish and on those who, concealing their origin, tried to avoid the tributes imposed on this nation. I remember seeing, when I was hardly an adolescent, a procurator examining a ninety-year-old man to see if he were circumcised" (Suetonius, *Life of Twelve Caesars*, "Domitian", VIII, 12).
**c. 85 (96?)–c. 110:** Gamliel assumes leadership in Jabneh. His policy is more "national," emphasizing ties with the diaspora communities and enjoying, at least *de facto*, recognition by the Roman authorities – a fact probably due to the fall of the Flavian dynasty in 96.

## The Travels of Rabbi Akiva, c. 120

Frontiers of the empire with Hadrian's accession (117)

**Rome** ⊚ Important community

• Community

Region with large Jewish population

400 km.

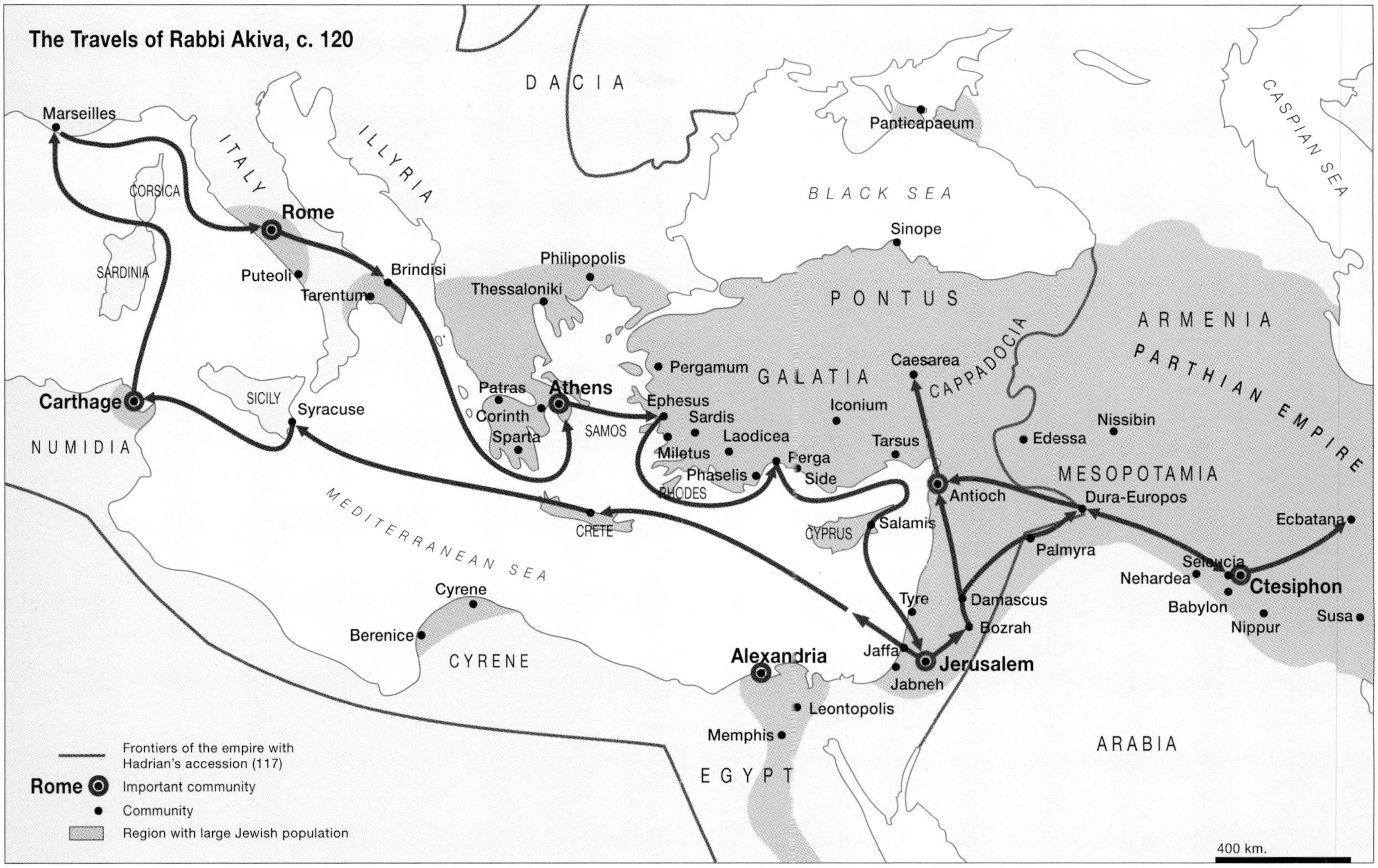

synagogue emerged as the focal point of community life, and prayer replaced sacrifice in the Temple. Hence the importance of local institutions grew steadily – new forms of social organization which would eventually fashion the patterns of medieval Jewry.

Interestingly, it was still in the land of Israel rather than in the diaspora that these developments took place. The success of the Jabneh generation ensured the continued obedience of diaspora communities to directives issued in Palestine. The best example was the Hebrew calendar, still

proclaimed in Palestine and followed by Jews throughout the world. Yet the two characteristics of the Palestinian leadership of that period – mobility and decentralization – would eventually corrode the supremacy of the Land of Israel. A second aborted attempt of the Jews of Palestine to free themselves from Roman rule – the Bar Kokhba revolt in 132 AD – completed the process. The leadership of the Jewish nation in religious, cultural, and social affairs was then transferred from the Land of Israel to the powerful community in Babylonia.

| Domitian | Nerva | Trajan |
|---|---|---|
| 81–96 | 96–98 | 98–117 |

**During the 90s:** Proliferation of "schools" around rabbis – a new term for the spiritual leaders in the era following the destruction of the Temple. In Lydda, Rabbi Eliezer ben Hyrcanus, succeeded by Rabbi Tarphon (Gamliel himself, who bore the title of *Rabban*, probably resided in Lydda before succeeding Johanan Ben Zakkai in Jabneh); in Bene-Berak, Rabbi Akiva, future spiritual leader of the Bar Kokhba revolt; in Sepphoris, Rabbi Halafta; in Peki'in, Rabbi Joshua ben Hanania, etc.
**96–98:** Reign of Nerva. A coin, minted after he abolished the extortionist procedure of taxing the Jews, bears the inscription: *Fisci iudaici calumnia sublata* ("to efface the shame of the Jewish tax").
**98–117:** Reign of Trajan.

*3. A Jew buried in Zoar (east of the Dead Sea) died, according to his epitaph, "in the 386th year after the destruction of the Temple." As late as the 5th century then, Jewish historical memory was ordered in reference to this event.*

*4. Lag ba-Omer (the annual festival commemorating the Bar Kokhba revolt) on Mt. Meron in the Upper Galilee, where tradition identified the burial place of Rabbi Simeon bar Yohai. This Palestinian scholar of the 2nd century AD was a disciple of Rabbi Akiva and an ardent supporter of the revolt.*

# The Synagogue

1. The synagogue in Baram, Upper Galilee, 3rd century AD.

2. A "Byzantine" mosaic in the synagogue of Bet-Shean, 6th century.

3. The synagogue of Bet Alfa. Mosaic pavement of the 6th century.

The Temple (*Bet ha-Mikdash*) in Jerusalem was a unique center and dominant symbol for the entire Jewish nation; the synagogue (*Bet ha-Knesset*) was an institution of a largely diversified and decentralized Jewry which had become accustomed to living with no political sovereignty. Despite one or two short-lived attempts to build a substitute *Mikdash* elsewhere (such as in Elephantine in Upper Egypt), a Temple could hold no real significance outside Jerusalem. By contrast, a synagogue exists in every Jewish community, no matter where. Moreover, the Temple in Jerusalem was a magnificent building, attended by a class of priests, and revolved around the sacrifice. A synagogue. which may be housed even in the simplest structure, is distinguished only by the fact that it contains the Torah scroll, acknowledges no authority other than that of the Scriptures, and maintains no sacrificial ritual whatsoever. The synagogue therefore is not a small Temple, for it has a completely different function in Jewish religious, social and cultural life.

The origin of the synagogue is not quite clear. During the time of the Talmud it was already so well established that the Babylonian sages (*amoraim*) attributed its emergence to the exile at the end of the First Temple period, identifying it with the "little sanctuary" mentioned in Ezekiel (11:16). The Talmud sages assumed that the synagogues founded in Babylon, and later in Palestine, were designed to fill the void left by the destruction of Solomon's Temple (586 BC). But, in fact, the synagogue was to fulfill this role only after the destruction of the Second Temple (70 AD). According to existing sources (Philo of Alexandria, Josephus Flavius, the New Testament), the synagogue initially served more as a multi-purpose community hall: a center for individual study or public reading of the Torah, an administration office, seat of the local tribunal, a place for making public announcements, collecting donations in aid of the poor, etc. It is quite possible that in the diaspora the synagogue fulfilled different functions to those it served in Palestine. In the Greco-Roman world, particularly in Egypt, the synagogue was sometimes referred to as *proseuxe* ("place of prayer"), while in Palestine it was always a *synagoge* ("place of assembly").

Archeological excavations have established that there were synagogues in the diaspora long before they were introduced into Palestine. In Egypt, for example, there is evidence of synagogues as early as the Ptolemaic

# 3rd Century BC–6th Century AD

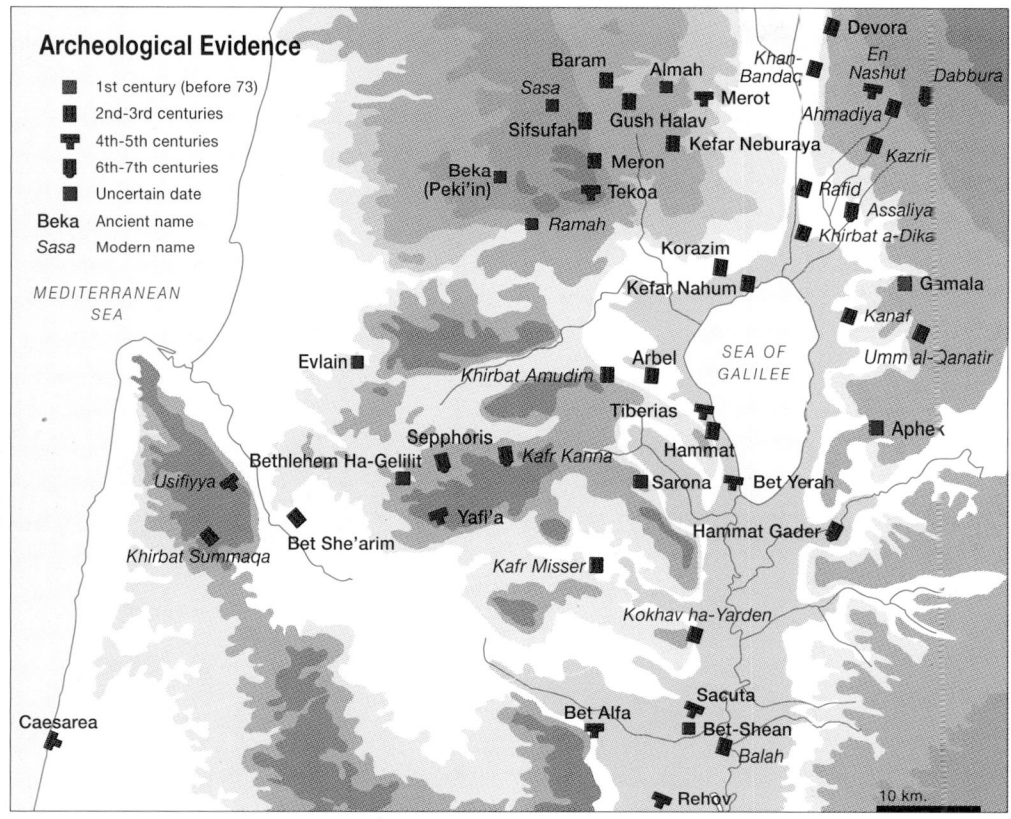

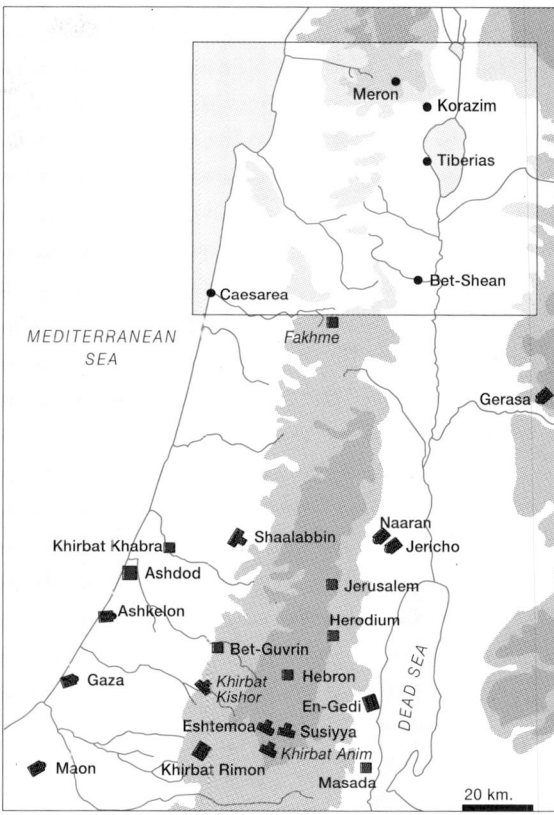

## Archeological Evidence

- 1st century (before 73)
- 2nd-3rd centuries
- 4th-5th centuries
- 6th-7th centuries
- Uncertain date

**Beka** Ancient name
*Sasa* Modern name

period (3rd century BC), at least three centuries before the first known synagogues in Palestine (such as those in Masada and Herodium in Judea, and the one recently excavated in Gamla on the Golan Heights) which date from the late Second Temple period. By the first century AD, however, the synagogue was the principal hallmark of every Jewish community. This is also evidenced by Paul's testimony, for wherever he went, the Apostle found an audience (of Jews or of "God-fearing" Gentiles) in the local synagogue.

With the fall of the Second Temple the synagogue became primarily a place of public prayer, although at times it still fulfilled other functions. In talmudic times, all Jewish communities consisting of several hundred families maintained a synagogue. The Talmud, in a text which lists institutions upon which the presence of Torah scholars is contingent, stresses the primary importance of the synagogue.

It is therefore not at all surprising that Church Fathers chose the *Synagoge* as their main target of attack. From the end of the fourth century on, Roman laws prohibiting the erection of new synagogues began to multiply, some decrees even demanding the demolition of those already existing, or the confiscation of the property. All these laws were decreed apparently as a result of pressure exerted by the Church. Although there were also laws protecting the right of Jews to maintain their own places of worship, these implicitly testify to the frequency of violent attacks by the masses or attempts to use the synagogue building as barracks for soldiers and officials.

Strangely enough, this was concurrently the golden age of synagogue construction and renovation in Palestine. Although inscriptions indicating the exact date of construction are rare, it is nevertheless clear that most of the ancient synagogues in Palestine were built between the fourth and seventh centuries. Architecturally, they fall into three distinct categories. Some were obviously magnificent edifices, often two-storied, built of large expertly-cut stones, with an imposing façade which could be seen from a distance. The most famous example of this type is the synagogue at Kefar Nahum (Capernaum), north of Tiberias, yet there are others like it in the Galilee (Baram, Meron, etc.). The entrance of these synagogues faces Jerusalem, but there was apparently no fixed place for the Torah ark, as attested by literary sources noting that the Torah was kept in an annex and brought into the central hall for public reading.

4. Mosaic of the synagogue in En-Gedi (detail). Judean Desert, 6th century.

Another model was the "basilica" type, which closely resembled eastern churches. This was an elongated building, with colonnades on both sides dividing it into a rectangular central nave and two aisles. The wall facing Jerusalem was in the shape of an apse (half circle), most likely suggesting that the Torah scroll was permanently kept there, and the entrance was through a door in the wall opposite the apse. The ability to pray while facing Jerusalem was probably the most important consideration in the choice of this architectural plan. It had been generally thought that the "monumental" edifice was the earlier type, and that the "basilica" came later. A third type, combining features of the other two, was therefore called the "transitional" type. This rigid chronological typology, however, has been abandoned by many archeologists who now attribute the styles to regional tastes rather than to different periods.

# The Bar Kokhba Revolt

*1. Domestic utensils found in the "Cave of [Bar Kokhba's] Letters." Nahal Hever, Judean Desert, 2nd century.*

The last armed attempt to overthrow the yoke of Roman rule in Palestine was the revolt led by a man whom Jewish tradition named "Son of the Star" (Bar Kokhba). This revolt marks the end of Jewish political activism in ancient times. Henceforth the Jews would resign themselves to national servitude. Many factors combined to provoke this uprising which in scope and vehemence was greater than all previous Jewish wars of liberation. Its outcome too was the most disastrous, even worse than the catastrophe brought about by the Great Revolt (66–73) that ended with the destruction of the Second Temple.

Politically the Jews regarded Roman rule as illegitimate, a Kingdom of Evil which had to pay for all the crimes and atrocities it had perpetrated since the conquest by Pompey in 63 BC. Activist messianic movements, which did not disappear with the destruction of the Temple but instead continued to grow, added an eschatological dimension to the conflict. For them the messianic era was an imminent political reality which could, through vigorous action, actually expel foreign occupation. The King-Messiah was to be a military commander who would lead the people on the battlefield and restore the Kingdom of David. His personage was not associated with any signs of supernatural spirituality, nor was his coming linked to a revolution in the cosmic order. This attitude best explains how

an earthly figure such as Bar Kokhba could have been perceived by many, including spiritual leaders of Rabbi Akiva's stature, as the Messiah incarnate. It is also possible that the beginning of the seventh decade after the destruction of the Temple gave rise to high expectations, for approximately seventy years had elapsed between the destruction of the First Temple and the erection of the Second.

When Hadrian became emperor in 117, the Jews rejoiced at first because it became known that he intended to reverse the conquest policy of his predecessor Trajan and help rebuild the towns which had been destroyed over the long years of devastating wars. There was even a rumor that he planned to rebuild Jerusalem, but, as it turned out, this was not at all in the manner expected by the Jews. On the ruins of their capital, the Roman emperor constructed a pagan city – Aelia Capitolina. According to the Greek historian Dio Cassius, this was the principal cause of the revolt. Other sources, however, emphasize the prohibition on circumcision. For Hadrian this measure was probably included in the general prohibition on castration; the Jews, however, regarded it as an abomination.

Whatever the cause, the revolt was not a spontaneous explosion. The Jews prepared long and hard for the war. They accumulated arms, dug subterranean hideouts, and planned their tactics and strategies. Dio Cassius gives a brief description of these preparations which are amply corroborated by archeological findings.

The insurrection began in 132 and lasted for three and a half years. The documents are sparse and fragmentary, and there is no account of the revolt to equal Josephus' history of the Great Revolt. Although of great importance, the letters and documents found near the Dead Sea and other archeological discoveries do not provide an overview of the whole war. Nevertheless, these documents provide much information on certain aspects of the period. For example, they reveal Bar Kokhba's real name: Simeon ben Kosevah, the very same as the *Shimeon ha-Nassi* ("Simeon, the prince of Israel") who appears on the coins minted during the revolt. These coins also provide valuable indications of the feelings of the rebels, their goals and hopes. They portray symbols linked to the ritual in the Temple, as well as inscriptions exalting in the "Redemption of Israel" and the "Freedom of Jerusalem."

Most of the war was conducted in the southern part of Palestine. Indeed, one outcome of the revolt was a shift in the Jewish population's center of gravity from devastated Judea to the Galilee. More significant, however, were the hundreds of thousands of Jewish victims, a decimation which demographically transformed the ethnic composition of the land. Although probably still the majority, the Jews were no longer dominant in large areas of Palestine. Towns and regions which had been exclusively Israelite now became mixed or even had a non-Jewish majority. Worse

| Accession of Hadrian | | Hadrian in Palestine | Beginning of the revolt |
|---|---|---|---|
| **117** | | **129** | **132** |

*3. Hadrian. Bronze, Tell Shalem near Bet Shean, 2nd century.*

**120–129:** Reconstruction of towns in the East raises false hopes that the emperor intends to rebuild Jerusalem. This may have given birth to the legend reported in a *midrash* (*Bereshit Raba*, 44): in the days of Rabbi Joshua ben Hananiah, the emperor had decided to build a Temple, but the Samaritans' opposition aborted the plan. The Jews then assembled in the valley of Rimmon, angrily demanding to revolt. Rabbi Joshua ben Hananiah calmed their turbulence with a fable about a bird who with its long beak had removed a bone stuck in a lion's throat; like that bird, he said, the Jews should be satisfied with the fact that they had entered the lion's jaw and came away unharmed. The lion (Rome) should not be expected to reward such a frail creature (the Jewish people). This legend vividly expresses the national and religious fermentation in Palestine, which persisted

*4. The Tenth "Fretensis" Legion. Inscription on a stone, Jerusalem, end of 1st century.*

even after the destruction of the Temple and the wars waged against Trajan.

**129–130:** Hadrian tours the East. Arriving in Phoenicia in 129, he travels to Syria, then to Arabia, spending the winter in Gerasa before visiting Petra on which he bestows the status of a Roman city (130), finally crossing

the Land of Israel (Jerusalem?) towards Gaza. Coins are minted in his honor in Gaza in 130. The emperor then continues to Egypt, but in 131 he returns to Syria. His departure from the region is the signal for the outbreak of the revolt.

**132:** Commencement of the revolt: first confrontations with Roman forces; the Jews capture territories in Judea and in the coastal plain within the triangle of Emmaus-Modi'in-Lydda. Issue of coins with the inscription "The First Year of the Redemption of Israel," and on the reverse side "Simeon, Prince of Israel."

**132–133:** The Romans organize their forces: detachments of legions are brought from Egypt, Arabia, Syria, Asia Minor, and the Danubian countries. Coins bearing the inscription "Second Year of the Freedom of Israel." Land-leasing contracts are dated "the 20th of *Shvat*, year II of the Redemption of Israel by Simeon ben Kosevah, prince of Israel."

**133–135:** The Romans' counter-offensive

2. Bar Kokhba's letter to one of his lieutenants, Jeshua ben Galgolah.

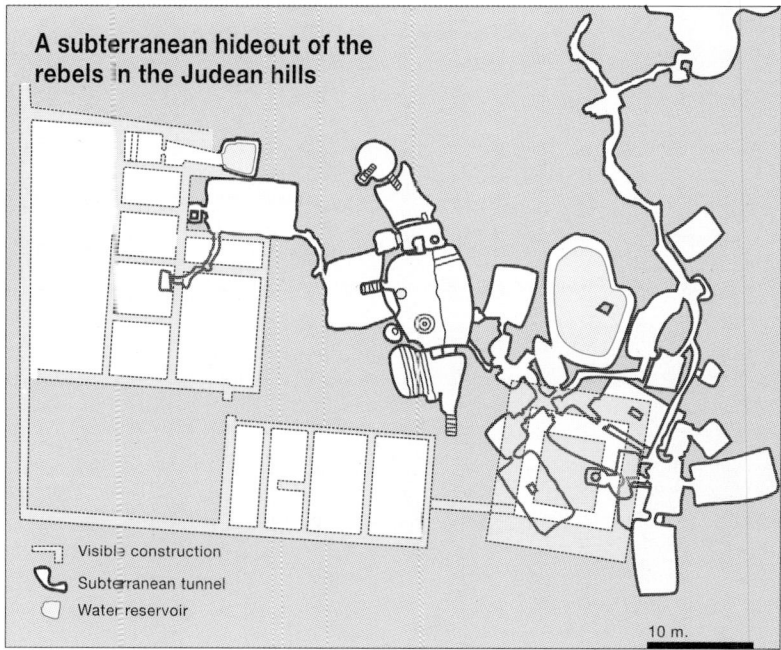

**A subterranean hideout of the rebels in the Judean hills**

Visible construction
Subterranean tunnel
Water reservoir

10 m.

still, the revolt's disastrous end created a real danger of mass emigration for the first time. The fears raised by this threat are explicitly expressed in the writings of the Palestinian Sages who thereby formulated the obligations of the Jew in regard to the Land of Israel. Furthermore, the revolt undermined the delicate balance between the Palestinian center and the diaspora. In the strong community of Babylonia, for example, several attempts were made to disengage from the spirtual leadership of Palestine and to attain spiritual independence and hegemony.

Finally, the religious leadership in Palestine suffered heavy blows from the Hadrianic persecutions which began towards the end of the war. Rabbinical sources testify to the long series of restrictive measures inflicted upon the Jews, designed not only to punish the rebellious nation, but probably also to destroy once and for all the oriental religion which had always had such a strong appeal for the inhabitants of the Empire. The Sages reacted by formulating the meticulous rules of *Kiddush ha-Shem*, "the Sanctification of God" or martyrdom. The legend of the Ten Martyrs, a group of sages tortured and put to death by the Romans, recurringly appeared in many different versions in later generations and became a symbol, in Jewish collective memory, of heroic sacrifice for the love of God.

5. A sela (tetradrachm) coin minted in 134. Bar Kokhba's name, Simeon, is inscribed around the façade of the Temple.

**Julius Severus in Palestine** — 133

**Fall of Bethar** — 135

his last stronghold in Bethar, Bar Kokhba complains bitterly: "From Simon bar Koseva to the men of En-Gedi, to Masbela and to Jonathan Bar Ba'ayann, peace! You are living well, eating and drinking off the property of the house of Israel, and care nothing about your brethren."

**135:** The crushing of the revolt is followed by a series of religious persecutions. Many choose to die for their faith. When Rabbi Hananiah ben Teradyon is asked by a Roman judge why he studied the Torah in defiance of the prohibition, his reply is: "I follow my God's commandment." The Romans immediately condemn him to be burned at the stake, his wife to be killed, and his daughter to be taken to the prostitutes (Babylonian Talmud, *Avoda Zara*, 17:12).Hananiah was but one of many martyrs; but, according to Dio Cassius, many Romans also perished in this war, so when Hadrian informed the Senate of his victory, he did not use the usual expression "I and my army are well."

begins with the arrival of Julius Severus, one of Hadrian's most able generals; the rebels are gradually forced back to a few isolated fortresses. Most of Bar Kokhba's surviving letters date from this last phase of the revolt. They reflect the desperate situation of the insurgents. In a letter probably written from

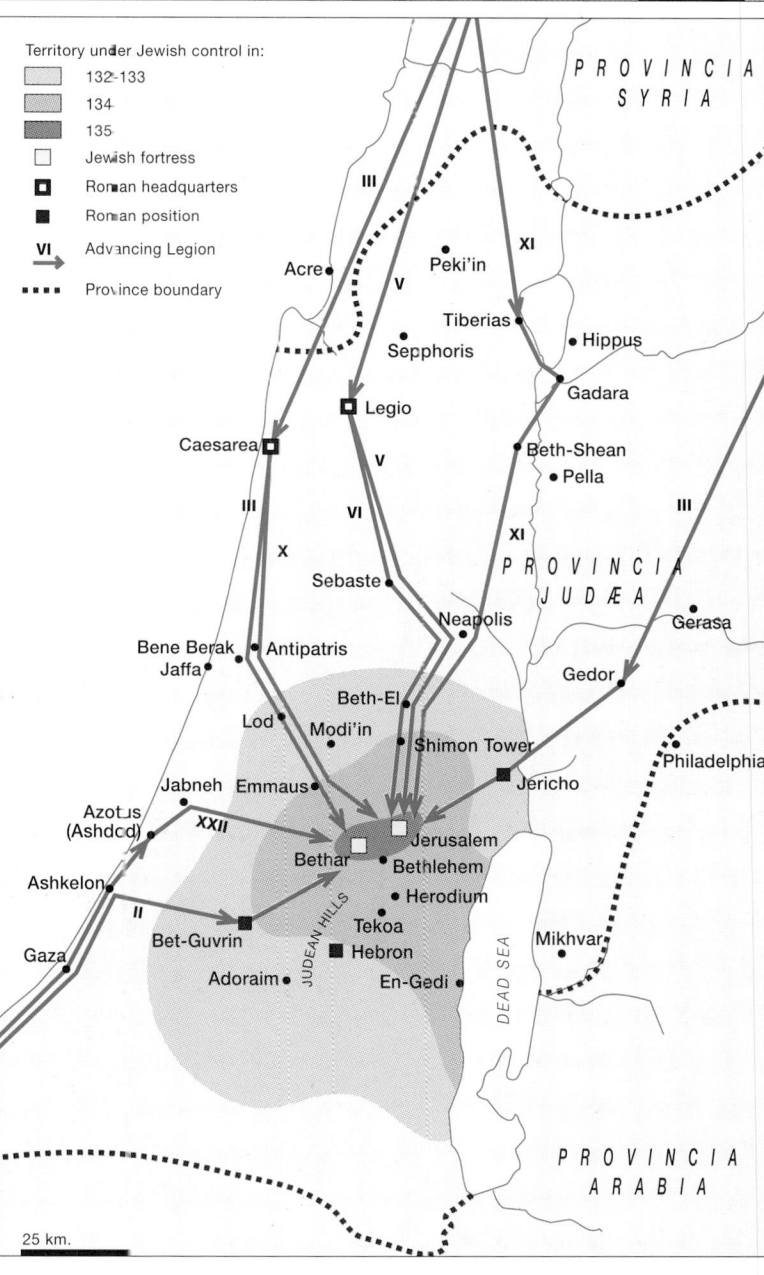

Territory under Jewish control in:
132-133
134
135
Jewish fortress
Roman headquarters
Roman position
VI  Advancing Legion
Province boundary

PROVINCIA SYRIA

Acre
Peki'in
Tiberias
Sepphoris
Hippus
Legio
Gadara
Caesarea
Beth-Shean
Pella
Sebaste
Neapolis
Gerasa
Bene Berak
Antipatris
Jaffa
Gedor
Beth-El
Lod
Modi'in
Shimon Tower
Philadelphia
Jabneh
Emmaus
Jericho
Azotus (Ashdod)
Jerusalem
Ashkelon
Bethar
Bethlehem
Bet-Guvrin
Herodium
Gaza
Tekoa
Mikhvar
Hebron
Adoraim
En-Gedi

PROVINCIA JUDÆA
JUDEAN HILLS
DEAD SEA

PROVINCIA ARABIA

25 km.

# Rabbinic Literature

During the first seven centuries of the Christian Era (the Period of the Sages, according to Jewish periodization) the intellectual and spiritual leaders of the Jewish nation studied, preached, and taught within two socio-cultural institutions: the synagogue (*Bet ha-Kenesset*) and the academy (*Bet ha-Midrash*). These sages produced several of the most central elements of Jewish civilization. They composed prayers and liturgy (*piyyutim*), translated the Bible into Aramaic, laid the foundations for Jewish esoteric mysticism, and, above all, created the *Halakhah* and the *Aggadah*.

The Halakhah (from the root *halokh*, meaning "to go" – the road which the observant Jew must follow) is a corpus of laws regulating every step in a man's life, from cradle to grave. The sages deliberated each and every matter; considered everything according to social, religious or technological developments; and reached a binding ruling. The Halakhah was elaborated on throughout the ages, each generation adding something of its own, always respecting continuity and tradition.

Unlike legal codices of other civilizations, the Jewish Halakhah is not simply a distilled corpus of laws and precedents, but is also a protocol of the entire debate preceding each decision. Rejected opinions, conflicting views, fragmentary propositions, support of arguments by biblical references – all these appear in the discussion of every subject in a succinct and precise style.

The major halakhic works are the *Mishnah* and *Tosefta* (1st–2nd centuries) and both Talmuds, the Jerusalem and the Babylonian (3rd–6th centuries). In the following centuries these works formed the basis of the teachings of Maimonides (*Mishneh Torah*, 12th century) and of Rabbi Joseph Caro (*Shulhan Arukh*, 16th century) which thereafter became the cornerstones of Jewish Law for all times.

Unlike the Halakhah, the Aggadah (from the root *hagged*, meaning "to say") has no normative authority. Its authors interpreted biblical stories, deriving from them a moral applicable to their own time. They coined metaphors and maxims, strengthened the faith of their people, admonishing and bolstering their pride and courage in troubled times. The Aggadah also discusses theological and ethical questions. Much of it is devoted to controversy, often petty and aggressive, against Israel's foes and adversaries, such as the Samaritans and Christians. While the Halakhah presents the serious face of the Sages, the Aggadah presents a lighter side. Containing many elements of exaggeration, fantasy, and satire, its style is fluent and popular, and, while it is amusing, its main purpose is nonetheless moral and didactic.

The Aggadah reached us in part through works of the Halakhah in which aggadic interpretations were added as illustrations to serious legal matters, but also in purely aggadic works called *Midrashim* (from the root *darosh*, meaning "to seek" or "to examine") as, for example, *Genesis Rabbah* or *Pesikta de-Rav Kahana*. This genre consists of works which vary greatly in form and content. Some interpret a single biblical text according to the order of its verses; others discuss a certain topic through references to verses chosen from different biblical chapters.

Both the Halakhah and the Aggadah were transmitted orally for

1. King David playing the harp. Psalter, northern Italy, 1450–1470.

generations – hence Oral Law – and were only written down long after they had been composed, sometimes several centuries after the period of the Sages. Teachers of the Halakhah in the Middle Ages were either *mefareshim* ("commentators," i.e., legal theoreticians) or *posekim* ("decision makers") who based their works entirely on the rabbinic literature which had been codified before the seventh century. Thus it may be said that the early Sages (the *Tannaim*, in Palestine) and their successors (the *Amoraim*, in Palestine and in Babylon) were, in fact, the men who laid the foundations of Jewish culture for all generations to come.

| Hillel the Elder | Mishnah | Jerusalem Talmud | Babylonian Talmud |
|---|---|---|---|
| C.1 AD | 200 | 425 | 500 |

**End of 1st century BC:** Hillel the Elder, the greatest of the sages of the Second Temple period, comes from Babylon to Jerusalem.

**1st–2nd centuries:** The period of the *Tannaim*: Beginning of compilation of materials from which the Mishnah and the *Tosefta* were developed in Palestine.

**c. 200:** The redaction of the Mishnah is completed by Rabbi Judah ha-Nasi (in the Galilee); the Mishnah is divided into six orders (*sedarim*): *zera'im* ("seeds") – on matters concerning agriculture; *mo'ed* – on festivals; *nashim* ("women") – the legal obligations of husband and wife; *nezikin* ("damages") – civil law; the order *kodashim* ("holy things") – on sacrifices in the Temple; and *tohorot* ("purities") – on purity and defilement.

**3rd century:** Tannaitic literature committed to writing in Palestine. Oral traditions from

2. An exceptionally rare illustration of a religious precept: a woman taking her ritual bath before rejoining her husband. German miniature, 1427.

the tannaitic period are contained in works such as the *Tosefta*, the *Mekhilta* (a discussion of the Book of Exodus), or the *Sifra* (mostly concerned with the Book of Leviticus).

**3rd–5th centuries:** The period of the *Amoraim* who compiled the legal materials to be included in the Jerusalem and the Babylonian Talmuds.

**End of 4th century:** The compilation of the *Tosefta* by an unknown editor, probably in Palestine. This is a collection of laws containing material excluded from the Mishnah, mostly unedited "raw material" including many conflicting teachings.

**5th century onwards:** Amoraic literature is transcribed in Palestine and Babylon.

**c. 425:** The "closing" of the Jerusalem Talmud (in Tiberias); its text is mostly a discussion of the orders of *zera'im*, *mo'ed*, *nashim*, and *nezikin* of the Mishnah. Composition of the *Midrash Genesis Rabbah* which interprets verses from Genesis in aggadic style.

**c. 450:** Composition of *Leviticus Rabbah* in the Galilee – a homiletic *Midrash* devoted mainly to the themes of reward and punishment, God's love for the poor, and the praise of peace.

**c. 475:** Composition of *Midrash Pesikta de-rav Kahana* in the Galilee – homilies for all the festivals, taken from various books of the Pentateuch or Prophets.

**c. 500:** The "closing" of the Babylonian Talmud which interprets the orders of *mo'ed*, *nashim*, *nezikin*, and *kodashim* of the Mishnah. Originally the Talmud consisted of two materials: a tractate from the Mishnah, written in Hebrew, and the *Gemara* which analyzes it, written in a mixture of Hebrew and Aramaic.

**6th century:** The period of the *Savoraim*, the Babylonian scholars who succeeded the *Amoraim*; they completed the ordering of the Talmud and introduced additional discussions and explanations.

**7th century:** Beginning of the period of the *Geonim*, heads of the academies in Babylon

A PAGE OF TALMUD. The *editio princeps* of the Babylonian Talmud printed by Daniel Bomberg (Venice, 1520–1523) determined the external form of the Talmud for all time. Thus, one cites the tractate, the folio, and the page (r or v). Here, the tractate *Eruvin*, fol. 3 r. (The tractate discusses symbolical acts which facilitate the accomplishment of otherwise forbidden acts on the Sabbath and festivals).

Titling the page: the name of the chapter, its number in the order of the chapters in the tractate, the name of the tractate, the folio.

The text of the Talmud proper is composed of two elements: the Mishnah, the legal code composed in Hebrew in Palestine between the 1st and 2nd centuries AD; and the *Gemara* – a summary in Aramaic of the debate over the Mishnah in the Babylonian academies between the 3rd and 6th centuries.

Rashi's commentary. Rashi (acronym for Rabbi Solomon ben Isaac), the 11th-century scholar from Troyes, was the most authoritative biblical commentator. His interpretation of the Babylonian Talmud is one of the great classics of rabbinical literature.

The commentary of the Tosafists. Disciples of Rashi, these "men of the additions" (*tosafot*) determined the tradition of the rabbinical schools in *Ashkenaz* (Germany and northern France) during the 12th to 14th centuries.

Systematization and codification of the *Halakhah*, such as Maimonides' *Mishneh Torah* (12th century), and Joseph Caro's *Shulhan Arukh* (Safed, 16th century).

The commentary of Rabbenu ("our teacher") Hananel ben Hushi'el. This great scholar from Kairouan was the first to compose a complete commentary on the Babylonian Talmud, inspired by *responsa* literature (11th century).

The commentary of Nissim ben Jacob ibn Shahin. Outstanding scholar and leader of the Tunisian community (Kairouan, 11th century), his talmudic commentary follows the method of the Babylonian sages.

The "proofs" of Joel Sirkes (named after the title of one of his works, *Bayit Hadash*, "New House"): brief "corrections" – or alternative readings – for the *Gemara* and Rashi's commentary (Poland, 16th century).

Annotations by Akiva Eger "The Younger" on the margins of the *Gemara*, Rashi's commentary, and the Tosafists' "additions" (Austro-Hungary, early 19th century).

The "Tradition of the Six Orders [of the Mishnah]," elaborated between the 16th and 19th centuries: a list of corresponding passages found in several places in the Talmud and in the literature of the Sages.

Biblical references for the text of the *Gemara* (16th–19th centuries); this brief reference has acquired the status of a commentary on the Talmud.

# Babylon, a Capital of the Jewish World

Long after the ancient city of Babylon and the kingdom of Babylonia had ceased to exist, the Jews continued to use the name "Babel" to designate Mesopotamia, the "land of the two rivers." Indeed, the Babylonian diaspora did not resemble any other. Its antiquity and the fact that it remained the only large Jewish community outside the Roman Empire made it a world apart. Since Mesopotamian Jewry was never embraced by the seductive and highly assimilative influence of the Greco-Roman civilization, it could develop its own original forms of social life and autonomous institutions.

The roots of the Babylonian community were very ancient, dating as far back as the end of the biblical period and the deportations from the Land of Israel, which both preceded and followed the destruction of the First Temple (586 BC). As it grew and prospered, the community tended to emphasize its antiquity. By the time it had produced its own version of the Talmud, it manifested a kind of "local patriotism." Was not Abraham, the Father of the nation, born "beyond the river" (Euphrates)? Were not

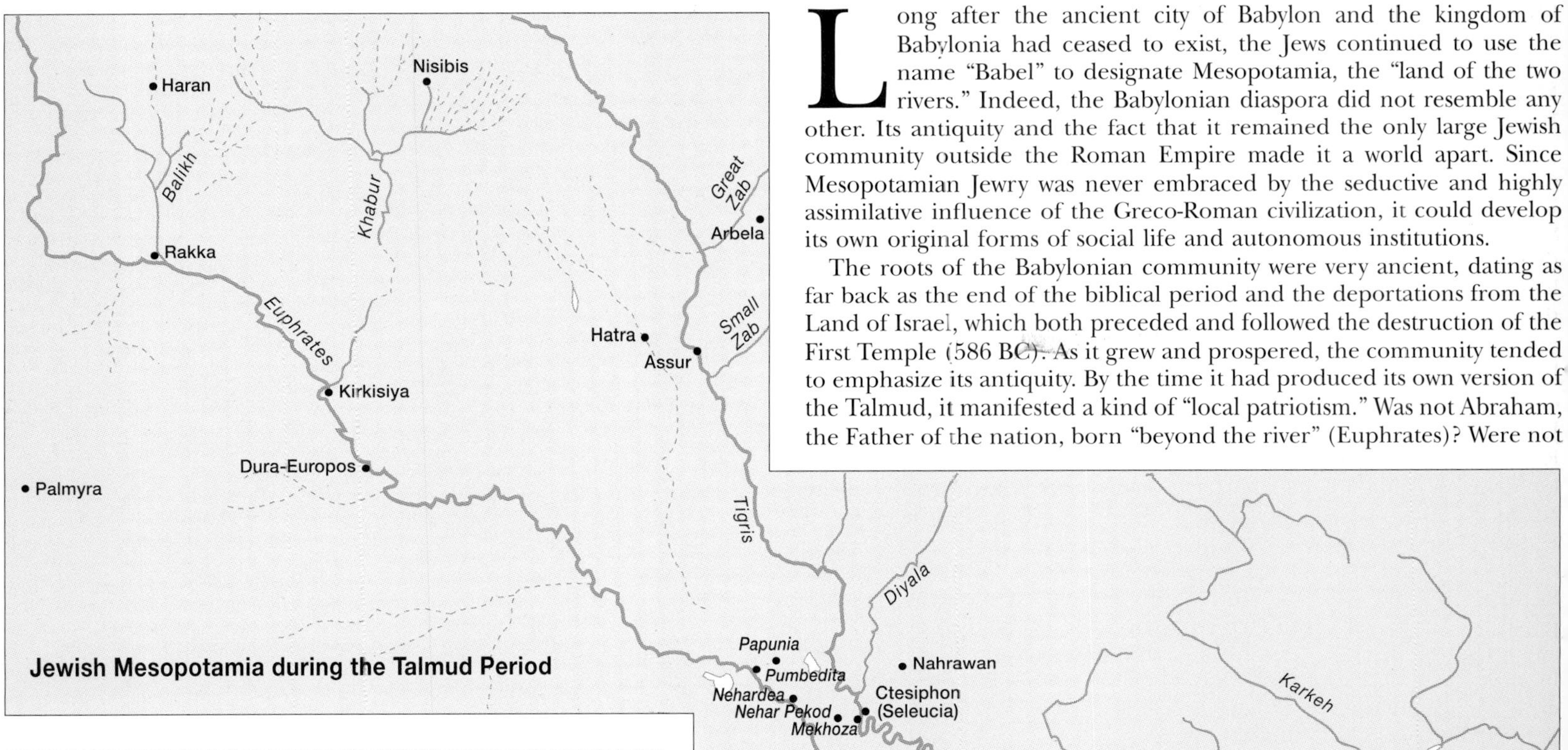

**Jewish Mesopotamia during the Talmud Period**

Map labels: Haran, Nisibis, Balikh, Khabur, Great Zab, Arbela, Rakka, Euphrates, Hatra, Assur, Small Zab, Kirkisiya, Dura-Europos, Palmyra, Tigris, Diyala, Karkeh, Papunia, Pumbedita, Nahrawan, Nehardea, Ctesiphon (Seleucia), Nehar Pekod, Mekhoza, Sikara, Shekanzib, Apamea, Mata Mekhassia, Sura, Pum Nahara, Humaniya, Susa, Kafri, Naresh, Karun, Spasinu Charax

*Kafri* • Talmudic name (unidentified site)

50 km.

1. *Rav Ashi (371–424) teaching at the Sura Academy. Reconstruction.*

3. *Ghosts engraved on incantation bowls. Babylonia, 5th–6th centuries.*

| Babylonian Exile | Hellenistic Babylonia | Parthian Babylonia |
|---|---|---|
| 586 BC | 331 BC | c. 150 BC |

**597 BC:** Exile of Jehoiachin; beginning of Jewish settlement in Mesopotamia.

**586 BC:** Fall of Jerusalem and destruction of the First Temple; beginning of the Babylonian Exile proper; the exiles seemed to comply with the advice given them by Jeremiah (29:5-7): "Build ye houses, and dwell in them; and plant gardens, and eat the fruit of them. Take ye wives, and beget sons and daughters; and take wives for your sons, and give your daughters to husbands, that they may bear sons and daughters; that ye may be increased there and not diminished. And seek the peace of the city." Their successful integration is best illustrated by the texts of the Murashu family in Nippur from the fifth century BC.

**331 BC:** Conquest of Alexander the Great. Until the middle of the second century BC, Babylonian Jewry was under Hellenistic domination; this was the last time prior to the Middle Ages that they were ruled by the same political regime as their brethren in Palestine.

**307 BC:** On the ruins of Babylon, Seleucus I Nicator founds the city of Seleucia.

**Middle of 2nd century BC:** Babylonian Jewry is now under Parthian domination; at the same time the Seleucids also lose their hold over Palestine (revolt of the Maccabees).

**20–35:** Two brothers, Hanilai and Hasinai (Anilaeus and Asineus), establish a short-lived "Jewish State" in the region of Nehardea.

**c. 36:** The conversion to Judaism of the kingdom of Adiabene (in the upper Tigris region), initiated by Queen Helena and her son Izates, marks the apogee of Jewish proselytizing in the Second Temple period both in the Parthian East and in the Greco-Roman world.

**c. 100:** Rabbi Akiva "goes down" to Nehardea to announce the Hebrew leap year; this is the first time that the sources mention a Palestinian sage active in the Babylonian diaspora.

**116–117:** Babylonian Jews take an active

the Euphrates and the Tigris the two rivers which flowed out of Eden according to Genesis (2:14)? The Jews of Babylonia, therefore, considered themselves the aristocracy of the Jewish people. Even the land of Mesopotamia acquired an aura of sanctity in their eyes, second to the Land of Israel of course, but holier than all other countries.

The history of this community during the first millennium of its existence remains obscure. Following the Hellenistic conquest of the East, the Jews of Babylonia, like their brethren in Palestine, came under Seleucid rule. From the second century BC until the third century AD, they were subjects of the Arsacid Parthians. The Parthian kingdom, a loose federation of "feudal" principalities, was a convenient structure for them. As long as they gave their support in times of war, the rulers kept out of the internal affairs of ethnic groups under their domination. The little that is known about the Jews there at the time comes from the quill of Josephus Flavius: they were very numerous, and their brethren in Judea sought their help while preparing their revolt against Rome. This Roman historian also mentions two episodes which he most probably learned from literary fragments: the adventure of two brothers from Nehardea who had founded a kind of thieves-state near the city of Seleucia, and the famous conversion of the kings of Adiabene to Judaism.

It is only after the fall of the Second Temple (70) and the Bar Kokhba Revolt (132–135) that one can truly follow the history of Babylonian Jewry, which becomes even clearer after the fall of the Parthian regime and the accession of the Sassanian dynasty (224). Sources relating to the first two centuries of the Christian era make no mention of any form of organized Torah studies in Babylonia and note hardly any Babylonian scholars. We do know that Rabbi Akiva, in his many travels, arrived in Nehardea where he announced the leap year. After Bar Kokhba's revolt we hear for the first time about groups of sages who "went down" to Babylonia, undoubtedly fleeing the religious persecutions which followed the crushing of the revolt. In Babylon the nephew of Rabbi Joshua, Hananiah, attempted to proclaim the order of the Hebrew calendar, a prerogative which until then had been indisputably reserved for the leadership in Palestine. Although Hanania was forced to make a retraction, it was nevertheless the first manifestation of Babylonian independence from the Palestinian center.

During the late second or the early third century, we hear about this community's political leaders for the first time: *Rosh ha-golah* (the *exilarch*, "prince of the exile"). Although nothing is known about the origins of this institution, it is certain that Babylonian Jews in the talmudic period regarded the *exilarch* as a scion of the House of David. Many talmudic texts compare his attributes to that of the *nasi* in the Land of Israel – another manifestation of the singular status of this Jewry.

The new Sassanian regime, unlike the Parthian, was far more central-

ized and strictly Zoroastrian. Certain Jewish sages were afraid that the king and clergy would interfere in community affairs. Others, on the other hand, hoped to find a *modus vivendi* with the Sassanians. The sage Samuel summarized this attitude in his famous saying: *Dina de-Malkhuta Dina*, the law of the land is law. On the whole, the Jews of Babylon adopted this point of view, which brought them an extensive period of prosperity and cultural blossoming.

It was during this period that Babylonia emerged as the great center of religious studies, which rivalled Palestine. Between the third and fifth centuries, Babylonian academies – the future *yeshivot* – established a method of commentary on the Bible which became the basis for the Babylonian Talmud. This tradition, later disseminated by the *Geonim* (heads of the Babylonian academies), was to be accepted by the entire Jewish world. Paradoxically perhaps, the sons of a community of which nothing is known prior to the third century, determined the norms and behavior of Jews throughout the world for fifteen centuries.

2. An incantation bowl inscribed with magical formulas and biblical verses in Aramaic. Babylonia, c. 600.

| Conversion of Adiabene | Accession of the Sassanians | End of the Talmudic period |
|---|---|---|
| c. 36 | 224 | 500 |

4. Sabbath at Nehardea. An emissary from Palestine with his Babylonian hosts. Reconstruction.

part in the Parthian resistance against the invasion of Trajan's troops.

**c. 150:** Hananiah attempts to order the Hebrew calendar in Babylonia; this Babylonian teacher was probably reacting to the consequences of Bar Kokhba's revolt, but he was rebuked by the spiritual leaders in Palestine who feared an irrevocable breach in the Jewish people; one of their emissaries reminds the Babylonian Jews of the famous prophecy by Isaiah (2:3): "For out of Zion shall go forth the law, and the word of the Lord from Jerusalem" – but he sarcastically substitutes Babylon for Jerusalem.

**219:** After a long period of study in Palestine, the Babylonian sage Rav returns to Babylon; in the tradition of the Babylonian sages, this date inaugurates a new era, the period of the Talmud: "When Rav came to Babylon, we became there like the Land of Israel" (Babylonian Talmud, *Gittin*, 1:1). According to them this date also marks the creation of the two great Babylonian *yeshivot*

– the Nehardea Academy (later transferred to Pumbedita) headed by Samuel, and that of Sura, founded by Rav himself.

**224:** Fall of the Parthian kingdom and accession of the Sassanians who will rule over all of Persia. After a brief period of uncertainty, the Jews establish cordial relations with the new regime.

**259:** Destruction of Nehardea during a Palmyrene invasion; the academy is transferred to Pumbedita.

**Late 3rd century:** The Babylonian community feels the oppression of the Zoroastrian church during its expansion.

**Late 4th–early 5th centuries:** Rav Ashi, head of the Sura Academy (till 424), is one of the principal redactors of the Babylonian Talmud.

**500:** Death of Ravina, head of the Sura Academy, considered to be the last of the *Amoraim* (the Babylonian sages of that generation); according to Jewish tradition beginning in the Middle Ages, this year marks the end of the Talmudic period.

# Daily Life in Palestine in the Talmudic Period

Jews living in Palestine in the early centuries of the Christian Era remained as they had been before the destruction of the Temple: an agrarian society. The process of urbanization of the Near East during the Roman and Byzantine periods only affected the Jewish population slightly. Although quite a few Jews resided in towns - Tiberias, Sepphoris, Caesarea, Lydda - which were even accorded legal urban status by the Roman authorities, the great majority were still living in modest-sized settlements of about 2000 to 5000 people, which Jewish sources describe as "villages." In the Byzantine period most of these communities were to be found in the Galilee and on the Golan, but there were some in the Hebron area in the south, and a few along the coastal plain and in the Jordan valley.

Thus, Palestinian economy in Talmudic times remained much the same as it had been in the Second Temple period, and could still be portrayed in the words of a second-century BC author: "Their love for tilling the soil is truly great. The country is plentifully wooded with numerous olive trees and rich in cereals and vegetables, and also in vines and honey. Date palms and other fruit trees are beyond reckoning among them. And for cattle of all kinds there is pasture in abundance" (*Letter of Aristeas*, 112).

The large number of presses found by archeologists almost everywhere confirm the existence of flourishing wine and oil industries (the latter being used for cooking, for illumination, and for skin lubrication). Fishing was an important industry in the northern part of the country. Crafts, however, were primarily an urban occupation. Jerusalem was apparently well known for the number and quality of its artisans. As more and more Jews moved to the coast, they began to engage in regional commerce. During this time many Jews in the north traded with port towns in Lebanon and Syria. Fishing also became a major economic occupation in the northern part of the country.

Patterns of community organization began to form in the Second Temple period. The Book of Judith, probably composed in the Hellenistic period (or even in the late Persian period), describes the communities as governed by *archons* who received their instructions from the central authorities in Jerusalem. According to Josephus Flavius, each village was administered by a group of seven judges. Josephus himself, appointed commander of the Galilee with the commencement of the Great Revolt, took these legal-administrative units in the region under his charge. It is possible that these convocations of seven judges provided the basis for the institution of the "seven town elders" mentioned in the Talmudic period. As the official representatives of the local community, they were empowered to buy and sell public property, including the synagogue. Both lite-

*1. Palm-decorated console from the synagogue at Capernaum. Galilee, 3rd century AD.*

rary sources and archeological findings refer to the leader of the local community as *archisynagogos*. It is still unclear whether he was actually the leader of the entire community or simply one of the synagogue directors, or perhaps in certain places these two functions were one and the same.

From the Talmud we also learn about the

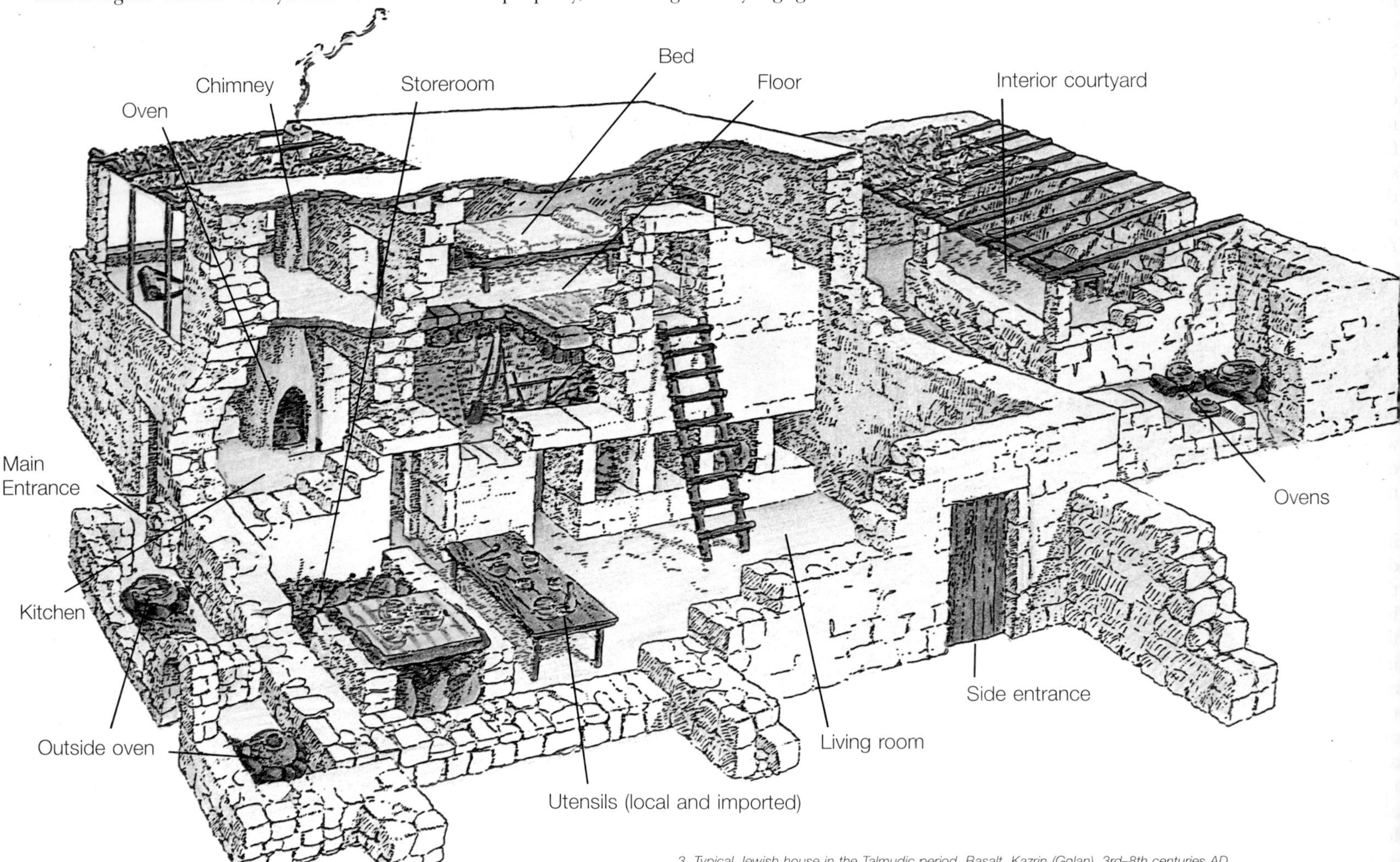

Oven
Chimney
Storeroom
Bed
Floor
Interior courtyard
Main Entrance
Kitchen
Outside oven
Utensils (local and imported)
Living room
Side entrance
Ovens

*3. Typical Jewish house in the Talmudic period. Basalt, Kazrin (Golan), 3rd–8th centuries AD.*

crystallization of a notion of "citizenship" among the Palestinian Jews: a distinction between permanent and transient inhabitants. The concept has even received legal formulation: "How long should one be in a town to be as the townsmen? Twelve months. And he who buys a house to dwell in, immediately becomes as the townsmen" (*Bava Batra*, 1:5). Even before completing a period of one-year's residence, the newcomer had to partake in certain obligations. After three months he was required to contribute to the communal charity fund; after twelve months he became a tax-paying citizen. Taxes were levied by the community in order to finance the construction of synagogues, buying Torah scrolls, maintaining public property, and paying the salaries of town officials. Among the latter were the *agronomos* (market inspector), the *Hazzan* (in the Talmudic period designating a synagogue officer, not a cantor), "city guards" (in charge of security but also of observance of municipal regulations such as opening hours of shops), and, finally, school teachers.

There is very little information about formal education prior to the destruction of the Temple, although later sources ascribe pedagogical programs to major figures of the Hasmonean years (Simeon ben Shetah) or of the close of the Second Temple period (Joshua ben Gamla). For the Talmudic period, however, there is definite evidence of the existence of permanent institutions for elementary religious instruction – mostly for teaching children how to read the Scriptures. These were very different from the Greco-Roman schools which primed adolescents for public careers. The young Jew, who in most cases would earn his living within the family circle, acquired the skill of reading (and sometimes, though not always, of writing), with the "teacher of infants." Only the very talented or affluent would advance to the study of the *Halakha* with a renowned master.

The entire educational system, needless to say, was designed only for boys. Although there are indications that some girls did receive a smattering of letters, public activity was reserved for men. Even if women went to the synagogue and heard the sermons, their role remained purely passive. Nonetheless, there was still no "women's gallery"; the segregation of the sexes in the synagogue was apparently not introduced until the early Middle Ages.

Another obscure matter is the extent of intervention of the central authorities in the daily life of the local community. All we know is that in Jerusalem the president of the Sanhedrin (*nasi*) and his "government" proclaimed the calendar, sometimes sent a commission to investigate the quality of teaching in the towns, and occasionally appointed a teacher or a spiritual leader when a community requested such assistance. One important institution was still absent in the Talmudic period: the "town rabbi," spiritual guide and pastor, respected by all and supported by public funds. This type of local leadership was to emerge only in later generations in diaspora communities.

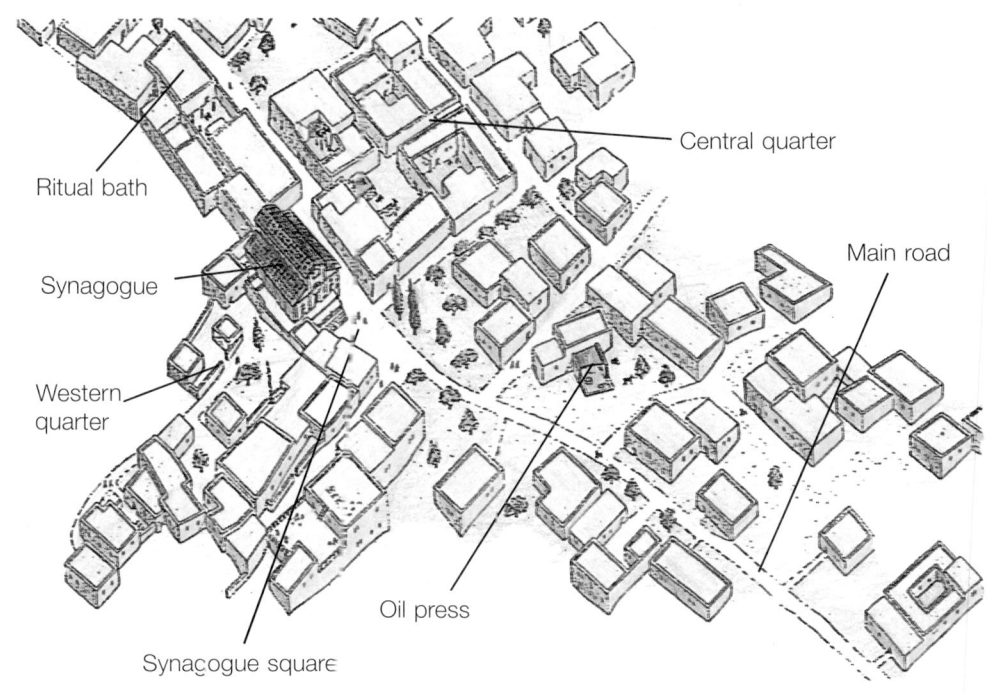

2. The village of Korazim in the Galilee (reconstruction). A halakhah in the Mishnah (late 2nd century AD) enumerates the essential institutions for a proper Jewish community: "... in a city in which the following ten things do not exist, it is not advisable for a scholar to reside, and they are: Five persons to execute what the court decides; a treasury of charity (which is collected by two and distributed by three); a prayer-house, a bath-house, lavatories, a physician, a barber, a scribe, and a teacher for children" (Babylonian Talmud, Sanhedrin, p.41).

4. Oil press. Tirat Yehudah (coastal plain), 2nd century BC.

# When the Roman Empire Became Christian

1. The church at Kursi in "the country of the Gadarenes" (Luke 8:26). By the Lake of Galilee, 5th century.

For over three hundred years, between Constantine's occupation of the eastern provinces in 324 and the Arab conquest in 634, Palestine was ruled by Byzantium's dual law: Roman and Christian. While still in majority at the beginning of the period, the Jews of Palestine were living alongside Samaritans, pagan Greco-Syrians, and a small Christian community. The change in demographic composition became noticeable in the early fifth century. This is clearly evident when comparing Eusebius of Caesarea's *Onomastikon*, a guide-book to the Holy Land composed in the early fourth century, to the Latin version edited by Jerome a century later. The first could only identify three biblical sites as "Christian villages," while the latter already refers to many places as such. By the sixth century the majority of the population was Christian. This transformation was the result of the permanent settlement of pilgrims, and the Christianization of large sectors of the pagan population. The success of evangelism was largely due to the efforts of the monasteries, which by then had become well-established and well-organized communities throughout the land.

Meanwhile, conciliar decisions and Roman legal codes – first those of Theodosius, then of Justinian – redefined the legal and social status of the Jews. To neutralize the influence which Judaism still exercised on the religious life of eastern Christian communities, the Byzantine rulers issued prohibitions on marriage, commercial exchange, and social relations between Jews and Christians. The Council of Nicaea (325), for example, decided to fix a constant date for Easter, a holiday which until then had been celebrated in the Orient on the same day as the Jewish Passover. While the bishops released their faithful from dependence on the Jewish proclamation of the festivals, civil authorities intercepted Jewish emissaries who were dispatched from Palestine to inform the diaspora communities of the order of the calendar. These circumstances were probably the cause for the decision taken by the patriarch (*nasi*) Hillel II in 359 to proclaim a permanent calendar calculated mathematically once and for all.

At the same time, the Roman legislature decided that there was no justification for the exemption of Jews from certain public offices which were supposedly linked to idolatry. Beginning with Constantine, several laws repeated the demand that Jews, like all other subjects of the empire, should perform municipal obligations. Nevertheless, certain exemptions, similar to those granted to church dignitaries, were accorded to the "princes and elders" of the community. While these laws may be seen as part of the effort to equalize the status of all subjects rather than as acts of discrimination, there were other, less innocent, decrees as well. A law promulgated in 329 forbade the Jewish communities' custom of punishing apostates to Christianity. Further measures were adopted to prevent conversions to Judaism, among them the law of 339 prohibiting the

**Constantine I** 306–337

**313:** "Edict of Milan": the two rulers of the empire, the Christian Constantine and the pagan Licinius, extend toleration to Christianity as to all other cults; this is an important first step towards the establishment of Christianity's dominance in the Roman Empire.
**324:** Constantine's victory over Licinius gives him possession of the eastern provinces of the empire; for the first time Palestine comes under the rule of a Christian monarch.
**325 onwards:** Construction of churches in Palestine; Constantine and his mother Helena order churches to be built in the most important Christian sites: Bethlehem, Jerusalem, Mount of Olives (inaugurated in 326), and Allonei Mamreh near Hebron.
**335:** Inauguration of the basilica of the Holy Sepulchre in Jerusalem on the site identified by Christian tradition as Jesus' burial place. The probable renewal of the interdict on Jews to reside in Jerusalem which has been in force since Hadrian's days. About the same time, an attempt was made by a

converted Jew known as Joseph the Apostate to build churches in the Galilee; his failure demonstrates that the Galilee is still a

3. Marble chancel screen found near Kibbutz Massuot Itzhak. Western Negev, 6th–7th centuries.

4. Madonna and child. Pottery figurine, Bet Shean, 4th–6th centuries.

**Julian the Apostate** 361–363

**Theodosius I** 379–395

predominantly Jewish region where, unlike Judea and the center of Palestine, Christianity has not yet taken root.
**351–352:** A Jewish uprising in the Galilee under the command of a certain Patricius; provoked by local conflicts with the representatives of the Roman regime rather than by a desire to overthrow the foreign yoke, the revolt broke out at Sepphoris and spread to other towns (Acre, Tiberias, Bet She'arim, and Lydda); it was crushed by an experienced commander Ursicinus, dispatched especially for this purpose. Ursicinus meets with Jewish sages, and he is mentioned, not unfavorably, in the Jerusalem Talmud.
**359:** Hillel II's permanent calendar: henceforth communities in the diaspora are less dependent on the spiritual leadership in Palestine.
**361–363:** Julian the Apostate: in his enterprise of anti-Christian restoration, the philosopher-emperor proposes to make Jerusalem a Jewish city and to rebuild the

2. *Monastery of the Temptation. Qarantal, north of Jericho, Byzantine period.*

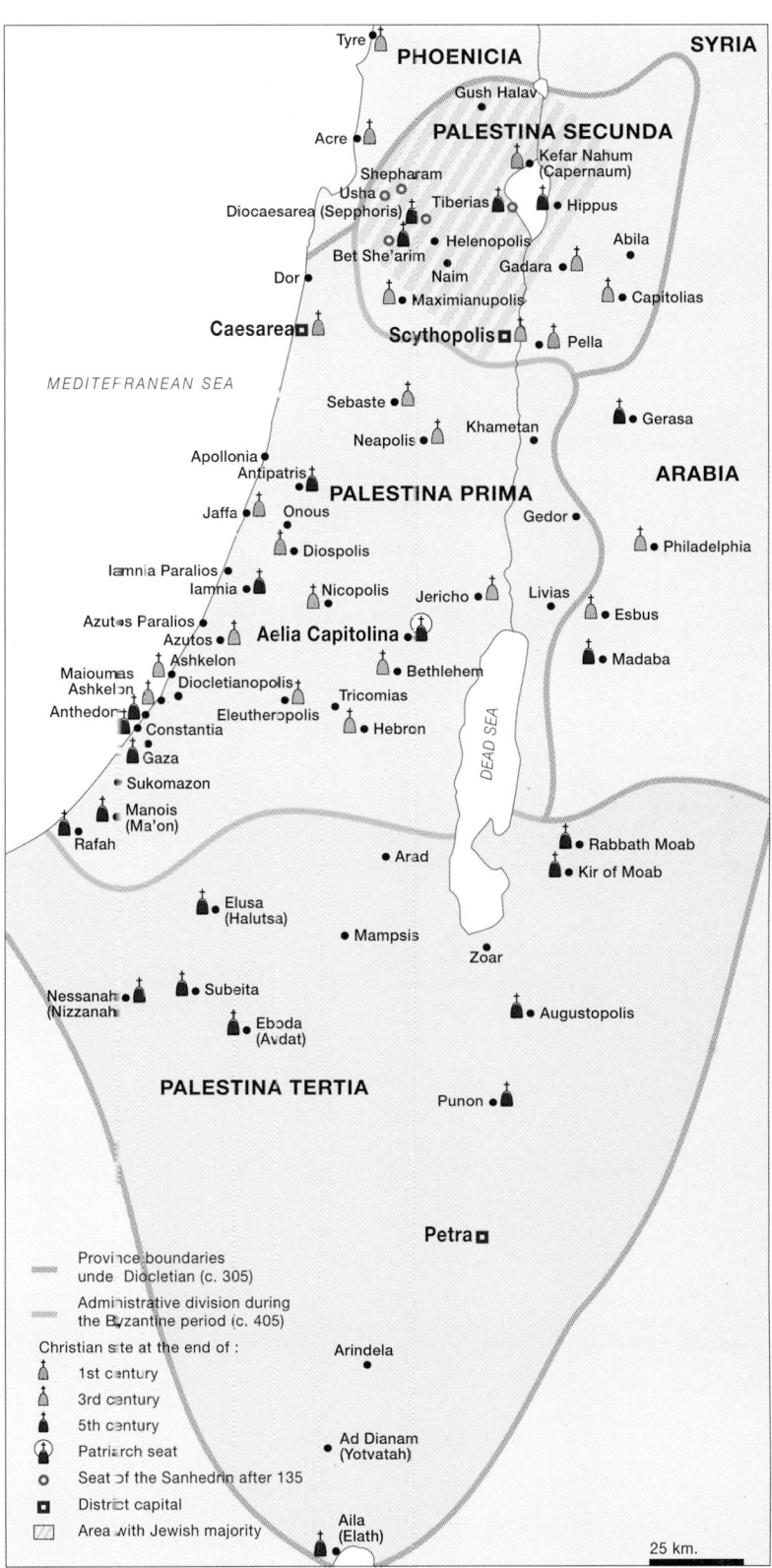

possession of Christian slaves by Jews. Since the foreign slave became a member of the Jewish people as soon as he was enfranchised, this law both harmed the Jews economically while contributing to their demographic decline.

During the second half of the fourth century, Roman legislature became concerned with Jewish prayer houses. Although initially the law was intended to protect such places from attack, in the early fifth century there were prohibitions on the construction of new synagogues. Admittedly, excavations have revealed that these laws were not always obeyed, but it is evident that the civil authorities were yielding to the pressures of a Church which was becoming increasingly less tolerant.

Finally, it was Church pressure which also led to the extinction of another Jewish institution – the patriarch in Tiberias. Symbol of "national" unity, recognized as such both in Palestine and in the diaspora which supported him by generous contributions, the *nasi* was above all a leader of the nation by virtue of being a scion of the "house of David." By representing the endurance of the dynasty, he served as a focus for national-messianic hopes – a phenomenon which the Church leaders viewed as an insufferable pretension. Thus, by 429 the Roman law speaks of the "extinguished" office of the *nasi*.

| Arcadius | Theodosius II | Zeno |
|---|---|---|
| 395–408 | 408–450 | 474–491 |

5. *An engraved plaque against the evil eye bearing distinctly-Jewish symbols. Provenance unknown, 5th century.*

Temple; in a letter to the Jews he asks them to pray to their God for his success in the war against the Persians, "So that I should restore the holy city of Jerusalem with my own money"; but Julian is killed during his Persian campaign and the reconstruction of Jerusalem is brought to a halt, probably also because of an earthquake which the Christians see as a manifestation of God's wrath at the apostate emperor.

**388. March 14:** A law prohibiting mixed marriages between Jews and non-Jews, defined as adultery (Theodosian Code III, 7, 2. The Code, compiled in 438, contained sixteen volumes of laws promulgated from the days of Constantine the Great, classified according to subjects).

**399. April 11:** A law prohibiting sending emissaries (*apostoli*) to collect donations on behalf of the *nasi*: "That the Jews should know that we have delivered them from this iniquitous tribute" (C.Th. XV, 8, 14).

**c. 425:** Abolition of the office of the patriarch (*nasi*) in Palestine.

6. *"And when ye see this, your heart shall rejoice, and your bones shall flourish like an herb" (Isaiah, 66:14). An unknown person inscribed these words on the Western Wall in Jerusalem, probably during the reign of Julian the Apostate, c. 360.*

Map legend:

- Province boundaries under Diocletian (c. 305)
- Administrative division during the Byzantine period (c. 405)

Christian site at the end of:
- 1st century
- 3rd century
- 5th century
- Patriarch seat
- Seat of the Sanhedrin after 135
- District capital
- Area with Jewish majority

25 km.

# The Jews of Byzantium

**Jewish Communities in the Byzantine Empire 9th - 10th centuries**

Caffa
Kherson
BLACK SEA
Sinope
Trebizonde
DALMATIA
BULGARIA
Ragusa
Siponto
Durazzo (Dyrrachium)
Constantinople
Nicea
Venosa
Bari
Oria
Kastoria
Thessaloniki
Tarentum
Otrante
Abydos
Amorion
Caesarea
Edessa
Rossano
Thebes
CHIOS
Synnada
Corinth
Ephesus
Miletus
Antalya
Tarsus
Antioch
RHODES
CYPRUS
Candia
Damascus
CRETE
MEDITERRANEAN SEA
Jerusalem

Borders of the Empire:
- - - in 976
——— in 1025
200 km.

**11th - 12th centuries**

HUNGARY
SERBIA
Sinope
Trebizonde
BULGARIA
Selymbria
Constantinople
Angora
Gangra
Durazzo
Drama
Rodosto
Nicea
SULTANATE OF ICONIUM (SELJUKS)
Kastoria
Gallipoli
Larissa
Thessaloniki
Abydos
Kotyaion
Afyon
CORFU
Arta
Lamia
Amorium
Konya (Iconium)
Lepanto
Chalcis
CHIOS
Synnada
Tarsus
Patras
Thebes
Ephesus
Khonai
LITTLE ARMENIA
Corinth
Miletus
Antioch
Mistra
Antalya
RHODES
CYPRUS
Candia
Damascus
CRETE

Borders of the Empire:
- - - in 1180
——— in 1204
200 km.

Reconstructing the history of Byzantine Jewry during the eleven centuries of the eastern Roman Empire is an impossible task. The sources are fragmentary, and the borders of the empire kept shifting. Justinian I (527–565) conquered vast territories in the West, but from the seventh century onward the empire suffered major territorial losses. Hence, the importance of Byzantine Jewry was progressively reduced, and its role in Jewish history was minor compared to the Jewries of the Christian West and the Muslim Orient.

In those regions which were still under Byzantine rule in the tenth century, there were many Jewish communities which could trace their origins back to pre-Christian times: in Asia Minor, in Greece (Salonika), in Cyprus, and in Rhodes. Some communities in northern Italy had existed from the fourth century, if not earlier, and that of Constantinople dated from the fifth century. In the eleventh and twelfth centuries the Byzantine communities re-established links with their brethren in Egypt and other Muslim lands. Spanish Jews began arriving in the late fourteenth century, but their massive influx came only after 1492, when Byzantium no longer existed.

Two fundamental traits characterized Byzantium: it was Christian and Greek. In the days of Constantine (324–337), a close alliance was established between church and state, and political unity became synonymous with religious unity. Consequently, the state supported the Christianization of the empire, legislating in religious matters and fighting against

heresy. Its attitude towards the Jews, determined by Justinian's legislative work, was always ambivalent. Judaism was tolerated, its rites and synagogues protected; and thus, paradoxically perhaps, the Jews enjoyed a better status than heterodox Christians. Yet at the same time, in order to encourage their conversion to Christianity, the Jews were made the target of discriminating and restrictive legislation which relegated them to the margins of society. They were excluded from the army and from public office and subjected to a selective tax. There were strict prohibitions on Jewish proselytizing and on polygamy. From the beginning of the eleventh century, residence of Jews was restricted to Constantinople, then to Salonika. The segregation of the Jews and their synagogues was undoubtedly motivated by religious considerations.

Latent anti-Judaism was often awakened by virulent attacks by the Orthodox church, which accused dissenting sects of being influenced by Jews and of "Judaizing." The Church was behind both popular anti-Jewish riots as well as official measures taken against the Jews. Nevertheless, outbreaks of hostility, persecutions, forcible conversions, and expulsions were quite rare, mostly local, and of short duration. On the whole, the situation of the Jews of Byzantium was decidedly better and more stable than that of the Jews in the Latin West.

The Greek nature of the empire was affirmed in the time of Justinian, becoming predominant after the loss of the eastern provinces in the seventh century. The "Romaniot" Jews ("Romania" was a synonym for

| Constantinople, capital of the Empire | Theodosian Code | Jerusalem captured by the Arabs |
|---|---|---|
| **330** | **435–438** | **638** |

**330:** Founding of Constantinople, the new capital of the Roman Empire, built by Constantine I and named after him.
**379–395:** Reign of Theodosius I. After an interval during Julian the Apostate's reign (361–363), the Christian mission to the Jews is renewed.
**387:** In Antioch John Chrysostom preaches eight virulent sermons against the Jews.
**415:** Temporary expulsion of Jews from Alexandria by Patriarch Cyril.
**435–438:** The Theodosian Code prohibits, among other things, the construction of new synagogues.
**442:** Jews congregate in the copperworkers' quarter of Constantinople, situated near the church of Hagia Sophia.
**527–565:** Reign of Justinian I.
**535–555:** Conquest of Italy, of the eastern part of the ancient Roman province in Africa, and of southeastern Spain. Justinian defines the legal status of the Jews in the Empire.
**End of 6th century:** Expulsion of Jews from Antioch; anti-Jewish riots in Syria and

Anatolia; the central authorities of the empire are too weak to protect the Jews nor can they force them to adopt Christianity.
**632:** Forced conversions ordered by Emperor Heraclius after the Jews were accused of collaboration with the Persian invaders, particularly in Jerusalem in 614.
**634–642:** Expansion of Islam: Palestine, Syria and Egypt – where the majority of Jews live – come under Arab domination.
**721–726 or 740:** Persecutions of heterodox Christian sects and of Jews ordered by Emperor Leo III.
**873 or 874:** Persecutions and forced baptisms by order of Emperor Basil I.
**932–c. 944:** Persecutions by Emperor Romanus I Lecapenus; community leaders are executed and Hebrew manuscripts are burned.
**Before 1060–1070:** A Jewish quarter and a "Jewish port" in the city of Constantinople,

2. Votive plaque with Greek inscription. Gold, Byzantine. c. 8th century.

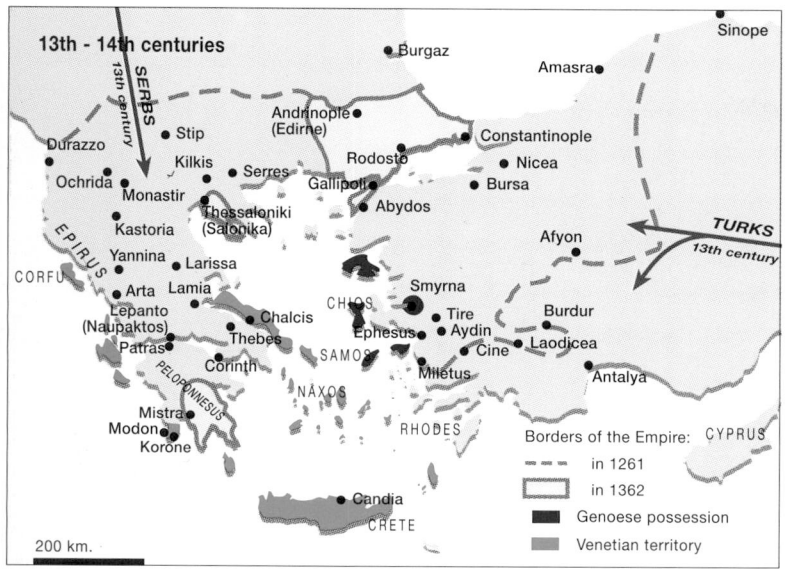

**13th - 14th centuries**

Borders of the Empire:
- – – – in 1261
- ☐ in 1362
- ■ Genoese possession
- ▒ Venetian territory

200 km.

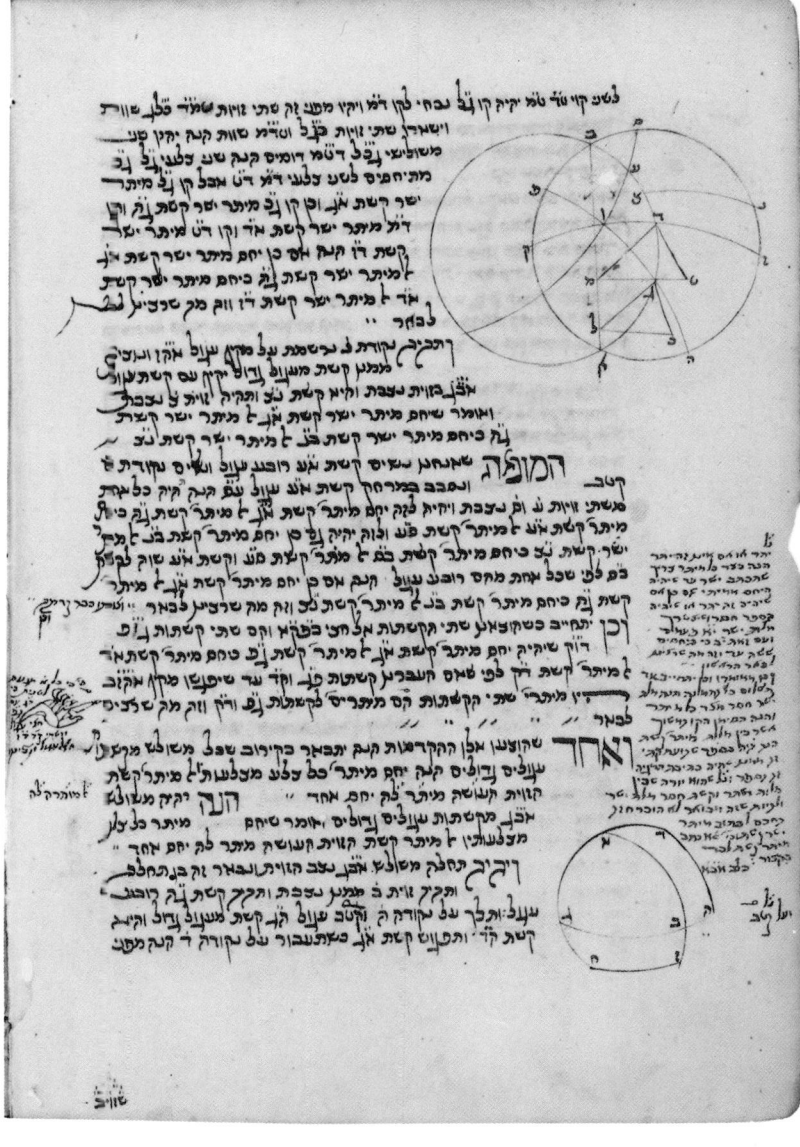

*1. Jaber ibn Aflah's abridgement of Ptolemy's Almagest translated into Hebrew by Jacob ben Makhir. Copy made by the Karaite Caleb Afendopoulo ben Eli ben Judah "for his personal use," Constantinople, 1482.*

Byzantium) yielded to the influence of their environment, differing from the Jews of Western Christendom and of Islam in their Greek names and language. They developed their own customs and rites which included reading the Bible in the synagogue in Greek translation. These distinctive traits were still preserved by Jewish communities which came under Western domination after the Fourth Crusade (for instance, in Crete and Corfu), and in certain cases they survived until the twentieth century when these communities were destroyed by the Nazis.

The presence of Jewish communities in the capital, in the commercial and industrial centers of Asia Minor, and along the Mediterranean coastline, ensured the active participation of Jews in the economic life of the empire. Jewish artisans played an important role in silk production, a state monopoly, as well as in the weaving and dyeing industries. They were to be found in Constantinople, Sparta, Corinth, Thebes, and Apulia. There were also a large number of Jewish tanners, particularly in Constantinople, and Jews had a large share in the local and regional commerce of the Byzantine Empire.

Byzantine Jewish culture was always influenced by the rabbinical centers in Palestine and in Babylon. It had, however, developed its own unique characteristics. The beginning of the ninth century witnessed a renaissance of Hebrew, which spread from southern Italy to other provinces of the empire. This revival found expression in religious poetry, biblical exegesis, historiography, and even in works on medicine.

**Fourth Crusade**
| | **Fall of Salonika** | **Fall of Constantinople** |
|---|---|---|
| 1204 | 1430 | 1453 |

near the districts inhabited by Venetian merchants on the southern shore of the Golden Horn.

**c. 1070–1203:** After their expulsion from Constantinople, the Jews reside in Pera, a suburb on the Golden Horn, where a wall separates Rabbanite from Karaite Jews. Benjamin of Tudela, the renowned Spanish Jewish traveller who provided precise information about so many Jewish communities throughout the Empire, visits Pera in 1165.

**1071:** End of Byzantine presence in southern Italy; the Jewish communities and the important rabbinical centers of the region come under Norman rule.

**End of 11th–15th centuries:** Asia Minor progressively comes under Turkish domination.

**1204:** End of the Fourth Crusade, led by Western knights and by Venice. The Jewish quarter in Constantinople is burned down by the Crusaders.

**1253–c. 1258:** Forced conversions are ordered by Emperor John III Vatatzes in his principality of Nicea (Anatolia), created after Constantinople was conquered by the Latin Crusaders.

**c. 1280–1453:** Concentration of Byzantine Jews, many of them tanners, in the district of Vlanga, burned down by the Turks in 1453; in Constantinople Jews from Venice reside in the Venetian quarter, and Jews from Genoa in the Genoese quarter established in Galata-Pera at the beginning of the 14th century.

**1430:** Salonika, the second largest city in the empire, falls to the Ottoman Turks.

**1453:** The conquest of Constantinople by the Ottomans ends the existence of the Byzantine Empire; only the Byzantine part of Peloponnesus maintains its independence from the Turks for another seven years. The downfall of the Byzantine Empire presents the Jews with a new lease on life; under Ottoman rule they will enjoy greatly improved conditions and will be able to absorb, forty years later, a huge wave of refugees.

*3. Jewish tombstone inscribed in Greek. Byzantine, provenance uncertain, c. 860.*

# Festivals

## THE HEBREW YEAR

The Jewish calendar is basically a lunar calendar of twelve months. The first day of the month (*Rosh Hodesh*), the birth of a new moon, marks the beginning of the monthly cycle and as such a further stage in the life of the individual and of society. The annual difference of eleven days between the lunar year and the solar year was adjusted by the intercalation (in Hebrew "*ibbur*," meaning "pregnancy") of an additional month, a "second *Adar*," to seven years in every cycle of nineteen years. In this manner the festivals celebrating agricultural events remained in their proper seasons.

In addition to the Sabbath, of prime importance among Jewish festivals, the calendar contains about twenty annual celebrations, both feasts and memorial days. Although the significance of some has been altered throughout the ages, the most important of these holy days – New Year, the Day of Atonement, Passover, Pentecost, and Tabernacles – were all commanded by the Pentateuch.

Other anniversaries marking certain events, some happy yet others largely tragic in the history of the Jewish people, were added in later periods: festivals of triumph and joy such as *Purim* and *Hanukkah*, days commemorating the destruction of the Temple, as well as purely national days marking recent events in the history of the State of Israel and incorporated into the calendar by the religious authorities.

## "THE SEVENTH DAY..."

The Hebrews invented the week. Without any connection to natural cycles which have served as time markers for all human civilizations since the dawn of mankind, the week was intended to break the sequence of days into regular series, each seventh day in contrast to the preceding six as rest is contrasted to work. While labor is considered as punishment ("In the sweat of thy face shalt thou eat bread," Genesis 3:19), rest is considered a blessing, a temporary but periodical return to the lost Paradise.

The origins of the Sabbath are obscure. The meaning of the Hebrew word *Shabbat* is related to the verb *shavat*, meaning "cease work" or "rest." According to Genesis, "God blessed the seventh day, and sanctified it; because that in it he had rested [*shavat*] from all his work which God created and made" (2:3). To the non-religious mind, the inverse process may seem more logical: the creation of the world was imagined according to the pattern of the week. Another hypothesis suggests that the myth of creation and the Sabbath both originate with the magical significance ascribed to the number seven. The Book of Exodus, however, prefers to link the Sabbath to the celebration of the departure from Egypt, when Israel's consecration to God was established (31:17). In Deuteronomy (5:12-15), on the other hand, emphasis is placed on the humanitarian rationale for the sabbatical rest, particularly significant for a people escaping slavery.

Among the rules concerning the abstention from work on the Sabbath, the strictest prohibition is on lighting a fire (Exodus, 35:3). Indeed, the process of kindling a fire for the purpose of preparing food involved a considerable amount of work in ancient times. But like many other prohibitions, in the process of building "a fence to the Torah" (a process of taboo-extension known in non-Jewish cultures as well), the ban was extended to any form of activity remotely connected with or vaguely resembling lighting a fire. Thus, the strictly orthodox Jews of today refrain from lighting cigarettes, turning on electricity, using the telephone, riding an elevator, or travelling by car.

Whatever its origins, the Sabbath is a ritual which throughout history has helped to humanize the onus of work. The rhythm of 6+1 is apparently the most agreeable to human nature for it was eventually adopted the world over, beginning with the Christians and the Muslims who made their sabbath the day after or the day before the Jewish *Shabbat*. Although the rhythm of 5+2 is today widely accepted in industrial societies, including Israel, the weekend sabbath is nonetheless a variation of the originally Jewish notion of a weekly day of rest.

"TEN DAYS OF PENITENCE" mark the beginning of the Hebrew year – an annual period during which one examines one's conscience, beginning on *Rosh Ha-Shanah* and ending on *Yom Kippur*.

ROSH HA-SHANAH (New Year) symbolizes the rule of God over the earth, a day of Judgement which inaugurates the new year. The origins of the festival are obscure. Celebrated "in the seventh month" of the Hebraic year (which began not in the month of *Tishri* but in the month of *Nisan*), it was "a sabbath, a memorial of blowing of trumpets" (Leviticus 23:24) – hence the custom of blowing the *shofar* (a ram's horn).

YOM KIPPUR (Day of Atonement): a day of fasting and mourning on which the Jew accounts for his deeds, an occasion for reflection on the previous year and the opportunity to start afresh with a clean slate. On this day, the only day considered holier than the Sabbath, man's fate is determined by the balance between his good and evil actions.

*1. A Yemenite Jew blowing the* shofar, *1947.*

THE THREE PILGRIM FESTIVALS were celebrated by the ancient Hebrews by going up to Jerusalem and offering sacrifices in the Temple. They symbolize the three essential phases of the agricultural year and at the same time commemorate the three central events of the exodus (a second day is added to each of these festivals when celebrated in the diaspora, a practice originating from the times when there was uncertainty in distant communities as to the precise day on which the New Moon holiday was announced in the Land of Israel).

PESAH (Passover): seven days which mark the beginning of the agricultural year and, more importantly, celebrate the departure from Egypt. Between Passover and Pentecost there are 49 days of the *Omer* (an ancient dry measure of new barley offered to the High Priest), and the 33rd of these (*Lag Ba-Omer*) commemorates Bar Kokhba's revolt in 132–135.

SHAVUOT (Pentecost): the harvest festival and the offering of the first fruits in the Temple. According to post-biblical tradition, it is also the festival commemorating the giving of the Torah.

SUKKOT (Tabernacles): eight days which mark the end of the annual agricultural cycle, also evoking the memory of the tabernacles or booths in which the children of Israel dwelt in the desert after the exodus from Egypt. The eighth and last day of *Sukkot* coincides with

Simhat Torah ("rejoicing in the Torah"), when the annual reading of the Pentateuch is concluded.

DAYS OF CELEBRATION of two "national" victories which occurred during the Second Temple period.

HANUKKAH (Inauguration): an eight-day festival dedicated to the purification and symbolic inauguration of the Temple (164 BC) after the victory of the Hasmoneans (Judah Maccabee and his followers) over the Syrian Seleucids.

PURIM: a gay and frivolous festival celebrating the triumph of the beautiful Queen Esther, consort of the Persian king Ahasueres (Xerxes I, 486–465) and of her uncle Mordecai ("The Jew Mordehai") over "Evil Haman," the vizier who plotted the annihilation of all Jews in the Persian Empire.

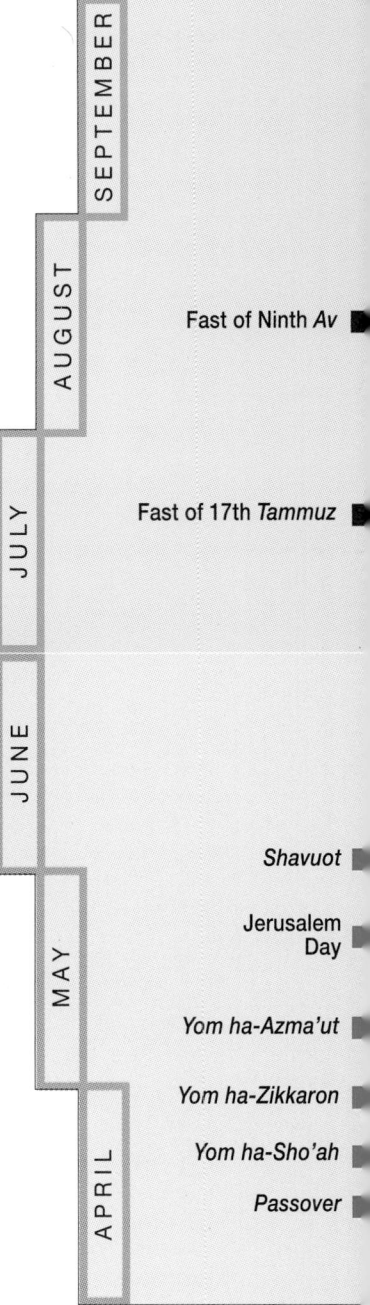

SEPTEMBER

Fast of Ninth *Av*

AUGUST

JULY

Fast of 17th *Tammuz*

JUNE

*Shavuot*

Jerusalem Day

MAY

*Yom ha-Azma'ut*

*Yom ha-Zikkaron*

*Yom ha-Sho'ah*

APRIL

*Passover*

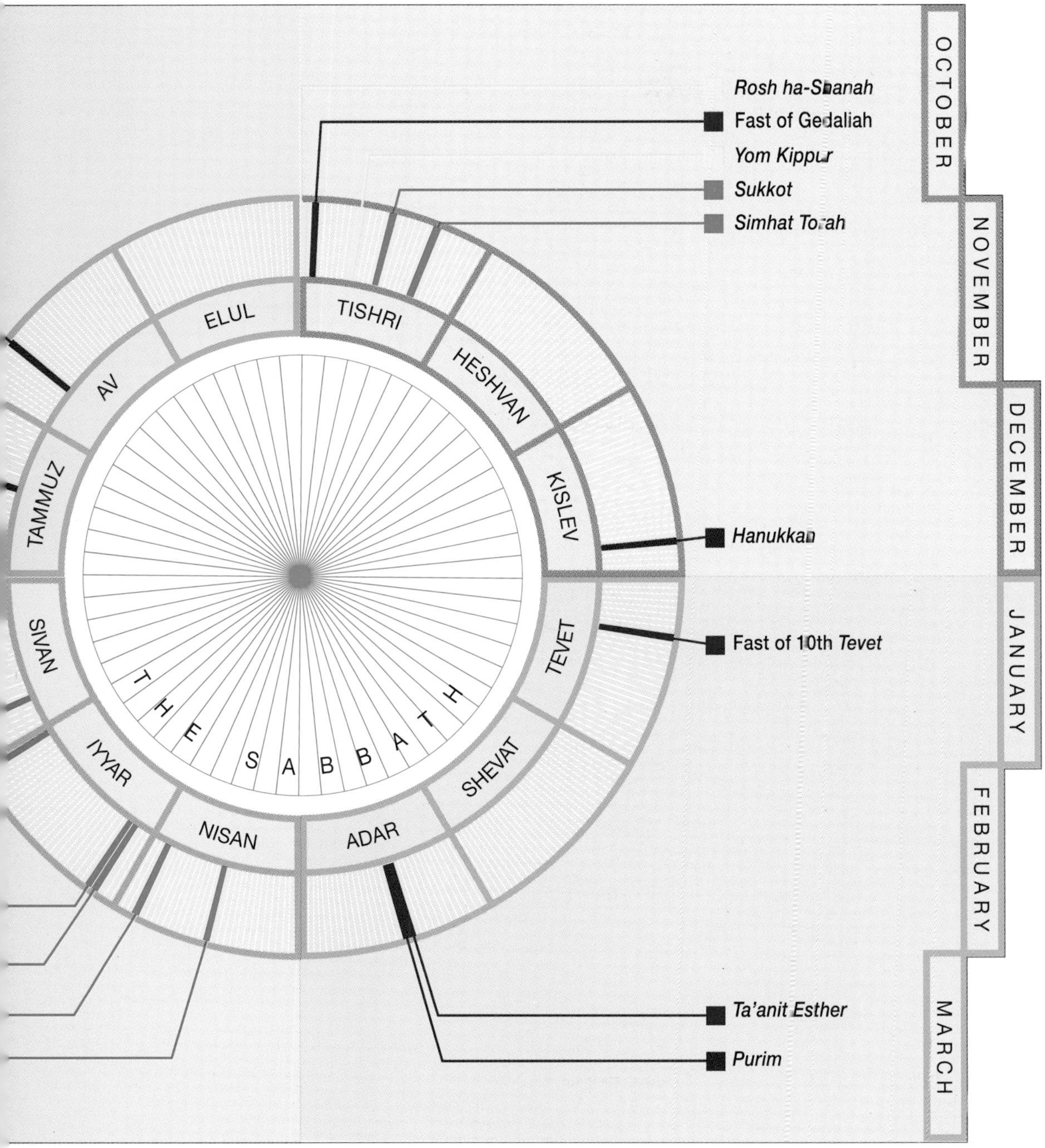

THE FAST OF 9 *AV*: over and above the destruction of the First and Second Temple, tradition adds other dramatic and traumatic events such as the defeat of Bar Kokhba in 135 AD.

Rosh ha-Shanah
Fast of Gedaliah
Yom Kippur
Sukkot
Simhat Torah

OCTOBER

NOVEMBER

DECEMBER

Hanukkah

Fast of 10th *Tevet*

JANUARY

FEBRUARY

Ta'anit Esther

Purim

MARCH

ELUL
TISHRI
HESHVAN
AV
KISLEV
TAMMUZ
TEVET
THE SABBATH
SIVAN
SHEVAT
IYYAR
NISAN
ADAR

*2. Shavuot: an illustration from the book by Ze'ev Raban, Our Festivals (in Hebrew).*

MODERN FESTIVALS established in the present century, commemorating the two major events in modern Jewish history, the Holocaust and the creation of the State of Israel.

YOM HA-SHO'AH, "The Holocaust and Heroism Remembrance Day": a day paying tribute to the victims of the Holocaust and to the anti-Nazi resistance fighters, it is celebrated in Israel on the 27th of *Nisan* and in the diaspora on April 19, the beginning of the Warsaw Ghetto uprising.

YOM HA-ZIKKARON, Remembrance Day for all the soldiers who fell in active service in Israel's wars. The day concludes with a siren blast which marks the beginning of Independence Day ceremonies.

YOM HA-AZMA'UT, Independence Day celebrates the end of the British Mandate and the establishment of the State of Israel (May 1948).

JERUSALEM DAY marks the re-unification of the City of Jerusalem under Israeli rule as a result of the Six Day War (June 1967).

*3. A Purim costume party. Safed, Palestine, 19th century.*

THE FAST OF GEDALIAH commemorates the death of Gedaliah ben Akhikam who had been nominated by Nebuchadnezzar to govern Judah after the fall of Jerusalem; the assassination of the governor brought the autonomy of Judah to an end.

THE FAST OF 10 *TEVET* marks the beginning of the siege on Jerusalem during the time of King Zedekaiah, at the end of the First Temple period.

*TA'ANIT ESTHER* (the Fast of Esther) commemorates, on Purim's eve, the fast observed by Esther before she presented herself to King Ahasueres to implore him to save her people and to chastise their enemies.

THE FAST OF 17 *TAMUZ* commemorates the fall of Jerusalem before the destruction of the First and the Second Temple. Tradition places both events on the same day.

THE FIVE FASTS – days of mourning in remembrance of tragic events, four of which mark the traumas of the destructions of the Temple (the First Temple in 586 BC, the Second Temple in 70 AD). The fast expresses the wish to repent for individual and collective sins in order to prevent similar catastrophes in the future.

*4. A Hanukkah candelabra. Iron, fabric, and glass. Mazagan, Morocco, c.1960.*

# Jews and Arabs: First Contacts

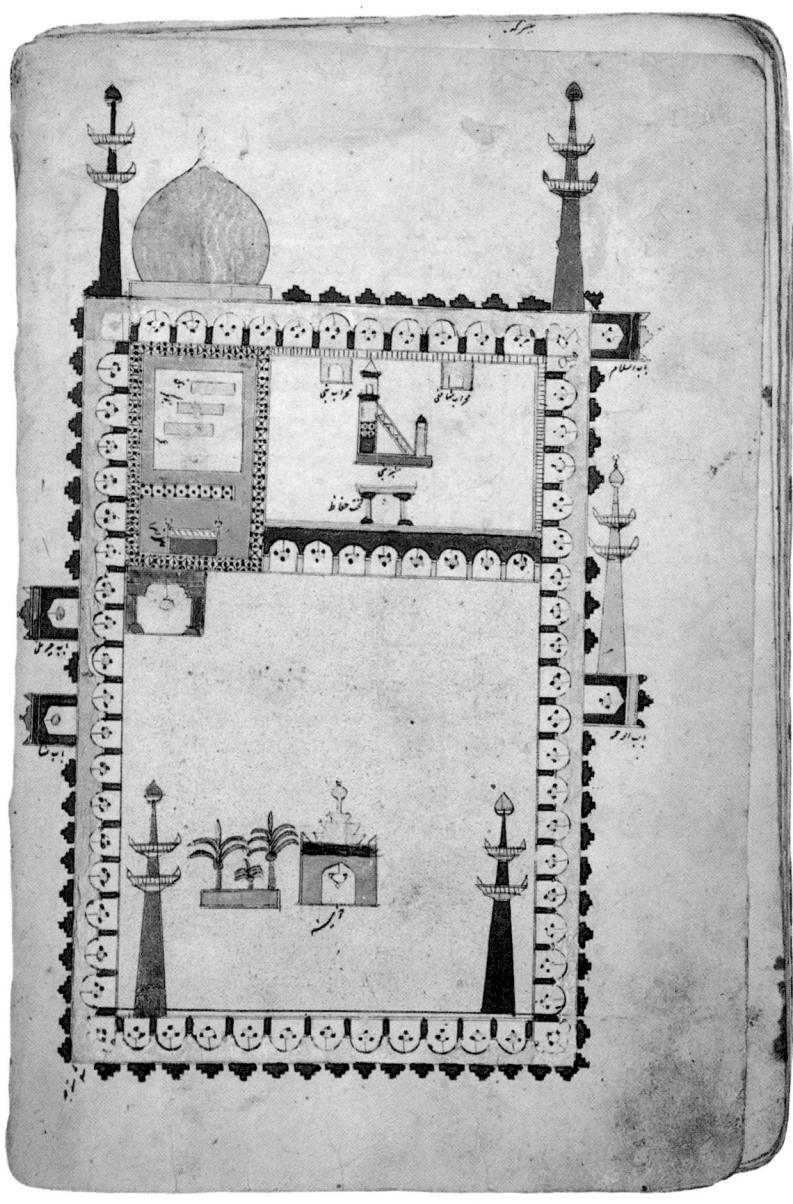

1. *The sanctuary in Medina. Iranian illuminated manuscript, 16th century.*

Jews had lived in Arabia since very ancient times. In the fifth century they were concentrated mostly in two regions: Himyar in the south and Hijaz in the north. Several sedentary tribes professing Judaism engaged in farming and crafts. They lived peacefully alongside Arab tribes who had become the predominant population in the peninsula shortly before the birth of Muhammad. Judaism, combined with Christianity of the oriental sects, must have had a certain influence on the Arab elites.

In the following century this influence was clearly evident in the self-perception of the Himyarite aristocracy. During the reign of King Yusuf As'ar Yath'ar – known by his epithet Dhu Nuwas – the Himyarites conducted an independent foreign policy in relation to the Byzantine and Persian Empires, and fought against the Christians of Najran in the name of a single god, referred to as "The Merciful One." Inscriptions on rocks in Arabia have preserved traces of this triple phenomenon: religious separatism, embryonic monotheism, and war against the Christians. Some Christians regarded this as part of a Jewish attempt to dominate the world. Yet the kingdom was not Jewish, and its monotheism was but an expression of Himyarite independence. Abandoned by his supporters,

2. *The Jews of the Nadir tribe surrender to Muhammad. Illuminated manuscript of the* Universal History *by Rashid al-Din. 13th century.*

Dhu Nuwas was killed in battle against a Christian Ethiopian army in 525. Himyar then came under Ethiopian rule, which lasted until the Persian conquest of southern Arabia in 575. Nevertheless, long after Dhu Nuwas' death, the inscriptions continue to mention the single "merciful" god of the Himyarites.

From about 610 Muhammad ibn Abdallah began proclaiming his monotheistic revelations. Analysis of their content clearly exposes ties

| The "Jewish" kingdom of Himyar | | The Hijra | Battle of Badr | Conquest of Mecca |
|---|---|---|---|---|
| 6th century | | 622 | 624 | 630 |

**327:** The Kingdom of Ethiopia adopts Christianity; Ethiopian missionaries sent to convert the Himyarites; the church historian Philostorgios remarks on the firm opposition of the Jews, thus offering the first evidence of a Jewish presence in the region.
**409, 458–459, 467:** Sabaean inscriptions engraved in stone refer to the Merciful One.
**518:** Accession of Yusuf As'ar Yath'ar Dhu Nuwas, King of Himyar.
**522:** Ethiopian Christian forces attack the capital Zafar, but are driven back by the Himyarite army; Dhu Nuwas conducts a campaign against the Christians of Najran.
**525:** Dhu Nuwas is killed in battle.
**Middle of 6th century:** The Arab tribes of Aws and Khazraj settle near Medina and are influenced by Jewish monotheism; they also adopt certain arts which until then were considered exclusively Jewish, such as the art of writing.
**c. 600:** Work of the Jewish poet Samuel ibn Adiya.
**c. 610:** Muhammad's first appearances.

3. *Arabic inscription on a tile in the church at Ruheibah (near Beersheba), 7th–8th centuries.*

**622:** The *Hijra* – Muhammad's flight from Mecca to Medina – marks the beginning of the Islamic era. About 8000–10,000 Jews inhabit the Medina region, most of them residing in the town itself.
**622–624:** Muhammad's unsuccessful attempts to win the support of the Jews of Medina; at this point there is little difference between Judaism and Islam; then, in disappointment, Muhammad changes the direction of the *qibla* from Jerusalem to Mecca.
**624. March 16:** Battle of Badr; expulsion of the Banu-Qaynuqa.
**625. March 24:** Expulsion of the Nadir; a member of this tribe, known for his hostility to Muhammad, the poet Ka'b al-Ashraf, is assassinated by Muslims.
**627:** Siege of Medina; the Qurayza probably remain neutral but are accused by Muhammad of conspiring against him

together with the men of Mecca; after 25 days of siege, the Qurayza ask to surrender on the same terms as the Nadir, but the Prophet demands unconditional surrender; arbitration of Sa'd ibn-Mu'adh, a leader of the Aws; liquidation of the tribe; the fate of these people will be evoked in Maimonides's *Epistle to Yemen*.
**628. May–June:** Conquest of Khaybar and treaty of the Jews surrender in the oasis.
**630. January:** Muhammad enters Mecca with 10,000 men and cleanses the shrine of the Ka'aba of its idols; he proclaims a general amnesty and forbids pillage; in the same month he attains victory over a large Bedouin army at Hunyan, demonstrating that he is the most powerful leader in the Arabian Peninsula; tribes all over Arabia ally themselves to him and become Muslim; the drive to the north begins.
**632. March:** Muhammad institutes the great pilgrimage, the *Hajj*.
**June:** Muhammad's death; Abu Bakr is the Prophet's successor, the first caliph.

between the new faith and the old traditions of local Jews and Christians. To the people of Mecca, Muhammad spoke of his revelation concerning the last day of judgement, of the necessity for man to be humble and grateful to the Merciful One and to worship Him alone, and of the obligation of generosity to the poor and the defenseless. The children of Israel, he insisted, could testify to the authenticity of his message. All these were elements directly influenced by the traditions and customs of the Jewish tribes of Medina. Like Jesus before him, Muhammad also claimed that he did not wish to abolish the tradition of Israel, but to update and adjust it in compliance with the new divine commandments revealed unto him.

In the formative stage of the new religion, the influence of Judaism was apparent not only in Islamic doctrines but also in its actual strategy of expansion. When the people of Mecca rejected Muhammad, he left town and migrated to Medina where he thought he would find a more receptive attitude to his gospel. He was particularly confident that the three Jewish tribes of the region – the Banu-Qaynuqa who were goldsmiths, and the Banu-Nadir and Banu-Qurayza who were date-farmers – would be the first to support him. He was, however, bitterly disappointed. Despite their

rivalries, which sometimes resulted in fratricidal wars and separate alliances with Arab tribes, the Jews of Medina unanimously rejected the Prophet. They criticized or mocked his revelations and in certain cases gave political support to his opponents. Muhammad therefore reversed his policy: his order to change the *qibla* – the direction of the Muslim prayer – from Jerusalem to Mecca, signified that he had abandoned all attempts to win over the Jews. He also decided to evict the Jews from the peninsula, and began by severing the alliances of each Jewish tribe with its Arab neighbors. The Qaynuqa were the first to suffer. After their surrender, they were forced to leave Medina and shortly afterwards migrated to Syria. The Nadir capitulated after their palm trees had been cut down, and the tribe proceeded to the oasis of Khaybar, 150 kilometers north of Medina. The Qurayza suffered the worst fate. All their men were put to death and the women and children sold into slavery.

The last Jewish opposition to Muhammad was in Khaybar, where the Jews formed a coalition with local Arabs. In June 628, however, Muhammad conquered the oasis. The Jews were allowed to remain there but had to pay heavy taxes. All religions previously existing in the Arabian Peninsula thus became minorities under the rule of Islam.

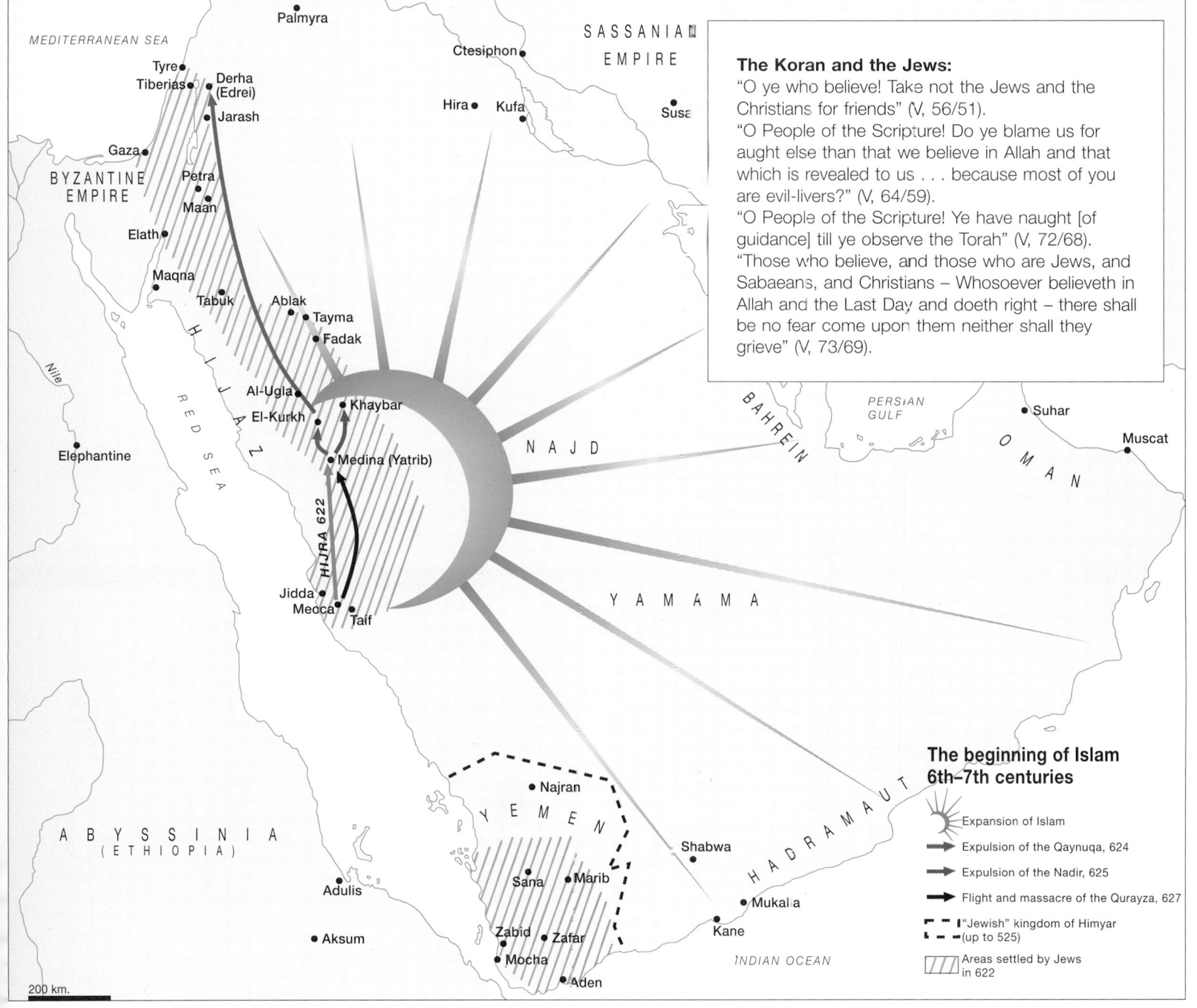

**The Koran and the Jews:**
"O ye who believe! Take not the Jews and the Christians for friends" (V, 56/51).
"O People of the Scripture! Do ye blame us for aught else than that we believe in Allah and that which is revealed to us . . . because most of you are evil-livers?" (V, 64/59).
"O People of the Scripture! Ye have naught [of guidance] till ye observe the Torah" (V, 72/68).
"Those who believe, and those who are Jews, and Sabaeans, and Christians – Whosoever believeth in Allah and the Last Day and doeth right – there shall be no fear come upon them neither shall they grieve" (V, 73/69).

**The beginning of Islam 6th–7th centuries**

Expansion of Islam
Expulsion of the Qaynuqa, 624
Expulsion of the Nadir, 625
Flight and massacre of the Qurayza, 627
"Jewish" kingdom of Himyar (up to 525)
Areas settled by Jews in 622

# Palestine Between Persians, Byzantines and Arabs

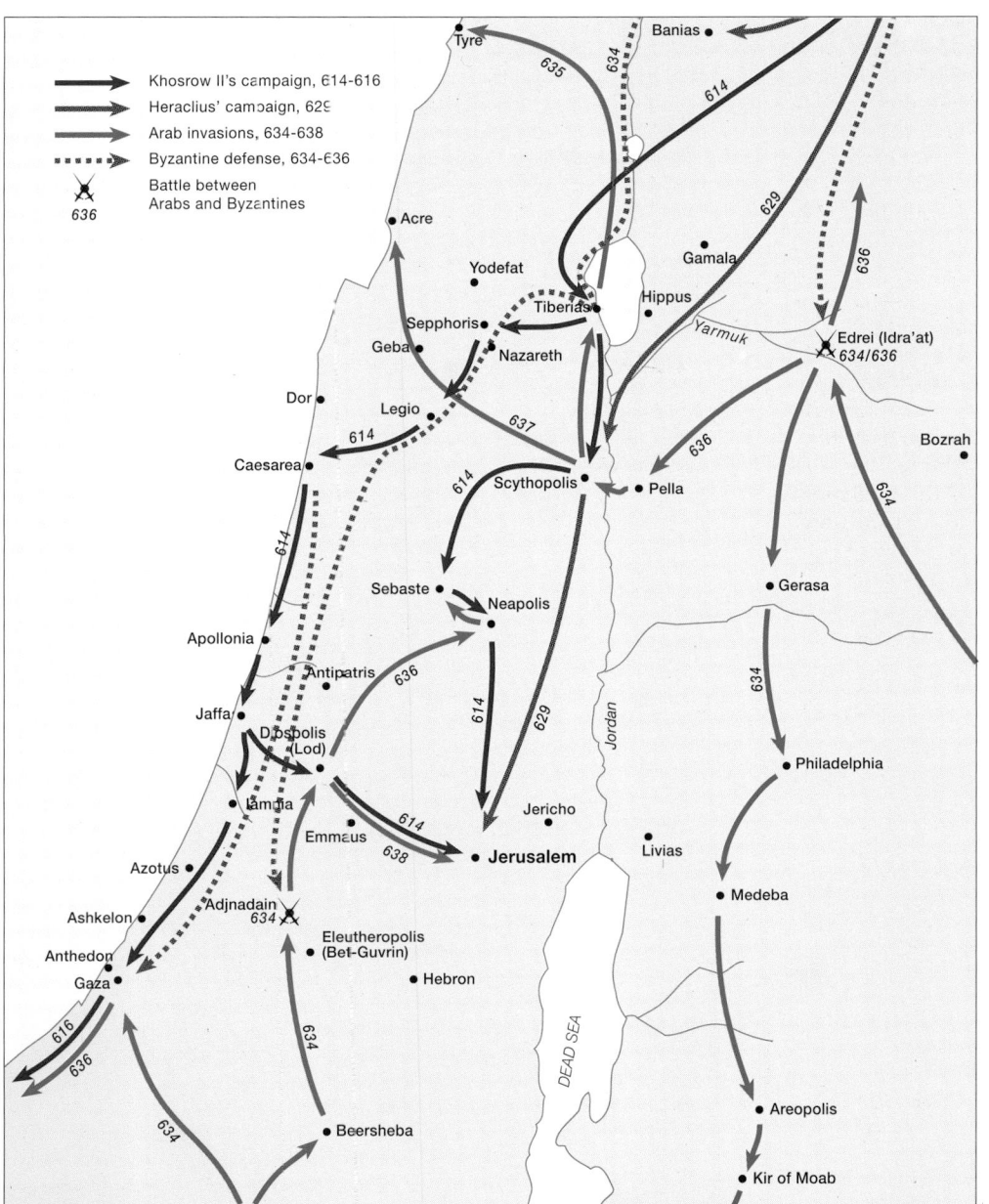

Khosrow II's campaign, 614-616
Heraclius' campaign, 629
Arab invasions, 634-638
Byzantine defense, 634-636
636 — Battle between Arabs and Byzantines

25 km.

Tyre
Banias
Acre
Yodefat
Gamala
Sepphoris
Geba
Nazareth
Tiberias
Hippus
Yarmuk
Edrei (Idra'at) 634/636
Dor
Legio
Caesarea
Scythopolis
Pella
Bozrah
Sebaste
Neapolis
Gerasa
Apollonia
Antipatris
Jaffa
Diospolis (Lod)
Jamnia
Emmaus
Jericho
Jerusalem
Livias
Philadelphia
Azotus
Adjnadain 634
Ashkelon
Eleutheropolis (Bet-Guvrin)
Anthedon
Gaza
Hebron
Medeba
Jordan
DEAD SEA
Beersheba
Areopolis
Kir of Moab
Elusa

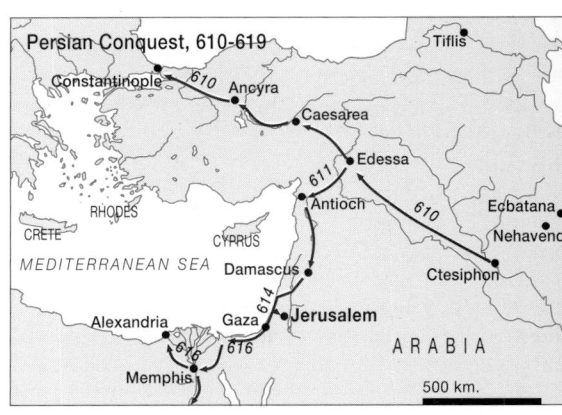

**Persian Conquest, 610-619**

Constantinople · Ancyra · Tiflis
Caesarea
Edessa
RHODES · CRETE · CYPRUS · Antioch · Ecbatana · Nehavend
MEDITERRANEAN SEA
Damascus · Ctesiphon
Alexandria · Gaza · Jerusalem
Memphis · ARABIA
500 km.

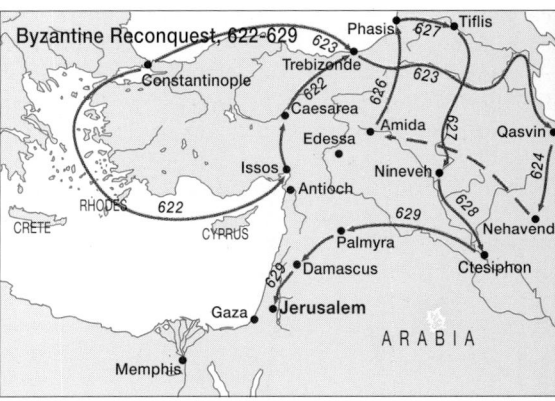

**Byzantine Reconquest, 622-629**

Phasis · Tiflis
Constantinople · Trebizonde
Caesarea · Amida · Qasvin
Edessa · Nineveh
Issos · Antioch · Nehavend
RHODES · CRETE · CYPRUS · Palmyra · Ctesiphon
Damascus
Gaza · Jerusalem
Memphis · ARABIA

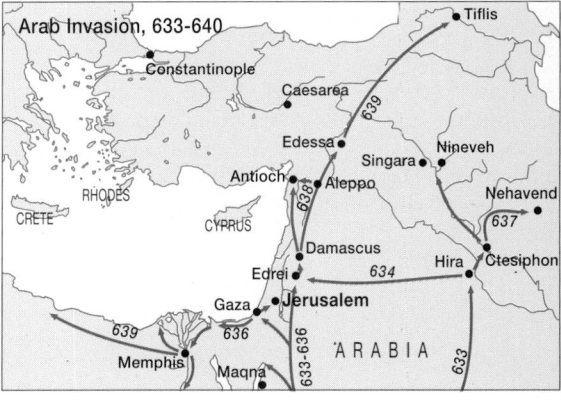

**Arab Invasion, 633-640**

Tiflis
Constantinople · Caesarea
Edessa · Singara · Nineveh
Antioch · Aleppo · Nehavend
RHODES · CRETE · CYPRUS · Damascus · Hira · Ctesiphon
Edrei
Gaza · Jerusalem
Memphis · Maqna · ARABIA

2. Mosaic pavement from a Byzantine church, discovered in the fields of Kibbutz Kissufim. Western Negev, 576–578.

**Persian Jerusalem**

**614**

**End of 5th–6th centuries:** Decline of Mediterranean commerce; weakening of trade links between India and the Mediterranean basin.
**602:** Death of the Byzantine Emperor Maurice; accession of Phocas, a military usurper.
**603:** Beginning of the last Persian war against Byzantium.
**609:** The Persians cross the Euphrates.
**610–641:** Reign of Heraclius I, emperor of the Christian orient.
**611:** The Persians take Antioch.
**613:** Damascus is captured by the Persians.
**614:** Jerusalem is captured after a brief siege; many Christians are killed, and others, including the patriarch Zacharias, are exiled.
**622:** Heraclius leaves Constantinople, reaching the mountains of Armenia by the Black Sea. This is the beginning of the

3. Hebrew manuscript of a lamentation, probably concerning the conquest of Palestine by Heraclius I in 629.

# 7th Century

The early decades of the seventh century AD comprised one of the most eventful periods in the history of the Land of Israel. Within twenty four years, between 614 and 638, the country changed hands three times. The four-centuries-long conflict between Rome and Persia was to come to an end in a final collision of Byzantine and Sassanid armies. Both these powers had attained great victories and suffered terrible defeats, and as they continued to enfeeble each other, they gave way to the rise of a new power, the Islamic forces, which would drive them both out of the region. The two monotheistic religions claiming Palestine as their holy land were joined by a third faith, newly born and extraordinarily vigorous. The Muslim conquest was destined to shape the character of the entire Middle East for the following thirteen centuries, down to this very day.

The events in Palestine during those years should be seen within the wider context of the relations between the powers in the Orient. Several centuries of struggle had created a sort of equilibrium: the Persians ruled east of the Euphrates, Rome ruled to its west, and the "buffer states" – Armenia, Syria, Mesopotamia and Palestine – constituted the battlefield for their frequent wars. This precarious balance persisted till the early sixth century when the sovereigns of these two empires, threatened by other enemies, began a correspondence that was meant to secure the frontier between them. The Byzantine emperor Maurice and the Persian Khosrow II Parviz (the "Victorious") finally signed an "eternal" peace accord which was to last for ten years. In 602 a soldiers' mutiny overthrew the Byzantine monarch and placed a junior officer named Phocas on the throne. Khosrow seized this opportunity to renew the war, leading the Persian armies into Byzantine territories in the Near East. In 613 his soldiers completed the conquest of Syria and captured Damascus. As the Persian armies were advancing, Jewish communities were rising in revolt against local Byzantine rulers and hailing the Persians as liberators.

In the early summer of 614 Khosrow's troops entered Jerusalem and massacred its Christian population. The role of the Jews during the Persian siege and conquest of Jerusalem remains unclear. Later Christian sources, however, accused the community of collaboration with the invaders and of the destruction of many churches in the city. On the other hand, there is clear evidence that the status of the Jewish population under Persian rule had deteriorated prior to 617. The Persians apparently realized that there was little to be gained from appeasing a small local minority. According to contemporary Jewish documents, a Jewish leader by the name of Nehemiah ben Hushi'el, probably a messianic figure, was executed: "And there was trouble in Israel as never before" (Book of Zerubbabel).

The Persian victory, however, was not to last. Following a victory in Nineveh in 627, the Byzantine Emperor Heraclius besieged the Persian

*1. A bowl from the Sassanid period, representing a hunting scene. The hunter is probably Khosrow II. Gilded silver, 7th century.*

capital of Ctesiphon. Khosrow was deposed and assassinated, and his son, who wished to end the war, died in 629. Heraclius reached an agreement with the Persian army commander who ordered his troops to withdraw from Mesopotamia, Egypt, Syria and Palestine, and also returned to the Byzantines the relics of the True Cross. On March 29, 629, as Heraclius triumphantly entered Jerusalem, Christians wept with joy at the miracle of the restoration of the True Cross. In his hour of glory, the emperor magnanimously refrained from taking reprisal against the Jews.

But the Christian restoration was also short-lived. In 634 the Arabs invaded the land and besieged Gaza. In 636 they defeated the Byzantines by the Yarmuk River, and two years later Jerusalem was conquered by the Muslim army. The Jews of Palestine looked on powerless as three empires fought over their land. With each upheaval, messianic expectations soared. Their hopes were expressed in religious hymns (piyyutim) which were recited on festivals in centuries to come: "When the Messiah son of David will come to his oppressed people, these signs will appear in the world... A king of the West and a king of the East will do battle and the western armies will grow strong. But from Yoktan [Arabia] another king will go forth whose forces will overrun the land... And the kohanim [temple priests] will officiate, and the Levites will preach from their pulpit [God] saying: I have returned to Jerusalem in mercy."

**Byzantine Jerusalem** / **Arab Jerusalem**

**629** / **638**

Byzantine counter-offensive against the Persians. In the same year, Muhammad's *hijra* (the flight from Mecca to Medina) marks the beginning of the Muslim era.
**622–630:** Muhammad deports and annihilates the Jewish tribes of Arabia.
**627–628:** Following Heraclius' victories in southern Armenia and in Persia, and the destruction of Ctesiphon (the future Baghdad), a peace treaty leads to the recall of Persian troops; Jerusalem and the rest of Palestine are returned to Byzantine rule.
**629. March 29:** Heraclius enters Jerusalem; in the same year the Byzantines are expelled from Spain.
**632:** Muhammad's death; Caliph Abu Bakr begins the conquest of Palestine.
**634:** Beginning of Omar's caliphate and the great Arab conquests; invasion of Palestine; victory in Gaza over governor Sergius. With the end of the war with the Arabs, Heraclius orders the enforced conversion of all the Jews in his empire and sends messengers to the kings of France and the

*4. A coin minted during the reign of Heraclius I, 7th century.*

Visigoths informing them of his decision.
**635:** The Arabs invade Syria from the Golan.
**636. August:** The decisive battle on the Yarmuk: Heraclius is defeated and the Arabs conquer Tiberias and all of the Galilee.

**637–638:** Omar besieges and captures Jerusalem; in the treaty which he signs with the patriarch there is a clause which confirms the prohibition on Jewish residence in the town. In 641 the treaty is revoked and Jews settle in the southern part of the town, after five centuries of absence.
**c.640:** Mu'awiya, future founder of the Umayyad dynasty, captures Caesarea after a seven-year siege.
**640:** Conquest of Egypt; founding of Fostat (the future Cairo).
**641:** The Arabs take Ashkelon, thus completing the conquest of Palestine.
**642:** Fall of Alexandria. The Arab victory in Nehavend opens the way to the Iranian hinterland.
**644–656:** The caliphate of Uthman; conquest of eastern Persia (Khorasan and Kirman) and of Cyrenaica (Libya).

*5. Muhammad designating Ali as his successor. A Chinese-style illumination from a manuscript of Al-Biruni's Chronology of Ancient Nations, 1307*

# The Beginnings of European Jewry

*1. Presentation of the Book to Pope Gregory. Rabanus Maurus, De Laude Crucis, 10th century.*

T he history of the beginnings of a Jewish presence in Europe cannot be thought of as a linear and continuous development. The evidence is fragmentary, random, and often inconsistent. The earliest recorded presence of Jews in medieval Europe is that of colonies of oriental or "Syrian" merchants in towns north of the Loire or in southern Gaul during the fifth and sixth centuries. In the historians' debate concerning the demarcation of periods, the existence of these colonies attests to the persistence of trade in the period of transition from the urban and Mediterranean world of Late Antiquity to the Middle Ages. It also indicates the contraction of commerce which was then limited solely to the import of luxury goods and carried out almost exclusively by non-indigenous groups which inherited the role of the Greek-speaking diaspora.

After an interruption of over 150 years, we encounter another group of Jewish merchants, new arrivals from the great centers of Jewish civilization in Palestine and Babylon. They were attracted to Europe not only by the profit to be made in distant lands but also by the policy of protection offered by the Carolingian kings who wished to encourage and control the suppliers of expensive textiles, spices, and other luxury articles consumed by the rich nobility.

In the ninth century some of these merchants were involved in long-distance trade encompassing the whole of Eurasia. From the Frankish kingdom they exported swords, slaves, and furs to the Muslim world; then, following the Silk Road to India and China and returning via Khazaria and the Slavic lands, they brought back spices and perfumes to Europe. A Muslim document refers to these great dealers as *radhaniya* (from the river Rhone or a region near Baghdad).

From several sources we learn of the existence of a community of prosperous Jewish merchants, protected by imperial agents, who enjoyed the social prestige which the Christian society was willing to accord to the descendants of the people of the Bible. When Agobard, the Archbishop of Lyons, conducted an intensive campaign against the Jews, his efforts to restrict their activities all failed.

It was only after the Carolingian period, however, that the Jewry destined to be known as "Ashkenazi" was formed and began to evolve its unique patterns of internal organization and cultural life. Large families, often led by rabbinical scholars, migrated from southern Europe, particularly from Italy, to establish communities in the Paris basin and the regions of Champagne and the Rhine. Quite small at first, these communities began to grow rapidly during the eleventh century. From about 4000 persons around the turn of the millennium, the number of Jews in German lands had reached almost 20,000 by the time of the First Crusade (end of eleventh century).

These new communities also dealt in long-distance trade. The first-generation immigrants recognized hereditary monopoly rights in relations with clients – a custom borrowed from Arabic-speaking communities such as that of Kairouan, and still practiced among Ashkenazi Jews as late as the seventeenth century. The new communities imposed internal discipline to prevent feuds between rival family firms and, while jealously guarding their independence, accepted an inter-communal system of control and intervention to ensure peaceful relations and harmony within their diaspora.

For historians who wish to organize the sporadic and uneven history of European Jewry into a convenient formula of a succession of dominant centers, the late eleventh century, "the age of Rashi," opens a new chapter. Henceforth, Ashkenazi Jewry would maintain its predominance in the Jewish world.

| Gregory the Great | Anti-Jewish legislation in Visigoth Spain | Muslim conquest of Spain | Agobard's letters |
|---|---|---|---|
| 590–604 | 613–694 | 711 | 820–828 |

**576:** Avit, Bishop of Clermont-Ferrand, forces the 500 Jews in his town to choose between conversion or expulsion.
**581:** King Chilperic I and Gregory Bishop of Tours conduct a disputation with the Jew Priscus, agent of the king. A year later Chilperic orders the forced conversion of the Jews in his kingdom.
**590–604:** The pontificate of Gregory the Great who adopts a "moderate" policy towards the Jews. He condemns forced conversions but approves of conversions attained by material inducements; he first formulates the principle which was reiterated from the twelfth century onwards in all papal bulls favorable to the Jews that "as one should not accord the Jews in their synagogues any liberty beyond what is fixed by law, thus they should not suffer, within what they were accorded, any infringement of their rights."
**613–694:** Anti-Jewish legislation in Visigoth Spain. 613: The Jews are made to prepare for the choice between conversion or exile.

633: The Fourth Council of Toledo (presided over by Isidore of Seville) condemns forced baptisms but confirms the validity of previously achieved conversions of children; converted children are to be taken from their families to protect them from returning to the false religion of their parents. 638: The Sixth Council of Toledo institutes a public confession for converted Jews who need to prove their loyalty to the Catholic faith. 653: The Eighth Council of Toledo demands that converted Jews sign a written promise not to marry within the forbidden degrees of family relations and that they themselves inflict the death penalty on any person who disobeys the observances of the Catholic faith. 681: The Eleventh Council is called upon to destroy "the Jewish pest"; prohibition on the celebration of all Jewish festivals; introduction of a system of surveillance on converted Jews. 694: Jews are accused of treason and reduced to "slavery."
**629:** Expulsion of the Jews by Dagobert I.

*2. Jewish tombstones in medieval Spain. Palencia, Old-Castile.*

**711:** Muslim conquest of Spain. According to Lucas de Tuy (13th century), the Jews delivered Toledo into the hands of the invaders. The accusation of "treason" during the Muslim invasion will be raised often against the Jews and *conversos* in the 15th century.
**797:** The Jew Isaac is included in a delegation sent by Charlemagne to Harun al-Rashid; he is the only one to return from the voyage.
**c. 820–828:** Letters of Agobard. The letter concerning "the superstitions of the Jews" reveals that the Jews of Lyons were familiar with the mystical writings of the ancient Orient.
**c. 825:** Louis I the Pious accords a bill of rights to "Rabbi Donatus" and his nephew, to Jews in Lyons, and to Abraham of Saragossa.
**838:** The Bodo-Eleazar affair: Bodo, a deacon at the court of Louis the Pious, befriended Jewish merchants who frequented the palace; in 838 he fled to

# 500–1096

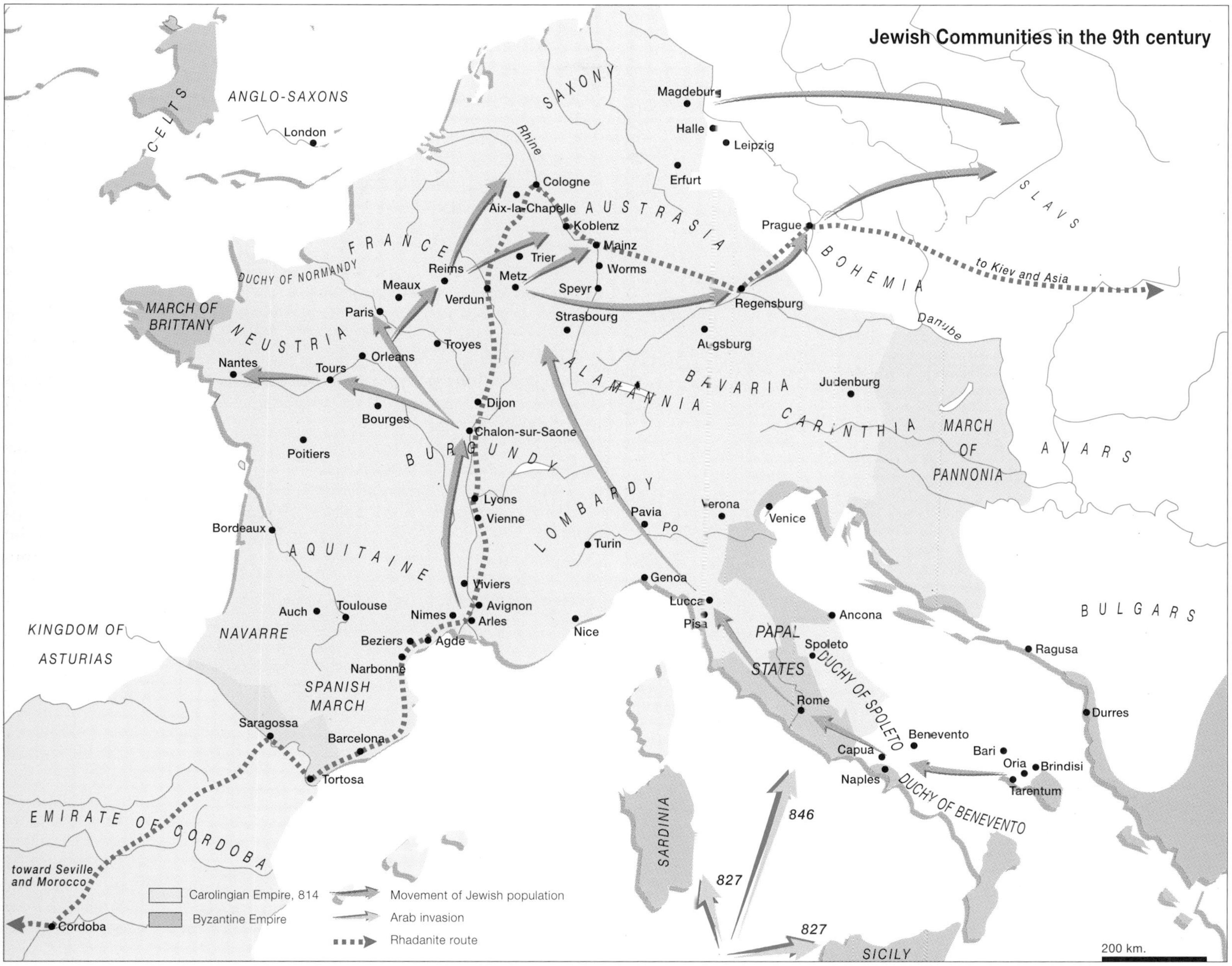

## Jewish Communities in the 9th century

[Map of Europe showing Jewish communities in the 9th century, with labeled regions including CELTS, ANGLO-SAXONS, SAXONY, FRANCE, NEUSTRIA, AUSTRASIA, ALAMANNIA, BAVARIA, BOHEMIA, SLAVS, AVARS, BULGARS, AQUITAINE, BURGUNDY, LOMBARDY, CARINTHIA, MARCH OF PANNONIA, NAVARRE, SPANISH MARCH, KINGDOM OF ASTURIAS, EMIRATE OF CORDOBA, PAPAL STATES, DUCHY OF SPOLETO, DUCHY OF BENEVENTO, SARDINIA, SICILY, DUCHY OF NORMANDY, MARCH OF BRITTANY]

Cities labeled: London, Magdeburg, Halle, Leipzig, Erfurt, Cologne, Aix-la-Chapelle, Koblenz, Mainz, Worms, Prague, Trier, Reims, Metz, Speyr, Regensburg, Meaux, Verdun, Strasbourg, Augsburg, Paris, Troyes, Dijon, Judenburg, Nantes, Tours, Orleans, Bourges, Chalon-sur-Saone, Poitiers, Lyons, Vienne, Pavia, Verona, Venice, Bordeaux, Turin, Viviers, Genoa, Auch, Toulouse, Nimes, Avignon, Arles, Lucca, Ancona, Nice, Pisa, Spoleto, Ragusa, Beziers, Agde, Narbonne, Rome, Benevento, Durres, Saragossa, Barcelona, Capua, Bari, Oria, Brindisi, Naples, Tarentum, Tortosa, Cordoba

Labels: Rhine, Danube, Po, to Kiev and Asia, toward Seville and Morocco, 846, 827, 827

Legend:
- Carolingian Empire, 814
- Byzantine Empire
- Movement of Jewish population
- Arab invasion
- Rhadanite route
- 200 km.

---

**Bills of Rights of Louis the Pious** | **The Bodo-Eleazar affair** | | **The First Crusade**
**825** | **838** | | **1096**

Muslim Spain, embraced Judaism, and adopted the name Eleazar; his works include missionary pamphlets extolling messianic expectations and describing the End of Days as the avenging of Israel's humiliation.
**Beginning of 10th century:** *The Book of Josippon*, a Hebrew version of Josephus Flavius, is composed in southern Italy by an unknown author.
**917:** The assumed date for the departure of the Kalonymus family from Lucca in Italy to Mainz in Germany. Hassidic sources from the 13th century influenced by the Carolingian legend attribute the migration to the initiative of a king called "Charles."
**982:** According to a Jewish story, a Jew called Kalonymus gives his horse to Emperor Otto II, thus saving the Emperor's life during a battle against the Muslims in Calabria, Italy.
**c. 1000:** In 992, according to a Hebrew source, the Jews of Limoges are accused of

witchcraft. In 1010 together with some Saracens from Spain, they are accused of inciting the Fatimid Caliph Al-Hakim to destroy the Holy Sepulchre in Jerusalem. Expulsion of the Jews of Limoges.
**1054:** In Capua, Italy, a certain Ahimaaz composes "The Ahimaaz Scroll," a splendid chronicle of his family, known for its prominent position in Byzantine Italy.
**1084:** The Bishop of Speyer grants privileges to the Jews according to the model of the letters of protection of Louis the Pious.
**1090–1095:** Gilbert Crispin, Abbot of Westminster and disciple of Anselm of Canterbury, writes a *Discussion between a Jew and a Christian*, presented as a transcript of a friendly disputation between Crispin and a Jew from Mainz; the Jew enumerates various objections which permit the author to expand on the fundamentals of Christianity in a rational manner.

*3. Florentius, Aaron in the tabernacle. Bible from Leon, 960.*

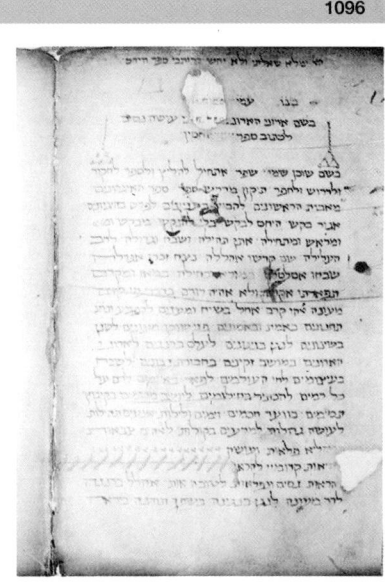

*4. First page of the Scroll of Ahimaaz. Oria, southern Italy, 11th century.*

# The Four Great Caliphs and the Umayyads

The legal status accorded to non-Muslims made the Arab conquest seem far more benevolent towards vanquished peoples than the previous rule of Persians, Byzantines, or Visigoths. Protected by the new rulers, Jews and Christians of all denominations found their situation considerably improved under the domination of the Crescent.

This was already evident in Muhammad's lifetime in the conditions of surrender offered to the Jews of Elath and Maqna in southern Palestine. The conditions included many of the elements which were later to appear in Islamic legal literature concerning war and conquest. In exchange for their military and political subjugation, which implied a series of specific obligations such as paying tribute, aiding the Muslim war effort, and not assisting the enemy, the Jews were offered physical security, religious and economic liberty, and autonomy for their community. Thus the Jews, formerly "tolerated," now became "protected" (*dhimmi*). In Palestine after the persecutions of Heraclius I in the 630s, this constituted a substantial improvement. The Jews therefore willingly accepted their new masters, and some traditions even claim that they delivered Caesarea and Hebron to the Muslims. Another significant change was the fact that the centuries-long prohibition on residing in Jerusalem, imposed on the Jews by both pagans and Christians, was lifted: several families were now allowed to settle in the town.

The Covenant of Omar, which was to regulate the relations between the Muslim power and the "Peoples of the Book" until the nineteenth century, is said to have originated with the conditions of surrender accepted by the Christians of Jerusalem in 637–638. The Covenant is a series of religious measures (prohibitions on building high prayer houses, conducting public religious ceremonies, studying the Koran) and certain humiliating restrictions (wearing distinctive clothes and a prohibition on riding horses), intended to mark the superiority of Islam over the infidels. But, since the second caliph, Omar I (634–644), was known for his tolerant attitude toward the protected subjects, most scholars agree that these discriminatory regulations, more consistent with a period of colonization than of conquest, should be attributed to Omar II (717–720) – a religious fanatic who adopted a harsher attitude towards all the minorities in his empire.

The largest concentration of Jews at this time was in Iraq and Iran. Badly treated during the century preceding the Muslim conquest, the Jews in these parts were also pleased with their new status, as well as with the ties they could now maintain with other communities throughout the Muslim Empire. Jewish traditions stress the excellent relations established between the first caliphs and the leaders of the communities.

The Berber tribes who resisted the Muslim conquest of North Africa were led by a woman, Cahina or Dahina, who is sometimes referred to as

*1. Muhammad's ride from Mecca to Jerusalem. Persian manuscript, 1494.*

| Founding of the Caliphate | Conquest of Jerusalem; Covenant of Omar (?) | Accession of the Umayyads |
|---|---|---|
| 632 | 638 | 661 |

**632–634:** Abu Bakr, Muhammad's brother-in-law and his companion on the flight from Mecca to Medina (Hijra, 622), is first caliph (*khalif* in Arabic means "successor"); first compilation of the Koran; first victories of Islam over Persians and Byzantines, particularly in Palestine (the battle of Adjnadain, near the future Ramleh).
**634–644:** Reign of the second caliph, Omar ibn al-Khattab, the Prophet's father-in-law, who conquers Egypt, Palestine, and Syria from the Byzantines, and Mesopotamia and large parts of Iran from the Persians; towards the end of his reign the Arabs reach the border of India. Omar prohibits the residence of non-Muslims in Arabia and (possibly) orders the expulsion of Jews from Khaybar in the northwest of the peninsula; on the other hand, a fragment found in the Cairo *Genizah* indicates that he authorized seventy Jewish families to settle in Jerusalem.
**635:** Conquest of Damascus.
**636:** A decisive battle against the Byzantines

near the Yarmuk River.
**637–638:** Conquest of Jerusalem after two years of siege.
**c. 640:** Conquest of Caesarea at the end of a seven-year siege, then of Ashkelon (641). Tiberias is the main Jewish center in Palestine till the end of the eighth century.
**644–656:** Reign of Uthman ibn Alfan, elected by a council designated by Omar; Uthman initiates the canonical compilation of the Koran; conquest of Armenia, Azerbaijan, vast territories in eastern Iran, and in North Africa and Nubia.
**652:** Destruction of the Byzantine fleet; incursions into Sicily.
**656:** Revolt in Egypt and death of Uthman (end of June); first civil war among Muslims as the Umayyads take revenge for the assassination of the caliph.
**656–661:** Ali ibn Abu Taleb, the fourth caliph, Muhammad's cousin and son-in-law; the

*2. The synagogue in Susiyya, south of Hebron, 6th century.*

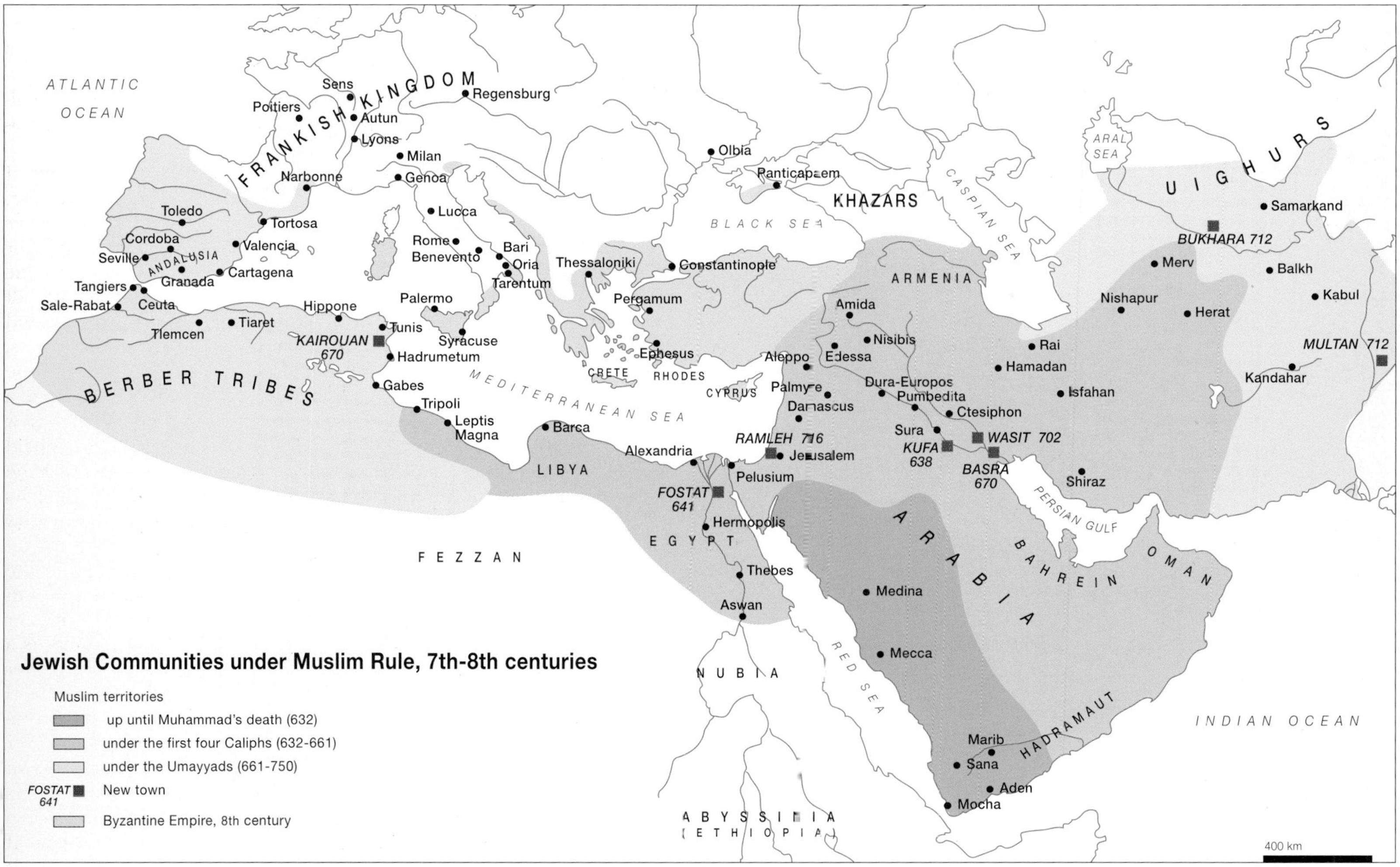

## Jewish Communities under Muslim Rule, 7th–8th centuries

Muslim territories
- up until Muhammad's death (632)
- under the first four Caliphs (632–661)
- under the Umayyads (661–750)

*FOSTAT*
*641* ■ New town

- Byzantine Empire, 8th century

400 km

"the Jewess." However, since the Jews of the Maghreb had been severely oppressed by the Byzantine rulers after they had reconquered the region from the hands of the Vandals, it is safe to assume (although there is no documentary evidence) that Jewish reaction to the Muslim conquest of North Africa was generally favorable.

Finally, in Spain, where the Visigoths had prohibited all manifestations of Judaism and had separated children from their families in order to bring them up as Christians, the Jews welcomed the Muslims as saviors from long persecution. Moreover, they actively collaborated with the invaders who rewarded them by leaving the defense of certain conquered cities to Jewish garrisons. Many Jews who had left Spain during the Visigothic persecutions returned there from North Africa.

The Muslim expansion had significant effects on the economic structure of the conquered population. In the early seventh century, in Palestine as throughout the Orient, Jewish economy was essentially agricultural. The tribute, both a poll tax and land tax imposed on the *dhimmi* by the Arab conquerors, led many Jews to leave the land and seek their fortune in the highly lucrative opportunities of commerce.

| Conquest of Spain | Battle of Poitiers | Accession of the Abbasids |
|---|---|---|
| 711 | 732 | 750 |

Shi'ites ("Shi'a" meaning "faction") regard him as Muhammad's only true successor. His reign is marked by constant wars, mainly with Mu'awiya, the governor of Syria, who proclaims himself caliph in Jerusalem in 660.
**658:** Caliph Ali enters Firuz-Shapur in Iran; the Ga'on of Pumbedita and thousands of Jews welcome him with enthusiasm.
**661–750:** The Umayyad Dynasty: conquest of all of North Africa, Spain, the Indus Valley, and Afghanistan. The center of power, transferred to Damascus, exerts a strong influence over the Jewish communities in Syria and Palestine.
**661–680:** The Caliph Mu'awiya, the first Umayyad caliph, transforms the Arab world into a secular state in which religion takes second place. For the first time leadership is in the hands of a person who was not one of the Prophet's associates. Mu'awiya settles Jews, whom he considers to be faithful allies

of the Arabs in Tripoli and Syria; a period of prosperity for the Jews and Christians in Palestine under a regime which is very tolerant toward the *dhimmi*.
**673–677:** Siege of Constantinople.
**691:** The Dome of the Rock (the "Omar Mosque" built by Caliph Abd al-Malik on the Temple Mount in Jerusalem.
**711:** Conquest of Spain. The Jews welcome the Muslims with great excitement.
**716:** Caliph Suleiman ibn Abd al-Malik builds Ramleh, the only town founded by the Arabs in Palestine; a quarter of the town is reserved for dyers – at the time, a distinctly Jewish profession.
**717–720:** Caliphate of Omar Abd al-Aziz; harsher attitude towards the *dhimmi*; it was presumably he who excluded the Jews from the Temple Mount and restricted them to praying at only one gate.
**732:** Battle of Poitiers: victory of Franks over Muslims.
**750:** Accession of the Abbasid Dynasty: founding of a new capital – Baghdad (762).

3. A decorative wood-panel in the Al-Aqsa Mosque. Jerusalem, 8th century.

4. An Arabic inscription mentioning the Umayyad Caliph Abd al-Malik and the governor of Palestine, Yahya ibn el-Hakam. Basalt, Galilee, 693.

# In the Abbasid Empire

In 750 an Abbasid coup d'etat removed the Umayyads from the caliphate. The new rulers transferred the seat of power from Syria to Iraq and established a new capital, Baghdad, which soon became the political and economic center of the empire, seat of all government institutions, hub of emissaries and messengers, spies and benefit-seekers, military units and commercial caravans, all busily coming and going. It was also the cultural capital, where the caliph and his court provided patronage for religious and artisitic activity, which was

1. Jewelry from the Fatimid period. Caesarea, 11th century.

faithful to Islam, yet touched with elements of Greek tradition.

This was undoubtedly a turning point in the history of the people of Israel. At the beginning of the ninth century, a new literary language emerged: Arabic written in Hebrew characters. In this language Jews began writing philosophical and scientific works in obvious imitation of contemporary Arabic literature. Even authors of religious works were affected by new discursive trends. The talmudic debate, dialectical in character and based on the association of ideas, was giving way to a form of thematic discourse. These texts were based on the authority of the Talmud, yet the very attempt to assemble, classify, and publish a "post-talmudic *Halakhah*" was clearly a sign of the authors' self-confidence and position of strength.

The Jewish accommodation of Muslim influences was, however, selective and partial. Although they adopted idiom and style from their Arab colleagues, Jewish writers still tried to preserve the specifically Jewish content of their teachings. Following the pioneering work of Saadia Gaon, Arabic became a legitimate vehicle for Jewish expression, and the structure of Arab texts its principal model. Gradually, particularly in fields where there was no previous Jewish tradition, words and concepts borrowed from the Islamic world began to penetrate Jewish texts in the form of titles of philosophical and scientific works, principles concerning laws of matrimony, regulations which at times contradicted Jewish legal traditions in commercial and financial spheres, and Arabic terms appearing in all *halakhic* literature.

The emergence of this Judeo-Arabic culture was linked to another aspect of Jewish life in the Abbasid caliphate: international trade. We have seen elsewhere how Jews shifted from agricultural work to dealing in commerce under Muslim rule. By the end of the eighth century the presence of Jews in all caravans connecting the East to the West was predominant. Known as the Rhadanites (probably after the name of the Jewish quarter in Baghdad), these Jewish merchants maintained the link

## The World of the Rhadanites

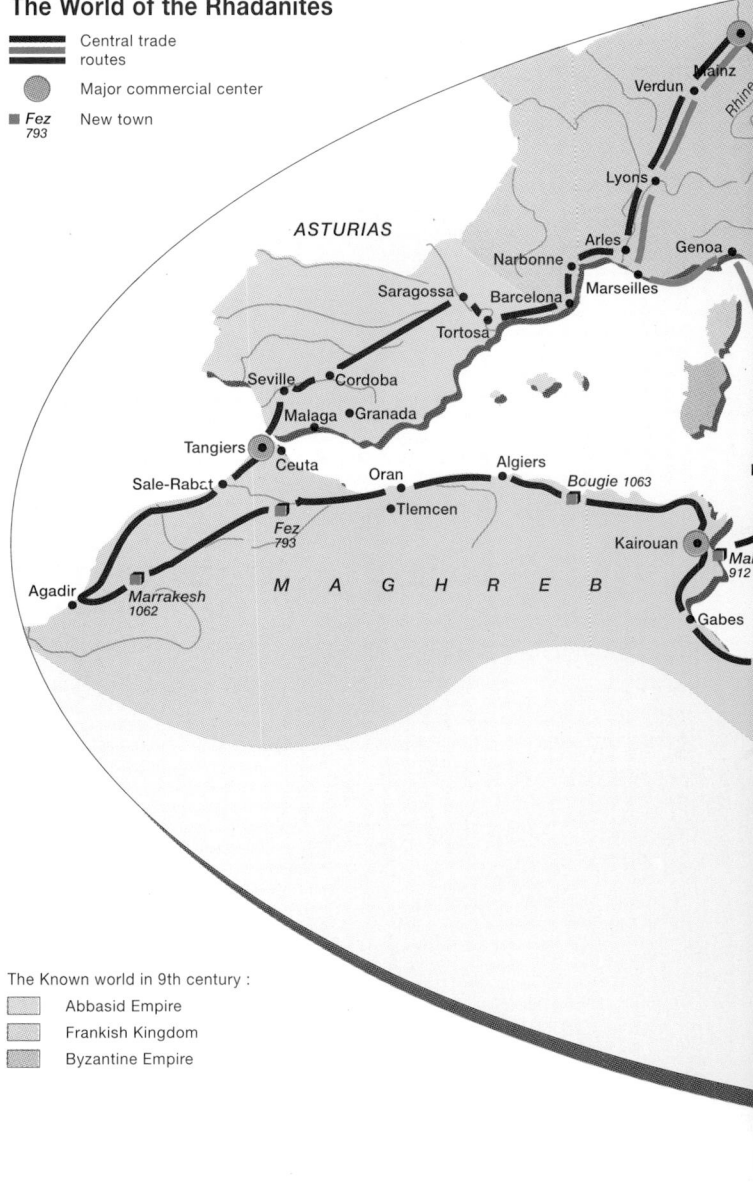

| | |
|---|---|
| ▬▬▬ | Central trade routes |
| ● | Major commercial center |
| ■ *Fez* 793 | New town |

The Known world in 9th century :

▢ Abbasid Empire
▢ Frankish Kingdom
▢ Byzantine Empire

| Accession of the Abbasids | Founding of Baghdad |
|---|---|
| 750 | 762 |

between trade stations on the Saharan frontier and the commercial centers of North Africa, and between these and the heart of the caliphate. They traversed the commercial routes in the Caspian region, frequented the Khazar kingdom, and reached as far as India by roads along the Red Sea and through the Arab Peninsula. They had certain advantages over all other traders: a unified legal code; supportive Jewish communities along the trade routes; and mastery of two international languages, Arabic and Hebrew. Thus they also became important cultural agents, bringing the teachings of the Babylonian center to all communities of the diaspora and contributing to its increasing authority.

For the Jews, as for Muslims, all roads led to Baghdad. The merchants' need for investment channels led to the emergence of a class of rich Jewish bankers who soon formed an affiliation with the courts of high Arab officials and potentates. By financing their military campaigns and luxurious lifestyle, these bankers became indispensable to the Muslim rulers, and in return were allowed to farm taxes. Their position in the princes' courts enabled them to protect their community's interests and they thus earend the awe and respect of their co-religionists who dubbed these influential men "the corners of the congregation."

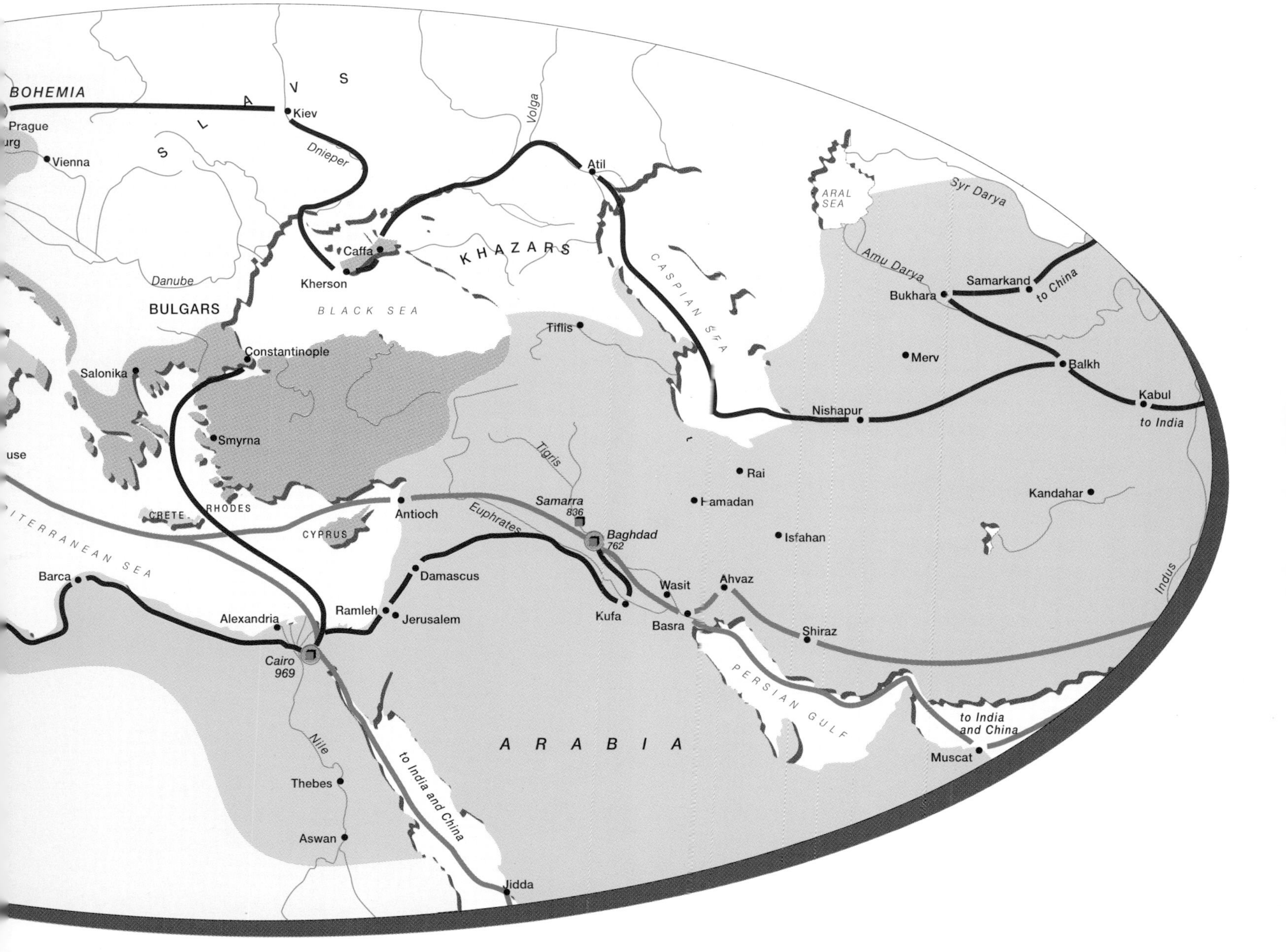

| Fatimid Caliphate in North Africa | Umayyad Caliphate in Spain | The Fatimids in Egypt |
|---|---|---|
| 910 | 929 | 969 |

**750:** Accession of the Abbasids; the center of the Muslim world is transferred from Syria to Iraq.

**797:** A Jewish interpreter named Isaac is a member of the delegation sent by Charlemagne to Caliph Harun al-Rashid.

**c. 800:** First evidence of Jewish emigrants from the East settling in North Africa.

**825:** David ben Judah and his brother Daniel, each supported by one of the two academies, fight bitterly over the title of Exilarch ("prince of the exile", political leader of the Babylonian community); the Abbasid Caliph El-Ma'mun authorizes the multiplication of religious sects among the *dhimmis*. The controversy and the caliph's decree both lead to a decrease in the Exilarch's prestige.

**c. 840:** The Babylonian Exilarch demands financial support from the communities in North Africa and Spain.

**c. 850:** According to the *Ahimaaz Scroll*, chronicle of an important Jewish family in Italy, a certain Aaron of Baghdad arrives in

*2. Piece of cloth. Palestine(?), c. 12th century.*

southern Italy and serves as a link between western and Babylonian Judaism.

**c. 880–930:** The prospering of the *jahbadhiyya*, rich Jewish bankers in Baghdad, influential at the caliph's court.

**890–898:** Hai bar Rav David Gaon transfers his *yeshiva* from Pumbedita to Baghdad.

**c. 900:** Isaac ben Solomon Israeli composes his works in philosophy and medicine.

**910:** Beginning of Fatimid rule in North Africa; emergence of the community of Kairouan (in Tunisia), destined to become an important center of the Jewish world.

**916:** Death of Netira, founder of an important Jewish banking firm in Baghdad.

**928:** Saadia ben Joseph, nominated Gaon of the Sura academy; Saadia Gaon was undoubtedly the greatest Jewish scholar in the Abbasid period.

**929:** The Umayyad prince of Spain proclaims himself Caliph.

**c. 950:** Dunash ibn Tamim composes his works in philosophy, mathematics, and astronomy; Baghdad and its wonders are

described by Nathan ben Isaac ha-Bavli ("the Babylonian") for the benefit of the Jews of North Africa.

**c. 960:** First manifestations of autonomy in the Spanish community: Hisdai ibn Shaprut founds a library, supports writers and linguists, and appoints Moses ben Hanokh to the rabbinical seat in Cordoba.

**969:** Conquest of Egypt by the Fatimids.

**983:** A group of rich Jewish merchants convenes in Mosul to debate questions of philosophy.

**990:** The legend of the "four captives": sold in four different countries and ransomed by their brethren, they establish four independent Jewish centers – in Egypt, Tunisia and Spain (the fourth is not named). Although the story is fictitious, it reflects a historical reality: the emergence of several Jewish centers which are gradually freed of Babylonian tutelage.

**c. 1000:** Said ben Babshad composes *piyyutim* (liturgical poems) which constitute a short encyclopedia of natural science.

# Jews in Muslim Palestine

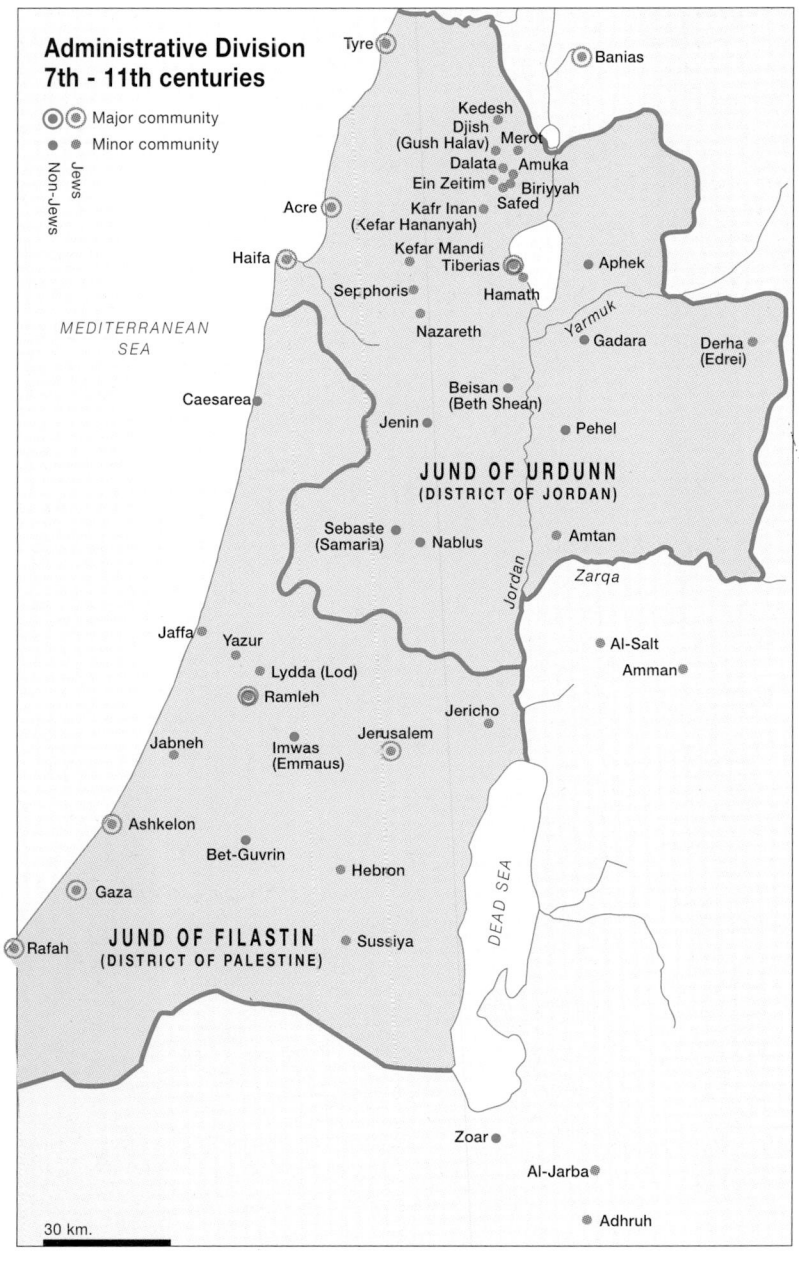

**Administrative Division 7th – 11th centuries**

◎◉ Major community
• • Minor community

Jews | Non-Jews

Tyre
Banias
Kedesh
Djish (Gush Halav)
Merot
Dalata
Amuka
Ein Zeitim
Biriyyah
Kafr Inan (Kefar Hananyah)
Safed
Acre
Kefar Mandi
Tiberias
Haifa
Aphek
Sepphoris
Hamath
MEDITERRANEAN SEA
Nazareth
Yarmuk
Gadara
Derha (Edrei)
Caesarea
Beisan (Beth Shean)
Jenin
Pehel
**JUND OF URDUNN (DISTRICT OF JORDAN)**
Sebaste (Samaria)
Nablus
Amtan
Jordan
Zarqa
Jaffa
Yazur
Al-Salt
Lydda (Lod)
Amman
Ramleh
Jericho
Jabneh
Jerusalem
Imwas (Emmaus)
Ashkelon
DEAD SEA
Bet-Guvrin
Hebron
Gaza
**JUND OF FILASTIN (DISTRICT OF PALESTINE)**
Sussiya
Rafah
Zoar
Al-Jarba
Adhruh

30 km.

The Arab conquest opened a new chapter in the history of the Jewish community in Palestine. The traditional hostility between Jews and Christians which had determined the condition of Palestinian Jewry during the Byzantine period was replaced by the relative tolerance of the new Muslim masters towards the "protected" minorities. It is therefore not surprising that the Jews accepted the change of regime with enthusiasm, even to the point of endowing the Arab conquest with a messianic significance.

After centuries of being barred from residing in the city, a small community was now formed in Jerusalem. Shortly afterward the academy (*yeshivah*) of Tiberias – the principal center of authority for Palestinian Jews – was moved to Jerusalem. Pilgrimage to the city was also renewed. Once a year, during *Sukkot*, the academy organized a celebration on the Mount of Olives, which attracted many Jews from all over the Orient. Jerusalem thus regained its status as a religious and spiritual capital.

Besides Jerusalem there were several important urban Jewish communities in Banias, Tyre, Acre, Haifa, Ashkelon and Gaza, and above all in Tiberias and Ramleh. Tiberias was a literary and religious center, renowned for the *masoretes*, the scholars responsible for the authorized version of the Bible (*Masorah*, "transmission"). Ramleh, founded in 716, was home to the largest community in Palestine during the tenth and eleventh centuries. At the same time, however, a process of Islamization

*1. Muslim mosaic representing a prayer alcove (mekhrab). Ramleh, 8th century.*

| Omar I captures Jerusalem | | Palestine under Fatimid rule | Seljuk conquest |
|---|---|---|---|
| **638** | | **970** | **1073** |

**636–641:** Arab conquest of Palestine.
**638:** Omar ibn Al-Khattab conquers Jerusalem; seventy Tiberian Jewish families settle in the city.
**c. 748:** An earthquake in the Jordan Valley; Tiberias suffers severe damage.
**Early 9th century:** Pirkoi ben Baboi, a Babylonian sage, attacks the tradition of the Palestinian academy; his polemical letter testifies to the influence of Palestinian customs on the Jews of North Africa.
**Late 9th century:** The Karaite community is established in Palestine; Jerusalem becomes a focus of attraction for Karaites throughout the Orient.
**895:** In Tiberias, Moses ben Asher copies and vocalizes a manuscript of Prophets, which may be found today in the Karaite synagogue in Cairo.
**912–933:** The Palestinian academy is headed by the Meir family: *gaon* Meir, his son Aaron, his grandson Abraham.
**921–923:** "The calendar dispute" between Aaron ben Meir and Saadia ben Joseph, the

*2. Torah page written according to the Tiberian Masorah. 10th century.*

future *gaon* of the Sura Academy.
**c. 930:** The Bible manuscript known as *Keter Aram Zova*, ("The Crown of Aleppo") is copied in Tiberias; the copy is attributed to Solomon ben Buya'a, and the vocalization to Aaron ben Asher.
**960:** The Rhine Valley communities send their halakhic questions to the Palestinian academy.
**970:** The Fatimids begin their conquest of Palestine.
**1009:** Beginning of anti-Christian and anti-Jewish persecutions by the Fatimid Sultan Al-Hakim; destruction of the synagogue in Fostat, which is reconstructed with a special room for its archives – the famous Cairo *Genizah*.
**1015–1025:** The academy is exiled to Ramleh.
**1024–1029:** Bedouin revolts (the "second war of the sons of Jarrah"); the Jewish

communities in Ramleh and Jerusalem are badly affected.
**1025–1051:** Solomon ben Judah is head of the Palestinian academy. Of the history of Palestine under Muslim rule, this is the period best documented by the *Genizah*.
**1033:** A severe earthquake hits the whole country, particularly the coastal plain; Jerusalem, Hebron, and particularly Ramleh, are badly damaged.
**1038–1042:** Solomon ben Judah and Nathan ben Abraham fight over the leadership of the academy, each supported by one of the Palestinian centers, Jerusalem and Ramleh; the communities in Fostat and Kairouan, as well as the strong Karaite communities in Jerusalem and Ramleh, take sides in the quarrel.
**1052–1062:** Daniel ben Azariah, a scion of the exilarchs, styles himself *gaon* and *nasi*; Daniel wins the leadership of the Palestinian community after a long dispute with members of the Ha-Kohen family.
**1062–1083:** Elijah ben Joseph Ha-Kohen

of the land emptied the Galilee of the peasants who had comprised the majority of the Jewish population during the Byzantine period. Unlike the villagers who were an indigenous population, the city inhabitants were immigrants from either Islamic countries of the Orient or from the Fatimid State interior. Among the newcomers, the immigrants from Babylonia were the most distinctive group; they continued to maintain ties with the exilarchs and with the Babylonian academies, and observed their ancient customs. In the major Palestinian centers, the two communities – *Shami'in* of Palestine and *Iraki'in* from Babylon – lived side by side. An additional group comprised the families of North African and Sephardi origin, who were active mainly in Jerusalem and Ramleh, and often became important dignitaries in their local Jewish society. Finally, there were the Karaites whose community was at the time large and important, and they enjoyed complete autonomy.

Jews throughout the districts formerly belonging to the Byzantine Empire upheld the authority of the Palestinian academy. The head of the academy, successor to the *nasi* of Byzantine times, was theoretically equal in status to the exilarch and the heads of the Babylonian academies; in fact, however, his status in the diaspora was inferior to theirs. The authority of the Palestinian academy was grounded mostly in the religious functions which it claimed as its prerogatives: organizing the pilgrimage ceremonies, and "proclaiming the festivals" (that is, determining the Hebrew calendar, a prerogative which was contested by the Babylonian center). On the other hand, in Palestine itself the academy was fully respected. Under Fatimid rule, the heads of the academy were recognized as "leaders of the Jews" throughout the caliphate. All community officials were elected from among its members. At the head of the large urban communities stood dignitaries who carried the title of *Haver* ("member of the academy"). Although they resided in Jerusalem, the importance of Ramleh was such that the head of the academy and the president of the rabbinical court regularly spent extended periods of time there.

The framework of the Fatimid state was also responsible for the strong ties between the Palestinian community and the community in Egypt – ties which would be continuously maintained albeit in different forms, till the end of the Mamluk period in the sixteenth century.

The eleventh century was a time of great hardship for Palestinian Jewry: famine, epidemics, two earthquakes, Bedouin incursions, flagging Fatimid power, and internal disputes within the academy. A final crisis culminated in the departure of the *yeshivah* from Jerusalem immediately after the Seljuk conquest in 1073. This move symbolized not only the decline of the Jerusalem community but the loss of the long-standing organizational and spirtual attributes of Palestinian Jewry as well. When the crusaders conquered the Holy Land in 1099, the Jewish community in Jerusalem came to an end.

**Fatimid reconquest**

**1089–1098**

*3. Earring. Beth Shean, 8th century.*

is head of the Palestinian academy.
**1073:** The Turkish Seljuks conquer Palestine; the Palestinian academy is transferred from Jerusalem to Tyre.

**The Crusaders in Jerusalem**

**1099**

**1078–1094:** David ben Daniel's time of activity, which culminated in 1082–1094 in his self-appointment as Exilarch in Fostat and attempt to impose his authority on the Palestinian communities. Supported by the Karaites and notables in Egypt, David ben Daniel attacks the head of the academy in Tyre, Abiathar ben Elijah Ha-Kohen. This affair, with its messianic overtones, gives birth to the *Scroll of Abiathar*.
**1081:** Celebration of *Sukkot* in Tyre, in imitation of the ceremony on the Mount of Olives in Jerusalem; on this occassion Abiathar ben Elijah Ha-Kohen is proclaimed *gaon* of the academy.
**1082:** Celebration of *Sukkot* in Haifa; the year is sanctified and the calendar proclaimed.
**1089:** The Fatimids capture the Palestinian coastal towns from the Seljuks.
**1098:** The Fatimids reconquer Jerusalem.
**1099:** The Crusaders enter Jerusalem, massacring the Muslim and Jewish population.

*4. Tower of the White Mosque, originally built by order of Caliph Suleiman ibn Abd Al-Malik in the new city of Ramleh (the ruins of the old mosque are seen on the left). Early 8th century.*

# The Period of the Geonim

The Muslim conquests were an important agent of unification for the Jewish communities throughout the diaspora. From the seventh century onwards the vast majority of Jews were under single rule and part of a large network of commercial ties connecting the different sectors of the Muslim empire. After the Arabs conquered the Maghreb ("the west" in Arab geographic terminology, designating North Africa and Spain), thousands of Jews immigrated there, mostly from the east (particularly from the areas of Iraq and Iran of today). The Jewish demographic map reflected a diversity largely due to incessant migrations. Nevertheless, there was a stable framework – a central authority which delegated some of its prerogatives to each community. Existing prior to the emergence of Islam, this structure was consolidated when the Muslim caliphate embraced a world of immense dimensions, obeying first Damascus and then Baghdad.

The seat of spiritual authority of the Jewish world was the yeshivah (academy). Between the eighth and eleventh centuries this was not simply a learning institute, but also the supreme court and source of instruction for all Jews. The head of the yeshivah, the *gaon*, was regarded as the highest religious authority, but his responsibilities also included organizing the courts, appointing judges and community leaders as well as scribes, ritual slaughterers and other officials. The *gaon* was authorized to dismiss any one of these, and it was he who exercised the powerful weapon of excommunication.

The *geonim* became incontestable leaders of the Jewish world as a result of two developments. The first was the conflict between the heads of the academies and *rosh ha-golah* (the exilarch) who officially represented the Babylonian community to the authorities. The two Babylonian academies, the yeshivah of Sura and the one in Pumbedita, were transferred to Baghdad in the early ninth century and continued to carry the names of their former locations. Before then the exilarch had held full authority, and he nominated the heads of the academies who were regarded as spiritual leaders only. But in time, the heads of the academies acquired more power; the office of exilarch persisted, but essential secular functions were taken over by the *geonim*.

The second development involved conflict between the center in Palestine and the Babylonian *geonim* over hegemony in the diaspora. The yeshivah in the Land of Israel had traditionally been responsible for the communities in Palestine, Syria, Lebanon and Egypt; the Babylonian center had jurisdiction over the communities in Iraq, Iran and Yemen. The North African communities were autonomous and solicited by both rival centers. Ties between the communities were bilateral: the communities sent their halakhic questions and donations to the *yeshivot*; and the heads of the academies in turn supplied answers and commentaries (*responsa*), as well as laudatory poems and honorary titles, tokens of respect for their supporters.

In the competition over North Africa the Babylonian *yeshivot* gained the upper hand. The centralized structure of the caliphate, the authority of the Babylonian Talmud, and the fact that many North African Jews had come from the east and preferred to address their questions and send money to their country of origin – all these combined to the advantage of the Babylonian *geonim*. In the tenth century the supremacy of the Babylonian center was unequivocally established, and the *geonim* were responsible for fashioning the thought of all the Jews within the Muslim world. More than any other, the figure of Saadiah ben Joseph (882–942) best

*1. Moses's canticle (Deuteronomy, 32). Page from an 11th or 12th-century Bible in a Babylonian or Persian hand. Called "Solomon's seal," the six-pointed star begins to appear in Hebrew manuscripts of that period, first in Muslim lands, then in Spain and Germany.*

| Accession of the Abbasids | Letter of Pirkoi ben Baboi | Paltoi bar Abbaye, *gaon* of Pumbedita | The calendar polemic | Saadiah, *gaon* of Sura |
|---|---|---|---|---|
| 750 | 810 | 842 | 921 | 928 |

**757–761:** Yehudai ben Nahman, *gaon* of Sura, suggests that the Jews of Palestine follow the Babylonian custom; the latter, however, prefer to maintain their own written traditions which were established in the Jerusalem Talmud.

**786:** Arguing that most Jews throughout the land no longer owned land, the heads of the Babylonian academies and the exilarch proclaim regulations which differ from those of the Talmud.

**c. 810:** Letter of Pirkoi ben Baboi to the Jewish communities in North Africa: he tries to convince them of the superiority of the Babylonian Talmud over the Jerusalem Talmud.

**842–855:** Paltoi bar Abbaye, *gaon* of Pumbedita, sends the Talmud and its commentaries to Jewish scholars in Spain.

**857–875:** Amram ben Sheshna is *gaon* of

*2. The Caliph of Baghdad receives the two rival leaders of the Jewish community, Saadiah Gaon and David ben Zakkai. Reconstruction.*

*3. Two pages of a manuscript containing a parashah (a portion of the Pentateuch according to the traditional order of reading the Bible in the synagogue). The text, from Numbers 13, is decorated in the style of 11th-century Egyptian Korans. Egypt, 1106–1107.*

## Between Baghdad and Jerusalem

```
┈┈┈  Country under Muslim rule
Fez ●  Major community
◁═  Influence of the two major
     cultural centers
⬤  Sphere of influence of the
     Palestinian center
```
600 km.

represents the geonic period. Born in Egypt, this original and innovative thinker immigrated to Babylon in 922. On his arrival he played a major role in the most significant medieval Jewish polemics: the debate over the calendar which revolved around the question of the precise date of Passover. Until then only the yeshivah in the Land of Israel proclaimed the dates of the festivals; using Saadiah's arguments, the Babylonian center now successfully established its authority. From 922 onwards, most Jewish communities in the diaspora were to celebrate Passover on the date decided upon by the Babylonian academy. This polemic, together with the conflict which arose a decade later between the *gaon* and the exilarch, made Saadiah ben Joseph the incontestable authority for all Jewish communities in the Muslim lands – a position which was to be overshadowed only by Maimonides three hundred years later.

| Letter of Sherira Gaon | End of the geonic Period |
|---|---|
| 987 | 1038 |

Sura. His *Seder* ("Order of Prayers and Blessings"), is the oldest extant order of Jewish prayers; it became influential in many communities in North Africa and Europe.
**882:** Saadiah ben Joseph is born in Faiyum, Egypt. During his years of study in Egypt (until 915) and in Palestine (until 922) he wrote several works, including a Hebrew-Hebrew dictionary (*Sefer ha-Agron*) and an anti-Karaite polemic.
**c. 920:** Following a dispute with the head of the academy who was supported by the court bankers, the exilarch Ukba is expelled by the caliph to Kairouan in Tunisia.
**921–923:** The polemic over the calendar, between the Ben Meir family, the Palestinian *geonim*, and the Babylonian community leaders supported by Saadiah ben Joseph. Summaries of the arguments are dispatched to the diaspora communities, most of whom accept the authority of the Babylonian center.
**926:** Saadiah ben Joseph writes his *Book of Documents and Deeds*, part of a larger

halakhic work which he intended to write; this is the first work on Jewish law written in Arabic, and the first divided according to topics rather than by association of ideas, in the manner of the Talmud.
**928:** Saadiah ben Joseph is appointed head of the Sura academy by the exilarch David ben Zakkai.
**c. 931:** A power struggle develops between Saadiah Gaon and the exilarch who appointed him: the exilarch nominates someone else as head of the Sura academy, Saadiah in turn appoints another exilarch, his adversary's brother. During these years Saadiah, forced to go into hiding for four years, wrote his major philosophic work, *Book of Beliefs and Opinions*: an attempt to find rational proof for the dogmas of the Oral and Written Law.
**937:** Saadiah returns to his position as head of the academy, where he will remain until his death in 942.
**987:** The famous letter by Sherira Gaon to the Jews of Kairouan listing the generations

of the Sages since the time of the Mishnah down to his own time; the ties between the Babylonian yeshivot and the North African communities are consolidated.
**1004:** Hai ben Sherira is nominated *gaon* of Pumbedita in his father's lifetime. Writing several halakhic works, he wishes to strengthen the ties between his academy and diaspora communities. In a letter written in 1006 he tries to no avail to impose his authority on the Spanish rabbi, Hanokh ben Moses.

**1005–1007:** Hushiel ben Elhanan, and later his son Elhanan (or Hananel), emigrate from Italy and settle in Kairouan.
**1015:** Hai Gaon confers the title of *nagid* on Rabbi Abraham ben Nathan; the latter, a physician at the Tunisian court, had collected large sums of money for the Pumbedita academy and sought to strengthen the ties between that yeshivah and the Maghreb communities.
**1038:** Death of Hai ben Sherira; end of the *geonim* period.

4. A Hanukah lamp. Bronze, Egypt or Syria, 12th–13th centuries.

# The Karaites

As in the west, so in the east, the Jewish community entered the Middle Ages well equipped with spiritual authority and institutional organizations sanctioned by ancient texts and traditions. The central current of Judaism continued to maintain and cultivate this heritage, but Judaism had other facets as well. New forces began to question the social institutions and fundamental dogmas of the rabbinical tradition. The Muslim conquest led to the emergence of two such forces, having more than one trait in common: Karaism and activist messianism. The Karaite "heresy" was to have a long history. Even today there are about seven thousand Karaites living in Israel, where they maintain their separateness by only marrying within their community. But it was only during the Middle Ages that they actually constituted an alternative to rabbinical Judaism.

The Karaites are first mentioned in written sources in the late eighth century. They themselves claim to be descendants of dissident sects of the First Temple period, and the rabbinical tradition traces them back to opposition trends of the Second Temple period. Although no direct affiliation to any particular sect in ancient times has been proven, they could have borrowed some of their customs and forms of organization from certain Jewish sects in Persia.

The beginnings of Karaite activity are associated with the figure of Anan ben David – a learned and aristocratic man, probably belonging to a family of exilarchs, the leaders of Babylonian Jewry. His immediate followers were a small group of intellectuals who formulated the sect's tenets and preached them in Jewish centers throughout the caliphate, including Palestine. In the tenth and eleventh centuries the Karaite communities were protected by eminent members of the sect who had reached influential positions in the ruler's court. Led by a *nasi* ("prince") claiming Davidic lineage, the Karaites attracted many scholars of distinction in biblical exegesis, law, Hebrew lexicography, and philosophy. The best part of the Karaite intellectual effort was directed at proving the errors of the Rabbanites. Their critical acuteness and thorough knowledge of rabbinical doctrines ensured the high level of their polemics. And their religious attack was accompanied by bitter social criticism of the Jewish leadership, the exilarchs, the *geonim*, and the dignitaries which surrounded them.

Islamic influence was apparent in all aspects of Karaism – in their philosophical outlook, in their spiritual views, customs, laws, and judicial processes. The main hallmark of the Karaites is their rejection of the authority of the Oral Law and the belief in the necessity of direct, independent, and critical study of the Bible. A "Karaite" reads the *Mikra* (the Pentateuch) and recognizes the Scriptures as the exclusive source of religious law. This biblical fundamentalism was the basis of their entire religiosity, and placed them irrevocably in opposition to talmudic Judaism. Some of the Karaite doctrines and customs distinguishing them from the Rabbanites are the literal interpretation of the biblical rules concerning the observance of the Sabbath, celebrating the festivals differently (they do not blow the *shofar* on *Rosh ha-Shannah*, nor do they

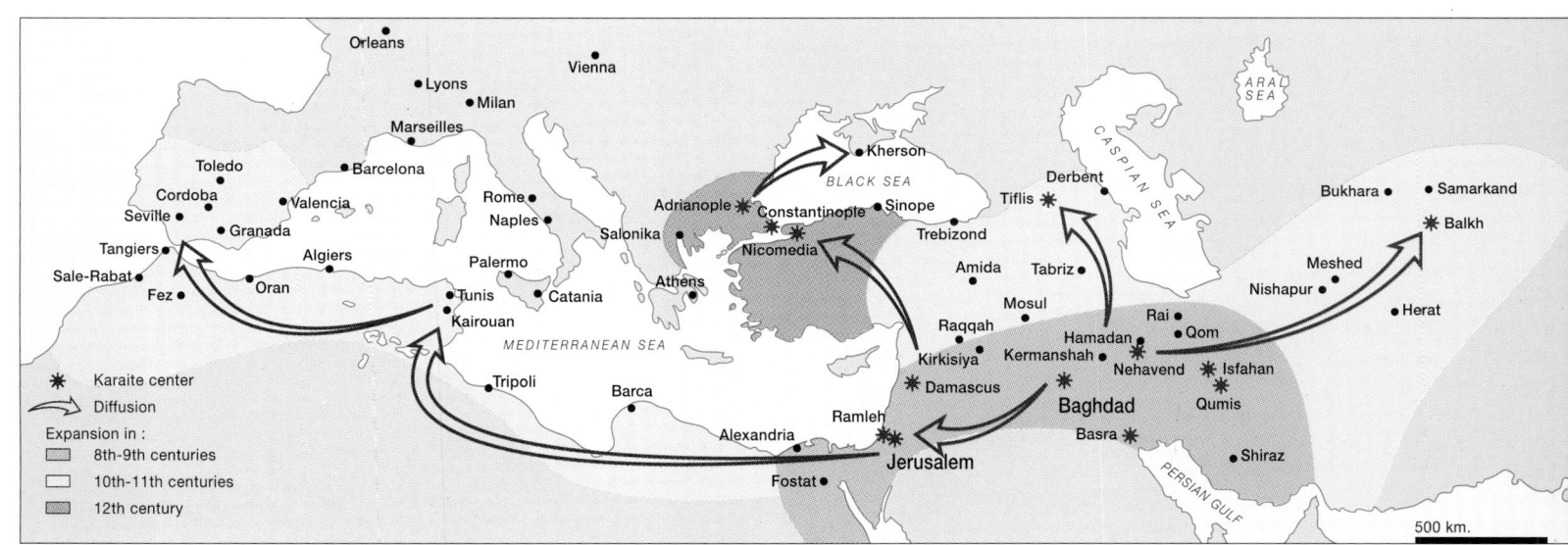

**Karaite center** ✳
**Diffusion** →
**Expansion in:**
8th-9th centuries
10th-11th centuries
12th century

500 km.

**Birth of Karaism** — c. 760

**Anti-Karaite polemics of Saadia Gaon** — c. 905

**The Karaites in Jerusalem** — 10th century

**c. 760:** Beginning of the activity of Anan ben David, founder of Karaism, and of his disciples – the Ananites. However, as rebels against all authority, they soon disintegrated into a plurality of groups.
**c. 830–860:** Benjamin ben Moses Nahawendi (of Nehavend) establishes a Karaite doctrine in Iran; through him the sect became known as Karaites or *Benei Mikra* ("sons of the Scriptures").
**873–875:** Daniel al-Qumisi – native of the town of Qumis, near Isfahan – brings the message of Karaism to Palestine.
**c. 905:** Saadia Gaon writes an attack on Anan ben David in Arabic; the future head of the Sura academy is the strongest opponent to the sect and the one most frequently cited in the writings of its adherents; his attack initiates the long and acrimonious quarrel between Karaites and Rabbanites.
**10th century:** An important community of Karaites exists in Jerusalem, where they regard themselves as *Avelei Zion* ("they who mourn in Zion," Isaiah, 61:3). During the first

3. A Karaite family observing the Sabbath in darkness, faithful to the literal wording of the biblical prohibition: *"You shall kindle no fire throughout your habitations upon the Sabbath day"* (Exodus, 35:3). Reconstitution.

half of the century, the most important figure of Karaism was Jacob al-Kirkisani. A great scholar, well versed in the theological sources of the three monotheistic religions, al-Kirkisani's works in Arabic include the *Book of Lights and Watch-Towers*, a code of Karaite law, and the *Book of Gardens and Parks* which is a commentary on the non-legal chapters of the Pentateuch.
**Second half of 10th century:** David ben Abraham Alfasi of Fez (Morocco), grammarian and biblical exegete, author of a Hebrew book of synonyms in which the language of the Bible is compared to Aramaic and Arabic. Towards the end of the century, Japheth ben Ali of Basra translates the Pentateuch into Arabic, adding his own commentary. In Jerusalem his son, Levi ben Japheth, composes a codex of religious laws, *The Book of Precepts*.
**First half of 11th century:** Period of activity of Abraham ha-Cohen ha-Ro'eh ("the Seer" – a euphemism, since the man was blind); a polyglot, a rationalist, and a great traveller,

# 8th–13th Centuries

*1. The Feast of Tabernacles (Sukkot) on the Mount of Olives, c. 1050. On the right stand the seven members of the Sanhedrin, proclaiming the dates of festivals, announcing new nominations to the Sanhedrin, and reiterating the excommunication of the Karaites. The latter, required to attend, stand on the far left, behind a Muslim soldier who interposes between the enemy groups. Painting on glass by John Frazer, based on literary sources.*

wave the "four species" in Sukkot; and they ignore Hanukkah since it is not mentioned in the Bible). In addition, they are particularly severe with regard to the law on marriage among relatives. Their liturgy is mostly biblical psalmody, and they practice different methods of ritual slaughter – a custom which widened the rift between them and the Rabbanites, as they cannot share the same food.

The Karaite attack was not powerful enough to demolish the rabbinical citadel, but it did succeed in breaching its walls, for the sect recruited many converts. Towards the end of the eleventh century the sect had adherents in most communities within the Muslim world and the Byzantine Empire: in the eastern parts of the caliphate, in Palestine and Egypt, in North Africa, in Spain, and in Asia Minor.

The Karaites, however, considered the dispersion a calamity. Their doctrine emphatically stressed the obligation to live in the Land of Israel. Residing in Jerusalem, praying at its gates, submitting to severe practices of purification – these concrete, measures were to hasten the End of Days; and without them there was no hope of Redemption. Hence the constant propaganda for a Return to Zion. And indeed, many of the sectarians were not content to preach, and sought to realize the ideal. Consequently, between the ninth and eleventh centuries the "roses" – as the Karaites called themselves in contradistinction to the rabbinical "thorns" – comprised the majority of the Jewish community in Jerusalem.

*2. A Karaite manuscript of the Bible. (Copy made in St. Petersburg, 1905). Egypt (?), 10th century.*

| Jerusalem taken by the Crusaders | Spread of Karaism in Europe |
|---|---|
| **1099** | **Beginning in the 12th century** |

he refutes Saadia Gaon's arguments against the sect, and contributes to the spread of Karaism.

**Second half of 11th century:** Due to the work of missionaries from Jerusalem, the Karaite center of activity gradually shifts to Europe. The authorities in Spain, forewarned by the Rabbanites, extirpate any sign of the sect; the situation is more favorable in the Byzantine Empire: an important center for the translation of Karaite works emerges in Constantinople around Tobias ben Moses *ha-Ma'atik* (the "copyist"), translator of Jeshua ben Judah, the last Karaite scholar in Palestine, and of the "Seer."

**1099:** The First Crusade destroys the Karaite community in Jerusalem; the Crusaders, making no distinction between Karaites and Rabbanites, drive them all together into a synagogue and burn them alive. Decline of Karaism throughout the East, with the exception of Egypt, where it will exercise some influence until the arrival of Maimonides in Cairo c. 1170.

**12th–14th centuries:** Golden age for Karaite literature in the Byzantine Empire. Judah ben Eli Hadassi writes *Eshkol ha-Kofer* ("The Cluster of Camphire," a title borrowed from the Song of Songs, 1:14), a theological summary and the most important Karaite work ever to be written in Hebrew. Aaron ben Joseph ha-Rofe ("the Physician"), called *ha-Kadosh* ("the Saint"), writes his classical commentary on the Bible, *Sefer ha-Mivhar*. Aaron ben Elijah, the "Karaite Maimonides," writes his *Gan Eden* ("Paradise"), a systematic codex of Karaite laws and beliefs.

**1354:** The poet Moses ben Samuel of Damascus, a native of Safed in Palestine who moved to Damascus and became a manager of the emir's estates, is forced to convert to Islam. Later he flees to Egypt and returns to Karaite Judaism.

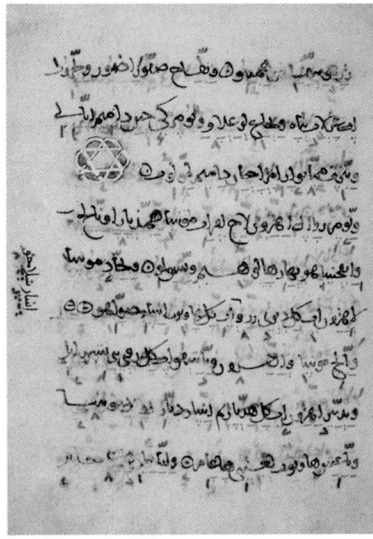

*4, 5. Karaite Pentateuch, written in Hebrew in Arabic characters. Palestine, 10th century.*

# The World of the Genizah

*1. Inscription in the Ben Ezra Synagogue at Fostat, Egypt. Carved wooden panel, 13th century.*

Derived from the root *g-n-z*, meaning "to conceal," the word *genizah* designated a place for depositing damaged bibles, torn prayer books, or ritual objects which could no longer be used. According to Jewish law, objects containing the name of God cannot be destroyed and therefore have to be preserved even when unusable. The depository could be within the synagogue or in a special storage room elsewhere; when full, the *genizah* would be transferred for burial in a cemetery. In some communities the burial of the *genizah* was a festive ceremony attended by a large crowd and accompanied by music and a ritual meal. It was an expression of joy at such evidence of the study of holy scriptures. Travelling scholars have always known that by searching such archives they could discover precious ancient documents.

In 1890, during repair work on the Ben Ezra Synagogue in Fostat (old

*2. Page from a children's reader, conserved in the Cairo Genizah. Egypt, 10th century.*

Cairo), old strata of its *genizah* were uncovered. Soon afterwards tattered pages of its old manuscripts began to circulate in the West, probably sold by the beadles of the synagogue through the mediation of Egyptian antique dealers. When the exceptional documentary value of these fragments came to the attention of scholar Solomon Shechter, he persuaded the community leaders to allow him to ship the entire content of the Cairo *Genizah* to Cambridge, England.

These archives, containing hundreds of thousands of pages, originating mostly from the eleventh to the thirteenth centuries, offer a detailed picture of the spiritual and material civilization of medieval Jewry. They contain rabbinical *responsa* and rare formulas of prayer, trial protocols and instructions of community authorities, books of linguistics, collections of poetry, treatises of *Halakhah*, science, philosophy and history, registers of merchants, books which had been in private and public libraries and portray the cultural profile of the community, bills of sale, letters, private notes, and other assorted papers.

Almost all these documents have one trait in common: no matter what language they use – Hebrew, Arabic, Persian, Spanish, Greek, and even Yiddish – they are written in Hebrew letters. Fortunately for us, the men responsible for the *Genizah* extended the definition of "sacred" to all that was written in Hebrew script, regardless of content. This was probably due to the decline in the use of Hebrew in everyday life, a process that turned it into a holy language and hallowed the letters themselves.

The custom of concealing texts may have been the result of mob attacks on Jewish funeral ceremonies. At the beginning of the eleventh century, a wave of anti-Jewish and anti-Christian riots swept over Palestine and Egypt. Churches and synagogues, including the great Palestinian synagogue of Cairo, were desecrated. The Jews therefore preferred to avoid public burial ceremonies and, while awaiting better times, to find a solution which they believed to be temporary. Reconstructed in the 1030s, the synagogue continued to house this treasury of documents in its attic until the late nineteenth century.

The reconstruction was financed by rich North African merchants who had settled in Egypt after the Fatimid center of power had been transferred from Tunisia to Cairo. As a rule, the Fatimids, who were Shi'ites

---

**The earliest dated document of the *Genizah***

**871**

**Letters of Judah Halevi**

**c. 1140**

**25:** The date attributed by legend to the founding of the Palestinian synagogue in Fostat (old Cairo). Although the synagogue may indeed have been founded during the Roman period, such an ancient date may have been selected in order to create the impression that it was established before the Muslim conquest and the introduction of the interdict contained in the Covenant of Omar on building new synagogues.

**871. October 5:** The oldest dated document of the *Genizah*: a *ketubbah* (marriage contract) written on Friday, 16th of the month of *Tishri*. The script resembles that of ancient Hebrew papyri. The scribe apparently noticed as he was working that he had erred with regard to the date, so he stopped in the middle

**969. August 5:** The Fatimids conquer Fostat.

**970. May:** Conquest of Palestine by the Fatimids; but another thirty years pass before this conquest is felt. The new masters of the land authorize the appointment of the

head of the Palestinian *yeshiva* and accept him as *nagid*: "head of the Jews." After the middle of the eleventh century they appoint a dignitary from the Egyptian community to that office. Among those who fulfilled the post were court physicians, public officials, heads of the Palestinian *yeshiva* (which was transferred to Egypt), Maimonides himself, and his descendants.

**973. October:** The capital of the Caliphate is transferred from the Maghreb to Egypt to a new city north of Fostat, Cairo, built especially for the new rulers.

**1003–1021:** Anti-Jewish and anti-Christian persecutions.

**1007 or 1009:** Destruction of the basilica of the Holy Sepulchre and the Church of the Resurrection in Jerusalem; desecration of Christian tombs; confiscation of church property.

**1012:** The Palestinian synagogue in Fostat is sacked; its wooden panels are torn out and sold by soldiers.

**1021–1039:** Major repair works on the

Palestinian synagogue of Fostat where the *Genizah* will be kept till the 19th century.

**c. 1025:** A dispute between the leaders of the Palestinian community and the Babylonian community in Fostat over questions of jurisdiction.

**1065–1082:** Judah ben Saadia ha-Rofe is the first *nagid* in Egypt.

**1082–1094:** David ben Daniel ben Azaria calls himself "head of the Jews" of Egypt.

**c. 1140:** Letters by Judah Halevi, discovered in the *Genizah*, clarify the circumstances of his writing the *Kuzari* ("The Book of the Khazars") and the reasons that led him to travel to Palestine. The greatest Hebrew poet of the "Golden Age" in Spain vows not to compose any more secular poetry, but he cannot resist the courtly atmosphere in the home of the *nagid*; his stay in Egypt delays his "ascent" to the Land of Israel until

*4. Sentence of a rabbinical tribunal in a divorce case, written in Judeo-Arabic. Damietta, Egypt, October 9, 1130.*

and thus themselves a minority within a predominantly Sunnite empire, treated religious minorities kindly. The Jews who came from the Maghreb, some of them closely allied to the Fatimid rulers, could therefore become dominant in the community which congregated around the Palestinian synagogue. The Genizah reflects their commercial activity, at first along the route from the Maghreb to Egypt, then along the more southern route connecting Egypt with India through Yemen.

The unparalleled richness of the Cairo Genizah can be explained by its location at the heart of three concentric circles: Egypt, land of immigration and a bridge between East and West; Cairo, capital of Egyptian Jewry; and the synagogue – a place of prayer as well as a tribunal and a school. The scholarly work of classifying, deciphering, editing, and publishing these treasures is still far from complete. To date research has yielded invaluable information on many fields in Jewish and general history such as relations between the Karaites and Rabbanites, relations with Muslims and Christians, the Crusades, medicine, the role of women, education, seafaring and warfare, and countless other subjects.

*3. Ketubbah (marriage contract). Parchment, Fostat, Egypt, 10th–11th centuries.*

**Maimonides in Egypt**

**1166–1204**

his death, announced in a letter conserved in the Genizah. This document makes it doubtful that Judah Halevi ever reached the Holy Land.

**1166–1204:** Maimonides in Egypt; his arrival in Fostat and his accession to the position of *nagid* are amply documented in the Genizah.

**1211:** The dignitaries of the Egyptian Jewish community reach an agreement concerning liturgy in the Palestinian synagogue; it is a compromise which preserves the old customs while conceding to the needs of the numerous immigrants who pray according to the Babylonian rite.

**1237:** Ten dignitaries of the Cairo community appeal to the synagogue at Fostat to appoint David ben Abraham Maimuni as *nagid*.

**1442:** Agents of the Mamluks inspect the synagogues of Cairo; they claim that the Jews had written the name of Muhammad on the floor of the synagogue in Fostat; consequently part of that synagogue is destroyed, many Jews are maltreated, and

other places of prayer are closed down.

**1473:** Muslim dignitaries inspect the Palestinian synagogue in order to find out whether any new additions were built contrary to Islamic law.

**1488:** Obadiah of Bertinoro describes his visit to the Palestinian synagogue in Fostat in a letter to his father. The synagogue, he writes, is attributed to Elijah the Prophet, and it contains a bible copied by Ezra himself.

**1734:** Visit by Moses Haim Capsuto of Italy who also attributes the synagogue to the prophet Elijah; he describes the courtyard and laments its poor condition.

**1752–1753:** Visit by Simon von Geldern who says he saw the synagogue of Elijah, explored its *genizah*, and donated many pieces of gold.

**1864:** Visit by Jacob Saphir who describes the synagogue and the opening of the Genizah in detail.

**1897:** Solomon Shechter transfers the documents of the Genizah to Cambridge, England.

*5. A genizah ceremony of damaged holy books in the cemetery of the community of Rietavas (Ritova), Lithuania, between the world wars.*

# A Golden Age in North Africa

1. A Spanish synagogue. Illuminated manuscript, c. 1350.

The Maghreb ("west" in Arabic, in contradistinction to the Mashrek, "east") in Arab geography designated North Africa as well as Spain. Indeed, for several centuries these two regions shared the same political and cultural features. While Jewish culture flourished alongside Arab culture in the Iberian peninsula, North African Jewry also enjoyed a period of brilliant economic prosperity and cultural creativity.

A natural bridge between east and west and hence a major thoroughfare for trade caravans, and a fertile region of temperate climate, North Africa had always attracted populations from the Mashrek. Among the immigrants from the East there were many Jews, and their influx transformed North African Jewry. From the ninth century onwards, these newcomers, who still had family, commercial and cultural ties in their countries of origin, began to dominate the Maghreb communities.

However, Baghdad, capital of the Arab-Muslim world, and the Babylonian centers of oriental Jewry, were geographically distanced from North Africa, thus forcing the Maghreb communities to find their own solutions to their everyday problems. From the tenth century onwards, for example, the Jewish community of Kairouan in Tunisia was governed by its own *nagid* (*rais al-yahud* in Arabic, meaning "leader of the Jews"; other *negidim* were to be found in Spain, Egypt and Yemen; in Morocco and Algeria the title *nagid* was bestowed on the leader of the community from the sixteenth to the nineteenth century). Furthermore, the Maghreb communities even developed a sense of superiority over their oriental brethren, since economic advantage enabled the more affluent ones to support the Babylonian academies by way of generous donations. Finally, the desire and ability to relax ties with the Jewish centers in the East were augmented by the political fragmentation of the Islamic empire. Chased out of Mesopotamia by the Abbasids, the Umayyads established an emirate in Spain, while in North Africa the Shi'ite Fatimids founded a caliphate in Ifriqiya (the future Tunisia) in the early tenth century.

The legend of the Four Captives illustrates the need of North African Jewry to demonstrate their independence: it recounts the story of four great sages who, captured by pirates and ransomed by four different communities, each founded an independent center of learning. Nevertheless, in reverence to the older, sanctified authority of the oriental centers, obedience and respect were preserved. Yet such tokens of subordination to the authority of the Palestinian or Babylonian centers did not prevent the new communities in the West from evolving their own patterns of public, spiritual and cultural life. Thus, although most surviving halakhic questions from the time of the *geonim* derive from the Maghreb, it appears that from the ninth century onwards many of the them were answered by local scholars. Their *responsa* were later collected and classified according to the subjects of the Talmud tractates, con-

| Idris I in Morocco | Founding of the Fatimid dynasty | The Fatimids in Ifriqiya |
|---|---|---|
| 789 | c. 862 | 909 |

**c. 800:** Earliest evidence of Jews participating in North African trade.

**c. 810:** Letter from Pirkoi ben Baboi to the Maghreb communities: the Babylonian sage encourages the North African Jews to accept the authority of the Babylonian academies rather than that of the Palestinian center. In fact, between 830 and 880, leaders of the North African community, Nathan ben Hananiah and Judah ben Saul, respond to certain halakhic questions themselves while addressing others to the Babylonian academies.

**825–1067:** Sicily is held by North African Muslims; strong institutional and commercial ties between the Jews of the island and the North African communities.

**c. 880:** Traveller Eldad Ha-Dani visits Tunisia.

**c. 900:** Families bearing names indicating Persian, Iraqi or Palestinian origin – Ben Ukal, Ben Shahun, Ha-Bavli ("the

Babylonian"), etc. – are prominent in Maghreb and Egyptian communities.

**909:** Creation of the Fatimid caliphate in the Maghreb marks the end of the first phase of expansion of this Shi'ite dynasty; themselves a minority in the Muslim world, the Fatimids appoint Jews and Christians to positions in which they have power over Sunnite Muslims.

**c. 930–1006:** Lifespan of Jacob ben Nissim ibn Shahun who wields spiritual authority over all the academies in the Maghreb.

**c. 940–1025:** Joseph ibn Abitur, member of an aristocratic Jewish family from Spain, translator of the Talmud to Arabic, finds refuge in Morocco and then in Egypt; he writes two hymns for the Palestinian synagogue in Fostat and participates in the leadership of the Egyptian and Palestinian communities.

**c. 950:** Hisdai ibn Shaprut is appointed

2. Manuscript by the poet Joseph ibn Abitur. Morocco, early 11th century.

3. Jewish tombstone. Tetuan, Morocco, 16th–17th centuries.

**North Africa and Andalusia 10th–11th centuries**

*Ifriqiya ("Africa") of the Zirides, 973-1135*
Hammadides, 1015-1152
Alawid invasion, c. 1050
Almoravid conquest
Almoravids, 1056-1147
915 ■ New town
Jewish emigration
Fez ◉ Jewish cultural center

stituting the basis for the earliest commentary on the Babylonian Talmud. The first Talmud commentator was a Tunisian rabbi from Kairouan, Hananel ben Hushi'el, who was followed by his pupil Nissim ben Jacob ibn Shahun. Extensive use of their work was made by Isaac Alfasi, and from Alfasi it passed on to scholars in Spain.

Other North African scholars entered the secular sciences. In the early tenth century, during the generation of Saadiah Gaon, Tunisian Isaac ben Solomon Israeli wrote treatises on medicine and philosophy, his disciple Dunash ibn Tamim wrote on mathematics, and another Dunash, a North African Jew who had studied with the *gaon* in Baghdad, brought Saadiah's theories on Hebrew poetry to North Africa. Indeed, medieval Hebrew poetry, born in the east, was developed and enriched in the west, and therefore labelled "Spanish." The first collection of stories in Judeo-Arabic was composed in Tunisia, and Hebrew philology was born in Fez, Morocco, spreading from there to Spain and Palestine. There was virtually no intellectual, spiritual or artistic sphere which was not explored and revitalized by medieval North African Jewry.

4. Latin edition of the works of Isaac ben Solomon Israeli, famous Jewish Tunisian physician in the 10th century. Lyons, 1515.

| End of the Spanish caliphate | The Almoravides conquer the Maghreb |
|---|---|
| **1031** | **1053–1056** |

counselor of the Umayyad caliph Abd al-Rahman III; patron of Jewish court culture, Hisdai surrounds himself with poets and scholars.

**969–973:** The Fatimids complete the conquest of Egypt where they establish their capital; the Zirids, a Berber dynasty loyal to the Fatimids, rule North Africa.

**c. 980–1062:** Lifespan of Nissim ben Jacob ibn Shahun, head of the talmudic school at Kairouan, author of talmudic commentaries and numerous halakhic works. The other leader of the Kairouan community after 1005–1007 is Hananel ben Hushi'el, author of the first complete commentary on the Talmud.

**993–1056:** Samuel ha-Nagid (Ismail ibn Nagrela), born in Cordoba and vizier of Granada, where he was military commander and author of halakhic treatises and collections of poems. Corresponding with contemporary Jewish scholars, Samuel emphasizes the Jewish nature of his deeds, presenting himself to the Muslim court as an emissary of the Jewish people.

**1015:** In Kairouan, Abraham ben Nathan, court physician to Zirid emir Badis (966–1016) and to his son Al-Mu'izz (1016–1062), receives the title of *nagid* in acknowledgement of his generous contributions to the Pumbedita academy in Babylonia.

**1031:** The Umayyad caliphate in Spain is split into small principalities, some founded by mercenary military commanders of Berber origin. In these courts, Jewish dignitaries attain positions of high authority.

**1053–1056:** The Almoravides conquer the cities in the Maghreb.

**1056–1066:** Succeeding his father at the Granada court, Joseph ben Samuel ha-Nagid is killed during a revolt which destroys the city's Jewish community.

**1057:** Death of Hananel ben Hushi'el. His commentary on the Talmud gained wide circulation and served as the main bridge between the teaching of the Babylonian *geonim* and the scholars of North Africa.

# Between the Cross and the Crescent

"They [Christians and Muslims] make war, and the ravages of combat bring about our ruin" (Judah Halevi). Indeed, in the second half of the eleventh century, after the demise of the Umayyad Dynasty and the fragmentation of Muslim Spain into small principalitites, the Christian kingdoms in the Iberian Peninsula launched the *Reconquista*. This was the great struggle to regain territories in Spain, a struggle which was viewed by European Christians as part of a larger crusade against Islam. The external threat forced the Arab and Berber principalities to forget their differences and to appeal to

*1. Coat-of-arms of the united kingdom of Castile and Leon. Spain, Soria (?), 1300.*

the Moroccan Almoravides for help. When the latter attained dominance over Andalusia, they formed a united empire "from the Ebro to Senegal." The Jewish communities found themselves caught between two powerful societies engaged in a deadly struggle.

In Granada as in Seville, the Almoravides expelled the Jews from all positions of influence. Poet Moses ibn Ezra, as he was wandering from place to place in Christian Spain, lamented the crudity of a society which lacked the refinement of the Andalusian courts. Between 1108 and 1111 Castile suffered a series of rural and urban uprisings similar to contemporary revolts of communes and peasants in other parts of Europe. A general economic depression, caused mainly by the drying up of the flow

of money from Muslim Spain, aggravated social unrest. This agitation was accompanied by anti-Jewish riots and massacres. Worse still, when the Almohads, another North African dynasty, replaced the Almoravides in Andalusia, they completely abolished the protection traditionally accorded by Muslim rulers to the Peoples of the Book, forcing everyone to profess Islam at least outwardly. The Jews then fled from Andalusia, some towards the Muslim Orient but the majority to the Christian kingdoms in Spain or to southern France.

The situation of the Jews who emigrated to the Christian part of the peninsula at first resembled the conditions they had enjoyed in Muslim Spain prior to the arrival of the Berber dynasties. The Christian monarchs of Castile and Aragon used the Jews in order to colonize regions reconquered from the Muslims. Also, in imitation of the Muslim princes, they developed the custom of employing Jews in the highest administrative and financial positions. Since Jews could not attain political power nor ally themselves with the nobility or the church, they became natural allies to the crown. The privilege charters (*fueros*) granted in the reconquered states were, however, suffused with ambiguities inevitable in a society where three ethnic-religious communities were forced to live together. While they did grant legal equality, the privilege charters also enforced submission to laws belonging in a non-mixed society.

The powerful Jewish families, who fulfilled functions for the Christian kings which were similar to those held by their fathers in Andalusian courts, naturally wielded considerable importance in the Jewish communities. For several generations the leadership of the community became a hereditary privilege of these dynasties of courtiers. Only in the early thirteenth century, and in connection with the Maimonidean controversy, did the first signs of a democratic reaction become apparent. The first power struggle took place in Barcelona in 1213 when the anti-Maimonidean party tried to dislodge the influential house of Sheshet, but failed. One generation later, in 1241, it succeeded. Henceforth the community was to be administered by a new type of urban Jewish patriciate.

---

**Reconquest of Toledo by Alfonso VI of Castile**   **The Almoravides in Spain**   **Capture of Saragossa by Alfonso I of Aragon**

**1085** **1086** **1118**

**1081:** Pope Gregory VII urges the King of Castile not to place any Jews in positions of influence.
**1085:** Alfonso VI of Castile captures Toledo: the first important stage in the reconquest of Spain from the Muslims.
**1090:** Granada is conquered by the Almoravides; the Jewish community is destroyed; the Ibn Ezra family is among the refugees.
**1099:** Death of Rodrigo Diaz de Vivar, the famous Spanish hero known as El Cid; miracles and conversions of Jews take place around his corpse. The poem *El Cid*, composed c. 1140, includes the story of two Jewish preachers from Burgos whose treacherous operations are foiled by the Christian knight.
**1106:** Conversion of Moses ha-Sefardi (Petrus Alfonsi), sponsored by the King of Aragon, Alfonso I the Battler. In his polemical

*2. Hispano-Moresque Passover Haggadah. Castile, c. 1300.*

works, Petrus Alfonsi attacks post-biblical rabbinical Judaism and denounces the anthropomorphic representations of divinity in Jewish homilies.
**1108:** Murder of Solomon ibn Ferrizuel, patron of Judah Halevi, and nephew of Joseph ha-Nasi Ferrizuel called "Cidellus" ("little Cid") who was counselor and physician to Alfonso VI.
**1109:** Jews are massacred in Toledo and in the Burgos region.
**1111:** Anti-Jewish violence erupts in the wake of the peasants' uprising in the Sahagun region.
**1118:** Capture of Saragossa by Alfonso I the Battler, King of Aragon. In November, King Alfonso VII of Castile, wishing to appease the townsmen of Toledo, introduces a law which excludes Jews and recent converts from public office in the city.

*3. The synagogue in Toledo of Samuel ha-Levi Abulafia, minister to Pedro I of Castile, built c. 1357; later the El Transito church, now a Jewish museum.*

## Reconquista Spain
## 11th–13th centuries

FRANCE

Lunel
Montpellier
Narbonne
Perpignan
Collioure
Gerona
Barcelona
Tarragona

Bayonne
Vitoria  Pamplona
NAVARRE
Jaca
Logroño  Sos
Huesca
Tudela
Tarazona  Saragossa  Lerida
Soria
Almazan
Calatayud
Siguenza  Alcañiz  Tortosa
Montalban
Castellon de la Plana
Sagunto (Murviedro)
Valencia
Alcira
Jativa  Denia
Palma
Ibiza

Gijon
Villalba
La Coruña
Oviedo
Santiago de Compostela
Leon
Vigo  Benavente
Tuy  Chaves  LEON
Braga  Braganza  Valladolid
Oporto  Vila Real  Zamora  Duero
PORTUGAL
Viseu  Ciudad Rodrigo  Avila  ARAGON
Coimbra  Covilha  CASTILE  Segovia  Guadalajara
Leiria  Plasencia  Tajo  Toledo  Cuenca
Tomar  Talavera de la Reina
Lisbon  Portalegre  Merida  Guadiana
Setubal  Estremoz  Elvas  Badajoz  Calatrava (Ciudad Real)
Evora  Llerena  Almaden
Beja  Serpa  Montoro  Ubeda  Orihuela
Lagos  Carmona  Cordoba  Guadalquivir  Murcia  Alicante
Olhão  Huelva  Ecija  Baena  Jaen
Faro  Palos  Seville  Lucena  Granada  Cartagena
Jerez de la Frontera  GRANADA
Cadiz  Malaga  Velez Malaga  Almeria
Algeciras  Oran
Tangiers  Ceuta
Tetouan
Mellila

Territories under Christian rule:
Late 10th century
Late 11th century
Late 12th century
Late 13th century
→ Berber advance (11th–12th centuries)
↪ Flight of Jews, 12th century

150 km.

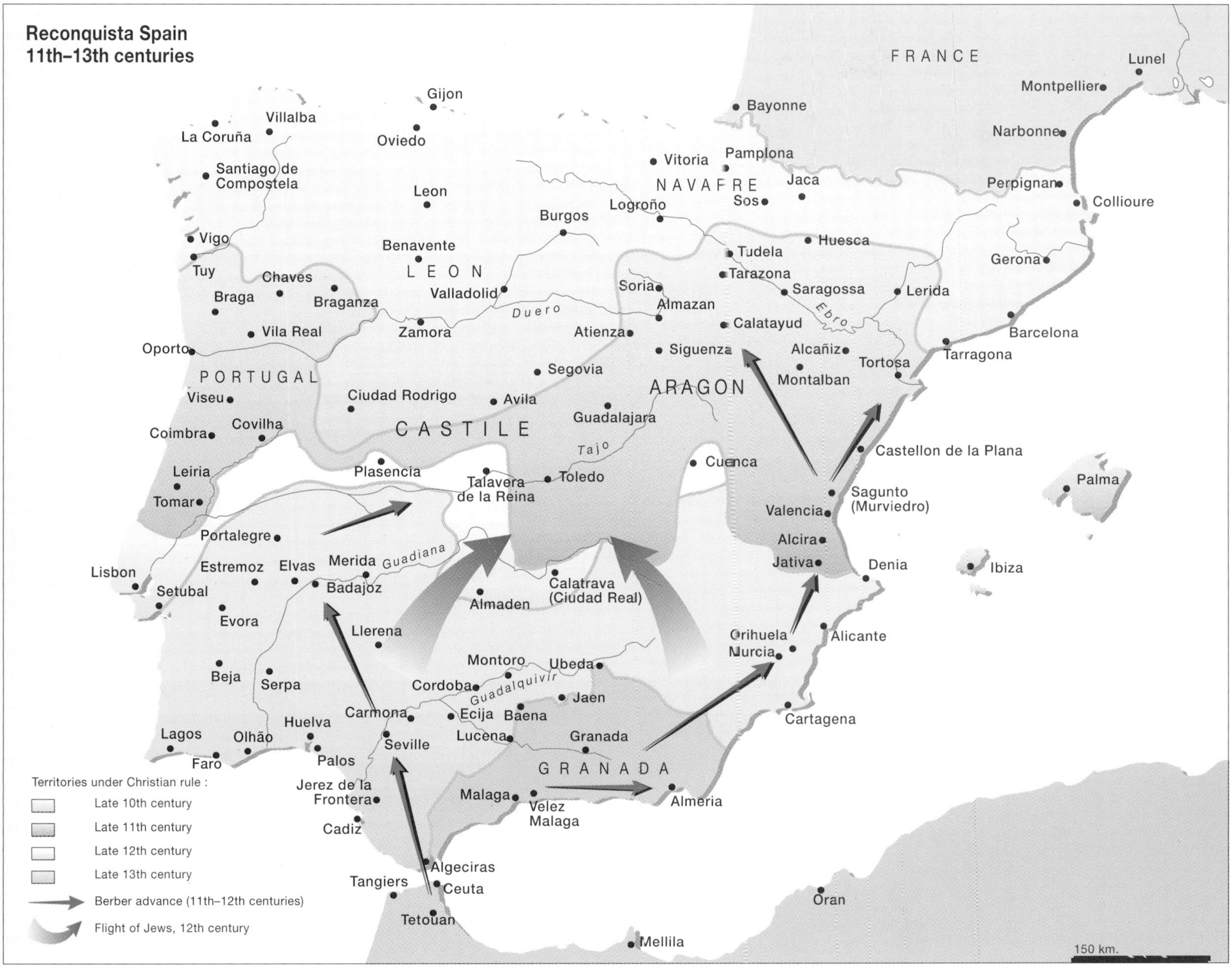

**The Almohads in Andalusia** | **Fuero of Teruel** | **Fourth Lateran Council**
1147 | 1176 | 1215

**1147:** Alfonso VII of Castile appoints Judah ibn Ezra (nephew of poet Moses ibn Ezra) commander of Calatrava (Ciudad Real), an important fortress on the Muslim border.
**1147–1148:** Most of Andalusia falls under Almohad rule.
**1151–1166:** John, Archbishop of Toledo, to whom "Avendahut Israelita philosophus" dedicated a translation from Arabic to Latin of Avicenna's *De Anima*. "Avendahut" was probably the philosopher and historian Abraham ibn Daud.
**1161:** Joseph Kimhi and Judah ibn Tibbon, both emigrants from Muslim Spain who settled in southern France, one in Narbonne and the other in Lunel near Montpellier, simultaneously translate the *Duties of the Heart* of the Jewish philosopher Bahya ibn Paquda from Arabic to Hebrew.
**1166:** Judah ibn Tibbon translates Judah Halevi's *The Book of the Kuzari* from Arabic to Hebrew.
**1176:** The *fuero* (privilege charter) of Teruel – Jews are made the property of the royal treasury.

**1202:** Meir ha-Levi Abulafia of Toledo asks the rabbis of Lunel to support his condemnation of Maimonides' theses which deny belief in the resurrection of the body. Sheshet Benveniste of Barcelona, physician, diplomat, and administrator at the Aragonese court, tries to dissuade the rabbis of Lunel from supporting Abulafia, arguing that the talmudic scholars of Castile opposed Maimonides' works only because his teachings undermine their judicial authority. This controversy will be rekindled a decade later, this time around the political issue of electing community leaders.
**1204:** Death of Maimonides in Egypt.
**1215:** Fourth Lateran Council, convened by Innocent III. Isaac Benveniste, Sheshet's nephew, heads a delegation of Jews from southern France who appeal to the Pope to prevent the adoption of anti-Jewish decisions. Nevertheless, the Council publishes a series of restrictive canons, particularly on Jewish money-lending.

4. The Jewish Quarter in Seville, viewed from the Cathedral.

# Scientists and Physicians in the Middle Ages

*1. The Astronomer. Illumination in a Jewish Italian manuscript of Meshal ha-Kadmoni (1291) – a collection of rhymed fables by Isaac ben Solomon ibn Sahula. Northern Italy, 1470–1480.*

Medieval science cannot be divided simply according to religious or ethnic categories. The same fields of knowledge, theories, practices, and learned controversies were shared by the three monotheistic civilizations. Defining a "Jewish science" is, in fact, a discussion of the Jewish contribution to scientific development in general.

This contribution was particularly significant in four areas: medicine; geography and cosmology; development of instruments for measurement, cartography, and navigation; and translation of works from Greek into Arabic and from Arabic into Latin and other European languages. The Jews therefore constituted an important link in the transmission of scientific knowledge from one culture to another and were thus crucial to the emergence of modern science; they also played a major role in the creation of the necessary tools for world exploration.

The first important center for medieval Jewish scientific activity in the eighth and ninth centuries was the Abbasid caliphate and particularly its capital, Baghdad. About a hundred years after the Muslim conquest of the Middle East, the name of the Jewish physician Masarjuwayh of Basra is mentioned as the first of a long list of men who translated Greek and Syrian works on medicine into Arabic. A Jewish convert to Islam, Rabban al-Tabari, was the first to translate Ptolemy's *Almagest* into Arabic. Isaac Judaeus (Isaac Israeli) is believed to have been the first medical author in Arabic whose works were brought to Europe.

It was in Muslim Spain, however, that Jewish science found the most fertile soil. In the early Middle Ages Andalusia was the greatest cultural center of Europe and of the entire Mediterranean basin. Its Muslim rulers, opulent and tolerant, offered the prosperous Jewish elite opportunities for complete social and cultural integration, which were not surpassed anywhere throughout the Middle Ages.

In Andalusia, as in the Muslim world at large, the Jews wrote their scientific treatises in Arabic, a language which they found best suited to this branch of human learning. Very early – in the mid-tenth century – Hisdai ibn Shaprut, a dignitary in the court of the caliph, leader of the Spanish Jewish community and an eminent physician, contributed to the construction of Arabic into a scientific vehicle, mainly by preparing the

final Arabic version of the *Materia medica*, the great pharmaceutical compendium by the Greek botanist Dioscrides (1st century AD).

The demise of the Spanish caliphate put an end to flourishing Jewish and Muslim science in Andalusia. First the Almoravids, a fanatic sect from North Africa who conquered southern Spain at the end of the eleventh century, and then the Almohads, who came in the twelfth century, totally changed the intellectual climate in Muslim Spain: scientific inquiry and philosophical rationalism could no longer exist. Moreover, most of the Jews were forced to leave. Some of them, including Maimonides, went to the east; the majority found refuge in Christian lands – northern Spain, southern France, Italy.

This was a turning point in the history of medieval science. As Muslim orthodoxy began stifling intellectual curiosity, the Latin West began to discover Greek science and its Arabic commentators. The Jews played a major role in this transition. Versed in Arabic and in European languages, they occupied a prominent place among the translators of important scientific works from Arabic into Latin, Spanish, and French. In Toledo and in the towns of Provence, numerous Jewish scholars translated a large number of works in philosophy, mathematics, geometry, physics, astronomy, astrology, medicine, and magic – a corpus of knowledge which constituted the basis for Latin science during the central and late Middle Ages.

At the same time another change was affecting Jewish science. Since the beginning of the twelfth century, Arabic was gradually being replaced by Hebrew as the sole language in which Jews wrote their scientific works. Translations from Arabic and Latin, as well as many original texts, were produced in Hebrew. Abraham ibn Ezra and Abraham bar Hiyya, philosophers and mathematicians, were the two most notable writers among these Hebrew-writing medieval scholars.

What was the attitude of Jewish religious authorities towards scientific inquiry? In Muslim Spain and in North Africa the orthodox were not particularly hostile to scientific studies, although there were disagreements among the scholars themselves as to what constituted proper science from the point of view of the *Halakhah* and of scientific validity. The rationalists, for example, eminently represented by Maimonides, rejected astrology and magic, even though most of their contemporaries considered these to be an integral part of scientific knowledge.

In the thirteenth and fourteenth centuries, however, Jewish society grew suspicious of all scientific activity. The condemnation culminated in a ban on the study of secular literature for persons under the age of 25, issued in 1305 by the rabbi of Barcelona, Solomon ben Abraham Adret (acronym Rashba), and other rabbis of southern France. However, even Rashba understood the importance of the study of medicine, and his ban did not restrict it in any way.

*2. An apothecary's shop in northern Italy. Jewish manuscript of Avicenna's Canon (980–1037). Lombardy or Venice, c. 1438–1440.*

# 7th–15th Centuries

**7th century (?):** *The Book of Remedies* by Asaph ha-Rofe (Asaph "the physician") – the oldest Hebrew work on medicine.

**850–c. 932:** Isaac ben Solomon Israeli (Isaac Judaeus), physician and philosopher, author of several medical works: *The Book of Remedies, The Book of Fever, The Ethics of Physicians.*

**882–942:** Sa'adiah Gaon, the illustrious leader of Babylonian Jewry and one of the first Jewish intellectuals in the Muslim orient to adopt Greco-Arabic philosophy; author of an Arabic commentary on *The Book of Creation* – an attempt to combine the principles of the Torah with Greek anatomy and physiology.

**913–983:** Shabbetai Donnolo, an Italian Jewish physician, the first author of Hebrew medical works in Europe; his most famous work, *Sefer ha-Yakar*, lists 120 different remedies and their compositions. His name is associated with the medical center in Salerno which was not influenced by Arab culture.

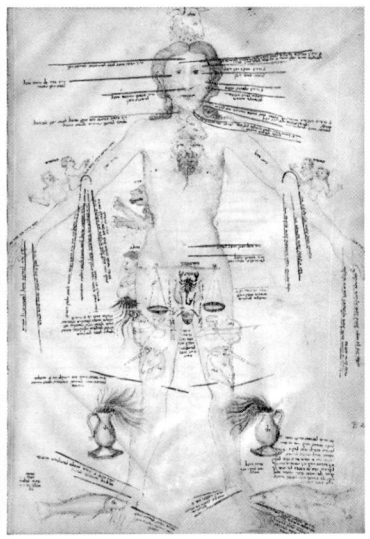

3. Zodiac and anatomy. Sephardi medical treatise. Italy, end of 14th century.

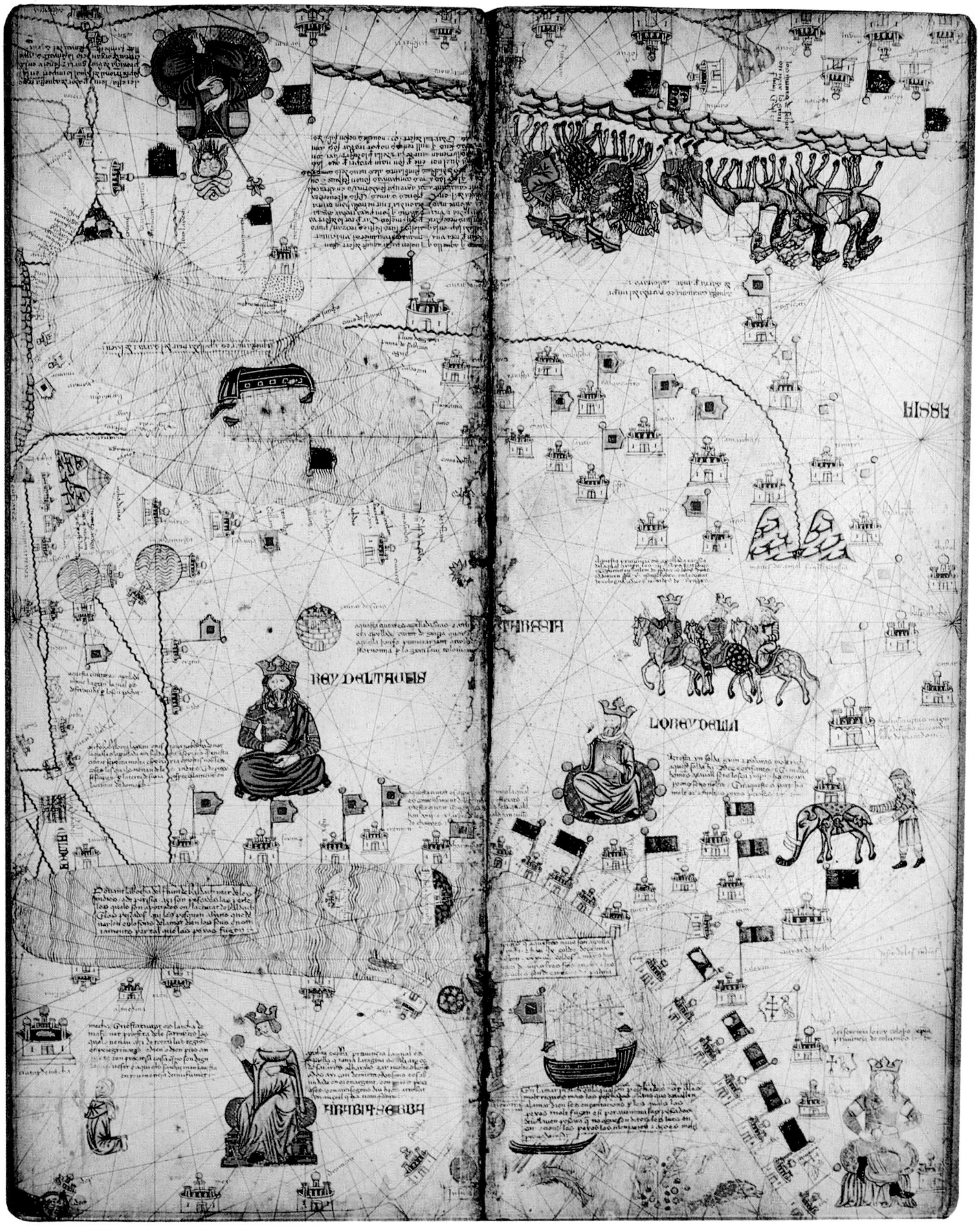

**c. 1110–1180:** Abraham ibn Daud (Johannes Avendahut Hispanus), active in Toledo under the protection of the archbishop Raymond, Maimonides' precursor in rationalist philosophy; author of books on instruments for measuring celestial bodies; translator from Arabic into Latin in all fields of scientific knowledge: astrology, astronomy, philosophy, medicine, and magic; author of books on instruments for measuring celestial bodies, on philosophy, and the occult. Because he was so prolific – his works span 23 titles – certain scholars attributed some of his works to other Jewish scientists.

**1135–1204:** Moses ben Maimon (Maimonides), the most important Jewish scholar in the Middle Ages; leader of the rationalist school, his work – particularly his *Guide of the Perplexed* – constitutes the greatest attempt at forming a synthesis between Jewish tradition and contemporary Aristotelian science. Maimonides' family fled from Almohad Spain to Egypt.

**First half of 12th century:** The Tibbonids, a family from Granada, settles in southern France; the family produces four generations of scholars and translators: Judah ben Saul ibn Tibbon known as the "father of translators"; Samuel ben Judah ibn Tibbon, translated into Hebrew Maimonides's *Guide of the Perplexed*; Moses ben Samuel ibn Tibbon, translator and famous physician; Jacob ben Machir ibn Tibbon, inventor of an original astronomical measuring instrument, the *Quadrans Novus* (*Quadrans Judaicus*).

**1252–1277:** Alfonso X ("the Wise"), King of Leon and Castille; patron of many Jewish scientists, including the astronomer Judah ben Moses ha-Kohen, author of the Alfonsine Tables, *Libros del saber de astronomia*, one of the important scientific achievements of the reign.

**1288–1344:** Levi ben Gershom de Bagnols, mathematician, astronomer, and inventor of navigation instruments; author of important scientific works which exerted a major influence on western science; his astronomical tables were based on sources found in Persia, Egypt, etc.

**Late 15th century:** Abraham ben Samuel Zacuto of Salamanca, mathematician and astronomer; his *Great Treatise*, written in Hebrew between 1473 and 1478 at the request of his patron Gonzalo de Vivero, bishop of Salamanca, and soon translated into Spanish and Latin; he develops important navigation instruments, particularly the astrolabe of copper, which are major contributions to the voyages of discovery. After the expulsion of 1492 he emigrates to Portugal and becomes court astronomer to John II and later to Manuel I; his advice is sought before Vasco da Gama's voyage to India (1496); but in the following year the forced conversion of the Jews of Portugal drives him to leave for Tunis; toward the end of his life he travels to the Holy Land.

4. Nautical atlas executed by Abraham and Judah Cresques for Pedro IV of Aragon. Spain, 1375–1377.

# Spiritual Trends in Ashkenaz

1. The so-called "Rashi's Chapel," adjoining the Worms Synagogue, built in the 17th century.

Between the post-Carolingian period and the First Crusade, the Jewish communities in the Rhine Valley were composed almost entirely of merchants engaged in long-distance trade. Yet it was at that time that the first Ashkenazi scholars made their debut: learned rabbis began producing exegetical works, biblical and talmudic commentaries, as well as *halakhic* prescriptions for everyday behavior. A high level of talmudic studies is noted in northern France and Germany from the late tenth century onward, the only non-Christian culture within an otherwise homogenous society.

Rashi (Solomon ben Isaac, c. 1040–1105) was undoubtedly the greatest biblical and talmudic commentator of all times. Under the influence of his work, the schools of Champagne and northern France would eventually supplant those of the Rhenish provinces. Based on a compromise between literal and midrashic interpretations, his biblical commentary, replete with original philological explanations, is characterized by its lucidity. His works also reflect eleventh-century circumstances by making

implicit references to the new kind of Christian aggression towards the Jews: his comments on biblical passages are often intended to refute christological interpretations which were offered by those converted Jews who placed their Judaic knowledge in the service of the Church. There are also frequent references to the tribulations of the Jews during the time of the First Crusade. Furthermore, Rashi's commentary on the Babylonian Talmud was to become the basis for all later literary activity in this field, particularly for that of the school of the *tosafot* ("additions").

The *tosafot* were glosses recording the oral, animated discussions held in the *yeshivot* of northern France in the twelfth century. In these schools a teacher and a small group of pupils would argue a talmudic question in dialectic fashion. These glosses were soon transformed into teaching material, eventually penetrating all the Jewish academies in France and Germany. This was an excellent example of the dissemination of ideas so characteristic of twelfth-century Europe. The tosafists set the intellectual standards for rabbinical scholarship and methods of teaching. The new qualities required from those transmitting rabbinical culture were mental agility, analytical abilities, and self-assured disputation. The intellectual jousts in the *tosafot* are distinctly different in tone from the sobriety of Rashi's commentaries.

The *Hasidei Ashkenaz* movement (the medieval "pietists of Germany"; not to be confused with eighteenth-century *Hasidism*) were the Jewish version of a phenomenon affecting twelfth and thirteenth-century European culture in general: religion wrestling with the values of a society undergoing rapid economic development and urbanization. *Hasidei Ashkenaz* responded to the pressure of Christian pietist movements and were also influenced by them. They stressed the special abilities of the learned and pious scholar to interpret Divine Will which, according to them, was only partially expressed in the scriptural commandments. Wonders and miracles, they believed, reveal God's nature; therefore, their literature is greatly concerned with the demonological and the magical. Like several contemporary Christian sects, these pietists felt that they were the bearers of a deeper religious awareness, and were thus subjected to stricter duties than the "simple folk." Mortification of the body, confession to a spiritual leader who could impose penitential punishment, humility, and the love of God through martyrdom – all these became hallmarks of this movement and earned them the respect of Jews outside their circles. However, as they were unable to impose their rigorous standards on the German communities, the *Hasidei Ashkenaz* considered various ways of sectarian secession.

The most important hasidic ethical work was *Sefer Hasidim* ("Book of the Pious"), which was composed largely by the great teacher Judah ha-Hassid (a figure often compared to Francis of Assisi). This is a collection of pragmatic and realistic ethical teachings covering every

| The *takkanot* of Rabbenu Gershom | Rashi | | The First Crusade |
|---|---|---|---|
| c. 1000 | c. 1040–1105 | | 1096 |

**Second half of 10th century:** Judah ha-Kohen Leontin, the first known German talmudic scholar.

**c. 950–1028:** Life of Rabbenu ("our master") Gershom. His name is associated with several *takkanot* ("directives"), such as the prohibition on polygamy and on the unauthorized reading of private letters, but there is no definitive evidence that these *takkanot* were really his.

**c. 1040–1105:** Lifespan of Rashi (Rabbi Solomon ben Isaac). Born in Troyes, he studied in Worms and Mainz, occasionally returning to these *yeshivot* after establishing his own school in Troyes.

**After 1100:** The generation of Rashi's disciples: Simhah of Vitry, Judah ben Nathan, Joseph Kara.

**First half of 12th century:** Composition of three chronicles recounting the persecutions during the First Crusade (1096).

**c. 1100–1171:** Lifespan of Jacob ben Meir Tam, called Rabbenu Tam, Rashi's grandson, the greatest of the tosafists. His nephew

Isaac of Dampierre was the most widely known tosafist in the late 12th century.

**After 1150:** Samuel he-Hasid, probable author of the first two parts of *Sefer Hasidim*, is regarded by all scholars as the founder of the *Hasidei Ashkenaz* movement.

**1171. May 26:** First blood-libel case in France: thirty two Jews are burnt at the stake in Blois after the disappearance of a Christian child. Rabbenu Tam institutes a fast on the date of that event; he apparently also coordinated attempts by the Jewish communities in Paris and in Champagne to convince King Louis VII and the Duke of Champagne to halt the spread of anti-Jewish allegations.

**1190:** Yom Tov of Joigny, a disciple of Rabbenu Tam and a synagogal poet, is said to have inspired the collective suicide of the Jews of York who took refuge in the royal castle to escape a crusaders' attempt to convert them by force.

**After 1196:** Death of Ephraim of Bonn, author of a chronicle recording the events

2. A teacher with a whip. In front of his disciple, the famous dictum of Hillel the Elder (1st century AD): "What is hateful to you, do not unto your neighbor." Coburg Pentateuch, 1395.

during the Second Crusade. He praises Bernard of Clairvaux for his endeavor to end anti-Jewish violence.

**c. 1200:** Time during which Judah he-Hasid, Samuel's son, who lived in Speyer and died in Regensburg in 1217, was active.

**1203–1204:** Meir Halevi Abulafia of Toledo writes to the French tosafists to enlist their support for his denunciation of Maimonides' position on the resurrection of the body. He receives an answer from Samson of Sens, the principal tosafist of his generation.

**1209–1211:** "The *aliyah* of three hundred rabbis" – the name given in Jewish historiography to the movement of migration to Palestine by many tosafists.

**c. 1230:** Death of Eleazar of Worms, signatory of the *takkanot* promulgated by the communities of Mainz, Worms and Speyer between 1200 and 1223. This disciple of Judah he-Hasid is better known to us than his predecessors because of his chronicle describing the attack on the Jews of Mainz during the Third Crusade (1189) and a poetic

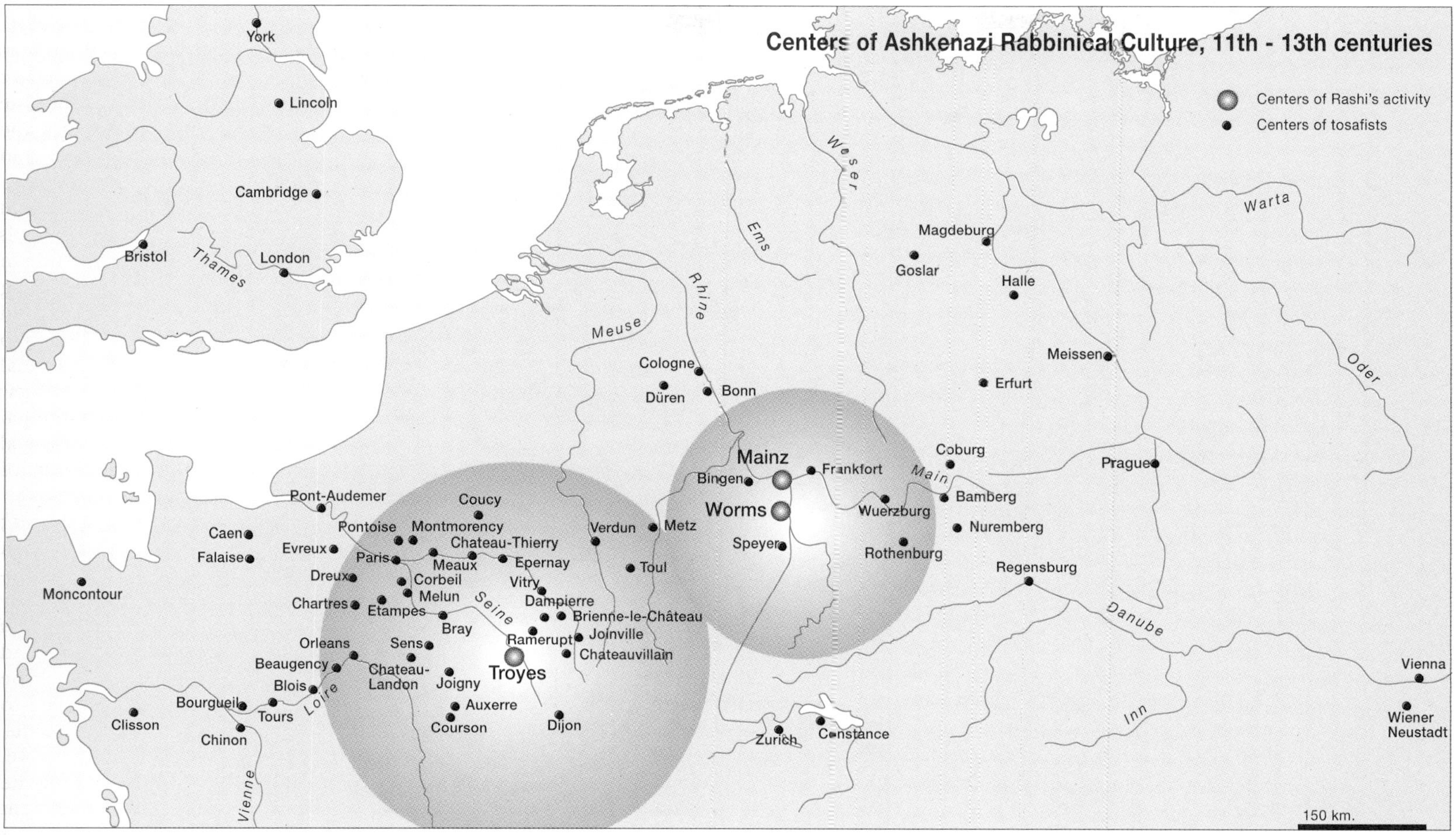

## Centers of Ashkenazi Rabbinical Culture, 11th - 13th centuries

- ◉ Centers of Rashi's activity
- ● Centers of tosafists

150 km.

aspect of life. The social doctrine of the *Hasidim* was essentially egalitarian, and perceived inequality to be the outcome of sin. Yet even in this respect, the movement's teachers related to the urban realities of the time, prescribing ways to mitigate the unjust distribution of riches by advocating virtuous ways, compassion, and charity. However, because they believed in a Heavenly law superseding the law of the Torah, their doctrine admitted certain moral modes of conduct which were unacceptable in orthodox morality. This pietist medieval movement disappeared during the second half of the thirteenth century. Ashkenazi Jewry adopted some of its ethical teachings and penitential practices; its esoteric theology, however, was overshadowed by the Sephardi Kabbalah.

| The Second Crusade | "The *aliyah* of three hundred rabbis" |
|---|---|
| 1147 | 1209–1211 |

composition describing the murder of his wife and children by crusaders in 1197.
**Before the summer of 1232:** Certain French tosafists threaten with excommunication those who study "Greek science" or read Maimonides' *Guide of the Preplexed* and his *Book of Knowledge*.
**1240:** Jehiel of Paris, head of the "talmudic academy" in Paris, is the main Jewish representative in the Disputation of Paris held at the court of Louis IX; in 1260 he emigrated to Palestine with a large number of his disciples.
**1475:** The first printed Hebrew book: Rashi's commentary on the Pentateuch, published in Reggio di Calabria.
**Early 17th century:** Printing in Yiddish of *Mayse Bukh*: didactic stories, translated from Hebrew, some of which center on the major figures of the medieval movement of *Hasidei Ashkenaz*.

*3. The Mikveh (Jewish ritual bath) in Worms, built in 1185.*

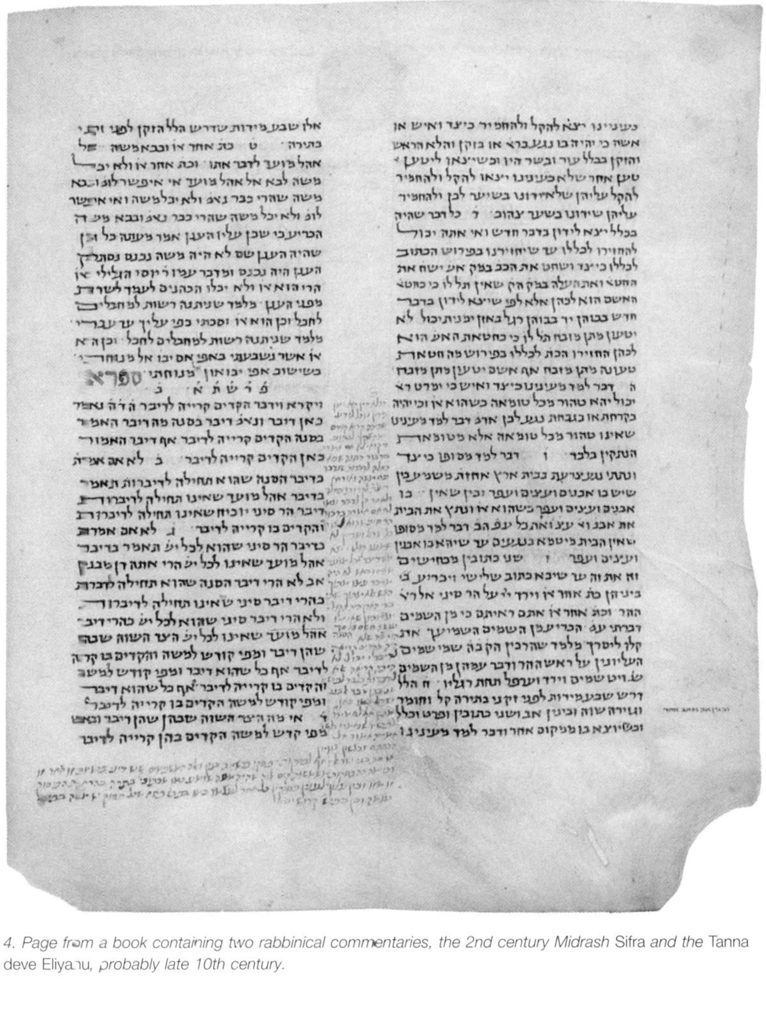

*4. Page from a book containing two rabbinical commentaries, the 2nd century Midrash Sifra and the Tanna deve Eliyahu, probably late 10th century.*

# Men of Letters in Medieval Spain

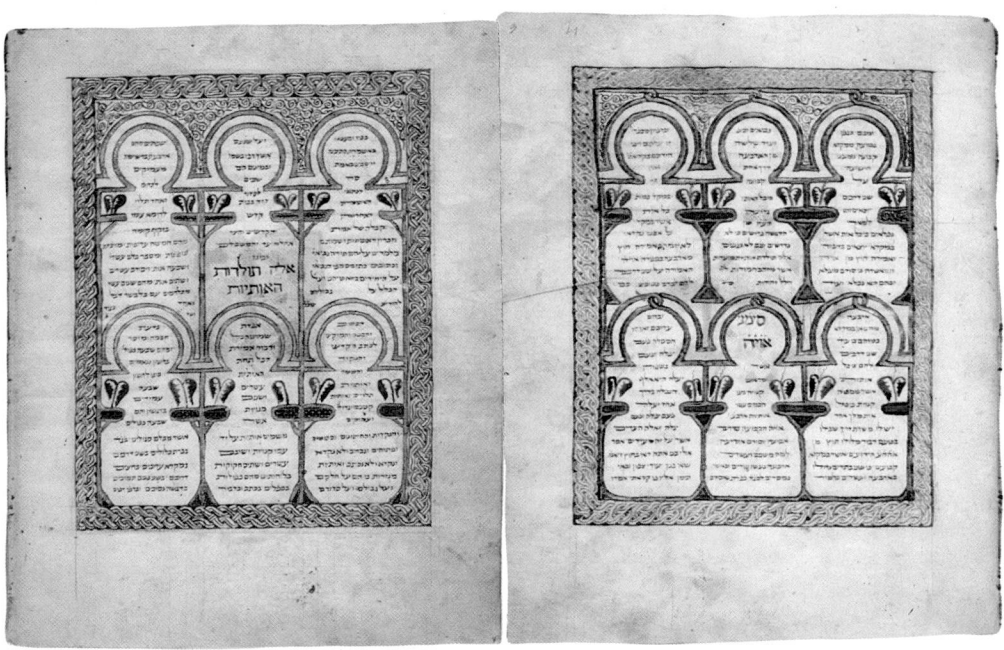

1. Sefer Dikdukei ha-Te'amin ("Rules of Accents"), a work which established the Massorah (rules of spelling and pronunciation of the biblical text), attributed to Aaron ben Asher (10th century). Spain, manuscript on animal skin, 14th century.

The Golden Age of Jewish literature in the Middle Ages was to a large extent the outcome of two centuries of interaction between Hebrew culture and the Arab-Muslim civilization. In Spain, however, the variety of literary creation was far richer than in the Abbasid caliphate of Baghdad or in North Africa. Strongly influenced by the Muslim renaissance of letters, the Jewish writers of Spain produced not only major works of philosophy and theology but also new genres of Hebrew literature.

Hebrew literature began to flourish in the Umayyad caliphate of Cordoba under Caliph Abd al-Rahman III and his Jewish vizier Hisdai ibn Shaprut during the tenth century. From the beginning, poetry and philosophy went hand in hand. Menahem ben Saruq, known for his profane poems, also compiled the first dictionary of biblical Hebrew roots, the *Mahberet*. This work provoked a fierce response from Dunash ben Labrat, leading to an extensive debate which was most beneficial to the advancement of biblical exegesis. The same Dunash ben Labrat revolutionized Hebrew poetry by introducing metrics and genres fashionable among Arab poets. At the same time, biblical exegesis and talmudic commentary were also flourishing in other Jewish intellectual centers – Lucena, Granada, Seville, Malaga, Saragossa, and Barcelona.

The fall of the Caliphate did not put an end to this brilliant culture, which continued to blossom in the small independent kingdoms that offered refuge to Cordoban exiles. The eleventh century was the age of Samuel ha-Nagid, Solomon ibn Gabirol, Moses ibn Ezra, and Judah Halevi, all of whom were great and versatile poets. Their secular poetry was concerned with love, friendship, nature, or war, while in their devotional poetry they composed hymns glorifying God and the covenant between God and his people. Their contemporaries, Judah Hayyuj and Jonah ibn Janah, laid the foundations for the scientific study of the Hebrew language. Comparative philology, in its turn, became an important tool for biblical commentators. Rabbinical scholars at Lucena were seeking ways to modernize talmudic

| Samuel ha-Nagid | Birth of Judah Halevi |
|---|---|
| 993–1056 | c. 1070 |

**929–961:** Caliphate of Abd al-Rahman III; Hisdai ibn Shaprut, physician and scholar, is vizier at the Caliph's court and a patron of Hebrew literature.

**958:** Menahem ben Saruq, secretary to Hisdai, writes his *Mahberet*, provoking the attack of Dunash ben Labrat.

**c. 1021:** The poet and philosopher Solomon ibn Gabirol (Avicebron in Latin) is born in Malaga.

**1031:** End of the Umayyad caliphate in Cordoba; the small Muslim kingdoms that take its place will survive until 1094.

**1038:** Samuel ha-Nagid (Ismail ibn Nagrela) is vizier to Badis, the Berber king of Granada; his writings begin the Golden Age of Jewish poetry in Spain.

**c. 1040:** Jonah ibn Janah, a philologist born in Cordoba c. 985, writes his *Kitab al-Tanqih* (Book of Grammar) in Saragossa.

**1055:** Moses ibn Ezra is born in Granada; a great poet and literary theoretician, dies in Castile after 1135.

**c. 1070:** Judah Halevi, the greatest Jewish poet in Spain, is born in Tudela (Navarre).

**1089:** Death of Isaac ibn Ghayyat; he is succeeded by Isaac Alfasi (1013–1103) and then by Joseph ibn Migash (1077–1114) as Talmud teachers in Lucena.

**1094–1145:** Andalusia is ruled by the Almoravides; many Jews escape to Christian Spain.

**1136:** Death of Abraham bar Hiyya from Catalonia, author of

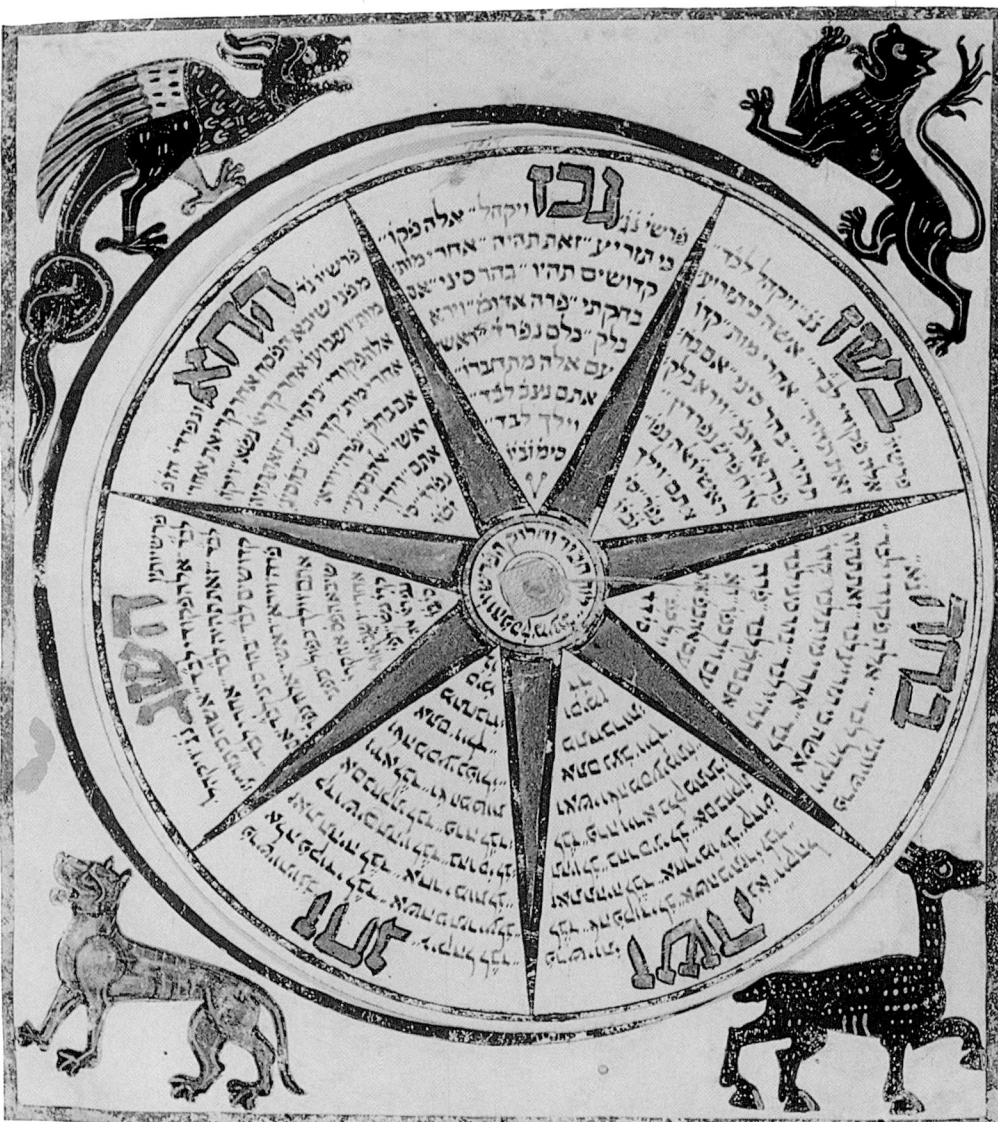

3. A liturgical calendar with a mobile parchment disk. Castile, 1300–1301.

law, while philosophers were critically comparing Jewish theology to other religious systems.

The accession of the Almoravides at the end of the eleventh century and of the Almohads fifty years later threatened the very existence of the Jewish communities. The decline of Jewish culture in Andalusia was swift and sudden. Henceforth its center would be in the northern part of the peninsula, in Christian Spain, which although less developed, was for a time more tolerant.

Jewish literature in the Christian kingdoms never reached the heights of the Andalusian period, but it had an important significance of its own. Emphasis now shifted to the sciences, medicine, and to the translation of scientific and literary works. By incorporating Arabic traditions, the art of narrative prose opened new avenues in works such as *Sefer Tahkemoni* by Judah Al-Harizi, with its use of the Arabic form of rhyming prose, or in the wide variety of historical chronicles and travel literature. Poetry, more realistic than in the Andalusian period, now included reflections on social and political issues.

The most animated intellectual debate, however, revolved around questions of philosophy and theology. In the first half of the thirteenth century, the problems raised by Maimonides evoked fierce antagonism between his disciples and their anti-rationalist opponents. Disputations with Christians were an important arena for incisive polemical arguments, but they were also a further expression of the deteriorating relations between the Jews and their neighbors. By accentuating differences between Judaism and Christianity, they often led to forced conversions. Some Jews escaped into mysticism and Kabbalah, cultivated mainly in Gerona and Leon, while Toledo and Catalonia remained centers of more traditional scholarship such as Hebrew law and talmudic commentary.

The gradual decline in Jewish cultural life was accelerated by the anti-Jewish outbreaks of 1391. The precarious situation of the communities was no longer conducive to intense intellectual activity, and the last century of Jewish life in Spain would leave very little for future generations to admire.

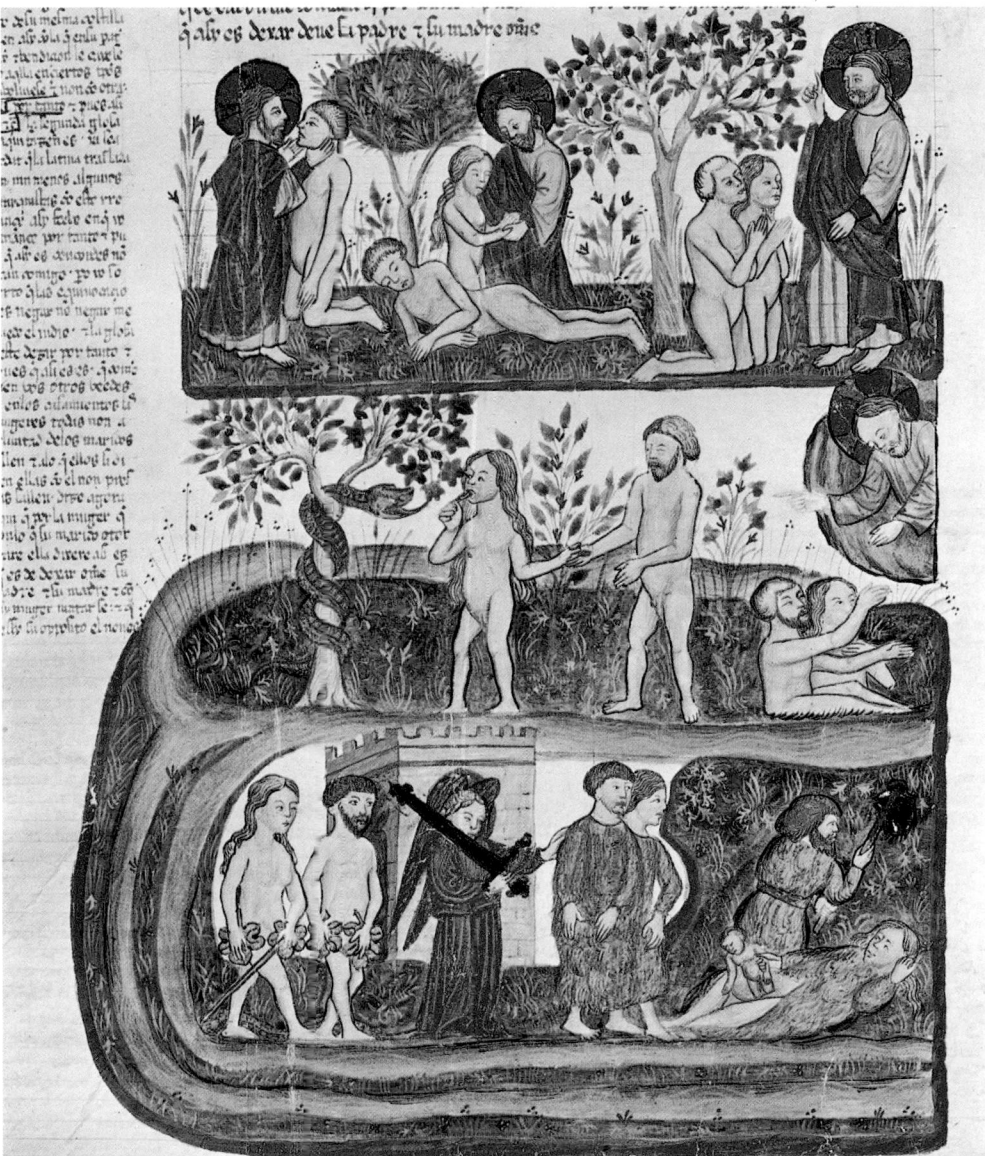

*2. The Alba Bible, translated from Hebrew to Castilian between 1422 and 1433 by Moses Arragel of Gudalajara. Commissioned by Luis de Guzman, Master of the Order of Calatrava. Illuminated by artists of Toledo.*

| Birth of Maimonides | The *Zohar* |
|---|---|
| c. 1138 | c. 1280 |

scientific works.

**1141:** Judah Halevi dies on his way to Jerusalem, or – according to tradition – is murdered near the city walls; end of the Golden Age.

**1147:** Rise of the Almohads; the major centers of Jewish culture in Andalusia are destroyed.

**c. 1150:** In Toledo Abraham ibn Daud composes his *Book of Tradition*, a history of talmudic scholarship.

**c. 1194–1270:** Moses ben Nahman (Nahmanides), philosopher and Kabbalist in Verona.

**1204:** Death of Moses ben Maimon (Maimonides) in Cairo.

**1230:** Death of Judah Al-Harizi, traveller, translator, and poet.

**1232:** End of Almohad rule; Granada remains the last Muslim principality on Spanish soil.

**1252–1284:** Alfonso X of Toledo encourages scientific translations, with the aid of Jewish scholars; Todros Abulafia (1247–1306) is court poet.

**c. 1280:** Moses de Leon composes the *Zohar* ("Book of Splendor") – the greatest work of Castilian Kabbalah.

**1412:** Death of Hasdai Crescas, anti-rationalist philosopher from Catalonia.

**1437–1508:** Isaac Abrabanel, statesman and biblical commentator.

**1452–c. 1515:** Abraham Zacuto, astronomer and author of scientific works.

**1492:** Fall of Granada and expulsion of the Jews from Spain.

*4. Commemorative tablet on the east wall of the synagogue in Cordoba, 1314–1315. The characters are of astonishingly modern form, resembling that of Hebrew printing today.*

# Maimonides

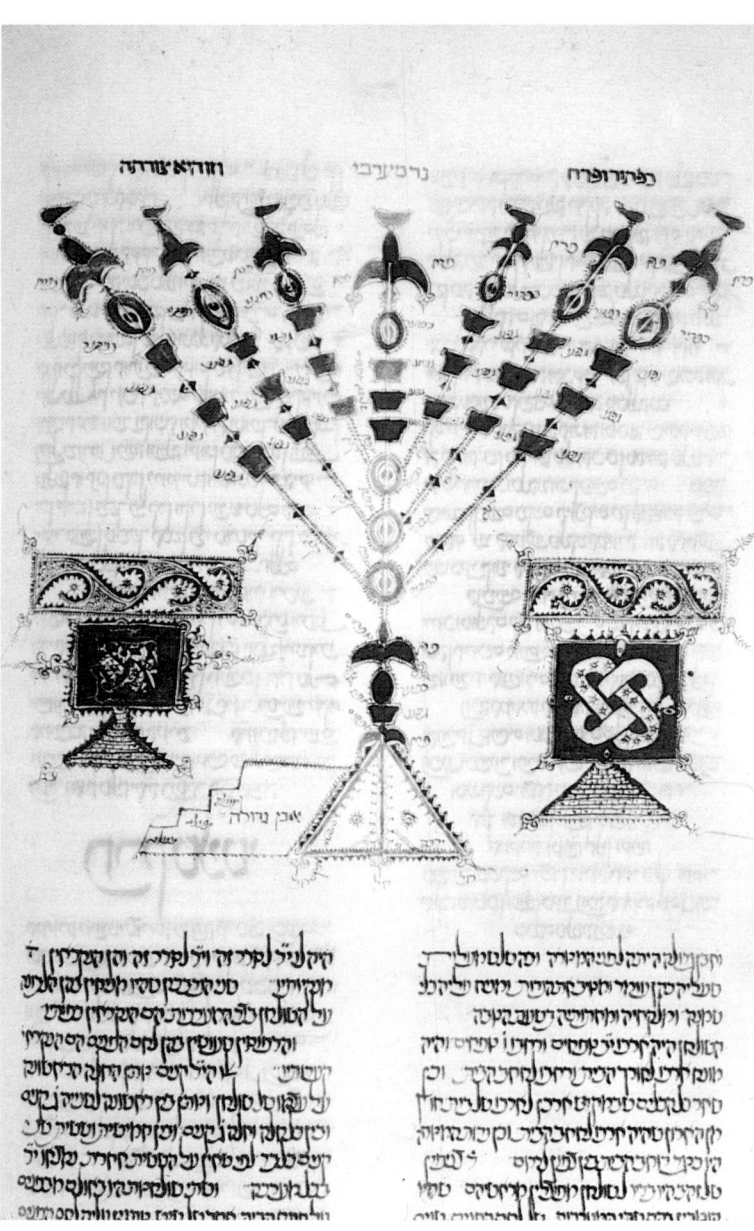

*1. Manuscript of Mishneh Torah. Spain, c.1460.*

aimonides (Moses ben Maimon, known by his Hebrew acronym "Rambam"), was the most illustrious figure in Judaism since the talmudic era. His influence on the future development of Judaism was incalculable, and his genius earned him the epithet "the Eagle." More than any scholar before him, Maimonides felt that it was incumbent upon him to play a decisive role in the culture to which he belonged: to give an account of its history, to offer a vision of its future, and to introduce by way of his own work an entirely new course of direction.

His commentary on the Mishnah in Arabic, completed in 1168, established his authority among the Jews in Islamic countries. But it was the Hebrew translation of his fourteen-book code, *Mishneh Torah* ("Repetition of the Law"), which gained him the reputation of the greatest rabbinical scholar in post-talmudic times. His status as a venerated spiritual guide enabled him to intervene in the affairs of many diaspora communities. To North African Jews, who had been forcibly Islamized, he offered advice on how to survive by secretly adhering to their Jewish faith, a kind of "marranism" *avant la lettre*. To the Yemenite community he sent his famous epistle of caution against messianic enthusiasm.

*Mishneh Torah* was an enterprise of immense proportions, motivated by complex reasons. Maimonides was pursuing, in fact, several aims simultaneously: recapitulating rabbinical legislation in a systematic and convenient exposition, without the cumbersome apparatus of quotations, "so that thus the entire Oral Law might become systematically known to all... so that all rules shall be accessible to young and old"; replacing the Talmud, the study of which should henceforth be reserved only to the intellectual elite; making an inventory of opinions and beliefs within their philosophical context – particularly in his *Sefer ha-Madda* ("Book of Science") which forms the first part of this work.

During the 1180s Maimonides wrote his major philosophical work, *Guide of the Perplexed*. As its title indicates, the book was intended for the Jewish intellectual who was firm in his belief, but having studied philosophy, was perplexed by biblical anthropomorphisms. Well aware of the dangers of teaching esoteric matters to the masses, Maimonides wrote enigmatically, making contradictory statements, employing paradoxes, leaving the perceptive reader to uncover the author's true ideas. Thus it is hardly surprising that this work has been a source of bewilderment to modern commentators no less than to its medieval students.

The Maimonidean controversy broke out during his lifetime. It concerned above all the question of the resurrection of the body which Maimonides seemed to deny. He apparently insisted on the immortality of the soul of the sage-philosopher, independently of any divine retribution. The dispute was then broadened to include other issues. In southern France, the question of whether the reading of the *Guide* should be

| Letter on Forced Conversion | | Mishneh Torah | Letter on the Resurrection of the Dead |
|---|---|---|---|
| c. 1160 | | 1168–1178 | 1190 |

**1138:** Moses ben Maimon is born in Cordoba to a family of scholars and dignitaries; in his own genealogical record he mentions *dayyanim* (rabbinical judges) like his father, Maimon ben Joseph, and talmudic scholars that go back seven generations.
**1147:** Conquest of Spain by the Almohads, a North-African Berber dynasty, who force the *dhimmis*, both Jews and Christians, to adopt Islam at least outwardly.
**c. 1156:** Maimonides writes *Millot Higgayon* ("Words of Logic"), a small treatise based on the works of the Muslim philosopher Al-Farabi (10th century).
**1159–1160:** The Maimon family flees to Fez in Morocco. Maimonides' father writes his *Iggeret ha-Nehamah* ("Letter of Consolation") to Jews under Almohad rule; Maimonides himself writes *Iggeret ha-Shemad* ("Letter on Forced Conversion") also named *Ma'amar Kiddush ha-Shem* ("Treatise on the Sanctification of the Divine Name [Martyrdom]").
**1161:** Maimonides begins his commentary

on the Mishnah.
**1165:** Maimonides leaves Fez for St. Jean d'Acre.
**1166:** Arriving with his family from Alexandria, Maimonides takes up residence in Fostat (Old Cairo).
**1168:** Maimonides begins writing *Mishneh Torah*, which was completed in 1178.
**1168–1169:** Weakened by the disintegration of Fatimid rule, Egypt is invaded by the Crusaders who attack the town of Bilbeis (eastern Egypt), capturing its inhabitants. Maimonides leads the operation in order to ransom Jewish prisoners.
**1170–1171:** Maimonides is mentioned in Arabic sources as *rais al-yahud* ("leader of the Jews").
**1171:** Accession of the Ayyubid (Sunnite) dynasty in Egypt. Maimonides becomes court physician to vizier Al-Fadil.
**1173:** Maimonides' brother, David, drowns in the Indian Ocean while on a business trip.
**c. 1185:** Maimonides becomes a regular adviser to vizier Al-Fadil and other dignitaries

in the entourage of the Ayyubid Sultan.
**1190:** *Iggeret Tehiyyat ha-Metim* ("Letter on the Resurrection of the Dead").
**1190–1191:** Maimonides completes the writing of *Guide of the Perplexed (Moreh Nevukhim)*.
**1194:** *Letter on Astrology* addressed to scholars in southern France.
**1198–1199:** Letters to the communities in Provence, particularly to the community of Lunel.
**1199:** Maimonides' letter to his Hebrew translator, Samuel ibn Tibbon of Provence, discussing the translation of *Guide of the Preplexed*, the philosophical works he consulted, and the daily fee the translator received for his work.
**1199–1200:** Maimonides is appointed personal physician to Al-Afdal, Saladin's son.
**1202:** Meir ha-Levi Abulafia of Toledo asks the rabbis of Lunel to condemn Maimonides' theses which, according to Abulafia, deny all

*4. Maimonides' house in Fez.*

allowed at all had wide ranging implications. The conflict reached such proportions that the "anti-Maimonideans" brought their accusations to the Inquisition, claiming that the *Guide* constituted a heresy. Copies of the work were indeed committed to the fire c.1233. This denunciation, however, brought such disgrace on Maimonides' opponents, that hence no one dared to attack openly the Master himself; the attacks were now directed at his disciples, who were accused of spreading dangerous philosophical teachings. During the third stage, a vehement dispute over the general legitimacy of philosophical studies and of allegorical interpretations of the Bible ended in compromise: men over the age of twenty-five were permitted to study philosophy, once they had completed their talmudic education (Barcelona, 1305).

In the long run, Maimonides and his oeuvre were not only accepted, they were even canonized. But the *Mishneh Torah*, appended with numerous glosses and commentaries, failed to replace the Talmud and became only one of the elements of talmudic studies. The *Guide*, while regarded as one of the great monuments of Judaism, did not generate further philosophical reflection. Maimonides had anticipated an immediate outcry, but believed he would be accepted by posterity. Ironically, what happened was quite the contrary: the work was well received, but the project failed.

3. Statue of Maimonides, erected in Cordoba, city of his birth, in 1964.

The Guide of the Perplexed *in Samuel ibn Tibbon's Hebrew translation. Manuscript copied and illuminated Barcelona in 1348.*

| Guide of the Perplexed | Letter on Astrology |
|---|---|
| 1190–1191 | 1194 |

elief in the resurrection of the body. Thirty ears later Abulafia was asked by Nahmanides to take part again in the controversy, but on this occasion he refused.
**1204:** Maimonides dies in Cairo.
**1230–1233:** The controversy over Maimonides' works rocks the Spanish and French communities; the rabbis of southern France pronounce an excommunication on anyone who reads the *Guide of the Perplexed* or seeks after "Greek wisdom" (the rabbis of Paris possibly burned the copies of Maimonides' works in their possession); a counter-excommunication is proclaimed by the Maimonidean camp of Provence" (southern France); letters of protest are sent to the rabbis of northern France; David Kimhi goes to Spain to gather the support of Spanish communities for the measures adopted by the pro-Maimonideans. In Spain, excommunication of anti-Maimonideans is proclaimed by the communities of Aragon (Summer, 1232); intervention of Moses ben Nahman

(Nahmanides), who obtains the retraction of the excommunication pronounced by the rabbis of northern France; the pro-Maimonideans refuse to retract their ban; their adversaries therefore denounce them to the Inquisition.
**1303:** Abba Mari of Montpellier writes to Solomon ben Abraham Adret of Barcelona asking him to take measures against the advance of "disbelief."
**1303–1305:** Correspondence concerning the proposals of Abba Mari between the communities of southern France and those of Spain.
**1305. July 31:** Excommunication pronounced in Barcelona against whoever reads works of science and metaphysics before the age of twenty-five, and against adherents of allegorical interpretations which reject the notion of revelation.
**July 1305–September 1306:** Excommunications and counter-excommunications between "rationalists" and "anti-rationalists" in southern France.

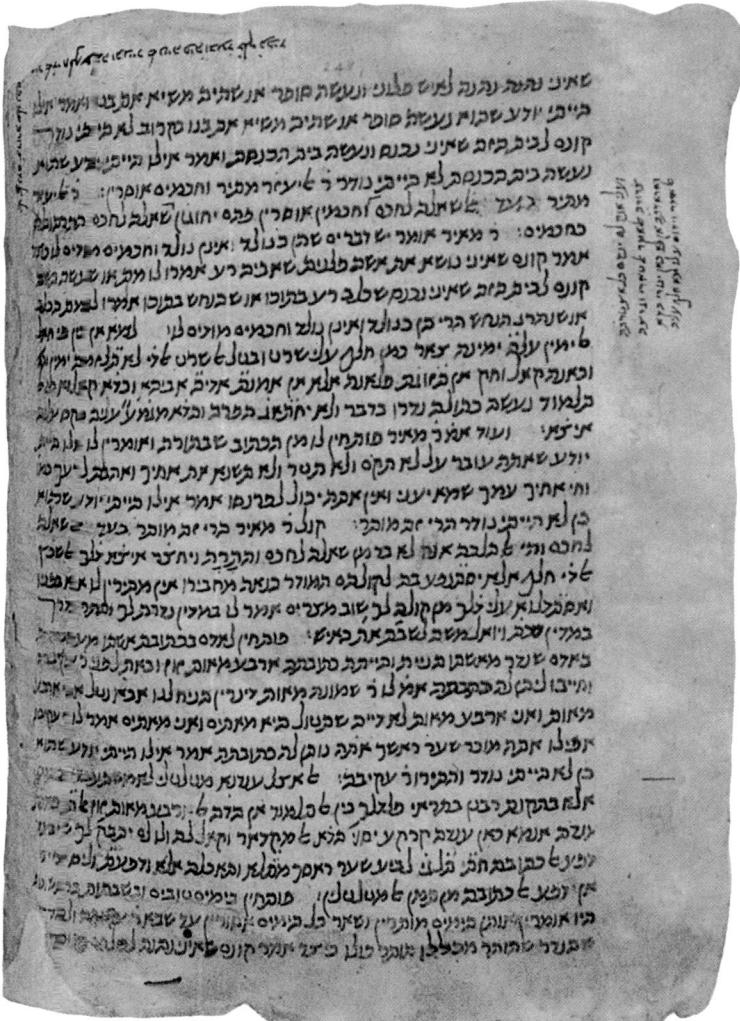

5. Maimonides' commentary on the Mishnah, written in Arabic in Hebrew characters. An autographed manuscript, Morocco or Egypt, 1161–1168.

# The Ruling Powers and the Jews

It was during the central Middle Ages, between the First Crusade and the Black Death, that the Catholic Church defined its policy towards the Jews. Its attitude was based on the Augustinian doctrine which ascribed an historical mission to the Jews as witnesses to the truth of Christianity. Their existence within Christendom was portrayed as double testimony. As the original recipients of God's messianic prophecies, and despite having rejected them out of blind wickedness, the Jews indirectly attested to the authenticity of these same prophecies. At the same time, their status as a despised nation, living in ignominy and misery, was testimony to God's wrath and to the intervention of Providence, constantly penalizing them for having rejected Christ.

This theological approach implied an acceptance of the continued presence of Jews. Yet many tried to undermine this relatively tolerant leaning. Talmudic texts which stressed the supremacy of the *Halakhah* as its decisions were not based on the dubious claim of supernatural inspiration were exploited by learned theologians. In the twelfth century, Peter of Cluny (the Venerable) and the instigators of the "trial" against the Talmud in the following century, fulminated against the pretensions of the Jewish Law, denouncing it as an illegitimate, even diabolical, addition to the Scriptures. Post-biblical Judaism, they said, could be defined as a form of heresy and therefore legitimately extirpated. But the

Papacy cut short such ideas. There was no way in which the Church could condemn the Jewish notion of Oral Law and Tradition without compromising its own claim of being the sole interpreter of the Holy Scriptures. Nevertheless, while it did adhere to the principle of toleration, the Church did not fully exercise its influence to ensure that tolerance was respected in practice. For example, although most popes during the twelfth and thirteenth centuries issued bulls prohibiting conversion by force, canon law, by distinguishing between absolute and conditional constraints, did not invalidate conversions obtained by threat. Furthermore, despite papal doubts concerning blood libels, the Church did not restrain the local clergy from spreading such accusations which resulted in the killing of many Jews.

Another aspect of Church doctrine concerned the social inferiority and subordination of the Jews. The rule of denying them power applied not only to public office but to every social relationship of an asymmetrical nature (master-servant, physician-patient), and to all daily-life situations which placed the Jew in a position of authority over a Christian. And since all contact between Christian and Jew posed the danger of undue influence, the Church recommended a policy of segregation. The obligation of wearing distinguishable garments or a special badge was imposed on Jews in order to prevent sexual relations between them and non-Jewish women. Popular fears of the Jew, although deriving from very different emotions than those guiding the theologians, were thus sanctioned by the official policy of the ecclesiastical authorities.

Throughout the High Middle Ages, Jews were considered to be the responsibility of the central secular authority in each country. The protection offered to the Jews by European monarchs while the crusading spirit was whipping up anti-Jewish propaganda and riots only increased their dependence. Emperor Frederick II, borrowing from the Church the notion of Jewish servitude, defined the condition of the Jew as that of slaves, or serfs, of the imperial treasury – a formula later used both in their defense as well as to justify the money exacted from Jews "belonging" to the sovereign. Some kings and princes, however, ultimately became scrupulous, fearing that revenue extracted from the Jew implicated them in the sin of usury. Hence the attempts at legislation intended to urge the Jews to forgo financial involvement in favor of "honest" manual labor or lawful trade. In 1230 Louis IX of France issued the Ordinance of Melun which forbade Jews to engage in moneylending. The King of England, Edward I, forbade the taking of interest in 1275. These anti-usury laws undoubtedly contributed to the impoverishment of the Jews, perhaps to the extent that they were no longer useful to the crown. The decisions to expel the Jews from England in 1290 and from France in 1306 (in circumstances which are still obscure), were the first steps in the process of purging Catholic Europe of Jews.

*1. Recognizable by their garments, Jews are depicted at the bottom of the medieval social hierarchy. Illustration from a German book of laws, 12th century.*

| Bernard of Clairvaux protects the Jews of the Rhine | The Fourth Lateran Council |
|---|---|
| **1146–1147** | **1215** |

**1096:** Massacres during the First Crusade.
**1097:** Emperor Henry IV allows Jews who were forcibly converted in the previous year to return to their faith.
**c. 1120:** The first *Sicut Judaeis* bull – a comprehensive act of protection for Jews; later renewed by Innocent III (1205) stipulating that it applies only to those Jews who refrain from subversive activity against Christianity.
**1146–1147:** Preparations for the Second Crusade. Peter of Cluny advises Louis VII to confiscate Jewish property to help finance the crusade. Bernard of Clairvaux goes to the Rhine Valley to stop the anti-Jewish campaign conducted by the monk Raoul.
**1182:** Frederick Barbarossa stresses the duty of the emperor, prescribed by justice and reason, to defend the rights of his subjects, including non-Christians.
**1198–1231:** Eighteen conventions between the King of France and his barons define their respective rights over "their" Jews.
**1205:** Pope Innocent III denounces the

ingratitude of the Jews who are "like a mouse in one's pocket, like a snake around one's loins."
**1215:** Decisions of the Fourth Lateran Council: obligation to wear a distinctive garment or badge and a prohibition on "immoderate" usury (implying the right to take "moderate" interest).
**1230:** Decree of Louis IX defining the subordination of the Jews to the king and to their lords "as if they were their serfs."
**1236. July:** Frederick II of Hohenstaufen refutes an accusation of ritual murder.
**1237. April:** Frederick II: "Imperial authority has from ancient times condemned the Jew to eternal servitude for their sins."
**1239:** The apostate Nicholas Donin presents Pope Gregory IX with a list of thirty-five indictments against the Talmud.
**June:** Letter from Pope Gregory IX to the bishops and to the kings of England, France, Castile, and Portugal, demanding the seizure of all copies of the Talmud for examination of their content; only Louis IX promptly

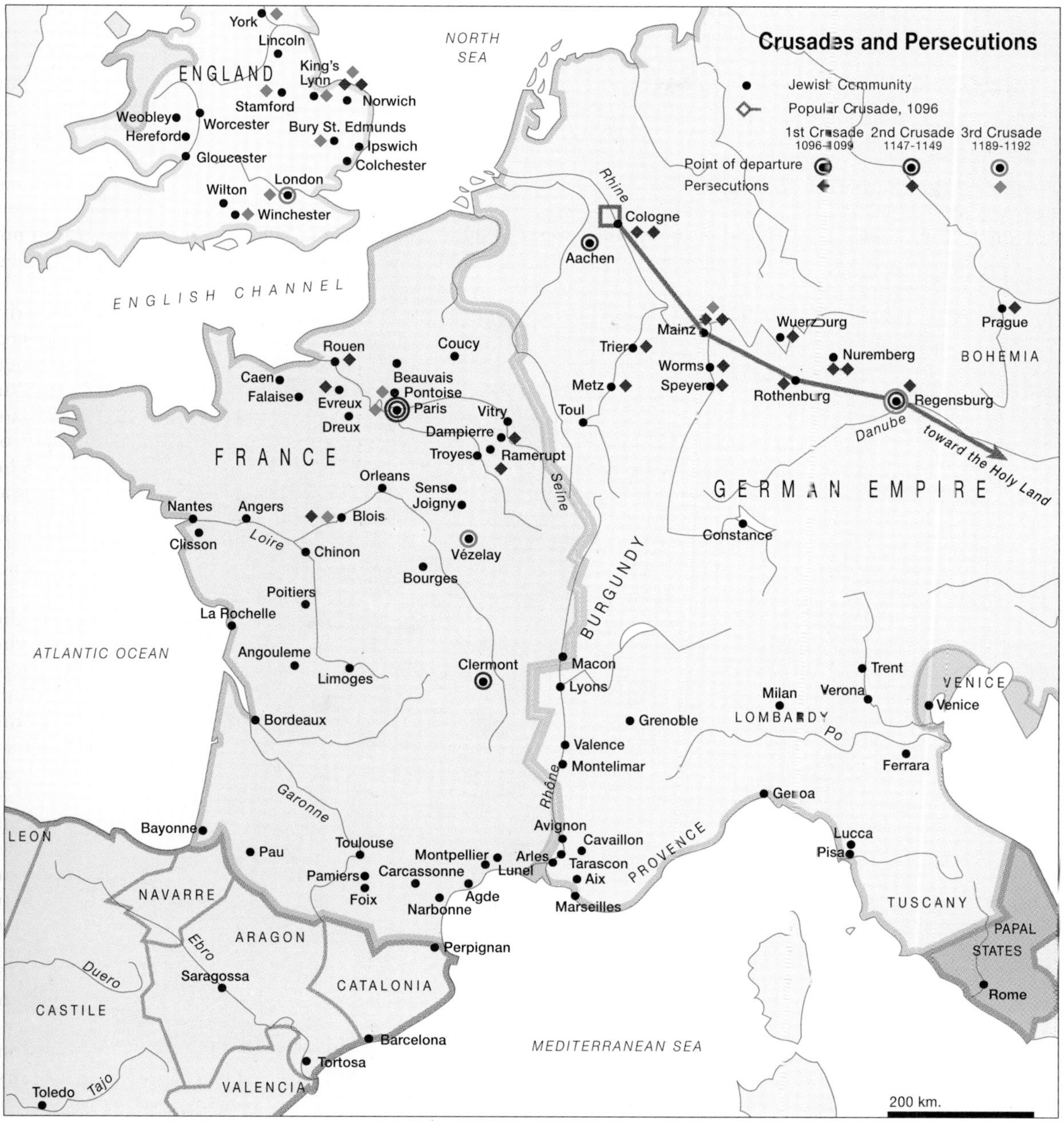

## Crusades and Persecutions

◆ Jewish Community
◇ Popular Crusade, 1096

| | 1st Crusade | 2nd Crusade | 3rd Crusade |
|---|---|---|---|
| | 1096-1099 | 1147-1149 | 1189-1192 |

◉ Point of departure
◆ Persecutions

### ENGLAND

York, Lincoln, King's Lynn, Stamford, Norwich, Weobley, Worcester, Hereford, Bury St. Edmunds, Ipswich, Gloucester, Colchester, Wilton, London, Winchester

NORTH SEA

ENGLISH CHANNEL

ATLANTIC OCEAN

### FRANCE

Rouen, Coucy, Caen, Beauvais, Falaise, Pontoise, Evreux, Paris, Dreux, Dampierre, Vitry, Troyes, Ramerupt, Orleans, Sens, Joigny, Nantes, Angers, Blois, Clisson, Chinon, Vézelay, Poitiers, Bourges, La Rochelle, Angouleme, Clermont, Limoges, Bordeaux, Macon, Lyons, Grenoble, Valence, Montelimar, Avignon, Cavaillon, Toulouse, Montpellier, Arles, Tarascon, Pamiers, Carcassonne, Lunel, Aix, Foix, Agde, Marseilles, Narbonne, Bayonne, Pau, Perpignan

Rhine, Seine, Loire, Rhône, Garonne

Cologne, Aachen, Mainz, Trier, Worms, Metz, Speyer, Toul, Wuerzburg, Nuremberg, Rothenburg, Regensburg, Constance, Trent, Verona, Milan, Venice, Ferrara, Genoa, Lucca, Pisa, Rome

### GERMAN EMPIRE

BOHEMIA — Prague
BURGUNDY
LOMBARDY — Po
VENICE
PROVENCE
TUSCANY
PAPAL STATES

Danube — toward the Holy Land

### LEON / NAVARRE / ARAGON / CATALONIA / CASTILE / VALENCIA

Bordeaux, Saragossa, Barcelona, Tortosa, Toledo

Ebro, Duero, Tajo

MEDITERRANEAN SEA

200 km.

2. The Jewish troubador Susskind von Trimberg (c. 1200–1250) performing before a bishop. Miniature, Zurich, 14th century.

3. The Franciscan Berthold of Regensburg (c. 1210–1272). Although he condemned the Jewish practice of usury, Berthold preached against attacks on Jews and forced conversions. Miniature, 1447.

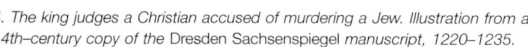

| Disputation of Paris | Thomas Aquinas' *De regimine Judaeorum* | Expulsion from England | Expulsion from France |
|---|---|---|---|
| 1240 | 1261 | 1290 | 1306 |

4. The king judges a Christian accused of murdering a Jew. Illustration from a 14th-century copy of the Dresden Sachsenspiegel manuscript, 1220–1235.

5. Trial and execution of a Jew accused of possessing Christian ritual objects. Detail from the copy of the Dresden Sachsenspiegel.

complies with the pope's request.
**1240. June:** Disputation over the Talmud, in the form of a trial, between Nicholas Donin and four rabbis, the most famous among them being Jehiel of Paris.
**1242:** Burning of the Talmud in Paris.
**1247. August:** Pope Innocent IV orders confiscated Talmud copies to be returned to the Jews.

**c. 1261:** Thomas Aquinas, *De regimine Judaeorum.* In his will the Duke of Brabant orders the expulsion of the Jews unless they renounced usury; his widow Aleyde, acting as regent, is reluctant to carry out the order and turns to Thomas for advice; the latter recommends mitigating the harsh fiscal policy towards the Jews and using the revenues obtained from their taxation on works for the common good.
**1263. July:** Disputation of Barcelona, in the presence of King James I, between the apostate Pablo Christiani and Moses ben Nahman (Nahmanides).
**1275:** Edward I's *Statutum de Judaismo,* prohibits Jewish moneylending.
**1281. January:** Alfonso X of Castile orders the wholesale arrest of Jews and demands an enormous ransom for their release.
**1290:** Expulsion of the Jews from England.
**1306:** Expulsion of the Jews from France.
**1315:** Louis X authorizes the return of the Jews to France under certain restrictive conditions. A new expulsion order is issued in 1322.
**1319–1321:** Renewed campaign against the Talmud.

# Christians and Jews

1. The Church Triumphant...

Historians usually regard the Crusades as a turning point in the persecution of Jews in Europe during the Middle Ages. Indeed, when the bands of crusaders passed through the Rhineland in 1096, they perpetrated massacres of Jews on an unprecedented scale. However, a chronological fact does not in itself constitute an explanation.

The first real "pogroms" occurred towards the end of the twelfth century. It is, of course, an anachronism to use the words "pogrom" and "antisemitism" in the context of the Middle Ages, but it helps to stress the radical novelty of the phenomenon. Hatred of the Jews was internalized, and had become part of a mental framework which was to last in different variations until the end of the Middle Ages. The impurity of the Jew, it was said, was a threat to the community and could contaminate its women, children, goods, and religion. Fear and disgust led to libels and imaginary tales: Jews poison wells, kill or devour children in their rituals, desecrate the Host, plot with the enemies of Christianity. Therefore, exclusion, expulsion, and massacres of Jews were seen as practical measures to safeguard public health. It was the co-existence of all these elements and their cumulative effect which determined the nature of medieval antisemitism after the end of the twelfth century.

The emergence of this new attitude could be attributed to a transition from a competition that had been resolved into a renewed process of acute rivalry. Before the twelfth century the Jew was perceived as an archaic representative of a religion which had been surpassed by Christianity. That perception engendered laws prohibiting proselytizing and led to social tension, riots, and sometimes even massacres against the "enemies of Christ." Actual rivalry, however, meant that the two populations were confronting one another and contending concurrently (and not in the distant past) with the same problems.

Two examples taken from the spheres of marriage laws and of biblical exegesis may serve to illustrate the transition from one conception to another. In the twelfth-century monasteries a new version of the Judas story emerged, grafted upon the Oedipal legend: before betraying Christ, Judas Iscariot killed his father and married his mother. The abundance of twelfth-century religious texts on incest reveal the obsession of European society at the time with marital and family problems. The Gregorian Reform of the eleventh century had prohibited marriage between cousins down to the seventh degree, calculated by a method more rigorous than ever before. In this manner the Church prevented all marriages of relatives, a practice which had been an important mainstay of feudal society. Only the Jews continued to practice endogamy (marriage within the extended family) since Church prohibitions did not apply to them and because their existence in closed and scattered communities limited their choice of spouses. Their Christian neighbors,

2. ...and the Synagogue blindfolded. Strasbourg Cathedral, c.1230.

| The first blood-libel case | | Burning of the Talmud in Paris | The ritual-murder allegation in Trent |
|---|---|---|---|
| **1144** | | **1242** | **1475** |

**Middle of 12th century:** The first Oedipal versions of the life of Judas appear in monastic circles.
**1144:** "Martyrdom" of young William of Norwich (East Anglia), supposedly killed by Jews. His remains were transferred to Norwich Cathedral in 1171. Although not officially canonized, the abundance of iconographic representations and the miracles recited by Thomas of Monmouth will perpetuate his memory. This is the first instance of the libel repeated until the 19th century: during Passover, the Jews have to kill a child, crucify him, and drink his blood as part of their ritual. The year 1144 also witnessed the first systematic attack on the Talmud (Peter the Venerable).
**1171:** The first pogrom caused by the new myth: the Jews of Blois are accused of killing a young Christian; thirty of them are burned at the stake.
**1179:** "Martyrdom" of young Richard of Pontoise or of Paris, recounted by Rigord and Guillaume of Breton; in the 15th century

Robert Gaguin will write the Passion of this Richard.
**1180:** "Martyrdom" of Herbert of Huntingdon (central England).
**1182:** Philip Augustus expels the Jews from the royal domain.
**1215:** The Fourth Lateran Council imposes a series of severe restrictions on the Jews.
**1242:** Burning of the Talmud in Paris by order of King Louis IX.
**1247:** Innocent IV's bull, *Lacrimabilem Judaeorum*, refutes the allegation that Jewish law prescribes the ritual consumption of a Christian child's heart; the same condemnation of the blood-libel will be reiterated in 1255 by Pope Alexander IV and again in 1272 by Gregory X.
**1250:** "Martyrdom" of Domingo of Val (Aragon); a Passion will be written about him in the 14th century, and a confraternity in Saragossa will be dedicated to him in the 15th century.
**1255:** "Martyrdom" of Hugh of Lincoln, recorded by Matthew Paris.

**1265:** The Oedipal version of the life of Judas is included in the *Legende dorée* of Jacques de Voragine.
**1287:** "Martyrdom" of young Werner of Oberwesel (the Rhineland); his cult was very popular at the end of the Middle Ages and in the 16th century. Throughout the 13th century accusations of the desecration of the Host by Jews are included in the *exempla* literature of the preachers.
**1290:** Edward I expels the Jews from England.
**14th century:** The ritual murder libel becomes more complex: the Jews kill Christian children in order to obtain the Host and desecrate it.
**1303:** "Martyrdom" of Conrade of Weisensee in Erfurt, central Germany.
**1306:** Expulsion of the Jews from France by Philip IV.
**1321:** Popular stories accuse the lepers of poisoning the wells in southeast France by the orders of Jews and Muslims from Spain.
**1348:** In southeast France the Black Death

epidemic is attributed to a Jewish plot.
**1429:** "Martyrdom" of Louis of Ravensburg (southern Germany).
**1462:** "Martyrdom" of André of Rinn (Tyrol).
**1475:** "Martyrdom" of Simon of Trent; a few days after the sermons of the Franciscan Bernardino da Feltre, the body of a young boy is found near the house of the leader of the Jewish community; after interrogation 17 Jews "confess" and are executed; despite the opposition of an emissary of Sixtus IV, the executions continue and a year later a papal bull confirms the verdict. Until the 18th century Jews were not admitted to Trent; Simon will be beatified and worshiped until 1965. It is undoubtedly the blood-libel case which exercised the greatest influence on Western collective memory, both Jewish and Christian.
**1485:** "Martyrdom" of Lorenzino de Sossio (northern Italy).
**1491:** "Martyrdom" of the holy child of La Guardia (Castille).
**1492:** Expulsion of the Jews from Spain.

# 12th–14th Centuries

shackled by ecclesiastical discipline, viewed Jewish customs as a mirror-image of their own social and individual frustrations.

At the same time, about 1144, the Abbot of Cluny, Peter the Venerable, composed a treatise against the Jews, quite traditional on the whole except for the last section which constituted the first explicit and comprehensive attack on the Talmud. A century later, in 1242, King Louis IX would order the burning of twenty cart-loads of Talmuds in Paris. In this matter sibling rivalry also seems to have been a crucial element: at the precise moment when Scholastic theology was reaching its greatest achievements, the Church also discovered the living traditions of Judaism. Medieval antisemitism was born when a distant contempt for the Jews was replaced by intimate hatred.

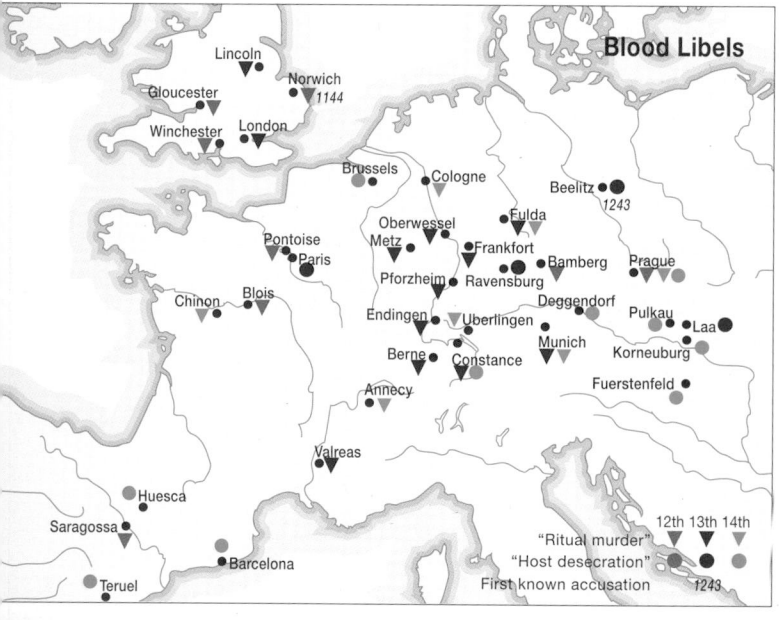

Blood Libels

Lincoln
Gloucester
Norwich 1144
Winchester London
Brussels Cologne
Beelitz 1243
Oberwessel Fulda
Pontoise Metz Frankfort
Paris Pforzheim Bamberg Prague
Chinon Blois Ravensburg
Endingen Überlingen Deggendorf Pulkau
Berne Munich Laa
Annecy Constance Korneuburg
Fuerstenfeld
Valreas
Huesca
Saragossa
Teruel Barcelona

12th 13th 14th
"Ritual murder"
"Host desecration"
First known accusation 1243

*The Jewish sacrifice. Master of the Manna, Haarlem (?), c. 1470.*

*4. The Italian John of Capistran preaches against the Jews, Bamberg, c. 1470.*

# Palestine in the Crusader Period

1. Acre, named St. Jean d'Acre by the crusaders. Aerial photograph.

"infidels." The legal status of Palestinian Jews was identical to that of other local populations, with a single exception: the crusaders revived the Byzantine edict that forbade Jews to live in Jerusalem.

The most important Jewish communities in Palestine during the twelfth century were located in the coastal cities: Tyre, Acre, and Ashkelon. Formed around a nucleus of native merchants, artisans, and talmudic scholars, they continued to conduct their lives according to traditional oriental customs and kept close ties with the spiritual leadership in Egypt. In the Galilee, once densely populated by Jewish peasants, there remained a few rural communities; a small congregation also existed in Tiberias, capital of the principality of the Galilee.

The Christian presence in the Holy Land and the improved maritime transportation between Europe and Palestine renewed the interest of Western Jewry in the land of their ancestors. Pilgrimage became frequent among members of the religious elites of the Western communities. Judah Halevi, philosopher and court poet in Spain, began the movement in 1140. Approximately forty years later, towards the end of the first crusaders' kingdom, another Spanish Jew, roving traveler Benjamin of Tudela, came to tour the land. His Ashkenazi counterpart, Pethahiah of Regensburg, followed in his footsteps two years later. Literary sources attest that among the pilgrims were *hasidim* ("devout") and *perushin* ("separated") – men of pietist and ascetic tendencies.

The movement of *aliyah* ("ascent") to the Land of Israel reached its peak in the thirteenth century, following the religious agitation provoked in Europe by the Ayyubid conquest of Palestine in 1187 and the Third Crusade of 1189–1192. In the early 1210s the desire to settle in the Land of Israel affected the center of Jewish intellectual life at the time – the French schools of the *Tosafists* (commentators on the *Halakhah*, followers of Rashi). This resulted in what is known as "the *aliyah* of the three hundred rabbis" from France and England. In the middle of the century they were joined by German rabbis who until then had been indifferent or even hostile to the movement.

The Ayyubids, thanks to the intercession of the *nagid* (head of the community) in Egypt, permitted Jews to resettle in Jerusalem, and the community was rebuilt with the assistance of Egyptian Jewry. Among the new settlers in the city were Jews from Yemen, the Maghreb, and France but in 1219 the Ayyubids destroyed the town and put an end to this endeavor. Ten years later the Christians regained the city, once more prohibiting the residence of Jews, only to lose it, for the last time, in 1244. Frequent changes of rule prevented the city from developing, so that in the second half of that century, Jerusalem was no more than a village on the periphery of historical events.

After losing Jerusalem, the capital of the crusaders' kingdom was transferred to St. Jean d'Acre. A cosmopolitan port-city, Acre attracted

The conquest of Palestine by the crusaders did not transform the life of the Jews there in any significant way. The land was not truly integrated into Christendom, and the traditional conflict between Judaism and Christianity had not yet erupted. Since the crusaders' continued existence in Palestine depended upon the non-Christian population, they needed to be fairly tolerant towards the

| The crusaders in Jerusalem | Capture of Acre | | Capture of Ashkelon | Battle of Hattin |
|---|---|---|---|---|
| 1099 | 1104 | | 1153 | 1187 |

**1095. November:** Council of Clermont; Pope Urban II calls a crusade for the liberation of the Holy Sepulcher from the Saracens.
**1096. March:** The peasants' crusade; massacres and forced conversions throughout northern France and in the Rhine and the Danube valleys.
**1099. July 15:** Conquest of Jerusalem by the crusaders. The Jews of Jerusalem participate in the defense of the northern wall of the city attacked by Godfrey of Bouillon. When the city fell, the Jews were burned inside the synagogue where they sought refuge. In the following years the crusaders will sell prisoners and prayer books for a high ransom to the oriental Jewish communities.
**1100:** The crusaders conquer Haifa. According to Albert of Aachen, the Jews defended the city and were slaughtered by the assailants.
**1104:** Conquest of Acre and massacre of its inhabitants.

**1123:** Siege and capture of Tyre. Its inhabitants, including Jews, are allowed to either leave with their belongings or to remain in the city.
**1140:** Judah Halevi sets out on his *Aliyah* to the Land of Israel; although tradition has it that he reached Jerusalem, he most likely died on the way.
**1153:** The crusaders take Ashkelon where a Jewish community will remain until 1191.
**1165:** Maimonides arrives in Acre, makes a pilgrimage to Jerusalem and Hebron, then leaves for Egypt.
**c. 1178:** Benjamin of Tudela in Palestine; his account is the only existing testimony of 12th-century Palestinian Jewry.
**c. 1180:** Pethahiah of Regensburg in Palestine.
**1187:** Battle of Hattin and end of the Latin Kingdom of Jerusalem. Saladin attacks Jerusalem; the Christian defenders capitulate; somewhat later a number of Jews are permitted to settle in the city.
**1191:** Saladin destroys Ashkelon; many of its

Jews leave for Jerusalem and constitute the nucleus of the Jerusalem community in the time of the Ayyubids.
**1205:** Maimonides is buried in Tiberias; his son Abraham is appointed *nagid* (head) of Egyptian Jewry.
**1211:** Samson of Sens settles in Acre.
**c. 1217:** Judah al-Harizi, poet and translator from Spain, visits Jerusalem
**1219:** The crusaders attack Egypt and capture Damietta; the Muslims destroy fortifications in Jerusalem.
**1229:** Treaty of Jaffa. Jerusalem is returned to the crusaders. Jews are once again prohibited from residing there.
**1236:** Jewish pilgrims are allowed to visit Jerusalem, and a single Jewish dyer is given permission to settle there.
**1244:** Called to the rescue by the Egyptians, the Khwarizmian Turks attack Jerusalem, massacre Christians, and sack the Holy

3. Seal of Nahmanides (1194–1270), found near Acre.

# 1099–1291

2. Siege of Tyre. Illumination in a crusaders' manuscript from St. Jean d'Acre.

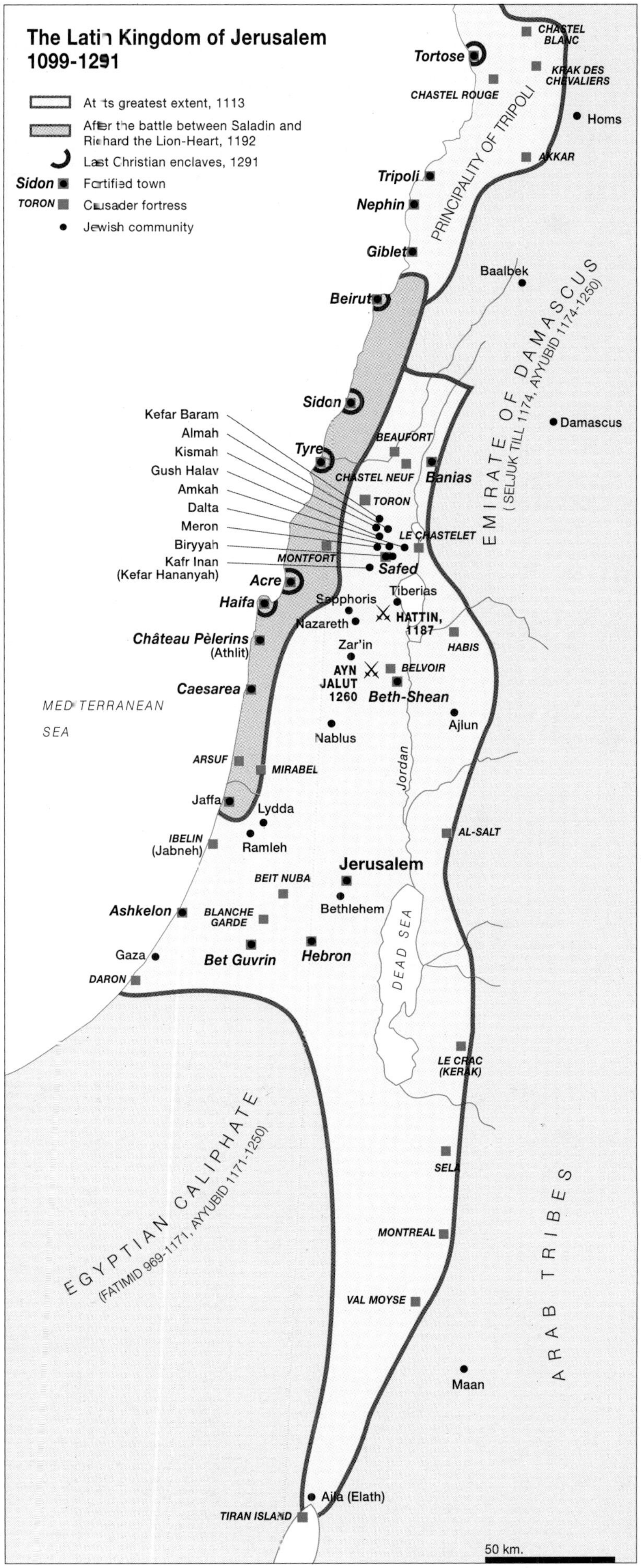

Jewish scholars from all over the diaspora. It became a meeting-point for French-German, Spanish, and Oriental spiritual leaders. Throughout the thirteenth century major figures either arrived or intended to come to Acre – from Samson of Sens, the first of the *Tosafists* to immigrate, down to the aborted attempts of Jehiel of Paris and of Meir of Rothenburg whose works concluded the *Tosafot* ("additions") period. The most illustrious Spanish scholar to settle in Acre during the thirteenth century was Moses ben Nahman (Nahmanides). The encounter with oriental Jewish culture made a deep impression on the European scholars, which was reflected in medieval Hebrew literature.

In 1286 this circle of learned immigrants was agitated by a dispute over Maimonides' works. It was the third and last of these battles in the Middle Ages. An attempt to prohibit the dissemination of Maimonides' writings was vehemently opposed by his descendants, and by oriental sages who would not tolerate any attack upon their greatest *halakhic* authority. Before the polemic was decided, however, the Mamluks captured Acre. The city which had been the European capital of the East was transformed into a mass of ruins and piles of rubble.

**End of crusaders' rule in Jerusalem**

| 1244 | 1291 |
|------|------|

**The Mamluks take Acre**

Sepulcher. End of the crusaders' domination of Jerusalem.

**1260:** The Mongols take Jerusalem and deport its inhabitants; the Jews transfer holy books to Nablus. Battle of Ayn Jalut: victory for Baybars I over the Mongols; beginning of Mamluk rule in Palestine.

**1267:** Nahmanides in Palestine; while visiting Jerusalem he encounters a small number of Jews grouped around a family of dyers which buys a resident permit from the Mamluks.

**1286:** The controversy in Acre concerning Maimonides' writings. The leader of the opponents of Maimonides' doctrines, the French scholar Solomon ben Samuel Petit, is excommunicated by the oriental scholars led by Rabbi David, Maimonides' grandson.

**1291:** The Mamluks capture Acre and kill many of its inhabitants; many victims among the Jewish community.

4. The Holy Sepulcher basilica in Jerusalem. Its façade was built in the crusader period.

## The Latin Kingdom of Jerusalem 1099-1291

- At its greatest extent, 1113
- After the battle between Saladin and Richard the Lion-Heart, 1192
- Last Christian enclaves, 1291
- **Sidon** ■ Fortified town
- TORON ■ Crusader fortress
- • Jewish community

CHASTEL BLANC
Tortose
KRAK DES CHEVALIERS
CHASTEL ROUGE
• Homs
PRINCIPALITY OF TRIPOLI
Tripoli
AKKAR
Nephin
Giblet
Baalbek
Beirut
• Damascus
Sidon
BEAUFORT
EMIRATE OF DAMASCUS (SELJUK TILL 1174, AYYUBID 1174-1250)
Kefar Baram
Almah
Kismah
Gush Halav
Amkah
Dalta
Meron
Biryyah
Kafr Inan (Kefar Hananyah)
Tyre
CHASTEL NEUF
Banias
TORON
LE CHASTELET
MONTFORT
Safed
Acre
Haifa
Sepphoris
Tiberias
HATTIN, 1187
Nazareth
Château Pèlerins (Athlit)
Zar'in
HABIS
AYN JALUT 1260
BELVOIR
Caesarea
Beth-Shean
Ajlun
Nablus
ARSUF
MIRABEL
Jaffa
Lydda
AL-SALT
IBELIN (Jabneh)
Ramleh
Jerusalem
BEIT NUBA
Bethlehem
DEAD SEA
Ashkelon
BLANCHE GARDE
Hebron
Gaza
Bet Guvrin
DARON
MEDITERRANEAN SEA
LE CRAC (KERAK)
SELA
EGYPTIAN CALIPHATE (FATIMID 969-1171, AYYUBID 1171-1250)
MONTREAL
VAL MOYSE
ARAB TRIBES
• Maan
• Aila (Elath)
TIRAN ISLAND
50 km.

# From the Black Death to the End of the Expulsions

1. Massacre of Jews, "poisoners of wells," as seen by Engelhart of Haselbach. The Egar Chronicle,

A round the year 1300, both France and England expelled their Jewish populations. Between the middle of the fourteenth and the first quarter of the sixteenth centuries, southern and central Europe evicted the Jews residing there.

The Black Death plague was followed by successive expulsions, burnings at the stake, and collective imprisonments – the largest wave of persecutions since the massacres of the Crusades. But the same towns which had driven out their Jews were soon forced to reinstate them in the course of reconstruction, although often under humiliating conditions which greatly reduced their status. Between 1450 and 1520, however, about ninety German cities expelled the Jews yet again. It appears that periods of renewed growth, during which the Jews were rendered economically marginal, were as bad for them as times of recession, during which they were perceived as scapegoats.

Marking the end of the era of expulsions in 1520 is basically correct, but is also to some extent arbitrary. The process of eliminating the Jewish presence in German lands was carried out piecemeal because of the fragmentation of the Empire. In fact, over the next fifty years the territorial princes in the German Empire, consolidating their rule over the cities, continued the policy of expulsion. It was only towards the end of the sixteenth century that changes in attitudes reversed this trend, permitting the resettlement of Jews in western Europe.

Whether a Jewish presence should be eliminated or tolerated was a question closely linked to perceptions of usury. In places which welcomed Jews, such as the towns of central and northern Italy during the second half of the fourteenth century, they were invited by communes or governments to fulfill the role of moneylenders, providing short-term loans to a poverty-stricken population. Charging interest was prohibited to Christians and reserved for Jews because it was defined by Christian ethics as an exaction, something permissible only to an enemy whose possessions and even person could be rightfully attacked.

This was an ambivalent justification for tolerating Jews: on the one hand it corresponded to market demands, on the other – it exposed the Jews to popular hostility. The established orders of society therefore considered it their responsibility to "protect" them. Yet even the great German humanist Johann Reuchlin, for example, despite opposing the confiscation of Hebrew books and regarding the Jews as "co-citizens" on the basis of Roman law, did not operate in any way to stop their persecution. He shared contemporary prejudices and supported the basic alternatives offered to the Jews: either to improve (i.e., convert to Christianity) or be expelled. And jurists who endorsed the charging of interest by Jews were forced to present it as a necessary evil. A frequently used analogy was that, in the same manner that it was expedient to authorize and to control the activities of prostitutes in order to defend the institution of marriage and prevent homosexuality, it was necessary to agree to Jewish moneylending under an official license in order to prevent the corruption of Christians. But the growing aspirations for social reform and a world free of vice led to an increased demand to extirpate the sin of usury altogether. Thus, moralistic religious fervor and the desire to remove the Jews from society sometimes overcame all considerations of economic expediency.

| The Black Death in Europe | Temporary return of Jews to France | The Simon of Trent affair | Expulsion from Spain |
|---|---|---|---|
| 1348 | 1361 | 1475 | 1492 |

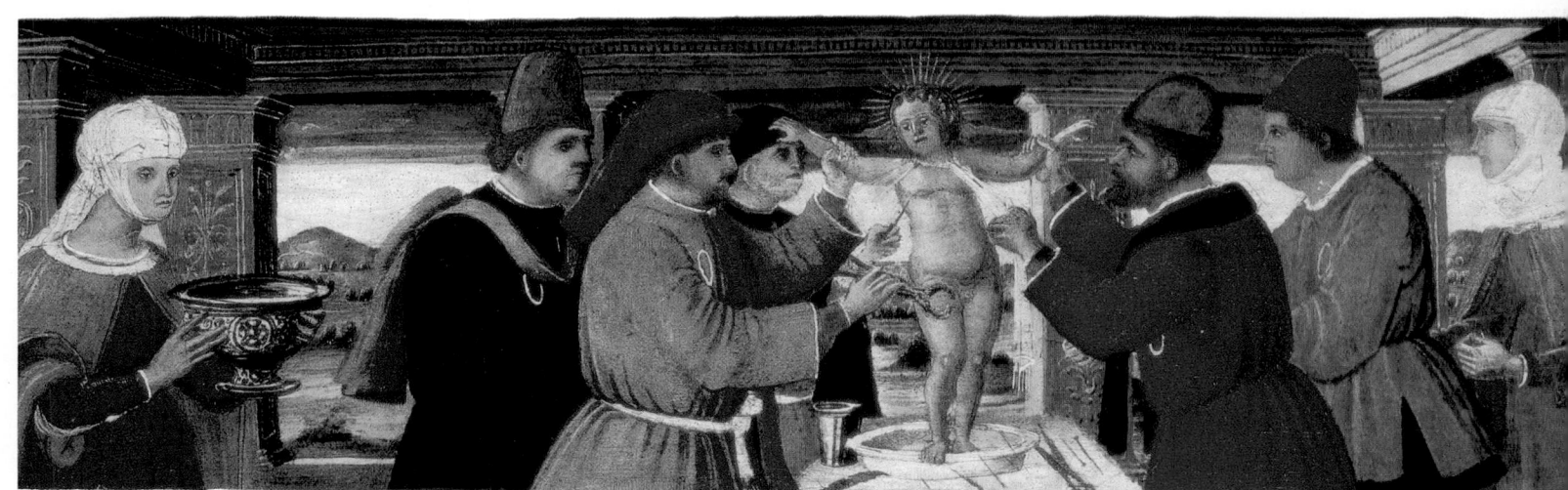

2. Glandolfino d'Asti, Martyrdom of Simon of Trent. Oil, late 15th century.

# 1348–1520

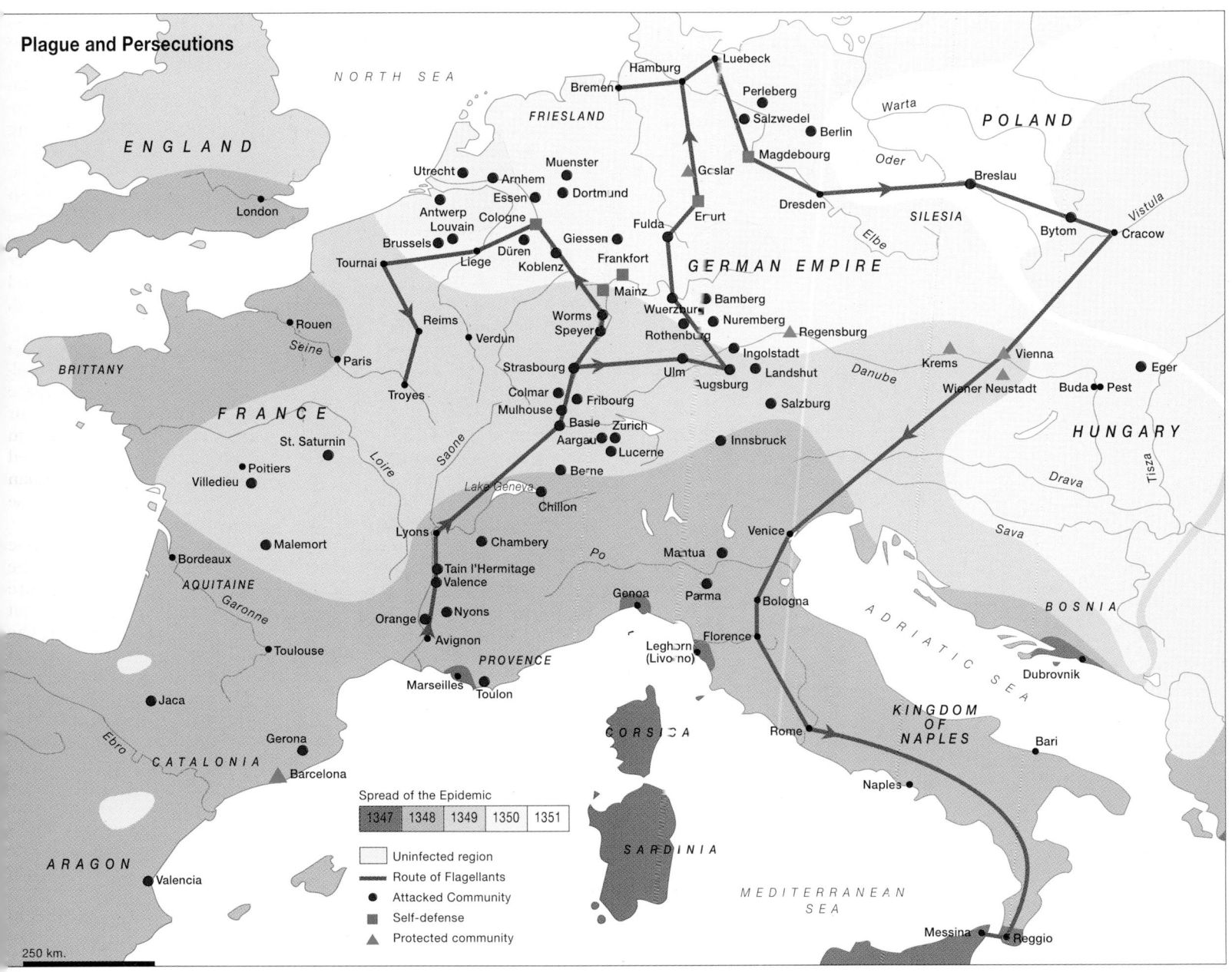

**Plague and Persecutions**

NORTH SEA

ENGLAND

London

BRITTANY

Rouen

Seine

Paris

FRANCE

St. Saturnin

Poitiers

Villedieu

Malemort

Bordeaux

AQUITAINE

Garonne

Toulouse

Jaca

Gerona

CATALONIA

Barcelona

ARAGON

Valencia

Ebro

FRIESLAND

Utrecht

Arnhem

Muenster

Dortmund

Essen

Antwerp

Louvain

Cologne

Brussels

Düren

Liège

Koblenz

Giessen

Frankfort

Tournai

Reims

Verdun

Troyes

Worms

Speyer

Strasbourg

Colmar

Fribourg

Mulhouse

Basle

Zurich

Aargau

Lucerne

Berne

Lake Geneva

Chillon

Lyons

Chambery

Tain l'Hermitage

Valence

Orange

Nyons

Avignon

PROVENCE

Marseilles

Toulon

Loire

Saone

Rhone

Hamburg

Bremen

Luebeck

Perleberg

Salzwedel

Berlin

Goslar

Magdebourg

Erfurt

Fulda

Mainz

GERMAN EMPIRE

Bamberg

Wuerzburg

Nuremberg

Rothenburg

Ingolstadt

Ulm

Landshut

Augsburg

Salzburg

Innsbruck

Regensburg

Warta

Oder

POLAND

Dresden

Breslau

SILESIA

Bytom

Cracow

Vistula

Elbe

Krems

Vienna

Wiener Neustadt

Eger

Buda

Pest

HUNGARY

Danube

Drava

Tisza

Sava

Venice

Mantua

Po

Genoa

Parma

Bologna

Florence

Leghorn (Livorno)

ADRIATIC SEA

BOSNIA

Dubrovnik

Rome

KINGDOM OF NAPLES

Bari

Naples

CORSICA

SARDINIA

MEDITERRANEAN SEA

Messina

Reggio

**Spread of the Epidemic**

| 1347 | 1348 | 1349 | 1350 | 1351 |

Uninfected region

Route of Flagellants

● Attacked Community

■ Self-defense

▲ Protected community

250 km.

---

**Expulsion from Provence**

1500–1501

**The Reuchlin-Pfefferkorn controversy**

1507

**Expulsion from Regensburg**

1519

**1348–1349:** The Black Death. Massacres in Provence and in Catalonia cause more deaths than the plague. In September 1348 the Jews of Chillon on Lake Geneva are arrested and "confess" to causing the plague by poisoning the wells in an attempt to destroy Christianity. Massacres in 1349 throughout northern Europe. The patricians of Strasbourg attempt to defend the Jews, but the establishment of a regime led by craftsmen is immediately followed by the burning of Jews on February 14, 1349. In Nordhausen (Thuringia) the Jews prepare for martyrdom and, led by their rabbi, throw themselves into the flames.

**1348. February:** The Cortes of Alcala adopts a law introduced by Alfonso XI of Castile prohibiting moneylending by Jews and encouraging them to acquire real estate. The law will be revoked in 1351.

**July 4, September 26:** Bulls of Pope Clement VI denounce the accusations which ascribe the plague to a Jewish plot.

**1349:** Clement VI prohibits Flagellant

processions which reach alarming proportions during the plague.

**1354. December:** An appeal by Jewish leaders in Catalonia and Valencia to the King of Aragon and to the Pope to help improve relations between Jews and Christians.

**1361:** King Charles V orders the recall of the Jews to France for a limited period.

**1366–1369:** Massacres of Jews in Castile during a civil war.

**1370:** An accusation of theft and desecration of the Host in Brussels; local Jews are burned at the stake. A cult of the miraculous Host will develop in the town in the 15th century in relation to this affair.

**1378:** *Il Pecorone*, a collection of stories by the Florentine writer Giovanni Fiorentino; the principal source for Shakespeare's *The Merchant of Venice*.

**1382:** The reign of Charles VI begins with anti-Jewish outbreaks in Paris and Rome.

**1385:** An agreement between Emperor Wenceslaus and 38 German towns: a moratorium on most debts owed to Jewish

moneylenders; city councils are to benefit from the money owed to the Jews.

**1394. September 17:** Final expulsion of the Jews from France.

**1418:** Pope Martin V revokes the anti-Jewish bull of Pope Benedict XIII; he also condemns the Franciscan campaign in Italy against the "usurious" Jews.

**1421:** The crusade against the Hussites. An anonymous Hebrew chronicle from the second half of the 15th century presents the King of Bohemia, Wenceslaus IV, as a disciple of Rabbi Avigdor Kara, and Huss himself as a Judaizer, yet complains of the iconoclasm and attacks on priests perpetrated by the Hussites.

**1437:** Cosimo de' Medici invites Jewish moneylenders to settle in Florence; they will be expelled with the fall of the Medici in 1494.

**1475:** The Jews of Trent are accused of the ritual murder of a Christian infant named Simon; the libelous affair leads to the expulsion of Jews from the town.

**1475–1495:** Anti-Jewish outbreaks in many towns in Provence. After its annexation to the kingdom of France in 1481, Jews are expelled from Arles (1493) and Tarascon (1496).

**1500–1501:** Edicts of expulsion of the Jews from Provence.

**1507:** The apostate Pfefferkorn demands the confiscation of the Talmud; Reuchlin takes on the defense of Hebrew writings. The polemic becomes the occasion for an open confrontation between the humanists and the "obscurantists."

**1509–1516:** When Venetian territories are invaded by the armies of the League of Cambrai, Jews from the mainland are admitted into the town. In 1516 the government of Venice encloses the Jews in a walled quarter (*getto* or *ghetto*) situated near a foundry.

**1519. February 21:** Expulsion of the Jews from Regensburg. After 1550 the only remaining important Jewish communities in German lands are Frankfort and Worms.

# The Art of the Hebrew Manuscript

In the manner of other Mediterranean civilizations, the ancient Hebrews first used scrolls made of papyrus and later of leather parchment. Abundant samples are provided in the collections of papyri from Yeb (Elephantine), Assuan and Edfu in Egypt, the Dead Sea Scrolls, and the fragments found in the Judean Desert. During the first centuries of the Christian era in the west and the Middle East, the scroll was gradually replaced by the codex: folded sheets sewn together in the middle – the book. The codex had obvious advantages over the scroll which was written only on one side of the parchment and was awkward to handle. By the fifth century AD the use of the scroll had disappeared almost entirely.

The Jews, however, were slow to adopt the codex; its spread is attributed to Christianity. There are no extant Hebrew codices dated prior to the ninth or tenth centuries. But from the late Middle Ages thousands of manuscripts were preserved, written in Hebrew in a wide variety of styles from all over the diaspora. These surviving texts of both religious and secular works are but a minute portion of Jewish literary production during those centuries. Outstanding proof of the enormous amount of Jewish writing is provided by the Cairo *Genizah* – the immense archive containing over 50,000 worn and damaged books produced by the single community of Fostat (Old Cairo) in 250 years.

A treasure of invaluable historical and literary importance, the *Genizah* manuscripts are also objects reflecting the material and artistic culture which produced them. In these hand-written books are harmoniously combined diverse technologies and handicrafts, the art of design and graphic creativity, the principles of two-dimensional architecture and aesthetic traditions, literary and calligraphic styles, the art of illustration and illumination – a magnificent introduction to Jewish cultural history of the early Middle Ages.

The dispersion of a literate Jewish population contributed to the particularly wide geographical dissemination of Hebrew writing. Hebrew characters were also used for texts in other languages such as Aramaic or Arabic and German Jewish dialects. Hebrew books were produced in Christian Europe, in Muslim Spain, in North Africa, in the Near and Middle East, and as far as central Asia. Each geo-cultural area produced

*1. The Spanish style: double carpet page from* Keter Damesek *("Crown of Damascus") - an annotated and illuminated manuscript of the Bible. Burgos, 1260.*

*3. The Italian style: David and Goliath, illustration in* Sefer Emet *(containing the Book of Psalms, Job, and Proverbs). Italy, Florence (?), 1460–1470.*

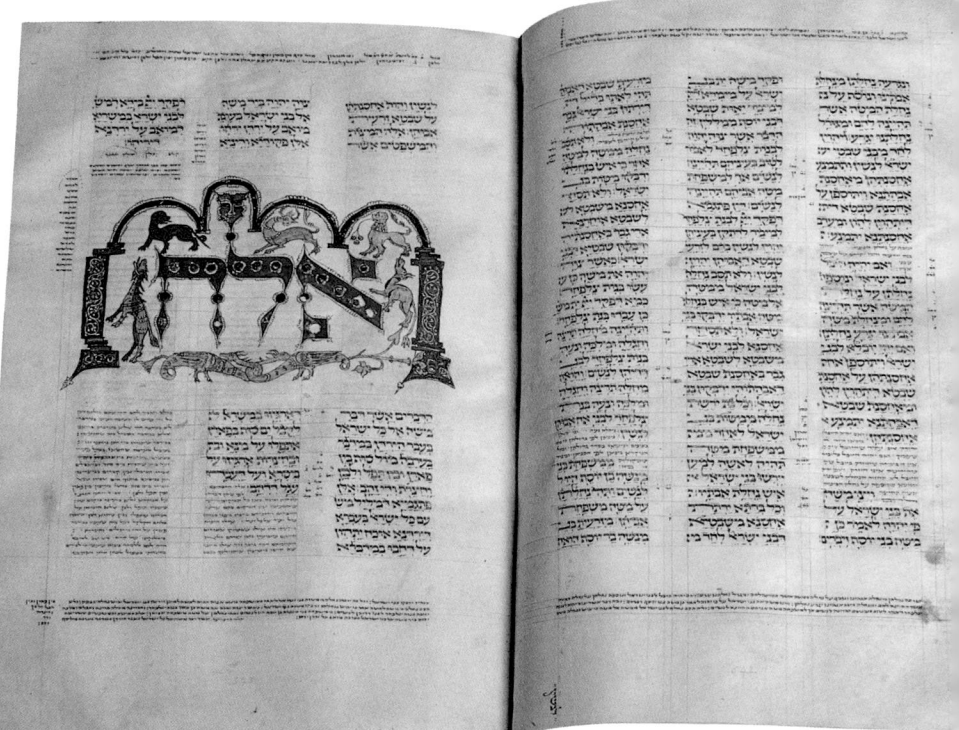

*4. The Ashkenazi style: from the "De Castro Pentateuch." Germany, 1344.*

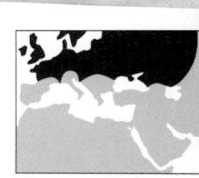

its own style in the art of the manuscript, exhibiting both the uniqueness and cohesion of the Jewish community as well as the influence of the local environment: Latin in western Christendom, Greek in the Byzantine sphere, Arab in the Muslim world. The rich variety is particularly evident in the three types of script – square, mashait (intermediate), and cursive – but is revealed in other material and aesthetic elements as well: the parchment and later the paper, the ink, the collation of the sheets, design of binding and title page, illumination, and illustration. Over time six principal types evolved: Ashkenazi (France, Germany, England, and central Europe); Italian; Spanish (Iberian peninsula, Provence, and North Africa); Byzantine; Oriental; and Yemenite.

The Second Commandment, prohibiting the making of "graven images," did not prevent illumination of manuscripts during the Middle Ages. The style of illumination was dependent on contemporary fashions in each region. Thus it is difficult to define a Jewish style, although there are certain distinctively Jewish motifs. For example, animal-headed figures became one of the main Jewish motifs in southern German Hebrew illumination of the thirteenth and fourteenth centuries. The absence of capital letters in the Hebrew script led to the decoration of initial words, or sometimes whole verses. Another peculiar Jewish element was the use of minute script to form geometric or floral design.

The spread of the printing press in the sixteenth century signaled the end of the manuscript as an independent art. Although unpublished texts – and in more impoverished regions even printed works – continued to be copied by hand until recent times, these were essentially imitations of printing. The traditional division into types of script disappeared not only because of the printed letter, but also as a result of the expulsion from Spain and the settlement of Iberian Jews in other places. Nevertheless, the art of the manuscript was revived in the eighteenth century in central Europe and in Germany with the fashion of copying illuminated Passover *Haggadot* and books of blessings.

The tradition of copying the Pentateuch on scrolls to be read in synagogues, as well as phylacteries, *mezuzot*, and divorce bills , continues to this day. Written in minute script, following strict rules, this work is done by specially trained expert scribes (*sofer setam*).

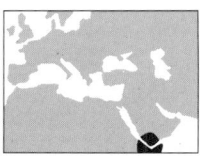

2. The Yemenite style: a Ketubbah (a marriage document) from San'a, Yemen.

5. The Byzantine style: manuscript of the Talmudic tract Pirkei Avot which relates the transmission of the Law from one generation to the next. Crete, end of 16th century.

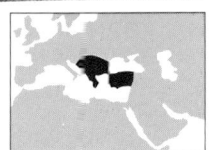

6. The Oriental style: a Jewish-Persian manuscript. Persia, 1686.

# Marranos, Conversos, New Christians

The year 1391 was a major turning point in Jewish history, for it inaugurated the era of the *anusim* ("forced converts"). In the summer of that year a wave of riots swept over Spain, from Andalusia in the south, to Catalonia and Majorca in the northeast. This was the Iberian version of urban and peasant revolts which plagued all of Europe in the late fourteenth century. However, in Spain this social unrest also marked the end of the *convivencia* – the relatively-peaceful cohabitation of three civilizations. During the riots, Jewish quarters were attacked, hundreds of Jews massacred, synagogues destroyed, and many thousands were forced to convert. The agitation which activated the riots of 1391 remained endemic, breaking out again

1. Torture chamber of the Inquisition. Engraving from the Atlas van Stolk, *Rotterdam, 1783.*

in 1412–1418 when the infamous friar Vicente Ferrer incited people to finish off what they had begun twenty years earlier.

The anti-pope Benedict XIII, hoping to impress all Christendom by accomplishing the conversion of Spanish Jewry, organized, in cooperation with the King of Aragon, a spectacular Christian-Jewish "disputation" in Tortosa, which from the outset was a missionary attack upon the Jews, carried out under threats and intimidation. Throughout the two years of this disputation, preachers everywhere incited the population to force Jews to convert. While theologians promised converts immediate acceptance to the fold as faithful Catholics, the Crown wished to secure the integration of the New Christians and to align their social status with that of "Old" Christians. The combination of intimidation with the promise of integration was indeed difficult to resist. Members of the Jewish intellectual elite, inclined to a certain philosophical indifference towards the external manifestations of religion, could thus justify their acceptance of baptism. Some apostates, with the zeal of neophytes, became ardent and sometimes vicious propagandists for Christianity. Others, on the other hand, tried to maintain an outward adherence to Christianity, while secretly clinging to their old faith. Thus, by the mid-fifteenth century, New Christians outnumbered those who continued to profess Judaism despite persecution and temptation.

Many Conversos benefited from this "proto-emancipation," swiftly rising in the ecclesiastical or political hierarchies. Mobilization of their cultural legacy and pent-up energies, the tenacity typical of men long subjected to conditional acceptance, and the swiftness by which they moved to the centers of power and prestige, all rendered the Conversos more conspicuous. Individual success and promotion therefore created a situation which undermined the intended result of collective effacement. Furthermore, the religious fervor of over-zealous converts produced a reaction of revulsion in the "Old" Christians who found such emotional manifestations unnatural and unnecessary. On the other hand, the "Judaizers" – Christians who secretly adhered to their former religion, named Marranos (a term of abuse probably derived from the Spanish word for "swine") – obviously aroused suspicion and hostility.

Before long, Spanish Christians generalized their envy and suspicion: all New Christians, they believed, enjoyed riches and high-ranking social positions; was this not adequate proof of their collective treachery? Such feelings motivated the rebels against the royal authority who seized power in Toledo in 1449 and introduced the first statute of "purity of blood," and the same resentments led to the attacks on Conversos in Castilian towns in 1471. Clearly, the "problem" of New Christians was becoming acute and creating disorder. Ferdinand and Isabella, the Catholic Monarchs, in the midst of the process of unifying Spain and centralizing its government, felt compelled to resolve it. Yet the 1478 decision to establish a new Inquisition was not necessarily inevitable. Prominent members of the open-minded cultured elites advised against it, believing that the residual attachment of some Conversos to their former religion was bound to disappear in time, with their complete integration. The Inquisition, however, was established nonetheless.

When the Spanish Inquisition began operating in 1481, the phenomenon it was determined to abolish was by no means an imaginary one. The inquisitors were sincerely concerned with saving the souls of "sinners" by separating Judaizers from true Christians; but as they tended to see duplicity and plots everywhere, none of the New Christians were safe from suspicion and persecution.

| Outbreaks against Jews | Disputation of Tortosa | "Purity of Blood" statute in Toledo | Marriage of the Catholic Monarchs | The Inquisition |
|---|---|---|---|---|
| 1391 | 1413–1414 | 1449 | 1469 | 1478 |

**1391:** Anti-Jewish violence throughout the Iberian peninsula, except for Portugal and Navarre.

**1391 (or 1390). July 21:** Conversion of Solomon Halevi, one of the leaders of Spanish Jewry, who assumes the name Pablo de Santa Maria; he later becomes Bishop of Burgos and Chancellor to the king of Castile. Joshua Lorki writes to Pablo de Santa Maria rejecting the latter's interpretation of the messianic role of Jesus; Lorki himself, however, converted in 1412, and became one of the leading Christian protagonists in the disputation of Tortosa.

**1412:** The laws of Valladolid directed against the Jews; the laws, formulated by Vicente Ferrer, were intended to hasten the conversion of the Jews.

**1413. February 7:** Opening of the disputation of Tortosa initiated by the anti-pope Benedict XIII; the first sessions revolved around the nature of the Messiah.

**Early 1414:** A wave of conversions.

**April–May:** During the second part of the

disputation of Tortosa, discussion of the "errors and blasphemies" in the Talmud.

**1415. May:** Decree of Benedict XIII ordering the expurgation of the Talmud.

**1434:** Alonso of Cartagena, Pablo de Santa Maria's son who succeeded his father as Bishop of Burgos, makes a speech at the Council of Basle praising the virtues of the Castilian nation, which has forsaken riches in order to fight "divine wars."

**1449. January 27:** A revolt against taxation in Toledo develops into attacks on rich Converso merchants. The rebel leaders take over the town.

**June 5:** The council of Toledo adopts a statute proclaiming that Conversos and their issue are not to hold any public office in the city; this is the first act of "racial" discrimination against New Christians.

**September 24:** Pope Nicholas V's bull denouncing the Toledan statute: "all Catholics constitute one body in Christ."

**End of October:** Fernan Diaz writes a memorandum explaining that the Toledan

statute was impossible to implement since "mixed" marriages between members of the aristocracy and families of Conversos were so frequent that any attempt to discriminate against men of Jewish descent would affect the entire upper class.

**1450:** Pedro de la Cavalleria, of Jewish descent, writes an anti-Jewish polemic entitled *The Zeal of Christ against the Jews, Saracens and Infidels*; in his effort to prove Christian dogmas, the author makes use of material from the Kabbalah.

**1451. November:** In response to a demand made by King John II, Pope Nicholas V approves in principle the establishment of an Inquisition tribunal in Castile.

**1460:** Juan Arias Davila, son of converso Diego Arias, who was Henry IV's treasurer, becomes bishop of Segovia.

**1460–1467:** A Papal Inquisition in Valencia conducts numerous trials against Conversos suspected of Judaizing.

**1465:** A solemn and secret ceremony of admitting a Converso back to Judaism

(accompanied by circumcision), conducted by Abraham Bilago, one of the most original thinkers in Aragon.

**June 5:** Henry IV of Castile is deposed and replaced by his half-brother Alfonso; the adversaries of the deposed king include the demand to reinforce the Inquisition.

**1467:** Renewed riots in Toledo; renewal of the statute of 1449.

**1473. March:** Attacks on Conversos in Cordoba and other towns in Andalusia; an edict in Cordoba prohibits New Christians from serving in public office.

**1478. November 1:** A bull of Pope Sixtus IV invests Ferdinand and Isabella with extraordinary powers to appoint inquisitors in every part of Castile. In 1482 the same pope will condemn the excessive harshness of the Spanish Inquisition.

**1480. September 24:** The Catholic Kings appoint Dominicans Juan de San Martin and Miguel de Morillo as inquisitors.

**October:** Establishment of the Inquisition tribunal in Seville.

2. Pedro de Berruguete (1450–1503), Auto-da-Fé.

**Anti-Jewish Riots, 1391**

→ Spread of riots

Palma
August 2 ⊙ Affected community

150 km.

---

**Fate of a Jewish Family in Spain**
**13th-15th centuries**

**JUDAH DE LA CAVALLERIA**
Bailiff of Saragossa, d. 1276

**ABRAHAM**
∞ BONOSA

**VIDAL** ∞ OROVIDA
d. 1373

**SOLOMON**

**JUDAH**
Not converted

**BONAFOS**
Converted in 1402

**BONAFOS**
(FERDINAND)
Converted Feb. 2, 1414.
Mentioned on Feb. 18 as
King's treasurer.

**JUDAH**

**BONAFILLA**

**JUDAH BENVENISTE** ∞ TOLOSANA
d. 1411
Farmed the revenues of the archdiocese of
Saragossa, then royal taxes. His home was a
meeting place for poets and scholars.

**SOLOMON**

**VIDAL**

**JUDAH**
Converted
(GASPAR)

**REINA**
Remained Jewish

LEONOR DE LA CABRA
∞ 2nd marriage

**VIDAL**
Negotiated in 1492
the admission to Portugal
of Jews expelled from
Spain.

**LEONARDO**

**TOLOSANA**

**PEDRO**
b. 1415, d. 1461
Adviser to Alfonso V; comptroller
general of Aragon; obtained in 1447 a
certificate that he was of pure
Christian descent. Author of an
anti-Jewish polemic.

4 children converted

2 daughters
remained Jewish

**VIDAL**
Author of Hebrew poetry.
One of the Jewish representatives
at the disputation of Tortosa.
After his conversion in 1414,
translated Cicero into Spanish.

**ALFONSO**
d. 1506
Vice-chancellor of Aragon.
Adviser to King Ferdinand,
entrusted with the administration
of the Kingdom.
Participated in the establishment of the
Inquisition in Barcelona.
Attempted to prevent the expulsion of 1492.

– Why are you so eager to make yourself a Christian, being so
learned in our [Jewish] law?
– Be silent, stupid. Could I as a Jew hope to rise to anything higher
than a rabbi? Now, for one crucified [Jesus], they grant me such
honors, and I give the orders in the town of Saragossa... If I wish to
fast on Kippur, who is to prevent me?
(An exchange between Pedro de la Cavalleria and a Jew according to the
latter's deposition when interrogated by the Inquisition in 1492)

# Berber North Africa and Mamluk Egypt

The golden age of the Jewish communities in Muslim lands ended between the twelfth and thirteenth centuries – first in North Africa, and later in the Levant. Their situations deteriorated as a result of major political upheavals in these regions: new regimes, which valued Islam well above older beliefs inherited from Greek antiquity, came into being. Intolerance towards religious minorites, Jewish and Christian, was one of the more bitter consequences.

In the Maghreb (which in contemporary Arab geography included Spain as well as North Africa), a new dynasty, the Almohad, came to power in the mid-twelfth century. Originating in the High Atlas mountains among the Berbers, adhering to a fundamental and fanatic form of Islam, the Almohads imposed their puritanical religious concepts on all Muslims who came under their rule. The protection traditionally accorded to the "Peoples of the Book" was severely restricted. Muhammad had given these nations, the Almohads claimed, five hundred years for their messiah to come forth; since the period of grace had elapsed, the whole world was now obliged to embrace Islam. Numerous Jews in Morocco refused to convert and chose martyrdom instead; others found refuge in Ayyubid Egypt; but the majority stayed on, hoping that the persecutions would soon subside. The Almohads, however, remained in power until 1269. North African Jewry was crushed under this brutal rule,

and survived only by virtue of religious dissimulation. This crypto-Judaism, however, could preserve none of the creative energies which had characterized the Jewish community prior to the Almohad conquest.

Many of those who converted to Islam did not return to Judaism even when the persecutions abated. Yet the converts did not fare very much better than those who maintained the religion of their ancestors. Suspected of "Judaizing," they were humiliated, spied upon, marked by distinctive clothes, prohibited from trading, and restricted to base occupations. Often their children were taken away by order of the authorities to be brought up in an orthodox Muslim environment. It was during this period that Maimon ben Joseph and his son Moses (the famous Maimonides), refugees themselves, wrote letters of advice and consolation from Egypt to the Maghreb Jews.

In the Orient, two major developments, both related to the Mongol invasion, transformed the conditions of Jewish existence. In Iraq the Mongols put an end to the Abbasid caliphate (Baghdad was captured and sacked in 1258); and in Egypt the Mamluks, after defeating the Mongols, formed their own kingdom. The Mongol wave destroyed the texture of urban life in Mesopotamia and ruined its trade. Although Jews attained important positions in administration at the beginning of the conquest, their situation was gravely affected when the Mongols adopted Islam. Delivered in to the hands of the vindictive mob, the Jewish communities paid dearly for their ephemeral success.

The Near East – Egypt, Palestine, Syria, and Lebanon – was under Mamluk domination for almost three centuries. A military aristocracy of slave origin, the Mamluks – mostly Turks or Balkan Christians taken from their families at a young age – were all the more devoutly Muslim since they were foreigners and recent converts. They formed an extremely centralized state. Its cadres were raised in religious schools (*madrasa*), and they made every effort to curry favor with the Muslim theologians. The Mamluk order was particularly resented by two strata of Muslim society: the urban middle classes which were excluded from government, and the city merchants who suffered from state intervention in the economy. Naturally, frustrations were vented against minority groups, mostly against Christians of the Coptic rite, still numerous in the high echelons of government and in commerce. However, in a period when the Covenant of Omar was increasingly interpreted in a narrower sense, and when the confrontation with the Crusaders intensified suspicion of non-Muslims, the Jews too had their share of tribulations.

Thus, it was a new era for the Jews throughout the Muslim world. They found themselves economically restricted, ill at ease in a civilization which had adopted a new spiritual direction, and ill-treated by the rulers who once had been their main source of security, but were now intent on alienating the minorities.

*2. The Fez Mahzor (prayer book). Late 15th century.*

| Almohad conquests in the Maghreb | Battle of Hattin |
|---|---|
| **Beginning in 1140** | **1187** |

**1140–1148:** The Almohads conquer cities in the Maghreb; the Jews are given the choice of either conversion or death. During the same years, the Jews of western Europe suffer a series of shocks in connection with the Second Crusade (1146–1147).

**1148:** In a letter to his father, Solomon ben Judah ha-Kohen describes the Almohad campaign of forced conversion.

**c. 1160:** Fleeing the Almohads, the Maimon family leaves Cordoba for Fez; then in 1165 they arrive in Acre, Palestine.

**1171:** The Kurdish Salah al-Din (Saladin), vizier of the last Fatimid caliph, founds the Ayyubid dynasty and re-establishes Sunna Islam in Egypt. According to Muslim sources, Maimonides becomes the *nagid* (head) of Egyptian Jewry.

**1184–1199:** Reign of Almohad Abu Yusuf Yaqub al-Mansur, during which the attitude towards the Jews is hardened.

**1187:** Saladin defeats the Crusaders at Hattin in the Galilee; end of the first Latin kingdom of Jerusalem.

*3. Jewish tombstone from southern Morocco, 1521.*

## The Muslim Mediterranean 12th -16th centuries

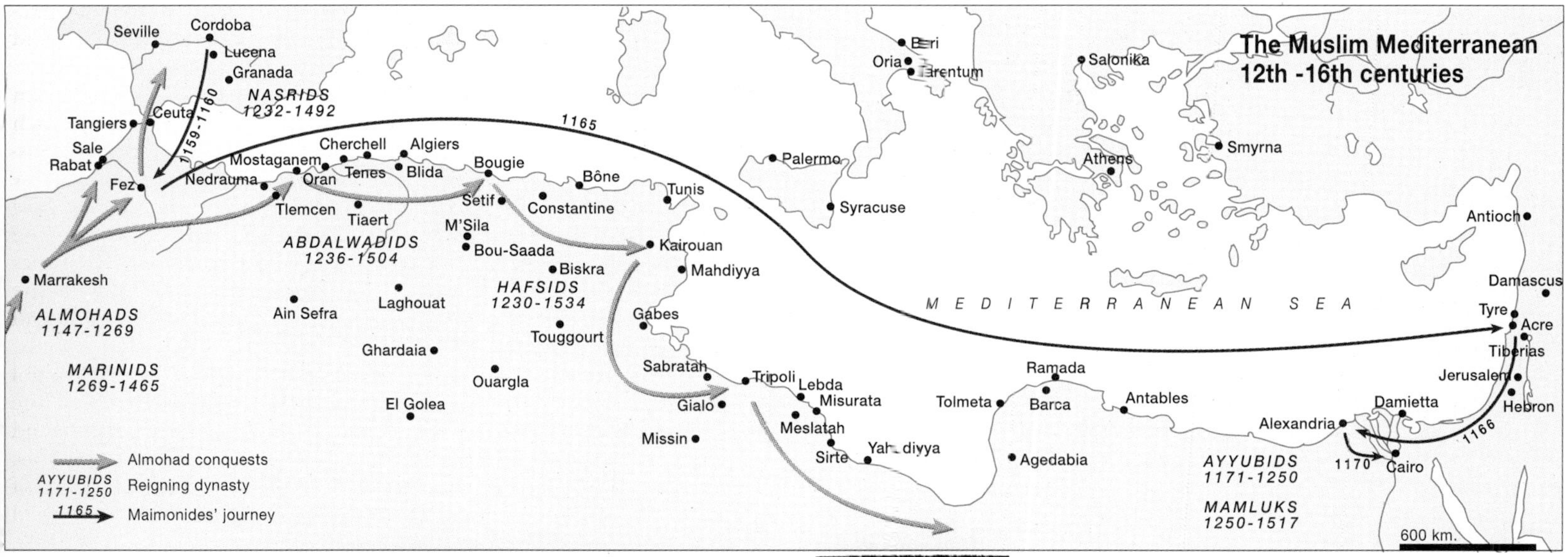

Seville · Cordoba · Lucena · Granada
Tangiers · Ceuta · Rabat · Sale · Fez · Nedrauma · Marrakesh
NASRIDS 1232-1492
ALMOHADS 1147-1269
MARINIDS 1269-1465
Mostaganem · Oran · Tlemcen · Tiaert
Cherchell · Algiers · Blida · Tenes
ABDALWADIDS 1236-1504
Bougie · Setif · M'Sila · Bou-Saada · Biskra
Constantine · Bône · Tunis
Kairouan · Mahdiyya
HAFSIDS 1230-1534
Ain Sefra · Laghouat · Ghardaia · Ouargla · El Golea
Gábes · Touggourt · Sabratah · Tripoli · Lebda · Misurata · Meslatah · Sirte · Yah diyya · Missin · Gialo
Oria · Beri · Brentum · Salonika
Palermo · Syracuse · Athens · Smyrna
MEDITERRANEAN SEA
Antioch · Damascus · Tyre · Acre · Tiberias · Jerusalem · Hebron
Ramada · Barca · Tolmeta · Antables · Agedabia
Alexandria · Damietta · Cairo
AYYUBIDS 1171-1250
MAMLUKS 1250-1517

Almohad conquests
*AYYUBIDS 1171-1250* Reigning dynasty
*1165* Maimonides' journey

600 km.

*1. Coptic tapestry. Egypt, 11th–12th century.*

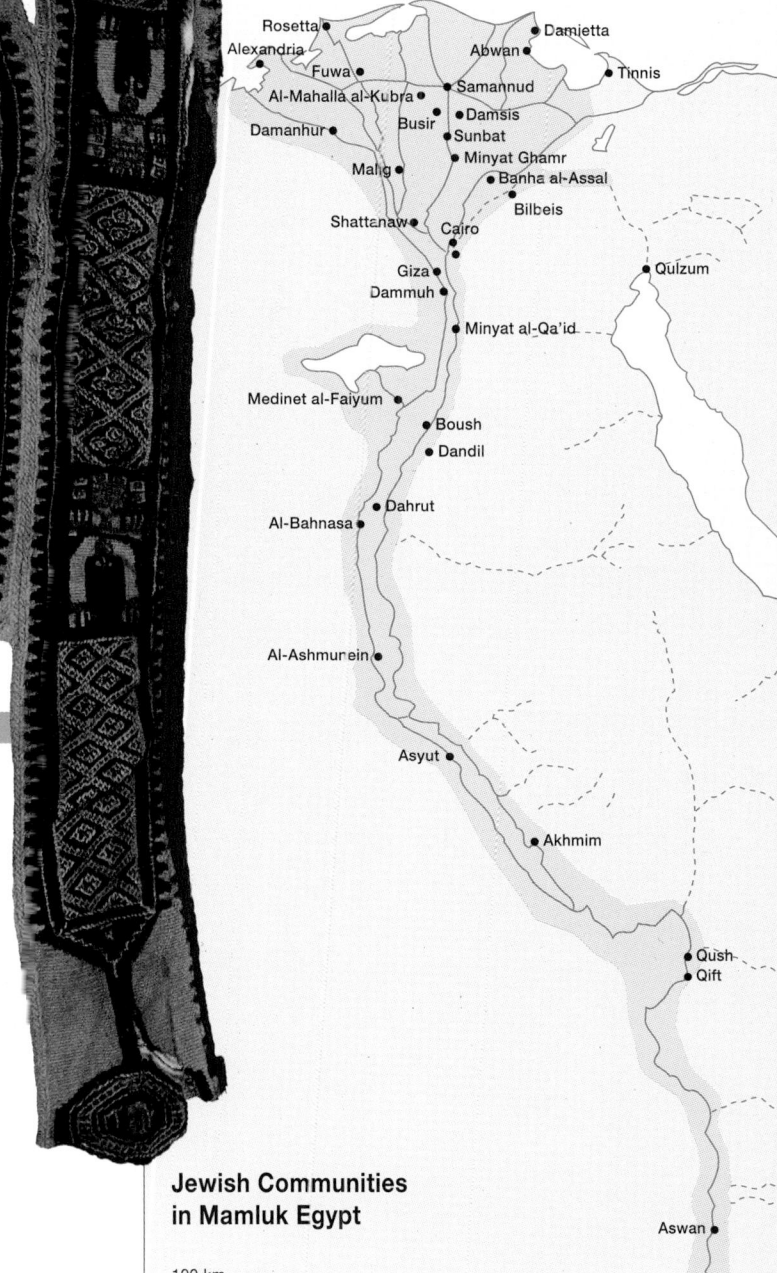

## Jewish Communities in Mamluk Egypt

Rosetta · Alexandria · Fuwa · Al-Mahalla al-Kubra · Damanhur · Malig · Shattanaw · Giza · Dammuh · Medinet al-Faiyum · Al-Bahnasa · Al-Ashmurein · Asyut · Akhmim · Qush · Qift · Aswan
Damietta · Abwan · Tinnis · Samannud · Damsis · Sunbat · Minyat Ghamr · Banha al-Assal · Bilbeis · Cairo · Minyat al-Qa'id · Boush · Dandil · Dahrut · Qulzum
Busir

100 km.

## The Mamluks in Egypt

### 1250

**1198–1201:** The Ayyubid sultan, al-Malik al-Muazzam Ismail, forces the Jews of Yemen to embrace Islam; Maimonides' *Epistle to Yemen*. After the assassination of the Sultan, persecutions cease and the Jews are able to return to their faith.

**1204:** After Maimonides' death, his son Abraham leads the Egyptian community; the title of *nagid* becomes hereditary in the Maimon family.

**1206:** Genghis Khan founds the Mongol empire; within half a century, he and his successors conquer China, Khwarezm, Afghanistan, the Caucasus, Russia, the Ukraine, Hungary, Iran, Iraq and Syria.

**1250–1517:** Mamluk rule in Egypt.

**c. 1250:** Messianic reactions among the Jews to the Mongol conquests.

**1258:** Under the command of Hülagü, Genghis Khan's grandson, the Mongols attack Baghdad, end the Abbasid dynasty and massacre the inhabitants.

**1259–1260:** The Mongols take Damascus, but are defeated by the Mamluks at Ayn

## The Mongols capture Damascus

### 1259–1260

Jalut (En Harod, in the Jezreel Valley).

**1284:** Anti-Jewish riots in Baghdad.

**1289–1291:** The Jew Saad al-Dawla is head vizier at the Khan's court in Baghdad; his fall entails the fall of many other Jewish courtiers.

**1291:** The Mamluks capture Acre from the Crusaders.

**1295–1304:** Reign of Rhazan Mahmud *ilkhan* (vassal of the Khan) in the Mongol kingdom of Iran and Mesopotamia; Rhazan imposes Islam on all his subjects, including Buddhists and Nestorian Christians.

**1301:** The Mamluks increase the pressure on all non-Muslims.

**1348:** The Black Death epidemic wreaks destruction throughout the Near East, before spreading to Europe.

**1354:** Restrictive legislation of the Mamluk sultan, Al-Malik al-Salih.

**1419:** Show trials in Egypt against non-Muslim officials.

**1448:** Sultan Jakmak prohibits Muslims from consulting non-Muslim physicians.

# The Formation of East European Jewry

*1. Arthur Szyk (1894–1951), an illuminated title page from the Statute of Kalisz.*

Jews had been present in Eastern Europe since the early centuries of the Christian Era. In Greek colonies on the shores of the Black Sea, there were Jewish settlers who were part of the Byzantine community. Then, in the eighth century, the ruling class of the Khazar kingdom in the steppes of southern Russia converted to Judaism. Some legends trace the origins of Polish Jewry to this Turkic people, but there is no historical evidence to corroborate such theories. There is ample evidence, on the other hand, that Jewish communities, both Rabbanite and Karaite, existed in many Slavic towns including Kiev, Russia's ancient capital. The sources, particularly a famous letter preserved in the Cairo *Genizah*, portray the Russian Jewish community as a branch of Byzantine Jewry, actively participating in the commerce between southern Ukraine and the Mediterranean. It seems most probable that Jews from Russian towns moved to Poland, and others became subjects of the Grand Duchy of Lithuania as it expanded to include regions where they were settled. As late as the seventeenth century we hear of Jews in Lithuanian towns who speak "Russian" and do not know any German, the "language of *Ashkenaz.*" This "Russian" nucleus was later joined by Jews from Italian colonies on the Black Sea.

All these elements, however, were to be submerged by large waves of immigrants which began arriving from Western Europe in the thirteenth century. By the late fifteenth century there were more than sixty Jewish communities in Poland, most of them founded by immigrants from Germany. Poland's Jewry is therefore essentially a product of immigration from the West, part and parcel of Ashkenazi Jewry. *Ashkenaz* was the Hebrew word by which Jews designated Germany (borrowed from the biblical name in Genesis 10:3). In the Middle Ages the term *Ashkenazi* was reserved for those Jews who either lived in German-speaking lands or had emigrated from the German Empire and settled elsewhere.

Information concerning Jewish life in Eastern Europe prior to the second half of the thirteenth century is scant and fragmentary. One thing, however, is certain. The social and cultural profile of the East European community was molded by Ashkenazi Jews who came to Poland in numbers which soon surpassed those of Jews who had arrived there earlier from other places. The Ashkenazi immigrants flocked to Poland for several reasons. First of all, their existence in German towns was becoming intolerable as endemic religious hostility was growing virulent, particularly during the Black Death years in the mid-fourteenth century. Poland seemed to be a haven of safety where, as the Jews would say till the sixteenth century, "their hatred does not overcome us as in the lands of *Ashkenaz.*" Moreover, Poland needed their special financial talents. The economic attraction of these regions was further augmented after the fall of Constantinople in 1453 when southern Poland became an important thoroughfare for commerce with the Ottoman Empire.

| The Statute of Kalisz | The Black Death | Privileges for Lithuanian Jews |
| --- | --- | --- |
| 1264 | 1348 | 1388 |

*3. Illuminated prayer book, Siddur of the Rabbi of Ruzhin. Poland (?), mid-fifteenth century.*

**1018:** Boleslaw I, Duke (later King) of Poland, plunders the Jewish community of Kiev.

**1177–1296:** Jewish mintmasters in Poland issue coins with Hebrew inscriptions – important evidence on the presence of Jewish financiers who probably constituted the core of the organized Jewish community.

**Early 13th century:** Letter of the rabbi and *tosafist* Eliezer ben Isaac of Prague concerning the communities of "Poland and Russia"; this is the earliest source testifying to the existence of organized communities in Poland, and it reveals the role played by the Ashkenazi rabbinical elite in the spiritual development of East European Jewry.

**Middle of 13th century:** Mongol invasions bring destruction to many towns in Poland; the need for reconstruction attracts immigrants from German towns.

**1264:** The Statute of Kalisz of Duke Boleslaw V the Pious: based on German charters, it is the oldest grant of privileges to the Jews of Poland.

**1304:** The earliest reference to a "Jewish quarter" in Cracow.

**1334:** Casimir III the Great ratifies the Statute of Kalisz.

**1388:** Grand Duke Vitold grants economic privileges to the Jews of Lithuania; it is an important signpost in the expansion of immigration to this principality.

**1495:** Expulsion of the Jews from Lithuania; according to some scholars it was related to the "Judaizing heresy." Poland at that time has a population of between 10,000 to 30,000 Jews.

**1505:** Jews are allowed to return to Lithuania subject to the condition that they finance army units.

*4. Coins from the Dukal Treasury with Hebrew inscriptions, issued by Jewish mintmasters in Poland in the reign of Prince Mieszko III the Elder (1195–1202).*

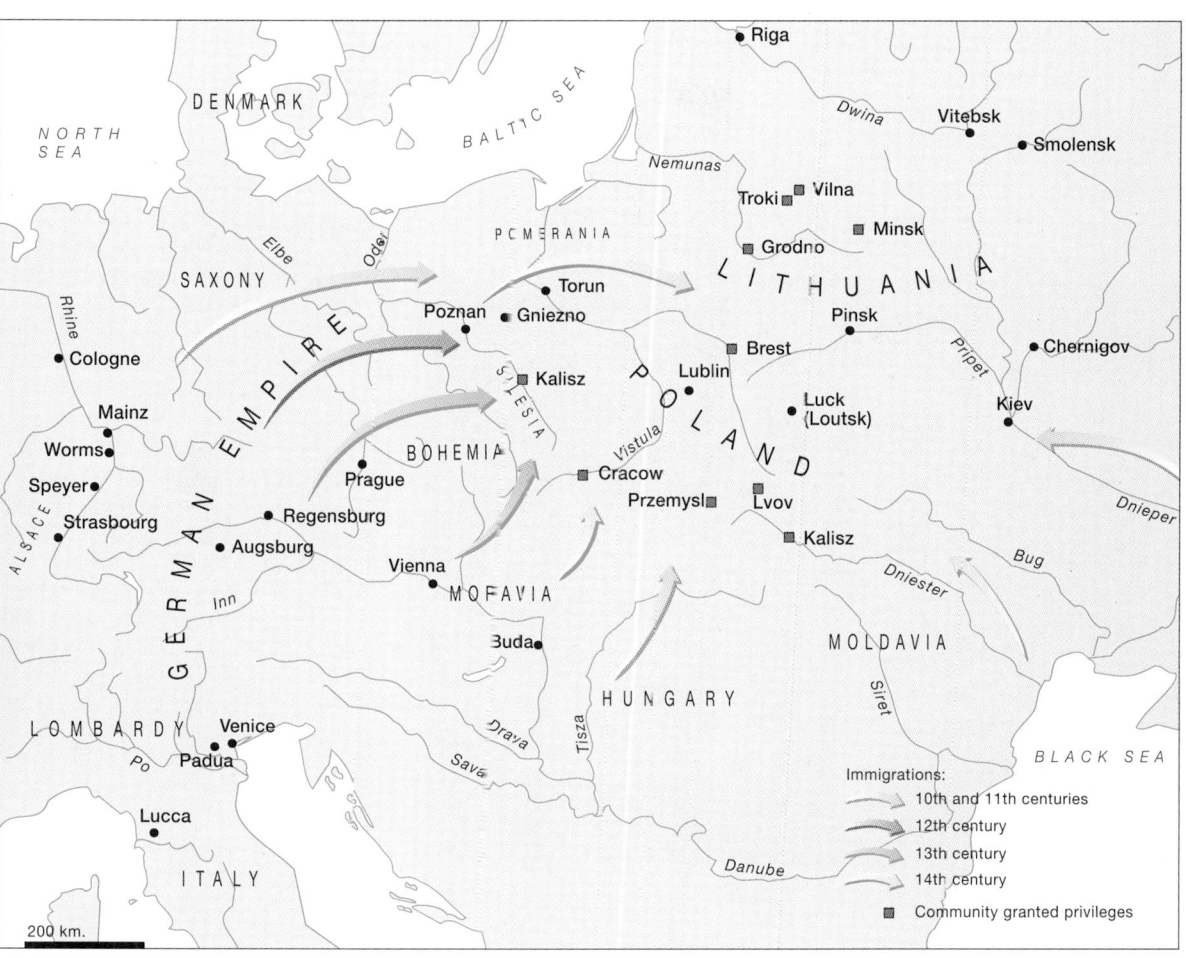

2. Torah finials (rimmonim) for decorating the Torah scroll and Yad (Torah pointer). Silver, Warsaw, mid-18th century.

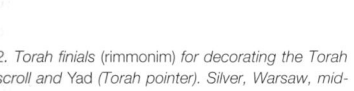

The demographic evolution of Poland's Jewry was accompanied by significant changes in their economic activity. While in Germany they specialized mostly in moneylending; in Poland they engaged in land-leasing from the nobles as well as in trade and crafts. These skills made them the ideal colonizers of border regions. Indeed, most of the new towns which grew on the frontiers of Poland and Lithuania were populated by a Jewish majority; but their movement to the eastern frontiers was also motivated by the growing hostility of the urban population in the old towns of the northwestern parts of the kingdom.

The Jewish expansion eastward was checked at the borders of the principality of Moscow. A Jewish presence in Russia became practically impossible after the panic aroused by the "Judaizing heresy" in the late fifteenth century. This religious event was crucial to the formation of the Russian rulers' attitude towards Jews, and they would not let them cross the Lithuanian border.

Thus, the colonization of the Ukraine, beginning with the unification of Poland and Lithuania and intensifying during the late sixteenth century, completed the dispersion of Ashkenazi Jewry. The geographical boundaries of the East European community would remain the same until the partition of Poland two centuries later.

| Expulsion of Lithuanian Jews | Return of the Jews to Lithuania |
|---|---|
| 1495 | 1505 |

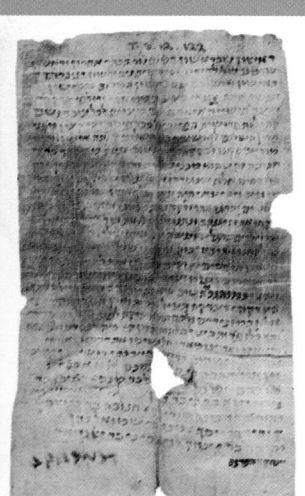

5. The "Kievan Letter" from the Cairo Genizah. On the bottom left corner, a word written in the Khazar idiom. 11th century (?).

DUKE BOLESLAW'S STATUTE, KALISZ, 1264 (excerpts)

1: In any cases concerning the property or person of a Jew, no Christian can be admitted against a Jew, unless the testimony of the Christian is accompanied by that of a Jew.

8: Municipal authorities shall have no jurisdiction in Jewish affairs, which shall remain in the hands of the prince or his count palatine . . .

9: If a Christian wounds a Jew, he shall be condemned . . . He shall bear moreover the costs of the damages and expenses sustained by the victim.

10: If a Christian murders a Jew, he shall receive due punishment, and all his goods shall be confiscated.

12: A Jew may go wherever he chooses. He shall be obliged to pay in each place the local taxes and duties bearing on his commerce, but he shall pay no taxes other than those laid upon the local citizens.

14: If a Christian commits a depredation in a Jewish cemetery, he shall be severely punished by the confiscation of all his goods.

15: If anybody attacks a Jewish synagogue with stones, he shall be condemned to pay two pounds of pepper to the count palatine.

20: If a Jew has been secretly murdered, and there is no witness to identify the murderer, and if certain Jews, upon inquiry, declare their suspicions, the duke as a mediator, will grant these Jews his protection of the court.

26: If anyone, man or woman, leads astray a Jewish child, he or she shall be punished as a thief.

29: Any Christian forcibly removing an article pawned with a Jew, or exercising violence in his house, shall be severely punished as a violator of justice.

30: Jews may be prosecuted only before their own courts or in places where Jews are customarily judged; exception alone is made for the duke or his count palatine, who can always summon Jews . . .

31: It is absolutely forbidden to accuse Jews of drinking human blood. If, nevertheless, a Jew is accused of the murder of a Christian child, such accusation must be proved by the testimony of three Christians and three Jews before the Jew can be condemned. If, however, the said witnesses and the innocence of the accused reveal the falsity of the charge, the accuser shall suffer the punishment that would have awaited the Jew.

35: If a Jew in dire straits calls for help in the night, and his Christian neighbors do not trouble themselves to succour him in his need, each of these Christians shall be fined 30 szelags.

# The Expulsion of the Jews from Spain

Early in 1492 Ferdinand and Isabella completed the *Reconquista* of Spain by defeating Granada, the last Muslim principality in the Iberian peninsula. At the end of that year Columbus informed the Spanish monarchs that he had discovered "the Indies." In between these two momentous events, the Catholic Kings signed the decree of expulsion of the Jews. The decision to banish the Jews was the culmination of a policy of repression adopted in Spain since the 1470s, a policy most clearly expressed by the establishment of a new Inquisition between 1478 and 1480, charged with the task of preventing "Judai-

1. Passover *Haggadah: the Hebrews fleeing from slavery pursued by the Egyptians. Catalonia, second half of 14th century.*

zation" among Christians. But was the expulsion decree a predictable and inevitable consequence of such a policy?

The Spanish inquisitors were indeed advocates of a "radical" solution: so long as there was a large and active Jewish community on Spanish soil, they said, all the Inquisition's attempts to deter and punish Judaizing Christians would be of no avail. The Jews were presumed responsible for the obduracy of the Marranos, who continued to practice Judaism clandestinely; the Jews were the ones who enticed New Christians back to their old faith. The Catholic Kings, on the other hand, were at first not inclined to bow to the inquisitors' directives. For quite some time they attempted to pursue the traditional policy of protecting both New

Christians and Jews. Not only a respect for precedent and a fear of disorder dictated this policy, but above all – material interest: the Jewish elites were, after all, indispensable to the economy of Spain.

Nevertheless, the Inquisition, genuinely convinced of the justness of its cause and obsessed with its own fears, was determined to attain its ends. In 1490–1491 it fabricated evidence of a Marrano-Jewish conspiracy, an allegation which made it possible to posit the expulsion of the Jews as a legitimate act of self-defense. No doubt, it was only the religious elation following the fall of Granada that persuaded the Spanish kings to agree to this extreme measure. Written by the Inquisition, signed by the sovereigns in March, and proclaimed a month later, the edict of expulsion ordered the Jews to leave Spain by the end of July. The great exodus proved such a terrible spectacle that even Spanish and Italian chroniclers who harbored no particular sympathy for the Jews, could not refrain from expressing horror and shock.

Most of the Jews found refuge in neighboring Portugal. Four years later the King of Portugal, under pressure by the Catholic Kings, proclaimed his own edict of expulsion. As the departures began, however, he reconsidered. His young and over-extended empire could not afford to lose a population which was so beneficial to the economy. He therefore decided to keep the Jews in the country by turning them into legal Christians. In 1497 all Jewish children were abducted and forcibly baptized; then the adults were assembled, ceremoniously baptized and declared equal citizens of the realm. In 1499 he withheld from these New Christians the right to emigrate. These blunt, uncompromising measures, however, did not lead to genuine integration: these converts continued to be regarded as Jews. Provoked by the plague and new taxes, riots in Lisbon in 1506 were accompanied by a massacre of New Christians. The Portuguese Crown was then forced to take this useful but victimized group under its protection, thus establishing with the *Conversos* the same kind of relationship that had existed between rulers and Jews in the Middle Ages.

In sixteenth-century Spain, "liberal" circles advocated an open policy towards the *Conversos*, believing that the superficial vestiges of their Jewish identity would eventually disappear. When the Jewish community was finally eradicated, the Inquisition was convinced that the New Christians had been completely integrated. Thus, by the 1520s or 1530s, the problem of "Judaizing" in Spain was practically resolved.

Nonetheless, the New Christians remained an integral part of Jewish history. Some *Conversos* found solace in the private sphere of literary creation; others sought refuge in ardent Christian piety. All these characteristics still set them apart from the "Old" Christian society and exposed them to various forms of discrimination. In some respects, the Jewish experience in early-modern Spain anticipated the dilemmas of emancipation which modern western Jewry was to face centuries later.

| First auto-da-fé in Seville | Torquemada is General Inquisitor | Fall of Granada |
|---|---|---|
| **February 6, 1481** | **October 1483** | **January 2, 1492** |

**1460:** In a work entitled *Fortress of the Faith*, Alfonso de Spina becomes the spokesman for "radical antisemitism": he proposes the establishment of a new Inquisition, denounces the "atrocious crimes" of the Jews, and cites the example of expulsions from other lands as precedents for the legitimacy and expediency of expelling the Jews and extirpating the "Jewish heresy."

**1481:** In an open letter to Cardinal Mendoza, royal secretary Hernando del Pulgar criticizes the actions of the Inquisition in Seville and proposes an alternative policy of "Christian education." In response, a defender of the Inquisition argues that the need to extirpate heresy justifies the occasional "stains" and persecution of innocents.

**February 6:** First auto-da-fé in Seville.

**1483. January 1:** Expulsion of the Jews of Andalusia.

**October:** Torquemada, Inquisitor General of Castile, is appointed Inquisitor General of Aragon; the entire Spanish Inquisition is henceforth under a single authority.

**1484:** First "instructions" for the Inquisition operations are issued by Torquemada.

**1485. September 15:** In Saragossa the inquisitor Pedro de Arbues is assassinated in the cathedral (he will be canonized by Pope Pius IX in 1867).

**1486. May:** The general chapter of the Hieronymite Order investigates Judaizing practices in its monasteries, and decides to prohibit the admission of New Christians. The General of the Order, who objected to the decision, is replaced. The Catholic Kings obtain a revocation of the rule, but in 1495 Pope Alexander VI ratifies a statute which prohibits the admission of all New Christians down to the fourth generation.

**1488:** The book *Alboraique* is written by an author close to Torquemada. The term "alboraique" signifies New Christians, portrayed neither as Christians nor Jews; they resemble the monstrosity of Borak, Muhammad's beast, which was neither horse nor mule. The *Conversos* have no place within a Christian society; being

2. *Alonso de Mena,* the Catholic Kings. *Royal Chapel, Granada, c.1630–1632.*

# 1492

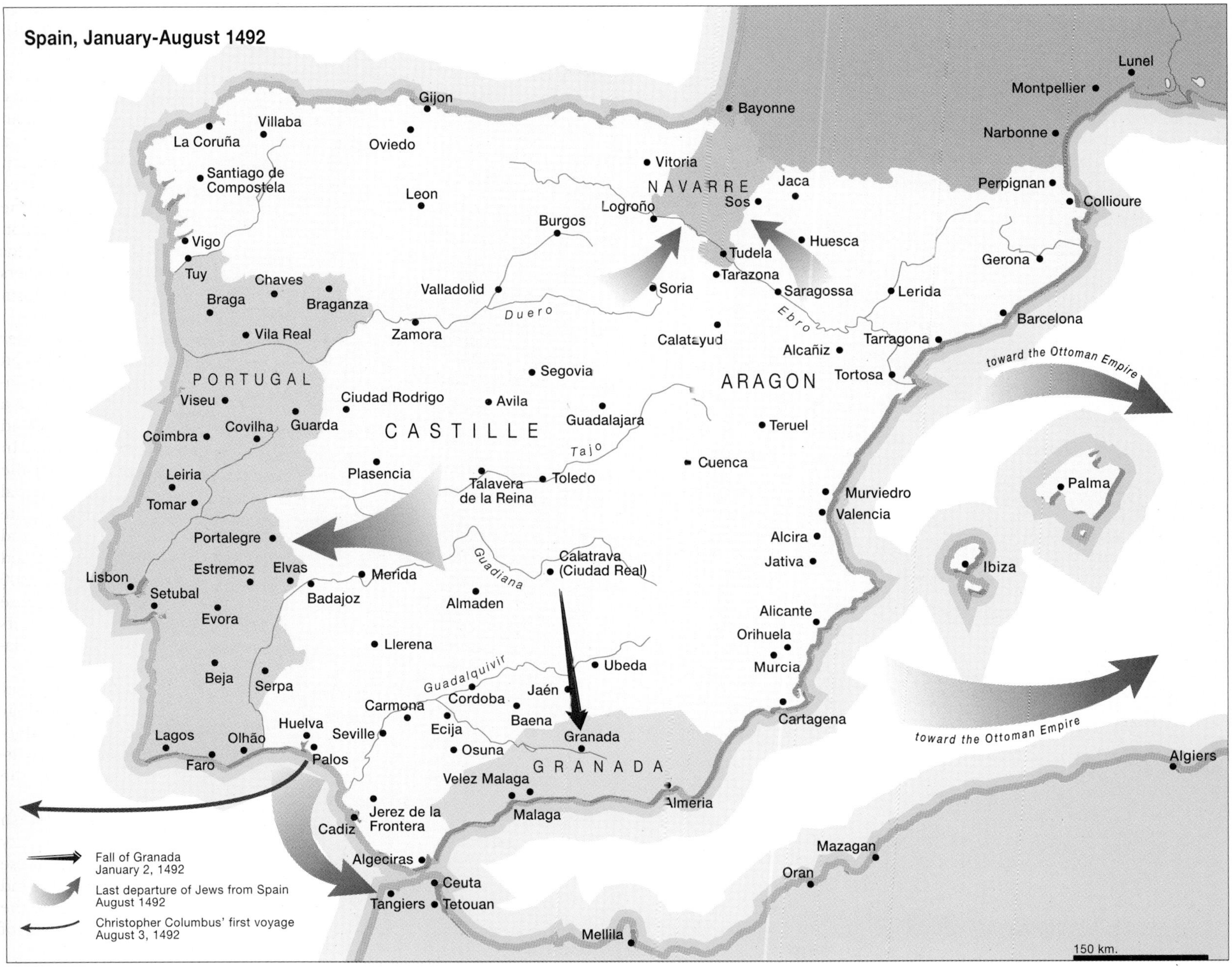

## Spain, January–August 1492

Lunel
Montpellier
Narbonne
Perpignan
Collioure
Gerona
Barcelona
Tarragona
Tortosa

Gijon
Bayonne
Villaba
Oviedo
La Coruña
Vitoria
NAVARRE
Jaca
Santiago de
Compostela
Leon
Logroño
Sos
Burgos
Vigo
Tudela
Huesca
Tuy
Soria
Tarazona
Saragossa
Lerida
Chaves
Valladolid
Braga
Duero
Calatayud
Alcañiz
Braganza
Zamora
ARAGON
Vila Real
Segovia
PORTUGAL
Viseu
Ciudad Rodrigo
Avila
Guadalajara
Teruel
Coimbra
Covilha
Guarda
CASTILLE
Cuenca
Leiria
Tajo
toward the Ottoman Empire
Tomar
Plasencia
Talavera
de la Reina
Toledo
Murviedro
Palma
Portalegre
Valencia
Estremoz
Elvas
Calatrava
(Ciudad Real)
Alcira
Lisbon
Merida
Guadiana
Jativa
Ibiza
Setubal
Badajoz
Almaden
Evora
Alicante
Llerena
Orihuela
Beja
Guadalquivir
Ubeda
Murcia
Serpa
Carmona
Cordoba
Jaén
Lagos
Huelva
Ecija
Baena
Cartagena
Olhão
Seville
Granada
Faro
Palos
Osuna
GRANADA
toward the Ottoman Empire
Algiers
Velez Malaga
Jerez de la
Frontera
Malaga
Almeria
Cadiz
Mazagan
Algeciras
Oran
Ceuta
Tangiers
Tetouan
Mellila

Fall of Granada
January 2, 1492

Last departure of Jews from Spain
August 1492

Christopher Columbus' first voyage
August 3, 1492

150 km.

| Decree of Expulsion | Departure of Christopher Columbus | Decree of Expulsion from Portugal |
|---|---|---|
| March 31, 1492 | August 3, 1492 | December 5, 1496 |

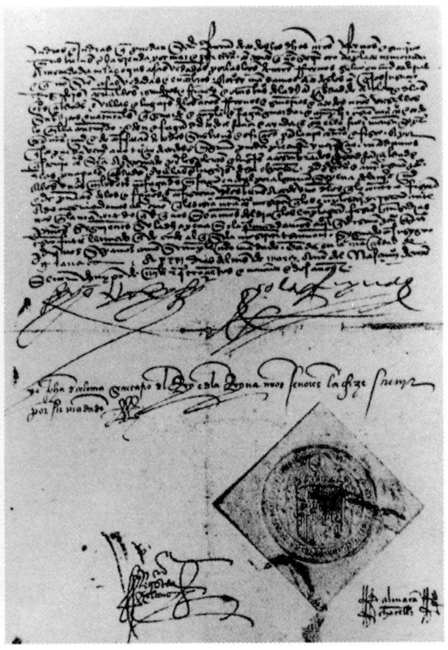

heretics, disloyal, and lazy, they can neither pray, fight, nor work.

**1490. December 17:** In Avila a trial takes place concerning the "child of La Guardia": Jews and *Conversos* are accused of crucifying a child and performing acts of sorcery designed to bring about the destruction of Christianity.

**1492. January 2:** The Catholic Kings enter Granada.

**March 20:** A plan for the expulsion of the Jews is presented to the Kings by Torquemada.

**March 31:** The Catholic Kings sign the edict of expulsion.

**April 29:** Publication of the edict.

**August:** Last departures of Jews.

**August 3:** Christopher Columbus sets sail from Palos.

**1493. January 12:** Last date set for the departure of the Jews from Sicily.

*3. Edict of expulsion, bearing seal and signature of the Catholic Kings. Granada, March 31, 1492.*

**1496. December 5:** Edict of expulsion of the Jews from Portugal.

**1497. April–October:** Expulsion from Portugal "commuted" to forced conversion.

**1504–1508, 1516–1522:** Two periods of crisis in Spain – one following the death of Isabella, and the other between the death of Ferdinand and the crushing of the *Communeros'* revolt, when strong objections are raised against the Inquisition.

**1506. April:** Attacks on New Christians in Lisbon.

**1507. March 1:** A law establishing "civil equality" between Old and New Christians in Portugal.

**June:** Diego Deza, a General Inquisitor known for the atrocities committed under his auspices, is dismissed and replaced by Ximenes de Cisneros.

**1510. November:** Partial expulsion of the Jews from the Kingdom of Naples.

*4. The Church of Santa Maria la Blanca, formerly a synagogue. Toledo, 13th century.*

# The Ashkenazi Mosaic

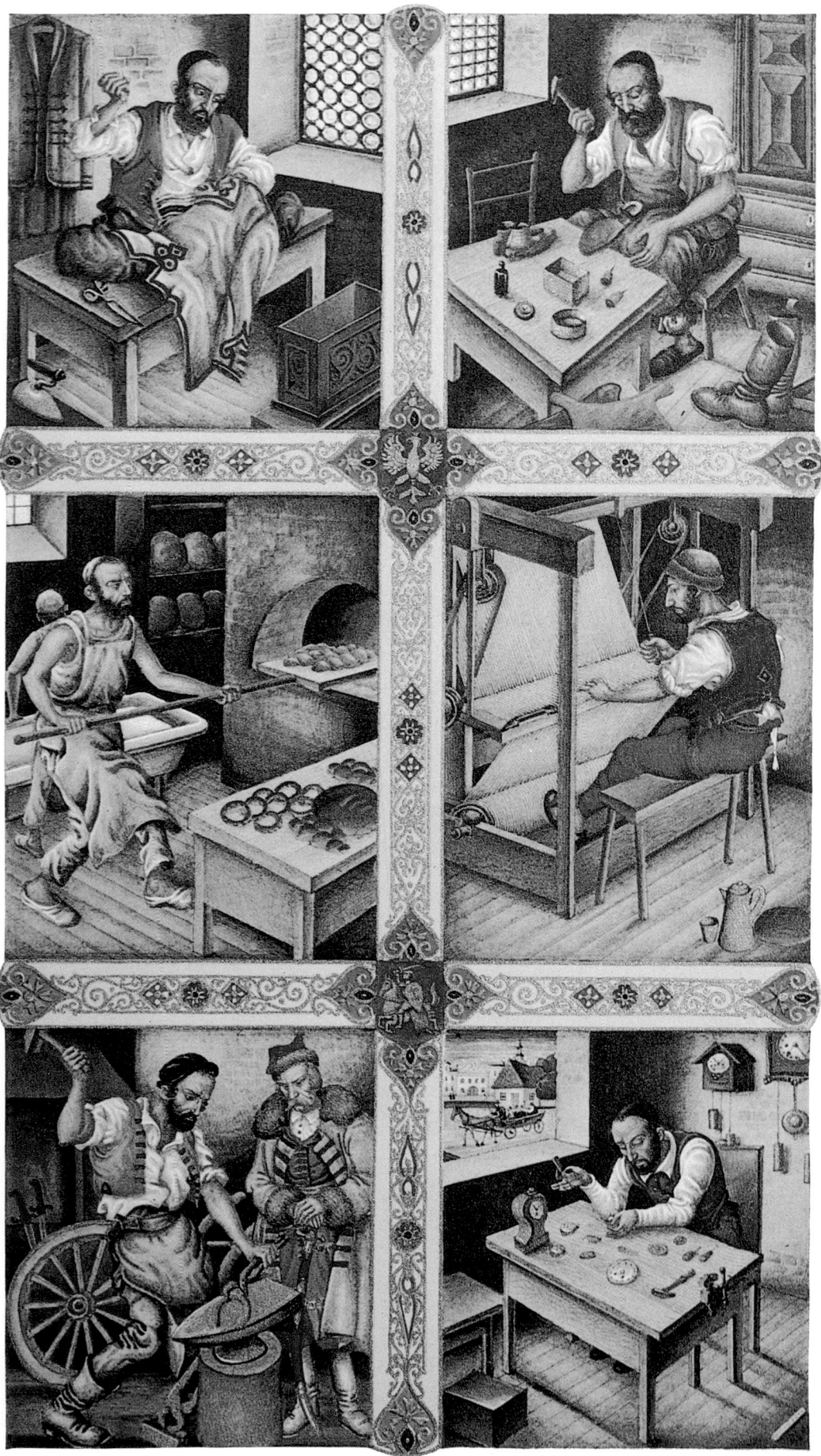

1. *Jewish occupations. A page from the illustrated edition of the* Kalisz Decree *(1264), by the Polish Jewish painter Arthur Szyk (1894–1951).*

During the late Middle Ages, the Jewish community in Poland, absorbing an influx of immigrants from Bohemia, Moravia, Italy and Germany, adopted customs which made it an integral part of the Ashkenazi diaspora. Ashkenazi culture, emanating from northern France and Germany, became dominant in East-European communities, and in Poland acquired some of its more characteristic features.

Jews settled in Poland at the same time as the Germans. The German urban model was transmitted to Eastern Europe, and the function of the Jew in the urban context was very similar to his previous role in German cities. Relations between Christian townsmen and Jews, both in the east and in the west, were determined primarily by rivalry and animosity.

Jews who immigrated to Poland imported forms of social organization which had evolved in the lands of *Ashkenaz*. Jewish communities throughout Eastern Europe were molded on these social structures: for instance, the structure of the *kahal* was almost identical in Alsace, Bohemia and Poland; and even the supra-structures ("Councils of the Lands"), normally associated with Poland and Lithuania, were not very different from those that had existed previously in Bohemia and Moravia.

The Jews of Germany brought with them the Judeo-German dialect, Yiddish, which was destined to become within a few generations the vernacular of Polish Jewry to the exclusion of all others. The "language of *Ashkenaz*" thus became the common idiom uniting the Jews of central and eastern Europe: Yiddish books printed in Basle, Amsterdam and Metz were sold in Cracow and Lublin; Yiddish literary works written in Italy became popular in Lithuania and the Ukraine. In Poland Yiddish became the Jewish language *par excellence*. An early seventeenth-century *responsum* of a rabbi to the inhabitants of a Lithuanian town clearly reflects this linguistic reality: "God willing, the earth will fill with knowledge and all will speak a single language, the tongue of *Ashkenaz*."

Finally, religious rites, formulation of prayers and methods of teaching in elementary talmudic schools (the *heder*, meaning classroom) as well as in the *yeshivot*, were also all transferred from Germany. It was this basic uniformity in Jewish religious life which for several centuries enabled students to move freely between the *yeshivot* of Poland, Germany and Alsace. Moreover, the intellectual elite of Polish Jewry was perfectly integrated in the Ashkenazi world: rabbis and talmudic scholars could travel with ease anywhere in the Ashkenazi domain, teaching or serving in communities which were distant from Poland, marrying into the Jewish oligarchies of Germany and Bohemia.

Polish Jewry was therefore an important member of a cohesive Jewish society. At the same time, it was also part (albeit a singular and an often despised part) of a German civilization that was spreading eastward. This fact helps to explain why Poland's Jews remained detached

# 14th–18th Centuries

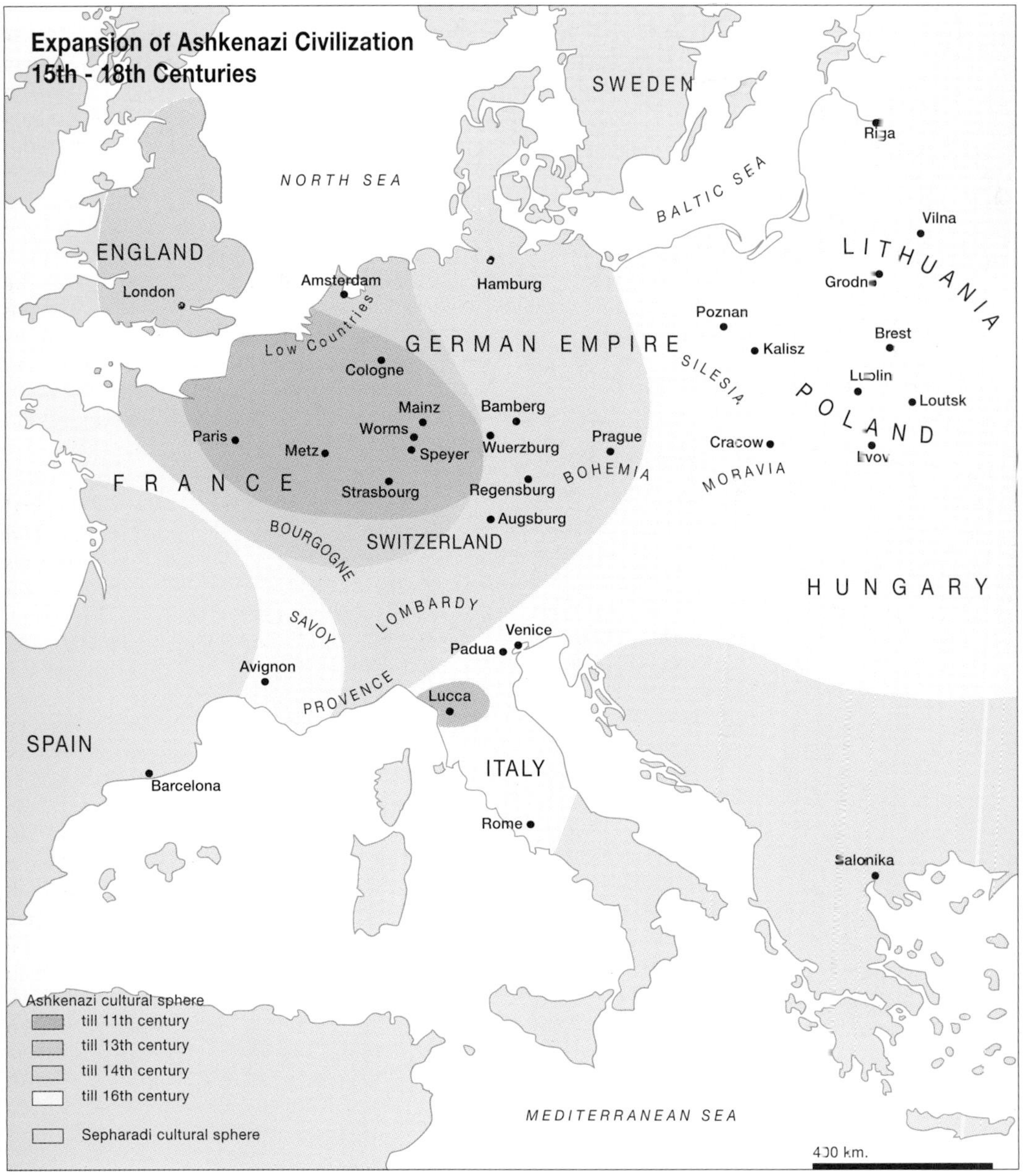
Expansion of Ashkenazi Civilization
15th - 18th Centuries
SWEDEN
NORTH SEA
BALTIC SEA
Riga
Vilna
LITHUANIA
Grodno
ENGLAND
London
Amsterdam
Hamburg
Low Countries
Poznan
Kalisz
Brest
GERMAN EMPIRE
SILESIA
Cologne
Lublin
Loutsk
POLAND
Mainz
Bamberg
Worms
Paris
Metz
Speyer
Wuerzburg
Prague
Cracow
Lvov
FRANCE
Strasbourg
Regensburg
BOHEMIA
MORAVIA
Augsburg
BOURGOGNE
SWITZERLAND
HUNGARY
SAVOY
LOMBARDY
Venice
Padua
Avignon
PROVENCE
Lucca
SPAIN
Barcelona
ITALY
Rome
Salonika
Ashkenazi cultural sphere
till 11th century
till 13th century
till 14th century
till 16th century
Sepharadi cultural sphere
MEDITERRANEAN SEA
400 km.

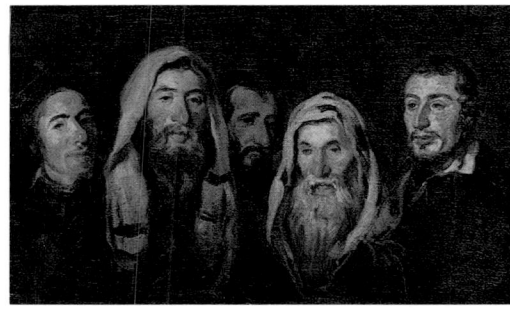

2. Piotr Mikhalowski (1800–1855), Jews.

SYNAGOGA·IVSTO
EST·EVERSA

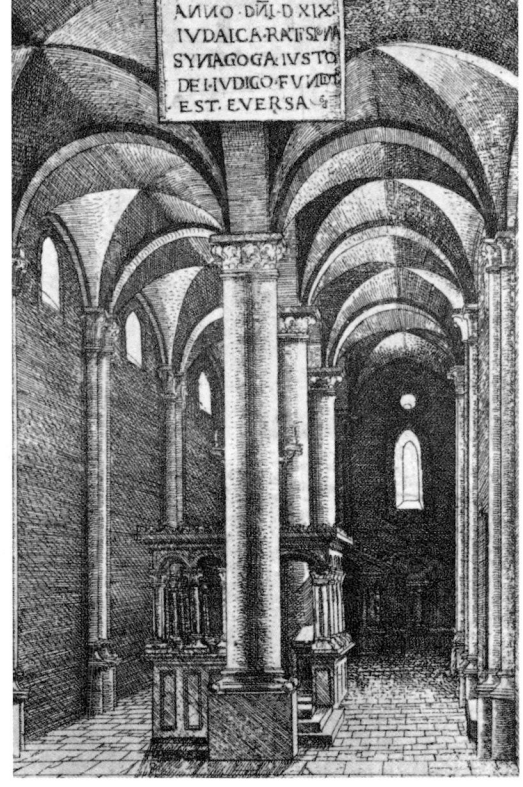

3. The synagogue in Regensburg. Engraving on copper, 1519.

from the Polish environment and were more influenced by intellectual developments in the west than in the east. Nevertheless, despite strong ties with German-Ashkenazi culture, the Jewish urban communites in Poland eventually developed their own local Ashkenazi tradition. Letters and other literary works from the seventeenth century indicate that local differences led to growing tension between Polish and German Jews. An anonymous satire dating from that period depicts a Polish Jew and a German Jew hurling terrible accusations at each other, thus revealing the diverging customs and ways of life which were gradually alienating these two communities.

The organizational, linguistic and cultural unity of the Ashkenazi diaspora survived until the second half of the eighteenth century. The advance of the Enlightenment in Germany, and the rise of enlightened despotism, drew the German Jews toward the modern urban civilization of the west, and weakened their ties with their fellow Jews in Poland.

ZYD
KRAWIEC
APTEKARZ
SZVNKARKA
MVZYK
ZLOTNIK
KVPIEC
CREDIT

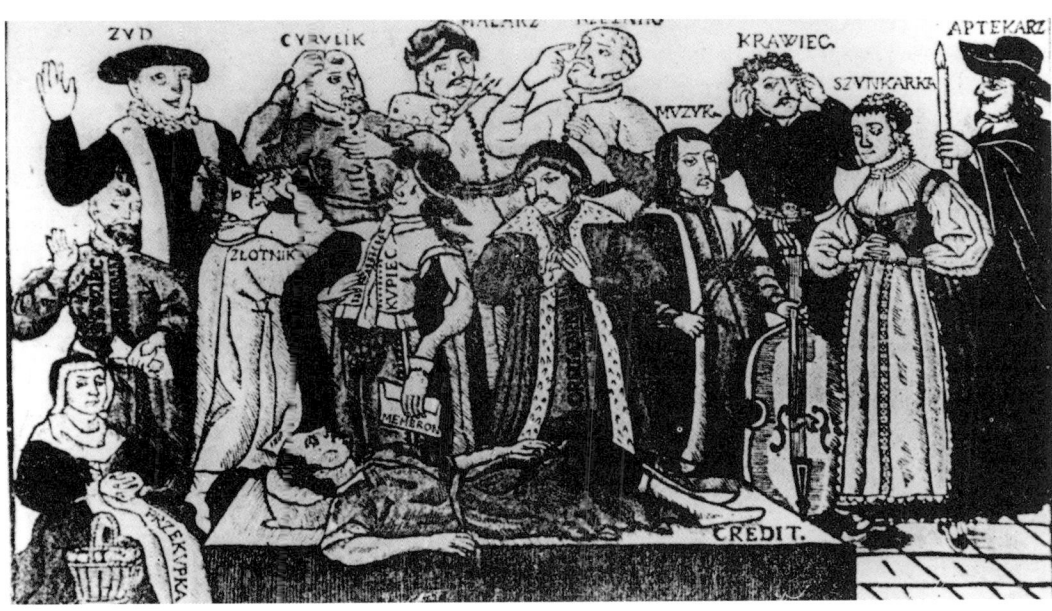

4. Allegorical painting depicting a Lamentation over the Death of Credit. Standing on the left is the Jew (ZYD). Engraving on wood, Poland, 17th century.

# Mamluk Palestine

1. Fountain of Sultan Qaitbay, Jerusalem, the Temple Mount, second half of 15th century.

When the Mamluks conquered Palestine, destroyed the coastal towns, and eliminated the last vestiges of crusader rule, the map of Jewish settlements in the land was radically changed. With the disappearance of the Acre community, which until then had been the most prominent, the inland communities of Safed, and especially Jerusalem, took its place. Gaza and Hebron harbored smaller communities, and several Jewish villages remained in the Upper Galilee. The Jewish villagers lived on agriculture, crafts, local trade, and rural peddling; the city-dwellers were artisans (weavers, saddlers, jewellers) and petty traders, mostly wine merchants – a trade prohibited to Muslims. Some European immigrants who specialized in what might be called a tourist industry supplied information, hostels, local products and money exchange to Christian pilgrims from their countries of origin. A tradition of Jewish pilgrimage to holy places in the Galilee as well as in Jerusalem, which began in the Ayyubid period, continued to bring many visitors from all over the Eastern diaspora, particularly in the spring months between Passover and Shavuot (Pentecost).

The leader of the Jews in the Mamluk state was the *nagid* in Cairo. Nominally he stood at the top of a hierarchy ruling over the communities of the three provinces – Syria, Palestine, and Egypt. A deputy leader represented the *nagid* in the provinces, at first in Damascus and from 1376 in Jerusalem. In practice, however, the Palestinian communities during the Mamluk period were self-governing, and the title of deputy-*nagid* was only honorary. The Mamluk authorities, fanatic and intolerant, harassed the Jewish population. At times there were outbreaks against the "protected people" followed by discriminatory legislation.

Immigration from the West continued regardless, but contacts with the source communities became extremely difficult after the collapse of the crusader state. Groups of scholars would prepare for *aliyah* to the Holy Land years before they undertook the journey itself, and on arrival in Palestine they formed communes based on a division of labor: some worked to support the whole group, while others studied the Torah.

In the second half of the fourteenth century, Palestine (this time Jerusalem rather than Acre) once more became a meeting place for three Jewish cultures – Ashkenazi, Sephardi, and Oriental. After the Black Death and the anti-Jewish violence which erupted in its wake, a group of scholars from the Rhineland, inspired by messianic expectations, founded an Ashkenazi *yeshivah* in Jerusalem which was active at least until the end of that century. Spanish Jews arriving at the same time were soon joined by Jewish intellectuals from Muslim countries and from Byzantium. Dozens of manuscripts produced in Jerusalem towards the end of the fourteenth century, some original and some copies of older works, on *Halakhah*, Spanish Kabbalah, Ashkenazi mysticism, and philosophy, attest to the rich blend and intensity of cultural life in this city.

**Battle of Ayn Jalut** — **1260**

**Mamluk conquest of Acre** — **1291**

**Anti-Jewish outbreaks in Spain** — **1391**

4. Tombs of the Just – Joseph in Shechem, Saul in Gilboa, Rabbi Akiva in Tiberias, etc. – in the eyes of a Jewish pilgrim. Manuscript dating from 1598.

**1260:** The Mongols take Jerusalem, slaughter part of the population, and expel the rest; Torah scrolls are transferred to Nablus; Baybars defeats the Mongols in the battle at Ayn Jalut and gradually conquers the land; beginning of Mamluk domination of Palestine.
**1267:** *Aliyah* of Moses ben Nahman (Nahmanides); he makes a pilgrimage to Jerusalem and describes the city in a letter to his son; he finally settles in St. Jean d'Acre, the major crusader port town.
**1286:** Temporarily removed from office as *nagid*, David ben Abraham Maimuni, Maimonides' grandson, settles for a while in Acre.
**1291:** The Mamluks take Acre, killing its inhabitants, including many Jews. The crusader period is over.
**1301:** Several violent anti-Jewish outbreaks throughout the Mamluk state.
**c. 1314:** Estori ha-Parhi, a Sephardi scholar, first settles in Jerusalem, then in Bet Shean; his *Sefer Kaftor va-Ferah* is the first

description of the topography and the population of medieval Palestine.
**1350:** *Aliyah* of Isaac ha-Levi Asir ha-Tikvah ("the hopeful"), the first Ashkenazi scholar to immigrate to Palestine after the Black Death.
**1354:** Anti-Jewish outbreaks, especially in Jerusalem.
**1377:** A deputy *nagid* is appointed in Jerusalem.
**1391:** Attacks on Jews in Spain lead to messianic agitation and emigration to Palestine.
**1391–1394:** The years covered by the "Documents of the Temple Mount" – archives of the Muslim tribunal in Jerusalem discovered in the al-Aqsa Mosque in 1975; these documents contain some information on the Jewish community in the city.
**1428:** The "interdict of the sea": following an attempt by the Jews of Jerusalem to seize a site on Mt. Zion known as the Tomb of David and held from 1335 by Franciscan friars, Pope Martin V prohibits Christian sea captains from transporting Jewish pilgrims to

2. Stone bridge. Ramleh, period of Sultan Baybars, 1260–1277.

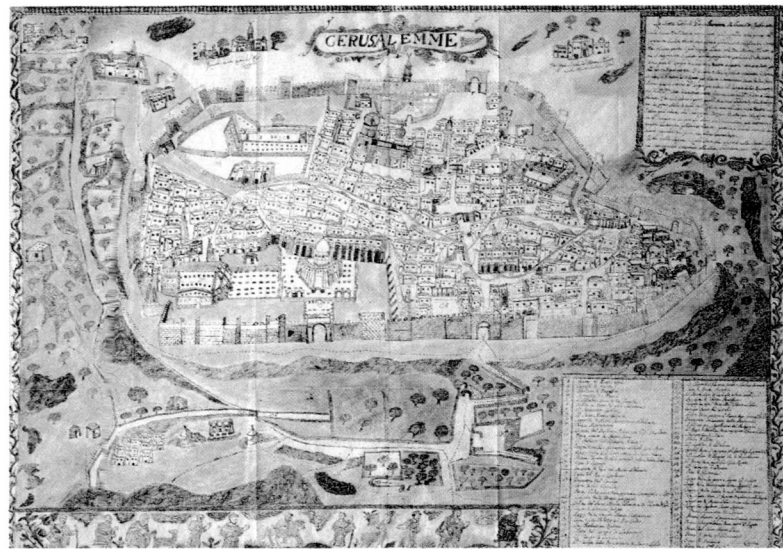

3. A map of Jerusalem. Anonymous, 16th century.

The 1391 anti-Jewish outbreaks in Spain, the fall of Constantinople in 1453, and the frequent expulsions from German cities formed an accumulation of disasters which aroused messianic tensions in Jewish society. The liquidation of the Byzantine Empire, for example, led many Jews who had suffered its persecutions and intolerance to believe that the end of Christianity was imminent. Such spiritual fermentation resulted in a continuous trickle of emigration from Europe to the Land of Israel. Those who announced their intention to "ascend" to the Holy Land enjoyed a privileged status within their communities, as these felt an obligation to aid and support such devout members. Nevertheless, when they came to Palestine, these immigrants, who in many cases were the religious elite in their former communities, encountered hostility on the part of the *parnasim* – the native secular leaders of the local communities – who were afraid of losing their authority.

Towards the end of the Mamluk period and particularly after the expulsion from Spain in 1492, it was the Spanish immigration (enthusiastically encouraged by the last *nagid*, Isaac ha-Kohen Sholal) which made its mark on Palestinian Jewry. Like all other communities in the Ottoman Empire, the community in the Land of Israel would be a predominantly Sephardi community until the nineteenth century.

| Expulsion of the Jews from Spain | Ottoman conquest of Palestine |
|---|---|
| **1492** | **1516–1517** |

Palestine; this quarrel is a pale reflection of fiercer strife between Jews and Christians in Europe, mostly in Spain, Germany, and Italy, often provoked by the mendicant orders. Jews from these communities, who were persecuted and consoled themselves with hopes of imminent redemption, comprised the majority of immigrants to Palestine. The papal interdict was strictly obeyed only by Venice and Naples.
**1453:** Constantinople is conquered by the Ottoman Turks.
**1456:** Abraham ben Eliezer ha-Levi, a *parnas* of the Jerusalem community, is the first emissary sent from the Jews of Palestine to the diaspora to inspire Jews to "ascend" to the Holy Land.
**1474:** Muslim zealots destroy the synagogue in Jerusalem; it was to be rebuilt that year by order of the Mamluk sultan Qaitbay. At about the same time Moses Esrim ve-Arba (meaning "twenty four"), a Yiddish writer and emissary from Jerusalem, embarks on a journey to Jewish communities throughout

the diaspora; signs of his visit have survived in Istanbul, Crete, Italy, and Germany.
**1481:** Pilgrimage of Meshullam of Volterra, a Florentine merchant, author of a remarkable travelogue particularly rich in detail about everyday life in Palestine.
**1483:** The "Elders affair": a severe conflict between local leaders and new immigrants, probably over financial matters, reduces the Jewish community in Jerusalem from 300 to 70 families.
**1484–1502:** Nathan ha-Kohen Sholal is the *nagid* of Jewry in Mamluk lands.
**1488:** *Aliyah* of Obadiah of Bertinoro from Tuscany, famous commentator on the Mishnah; the three letters which he sent from Jerusalem to Italy constitute a valuable source of information about Palestine at the end of the 15th century.
**1503–1517:** Isaac ha-Kohen Sholal is the last *nagid* under Mamluk rule.
**1516–1517:** The Ottomans conquer Palestine; end of the Mamluk period n the Land of Israel.

# The Jews of Italy

The self-governing medieval towns (communes) of central and northern Italy began to attract Jewish financiers from Rome and from lands beyond the Alps at the end of the thirteenth century. This migration constituted the original nucleus of most Italian Jewish communities surviving to this day. Jewish merchants and moneylenders had made themselves indispensable to the ecclesiastical authorities in Rome. Then, during the Avignon exile of the Papacy, many of them made their way to the north and settled wherever they found security for their investments, a convenient fiscal policy, and a need for the liquid capital they brought with them. A closely knit network of small Jewish communities was thus formed in the center of the peninsula, while other Jewish families migrated further north.

In the second half of the fourteenth century, Roman Jews reached the Po Valley. At the same time numerous Jews crossed the Alps into northern

1. A decorated coffer, marriage gift to the fiancée. Northern Italy, 15th century.

Italy after being chased out of German lands by the wave of pogroms provoked by the Black Plague of 1348–1349. For them too Italy was the obvious destination since the communes offered relative security and economic opportunities. A third wave, smaller in number, arrived in northern Italy after the expulsion of the Jews from France by Charles VI (1394). These Jewish merchants settled mostly in Piedmont and Savoy.

Jewish merchants and loan bankers were active in Italian lands throughout the communal period; but the most favorable period for Italian Jews was the Renaissance, when their community reached the zenith of its demographic curve: approximately 50,000 persons. Widely dispersed throughout the peninsula and distinguished by great geographical and social mobility, it was essentially a prosperous community and well integrated into local society which was, on the whole, surprisingly well-disposed towards the Jews.

As all moments of prosperity during the history of the diaspora, the Renaissance was also a time of brilliant cultural achievement: Jews participated actively in the general intellectual revival (the musician Salomone de'Rossi being perhaps the most illustrious example), but also vastly enriched their own particular culture. The spirit of the Renaissance deeply affected all fields of Jewish studies. It gave birth to Jewish historiography (Azariah de'Rossi); to Jewish biblical exegesis (Obadiah ben Jacob Sforno, who taught Hebrew to the German humanist Johannes Reuchlin); as well as to Jewish drama (Leone de'Sommi Portaleone).

Nevertheless, relatively tolerant though it may have been, Italian Renaissance society was still devoutly Christian, and thus by definition hostile to Jews. The Franciscan propaganda against usury, particularly ferocious during the fifteenth century, led to the founding of charitable loan banks (*monti di pietà*) throughout Italy. These were explicitly designed to chase the Jews out of the financial market where they had been especially numerous as a result of church prohibitions on Christians to engage in certain financial activities. Anti-Jewish sentiments were inflamed in 1475 by a ritual-murder libel in Trent which led to the destruction of the local Jewish congregation. Furthermore, when the Spanish monarchs decided to expel the Jews from Spain, their policy was also extended to their Italian possessions. Jews were ordered out of Sicily and Sardinia in 1492, and from the Kingdom of Naples in 1510; in 1515 the edict of expulsion was extended to the New Christians and their descendants. Renaissance toleration was being replaced by an age of segregation and expulsions.

The atmosphere surrounding the Jews became even more oppressive during the second half of the sixteenth century. The Catholic Church during the Counter-Reformation, in its efforts to protect Catholics from the possibility of religious contamination, invested great efforts in the process of pushing the Jews to the margins of Italian society. Their community, until then an integral and important part of the social, economic, and cultural life of Italy, was now turned into a persecuted pariah caste by the legislation and propaganda of popes and princes. The establishment of the Roman Inquisition, the burning of the Talmud in 1553, the creation of the ghetto in Rome by Pope Paul IV in 1555, the expulsion of the Jews from the Papal States in 1569 – all these were signposts in a process which would continue for over two centuries, until the French entered Italy in 1796.

| Jewish communities in the Po Valley | | The Bank of Pisa in Florence | The first *monte di pietà* |
|---|---|---|---|
| c. 1275 | | 1438 | 1463 |

**1255:** Pope Alexander IV nominates a group of Roman Jewish bankers as *mercatores Romanam Curiam sequentes* – official merchants of the papal curia.
**1275–1400:** Jews from Rome settle in central and northern Italy.
**1275–1475:** The rise of Jewish banking.
**1350–1420:** Establishment of Ashkenazi Jewish communities in northern Italy.
**1388–after 1460:** Moses ben Isaac da Rieti, rabbi of the Rome community, physician of Pope Pius II and poet, author of *Mikdash Me'at* – a Hebrew poem inspired by Dante's *Divine Comedy*.
**1390–1430:** Communities of French Jews are founded in Piedmont.
**1419, 1429:** Two bulls of Pope Martin V attempt to put a stop to the anti-Jewish activities of the Franciscans.
**1438:** Founding of the Pisa bank in Florence, the largest Jewish bank in Renaissance Italy.
**c. 1450–before 1515:** Obadiah ben Abraham Bertinoro, author of a commentary on the Mishnah, published in Venice in 1548–49; it will become the standard commentary on the Mishnah as is Rashi's on the Talmud.
**1463:** The first *monte di pietà* is established in Perugia.
**1468–1549:** Eliyahu Levita, called Bahur, philologist and lexicographer, compiler of dictionaries of Hebrew words in the Talmud, of Aramaic, and the first Hebrew-Yiddish dictionary.
**1475:** A ritual-murder libel in Trent.
**1486:** Giovanni Pico della Mirandola's *Oratio de dignitate hominis*; associated with the humanistic circle of this Florentine Hebraist and Christian Kabbalist, are the Jewish philosophers Elijah Delmedigo and Johanan Alemanno.
**1493:** Following the expulsion from Spain, Jews are forced to leave Sicily and Sardinia which are under Aragonese rule.
**1516:** The first ghetto is created in Venice.
**1524:** Pope Clement VII receives David Reubeni – a mysterious figure from the east

3. "La Schola Spagnola," the Spanish synagogue in Venice, completed in 1555, reconstructed in 1654 by the architect Baldassare Longhena, remains unchanged to this day.

claiming to be a prince of a Jewish kingdom of the lost tribes, seeking Christian aid against the Muslims in the Holy Land.
**1535:** Judah Abrabanel (Leone Ebreo) writes *Dialoghi d'amore*, a classic of Italian philosophic literature.
**1541:** Expulsion of the wealthy Jews of Spanish southern Italy who had been allowed to remain under previous edicts.
**1545–1563:** The Council of Trent – the Catholic Church defines its dogmas and adopts a harsh line against non-Catholics.
**1553:** Pope Julius III orders the burning of the Talmud in Rome and throughout Italy.
**1554:** All Hebrew books are submitted to censorship.
**1555–1796:** The Age of the Ghetto.
**1555:** Pope Paul IV orders the segregation of the Jews of Rome.
**1556:** The burning of *conversos* in Ancona.
**1569:** Pius V expels the Jews from all papal states, except Rome and Ancona.
**1571:** Expulsion of the Jews from Tuscany, except the ghettos in Florence and Sienna.

### The Ghettos of Italy, 16th - 18th centuries

Jews expelled from Spain (1492) and from Portugal (1496-1497)

Jews expelled from Spanish territories in Italy (1492-1493)

Expulsion to the interior of Italy

Ghetto

SAVOY
PIEDMONT
1575
MILAN
1597
Turin
Milan •
1489 Cremona
PO
GENOA
Genoa
1515
1550
Pisa
Leghorn
(Livorno)
1571
Sienna
TUSCANY
Florence
CORSICA
Trent
VENICE
1550
Mantua
Padua
Venice
Modena
Bologna
1593
Ravenna
• Rimini
Ancona
PAPAL
STATES
1569
Rome
ADRIATIC SEA
1515
1541
Naples
KINGDOM
OF NAPLES
Brindisi •
Tiber
• Sassari
• Alghero
SARDINIA
Cagliari •
MEDITERRANEAN SEA
• Palermo
Marsala •
SICILY
• Nicosia
• Paterno
Agrigento •
Ragusa
Scicli
Messina •
• Reggio
• Syracuse

150 km.

---

**The Ghetto of Venice**

**Burning of the Talmud in Rome**

**Expulsion of the Jews from papal states**

| 1516 | 1553 | 1569 |

**1583–1663:** Simone Luzzato, rabbi of the Venetian community, philosopher and mathematician, is the first to advance economic arguments in favor of toleration towards the Jews.

**1589–1628:** Solomon de'Rossi composes his major musical works: *Ha-Shirim asher li Shelomo* ("Solomon's Songs") – the first musical composition destined for liturgy in the synagogue.

**1593:** Portuguese *conversos* establish a community in Livorno (Leghorn), to become the most important of Italian Jewish communities.

**1597:** Philip II of Spain orders the expulsion of the Jews from the Duchy of Milan.

**1682:** Innocent XI orders the closing of the Jewish banks in Rome and throughout the papal states.

**1684:** During the siege of Buda in Hungary, the Jews are accused of aiding the Turkish defenders of the city; pogroms in Italy; the Padua Ghetto is attacked and pillaged.

**1777:** The Republic of Venice imposes heavier restrictions on the Jews living in the ghetto.

**1782:** In Italian territories under Austrian rule the Jews are granted religious freedom and other privileges.

**1796:** Bonaparte's Italian army puts an end to the Age of the Ghetto and proclaims the emancipation of Italian Jewry.

*4. Jewish Funeral, by the Venetian painter Pietro Longhi (1702–1785).*

# Jewish Music

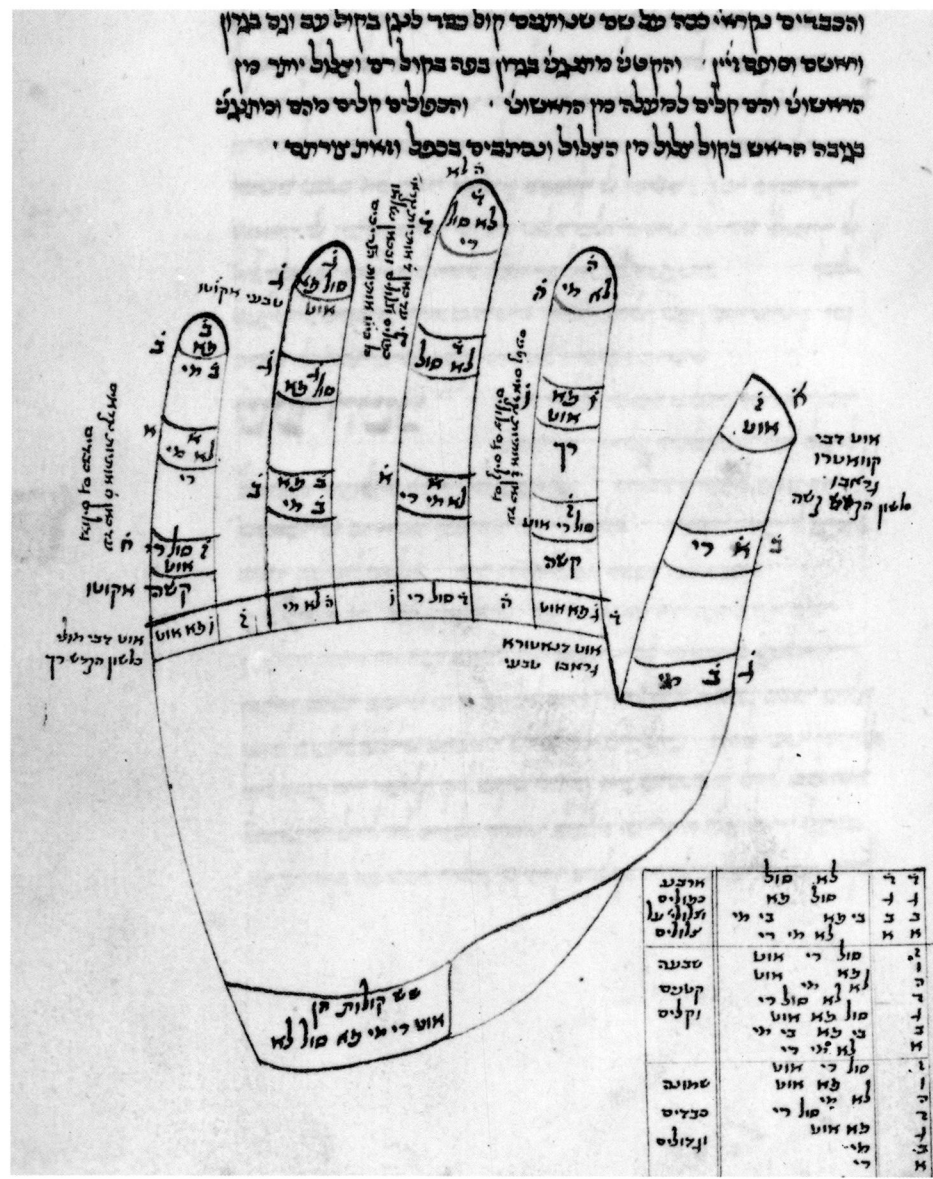

*1. Hebrew version by Judah ben Isaac (13th century) of the "Guidonian Hand," named after Guido of Arezzo, the 11th-century Benedictine monk to whom we owe the names and order of the notes.*

Were it possible to hear in modern melodies traces of levitical singing in the Temple, or the playing of instrumental music by both elite and simple folk in biblical times, it might be said that Jewish music is one of the oldest musical traditions in the world. However, ancient Hebrew music was transmitted solely by way of an oral tradition, leaving no written records. Furthermore, the destruction of the Temple, exile, and dispersion, have fragmented this musical heritage into a multitude of regional traditions which over time have absorbed different local influences. Scholars attempting to uncover common roots underlying the elements accumulated over the centuries, have proposed interesting, but entirely unfounded, hypotheses.

There is however sufficient evidence to describe certain stages in the evolution of Jewish music after the destruction of the Temple. The first basic change occurred in the transition from a ceremonial ritual of singing and playing by a professional order of musicians – the levitical singers in the Temple – to the more intimate and simple form of unaccompanied chanting in the synagogue. The text and its message were the primary object of prayers and biblical readings chanted in a simple melodic pattern. Therefore, any member of the congregation could lead in prayer as a "delegate of the community" (*sheliah zibbur*). After the completion of the Talmud, a system of accents and vocalization indicators (*ta'amei mikra*), prescribing how the reader was to organize his recitation, was gradually established. Most of the diaspora followed the musical intonation invented in Tiberias in the tenth century, but the style was gradually transformed in each region through the influence of local musical traditions. This "learned art" of biblical chanting became one of the driving forces of Jewish musical evolution. The Ashkenazi style was the first to be transcribed into musical notes by Christian humanists in the early sixteenth century.

The introduction of the hymn (*piyyut*) into synagogue liturgy is ascribed to sixth-century Palestine. Initially intended to embellish prayers on Sabbaths and festivals, liturgical hymns soon emerged out of the synagogue and became prevalent in all spheres of Jewish life, the communal as well as the private. A key element in the evolution of Jewish music was thus the composition of *piyyutim*, with melodies based primarily on local traditions. The

| Levitical singers | The Palestinian *Piyyut* | Golden Age of Spanish music |
|---|---|---|
| 10th–6th centuries BC | 6th–7th centuries AD | 10th–13th centuries |

*3. Liturgical chant for a synagogue service. The Hebrew text is the beginning of Psalm 86 and the musical notes conform to the usual notation of the period. Italy, late 13th century.*

**First Temple Period:** Elaborate sacerdotal music, reserved for a specific order of Temple musicians – the levitical singers. Sixteen different musical instruments are mentioned in the Bible.

**1st–2nd centuries AD:** The Mishnah contains eyewitness descriptions of music in the Temple; the Dead Sea Sect develops public chanting of Psalms and composes a rudimentary musical theory; Hellenistic

influences on secular Jewish music.
**6th–7th centuries:** Beginning of the *piyyut* in Palestine.
**9th–11th centuries:** The *hazzan* as a professional musician; adoption of the Tiberian system of accents and musical intonation; rudimentary musicology under Arab influence. Before 942, Saadiah Gaon writes a treatise on rhythmic science influenced by the Arab philosopher Al-Kindi.
**10th–13th centuries:** The Spanish Golden Age: Dunash ben Labrat adapts Arab metrics to Hebrew poetry. Jewish musicians, minstrels and jugglers, perform in Spanish courts and before high-class audiences elsewhere in Europe. The earliest notation of Jewish music by Obadiah the Norman Proselyte (12th century), found in the Cairo *Genizah*.
**14th century:** Levi ben Gershon

*4. Salamone de' Rossi (c. 1570–1628), The Songs of Solomon, the first synagogal composition to be printed. Venice, 1622–1623.*

*hazzan-paytan* ("cantor-poet") was the composer of both text and tune and the solo singer of his own creations. The growing importance of the musical element in the synagogue was regarded with suspicion by the rabbis. Rabbinical prohibitons (on playing instruments in the synagogue or on imitating foreign rites) undoubtedly impeded the development of Jewish music.

The classical tradition of liturgical hymns was continued in Italy and Germany, while in Spain new forms were developed between the tenth and fifteenth centuries under the influence of Arab and Spanish poetry. Particularly stimulating was the adoption of strophic forms in the order of the rhymes which are more easily integrated with music and enable audience participation in singing the unchanging refrain. The Spanish heritage also fostered a repertoire of secular folk songs, popular ballads or *romanceros*, preserved by Ladino-speaking communities down to this day.

The expulsion from Spain and the mass migration of Ashkenazi Jews to the east in the sixteenth century created a new map of Jewish communities. During the same period there was an increase in the spread of the Safed Kabbalah, which emphasized singing as a means of elevating man's spirit to the celestial. The joyous reception of the Sabbath (on Friday evening), supplications, psalmody, and wordless coloraturas of the mystics, considerably enriched the Jewish musical repertoire. The musical ideas of the mystical Kabbalah had a strong influence on the sacred and secular poetry of Yemenite Jewry, and on the singing and dancing of the Ashkenazi Hasidic movement. From the early eighteenth century the *niggun* ("melody") was a major element in the life of the *hasid*, helping him to ascend to higher levels of mystical enthusiasm.

When emancipation enabled Judaism to emerge from its relative isolation, integration into European music became all the more pronounced. The Reform movement, attempting to modernize German Jewry by adopting European customs and aesthetic values, introduced the organ, a professional choir, and chorale-like music into the synagogue. With its encounter with modernity in both western and oriental communities, the characteristic features of Jewish music were gradually depleted. The one remaining distinctive trait of contemporary Jewish music is its profusion of styles.

2. *The Barcelona Haggadah. Barcelona, mid-14th century.*

---

**Hazzanut in Eastern Europe** | **Music of the Hasidim** | **Reform of synagogue service in Germany**

| 17th century | 18th century | 19th century |

**Hazzanut in Eastern Europe**

5. *Fragment of a Hebrew hymn with musical notation from the Cairo Genizah, early 12th century.*

(1288–1344), *De numeris harmonicis.*
**14th–15th century:** The spread of the Kabbalah among Spanish, Provençal and Italian Jews endows music with special importance; integration of Italian Jews in Renaissance culture.
**15th–16th centuries:** Transcription of *ta'amei ha-mikra* by Solomon Minz (1483) and by the Christian humanists J. Boeschenstein, J. Reuchlin and S. Munster.
**16th century:** Due to the Safed Kabbalah, singing penetrates every aspect of Jewish life; in Italy, first attempts to introduce "classical" music to liturgy; a similar process takes place among Spanish and Portuguese exiles in the West, while the oriental Jews adopt Arab and Turkish music.
**c. 1650:** First information about synagogue singing (*Hazzanut*) in Eastern Europe, and about *Klezmerim*, musicians who perform for Jews and gentiles on festive occasions.
**1730–1750:** *Hasidim* exalt singing and dancing as essential elements in their religious practices. Ashkenazi *hazzanim*

6. *Detail from the Golden Haggadah. Barcelona, c. 1320.*

begin to note their music.
**1804–1807:** In Germany, the Reform movement introduces organ music and professional choir singing to the synagogue service.
**1822–1845:** East European *hazzanut* emphasizes the virtuosity of the singer under the influence of opera.
**After 1850:** Traditional *hazzanut* loses its importance; compilation, notation and publication of works on Jewish music.
**1880:** Ashkenazi *hazzanut* first appears in the United States.
**1896:** Systematic collections of Judeo-Spanish *romanceros*.
**1905:** In Jerusalem, an American, A.Z. Idelsohn, collects and records the musical traditions of the oriental communities, and publishes a *Thesaurus of Hebrew Oriental Melodies* in ten volumes.
**1908–1922:** In St. Petersburg, a society for Jewish folklore music begins to collect popular songs; the appearance of the idea of a "national Jewish style."

# Jews in the Ottoman Empire

The Ottomans began to emerge as a great political and military power from the early fourteenth century. Uthman, founder of a dynasty, came from a small Turkish principality, which in time grew into a vast empire. The swords of his successors brought to an end the centuries-long Greek influence in the south of the Mediterranean basin, replacing it with Muslim domination. Extending deep into the European continent, Ottoman expansion turned Vienna into an outpost of Christendom.

The Greek-speaking Jewish communities, which the immigrants from Spain and Portugal later called "Romaniots" or "Gregos," were all under Ottoman rule at the time of the fall of Constantinople – renamed Istanbul – in 1453. The Arabic-speaking Jews ("Mustarabs" in the idiom of the Iberian refugees), were the other important indigenous group. They lived in "Arabistan" – countries conquered mainly during the reign of

1. The "Ochrida" synagogue in Istanbul, founded after the Ottoman conquest of the town.

Selim I (1512–1520) and of his son Suleiman the Magnificent (1520–1566). For all the Jews the conquest was a salvation, as their situation in the fourteenth and fifteenth centuries under Byzantine and Mamluk rule had been extremely difficult.

Then, in the wake of the expulsion from Spain (1492) and the forced conversion in Portugal (1497), tens of thousands of Iberian Jews arrived in Ottoman territories. As all that was required of them was the payment of a poll-tax and acknowledgement of the superiority of Islam, the empire became a haven for these refugees. From early in the sixteenth

century, the Jewish community in the Ottoman Empire became the largest in the world. Constantinople and Salonika each had a community of approximately 20,000 people. Immigration from the Iberian peninsula, arriving in several waves throughout the sixteenth century, also transformed the character of Ottoman Jewry. Far more numerous than the local Jews, the Spaniards and the Portuguese soon submerged the Romaniots, and the indigenous population was assimilated into the culture and community of the new immigrants.

After the conquest of Constantinople, Muhammad II, wishing to aggrandize the city and make it into a capital befitting a great empire, brought into it many people from the provinces. This migration affected the Jewish community and changed the character it had acquired during the Byzantine period. The economic and religious situation was indeed ameliorated; but many of the older Romaniot congregations disappeared, their memory preserved only in the names of several synagogues in Istanbul. The congregations which replaced them in the capital, as well as in Salonika or in Tiriya in western Anatolia, were purely Spanish.

Within the communities the congregations were organized according to the geographic origin of their members. Grouped around the synagogues, the Jewish organizations provided all the religious, legal, educational, and social services, thus creating an almost autonomous society. Until the end of the sixteenth century, these institutions were very flexible, allowing significant mobility within them. The geographic origin of its members soon lost its importance, and the development of the congregation was determined by power struggles between rich individuals or groups with conflicting interests.

Throughout the sixteenth century the Jews in the Ottoman Empire enjoyed remarkable prosperity. The empire was rapidly expanding, and economic demand rose accordingly. Thus the Jewish population could easily enter into trade with Christian Europe and into industries such as wool weaving which were only then beginning to evolve. Under the leadership of figures like Don Joseph Nasi and Solomon ibn Yaish, they could take advantage of their world-wide network of family connections and their knowledge of European affairs in order to promote the concerns of the Sublime Porte, as well as to protect their personal interests and those of their community.

This was also a time of cultural blossoming: Hebrew Law was enriched by Joseph Caro's *Shulhan Arukh* (the "Prepared Table") which was to become the authoritative code for the entire Jewish nation; while from Safed in Palestine emerged the Lurianic Kabbalah of Ha-Ari, one of the most influential trends in Jewish mysticism. It seems that these communities of exiles, suddenly liberated from the danger of extinction, could give expression to an outburst of cultural forces which had been stifled by centuries of persecution.

| Timur Lang in Anatolia | Conquest of Constantinople by Muhammad II | Expulsion from Spain |
|---|---|---|
| 1402–1413 | 1453 | 1492 |

**1394:** Expulsion of the Jews of France and the beginning of their emigration to territories under Ottoman occupation.
**1402–1413:** The Mongols of Timur Lang conquer the Ottoman principality.
**1413–1450:** Reign of Muhammad I and Murad II: a new era of conquest.
**1426–1450:** Expelled from the Rhineland and Bavaria, the Jews migrate to Ottoman lands.
**1453:** Constantinople is captured by Muhammad II, the Conqueror; deportation of Jewish communities of western and southern Anatolia, of the Black Sea, of Macedonia, Thracia, and Bulgaria to the new capital of the empire; establishment in Istanbul of congregations of the expelled (*surgun*); Rabbi Moses Capsali – rabbi of the Romaniots in Istanbul.
**1492:** Expulsion of the Jews from Spain, many of whom migrate to Ottoman lands; establishment of congregations of immigrants who "came of their own free will" (*kendi gelen*) in Istanbul, as well as in all other important towns throughout the

empire; beginning of the wool industry in Salonika.
**1497:** Beginning of the immigration from Portugal.
**1501:** Expulsion of the Jews from Provence.
**1504:** First Hebrew printing press in Istanbul.
**1506:** Pogroms against "New Christians" in Lisbon and beginning of a "period of grace" when they are allowed to leave Portugal; immigrants continue to flock to Ottoman lands.
**1512–1520:** Reign of Selim I; incursions into Iran and conquest of the Near East.
**1513:** Beginning of Hebrew printing in Salonika.
**1516:** Conquest of Palestine; accelerated immigration to the two centers of the country – Safed and Jerusalem.
**1520–1566:** Reign of Suleiman II, the Magnificent; conquests in Iran, Hungary, Transylvania; building of the present walls of Jerusalem.
**1525:** Wool industry flourishes in Safed which becomes the most important Jewish

2. A Jew from Istanbul, painting on paper, 1618.

center in Palestine and, after Istanbul and Salonika, the third in importance in the empire.
**1531:** End of the "period of grace" in Portugal.
**1538:** Rabbi Jacob Berab renews the ordination of sages in the Land of Israel, interrupted since the suppression of the Sanhedrin.
**1542:** In Safed Rabbi Joseph Caro completes his work *Bet Yossef* ("The House of Joseph").
**1553–1554:** Don Joseph Nasi and Dona Gracia settle in Istanbul; beginning of Don Joseph's activities at the sultan's court.
**1554:** Moses Hamon, the sultan's physician, obtains a *firman* (decree) against those who accuse Jews of ritual murder.
**1555:** Joseph Caro completes the writing of *Shulhan Arukh*, an abridgement of *Bet Yossef*.
**1556–1557:** Burning of Conversos in Ancona and an abortive attempt by the Nasi family to organize a boycott of this port by all the

## Migration within the Ottoman Empire
### 15th - 16th centuries

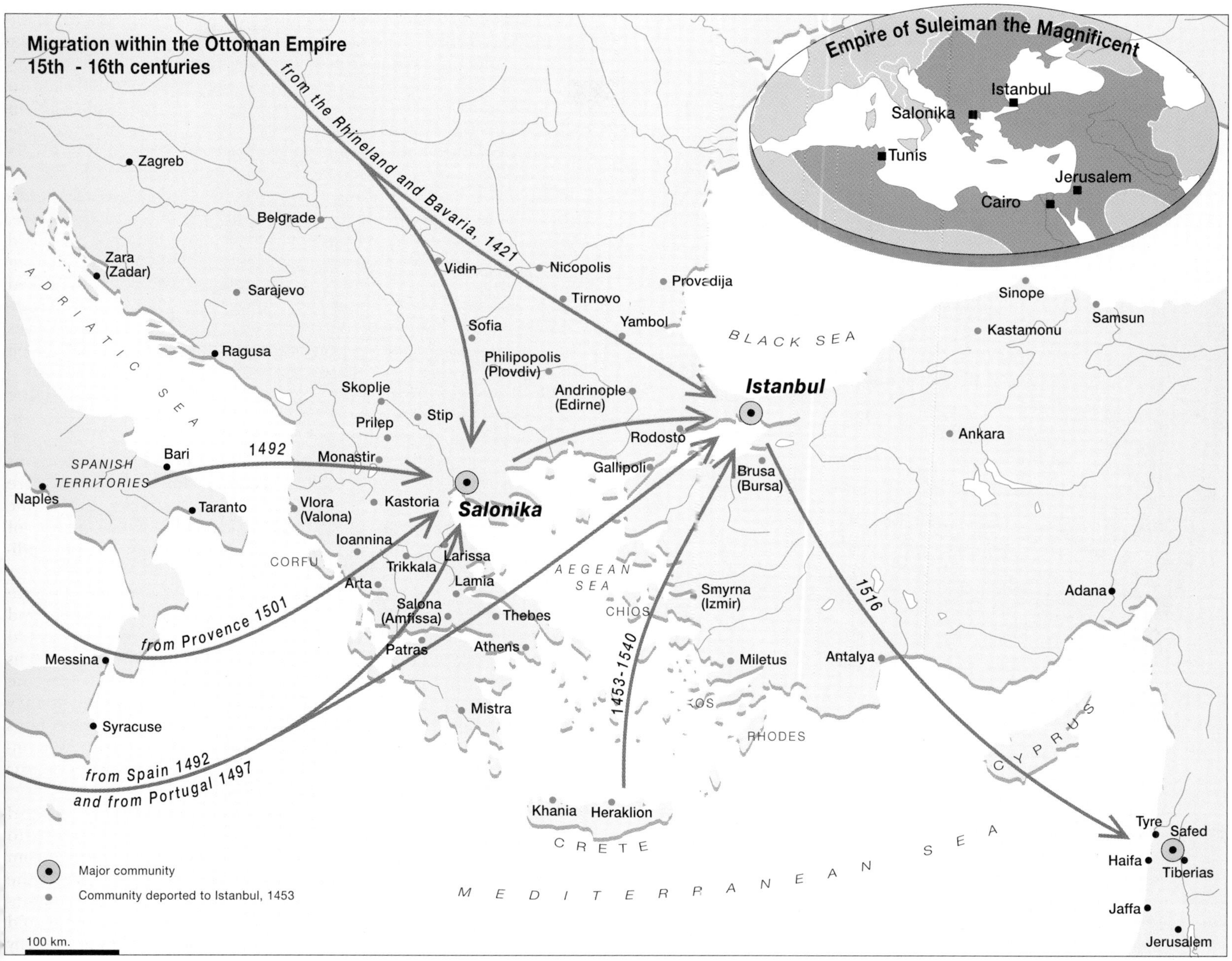

**Empire of Suleiman the Magnificent**

*(Map labels:)*

Zagreb
Belgrade
Zara (Zadar)
Sarajevo
Vidin · Nicopolis · Provadija
Tirnovo
Yambol
Sofia
Philipopolis (Plovdiv)
Andrinople (Edirne)
Skoplje
Prilep · Stip
Rodosto
Monastir
Gallipoli
Vlora (Valona) · Kastoria
**Salonika**
Ioannina
Larissa
Trikkala
Arta · Lamia
Salona (Amfissa)
Thebes
Patras
Athens
Mistra
Khania · Heraklion

*from the Rhineland and Bavaria, 1421*
*1492*
SPANISH TERRITORIES
Bari
Naples
Taranto
Messina
*from Provence 1501*
Syracuse
*from Spain 1492 and from Portugal 1497*

CORFU
ADRIATIC SEA
Ragusa

**Istanbul**
Brusa (Bursa)
BLACK SEA
Sinope
Kastamonu · Samsun
Ankara
Smyrna (Izmir)
Miletus
Antalya
Adana
*1516*
*1453-1540*
AEGEAN SEA
CHIOS
RHODES
CRETE
CYPRUS
MEDITERRANEAN SEA

Tyre · Safed
Haifa · Tiberias
Jaffa
Jerusalem

Istanbul
Salonika
Tunis
Cairo
Jerusalem

⊙ Major community
• Community deported to Istanbul, 1453

100 km.

---

**Selim I conquers Palestine** | **Accession of Suleiman the Magnificent** | **Don Joseph Nasi in Istanbul**
1516 | 1520 | 1553

*3. The walls of Jerusalem erected by Suleiman the Magnificent. Photograph by Auguste Salzmann, 1854.*

Jews in the empire.

**1560:** On the initiative of Dona Gracia Nasi, Jews begin to resettle in Tiberias.

**1566:** Death of Suleiman the Magnificent and ascent of Selim II; Don Joseph Nasi becomes Duke of Naxos.

**1568** A delegation of Jews from Salonika obtains a convenient tax arrangement from the sultan.

**1569:** A great fire in Istanbul causes grave damage in the Jewish quarter; death of Dona Gracia Nasi; capitulations to France. The import of French cloth competes with the products of the Jewish-owned industry.

**1570–1572:** Ha-Ari (Rabbi Isaac Luria Ashkenazi) is leader of the kabbalists of Safed.

**1579:** Death of Don Joseph Nasi.

**1580:** Capitulations to England; the Ottoman markets are flooded with English cloth which seriously harms the industry of Salonika.

**1585:** Don Solomon ibn Yaish arrives in Istanbul and begins his political activities.

**1603:** Death of Don Solomon ibn Yaish.

*4. Selim I at the battle of Chaldiran (1514). Oil on wood, Iran, 19th century.*

# The Marrano Diaspora

*1. Ex-libris used by Manasseh ben Israel between 1635 and 1650.*

**P**ortugal, pressured by Spain to rid itself of its Jewish population but reluctant to lose economic benefits, chose in 1497 to solve the problem by mass conversion rather than by expulsion. But, by creating a large class of New Christians, the Portuguese authorities now had to contend with the emergence of Crypto-Judaism, a problem for which they were ill-equipped. The model of the Spanish Inquisition offered a "solution."

The establishment of the Portuguese Inquisition between 1536 and 1539 accelerated the exodus of New Christians from the Iberian peninsula, a tide which frequent prohibitions on emigration could not stem. Some of the emigrants went to join the prosperous communities in the Ottoman Empire where they could openly return to Judaism. Many others, however, preferred to remain in western Europe either for economic and social reasons, or simply in order to stay in familiar surroundings. The Conversos who settled in Catholic countries outside the control of Spain and Portugal were not completely free from molestation, and depended on the good will of rulers for protection. In France they had to maintain some semblance of Catholicism for more than two centuries, but their Jewishness was an open secret. Thus, there was now a diaspora of men and women for whom Judaism, although retained as an identifying frame of reference, was reduced to a private ceremonial practice. In Protestant places too, many Marranos continued this double life long after these areas had broken ties with Rome. It was only at the very end of the sixteenth century that Jewish communities of former Marranos, unambiguously returned to their Jewish identity, were constituted in certain European Mediterranean and Atlantic port cities.

There was no Marrano presence in Amsterdam until the 1590s and, although they openly practiced Judaism almost from the moment of their arrival, they had to wait until 1615 for Jewish settlement to be officially authorized. Thanks to the Marranos, Amsterdam became one of the greatest Jewish centers in the seventeenth century and a haven for persecuted Jews from other places. The most remarkable feature of this community was the ease and swiftness with which erstwhile Marranos shed their Christian identity and returned to full intellectual, religious and communal Jewish life. On the other hand, the Marrano experience composed of dissimulation, double life and split personality, grafted upon the "philosophical" tendency of Spanish Jewry, produced a wide variety of dissidence, libertarianism, and individualistic free thinkers. The Amsterdam community was therefore split by tensions between the orthodox rabbis on the one hand, and an influential group of intellectuals of critical inclinations on the other hand.

The ferment aroused by Shabbetai Zevi in the mid-seventeenth century can be explained in part by Marrano history. Shabbatean messianism could be seen as a form of penitential catharsis, a way to appease the guilt which was still plaguing those who had been forced to lead a double life. Shabbetai Zevi's apostasy, explained by his followers as an outward submission to evil in order to carry on his mission of redemption from within, could be interpreted to endow the Marranos' humiliating past experience with a glorified mystical significance. Both these trends, the philosophical and the mystical, were the routes by which many Jews of Marrano origin distanced themselves from orthodox Judaism.

| The Portuguese Inquisition | Religious liberty in Venice | Beginning of the Amsterdam community | Rembrandt, *The Synagogue* |
|---|---|---|---|
| **1536** | **1589** | **1595–1600** | **1648** |

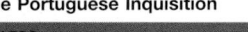

**Kraan**
*Scheeps-kraan; dit is 't Model van de Groote Kraan, tegenwoordig in 't Ivoir deeze Stad Amsterdam*

*2. David Franco Mendes' multilingual marine dictionary (French, Dutch, Portuguese, and Spanish). Amsterdam, 1780.*

**1525–1528:** David Reuveni's stay in Portugal; presenting himself as an ambassador from the kingdom of the Lost Tribes, Reuveni was regarded by New Christians in Portugal as a harbinger of the Messiah.
**1536. May:** Pope Paul III institutes the Portuguese Inquisition.
**1547. July:** The Church of Toledo adopts a 'purity of blood' statute.
**1550. August:** Letters patent of Henri II allowing Portuguese New Christians to settle in France.
**1589:** Venice accords full liberty of religious practice to former Marranos from Spain and Portugal.
**1595–1600:** Beginning of a Jewish presence in Amsterdam.
**1615:** Hugo Grotius presents his report concerning the admission of Jews to the

Estates of Holland.
**1621:** With the renewal of the war against the United Provinces, Spain prohibits all traffic with Dutch nationals; about a quarter of Amsterdam Jews (between 300 to 500 persons) whose livelihood depended on the import of goods from the Portuguese colonial empire, leave Amsterdam and settle in Hamburg.
**1627:** After the bankruptcy which ruined many Genoese bankers, Count-Duke Olivares, Philip IV's all-powerful minister, recalls "New Christian" Portuguese financiers. His fall in 1643 also leads to their downfall.
**1639:** Founding of a unified Portuguese Jewish community in Amsterdam.
**1640. April:** Suicide of Uriel da Costa, a Portuguese Marrano who had returned to Judaism, but to a heterodox faith which led to his excommunication by the rabbis of the Amsterdam community.
**1648:** Fleeing the Spanish Inquisition, brothers Fernando and Miguel Cardozo,

*3. Marriage contract (Kettubah), Rome, 1627.*

# 16th–18th Centuries

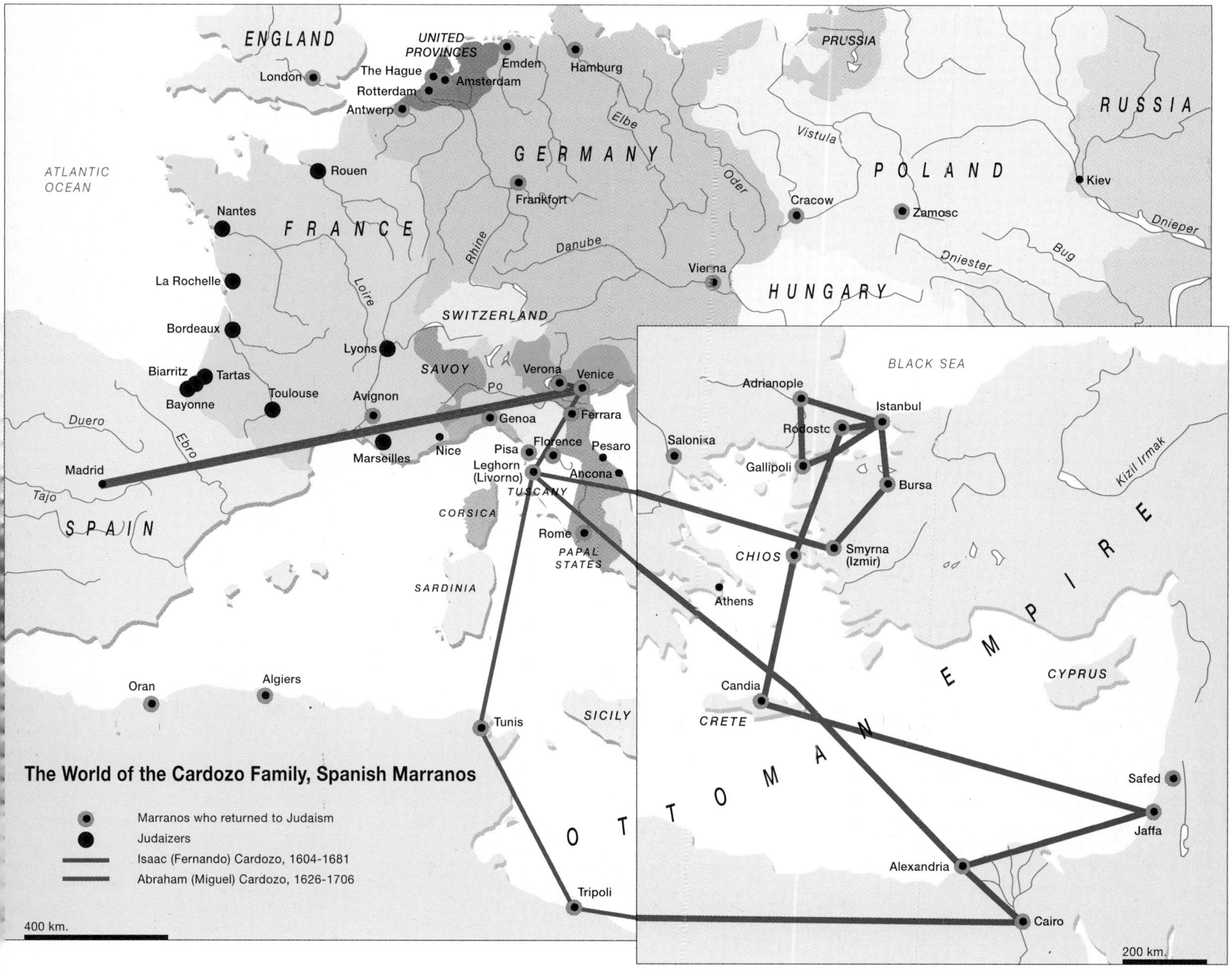

## The World of the Cardozo Family, Spanish Marranos

ENGLAND

UNITED PROVINCES

PRUSSIA

RUSSIA

London
The Hague
Emden
Hamburg
Rotterdam   Amsterdam
Antwerp

GERMANY

POLAND

ATLANTIC OCEAN

Rouen

Frankfort

Elbe
Vistula
Kiev

FRANCE

Nantes

Oder

Cracow
Zamosc

Dnieper

La Rochelle

Rhine   Danube

Vienna

Dniester   Bug

Bordeaux
Lyons

Loire

HUNGARY

Biarritz   Tartas
Bayonne
Toulouse

SWITZERLAND
SAVOY

Verona   Venice

BLACK SEA

Avignon

Po   Ferrara

Adrianople

Istanbul

Duero

Marseilles   Nice

Genoa

Pisa   Florence   Pesaro

Rodosto

Madrid

Ebro

Leghorn (Livorno)   Ancona

Salonica

Gallipoli

Bursa

Tajo

TUSCANY

CORSICA

Smyrna (Izmir)

SPAIN

Rome

CHIOS

Kizil Irmak

SARDINIA

PAPAL STATES

Athens

CYPRUS

OTTOMAN EMPIRE

Oran   Algiers

Candia
CRETE

Safed

Tunis   SICILY

Jaffa

• Marranos who returned to Judaism
● Judaizers
— Isaac (Fernando) Cardozo, 1604-1681
— Abraham (Miguel) Cardozo, 1626-1706

Alexandria

Tripoli

Cairo

400 km.

200 km.

Spinoza's excommunication | Spinoza's *Tractatus Theologico-Politicus* | Isaac de Pinto's controversy with Voltaire

1656 | 1670 | 1762

physicians of Marrano-Portuguese origin, arrive in Venice. Returning to Judaism, they each take a different route: the first brother, now named Isaac, becomes an adherent of rationalist Judaism, hostile to the Kabbalah and to Shabbateanism; the second, Abraham, becomes an apostle of the false messiah from Izmir.

**1650:** Manasseh ben Israel, *Hope of Israel*.
**1656. July 27:** Excommunication of Baruch Spinoza.
**1684:** A theological "amicable discussion" between Orbio de Castro and Philippe van Limborch, one of the leading representatives of liberal Arminian Calvinism in Amsterdam. In 1687 he publishes a written version of the discussion, with an appendix containing Uriel da Costa's *Autobiography*; in reference to Da Costa's case, he denounces the right to excommunicate accorded to the Jewish community as permission to maintain "a state within a state."
**1687:** Posthumous publication of Uriel da Costa's *Exemplar Humanae Vitae*.

**1703:** David Nieto, rabbi of the Sephardi community of London, is accused of Spinozism.
**1707:** Moses Khaghiz, emissary of the Jewish communities in the Holy Land, visits Amsterdam. Some of his interlocutors reject the notion of the special merit attached to residing in the Land of Israel, and see no point in a "return" except for "the poor Jews of Poland, Germany, and Turkey."
**1723:** Letters patent accorded to the Portuguese of Bordeaux, for the first time addressed explicitly as Jews.
**1762:** In his *Apology for the Jewish Nation*, Isaac de Pinto, an economist and philosopher of Portuguese-Marrano origin, attacks Voltaire's anti-Jewish remarks, calling him to admit that he "owes an apology to the Jews, to truth, and to his century."

*4. The Portuguese synagogue (left) and the Ashkenazi synagogue (right) in Amsterdam, as they were in Spinoza's lifetime.*

# Autonomous Subjects of the King of Poland

1. Ukrainian woodcutters in a Jewish tavern. Color print by F. Lewicki, Podolia, 1870.

J ewish life in the Polish kingdom was conducted within the framework of a community (in Hebrew, *kehillah*): a corporation of people sharing particular religious and ethnic origins, and possessing recognized legal status in the feudal Polish state. In many respects the Polish Jewish community resembled other Ashkenazi communities in western and eastern Europe. Its wide social, economic, and cultural autonomy was defined by "charters" of the same kind as privileges granted to towns of German settlers in Poland (such as Magdeburg). Demographic growth and close relations with the nobility, however, eventually produced unique forms of social organization.

The community leadership was oligarchic: only a small group of the wealthy and the educated took an active part in public life. Government of the community was in the hands of the *kahal*, a body which elected the *parnasim* – notables who had executive powers. Religion, of course, was omnipresent and all-powerful: leaders of the community were regarded as representatives of God's will; and the laws which regulated economic and social activity were based on the *Halakhah* as determined by the rulings of the rabbi and his court of justice. On the surface, it seemed as though this closed self-sufficient Jewish world had nothing in common with the non-Jewish environment.

In fact, however, the community maintained close legal and administrative relations with the Polish authorities, whether local, regional, or "national." Not only did the community provide its devout members with their daily needs, from ritual slaughtering and ritual baths, to support for the synagogue and the school – it also controlled their economic life, which was based on the feudal system of leasing land and means of production. Frequently the *kahal* behaved as though it were an independent economic agent, leasing property or rights from the noblemen in order to sub-lease them to community members, or borrowing money from the church, monasteries, and religious colleges and lending it to individuals, as would any banking institution.

The Jews, on the other hand, provided the aristocracy with a variety of economic services, and constituted the principal source of credit and capital. The Polish government regarded the poll tax levied on the Jews as its main source of revenue for financing the army; it thus aspired to collect this tax most expediently within the confines of the cumbersome feudal administration. Organizing a central autonomous Jewish body was the only way to spread the financial burden among the kingdom's hundreds of communities. The Jews, on their part, needed a superstructure free of local prejudices which could deal with problems that the individual community was incapable of solving. Such central organizations, provincial and general, emerged in the sixteenth century. "The Council of the Four Lands" and the "Council of the Land of Lithuania," tacitly authorized by the authorities, continued to function as central institutions of Jewish self-government until 1764. The crown regarded them as responsible only for the collection of taxes, but their full range of activities was in fact much wider: they censured publications, negotiated with the Sejm, made social and economic legislations, and adjudicated in disputes which the local tribunals could not settle. Organized on the model of the single community, the councils, however, did not influence the life of Poland's Jews to the same extent as the *kahal*. They were federal bodies composed of representatives of the major communities, but lacked coercive power. All their decisions had to be ratified and implemented by the local community authorities.

## The Union of Lublin

### 1569

**1569:** The Union of Lublin, between the kingdom of Poland and the Great Duchy of Lithuania, inaugurates a period of intensive colonization in the southeast of the new state; Jews take an active part in the founding of new towns in the frontier regions, thus contributing to the development of an economy based on the export of grain to western Europe.

**1580. November 22:** The earliest detailed ordinance of the Council of the Four Lands to have been preserved: the council limits the extent of land-leasing (arenda) that is permitted to any individual. The prevention of competition for arenda was one of the Council's major concerns.

**1606:** The Council of the Four Lands asks the rabbinical authorities to write a detailed code of ordinances regulating the economic activities of Poland's Jews, particularly the permissibility of charging interest.

**1623:** The earliest remaining ordinances of the Council of the Land of Lithuania: they concern various economic activities,

2. Wincenty Smokowski (1797–1876), a Jewish wedding.

## Accession of John Sobieski

### 1674

distribution of the fiscal burden, and questions pertaining to the social organization of the Lithuanian communities.

**1649–1660:** The Councils of Poland and Lithuania adopt measures to aid victims of Cossack pogroms: ransoming of prisoners sold to the Tatars or deported to Lithuania during the Russo-Polish war, and solving the problem of *agunnot* – women whose husbands had disappeared and could not remarry until declared widows.

**1652:** The Lithuanian council rules that every community should maintain a *Yeshivah*.

**1670–1672:** The Council of the Four Lands excommunicates twice all adherents of the false messiah Shabbetai Zevi.

**1674:** The Councils of Poland and Lithuania prevent the expulsion of the Jews from these lands following the coronation of John III Sobieski; the enormous cost of the operation leads to friction between the Council of the Four Lands and the Council of Lithuania.

**1717:** Following depreciation of the currency the Sejm imposes a poll tax totalling

## Jewish Autonomy: Territory of the Four Lands

*BALTIC SEA*

PRUSSIA

DUCAL PRUSSIA

LITHUANIA

SILESIA

MORAVIA

AUSTRIA

RUSSIA

OTTOMANS

Vilna (Vilnius)
Grodno
Tykocin
Vysokoye
Ciechanow
Wegrow
Brest
Pinsk
Slutsk
Gniezno
Poznan
Torun
Grodzisk
Leczyca
Leszno
Kalisz
Krotoszyn
Lublin
Leczna
Belzec
Chelm
Checiny
Opatow
Sandomierz
Wodzislaw
Szydlowiec
Zamosc
Vladimir Volynski
Kovel
Loutsk
Pinczow
Belz
Ostrog
Olkusz
Dubro
Izyaslav
Cracow
Zolochev
Kremenets
Jaroslaw
Brody
Lvov
Satanov

■ Important community
● Average-size community
⬤ Market town
━ Administrative division of the Council of the Four Lands

100 km.

London
Hamburg
Vilna
Amsterdam
Paris
Prague
Vienna
Kiev
Venice
Salonika
Istanbul
Tunis
Jerusalem

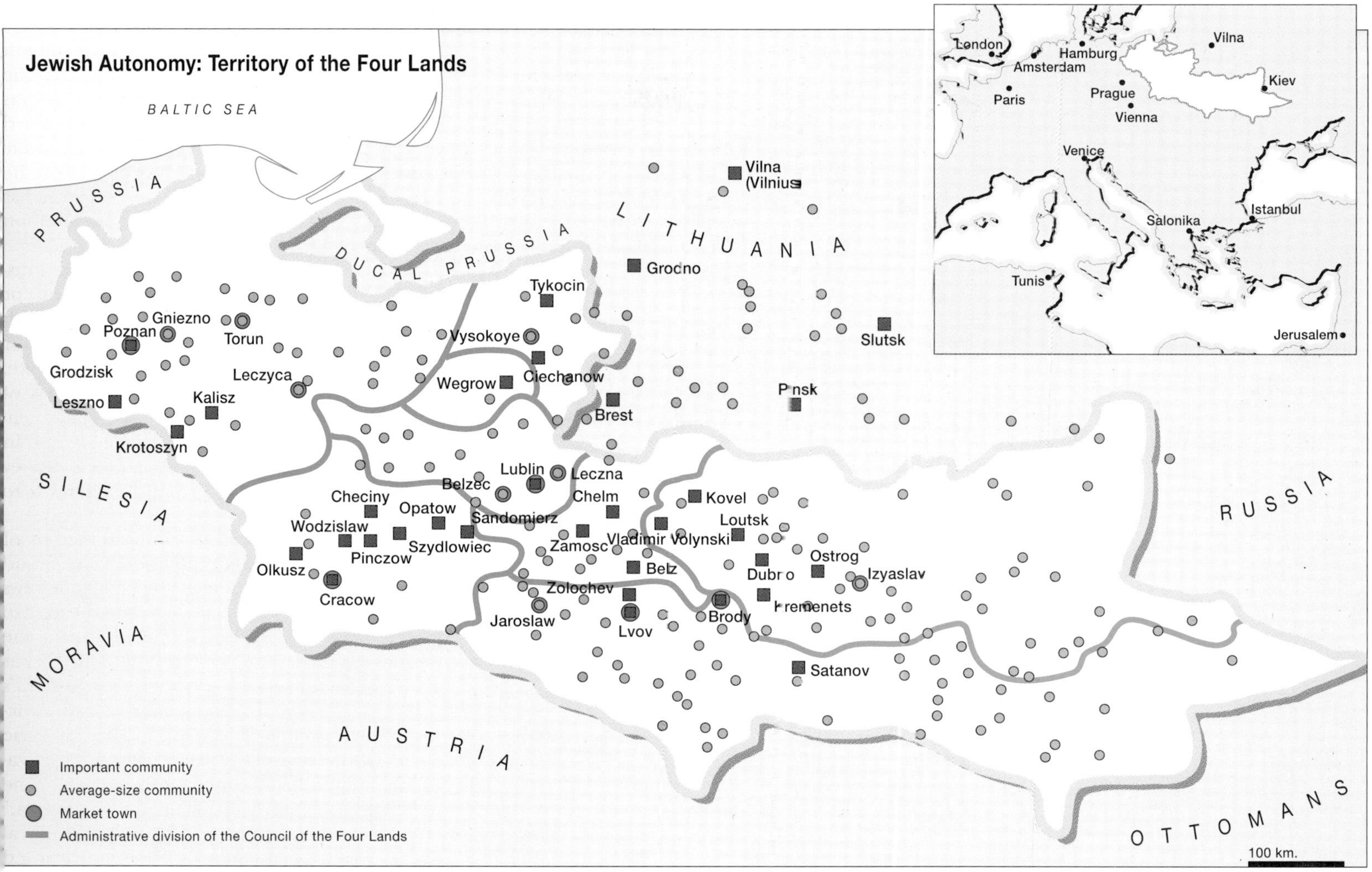

Furthermore, the authority of the two central councils in Poland-Lithuania was diminished because they did not always concur over questions of general policy. Nevertheless, in later generations these councils became idealized symbols for many Jewish "autonomist" movements.

The map of Jewish autonomy – i.e., the zones of jurisdiction of the provincial and central councils – roughly corresponded to the administrative division of the kingdom. Changes in this map sometimes resulted from disputes between communities over their dependent boroughs (*sevivot*) or from transfers of ownership of towns from one noble to another. A further cause of change was the great geographical mobility of the Jewish population. In the second half of the sixteenth century, the colonization of the Ukraine added vast territories to the map of Jewish settlements. The vast grain-growing estates fostered by the Polish magnates in the southeastern regions attracted many Jewish settlers to the new towns and villages, and thus considerably enlarged the dissemination of East European Jewry.

| Abolition of the Council of the Four Lands | Last partition of Poland |
|---|---|
| 1764 | 1795 |

*Market-day in a Lithuanian town between the two world wars.*

220,000 gold zlotys on the Jews of Poland.
**1739:** The Polish Treasury issues regulations which subject the Council of the Four Lands to stricter control by the state authorities.
**1753:** The Polish Treasury appoints an inspector to supervise the activities of the Council of the Four Lands.
**1764. June 1:** The Sejm abolishes the Council of the Four Lands, the supreme body of Jewish self-government in Poland; the motivation for the suppression of the Council was the wish to reorganize the system of taxation; henceforth the poll tax would be collected directly from each individual rather than through a body of community representatives. A special government committee is set up to settle the problem of debts which the defunct council had accumulated.
**1768:** Haidamack massacres.
**1795:** Over thirty years after its abolition, the council's debts are still being discussed; the third and final partition of Poland solves the problem by default.

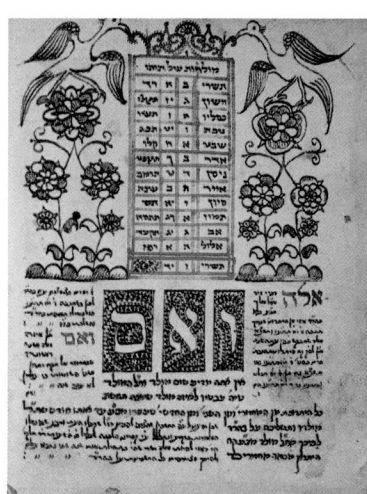

*4. List of the months. An illustrated page from the book* Evronot, *Poland, 1640.*

# Jewish Printing

1. *Page of Genesis. The Hebrew Bible of Gershom ben Moses Soncino, illuminated by a Christian artist. Brescia, May 1494.*

The appearance of the printing press in Europe coincided with a major turning point in Jewish history. Two great centers of medieval Jewish culture – in the Iberian Peninsula and in German cities – were wiped out by expulsions. New centers were emerging in their place: in northern Italy, Bohemia, Moravia, and Poland for Ashkenazi Jewry; in central Italy and in commercial cities in western Europe and the Ottoman Empire for Sephardi Jewry. The printed letter arrived at precisely the right time, as the classification and organization of the enormous literary corpus inherited from the Middle Ages was becoming an urgent task. The medieval canon of texts was primarily based on local traditions; now this was changed and a new canon was created, based on the printed word. Furthermore, the Hebrew printing press increased the Hebrew readership, transforming the composition of the intellectual elite. In short, as in non-Jewish society, printing caused a major revolution which was social as well as intellectual.

Conceptually, the Hebrew incunabula ("cradle books," printed in the fifteenth century) still reflected the era of manuscripts. Early books were printed with no title page or pagination, and in small editions. The majority consisted of books needed for daily use, such as prayer books for various rites, collections of religious precepts, Talmud tractates, and biblical commentaries – above all, Rashi's commentary. The latter, a monumental work by the eleventh-century erudite scholar from Troyes became the principal textbook for Torah study throughout the Jewish world, and was printed in at least six editions before 1500. Hebrew printing shops mushroomed within a very short time. Italy was the earliest and largest center of Hebrew book production, supplying intellectual nourishment to the entire diaspora. Istanbul and Salonika, where refugees from Spain established the first Hebrew presses in the Ottoman world, and Prague, Cracow, and Lublin in *Ashkenaz*, produced works intended mainly for local consumption. In addition to religious handbooks, the printing press in each of these places issued a wide variety of works which reflected the local tastes of the time.

In the first half of the sixteenth century the Venetian presses were those who determined the new canon of Hebrew literature. Most of these were Christian establishments which employed Jews or apostates in the production of Hebrew books. It was their selection which decided the fate of a book – immortalization in print or relegation to oblivion. It was in sixteenth-century Venice, therefore, that the classical Jewish library was established. By flooding the market with enormous quantities of low priced books (particularly the Pentateuch and prayer books) for the general public, Italian printers secured the capital necessary for the production of expensive editions for which there was less of a demand. The Jewish book market was thus considerably enlarged and its products standardized. Moreover, this mass production of Hebrew books for daily

| First Hebrew printing press | Beginning of the Soncino firm | Hebrew press in Istanbul | Hebrew press in Prague |
|---|---|---|---|
| **c. 1470** | **1483** | **1504** | **1512** |

**1469–1500:** The incunabula period: approximately 180 Hebrew titles printed at that time have survived. In 1470, one generation after the appearance of the first book ever printed (the Mainz Bible, 1454), three Hebrew titles were apparently printed in Rome; the first was probably Rashi's commentary on the Pentateuch.

**1475:** Rashi's commentary is printed in Reggio di Calabria by Abraham ben Isaac ben Garton – the first Hebrew book bearing the printer's mark, date, and place of publication.

**1483–1546:** The period of activity of the Soncino family of printers, producers of over 200 titles in the town of Soncino itself, in other towns in Italy, and in Salonika and Cairo.

**1484:** Joshua Solomon, founder of the Soncino dynasty of printers, publishes the first tractate of the Babylonian Talmud ever to be printed.

**1488:** The Soncino firm publishes the first printed Hebrew Bible.

3. *Mark of the printer Marco Antonio Giustiniani, a representation of the Temple. Woodcut, Venice, 1547.*

**1489–1534:** Period of activity of Gershom Soncino, the most important printer of the family who produced over one hundred works, among them, for the first time, books of secular Hebrew prose and poetry.

**1504:** Founding of a Hebrew printing press in Istanbul, the first in the Orient.

**1509:** The first Hebrew book to have numbered folios is Maimonides' *Mishneh Torah*, printed in Istanbul in 1509.

**1512:** Founding of a Hebrew printing press in Prague, the first in Ashkenazi Europe. Gershom Kohen, founder of a line of printers which would be active till the middle of the 17th century, is the principal Jewish printer in that city from 1526.

**c. 1513:** Beginning of Hebrew printing in Venice.

**1516–1522:** Hebrew books are printed in Fez, Morocco, using Lisbon type.

**1513–1548:** Period of activity of Daniel Bomberg, a Christian humanist from Antwerp, founder of the first Hebrew printing press in Venice.

4. *Two magic formulas from Sefer Raziel ("The Book of Raziel"), a kabbalistic work printed in Amsterdam in 1701.*

religious use resulted in a social transformation similar to that which was accomplished in Christian society by the translation of the Bible into vernacular languages: it made the Scriptures accessible to all, enabled everyone to understand the prayers and follow the reading of the Torah in the synagogue, thus becoming an active participant. For the middle and lower classes, this constituted a veritable revolution.

In the second half of the seventeenth century, the center of Jewish printing moved to northwestern Europe in accordance with the general trend of the European economy. Amsterdam, a commercial metropolis and a meeting place for Sephardi and Ashkenazi Jewry, replaced Venice as the major center of Hebrew printing. But soon other centers began to emerge in Germany: in Frankfort on the Oder, Frankfort on the Main,

Berlin, Hamburg, and other cities. The decline of the printing industry in eastern Europe caused by the Thirty Years' War and the massacres of 1648–1649 brought experienced workers to these new establishments as well as many a Jewish author in search of a publisher. In the west as in the east, printing in the seventeenth and eighteenth centuries was less important to the literary elite who had done quite well in the era of the manuscript, than to the second-rank intelligentsia. Itinerant preachers, half-learned teachers, and pen-pushers of all kinds, were intoxicated by the printing revolution. The massive output of works composed by men who despite modest intellectual abilities, were enthusiastic, imaginative, and creative, gave birth to new literary genres which radically transformed Jewish culture.

**First Printings of the Talmud
15th - 18th Centuries**

Shklov
Hamburg
Amsterdam
Grodno
Dessau
Berlin
Frankfort on the Oder
Halle
Jessnitz
Frankfort
Hanau
Lublin
Metz
Offenbach
Cracow
Zolkiew
Sulzbach
Prague
Turka
Lvov
Vienna

Trent
Brescia
Venice
Soncino
Piove di Sacco
Cremona
Ferrara
Casalmaggiore
Cesena
Guadalajara
Mantua
Rimini
Pesaro
Toledo
Leghorn
(Livorno)
Fano
Ortona
Ancona
Istanbul
Naples
Salonika

MEDITERRANEAN SEA

- Late 15th and 16th centuries
- 17th century
- 18th century
- Printing press founded by a member of the Soncino family

2. Sefer Kol Bo ("everything within"), an anonymous compilation of halakhic rulings. Printed by Gershom Soncino, Rimini, c. 1524–1525.

| Hebrew press in Venice | Printing of the *Zohar* | Printing of *Shulhan Arukh* | Hebrew press in Amsterdam |
|---|---|---|---|
| c. 1513 | 1559–1560 | 1565 | 1623 |

**1520–1523:** Bomberg produces the first printed edition of the Babylonian Talmud. The form of this elegant edition, its pagination, additions, and titling, will determine the manner of Talmud study for the entire Jewish nation.
**1523:** Bomberg prints the Jerusalem Talmud.
**1534:** The Hellitz brothers establish the first Hebrew printing press in Cracow. Active till 1541, they produced over twenty titles before converting to Christianity.
**1540:** Christian Hebraist Paulus Fagius, in conjunction with Eliyaha Levita, sets up a Hebrew press at Isny, Wuertemberg, and later at Konstanz where some books are printed in separate editions for Jews and Christians.
**1553:** Pope Julius III orders the burning of the Talmud in the Campo di Fiori in Rome; burnings of this kind were recurrent throughout Italy till 1559.
**1559–1560:** Two editions of the *Zohar* appear in Mantua and in Cremona simultaneously. The publication provokes a

5. A German Haggadah: the copyist attempted to imitate printed typography. Hamburg, 1768.

fierce debate among Jewish Italian scholars over whether or not Kabbalistic works should be printed and made available to everyone.
**1565:** Joseph Caro's *Shulhan Arukh* ("the prepared table"), a code of all Jewish religious precepts, is published in Venice. Five years later it is printed in Cracow with changes and additions modifying it to Ashkenazi custom. Caro's text was soon to become the basic guide for world Jewry, contributing more than any other printed text to the cultural cohesion of the nation.
**1566:** Pope Pius V authorizes the printing of Hebrew books on condition that they do not contain offensive references to Christianity. following this decision, the Roman Inquisition introduces the censorship of Hebrew books, which is carried out by converted Jews and Christian Hebraists. Later the Italian Jewish communities censure all books issued by their presses.
**1577–1587:** Eliezer Ashkenazi, native of Prague and formerly a printer in Lublin and

Istanbul, founds a Hebrew press in Safed.
**1605:** Beginning of the activity of the Bak family, printers in Prague till the end of the 19th century.
**1623:** Manasseh ben Israel founds a Hebrew printing press in Amsterdam.
**1658:** Beginning of Joseph Athias' printing press in Amsterdam. In 1679 Athias publishes a translation of the Bible in Yiddish, competing with a version published in the same year by the printer Uri (Phoebus) ben Aaron Halevi.
**Second half of 17th century:** Spread of Hebrew printing in Germany following the destruction of the Lublin and Cracow firms in the 1648 pogroms and the decline of the Prague presses during the Thirty Years' War. The Hebrew press in Poland, however, was soon to be revived: in 1692 Uri Halevi, from Amsterdam, founds an important firm in Zolkiew (Galicia) which would be the only one in Poland till 1760. Many other firms would later be established throughout eastern Europe.

# The Return to Western Europe

*1. "Thus shall it be done to the man whom the king delighteth to honour" (Esther, 6:9): the triumph of Mordecai over evil Haman. Purim plate, Fayence, 18th century.*

biting in 1544 all banishments not explicitly approved by him. After his abdication in 1556, however, the expulsions were renewed.

An apparent reversal of the process seems to have been introduced during the last three decades of the sixteenth century, when in several places initiative was taken towards readmitting the Jews. Although each individual case may have been of limited consequence, the accumulative effect of such policies marked a significant change: henceforth almost every European society considered the advantages of a Jewish presence. Venice, after a long period of hostility towards the Marranos, whose Catholicism was suspect, began to encourage the immigration of Sephardi Jews who were expected, because of the experience they had acquired in other western countries or in the Ottoman Empire, to revive the deteriorating trade with the Levant. Frankfort invited Jews as well as Dutch Calvinists. Portuguese New Christians established self-governing Jewish communities in Holland and Italy, and were allowed to settle in French port cities (Bordeaux, Nantes, Rouen) as long as they did not publicly reveal their former Jewish identity. In Spain itself, many reform programs recommended, among other corrective measures intended to remedy the kingdom's afflictions, the mitigation or even the revocation of the laws concerning purity of blood. Olivares invited New Christian financiers to replace the Genoese bankers, and there was even a rumor that he intended to revoke the expulsion decree of 1492.

The movement for the "readmission of the Jews" attained greater momentum after 1650. In England, the commission convened by Oliver Cromwell dispersed without reaching a decision, but Jews were unofficially readmitted. In France, the privileges of the Jews of Metz were confirmed, and then extended to their brethren in royal Alsace; the New Christians of Bordeaux openly established a Jewish community towards the end of the century. In central Europe devastated by the Thirty Years War, the Great Elector of Brandenburg invited Jews expelled from Vienna to settle in his land, and other German princes pressed by the need for reconstruction soon followed suit. During the war itself, Jewish communities enjoyed the protection of army generals who had an interest in maintaining the competition between munition suppliers, as this kept the prices down. Indeed, it was the enterprise of such army suppliers which constituted the first stage in the emergence of "Court Jews," particularly after 1672 in the countries which formed a coalition against Louis XIV.

A fter 1520 there remained only fragments of Jewish communities in western Europe. Moreover, the eradication of Jewish presence from the German Empire, a process that had begun in the mid-fifteenth century, continued until about 1570. The Protestant Reformation did not bring about any immediate change of policy or revised attitudes. Although Martin Luther, in his all-embracing rejection of church tradition, initially condemned the theory of Jewish servitude and social degradation, he soon changed his mind. In 1536 he expressed approval of the expulsion of the Jews by the Elector of Saxony, and viciously attacked Jews and Judaism between 1542–1543. Thus, while the Protestant princes adopted an active anti-Jewish policy, it was the Catholic emperor, Charles V, who accorded them protection, prohi-

---

| "Great Privilege" of Charles V | Privileges by Emperor Rudolf II | Luzzatto's *Discourse on the State of the Jews of Venice* |
|---|---|---|
| **1544** | **1577** | **1638** |

*3. "Chair of Elijah," used in circumcision ceremonies. Dermbach, Thuringia, 1768.*

**1530:** A disputation between Joselmann of Rosheim and the apostate Anton Margarita is conducted during the Diet of Augsburg in the presence of Charles V; convicted of imposture, Margarita is imprisoned and then banished from Augsburg.
**1536:** Expulsion of the Jews from Saxony.
**1538:** Reformer Martin Bucer, in his proposal concerning the status of Jews in the principality of Hesse, insists that they should be confined to the lowest estate.
**1544:** The "Great Privilege" granted by Charles V to the Jews of the German Empire.
**1565:** Several Jewish families are allowed to settle in Metz, one of the three bishoprics held by the King of France since 1552.
**1572:** The Duke of Savoy considers giving the Jews permission to settle in Nice, but renounces this plan under pressure from Spain and the Pope.

**1574:** Henri III renews the letters patent of 1550 which accorded to Portuguese New Christians the right to settle in France.
**1575:** Expulsion of the Jews from the Calvinist Palatinate.
**1577:** Rudolf II confirms the ordinance of 1567 permitting the residence of Jews in Prague and grants privileges to Jewish craftsmen, thus attempting to break the monopoly of the guilds.
**1589:** A Venetian charter is issued, and regularly renewed in the future, granting Levantine and Western Jews ten-year residence permission.
**1593:** The Grand Duke of Tuscany issues a charter in favor of the Jews who have recently settled in Livorno, protecting them from persecution by the Roman Inquisition.
**1614:** Agitation of the guild craftsmen in Frankfort is followed by anti-Jewish riots.
**1615:** The Estates of the province of Holland ask Hugo Grotius and another lawyer, Adriaan Pauw, to draw up regulations for the admission of Jews and the conditions of

# 16th–18th Centuries

The seventeenth century, an interim period between the disappearance of medieval traditions and the crystallization of "enlightened" anti-Judaism, witnessed various manifestations of a novel phenomenon – philosemitism. Advocates of mercantilism attributed to Jews collective virtues of diligence and thrift, qualities which they wished to see fostered by the whole of society. The cultured elites displayed an intellectual curiosity towards Judaism and post-biblical Jewish history: Jewish and Christian scholars developed friendly relations of a kind that would not be matched in the following century. Both Catholic and Protestant millennarians assigned an important role to the conversion of the Jews in their expectations for the coming of a new age, thus expressing in theological terms a demand, albeit equivocal, for Jewish integration. All these motivations combined to create a more favorable atmosphere. The gradual acceptance of the presence of Jews in western Europe was a linear process, however fraught with obstacles, which culminated in their full legal emancipation at the end of the eighteenth century.

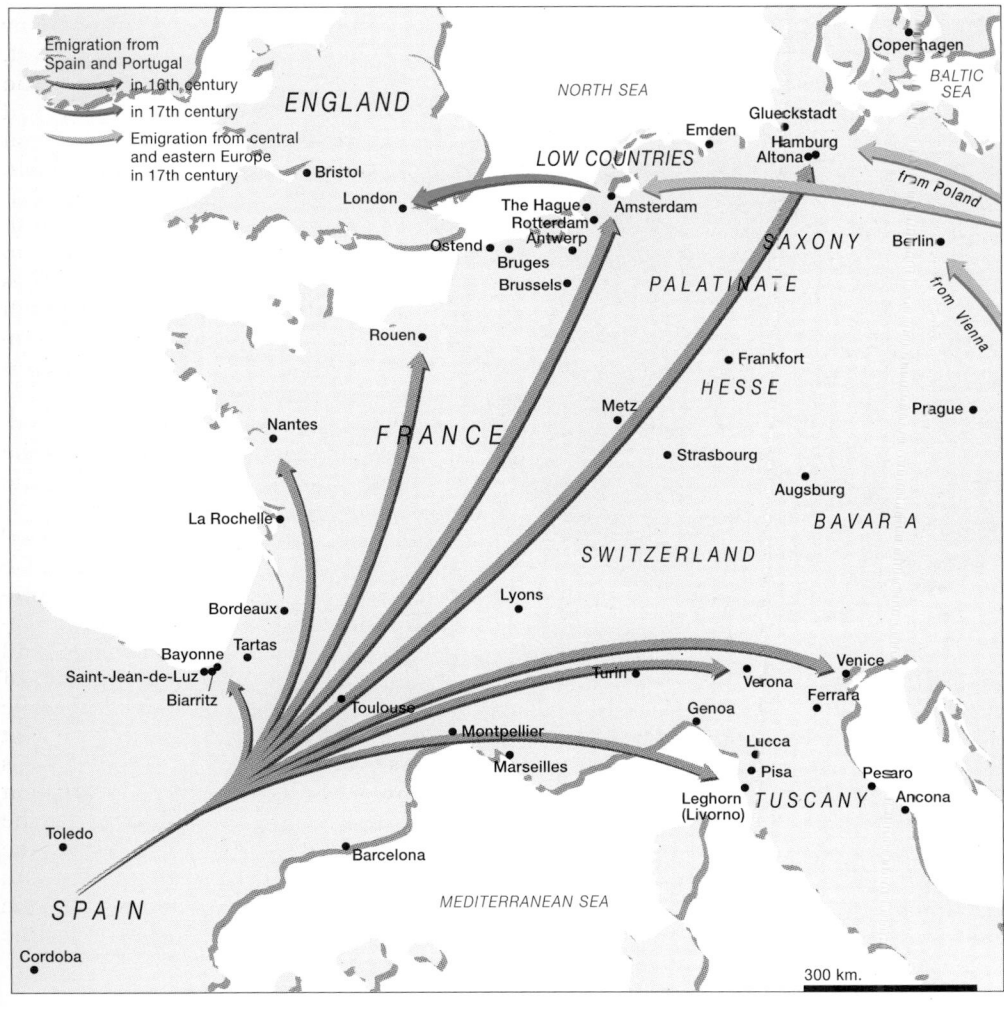

2. Parokhet (Ark curtain). Damascus silk, Italy, 18th century.

| Manasseh ben Israel's *To the Lord Protector* | Privileges to the Jews of Metz | Toland's *Reasons for Naturalizing the Jews* |
|---|---|---|
| 1655 | 1657 | 1714 |

their settlement, but decide to allow each city to make its own policy towards the Jews. Louis XIII reiterates the interdict on Jewish residence in the kingdom of France.
**1633:** With the intervention of Richelieu, the King's Council acquits "Portuguese" merchants in Rouen who were accused of Judaizing.
**1634–1641:** Rumors circulate in Spain that Count-Duke Olivares, Philip IV's all-powerful minister, is trying to obtain permission for Jews to return to the Iberian peninsula.
**1637:** Leone Modena writes his *History of Hebrew Rites* (in Italian) at the request of the English ambassador to Venice for presentation to King James I.
**1638:** Simone Luzzatto's *Discourse on the State of the Jews in Venice* argues for toleration towards them, especially on economic grounds.
**1646–1647:** Antonio Vieira, a Portuguese Jesuit statesman, meets with Manasseh ben Israel in Holland; in 1646 Vieira advocates abolishing the disabilities of New Christians

in Portugal.
**1655:** Manasseh ben Israel's *To the Lord Protector [Oliver Cromwell]... Humble Address in Favour of the Jewish Nation.*
**1657:** Letters patent confirming the privileges of the Jews of Metz.
**1670:** The Great Elector invites Jews expelled from Vienna to settle in Brandenburg. Baruch Spinoza publishes his famous *Tractatus Theologico-Politicus.*
**1699:** Founding of an openly-Jewish charity organization in Bordeaux.
**1714:** John Toland's *Reasons for Naturalizing the Jews in Great Britain and Ireland*; Toland advocates the naturalization of foreign-born Jews and admitting Jews to public office (half a century later, in his *On the Improvement of the Jews*, the German Christian Wilhelm von Dohm, while repeating some of Toland's arguments, suggests that Jews should not be allowed to enter into public service until properly reformed).

4. Scroll of Esther (detail). Alsace, 18th century.

# The Jews of England

Although individual Jews could be found in England even after their expulsion in 1290, it was only in the sixteenth century that they returned in small but traceable numbers. Henry VIII used Jewish scholars to justify his divorce from Catherine of Aragon and his marriage to Anne Boleyn, but was unaware that a secret Jewish community existed in England, including over twenty Jews who were court musicians. But the trial and execution of Dr. Rodrigo Lopez, a Marrano indicted for treason and for his involvement in a Spanish plot to assassinate Queen Elizabeth I (1594), scattered Tudor Anglo-Jewry, which subsequently found shelter mainly in the Low Countries, disguised as Spanish or Portuguese Roman Catholics.

The rise of the Puritans placed English interest in the Jews on a new footing. These adherents of a militant brand of Calvinism were intrigued by the idea of the Jews – guardians of the language and tradition of the Old Testament, so fundamental to Puritan theology – without even having met any. Their millenarian outlook required the conversion of the Jews to Protestant Christianity and the return of the Lost Ten Tribes to the Holy Land as necessary prerequisites of the Second Coming of the Messiah. Oliver Cromwell's accession to power in the mid-seventeenth century signalled that the readmission of the Jews to England was now only a matter of time.

Cromwell's agents made their initial overtures to the famous Rabbi Menasseh ben Israel of Amsterdam, who in fact functioned as the Jewish ambassador to the gentiles, and was certainly one of the most well-known Jews of his day. Although he had long been in touch with the dramatic events in England, Menasseh only began to focus on the practical implementation of the readmission of the Jews after several of his other projects had failed. Most notable among these was his attempt to become the Jewish Descartes in Queen Christina's Sweden. After several postponements, Menasseh arrived in London in September 1655 and began negotiating the return of the Jews to England.

Cromwell, for his part, hoped that most of his compatriots would be as enthusiastic as he was, and took the extraordinary political risk of calling a conference to approve Jewish readmission. But this Whitehall Conference of 4–18 December 1655 gave vent to a broad range of attitudes, and the merchants questioned the practical commercial wisdom of putting this millenarian goal into practice. Cromwell angrily dismissed them, and resolved to authorize the tacit and unofficial readmission of the Jews, regardless. Menasseh ben Israel, who had always dreamed of obtaining official permission in writing, returned to Holland a self-imagined failure, expiring before he reached his destination.

The secret Jews of England, however, had never supported Cromwell's and Menasseh's extravagant plans, and were far from happy about the fact that their very existence in London had been revealed. Only the English war with Spain in 1656 forced them to jump on the bandwagon, for by declaring themselves refugee Jewish Marranos they were able to avoid the confiscation of property which was the fate of enemy Spaniards in London. To their surprise, they were now able to lead their lives as Jews openly, and thanks to several royal declarations after the Restoration, the community was able to expand and to enjoy the religious toleration that soon became the hallmark of English life.

The number of Jews in London was increased by immigration, principally from Amsterdam, or else directly from Spain and Portugal. The only other Jewish community in the British Isles was a small Sephardi group in Dublin. Jews also began to figure increasingly in the growing colonial empire. In the course of the second half of the eighteenth century several congregations sprung up in country towns. Gradually the Sephardi community had to yield pride of place to the Ashkenazim who came from Amsterdam, Germany, and later from Eastern Europe.

The history of Anglo-Jewry after 1655 became a series of "firsts": from the first Jewish knight (1700), through the first Jewish Lord Mayor of London, to the so-called "Emancipation of the Jews" (1858), which was merely the result of the emendation of the Christian oath required of all members of Parliament. The day that Baron Lionel de Rothschild took his seat in the House of Commons (26 July 1858) was the almost-inevitable consequence of the deliberately vague terms on which the Jews had been readmitted to England two centuries before.

*1. The festival of Tabernacles celebrated at the New Synagogue in London. Papier-mâché tablecloth, c.1850.*

| Expulsion of the Jews from England | The Commonwealth | Menasseh ben Israel in London |
|---|---|---|
| 1290 | 1649 | 1655 |

*2. A Jewish peddler and his wife. Porcelain, England, c. 1760.*

**1290:** Expulsion of the Jews from England by Edward I.
**1494:** First evidence of Jews in Tudor England.
**1594. June 7:** Execution of Dr. Rodrigo Lopez on charges of treason and plotting to poison Queen Elizabeth I.
**1609:** On suspicion of being Jewish, Portuguese merchants are expelled from London.
**1649–1660:** The Commonwealth, ruled by Oliver Cromwell (1599–1658).
**1655. September:** Menasseh ben Israel arrives in London.
**October 31:** Menasseh presents a 7-point petition to the Council of State calling for the readmission of the Jews to England.
**November 14:** Cromwell selects the members of the Whitehall Conference to discuss Jewish readmission.
**December 4–18:** The Whitehall Conference meets, but fails to come to a decision, and is angrily dismissed by Cromwell, who resolves to settle the issue informally.

**1656. March:** The Anglo-Spanish war.
**March 24:** English Jews petition Cromwell, declaring themselves Marranos rather than enemy Spaniards; Cromwell declines to issue a written reply, but tacitly permits them to remain in England and to live and worship freely.
**1657. September:** Menasseh ben Israel dies in Middleburg on his return journey to Holland.
**1660:** Restoration of Charles II.
**1664. August 22:** Jews petition Charles II, who grants a formal written statement of toleration.
**1673:** Religious liberty is granted to the Jewish community.
**1674, 1685:** Further royal declarations confirming the promises of 1664. 1685 is the year when Louis XIV in France revoked the toleration granted to Huguenots in France by the Edict of Nantes.
**1687:** Newton's *Principia mathematica*.
**1689:** William and Mary, enthroned by the Glorious Revolution, adopt the Bill of Rights

## Jews in England

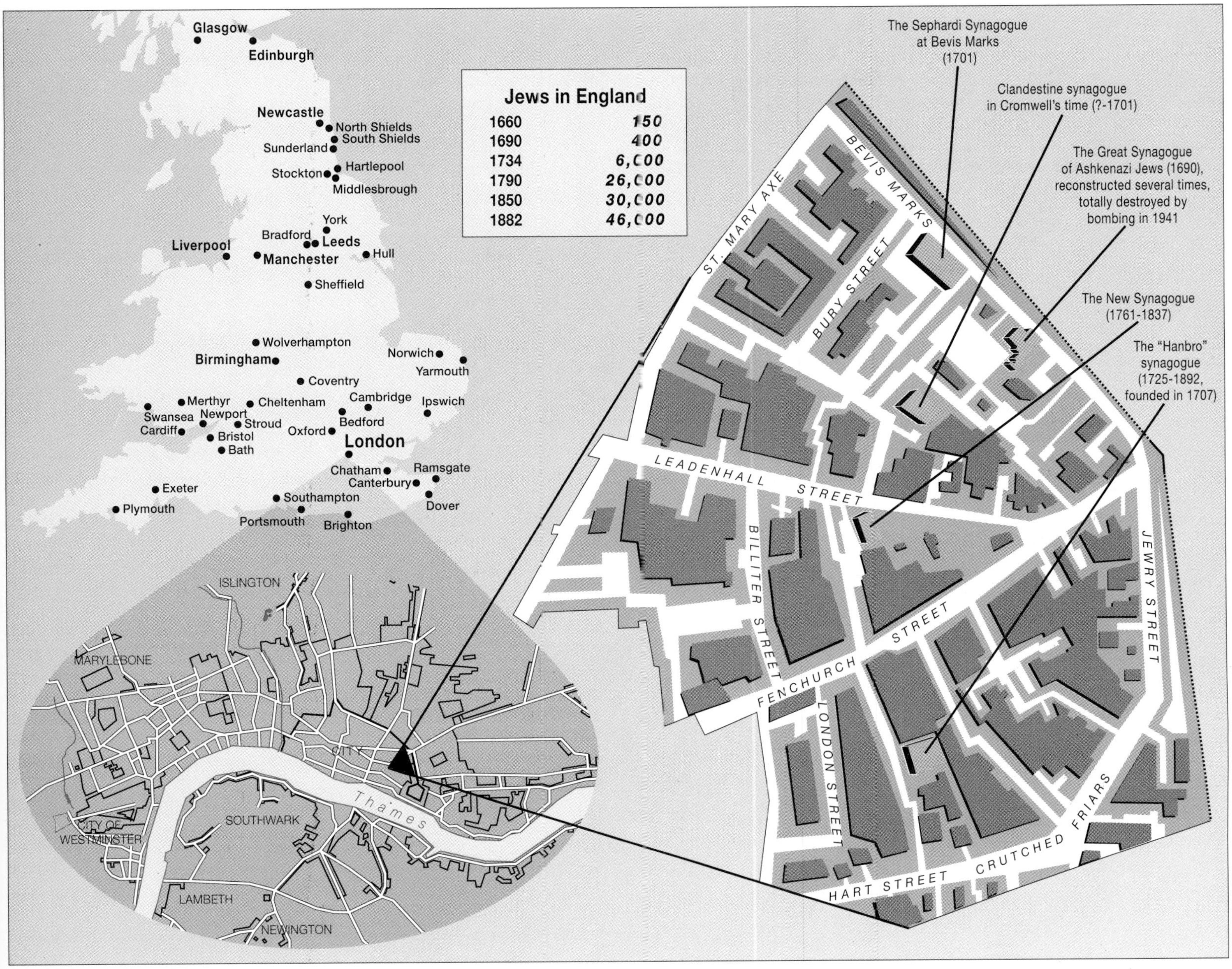

| Year | Number |
|------|--------|
| 1660 | 150 |
| 1690 | 400 |
| 1734 | 6,000 |
| 1790 | 26,000 |
| 1850 | 30,000 |
| 1882 | 46,000 |

The Sephardi Synagogue at Bevis Marks (1701)

Clandestine synagogue in Cromwell's time (?-1701)

The Great Synagogue of Ashkenazi Jews (1690), reconstructed several times, totally destroyed by bombing in 1941

The New Synagogue (1761-1837)

The "Hanbro" synagogue (1725-1892, founded in 1707)

**The Glorious Revolution**

1688–1689

**First Jewish mayor of London**

1855

**Disraeli Prime Minister**

1874

*3. Menasseh ben Israel (1604–1657), painting by Rembrandt.*

promulgated by Parliament; the Toleration Act permits everyone except Catholics, Jews and Unitarians to worship as they please.
**1697:** Limitation of the number of "Jew Brokers" in the City of London to 12.

**1698:** The Act for Suppressing Blasphemy grants implicit recognition to the legality of the practice of Judaism in England.
**1700. June 23:** Solomon de Medina is knighted by William III.
**1701:** The stately Sephardi synagogue at Bevis Marks is opened.
**1705:** A Hebrew printing press is opened in London.
**1753:** The "Jew Bill," which would have given limited emancipation to a small number of wealthy Jews, is issued.
**1831:** The Jews of London receive the Freedom of the City.
**1837:** Moses Montefiore is knighted by Queen Victoria.
**1841:** Isaac Lyon Goldsmid is made baronet; the first Jew to receive a hereditary title.
**1855:** First Jewish Lord Mayor of London.
**1858. July 26:** "Emancipation of the Jews"; Lionel de Rothschild takes seat in the House of Commons (but never speaks).
**1874:** Benjamin Disraeli becomes Prime Minister.

*4. Benjamin Disraeli (1804–1881) by the caricaturist William Bowcher, August, 1876.*

# Poland as a Cultural Center

Ashkenazi culture first emerged in the urban centers of German-speaking lands of the Holy Empire. Rabbis and talmudic scholars in those communities formed the nucleus which would evolve through the ages into a distinguished tradition of erudition. Until the 15th century, young Jews from Poland would complete their education in German *yeshivot*, and scholars were sent from Germany to Poland to serve there as rabbis and teachers. However, immigration from Germany in the sixteenth century transmitted this cultural legacy to the new communities in Poland. In the newly-founded *yeshivot* in the east, the Talmud was studied according to the Ashkenazi tradition of commentary, established by Rashi and the tosafists (the French scholars who composed the *tosafot*, "additions"). An age-old trend was thus reversed: German Jews now began to travel eastward, to the rabbinical academies in Poland.

Furthermore, rabbis throughout the diaspora now revealed a changed attitude towards Polish Jews, which reflected the growing prestige of this new intellectual center of Ashkenazi Jewry. In the fifteenth century a German rabbi could have still said about the Jews of Cracow that "they are unlearned in the Torah"; several decades later, the Jews of Istanbul were directing their questions concerning the Halakhah (talmudic law) to a rabbi in the very same Cracow. The Ashkenazi cultural heritage, with its unique mixture of legal studies and mysticism, created an ideal type of Jewish scholar who was ascetic and severe, withdrawn from the world and entirely devoted to studying, mostly ignoring non-Jewish learning, and hostile to rationalist philosophy. This type of Talmud scholar and his cultural heritage were brought to Poland by the huge wave of immigration from Germany, Bohemia and Moravia.

In Poland, however, the Ashkenazi tradition came into contact with and absorbed other currents stemming from Sephardi centers and from other Jewish communities located outside the Ashkenazi sphere. While Spanish refugees were settling in Italy and influencing the culture of Italian Jews, the spirit of the Renaissance and rationalist philosophy began to penetrate the world of Polish Judaism.

The spread of printing and the publication of fundamental works of Halakhah, philosophy and mysticism in the second half of the sixteenth century, intensified the Sephardi tendency to condense rabbinical legislation into works of codification. The Ashkenazi tradition of Talmud study, which was based on theoretical analysis and not directed at reaching halakhic rulings, was dramatically changed when it encountered the esteemed systematic code of Sephardi law and custom: the *Shulhan Arukh* by Joseph Caro. Composed in Safed and printed in Venice in 1565, the code was quickly adopted in Poland where it was enriched with additions, commentaries and corrections designed to accommodate it to Polish-Ashkenazi custom. In 1570–1571, only five years after its original publication, the *Shulhan Arukh* was published in Cracow with modifications introduced by Moses Isserles (1530–1572). This was indeed a momentous occasion, for the "tablecloth" (*Mappa*) which was spread by the Polish rabbi over the "prepared table" (the literal meaning of *Shulhan Arukh*) belonging to his illustrious colleague from Safed, was the most important agent of unification of the Sephardi and the Ashkenazi branches of the Jewish people. Henceforth a single text would become the only practical guide to religious behavior for the entire diaspora. "In all the lands of *Ashkenaz*", they said in Poland, "we accept and obey the words of our master Rabbi Moses Isserles."

| Founding of the Cracow *yeshivah* | First Polish edition of a talmudic tractate |
|---|---|
| c .1494 | 1559 |

**1474:** Moses Mintz, a spiritual leader of the Ashkenazi diaspora and rabbi of several major communities in Germany, comes to Poznan and describes the customs of Polish Jewry.
**c. 1494:** Jacob Pollack, native of Bavaria and the leading scholar in Poland in the 15th century, founds a yeshivah in Cracow which he heads till 1522. It was Pollack who transferred to Poland the method of talmudic argumentation known as *hilukim*.
**c .1495–1558:** Life of Shalom Shakhna, Pollack's disciple and the first among Poland's talmudic scholars who was not an immigrant from Germany; as head of the yeshivah in Lublin, he educated the best Jewish scholars of 16th-century Poland.
**1503:** King Alexander I appoints Jacob Pollack as chief rabbi for the whole of Poland.
**1510–1573:** Life of Solomon Luria, first great

talmudic scholar in Lithuania; his Talmud commentary was in the Ashkenazi tradition, hostile to the Sephardi method disseminated by the writings of Joseph Caro, opposed to Isserles's use of Aristotle's writings. His criticism reveals the influence of rationalist tendencies among Jewish scholars.
**c .1525–1609:** Lifespan of Judah Loew ben Bezalel, known as the Maharal of Prague, philosopher, mathematician, important Ashkenazi rabbi and founder of the yeshivah in Prague (1573); in 1592 he was consulted by Emperor Rudolph II – this meeting gave rise to the legend that the Maharal was an alchemist and dealt in magic.
**1555–1614:** Lifespan of Joshua Falk, head of the Lvov yeshivah and author of a famous commentary on the *Shulhan Arukh*. Falk was also actively involved in 1605 in the composition of the decrees of the Council of the Four Lands, the central institution of Polish Jewry.
**1559:** In Lublin, first printing of a Talmud tractate in Poland; when the Roman

*2. Torah-Ark Doors. Painted wood, Cracow, early 17th century.*

# 15th–17th Centuries

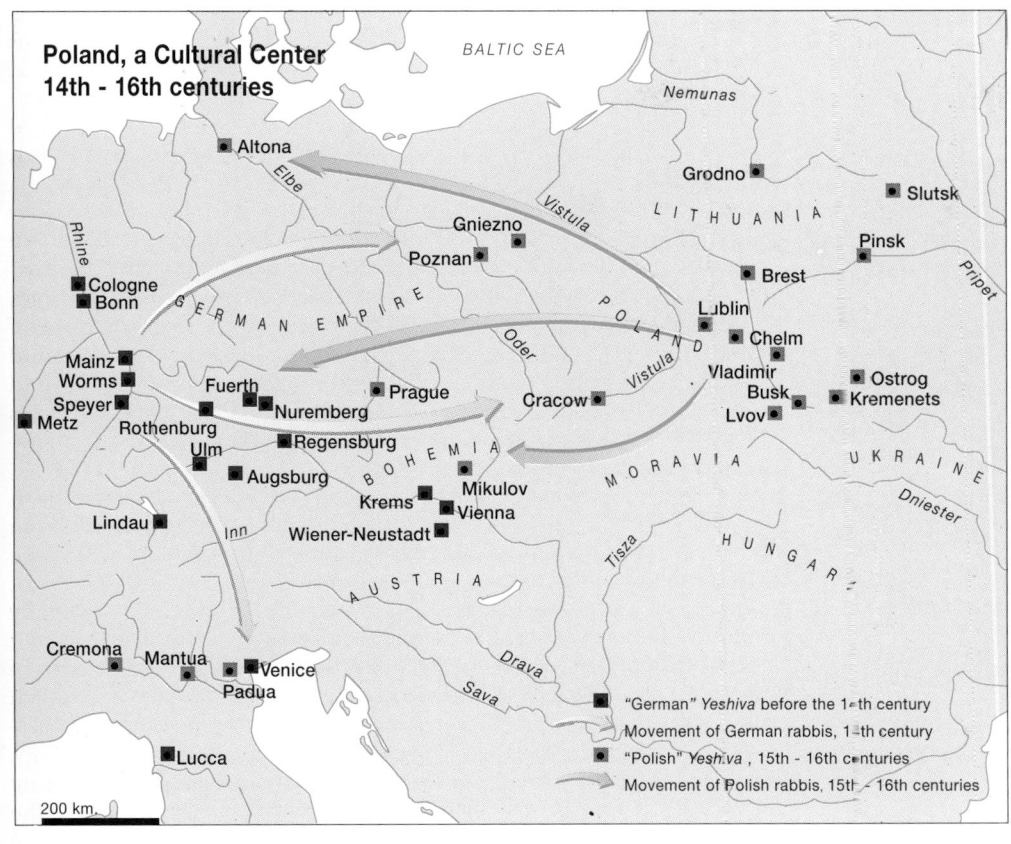

**Poland, a Cultural Center 14th - 16th centuries**

- ◼ "German" *Yeshiva* before the 14th century
- → Movement of German rabbis, 14th century
- ◼ "Polish" *Yeshiva*, 15th - 16th centuries
- → Movement of Polish rabbis, 15th - 16th centuries

200 km.

*1. Hanukkah lamp. Brass, Poland, 18th century.*

The *yeshivot* founded in Poland in the sixteenth century, maintained by community funds and headed by the greatest Polish rabbinical scholars, attracted students from all over the kingdom as well as from abroad. These institutions developed a unique dialectical method of study – the casuistic *pilpul* based on *hillukim* ("fine distinctions") which were a series of questions and answers concerning a talmudic text. This was undoubtedly an excellent method for sharpening the student's mind, yet it often aroused opposition amongst some rabbis who regarded it as a sterile, hair-splitting method which distracted students from the proper study of the Halakhah.

Nonetheless, graduates of these *yeshivot* constituted the cultural elite of Polish Jewry. They were the most sought after bridegrooms for the daughters of the Jewish oligarchy and the best candidates for rabbinical positions in Poland and in neighboring countries. The yeshivah was the best channel for social mobility: every poor but talented student could expect to marry the daughter of a rich merchant and thus improve his social position. Nathan Nata Hanover, idealizing Jewish society as it had been before the terrible disasters of 1648, writes in his *Yeven Mezullah* ("Abyss of Despair"): "In each fair there were several hundred heads of *yeshivot* and several thousand students and hundreds of thousands of young men and Jewish merchants... as the sands upon the seashore... and whoever had a son or a daughter to marry, went to the fair to find a match, for everyone could find there his heart's desire."

Indeed, Jewish intellectual life in Poland was disrupted and gravely impaired by the Cossack invasions and the mid-seventeenth century wars, but the strength and vitality of Polish Judaism continued to sustain it as the principal cultural center of Ashkenazi Jewry-from France in the west to Russia in the east-for many generations to come.

| Privileges to the *yeshivah* of Lublin | Publication of the Ashkenazi version of *Shulhan Arukh* | First *imprimatur* of the Council of the Four Lands |
|---|---|---|
| 1567 | 1570–1571 | 1603 |

*3. Ch. Burstin, A Theological Disputation, 1933.*

Inquisition starts burning the Talmud and forbids its study in Italy, the center for talmudic publications is transferred to Poland.

**1561–1640:** Lifespan of Joel Sirkes, rabbi of Cracow from 1619 and author of a treatise rejecting the *Shulhan Arukh* as a work of normative Halakhah.

**1567:** Sigismund II August Jagellon authorizes the founding of a second yeshivah in Lublin; the head of the yeshivah is not subordinate to the authority of the community rabbi, and the yeshivah itself is granted privileges including exemption from taxation and immunities similar to those granted to universities.

**1570–1571:** The Ashkenazi version of *Shulhan Arukh*, Moses Isserles's *Mappa*, is published in Cracow; the rapid spread of the *Shulhan Arukh*, its immediate adaptation to Ashkenazi custom, as well as the spread of Jewish mysticism emanating from the circle of kabbalists in Safed, are all manifestations of the enormous effects of the cultural revolution triggered off by the invention of printing. Poland's Jewry, having been a major consumer of Italian books, soon establishes its own printing shops, which are able to satisfy the local demand for works of religious law, ethics and Kabbalah.

**1603:** First *Haskamah* ("agreement", "approbation") of the Council of the Four Lands for the printing of a book. Until the second half of the 18th century, the Council, wishing to control the spread of printing and to prevent the publication of undesirable works such as Shabbatean-inspired books of Kabbalah, gave its *imprimatur* to dozens of different titles.

**1631:** Yom-Tov Lipmann Heller, rabbi of Prague, settles in Poland where he becomes one of the prominent figures in the Council of the Four Lands; after the 1640s he serves as rabbi of Cracow and head of its yeshivah. His most important book is a commentary on the Mishnah.

# The Spiritual Adventure of the Kabbalah

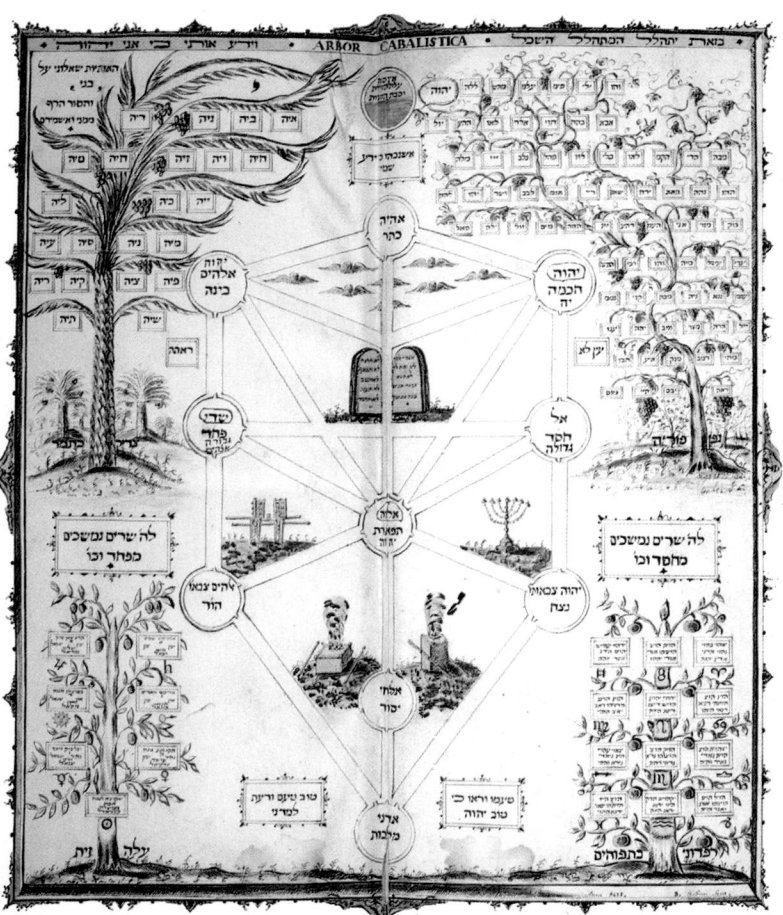

*1. Ilan Sefirot ("Tree of Divine Emanations") in a book by the Kabbalist Abraham Cohen Herera (c. 1570–c. 1635). Copy of 1675.*

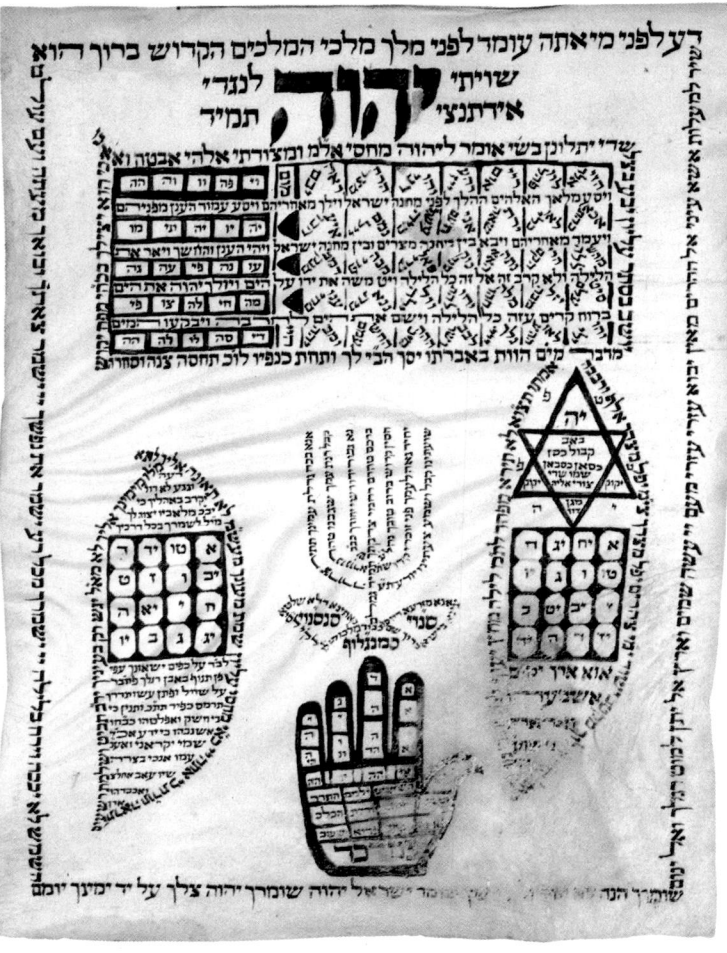

*2. Kabbalistic amulet. Ink on parchment. Palestine, 18th century.*

**T**he Kabbalah (Hebrew for "handed down by tradition") made its appearance in the twelfth century in Provence, southern France, which at the time was the scene of the Cathar heresy. It reached maturity, however, in thirteenth-century Spain, with the composition of *Sefer ha-Zohar* ("Book of Splendor"). Henceforth, the Kabbalah became the main trend of Jewish mysticism, theosophy and esotericism, comprising many different, at times contradictory, approaches. Basically, kabbalists wanted to transform Judaism into a more profound inner experience; an experience, so they believed, that could not be attained through a rational and intellectual approach to religion. For them Judaism was a system of mystical symbols reflecting the mystery of God and the universe, and their aim was to discover keys to the understanding of this symbolism. The *Zohar*, generally attributed to Moses de Leon, sought to revive a "communion" between the faithful and divinity. The Divine manifests itself in ten *Sefirot* (emanations) representing an intermediate stage between God and creation. Just as these emanations are contained within the Godhead, so they impregnate all beings outside it. Man is capable, by practising precise rites, of influencing the *Sefirot* which determine the span and progress of the world. The theory of *Sefirot* became the backbone of Spanish kabbalist teachings, represented by a great number of images.

In time, two attitudes emerged: one esoteric, which tried to restrict the secrets of kabbalist wisdom to a small circle of initiates; and a second which insisted that it should be widely-spread, benefitting everyone. Rabbinical Judaism received the Kabbalah with mixed feelings: some rabbis regarded the kabbalists as brave defenders of tradition, whose insistence on a meticulous observance of the commandments was more than praiseworthy; others saw in them dangerous innovators, whose introduction of non-Jewish elements must be arrested at all costs.

The expulsion of the Jews from the Iberian peninsula destroyed one of the most important kabbalist centers. The dispersion of kabbalists in three continents, however, soon led to the establishment of new schools. Four new centers emerged during the sixteenth century. In North Africa refugees from the peninsula preserved the Spanish tradition in its original purity. In Italy the encounter between the Kabbalah and the Renaissance led to its infusion with strong neoplatonic elements. In the Ottoman Empire Spanish kabbalists came into contact with earlier kabbalistic trends, giving precedence to ecstatic components of the Kabbalah, to theories relating to the transmigration of souls, cosmic cycles, and calculations of the End of Days. And finally, in Palestine, where the Kabbalah had two successive centers – first in Jerusalem, where there existed from the thirteenth century an ecstatic tradition with strong messianic tendencies; then in Safed, which witnessed in the mid-sixteenth century a great revival of mysticism.

| Provençal Kabbalah | Spanish Kabbalah |
|---|---|
| **12th century.** | **13th–15th centuries.** |

**Early 12th century:** Beginnings of the Kabbalah in southern France, contemporary with the Ashkenazi pietist movement of the *Hasidim*. The vocabulary of the Kabbalah proper, however, would emerge only in the following century.

**Middle of 12th century:** Extensive kabbalist activity in Provence: Abraham ben Isaac of Narbonne, his son-in-law Abraham ben David of Posquieres (today Vauvert), Jacob Nazir of Lunel, and others. This circle was influenced by Judah Halevi's *Kuzari*, in the Hebrew translation of Judah ibn Tibbon.

**Early 13th century:** Emergence of the kabbalist center in Gerona, Catalonia: its most illustrious member is Nahmanides (c. 1194–1270) who will become the greatest rabbinical authority of his generation.

**c. 1280–1286:** Moses de Leon composes the bulk of the *Zohar*. Intense kabbalistic activity in the region of Toledo.

**Early 14th century:** Appearance of *Ma'arekhet ha-Elohut* ("The Order of God"), an anonymous work which was to exercise a

*3. Diagram of the ten Sefirot, composed of the initial letters of their names. From Moses Cordovero, Pardes Rimmonim, Cracow, 1592.*

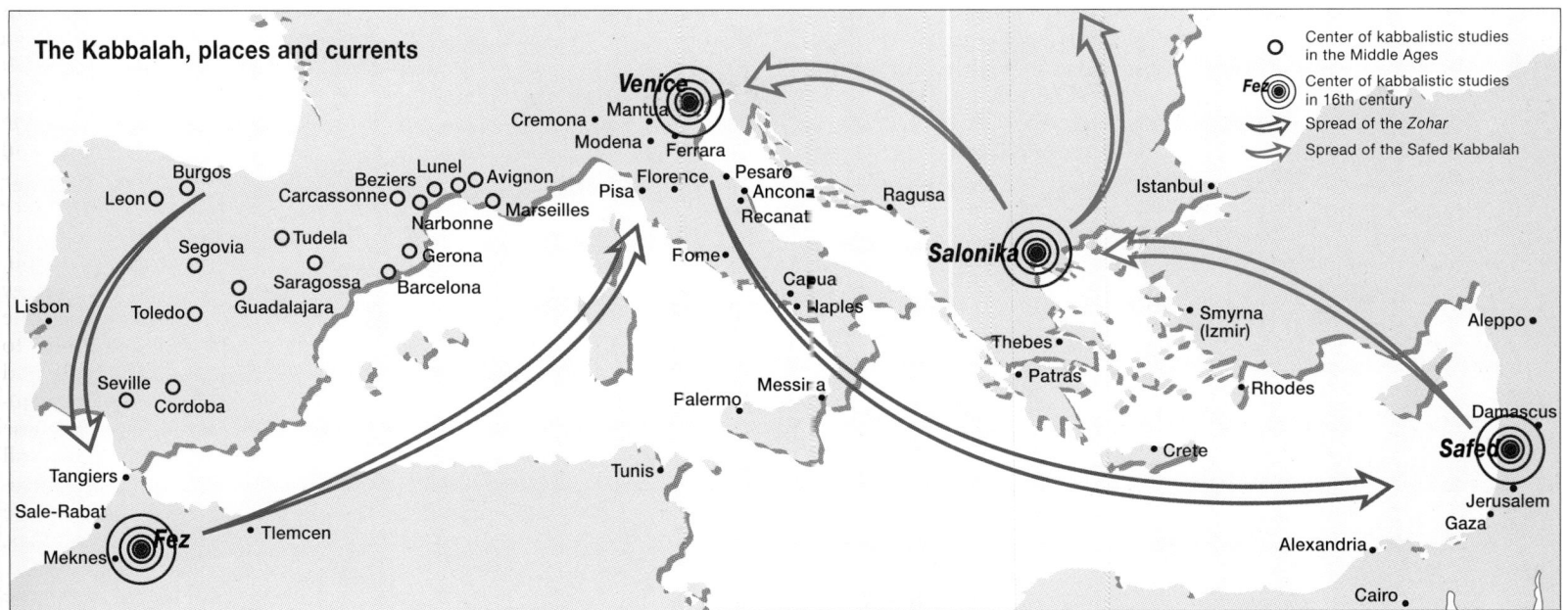

**The Kabbalah, places and currents**

○ Center of kabbalistic studies in the Middle Ages

◉ *Fez* Center of kabbalistic studies in 16th century

⇨ Spread of the *Zohar*

⇨ Spread of the Safed Kabbalah

The Kabbalah in Safed developed in two stages. The doctrine introduced by Moses Cordovero was a concise synthesis of the trends prevalent up to his time, whereby he sought to construct a speculative kabbalistic system which he later presented in his works, particularly in *Pardes Rimmonim* ("Garden of Pomegranates"). Then, after Cordovero's death, Isaac Luria Ashkenazi founded his own school, teaching extremely complicated theories intended only for a small circle of initiates.

The study and teaching of Lurianic Kabbalah continued throughout the seventeenth century in Jerusalem and Damascus. The form in which we know it today was presented in *Sefer Ez ha-Hayyim* ("Book of the Tree of Life") by Hayyim Vital, Luria's greatest disciple. This version of the Kabbalah was disseminated in Italy at the end of the sixteenth century by Israel Sarug, and from there spread to the rest of Europe. By the end of the following century, this corpus of teachings, edited by Vital and his successors, was a major influence on kabbalists everywhere.

Lurianic Kabbalah, mostly as a philosophical system, became known to the Christian world in a Latin translation, *Kabbala denudata* (1677–1684), by Christian Knorr von Rosenroth. Meanwhile, in the Jewish world, the Kabbalah broke out of the narrow circles of mystic intellectuals and became the property of ever growing numbers of people, affecting the behavior, attitudes and beliefs of a large part of the Jewish nation.

4. Michail Grobman. *Gate of Heaven*, 1977.

### Safed Kabbalah

**16th century.**

profound influence on the Kabbalah till the 16th century; spread of the Kabbalah throughout the Spanish communities; beginning of its penetration into Italy and the Orient.

**1500–1502:** Asher Lemlein, an ecstatic kabbalist active in northern Italy, presents himself as the Messiah and stimulates a movement of repentance among the Jews.

**1510–1532:** Treatises and letters by the apocalyptic kabbalist Abraham ben Eliezer ha-Levi, predicting the coming of the Messiah in 1540, are circulated in Jerusalem and Italy. David Reubeni, presenting himself as an oriental Jewish prince on a mission in Europe to raise an army against the Turks, meets Solomon Molkho, a Portuguese Marrano who returns to Judaism, studies the Kabbalah and regards himself as a messiah.

**1522–1570:** Moses ben Jacob Cordovero, founder of the kabbalistic school in Safed, a disciple of the mystic poet Solomon Alkabez and of the great codifier Joseph Caro, and teacher to Isaac Luria.

### Diffusion of the Kabbalah

**17th century.**

**Middle of 16th century:** Fierce disputations over the publication of the *Zohar*, printed for the first time in Mantua and Cremona simultaneously (1558). Both editions are disseminated throughout Europe and contribute to the acceptance of the Kabbalah as normative literature. The kabbalists of Safed begin interpreting the *Zohar* which becomes the canonical text of the discipline.

**1570:** *Sefer Reshit Hokhmah* ("Book of Initial Wisdom") by Elijah de Vidas, disciple of Cordovero; published in Venice, the book was aimed at a popular audience and accepted as one of the most important kabbalist works.

**1592:** Arriving in Venice from Egypt, Israel Sarug propagates his version of the Lurianic Kabbalah and influences the greatest Italian kabbalist of the time, Menahem Azariah Fano.

**Early 17th century:** A special brand of the Kabbalah begins to emerge in Poland; its principal representatives, Samson ben Pesah Ostropoler and Nathan Shapira of Cracow, were deeply concerned with demonology and messianism.

**1620:** After leaving Safed and serving as rabbi in Jerusalem, Hayyim Vital dies in Damascus; he bequeaths to his son, Samuel Vital, the largest collection of Lurianic teachings, written as annotations to the master's lessons.

**c. 1630:** Leone (Judah Aryeh) Modena, rabbi of Venice, writes *Ari Nohem* ("Growling Lion") – the first comprehensive polemic against the Kabbalah; although he does not dare publish it, his work provokes bitter polemics.

**c. 1665:** Shabbetai Zevi's messianic mission is connected to the Lurianic Kabbalah.

# The Jews of Poland between the Nobles and the Church

The mass immigration of Ashkenazi Jews into Poland during the sixteenth century greatly affected their economic life. While in German towns they had been mostly moneylenders, in Poland they entered a far greater variety of commercial activities. A hostile description from the early seventeenth century presents them as monopolizers of exports and imports, of both wholesale and retail trade: "They go to the lands from whence one brings diverse merchandise . . . When goods arrive in Poland, the Jews hurry and buy them all . . . Moreover, they send the merchandise out . . . to Hungary, to Moravia . . . There is no object, from the dearest to the cheapest, in which the Jews do not trade . . . they are not satisfied to do business in their shops, but they peddle everywhere, in the markets, in the houses, and in the courtyards."

The economic success of the Jews was due mainly to the support of the Polish nobility whose power in the kingdom was continuously rising. The townspeople, however, regarded them as competitors and attempted to limit their freedom of movement and to chase them out of the towns. Expelled from the old royal cities, and settling in the new "private" townships which had begun to emerge on the magnates' estates, it was only natural that the Jews should regard the nobles as their allies.

Furthermore, Poland's unification with Lithuania (1569) opened new economic opportunities for the Jews. The Polish nobility initiated vast colonization enterprises in the steppes of the Ukraine, but had little interest in the administration and commercialization of their vast and remote estates. Therefore they turned to the Jews. A leasing system was devised, the "agricultural arenda": in return for a fixed rent, the Jewish lessee administered the estate and controlled all means of production, including the serfs. Consequently, the Ukrainian Orthodox peasant began to see the Jew as the representative of the oppressing and Catholic Polish noble. Becoming an object of hatred for the rural population, the Jewish leaseholder was often the first victim of popular revolts. Caught between the hatred of the burghers and that of

1. "I am Jewish, my father is Jewish... I amass thalers by the sacks," an "arenda jug" for alcoholic beverages shaped in the figure of a Jewish innkeeper. Poland, 17th century.

the peasants, his physical security depended entirely on his relations with the nobleman.

In 1648 the Ukrainian volcano erupted. In the course of a major revolt, dozens of Jewish communities were destroyed and thousands of Jews were massacred. Allied to the serfs, the Cossacks, warriors from the Polish frontier regions, ravished the southeastern parts of the kingdom. Here and there, Jews took up arms and participated in the defense of the towns (Tulchin, Nemirov); but most of them fled, or preferred to fall into the hands of the Tatars, allies of the Cossacks, in the hope of being ransomed by their brethren. After 1648 many Jews returned to Poland; but wars and hardship continued to endanger their communities till the 1660s.

During the second half of the seventeenth century, the Jews also encountered the hostility of the Church – an age-old hostility, it is true, yet becoming increasingly more vehement as the religious orders, particularly the Jesuits, consolidated their positions. In addition, in the villages on the estates which they administered, the Jews were accused of interfering with the affairs of the Orthodox church.

Graver still, accusations of murdering adolescent Christians for the use of their blood in the preparation of the Passover unleavened bread were multiplying, becoming in the following century almost an annual event. The Church even intervened in the affairs of Frankism – the post-Shabbatean messianic movement of Jakob Frank – by offering protection to followers of the false messiah. In return, the Frankists "authenticated" the blood libels.

In order to defend themselves, the Jews turned to Rome, or once more requested the assistance of the Polish nobility. Such protection was expensive and depleted the communities' funds and weakened their councils. All this however did not prevent abbeys and religious orders from maintaining financial relations with Jewish communities. Thus, although Polish Jewry eventually recovered from the convulsions of the seventeenth century, much of its former dynamism was lost.

---

**Cossack pogroms**

**1648–1649**

**1648–1649:** The great Cossack and peasant revolt led by the hetman Bogdan Chmielnicki. This minor Ukrainian noble leads the Dnieper Cossacks against Polish domination in the hope of achieving, if not an independent, at least an autonomous Ukraine. The long march of "Chmiel the Wicked," as he is branded in Jewish annals, destroys numerous Jewish communities. On June 10, in the single community of Nemirov, about 6000 Jews are massacred; in this town in southeastern Poland, where many Jews from surrounding unfortified villages sought refuge, the massacre is perpetrated in collaboration with the Polish defenders (this day will be commemorated by Jews in Eastern Europe until the 20th century). In September the Cossack army of Bogdan Chmielnicki arrives in Lvov; the hetman, great butcher of Jews, lifts the siege the town in return for a ransom paid in part by the local Jewish community.
**1653:** Nathan Nata Hannover, *Yeven Mezulah* ("The Abyss of Despair"): written by

**"Ritual murder" in Sandomierz**

**1698**

a survivor, it is the most detailed chronicle of the horrors of the immense pogrom during the Cossack revolt of Bogdan Chmielnicki. Hannover glorifies the figure of Jeremi Wisniowiecki, a Polonized Russian prince, owner of enormous domains in the Ukraine and a private army of 3000 men, who in 1648–1651 led several battles against Chmielnicki's Cossack and Tatar bands and defended the Jews living on his lands.
**1654–1656:** Immediately after the end of the revolt, the Russo-Swedish war brings the Russian armies to the northeastern parts of Poland-Lithuania; the Russians chase the Jews of the region's towns; in Moghilev, the Cossacks massacre the Jewish population; in other places forced conversions are followed by deportations to interior Russia. As the Swedes advance, Jews are accused

2. A pro-Frankist "book-burning" bishop receives his just deserts, drowning in the river like Pharaoh's chariots. Caricature in Jacob Emden's anti-Frankist *Sefer Shimush*, 1758–1762.

## The Cossack Revolt

ESTONIA

SWEDEN

LIVONIA

• Ostrow

• Riga

BALTIC SEA

RUSSIA

Volga

• Moscow

Dwina

• Polotsk

L I T H U A N I A

Kaunas •

• Vitebsk

• Smolensk

Gdansk
(Danzig) •

PRUSSIA

Troki •

• Vilnius

• Shklov

• Mogilev

Grodno •

Minsk •

Nemunas

Vistula

Torun •

• Plock

Slutsk •

• Orel

• Poznan

P O L A N D

Warta

• Kalisz

Bog

Brest •

Pinsk •

Pripet

• Gomel

• Starodub

• Kursk

Piotrkow •

Lubecz •

Chernigov •

Kovel •

Kiev •

Chelm •

Wlodzimierz
(Vladimir) •

Opatow •

Lublin •

• Pereyaslav

Sandomierz •

Zamosc •

Loutsk •

• Rovno

Zhitomir •

• Lubny

• Kharkov

Cracow •

Belz •

Dubno •

Izyaslav •

Luban •

Berdichev •

Boguslav •

• Poltava

Jaroslaw •

Brody •

Konstantinov •

Korsun •

Kremenchug •

Przemysl •

Lvov •

Zbarazh •

Medzibozh •

Tarnopol •

Letichev •

Vinnitsa •

Dnieper

Satanov •

Bar •

Nemirov •

Bratslav •

Yambol •

Dniester

Bug

O T T O M A N   E M P I R E

Jassy •

SEA OF AZOV

BLACK SEA

| | |
|---|---|
| ▨ | Extent of the revolt |
| → | Route of Cossack bands |
| ▬ | Borders of the Kingdom in 1634 |
| ▬ | and in 1667 |
| ▪▪▪ | Lithuanian - Polish line of demarcation |

200 km.

---

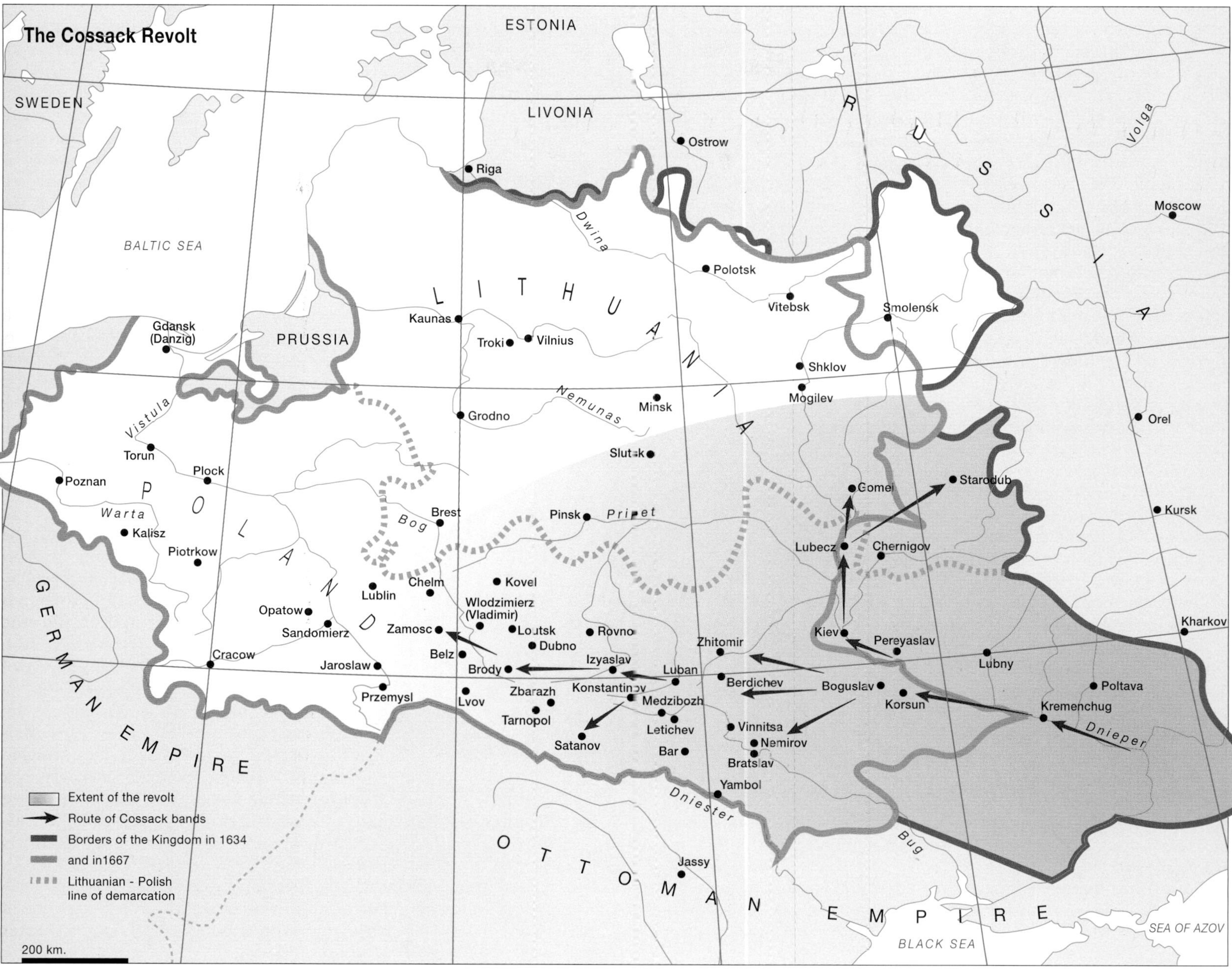

### "The Northern War"
**1700–1721**

### The Haidamacks
**1734–1768**

of collaborating with the invaders and are victimized by the local population.

**1664:** Anti-Jewish riots in Lvov.

**1666:** The appearance of Shabbetai Zevi arouses great messianic hopes throughout the suffering Jewish communities of Eastern Europe. The Polish Kabbalist Nehemiah ha-Kohen, after meeting with Shabbetai Zevi in Gallipoli, is convinced that Shabbetai is a false messiah and denounces him to the Ottoman authorities. His activities cause an uproar throughout Poland.

**1670:** In Lublin, the Council of the Four Lands proclaims the excommunication of the false messiah Shabbetai Zevi.

**1680:** Anti-Jewish riots in Brest-Litovsk.

**1687:** Jews of Poznan attacked.

**1698–1704:** The blood-libel affair in Sandomierz. A dignitary of the community is accused of the murder of a Christian child and executed; this affair becomes the model

*3. Jan Piotr Norblin, a Jewish family. Poland, 19th century.*

for dozens of similar accusations throughout the 18th century.

**1700–1721:** The Great Northern War: Russia and Sweden intervene in the conflict over the throne of Poland; the communities in northwestern Poland, Lithuania, and the Ukraine are affected most of all.

**1728:** In Lvov two Jews are tried and condemned to be burned at the stake for having aided a converted Jew's return to Judaism.

**1734, 1750, 1768:** Pogroms of the Haidamacks. Bands of escaped serfs, together with Zaporozhian Cossacks, poorer urban elements, heretics of all kinds, and some renegade Jews, terrorize the eastern regions of Poland with the tacit approval of the Russians. Their slogan: "[Polish] Lords and Jews, out of the Ukraine!".

**1759:** Frank's disciples convert to Christianity.

*4. Hondius, The hetman Bogdan Chmielnicki. Engraving, Danzig, 1651.*

# The Era of False Messiahs

Messianic agitation was widespread among Spanish Jews even before the expulsion, and it certainly grew stronger in its aftermath. In the sixteenth century many kabbalists, among them Abraham ben Eliezer ha-Levi and Solomon Molkho, became obsessed with eschatological themes. With the approach of the year 5335 (1574 of the Christian Era), the Jewish world witnessed a new upsurge of messianic fervor. Some regarded Isaac Luria, the great Safed kabbalist, as the Messiah; while Hayyim Vital, Luria's disciple, preferred to see himself as the hero of a messianic drama. Eschatological tension apparently abated somewhat in the first half of the seventeenth century, but in the second half of that century expectations for imminent redemption seemed to reach a new peak.

Several historical developments account for this renewed wave of messianism: the intensification of eschatological tension among certain radical Protestant groups in Europe, particularly in Holland and England; the massacres of 1648–1649 which destroyed hundreds of communities in Poland and the Ukraine; recent memories of Solomon Molkho's messianic activity; and finally, the diffusion of kabbalist literature which was permeated with calculations for the End of Days.

Yet even within this context, the momentous success of Shabbateanism was a remarkable phenomenon. Born in Smyrna (Ismir), Shabbetai Zevi moved to Jerusalem, then to Gaza where he met with an adept of Lurianic Kabbalah – Nathan Ashkenazi, called Nathan of Gaza. Nathan, receiving a revelation about the messianic role of his companion, became the prophet of the new Messiah. The terminology he used was derived from Lurianic Kabbalah as well as from concepts of popular Jewish messianism. Although Shabbetai Zevi himself studied other kabbalistic trends and was averse to Lurianic theosophy, this did not affect the enormous success of Nathan's propaganda. Within a very short time its impact was felt throughout the diaspora in processions of joy, acts of extreme mortification, and innumerable delegations who came to behold the Messiah.

*1. Shabbetai Zevi "King of the Jews," by Ioannes Meyfsens. Engraving, 17th century.*

This messianic agitation soon alarmed the Ottoman authorities. Summoned to appear before the sultan, Shabbetai Zevi was given a choice of apostasy or death. To the amazement of all his believers, the Messiah converted to Islam. His prophet Nathan immediately came up with an audacious kabbalist explanation: the Messiah has descended into the depths of the *kelippah* – the realm of evil – to conquer it from within. And so strong was the aspiration for redemption that neither the apostasy nor the death of Shabbetai Zevi destroyed the belief of his followers. Among them we may distinguish two radical currents. In Greece the sect of the Doenmeh (Turkish for "converts" or "apostates") professed Islam in public but adhered to a mixture of traditional and heretical Judaism in secret, believing in the divinity of Shabbetai Zevi and practicing sexual license. This sect survived in Greece till 1924 and then moved to Turkey.

In eighteenth-century Europe a last burst of Shabbateanism occurred with the appearance of Jacob Frank, a former disciple of Shabbetai Zevi who came under the influence of radical Shabbatean trends in the Balkans. Frank declared himself to be an incarnation of divinity and the successor of the Messiah from Smyrna. Frankism advocated outward adherence to Catholicism while secretly believing in a nihilistic version of heretical Judaism. Spreading from Poland to central Europe, the influence of the Frankists persisted well into the nineteenth century.

Shabbateanism in its various forms weighed heavily on the Jewish conscience. Its immense success could be attributed partly to the phenomenon of marranism. Communities of Jews who had been forcibly converted and returned to Judaism, without fully assimilating its rigid normative system, were naturally more inclined to accept the antinomian tendencies of Shabbatean messianism. Another factor was the great social and intellectual mobility which facilitated the rapid transmission of ideas. The general crisis of the mid-seventeenth century also precipitated a great wave of millenarianism in Europe, and Shabbateanism was the Jewish expression of this general outburst.

| Shabbetai Zevi proclaims himself the Messiah | Shabbetai Zevi's apostasy | Shabbetai Zevi's death |
|---|---|---|
| 1665 | 1666 | 1676 |

*2. Solomon Molkho's banner. Italy (?), before 1628.*

**1626:** Birth of Shabbetai Zevi in Smyrna. His father Mordecai was born in the Peloponnesus to a family of Ashkenazi origin; first a small merchant, he later became a commercial agent for western traders, benefitting from the economic rise of Smyrna. Exceptionally talented, young Shabbetai seemed destined to become a member of the rabbinical elite.

**1642–1662:** Shabbetai Zevi's years of kabbalistic studies, revelations, "strange acts" (contrary to religious law), and travels throughout the European regions of the Ottoman Empire.

**1648–1649:** Chmielnicki's massacres in the Ukraine.

**1665:** Shabbetai Zevi's meeting in Gaza with Nathan Ashkenazi; the latter has a revelation concerning Shabbetai's messianic vocation; Shabbetai is persuaded to proclaim himself the Messiah and begins to cultivate majestic pomp. Nathan spreading the tidings of imminent redemption and calling for repentance. Returning to Smyrna, Shabbetai arouses messianic enthusiasm in many Jewish communities. Arrested by the grand vizier, he is imprisoned in Gallipoli.

**1666:** After a disputation with a Polish kabbalist Nehemiah ha-Kohen, Shabbetai Zevi is accused of fomenting sedition among the Jews. Brought before Sultan Mehmed IV, he denies ever making messianic claims and accepts conversion to Islam in order to escape execution. Together with Shabbetai (now called Aziz Mehmed Effendi), his wife and dozens of his disciples convert as well.

**1673–1676:** Deported to Dulcigno in Albania following a denunciation, the false messiah dies on the Day of Atonement.

**1680–1700:** Period of intense Shabbatean agitation in northern Italy; missionary activities of Abraham Miguel Cardozo, one of the principal leaders of the movement.

**c. 1700:** Emergence of the radical current within the Doenmeh movement led by Baruchiah Russo (Osman Baba), who abolishes many biblical prohibitions, presenting them as contrary to the new

# 17th–18th Centuries

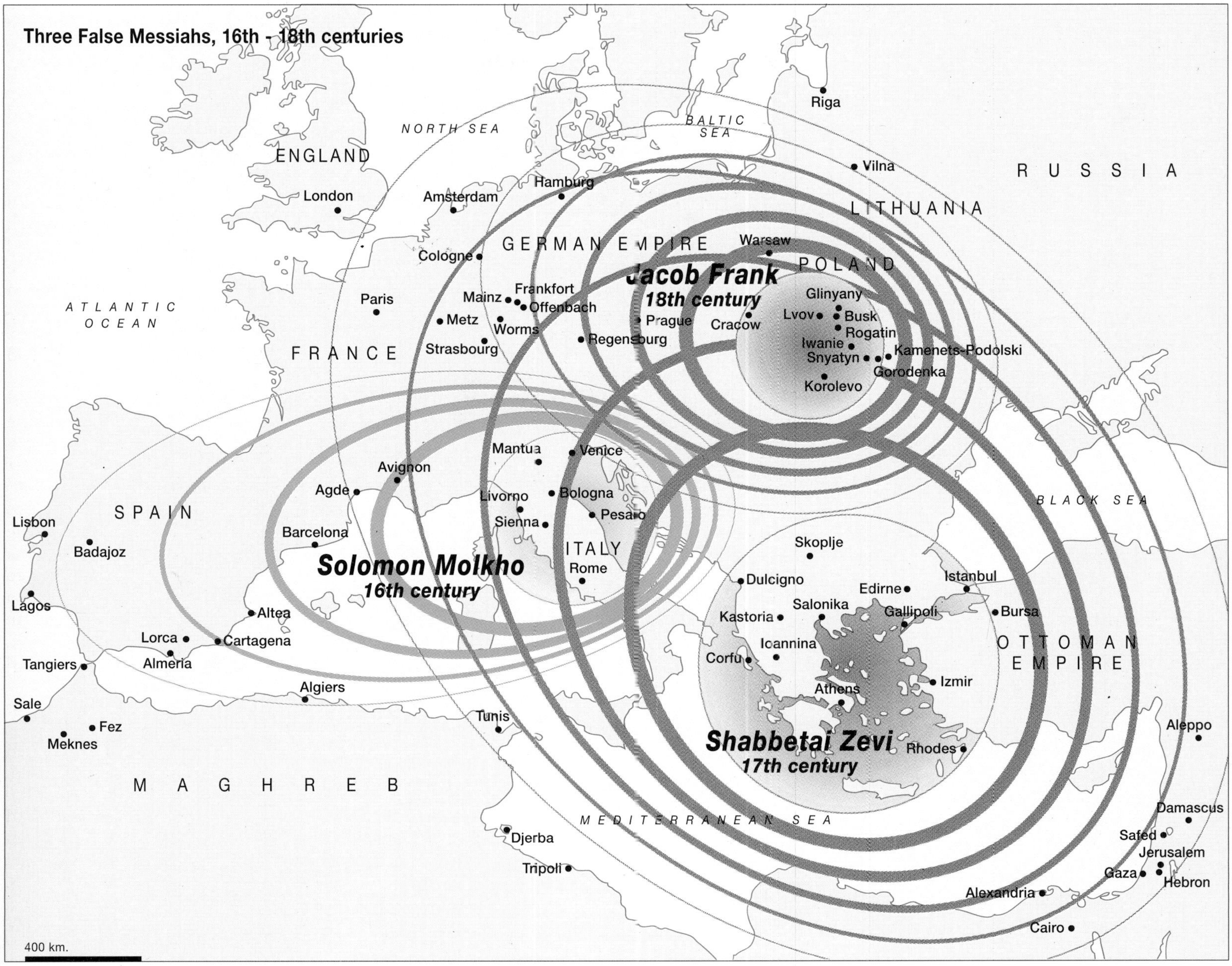

## Three False Messiahs, 16th – 18th centuries

Riga
ENGLAND
NORTH SEA
BALTIC SEA
Vilna
RUSSIA
London
Amsterdam
Hamburg
LITHUANIA
Cologne
GERMAN EMPIRE
Warsaw
POLAND
**Jacob Frank**
**18th century**
Glinyany
Paris
Mainz Frankfort
Offenbach
Prague Cracow
Lvov Busk
Rogatin
ATLANTIC
OCEAN
Metz
Worms
Regensburg
Iwanie Kamenets-Podolski
Strasbourg
Snyatyn
Gorodenka
FRANCE
Korolevo
Mantua Venice
Agde Avignon
BLACK SEA
SPAIN
Livorno Bologna
**Solomon Molkho**
Barcelona Sienna Pesaro
**16th century**
Lisbon
ITALY
Badajoz
Rome
Skoplje
Istanbul
Lagos
Altea
Dulcigno
Edirne
Lorca Cartagena
Salonika Gallipoli
Bursa
Tangiers
Almeria
Kastoria
Icannina
OTTOMAN
Sale
Algiers
Corfu
Izmir
EMPIRE
Fez
Athens
Aleppo
Meknes
Tunis
**Shabbetai Zevi**
Rhodes
MAGHREB
**17th century**
Damascus
MEDITERRANEAN SEA
Safed
Djerba
Jerusalem
Tripoli
Gaza Hebron
Alexandria
Cairo

400 km.

---

**The Emden-Eybeschuetz disputation**

**1750–1764**

**Conversion of Jacob Frank**

**1757**

3. Nathan of Gaza leads his people to the Promised Land. Engraving, Germany, 1666.

spiritual message of the Messiah.

**1700:** Led by Judah Hasid and Hayyim ben Solomon Malakh ("Angel"), Shabbatean groups from Poland "ascend" to the Land of Israel.

**1700–1760:** Shabbateanism is spread in central Europe and in northern Italy by several "prophets" and "believers" such as Judah Leib Prossnitz, Meir Eisenstadt, Nehemiah Hayon, Jonathan Eybeschuetz and his son Wolf Jacob Koppel, and Moses Hayyim Luzzatto and his circle. The same years witness the appearance of anti-Shabbatean literature, notably the writings of Jacob Emden who violently attacks Eybeschuetz.

**1726–1791:** Life of Jacob Frank, Shabbatai Zevi's greatest successor.

**1759:** Founding of a Frankist sect in Iwanie, Podolia (the Ukraine).

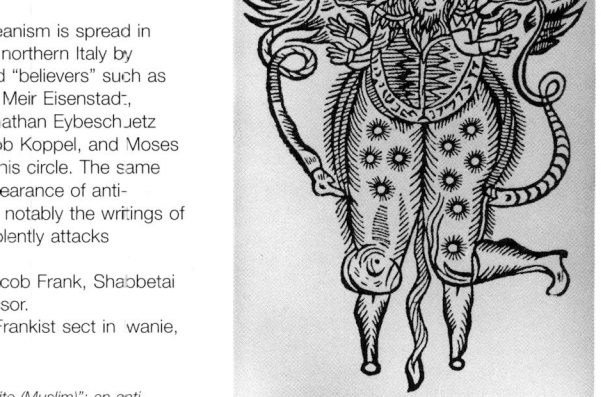

4. "Christian-Jew-Ishmaelite (Muslim)": an anti-Frankist caricature in Sefer Shimmush by Jacob Emden. Altona, 1758–1762.

# A New World: Latin America

### The First Communities 16th-18th centuries

- ●●●● Jewish Migration
- ● Jews
- • Judaizers
- 1569 ◆ Inquisition Tribunal

Territory:
- ☐ Portuguese
- ☐ Spanish
- ☐ Dutch
- ☐ French
- ☐ English
- ☐ Dutch between 1630 and 1654

1,000 km.

On the borderline between the Middle Ages and Modernity, at the precise moment western Europe was either expelling its last remaining Jews or confining them to ghettos, a Genoese navigator in the service of the Spanish Crown inadvertently stumbled upon a new continent.

Among those who accompanied Christopher Columbus, sailing with him to discover a new route to the Indies, were at least four descendants of Spanish Jews. On October 12, 1492, one of them, interpreter Luis de Torres, was among the first to set foot on the shores of the island of Guanahani (San Salvador). Was Columbus himself of Marrano extraction? Some historians ardently defend this theory on the basis of Columbus' signature and several of his letters. One thing, however, is certain: his voyage was made possible by the political and financial support of courtiers of Converso origin, and it was to them that he sent his first reports.

Another converted Jew, also an interpreter, participated in the expedition of Pedro Alvares Cabral which led to the discovery of Brazil. There were several Conversos among the *conquistadores* of Mexico, Peru, and Chile. However, from 1507 on, and throughout the colonial period, all those who could not prove their "purity of blood" were not permitted to travel to the Americas. Nevertheless, numerous New Christians in flight from the Inquisition and the policy of expulsions, eventually settled in the New World, legally or illegally.

The Spanish Inquisition continued to persecute New Christians even in these distant lands. In the late sixteenth and early seventeenth centuries, tribunals of the Holy Office were established in Lima, Mexico, and Cartagena. The younger Portuguese Inquisition (founded in 1536) was never formally introduced into Brazil, but inquisitors who came from the metropolis sent suspects to stand trial in Lisbon. Officially, Brazil did not permit the entry of New Christians, but this restriction was even less rigorously observed there than in the Spanish colonies. New Christians were crucial to the development of the sugar industry in Brazil, just as

---

| The Inquisition in America | Brazil under Dutch rule | Equal rights in Surinam |
|---|---|---|
| **1569** | **1637–1644** | **1667** |

**1492. August 3:** Four days after the final day fixed for the departure of the Jews from Spain (July 31), Christopher Columbus sailed from the port of Palos de Moguer on his voyage to the "Indies"; he reached American land – the island of Guanahani in the Bahamas – on October 12.

**1497:** The forced conversion of Portuguese Jews.

**1528:** The first auto-da-fé in Mexico: two Judaizers – one of them a companion of Cortes – are executed.

**1569. January 25:** Philip II of Spain orders branches of the Inquisition to be established in America.

**1570:** The Inquisition in Peru.

**1591–1596:** Judaizing Marranos are expelled from Brazil.

**1593:** Beginning of the Jewish community in Amsterdam.

**1596:** In Mexico, Luis de Carvajal the Younger is burned at the stake.

**1636:** *La Complicidad Grande*: some Jews are discovered among the Portuguese

merchants in Lima; 161 are arrested and interrogated by the Inquisition.

**1637–1644:** Seven good years for the 1,500 Jews under Dutch rule in northeastern Brazil.

**1639. January 23:** Epilogue of the "Great Complicity": in an immense auto-da-fé scores of condemned are humiliated in public; seven are burned at the stake, among them Manuel Batista Perez, known as *El Capitáno grande*, the richest merchant in the province, and a famous physician, Francisco Maldonado da Silva (Eli Nazareno).

**1649:** A collective auto-da-fé in Mexico.

**1654:** The Portuguese reoccupy Recife; part of the Jewish community escapes to other Dutch colonies, including twenty-three who migrate to New Amsterdam, the future New York.

**1661:** The first Jews are authorized to settle in Barbados.

**1667:** Surinam, an English colony, is ceded to the Dutch; for the first time in the history of the diaspora, Jews are granted full legal equality.

*2. Shop belonging to Isaac Abraham Levy Aron in Surinam, by French painter Benoît. Watercolor, 1839.*

in the early decades of the sixteenth century they had been important to cultivating the brazil wood after which the colony was named.

Between 1580 and 1640 the kingdoms of Portugal and Spain were united under one crown, and thus many "Portuguese" – that is, descendants of Jews who had been forcibly converted by Manuel I in 1497 – found themselves under Spanish rule. Persecutions in Brazil intensified during the years 1591–1596 and 1618, and then once more in the first half of the eighteenth century. By that time, however, the descendants of the Conversos were no longer aware of their particularity, and it became evident that class interests rather than questions of true faith were the real cause of their persecution. Thus, the Marquis of Pombal, the liberal Prime Minister of Joseph Manuel I (1750–1777), ordered the destruction of all lists of New Christians.

In Spanish territories persecutions first reached a peak towards the end of the sixteenth century. Then, after a brief respite, inquisitorial activity was renewed with vigor in 1624. All in all, the Spanish Inquisition in Latin America sent about a dozen persons accused of Judaizing to their deaths, and scores of others were tried and penalized in various ways. In the second half of the seventeenth century, autos-da-fé became increasingly rare, although the Inquisition continued till its last days to organize special ceremonies designed to encourage the denunciation of Judaizers.

An interesting chapter in the history of Latin-American Jewry concerns the small Portuguese community in Holland. Soon after the official constitution of the Amsterdam community (1597), Jewish merchants comprised some of the principal founders of the West India Company (1621). In Recife, conquered by the Dutch in 1630, the first openly Jewish community in America was founded. Twenty-four years later, when this Dutch enclave in Brazil was reconquered by the Portuguese, its Jews moved to Guyana, Surinam, and Curaçao, enlarging their European population. It was in these Dutch colonies that Jews received full equal rights for the first time in the history of the diaspora.

1. The synagogue in Curaçao, inaugurated in 1732.

| Equal rights in Barbados and Jamaica | Emancipation of New Christians in Brazil | Wars of liberation in Latin America |
|---|---|---|
| 1740 | 1773 | 1808–1826 |

**1732:** The synagogue in Curaçao is founded.
**1740:** The English colonies in Barbados and Jamaica grant Jews full equal rights long before the metropolis.
**1773:** Emancipation of the New Christians in Brazil.
**1804:** In Corrientes, Argentina, the Inquisition organizes a traditional ceremony designed to expose Judaizers and other heretics – one of the last public manifestations of Inquisitorial activity in Latin America.
**1808–1826:** Wars of independence in Latin America.
**1811:** Abolition of the Inquisition in New Granada (Colombia) and in Paraguay.
**1813:** Abolition of the Inquisition in Argentina, Mexico, Peru, Chile, and Uruguay.
**1815:** The Inquisition is re-established, only to be suppressed once again when the Latin American countries gain independence.

3. A tombstone in the old Jewish cemetery in Cassipoera, Surinam.

4. Torture chamber. The Inquisition Palace in Cartagena, Colombia, 17th century.

# The Beginnings of American Jewry

1. George Washington with two eminent members of the American Jewish community. Monument erected in Chicago celebrating the Jewish support for the patriotic cause.

I n their colonies in both South America and North America (New Amsterdam), the Dutch offered all immigrants the same religious freedom as was offered in Holland itself. Recife, capital of Dutch Brazil (1630–1654), was home to a flourishing Spanish-Jewish community which practiced Judaism openly until the region was reconquered by the Portuguese after several years of fighting. Part of the community preferred to follow their former rulers to New Amsterdam, soon to become the city of New York.

Thus, like the English Puritans, the Jews arrived in America in search of religious toleration and new economic opportunities. In 1664 the English drove out the Dutch by conquering the province of New Netherland. The Jews living in the British colonies during the eighteenth century numbered no more than 2,000 (out of a total population of approximately two million). They came from the Antilles, Amsterdam, and London, but also directly from Spain and Portugal. During the course of that century, Ashkenazi Jews made their way to America as well, mostly from Germany and Poland. By the 1730s Jews from Central and Eastern Europe already constituted a majority, although the community retained distinct marks of its Sephardi origins, particularly in its liturgy. Spanish, Yiddish, and German were the spoken languages, but English was soon to replace them.

Most American Jews at the time were small shopkeepers. When successful, they became merchants, importing consumer goods from their countries of origin and exporting raw materials; some engaged in buying and selling furs, others in the slave trade. At the top of the economic ladder were those merchants who manufactured fabrics out of raw materials for export to Europe.

On the whole, North American Jews enjoyed fundamental civil liberties. Only participation in the colonies' government – reserved exclusively for Protestants – was provisionally closed to them. Generally, however, the North American Jew was free, more free than his Catholic compatriots and in a far better position than his co-religionists anywhere else. There were very few anti-Jewish incidents. Vast spaces for colonization, a land of immigrants unencumbered by historical memories, and a young but already well-established tradition of offering refuge to victims of religious persecution – all these elements created ideal conditions for painless integration.

It is therefore not surprising that American Jews were wholeheartedly committed to the fight for independence. A long history of political deprivation and the individual liberties they enjoyed in America made them sympathize with the rebels' cause. Their economic activities made them primary victims of the restrictive commercial laws enacted in Westminster. Thus many Jewish soldiers and officers participated on all fronts in the American War of Independence.

3. The Touro synagogue in Newport, designed by architect Peter Harrison, completed in 1763.

| First Jewish immigrants in New Amsterdam | First synagogue in North America |
|---|---|
| 1654 | 1729 |

**1620. December 26:** The Mayflower, ship of the Pilgrim Fathers, anchors in Plymouth.
**1654. August:** The first Jewish immigrants arrive in New Amsterdam, the future New York; one month later they are joined by 23 Ashkenazi and Sephardi Jewish refugees from Brazil, who had participated in the war against the Portuguese. By the end of the 17th century, the second Jewish community on the North American continent had already been established in Charleston, South Carolina.

**First half of 18th century:** First Jewish immigrants in Philadelphia, Pennsylvania, as well as in Savannah, Georgia – a town which suffers great difficulties until it is refounded in 1760. In the middle of the century a Jewish center is established in Newport, Rhode Island. Until the end of the colonial period the Jews remain concentrated in these five communities, all situated along the eastern seaboard. From these centers they will begin to disperse inland.
**1729:** The first – and very modest –

4. Sheftall Sheftall, from Georgia, dressed in the revolutionary army uniform, which he wore till his death in 1847. Silhouette, late 18th century.

2. Ezra Stiles (1727–1795), president of Yale College, theologian and scholar. Stiles led friendly relations with the Newport community.

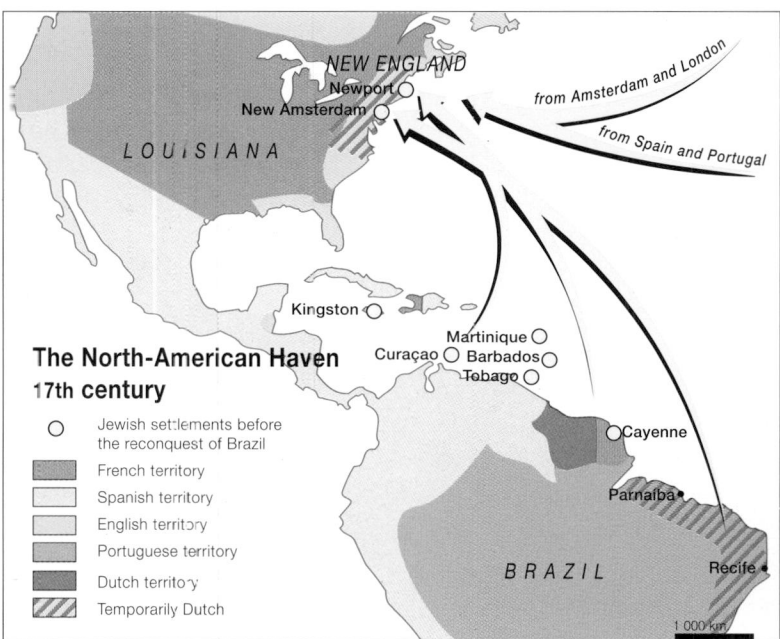

**The North-American Haven**
**17th century**

○   Jewish settlements before the reconquest of Brazil

     French territory

     Spanish territory

     English territory

     Portuguese territory

     Dutch territory

     Temporarily Dutch

The years of battle against the British constituted a formative period in the consolidation of principles of government and of American political thought: separation of church and state, freedom of conscience, equality before the law. Consequently, American Jews gained emancipation almost without a struggle, and they benefited from equal rights before liberal thinkers began advocating the emancipation of Jews in European countries. By the late eighteenth century, the small Jewish community of about 4,000 was an integral part of American society.

| Independence | The Constitution |
|---|---|
| **1776** | **1787** |

synagogue in North America, is founded in New York, serving both as a prayer house and a community center; thirty years later the Newport community erects a splendid synagogue, preserved to this day as part of the American national heritage.

**1739–1763:** The last colonial wars in America are concluded with the treaties of Aix-la-Chapelle and Paris which confirm British imperial superiority.

**1740:** British Parliament adopts a law according civil rights to Jews and Christian Dissenters after a seven-year period of residence, giving Jews a dispensation from the obligation to take an oath "according to the true Christian faith."

**1746, 1751, 1775:** Desecration of Jewish cemeteries in New York, Philadelphia, and Newport.

**1755:** The first Jewish school in New York becomes an all-day institution.

**1765–1781:** Beginning of the American Revolution in 1765 with the colonies' refusal to pay the new prohibitive British taxes ("no

taxation without representation"); followed by the Declaration of Independence on July 4, 1776; ends with the military victory of the rebels in 1781. The minute Jewish community actively participates in the Revolution.

**1776:** The Declaration of Independence on July 4 – the "Great Promise" that fascinates the Jews. Francis Salvador, the first Jew elected to an American legislative body – the revolutionary provincial Congress of South Carolina – joins the patriotic forces against the British Army besieging Charleston; killed in an ambush, he is scalped by Indians.

**1787:** First adopted in Virginia, Jefferson's law on the separation of church and state serves as a model for Congress when it writes the Federal Constitution granting Jews equality on the federal level.

**1791:** The First Amendment of the Constitution, incorporated as part of the Bill of Rights, stresses two principles: the separation of church and state and freedom of religion.

**Settlement in North America**
**17th–19th centuries**

     Colonized c. 1775

     Colonized c. 1800

[1750]   Jewish community

– · –   Frontier of the 13 colonies

· · · ·   Frontier of the United States in 1783

300 km.

# The Breakup of Polish Jewry

1. Henryk Pillati, *The Death of Berek Joselewicz in Kotsk, 1867.*

The kingdom of Poland, where approximately 800,000 Jews resided in the second half of the eighteenth century, ceased to exist as an independent entity in 1795. Within less than twenty-five years this large state had been partitioned three times (in 1772, 1793 and 1795) by neighboring powers – Russia, Prussia, and Austria. The Jews of Poland now became subjects of three different crowns and exposed to the regime of "enlightened despotism." Policies of centralized administration, drastic curtailment of the authority of autonomous bodies, and tight control of the subject, were adopted with the professed intent of ameliorating the subjects' well-being, revamping the economy, and educating the masses in the spirit of the Enlightenment.

Before being partitioned, Poland had embarked upon the road to reform, which included the "reformation" of the Jews who constituted a large part of the urban population, and were of prime economic importance. The years 1764–1765 during the reign of Stanislaw August Poniatowski, the last king of independent Poland, saw the abolition of two important institutions of Jewish self-government: "The Council of the Four Lands" (in existence since the sixteenth century) and "The Council of Lithuania." These establishments had formed the real government of the communities, exercising authority in legal and fiscal matters and representing Polish Jewry to the central authorities. The official justification for their abolition – the reform of the fiscal system – was typical of the general policy of centralization.

The absolutist monarchs who annexed parts of Poland in 1772 soon realized that the large Jewish population, with its unique socioeconomic profile, would not be easily integrated into the "State of Orders" which these monarchs were trying to create; nonetheless efforts were made to do so. In Russia, despite the age-old prohibition on the admission of Jews, Catherine II issued in September 1772 a declaration affirming the rights of Jews in the annexed territories. In Austria Maria-Theresa initiated a process of abolishing Jewish self-government, completely subordinating the Jews to the central administration (even including a government-appointed Grand Rabbi). Her successor, Joseph II, made far-reaching changes in the status of the Jews in Galicia. He established state schools for Jewish children, ordered their compulsory enlistment in the army, and finally issued the Edict of Toleration in 1789 – all with the intention of turning the Jews into "useful" ordinary citizens.

The Sejm (Parliament of Nobles) in truncated Poland had similar intentions. During the years 1788–1792 it discussed major reforms in which the Jews loomed large. Yet the constitution produced at the end of this four-year period failed to affect the status of the Jews in a significant way. Moreover, before any of the proposed reforms could be implemented, Poland was wrecked by invasions and wars. The kingdom was partitioned for a second and then a third time, and most of its Jews became Russian subjects.

The Russian government now needed to define its policy concerning the "Pale of Settlement" – the areas where Jews were allowed to reside permanently. The Pale was the area inhabited by the majority of Poland's Jews and annexed to Russia in 1772. The czarist government was prepared to encourage Jewish settlement in the sparsely inhabited southern regions which it wished to colonize, but strictly controlled the admission of Jews into central Russia.

At first, the new borders created by the partitions hardly affected the social structures and cultural cohesion of East European Jewry. With time, however, as evidenced by the rapid "westernization" of Prussian Jews, differences among the various sectors of divided Polish Jewry grew deeper and wider.

---

**First partition**

**1772**

**1764:** Accession of Stanislaw II August Poniatowski, last king of Poland. The Sejm abolishes the "Council of the Four Lands" and imposes a poll tax on the Jews. In a general census in Poland and Lithuania, the number of Jews is given as 587,000, but is generally believed to have been much higher.
**1772:** First partition of Poland. Maria-Theresa, Empress of Austria, annexes Galicia and promulgates a series of laws on Jewish affairs (August); Catherine II of Russia annexes regions in east Lithuania (Mogilev, Polotsk, and Vitebsk) and issues a declaration concerning the rights of Jews in her new territories (September). Shklov, an important commercial town on the new border between Russia and Poland, becomes a major intellectual center of Ashkenazi Jewry. Death of the *Maggid* of Mezhirech, leader of the Hasidic movement. Beginning of the struggle between the *hasidim* and their orthodox opponents; beginning of the East European *Haskalah*. Both movements spread in all regions of

partitioned Poland.
**1775:** "Reform of the regions" in Russia: the central authorities strengthen their control over annexed territories inhabited by a large Jewish population.
**1780:** Death of Maria-Theresa and accession of Joseph II.
**1781:** Edict of Toleration addressed to Austria's Jews. Similar edicts are proclaimed in Russia and Poland during the following decades.
**1782:** *Words of Peace and Truth* by the *maskil* Naphtali Herz Wessely applauds the government's centralizing policies. This work had a profound influence on the *Haskalah* movement in eastern Europe and raised fierce objections among the Polish rabbis.
**1784:** Joseph II imposes severe restrictions on *arenda* (a system of leasing property and privileges) in Galicia.
**1785:** As part of major reforms in the administration of the Orders, Russian Jews are included in the urban order of Russia. Nevertheless, the autonomy of the Jewish

**The four-year Sejm**

**1788–1792**

2. Parokhet *(curtain concealing the doors of the Ark of the Law in the synagogue, where the Torah scroll is kept) made from a Polish military banner used during the Napoleonic wars. Silver and gilded-silver embroidery on silk. Czestochowa, early 19th century.*

# 1772–1795

## Principal Communities in the Polish Sphere 1772

*Map labels:*

COURLAND
BALTIC SEA
Riga
Memel (Klaipeda)
Kiejdany
Polotsk
LITHUANIA
Vitebsk
Smolensk
Koenigsberg
Kovno
Vilna
Vilija
Dwina
Nemunas
Borisov
Shklov
Mogilev
Minsk
Gdansk (Danzig)
POMERANIA
DUCAL PRUSSIA
Grodno
Novogrudok
BELORUSSIA
Dnieper
Chelmno
Tykocin
MAZOVIA
Poznan (Posen)
Plock
Bog
Ciechanow
POLESIA
Slutsk
Bobruisk
Warta
Warsaw
Wegrow
Brest
Pinsk
Pripet
Mozyr
Desna
Volga
Leszno
Krotoszyn
Kalisz
GREATER POLAND
Vistula
Lublin
Kovel
RUSSIA
PRUSSIA
LITTLE POLAND
Opatow
Chelm
Zamosc
Vladimir
Rovno
Ostrog
Zhitomir
Kiev
Breslau
Pinczow
Szydlowiec
Belz
Loutsk
Wodzislaw
Olkusz
Brody
Izyaslav
Kremenents
UKRAINE
Dnieper
Cracow
Przemysl
Lvov
GALICIA
VOLHYNIA
AUSTRIA
Satanov
PODOLIA
Bratslav
Bug
Tisza
Dnieter
BESSARABIA
JEDISAN
Danube
HUNGARY
BUCOVINA
OTTOMAN EMPIRE
Odessa
Jassy
MOLDAVIA

▬ Poland's borders in 1772
░ Outline of final partition, 1795

100 km.

### The Contraction of Poland

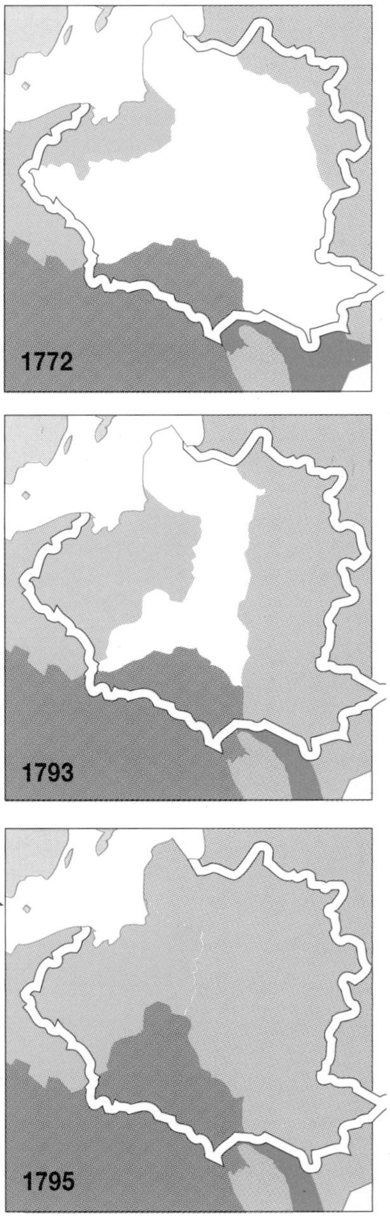

**1772**

**1793**

**1795**

---

| "Pale of Settlement" | Second partition | Kosciuszko's insurrection | Third partition |
|---|---|---|---|
| **1791** | **1793** | **1794** | **1795** |

community is preserved. Modern research considers this the beginning of Jewish civil emancipation in eastern Europe.

**1788:** First session of the four-year Sejm which was to debate, among other things, the "reform" of Poland's Jews. Influences of enlightened absolutism and the French Revolution, as well as the interests of the Polish nobility, determine the various reform programs of several leading Polish thinkers of the time: Hugo Kollantaj, Stanislaw Staszic, Tadeusz Czacki.

**1789:** *A Way to Reform the Jews of Poland and Make Them Useful Citizens of the State*, by Mateusz Butrymowisz is published in Warsaw; the Rabbi of Chelm responds with a refutation. Joseph II's Edict of Toleration to the Jews of Galicia.

**1791:** The *maskil* Menahem Mendel Lefin (Levin) publishes a pamphlet in French advocating the reform of the Jews; he attacks the *hasidim* whom he accuses of opposing integration.

**May 3:** The new Polish constitution is proclaimed by the four-year Sejm; Poland's Jews are granted emancipation.

**December 23:** Catherine II defines the "Pale of Settlement" in Russia.

**1793:** The second partition of Poland. Russia annexes Polish Ukraine and the rest of Belorussia; Prussia enlarges its territories in to western Poland.

**1794:** Kosciuszko's insurrection. The Poles turn to the lower social strata and the Jews for support, promising future political rewards; the Jewish cavalry unit is established under the command of Berek Joselewicz. The Russians crush the insurrection with fierce cruelty, and massacre the Jews of Praga, a suburb of Warsaw.

**1795:** Third partition of Poland. Russia annexes the rest of Lithuania, including Vilna, the largest Jewish community in eastern Europe at the time. Prussia receives Warsaw and its environs. *Finis Poloniae.*

*3. Model of the wood synagogue of Zabludow, Poland, 17th century.*

# Under Ottoman Law

During the sixteenth century, many Jews, mostly refugees from Europe with valuable skills and knowledge, made themselves very useful to the Turks. The ruling Muslim elite was primarily military, administrative, and religious, its wealth derived mainly from land property. Though some of them invested in commerce and industry, they were usually content to leave the running of these ventures to non-Muslims, with a marked preference for Jews who, unlike Christian subjects, were not suspected of being sympathetic toward the European enemies of the Empire. Because of their close association with the Turks, the Jews both rose and fell with their Turkish patrons. When the Turks conquered Hungary, they brought their Sephardi Jews from Istanbul with them; when they left in 1686, they took them back again.

At the beginning of the seventeenth century, the Ottoman Empire and its Jewish community entered a period of decline. The loss of power, wealth, and prestige of the Jewish *millet* (autonomous community) corresponded with the rise of the Christian minorities – first the Greeks, then the Armenians, and finally the Arabic-speaking Christians. The Christians were in many ways better placed than the Jews: far more numerous, educated in European schools which Jewish children could not attend, and active in shipping, from which the Jews were almost entirely absent. The Christians' greatest advantage was their European connection, and the preference shown to them by European governments and trading companies. Thus, although the Turks continued to favor the Jews, Jewish

1. Purim *image: King Ahasuerus' soldiers dressed in Ottoman uniforms. Painting on glass by Yossef Geiger. Safed, 1843.*

merchants and middlemen were gradually replaced by Christian competitors. In 1826, the destruction of the Corps of Janissaries was the last blow to the position of the Jews in the Empire in general, and to the status of the veteran Jewish leadership in particular. A small group of Jewish families had long-standing ties with the Corps, and owed their wealth and position to this connection. The void left by the massacre of the Janissaries was soon filled by Greeks and Armenians.

The situation of the Jews deteriorated even further as a result of specific changes within the community. In the seventeenth century immigration from Europe practically came to a standstill. Europe, richer now and more tolerant, could offer the Jews better opportunities. The Jews of the Ottoman Empire subsequently lost contact with Europe, no longer had access to its science, technology, and commerce. Jewish physicians and merchants found themselves outclassed by more qualified and better connected Christian competitors. Finally, the Ottoman Jewish communities paid a heavy price for the Shabbatean affair. The ignominious ending of Shabbetai Zevi left the community in a state of despair; it also reinforced the authority of the rabbis to an unprecedented extent. Thus, when the incursion of new ideas from Europe provoked, in the Jewish as in the Muslim and Christian communities, a quarrel between "ancients" and "moderns," the upper hand was readily gained by the conservatives and the traditionalists within the Jewish community.

The growing intervention of European powers transformed the structures of the Empire, affecting all its communities. The most obvious change was the loss of territory, first to European powers, then to Iran, and finally to independent states formed by peoples who had formerly been subjects of the Sublime Porte. All these countries – in the Balkans,

2. *A Jewish woman. Turkey, late 18th century.*

| Selim II | Mahmud I |
|---|---|
| 1566–1574 | 1730–1754 |

**1579:** Death of Don Joseph Nasi, duke of Naxos.
**1626–1676:** Lifespan of Shabbetai Zevi, the false messiah whose undertaking had a profound effect on the Ottoman Empire's Jewish communities.
**1686:** After a century and a half of Turkish domination in Hungary, the Habsburgs chase the Ottomans out; Jews serving the Turks leave with their masters.
**1703:** The Shabbatean propagandist, Miguel Cardozo, settles in Egypt.
**1774:** The Kutchuk Kainarji Treaty ends Ottoman suzerainty over the southern shores of the Black Sea.
**1783:** Russia annexes the Crimea.
**1812:** Russia annexes Bessarabia.
**1830:** France occupies Algeria. Greek independence. Ishak Effendi, a Greek Jew from Yannina who converted to Islam, becomes chief instructor in the military

3. *Sign of European influence in the Empire: a cigarette box. Turkey, 19th century.*

college of engineering; through his teaching, and still more through his translations into Turkish of European scientific works, he becomes one of the pioneers of modern science in Turkey.
**1835:** Mahmud II, reforming sultan, officially invests the *Hakham Bashi* – chief rabbi – with jurisdiction over the entire Jewish population in the Empire.
**1839:** Great Britain occupies Aden.

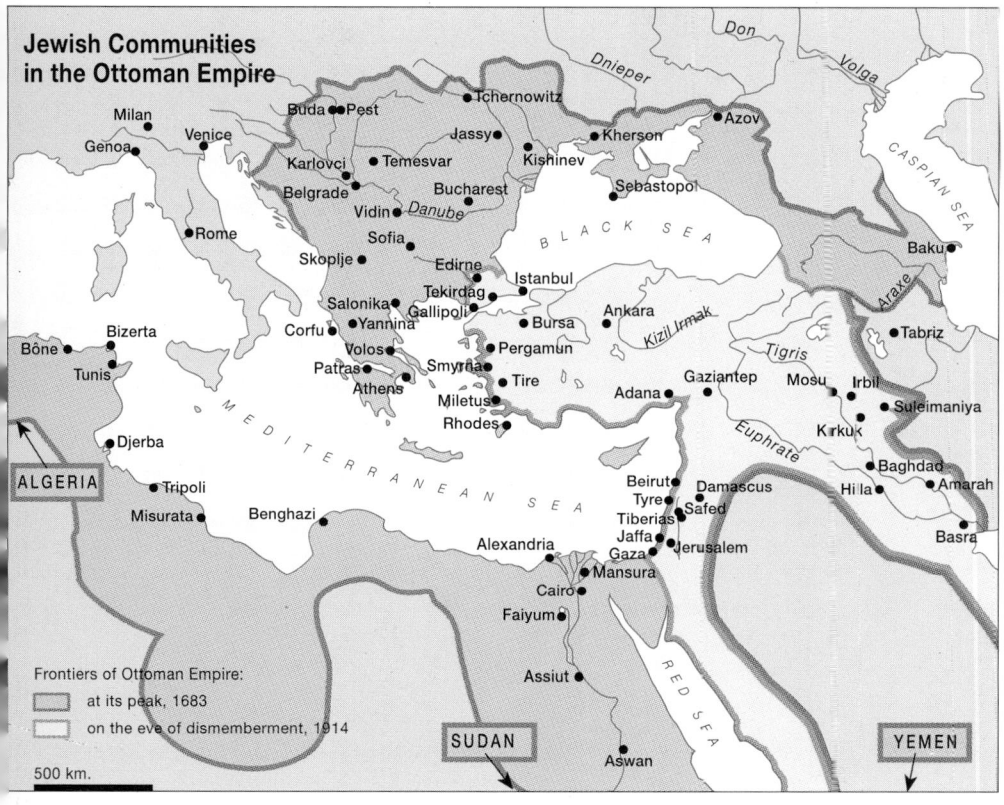

**Jewish Communities in the Ottoman Empire**

Frontiers of Ottoman Empire:
- at its peak, 1683
- on the eve of dismemberment, 1914

500 km.

**Ottoman Heritage in Turkey, 1930**

250 km.

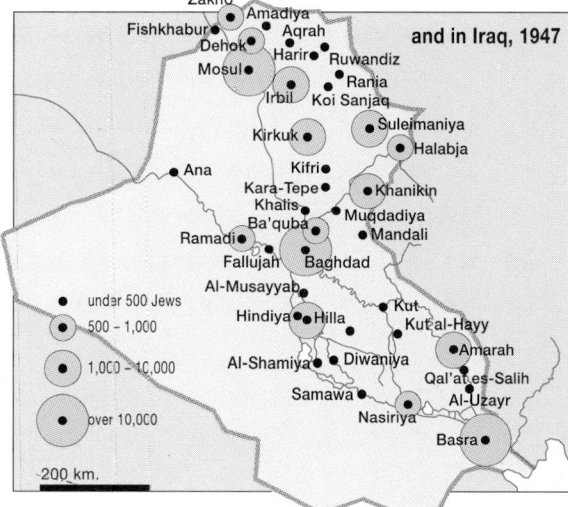

**and in Iraq, 1947**

- under 500 Jews
- 500 – 1,000
- 1,000 – 10,000
- over 10,000

200 km.

in North Africa, and in the Near East – contained important Jewish communities whose future evolution was to be shaped by influences vastly different from the Ottoman rule and the rabbinical hierarchy. Even the Jews of Turkey proper were ultimately affected by these new trends, either through reformed government schools, or through foreign educational establishments, above all the network established by the *Alliance Israelite Universelle*. Indeed, it was through the French language that the Alliance pupils gained access to the modern world.

Gradually, the Ottoman Jews emerged from their isolation, sometimes participating themselves in the shaping of events. Towards the end of the nineteenth century Jews began to play a role in the bureaucracy, in the parliaments, and, inevitably, in the opposition of the Young Turks. European influence, however, also had its darker side, namely the introduction of European-style antisemitism. The Muslim majority, painfully aware of the decline of the Empire and embittered by European

intervention, projected its hostilities on the non-Muslim population, particularly onto the Christians, but on the Jews as well. At the same time, The Christian population, sometimes with the encouragement of foreign consuls and ecclesiastical patrons, began to disseminate antisemitic propaganda and to translate anti-Jewish literature. Blood libels, unknown to classical Islam, rare in the Ottoman territories and previously always condemned by the authorities, became commonplace in the nineteenth century, and were often followed by outbreaks of violence.

Troubles in eastern and southeastern Europe, the independence attained by the Balkan states, and the persecution of the Russian Jews, all led to the resumption of Jewish immigration to Turkey in the late nineteenth century. The increase in the Jewish population, however, was modest. Many of the refugees moved on to other countries, notably in North or South America, and quite a few native Turkish Jews took the same route.

| Mahmud II | Abd al-Majid I | Abdu-l-Hamid II |
|---|---|---|
| 1808–1839 | 1839–1861 | 1876–1909 |

Beginning of reforms set by Sultan Abd al-Majid I: *hatt-i-sherif* of the *Gul-Khane* ("The Rescript of the Rose Chamber"), promulgated on November 3, inaugurates a series of laws and regulations which together constitute the *Tanzimat* ("reforms"); the sultan vouched for the security of the lives and property of all his subjects and guaranteed equality of rights and military service for non-Muslim citizens.

**1840:** The Damascus ritual-murder libel. Inspired by the example of Greece and Serbia, Judah Alkalai, a rabbi from Bosnia, proposes a novel solution to the Jewish question: restoration of Jewish sovereignty in the Land of Israel by human efforts alone.

**1842:** In Izmir, publication of *Buena Esperanca*, the first weekly in Ladino, to be followed by about 300 other newspapers and journals in the following century.

**1854–1856:** The Crimean War.

*Ketubbah. Istanbul, 1853.*

**1856:** The *hatt-i-humayun* by Abd al-Majid confirms the *hatt-i-sherif* of 1839; this imperial decree is equivalent to a toleration charter for the non-Muslim subjects of the Empire.

**1857:** In Tunisia, the "Pact Fondamental" proclaims the equality of all Tunisian subjects, regardless of religion.

**1860:** Founding of the Alliance Israelite Universelle in Paris.

**1862:** An Alliance school is opened in Tetuan, Morocco.

**1864:** Alliance school set up in Baghdad.

**1865:** Alliance school set up in Volos, Greece.

**1867:** Alliance school set up in Edirne.

**1869:** Inauguration of the Suez Canal.

**1876:** Constitution of the Ottoman Empire.

**1877–1878:** Russo-Turkish War.

**1878:** Congress of Berlin. Serbia, Rumania, Bulgaria, and Tunisia gain independence.

**1881:** France occupies Tunisia.

**1882:** Great Britain occupies Egypt; pogroms in Russia.

# Emancipation in Western Europe

Recognizing that Jews were equal to other citizens and the legal abolition of disabilities and inequities were ideals that began to materialize in Western Europe only two centuries ago. The Declaration of the Rights of Man and of the Citizen, the manifesto of the French Revolution, inspired by the spirit of the Enlightenment, implied Jewish equality. The law passed by the Constituent Assembly on September 27, 1791, the first act of full emancipation by a Christian state, was perceived by the Jews as an historic turn which heralded a future of happiness. "France... is our Palestine, its mountains are our Zion, its rivers our Jordan. Let us drink the water of these sources; it is the water of liberty...!" (a letter to *La Chronique de Paris*, 1791).

After the French Revolution, emancipation became the central issue for Jews everywhere, but each community had to maintain its own struggle for emancipation. In most places the legal decision was the crowning achievement of a lengthy process of economic and social integration. However, in some cases – as in France itself – emancipation preceded the renunciation of traditional Jewish society: it was the liberals' struggle for the universal application of "natural rights" which ensured the civil equality of the Jews. Comte de Clermont-Tonnere, in his famous speech to the National Assembly (December 1789), explicitly demanded that the Jews not be excluded from article X of the Declaration of Rights ("No man ought to be molested because of his opinions, including his religious opinions"). Therefore, he said, "The Jews should be denied everything as a nation, but granted everything as individuals." The revolutionary French armies were to export this type of emancipation to all the countries they conquered.

Whether it was the result of a deliberate choice (as in France), or imported and enforced (as in Italy and Germany), or a product of an extended process of socio-cultural maturation (as in Austro-Hungary) emancipation was never a linear nor a painless process. The customary religious hostility toward the Jews, characteristic of traditional pre-industrial societies, was reinforced by modern ideologies and political forces, both conservative and revolutionary, which regarded Jewish equality with fear and antagonism. These animosities often merged with the opposition to Napoleon who extended the scope of emancipation with his military victories. Thus, Jewish emancipation in Europe suffered major regression during the years following the Congress of Vienna (1814–1815), which ended the age of the Revolution and sought to reestablish peace in Europe based on the restoration of the old order. Nevertheless, liberal and democratic forces everywhere took up the cause of Jewish emancipation and turned it into a central issue in their political campaign. On the eve of the revolution of 1848, the idea of Jewish equality could no longer be ignored anywhere in the west.

The upheavals which rocked Europe in the mid-nineteenth century

1. "A wise government protects all religions." Bonaparte proclaims freedom of worship, 1802.

| Emancipation in France | ... in the Netherlands | ... in Prussia |
|---|---|---|
| **1791** | **1796** | **1812** |

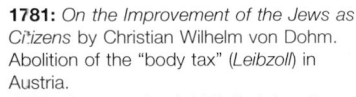

**1781:** *On the Improvement of the Jews as Citizens* by Christian Wilhelm von Dohm. Abolition of the "body tax" (*Leibzoll*) in Austria.
**1784. January:** Louis XVI abolishes the "body tax" that was levied on the Jews of Alsace.
**1785:** In an essay competition in 1787, the Academy of Metz sets the following subject: "Are there any ways of making the Jews of France happier and more useful?" Abbé Henri Gregoire wins the prize for his *Essay on the physical, moral and political regeneration of the Jews* (1789).
**1787:** Comte de Mirabeau publishes his book *On Moses Mendelssohn and on the Political Reform of the Jews*.
**1790. January 28:** The decree according active civil rights to "Spanish," "Portuguese" and "Avignonese" Jews in France.
**1791. September 27:** Emancipation decreed for all Jews in France.
**1796. September 9:** The National Assembly of the Batavian Republic accords equal

rights to the Jews of the Netherlands – a typical example of the application of revolutionary ideals in republics established with the help of the French armies; the same step will be taken in Italy, Belgium, and German states.
**1801. July 15:** Signing of the Concordat: the French government recognizes Catholicism as the religion of "the great majority of Frenchmen".
**1808:** The consistorial system imposed by Napoleon on the Jews of France represented a step backward in revolutionary ideals; the *decret infâme*, determining Jewish activities, was not renewed after the expiry of its ten-year time limit.
**1812. March 11:** The Prussian decree of emancipation accords the Jews civil rights, but excludes them from government service; similar to the formulation of Jewish emancipation in Baden (1809), this decree remained one of the most liberal texts in Germany until 1848.
**1814. March 29:** The King of Denmark

3. The crucifix on Charles Bridge in Prague. In expiation for a blasphemous act by a Jew in 1696, the community had to finance the Hebrew inscription in gold letters: "Holy, holy, holy is the Lord of Hosts."

4. Gabriel Riesser, by Moritz Oppenheim, between 1838 and 1840.

**Emancipation in the late 19th century**

Emancipation by decree or constitution:

| 1791 | End of 18th century |
| 1821 | 19th century |

Territory under French *Code Civil*, 1804-1814

No equal rights before 20th century

600 km.

2. One hundred years of Philathropin, a modernized Jewish school founded in Frankfort in 1804.

resulted, admittedly, in only a few formal changes. Popular anti-Jewish feelings, the reticence of governments, and nationalist fermentation in multi-national empires, all still played a central role in restricting the full and legal admission of the Jews into society. But as the West was shedding, at an uneven but irreversible pace, its feudal and traditional structures, and entering a liberal, bourgeois, individualist and industrial age, the equality of all citizens was becoming an essential condition of modernity. When Switzerland granted the Jews equal rights in 1874, the process that had begun in Paris almost a century earlier was completed: Jewish emancipation in the West was by now an established political and legal fact. This nineteenth-century achievement, however, was rather fragile, and was therefore easily destroyed in certain European countries with the rise of twentieth-century racist ideologies. This goes to show that legal equality and full political participation do not necessarily lead to social acceptance and recognition.

**.. in Denmark** | **... in Sweden** | **... in Austria**

1849 | 1865 | 1867

authorizes the Jews in his kingdom to engage in all professions.

**1819. August:** To the rallying cry *hep! hep!* derived perhaps from the initials of *Hierosolyma est perdita*) anti-Jewish riots break out in Wuerzburg, quickly spreading to neighboring states. The riots expressed the anger of many Germans at the improvement in the situation of the Jews.

**1830:** Louis Philippe is king of France; the 1830 charter abolishes the notion of "state religion" which was introduced by the Restoration.

**1831:** Gabriel Riesser (1806–1863), a Jewish notary from Hamburg and a champion of emancipation, begins publishing his journal *Der Jude* ("The Jew"). Publication of the journal ceased in 1833, but Riesser continued his struggle to attain equal rights for German Jews.

**1837:** Danish Jews become eligible for municipal election.

**1848:** Demolition of the Ghetto walls in Rome. The German National Assembly proclaims the emancipation of the Jews.

**1849. March 4:** The Imperial government introduces a constitution guaranteeing equal rights to the Jews of Austria; suppressed in 1851, emancipation will be re-introduced in 1867 and henceforth maintained.

**June 5:** Adoption of a liberal constitution in Denmark: article 84 implies emancipation of the Jews.

**1865:** The Jews of Sweden are accorded the right to vote.

**1866:** Deletion by law of the Christian portion of the oath of loyalty enables Jews in England to be elected to public office.

**1871. April 22:** Granting of equal rights to the Jews of Bavaria completes the process of emancipation in the German Empire.

**1874:** The granting of equal rights to the Jews in Switzerland completes the process of emancipation in Europe.

5. *The Jew, a member of the National Guard but still a coward. Antisemitic lithograph by H. Gerhart, Vienna, 1848.*

# French Patriots

*1. Sukkah decoration. A man carrying the symbols of the Festival of Tabernacles on his way to the synagogue. Bischwiller (Haut-Rhin), 18th century.*

When the French Revolution brought about the downfall of the Ancien Régime, there were approximately 40,000 Jews living in France, more than half of them in Alsace and Lorraine. Theirs was a highly heterogeneous population: well-integrated "Portuguese" Jews in Bordeaux and Bayonne, and "Papal Jews" in Avignon, barely tolerated their Yiddish-speaking Ashkenazi brethren who had acquired nothing of French culture. They were further divided over attitudes towards the Revolution. On the whole, however, French Jews supported the Revolution but did not actively participate in it. Nevertheless, although not immediately felt, the outcome of the Revolution marks the beginning of the history of modern French Jewry. Extracted with great difficulty by the more advanced elements in the National Assembly and based on broader arguments than the Jewish question, the principle of equal civil rights granted the Jews the legal emancipation that enabled their integration into French society.

It was Napoleon who made them realize the full significance of their new citizenship. Faithful to his policy of centralization, the Emperor created institutions designed to integrate the Jews into the French state system. In 1808 he set up a special body which was fashioned on the arrangements introduced for French Protestants: a Central Consistory, a vehicle guaranteeing state supervision of religious affairs. Brandishing the banner of "Religion and Homeland," the Consistory attempted to accelerate the modernization of French Jewry. Its success was undeniable even though in certain parts of France, particularly in Alsace and Lorraine, a traditional Jewish existence persisted until the end of the nineteenth century.

Legal emancipation led to a profound transformation of Jewish society. Jews became fluent in the French language, flocked to the cities (Paris above all), entered into new careers and professions, became involved in political life, and enthusiastically welcomed the values of French civilization, its culture and education. Relations with the non-Jewish society varied according to social and geographical distribution. Hostile manifestations persisted: traditional anti-Judaism persisted in eastern France while modern antisemitism, evidence of the growing integration of the Jews, was rearing its ugly head in Paris and other large urban centers. All these, however, could not reverse the progress of emancipation, acculturation, and assimilation.

The unlimited trust which Jews placed in the French system survived even after the 1870 defeat, and the annexation of Alsace-Lorraine to Germany. Moreover, thousands of Jews migrated to France after the disastrous Franco-Prussian war. Their love for France was further augmented by the establishment of the Third Republic, which was explicitly committed to the principles of 1789. The emergence of an antisemitic political movement in the 1880s following the tragic Dreyfus affair, failed to change these sentiments. Thus, the nascent Zionist movement had few adherents among French Jews.

The two dominant traits of Jewish society in France – its strong attachment to the promises of the Revolution and the homogeneous character it acquired after a century of acculturation – were seriously challenged in the twentieth century. Prior to World War I, and particularly in its aftermath, a wave of Jews from eastern Europe flooded France, soon becoming the majority of French Jewry. Adopting French culture was not their first priority. They remained foreigners, on the margins of the "old" community, evoking the same attitude that the "Portuguese" of Bordeaux had displayed towards Ashkenazi citizens of France 150 years earlier. Even in its darkest hour, facing persecution and extinction, the French community was incapable of surmounting its differences. The Nazi occupier and the Vichy regime, however, made no distinction between "old" and "new" French Jews.

| Emancipation | The Consistory | French citizenship to Algerian Jews | Drumont's *La France juive* |
|---|---|---|---|
| 1790–1791 | 1808 | 1870 | 1886 |

*2. "I gain from all of you," says the Jew at the top of the "real" social hierarchy. An antisemitic caricature, France, c. 1880.*

**1789. August 26:** The Declaration of the Rights of Man and of the Citizen.

**1790. January 28:** Jews of Portuguese, Spanish, and Avignonese origin are granted equal rights.

**1791. September 27:** The National Assembly grants civil rights to the Jews of Alsace and Lorraine; the process of emancipation of French Jews is now complete.

**1799. November 9:** A *coup d'etat* brings Napoleon Bonaparte to power.

**1806. October 6:** The Assembly of Jewish Notables is required to answer twelve questions, intended to inform the authorities about the nature of Judaism and to test the knowledge of French among the Jews.

**1807. February–March:** The "Grand Sanhedrin" meets in Paris, presided by David Sintzheim of Strasbourg; it was convened by Napoleon in order to codify the decisions of the Assembly of Notables.

**1808. March 17:** Establishment of the Central Consistory of French Jews.

**1830:** Conquest of Algeria.

**1840:** A blood libel affair in Damascus; Adolphe Cremieux and Salomon Munk are members of a delegation sent to Damascus to free the prisoners.

**1848:** Adolphe Cremieux is appointed Minister of Justice.

**1852. December 2:** Napoleon III is crowned emperor.

**1860:** Founding of the *Alliance Israelite Universelle*, an organization based on the French ideal of "regeneration" and on the Jewish notion of solidarity, dedicated to the modernization of Jewish communities in North Africa and the Near East.

**1869:** Zadoc Kahn is appointed *Grand Rabbin* of France.

**1870:** The Franco-Prussian war. The Cremieux Decree: the Jews of Algeria receive French citizenship (from 1865,

## Major Jewish Communities in France

- Since 1945
- From 1500 to 1940
- From inception to end of Middle Ages

Lille 3,000
Le Havre
Beauvais
Rouen
Creil
Caen
Pontoise
Evreux
Paris 350,000
Falaise
Dreux
Chartres
Melun
Etampes
Le Mans
Orleans
Blois
Nantes
Angers
Clisson
Tours
Chinon
Bourges
Poitiers
Niort
Limoges
Angouleme
Bordeaux 6,000
Feims
Verdun
Thionville
Metz 2,500
Chateau-Thierry
Meaux
Bar-le-Duc
Nancy 2,000
Haguenau
Toul
Luneville
Strasbourg 12,000
Provins
Fontainebleau
Sens
Troyes
Selestat
Colmar
Auxerre
Vesoul
Mulhouse
Dijon
Belfort
Nevers
Besançon
Macon
Bourg-en-Bresse
Vichy
Roanne
Trevoux
Lyons 30,000
Clermont-Ferrand
Vienne
Saint-Etienne
Grenoble 5,000
Valence
Largentiere
Montelimar
Valreas
Orange
Carpentras
Nice 25,000
Ales
Avignon
Forcalquiers
Albi
Nimes
Tarascon
Toulouse 25,000
Lunel
Beaucaire
Draguignan
Cannes
Bayonne
Montpellier
Arles
Aix-en-Provence
St. Jean-de-Luz
Pau
Capestang
Beziers
Marseilles 70,000
Toulon
Carcassonne
Pamiers
Narbonne
Agde
Foix
Limoux
Perpignan

100 km.

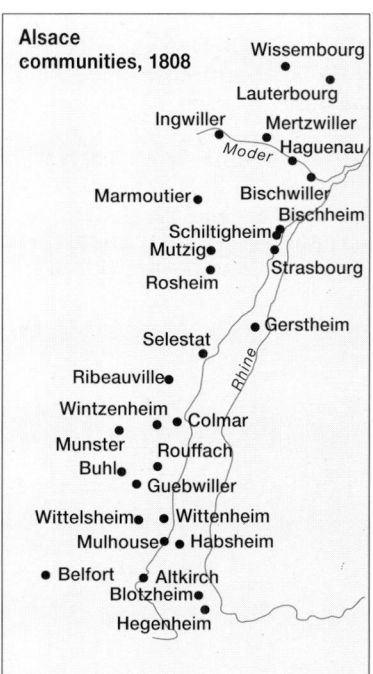

## Alsace communities, 1808

Wissembourg
Lauterbourg
Ingwiller
Mertzwiller
Moder
Haguenau
Marmoutier
Bischwiller
Bischheim
Schiltigheim
Mutzig
Strasbourg
Rosheim
Gerstheim
Selestat
Rhine
Ribeauville
Wintzenheim
Colmar
Munster
Rouffach
Buhl
Guebwiller
Wittelsheim
Wittenheim
Mulhouse
Habsheim
Belfort
Altkirch
Blotzheim
Hegenheim

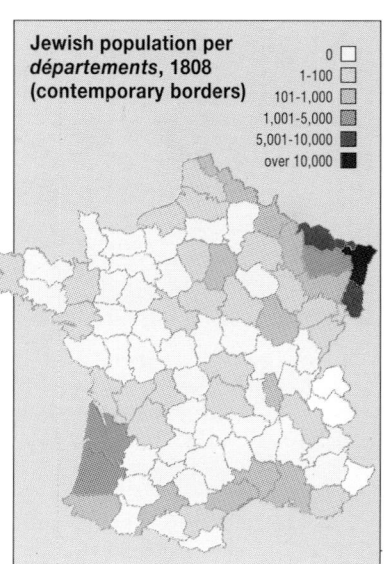

## Jewish population per *départements*, 1808 (contemporary borders)

- 0
- 1–100
- 101–1,000
- 1,001–5,000
- 5,001–10,000
- over 10,000

| Emile Zola's *"J'accuse"* | Dreyfus' rehabilitation | The Popular Front | The *Statut des Juifs* |
|---|---|---|---|
| **1898** | **1906** | **1936** | **1940** |

LOGIQUE

Traitre dehors patriote dedans

*3. Alfred Le Petit, ironic caricature entitled "Logic": Paul Déroulède, a true patriot, remains in prison while the traitor Dreyfus is released. Paris, 1899.*

following Napoleon III's visit to Algeria, Jews and Muslims were entitled to citizenship on an individual basis).
**1871. March–May:** The Paris Commune.
**1875:** Establishment of the Third Republic.
**1878:** A delegation representing the central committee of the Alliance participates in the Congress of Berlin; this is the first time that a Jewish delegation takes part in an international congress.
**1886:** Publication of Edouard Drumont's *La France juive*, to become the central text of French antisemitism.
**1894:** Bernard Lazare's book, *Antisemitism, Its History and Its Causes*. Alfred Dreyfus is arrested for alleged treason.
**1897:** The first French version of Herzl's *The Jewish State* is published in Paris.
**1898:** Emile Zola publishes his letter

*4. Leon Blum (1872–1950).*

*"J'accuse"* in *L'Aurore* (January 13). Drumont is Algerian deputy to the National Assembly; anti-Jewish leagues and pogroms in Algeria.
**1905. December 9:** Separation of church and state.
**1906. July:** Rehabilitation of Dreyfus.
**1923:** Founding of the *Fédération des Sociétés juives de France*, a body which united the immigrants' aid organizations; the Federation supports the Zionists, and in 1938 the organizations with Communist leanings secede and form the Union of Jewish Societies.
**1936. May:** Victory for the Popular Front; Leon Blum becomes the first Jewish Prime Minister of France (June 4).
**1938:** The Evian Conference.
**1940. August 7:** Abrogation of the Cremieux Decree: the Jews of Algeria lose their French citizenship.
**October 3:** The Vichy regime promulgates the *Statut des Juifs*, racial laws which in practice abolish the emancipation of French Jews.

# "Pietists" and "Opponents"

In the eighteenth century East European Jewry witnessed a great religious awakening. The upheaval following the collapse of the Shabbatean movement, the spread of kabbalistic mysticism among the scholars, as well as popular traditions of mass enthusiasm, provided the background for the emergence of a new spiritual movement: Hasidism (from *hasidut*, meaning "piety").

The father of Hasidism was a rabbi from Podolia in southeast Poland – Israel Ba'al Shem Tov (c. 1700–1760). A miracle-worker and a healer, an ecstatic mystic and a charismatic leader, the man drew followers and admirers from among kabbalists, rabbis, and leaders of groups devoted to occult studies. His religious teachings concerning the best methods to avoid sinful "undesirable" thoughts attracted all manner of rabbis and

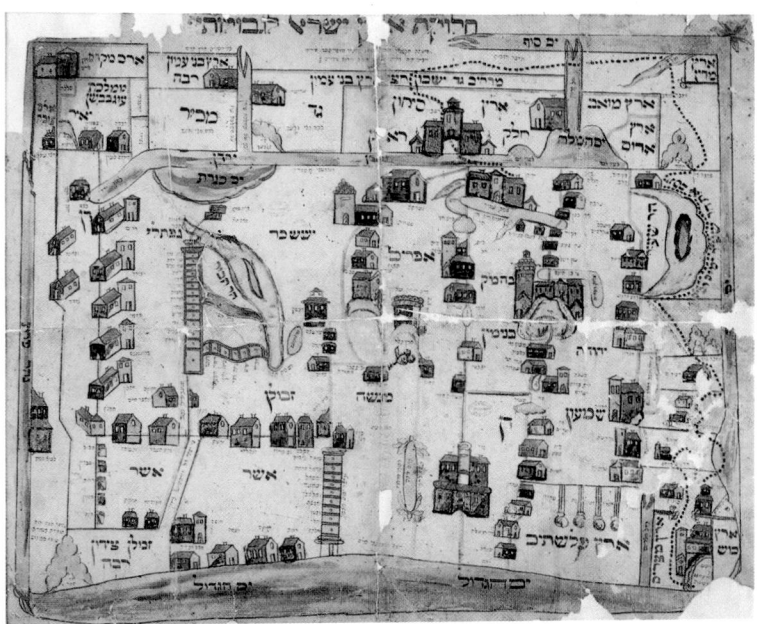

*1. The Land of Israel divided into tribes. Map attributed to the "Gaon of Vilna," c. 1802.*

scholars from the elite of Jewish society. At the beginning of the 1730s he settled in Medzibozh, in Podolia, where he headed a community of disciples, some of whom were to become in their turn leaders of small mystical groups.

After his death in 1760 he was succeeded by Dov Baer of Mezhirech (1704–1772), who spread the teachings of the master and transformed

the small community into a real movement. Within a few decades, Eastern Europe was dotted with hundreds of Hasidic communities.

The disciples of Dov Baer, the *Maggid* ("preacher"), became leaders of these groups. In a complex process of decentralization, the movement split into numerous currents, each adhering to its particular doctrine, ritual, and organization. Certain elements, however, were common to all the various groups: belief in the supernatural powers of the leader (the *Zaddik*, the "righteous," or the *Rebbe* in the affectionate and respectful meaning which the *Hasidim* gave to that title), and the conviction that he had direct links with the divine world.

The movement began to spread precisely while Poland was undergoing the tribulations of partition; but the new political frontiers, although separating the Jews of the Ukraine from their brethren in Lithuania and central Poland, did not prevent the advance of Hasidism. Moreover, it soon emerged as a cohesive force, unifying traditional Judaism and ensuring its survival in difficult times, when the absolutist princes were beginning to curb Jewish autonomy and to interfere in community affairs. Congregated around the *Zaddik*, the Hasidic community, although lacking official authority, offered an alternative to the former corporation and also constituted a bastion against Western influences which were beginning to threaten orthodox Jewry.

From its very early stages, however, the movement encountered internal opposition: at least part of the traditional rabbinic elite regarded the Hasidic enthusiasts as dangerous innovators. At the head of these *Mitnaggedim* ("Opponents") stood a great Lithuanian scholar, Elijah of Vilna (the "*Gaon* of Vilna," 1720–1797). The battle was waged with great ardor and knew no restraints. There were mutual excommunications and even denunciations to the authorities. A veritable war of religion developed in Vilna itself, each party trying to obtain the support of the rulers. After the death of the *Gaon*, the feud abated. The rival brethren eventually resigned themselves to each other's existence; after all, a common enemy was appearing on the horizon: the European *Haskalah*.

While Hasidism was spreading in central Poland, crossing the Carpathian Mountains into Hungary and reaching as far as Palestine itself, the arduous labors of talmudic scholarship continued uninterrupted in Lithuania. At the beginning of the nineteenth century, this very old tradition produced a new socio-religious phenomenon which was to some extent a positive reaction to the brilliant success of Hasidism: the "Moral" (*Musar*) movement, combining strict ethical behavior with an intensive study of the *Halakhah*.

Hasidism, Lithuanian scholarship, and the *Musar* movement were all manifestations of a vigorous religious revival which checked the growing influence of the *Haskalah* and eventually became the pivot of resistance of a traditional society to the challenge of modernity.

| The Ba'al Shem Tov | The birth of the *Habad* movement | Death of the *Gaon* of Vilna |
|---|---|---|
| c. 1700–1760 | 1788 | 1797 |

**c. 1736:** Israel Ba'al Shem Tov is revealed as a *zaddik* ("righteous man") and settles in the town of Medzibozh.
**1760:** Death of the Ba'al Shem Tov; Dov Baer of Mezhirech, the *maggid* ("preacher") succeeds him as leader of the movement.
**1772:** First partition of Poland. Death of the *Maggid*. In Vilna, then in Brody, the first pronouncements against the *Hasidim* are made; a violent anti-Hasidic pamphlet provokes a wave of persecutions against the movement's adherents, mostly in Lithuania. Pinhas Horowitz, the *Maggid*'s disciple, settles in Frankfort – he is the first Hasidic leader to cross into Germany and serve there as a rabbi.
**1773:** Rabbi Menahem Mendel of Minsk settles in Vitebsk and propagates Hasidism throughout Belorussia.
**1777:** Dozens of *Hasidim* led by Menahem Mendel leave for Palestine.

*2. The seat of Rabbi Nahman of Bratslav (1772–1811).*

*3. Box of Shemirot, coins offered by the zaddik to his disciples as good-luck charms. Austria, 19th–20th century.*

**1780:** Following the appearance of the first book of Jacob Joseph of Polonnoye, who wrote down the teachings of the Ba'al Shem Tov, the leaders of the Vilna community pronounce a new excommunication against the *hasidim*.
**1784:** Rabbi Levi Isaac settles in Berdichev where he served as rabbi till the beginning of the following century.
**1786:** Death of Rabbi Elimelech of Lyzhansk, teacher of Hasidism throughout Austrian Galicia.
**1788:** Rabbi Shneur Zalman of Lyady, a Hasidic leader in Belorussia, founds *Habad* Hasidism.
**1796–1801:** Bitter polemics between *Hasidim* and *Mitnaggedim* in Lithuania; denounced by the "Opponents," Shneur Zalman is imprisoned twice in St. Petersburg.
**1797:** Death of Elijah of Vilna (the "*Gaon* of Vilna"), the greatest opponent of the Hasidic movement.
**1799:** The voyage of Rabbi Nahman, great-

## Hasidim and Mitnaggedim
### 18th - 19th centuries

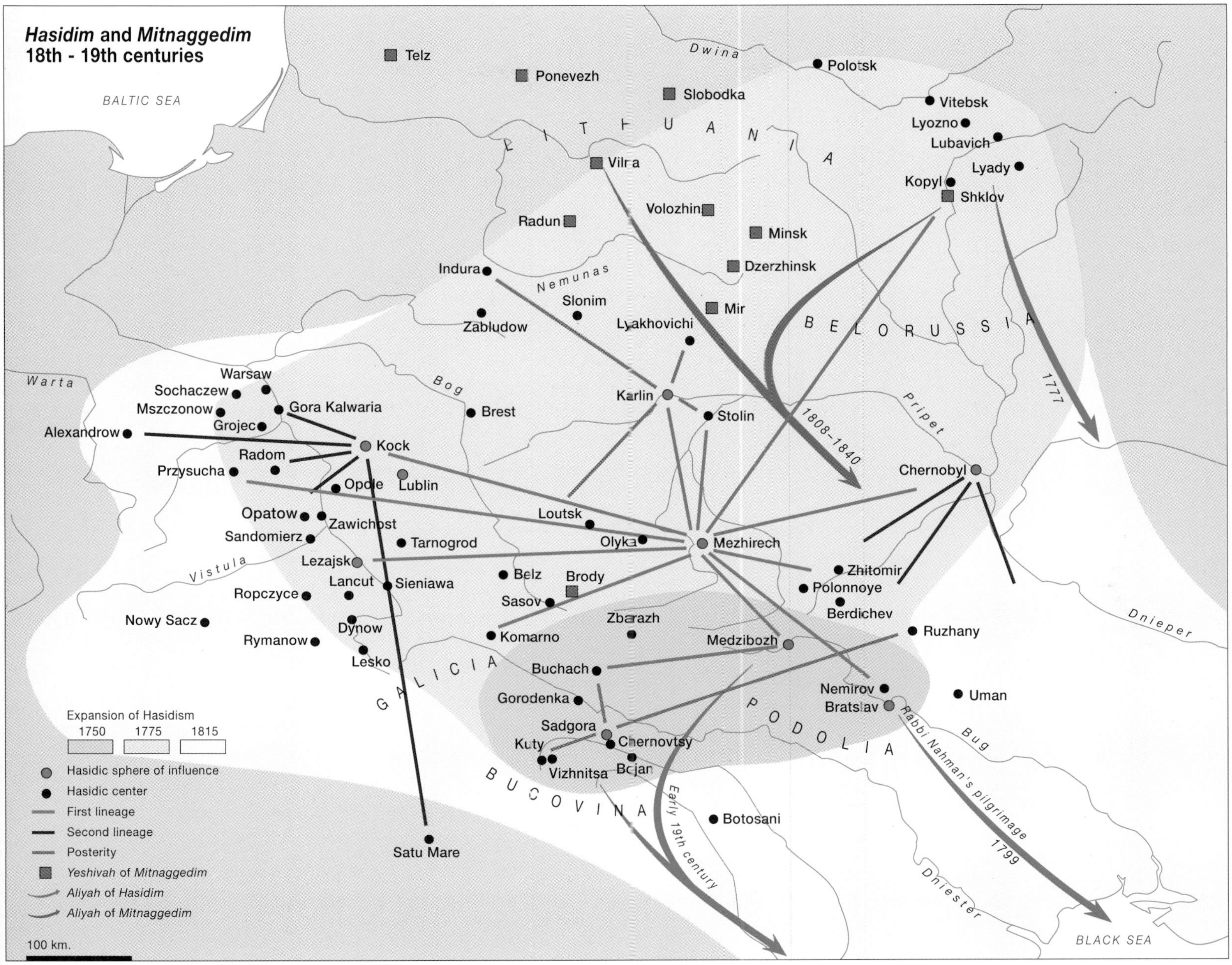

BALTIC SEA

Telz

Ponevezh

Slobodka

Polotsk

Vitebsk

Lyozno

Lubavich

Vilra

Kopyl

Lyady

Shklov

Volozhin

Radun

Minsk

Dzerzhinsk

Indura

Nemunas

Slonim

Mir

Zabludow

Lyakhovichi

BELORUSSIA

Warsaw

Sochaczew

Mszczonow

Gora Kalwaria

Brest

Karlin

Stolin

Pripet

1777

Alexandrow

Grojec

Radom

Kock

Przysucha

Opole

Lublin

Loutsk

Olyka

Mezhirech

Chernobyl

1808–1840

Opatow

Zawichost

Sandomierz

Tarnogrod

Dniepe

Lezajsk

Lancut

Sieniawa

Belz

Brody

Sasov

Zhitomir

Polonnoye

Berdichev

Ropczyce

Nowy Sacz

Dynow

Komarno

Zbarazh

Medzibozh

Ruzhany

Vistula

Rymanow

Lesko

Buchach

Nemirov

Uman

GALICIA

Gorodenka

Bratslav

Sadgora

PODOLIA

Bug

Kuty

Chernovtsy

Rabbi Nahman's pilgrimage

Vizhnitsa

Bojan

BUCOVINA

Early 19th century

Botosani

1799

### Expansion of Hasidism
1750   1775   1815

● Hasidic sphere of influence
● Hasidic center
— First lineage
— Second lineage
— Posterity
■ Yeshivah of Mitnaggedim
⇢ Aliyah of Hasidim
⇢ Aliyah of Mitnaggedim

100 km.

Dwina

LITHUANIA

Bog

Warta

Dnieper

Dniester

BLACK SEA

---

**Rabbi Nahman of Bratslav**

**1802**

**Praises of the Ba'al Shem Tov**

**1815**

**Beginning of the Musar movement**

**1849**

grandson of the Ba'al Shem Tov, to Palestine; in 1802 he settles in Bratslav where he founds a new Hasidic trend.
**1808:** A first group of Lithuanian scholars settles in Palestine and establishes a yeshivah in Safed following the doctrines of the "Gaon of Vilna."
**1815:** The Praises of the Ba'al Shem Tov appears in Kopys, Belorussia – it is a collection of stories recounting the deeds of the founder of Hasidism and his disciples; death of Jacob Isaac, the "Seer of Lublin."
**1819:** Joseph Perl, a Galician maskil (an adherent of the Haskalah), publishes a fierce anti-Hasidic pamphlet in Vienna aimed at alerting the Austrian authorities to the anti-government attitudes of the Hasidim.
**1821:** Death of Rabbi Hayyim, founder of the yeshivah in Volozhin which was established to serve as a barrier against the spread of Hasidism.
**1823:** The authorities in Congress Poland

conduct an inquiry into the Hasidic movement which is suspected of working against the state and society.
**1838:** The Hasidic leader, Israel Ruzhin, is arrested by the Russian authorities following a denunciation; released after two years, he eventually settles in Sadgora in Austrian Bukovina.
**1843:** Rabbi Isaac, head of the Volozhin Yeshiva, and Rabbi Menahem Mendel of Lyubavitchi, leader of Habad, participate in a congress convened by the Russian authorities for the purpose of reforming Jewish education; faced with the dangers of governmental reforms and of modernity in general, Hasidim and Mitnaggedim forget their differences.
**1849–1857:** From Kovno in Lithuania, Rabbi Israel Salanter disseminates the ideas of the Musar movement.

*4. A Lithuanian Jew with his wife and daughter...*

*5. ...and a couple of Hasidim. Engraving according to L. Hollanderski, The Israelites of Poland, Paris, 1846.*

# Jews in Modern Economy

1. Coat-of-arms of Joachim Popper, a merchant from Prague and leader of the Bohemian Jewish community, ennobled by Leopold II.

2. A Jewish exodus from Russia. An antisemitic German caricature, 1899.

**The first 200 millionaires in Prussia, 1908**

| 31 | 19 | 10 | 55 | 26 | 59 |
|----|----|----|----|----|----|

| | | | 8 | | |
| | | | 47 | | |

**NON-JEWS : 145**          **JEWS : 55**

| Mines | Agri. | Misc. | Manufactured Products | 14 | 33 |
| | | | | 12 | 26 |
| | | | | Commerce | Finance and Banking |

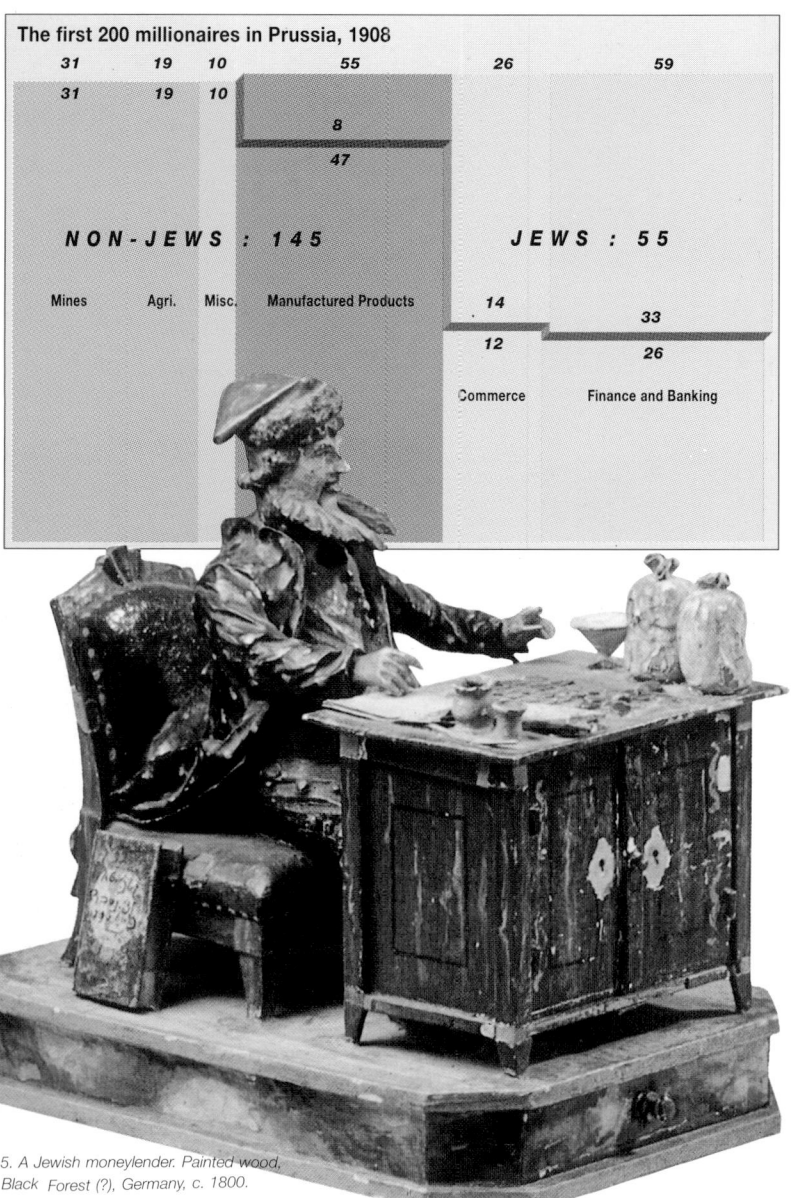

5. A Jewish moneylender. Painted wood. Black Forest (?), Germany, c. 1800.

I n the second half of the seventeenth century, the small Jewish population in western Europe began to grow. The Thirty Years War, Bogdan Chmielnicki's massacres in Poland and the Ukraine, inquisitorial persecutions of New Christians in the Iberian Peninsula – all these encouraged the Jews to move from danger zones to the more receptive countries in central or western Europe. New communities emerged, and older communities began to flourish. In the demographic and economic history of European Jewry, this initial westward migration towards the major centers of early capitalism constituted a major turning point. Henceforth, the role played by Jews in European economy would steadily increase.

During the seventeenth and eighteenth centuries, Jews settling in western Europe engaged in economic activities which were quite different from the occupations of their co-religionists in the east. Sephardi Conversos, for example, whether nominally Christian or openly returned to Judaism, participated in the great colonial enterprise, and thus contributed to the rise of new centers of a world economy located along the Atlantic coast – Antwerp, Amsterdam, Hamburg, Bordeaux – as well as to

| Bank of Hamburg | Mayer Amschel, first of the "great" Rothschilds |
|---|---|
| **1619** | **1743–1812** |

**1635:** Ashkenazi Jews form a separate congregation in Amsterdam.

**1645–1724:** Lifespan of Glueckel of Hameln. A Jewess born in Hamburg, widowed by a rich merchant from Hamlen, then re-married to a banker from Metz, Glueckel was an extraordinary woman who, while raising 12 children, also managed the family business and financial enterprises. Her memoirs, written in Yiddish between 1699 and 1718, portray a Jewish commercial network which extended throughout Europe, from Prague to Amsterdam and from Vienna to Copenhagen.

**1655:** Diego Teixeira (Abraham Senior, 1581–1666), a banker from Artwerp of Sephardi origin, is appointed by Queen Christina as Sweden's crown agent in Hamburg. It was there that Teixeira openly returned to Judaism; his family was to attain a great fortune and an eminent position.

**1670:** The elector of Brandeburg invites "forty or fifty" affluent Jewish families to settle in his principality.

**1699–1738:** Lifespan of Joseph Suess Oppenheimer, better known as *The Jew Suess*, hero of the famous novel by Leon Feuchtwanger (1925). This Court Jew served Duke Charles I Alexander of Wuerttemberg as manager of large business enterprises. After the duke's death he was imprisoned and executed.

**1744–1745:** Concerted effort by Court Jews throughout Europe to persuade Maria-Theresa to abrogate the edict of expulsion proclaimed on the Jews of Prague.

**1812:** Founding of the Parisian branch of the Rothschild Frères firm. The French Rothschilds were engaged, among other things, in railroad construction (*Chemin de Fer du Nord*); two of them would become regents of the Banque de France.

**1831–1896:** Lifespan of financier and philanthropist Baron Maurice de Hirsch, descended from a family of Jewish court bankers.

**1845:** Alphonse Toussenel publishes a two-volume antisemitic work entitled *Les Juifs,*

*3. A Jewish street in Frankfort, 1884.*

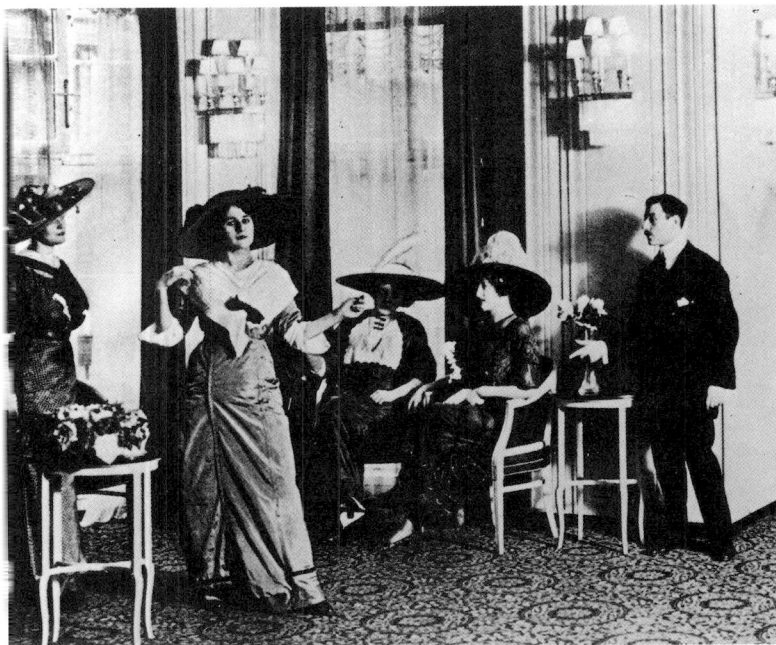

*4. A fashion show in the Gerson salon. Berlin, c. 1910.*

the growth of Mediterranean ports such as Leghorn (Livorno). Relying on widespread family networks and controlling certain markets, they assisted in the transition of European society to capitalism. The governments could only welcome these newcomers, who were innovators by definition, since they had no roots in traditional social structures which had hindered economic growth and modernization. The German states, whose absolutist rulers were engaged in fostering a mercantile economy, encouraged Jews to settle in their lands and assume various functions in the service of the state. As army and court suppliers, bankers, minting administrators, diplomats and entrepreneurs, these Court Jews wielded considerable influence which also enabled them to become protectors of their fellow Jews – obviously arousing the envy and hostility of large sectors of non-Jewish society.

Spectacular though it was, this evolution was but the beginning of greater upheavals. Partly due to the amelioration of their social and political situation, European Jewry was to experience remarkable demographic growth, reaching approximately 7.5 million people at the end of the nineteenth century. Driven to emigration by their precarious exist-

ence in eastern Europe, great waves of Jewish immigrants periodically inundated western and central Europe. Most of them soon integrated into the new environment. This demographic expansion accelerated the urbanization of the Jews and diversified their economic activities. Concentrated more and more in the largest cities, they entered the world of business, banking, export-import, the liberal professions, and various industries – particularly those of construction and transport. It should be remembered, however, that only a small minority of Jewish families attained wealth and prominence, while the majority – uprooted and urbanized – remained part of the lower classes.

Traditional Jewish life underwent a radical transformation. City life accelerated the integration of Jews into the dynamic European society, and these integrated Jews in turn became agents of modernization. Crumbling, fragmented by extreme economic inequality, deprived of its former internal cohesion, the traditional Jewish community was fast disappearing. Demographic growth, migration, urbanization, industrialization – all these processes, for better or for worse, carried west-European Jewry over the threshold into the modern capitalist era.

| Isaac Pereire, *Lectures on Industry and Finance* | First railroad in France, Paris-Saint-Germain | Alphonse de Rothschild, regent of the Banque de France |
|---|---|---|
| **1832** | **1837** | **1855** |

*6. Tadeusz Epstein (1870–1939), an industrialist from Cracow, by Leopold Buczkowski, c. 1930.*

*rois de l'epoque; histoire de la féodalité financière*, a tirade provoked by the economic success of Jews in Paris.
**1853:** Founding of the Darmstaedter Bank; the Oppenheims of Cologne play a leading role in the establishment of this first joint stock bank in Germany.
**1872:** Gerson Bleichroeder, Bismarck's confidant and financial agent, becomes the first non-converted Jew in Prussia to receive a hereditary title of nobility.
**1881–1882:** In Berlin, 11–12% of physicians and 8–9% of journalists are Jews.
**1900:** The distribution of Austrian Jews according to their occupations: 27.8% – in industry; 16.2% – professions and state administration; 11.4% agriculture; 43.7% – business and transport.
**1913:** Founding of the Federation of Jewish Societies in Paris, comprising over twenty organizations of East-European immigrants.

*7. The Orient Express (1884) constructed by Baron Maurice de Hirsch (1831–1896).*

# The Jews of China

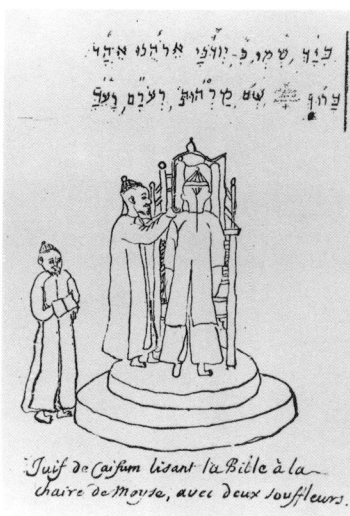

*1. The synagogue in Kaifeng as it was in the 18th century. Reconstruction according to sketches drawn by Italian Jesuits.*

Jewish merchants arrived in China together with other traders from the west when the famous Silk Road was open and safe, perhaps as early as the second century BC. The oldest extant testimony to their presence there, however, dates from the beginning of the eighth century AD (Tang Dynasty). It is a business letter, written in Persian using Hebrew script, discovered by Sir Aurel Stein at Khotan, a western outpost of the Chinese Empire. It is safe to assume that Jewish and Muslim merchants also lived in the port towns of southeastern China – Canton, and perhaps Ningpo and Chuanchow – but never permanently settled there. During the Mongol period (Yuan Dynasty), Jews and Muslims are mentioned together in decrees pertaining to taxation, prohibitions on ritual slaughtering, and levirate marriages (the custom of marrying the widow of one's deceased brother). Since no traces of these communities remain, it is impossible to estimate their size; all we know is that Marco Polo, who visited China toward the end of the thirteenth century, recounts meeting many Jews in Khanbalik (Peking) and in Hangchow.

In fact, the only real Jewish community in China was the one in Kaifeng. Its origins date back to the 11th century AD, when approximately 1000 Jews, bringing cotton from either Persia or India, received permission to settle in this town in central China. In 1163 a synagogue was built in Kaifeng which was rebuilt several times over the years. Three steles, erected in the years 1489, 1512, and 1663, attribute different dates to the first arrival of Jews in China; the very early dates which the two latter steles suggest – the beginning of the first century or even earlier – should be regarded circumspectly. The inscriptions, in an attempt to reconcile Jewish and Confucian beliefs, recount in detail the genealogy of the Jews from Adam, who is none other than the Chinese Pan Ku.

Chinese sources make no mention at all of the Jews of Kaifeng, but in 1605 the well-known Jesuit missionary, Matteo Ricci, met in Peking a man

| Recorded presence of Jews in China | Beginning of the Kaifeng community | Construction of the synagogue in Kaifeng |
|---|---|---|
| **Early 8th century** | **End of 10th century** | **1163** |

*2. A Chinese Jewish family, Kaifeng, 1910.*

**1000-256 BC:** The Chou Dynasty – when China's first true civilization was formed; a time of enormous intellectual ferment, producing China's oldest surviving literature and giving rise to China's golden age of philosophy; according to a late source (1663), the first Jews arrive in China during this period.

**479 BC:** Death of Confucius.

**206 BC-220 AD:** The Han Dynasty: China forms links with Western Asia via the Silk Road; a late inscription (1512) dates the arrival of the first Jews in China to this period.

**718:** The date of the letter found by Sir Aurel Stein in Khotan in the Sinkiang Province on China's western frontier.

**878–879:** According to the testimony of the Muslim traveller Abu Zayyd, 120,000 people – Muslims, Christians, and Jews – are massacred during a rebellion in Canton.

**960–1280:** The Sung Dynasty: its capital remains Kaifeng until 1127 and is then transferred to Hangchow after the

conquest of northern China by the Tatar Jürchen Dynasty; it is probably during this period that Jews arrive in China and settle in Kaifeng.

**1131–1200:** Chu Hsi, the philosopher who reformulated Confucianism and made it the official ideology of the Empire, determining its spiritual character up to the beginning of the 20th century; Chinese Jews have always tried to minimize the differences between this doctrine and their own faith.

**1163:** Construction of the synagogue in Kaifeng.

**1260–1294:** Reign of Kublai Khan, Emperor of China, one of the most enlightened monarchs in human history; his court is visited by foreigners of all religions (Marco Polo among them), including some Jews.

**1300:** In a letter to his superiors in Rome, a Catholic missionary complains that he has

*3. "A Jew of Caifum (Kaifeng) reading the Bible from Moses' pulpit, with two prompters." A drawing by Father Domenge, 1722.*

# 11th–20th Centuries

from Kaifeng called Ai Tien who told him about his community. According to Ricci, there was a Hebrew Pentateuch in the Kaifeng synagogue, and the Jews there practiced circumcision and refrained from eating pork. But apart from the steles, the only tangible evidence of the Kaifeng community are several prayer books discovered by Christian missionaries in the nineteenth century, as well as a community register from the middle of the nineteenth century written in Hebrew and Chinese.

Over the years the Jews of Kaifeng have been dispersed or assimilated into the local environment; they adopted Chinese surnames and customs, and some attained prominent positions in the mandarinate and in the army. By the beginning of the nineteenth century the community had no rabbi and had virtually ceased to exist.

Today there are still a handful of Chinese who consider themselves descendants of the Kaifeng Jews (rumor has it that China's former president, Liu Shao Chi, was one of them); but, to all intents and purposes, their Jewish identity has been lost.

Modern Jewish communities were formed in China during the nineteenth and twentieth centuries. In Hong Kong the Jews were predominantly British subjects, many from India and Iraq. By 1937 about 10,000 European Jews were living in China. The Russian Jewish population in Harbin numbered some 5,000 people, most of them refugees from the Russian Revolution of 1917. The greatest influx of Jews to China was, however, prompted by World War II. Very few of them made the effort to study Chinese culture, and most left for other parts of the world soon after the war. Today there is a small Jewish community in Hong Kong – the only remnant of Jewish existence in the vast Chinese world.

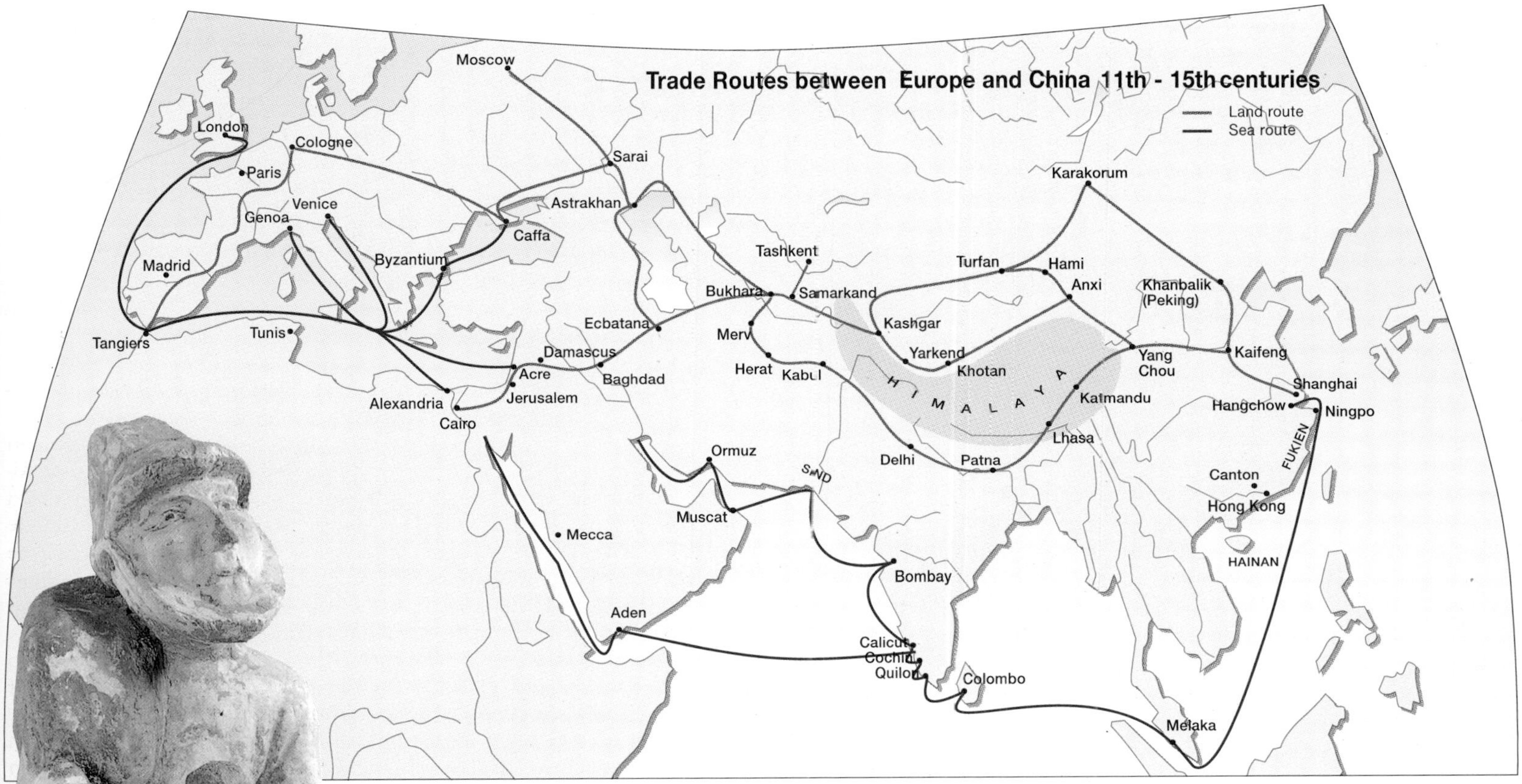

**Trade Routes between Europe and China 11th - 15th centuries**

| | Disputation of Peking | Three Jewish steles in Kaifeng | Death of the last rabbi of Kaifeng |
|---|---|---|---|
| | 1342 | 1489, 1512, 1663 | c. 1800 |

not managed to convert even a single Jew in Fukien Province.
**1340:** Imperial decrees forbidding levirate marriages mention both Jews and Muslims.
**1342:** A theological disputation between Jews and the priest Mariniolli in Peking.
**1489, 1512, 1663:** Dates of the steles in Kaifeng describing the history of the Jews: the first dates the arrival of Jews to Kaifeng during the Sung Dynasty period; the second, engraved on the back of the stele of 1489, ascribes it to the Han Dynasty; the third claims the Jews arrived during the Chou Dynasty and describes their beliefs in Confucian terms.
**1605:** Ai Tien of Kaifeng tells the Jesuit missionary Matteo Ricci about his community.
**1642:** The synagogue of Kaifeng is destroyed during an anti-imperial revolt.
**1663:** The Kaifeng synagogue is reopened.

**c. 1800:** Death of the last rabbi of Kaifeng.
**1867:** A Jew called Lieberman arrives in Kaifeng and discovers the community's descendants.
**1898:** The first Jews settle in Harbin.
**1905:** Following the Russo-Japanese War and pogroms in Russia, the Harbin community grows from 500 to 8000.
**1938–1941:** Approximately 20,000 Jewish refugees from Europe find shelter in Shanghai.
**1948:** Mao Tse-tung, leader of China's Communist Party, proclaims the People's Republic; the Nationalists retreat to Taiwan.
**1955:** A Chinese exile in Taiwan claims he is the last Chinese Jew.
**1959:** Liu Shao Chi is elected president of the People's Republic of China; rumor has it that his ancestors were Jews from the Kaifeng community.

4. A Jewish peddler (?). A miniature terracotta sculpture from the Tang period (618–907 AD).

5. Cover page of a special edition of the journal Jewish Life, dedicated to the first conference of the Jewish communities in the East. Harbin, 1939.

# In the Habsburg Empire

Die Juden geh'n im Gänsemarsch
Was haben sie im Sinn?
So zog'n sie übers rothe Meer
Der Wolf, der Fuchs, der Löw, der Bär
Die Juden geh'n im Gänsemarsch
Zum Lueger nach Wien.

*1. "Towards Lueger in Vienna." Antisemitic postcard, Germany, 1898.*

In the multi-national mosaic of the Habsburg empire, the Jews were generally considered the most reliable and loyal subjects of the dynasty, supporting, together with other mainstays (the army, the bureaucracy, the nobility, and the Catholic church) the unity of the Empire. The monarchist loyalty of the Jews was founded on an ardent wish to integrate and on interests shared with the Crown. The Crown in its turn saw in these authentic "Austro-Hungarians" the sole defenders of an "identity" which it was trying to instill throughout the realm. In return, the Crown defended the Jews against the tides of nationalism and antisemitism which rose in the late nineteenth century.

The Jews of the Habsburg "Monarchy" (as the Austro-Hungarian empire was officially known from 1867 on) did not constitute a homogenous entity. They were, in fact, an assortment of diverse communities which were encompassed in the expanding empire at different times. Thus, even by World War I, which heralded the end of this large empire, there was still little in common between, for example, the Jews of Bosnia-Hercegovina annexed in 1908 and the Jews of Polish Galicia who had become Austrian subjects in 1772. The status of the Jews was determined by a combination of the orders given at the center in Vienna and the prevailing conditions on the local level.

At the end of the eighteenth century, the Austo-Hungarian empire harbored the largest Jewish population in Europe. It was therefore both the laboratory for the process of emancipation, as well as a hotbed for the emergence of political antisemitism. Joseph II's Toleration Edict in 1781 opened to the Jews the gateway to society. Although there was a certain deterioration in their situation after the Emperor's death, on the whole the Jews of the Habsburg Empire now entered a new phase in their history. A century later, with legal equality firmly established, the Jewish elites were fully integrated into the dominant German culture, and instrumental in the expansion of industry, transportation, commerce, and banking in the Empire. They even successfully penetrated the army, the bastion of social conservatism.

The Jewish map became extremely diversified, ranging from the assimilated bourgeoisie of cosmopolitan Vienna to the traditionalist communities in the townlets of Galicia, through the whole gamut of social, cultural, "national" and regional nuances. Apostasy and marriage to non-Jews became a widespread phenomenon among the Jewish elites both in Vienna and Budapest. On the other hand, Orthodox communities, particularly in Hungary, developed a large number of ultrareligious factions centered on certain Hasidic dynasties.

A perennial consort of such efflorescence, antisemitism in a variety of forms – Catholic anti-Judaism, nationalist xenophobia, racism – threw an alarming shadow over the achievements of Austro-Hungarian liberalism. This was the time of the blood-libel affair in Tisza-Eszlar (1882), the

---

| Joseph II's Edict of Toleration | Democratic revolutions | Equal Rights |
|---|---|---|
| **1781** | **1848** | **1867** |

**1772:** The annexation of Galicia doubles the Jewish population of Austria.
**1774:** Annexation of Bukovina.
**1781:** *Toleranzpatent* (Edict of Toleration) of Joseph II.

*3. A medal commemorating Joseph II's Edict of Toleration. Vienna, 1782.*

**1784:** Abolition of Jewish jurisdictional autonomy.
**1792:** The accession of Franz II marks a deterioration in the situation of the Jews in the empire; the emperor attempts to "modernize" his Jewish subjects, demanding that they abandon their "superstitions" and "vain rabbinic argumentation." Nevertheless, the edict of toleration remains in force, and the Jews contribute to the economic prosperity of Austria (Solomon de Rothschild, for example, builds the first railroad in Austria), while others enter the world of journalism, literature and the arts.
**1815:** Congress of Vienna; a delegation of Jews demands, but fails to attain, equal rights from the Emperor. Approximately 14,000 Jewish families reside in Bohemia and Moravia, mostly in Prague.
**1846:** The oath *more judaico*, considered as particularly humiliating, is abolished.
**1843:** Numerous Jews participate in the revolution: in Vienna, Adolf Fischoff heads the revolutionary Security Council, and five

*4. Emperor Franz Joseph visits the Goldberger textile factory in Buda. Ilustrietes israelisches Jahrbuch, 1780.*

Jewish deputies – two from Vienna, including Fischoff himself, one from Stanislawow, one from Cracow and one from Brody – are elected to the revolutionary parliament of Kromeriz. In Hungary, about 20,000 Jews serve in the national army; the Jews support the Hungarian national cause represented by Lajos Kossuth, who comes to the synagogue to ask the Jewish people for forgiveness for past persecutions.
**1848–1916:** Reign of Franz-Joseph I; in 1867 he accords Jews full equal rights; but the emperor's good will cannot stem the tide of rising antisemitism.
**1882:** Founding in Vienna of the *Kadimah* ("Forward") society, the first national society of Jewish students.
**1891:** Karl Lueger founds the antisemitic Social-Christian Party.
**1896:** Herzl's *The Jewish State* is published in Vienna.
**1897:** Lueger's election as mayor of Vienna is confirmed by the Emperor (who had previously denied it on several occasions).

emergence of an antisemitic party in Hungary, and Karl Lueger's accession to the position of mayor of Vienna by means of an antisemitic platform. Budapest, where Herzl was born, and Vienna, the city he adopted as his own, were the background for the birth of Zionism – the Jewish national reaction to the ineffectiveness of assimilation in the face of antisemitism. Although Zionism did not become a major driving force among the Jews of the Empire prior to World War I, its roots were deeply embedded in the culture, mentality and extreme complexity of the national problem within it. Jewish socialism was also, to a large extent, born in the Habsburg Empire. In Austria, many prominent figures in the Socialist Party were Jews, most of whom supported assimilation; Vienna, a magnet attracting Jewish intellectuals from all parts of Eastern Europe, was the birthplace of several Zionist socialist movements.

With the collapse of the empire, the Jews of the Monarchy became subjects of new states. Yet they continued to maintain a heritage all of their own. In the dark years that later awaited them, this "Habsburgian" heritage was a source of nostalgia and deepened their sense of tragedy. An old-age home in Tel Aviv which houses Austro-Hungarian Jews is probably the only place in the world in which a portrait of Emperor Franz-Joseph still hangs on the wall.

*2. A Jewish peddler in an Hungarian market. Lithograph, 1840.*

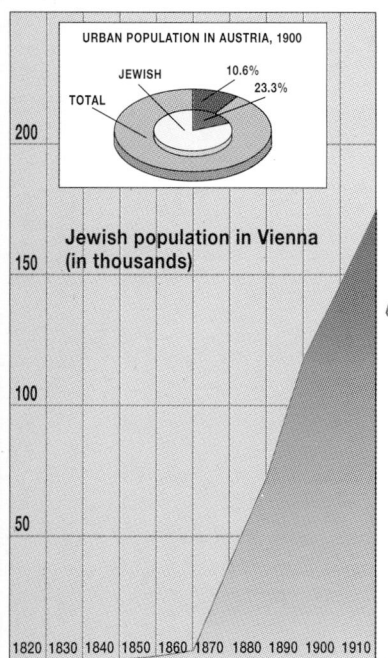

URBAN POPULATION IN AUSTRIA, 1900
JEWISH 10.6%
TOTAL 23.3%

**Jewish population in Vienna (in thousands)**

200 — 150 — 100 — 50

1820 1830 1840 1850 1860 1870 1880 1890 1900 1910

**Between Vienna and Budapest**

RUSSIA

Prague — Elbe
Vistula
BOHEMIA
Jaroslaw — Lemberg (Lvov) — Brody
Cracow — Tarnow
Brno — Morava
Przemysl — Dniester — Tarnopol
MORAVIA — GALICIA
BAVARIA — Danube — Moldau — Znojmo — Nitra — Stan slav — Kolomyya
Munkacs — Chernovtsy
Vienna — Pressburg — Szigetvar — Radauti
Linz — Eger — Nyiregyhaza — BUCOVINA
Salzburg — Sopron — Gyor — Debrecen — Szatmar (Satu Mare)
TYROL — Budapest — Tisza
AUSTRIA — HUNGARY — Kolozsvar (Cluj)
Nagykanizsa — Kaposvar — Bekesccsaba — TRANSYLVANIA
Drava — Pecs — Baja — Szeged — Maros
Trieste — Zabadka (Subotica) — Zenta — Temesvar (Timisoara)
ITALY — Zagreb — SLAVONIA — Ujvidek (Novi Sad)
Po — Osijek — Sava — RUMANIA
CROATIA — Olt
ADRIATIC SEA — Banja Luka — BOSNIA-HERCEGOVINA — Belgrade — Danube
Travnik
Jewish communities, 1910 — Sarajevo
• 5,000 - 10,000 Jews — SERBIA
◉ 10,000 - 50,000 — BULGARIA
◉ Over 50,000

100 km.

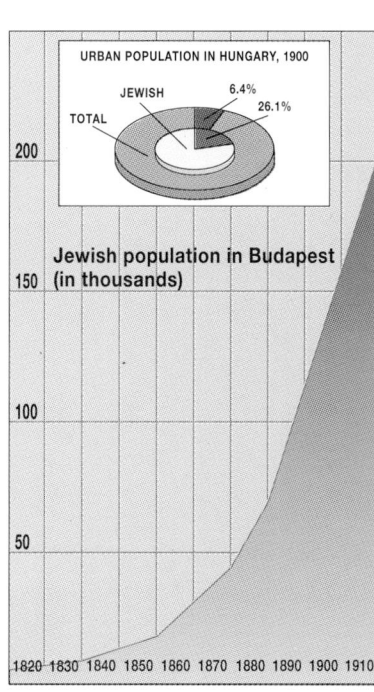

URBAN POPULATION IN HUNGARY, 1900
JEWISH 6.4%
TOTAL 26.1%

**Jewish population in Budapest (in thousands)**

200 — 150 — 100 — 50

1820 1830 1840 1850 1860 1870 1880 1890 1900 1910

**Herzl's *The Jewish State***
**1896**

**Karl Lueger is mayor of Vienna**
**1897**

**Assassination in Sarajevo**
**June 28, 1914**

Another antisemitic agitator, Georg von Schoenerer, returns to parliament after a stretch in prison.
**1899:** The first Zionist meeting in Prague is dispersed by the police. Thomas G. Masaryk, the future founder of the Czechoslovak republic, denounces a blood libel in Bohemia.
**1907:** Four representatives of the Jewish National Party are elected to the Austrian parliament. Otto Bauer's *The Question of Nationalities and Social-Democracy*. Bauer, son of a Jewish industrialist, one of the leaders of Austrian socialism and the first foreign minister of the Austrian Republic (November 1918 and July 1919), advocated assimilation and argued that the Jews could not be regarded as a nationality.
**1914:** On the eve of war, about 200,000 Jews live in Vienna, of whom 18% are immigrants from Galicia.

*5. "After the Burial" by an unkown painter. Prague, c. 1780.*

# The Legend of the Wandering Jew

1. One of many versions of the Laments of the Wandering Jew. Postcard, France, c. 1910.

**W**ell over 120 different oral legends collected by folklorists all over Europe, from Spain to Finland and from England to Sicily, relate to the figure of the Wandering Jew. But, although enhanced by elements borrowed from earlier traditions, the character of the Wandering Jew in these orally-transmitted legends is not a figure derived from ancient European folktales – he made his first debut only in 1602. Several German chapbooks issued in that year under different imprints relate how the recently deceased Bishop of Schleswig met in his youth, during a visit to Hamburg, a tall man, dressed in threadbare garments, who proclaimed he was none other than Ahasuerus, a Jewish shoemaker from Jerusalem. He had prevented Jesus, carrying the cross on his calvary, from leaning on his house to rest, and was therefore condemned to wander eternally without respite. This

2. R.B. Kitaj, The Jewish traveller, 1984–1985.

| A Short Description... | The Admirable History of the Wandering Jew |
|---|---|
| 1602 | c. 1740 |

**After 1235:** Matthew Paris, a monk from St. Albans, reports in his *Chronica Majora* how during a visit to England an Armenian archbishop recounted the story of an eyewitness to the Passion of the Lord, Joseph Cartaphilus – an official of Pontius Pilate who had struck Jesus and said: "go, go," and to whom Jesus had replied: "I go, and you will await me until I come again."

**Mid-15th century:** Antonio di Francesco di Andrea reports that a certain Giovanni Buttadeo who passed through Florence c. 1411–1416 was the man who had pushed Jesus on his calvary and told him to go to his death.

**1547:** The Inquisition in Toledo condemns a vagrant who calls himself "Juan Espera en Dios," claiming to be the shoemaker who had struck Jesus.

**1586–1587:** A German version of Matthew Paris's chronicle appears in Zurich.

4. The Wandering Jew as a village vagrant. Postcard, France, c. 1901.

5. Ahasuerus facing the might of Rome. Postcard, Austria, 1897.

AHASVER in ROM

sinner against Christ had long since repented, becoming an exemplary Christian, renowned for his charitable work.

Ahasuerus, a new Cain, personifies the history of the Jewish people, and his tale incorporates the same ambiguity embedded in contemporary attitudes towards the Jews. On the one hand testifying to the Christian gospel by bearing the punishment incurred by his incredulity, the figure of Ahasuerus evokes empathy and pity on the other. This duality can be explained by the strange mixture of medieval theological anti-Judaism still prevalent in the seventeenth century, and more recent attitudes, based on an eschatological expectation for the regeneration of the Jews through conversion. Inversely, it could be attributed to the novel idea that such a terrible destiny was preordained and inevitable and could not be avoided even by conversion. However, the root of the ambivalence more probably lies in the wide range of sources from which the figure of Ahasureus was borrowed, as well as in the specific circumstances under which it was constructed. The figure of the immortal wise pilgrim and the offender of Christ have in fact been fused into one figure. Later, in times of legislation against mendicancy, this figure was exploited by imposters posing as pilgrims testifying to the Passion of the Lord, whose act of deep contrition was but an attempt to extract money from the gullible.

The pocket-sized books peddled in the eighteenth century ensured the legend's wide circulation and embellished it with elements of the supernatural. Yet at the same time the legend's transmission by way of popular literature discredited it in more enlightened circles. In the nineteenth century, on the other hand, the literary and political climate was conducive to the rediscovery of the Wandering Jew, who became a vehicle for certain notions which, although in some ways contemporary, could nevertheless be retraced to the original legend. The Romantics included Ahasuerus in their gallery of great tragic figures. At the same time this vagrant, whose longevity caused him to traverse centuries, conveniently lent himself to sentiments evoked by the upheavals of the "era of revolutions." Ahasuerus' purgatorial ordeals could be perceived as tokens of the trials and tribulations endured by mankind ascending the ladder of progress. In Edgar Quinet's epic drama, Ahasuerus, accompanied in the manner of the Romantic theosophies by a feminine redeemer, was called upon to "exhaust all suffering" just like Christ. In Eugène Sue's *Le Juif errant*, Ahasuerus makes only brief episodic appearances, but portrays both the tale's original ambiguity and the characteristic tendency of the author's era to inflate symbolic meanings. The shoemaker who had spurned Christ was ignorant in the teachings of Love, because, as an artisan, he was a victim of social injustice; yet he also belonged to the "race of workers" who were to be redeemed from "modern slavery" by virtue of their suffering. Ahasuerus, to whom death was denied, and who was doomed to perpetual and endless solitude, was seen by the German

3. Maurycy Gotllieb, Ahasuerus (self-portrait). Poland, 1876.

Romantics as a paragon of wretchedness. Richard Wagner projected this exaggerated image of the Wandering Jew onto the Jewish collective: death hovering over a ghost nation which ultimately outlives all other nations. Whilst other peoples experience the natural cyclical process of birth and death (and so replicate the natural life-cycle of the individual), the Jews, especially since the Emancipation which severed their ties with their own traditions, are destined to exist forever as parasites who feed off other national bodies. Their only hope of salvation lies in attaining what Ahasuerus most desired – extinction. Readers familiar with the vocabulary of German radicals in the 1840s read this obscure formulation as a call for the obliteration of Jewish self-identity, and the merging of the Jews into the collective struggle for human emancipation. Less subtle minds, however, interpreted it as an appeal for annihilation.

| Wordsworth, *Song for the Wandering Jew* | Goethe, *Der Ewige Jude* | Eugène Sue, *Le Juif errant* | |
| --- | --- | --- | --- |
| 1800 | 1771–1775 | 1844–1845 | |

6. Wood engraving, France, 19th century.

**1602:** Appearance of German chapbooks on Ahasuerus, one entitled *A Short Description and Story of a Jew Named Ahasuerus*, another entitled *A Marvelous Tale of a Jew Born in Jerusalem*.
**1605:** Appearance of the French translation of the *Short Description* by P. Cayet, who was also the translator of *The History of Doctor Faustus*.
**1623:** A deserter from the Spanish army in Flanders pretending to be the Wandering Jew is exposed and tried.
**c. 1740–1813:** *The Admirable History of the Wandering Jew* is printed in Rouen; it was later included in the *Bibliothèque bleue*.
**1777:** The appearance of *Memoirs of the Wandering Jew on his Seventeen Voyages Around the World (One in Each Century)*.
**1797:** *The Wandering Jew or Love's Masquerade*, a comedy by Andrew Franklin, produced at Drury Lane, London.
**1813:** Appearance of *Queen Mab* by Percy

Bysshe Shelley: the Wandering Jew as a rebel against a tyrannical deity
**1823:** Edger Quinet's *Les Tablettes du Juif errant*.
**1833:** Quinet's *Ahasuerus*. Beranger's *Lament of the Wandering Jew*, later to be put to music by Gounod.
**1834:** *Le Juif errant, journal, revue mensuelle du progres* (three issues): "[the Wandering Jew] is humanity on the road, it is progress on the march."
**1844–1845:** Eugène Sue publishes a feuilleton, "The Wandering Jew" in *Le Constitutionnel*.
**1847:** Hans Christian Andersen's drama *Ahasuerus* staged in Danish.
**1852:** *The Wandering Jew* – an opera by Eugène Scribe to music by Halevy.
**1869:** Mark Twain in his *Innocents Abroad* summarizes a version of the legend told in Jerusalem by his guide in the Via Dolorosa.

7. A character in Karagoz, the popular Turkish shadow puppet theater. Leather, late 19th century.

# German Jewry

1. Moritz Daniel Oppenheim (1800–1882), Lavater and Lessing Visit Moses Mendelssohn. *A very personal view by the first Jewish painter in Germany of the famous controversy between the Jewish philosopher (seated on the left) and the Lutheran clergyman. Standing is the author of* Nathan the Wise, *playwright Gotthold Ephraim Lessing. Oil, 1856.*

Between the end of the Thirty Years War and the rise of National Socialism, German Jewry was the pivot of modern European Judaism, the community that pioneered cultural, religious, and social innovations. What had been a small and peripheral community, traditional and homogeneous, gradually developed into a pluralistic society adhering to a wide spectrum of beliefs, political attitudes, and social ideals manifesting astonishing creative powers in the cultural sphere and astute prowess in economic affairs. Despite recurring outbursts of hostility and discrimination, it was remarkably well integrated into German society at all levels.

In the history of Jewish-German relations, the modern era begins with the emergence of absolutism and its mercantile economy. Regarding interests of state as a supreme value, the princes in the fragmented Empire discovered the economic benefits to be gained from a Jewish presence. Reversing the restrictive policy of the past, they would henceforth encourage the settlement of Jewish entrepreneurs who could provide the rising modern state with the capital and economic experience it so desperately needed. In return, the Jews were granted protection, religious freedom, and commercial liberties. Some of them, particularly the Court Jews, attained positions of prominence thanks to their personal contacts with the ruler, thus offering their community a glimpse of a world which the rabbis were generally trying to shut out. These glimpses, however, did not in any significant manner affect the austere and rigid pattern of traditional Ashkenazi society.

It was only in the eighteenth century that the emergence of new trends within Jewish society in Germany became apparent. Growing disaffection led many members of the intellectual elite, encouraged by the promise of toleration, to seek new answers within the currents of modernization. They became advocates of greater openness, seeking to converge Judaism and German culture in a symbiosis that would nonetheless retain the unique and rich character of their heritage.

The person who best exemplified this ambition, the greatest philosopher of the Jewish Enlightenment (*Haskalah*, "learning"), was Moses Mendelssohn. Like Nathan the Wise in Lessing's play, Mendelssohn had to fight on two fronts: with traditionalist rabbis who feared losing the purity of Judaism and the nation's cohesion, and with Germans who opposed Jewish emancipation.

The French revolutionary armies carried the promise of emancipation into Germany, but the fall of Napoleon and the victory of the Holy Alliance resulted in the almost total withdrawal of the equality that had been achieved by the Jews. The 1812 Prussian Edict of Emancipation remained the only act of its kind in German principalities for over a generation. Anti-Jewish feelings were revived in the post-Napoleonic period as part of a Christian-Teutonic, romantic, and nationalist reaction. But a growing numbers of Jews persisted in trying to force their way into German society. Some followed the path of assimilation to its logical end – conversion to Christianity. Throughout the nineteenth century, later than in the West but at a quicker pace, German society was engaged in freeing itself from the last vestiges of feudalism, and entering a rapid process of industrialization and liberalization – a process which was very attractive to the Jews. Most Jews carried on living in the rural areas where the older, more traditional ways were still upheld; but many moved to the cities, taking up new careers, repressing their religious beliefs and ethnic affiliation, thereby increasing their accord and association with the values of German culture and society. Some Jews, faithful disciples of Mendels-

---

| Founding of the Jewish community in Berlin | Execution of the "Jew Suess" | Moses Mendelssohn, *Jerusalem* |
|---|---|---|
| 1671 | 1738 | 1783 |

**1670:** The Elector of Brandenburg invites several dozen wealthy Jews to settle in Berlin; a Jewish community is founded the following year.
**1714:** Death of Leffman Behrends, one of the most important Court Jews in northern Germany, who served Ernest Augustus of Hanover.
**1729–1786:** Lifespan of Moses Mendelssohn, "father of the *Haskalah*," the Jewish version of the *Aufklärung* (German Enlightenment).
**1769–1770:** The famous dispute between Mendelssohn and the Swiss pastor Johann Kaspar Lavater in which Mendelssohn was compelled to defend his loyalty to Judaism.
**1778:** A "Jewish free school" is founded in Berlin using modern methods and omitting Talmud studies from its curriculum.
**1780–1783:** Mendelssohn translates the Pentateuch into German and publishes it in

Hebrew characters; his *Biur*, a commentary in Hebrew, follows rabbinical tradition but introduces modern concepts of exegesis.
**1781:** Christian Wilhelm von Dohm, a Prussian intellectual and government official, publishes *On the Improvement of the Jews as Citizens* – which later influences the process of emancipation.
**1782:** Naphtali Herz Wessely (1725–1805) publishes his *Divrei Shalom ve-Emet* ("Words of Peace and Truth") in Berlin, the first Hebrew work concerned with the education of the Jews in the spirit of the Enlightenment.
**1783:** Moses Mendelssohn publishes *Jerusalem* – an exposition of his philosophy of Judaism in relation to the State.
**1815:** Congress of Vienna permits the abolition of emancipation laws in the German states.
**1818. October 18:** The dedication of the Hamburg Temple – a synagogue of the Reform movement – marks the beginning of the open conflict with Orthodox Jewry.

3. Heinrich Heine and his wife Mathilde, *by Ernest Benedikt Kietz. Oil, 1851.*

## The Mendelssohn Family

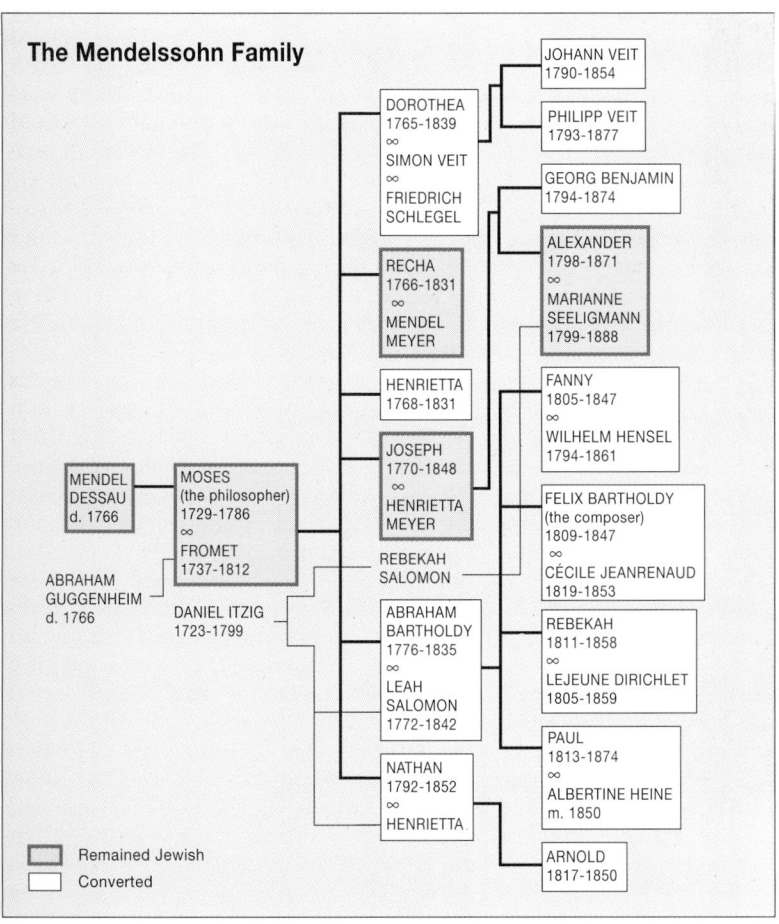

Remained Jewish
Converted

2. Ceiling of the synagogue in Horb near Bamberg. Painted wood, Germany, 1735.

sohn, tried to cling to their Jewish heritage, adjusting it to modern custom and requirements. It is therefore not surprising that innovations such as Reform Judaism, the Science of Judaism, and changes in traditional synagogue rites and ceremonies were all introduced by German Jews. A number of community associations propagated Jewish principles which embraced German ideas, and many Jews became politically involved in order to defend liberal causes pertaining to emancipation.

When emancipation finally came following the unification of Germany in 1871, the 470,000 Jews of the Reich envisaged the future as a straight road leading directly to full integration into German society. The emergence of a strong antisemitic movement at the end of the 1870s did raise apprehension in the hearts of some, but most Jews saw it as a one-time aberration which posed no serious threat to the process of their integration. Others, deeply distressed by the fact that their love for Germany was rejected by some members of its society, found solutions either in conversion (which at the beginning of the nineteenth century assumed dimensions of a mass movement) or in one form or another of a more zealous Jewish lifestyle. Nonetheless, complete acculturation remained the ultimate hope of the majority of German Jews. This hope survived the adversities of the Great War and the growing shadows during the Weimar Republic. Only the rise of National Socialism in the 1930s would finally shatter it completely.

| Emancipation in Prussia | Baptism of Heinrich Heine | Emancipation in Bavaria |
|---|---|---|
| 1812 | 1825 | 1871 |

**1819:** A group of seven students (among them Leopold Zunz and Eduard Gans, promoters of modern Jewish historiography) found a Society for the Culture and Science of the Jews (*Verlein fur Kultur und Wissenschaft der Juden*) in Berlin; their idea is to improve the image of Judaism in the eyes of both Jews and Gentiles by way of scholarship.
**1825:** Heinrich Heine (1797–1856) is baptized as a Lutheran, his "admission ticket," he would say, to European culture. A quarter of a century later the poet declares: "I make no secret of my Judaism, to which I have not returned, because I never left it."
**1836:** Samson Raphael Hirsch (1808–1888) publishes *Nineteen Letters on Judaism*; Hirsch defends traditional Judaism against the Reform movement and the modernists, yet his neo-orthodoxy takes certain modern norms of behavior into account.
**1845:** Reform Society formed in Berlin.
**1854:** Zacharias Frankel becomes director of the newly founded Jewish theological seminary in Breslau.

**1878:** Wilhelm Marr publishes *The Victory of Judaism over Germandom*, a violently racist pamphlet. It was Marr who introduced the term "antisemitism" into the political vocabulary. The following year he founded the League of Anti-Semites and a short-lived monthly.
**1882:** Heinrich Keller publishes the first complete edition of the paintings of Moritz Oppenheim, *Family Scenes from Jewish Life of Former Days*, which was to become one of the most popular Jewish books in Germany.
**1893. March 26:** Founding of the Central Society of German Citizens of the Jewish Faith: a defense organization intended to protect German Jews from antisemitism, it evolved into a central body of German Jewry in future generations.

4. Jewish merchants selling a milking cow to a Gentile. Antisemitic statuette. Bronze, Zizenhausen, Germany, c. 1840.

# American Jews: The "German" Period

The United States, land of freedom and economic opportunity, attracted immigrants from the Old World like a magnet: within half a century the American population grew from less than ten million to more than fifty million people. This phenomenal growth was due largely to immigration from the British Isles, Germany, and Austria. The German-speaking arrivals included many Jews, and the Jewish population, which reached approximately 280,000 by the end of the period under discussion, thus became an important part of the American nation.

All forms of legal discrimination disappeared by the beginning of the nineteenth century. The last affair of any significance – the disqualification of Jewish candidates to the legislative assembly of Maryland – was settled by law in 1826. Typically, the Jewish question was not on the agenda of debates which revolved around the issue of church-state relations. Manifestations of antisemitism were rare, and hatred was more often directed against the Catholics, mostly against Irish immigrants. Moreover, there were frequent cases of philosemitism: qualities attributed to the Jews such as diligence, ambition, civic involvement, and community responsibility were regarded as precisely the qualities upon which the American spirit was based.

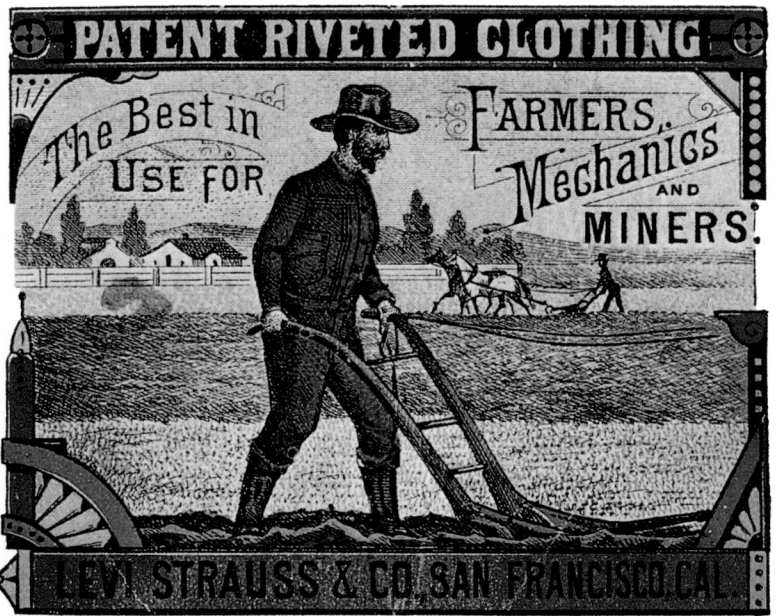

1. The original jeans: advertisement for denim work clothes produced by Levi Strauss & Co., San Francisco after 1875.

The social status of the Jews, however, was far from brilliant. With the exception of a few physicians, and contrary to their later image, the Jews played but a minor role in the professions. By the mid-nineteenth century, most Jews in America were earning their living as itinerant traders, even those among them who had been professionally trained in the old country. The typical Jewish peddler bought merchandise on credit from the Jewish wholesalers in the cities, and sold it to people living in farms scattered throughout the countryside. During the second half of the nineteenth century, the Jewish travelling salesman began providing essential goods to the growing communities of gold-diggers in the West, in the Rocky Mountains, and in the southwest.

The cultural characteristics of the American Jewish community had been radically transformed since the eighteenth century. German culture penetrated most communities. Theatrical and musical societies, newspapers in German, courtesy, manners, and their overall lifestyle were all transposed from Central Europe. This strong German influence, combined with the pluralism and liberalism of American society, formed the basis for the emergence of the Reform movement within American Judaism. The German synagogues, originally orthodox, gradually abandoned prayers which they considered inappropriate for social or moral reasons. They replaced Hebrew with English or German in the liturgy, and the men ceased to cover their heads. This process culminated, in the 1870s and 1880s, with Reform Judaism encompassing practically the entire American community. In the Reform synagogue, called a "temple," the central role was played by the rabbi, whose sermons were the focus of the service. An abridged version of prayers was recited only on the Sabbath and on major festivals and holy days. Rejecting the concept of the Exile and the eschatological ideal of the Return, the Pittsburgh Platform (1855) defined the movement's ideology. It retained only *mitzvoth* (commandments) which seemed reasonable and which were in keeping with modern morality: "We recognize, in the modern era of universal culture of heart and intellect, the approaching of the realization of Israel's great messianic hope for the establishment of the kingdom of truth, justice and peace among all men. We consider ourselves no longer a nation, but a religious community." These principles remained the basic tenets of Reform Judaism till 1937.

In opposition to such radical tendencies, more moderate religious currents also emerged, and these, while willing to embrace modernity, wished at the same time to respect tradition. They retained the exclusive use of Hebrew in the prayers, the full observance of the Sabbath, the rules of alimentary purity, and the messianic expectation for the Return. Thus, two years after the Pittsburgh Platform, the Jewish Theological Seminary of America was established in New York by Conservative rabbis seeking to preserve traditional values..

| American Reform Judaism | "Jacksonian Democracy" | Jewish immigration from Germany | Founding of *B'nai B'rith* |
|---|---|---|---|
| 1824 | 1829–1837 | 1834 | October 1843 |

4. Advertisement for the tobacco "Love," produced by Myers Bros. & Co. Richmond, Virginia, c.1865.

**First half of 19th century:** Expansion of U.S. Jewry throughout the North American continent. Jews settle in towns in the Great Lakes district, in Ohio, and Mississippi. Jewish communities in the large cities experience rapid growth; Cincinnati's community is second only to New York; in Louisville, Minneapolis Saint Louis, and New Orleans, Jews play an important role in the transformation of these cities into the economic capitals of their respective regions. Small numbers of Jews even penetrate the deep South and the West. On the Atlantic coast, the communities of Charleston and Newport are dwindling, but those of Philadelphia and Baltimore are beginning to grow. New York, however, with its tens of thousands of Jews, holds the largest concentration of American Jews, and remains the most important center of American Jewry to this day.
**1824–1833:** The American Reform movement, in its early Sephardic form, is born in the Charleston community.

5. Jewish soldiers in the Northern army in the company of their co-religionists from the South. Dougherty, Georgia, c.1865.

2. Herbert H. Lehman, from a Jewish Bavarian family which came to America in the early 19th century, elected governor of New York State in 1932.

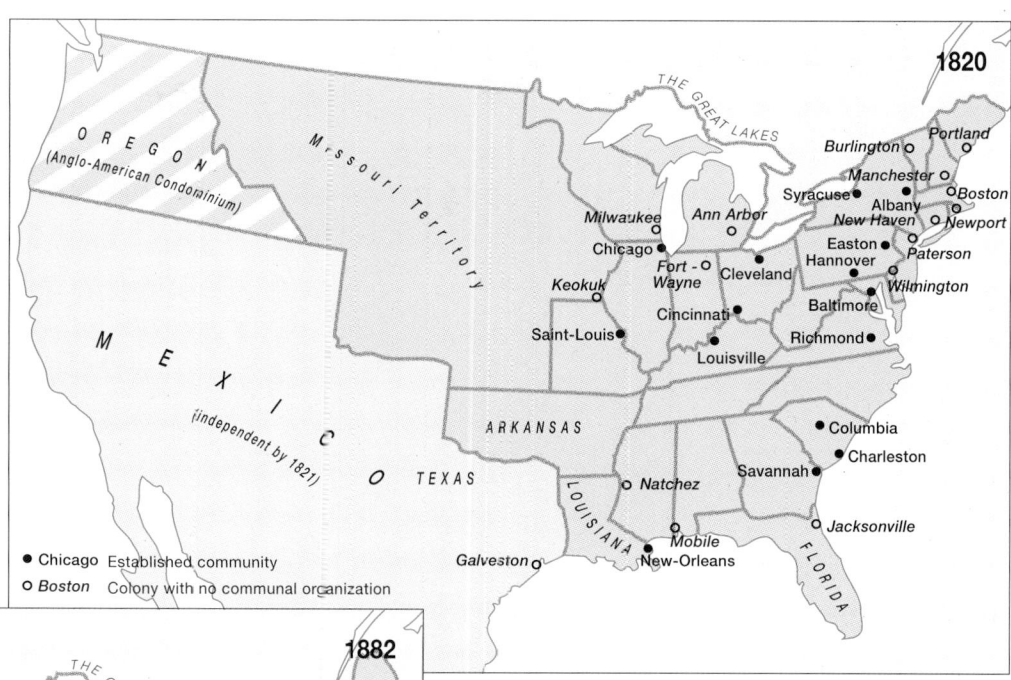

- ● Chicago — Established community
- ○ Boston — Colony with no communal organization

- The United States in 1853
- The Confederacy after secession, 1861
- 1841 — Communities established by German Jews
- ① — Number of organized communities in 1860

3. The merchant Julius Meyer in the company of Indian chiefs. Omaha, 1869.

**Abolition of Slavery. Lincoln's Assassination** — 1865

**Founding of the Ku Klux Klan** — 1867

**Beginning of Jewish immigration from Eastern Europe** — 1881

**1826:** Jews settle in New Orleans. The Jews of Maryland obtain political equality: the "Jew Bill" allows them to fulfill all public functions without taking a Christian oath.
**1834:** Beginning of the mass immigration of German Jews.
**1837:** Jews settle in Cleveland.
**1841:** Jews settle in Chicago.
**1843. October 13:** In a cafe in the Lower East Side of New York, twelve men establish a fraternal organization which still exists today: B'nai B'rith. At this time American Jewry numbers 15,000.
**1854:** Isaac Mayer Wise, an immigrant from Bohemia who came to the U.S. in 1846, settles in Cincinnati; a remarkable organizer and a major influence on the nature of the Reform movement in the United States, he seeks to fashion American Judaism according to the dominant Protestant pattern.
**Second half of 19th century:** Public schooling, non-confessional and free, is established throughout the United States,

and most Jewish children are integrated into this educational system. Relegated to afternoons and Sundays, proper Jewish education assumes only a complementary role.
**1861–1865:** Approximately 10,000 Jews participate in the Civil War, 3000 of them in the Confederate Army.
**1862:** The Northern army begins to appoint Jewish military chaplains.
**December 17:** The most serious manifestation of antisemitism of that time: General Grant, accusing the Jews of trafficking with the Confederation, gives an order to expel Jewish cotton traders behind the lines; the order is revoked by President Lincoln.
**From 1865:** The decades after the end of the Civil War are a time of prosperity for American Jews of German origin, since many of them are army purveyors,

6. Charles Strauss c. 1880. Strauss became mayor of Tucson, Arizona, in 1883.

manufacturers of and traders in uniforms, financiers, and money changers. Bankers such as Joseph Seligman (1820–1880) and his brothers, Jacob Schiff (1847–1920), and several others, play an important role in the economic history of the United States and of their own community. In 1869 President Grant offers Joseph Seligman the position of Secretary of the Treasury, but Seligman declines.
**1873–1889:** The organization of Reform Judaism is completed by the establishment of three institutions: the Union of American Hebrew Congregations, the Hebrew Union College, and the Central Conference of American Rabbis.
**1885:** The Pittsburgh Platform, composed by the radicals of the Reform movement.
**1887:** The Jewish Theological Seminary of America is founded in New York, dedicated to the "preservation in America of the knowledge and practice of historical Judaism." It remains to this day a most important spiritual and educational center.

# Modernization in Eastern Europe

1. Burial of five victims of Russian repression in Warsaw in 1861, by Alexander Lesser (1814–1884). A manifestation of Polish patriotism, showing a bishop flanked by a pope and a rabbi.

The officials of the absolutist "enlightened" state were naturally ill-disposed towards the autonomy of the Jews, and their desire was to turn them all into loyal and "useful" subjects. "Useful" in the sense of the Physiocrats meant having productive occupations: agriculture and crafts. The method adopted was that of "the carrot and the stick": those who showed themselves willing to change were encouraged, while the others were bullied to enter, step by step, into a modernized mold. In this process of enforced acculturation, the Jewish state schools (established in Galicia during the late eighteenth century and in Russia during the 1840s) played a major role in the forming of westernized elites.

This authoritarian policy was pursued in eastern Europe until the mid-nineteenth century. The Russian and Austrian authorities invested considerable effort in modernizing the Jews, but they encountered fierce resistance among the Jewish masses and attained negligible concrete results. Westernizing influences affected only small and isolated circles of *maskilim* (those who adopted the ideas and values of the *Haskalah*, the Jewish version of the Enlightenment) and some wealthy merchants in the larger cities. Moreover, these effects were due to direct contacts with the German *Haskalah* rather than to the reforming zeal of the authorities.

The *Haskalah* was indeed an all-Ashkenazi phenomenon. Jews from eastern Europe played an important part in the emergence of the movement in Berlin. A second *Haskalah* center developed in Koenigsberg in eastern Prussia near the Lithuanian border. Members of the eastern communities participated in Moses Mendelssohn's enterprise of religious and intellectual revival (for example, the translation of the Bible into German accompanied by a rationalist commentary in Hebrew). *Maskilim* who had lived for a time in Germany returned to Poland and disseminated the ideals of the movement. Meanwhile, in the large cities – Warsaw, Cracow, St. Petersburg – the Jewish economic elite adopted the cultural values of its social milieu. The entire phenomenon – secular studies, loyalty to the modern centralized state, integration into society and cultivation of Hebrew – was, however, very limited in scope; and in the second or third generation the emphasis on assimilation often led to conversion to Christianity.

It was only in the second half of the nineteenth century that Jewish society in eastern Europe was truly transformed. This metamorphosis, however, occurred not due to government coercion, but as a result of overall modernizing processes. Within a few decades the economic and social upheavals liquidated the traditional way of life and caused the displacement of hundreds of thousands of Jews.

Alexander II's accession opened an era of reform in Russia. Serfdom was abolished and the empire was opened to capitalist enterprise. The former seignorial system which had incorporated the Jews for centuries was crumbling, and the Jewish townlet (the *shtetl*) was thus cut off from it

I n the second half of the eighteenth century, western winds brought changes to eastern Europe. For the Jews of "Poland" – Lithuania, Volhynia, Galicia – the agent transmitting foreign influences was the government itself. The "enlightened despots" who had inherited hundreds of thousands of Jews with the partition of Poland, wanted to "reform" their new subjects according to the fashionable ideas of the French *philosophes*.

| First partition of Poland | Emancipation of French Jews | The "Jewish Statute" in Russia |
|---|---|---|
| 1772 | 1791 | 1804 |

3. Alexander II, reforming czar (1818–1881).

**1783:** Moses Mendelssohn publishes his German translation of the Pentateuch with a Hebrew commentary known as the *biur*. The prospectus for this project was prepared in 1778 by Solomon Dubno.
**1784–1811:** The first Jewish periodical, *Me'assef* ("Collector"), intiated by the Mendelssohn circle and published in Koenigsberg, encourages secular studies, integration in the surrounding society, and the increased use of the Hebrew language.
**1787:** The *maskil* Herz Homberg, inspector of Jewish state schools in Galicia, creates a network of schools based on European (mostly German) culture. His success is limited because of the rapid spread of Hasidism.
**1804:** The first "Jewish Statute": Russian Jews are permitted to enter learning institutions of all levels.
**1840:** Nicholas I founds a "Committee for establishing means to reform the Jews of Russia," which is inspired by western models.

**1841–1845:** Uvarov, Russia's minister of education, invites a young *maskil* from Riga, Max Lilienthal, to create a network of Jewish state schools; his project encounters strong opposition among the Jews, including modernists. Lilienthal eventually emigrates to the U.S.
**1845:** The Russian government opens two rabbinical seminaries in Vilna and in Zhitomir, designed to produce rabbis educated in the Russian and European cultures.
**1846:** Sir Moses Montefiore, the British Jewish philanthropist, is received in St. Petersburg by Nicholas I; this visit was meant to improve the situation of Russian Jewry, but it is mainly used for czarist propaganda.
**1856:** Alexander II ends the Crimean War and inaugurates an era of reform. In Lyck in eastern Prussia, the Hebrew newspaper *Ha-Maggid* ("The Declarer") is founded by

4. Polish Jews in the uniform of the national guard, 1830–1831. Contemporary engraving.

economic roots. At both ends of the social ladder, as both proletarians and as capitalists, the Jews gradually entered into the new socioeconomic system. The political liberalization introduced by Alexander II's reforms was a catalyst for the emergence of a prosperous Jewish bourgeoisie; and a new Jewish intelligentsia was graduating from Russian high schools and universities. In the 1850s and 1860s Jewish periodicals in Hebrew, Russian, and Polish began to appear in St. Petersburg, Odessa, Kiev, Warsaw, and Lvov, weaving a network of communication across eastern Europe.

Modernization, obviously, is never a painless process. The westernization of Russo-Polish Jewry was no exception. Two major developments reflected the difficulties: first, the rise of radical ideologies; second, mass migration, both internal (from Lithuania to southern Russia and western Poland) and external, towards the West.

2. Emblem of the Jewish tailors' guild in Prague, 18th century.

**Spread of the *Haskalah* in Eastern Europe**

- Until 1800
- 1800–1860
- 1860–1900
- ● Major center
- ● Secondary center
- ■ School or seminary
- ■ Publication of journals

| Columns / labels on map |
| --- |
| St. Petersburg |
| Berlin |
| Lvov |
| Riga |
| BLACK SEA |
| LITHUANIA |
| RUSSIA |
| Kaunas |
| Koenigsberg |
| Vilna |
| Ilya |
| Shklov |
| Lyck |
| Nemunas |
| Minsk |
| PRUSSIA |
| Slonim |
| BELORUSSIA |
| Berlin |
| Frankfort-on-the-Oder |
| Oder |
| Vistula |
| Warsaw |
| Brest |
| Elbe |
| Breslau |
| POLAND |
| Zhitomir |
| Kiev |
| Dnieper |
| Zamosc |
| Dubno |
| Berdichev |
| Tarnow |
| Lvov |
| Brody |
| Kremenents |
| Prague |
| Prostejov |
| GALICIA |
| Tarnopol |
| Uman |
| BOHEMIA |
| Mikulov |
| MORAVIA |
| Satanov |
| Vienna |
| Chernovtsy |
| Dniester |
| Pressburg |
| AUSTRO-HUNGARY |
| MOLDAVIA |
| Botosani |
| Budapest |
| Kishinev |
| Jassy |
| Odessa |
| Szeged |
| BLACK SEA |

200 km.

| Modernist rabbinical seminaries in Russia | Reforms of Alexander II | First weekly Hebrew journal in Russia |
| --- | --- | --- |
| **1845** | **1856** | **1860** |

Eliezer Lipmann Silbermann; his intention was to distribute it in Russia (where censorship prevented its publication), offering readers news from Europe, and disseminating moderate *Haskalah* ideas.

**1860:** Edited by Alexander Zederbaum, the first Hebrew weekly in Russia appears in Odessa: *Ha-Melitz* ("The interpreter between the people of Israel and the authorities, between faith and *Haskalah*"). The same year saw the publication of the weekly Russian periodical *Razsvet* ("Dawn") in Odessa, propagating the ideas and ideals of the *Haskalah*.

**1863:** Judah Leib Gordon (1831–1892) publishes his poem *Hakitsa Ammi* ("Awake, my people") which becomes the credo of the Hebrew *Haskalah*. In the same year a group of affluent Jews in St. Petersburg found the Society for the Promotion of Culture Among the Jews; the Society finances the translation of Russian works into Hebrew, distributes foreign books to the Jewish public, and offers scholarships; in 1867 it opens a branch in Odessa.

**1869–1872:** The Yiddish journal *Kol Mevasser* ("Announcing Voice"), founded in 1862 as a supplement to the Hebrew weekly *Ha-Melitz*, disseminates scientific information in western style. The *maskilim* disparage Yiddish, yet they have no choice but to address the Jewish masses in the only language they know.

**1879:** Denounced to the authorities, probably by *Hasidim*, J.L. Gordon is arrested for conspiring with revolutionary elements.

5. Pithom and Ramses, the two towns built by Hebrew slaves in Egypt (Exodus 1:11), seen through the prism of the industrial revolution. Passover Haggadah, Warsaw, 1879.

# Mediterranean Capitalism

*1. A Jewish wedding in Tangier, according to a painting by Delacroix, c. 1832.*

Towards the end of the eighteenth century, when North Africa and the Near East began opening up to European commerce, it was only natural that the local rulers should turn to Jewish merchants who had always been active in Mediterranean trade. They made them their commercial agents in European countries, and granted them privileged licenses for import and export. During the nineteenth century, the political and military decline of these countries facilitated the economic penetration of European powers. Local rulers were forced to sign "capitulations" granting special rights to European businessmen, entrepreneurs, bankers, and engineers who settled in growing numbers in all North African and Near Eastern cities.

By transferring the centers of economic activity and the main trade routes to the coastal areas, where the population of merchants, consuls, and immigrants was concentrated, European expansion influenced the entire political and economic orientation of the region. Inevitably, many Jews from the interior flocked to these new centers, where they were protected by the presence of representatives of European states, and where contact with immigrants promoted rapid acculturation. Indeed, many of the immigrants were themselves Jewish, particularly in Tunisia where hundreds of Jewish Italian subjects were absorbed, and in Egypt,

which after the opening of the Suez Canal attracted thousands of Jews from Mediterranean countries, the Balkans, and Eastern Europe.

Thus, although most Jews carried on their traditional occupations, the period witnessed the rise of a new bourgeoisie. As merchants, industrialists, and financiers, these Jews played an important role in the transformations which preceded the colonial conquest of the Near East and North Africa. Well-disposed towards the Europeans and the reforms which were introduced under their influence; well acquainted with the region, its languages and customs; skilled in international commerce and in possession of family connections throughout the world, the Jews were well qualified to become agents of European companies, associates of local authorities, or independent entrepreneurs. Members of this new bourgeoisie prospered as they learned to diversify their assets, to invest in real estate at home and abroad, and to benefit from the protection of diplomatic immunity or foreign citizenship.

In Morocco, the "king's merchants" (*tujjar al-sultan*) – the aristocracy of this new class – enjoyed special privileges which permitted them to build vast commercial enterprises. They imported textiles, candles, sugar, and tea (which from the eighteenth century onward became the national drink of Morocco) and exported wheat, oil, hides, ostrich feathers, and corals. Their commercial activity ranged from the Sahara to the Mediterranean shores, and from there to Leghorn (Livorno), Marseilles, Gibraltar, and Manchester. European businessmen, impressed by the Jews' success, tried to involve them in their enterprises. When the French company Paquet opened its maritime line to Morocco, several local Jewish families (Corcos, Elmaleh, Benchimol) were among the first shareholders; when the Pereire brothers established their Transatlantic Bank, they chose local *tujjar* as their representatives in Mogador, Marrakesh, and Tangier. In other North African countries, on the other hand, the new economic elite comprised mainly immigrants, the best example being the *Gorni* – Jewish families from Leghorn, such as Castelnuovo, Lumbroso, and Guttieres, who settled in Tunisia.

The emergence of Jewish capitalism in Egypt and elsewhere in the Middle East followed a similar pattern, but the Jews there had to compete with other minorities – local Christians, Greeks, and Armenians. In Turkey and Syria, Christians occupied most of the key positions in banking and international commerce, although certain "Frankish" Jewish families – Di Figiotto, Carasso – did rise to prominence.

Finally, one can not but mention the "Rothschilds of the East" – those Jewish merchants from Iraq and Syria who rose to great fame and affluence in India: the Sassoon family, originally from Baghdad, who directed an enormous commercial empire from Bombay; and the Ezra family who immigrated from Aleppo to Calcutta in the early nineteenth century, and established a trading network spanning three continents.

| The "King's merchants" in Morocco | | Napoleon in Egypt | The Sassoons in Bombay |
|---|---|---|---|
| 1764 | | 1798 | 1820 |

**1764:** Muhammad III of Morocco orders several families of Jewish merchants to settle in the new town of Mogador; the beginnings of the *tujjar al-Sultan* – the privileged group of the "King's merchants."
**1781–1817:** Sheikh Sassoon, president of the Jewish community in Baghdad, is chief treasurer of the Ottoman pashas.
**1798:** Napoleon's conquest marks the beginning of the modern era in Egypt.
**1805:** Accession of Muhammad Ali in Egypt. The "Black Sabbath" in Algiers: hundreds of Jews are killed by Janissaries who also assassinate Naphtali Busnach, the Jewish counselor of the Dey.
**1807:** The Sultan of Morocco, Mulay Suleiman, orders Jews out of the city centers and instructs them to settle in special quarters – the *mellahs*.
**1820:** David Ezra of Aleppo settles in Calcutta, India, where he becomes a leading opium trader; the drug was purchased in China and sold in Europe. During the 1820s, the Sassoon family from Basra in Iraq settles

in Bombay where, in association with several other Iraqi and Iranian Jews, they become the chief suppliers of indigo to Great Britain. At the end of the 19th century some of these "Rothschilds of the East" settle in England.
**1823:** The "hats affair" in Tunisia: a Jewish-British subject is arrested for wearing a European hat rather than the special headgear reserved for Jews. The English react sharply; the man is released and henceforth all foreign nationals are exempted from this law.
**1826:** Dissolution of the Janissary army in Turkey.
**1830:** France conquers Algeria.
**1830–1840:** Muhammad Ali conquers Syria and Palestine.
**1832:** Greece becomes independent.
**1838:** Britain conquers Aden; Captain Haines annuls the discriminatory laws against the Jews.
**1840:** The blood-libel affair in Damascus: the leaders of the Jewish community are

*2. A five centimes stamp used by the local postal service established in Morocco in 1896 by M. Ben Chimol. Letter from Tetuán to Chechuan, July, 1897. (In 1891 the first postal service connected Mazagan with Marrakesh.)*

accused of murdering an Italian Capuchin friar and his Muslim servant in order to use their blood for Passover; leading western Jewish figures – Moses Montefiore, Adolphe Cremieux, the brothers Jacob and Solomon Rothschild – to take up their defense.
**1853–1856:** The Crimean War: Doctor Lumbroso, in charge of the health service of the Tunisian army, helps many Jews attain important positions in the country's economy. During the 1860s when Tunisia finds itself on the verge of bankruptcy, Lumbroso is elected to the commission responsible for regulating its public debt. Another Jew, Jacob Guttieres, is one of the main creditors of the bey. Approximately 70% of Tunisia's public debt is in the hands of Jewish businessmen.
**1859:** The French-Moroccan War: several hundred Jews from Tetuan leave for Algesiras, Gibraltar, and Oran; many of them then continue to London and Manchester.
**1860:** Founding of the *Alliance Israelite*

# 18th–19th Century

## Principal Migrations of North African Jews, 18th-19th centuries

### To the Coastal Cities

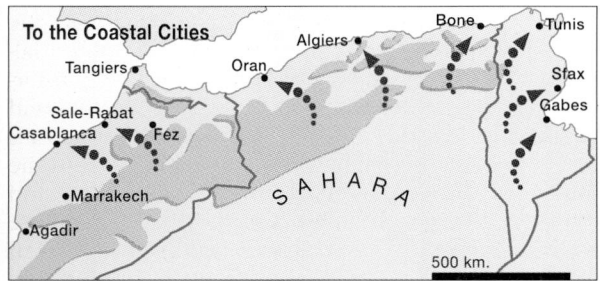

Tangiers · Oran · Algiers · Bone · Tunis · Sfax · Gabes · Sale-Rabat · Casablanca · Fez · Marrakech · Agadir

SAHARA

500 km.

### To the Eastern Mediterranean

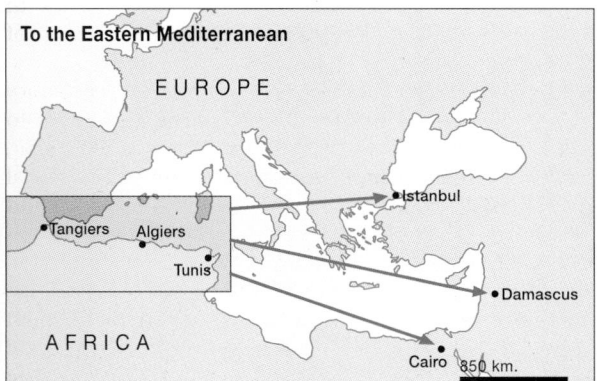

EUROPE

Tangiers · Algiers · Tunis · Istanbul · Damascus · Cairo

AFRICA

850 km.

### To New Worlds

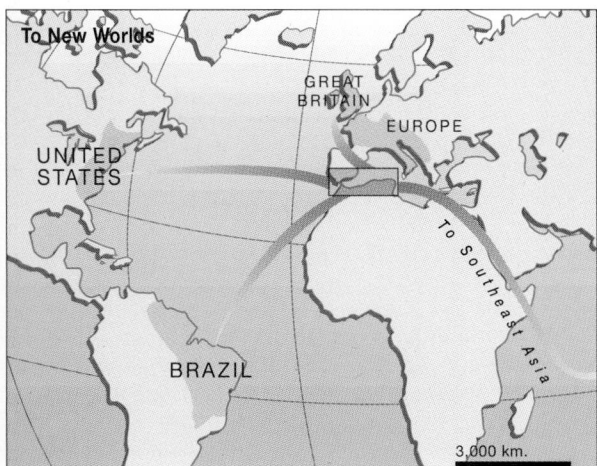

GREAT BRITAIN · EUROPE · UNITED STATES · To Southeast Asia · BRAZIL · SAHARA

3,000 km.

## Commercial Networks Across Three Continents

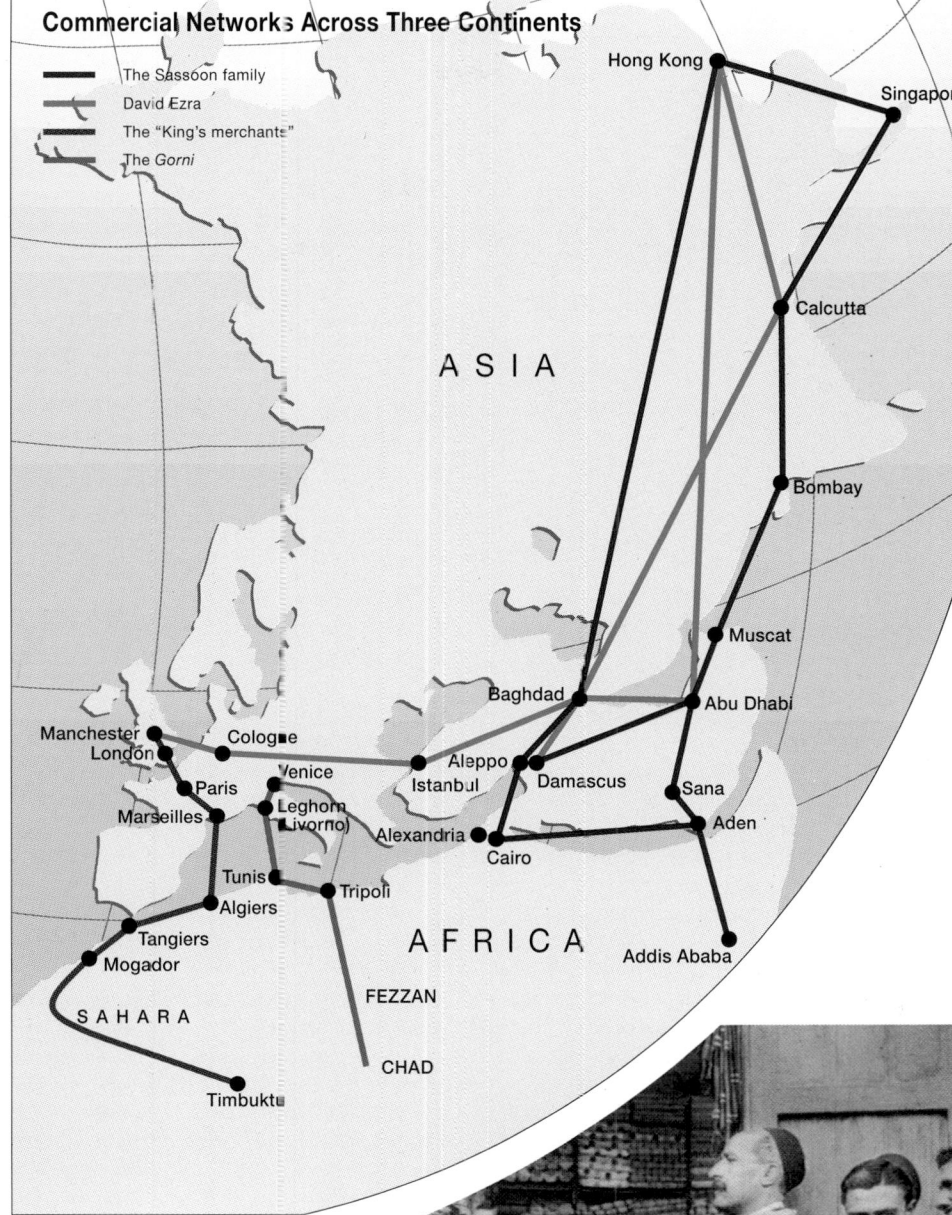

Legend:
— The Sassoon family
— David Ezra
— The "King's merchants"
— The *Gorni*

ASIA · AFRICA

Hong Kong · Singapore · Calcutta · Bombay · Muscat · Baghdad · Abu Dhabi · Aleppo · Damascus · Sana · Istanbul · Aden · Alexandria · Cairo · Addis Ababa · Manchester · London · Cologne · Paris · Venice · Leghorn (Livorno) · Marseilles · Tunis · Tripoli · Algiers · Tangiers · Mogador · FEZZAN · CHAD · Timbuktu

**Conquest of Algeria** — 1830

**The Suez Canal** — 1869

**Tunisia becomes a French protectorate** — 1881

*Universelle* in Paris.
**1868:** Jacopo Castelnuovo, a Jew originating from Livorno, represents the Tunisian authorities in negotiations with Italy concerning Tunisia's debt.
**1869:** Opening of the Suez Canal.
**1870:** Castelnuovo founds the *Societa anonima commerciale, industriae e agricola per Tunisia*, an immense investment company which includes certain Florentine bankers among its main shareholders.
**1871:** The Anglo-Jewish Association is founded in London.
**1872:** Turkey conquers Yemen.
**1881:** Tunisia becomes a French protectorate.
**1882:** Britain conquers Egypt.
**1891:** Beginning of the revolt in Yemen against Turkey.
**1896:** Assassination of Iran's Shah Nasr-el-Din.

3. David Sassoon and three of his sons, c. 1850.

4. Jewish merchants from Mazagan, Morocco. Postcard, end of 19th century.

# Jewish Settlement in Latin America

1. Frieda Kahlo, daughter of Jewish immigrants in Mexico, My grandparents, my parents, myself, 1936.

O n June 11, 1808, Napoleon deposed King Ferdinand VII of Spain and replaced him with his brother Joseph Bonaparte. Two years later, the repression of the anti-French rebellion in Spain ignited the revolt of the Spanish colonies in Latin America, seemingly out of loyalty to the legitimate monarch. Yet when Napoleon was defeated and Ferdinand VII returned to the throne, the pretense was dropped, and the revolt continued in the name of the right to self-determination. The wars of independence were fought intermittently until December 1824, when the battle of Ayacucho in Peru brought three centuries of Iberian colonialism in South America to an end.

The new republics, from Mexico in the north down to Argentina and Chile, abolished the Inquisition – a distinct symbol of Spanish oppression. Without going so far as a separation of church and state, for the first time the new republics allowed non-Catholics to settle in their territories. Brazil gained its independence without bloodshed: On September 7, 1822 Dom Pedro, who remained in Rio de Janeiro when the royal family went back to Portugal, proclaimed the independence of Brazil and the estab-

lishment of a constitutional empire. According to the constitution of March 25, 1824, Roman Catholicism officially remained the state religion, but freedom was granted to other religions. These conditions created the legal basis for Jewish life in Latin America.

The Jewish immigrants who came in the early nineteenth century arrived either from "Portuguese" communities in the Caribbean islands, from western and central Europe, or from Morocco. The settlers in Coro, in north Venezuela, came from the small nearby community of Curaçao. It was there, on July 13, 1829, that a Jew first received citizenship of a Latin American country – from Simon Bolivar, the liberator of Venezuela. Coro is also where the oldest Jewish cemetery on the continent is located, its earliest tombstones dating from the 1830s. Jewish settlers from the Caribbean islands also arrived in Cartagena, Colombia, and a few years later, in 1876, the Shearith Israel community was founded in Panama by Jews from St. Thomas and Curaçao.

Jews from Germany, France, and England came individually, and were indistinguishable from their non-Jewish immigrant compatriots. Recent studies indicate that there were west-European Jews in Brazil from 1808, in Mexico from 1830, in Peru from 1833, in Argentina from 1834, and in Chile from 1842. Jewish organizations were founded much later, and then only in large urban centers: Buenos Aires (1862), Lima (1870), and Rio de Janeiro (1840, and again in 1873).

The deteriorating situation of the Jewish communities in Morocco, and the increasing production of caoutchouc (natural rubber) in northeastern Brazil, drove young Moroccan Jews to migrate to the Amazonas. The first synagogue in Brazil was founded in Belém in the state of Para as early as 1828 (and perhaps even in 1824). These immigrants settled in trading posts and villages along the Amazon River and its tributaries. Their principal communities were at Belém, Manaos, and Iquitos in Peru. Some of these Moroccan Jews also arrived in Rio de Janeiro, Caracas, and Buenos Aires.

Jewish immigration from Russia began in the 1880s, but Latin America first became the destination of Jewish migration from eastern Europe in 1891, when Baron de Hirsch established his agricultural settlements in Argentina. By World War I Argentina and, to a lesser extent, Uruguay and Chile, had become important centers of Ashkenazi Jewry.

Finally, the decline of the Ottoman Empire precipitated the exodus of Ladino-speaking Jews from Turkey and the Balkans, and Arabic-speaking Jews from the Syrian communities of Aleppo and Damascus. These immigrants formed the nuclei of the first Sephardic communities in Buenos Aires (1904 and 1910) and in Temuco, Chile (1916).

All in all, the Jewish diaspora in Latin America by the end of World War I numbered approximately 150,000 people, the largest community being in Argentina.

| Abolition of the Inquisitions | The Battle of Ayacucho | The Argentinian Constitution | Founding of the Jewish Congregation of Argentina |
|---|---|---|---|
| 1811–1813 | December 1824 | May 1853 | 1868 |

**1811:** Abolition of the Inquisition in New Granada (Colombia) and in Paraguay.
**1813:** Abolition of the Inquisition in Argentina, Mexico, Peru, Chile, and Uruguay. Although re-established almost everywhere in 1815, it would be finally suppressed when these countries gained independence.
**1825:** England signs treaties with Brazil, Venezuela, and Argentina which contain a clause granting freedom of religion to non-Catholics.
**1853. May 2:** The Argentinian Constitution promises freedom of religion and immigration.
**1857:** Constitutional reform in Mexico establishes the separation of church and state.
**1864–1867:** Mexico under French rule; many Jews arrive from France, Belgium, and Austria.
**1868:** Founding of the Congregacion Israelita de la Republica Argentina.
**1876:** First Jewish community in Panama.
**1881. August 6:** The government of

Argentina appoints a special agent to attract Jewish immigration from Russia.
**1889:** Beginning of large-scale immigration and agricultural settlement in Argentina.
**1890:** Inspired by La France juive of Edouard Drumont (1886), Argentinian José Maria Miró inserts several antisemitic passages in

his novel La Bolsa; originally published by the influential newspaper La Nación, the book has been reprinted many times.
**1891:** Establishment of ICA by Baron Maurice de Hirsch.
**1897:** Zionist organizations in Argentina are formed.

**1898:** The Spanish-American War; after the war, demobilized Jewish American soldiers settle in Cuba. Three Yiddish journals are published in Argentina. First Syrian Jews immigrate to Mexico; the literary weekly El sábado secreto (later La luz del sábado), dedicated to the language and history of Sephardic Jewry, appears in Mexico.
**1908:** The revolution of the Young Turks precipitates the emigration of Jews from the Ottoman Empire.
**June 24:** Rabbi Martin Zielonka from El Paso, Texas, helps the Jews of Mexico organize their community.
**1909. May 1:** The Jewish anarchist, Simon Radowitzki, attempts to assassinate the Argentinian chief of police, Ramon Falcon.
**August:** Founding of Sociedad Unión Israelita de Chile and of Juventud Israelita Argentina, an organization of Jewish students; its journal – Juventud – is the organ of Argentinian Jewish intellectuals.
**August 8:** The first community organization is founded in Santiago, Chile.

2. Bolivar in the company of Mordechai Ricardo, on the latter's property in Curaçao, stamp, 1988.

**Jewish population in 1917**

ARGENTINA 110,000

BRAZIL 4,000
DUTCH GUIANA. 882
CURAÇAO 600
PERU 300
URUGUAY 300
VENEZUELA 475
CUBA 2,000
JAMAICA 1,490
MEXICO 300
TRINIDAD and BARBADOS 50

**Jewish immigrations**

| | ARGENTINA |
| | BRAZIL |
| | OTHER |

1840-1880
1881-1900
1901-1920

0  10,000  20,000  30,000  40,000  50,000  60,000  70,000  80,000  90,000  100,000

Community of under 2,000
Over 2,000
Over 50,000

MEXICO — Mexico City
Havana CUBA
JAMAICA Kingston
Port-au-Prince
HAITI Santo Domingo
DOMINICAN Rep.
San Juan PUERTO RICO
CURAÇAO
TRINIDAD and BARBADOS
San José COSTA RICA
Panama PANAMA
Cartagena Coro
Caracas
Georgetown Paramaribo Cayenne
Bogota
VENEZUELA
COLOMBIA
GUYANAS
PACIFIC OCEAN
Quito
ECUADOR
Iquitos
PERU
Lima
Manaos
Belem
B R A Z I L
Recife
La Paz
BOLIVIA
PARAGUAY
CHILE
Asuncion
Rio de Janeiro
São Paulo
Porto Alegre
ARGENTINA
Cordoba
Mendoza Rosario
Santiago
Temuco
URUGUAY
Montevideo
Buenos Aires
ATLANTIC OCEAN

---

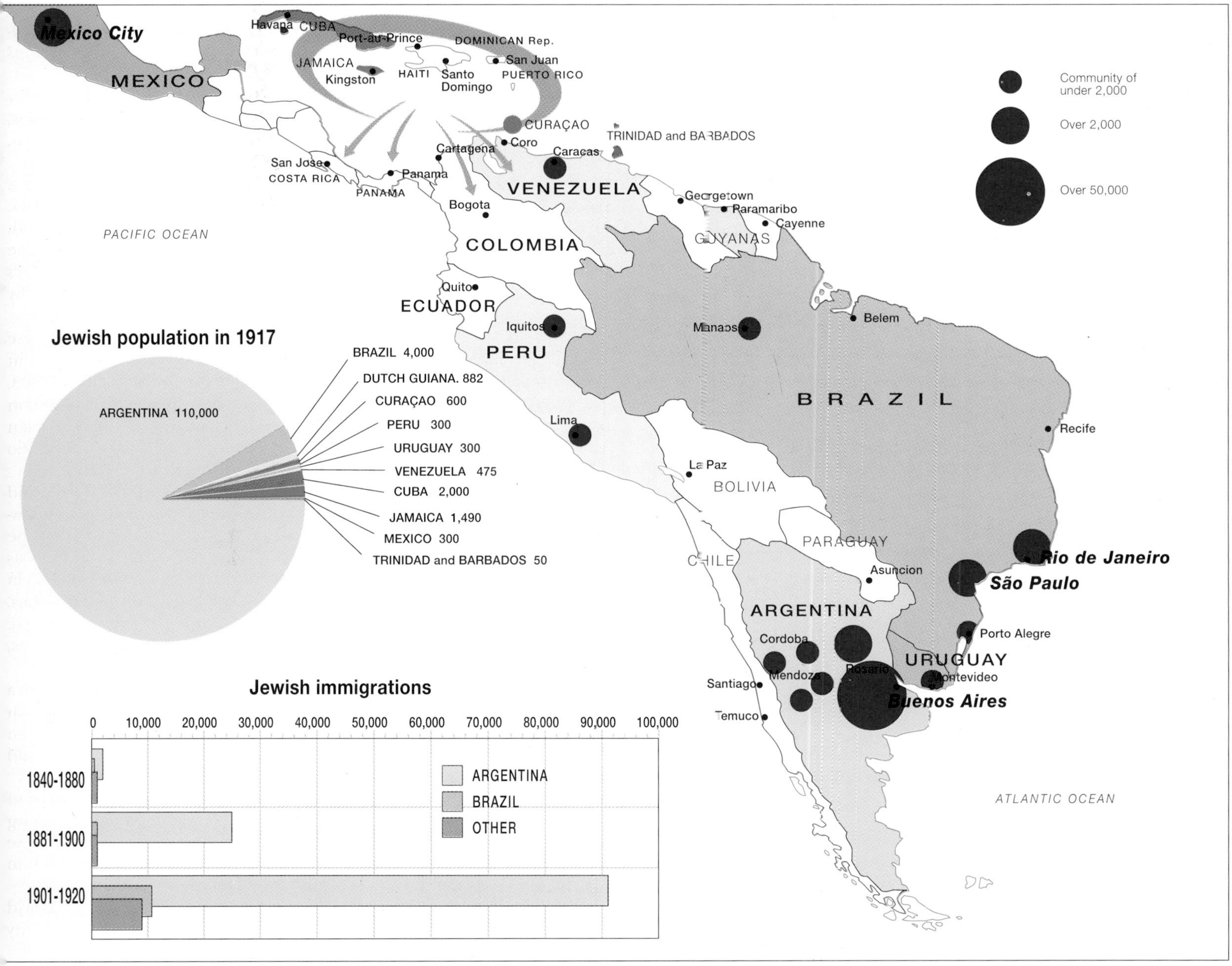

**Founding of ICA**
**1891**

**The Mexican Revolution**
**1910**

**The Community of São Paulo**
**1915**

**General Congress of Argentinian Jewry**
**February 1916**

*3. A silver cup awarded to Moses Delgado in recognition of services rendered to the cause of equal rights for Jews in Jamaica, 1831.*

**September 21:** "Ezrah," the first Ashkenazi community organization, is founded in Montevideo.

**1910. May 14:** A pogrom is perpetrated by a nationalist organization against the cultural institutions of the "Russian" Jews in Buenos Aires.

**1912:** Congregation *Alianza Monte Sinai* is founded in Mexico – one of the rare "mixed" congregations; due to their small number, the Jews were forced to overcome their tendency to group solely according to their places of origin.

**1913:** Establishment of the Sephardic congregation in Montevideo.

**1914:** Founding of a community organization in Cuba (*Sheveth Ahim*).

**1915:** Founding of the congregation in São Paulo; the first Yiddish journal in Brazil is published in Porto Alegre.

**1916. February 26–29:** The Congress of Argentinian Jewry drafts the demands of the Jewish people from the peace conference to decide on post-war arrangements.

*4. A road in the Jewish agricultural colony of Moisesville, Argentina, 1904.*

# The Jews of India

כדיני החמים ושחיתם למצות וכדיני אפיית המצה וכו׳

*1. Preparing the* mazzah *(unleavened bread) according to Bene Israel custom. Two pages of a Passover* Haggadah *with Marathi translation. Poona, 1874.*

**B**efore the colonial period there were two distinct and separate Jewish communities in India: Bene Israel ("Sons of Israel") in the Konkan region in the present-day state of Maharashtra; and in Kerala, the Jews of Cochin. Bene Israel, the largest group of Indian Jews, regard themselves as descendants of refugees from the Galilee who fled the persecutions of Antiochus Epiphanes in the second century BC; but they are not mentioned in any external sources prior to their first contact with the Jews of Cochin in the eighteenth century.

Closely resembling their Maratha neighbors in appearance, customs, and language, Bene Israel engaged in agriculture and oil production. They practiced circumcision and observed the Sabbath and Jewish dietary laws. Within the rigid Indian caste system, it was natural for these "Sabbath-observing oilmen" (*Shanwar Telis*) to maintain their distinctiveness and to remain separate.

During the British Raj, many Bene Israel moved from their villages to Bombay and excelled as officials and soldiers. Following the encounter with other Jewish communities – first with the Cochin Jews, and at the beginning of the nineteenth century with Arabic-speaking Jews from Baghdad – Bene Israel extended their Jewish education and built a few synagogues. They translated prayer books and the Passover *Haggadah* into the Marathi language, and for a time published several Jewish periodicals. The more prosperous and educated families sent their sons to English schools. Attracted by the opportunities offered in the civil service, many of them moved to other cities such as Ahmadabad, Baroda, Poona, Ajmer, Delhi, and Calcutta, where they lived alongside other Jewish communities but did not inter-marry with them.

From the 1920's many Bene Israel became Zionists due to the activities of emissaries sent by the movement. After the establishment of the State of Israel, most of them emigrated there, while others went to England. From the 24,000 persons who constituted the community in 1947, only a few thousand still remain in India today. When they emerged from their isolation, Bene Israel found it difficult to be recognized as legitimately Jewish. The controversy concerning their status was only resolved in 1964 when the Israeli government issued a statement to the effect that Bene Israel are Jews in every respect.

The history of the Jews in Kerala is also obscure. This tiny community – about 2500 persons at the beginning of this century, of whom 1000 lived in Cochin itself and 500 in the nearby town of Arankolam – was divided into three distinct groups: "White Jews" (*Paradesi*, meaning foreigners), "Black Jews," and "Freedmen"; the latter integrated into the "Blacks" at the beginning of the present century.

Legend and tradition trace the history of the Jews on the Malabar Coast to King Solomon's times, but the earliest historical evidence of their existence dates from c. 1000. Two copper plates inscribed in Tamil record the privileges granted by the Hindu ruler of Malabar, Bhaskara Ravi Varman, to one Joseph Rabban (Issuppu Irappan) from the village of Angivanam. Accounts of various travellers – Marco Polo, Ibn Batuta, and the Jew Benjamin of Tudela – confirm the existence of small Jewish communities dotting the Indian coast from Quilon in southern Cochin to Calicut in the north.

The Portuguese conquest brought many Jews to India, but it also introduced the first religious persecutions. The Rajah of Cochin offered them asylum in his city, granted them freedom of worship, and even appointed them a community leader (*mudaliar*), who was to serve as their spokesman and arbitrator.

Dutch rule (1663–1795) was a time of freedom and prosperity for the community. The "White Jews" maintained commercial and cultural links with Jewish communities in Amsterdam and other places. The famous *Paradesi* synagogue of Cochin, built in 1568 and partly destroyed by the Portuguese, was rebuilt in 1760.

The community retained its independence under the British Raj, but after the establishment of Israel most Cochin Jews emigrated there, and the community in India virtually ceased to exist.

Finally, some mention must be made of small groups of Jewish merchants who settled in India at various times: traders from Persia who came to northern India during the Mogul period; and in the seventeenth century, European and Iraqi Jews, involved in the trade of the European East India companies, settled in India's larger cities.

**Earliest evidence for a Jewish presence near Cochin**

**Visit of Benjamin of Tudela in Malabar**

**10th century**

**1167**

*4. Preparing the* mazzah, *Cochin, 1983.*

**11th century BC:** The assumed period of the arrival of Aryans to the Ganges and Indus valleys; writing of the Rig Veda, the oldest sacred text of Indian culture.
**10th century BC:** Reign of Solomon in Israel; some slim evidence suggests commercial links between the Kingdom of Israel and southern India; legend and tradition trace the Jewish settlement on the coast of Malabar back to this period.
**546–466 BC:** Life of Buddha; the religion he founded spread throughout eastern Asia but disappeared from India itself during the 10th century AD.
**962–1019:** Reign of Bhaskara Ravi Varman; the Jew Joseph Rabben is granted the right to live in Cranganore on the Malabar Coast, 35 km north of Cochin.
**1167:** Benjamin of Tudela arrives in India; evidence of a Jewish settlement on the Malabar Coast.
**1288:** Marco Polo visits India.
**1333:** The Arab traveler from Tangiers, Ibn Batuta, visits India.

*5. A family of Bene Israel, 1983.*

*A family of Bene Israel in Bombay, 1890.*

*The Paradesi synagogue in Cochin, built in 1568.*

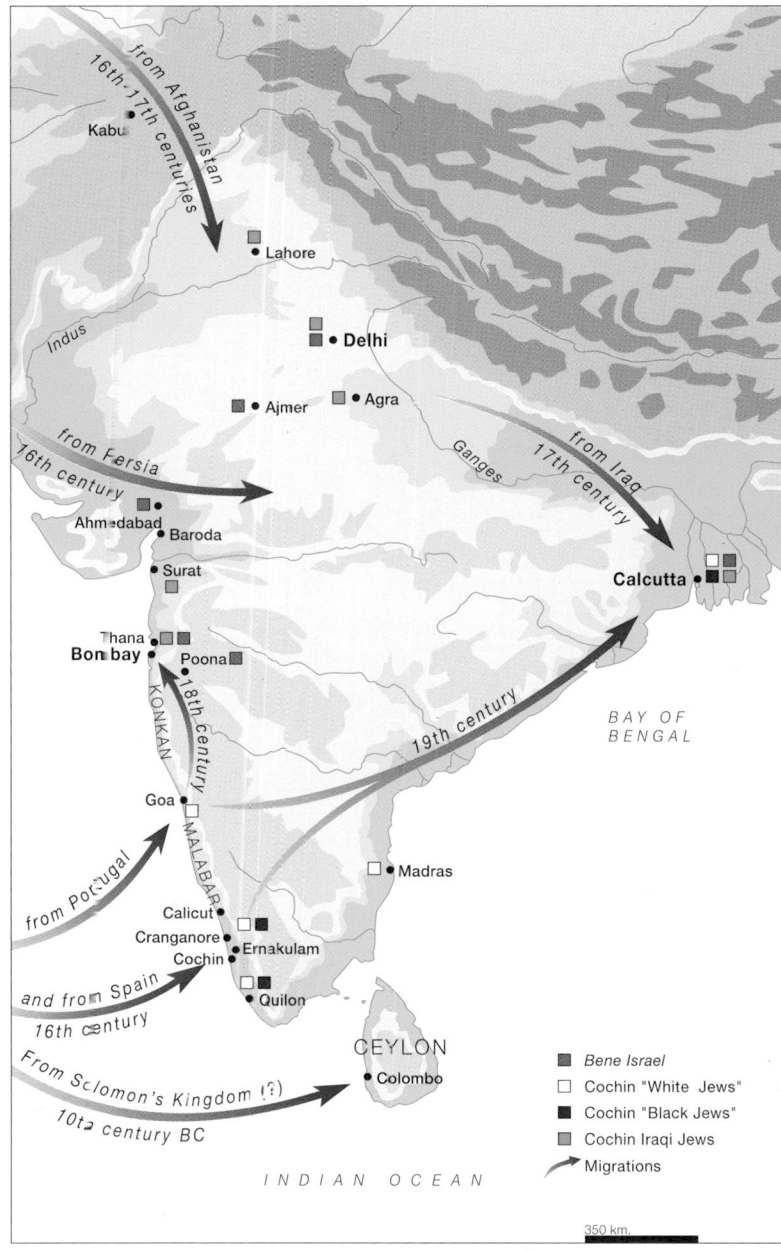

| The *Paradesi* synagogue in Cochin | The first synagogue of Bene Israel in Bombay | The first Jewish printing press in India | Jewish emigration from India |
|---|---|---|---|
| **1568** | **1796** | **1840** | **1948** |

**510:** The Portuguese conquer Panjim and establish Goa as the seat of the viceroy; many Jews and Marranos among the settlers.

**523:** The Portuguese capture Cranganore; the Jews find refuge in Cochin.

**556–1605:** Reign of Akbar the Great, third Mogul emperor: a period of religious toleration.

**560:** The Inquisition established in Goa.

**568:** The *Paradesi* synagogue in Cochin is built.

**663–1795:** The Dutch rule Cochin; a period of prosperity for the Jews.

**674:** The English East India Company transfers its center from Surat to Bombay, which becomes in subsequent centuries the largest Jewish center on the Indian subcontinent.

**686:** The first delegation from the Jewish Portuguese community of Amsterdam arrives in India and establishes contacts with Indian Jewry.

**1750:** Missionaries discover the Jewish congregations of Bene Israel in Konkan, Maharashtra; first meeting between a Cochin Jew (David Rahabi) and a Jewish army officer, Samuel E. Divekar.

**1772:** Calcutta becomes the official capital of the British government in India; in the following century a flourishing Jewish community will develop there.

**1796:** The first synagogue of Bene Israel in Bombay: *Sha'ar ha-Rahamim* ("Gate of Mercy").

**1799:** The last battle of Tippu Sahib, Sultan of Mysore, against the British who consolidate their rule over southern India.

**1810:** The American Mission Society is founded in Bombay and opens a school in the Marathi language for Bene Israel.

**1832:** A Hebrew grammar book in Marathi is published.

**1840:** A Cochin Jew establishes the first Hebrew printing press in India.

**1846:** Translation of the *Haggadah* into Marathi.

**1875:** The Sassoon family establishes a

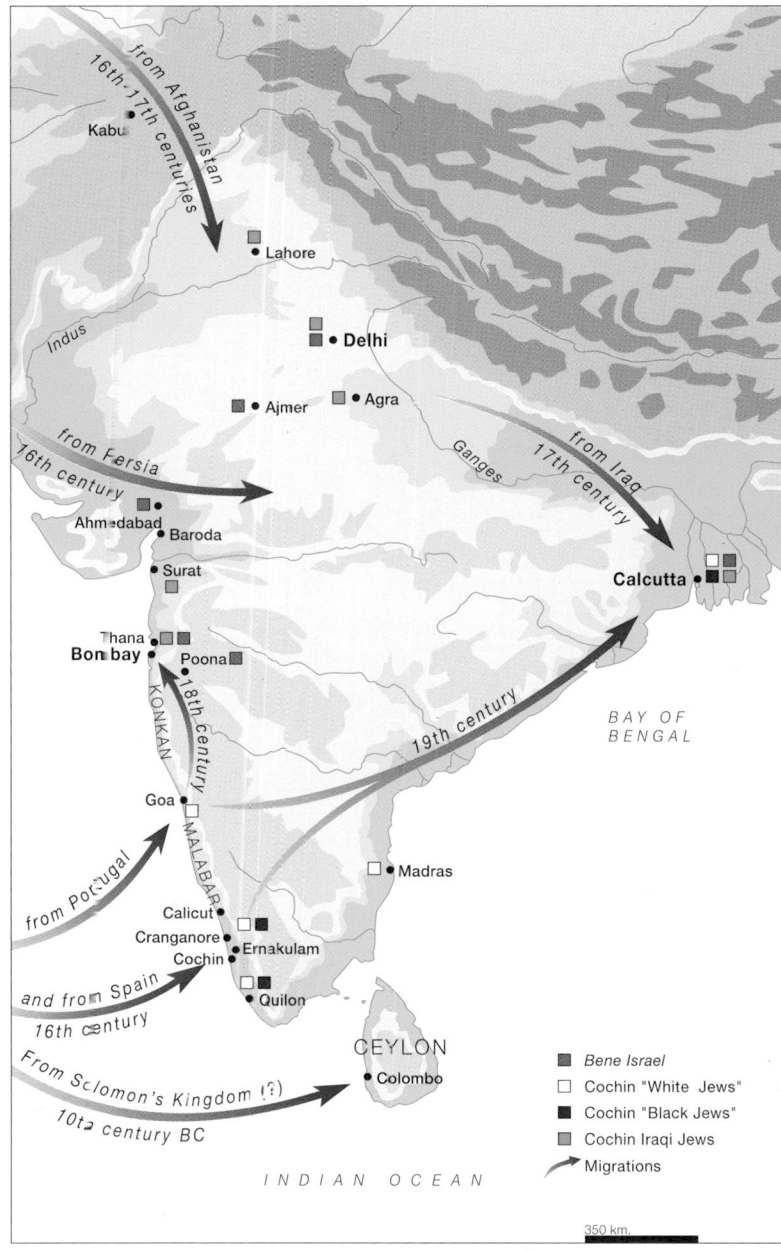

*6. An inscription in Tamil concerning the Jews of Malabar. End of 10th century.*

special school for Bene Israel in Bombay.

**1884** "Maghen David," the largest synagogue in the Far East, is built in Calcutta.

**1918** The first Zionist organization of Bene Israel founded in Bombay.

**1937–1938:** E. Moses, a Bene Israel Jew, is mayor of the City of Bombay.

**1948:** Widespread emigration of Indian Jews to Israel, England, and other countries.

# Jewish Emancipation in Muslim Lands

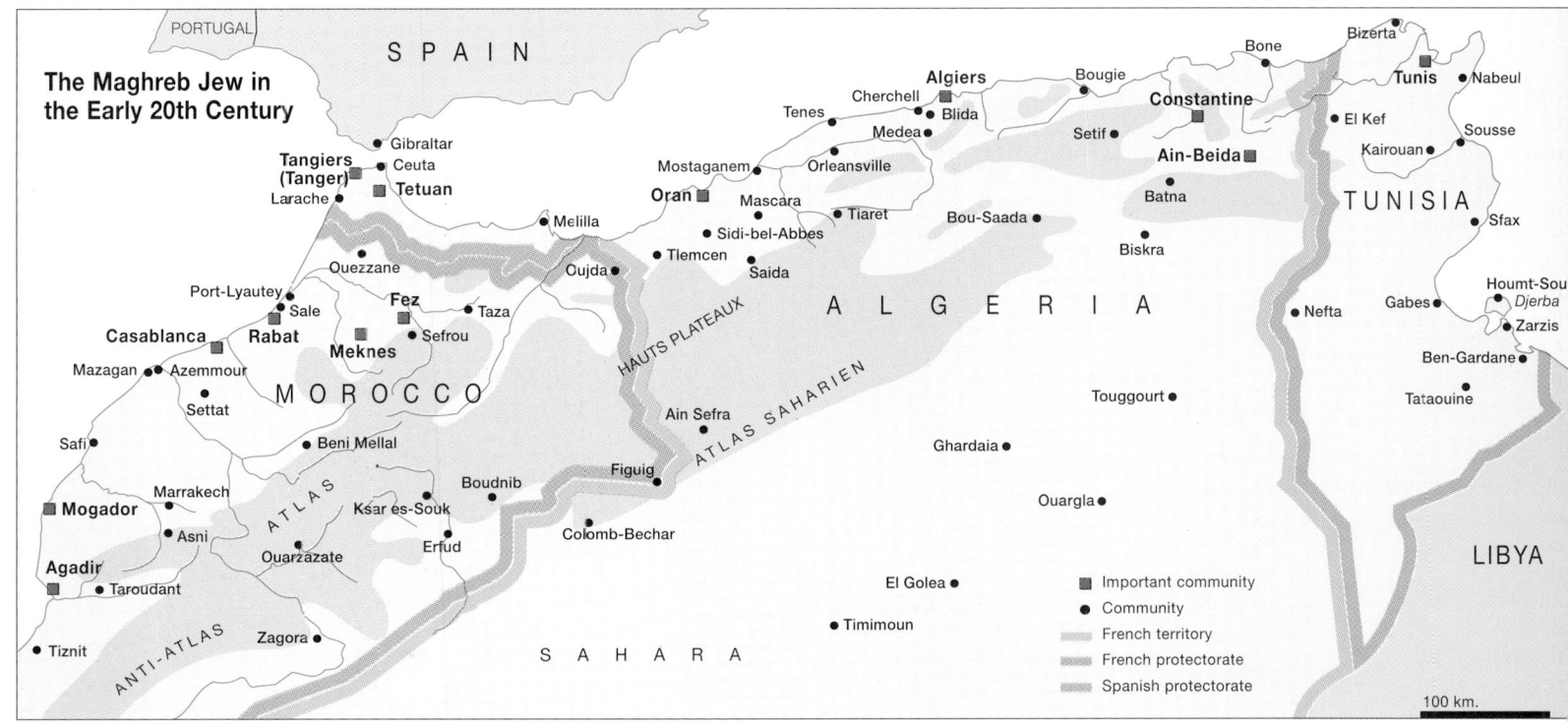

**The Maghreb Jew in the Early 20th Century**

PORTUGAL · SPAIN · Gibraltar · Ceuta · Tangiers (Tanger) · Tetuan · Larache · Melilla · Ouezzane · Port-Lyautey · Sale · Fez · Taza · Casablanca · Rabat · Sefrou · Meknes · Mazagan · Azemmour · Settat · MOROCCO · Safi · Beni Mellal · Marrakech · ATLAS · Ksar es-Souk · Boudnib · Figuig · Mogador · Asni · Ouarzazate · Erfud · Colomb-Bechar · Agadir · Taroudant · Tiznit · Zagora · ANTI-ATLAS · SAHARA

Algiers · Cherchell · Blida · Tenes · Medea · Mostaganem · Orleansville · Oran · Mascara · Tiaret · Sidi-bel-Abbes · Tlemcen · Saida · Oujda · Bou-Saada · HAUTS PLATEAUX · ALGERIA · ATLAS SAHARIEN · Ain Sefra · Touggourt · Ghardaia · Ouargla · El Golea · Timimoun

Bougie · Bone · Bizerta · Constantine · Setif · Ain-Beida · Batna · Biskra · Nefta · TUNISIA · Tunis · Nabeul · El Kef · Kairouan · Sousse · Sfax · Gabes · Houmt-Souk · Djerba · Zarzis · Ben-Gardane · Tataouine · LIBYA

■ Important community
● Community
French territory
French protectorate
Spanish protectorate

100 km.

*2. North African jewelry, 19th–20th centuries.*

The change in the legal status of the Jews in Muslim countries was part of a general process of westernization which took place in these societies between the end of the eighteenth century and World War I. Basically, this meant the revocation of the Covenant of Omar – the series of regulations applied to the *dhimmis* (protected Christians and Jews) from the days of the first caliphs. Indeed, the advent of European-influenced reform, which left its mark on all countries in the Middle East and North Africa (except Yemen and Iran), brought with it considerable improvement in the social and political status of the Jews throughout the Muslim world. The western powers concerned themselves with the "Jewish question" in the Islamic countries as they did with the Christian or Greek minorities, not only out of pure humanitarian considerations. Dealing with these minorities conveniently served as a means of intervention and control in regions of great strategic and economic importance. Sultan Abd Al-Majid's proclamation of two important decrees: the *Hatt-i-Sherif* (1839) and the *Hatt-i-Humayun* (1856), which inaugurated a whole series of measures granting equal

| Ottoman reforms | Blood-libel affair in Damascus |
|---|---|
| **1839** | **1840** |

**1830:** Conquest of Algeria; the Jewish population numbers about 17,000; many emigrate to Palestine.
**1839:** The first reform declared by Abd al-Majid, sultan of Turkey – the *Hatt-i-Sherif* – proclaims the equal rights of non-Muslims; at the same time, however, it limits the autonomy of the communities by reinforcing state control over their institutions, for example by nominating the chief rabbi (*Hakham Bashi*). The conversion of Meshed: Jews of this Iranian town are forced to embrace Islam.
**1840:** Sir Moses Montefiore and Adolphe Cremieux visit the Middle East following the blood-libel affair in Damascus.
**1845:** Abolition of the traditional organization of the Algerian communities and their replacement by consistories according to the French model.
**1856:** The Batto Sfez affair in Tunisia. The second reform declaration in the Ottoman Empire – the *Hatt-i-Humayun* – promises religious freedom to all communities, the

*3. Adolphe Cremieux (1796–1880).*

right to build new houses of prayer, open schools and charity institutions; it also ordered the omission of all humiliating references in official documents, and, most importantly, the abolition of the *Jizya* – the special poll

rights for all communities (*millets*) in the Ottoman Empire, were issued as a concession to European pressure.

Emancipation in Tunisia was precipitated by the Batto Sfez affair, which concerned a Jewish coach-driver executed in 1856 for having blasphemed Islam. Scandalized, Jews and Europeans in Tunisia sent a delegation to Napoleon III requesting his protection. The Emperor responded immediately: he sent a squadron ordering the commander to instruct the bey to implement the principles of the *Hatt-i-Humayun*. On September 9, 1857, the "Pacte Fondamental" proclaimed equal rights to all Tunisian subjects, freedom of religion, and the abolition of the *jizya* – the humiliating poll tax imposed on the *dhimmis*. The Muslim masses, however, regarded the pact as further evidence of capitulating to the Christian west, and an insurrection of tribes broke out. While it did manage to suspend the pact, the revolt also led to increased European pressure and eventually to the establishment of the French Protectorate in Tunisia in 1881.

In Morocco the situation was even worse. The reigns of Mulay Abd al-Rahman (1822–1859) and his successors were marked by the pressure of the Christian powers, and by increased Jewish involvement in the economic and diplomatic spheres. As a result, Moroccan hostility towards the Jews only increased. During the Spanish-Moroccan War of 1860, anti-Jewish pogroms took place in several towns. Prohibitive measures even more severe than the restrictions of Muslim law were imposed upon the Jewish populace in the interior. Although Mulay Muhammad IV, in response to a plea by Sir Moses Montefiore, promulgated a *dahir* (royal decree) granting the Jews equal rights in 1864, there was no significant change in their status, which continued to be determined by the terms of the Covenant of Omar. The royal decree was ignored by local magistrates and pashas who accused the Jews of being agents of European influence. As the date of the imposition of the French Protectorate approached (1912), attacks on Jewish communities intensified.

The Jews in all Muslim lands, caught in the vicious circle of pervasive European influence and the rise of hostility against it, had no alternative but to seek the protection of the western powers. Therefore, the emancipation of these communities was entirely different from the process in Europe. Rather than aspire to citizenship and integration with the local society, the "Jews of Islam" measured their social success and emancipation by the distance placed between themselves and the native population. From this point of view, Algeria constitutes a perfect model. Forty years after the conquest, the Cremieux Decree (1870) granted the Jews of Algeria French citizenship with all its rights and obligations. Thus France erased at a stroke their previous humiliating status as *dhimmis*, elevating them to the status of European colonists, and completely distinguishing them from their Muslim neighbors, who remained simple "subjects."

17 — CONSTANTINE. Une Rue du Quartier des Juifs. ND Phot.

1. In the Jewish quarter of Constantine, Postcard, early 20th century.

| The Tunisian "Pacte Fondamental" | The Cremieux Decree | Morocco becomes a French protectorate |
|---|---|---|
| **1857** | **1870** | **1912** |

tax on non-Muslims; the latter, however, was immediately replaced by a special tax in lieu of conscription.
**1857:** The "Pacte Fondamental" in Tunisia grants equal rights to Jews.
**1862:** Founding of the first *Alliance Israelite Universelle* school in Morocco.
**1863:** The first Alliance school in Istanbul.
**1864:** Montefiore's visit to Morocco. Suspension of the "Pacte Fondamental" in Tunisia. Reorganization of the Jewish courts in the Ottoman Empire (*Hakham Khane*). First Alliance school in Baghdad.
**1869:** The Alliance begins its activities in Aleppo and Beirut.
**1870:** The Cremieux Decree grants French citizenship to the Jews of Algeria.
**1876:** Founding of the mutual-aid organization of the Jews of Tunisia; restriction of their autonomy. The establishment of the Ottoman parliament; the Jews are represented in the parliament and in local councils, and admitted to high positions in the government.

Les Affaires sont les affaires

Simon! Simon!... Vas-tu rentrer, Ti en as pas honte, de jouer comme ça l'argent... dans la rue... vie dès petit: voious?
Mai papa... ji gagne.
Tu gagnes!... mon fils... continue!... autrement j'ti donne un coup de souf-flet!...

4. An antisemitic caricature.

**1877:** Anti-Jewish riots in southern Morocco.
**1878:** First Alliance school in Tunisia.
**1880:** The Madrid Conference imposes restrictions on the system of granting European protection to Moroccan Jews.
**1895:** The opening of an Alliance school in Libya is resented by some of the more orthodox Jews in Tripoli.
**1897–1901:** Anti-Jewish riots in Algeria.
**1897:** The First Zionist Congress in Basle marks the beginnings of Zionist activities in North Africa and the Near East.
**1901:** The Alliance opens an agricultural school in Djedaida in Tunisia.
**1906:** The Conference of Algeria defines the demarcation lines between the French and the Spanish zones of influence in Morocco.
**1908:** Jews take an active part in the revolution of the Young Turks.
**1911:** B'nai B'rith establishes its first lodges in Istanbul.
**1912:** On the eve of the proclamation of the French Protectorate in Morocco, anti-Jewish riots break out in Fez.

# Modern Antisemitism

In a pamphlet published in 1873, *Der Sieg des Judentums uber das Germanentum* ("The Victory of Judaism over Germandom"), Wilhelm Marr, the German political agitator, coined the term "antisemitism." Fortuitous though it may have been, the coincidence of the invention of the word and the manifestations of what could be considered early modern antisemitism, was certainly very symbolic. Themes and notions of a whole new kind were now grafted upon traditional anti-Judaism.

It should be emphasized, however, that anti-Jewish attitudes based on traditional theological and economic reasons were still widespread throughout European society, mostly among the peasant population. They were still voiced in western and central Europe, but were particularly prevalent in eastern Europe and the Balkans. Modern antisemitism, on the other hand, was especially potent in those lands and those sectors of society which were undergoing a rapid process of industrialization and urbanization. Without actually supplanting the older hatreds, it was the new themes which now came to the fore in the more advanced societies. The early 1870s constituted the formative years of the novel phenomenon.

Several socio-economic, cultural, and political elements converged to give birth to modern antisemitism. The process of desegregation of the Jews in western and central Europe was undoubtedly an important factor. The growing presence of Jews in the larger urban centers, their rapid social ascent, their visibility in the liberal professions, in the world of finance, in the press, and in the arts, as well as in left-wing political movements, provoked violent reactions. These reactions were exacerbated by fantasies entirely divorced from reality: the Jewish minority, representing between 0.3% to 1% of society at large, was described as an occult force, manipulating both capitalism and revolution in order to achieve domination over all nations. This was the central theme of *La France juive* by Edouard Drumont (1886) and of the "pioneering" work of

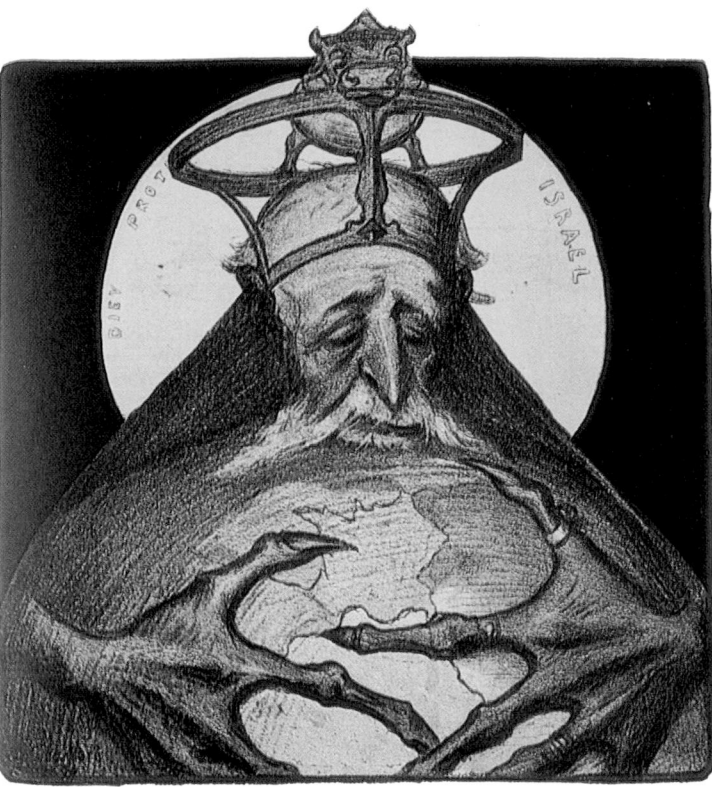

1. Rothschild, a French caricature by C. Leandre. 1898.

the Fourierist Alphonse Toussenel, *Les Juifs, rois de l'epoque* ("The Jews, Kings of the Era," 1845). The negative, often diabolical, stereotype of the Jew inherited from medieval Christian anti-Judaism, far from disappearing in modern times, reemerged in secularized versions.

The multiple forms of modern antisemitism could be grouped in two general categories. Animosity against the Jews based on the economic, social, and cultural reasons mentioned above, was translated into political terms: the demand to curb the alleged influence of the Jews by forcing them to assimilate into the local society was tantamount to a call for their complete disappearance as a separate entity (religious, ethnic, and cultural). French antisemitism, repeatedly boosted by the crash of the *Union Générale* (1882), the Panama scandal (1889), the Dreyfus affair, and the agitation of the *Action Française* and other antisemitic movements, remained confined, on the whole, to this first category.

Germany, on the other hand, witnessed the appearance of racial antisemitism. Although still marginal, and often still based on older arguments, this was nonetheless a phenomenon in its own right. Racist theories, originating in various national constellations, seemed to offer a neat solution to the perennial "Jewish question." The Jews could now be depicted as an inherently destructive race, and the struggle between Aryans and Jews as an inexorable and merciless war. The better-known ideologists of racial antisemitism in imperial Germany were Eugen Duehring, Theodor Fritsch, Houston Stewart Chamberlain and Steinrich Class. Their political influence before World War I was minimal, but their ideas soon infiltrated social groups of every kind.

The Bolshevik menace, German defeat, economic chaos following World War I – all these constituted fertile soil for the growth and radicalization of antisemitic theories. These finally culminated in an exceptionally virulent form, in Nazi ideology.

| Alphonse Toussenel, *The Jews, Kings of the Era* | Arthur Gobineau, *Essay on the Inequality of Human Races* | Eugen Duehring, *The Jewish Question* |
|---|---|---|
| 1845 | 1853–1855 | 1881 |

3. Ein Gigerl kaufte nicht beim Schneider,
Sondern beim Händler seine Kleider,
Sehr billig, englische Fasson!
Doch bald zeigt sich der Schaden schon;
Der Stoff geht ein, Farb' ist nicht echt —
Na ja, dem Esel g'schieht ganz recht;
Er ist blamiert, wie 's jedem scheint — — —
Der Händler lacht — das Gigerl weint!

3. The swindling Jewish merchant and a gullible dandy. The illustrated Kikeriki, Vienna, 1897.

**1850:** Richard Wagner, *Das Judentum in der Musik* ("Judaism in Music"), a virulently antisemitic pamphlet.
**1853–1855:** Arthur de Gobineau, *Essai sur l'inegalite des races humaines* ("Essay on the inequality of the human races").
**1863:** Wilhelm Marr, *Der Judenspiegel* ("The Jews' Mirror").
**1867:** Creation of the double-headed monarchy of Austro-Hungary.
**1869:** Henri Gougenot des Mousseaux, *Le Juif, le judaisme et la judaisation des peuples chretiens*. This pamphlet by a "soldier of Christ," obsessed with Jews and demons, influenced the works of Eduoard Drumont.
**1878:** Congress of Berlin; in Germany, Adolf Stoecker founds the Christian Social Workers' Party; founding of the Antisemitic League, modeled upon similar organizations in Austria and Hungary.
**1879:** Wilhelm Marr founds the League of Antisemites which achieves little success.
**1879–1880:** A public disputation concerning the Jews and their role in the history of

4. Postcard. France, c. 1900.

# 19th Century

2. Amschel Rothschild financing the two parties in the Napoleonic wars. Frankfort, 1845.

---

**Edouard Drumont, *La France juive***

**1886**

**Houston S. Chamberlain, *The Foundations of the Nineteenth Century***

**1899**

***Protocols of the Elders of Zion***

**1903**

---

German culture takes place between the Jewish historian Heinrich Graetz and his antisemitic colleague Heinrich von Treitschke (*Ein Wirt uber unser Judentum*, "A word about our Judaism").

The great classical historian, Theodor Mommsen, reacts with *Auch ein Wort uber unser Judentum* ("Another word about our Judaism") in which he accuses Treitschke of creating a public disturbance.

**1881:** Mommsen and other intellectual celebrities sign a petition protesting against antisemitism (The Declaration of the Notables, published in the *National Zeitung* on November 14, 1888). At the same time, an antisemitic petition, bearing 225,000 signatures and calling for the "liberation" of the German people from Jewish domination, is presented to Bismarck. Eugen Duehring, economist, philosopher and antisemitic writer, publishes his *Die Judenfrage als Rassen-Sitten-und Kultur-Frage* ("The Jewish Question as a racial, moral, and cultural question").

5. Jewish women. German postcard, 1900.

**1881–1882:** Wave of pogroms in Russia and the Ukraine following the assassination of Alexander II.
**1882:** The first international antisemitic congress meets in Dresden.
**1886:** First edition, to be followed by innumerable others, of Edouard Drumont's *La France juive*.
**1887:** The first antisemitic deputy in the Reichstag, folklorist Otto Boeckel, publishes *The Jews, Kings of Our Time*, a pamphlet which sells a million and a half copies; three

years later, he founds an antisemitic popular party. Orientalist Paul Anton Boetticher, known as de Lagarde, publishes *Juden und Indogermanen* ("Jews and Indo-Germans").
**1889:** Bankruptcy of the Universal Company of the Interoceanic Canal; Drumont, who in the same year founds his Antisemitic League, stresses the role played by Jewish financiers in this "Panama scandal."
**1892:** Drumont launches the antisemitic journal *La Libre Parole* ("The Free Word").
**1893:** Theodor Fritsch, *Antisemiten-*

*Katechismus*; the Nazis would acknowledge Fritsch as one of their mentors.
**1894–1906:** The Dreyfus affair.
**1897:** Karl Lueger is elected mayor of Vienna on an antisemitic platform.
**1898:** Emile Zola publishes his famous *"J'accuse"* in *L'Aurore*. A National-Socialist Party is created in Bohemia.
**1899:** Houston Stewart Chamberlain, *The Foundations of the Nineteenth Century*; English by birth, French by culture, and German by sentiment, this champion of the Aryan race, Wagner's son-in-law, is one of the spiritual fathers of Nazism.
**1903:** First publication, in Russian newspapers, of *The Protocols of the Elders of Zion*: a document forged by the czarist secret police (the *Ochrana*), based on a French pamphlet directed against Napoleon III (*Dialogue in Hell between Machiavelli and Montesquieu* by Maurice Joly, 1864).
**1903–1906:** Second wave of pogroms in Russia and the Ukraine; Kishinev and Gomel (1903), Zhitomir (1905), Odessa (1906).

# Colonialism and Modernization

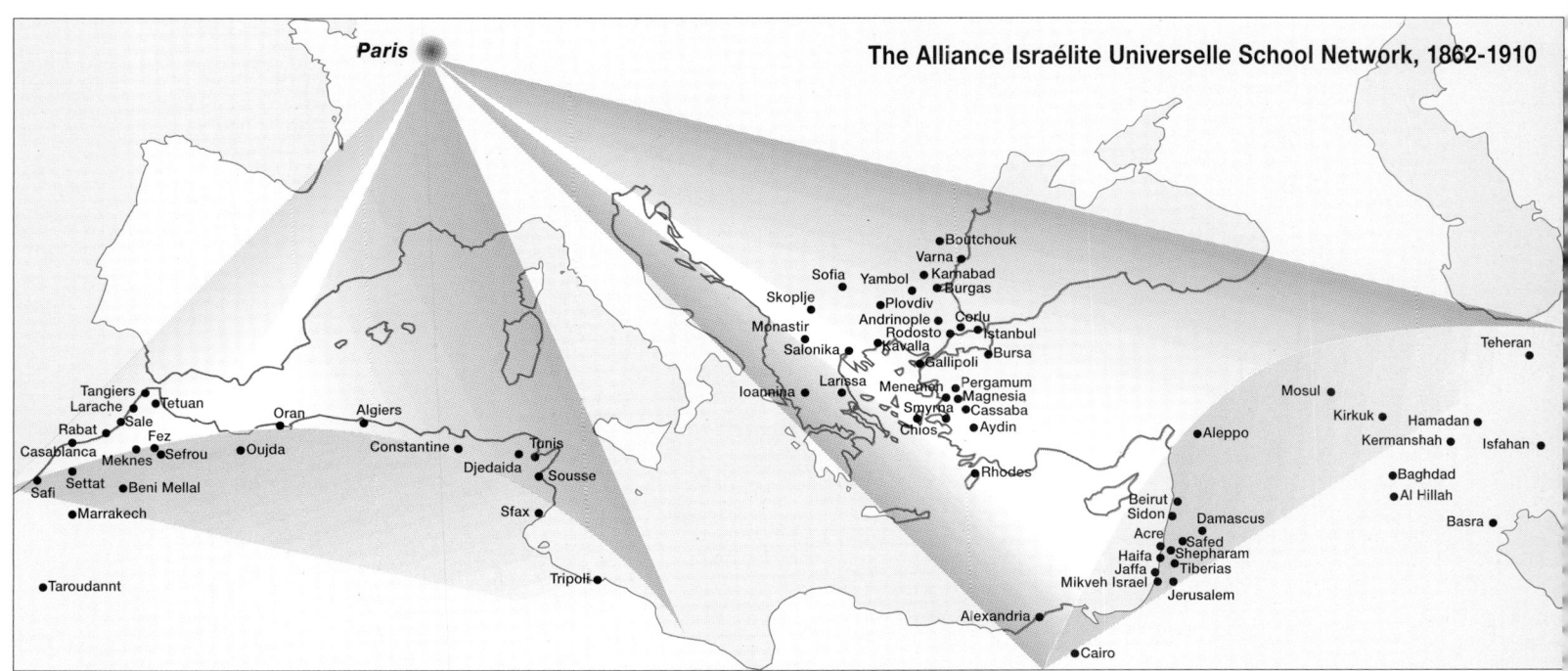

The Alliance Israélite Universelle School Network, 1862-1910

**M**odernization, brought to the Mediterranean world by the expansion of European colonialism from the early nineteenth century, affected all oriental Jewish communities with the possible exception of Yemenite Jewry. However, not all communities were affected in the same manner: enormous differences separated a community existing in a forcibly-secularized state such as Ataturk's Turkey from a community in a country like Iran, modernized only at a much later stage under the Pahlavi dynasty. Furthermore, there were significant differences between communities which found themselves under British colonial rule (Egypt, Iraq) and those under French domination (North African countries, Syria and Lebanon). In the latter, the transformation of social structures and lifestyle conditions of the Jews was far more drastic than in the former.

In Algeria, conquered in 1830, the encounter between Mediterranean Jewry and the West was accompanied by the most remarkable transmutation. In 1841 the 30,000 Jews of Algeria lost their traditional self-government in legal matters; community institutions were then replaced by consistories based on the model of this organization in the metropolis; chief rabbis were brought from France and paid by the government to assist in the process of acculturation; finally, in 1870, Algerian Jews were

1. Typing class in a Jewish vocational-training school in Casablanca, Morocco, c. 1950.

| Conquest of Algeria | Conquest of Egypt | Revolution of the Young Turks | French Protectorate in Syria and Lebanon | British Protectorate in Iraq |
|---|---|---|---|---|
| 1830 | 1882 | 1908 | 1920 | 1922 |

**1841:** Abolition of the rabbinical courts in Algeria.
**1845. November 5:** Establishment of consistories in Algeria.
**1854:** A new regulation in Alexandria separates religious affairs, reserved for rabbinical jurisdiction, from general administrative matters reserved for an elected committee. From 1872 onwards, the rabbi himself is elected by an assembly of community members, an example soon to be followed by the Cairo community.
**1857. January 1:** Inauguration of the railway between Cairo and Alexandria.
**1862:** Founding of the first school of the *Alliance Israelite Universelle*, in Morocco.
**1863:** The *Alliance Israelite Universelle* establishes its first school in Istanbul.
**1869:** Opening of the Suez Canal; thousands of Jewish immigrants from the Near East, the Balkans, and Eastern Europe flock to Egypt. In the same year, the Alliance begins its activities in Aleppo and Beirut.
**1870. October 24:** The Cremieux Decree

confers French nationality on Algerian Jews.
**1872:** The Turks conquer Yemen.
**1878:** First Alliance school in Tunis.
**1881. May 12:** The Bardo treaty institutes the French Protectorate in Tunisia.
**1882. July-September:** The British occupy Egypt and crush a nationalist revolt led by Colonel Urabi.
**1895:** The opening of an Alliance school in Libya provokes a split in the Jewish community in Tripoli.
**1896–1898:** Numerous municipal councils in Algeria fall into the hands of antisemitic parties.
**1901:** The Alliance opens an agricultural school in Djedeida, Tunisia.
**1908:** Revolution of the Young Turks.
**1910:** Tunisian Jews are authorized as individuals to adopt French citizenship.
**1911:** Italy conquers Libya. The first 25 years of Italian rule are a time of prosperity and

4. Apprentices at an Alliance Israelite Universelle school in Tunis, 1901.

2. Shiviti, *an inscription in the synagogue, named after the first words in the verse "I have set the Lord always before me" (Psalms, 16:8). Paper, Izmir, 1878.*

3. Jewish Moroccan needlework. Chameleon embroidered in gold and silver on a velvet cushion-cover. Fez, mid-20th century.

granted French citizenship in keeping with the terms of the Cremieux Decree. Naturalization led to complete emancipation, obliterating their ancient status as *dhimmis*, granting the Jews equal rank with the masters of the colony, a status much higher than that of most other European inhabitants of the country. As a result, the latter, regardless of their political orientation, were united by a virulent antisemitism. The 1880s witnessed a wave of pogroms and the rise of an antisemitic party. Such sentiments were given free reign under Vichy, when the Jews of Algeria lost their French nationality and were submitted to the yoke of the *Statut des Juifs* in the same manner as their brethren in France.

Admittedly, the French – like the English or the Italians elsewhere – had never intended to transform the position of the Jews to such a radical extent. Nevertheless, from Morocco to Libya and from Egypt to Iraq, the Jews' standing was completely altered. In all these lands they gradually abandoned their traditional occupations, and a new middle class emerged, initially comprised of graduates of the European schools. Established primarily by international Jewish organizations such as the *Alliance Israelite Universelle*, these schools were not open equally to all social groups: as a rule, they were founded chiefly in the larger urban centers, and served the more affluent classes of Jewish society who were able to afford proper education for their children.

By contrast, on the legal level, all the Jews benefited from the abolition of their traditional status as *dhimmis*, as the notorious Covenant of Omar was suppressed practically everywhere. Furthermore, although they did not all enjoy equal civil and political rights, all Jews in Islamic lands now enjoyed freedom of movement and had a choice of occupation. Yet, at least until the emergence of Zionism which changed their cultural orientation, the Jews tended to distance themselves from their Muslim compatriots, affiliating themselves to the colonial European minority, adopting its culture, language and behavioral practices. Therefore, with the notable exception of Jewish youth in Iraq, one rarely found Jews among the nationalist movements fighting for the independence of their countries. As these movements adopted pan-Arab and pan-Islamic orientations, they became even less open or attractive to the Jews.

Thus, contrary to what happened in Europe, in Islamic lands emancipation and modernization, both introduced by the colonizing powers, were acquired by the Jews at the cost of estrangement from the local population and of being identified with the foreign colonizer. This constituted an adequate reason in itself for the majority of Jews to decide to leave these countries once the process of decolonization had begun.

| The Pahlavi in Iran | Racist legislation in North Africa | Independence of Morocco and Tunisia | Independence of Algeria |
|---|---|---|---|
| 1925 | 1940–1942 | 1956 | 1962 |

progress for the Jewish community. In 1936 the Italians begin to enforce anti-Jewish legislation.
**1912:** France and Spain divide Morocco between them.
**1912–1913:** The first war in the Balkans; the Turks relinquish Salonika.
**1917:** Bloody scuffles between Jews and Arabs in the main towns of Tunisia.
**1918–1923:** Greco-Turkish war. The Turks abandon Iraq and Yemen.
**1920:** French Protectorate in Syria and Lebanon.
**1921:** Faisal is king of Iraq.
**1922:** British Protectorate in Iraq.
**1925:** The Pahlavi's accession in Iran. Kemal Ataturk institutes a secular state in Turkey.
**1932:** Iraq gains independence.
**1934. August:** A pogrom in Constantine.
**1936–1939:** The Arab Revolt in Palestine.
**1938:** Abolition of the capitulations regime in Egypt. Promulgation of the racist Manifesto in Rome.
**1940–1942:** Anti-Jewish legislation in all North African countries.
**1941:** Rashid Ali's pro-German *coup d'etat* in Iraq; in June, massacre of Jews in Baghdad and Basra.
**1948:** Proclamation of the State of Israel. Mass emigration of Jews from all Islamic countries in the Near and Middle East.
**1952:** Revolution of the "Free Officers" in Egypt.
**1953:** Beginning of Morocco's war of independence.
**1954. November:** Beginning of the war in Algeria.
**1956:** Morocco and Tunisia gain independence; The Suez Campaign and the Israeli-Egyptian war; deportation of thousands of Jews from Egypt.
**1957:** Habib Bourguiba institutes the Republic of Tunisia.
**1962:** Mass emigration of Jews from Algeria as the country gains independence.

5. Young Moroccan Jews on a picnic. Tangier, Spanish Morocco, c. 1910.

# State Antisemitism in Eastern Europe

After the partition of Poland, the Jews of Russia constituted the largest Jewish community in the world. Their legal situation during the nineteenth century was entirely subject to the capriciousness of the czarist regime. A traditionalist czar like Nicholas I, who wanted to confine the Jews to the Pale of Settlement, interpreted "integration" as "conversion." An "enlightened despot" like Alexander II, by contrast, wished to "reform" the Jews in order to integrate them completely into the empire's economy.

Until the mid-nineteenth century, hatred of the Jew in Russia was rooted in Christian tradition; after the 1850s it acquired new dimensions of modern antisemitism. The role played by Jews in the rise of capitalism, their penetration into inner Russia and their cultural integration, the emergence of radical ideologies and nationalist movements – all these combined into a strongly antisemitic climate of opinion, increasingly voiced after the Polish insurrection of 1863. Antisemitic slogans were regurgitated daily by the press, in literature, and in political discourse, representing the Jew as a parasite and exploiter of the peasants – an image accepted by radicals and conservatives alike. The great Fyodor Dostoyevski himself published a series of virulently antisemitic articles, describing the Jew as *piccola bestia* – a repulsive and venomous insect. And the czarist regime, which in the early days of Alexander II's reign had encouraged assimilation and even attempted to make use of the Jews as a "russifying" element in the western regions of the empire, now began reversing its policies. Nationalist and Slavophile tendencies were rife among imperial officials who openly encouraged antisemitic publications. Indeed, the word "pogrom" (Russian for "thunderstorm") was first used in 1871 to describe an attack upon Jews perpetrated by the Greek minority in Odessa. Nevertheless, the government still refrained from actually adopting blatantly antisemitic measures.

However, the assassination of Alexander II on March 1st, 1881, aggravated the Jewish situation even further. Anti-Jewish riots immediately broke out in southwest Russia and spread to the Ukraine. There is no clear evidence as to who actually instigated these pogroms; according to some they began upon the incitement of court agents. It seems that certain conservative circles in St. Petersburg took advantage of the czar's murder in order to attack the revolutionary movement by playing on the deep-seated hatred of Jews prevalent in the Ukraine. Ignatyev, Russia's minister of the interior, blamed the riots on Jewish control over commerce and industry. Alexander III, deciding "to defend the principal population from Jewish exploitation," imposed on the Jews severe economic restrictions through "Temporary Laws" promulgated on May 3rd, 1882 (and enforced till the revolution in 1917). Additional prohibitions were decreed during the last two decades of the century.

State and popular antisemitism reached unprecedented heights during the reign of the last czar, Nicholas II, in reaction to the rise in revolutionary activity. This was the time of the fabrication of the "Protocols of the Elders of Zion" by *Okhrana* (secret police) officials in Paris. These were also the years of major outbreaks of violence orchestrated by the "Black Hundred" – an antisemitic movement supported by the government. The pogrom perpetrated in Kishinev in April 1903 was far more savage and atrocious than any of the attacks in the 1880s. With the intention of deflecting revolutionary agitation, local and central authorities continued to encourage this anti-Jewish violence even after Russia's defeat in the war with Japan and the revolution of 1905. The pogroms did not abate until 1907, when the minister of the interior, Peter Stolypin, began to fear that matters were getting out of hand. An embryonic Jewish self-defense movement, and some loudly-voiced protestations by Russian and foreign liberals, also played a part in putting a stop to the massacres.

But although the pogroms ceased, a vicious antisemitic campaign persisted, culminating in the Beilis affair in 1913 – a ritual murder charge against a Jew from Kiev, carefully prepared by the ministry of justice. Turning into an international *cause celebre*, the Beilis affair became a symbol of the corrupt and reactionary nature of the czarist regime.

1. A caricature in Pluvium, a short-lived antisemitic journal. St. Petersburg, February 1907.

| Alexander II's reforms | Alexander II assassinated | H.N. Bialik, *In the City of Slaughter* |
|---|---|---|
| 1856–1863 | March 1, 1881 | 1904 |

**1825–1855:** Reign of Nicholas I.
**1827:** Jews are forcibly conscripted into the army under the Cantonist system: those aged under 18 are sent to military schools; children are delivered to the authorities by the community or "snatched" by special agents. Military and Christian education are some of the measures adopted by Nicholas I to solve the "Jewish Question."
**1835:** The "Constitution of 1835" limits the settlement of Jews to villages in certain regions and to some larger cities, prohibiting their residence near the western borders.
**1844:** Abolition of the *Kahal*, the Jewish self-government institution in Eastern Europe, and its replacement by government-appointed officials.
**1856–1863:** Alexander II's reforms: "useful" Jews are granted special privileges; admission of Jews to public office; encouragement of cultural assimilation and of economic activity outside the Pale of Settlement. Although intended only for the upper stratum of Jewish society, Alexander's

2. Destruction in a Jewish street after the pogrom. Ukraine, 1881.

reforms attract tens of thousands of Jews to towns in Russia's interior.
**1863:** The Polish Revolt persuades the czar to moderate his reforms, but strengthens his resolve to use the Jews as a russifying element against Polish nationalism.
**1869:** Jacob Brafman, an apostate from Minsk, publishes "The Book of the Kahal" – a Russian translation of the protocols of the Minsk community; the book provides ammunition for antisemitic accusations to the effect that the Jews are maintaining a "state within a state."
**1871:** A pogrom in Odessa; many assimilationist Jews begin to doubt the possibilty of integration.
**1877–1878:** The Russo-Turkish war; the press accuses the Jews of profiteering.
**1878:** A blood-libel affair in Kutais in the Caucasus.
**1881. March 1:** Alexander II is assassinated by revolutionaries.
**April:** Anti-Jewish riots begin in Yelizavetgrad and spread to other towns and townlets.

## Pogroms in the "Pale of Settlement" 1881-1906

Emigrations

1,500,000 to America and Western Europe

40,000 to Palestine

▼ First wave (1881-1884)
▼ Second wave (1903-1906)
→ Pogromists
☐ Self-defense

200 km

**First Russian Constitution**

**The Beilis trial**

**Revolutions**

**May:** Anti-Jewish riots in Odessa. Jewish students organize self-defense operations.
**August:** Special commissions are set up in each region within the Pale of Settlement to investigate the harm caused to the "principal" population by Jewish economic activities.
**December:** A pogrom in Warsaw. Members of the Polish nobility denounce the violence since they believe it aids the Russian cause.
**1882. January:** Count Ignatyev, minister of the interior, declares that Jews are allowed to leave Russia: a huge wave of emigration to the West.
**May:** A pogrom in Balta. The "Temporary Laws" are ratified by the czar, resulting in severe limitations on Jewish economic activities. Yielding to public pressure, the czar dismisses Ignatyev.
**1887. July:** A *numerus clausus* (quota) is introduced in secondary schools and universities.
**1889:** Jewish lawyers are forbidden to practice law without special permission from

the ministry of justice.
**1891:** The expulsion from Moscow.
**1903. April:** The pogrom in Kishinev: many Jews are killed, hundreds injured.
**1904–1905:** The Russo-Japanese war.
**1905. October:** The revolution compels the czar to proclaim a constitution. The Black Hundred, a government-supported antisemitc organization, instigates anti-Jewish riots.
**1906:** A pogrom in Bialystok, in northeast Poland; the army and the police collaborate with the rioters.
**1913:** The Beilis trial: the Russian ministry of justice tries to prove that the Jews use Christian blood in their rituals.
**1915. July 5:** Prohibition on Hebrew and Yiddish publications.
**1917. February:** The revolution radically changes the relations between the Jews and the regime; a wave of enthusiasm engulfs Russian Jewry.

*3. Krestin Lazar (1868–1938), Self-Defense.*

# Yiddish: The Dialect of Ashkenazi Jewry

*1. A pupil in an Agro-Joint school in the U.S.S.R in the 1920s or 1930s.*

Y iddish is the language which has been used by Ashkenazi Jews for the past nine or ten centuries. Drawing primarily upon a unique combination of German medieval city dialects, it has absorbed several other stocks (Hebrew, Aramaic, Romance and Slavic), often modifying them in an ongoing process of innovation. Named in the beginning *ioshn Ashkenaz* ("Language of Germany") or *taytsh* ("Deutsch"), Yiddish accompanied those who spoke it wherever they migrated to beyond the German-speaking lands of its origin. Despite its diversity in pronunciation, vocabulary, grammar, etc. resulting from contacts with new and variegated languages and cultures, Yiddish became primarily the hallmark of Ashkenazi Jewry everywhere and the vehicle for its folklore and cultural traits.

Until the end of the eighteenth century, Yiddish was the sole means of oral communication among Ashkenazi Jews. However, it also became an important medium of written communication. Alongside Hebrew, and using its alphabet, it produced an enormous range of literary genres: translations of scriptures and liturgy, biblical epics and drama, homiletic prose, religious poetry, fables, stories and legends, songs commemorating current events, historiography, memoirs, adaptations of non-Jewish literature. In order to be understood by Yiddish readers throughout the Ashkenazi diaspora, Yiddish writers developed a fairly uniform literary language based on Western Yiddish which did not reflect distinctions on the local level.

In the late eighteenth century, the *Haskalah* movement (the Jewish Enlightenment) began a drive aimed at persuading Ashkenazi society to use national languages. The campaign succeeded in most German-speaking countries, leading to an almost fatal decline in the use of Yiddish in the West. At the same time, however, the number of Yiddish speakers in Eastern Europe was growing rapidly. The old literary standard, increasingly remote from the living speech of the East European majority, finally collapsed in the 1820s and was replaced by a new standard based on Eastern Yiddish, enabling an effloresence of literary activity. Several Hasidic works, and some anti-Hasidic *Haskalah* literature, preceded the turning point marked by the emergence of the great "classical" Yiddish writers such as Mendele Mokher Seforim, Y.L. Peretz, and Shalom Aleichem. These were followed, in Eastern Europe as well as in the new centers of Ashkenazi Jewry, America and Israel, by a tremendous proliferation of Yiddish writers. This modern corpus of literature deals, through the entire spectrum of genres, with all aspects of life in general, the predicament of Jews, and the overall dilemmas of modernity.

Active printing presses and publishing firms, the emergence of a vigorous theater, secular educational networks, teacher-training schools and research institutes, all used Yiddish in a wide variety of new functions. The estimated number of Yiddish speakers on the eve of World

*2. Eliezer Lissitzy (1890–1941), illustration for "Had Gadya," an allegorical song in the Passover* Haggadah. *Watercolor and pencil on paper, c. 1918.*

War II amounted to 11 million, of whom about 7 million lived in central and eastern Europe and approximately 3 million in North America.

The Holocaust, the intentional annihilation of Yiddish cultural life in the Soviet Union, the acculturation of Jews in the West, and the renaissance of Hebrew as a national language, all led to a drastic reduction in the number of Yiddish speakers. Today Yiddish is still used as a vernacular mainly in Orthodox communities. Some Ashkenazi Jews, traditionally multilingual, have retained a knowledge of Yiddish, at least as their second language. However, while its use as a primary vernacular has almost disappeared, Yiddish literature is still being written, and the study of Yiddish language and culture is flourishing.

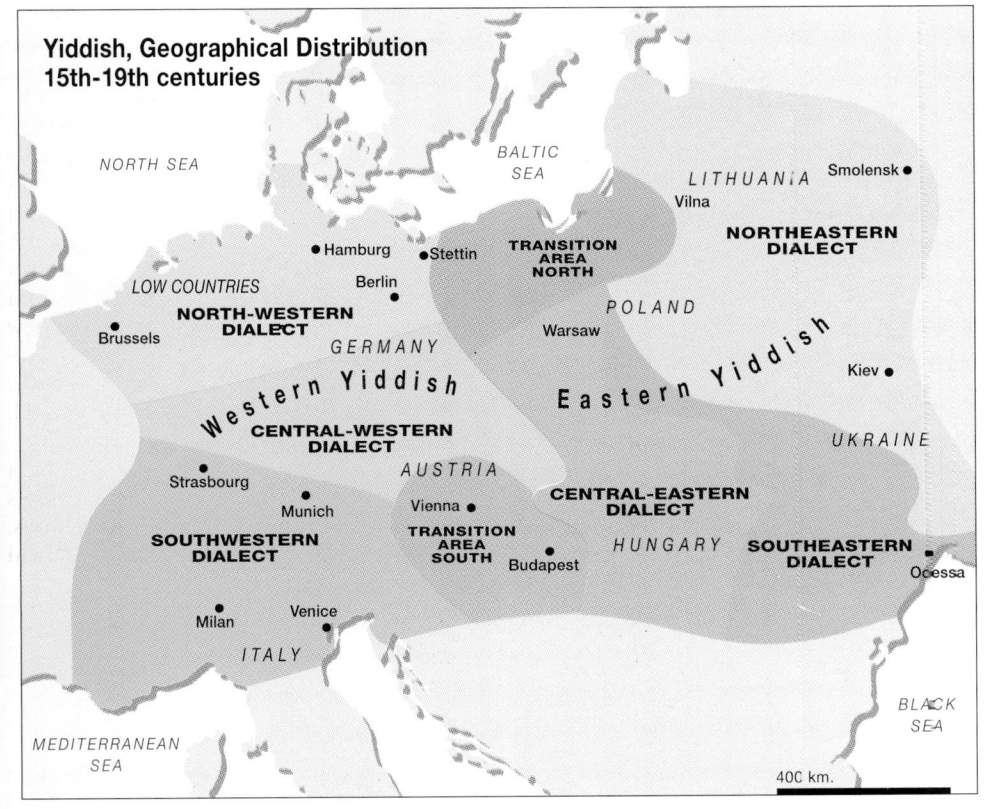

**Yiddish, Geographical Distribution 15th–19th centuries**

NORTH SEA

BALTIC SEA

LITHUANIA · Smolensk

Vilna

TRANSITION AREA NORTH

NORTHEASTERN DIALECT

· Hamburg · Stettin

LOW COUNTRIES

Berlin ·

POLAND

· Brussels

NORTH-WESTERN DIALECT

GERMANY

Warsaw ·

*Western Yiddish*

*Eastern Yiddish*

Kiev ·

CENTRAL-WESTERN DIALECT

UKRAINE

AUSTRIA

CENTRAL-EASTERN DIALECT

· Strasbourg

Vienna ·

Munich ·

TRANSITION AREA SOUTH

HUNGARY

SOUTHEASTERN DIALECT

SOUTHWESTERN DIALECT

Budapest ·

Odessa ·

· Venice

Milan ·

ITALY

BLACK SEA

MEDITERRANEAN SEA

400 km.

ל. קוויטקא

קארל און מיזרא

ביב

3. Leib Kvitko, "Karl and Mizra," From the Pioneer Book series. Kharkov. c. 1927.

| Period | Yiddish-speaking Communities | Historical Background | Linguistic Characteristics | Important Dates |
|---|---|---|---|---|
| Early Yiddish (before 1250) | Valleys of the Moselle, Rhine, Main and the Upper Danube Rivers. | In the Carolingian period, Jews settle in the valleys of the Moselle and Rhine rivers; the Crusades. | Western Yiddish composed of: Hebrew-Aramaic, Romance, German. | No written documents. |
| Old Yiddish (c. 1250–c. 1500) | Spreads to Bohemia and Moravia, Poland and Lithuania, northern Italy, Palestine and Egypt. | European expansion eastward; Slavic lands are opened to Jewish colonization, driven by the Black Death and expulsions from the large towns of Germany and Austria. | Appearance of a fourth component: Slavic; written language based on Western Yiddish. | **1272:** The earliest known Yiddish text: a two-line rhyming blessing from the Worms *Mahzor* (prayer book). **1382:** The oldest literary documents in Yiddish: a fable, and four short epics on biblical themes, found in the Cairo Genizah. |
| Middle Yiddish (c. 1500–c. 1750) | Spreads to western Alsace, Holland, northern Germany, and eastern Courland. | The Union of Lublin: southern and western Lithuania are annexed to Poland; the Thirty Years War; Chmielnicki's massacres and the Swedish Wars; dispersion of the Jewish population westward (*Landjuden*) and eastward (*shtetls*, villages). | Formation of Eastern Yiddish dialects which are distinct from Western Yiddish; yet the written language is still in the Western idiom. | **1469–1569:** Elijah Levita, called Bahur, born in Germany but lived in Italy, Yiddish writer, author of the first Hebrew-Yiddish dictionary. **1534–1535:** First printed books in Yiddish. **1622:** The fourth edition – and the earliest extant – of the *Zena u-Rena*: written in the late 16th century for women, this collection of commentaries and stories is the most popular book in the history of Yiddish literature (over 300 editions to date). |
| New Yiddish (c. 1750–) | Declines in western Europe, spreads in eastern Europe, Palestine and the Americas. | Spread of the *Haskalah* and of Hasidism; urbanization, secularization, waves of migration to the West and to Palestine; progressive political emancipation; World War II and genocide; liquidation of Yiddish culture in the Soviet Union. | Considerable enrichment of the language due to its use in new social situations (political movements, modern literature, newspapers, theater schools, science); a written language based on Eastern Yiddish; emergence of a Yiddish literary culture. | **1790–1860:** Abundant *Haskalah* literature: M. Lefin, J. Perl, A.B. Gotlober, I. Aksenfeld. **1815:** First edition of the *Stories of Nahman of Bratslav* and of the *Praise of the Baal Shem-Tov*, the principal Hasidic works in Yiddish. **1862:** First Yiddish journal (with a Hebrew title: *Kol Mevasser*, "Announcing Voice"). **1870–1917:** The period of the "Classics." **1908:** A Yiddish conference in Chernowitz. Between the World Wars, an effloresence of modern Yiddish literature in Poland, the Soviet Union and the United States. |

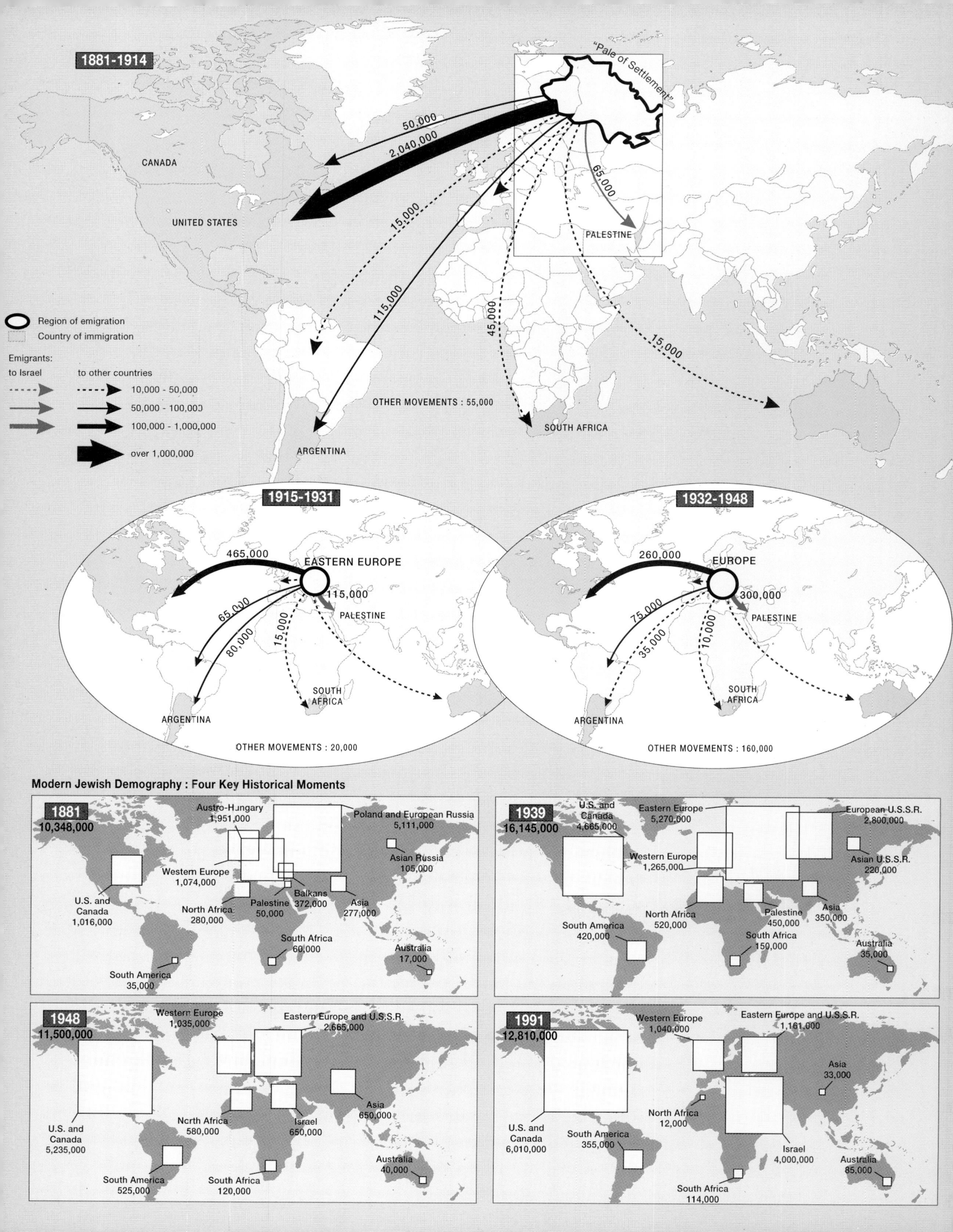

**1881-1914**

"Pale of Settlement"

CANADA

50,000

2,040,000

UNITED STATES

15,000

115,000

45,000

15,000

65,000

PALESTINE

ARGENTINA

SOUTH AFRICA

OTHER MOVEMENTS : 55,000

Region of emigration
Country of immigration

Emigrants:

to Israel | to other countries
--- | ---
 | 10,000 - 50,000
 | 50,000 - 100,000
 | 100,000 - 1,000,000
 | over 1,000,000

**1915-1931**

465,000

EASTERN EUROPE

115,000

PALESTINE

65,000

80,000

15,000

SOUTH AFRICA

ARGENTINA

OTHER MOVEMENTS : 20,000

**1932-1948**

260,000

EUROPE

300,000

PALESTINE

75,000

35,000

10,000

SOUTH AFRICA

ARGENTINA

OTHER MOVEMENTS : 160,000

## Modern Jewish Demography : Four Key Historical Moments

**1881**
10,348,000

Austro-Hungary 1,951,000

Poland and European Russia 5,111,000

Western Europe 1,074,000

Asian Russia 105,000

U.S. and Canada 1,016,000

North Africa 280,000

Palestine 50,000

Balkans 372,000

Asia 277,000

South Africa 60,000

Australia 17,000

South America 35,000

**1939**
16,145,000

U.S. and Canada 4,665,000

Eastern Europe 5,270,000

European U.S.S.R. 2,800,000

Western Europe 1,265,000

Asian U.S.S.R. 220,000

North Africa 520,000

Palestine 450,000

Asia 350,000

South America 420,000

South Africa 150,000

Australia 35,000

**1948**
11,500,000

Western Europe 1,035,000

Eastern Europe and U.S.S.R. 2,665,000

North Africa 580,000

Israel 650,000

Asia 650,000

U.S. and Canada 5,235,000

South America 525,000

South Africa 120,000

Australia 40,000

**1991**
12,810,000

Western Europe 1,040,000

Eastern Europe and U.S.S.R. 1,161,000

Asia 33,000

North Africa 12,000

U.S. and Canada 6,010,000

South America 355,000

Israel 4,000,000

Australia 85,000

South Africa 114,000

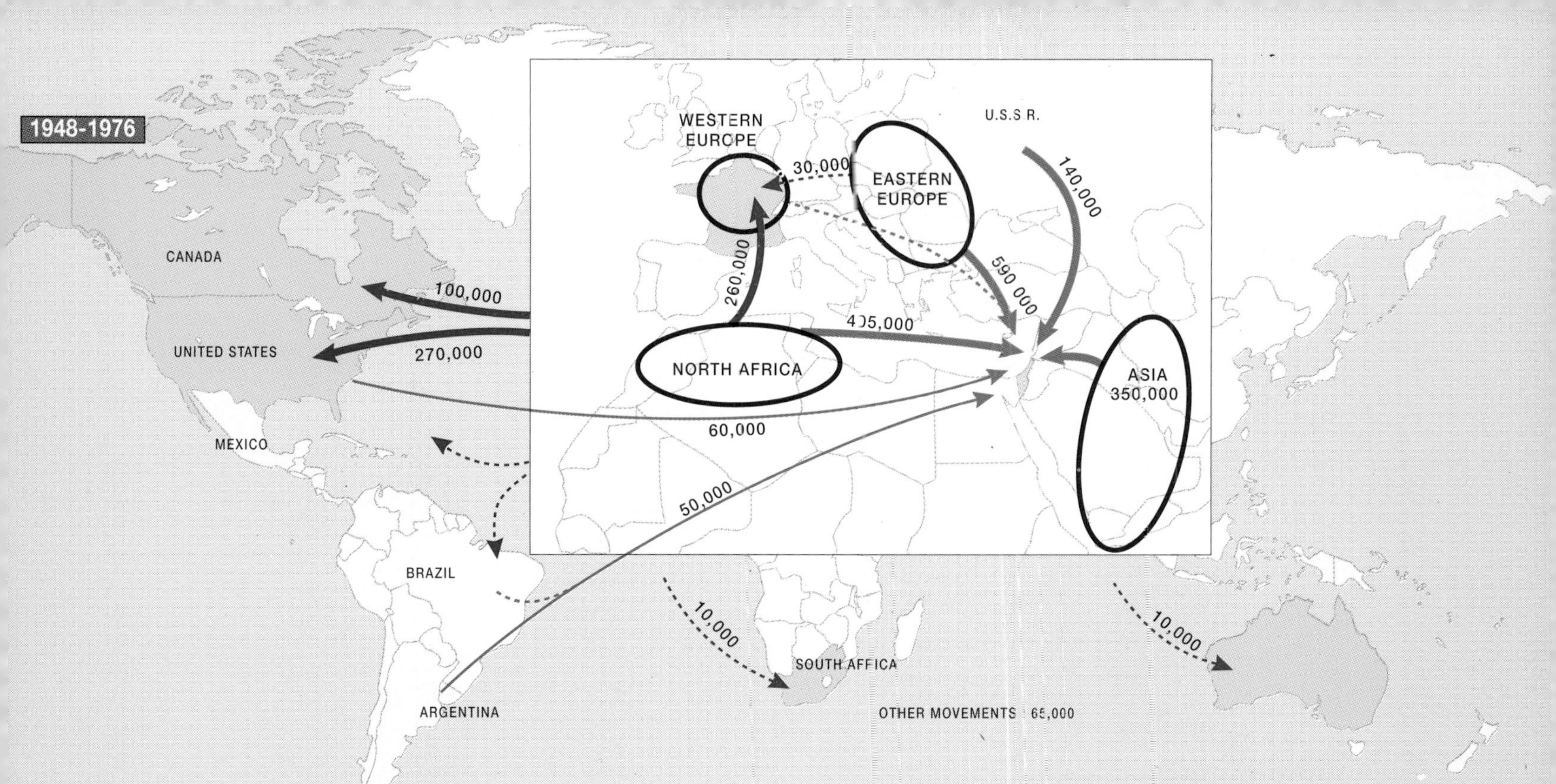

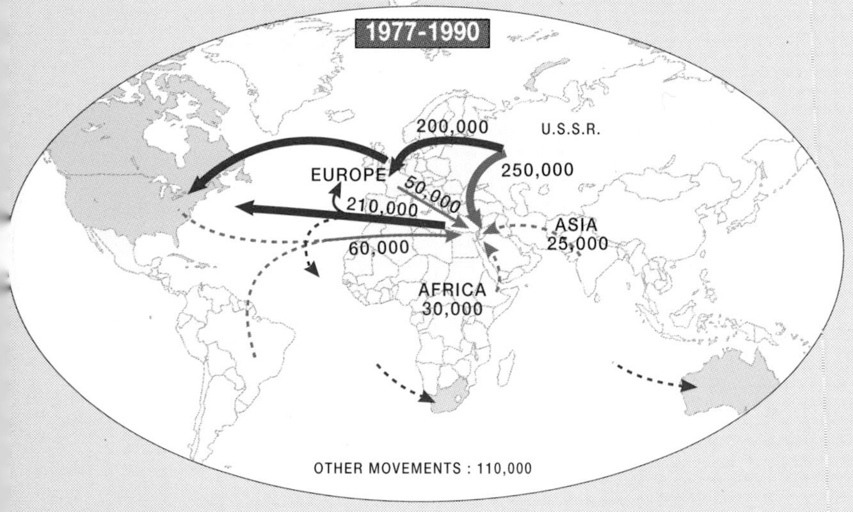

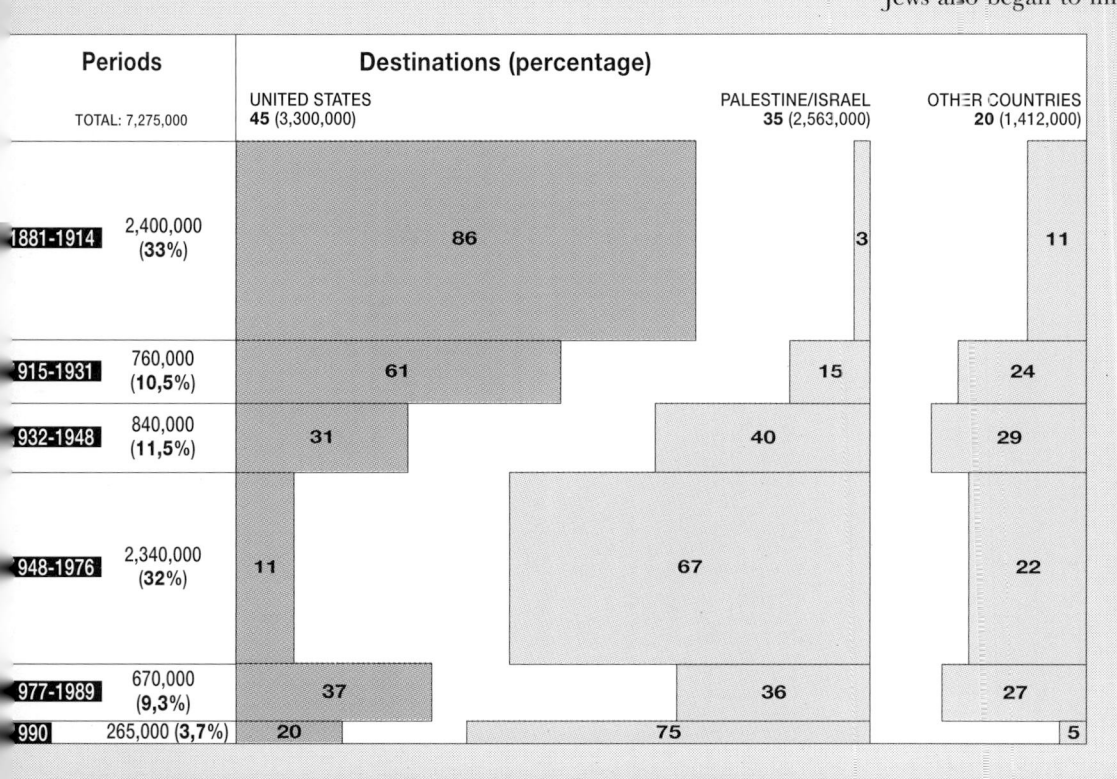

**1948-1976**

CANADA — 100,000
UNITED STATES — 270,000
MEXICO
BRAZIL
ARGENTINA

WESTERN EUROPE — 30,000 — EASTERN EUROPE
U.S.S.R. — 140,000
260,000
590,000
405,000
NORTH AFRICA — 60,000
50,000
ASIA 350,000

SOUTH AFRICA — 10,000
10,000
OTHER MOVEMENTS : 65,000

**1977-1990**

200,000
U.S.S.R.
EUROPE — 250,000
50,000
210,000
60,000
ASIA 25,000
AFRICA 30,000

OTHER MOVEMENTS : 110,000

# Migrations:19th–20th Centuries

O ver the last 150 years, about 7.5 million Jews have moved from one continent to another. In addition, there was considerable Jewish migration within continents. The mobility of the Jewish population was at first mainly within Europe, where the modern state gradually abandoned geographical restrictions traditionally imposed on Jews. From the mid-nineteenth century onwards, rapid demographic growth resulted in new tensions. Growing numbers impoverished the community which had, at the same time, to contend with the rising hostility of the environment, particularly in Eastern Europe. The combination of demographic, economic, social, and political factors resulted in large waves of emigration at the end of the century. In the 1880s immigration to America reached proportions of a massive transfer of population. A small percentage of European Jews also began to immigrate to Palestine.

In the 1920s and 1930s, however, the curve of Jewish emigration began to decline. The quotas in America, then the White Paper policy restricting immigration to Mandatory Palestine, closed the traditional havens precisely when emigration from Europe was becoming imperative. Until World War I, the United States had absorbed between 80 to 90% of the Jews emigrating from Europe; in the interwar years about a third went to Palestine, while growing numbers sought refuge in other countries of immigration: Canada, Latin America, South Africa.

When the "national home" in Palestine became a sovereign state, it was able to absorb the influx of Jews departing from postwar Europe and from all Muslim countries undergoing decolonization. Between 1948 and 1990, Israel received two million new immigrants. Finally, since the late 1960s, a large percentage of Soviet Jewry has been on the move. In 1989, the pace of departures from the Soviet Union and other East-European countries was accelerated, once more reaching the dimensions of the huge waves of nineteenth century emigration.

| Periods | Destinations (percentage) | | |
|---|---|---|---|
| TOTAL: 7,275,000 | UNITED STATES 45 (3,300,000) | PALESTINE/ISRAEL 35 (2,563,000) | OTHER COUNTRIES 20 (1,412,000) |
| 1881-1914 2,400,000 (33%) | 86 | 3 | 11 |
| 1915-1931 760,000 (10,5%) | 61 | 15 | 24 |
| 1932-1948 840,000 (11,5%) | 31 | 40 | 29 |
| 1948-1976 2,340,000 (32%) | 11 | 67 | 22 |
| 1977-1989 670,000 (9,3%) | 37 | 36 | 27 |
| 1990 265,000 (3,7%) | 20 | 75 | 5 |

# Jews and Social Utopia

1. *"The Jewish Worker,"* organ of the Pcalei Zion *party in Austria and Galicia, appearing in German and Yiddish. Vienna and Cracow, 1904.*

The remarkable prominence of Jews in all socialist movements, whether revolutionary or reformist, universalist or nationalist, is a phenomenon which requires explanation. Every generation during the past two centuries has produced a small but select group of Jewish youths who fought for the establishment of one form of utopia or another. Some scholars regard this utopian impulse as a modern secular version of the messianic tradition and of the promise for an ideal future implied in biblical prophecy. But it seems more reasonable to seek an explanation in more recent times. With the beginning of emancipation in the wake of the French Revolution, many Jews became impatient with the slow advance of liberalism. The universalist message, the vision of a just society, obviously appealed to members of a persecuted minority anxious to liberate themselves from the status of pariah and to join the "Brotherhood of Man." Rising expectations, frustrated by early manifestations of modern antisemitism, combined with demographic growth and expanding circles of secularly-educated youth intoxicated with the heady wine of new ideals, probably account for the fact that utopian aspirations became an intellectual hallmark of Jewish society.

Saint-Simon, founder of the earliest utopian socialist movement, considered the emancipation of the Jews an essential prerequisite for the liberation of humanity. It is therefore not surprising that among his supporters were many Jewish intellectuals and financiers. But it was in Germany that Jews became the pioneers of the first real socialist workers' movement. It was Moses Hess who converted Karl Marx and Friedrich Engels to the concept of historical materialism upon which communism was based (although Hess himself later became a precursor of socialist Zionism); and in 1863 another Jewish intellectual, Ferdinand Lassalle, founded the first actual workers' party in Germany.

In Russia, the socialist movement emerged when Jewish workers established the Bund – the General Jewish Workers' Union of Lithuania, Poland and Russia – in 1897. At the turn of the century there were numerous Jews among the leadership and cadres of all major revolutionary movements. Many of them, however, were assimilated individuals from multinational regions, and they honestly believed that once their utopia materialized, all ethnic differences would disappear.

There is no doubt that the disproportionately large presence of Jews in revolutionary movements served to aggravate anti-Jewish feelings among those sectors of European society who, as adherents of the old order, had every reason to fear a "brave new world." It was easy to pin these apprehensions on persons belonging to a people which had always been regarded as foreign among the European family of nations. The role played by Jews in the communist enterprise was to result in terrible

| First International | First Russian Revolution | October Revolution | Third International |
|---|---|---|---|
| 1864 | 1905 | 1917 | 1919 |

4. *Rosa Luxemburg speaking at a ceremony in memory of Ferdinand Lassalle during a Socialist Congress at Stuttgart, 1907.*

**1837:** Moses Hess publishes the first communist work in Germany: *The Sacred History of Humanity by a Disciple of Spinoza*.
**1848:** Marx and Engels publish the *Communist Manifesto*.
**1862:** Moses Hess, *Rome and Jerusalem* – a Zionist work inspired by the unification of Italy.
**1863:** Ferdinand Lassalle founds the General German Workers Association.
**1864:** The First International led by Karl Marx.
**1885:** *Ein Zukunftsbild* ("An Image of the Future") by Edmund Menachem Eisler, published in Vienna, is the first Zionist literary utopia.
**1892:** "A Journey to the Land of Israel in the year 2040," published by E.L. Lewinsky in Odessa, is the first Hebrew utopia.
**1897:** Founding of the Bund, an autonomist

Jewish party, which is also the first socialist workers'organization in Russia and the nucleus of the Social Democratic Party.
**1898:** Under the influence of Owen and Bellamy, Herzl begins writing *Altneuland*: a portrayal of the imaginary outcome of his Zionist efforts.
**1905:** The first Russian revolution; Trotsky leads the St. Petersburg Soviet; the *Ha-Po'el Ha-Tsa'ir* movement is founded in Palestine.
**1907:** Gustav Landauer, "The Call to Socialism," a manifesto of socialists who reject any form of government authority.
**1910:** Founding of the first kibbutz – Deganyah.
**1916:** The Zionist socialist movement, *Hashomer Ha-Tsa'ir*, is founded in Poland.
**1917:** The October Revolution; Trotsky is People's Commissar for Foreign Affairs.
**1918:** Revolution in Germany and proclamation of a Republic; Ernst Bloch writes "The Spirit of Utopia."
**1919:** Trotsky organizes the Red Army. The Third International is founded in Moscow. A

consequences: on the one hand, it gave credence to the antisemitic slogan of "Judeo-Bolshevism"; on the other hand, within the Communist world itself, thousands of Jews, regardless of whether they had been Communist activists themselves or simply supporters of Communism as the enemy of Fascism, were sacrificed to the Leninist-Stalinist Moloch.

Social utopianism also colored various Jewish nationalist movements. "If you will it, it is no fairy-tale" was Theodor Herzl's motto for *Altneuland* – the most famous of early Zionist literary utopias. Although considered "bourgeois" by Moses Hess and other committed socialists, there is no doubt that Herzl, and some of his predecessors in the Zionist utopian genre, were influenced by socialist ideologies prevalent in Europe during the second half of the nineteenth century: they shared the dream of creating in the Land of Israel a society based on social justice, enlightenment, and tolerance. The kibbutz, a concrete and lasting expression of the agrarian social utopia, was the creation of Zionist movements originating in eastern Europe, such as *Ha-Po'el Ha-Tsa'ir* ("Young Worker") and *Ha-Shomer Ha-Tsa'ir* ("Young Guard"). The utopian bent inherent in Zionism was manifested not only in the socialist movements which were predominant in the Palestinian *yishuv*, but also in the philosophies of major thinkers such as Martin Buber, spiritual leader of his generation and a partisan of a Jewish-Arab dialogue. The present collapse of Communism does not necessarily signify the death of social utopia – however, only the future will tell what form it will take and whether Jews will continue to play a prominent role in bringing it about.

2. "Down with the Czar's Constitution! Long Live the Democratic Republic!" A Yiddish poster, Russia, 1905.

3. "Long Live the October Revolution!" – a poster of the Socialist League of Ha-Shomer Ha-Tsa'ir.

| Moscow Trials | Fourth International | Establishment of the State of Israel | Students' revolution in Paris | Collapse of Communism in Eastern Europe |
|---|---|---|---|---|
| **1936** | **1938** | **1948** | **1963** | **1989–1991** |

year of revolutions in Central Europe: in Budapest (Bela Kun), in Munich (Ernst Toller and Eugene Levine), in Bavaria (Gustav Landauer), and in Berlin – the failure of the "Spartakusbund" revolution in this city leads to the assassination of Rosa Luxemburg and Leon Jogiches.
**1921:** Walter Benjamin, *Critic of Violence*.
**1922:** Ernst Bloch *Thomas Muentzer, Theologian of the Revolution*.
**1923:** Georg Lukacs, *History and Class Consciousness*.
**1930:** Beginnings of the Frankfort School – Max Horkheimer, Walter Benjamin, Herbert Marcuse, Theodor Adorno.
**1931:** Emma Goldman, an American-Jewish anarchist of Russian origin publishes her autobiography *Living My Life*.
**1933:** Hitler is Chancellor of the Third Reich; exile and deportation decimate the German-Jewish intellectual elite.
**1936:** Beginning of the great show trials in Moscow; Bolshevik leaders, many of them Jews, are executed.

5. *Karl Marx, a "modern Moses" descending from Mount Proletariat holding "New Tablets of the Law" (The Capital and the Communist Manifesto). Postcard, Paris, 1918.*

**1936–1939:** Civil War in Spain; among the 35,000 volunteers to the International Brigades, coming to fight for "your liberty and for ours," 7,000 are Jews from all over the world, including from Palestine (at the time in the throes of the Arab Revolt).
**1938:** Trotsky founds the Fourth International, some of whose leaders are Jews (Max Schachtmann, Pierre Frank).
**1940:** Walter Benjamin, having recently completed his *On the Concept of History*, commits suicide (?) in Spain. Trotsky is assassinated in Mexico by an agent of the G.P.U. (the Soviet secret police).
**1943:** The Warsaw Ghetto uprising led by young Zionists, Bundists and Communists.
**1945:** Martin Buber, *Paths in Utopia*.
**1948:** A utopia is realized: the procalmation of the State of Israel.

**1949:** Ernst Bloch, *The Principle of Hope*.
**1964:** Herbert Marcuse's *One-Dimensional Man*, which becomes essential reading for the new generation of students.
**1968. May-June:** Some of the leaders of the students' revolution in Paris – Daniel Cohn-Bendit, Alain Krivine, Benny Levi, and others – are young Jewish intellectuals.
**1969:** Death of the Hungarian Marxist historian, Georg Lukacs, who believed that he could "sacrifice his soul in order to redeem it."
**1977:** Ernst Bloch, "the Marxist philosopher of hope" dies in Tübingen. He had hoped to work for the moral revival of Marxism as a humanist teaching by integrating it with Christian eschatology and Jewish messianism.
**1981–1991:** Collapse of the ruling Communist parties in Eastern Europe. Modest beginning of Glasnost.
**1990:** In Barcelona, inauguration of a memorial to the Jewish fighters in the Spanish Civil War.

# Zionism

The roots of Zionism in its most potent form lay in Eastern Europe, notably within the confines of the Russian Empire. It was there, towards the end of the nineteenth century, that the largest and, in many ways, the most dynamic of Jewish communities was located – though it was also the most troubled. Conceived by the czarist autocracy as a major obstacle to its drive to transform the Russian population into a uniform and malleable society, Russian Jewry was subjected to extremely severe pressures to change its customs, culture and religion. In their customary way, the Jews tended to bear with the laws regulating their daily lives and cumulatively humiliating and impoverishing them. But when wholesale expulsions from certain areas and successive waves of physical attack were added to the long-familiar misery, life under Russian rule in the 1880s began to be judged intolerable.

The Jewish predicament precipitated several reactions, all with a view to finding a lasting solution: a vast movement of emigration, chiefly to the west; the radicalization and politicization of great numbers of young Jewish people, many bending their energies to the overthrow of autocracy; and, among the increasingly secularized *intelligentsia*, a rise in modernist national consciousness. It was the latter tendency – Zionism – that bore the most radical implications and was to have the most remarkable results.

The Zionist analysis of the nation's afflictions and its prescription for relief consisted of four inter-connected theses. First, that the fundamental vulnerability of the Jews to persecution and humiliation required total, drastic and collective treatment. Second, that reform and rehabilitation – cultural, no less than social and political – must be the work of the Jews themselves, i.e., that they had to engineer their own emancipation. Third, that only a territorial solution would serve; in other words, that establishing themselves as the majority population in a given territory was the only way to normalize their status and their relations with other peoples and polities. Fourth, that only in a land of their own would they accomplish the full, essentially secular, revival of Jewish culture and of the Hebrew language.

These exceedingly radical theses brought the Zionists into endless conflict with an array of hostile forces, both Jewish and non-Jewish. On the one hand, Zionism implied a disbelief in the promise of civil emancipation and a certain contempt for Jews whose fervent wish was assimilation into their immediate environment. On the other hand, by offering a secular alternative to tradition, Zionism challenged religious orthodoxy as well – although, given the orthodox view of Jewry as a nation, the two had something in common after all. The Zionists were thus condemned from the outset to being a minority among the Jews and lacking the support that national movements normally receive from the people to whose liberation their efforts are directed.

The other struggle which the Zionists had to face resulted from their political and territorial aims. They had to fight for international recognition and for acceptance as a factor of consequence, however small, by the relevant powers. In the course of time they have had to contend with the political and, eventually, armed hostility of the inhabitants and neighbors of the particular territory where virtually all Zionists desired to re-establish the Jewish people as a free nation: Palestine, or in Hebrew, *Eretz Yisrael*, the Land of Israel.

In the event, they were to be more successful in the broader international arena than on the

1. Three Zionist leaders. The farmer and the Western Wall symbolize the two aspirations of the Zionist dream. Children's sticker, 1906.

local front. Ottoman opposition hobbled the movement almost fatally in its early years; and the violent opposition mounted by Arab states and peoples has to this day shaped the physical and political landscape in which Zionism has implemented its ideals. In the final analysis, it is nonetheless the reluctance of the majority of Jews world-wide to subscribe to its program in practice that has presented the strongest challenge to Zionism, and has proved the greatest obstacle to its ultimate triumph.

| Leon Pinsker's *Autoemancipation* | Theodor Herzl's *The Jewish State* | First Zionist Congress | The Uganda Scheme |
|---|---|---|---|
| 1882 | 1896 | 1897 | 1903 |

**1881:** Serious aggravation of hostility, both popular and governmental, towards the Jews of Russia and Rumania, leading to a wave of physical attacks encouraged in most cases by the authorities.
**1882:** Leon Pinsker's pamphlet *Autoemancipation!*, calling the Jews to assume responsibility for their own destiny and to re-make themselves as a territorial nation, precipitates the founding of the proto-Zionist *Hibbat Zion* movement.
**1897:** The foundation of Zionism proper at the first Congress, convoked in Basle by Theodor Herzl: an unprecedented supra-communal parliamentary institution setting national goals to be pursued by political and diplomatic means. At the same time, however, it leads to the emergence of a wide spectrum of parties, groups and trends, ranging from the ultra-orthodox to atheistic socialism, from political pragmatism to moralist "spiritualism."
**1903–1905:** The first and greatest crisis of Zionism provoked by the "Uganda Scheme"

– the proposal made by the British government to establish an autonomous Jewish colony in East Africa (now Kenya). An opposition led by Menahem Ussishkin and Ahad Ha-Am, strongly objecting to such a departure from the established course, proved a stronger party than Herzl and his "political Zionists" and set the ethos of mainstream Zionism from that time on.
**1914–1918:** Concerned above all for the fragile *yishuv* in Palestine, the official Zionist leadership proclaims neutrality upon the outbreak of World War I. It is left to the movement's mavericks, such as Chaim Weizmann and Vladimir Jabotinsky, to see that the war and the interest of the belligerent powers in small nations have opened new political opportunities for the Jewish people.
**1917:** The Balfour Declaration: Britain's formal undertaking of support for the Zionist

3. Carpentry shop of the Zionist movement He-Halutz ("The Pioneer"). Galati, Rumania, 1922.

## Alternative Homelands

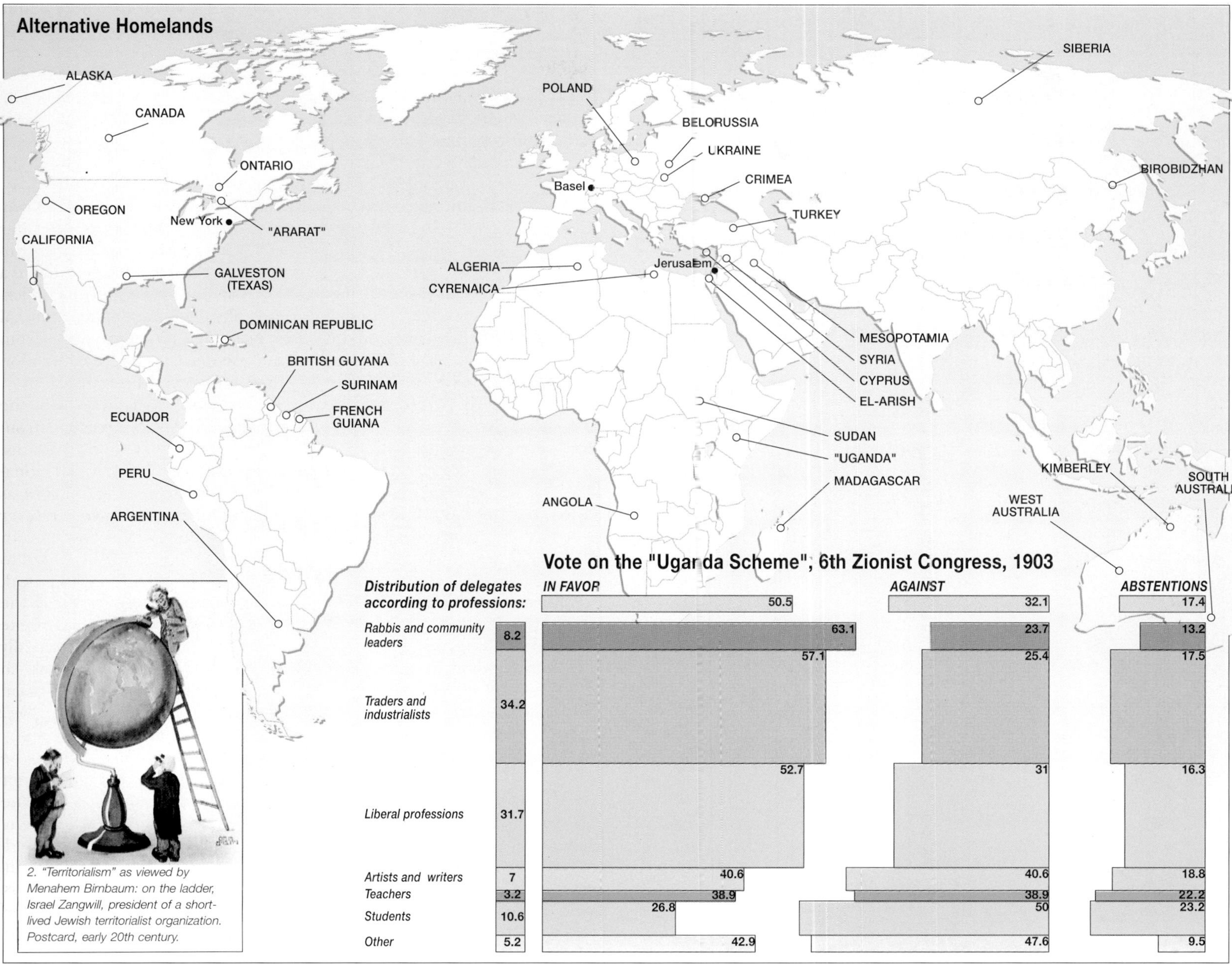

*(World map with labeled locations:)*

ALASKA, CANADA, ONTARIO, OREGON, New York, "ARARAT", CALIFORNIA, GALVESTON (TEXAS), DOMINICAN REPUBLIC, BRITISH GUYANA, SURINAM, FRENCH GUIANA, ECUADOR, PERU, ARGENTINA, POLAND, BELORUSSIA, UKRAINE, Basel, CRIMEA, TURKEY, SIBERIA, BIROBIDZHAN, Jerusalem, ALGERIA, CYRENAICA, MESOPOTAMIA, SYRIA, CYPRUS, EL-ARISH, SUDAN, "UGANDA", MADAGASCAR, ANGOLA, KIMBERLEY, WEST AUSTRALIA, SOUTH AUSTRALIA

2. "Territorialism" as viewed by Menahem Birnbaum: on the ladder, Israel Zangwill, president of a short-lived Jewish territorialist organization. Postcard, early 20th century.

### Vote on the "Uganda Scheme", 6th Zionist Congress, 1903

| Distribution of delegates according to professions: | | IN FAVOR | AGAINST | ABSTENTIONS |
|---|---|---|---|---|
| | | 50.5 | 32.1 | 17.4 |
| Rabbis and community leaders | 8.2 | 63.1 | 23.7 | 13.2 |
| | | 57.1 | 25.4 | 17.5 |
| Traders and industrialists | 34.2 | | | |
| | | 52.7 | 31 | 16.3 |
| Liberal professions | 31.7 | | | |
| Artists and writers | 7 | 40.6 | 40.6 | 18.8 |
| Teachers | 3.2 | 38.9 | 38.9 | 22.2 |
| Students | 10.6 | 26.8 | 50 | 23.2 |
| Other | 5.2 | 42.9 | 47.6 | 9.5 |

---

### The Balfour Declaration
**1917**

### The British Mandate
**1920–1922**

### First partition plan
**1937**

### Last Zionist Congress before the War
**1939**

4. Poster for the Palestine Exhibition organized in Vienna during the 14th Zionist Congress, August 1925.

cause, a typical piece of war-time calculation and a product of the rivalry between two powers over control in the region, transforms the prospects of the movement.
**1920–1922:** The Jewish *yishuv* in Palestine is allowed to grow and develop socially and culturally under the British Mandate; its Arab and, increasingly, its British opponents, see and fear it as a state within a state.
**1923–1925:** Publication of Ahad Ha-Am's collection of essays, *Al Parashat Derakhim*. Ahad Ha-Am, ("One of the People," pseudonym of Asher Ginsberg, 1856–1927) represented the pragmatic opposition to Herzl's Zionism: he distrusted the attempt to carry out the great Zionist enterprise prematurely; he did not present the vision of the ingathering of the exiles even as an ultimate long-term goal; he believed that those who would settle in Palestine would

5. "They that sow in tears shall reap in joy" (Psalms 126:5). Emblem of the 6th Zionist Congress held in Basle in 1903

serve as a "spiritual center" for the diaspora; one of the reasons for his limited program was consideration for the national rights of the Palestinian Arabs. Ahad Ha-Am prompted debates and influenced every stream of Zionism.

**1936–1937:** Upon the outbreak of a large-scale Arab rebellion, the sense of endemic conflict is pervasive. The proposal of the Royal (Peel) Commission to divide the country into an Arab state, a Jewish state and areas to be retained by the British. The proposal, the most serious of the many attempts to resolve the conflict, is reluctantly accepted by the official Zionist leadership, rejected by the Arabs and ultimately by the British government as well.
**1939:** British policy is decisively reversed: drastic limitations on Jewish immigration and purchase of land.
**August:** The Zionist Congress convenes in Geneva: it is the last Congress to reflect the Zionist movement in its original form – a national movement rooted above all in the historical background of East European Jewry. The Congress disperses in haste: in addition to all previous clouds hanging over the Zionist movement, the large majority of the Jewish people are facing dangers of an unprecedented kind.

# Hebrew: A Sacred and Secular Language

*1. Direction: "Hebrew." Poster of the cultural services of the Israeli Army in the 1950s.*

*3. A Hebrew book fair. Tel Aviv, 1926.*

**H**ebrew belongs to the family of Semitic languages. Although its origins are obscure, the Bible testifies to its antiquity: by the late second millennium BC, it was already completely formed. The Bible, however, is a collection of literary texts of diverse genres, and thus we may only conjecture how Hebrew was spoken in biblical times. We know much more about the second stratum, Mishnaic Hebrew, which evolved from the biblical language during the Second Temple Period. This "language of the Sages" was both written and spoken till about 200 AD when, it apparently, ceased to be used as a vernacular. But, while it was succeeded by both Aramaic and Greek as a spoken language, Hebrew continued to evolve as a literary vehicle. The Middle Ages in Spain, North Africa and Provence were a period of extensive literary and scientific creation in Hebrew. Throughout the Exile, however, at least till the end of the nineteenth century, it was exclusively a written language and a sacred tongue: the language of the Torah, of rabbinical studies and of the Halakhah, of prayer and liturgy.

The transformation of Hebrew into a modern language was the work of the *Haskalah*, first in Germany in the early eighteenth century, then in Russia and Poland. The *maskilim*'s desire to bring the Enlightenment to the Jewish masses coincided with the rise of nationalism in Europe in the mid-nineteenth century. The *maskilim* preferred Hebrew, the language spoken in times of national sovereignty, and despised Yiddish, the jargon of the Exile. Wishing to make Hebrew a vehicle of expression for all fields of knowledge, the *maskilim* refined its forms and enriched its vocabulary. At first they attempted to write in a "pure" biblical style. The first modern Hebrew novel, *Ahavat Ziyyon* ("The Love of Zion," 1853) by Abraham Mapu, takes the reader on a fascinating journey to the Land of Israel during the First Temple Period, in the language of the Judges, the Kings, the Levites, and the prophets. Yet, since there was a need to write texts other than literature and poetry, the *maskilim* had to innovate and coin new words. Towards the late nineteenth century, a "synthetic" Hebrew emerged, integrating the different strata of the language – biblical, Mishnaic, medieval – as well as foreign idioms.

Nonetheless, it was still only a written language. The invention of a living spoken Hebrew was the pioneer work of Eliezer Ben-Yehuda. In 1879, this Lithuanian Jew born in an Orthodox environment, published an article entitled "A Burning Question" in the journal *Ha-Shahar* ("Dawn"). For the first time the idea of a national spiritual center in the Land of Israel was clearly propounded, linking the return to the ancestral soil with the revival of Hebrew as a written *and* spoken tongue. But reviving a "dead" language was not an easy project. The first problem was pronunciation – should it be spoken in the Ashkenazi, the Sephardi or the Yemenite way? Eventually, the Sephardi pronunciation was chosen. A courageous decision, bearing in mind that the debate took place within

| First biblical texts | Final redaction of the Pentateuch |
|---|---|
| **13th century BC (?)** | **5th century BC** |

**Late 15th century BC:** The Tell el-Amarna letters (from lower Egypt), written in Akkadian, contain words and phrases later found in the Bible.
**13th century BC:** Exodus from Egypt; crystallization of Hebrew as a language particular to the tribes which invade Canaan. Several of the earliest biblical texts – Jacob's benediction (Genesis 49), Deborah's song (Judges 5) – are probably composed in this period.
**Mid-5th century BC:** The ancient Hebrew letters are replaced by the Aramaic "square" characters still in use today; according to the Talmud, this change can be attributed to Ezra the Scribe, one of the leaders of the Return to Zion (c. 458). Final composition of the Pentateuch.
**3rd century BC:** The Dead Sea Scrolls, mostly written in "square" letters, but in biblical style.
**200 BC–500 AD:** Mishnaic Hebrew, greatly influenced by Aramaic, the lingua franca of the Fertile Crescent, which also contained

many Greek and a few Latin words.
**c. 200:** Judah ha-Nasi completes the redaction of the Mishnah, the most important corpus written in the "language of the Sages."
**From the late fifth century:** Appearance of *piyyutim* in Palestine, religious hymns partly composed of biblical verses, constructed in their own particular literary and linguistic forms.
**c. 750–950:** In order to perpetuate the correct pronunciation of the Torah, the Tiberias scholars invent the system of Hebrew vocalization (*nikkud*), since previously written Hebrew had no marks for vowels.
**c. 902:** Saadiah Gaon composes the first Hebrew dictionary arranged alphabetically. Beginnings of systematic Hebrew grammar.
**10th–12th centuries:** "Golden Age" of Hebrew poetry in Spain; strong Arab influences reflected in its themes as well as in its literary forms; works on Hebrew grammar and lexicography.
**12th–13th centuries:** Emergence of

*Haskalah* circles which were purely Ashkenazi. Then the question of grammar arose, which Ben-Yehuda wanted to base on the Bible; but he was overruled. Modern Hebrew, at least in its system of tenses, is based primarily on Mishnaic Hebrew whose morphology is closer to European languages. Finally, the major difficulty was in the realm of vocabulary. Ben-Yehuda's rule was to search for an appropriate word first of all in the various strata of Hebrew, if necessary exploiting the lexicons of other Semitic languages (Aramaic, Arabic, etc.) by casting their roots in a Hebrew mold. Borrowing from non-Semitic languages was strictly forbidden, with the exception of words with Hebrew-like form, or those already in frequent use.

Disembarking in Jaffa in 1881, Ben-Yehuda anounced to his family that henceforth they would converse only in Hebrew. Having imposed this ruling on his household, he then sought to impose it on his people. But the road was far from smooth, and he met with opposition from various quarters. Numerous Zionist leaders, including Herzl himself in his *Jewish State*, refused to believe that Ben-Yehuda's dream was feasible. Objections were also voiced by Yiddish writers, including the greatest of them all, Mendele Mokher Seforim (who nevertheless was to become one of the great writers in modern Hebrew). And, of course, the Orthodox, who regarded

*2. A linguistic game invented by Levin Kipnis. Tel Aviv, c. 1922.*

the secularization of the sacred tongue as a profanation – how could they tolerate addressing a dog in the language of the Bible?

The principal arena of this struggle took place in the schools where Hebrew had to compete with German and French. In 1913, the "language conflict" which developed in the Technion, the technical college founded in Haifa by the *Hilfsverein* (the German equivalent of the *Alliance Israelite Universelle*) ended with the triumph of Hebrew. The monumental "Complete Dictionary of Ancient and Modern Hebrew," undertaken by Ben-Yehuda shortly after his arrival in Palestine, was completed only in 1958; but Hebrew was firmly established as a spoken language long before then. In 1922, the Mandate government proclaimed Hebrew one of Palestine's three official languages, alongside English and Arabic.

The Hebrew revival is a unique phenomenon in the history of nations. Ben-Yehuda and his followers have accomplished what others – Irish, Welsh Bretons and Occitans, who never left their native soil – failed to do. An amazing cultural achievement, the revival of the Hebrew language is also a major victory of the Zionist ideal: in a land of immigrants coming from the four corners of the earth, a national language is a paramount tool of unification. Adequate proof of this is the sight of a Russian child playing with an Ethiopian child, barely six months after their *aliyah*, talking to each other in Hebrew, their common language. In the words of Ephraim Kishon, an Israeli humorist of Hungarian origin: "Israel is the only country in the world where mothers learn their mother-tongue from the mouths of their children."

| Redaction of the Mishnah | "Golden Age" in Spain | Haskalah | Spoken Hebrew |
|---|---|---|---|
| c. 200 | 10th–12th centuries | 18th–19th centuries | 20th century |

*4. Eliezer Ben-Yehuda at his desk, photograph by Ya'akov Ben Dov. Jerusalem, c. 1912.*

Hebrew as a scientific language; translations into Hebrew by the Tibbonids of Provence; original Hebrew works by Abraham ibn Ezra and Abraham bar Hiyya.

**Late 15th century:** The invention of printing enriches the Hebrew library.

**18th–19th centuries:** The Jewish *Haskalah* in western and central Europe leads to a renaissance of Hebrew as a secular language.

**c. 1750:** Moses Mendelssohn's *Kohelet Musar* ("Moral Ecclesiastes"), a collection of texts regarded as a milestone in the emergence of modern Hebrew.

**1856:** *Ha-Maggid* ("The Declarer"), the first Hebrew newspaper, appears in Lyck, eastern Prussia.

**1860:** Founding of the organ *Ha-Meliz* ("The Advocate") in Odessa.

**1881:** Ben-Yehuda settles in Jerusalem.

**1886:** The first Hebrew daily newspaper appears in St. Petersburg: *Ha-Yom* ("The Day"), revolutionizing journalistic Hebrew – its style simple and precise rather than literary and stilted.

**1889:** Ben-Yehuda begins composing his great Hebrew dictionary.

**1892–1901:** Founding of Hebrew publishing houses in Poland and Russia.

**1913:** Ben-Yehuda's "party" wins the "language conflict" at the Technion.

**1922:** Hebrew is proclaimed one of the three official languages in Palestine.

**1949:** The first *Ulpan* – new immigrant adult center for the study of Hebrew.

**1953:** *Va'ad ha-Lashon* (The Hebrew Language Committee) founded by Ben-Yehuda becomes the Academy of the Hebrew Language whose functions include deciding on terminology and spelling, decisions which are accepted as binding for State institutions. The Academy also begins preparing an exhaustive Hebrew dictionary.

**1970:** D. Ben Amotz and N. Ben Yehuda publish the first dictionary of Hebrew slang.

*5. Hebrew Speech: a manual for the study of Hebrew by the natural method." Warsaw, 1905.*

# The Revival of Jewish Palestine

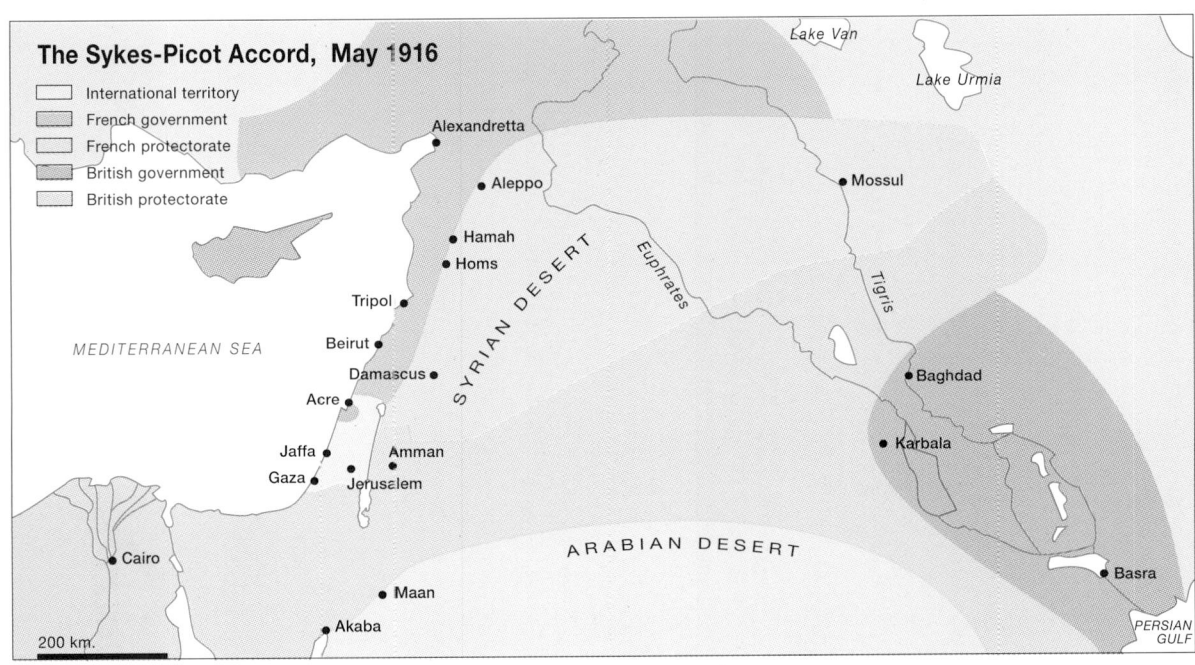

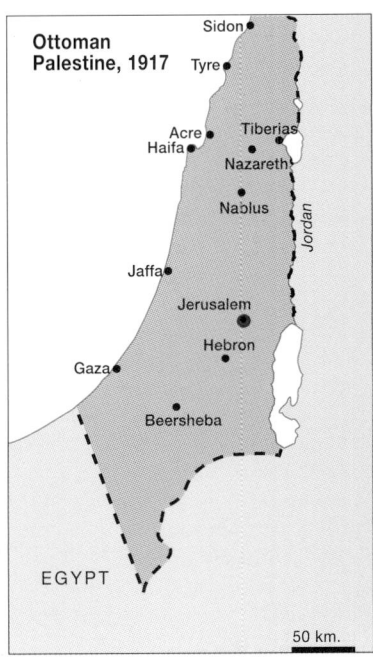

Strange though it may seem today, Palestine was not always considered the only possible site for the creation of a Jewish state and the ingathering of the exiles. From East Africa to Argentina, from Madagascar to New Caledonia, one could name thirty six regions throughout the world which at one time or another were regarded as possible territorial solutions to the "Jewish problem." Faced with the Ottomans' animosity and intensifying persecutions of East-European Jewry, even Herzl resigned himself to the idea of Uganda (Kenya, in fact) as a substitute for Palestine, a solution officially proposed by Lloyd George's government. Only after Herzl's death in 1904 the Seventh Zionist Congress in Basle finally discarded the African project, provoking by its decision the secession of an Independent Territorial Organization (I.T.O.), which was eventually disbanded in 1925. Henceforth, all Zionist efforts were centered on Palestine.

Between 1882 and 1948, the historical revolutionary process of recreating an incontestable Jewish center in the Land of Israel, was completed. The feeble trickle of settlers who began arriving in the 1880s managed within two generations to transform the *yishuv* (the Jewish community in Palestine) from a "national home" into a sovereign state.

Most striking was its demographic growth which increased rapidly as a direct result of Palestine's new status in Jewish history. Indeed, from the 1880s, this neglected province of the Ottoman Empire became a focus for Jewish immigration, which originated mostly from Eastern Europe: between 1881 and 1948, several *aliyot* (waves of immigration, literally meaning "ascents") radically transformed the composition of the population – from 24,000 the Jewish population grew to 630,000, over a third of the total population in Palestine.

Two principal processes led to the metamorphosis of Palestine. First, the Jews were rapidly losing faith in the possibility of integration into East-European societies, their hopes shattered by the rise of a nationalist fervor among the autochthonous populations, the increase of official and popular antisemitism, and the overall predicament of the Jewish masses. Indeed, after the extensive pogroms of 1881–1882 in Russia, each new wave of persecutions drove hundreds of thousands of Jews to emigrate.

The second process was the outcome of changes which had been affecting the Jewish elites since the emancipation. Zionism transformed messianic expectations and the religious "remembrance" of Zion into modern secular nationalism, which posited the Land of Israel as the "homeland," the concrete territory upon which the national and cultural unity of the Jewish people could be materialized.

| Balfour Declaration | British Mandate | U.S. immigration quotas |
|---|---|---|
| November 2, 1917 | April 1920 | 1921, 1924 |

**1881–1882:** Pogroms in Russia; beginning of mass emigration.
**1882–1903:** First *Aliyah* (wave of immigration).
**1882:** Leon Pinsker's *Autoemancipation*.
**1890–1913:** Ottoman restrictions on Jewish immigration to Palestine.
**1894:** Beginning of the Dreyfus affair.
**1896:** Theodor Herzl publishes *The Jewish State*.
**1897:** The First Zionist Congress convenes in Basle.
**1903:** Pogrom in Kishinev.
**1904–1914:** Second *Aliyah*.
**1906:** An Anglo Turkish agreement regarding the southern border of Palestine.
**1913:** The American women's organization, *Hadassah*, begins operating in Palestine.
**1916:** The Sykes-Picot agreement partitions the Ottoman Empire into British, French and Russian zones of influence; the "creation" of the Near East.
**1917 October:** General Allenby's troops invade Palestine; in December Jerusalem

surrenders.
**November 2:** The Balfour Declaration: the British government recognizes the right of the Jewish people to a National Home in Palestine.
**1918:** A Zionist Commission, headed by Chaim Weizmann, is sent to Palestine to assist the British in implementing the Balfour Declaration. In 1921 the Commission is replaced by the Zionist Executive.
**September 25:** Ottoman capitulation; Palestine is separated from other regions of the defunct Empire.
**December:** The third Constituent Assembly of the *yishuv* ensures the representation of the entire Jewish community in Palestine.
**1919–1923:** Third *Aliyah*.
**1920. April:** The San Remo Conference grants Great Britain the mandate on Palestine; this decision is ratified in July 1922 by the League of Nations.
**July:** End of the military regime in Palestine.

*2. Dinner at Kibbutz Kefar ha-Horesh, 1930.*

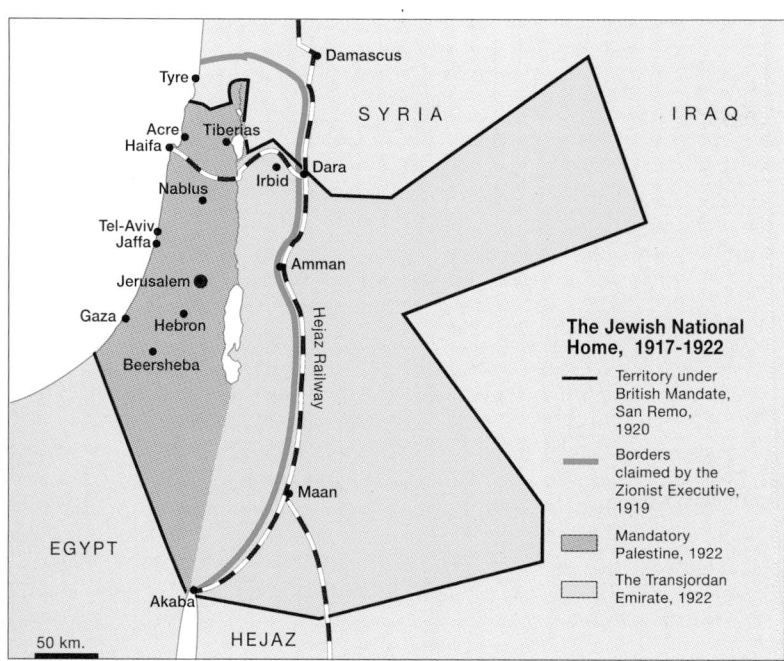

Admittedly, only a tiny minority (2–3%) of the 2.5 million European emigrants between 1882 to 1914 chose to go to Palestine. But these pioneers established a vital core for the absorption of future waves of immigrants who were less ideologically motivated. The British conquest, the economic prosperity that came in its wake, and the Balfour Declaration, all made Palestine seem like an attractive option. The advent of Nazism and the subsequent shutting of the gates of most western democracies, rendered Palestine the only safe haven for those fleeing Europe. When the United States, a major destination for many European emigrants, imposed immigration quotas, the percentage of Jews who now elected to settle in Palestine increased considerably. During the interwar years, 36% of Jewish emigrants went to the U.S., yet 30% found refuge in the Land of Israel.

The Zionist movement, whose weight was substantially increased as a result of all these developments during the interwar years, thus managed to transform the *yishuv* into a structured national entity. The importance of Palestine for the Jewish nation was constantly highlighted during the British Mandate, and became self-evident especially during, and immediately after, World War II. In this respect, the establishment of the State of Israel was simply the sanctioning of an already established fact.

1. Sports in the service of state building: poster of the Maccabi sports federation, 1936.

## "Illegal" immigration

### 1934–1939, 1945–1948

The country is now placed under the authority of the "Government of Palestine-Eretz Yisrael"; Sir Herbert Samuel is first High Commissioner in Palestine.
**1921, 1924:** Strict immigration quotas in the United States.
**1922. June 3:** Unable to honor their commitment towards a great Hashemite kingdom in Syria, the English separate Transjordan from the Palestinian entity, giving it to Emir Abdullah. The Churchill White Paper further reduces in size the territory intended for the Jewish National Home. Moreover, this document stresses the economic viability of the land as a determinate of the volume of Jewish immigration.
**1923:** The southern border of Palestine is finally determined.
**1924–1928:** Fourth *Aliyah*.
**1925:** General implementation of the "certificates" system and the immigration quotas.
**1929–1930:** Arab riots in Palestine; a report

## Independence

### 1948

by a British inquiry delegation, the Shaw Commission, blames the unrest on Jewish immigration.
**1933–1939:** Fifth *Aliyah*.
**1934:** Beginning of *Aliyyat Yeladim va-No'ar* ("Youth *Aliyah*"), immigration of young people without their families.
**1934–1939:** "Illegal" immigration, in breach of British restrictive regulations (mostly the 1936 White Paper); in January 1938, the *Mosad le-Aliyah Bet* ("the Institution for Immigration B") is established for organizing illegal immigration. Clandestine immigration will be renewed in the final years of the war and continue till the establishment of the State.
**1936–1939:** The anti-British and anti-Jewish Arab Revolt in Palestine.
**1948. March:** A corps of Jewish volunteers from abroad is founded who participate in the War of Independence.
**1948–1950s:** Large waves of immigration during the first years following Independence.

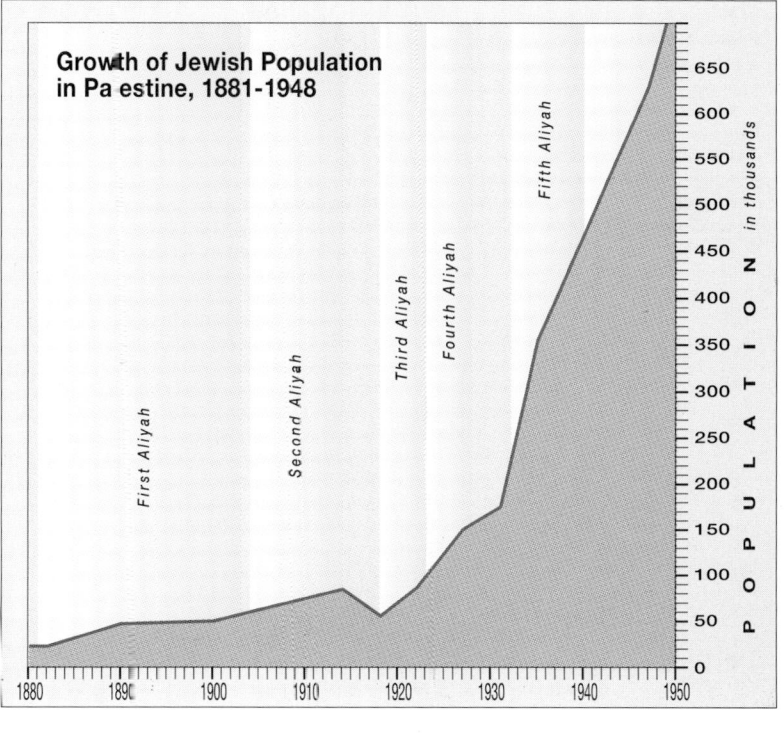

# The New Promised Land: The United States

1. "Hide me under the shadow of thy wings" (Psalms, 17:8): American Jews open their arms to their East European brethren. Naive painting, early 20th century.

I n 1880, in a Jewish population of approximately 250,000, only one out of six American Jews was of East European extraction; forty years later, in a community which had reached four million, five out of six American Jews came from Eastern Europe. Indeed, at that time over a third of East European Jewry had left their countries of origin, and 90% of them emigrated to the United States. Such an enormous wave of immigration had a tremendous effect on the American Jewish community.

The newcomers tended to cluster in the poorer districts of the metropolises. Most of them settled in the great commercial, industrial, and cultural centers of the northeast (New York in the first place, then Philadelphia, Boston, and Baltimore) and of the Midwest (particularly Chicago). Certain neighborhoods in these cities became almost exclusively Jewish, congested and bustling with a rich, typically Jewish way of life. Through hard work and under extremely difficult conditions, these Jews established themselves in the garment industry, petty trade, cigarette manufacture, construction, and food production. About thirty years after the beginning of the mass immigration, and not without bitter struggles, the Jewish trade union movement emerged as a formidable force, supported by over a quarter of a million workers. A flourishing Yiddish culture – poetry, prose, and drama – revolved mostly around the themes of the hardships of the Jewish worker's life, expressing the reality of daily existence within a community of immigrants.

Although the majority of the immigrants were Orthodox and attached to the congregational traditions of their forefathers, life in America soon transformed them. The number of those volunteering to organize the corporative bodies of the congregation dwindled rapidly, former Eastern European institutions were replaced by a host of other organizations – ideological societies, confraternities, trade unions, lay charitable institutions, cultural centers, clubs, and leisure enterprises. Economic pressures, opportunities for social promotion, the cult of liberty and individualism – all these contributed to the disintegration of Orthodox Jewry. How, for example, could one join the American race for success while observing the Sabbath? Nevertheless, Reform Judaism, although it remained dominant, did not encompass the entire American Jewish community. Rivalry between Reform, Conservative, and Orthodox Judaism was a major contribution to the emergence of a religious pluralism unique to American Jewry.

All these ideological movements, social tensions, religious currents, institutions, and organizations, however, did not prevent the development of solidarity and a strong group consciousness among American Jews. Charitable organizations constituted a pivotal axis for identification with the entire community. Between 1895 and 1920 many of these bodies formed large "federations" which eventually became the most influential factors in community consolidation, as well as a symbol of Jewish continuity.

The avalanche of disasters which befell East European Jewry during World War I and its aftermath precipitated this development. The principal Jewish aid organization, the Joint (American Jewish Joint Distribution Committee), established in November 1914, organized large-scale financial, medical, and social relief for their Jewish brethren in Europe, whereas the American Jewish Committee, the oldest Jewish defense

**Theodore Roosevelt is President**

**1900**

**Woodrow Wilson is President**

**1912**

3. "Share": poster of an American-Jewish aid organization, c.1915.

**End of 19th century:** About one third of the Jewish workers in the large cities are engaged in the garment industry; entrepreneurs and sub-contractors employ men, women, and children in sweatshops situated in the city slums; a typical work week consists of seventy hours. Nevertheless, these terrible conditions do not prevent the fittest from attaining economic independence relatively quickly.
**1897:** Founded and edited by Abraham (Abe) Cahan, the Yiddish journal Forverts ("Advance") soon becomes the organ of the Jewish workers' movement and a powerful element within the community; the journal supports the Jewish trade unions but does not commit itself to any ideological dogma.
**1902:** The Jewish Theological Seminary, founded in 1887, is headed by Solomon Shechter who came to the U.S. from Cambridge University; under his direction

the Seminary becomes the national center for the ordination of modern rabbis, education of teachers for Jewish schools, and promotion of Jewish studies; Shechter also initiates a union of Conservative synagogues.
**1910:** Abraham Lincoln Feilin, a department store owner in Boston, seeks the intervention of lawyer Louis Brandeis in the strike movement that agitates the Jewish garment industry in New York; Brandeis achieves a "protocol of permanent peace" between workers and employers according to the principle of the "preferential shop," lowers the number of weekly working hours to an average of 50, abolishes the piece-work system in the sweatshops, and creates a system of arbitration by representatives of workers, employers, and independent persons; Brandeis' system later spreads to other industries.

4. "Grandmother's Heritage." Playbill of a Yiddish theater, 1920.

organization in the U.S., afraid of being accused of dual loyalty, was content to practice a policy of discrete diplomacy.

The same postwar period witnessed the growth of the American Zionist Movement which was developing a spirit entirely different from the radical brand of European Zionism. Led from August 1914 by Louis D. Brandeis, it combined Zionist allegiance with respect for American ethnic pluralism and for the democratic and progressive ideals of American culture at large.

Antisemitism began rearing its ugly head in America in the 1890s. The well-established white Christian community despised the masses of poor immigrants who flocked to the United States, including the East European Jews, and regarded them as a threat to the American way of life and mode of government. The success of the German Jews, on the other hand,

2. Jewish workers sew suspenders in a New York sweatshop. c.1910.

aroused envy and antagonism. A prolonged propaganda campaign with strong antisemitic undertones led to the 1921–1924 legislation which drastically limited immigration and revealed an explicit preference for the "Nordic race."

Yet the fundamental characteristics of American society were too strong to permit the arrest of integration, and Jews continued to advance in every field. Bankers, scholars, judges, artists, and writers continued rising to prominence and making their impact on American life.

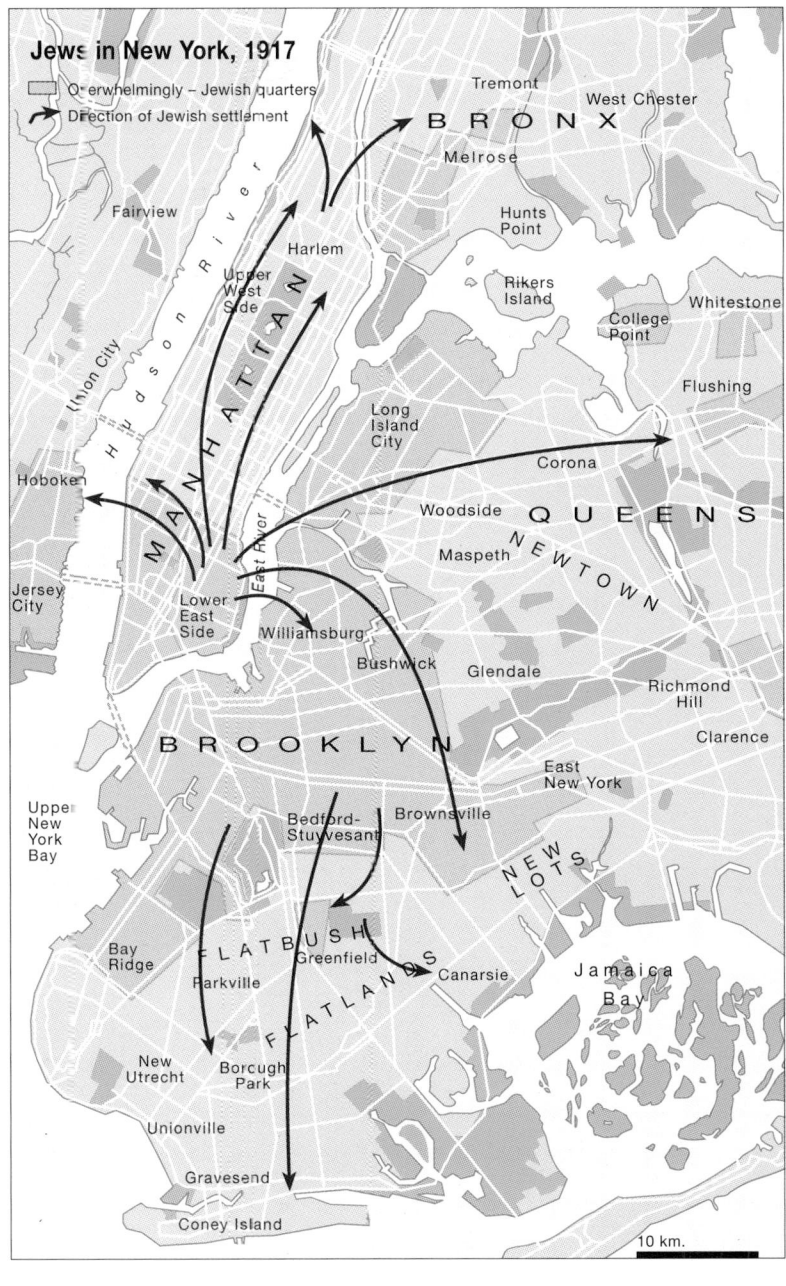

**Jews in New York, 1917**

☐ Overwhelmingly – Jewish quarters
→ Direction of Jewish settlement

10 km.

---

**The United States at war**

**1917**

**Immigration quotas**

**1921, 1924**

**1912:** Henrietta Szold founds the Women's Zionist Movement, *Hadassah*, which devotes itself mainly to the establishment of medical facilities in Palestine; in 1920, with the encouragement of Louis Brandeis, she settles in Palestine where she directs her organization and, from 1933, the Youth *Aliyah*, until her death in 1945.

**1914–1921:** American Zionism under the leadership of Brandeis and his friends – Reform Rabbi Stephen Wise (1874–1949), liberal jurists Julian Mack and Felix Frankfurter, and founder of *Hadassah* Henrietta Szold. The distinctly American spirit of the movement is best expressed in Brandeis's words: "In order to be good Americans, we must be better Jews, and to be better Jews, we must become Zionists."

**1915:** Yeshiva University, the first important Orthodox education institute in the United States, founded in 1897 as the Rabbi Isaac Elhanan Theological Seminary, now includes an elementary school, high school, college, and teachers' institute.

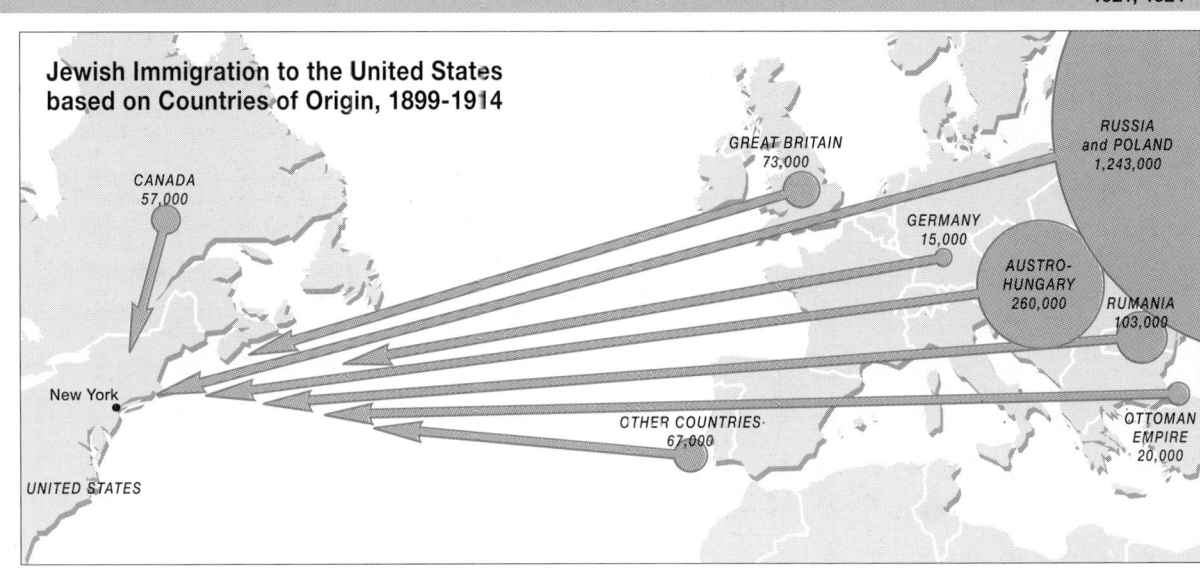

**Jewish Immigration to the United States based on Countries of Origin, 1899-1914**

CANADA 57,000

GREAT BRITAIN 73,000

GERMANY 15,000

RUSSIA and POLAND 1,243,000

AUSTRO-HUNGARY 260,000

RUMANIA 103,000

OTTOMAN EMPIRE 20,000

New York

OTHER COUNTRIES 67,000

UNITED STATES

# Jewish Culture in Eastern Europe

During the last two decades of the nineteenth century there was an astonishing cultural and social renaissance within East-European Jewry. The pogroms of 1881–1882 constituted a major turning point. Disillusioned with the czarist regime, members of the *Haskalah* movement turned to radical nationalist and socialist activities. Zionism, autonomist socialism (The Bund and Herzl's World Zionist Organization were both founded in 1897), nihilism, and revolutionary socialism, all acquired many thousands of young Jewish adherents. Political activism was also accompanied by dynamic cultural creativity. Several important cultural centers emerged all over the Russian Empire (St. Petersburg, Odessa, Warsaw) and in Austrian Galicia (Lemberg). This was essentially a secular culture. Vehicles formerly used for religious expression were now mobilized for spreading secular ideals: political propaganda, European aesthetic values, the glorification of national history, hopes and aspirations of the oppressed masses.

The new Jewish culture that flourished between 1881 and 1914 was trilingual: Hebrew, Yiddish and the native tongue, whether Russian, Polish or German. Writers and poets often used two or three languages to address a multilingual public. But this plurality of languages was often rife with conflicts, particularly between Hebraists and Yiddishists. When Shalom Rabinovitz (1859–1916) published his first stories in Yiddish, he hid behind the pseudonym Shalom Aleichem ("Peace be upon you," a

form of greeting) in order to avoid antagonizing his own father who was a fervent partisan of Hebrew. The Czernowitz Yiddish Writers Conference held in 1908, proclaimed, after an acrimonious debate, that Yiddish was *a* national language of the Jewish people, rather than *the* national Jewish language. The writer and poet I.L. Peretz (1852–1915), who was deputy chairman at that conference, best exemplifies the dilemmas and conflicts of his generation: he first wrote Hebrew literature in the *Haskalah* style, then wrote in Polish, then Yiddish works in which he empathized with the unprivileged, while in his later years he turned to neoromanticism and symbolism in both Hebrew and Yiddish. His work represents the language dispute as well as the tension between the desire to contend with a concrete social and political reality on the one hand, and pure artistic aspirations on the other.

When an independent Poland was reconstituted at the end of World War I, and particularly after the Russian Revolution, the center of gravity of East-European Jewry shifted to the new Polish republic whose three million resident Jews constituted the second largest Jewish community in the world. Despite the population's hostility and the difficult economic conditions (on the eve of World War II, one out of three Polish Jews was dependent on Jewish welfare organizations), Polish Jewry managed to develop an exceptionally rich and vibrant culture. In the 1930s, about 250 Jewish journals were issued regularly, and hundreds of Hebrew and Yiddish works were published each year.

Moreover, unlike their brethren in western Europe, the Jews in Poland felt no need to adopt the behavioral norms of the surrounding society. A vehement ideological war evolved in Poland between Zionists – who wished to increase Jewish national consciousness, the attachment to the ancestral homeland, and to Hebrew as the national language – and Bundists who sought to develop a secular culture in Yiddish, the *Jargon* of the masses. Hebrew was predominant in the Zionist press and in Jewish schools. Hundreds of thousands of children attended schools belonging to the *Tarbut* ("Culture") society founded by the World Zionist Organization. Yiddish, however, retained its hegemony as the vernacular: In 1931 about 80% of both Orthodox and "secularized" Polish Jews declared Yiddish their mother tongue. Maintained by workers' parties, particularly the Bund, a network of secular Yiddish schools operated in competition with *Tarbut* classes. Furthermore, during the interwar period in Poland Yiddish literature, Yiddish theater, and even the beginnings of a Yiddish film industry blossomed and flourished.

In Yiddish or in Hebrew, then, Poland during the first third of the twentieth century was the incontestable spiritual center of Ashkenazi Jewry. In the words of one of its leaders shortly before the catastrophe that was to destroy this entire civilization: "We are... the spine, the heart and the mind [of the Jewish people]."

*3. A May-Day march of Zionist Socialists in Chelm, Poland, 1932.*

## Leon Pinsker's Autoemancipation

**1882**

## Founding of the Bund

**1897**

**1881–1890:** Appearance of the Yiddish weekly *Yidishes Folksbiat* ("Journal of the Jewish People") in which Shalom Aleichem publishes his first stories (July-August 1883).
**1883:** The proto-Zionist movement *Hibbat Zion* ("Love of Zion") begins publishing numerous periodicals and writings in Hebrew, Yiddish and Russian. In 1884, during its first congress, the movement elects Leon Pinsker, author of *Autoemancipation*, as its leader. The first Yiddish socialist paper, *Dos Poylisher Yidl* ("The Polish Jew"), appears in London.
**1886:** The first Hebrew daily newspaper, *Ha-Yom* ("The Day"), is issued in St. Petersburg.
**1889:** Asher Ginsberg, dubbed Ahad Ha-Am ("One of the People"), advocate of "spiritual" Zionism, publishes an article entitled "The Wrong Way," and founds in Odessa the *Benei Moshe* ("Sons of Moses") movement.
**1897:** Founding of the Bund in Vilna. The following year the Bund joins the Russian Social-Democratic Party, only to leave it a

few years later when the party refuses to accommodate a national faction.
**1905:** Following the revolution in Russia, censorship is abolished and the Jewish press flourishes.
**1905–1907:** *Der Weg* ("The Road"), the first Yiddish daily in Warsaw.
**1918:** Birth of the Polish state. National minorities constitute one-third of its population, and whether it should be considered a Polish or a multinational state is therefore fiercely debated. The Versailles Conference hinges its recognition of Poland upon the latter's agreement to sign the Minorities Charter; the Poles regard this as an encroachment on their sovereignty.
**1918. November 12:** Jozef Pilsudski, head of the newly-born Polish state, receives a delegation of Jewish leaders. Yizhak Gruenbaum, prominent Zionist, demands autonomy for Poland's Jews. Pilsudski promises to take measures against anti-Jewish violence.
**November 1918–April 1919:** A wave of

# 1881–1939

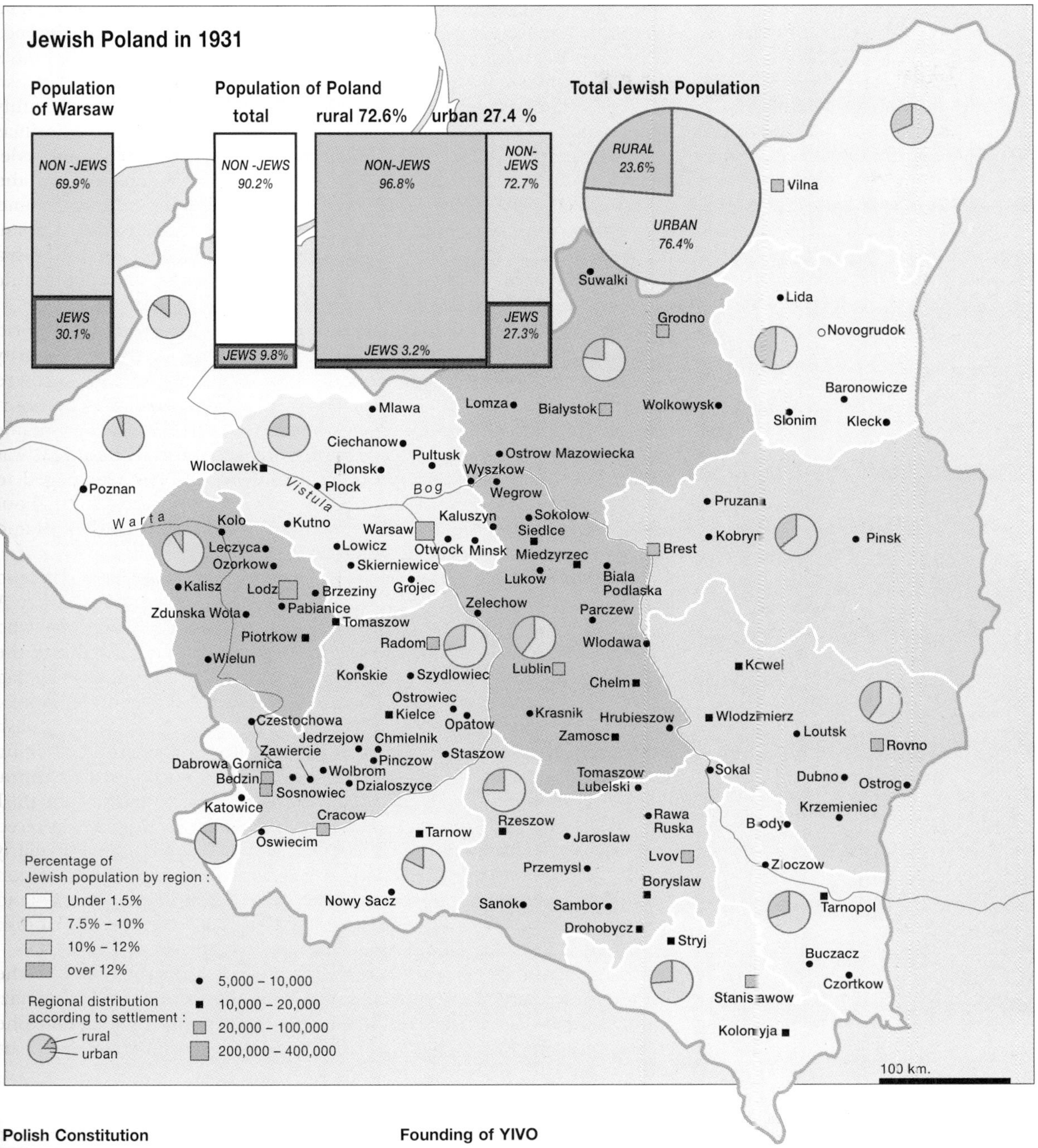
Jewish Poland in 1931
Population of Warsaw
NON -JEWS 69.9%
JEWS 30.1%
Population of Poland
total
NON -JEWS 90.2%
JEWS 9.8%
rural 72.6%
NON-JEWS 96.8%
JEWS 3.2%
urban 27.4 %
NON-JEWS 72.7%
JEWS 27.3%
Total Jewish Population
RURAL 23.6%
URBAN 76.4%
Vilna
Suwalki
Lida
Grodno
Novogrudok
Baronowicze
Slonim
Klecko
Lomza
Bialystok
Wolkowysk
Mlawa
Ciechanow
Pultusk
Ostrow Mazowiecka
Plonsk
Wyszkow
Wloclawek
Plock
Bog
Vistula
Wegrow
Poznan
Pruzana
Warta
Kolo
Kutno
Kaluszyn
Sokolow
Siedlce
Warsaw
Lowicz
Otwock
Minsk
Miedzyrzec
Brest
Kobryn
Pinsk
Leczyca
Ozorkow
Skierniewice
Lukow
Biala Podlaska
Kalisz
Lodz
Brzeziny
Grojec
Pabianice
Zelechow
Zdunska Wola
Parczew
Tomaszow
Piotrkow
Radom
Wlodawa
Wielun
Konskie
Szydlowiec
Lublin
Kowel
Chelm
Ostrowiec
Czestochowa
Kielce
Opatow
Krasnik
Hrubieszow
Wlodzimierz
Jedrzejow
Chmielnik
Zamosc
Loutsk
Zawiercie
Staszow
Rovno
Pinczow
Dabrowa Gornica
Wolbrom
Sokal
Bedzin
Tomaszow Lubelski
Dubno
Ostrog
Sosnowiec
Dzialoszyce
Katowice
Krzemieniec
Cracow
Rzeszow
Rawa Ruska
Tarnow
Jaroslaw
Brody
Oswiecim
Lvov
Przemysl
Zloczow
Boryslaw
Nowy Sacz
Sanok
Sambor
Tarnopol
Drohobycz
Stryj
Buczacz
Czortkow
Stanislawow
Kolomyja
Percentage of Jewish population by region :
Under 1.5%
7.5% - 10%
10% - 12%
over 12%
5,000 - 10,000
10,000 - 20,000
20,000 - 100,000
200,000 - 400,000
Regional distribution according to settlement :
rural
urban
100 km.

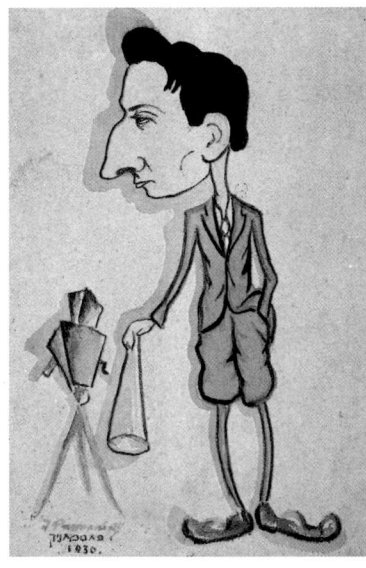

1. Jonas Turkow, a famous Yiddish actor, by Joseph Pasmanik. Poland, 1930.

יונג-ווילנע

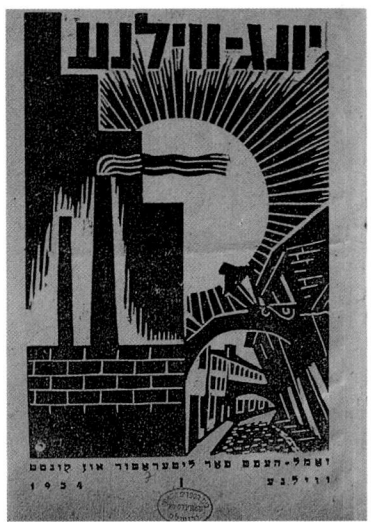

2. Yung Vilne ("Young Vilna"), a short-lived journal founded in 1929 by a Yiddish literary group numbering more then three dozen writers.

| Polish Constitution | Founding of YIVO | Germany invades Poland |
|---|---|---|
| March 1921 | 1925 | September 1939 |

POPIERAJCIE KEREN KAJEMET LEISRAEL!
קרן קימת לישראל
EMEK-JEZREEL
עמק-יזרעאל
GDZIE SIĘ OSIEDLIMY
הבה נגאל את העמק
WYZWÓLMY EMEK
לאמיר אויסלייזן דעם עמק

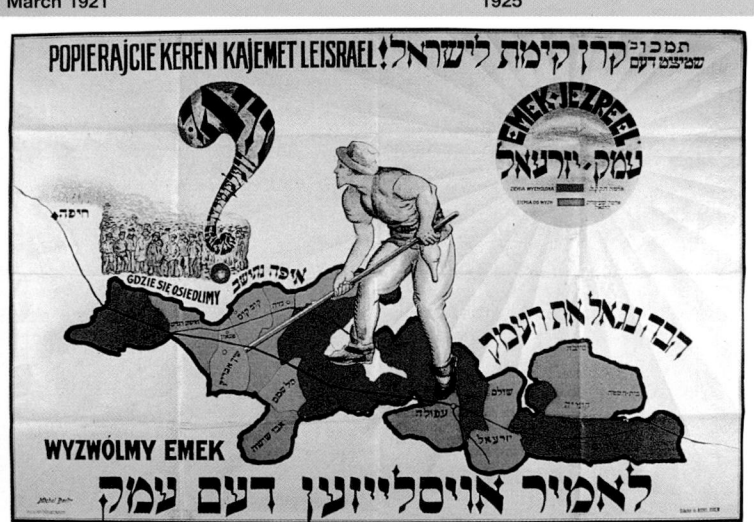

4. "Let us redeem the [Jezreel] Valley." A trilingual (Yiddish, Hebrew, Polish) poster of the Jewish National Fund (K.K.L.). Poland, 1930s.

pogroms in Poland, perpetrated mainly by army units who accuse the Jews of collaboration with Poland's enemies.
**1919. January 26:** Elections to the Constituent Assembly; Jewish parties receive about 10% of the votes, but the electoral system grants them only 11 out of 394 seats
**November 14:** The Constituent Assembly declares Sunday as the official day of rest.
**1921. March 17:** The Assembly ratifies the constitution of the Polish Republic; Jews are granted equal rights.
**1922. December 16:** Poland's president, Gabriel Narutowicz, elected thanks to the support of the minorities' bloc, is assassinated by a nationalist; right-wing parties regard the victim as the "president of the Jews."
**1925. August 12:** The Institute for Jewish Research (YIVO) is founded at a conference of Jewish scholars in Berlin; the conference selects Vilna as the center and Yiddish as the language of research
**1925–1939:** An efflorescence of Yiddish theater: about 20 different troupes perform throughout Poland.
**1926–1935:** Marshal Pilsudski's dictatorship.
**1934. January 26:** Poland signs a non-aggression pact with Hitler's Germany.
**September 13:** Poland officially renounces the Minorities Charter.
**1936. March 9:** Three Jews are killed during a pogrom in the small town of Przytyk; in a Jewish self-defense operation one Pole is killed, and the Jew convicted of killing the Pole receives a heavy sentence; the Bund declares a general strike which is observed by most of the Jews; the Polish Socialist Party expresses its solidarity.
**June 4:** The Prime Minister, F. Slawoj-Skladkowski, declares his support for the "economic war" against the Jews.
**1938. May 21:** The ruling party adopts "thirteen articles pertaining to Jewish affairs," stating that the Jews are "an element which hinders the normal development of the forces of the Polish nation and state."

# Modern Palestine

The modernization of Palestine did not begin with the arrival of the English. During the brief period of Egyptian administration (1832–1840) which was highly centralized and eager for innovations, and after the return of Ottoman rule, Palestine, particularly Jerusalem and the Coastal Plain, was opened to western influences. Palestine, for a long time a neglected province of a disintegrating empire, gradually became part of the international economic system and a focal point for world politics.

While the small Jewish community, poor and very pious (the old *yishuv*), resisted the process of modernization, the immigration wave of 1882–1903 (the First *Aliyah*) was a powerful force of acceleration. This first nucleus of the "new *yishuv*" brought with it methods of colonization which completely transformed the Palestinian countryside and precipitated the industrialization and urbanization of the land. From the beginning of the 1880s, the "dormant Orient" was awakening and undergoing radical changes.

Nonetheless, the real leap into modernity was made possible only

with the British conquest and the mandate for Palestine assigned to Great Britain by the League of Nations. The modern Near East, and within it the territorial entity named Palestine, came into being on the ruins of the Ottoman Empire.

The dismemberment of that empire created an urgent need for the demarcation of political boundaries. This difficult task, determined by strategic rather than historical or cultural considerations, was completed in 1923 with the first partition of the land creating two separate entities: Transjordan and Western Palestine. The latter, under an increasingly oppressive mandatory rule, became the basis for the Jewish national home promised in 1917 by the famous Balfour Declaration (named after the British foreign minister at that time). The participation of this region in the modern world and the emergence of the Zionist enterprise became possible only with its transformation into an autonomous entity.

General Allenby's campaign in 1917–1918, which forced Turkey out of the war, constituted a major turning point. For the first time in many centuries the country was governed by a Christian power ruling over the greatest colonial empire that ever existed. Yet Palestine was not simply one of the British colonies enjoying the fruits of western technology. The Balfour Declaration recognized the national right of the Jews in Palestine, their right to settle there with the full cooperation of the British authorities, and to develop it into an autonomous national and political entity. Moreover, the international community, through the voice of the League of Nations, endorsed the Declaration and included it as an obligation in the Mandate Charter.

British rule indeed proved to be a powerful catalyst for the process of modernization. The Mandatory authorities invested considerable sums in developing services such as education and health, as well as in laying an infrastructure: roads and railways, communication systems, and construction of airports and ports. The port at Haifa, built during 1929–1933, was soon to become one of the most important in the region.

It was mostly the Zionist movement, however, that built the technological infrastructure, particularly the electrification of the entire country. The *yishuv* first imported, but soon produced, a large quantity of machine-tools and mobilized all its energies and resources to contribute to the British war effort against Nazi Germany. During the Mandate period it went through all the stages of a classical industrial revolution, only at an extraordinarily rapid pace.

Obviously, technological modernization brought about changes and advancements in every sphere of life, including labor methods, social organization, cultural expression, hopes, and ideologies. Thus, it was the combination of the British Mandate, the pioneering spirit of the Zionist community, and the needs of World War II, which completely transformed the land within a very short time.

*1. Siona Tagger, The Train in Herzl Street. Oil Painting, Tel Aviv, 1924.*

| Jaffa-Jerusalem railway | Creation of the Anglo-Palestine Company | Founding of the Technion |
|---|---|---|
| 1892 | 1903 | 1912 |

**1869–1870:** The first modern road: from Jaffa to Jerusalem.
**1882–1900:** Baron Edmond de Rothschild invests about £1,600,000 in the modernization of agriculture and industry (wine in Rishon le-Zion and Zikhron Ya'akov, perfumes in Yesud ha-Ma'alah, silk in Rosh Pinnah).
**1892:** The first railroad from Jaffa to Jerusalem.
**1899:** Baron Edmond de Rothschild transfers the administration of the settlements to the Jewish Colonization Association (ICA).
**1903:** Creation of the Anglo-Palestine Co.: the beginning of modern banking.
**1906:** The first Hebrew secondary school, Gymnasia Herzliyah.
**1909–1910:** Founding of the first Jewish town in modern Palestine: Ahuzzat Bayit, the future Tel Aviv.
**1910:** Founding of Pardes, the citrus growers' association in Petah-Tikvah.
**1912–1913:** The foundation stone of a

college of technology, the Technion, is laid in Haifa; it will open in 1924, a year before the opening of the second great institution of higher learning, the Hebrew University in Jerusalem.
**1917–1918:** Beginning of an urban and interurban telephone system; by 1948, 1.3% of the population will be subscribers.
**1918. May 8:** Inauguration of the Haifa-Egypt railway.
**1918–1919:** Construction of modern hospitals in Tiberias, Safed, Jaffa, Haifa, Jerusalem.
**1920:** First Jewish archeological excavations in Tiberias.
**1920–1922:** Rapid development of roads, particularly in the Galilee.
**1921:** Founding of Bank Ha-Poa'lim (the Workers' Bank) – the financial company of the Histadrut, the labor federation of Palestinian workers; creation of the Histadrut's Public Works and Building Office, renamed Solel Boneh in 1924.
**1921–1922:** Beginning of many new

*3. The Shemen factory in Haifa in 1935.*

industrial enterprises such as Shemen (oil) and Nesher (cement).
**1921–1932:** Pinhas Rutenberg establishes the Palestine Electric Company; power plants are constructed in Tel Aviv, Haifa, Tiberias, and Jerusalem (1922–1926), in Naharayim (1928–1932) – a hydroelectric station utilizing the waters of the Yarmuk and Jordan rivers, inaugurated by Rutenberg and Emir Abdullah of Transjordan – and the first steam-power plants in Haifa and Tel Aviv.
**1924–1926:** Rapid advancement in the construction of Tel Aviv; beginnings of private investments in industry by entrepreneurs who came with the Fourth Aliyah.
**1925–1927:** Draining of the marshes near Haifa in the fight against malaria.
**1926:** Founding of Tnuva, a cooperative for distribution of the products of agricultural collectives.
**1929–1933:** Creation of the Dead Sea Potash Works.
**1933:** Inauguration of the deep-water port at Haifa; founding of the inter-city transportation

## Roads

### 1917

— Tarred road
— Unpaved road

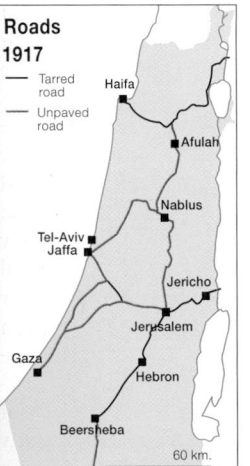

Haifa
Afulah
Nablus
Tel-Aviv
Jaffa
Jericho
Jerusalem
Gaza
Hebron
Beersheba

60 km.

### 1922

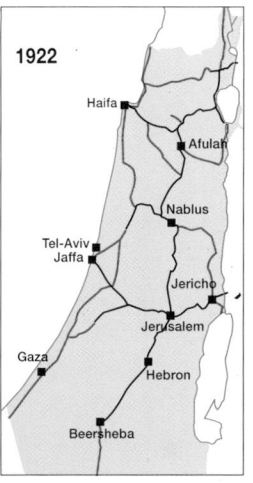

Haifa
Afulah
Nablus
Tel-Aviv
Jaffa
Jericho
Jerusalem
Gaza
Hebron
Beersheba

### 1929

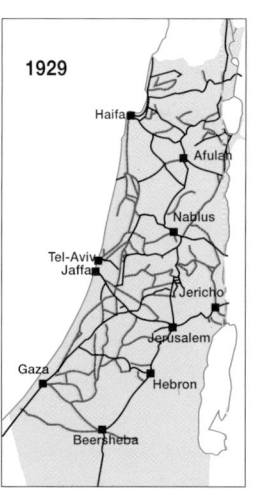

Haifa
Afulah
Nablus
Tel-Aviv
Jaffa
Jericho
Jerusalem
Gaza
Hebron
Beersheba

## Infrastructure

🏭 Factory
✈ Civilian airport
⌁ Electric power station
— Telephone line
▪▪▪ Railroad

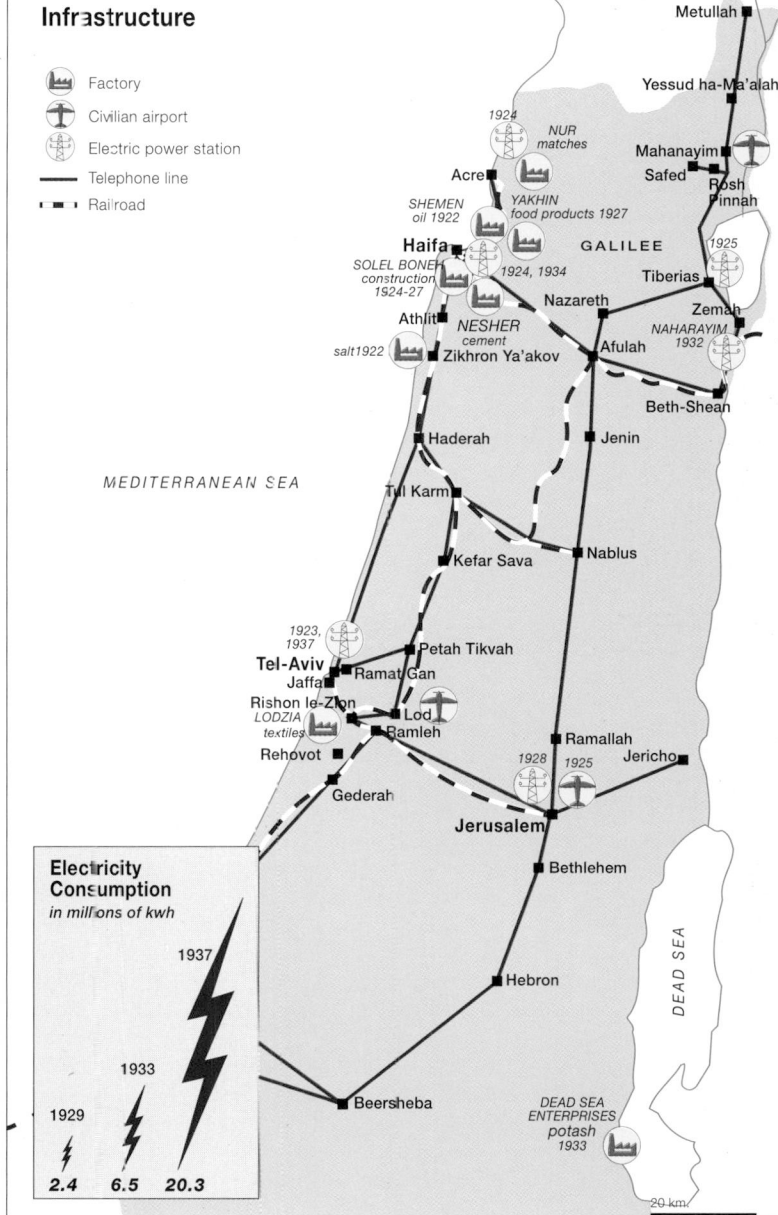

Metullah
Yessud ha-Ma'alah
1924
NUR matches
Acre
Mahanayim
Safed
Rosh Pinnah
SHEMEN oil 1922
YAKHIN food products 1927
Haifa
GALILEE
1925
SOLEL BONEH construction 1924-27
1924, 1934
Tiberias
Athlit
Nazareth
Zemah
NESHER cement
Afulah
NAHARAYIM 1932
salt 1922
Zikhron Ya'akov
Beth-Shean
Haderah
Jenin

MEDITERRANEAN SEA

Tul Karm
Kefar Sava
Nablus
1923, 1937
Petah Tikvah
Tel-Aviv
Jaffa
Ramat Gan
Rishon le-Zion
LODZIA textiles
Lod
Ramleh
Ramallah
Rehovot
1928
1925
Jericho
Gederah
Jerusalem
Bethlehem
Hebron

DEAD SEA

Beersheba
DEAD SEA ENTERPRISES potash 1933

### Electricity Consumption
*in millions of kwh*

1937
1933
1929
2.4    6.5    20.3

20 km.

2. "Ships of the Desert" in Tel Aviv, in 1946.

| The first telephone lines | The first power station in Tel Aviv | Inauguration of Haifa port |
|---|---|---|
| 1917–1918 | 1922–1923 | 1933 |

cooperative, Egged.

**1934:** 600,000 visitors come to the sixth Levant Fair – an international agricultural exhibition: 36 countries and 2200 companies, 700 of which are Palestinian, participate; founding of the Daniel Sieff Institute for agricultural research in Rehovot, to become part of the Weizmann Institute in 1949.

**1935:** Beginnings of a commercial fleet.

**1936:** Creation of a broadcasting service; Palestine is the third largest exporter of citrus fruit in the world.

**1937:** The Jewish Agency and the Histadrut create *Mekorot* ("sources") Water Company; the Jaffa-Haifa highway is completed.

**1940–1943:** World War II provokes a real industrial revolution in Palestine, particularly in metallurgy. The Board of Scientific and Industrial Research (BSIR) is founded in 1942 to further the war effort.

4. "Our Products" – a poster of the agricultural cooperative Tnuva.

5. Construction of Haifa port.

1. *Jewish soldiers and officers of the Austro-Hungarian army in prayer. Painting by Joseph Ehrenfreund.*

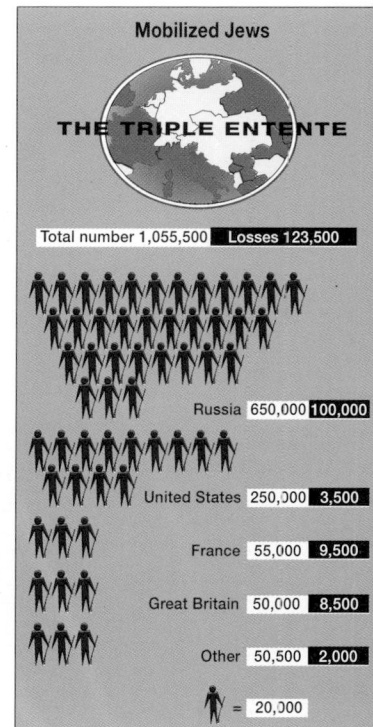

**Mobilized Jews**

**THE TRIPLE ENTENTE**

| Total number 1,055,500 | Losses 123,500 |
|---|---|

| | Russia 650,000 | 100,000 |
| | United States 250,000 | 3,500 |
| | France 55,000 | 9,500 |
| | Great Britain 50,000 | 8,500 |
| | Other 50,500 | 2,000 |

= 20,000

The First World War, the most appallingly savage international conflict in all preceding history, had a profound impact on world Jewry. This was due to the existence of a large concentration of Jews within one of the principal arenas, the enlistment of unprecedented numbers of Jews to the armies of the belligerent nations, and the success of Jewish leaders in influencing the political policies of the major powers. Furthermore, increasing tensions during the war years deepened the hostile attitudes towards the Jews, particularly in Germany and in Eastern Europe.

The war on the eastern front between Russia and the Central Powers (Germany and Austria) was conducted on territories which were home to almost four million Jews. In the autumn of 1914 and the winter of 1915, Russian forces occupied Austrian Galicia, and in the spring and summer of 1915 Germany and Austria conquered Congress Poland (the duchy annexed by Russia according to the treaties of 1815), Volhynia, Lithuania, and western Belorussia. Under Russian rule the Jews were suspected of collaboration with the enemy, and 600,000 of them were banished from the front by the czarist army – a traumatic experience and an economic catastrophe which was still felt long after the war. To aid their displaced and impoverished brethren, Jews around the world established welfare organizations on a scale previously unknown.

At the outbreak of the war, the Jews, eager to demonstrate their loyalty to their respective countries, rallied to the war effort. Initially the Jews in Russia were no exception, but when the policy of deportation was implemented, many Jews began to pray for the victory of the Central Powers. Nevertheless, about half a million Jews donned Russian uniforms. On the opposite side, almost 100,000 Jews were serving in the German army. Yet despite this massive enlistment, accusations of evasion and of profiteering were brought against the Jews in both countries, and official investigations were instigated. Although the conclusions of these inquiries were never published, the statistics indicate that the percentage of Jewish losses was in no way smaller than that of the non-Jewish population. Suspicions concerning their loyalty were even voiced in England and the United States, since the Jews did not hide their hostility toward

**The assassination in Sarajevo**

**June 26, 1914**

**Deportations to the East**

**1914–1915**

POUR LA PATRIE

2. *"Death of Rabbi Abraham Bloch." Serving as chaplain in the French army during the Great War, the rabbi, in the absence of a priest, offers the crucifix to a wounded Catholic, and is struck by canon shell. French postcard.*

**1914. August 1:** Outbreak of World War I: Russian troops advance westward against the armies of Austria and Germany; Jews in all belligerent countries enlist.

**August 17:** In a proclamation addressed to Russian Jews, the General Staff of the German army calls for an uprising against the czarist regime and promises full equal rights to the Jews in any territory conquered by the Germans.

**August–September:** Russian attack on Lvov (Lemberg) drives the Austrian troops out of eastern Galicia. Hundreds of thousands of Jews subjected to Russian rule.

**November 27:** Establishment of the American Jewish Distribution Committee (the Joint), for aid and assistance to Jewish war refugees.

**1915. March–September:** Mass deportations of Jews from the areas on the eastern front.

**March 22:** Jewish exiles from Palestine and Russia form the "Zion Mule Corps" in Egypt and offer to aid the British army in the conquest of Palestine from the Turks; Joseph Trumpeldor commands a corps of 562 soldiers who fight alongside the English in the battle of Gallipoli.

**April–August:** Deportation and massacre of Armenians in Turkey.

**July–September:** A combined German-Austrian offensive from Lithuania in the north to Bukovina in the south: eastern Galicia is returned to Austrian rule; most of the Jewish Pale of Settlement in Russia is occupied by the German army.

**September:** Kurt Blumenfeld, Secretary of the Zionist Federation, publishes an article in the prestigious German periodical *Preussische Jahrbücher*: "Zionism – a question of German policy in the east," in which he claims that the Zionist Movement might play a major role in strengthening the Ottoman Empire and increasing German influence within it. The article arouses a furious public debate in Germany about the Jewish question, and accusations of

# 1914–1918

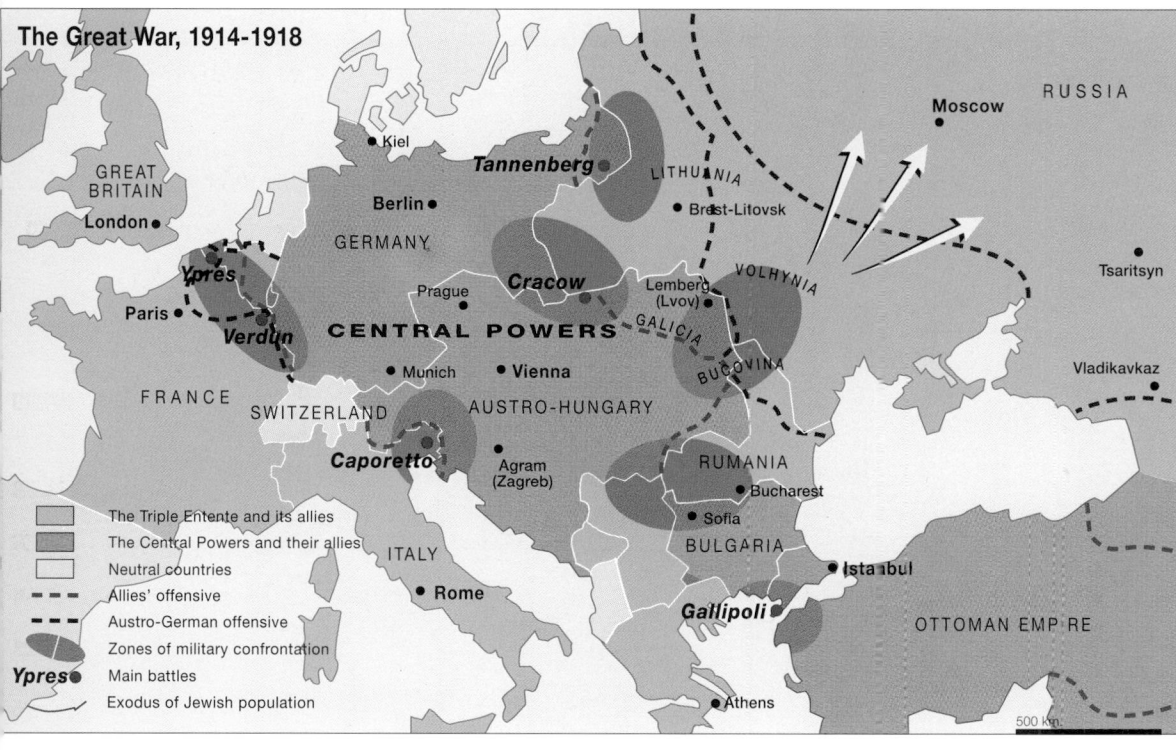

### The Great War, 1914-1918

RUSSIA

Moscow

Kiel
Tannenberg
LITHUANIA
Berlin
Brest-Litovsk
GERMANY
GREAT
BRITAIN
London
Tsaritsyn
VOLHYNIA
Lemberg
(Lvov)
Prague
Cracow
Ypres
GALICIA
Paris
CENTRAL POWERS
Verdun
BUCOVINA
Vladikavkaz
Munich
Vienna
FRANCE
SWITZERLAND
AUSTRO-HUNGARY
Caporetto
RUMANIA
Agram
(Zagreb)
Bucharest
Sofia
ITALY
BULGARIA
Rome
Istanbul
Gallipoli
OTTOMAN EMPIRE
Athens

500 km.

The Triple Entente and its allies
The Central Powers and their allies
Neutral countries
Allies' offensive
Austro-German offensive
Zones of military confrontation
**Ypres** Main battles
Exodus of Jewish population

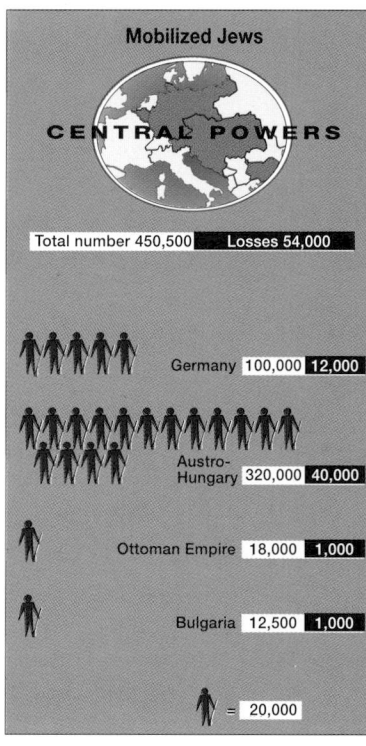

### Mobilized Jews

**CENTRAL POWERS**

| Total number 450,500 | Losses 54,000 |

Germany 100,000 12,000
Austria-Hungary 320,000 40,000
Ottoman Empire 18,000 1,000
Bulgaria 12,500 1,000

= 20,000

the oppressing Russian autocracy, the ally of these two powers; and indeed, there were those among the recently-arrived immigrants from Russia who refused to enlist. In both countries, Jews of German origin were required to sign humiliating public declarations of loyalty.

While the loyalty of Jewish individuals was torn between the opposing camps, Jewish international associations, including the World Zionist Organization, declared themselves neutral. But in view of the nature of the czarist regime and the large proportion of Polish and Russian Jews, the sympathy of most Jewish leaders lay with Germany and the Austro-Hungarian Empire. The German Foreign Office was aware of this, and during the first years of the war tried to exploit this to further German interests. German Jews all over the world founded the "Committee for the East" which disseminated pro-German propaganda among the Jews of Poland. Zionists in Germany conducted negotiations with the Foreign Office concerning cooperation over Palestine, and in 1915 the Jewish philosopher, Hermann Cohen, went to the United States to ask the Jews there to try to persuade the American government to enter the war

on Germany's side. These efforts undoubtedly spurred the British government to make advances to the pro-English minority within the Zionist Organization, which contributed to the publication of the Balfour Declaration in November 1917.

Despite this first diplomatic victory for political Zionism, by the end of the war the majority of Jews found themselves confronting hatred and trouble. In Germany, the Jews were identified with the republican regime imposed on the country by the victors; vanquished and humiliated, many Germans consoled themselves with the "stab in the back" myth, counting the Jews among the chief traitors. As the perennial scapegoat, the Jews were also blamed by many for the Bolshevik *coup d'etat* of October 1917: approximately 100,000 Jews were killed in the anti-Bolshevik campaigns conducted by Ukrainians, Poles, and Russians.

The war's great upheavals changed the demographic map of the Jewish people. During the war, intercontinental migration dwindled, but there were large movements of refugees within Europe. Once the war was over, hundreds of thousands of Jews began leaving Europe again.

---

**Martin Buber founds the monthly *Der Jude***

**1916**

**Revolution in Russia**

**1917**

**Creation of the Jewish regiment in the British army**

**August 1917**

"England has been all she could be to Jews; Jews will be all they can be to England" — Jewish Chronicle Aug 7 1914

"Blessed be the Lord my Rock, who teacheth my hands to War, and my fingers to fight." Psalm CXLIV

ESTᵈ 1841 ESTᵈ 1841

# The JEWISH CHRONICLE
## WAR NUMBER

*A special edition of the Jewish Chronicle, London, November 1915.*

...vasion are voiced.
**1916. October 11:** The German War Office, under pressure from the right-wing parties, orders a census according to the function

formerly held by Russia. The Jews are granted freedom of association and community self-government.
**1917. March 12:** The February Revolution in Russia.
**April 2:** The Russian Provisional Government, formed after the abdication of the Czar, grants full equal rights to the Jews of Russia.
**August 23:** The British government permits formation of a Jewish regiment – "The 38th Battalion of the Royal Fusiliers"; about 800 Jews enlist in the regiment; it was dispatched to Palestine in February 1918.
**November 7:** The October Revolution in Russia.
**1918. March 3:** The Peace of Brest-Litovsk ends Russia's participation in the war and ensures Germany's hegemony in eastern Europe.
**November 11:** End of World War I.

of Jews serving in the Imperial Army.
**November 1:** Germany and Austria declare the establishment of a semi-autonomous Polish state on territories

*4. Jabotinsky, founder of the Jewish Legion, in a poster of the Zionist Fund, Keren ha-Yesod.*

WELCOME JABOTINSKY FOUNDER OF JEWISH LEGION

Contribute to KEREN HAYESOD
קרן היסוד

# The Balkan Communities

The political, economic, and social features of the Jewish communities in the Balkans were shaped by many centuries of Ottoman rule, while their religious and cultural traits were determined by Sephardi traditions. Although there were in the region some very ancient local communities (such as the Jews of Macedonia), most of the Balkan Jews were, in fact, descendants of exiles from the Iberian communities who had found refuge in the Ottoman Empire after 1492. More recent newcomers arrived during the nineteenth century: Bavarian or Hungarian Jews who settled in Bulgaria, Polish and Hungarian Jews who settled in Greece.

The nature of the Balkan communities was also determined by modern political developments in the region. As the Ottoman Empire disinte-

1. Jewish women in Salonika, 1913.

Borders of Ottoman Empire, 1878

Borders of Balkan states, 1919

Jewish communities
- Under 2,000
- 2,000 – 5,000
- 5,000 – 10,000
- over 10,000

| Congress of Berlin | Creation of Yugoslavia | Greco-Turkish war |
|---|---|---|
| 1878 | 1918 | 1923 |

3. Opening ceremony of the second national gathering of the Maccabi sports federation in Bulgaria. Sofia, 1930.

**1821:** The Greek Revolt. Accused of entertaining cordial relations with the Turkish oppressor, the Jewish communities are subjected to persecutions; the massacre in the Peloponnesus claims 5,000 victims; many Jews flee to Corfu.

**1845:** The Jews in Serbia are prohibited from working as tailors and shoemakers.
**1876:** Jews in the Ottoman Empire are granted equal rights; there are Jewish deputies in the Parliament.
**1878:** Jewish self-defense is organized in

Sofia in order to protect the community during the Turks' retreat.
**1884:** La Alborada ("Dawn"), the first Ladino, newspaper (the Jewish-Spanish language of Sephardi Jews) appears in Bulgaria.
**1885:** Jews are drafted for the first time to the Bulgarian army.
**1889:** Emancipation of the Serbian Jews.
**1891:** A blood libel affair in Corfu.
**1906:** The Austro-Hungarian government legally defines the status of the Jewish communities in Croatia, Slavonia, and Dalmatia.
**1912–1913:** Following the Balkan War, with the annexation of territories, the Jewish population in Greece grows to 100,000.
**1918:** Creation of Yugoslavia whose population includes some 70,000 Jews.
**1919:** Founding of the Federation of Jewish Communities in Yugoslavia, a body recognized by the state. In 1924, Isaac Alkalai is appointed chief rabbi by the king; as a member of the Yugoslav senate, his status is similar to that of spiritual leaders of

other communities.
**1936:** A small antisemitic movement – Ratnik ("Warrior") – is founded in Bulgaria; in Croatia, the Fascist movement of the Ustashe enjoys wide popular support.
**1941. April:** German invasion of Yugoslavia and Greece; beginnings of the genocide in the Balkans. 46,000 Jews of Salonika are deported, most of them to Auschwitz – this brings the largest Sephardi center in Europe to an end. A total of 65,000 Greek Jews, 85% of the entire Greek Jewish population, are sent to extermination camps. Over 11,000 Jews from Thrace and Macedonia are deported by the Bulgarians to Poland; about 2,200 of them survive. About 60,000 Jews from the different regions of Yugoslavia later disappear. On the other hand, Jews take an active part in the Yugoslav Resistance movement; over 2,000 fight in Tito's army, among them Mosa Pijade who becomes one of Tito's four vice-presidents after the liberation.
**1944. December:** Ben-Gurion's visit to

grated, the Jews felt a need to suppress their history of reasonable relations with the Turks and prove their loyalty to the nascent nation-states which emerged in the nineteenth and twentieth centuries. Furthermore, territorial changes which occurred with the creation of independent Bulgaria or Yugoslavia formed new Jewish entities out of communities which had previously belonged to different political frameworks. Thus, the "Yugoslav" community comprised Jews who for centuries had been subjects of the Austro-Hungarian Empire, Serbia, or the Ottoman Empire. Admittedly, these changes initially had little effect on the socio-economic structure of the Jewish community: the Jews remained primarily merchants and tradesmen, extending the long tradition of commerce with neighboring regions such as the Danubian Principalities (the nucleus of the future Rumania) or with more distant lands such as Central Europe and the Mediterranean shores.

In the new and, on the whole, more favorable environment, the Jews were now able to develop richer forms of spiritual and cultural life based on their Sephardi traditions. Jewish folklore in the Ladino language endowed these Balkan communities with a unique flavor, passed on from generation to generation. The emergence of modern Jewish nationalism, however, affected all these communities from an early stage. Three Bulgarian delegates participated in the First Zionist Congress in 1897, and large and vigorous Zionist federations and youth movements were established almost everywhere.

Political upheavals were followed by legal emancipation. Bulgaria, for example, was urged to grant the Jews political rights by the Congress of Berlin. Although there were occasional attacks on Jews for economic reasons – as, for instance, when the war with Turkey in 1923 brought an influx of Greek refugees from Anatolia to Salonika – on the whole, antisemitism was never a major political factor in the Balkans. In interwar Bulgaria, for example, discrimination against Jews never reached the same level of virulence as in other European countries at the time.

Here as elsewhere throughout Europe, World War II totally changed the course of Jewish history. The genocide perpetrated by the Nazis hit the Balkan communities in varying degrees: Yugoslav and Greek Jewry was practically annihilated, while the Jews of Bulgaria, protected by their compatriots, were largely spared. Then, while the British prevented Greece from falling into the Soviet orbit, Bulgaria and Yugoslavia became Communist countries. And, although less intolerant than the Soviet Union, they also neutralized the cultural autonomy of their Jewish communities. In the early 1950s, the majority of Bulgarian and Yugoslav Jews emigrated to Israel. Those who remained, approximately three to five thousand Jews in each respective country, continued to cultivate certain traits of Jewish cultural and communal life which were still important to the older generation.

2. The Jewish community of Monastir welcomes Mehmet V. (The Ottomans held Macedonia until 1913). Postcard, 1910.

Although Greece's overall fate was different, a similar outcome was in store for its Jews: in a community of approximately six thousand, which has never been troubled by the government, the synagogues are nonetheless filled only on major festivals – a sad remnant of a glorious past.

And in conclusion, the tiny community of Albania. After long decades of silence, the Albanian Jews were finally able to benefit from recent political developments. In 1991, about five hundred Albanian Jews arrived in Israel – practically the entire Jewish community.

| German invasion | Jewish emigration from Bulgaria and Yugoslavia |
| --- | --- |
| 1941 | 1949–1950 |

Bulgaria; between September 1944 and October 1948, 7,000 Bulgarian Jews emigrate to Palestine.
**1947:** Founding of a Hebrew Science Institute in Sofia.
**1949–1952:** Mass immigration to Israel of Bulgarian (44,300) and Yugoslav (8,000) Jews.
**1958–1960:** A. Hananel and E. Eskenazi publish *Fontes Hebraici*, a corpus of responsa concerning the economic life of the Balkan Jews, under the auspices of the Bulgarian Academy of Science.
**1985–1990:** As the Communist regimes decline, finally succumbing to popular pressure, the Jewish communities in Bulgaria and Yugoslavia are able to maintain relations with Israel and the Jewish world.
**1991:** The tiny Jewish community of Albania immigrates to Israel.

4. Joseph Jakoel, author of a history of Albanian Jewry, holding an ancient Ketubbah (marriage contract). Tirana, March, 1991.

5. The old Jewish cemetery in Sarajevo.

# Soviet Jewry Between the Wars

The democratic February Revolution (March 1917) raised great hopes among Russian Jews. The Provisional Government, declaring that citizen's rights would no longer be determined by national or religious identity, accorded to the Jews long-awaited civic emancipation and abolished about 150 discriminatory laws, including the prohibition on residence outside the Pale of Settlement. All the Jewish parties united jointly to prepare an "All-Russian Jewish Convention" which was to establish a politico-cultural autonomous organization and provide the central representative body for all the Jews in Russia.

The convention, however, never took place. The Bolshevik coup in November 1917 (the October Revolution) ended Soviet Jewry's brief springtime. Most Jewish organizations, well aware that the new rulers intended to centralize all political power in their own hands, felt little sympathy for Lenin's party. At the same time, however, a significant number of members of the Bolshevik leadership (around 25%) were of Jewish origin. This is why the Jews were automatically identified with the new regime. During the civil war (1918–1921), those loyal to the old regime used this false identification as another excuse to massacre Jews. The "White Army" of Anton Denikin killed thousands in pogroms perpetrated in over 160 Jewish settlements; about 100,000 Jews were murdered in the Ukraine alone.

Meanwhile, while the Bolsheviks repudiated antisemitism and severely punished soldiers who attacked Jews, they were ideologically committed to the destruction of Jewish religion, culture, and national identity. In early 1918 many Jewish organizations were liquidated. The Zionist movement and the socialist and autonomist Bund ("Zionists who suffer from sea sickness," according to Plekhanov) were outlawed, publication of Hebrew books and journals was forbidden, and Yiddish publications were placed under strict control. A Jewish commissariat, active between

1. "Build a communist life on the fields of the USSR," a lithograph extolling the virtues of working the land, c.1926.

1918 and 1923, dealt with Jewish affairs. "Jewish Sections" were also set up in branches of the Communist Party. A violent campaign against the Jewish religion and its leaders was conducted, and heavy taxes were imposed on rabbis and other religious officials.

The regime also sought ways of transforming the economic structure of Jewish society – a society composed mostly of "petty bourgeoisie," hence considered non-productive. An attempt was therefore made to transfer as many Jews as possible to agriculture and heavy industry. In the Ukraine and Crimea the Soviet authorities, supported by western Jewish organizations, created agricultural colonies for Jews. Indeed, the combined effect of World War I, the Revolution, the civil war, as well as government pressure, undermined the economic structure of Jewish society and forced many to seek new occupations. By 1930, 11% of Jewish families worked in agriculture, 16% in industry, and many others in administration or in the professions. These changes were accompanied by internal migration from the western frontier areas into Russia.

In order to hasten the process of "productivization" of the Jews, the Soviet authorities created a "Jewish Autonomous Region" in 1928 in Birobidzhan, near the Chinese border. Since they did not establish a proper infrastructure, however, the area did not attract many settlers; and out of the 20,000 Jews who came between 1928 and 1933, over 11,000 soon left the region.

During the 1930s the Soviet regime began abolishing the Jewish institutions it had created in the previous decade. The Jewish section of the Communist Party (the *Yevsektsiya*), for example, was disbanded. Then, in the purges of 1937–1938, thousands of Jews were arrested, deported, and killed. Thus, by the time the German invasion began in 1941, the first stage in the liquidation of the national life of the Jews in the Soviet Union had been completed.

---

| Revolutions in Russia | Creation of the *Yevsektsiya* | Stalin becomes First Secretary |
|---|---|---|
| March, November 1917 | January 1918 | April 1922 |

**1917. March 9:** The February Revolution.
**March 16:** The Provisional Government abolishes all restrictions imposed on the Jews by the czarist regime.
**June 5:** The seventh Zionist conference in Russia is held in Petrograd, headed by Tschlenow and Ussishkin; founding of the movement *He-Halutz* ("The Pioneer") which prepares its members for emigration to Palestine.
**September:** Election campaign for an all-Russian Jewish convention; though the elections were held, the convention itself never convened due to the Bolshevik Revolution.
**November:** With news of the Balfour Declaration (November 2), large-scale Zionist demonstrations and meetings are held in Kiev, Odessa, and Moscow.
**November 7–9:** The Bolshevik Revolution; Russia declares its withdrawal from the war.
**1918. January 18:** Simon Dimanstein heads the commissariat for Jewish affairs; under his direction, the Jewish section of the

2. Mendele Mokher Seforim, The Travels of Benjamin III, directed by Alexander Granovski, The Jewish State Theater, Moscow, 1927.

Communist Party (*Yevsektsiya*) – created "to impose the proletarian dictatorship among the Jewish masses" – intervenes in all aspects of Jewish life in the Soviet Union.
**March 3:** Treaty of Brest-Litovsk ends the war with Germany.
**1919:** The authorities begin the systematic liquidation of Jewish autonomy: suppression of community organizations, prohibition on teaching Hebrew and publishing Hebrew books, dissolution of the Bund (the socialist autonomist Jewish party); the Zionist movement is forced underground.
**March 2:** Founding of the Comintern.
**June:** Stalin, as Commissar of Nationalities, signs a decree which abolishes the legal status of the Jewish communities.
**November 15:** Lenin promises liberty and self-determination to all nationalities in the empire.
**1919–1920:** Devastating pogroms in the Ukraine; Zionists and Bundists attempt self-defense, but these are mostly undermined by Communists.

## Demographic and Professional Distribution in the late 1930s

Moscow — Over 100,000
Minsk — 50,000 to 100,000
Riga — 30,000 to 50,000
Rostov — 20,000 to 30,000
Mozyr — 5,000 to 20,000

**U.S.S.R.**

Moscow · Saratov · Astrakhan · Derbent · Baku · Samarkand · Irkutsk · Tchita · Khabarovsk

OTHER — 3.8 % · 0.2 %
FARMERS — 5.8 %
ARTISANS — 46.4 %
20.1 %
3.8 %
WORKERS — 30.6 % · 32.6 %
OFFICIALS — 40.6 % · 17.2 %

Jews / Non-Jews

**Number of Yiddish books sold, 1923–1932**

| 1923 | 1928 | 1932 |
|---|---|---|
| 156,000 | 875,100 | 2,218,600 |

### Regional map (top left)

Leningrad · Yaroslavl · Riga · Siauliai · Kaunas · Vitebsk · Polotsk · Smolensk · Moscow · Borisov · Mogilev · Bryansk · Minsk · Bobruisk · Voronezh · Slutsk · Kursk · Mozyr · Gomel · Zhitomir · Kiev · Kharkov · Berdichev · Kremenchug · Poltava · Sverdlovsk · Vinnitsa · Uman · Dnepropetrovsk · Donetsk · Rostov · Odessa · Melitopol

BLACK SEA
500 km.

### POPULATION IN CRIMEA 713,800

JEWS 45,900

### Jewish agricultural colonies in Crimea in the 1930s

CRIMEA · Mishmar · Kadimah · Tel Hai · Ma'ayan · Dzhankoi · Avodah · Haklai · Kolai · Korman · Kameltchi · Herut · Ahdut · Beit Lahm · Yevpatoriya · Zemlerov · Osnova · Zemledeletz · Rabotnik · Povida · Simferopol · Feodosiya · Kerch · Sevastopol · Yalta

SEA OF AZOV · BLACK SEA
50 km.

Jewish agricultural colony
Osnova — Russian name
*Kadimah* — Hebrew name

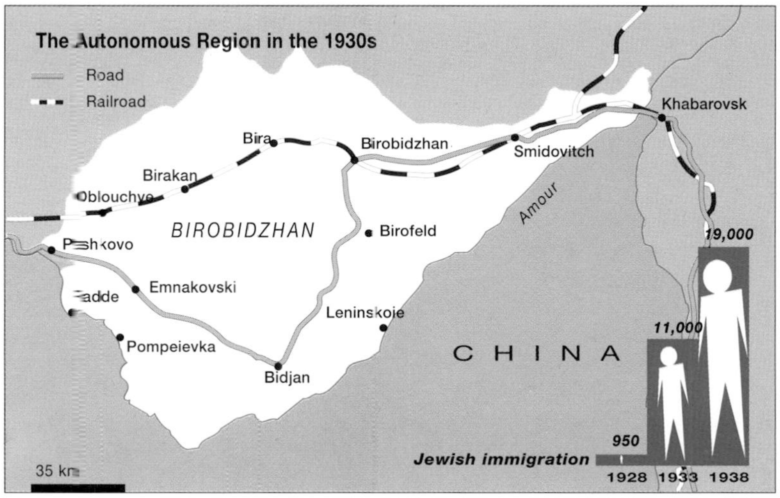

### The Autonomous Region in the 1930s

Road
Railroad

BIROBIDZHAN · Khabarovsk · Bira · Birobidzhan · Smidovitch · Birakan · Obluchye · Birofeld · Pashkovo · Amour · Fadde · Emnakovski · Leninskoje · Pompeievka · Bidjan · CHINA

**Jewish immigration**

| 1928 | 1933 | 1938 |
|---|---|---|
| 950 | 11,000 | 19,000 |

35 km.

---

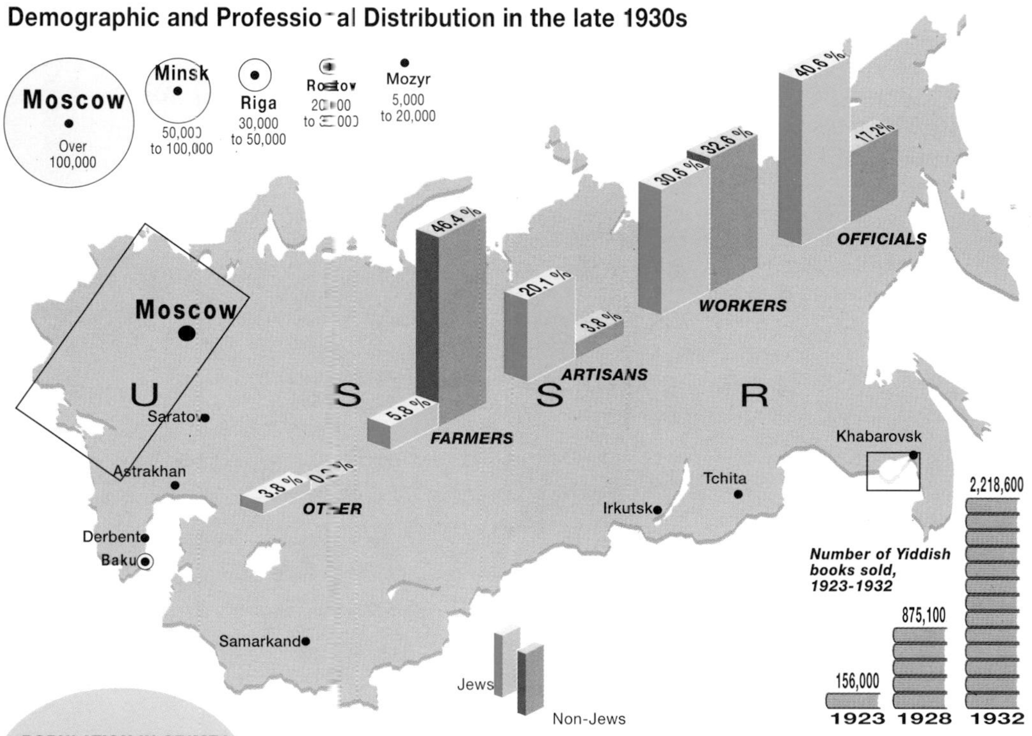

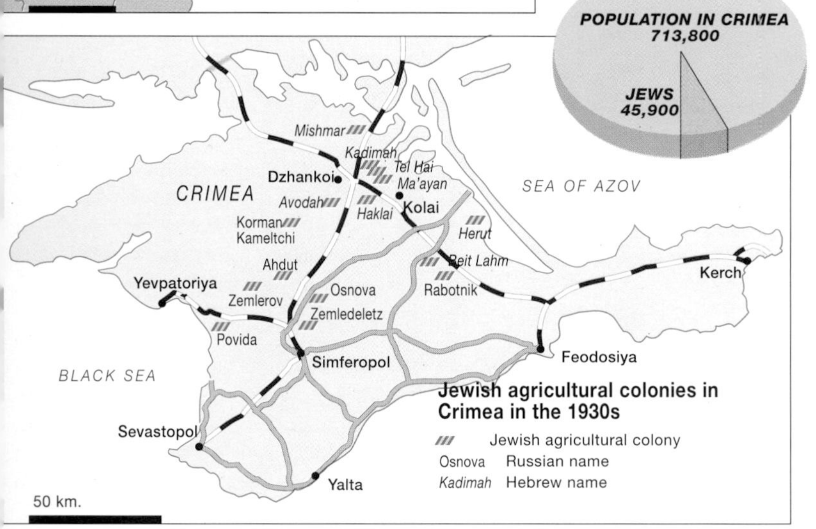

**Birobidzhan, a Jewish autonomous region** — May 1928

**The first Five-Year Plan** — 1928–1933

**The Moscow Trials** — 1936–1938

**1921. March 17:** The Party Congress proclaims the NEP – the New Economic Policy.

**1921–1927:** Introduced by Lenin in order to save the country from disaster, the NEP restores a liberal economy for a while; the pressure for "productivization" exerted on the Jews is eased off, but the burden of taxation brings impoverishment and destruction; at the same time the image of the Jewish merchant as "exploiter of the peasants" is still dominant.

**1921. June:** A group of Hebrew writers, led by the poets Hayyim Nahman Bialik and Saul Tchernichowsky, leaves Russia for Palestine.

**1922. April:** Stalin is made First Secretary of the Russian Communist Party.

**1925:** A Yiddish theater network, under the direction of Alexander Granovski, becomes the Jewish State Theater of the Soviet Union; it produces adaptations of Yiddish classics by authors such as Mendele Mokher Seforim, Shalom Aleichem, and I.L. Peretz, as well as pieces of Soviet propaganda; in

1929 Granovski is replaced by the actor Solomon Mikhoels.

**1925–1936:** Jewish Communists attempt to develop a "Jewish proletarian culture" which was to be according to Stalin's slogan, "national in form and socialist in content," based on the promotion of the Yiddish language and its literature; founding of Yiddish journals (such as *Der Emes*, "Truth," in Moscow) and "faculties of Jewish culture" in the universities of Minsk and Kiev, all subject to the control of the *Yevsektsiya*; development of a large network of Yiddish schools, particularly in the Ukraine and Belorussia; at the height of this period, in 1932, 160,000 pupils (over one-third of all Jewish children of elementary school age) attend these schools.

**1927. November:** Leon Trotsky, (Lev Bronstein) is expelled from the Party, then banished from the Soviet Union (1929).

*3. Chaim Typin, from a Birobidzhantzi Kolkhoz, Stalindorf (the Ukraine), 1930s.*

The leader of *Habad* Hasidism, Rabbi Joseph Schneersohn, is imprisoned and then expelled from the Soviet Union.

**1928–1933:** The introduction of the first Five-Year Plan ends the NEP and liquidates the entire class of Jewish merchants; five autonomous Jewish regions are established.

**1930:** Abolition of the *Yevsektsiya*.

**1934:** At the first conference of Soviet writers about 20% of the delegates are Jews; a minority among them write in Yiddish, the rest – including Ilya Ehrenburg, Boris Pasternak, Isaac Babel – in Russian.

**1935–1937:** The regime begins an attack on cultural activities in Yiddish: journals are closed down; all of Soviet Jewish culture is to be concentrated in the Autonomous Region in Birobidzhan; many Jewish writers, among them the poet Moses Kulbak, are imprisoned and later executed.

**1936–1938:** The Moscow Trials: many of the victims (such as Grigori Zinoviev and Lev Kamenev, leaders of the so-called "left opposition") are of Jewish origin.

# Jewish Agriculture in South America

In Latin America, which was basically agrarian and industrially underdeveloped, agricultural settlement was an important avenue of immigrant absorption. During the sixteenth and seventeenth centuries many New Christians were engaged in exploiting the natural resources of Brazil and the Caribbean Islands and in exporting them to Europe. A second period of Jewish agriculture in Latin America began following the mass immigration of Russian Jews in the late nineteenth century. Individual Jews began farming in Argentina during the 1880s, and in 1888 a group of eight Jewish families settled in the north of Santa Fé Province. But it was the fate of eight hundred persons who arrived in Argentina in August 1889 and established a colony named Moisesville in the same region, that attracted the attention of Jewish organizations in France and Germany, and convinced Baron Maurice de Hirsch to choose Argentina as the major objective of his colonization enterprise. Maurice de Hirsch had ambitious plans to solve the problem of Russian Jews by settling them in agricultural land, aided by western European affluent Jews. In 1891 he founded the Jewish Colonization Association (ICA) in Paris, which was incorporated in London with a basic endowment of two million pounds sterling.

Baron Hirsch hoped to concentrate hundreds of thousands of Jews in a large and autonomous area. But at the time of his death in 1896, ICA had purchased only 500,000 acres in three separate and far off provinces where five colonies were established, comprising 910 farms with a population of 6757 persons. Half a century later, on the eve of World War II, the Association possessed 1,500,000 acres in thirteen colonies, the largest among them (Moisesville, Baron Hirsch in Buenos Aires Province, Clara in Entre Rios Province) owning at least 250,000 acres of farmland, villages, and townlets. In 1925 the size of the population in the colonies reached its peak – 33,135 persons – of whom 20,382 were farmers. In addition to the ICA settlements, a few independent colonies developed in four provinces, numbering about 200 family holdings in 1925.

Recurring economic crises, the fact that most of these farms were located on the periphery of fertile regions and were badly afflicted by natural disasters, industrialization, modernization of agriculture, the inferior social status of the Argentinian peasant, the development of an urban Jewish community, and emigration to Israel, all contributed to the gradual disintegration of Jewish agriculture. In 1989, when Argentinian Jewry celebrated a centenary of agricultural settlement, most of the colonies' land was still under Jewish ownership, but very few Jews were actually engaged in farming.

ICA was active in other Latin American countries as well. In 1903 it founded Philippson, a small agricultural colony in the state of Rio Grande do Sul in Brazil. Six years later it acquired 230,000 acres in Quatro Irmãos where settlement began in 1914; but neither of these colonies prospered. The modest size of the family holdings, the small number of settlers, and the attraction of easier occupations in nearby towns led to the desertion of the first colony; dense forests, isolation, and a civil war which raged in the area after World War I, prevented the development of the other. Although groups of new colonists were brought by ICA to Quatro Irmãos in 1926, five years later there were only 464 Jews among 2080 non-Jews. During World War II, there were attempts to relocate Jewish refugees to these colonies as well as to Rezende, a newly

1. "He that tilleth his land shall be satisfied with bread" (Proverbs 12:11) – a poster celebrating the fiftieth anniversary of Jewish agricultural colonies in Argentina.

**The first ICA colony**

**1891**

**Death of Baron Maurice de Hirsch**

**21 April 1896**

**1876. October 19:** Argentina completes legal reforms pertaining to immigration and land colonization; the new laws permit the establishment and consolidation of Jewish agricultural settlements.

**1881. August 6:** Argentina's government, by presidential decree, nominates an agent in Europe to promote the immigration of Russian Jews.

**1889. August 14:** The ship Weser docks in Buenos Aires with 820 Jewish immigrants from Podolia (western Russia), most of them orthodox Jews.

**1891:** Founding of Mauricio, ICA's first colony.

**1893–1894:** Nine groups of fifty families each are transferred from Russia to Entre Rios Province in Argentina.

**1896. April 21:** Death of Baron Maurice de Hirsch.

**1900:** The first agricultural cooperative in

2. Orange picking in Sosúa, the Dominican Republic, 1941.

Argentina is founded in the Jewish colony of Lucienville. From its beginnings to the present, Jewish agricultural settlement in Argentina is characterized by an important cooperative movement.

**1902–1903:** First acquisitions of land in Brazil, mostly in the south, in Rio Grande do Sul, where ICA buys 250,000 acres.

**1904:** Founding of the Baron Hirsch colony in the south of the Buenos Aires Province.

**1910:** The governor of Entre Rios declares: "We owe the prosperity of our province

charted settlement occupying 5000 acres of land near Rio de Janeiro bought by ICA in 1936, but these were frustrated by the refusal of the Brazilian government to admit Jewish immigrants.

Colonization attempts were also made in Uruguay, Mexico, Ecuador, Bolivia, and in the Dominican Republic, where the dictator, Leonidas Trujillo, surprisingly announced that he was willing to accommodate 100,000 Jewish refugees in the country's agricultural areas. However, poor conditions for agricultural production, the lack of adequate train-

ing, insufficient funding, and a general lack of determination on the part of the settlers themselves, who after all came from European urban environments, doomed these attempts to failure.

Agriculture has always played an important role in the relations obtaining between the State of Israel and the Latin American countries, particularly since the 1960s. Ironically, many agricultural experts sent by Israel to serve in these countries as land-development instructors had previously been members of the Jewish agricultural colonies in Argentina.

**SE SACIA DE PAN**

עבודת ישראל

**NIZACION ISRAELITA**

**A ARGENTINA**

| NIA BARON HIRSCH<br>IRES y GOB. de la PAMPA<br>1905<br>4 COLONOS | COLONIA DORA<br>PROV. SANTIAGO DEL ESTERO<br>1911<br>20 COLONOS | MEDANOS. LA PAMPA<br>1902<br>77 COLONOS |
|---|---|---|
| | | GOB. RIO NEGRO<br>1906<br>21 COLONOS |
| NIA NARCISSE LEVEN<br>NACION DE LA PAMPA<br>1909<br>5 COLONOS | COLONIA MONTEFIORE<br>PROV. DE SANTA FE<br>1912<br>100 COLONOS | GOB. DEL CHACO<br>1917<br>34 COLONOS |

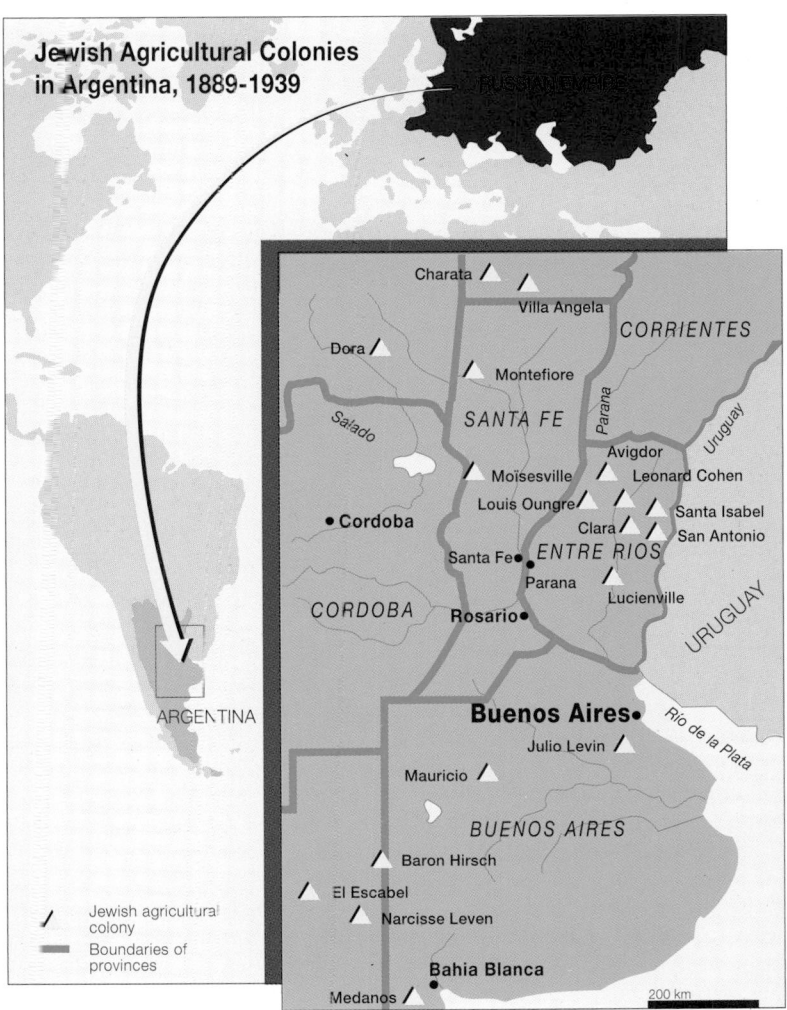

**Jewish Agricultural Colonies in Argentina, 1889–1939**

RUSSIAN EMPIRE

Charata
Villa Angela
CORRIENTES
Dora
Montefiore
Parana
SANTA FE
Salado
Avigdor
Moisesville    Leonard Cohen
Louis Oungre
Santa Isabel
• Cordoba
Clara    San Antonio
Santa Fe•    ENTRE RIOS
Parana
Lucienville
CORDOBA    Rosario•
Uruguay
URUGUAY

ARGENTINA

**Buenos Aires**•
Julio Levin
Mauricio
Rio de la Plata
*BUENOS AIRES*
Baron Hirsch
El Escabel
Narcisse Leven
**Bahia Blanca**
Medanos
200 km

↗ Jewish agricultural colony
▬ Boundaries of provinces

**Jewish colonies in Chaco, Argentina** — 1922

**The Avigdor colony in Argentina** — 1936

Arroyos with the help of the Jewish Communist Bank in Montevideo. none of these ventures survived.

**1917:** First appearance of the monthly *Colono Cooperador*, the official organ of the Jewish cooperatives, published to this day in Spanish and Yiddish.

**1922:** A colony of Jewish cotton growers was founded in Chaco, Argentina.

**1925:** A congress of the cooperatives of the Jewish agricultural colonies in Argentina establishes a national organization, the *Cooperativa de Cooperativas*.

**1928:** Philippson, the colony in Rio Grando do Sul in Brazil, is abandoned by most of its settlers who move into the cities.

**1936:** Founding of the Avigdor colony in Argentina for refugees from Germany. The Brazilian government prohibits the admittance of Jews into the colony of Rezende.

**1937:** ICA's colony Leonard Cohen is established in Entre Rios, Argentina.

**1938:** Jewish immigrants begin to lease or

buy land in Ecuador where they develop successful dairy farms.

**1939–1940:** The Mexican *Comite Central Israelita* helps to settle a number of Jews in Coscapa, in the state of Vera Cruz, as well as in farms near the city of Monterrey.

**1940:** In Bolivia the American Joint Distribution Committee and a mining magnate, the German Jew Mauricio Hochschild, establish Buena Tierra, which is perched at an altitude of 4000 meters in the Andes. In Chile an attempt at colonization is made on the large island of Chiloe. Large sums of money are invested in the famous colony at Sosua in the Dominican Republic organized by the American Agro-Joint; of 433 settlers, 136 are refugees from Nazi-occupied countries; only ten Jews remain there today.

**1964:** After 75 years of colonization, approximately 2000 persons still earn their livelihood from agriculture; the overall Jewish ownership of agricultural land is approximately 1,100,000 acres.

solely to the Jewish colonists"; Alberto Gerchunoff (1884–1950) publishes *Los Gauchos Judíos* – a collection of articles describing in vivid colors the life of Jewish colonists in Entre Rios during the last decades of the 19th century; congress held by representatives of the cooperative movement establishes the *Confederación Agrícola Israelita Argentina*.

**1913:** Acquisition of Quatro Irmãos in Southern Brazil.

**1915:** Thirty-eight families in Uruguay establish the colony 19 de Avril on government-owned lands in the district of Paisandu (by 1950, only one family remained there); another group attempts to settle by its own resources in the district of Mercedes; in 1938 a third group founds the colony Tres

# American Jewry: Integration and Distress

1. Max Weber (1881–1961), "Latest News." Oil, 1940. Born in Bialystock, Poland, Weber immigrated to the U.S. in 1891.

The Johnson Act of 1924 reduced Jewish immigration to a trickle of several thousand refugees a year. Constituting a terrible tragedy for the Jews of Eastern Europe, who were thus deprived of their principal haven, it also hastened the integration and acculturation of those already settled in America. Families which belonged to the industrial proletariat in the first generation, attained middle class status in the second. Fathers worked hard in order to put their children through college – the gate to success in business, managerial employment, and the liberal professions. Although their regional dispersion remained the same as before, there was considerable mobility within the cities as families moved from old slums downtown into more affluent districts. Some suburbs became typical Jewish neighborhoods, built around the synagogue and the community center. By the same token, many Jews were climbing up the social ladder within their respective communities. East European Jews joined the Reform temples, fulfilled central community functions, and infiltrated the old clubs of the "German" Jews. This process of internal integration was a primary reason for the "Zionization" of Reform Judaism. Yet the majority still preferred the Conservative Movement which offered a seductive combination of Hebraic tradition, openness to the modern world, and respect for the values of the American middle class. By the end of World War II, the Conservatives emerged as the strongest and most important current within American Jewry.

Admittedly, the situation of America's Jews was not all rosy. The eruption of xenophobia and "nativism" in the 1920s provided a new impetus for antisemitism. Racist theories flourished, translated into social practices by various forms of discrimination: restrictions on places of residence, places of work and leisure, and on acceptance of Jewish students to certain universities. European Nazism and the economic depression aggravated the poisonous atmosphere. Pro-Nazi organizations (such as the notorious Ku Klux Klan), Catholic and nativist preachers, and isolationist politicians combined forces in an attempt to intimidate and marginalize the Jewish community. In such an atmosphere all attempts to modify the harsh laws on immigration were bound to fail. The State Department was not only doing its best to shut the gates of America against the flood of European Jews fleeing the expansion of Nazism, but it also persistently refrained from pressurizing Great Britain to open the gates of Palestine. It even went so far as to withhold for many months reliable information about the mass extermination of European Jewry. The Jewish community itself, lacking self-confidence, contributed little towards the rescue of their European brethren.

Nevertheless, American democracy, which was never seriously placed in question, enabled the Jews to fight openly against manifestations of antisemitism. In this struggle the Jews found many allies among intellectuals and the political elite (Franklin D. Roosevelt's intolerance of antisemitism earned him and the Democratic Party the support of the great majority of American Jews). Well-integrated despite everything, their successsful acculturation was the main cause for the failure of the emergence of a mass Zionist movement in America. Thus, ideological Zionism only began to exert influence towards the end of World War II, although the pragmatic and philanthropic bodies, such as the women's organization *Hadassah*, enjoyed stability and widespread support. On the whole it was the non-Zionist – or the moderately Zionistic – organizations which were most successful in the United States during the first half of the twentieth century: the Joint, the United Jewish Appeal, and the order of B'nai B'rith. After the Holocaust, however, very few American Jews remained uncommitted to the Zionist cause.

| Law on immigration | The Stock Exchange Crash | The New Deal |
|---|---|---|
| 1924 | October 24, 1929 | 1933 |

**1918–1941:** Between the end of World War I and America's entry into World War II, antisemitic manifestations increase: the extremely racist Ku Klux Klan organization accuses the Jews of being agents of international Bolshevism; Henry Ford, the automobile magnate from Detroit, identifying all Jews with New York high finance, publishes an American edition of the *Protocols of the Elders of Zion*; more serious still, some prestigious American universities, such as Harvard, impose a *numerus clausus* (quota) on Jewish students; most rigorous in the faculties of medicine, this discrimination leads community authorities to promote the founding of its own medical institutions (such as the Mount Sinai hospitals).
**1920–1945:** Construction of thousands of synagogues which, in order to attract young families, open schools and elect young modern rabbis who speak perfect English. The Conservative synagogues are the ones fulfilling the greatest variety of civil, social, and cultural functions. The community

3. The Jew, last master of the land; an antisemitic caricature in Life Publication, 1909.

centers which spring up in all the suburbs of the large cities are opened equally to non-Jews.
**1929:** Beginning of the Great Depression.
**1930s:** From 60% in 1900, the proportion of Jews working in industry drops to 20% during the 1930s – a proportion two or three times lower than in the non-Jewish population; in the same period, the proportion of Jews in commerce and public services follows the inverse curve (25% in 1900, 60% in the 1930s, which is double the percentage of non-Jews); finally, the proportion of East European Jews engaged in the professions rises from 3% to 15%. This spectacular transformation of the socio-economic position of the Jews is best illustrated by the fact that all the big film companies, bar just one, were owned at that time by Jews, and the Kuhn-Loeb Bank was for a long time the principal financier of the American film industry.
**1932–1938:** Many German Jewish intellectuals settle in the United States; to

# 1924–1945

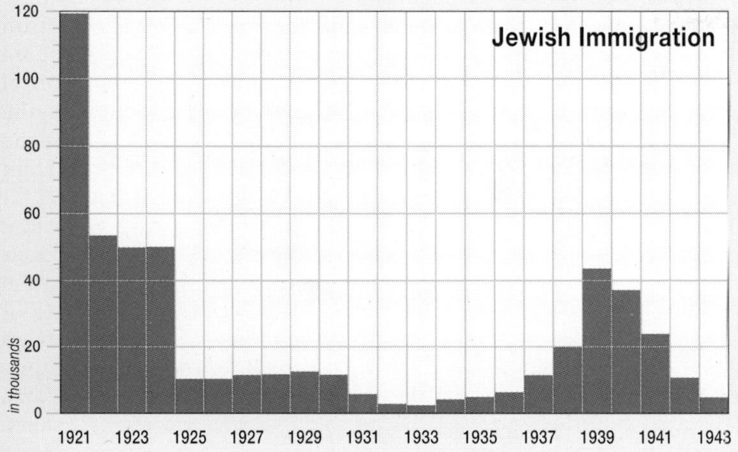
Jewish Immigration
120
100
80
60
40
20
0
in thousands
1921 1923 1925 1927 1929 1931 1933 1935 1937 1939 1941 1943

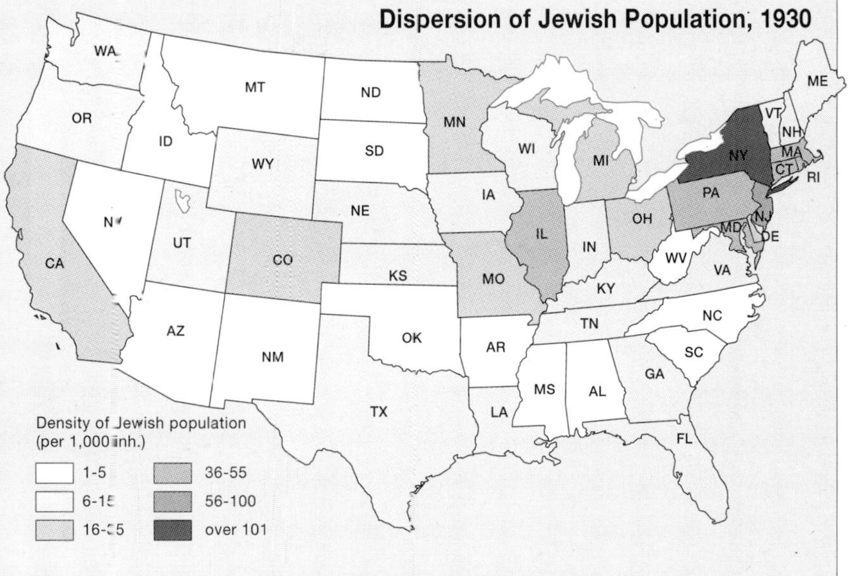
Dispersion of Jewish Population, 1930
WA
OR
ID
MT
ND
SD
WY
NV
UT
CO
NE
KS
CA
AZ
NM
OK
TX
MN
IA
MO
AR
LA
WI
IL
MI
IN
OH
KY
TN
MS
AL
GA
FL
SC
NC
VA
WV
PA
NY
VT
NH
ME
MA
CT
RI
NJ
MD
DE
Density of Jewish population (per 1,000 inh.)
1-5
6-15
16-35
36-55
56-100
over 101

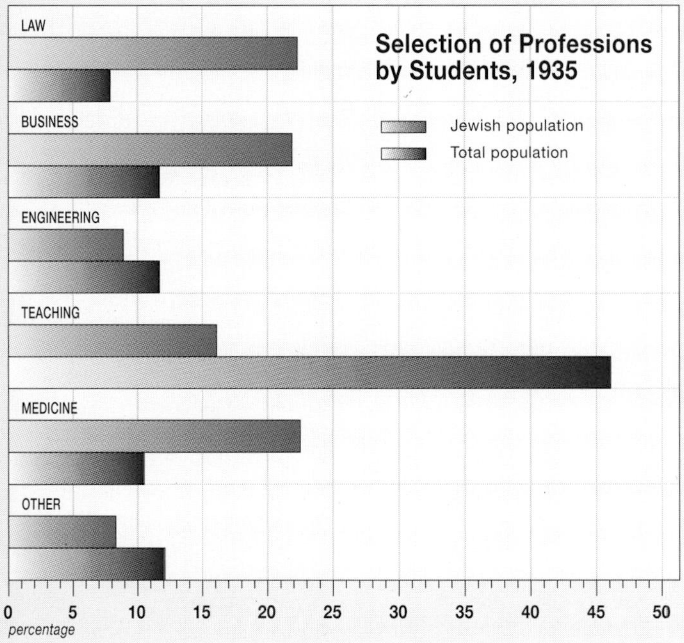
Selection of Professions by Students, 1935
Jewish population
Total population
LAW
BUSINESS
ENGINEERING
TEACHING
MEDICINE
OTHER
0 5 10 15 20 25 30 35 40 45 50
percentage

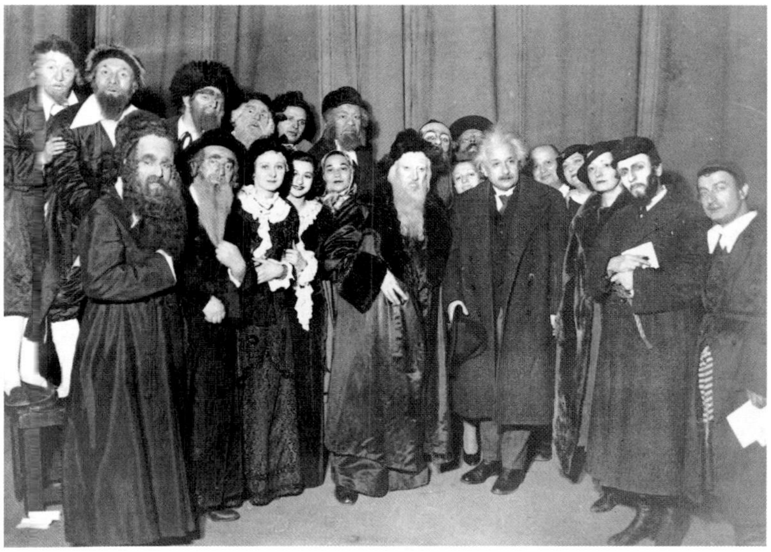

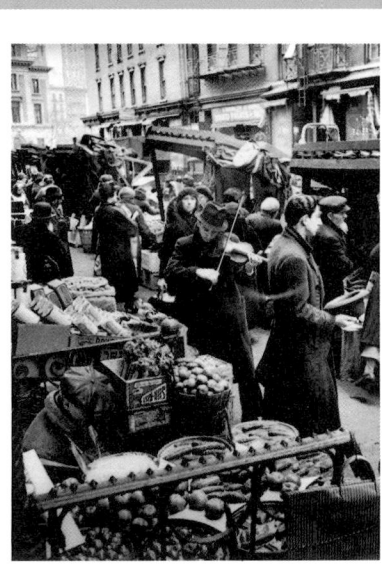

2. Albert Einstein in the company of a Yiddish theater troupe. New York, c. 1935.

| New platform of Reform Judaism | The United States at war | The Biltmore Program | The War Refugee Board |
|---|---|---|---|
| 1937 | 1941 | May 1942 | 1944 |

mention but a few: Albert Einstein (1932), and the leading figures of the Frankfort School – Erich Fromm (1933), Herbert Marcuse (1934), Theodor Adorno (1938).
**1933, 1936:** The two phases of Roosevelt's New Deal; American Jews support it to the extent that the antisemites soon label it the "Jew Deal," particularly as the Secretary of the Treasury from 1934 was Henry Morgenthau Jr.
**1934:** Mordecai M. Kaplan, founder of the Reconstructionist Movement, influences generations of Conservative rabbis with his conception of Judaism as a civilization encompassing of all aspects of individual and collective life; religion is the expression of the collective Jewish consciousness, the revival of *Eretz Yisrael* – an expression of the renaissance of the Jewish people.
**1937:** The Reform Movement replaces the "Pittsburgh Platform" with the "Columbus Platform" which is more open to traditional observance and to the Zionist enterprise: "the obligation of all Jewry to aid in

4. The Lower East Side in the late 1930s.

[Palestine's] upbuilding as a Jewish homeland by endeavoring to make it not only a haven of refuge for the oppressed but also a center of Jewish cultural and spiritual life [...] Judaism as a way of life requires, in addition to its moral and spiritual demands [...] the use of Hebrew, together with the vernacular, in our worship and instruction."
**1939:** The British White Paper practically closes Palestine to Jewish immigration. Founding of the United Jewish Appeal following the news about *Kristallnacht*.
**1941–1945:** The United States at war. About 550,000 Jews join the ranks of the American army; 10,500 are killed, 24,000 wounded, 36,000 decorated for bravery.
**1942. May:** The Biltmore Program defines what the Zionist Movement expects to attain after the war: a Jewish commonwealth in Palestine. Most American Jews are won over to the Zionist cause.
**1943:** The American Jewish Conference, convened in order to decide how to save European Jewry and to discuss the question of Palestine, representing the majority of American Jewish communities, clarifies its positions. Under the influence of the radical Zionist, Abba Hillel Silver, and despite opposition from the anti-Zionist organizations – the Jewish Workers Committee and the American Jewish Committee – a resolution is adopted in favor of creating a sovereign Jewish entity in Palestine. However, the resolutions concerning the rescue of European Jewry are not translated into action and have little effect on public opinion.
**1944:** Under strong pressure, Roosevelt creates a War Refugee Board; under the direction of Henry Morgenthau Jr., the Board manages to save about 200,000 Jews, mostly Hungarian from death in the concentration camps ("too little and too late").
**1945:** When the war ends, U.S. Jewish communal life is dominated by concern for the Holocaust survivors.

# The Emergence of a New Society

1. *"The General Federation of Hebrew Workers in Eretz Yisrael." Propaganda poster of the* Histadrut, *December 1948.*

In the history of Jewish Palestine the year 1881 inaugurated a new era. For many centuries Jews from all over the diaspora had been "going up" to the Land of Israel, to live and die there, but the immigration of 1881 did not resemble any other. Inspired for the first time by an essentially modern national movement, this *aliyah* laid the foundations for the national rebirth of a Jewish society.

Everywhere else society preceded the nation; in this case, the national sentiment came first, and then, in order to be transformed into reality, it needed to go through a stage of immigration to an ancestral homeland where the nation-building process could begin. This was a unique case of a society of potential immigrants who felt they belonged in a specific land long before they had set foot on its soil, and in less than two generations succeeded in forming a nation endowed with all the attributes of national "normality." Thus, although a minority in the demographic sense, the Jews of Palestine were not a minority in the national sense: the mandate of the League of Nations represented them as a national community aspiring to independence, and the relations between the mandatory authorities and the *yishuv* (the Jewish community in Palestine) did not resemble the usual interaction between a ruling power and ethnic minorities.

The nature of this new society, its structures, and the pace of its growth were determined by several factors. First, the magnitude of each wave of immigration and its social composition, both largely determined by the immigration policy of the Mandate and the division of the immigrants into categories – workers, capital holders, and professionals. Second, the financial resources available to the colonizing institutions and the volume of private investment (between 1918 and 1945, the investment of foreign capital amounted to 153 million pounds, 109 million of which were private funds). This enabled the leaders of the *yishuv* to establish a network of agricultural settlements embodying the predominant collectivist ideology, and marking the borders of the future state. Third, the nature and this emerging society was shaped also by political tensions within the Zionist leadership, and ideological conflicts among the immigrants who perceived the Zionist enterprise in vivid utopian colors.

Therefore, dividing the history of modern Jewish Palestine according to the successive *aliyot* is well justified, since each wave of immigration brought with it specific ideological and social characteristics which shaped the development of the *yishuv*. The First *Aliyah* (1881–1903) created the *moshavot*, villages of independent farmers; the Second (1904–1914) brought the collective settlement (the *kibbutz*); the Third (1919–1923), Fourth (1924–1928), and Fifth (1933–1939) were responsible for spectacular urban and industrial growth.

In 1880 the total number of Jews in the country was 20,000–25,000, two-thirds of whom were in Jerusalem; on the eve of independence they numbered about 650,000, in old new towns and in hundreds of settle-

| Petah Tikvah, the first *moshavah* | Deganyah, the first kibbutz; Ahuzzat Bayit, Tel Aviv's first quarter | Founding of the *Histadrut* | Nahalal, the first *moshav* |
| --- | --- | --- | --- |
| 1878 | 1909 | 1920 | 1921 |

**1878:** Petah Tikvah, "mother of the *moshavot*, is founded."
**1881–1903:** The First *Aliyah*: small groups of pioneers from Russia and Rumania begin settling the land.
**1882:** Founding of Rishon le-Zion; by the end of the year the Jews possess 5500 acres of land.
**1883:** Founding of Yesud ha-Ma'alah and Ekron.
**1884:** Founding of Gederah.
**1890:** Founding of Rehovot and Haderah.
**1901:** Creation of the *Keren Kayemet le-Israel*, the Jewish National Fund.
**1904–1914:** The Second *Aliyah*.
**1905:** Founding of the leftist Zionist party, *Hapo'el ha-Tsair*, the "Young Worker."
**1906:** Founding of *Po'alei Zion*, the "Workers of Zion" party.
**1908:** Arthur Ruppin establishes the Palestine Office in Jaffa, an association for the purchase of buying land intended for agricultural settlement.
**1909:** A self-defense organization, *Ha-*

2. *Kibbutz Ein-Harod at its establishment, 1921.*

*Shomer* ("The Watchman") is founded by pioneers of the Second *Aliyah*.
**1909–1910:** Acquisition of lands in the Jezreel Valley; the first Jewish settlement in the valley – Merhavyah – will be founded in 1911.
**1913:** *Hadassah*, organization of Zionist American women, begins its activities in Palestine.
**1917. November 17:** The Balfour Declaration: the British Government recognizes the right of the Jewish people to a national home in Palestine.
**1919–1923:** The Third *Aliyah*.
**1919:** Two workers' parties are established: *Ahdut ha-Avodah* ("Unity of Labor") and *Ha-Shomer ha-Tsair* ("The Young Watchman").
**1920–1945:** Over 250,000 immigrants arrive; about 171,000 – category A – "workers" – and 84,000 – category B – "capitalists" and "professionals." These categories determine the distribution of immigration certificates by the Mandatory authorities.
**1922:** Churchill White Paper.

# 1881–1948

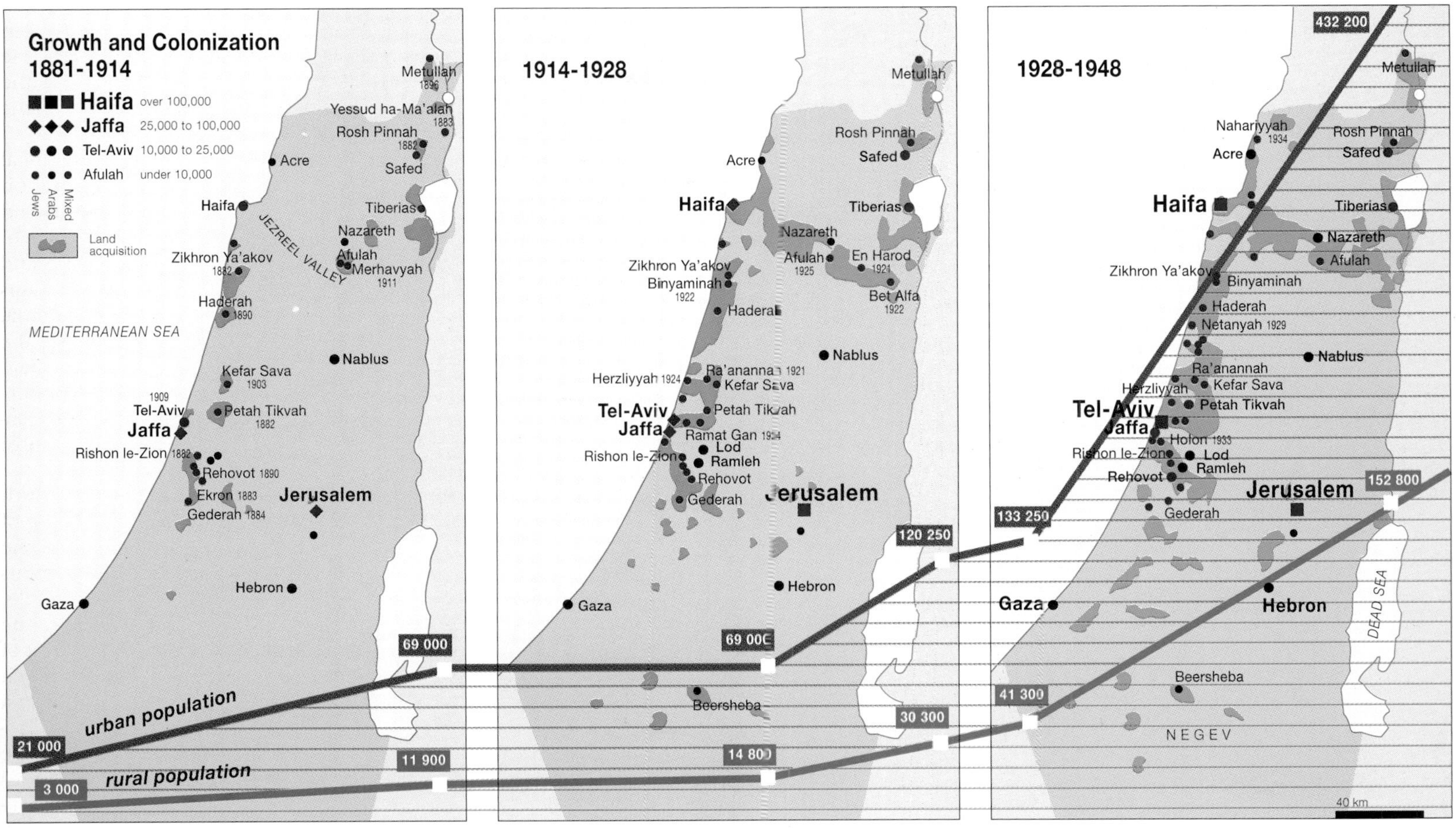

## Growth and Colonization 1881-1914

■■■ **Haifa** over 100,000
◆◆◆ **Jaffa** 25,000 to 100,000
●●● Tel-Aviv 10,000 to 25,000
• • • Afulah under 10,000

Mixed / Arabs / Jews

Land acquisition

Metullah 1896
Yessud ha-Ma'alah 1883
Rosh Pinnah 1882
Safed
Acre
Haifa
JEZREEL VALLEY
Tiberias
Nazareth
Afulah
Merhavyah 1911
Zikhron Ya'akov 1882
Haderah 1890
MEDITERRANEAN SEA
Kefar Sava 1903
• Nablus
1909 Tel-Aviv
**Jaffa** Petah Tikvah 1882
Rishon le-Zion 1882
Rehovot 1890
Ekron 1883 **Jerusalem**
Gederah 1884
Gaza
Hebron

urban population
21 000
69 000
rural population
3 000
11 900

### 1914-1928

Metullah
Rosh Pinnah
Acre Safed
**Haifa** ◆
Nazareth Tiberias
Afulah 1925 En Harod 1921
Zikhron Ya'akov
Binyaminah 1922 Bet Alfa 1922
Haderah
Herzliyyah 1924 Ra'anannah 1921
Kefar Sava
Tel-Aviv Petah Tikvah
**Jaffa** Ramat Gan 1924
Rishon le-Zion Lod
Ramleh
Rehovot
Gederah
• Nablus
**Jerusalem**
Hebron
Gaza
Beersheba
120 250
69 000
30 300
14 800

### 1928-1948

432 200
Metullah
Nahariyyah 1934 Rosh Pinnah
Acre Safed
**Haifa** ■
Nazareth
Afulah
Zikhron Ya'akov Binyaminah
Haderah
Netanyah 1929
Ra'anannah
Herzliyyah Kefar Sava • Nablus
Tel-Aviv Petah Tikvah
**Jaffa** Holon 1933
Rishon le-Zion Lod
Rehovot Ramleh
Gederah **Jerusalem**
133 250 152 800
Gaza Hebron
Beersheba
41 300
NEGEV
DEAD SEA
40 km

ments throughout the land. There were 44 Jewish agricultural settlements, mostly *moshavot*, when the British conquered Palestine in 1917; by the time the State of Israel was established in 1948, the pioneering ideology of "conquest of soil and labor" of the Second and Third *Aliyot* added another 148 *kibbutzim* and 94 cooperative villages (*moshavim*). Even more impressive was the development of the urban sector, which absorbed more than three-quarters of the immigration. Tel Aviv, the "first Hebrew city," numbered 40,000 inhabitants in 1931, 135,000 at the end of the Fifth *Aliyah*, and 200,000 in 1945.

From the beginning the Zionist movement considered the *yishuv* as a territorial political entity, a united, autonomous, and democratic community. Indeed, even before the British conquest and at an accelerated pace afterwards, the Palestinian Jewish community created governmental institutions based on universal suffrage and principles of western democracy – notably the Assembly of Deputies and the National Council – which had departments corresponding to government ministries.

However, the most typical feature of political life in Palestine was the central role played by the parties – comprehensive political societies with networks of clients, colonization federations, as well as economic, cultural, and sports institutions, even para-military units. And first among them was the left-wing Labor Party which held sway over the *yishuv* and later over the State of Israel for several decades.

| The Labor Party (*Mapai*) | The White Paper | The proclamation of the State of Israel |
|---|---|---|
| 1930 | 1939 | 1948 |

**1920:** Founding of the *Histadrut*, the General Federation of Jewish Labor; the *Haganah* ("Defense") – the nucleus of a nationwide defensive militia; *Gedud ha-Avodah* ("Labor Legion") a voluntary Socialist-oriented organization which aspired to transform the country into a large commune.
**1921:** The Labor Legion founds Kibbutz En Harod in the Jezreel Valley.
**1922:** Bet Alfa, the first kibbutz founded by *Ha-Shomer ha-Tsair*.
**1924–1928:** The Fourth *Aliyah*.
**1925:** Founding of the nationalist right-wing Zionist Revisionist Organization.
**1929:** Creation of the enlarged Jewish Agency which for the first time includes non-Zionist personalities such as Albert Einstein and Leon Blum.
**1930:** Lord Passfield's White Paper inaugurates the policy of restriction on land purchase by Jews; with the merger of two labor parties, *Mapai* – the Workers' Party of Eretz Yisrael – is formed, led by Ben Gurion.
**1933–1939:** The Fifth *Aliyah*.

*3. Aerial view of Tel Aviv, 1947.*

**1934:** Creation of the National Federation of the Workers of Eretz Yisrael – the right-wing equivalent of the *Histadrut*.
**1936–1939:** In order to overturn British restrictions on Jewish colonization, the *yishuv* adopts the method of "Stockade and Watchtower" – the erection of a new settlement overnight; 52 settlements are established in this manner within the three years which also witness the Arab Revolt.
**1937:** The Peel Commission, sent to Palestine to inquire into the causes of the Arab Revolt, proposes the partition of Palestine; the Mandatory authorities prohibit the purchase of land by Jews in territories allocated to the Arab state.
**1939:** Ramsay MacDonald's White Paper imposes new restrictions on land acquisition.
**1945:** Split within *Mapai*.
**1946:** Eleven settlements are created in the northern Negev; intensive colonization throughout the land.
**1947:** 450,000 acres of agricultural land are in Jewish hands.

# The Jews of Persia

The origin of the Jewish community in the Persian empire (whose center was located in what today is the province of Fars in Iran) is obscure. Tradition traces it back either to the deportation of the Israelites from Samaria by the Assyrians Tiglath-Pileser III and Saragon II in the eighth century BC, or to the destruction of the First Temple by Nebuchadnezzar in the mid-seventh century BC. In any case, it would appear that when Cyrus II permitted the exiles to return to their homeland (538 BC), some of them preferred to remain in the diaspora. Gradually the Babylonian communities expanded to the provinces and cities of Persia. The tolerance of the Persian rulers enabled many Jews to rise to prominent positions at the royal court: the Bible has preserved the names of Zerubbabel, Ezra, Nehemiah, Daniel, Mordecai and his niece Esther (probably in the reign of Xerxes I). Alexander the Great's conquest of Persia (331 BC) and Seleucid rule over the eastern provinces of Alexander's empire, apparently did not affect the Jewish communities. Sources dating from the period of Parthian rule in the east (247 BC–224 AD), testify to the existence of large and prosperous Jewish communities beyond the Euphrates, which enjoyed religious and legal autonomy. Only during the centuries of Sassanid rule (224–651) and with the intervention of Zoroastrian priests in affairs of government, did the situation of

1. A man's headgear. Jewish craftsmanship, Iran 19th or 20th century.

Persian Jews begin to deteriorate. In the mid-seventh century the Persian state became a province of the Arab-Muslim empire. The Arab conquest replaced one state religion with another, but for the Jews this was a change for the better. As *dhimmis* they were deprived of equality, but were protected by the rulers according to the regulations of the "Covenant of Omar." Economically, they were free to engage in any occupation, and the sources indicate that Persian Jews were active as artisans, shopkeepers, merchants and manufacturers. The growing urbanization of the Muslim Orient and the growth of international commerce led to the emergence of a wealthy class of merchants and bankers in the large cities: Baghdad, Ahwaz, Isfahan, and Shiraz. Economic prosperity was accompanied by religious and intellectual fermentation: during these early centuries of Muslim rule the Jewish communities produced a large number of sects, freethinkers, heretical and messianic movements of all sorts, the most notable among them being the Karaites who emerged during the eighth century and spread throughout

2. A Hebrew zodiac. Illuminated manuscript, Iran, 19th or 20th century.

the Persian provinces. The conquest of Baghdad by Hulagu Khan's Mongols in 1258 ended the Abbasid caliphate. Once again the Jews underwent a radical change: the new overlords abolished the status of *dhimmi*, and all religions were acknowledged as equal. This was a golden age for Persian Jews who became more involved than ever in the economic and political life of the empire. The cultural climate which enabled them to attain political integration also gave birth to a rich Judeo-Persian literature.

Another dramatic turning point occurred with the accession of the Safawid dynasty (1501) which tried to introduce Shi'ism as the state

| Achaemenid dynasty | Seleucid domination | Parthian domination | Sassanid dynasty | Arab conquest |
|---|---|---|---|---|
| 559–330 BC | 312–247 BC | 247 BC–224 AD | 224–561 | Beginning in 636 |

**722 BC:** Shalmaneser V, king of Assyria, deports the inhabitants of Samaria to northern and eastern Persia.
**586 BC:** Nebuchadnezzar I destroys the Temple and deports the Judeans to Babylonia; some of the exiles later emigrate to Persian towns; according to tradition, a town named Yahudiya, later Isfahan, was founded by Jews at the time.
**559–330 BC:** The Achaemenid dynasty.
**538 BC:** Babylon is conquered by Cyrus the Great; the Cyrus Declaration.
**c. 470 BC:** Probable date of the events described in the Book of Esther.
**247 BC–224 AD:** Parthian rule.
**224–651:** The Sassanids.
**459–484:** Reign of the Sassanid King Peroz; persecutions of Jews.
**590–628:** Reign of Khosroes II; in 614 he conquers Jerusalem with the help of the Jews, but later he turns against them.
**636:** Beginning of the Arab conquest of Iran.
**c. 750:** Abu Isa, a Jew from Isfahan, proclaims himself a messiah and leads an

armed revolt; he is killed in battle and his army destroyed.
**From 1100 onwards:** Jewish merchants establish communities along the trade routes to the Far East.
**1221–1258:** Mongol conquest of Iran; an era of tolerance towards religious minorities; Jews rise to prominent positions. Under the Mongol dynasty of the Il-Khans, beginning in 1335, the Jews produce a rich Judeo-Persian literature: Bible translations and original poetry; the greatest Jewish poet of the time is Shahin whose writing is based on biblical themes.
**1501–1736:** The Safawid dynasty imposes Shi'ite Islam by force; severe persecutions of Jews.
**1747:** During the reign of Nadir Shah, Jews settle in the holy city of Meshed.
**c. 1797:** Destruction of the community of Tabriz.
**1839:** Forced conversion of the Jews of

4. Jewish weavers. Hamadan, early 20th century.

religion. Massacres and forced conversions brought Persian Jewry to the brink of destruction. The Kajar dynasty (1794–1925) carried on the same political and religious policies as the Safawids, only with greater diligence. Only towards the late nineteenth century did the European powers, Jewish organizations, prominent Jewish figures such as Sir Moses Montefiore and Adolphe Cremieux, and the Zionist movement, begin to concern themselves with the plight of Iranian Jewry and to put pressure on the Iranian government.

The accession of the Pahlevi dynasty in 1925 changed the course of Iranian history. The policy and reforms introduced by Riza Shah and his son Muhammad Riza were all directed at bringing westernization and secularization to Iran, and at overthrowing the fanatical power of the Shi'ite clergy by reviving Iran's pre-Islamic heritage. The political emancipation of the Jews was an obvious and integral part of such policies. Persian Jews also benefited from the close relations, established in the early 1950s, between Iran and the State of Israel. Enforced modernization, however, proved to be a somewhat fragile accomplishment. The Islamic revolution which overthrew the Shah in 1979 was a reaction to over fifty years of submission to imported ideals and tyrannical rule. The Iranian Jews fell prey to the passions unleashed by the new regime.

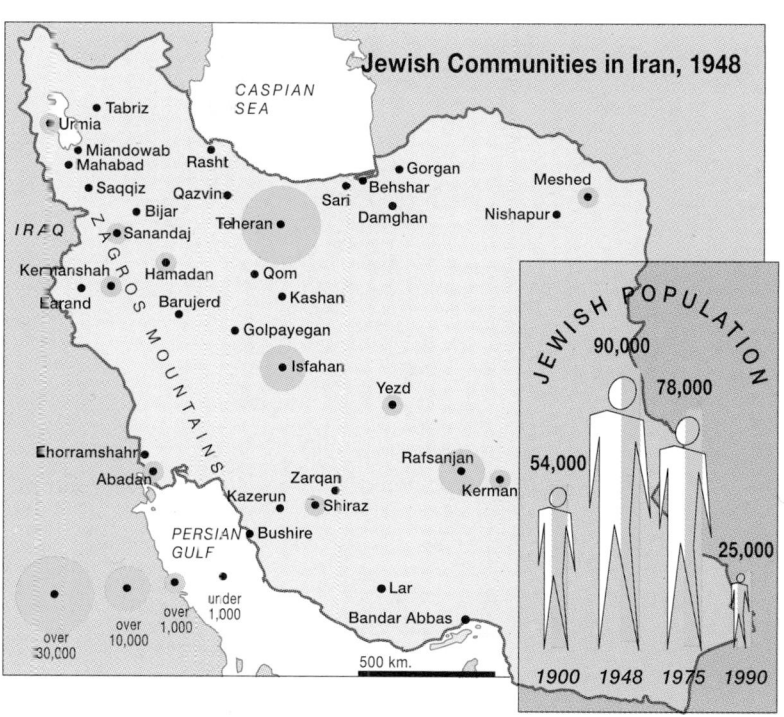

Jewish Communities in Iran, 1948

3. Ketubbah *(marriage contract). Iran, 1847.*

| Safawid dynasty | Accession of the Pahlevi | Islamic Revolution |
|---|---|---|
| 1501–1736 | 1925 | 1979 |

Meshed; thirty Jews are assassinated and hundreds wounded; the converts secretly adhere to Judaism until the 1930s.
**c. 1850:** European Jews begin to take an interest in their Iranian counterparts.
**1865:** Massacre of Jews in Barforush.
**From 1884 onwards:** Emigration to Palestine.
**1896–1907:** Reign of Shah Muzaffar-ed-Din; an important stage in the emancipation of Iranian Jews; in 1906, election of the first Persian parliament (*madjlis*) which officially expresses gratitude to the Jewish community for its contribution to the modernization of Iran; the *Shari'a* (religious Law) is replaced by civil legislation, and all discriminatory regulations are revoked; nevertheless, members of religious minorities are not themselves admitted to parliament but must be represented by Muslim deputies.
**1898:** The *Alliance Israelite Universelle* opens its first school in Teheran, and others follow shortly afterwards in many other provincial

towns.
**1918–1926:** Zionist activities. Aziz ben Jonah Naim writes a history of the Zionist movement in Persian written in Hebrew characters (1920); Zionist periodicals, translations of modern Hebrew literary works.
**1925–1941:** Reign of Riza Shah, bent on the modernization of Iran.
**1948:** When the State of Israel is established, about 20,000 Iranian Jews live in Palestine, and about 100,000 in Iran; by 1968, 70,000 of them have left for Israel, but 10,000 later return to Iran.
**1960:** The Shah publicly confirms his country's recognition of Israel, an act which places a strain on Iran's relations with Arab states.
**1979:** The Islamic Revolution of Ayatollah Khomeiny; exodus of Iranian Jews: by 1990 about 55,000 have left the country, 30,000 of them to the U.S.A, 20,000 to Israel, 5,000 to Europe; in the Islamic Republic of Iran there remain about 25,000 Jews.

5. Passover plate. Painted ceramic, Iran, 15th century.

# The Invention of Modern Hebrew Culture

גשפי פורים המאוחדים
אהל-פורים גשפי אגדתי
בהפרשה לקהקל

דפוס מסדר

בכל אולמי התערוכה והגן

*1. Purim carnival in Tel Aviv during the 1930s. A poster.*

Rooted in the *Haskalah*, the Jewish Enlightenment of the late eighteenth century, and nourished on nationalism and modernization, the new culture which emerged in Palestine has been labeled "national," "Israeli," but mostly a "Hebrew" culture. All these terms are intended to emphasize the demarcation line between the new phenomenon and the "old" Yiddish culture, traditional and orthodox, which characterized the townlets of Eastern Europe. Insisting on Hebrew stemmed from a desire to plant this new culture firmly in the soil of the ancestral homeland. Attempting to integrate harmoniously all past traditions of the Jewish people – religious and secular, European and Oriental, ancient and modern, universalist and national – Hebrew was thought to contain all the necessary ingredients of a collective identity option, and to form a bridge between the diaspora and the newly-found land. It was above all a "national" phenomenon. Henceforth its historical role was well defined: to determine the spiritual nature of the newly-born Jewish society and to endow it with a system of values and with a vehicle for unification. In other words, it offered a legitimate alternative to the older religious system of values and concepts.

The language was first to be created. The process of transforming Hebrew into the exclusive tongue of the society at large, for every possible need and on all strata, began in the 1880s. This was accomplished mainly through the schools: when the State was established, the Hebrew school network comprised 65% of all schools and about 100,000 pupils, ten times more than it had a generation earlier, in 1918. The revival of the language made it possible to create an original Hebrew culture and to translate features of other cultures into Hebrew properties. It also constituted a powerful unifying tool. A new, doubly motivated mentality emerged, based on notions of a "new society" (collective) and a "new man," (individual), rooted in the land itself, and in the idea of toiling the land with one's own hands, nourishing its soil with one's sweat and blood. This "new man" was actively involved in the making of history, and no longer a mere object; he was to be a hero in a modern saga which at once glorified the past while depleting it of religious significance. Orthodoxy was to take its revenge one day, but meanwhile, although religious institutions were officially recognized by the state, religion as a value system had only a minor influence on the culture of the new Jewish society in Palestine.

The "new society" and the "new man" were inseparable from the new-old homeland, valorized by poets, artists, and romantics. The Land of Israel, its landscape, its archeological sites (the evidence of origins produced by archeology was to play a unique role in the formation of an Israeli consciousness), constituted the material from which new myths, folklore, festivals and ceremonies were created. Excursions and hikes organized by schools and youth movements were tantamount to a sym-

| The Hebrew Language Committee | Herzliyah high-school | First volume of Ben-Yehuda's dictionary | | The Technion in Haifa | The Hebrew University |
|---|---|---|---|---|---|
| **1890** | **1906** | **1908** | | **1912** | **1925** |

**1881:** Eliezer Ben-Yehuda, the "father" of modern Hebrew, arrives in Jerusalem. This marks the beginning of a long struggle to impose Hebrew as the exclusive language of the Jews in Palestine.
**1890:** Establishment of the Hebrew Language Committee.
**1892:** The National Library is founded in Jerusalem.
**1896:** Ahad Ha-Am ("One of the People," pen-name of the essayist Asher Ginzberg) founds the literary monthly *Ha-Shilo'ah*. Establishment of the first Hebrew publishing firms (*Ahi'asaf* and *Tushiyyah*) and the first Hebrew-speaking elementary school in Jaffa.
**1898:** The first Hebrew-speaking kindergarten, in Rishon le-Ziyyon.
**1906:** Founding of the first Hebrew high-school, Herzliyah; three years later, it was transferred to a new site north of Jaffa, where "the first Hebrew city," Tel Aviv, rose out of the sands. An arts school, Bezalel, is founded in Jerusalem.
**1908:** Publication of the first volume of

Ben-Yehuda's dictionary, the first great dictionary of the Hebrew language. Shemuel Yosef Agnon, the future Nobel Prize winner, publishes his first novel *Agunot* ("Forsaken Wives").
**1910:** Founding of the first Hebrew daily newspaper in Palestine – *Ha-Doar* ("The Post').
**1912:** Founding of the *Technicum* (later named Technion) in Haifa – the first engineering college in Palestine.
**1919:** The newspaper *Hadashot ha-Aretz* ("News of the Land," the future *Haaretz*) is issued.
**1920:** First "Hebrew" archeological excavations, in Tiberias.
**1921:** Establishment of the Hebrew Writers Association in Palestine. The writer Joseph Hayyim Brenner is assassinated in Jaffa during Arab riots.
**1922:** Death of Eliezer Ben-Yehuda.
**1923–1931:** An upsurge of Hebrew publishing in Palestine.
**1924:** The poet Hayyim Nahman Bialik,

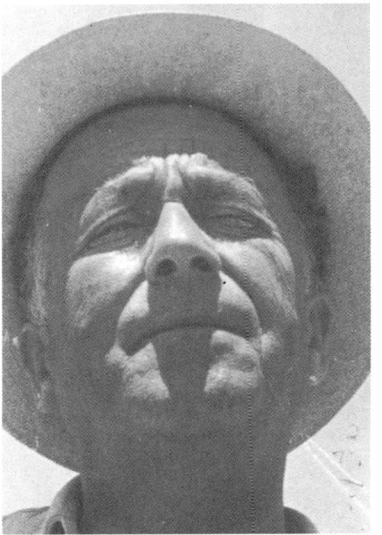

authorized to leave Russia three years earlier, following the intervention of Maxim Gorki, settles in Tel Aviv. Uri Zvi Greenberg, nationalist poet, arrives in Palestine.
**1925:** The workers' leader, Berl Katzenelson, founds the daily newspaper *Davar*, the voice of the *Histadrut*. The coeditor of the literary journal *Ketuvim* ("Writings"), poet Abraham Shlonsky, challenges Bialik's literary authority. Poet Nathan Alterman arrives in Palestine. Inauguration of the Hebrew University of Jerusalem.
**1925–1928:** Emergence of the Hebrew theater in Palestine; in 1928 the *Habimah* group, founded in Moscow in 1917, settles in Tel Aviv where it functions as the national theater to this day.
**1926:** Violinist Yasha Hefetz performs in the Jezreel Valley.
**1931:** Inauguration of the art museum in Tel Aviv; Menahem Shemi, Reuven Rubin, Israel

*3. S.Y. Agnon photographed by poet Shimshon Meltzer, 1950.*

*2. The Technion in Haifa 1934.*

bolic "conquest" of the land. "Hebraization" meant the rebirth of all the original facets of a civilization that had been uprooted from its natural soil. This trend, whose extreme manifestations took the form of Canaanite primitivism, predominated well into the 1930s. Later years witnessed a return to the more modernist and universalist outlook.

From its very early stages, the community of idealistic immigrants created an impressive array of cultural institutions: journals, periodicals, libraries, museums, publishing houses, and theaters. The small dimensions of the *yishuv* did not prevent Palestine – and Tel Aviv above all – from becoming a lively intellectual and artistic center, the only Hebrew civilization in the world.

It was literature which dominated spiritual and cultural life in Jewish Palestine. Ideologically committed, Hebrew writers in the early years were invested with national importance and authority. In its secular and national garb, the literary elite in the *yishuv* continued, in fact, to play the central role it had always played in Jewish culture. A new poem by Nathan Alterman, to take but the most famous example, was regarded as an important political event. Although at a later point the State would drive writers out of the central political arena, modern Palestine was, in a sense, largely an invention of the writers.

This new Hebrew culture was no doubt founded on eclecticism, provincialism and nationalism. Artificially created by East-European Zionists, it conveyed but little of Jewish oriental heritage. However, the combination of national traditions with acquisitions from western modernity eventually produced a truly novel Jewish civilization. Full of conflicts and contradictions, like any living culture, it finally did accomplish the role for which it was designed: welding together a society in the process of transformation, thus providing a new frame of reference for an ancient people now emerging as a modern nation.

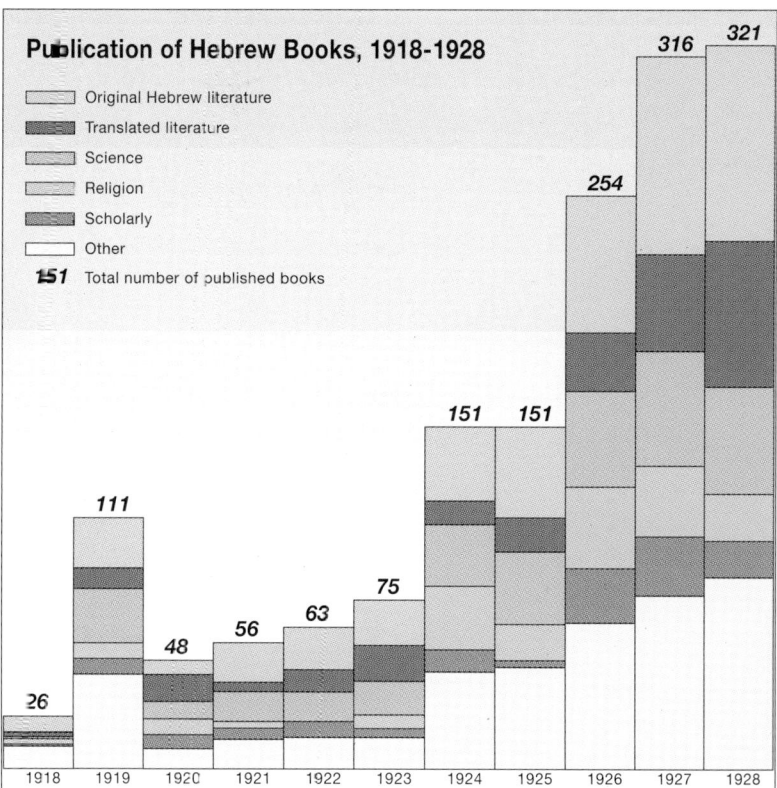

**Publication of Hebrew Books, 1918-1928**

- Original Hebrew literature
- Translated literature
- Science
- Religion
- Scholarly
- Other

**151** Total number of published books

Values: 26 (1918), 111 (1919), 48 (1920), 56 (1921), 63 (1922), 75 (1923), 151 (1924), 151 (1925), 254 (1926), 316 (1927), 321 (1928)

**Habimah theater in Tel Aviv**
**1928**

**The Palestine Symphony Orchestra**
**1936**

Paldi and Nahum Gutman are the principal representatives of this generation of artists. The poet Saul Tschernichowski settles in Palestine.
**1932:** Beginning of the excavations in Masada.
**1936:** First concert of the Palestinian Symphony Orchestra, founded by violinist Bronislaw Huberman, conducted by Arturo Toscanini.
**1936–1937:** The Palestine Broadcasting Service transmits in Hebrew, English and Arabic; founding of the Broadcasting Symphony Orchestra.
**1938:** Philosopher Martin Buber settles in Jerusalem.
**1939:** Founding of the evening daily *Yediot Aharonot* ("Latest News"), which today has the largest circulation in Israel.

*4. "Artists of Tel Aviv," a series of portraits by David Tartakover, 1983–1984. In the center here is the celebrated actress Hanna Rovina.*

לְשׁוֹן אַחַת־עַם אֶחָד

לְמַעֲנֶךָ וּלְמַעַן יְלָדֶיךָ

לְמַד עִבְרִית

לְמַד עִבְרִית!

הַרְשֵׁם הַיּוֹם

בְּשִׁעוּרֵי הָעֶרֶב לְעִבְרִית

*5. "For your own sake, and for the sake of your children, learn Hebrew!." A poster.*

# Prelude to the Holocaust

**Europe on the Eve of World War II**
- Liberal democracies
- Communist regime
- Authoritarian regime
- Fascist regime

The 1920s, a decade of hope, economic prosperity, rise of democratic governments, and attempts to ensure stability and peace, ended with the great economic crash of October 1929. This crisis not only caused the collapse of world economy, it also led to a deep disillusionment with Western civilization and the values of the Enlightenment. Europe was ravaged by extremist ideologies and violent tyrannies; young democracies were collapsing one after the other, being replaced by dictatorships and totalitarian regimes. Political polarization, endemic violence, persecution of minorities, and civil wars between liberal, democratic forces on the one hand, and militaristic, often racist, nationalists on the other, characterized the 1930s – "a low, dishonest decade," in the words of W.H. Auden.

In central and eastern Europe, where the largest Jewish population resided, the 1930s brought a rapid deterioration in the circumstances of the Jews. Despite legal equality and various commitments to protect minorities contained in the treaties concluding World War I, the Jews suffered discrimination in all walks of life. They were excluded from most economic activities, barred from public office, and gradually removed from all positions of authority. A *numerus clausus* for Jewish students was introduced in all universities. In Poland, where part of the intelligentsia

opposed such official discrimination, the authorities introduced instead a system of "ghetto benches" for Jewish students. Gradually whole towns were "purged" of Jews.

By the mid–1930s discrimination had evolved into violent persecution: pogroms, pillage, and massacres raged through Poland as the Nazi menace loomed large. The sizeable Jewish community in Poland was in a desperate situation even before the outbreak of the war. In Rumania, home of the third largest Jewish community (after Russia and Poland), race laws were enacted in 1938. Physicians' and lawyers' associations expelled their Jewish members, and the "Rumanization" of industries owned by Jews was intensified. Similar developments were taking place in the Baltic countries, in Hungary, Austria, and throughout central and eastern Europe. Even Italy, a country which did not have an antisemitic tradition, adopted Nazi racist principles in 1938, while in France anti-Jewish propaganda ran wild.

But Nazi Germany itself exemplified the worst oppression and persecution of the Jews. Hitler's plan to rid Germany of all Jews, outlined in *Mein Kampf* (1925), was immediately put into practice with the rise to power of the National-Socialist party in 1933. In full view of an indifferent world and ineffectual Jewish protests, Jews were deprived of their German citizenship, eliminated from the civil service, from the professions and from the intellectual and artistic life in which their proportional importance had far exceeded their percentage in the population. Attacks, dismissals, arrests, burnings of books and shops – all these became a daily routine. Famous Jewish scientists, physicians, lawyers, artists and musicians departed by the thousands, creating a deep void in Germany's cultural and intellectual life.

The German press daily published vicious attacks against the Jews: the physicians' journal in June 1935, for example, likened the Jews to tuberculosis bacilli. The Nuremberg Laws of September 15, 1935 classified the Jews as "subjects" deprived of all political rights. Many additional decrees and regulations enacted soon after further reduced their freedom, until they had no legal status whatsoever. By 1939, the 220,000 Jews who remained in Germany were totally unprotected by law and exposed to all forms of terror.

The organized and systematic Nazi pogrom on the night of November 9–10, 1938, was ostensibly an act of retaliation for the assassination of a German diplomat in Paris by a young Jew. Hundreds of synagogues throughout Germany and Austria were burnt down, about 7,500 Jewish businesses were destroyed, and at least 36 Jews were killed by the mob. This outrage obliterated any remaining hopes that the symbiosis which had once existed between Jews and Germans could ever be restored. It soon became obvious that this *Kristallnacht* was but a pale prelude to the darkness that was to descend on the entire continent.

| Dachau | Nuremberg Laws | Evian Conference |
|---|---|---|
| **March 1933** | **September 1935** | **July 1938** |

**1933. January 30:** Adolf Hitler is appointed Chancellor of the Reich.
**March:** Dachau, the first concentration camp for political opponents, is set up near Munich.
**March 9:** A pogrom on German Jews perpetrated by the S.A. and the *Staahlhelm* ("Steel Helmets").
**March 27:** Demonstration in New York organized by the American Jewish Congress, protesting against the persecution of Jews in Germany.
**April 1:** A day-long boycott against German Jews. The German-Jewish newspaper, *Jüdische Rundschau*, exhorts the Jews "to wear the yellow badge with pride."
**April 7:** Law forbidding Jews to be members of the government administration.
**April 21:** A law forbidding ritual slaughtering.
**May:** Petition against anti-Jewish discrimination in Germany presented to the League of Nations by the Committee of Jewish Delegations; anti-Nazi demonstrations organized by Jews in Paris.

*2. A Belgian antisemitic poster. Brussels.*

**May 10:** Public burnings of books written by Jews and anti-Nazi authors.
**August 20:** The American Jewish Congress declares a boycott on Germany.
**1934. July 25:** Nazi attempt to seize power in Austria; Chancellor Dollfus assassinated.
**August 2:** Death of President Hindenburg; Hitler assumes power as head of state.
**1935. March 16:** Compulsory military service resumed in Germany, in breach of the Versailles Treaty.
**May 31:** Prohibition on German Jews enlisting.
**June:** Wave of pogroms in Poland.
**September 15:** The Nuremberg Laws.
**December:** Attacks on Jewish students in Poland's universities.
**1936. March 3:** Prohibition on Jewish physicians working in German public medical centers.
**March 17:** In Poland, Jews and liberal non-Jews demonstrate against antisemitic persecutions.
**June 17:** Himmler appointed chief of

*3. "Jews undesired." A sign in a Corbach tavern, Prussia, 1936.*

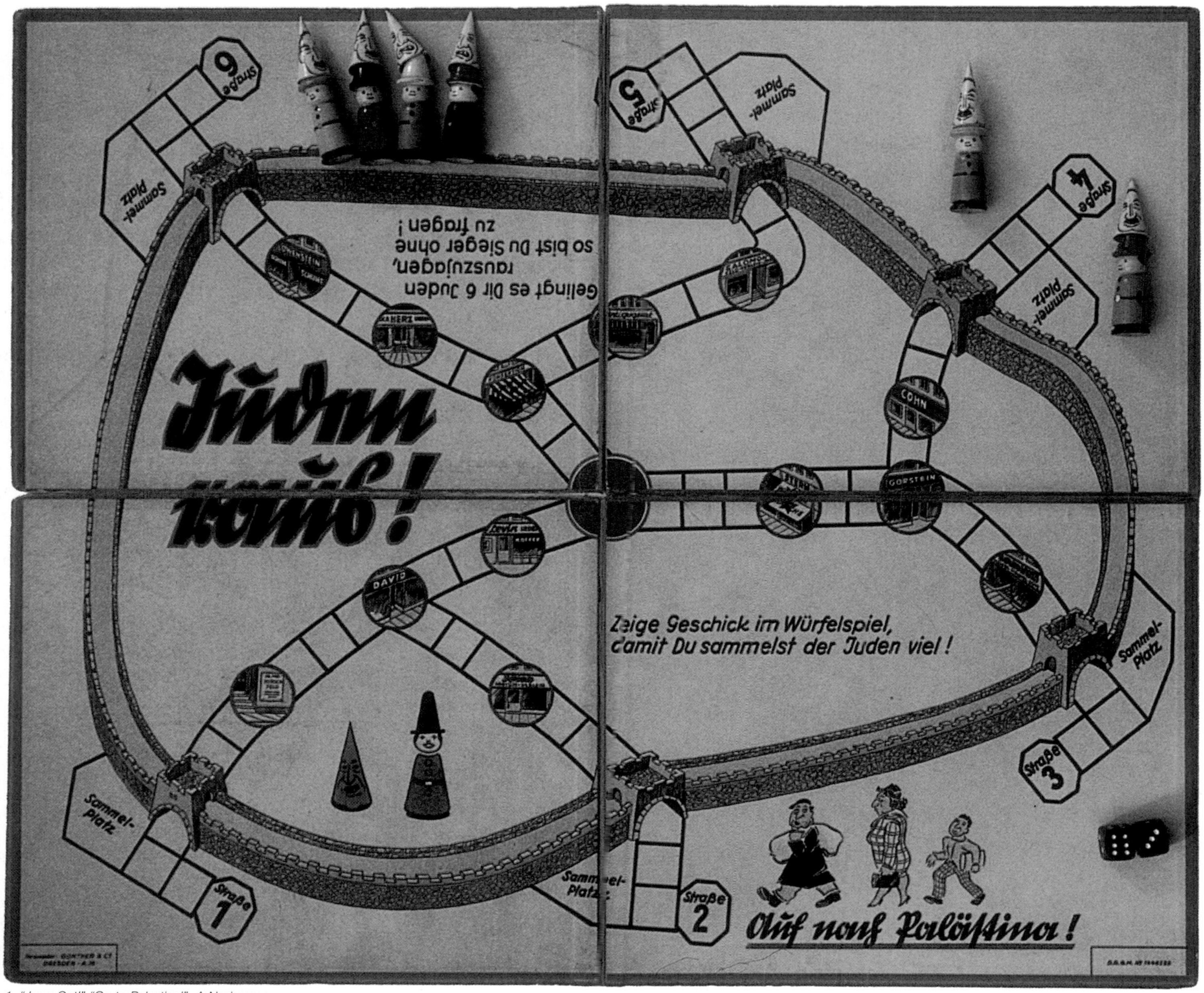

1. *"Jews Out!" "Go to Palestine!". A Nazi game.*

**Racist laws in Italy and Eastern Europe**

**1938**

German police.
**July 16:** Civil war breaks out in Spain.
**1937. July:** Concentration camp set up in Buchenwald.
**October:** Jewish property confiscated and transferred to "Aryan" owners.
**1938. January 21:** Rumanian Jews are deprived of their citizenship.
**March 12–13:** The "Anschluss" – Austria is annexed to the German Reich; 135,000 Austrian Jews are now subjected to Nazi race laws.
**July 16:** The Evian conference fails to find a solution for the problem of German refugees.
**August 1:** Establishment of the Center for Jewish Emigration headed by Adolf Eichmann.
**September 29–30:** The Munich agreements.
**October 5:** German Jews are deprived of their passports.
**October 28:** 20,000 Jews of Polish nationality are deported to the Polish border station at Zbaszyn.
**November 6:** In Paris, Herschel Grynszpan,

**Kristallnacht**

**9–10 November 1938**

4. *Registration of prisoners in Dachau, 1938.*

**Invasion of Poland**

**1 September 1939**

son of Jewish refugees, assassinates Ernst vom Rath, German Embassy secretary.
**November 9–10:** *Kristallnacht* ("Crystal Night"), a Nazi organized pogrom held in Germany and Austria, is followed by the deportation of tens of thousands of Jews to concentration camps.
**1939. January 24:** Reinhard Heydrich appointed head of the Berlin Center for Jewish Emigration .
**March:** The St. James Conference (British-Jewish-Arab) ends in failure: the White Paper closes the gates of Palestine to the rescue-immigration of European Jews.
**March 15:** The Germans occupy Czechoslovakia and establish the Bohemia-Moravia Protectorate.
**April 18:** Racist anti-Jewish legislation in independent Slovakia.
**May 3:** The "First Jewish Law" in Hungary restricts the number of Jews in the liberal professions.
**September 1:** 2,700 German Panzer tanks cross the border into Poland.

# The Holocaust: First Act

1. Children in the Warsaw Ghetto. Photo taken by the German soldier Heinz Joest on September 19, 1941.

There is no explicit mention of the systematic physical annihilation of human beings in general, and of the Jews in particular, in official Nazi documents, with the exception of the agreement between Himmler and Thierack (Reich minister of justice) dated September 18, 1942 stating that men and women were to be "worked to death" (*Vernichtung durch Arbeit*). The absence of written and explicit orders of extermination bred a rich literature denying the Jewish Holocaust. But even without such an order, Hitler's plan for the total destruction of European Jewry was clear to all members of the Nazi leadership, put into action from the first days of the war, and accelerated as the war progressed.

Occupied Poland became a laboratory for the Final Solution. Less than a month after the German occupation, on September 21, 1939, Heydrich, the Reich chief of security, issued orders to the special Nazi units (*Einsatzgruppen*) instructing them to gather all Polish Jews into cities located near major railways, and within these cities to confine them in closed quarters – the ghettos. Small communities of less than 500 people were marked for immediate extermination. The provinces Danzig, East-ern Prussia, Poznan and Upper Silesia were to be "promptly cleaned" of all Jews. Finally, Jewish councils (the *Judenraete*), comprising rabbis and community leaders, were appointed and made responsible for the enforcement of Nazi orders concerning the Jews. The Heydrich letter, containing an absolute-secrecy directive, constitutes the fundamental document for the first stage of the Final Solution.

During the months of October and November, 3.3 million Polish Jews were forced to wear bands of identification; their enclosure in ghettos began in November 1939 – Lodz Ghetto was sealed in May 1940, Warsaw Ghetto in November – and was completed by the summer of 1941 with the occupation of Galicia. By then half a million Polish Jews had died of starvation, disease, forced labor or terror – "natural causes," according to Nazi terminology.

On June 22, 1941, Hitler attacked the Soviet Union: within weeks of the German invasion, hundreds of thousands of Jews disappeared in Vilna, Kovno, Riga, Bialystok, Minsk, and every other town where the *Einsatzgruppen* arrived as the army advanced along the front ranging from the Baltic to the Black Sea. 20,000 Vilna Jews were massacred in Ponary forest and buried in a mass grave; in September, 34,000 Kiev Jews were murdered in Babi-Yar; and in October – 19,000 Odessa Jews. German statistics show that 250,000 Baltic and Belorussian Jews had been killed by the end of that summer. "The [German] soldier is not only versed in the art of war, but is a bearer of a ruthless national ideology, and thus must understand the necessity of a cruel but just revenge against sub-human Jewry" – proclaimed Fieldmarshal von Reichenau on October 10, 1941, in his order of the day to the soldiers of the sixth battalion.

October 1941 was one of the darkest months in this first stage of the Holocaust: the camps of Birkenau (Auschwitz II) and Jasenovac, and the ghetto at Theresienstadt were set up; deportation of the Jews of Germany and Austria began to the ghettos of Lodz, Kovno, Riga and Minsk; the Jews of Odessa and many of the Jews of Belgrade were murdered.

Terror spread with the advance of German troops; it was perpetrated by soldiers, by the S.S. which followed the army, and by local collaborators. In Rumania the massacre of Jews began concurrently with the invasion of the Soviet Union by the German army: in June 1941 7,000 Jews were most cruelly murdered in Jassy; Ukrainians slaughtered Jews in the regions of Bessarabia and Bukovina; Transnistria, the area between the Dniester and the Bug rivers, was turned into an enormous concentration camp for the Jews of Rumania.

By this stage, developments in western Europe, although less violent, already bore the mark of the catastrophe to come: anti-Jewish legislation, confiscations, deportations and concentration camps were the lot of Jews in Norway, the Netherlands, Belgium, and Luxembourg. Less than a month after the armistice between France and Germany (June

| The Wehrmacht in Poland | First ghetto in Poland | Construction of Auschwitz |
|---|---|---|
| **September 1, 1939** | **November 28, 1939** | **May 1940** |

**1939. August 16–26:** The 21st Zionist Congress convenes in Geneva – the last conference of world Jewry before the war.
**August 23:** The German-Soviet Pact.
**September 1:** The German army invades Poland.
**September 3:** England and France declare war on Germany.
**September 17:** The Red Army invades eastern Poland.
**September 21:** Heydrich's letter ordering the segregation of Polish Jews in ghettos and the establishment of Jewish councils (*Judenraete*).
**September 27:** The Polish army surrenders in Warsaw.
**October 10:** Establishment of the General Government in central Poland; western Poland is annexed to the Reich.
**October 12:** Beginning of deportations of Jews from Vienna and Czechoslovakia to Poland.
**October 26:** Beginning of forced labor in the General Government.

2. A German passport. On the left, the letter "J" affixed in 1939 indicates the Jewish origin of the bearer.

**October-November:** Tens of thousands of Jews in Poland flee the German-occupied zone in favor of the Soviet zone.
**November 23:** Jews in the General Government are ordered to wear a band of identification on their sleeves.
**November 28:** Hans Franck, governor of the General Government, orders a *Judenrat* to be established in the territory under his jurisdiction; the first Polish ghetto is set up in Piotrkov.
**1940. January-February:** First resistance and anti-German activities organized by Zionist youth movements in Poland.
**February 8:** Construction of the Lodz Ghetto begins.
**April 27:** Himmler orders the construction of a concentration camp at Auschwitz; work begins on May 20.
**May 1:** Lodz Ghetto is sealed.
**June 4:** End of the British army evacuation

3. The S.S. amuse themselves. Plotsk, Poland, October 1939.

## Einsatzgruppen, 1941-1942

FINLAND

NORWAY

SWEDEN

DENMARK

BALTIC SEA

| Legend |
| --- |
| ▬▬ Frontiers of the Third Reich in September 1939 |
| ▬▬ Frontline in November 1942 |
| ⇨ *Einsatzgruppen* operation zone |
| ○ Massacre |
| ■ Concentration camp |

• Leningrad

• Tallinn

ESTONIA

• Pskov

• Moscow

Riga

LATVIA

Kiev

U. S. S. R.

○ Chiaouliai  Daugavpils

LITHUANIA

○ Vitebsk

• Tula

○ Polotsk

• Hamburg

Danzig ●

EASTERN PRUSSIA

○ Kovno
○ Vilna

Orcha ○   Smolensk ●

Brichany ○
• Orel

• Stettin

Grodno ●
Bialystok ●

○ Ponary  • Minsk  Mogilev ●

○ Borisov

• Berlin

Poznan ●

MAZOVIA
Warsaw ●

Baranovichi ○  Bobruisk ●

B E L O R U S S I A

Kursk ○

THE THIRD REICH

Chelmno ■
Lodz ●

• Brest

○ Pinsk

○ Gomel

Stalingrad ●

Buchenwald ■  Leipzig ●

Piotrkow ●  Chelm ●

GENERAL GOVERNMENT

Zhitomir ○  ○ Kiev

Kharkov ●

Theresienstadt ■

SILESIA

Auschwitz-Birkenau ■  Cracow ●

Babi Yar

Dnieper

Don

Prague ●

Lvov ●

Rovno ○  Poltava ○

Dnepropetrovsk ○  Donetsk ○

• Nuremberg

GALICIA
Tarnopol ○

U K R A I N E

Zaporozhe ○  Rostov ○

Munich ●

Vienna ●

SLOVAKIA

Kamenets Podolski ○

Krivoi-Rog ○  Taganrog ○

Stavropol ○

ITALY

Chernowitz ○

BUCOVINA

T R A N S N I S T R I A

Nikolayev ○
○ Kherson

SEA OF AZOV

Krasnodar ○  ○ Armavir

HUNGARY

BESSARABIA

Jassy ○

MOLDAVIA

Odessa ●

Novorossisk ○  ○ Piatigorsk

YUGOSLAVIA

R U M A N I A

Simferopol ○

CRIMEA

Feodosiya ○

Sevastopol ○

BLACK SEA

200 km

---

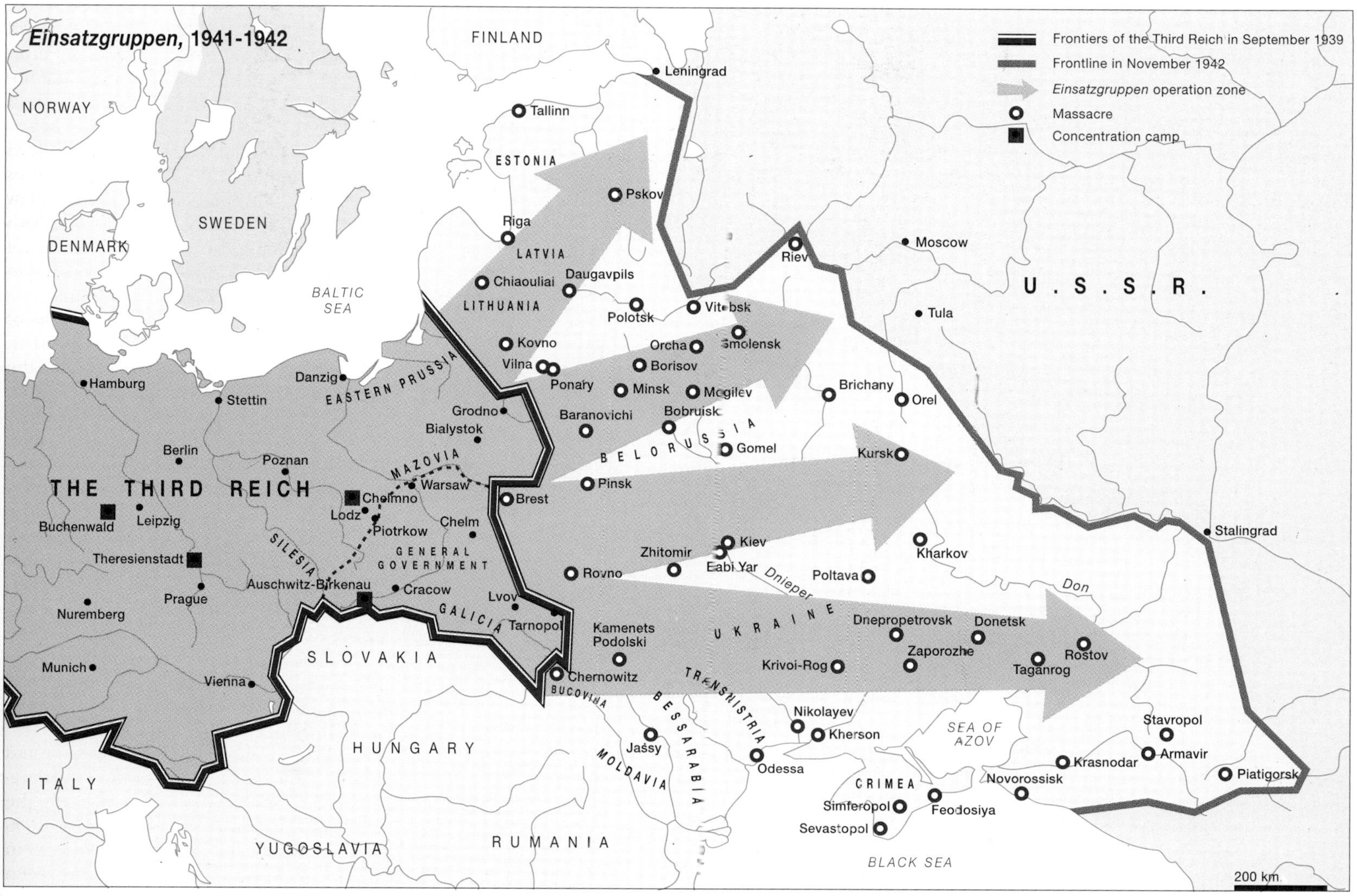

1940), Alsace-Lorraine Jews were deported to southern France, and anti-Jewish legislation (*Statut des Juifs*) inaugurated their persecution which was fully supported by the Vichy government. In reaction, the first Jewish underground group in France was organized in November 1941. The Dutch, on the other hand, did their utmost to save the Jewish community in their country.

By the end of 1941, approximately one million Jews in Nazi-dominated Europe had been exterminated by "conventional" means – famine, forced labor, shooting, bombing and gassing. The creation of a death camp in Chelmno in December 1941 signalled the beginning of a new phase in the systematic annihilation of European Jewry – an industrial genocide of a kind unknown in human history.

---

| *Statut des Juifs* in France | Adolf Eichmann, in charge of Jewish affairs in the Gestapo | Operation Barbarossa |
| --- | --- | --- |
| October 3, 1940 | March 1941 | June 22, 1941 |

from Dunkirk in France.

**June 10:** Italy enters the war on Germany's side; the searoutes from Europe to Palestine are closed.

**June 14:** The German army enters Paris. The European center of the Joint is transferred from Paris to Lisbon; the beginning of rescue operations through Portugal.

**June 22:** The French army surrenders; Petain signs an armistice agreement with Germany.

**July:** Pogroms in Rumania. Rescue operation of several thousand Polish Jews via Lithuania, the Soviet Union and Japan.

**August 17:** Mass demonstrations in the Lodz Ghetto are provoked by starvation. A Jewish underground resistance is organized in France – *l'Armée juive*.

**September 27:** The Berlin-Rome-Tokyo axis is established.

**October 3:** Anti-Jewish legislation of the Vichy government – the *Statut des Juifs*.

**October 28:** Anti-Jewish legislation in

Belgium.

**November 15:** Warsaw Ghetto is sealed.

**December:** In the Warsaw Ghetto, historian Emanuel Ringelblum keeps a secret archive, *Oneg Shabbat*, containing reports on events under Nazi occupation. The archive was recovered after the war.

**1941. January 20:** The Jews of western Mazovia are deported to the Warsaw Ghetto which now holds 130,000 refugees.

**January 21–22:** Insurrection of the Iron Guard in Rumania; pogroms against the Jews.

**February 22–23:** Jews in Amsterdam are rounded up and deported to Buchenwald.

**March:** Adolf Eichmann is appointed head of the section for Jewish affairs in the Gestapo.

**May:** The *Einsatzgruppen* conduct a mass murder of Jews in Pretzch in Saxony.

**June 22:** Operation Barbarossa – German surprise attack on the Soviet Union.

**June 25:** Massacre of Jews in Jassy by the Rumanian army.

*4. Jews from the villages around Cracow are led to the ghetto in the city. March 1941.*

# Palestine During World War II

World War II was the first major international conflict in which Jewish loyalty was undivided: all Jews everywhere were united in the commitment to fight Hitler and Nazism. Initially, the *yishuv* (the Jewish community in Palestine) was not under direct threat itself, but its relative security was shattered in June 1940. When Italy joined the war, the Mediterranean became a central arena of military operations; and when France capitulated, the French forces in Syria and Lebanon were placed under the authority of the Vichy government. The pro-German *coup* in Iraq, in April of the following year, made matters graver still. Finally, peril began looming in North Africa, becoming acute with the arrival of Rommel's *Panzerarmee Afrika* at El-Alamein in June 1942. Palestine now faced the danger of a simultaneous invasion from the north and the south, together with a possible Arab attempt to take advantage of the situation and destroy the Zionist enterprise from within.

For the High Command of the *Haganah* (the defense forces of the Jewish community in Palestine, first established in 1920), Rommel's advance towards the Nile Valley signified the need to prepare for the eventuality of British evacuation. The "Carmel Plan" – to concentrate the Jewish population in the hills around Haifa where, armed with ammunition provided by the British and aided by the Royal Air Force and the Navy, they would defend themselves to the end – was conceived with this ominous possibility in mind.

Thus, despite Jewish-British antagonism fostered by the anti-Zionist policy of the London government, the German menace finally enforced cooperation. Indeed, with the exception of a handful of extremists, the Jews in Palestine immediately suspended all hostile operations against the British and actively supported the war effort against Nazi Germany. They aspired, however, to create an autonomous Jewish fighting force under the Zionist flag – a desire which the British, for obvious political reasons, denied them, insisting on mixed Palestinian units consisting of both Jews and Arabs fighting side by side.

However, as Arab volunteers were relatively few, necessity eventually obliged the Mandatory authorities to consent: separate Jewish infantry companies were attached to the East Kent Regiment (the "Buffs") in

1. *"A Jewish Army." A propaganda poster of the Palestinian yishuv.*

September 1940. Two years later, these companies formed three Palestinian battalions. Finally, in September 1944, the prolonged attempt by the *yishuv* for recognized representation in the war was rewarded by the establishment of the Jewish Brigade Group (*Hayil*). The Brigade saw service in Egypt, on the north Italian front, and in northwest Europe between 1944–1946. These Palestinian Jewish soldiers, most of whom were *Haganah* members in British uniform, became actively engaged in the rescue of Holocaust survivors at the end of the war. Yet this Zionist activity which was resented by the British led to the disbanding of the Brigade in July 1946.

Meanwhile the *yishuv*, not wishing to rely solely on British defense, clandestinely strengthened its own forces by forming the *Palmah* – the assault companies of the *Haganah* – whose units were located in *kibbutzim* all over the country. The Mandatory authorities clashed with these units when searching for arms, and arrested several *Haganah* members. Yet as the situation grew more and more critical, with the German army standing on Egypt's doorstep, the British were forced to comply with this "illegal" army: hundreds of *Palmah* members received commando training by British officers, participated in the invasion of Vichy Syria and sent a detachment to sabotage oil refineries in Lebanon. For similar reasons of expediency the English agreed to dispatch Jewish paratroopers into Nazi-occupied Europe: the desire of the Jews to assist their suffering fellow-Jews coincided with the need of British Intelligence to establish contact with anti-Nazi underground movements.

Finally, less dramatic but just as crucial was the economic cooperation. The whole *yishuv* rallied to the British war effort: industry was militarized to produce armaments and ammunition, tents and uniforms, food supplies and chemicals; high technical skills were recruited to produce and maintain sophisticated optical and electronic equipment; construction companies were engaged in the construction of military installations, airfields and roads all over the Middle East. In sum, Great Britain found in Jewish Palestine an important logistic base for its war against Hitler. But as soon as the war ended, the British renewed their White Paper policy, and the *yishuv* resumed its struggle for independence.

| England enters the war | Jewish infantry units | Founding of the *Palmah* | The English and the Gaullists in Syria |
|---|---|---|---|
| September 1939 | September 1940 | May 1941 | June 1941 |

**1939. September 1:** Hitler invades Poland. Chaim Weizmann, president of the World Zionist Organization, promises the British Prime Minister every possible assistance from the Jewish people in the war against Nazism. The principal anti-British resistance movements in Palestine cease all hostilities against the Mandatory government. It was Ben-Gurion who laid down the policy: "To fight the war as if there were no White Paper [which prohibited almost all Jewish immigration to Palestine], and to fight the White Paper as if there were no war."
**September 11:** The *yishuv* proclaims a "Volunteers' Muster for National Service."
**December 12:** The Mandatory government announces the enlistment of mixed Arab-Jewish units to the British Army. These units later participate in the Battle of France.
**1940. June 10:** Italy joins the war.
**June 22:** German-French armistice signed;

2. *"Put on thy beautiful garments" (Isaiah, 52:1). Poster of the A.T.S., 1942.*

3. *Yizhak Sadeh with two of his lieutenants, Moshe Dayan (left) and Yigal Allon, in 1938. Sadeh, one of the Haganah leaders, becomes the first commander of the Palmah.*

# 1939–1945

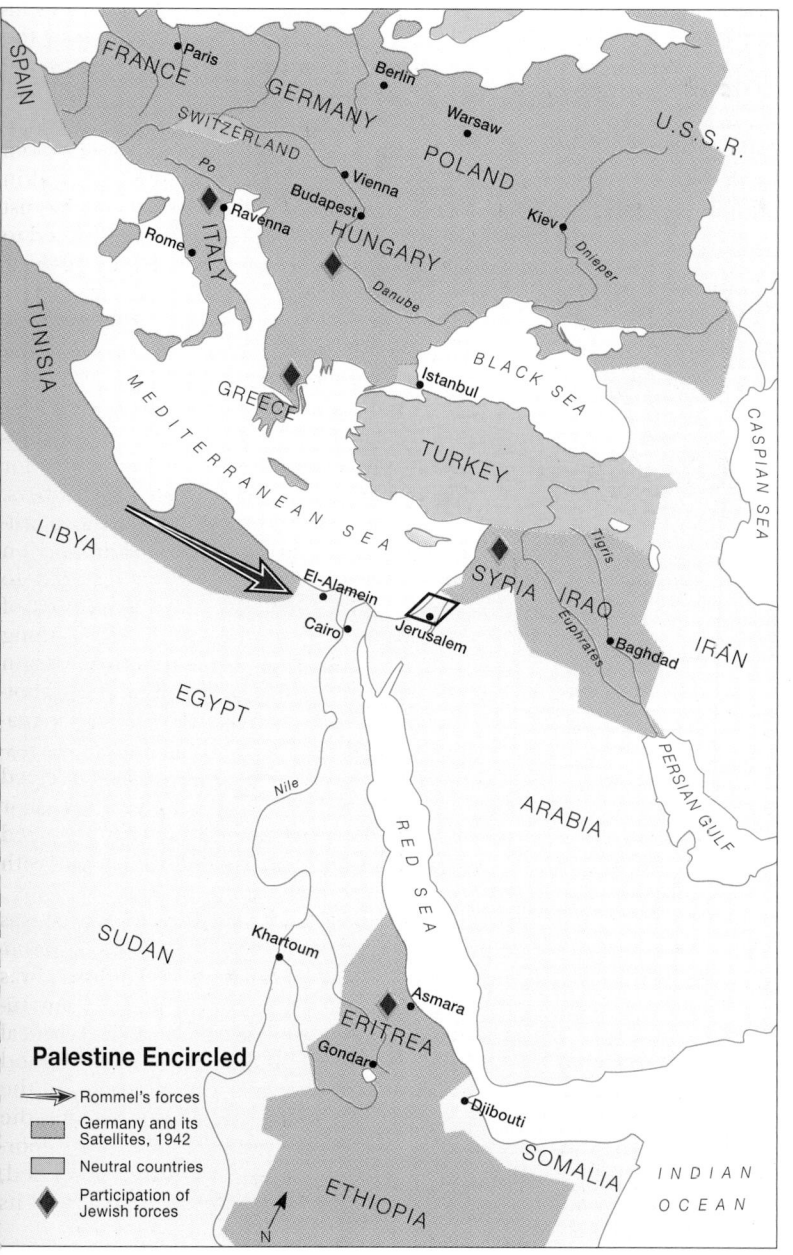

## Palestine Encircled

→ Rommel's forces
▨ Germany and its Satellites, 1942
▨ Neutral countries
◆ Participation of Jewish forces

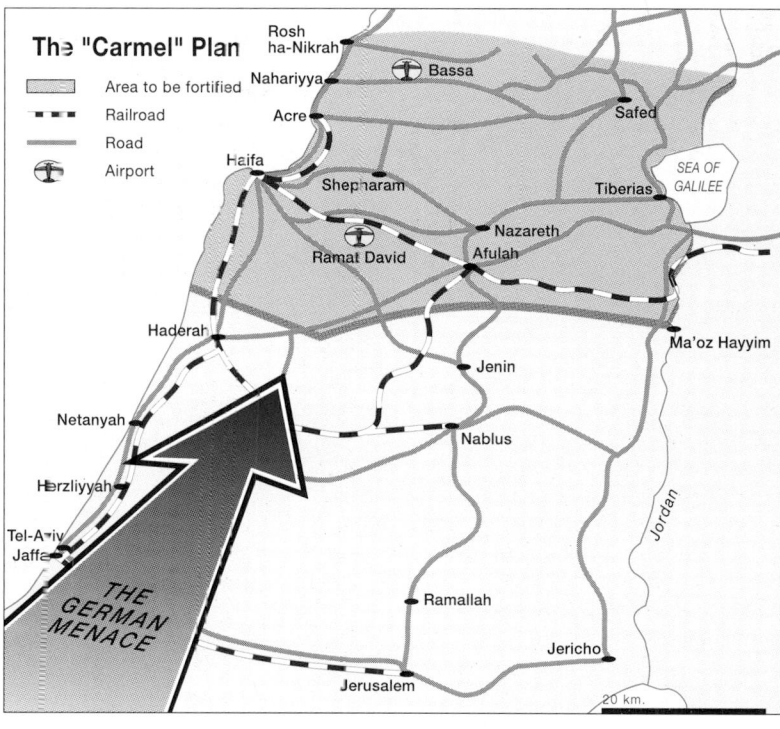

## The "Carmel" Plan

▨ Area to be fortified
- - - Railroad
— Road
✈ Airport

THE GERMAN MENACE

20 km.

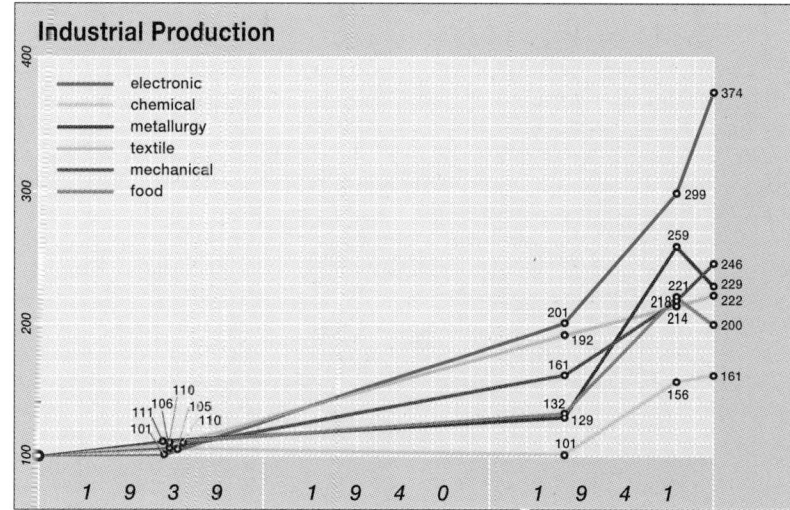

## Industrial Production

— electronic
— chemical
— metallurgy
— textile
— mechanical
— food

374
299
259
246
229
221
222
218
214
201
200
192
161
161
156
132
129
110 110
106 105
101
111
101

1 9 3 9      1 9 4 0      1 9 4 1

| Rommel in El-Alamein | Rommel's retreat | Formation of the Jewish Brigade | The Brigade in Italy |
|---|---|---|---|
| **June 1942** | **November 1942** | **September 1944** | **November 1944–June 1945** |

Syria becomes part of Vichy France.
**July 29:** Creation of the *yishuv's* "Security Committee."
**July–September:** Several Italian Air Force bombardments of Haifa and Tel Aviv; almost 200 people killed, hundreds wounded.
**September 15:** Formation of Jewish infantry companies (Palestine "Buffs").
**1941:** Jewish volunteers join the British Commandos in the East African campaign.
**April:** Jewish Palestinian volunteers take part in the campaign in Greece. Over a thousand of them, abandoned by the English, are taken prisoner by the Germans on April 29.
**April 3:** "Mobilization Order No. 1" of the Jewish institutions in Palestine. The pro-German rebellion of Rashid Ali in Iraq.
**May 2:** The British attack the insurgents in Iraq; David Raziel, commander of the *Irgun Zeva'i Le'ummi*, is sent by the British to sabotage the oil depots on the outskirts of Baghdad.
**May 15:** Twenty three *Haganah* members carry out a naval commando mission to

Vichy Syria and all are killed. The *Haganah* decides to form a striking force – the *Palmah*.
**June 7:** British invasion of Syria; *Palmah* units participate as guides, saboteurs and intelligence men.
**June 11:** Night bombardment of Tel Aviv by the German Luftwaffe and by Vichy French Air Force.
**November 9:** Weizmann announces the failure of negotiations with the British over the creation of a Jewish Army.
**1942:** The British agree to dispatch Jewish parachutists to Nazi-occupied Europe.
**February 2:** Jewish women begin to volunteer to the A.T.S. (Auxiliary Territorial Service).
**June 30:** Rommel's forces reach El-Alamein.
**August 6:** The British announce the formation of Jewish battalions.
**August 23:** Beginning of the battle at El-Alamein.
**November 5:** Defeated by Montgomery, the Axis forces retreat from El-Alamein.

*4. Soldiers of the Jewish Brigade in Rome*

**1943. May 22:** The first Jewish parachutists jump in Yugoslavia.
**1943–1945:** Of the 250 Palestinian Jews who volunteered for such missions, only thirty two (including three women) are actually dispatched to Europe; twelve are captured, seven (including two women) are executed by the Nazis.
**1944. September 20:** Formation of the Jewish Brigade Group (*Hayil*), placed under the command of the Jewish Canadian-born Brigadier Ernest Frank Benjamin; on November 1 the Brigade leaves for Italy where it will hold Ravenna till March 24, 1945, and is later deployed along the Senio River.
**1945. April 3:** The Jewish flag is officially raised in Brigade headquarters.
**April 11:** The Brigade, comprising approximately 5,000 fighting men, cross the Senio in the Allies' final offensive. In May, when transferred to northeast Italy, it encounters for the first time survivors of extermination camps.

# The Final Solution

1. Accompanied by the prisoners' orchestra, an inmate caught trying to escape is led to execution. Mauthausen, Austria.

Historians of the Holocaust are divided into two schools: the "intentionalists" insist on the central role of Nazi ideology and believe that there was a carefully prepared plan for the extermination of European Jewry; the "functionalists," or "structuralists," by contrast, stress the chaotic nature of the Nazi system, a nondesign reflected in their foreign and economic policies as well. According to the latter school, it was this inherent disorder rather than premeditated design which led, through a process of cumulative radicalization, to the systematic extermination of European Jewry.

On January 20, 1942, Reinhard Heydrich, head of the Reich Security Head Office, convened all secretaries of state of the major German ministries to the Wannsee Conference. This conference is generally held to have been a major turning point, whereby the "final solution of the Jewish question" in Europe by "evacuation" to the East and by other "means" was decided upon. But in fact, the mass extermination of the Jews on an industrial scale, made possible by the creation of death camps, was launched prior to this notorious conference. Executions by the *Einsatzgruppen* were abandoned for practical reasons. Although approximately 1.5 million Jews had been shot by the winter of 1941, the Nazis felt that the efficiency of this slow and cumbersome method left much to be desired. Moreover, they found it was bad for the soldiers' morale. Himmler himself, commander of the S.S. and as such responsible for the annihilation of the Jews, was persuaded, after having witnessed such an execution, that it badly affected the mental health of those carrying out the execution. The institutionalization of organized murder, founded on a division of labor and carried out in special installations expressly designed for this purpose, distanced the executioner from the victim – an indispensable psychological advantage in an enterprise of annihilation of such a huge scale.

The murder industry began in the Chelmno Camp, built in December 1941. Work was carried out in special trucks, where the victims were asphyxiated by exhaust fumes – a method which had been tried before on those whose lives were deemed useless (the "Euthanasia Program"). From September 1939, about 100,000 "Aryan" Germans were assassinated in this manner, in what was named "Operation T4." Two years later, the personnel responsible for the "euthanasia" program was called upon to apply its expertise to murdering Jews. In the

single camp of Chelmno, 150,000 human beings were gassed to death, most of them brought to the camp from annexed territories, the Warthegau district in western Poland, and the Lodz Ghetto.

Majdanek, set up in September 1941 as a camp for Soviet prisoners-of-war and as a concentration camp for Polish Jews and non-Jews, became the base for the S.S. advancing in the East and a reservoir of slave-labor for factories in the Lublin region. Extermination installations were built there in the autumn of 1942, but it was only in the winter of the following year that the Zyklon B gas chambers and the crematorium were used for the first time. Of the 200,000 persons killed in Majdanek about 50,000–60,000 were Jews.

Belzec, Sobibor and Treblinka formed part of what the Nazis called "Operation Reinhard," whose sole purpose was the systematic massacre of Jews. A labor camp existing in Belzec since 1940 was turned into an extermination camp in the autumn of 1941, becoming operative in March 1942. In the same month the camp at Sobibor was set up to alleviate the overburdened camp of Belzec. The third, Treblinka, received the Jews from Warsaw and the Radom district.

These three extermination factories – with Belzec responsible for about 600,000 victims, Sobibor 200,000 Treblinka 900,000 – shared certain features: like Auschwitz at a later stage, they were equipped with railroad terminals which the trains entered in reverse. The victims were ordered to undress and then led through a corridor to the gas chambers; the gas was composed of carbon monoxide produced by diesel motors. At first, the corpses were buried in mass graves; later they were burnt in crematoria. The similarity to the "euthanasia" program was evident here too: in August 1941 the camps inspector was S.S. *Sturmbannführer* Christian Wirth who, like dozens of other specialists of "Operation T4," was placed under the commander of the S.S. for the region of Lublin, Odilo Globocnik.

However, the capital of this bureaucratized and industrialized world of mass murders was Auschwitz. An operative concentration camp since May 1940, in the autumn of 1941 it was equipped with gas chambers. According to latest estimates, the number of Jews killed in this camp approximated 1.5 million. In Auschwitz II (Birkenau), symbol and synonym for the Holocaust, the Nazi program of mass extermination reached the highest level of perfection.

2. Human debris at Buchenwald after the liberation. April 1945.

# 1941–1945

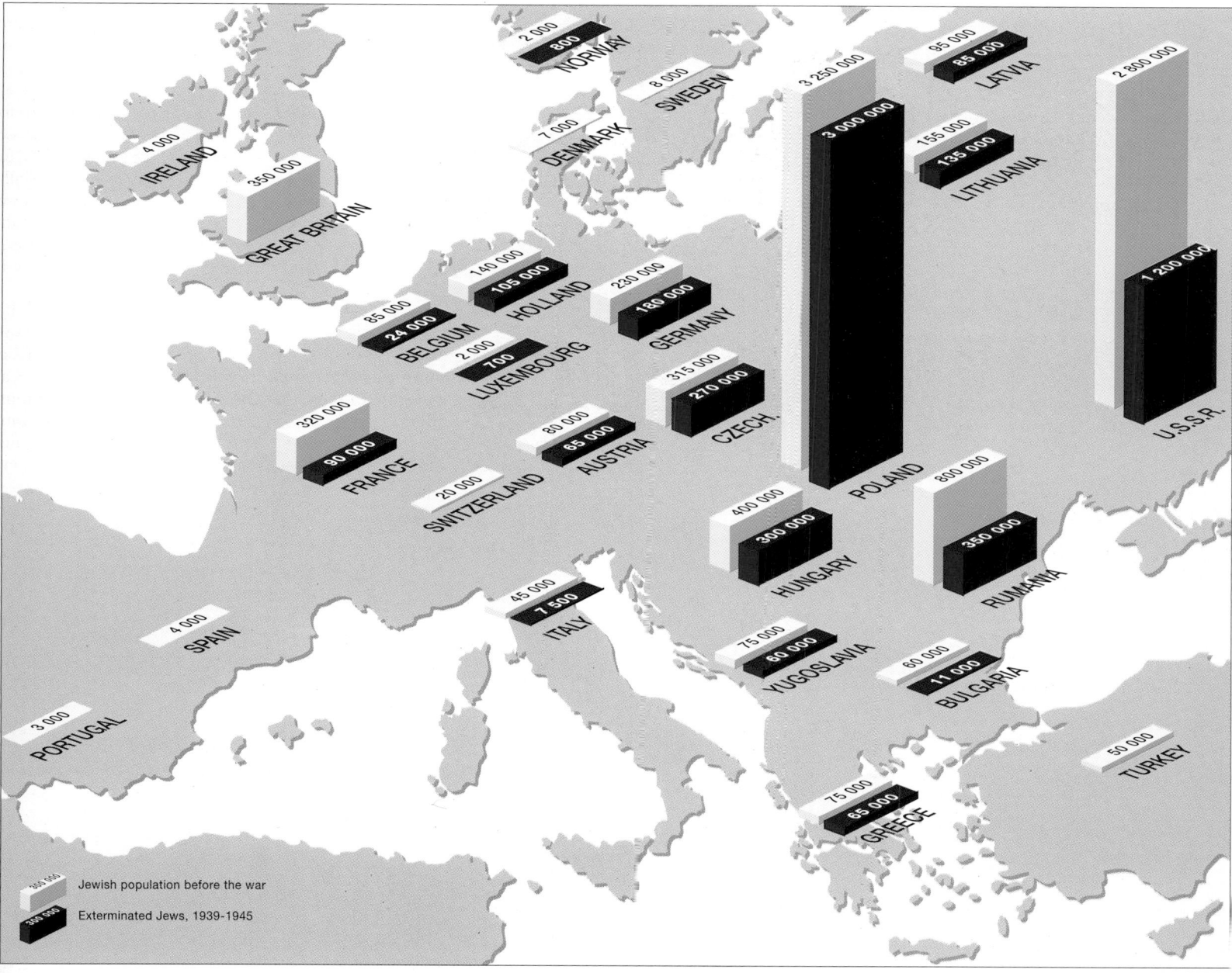

2 000 / 800 NORWAY

8 000 SWEDEN

7 000 DENMARK

95 000 / 85 000 LATVIA

3 250 000 / 3 000 000 POLAND

155 000 / 135 000 LITHUANIA

2 800 000 / 1 200 000 U.S.S.R.

4 000 IRELAND

350 000 GREAT BRITAIN

140 000 / 105 000 HOLLAND

85 000 / 24 000 BELGIUM

2 000 / 700 LUXEMBOURG

230 000 / 180 000 GERMANY

315 000 / 270 000 CZECH.

320 000 / 90 000 FRANCE

20 000 SWITZERLAND

80 000 / 65 000 AUSTRIA

400 000 / 300 000 HUNGARY

800 000 / 350 000 RUMANIA

4 000 SPAIN

45 000 / 7 500 ITALY

75 000 / 60 000 YUGOSLAVIA

60 000 / 11 000 BULGARIA

3 000 PORTUGAL

75 000 / 65 000 GREECE

50 000 TURKEY

Jewish population before the war

Exterminated Jews, 1939-1945

**"Euthanasia Program"** — September 1939

**Auschwitz-Birkenau** — November 1941

**The Wannsee Conference** — January 1942

**Liberation of Auschwitz** — January 1945

**1939. January 30:** Hitler's speech in which he predicted that if a world war breaks out, "the Jewish race in Europe will be extirpated."
**September 1:** Hitler's order to launch the "euthanasia" ("mercy-killing") program is attributed to this date.
**1941. June:** Himmler orders Rudolf Hoess to establish in Auschwitz a camp for extermination by gas.
**July:** Creation of the Majdanek camp.
**July 21:** Hitler announces to the Croatian minister of defense his plan for "ridding" Europe of its Jews.
**July 31:** Goering's letter commissioning Heydrich to prepare the "complete solution of the Jewish question."
**August:** Officially interrupted, the "euthanasia" program continues in secrecy.
**September 19:** Jews in Germany are forced to wear the yellow badge.
**October 14:** Order of deportation of the Reich Jews to the ghettos of Kovno, Lodz, Minsk, and Riga.

**November 1:** Construction of the extermination camp in Belzec.
**November 10:** Beginning of the construction of the "model camp" at Theresienstadt.
**November 26:** The gas installations in Auschwitz II (Birkenau) begin to function.
**December 8:** Beginning of the killing of Jews in gas trucks at Chelmno.
**1942. January 20:** The Wannsee Conference.
**March 1:** Beginning of the construction of the extermination camp at Sobibor.
**March 17:** Beginning of "Operation Reinhard."
**March 28:** First transport of French Jews to Auschwitz.
**June 1:** Treblinka becomes an extermination camp.
**July 19:** Himmler orders the annihilation within one year of all Jews in the General Government (Poland).
**July 21–22:** First transports of Warsaw Jews to Treblinka.

**August 13–20:** Most Croatian Jews are sent to Auschwitz.
**Autumn:** Majdanek becomes an extermination camp.
**October 2:** Transport of Dutch Jews is accelerated.
**October 16:** The Jews of Rome are sent to Auschwitz.
**December 10:** The Polish government in exile tries to persuade the Allies to react to the mass extermination in Poland.
**1943. January 14:** in Casablanca, Churchill and Roosevelt decide to impose an "unconditional surrender" on Germany.
**February 2:** German forces capitulate in Stalingrad; a major turning point in the war.
**February 26:** First transport of Gypsies to Auschwitz.
**March 20:** First transport of Jews from Salonika to Auschwitz.
**May 19:** Berlin is proclaimed *Judenfrei* (free of Jews).
**July 21:** Himmler orders the liquidation of the ghettos in the East (*Ostland*); the Minsk

Ghetto is evacuated on September 11, the Vilnius (Vilna) Ghetto on September 23.
**October 1:** The Danes save the entire Danish Jewish community by transferring them to neutral Sweden.
**November 3:** Liquidation of the camps of Poniatowa and Trawniki, as well as of the remaining Jews in Majdanek; this operation called by the Germans the "Harvest Festival," brings about 43,000 Jews to their deaths.
**1944. March 19:** The Germans conquer Hungary.
**May 15:** First transports of Hungarian Jews to Auschwitz.
**End of October:** Killings by gas in Auschwitz are stopped.
**November 26:** Himmler orders the dismantling of extermination installations in Auschwitz.
**1945. January 17:** The S.S. evacuate Auschwitz; 60,000 prisoners are marched towards other camps.
**January 27:** A Soviet army unit liberates Auschwitz, where it finds 7,650 prisoners.

# Why Was Auschwitz Not Bombed?

The Nazi program of genocide was carried out in total secrecy. On Hitler's explicit orders the organizers contrived ingenious methods of camouflage and deceit, including the manipulation of the language (*Sprachregelung*), to conceal their murder industry from the world and from the victims themselves. Nevertheless, information filtered through. Men of good will risked their lives in order to inform the free world of the atrocities committed behind the barbed wire in the ghettos and camps. And thus during 1942, when the systematic extermination was in full motion, the truth became known to those who wished to know.

Historical research today can accurately trace the route by which reports travelled to the west, the dates they arrived, and the persons they reached, as well as the responses they evoked. What research cannot explain, however, are the limits of human understanding, the ideological and political inhibitions, the depths of the crisis, and the failings of morality – all the elements which caused the lack of action in response to the news of the destruction of European Jewry.

The common response of persons who received the reports, which were becoming more detailed and explicit, was denial, refusal to believe the unbelievable. The free world, waging all-out war against the Nazi dictator-

ship in order to save a civilization which held human freedom as its supreme value, was incapable of believing that one human society could exterminate another for no reason and no purpose. According to a survey conducted in the U.S. in December 1944, only 4% of Americans believed that over a million Jews had already been murdered, although the existence of the death camps had been common knowledge for over two years. The report of S.S. officer Kurt Gerstein about his service in three extermination camps was relayed by one of the leaders of the Dutch Resistance who himself later admitted that he did not believe it. Worse still, the American Deputy Secretary of State Sumner Welles decided not to disclose the contents of a telegram from the World Jewish Congress representative in Geneva, Gerhart Riegner, on August 8, 1942, detailing the German plan for the extermination of 3.5–4 million Jews in German-occupied Europe because it seemed to him unfounded.

However, by the winter of 1942 the flow of information was becoming so heavy that the west could no longer ignore it. On December 17, 1942, the Allies, together with governments in exile (those of France, Belgium, Czechoslovakia, Greece, Holland, Norway, Poland, Yugoslavia, and Luxembourg), issued a vehement condemnation of Nazi atrocities. And that was the extent of their attempts to save European Jewry. The Pope,

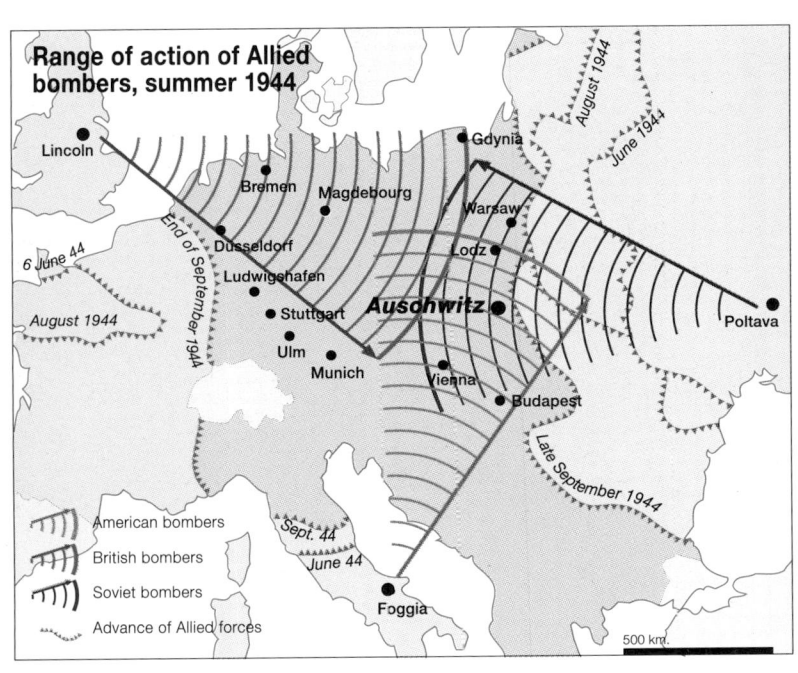

**Range of action of Allied bombers, summer 1944**

American bombers
British bombers
Soviet bombers
Advance of Allied forces

500 km.

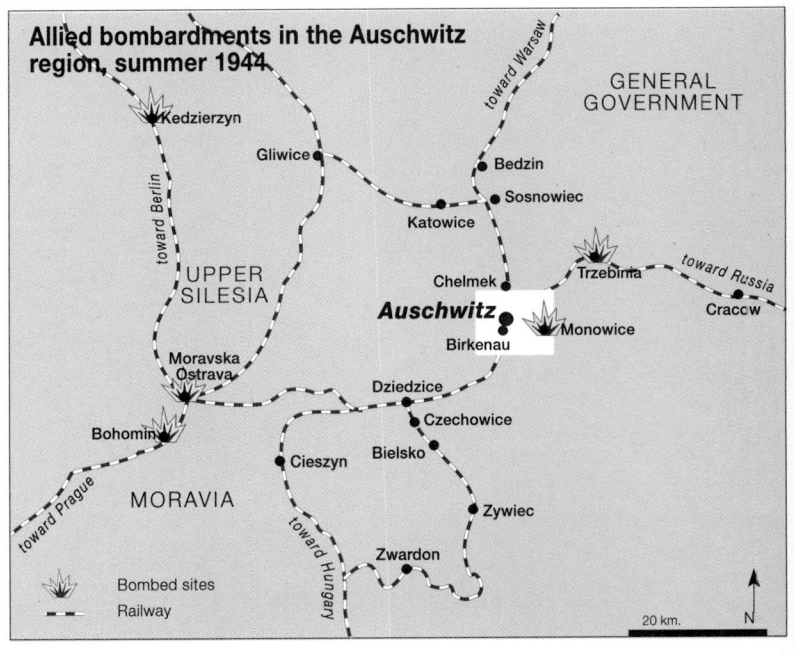

**Allied bombardments in the Auschwitz region, summer 1944**

GENERAL GOVERNMENT

UPPER SILESIA

MORAVIA

Bombed sites
Railway

20 km.

N

**First reports of massacres**

**March 1942**

**1942. March 16:** The Jewish press in Palestine reports the massacre by the Gestapo of 250,000 Jews in the Ukraine and the murder of tens of thousands more in other territories conquered from the Soviet Union.
**June:** The London media report information which reached the Polish government in exile about the massacre of 700,000 Polish Jews.
**June 30:** A spokesman of the World Jewish Congress broadcasts on American radio the reports about the extermination of a million Jews in Nazi-occupied Europe.
**August 8:** Riegner's telegram is received, which the State Department refuses to publish.
**November 1942–September 1943:** The "Europa Plan" to save the Jews of Slovakia by paying huge bribes to Himmler's representative in Slovakia, Dieter Wisliceny; it delays, but fails to prevent, the extermination of Slovakian Jewry.
**November 22:** First official communication of the Jewish Agency in Palestine about the

*2. A "righteous of the nations": Raoul Wallenberg.*

liquidation of Polish Jewry and of the Jews from eastern and central Europe deported to Poland.
**November 30–December 2:** "Days of Protest and Alarm" in the *yishuv*.
**1943. January 31:** The Rescue Committee of the Jewish Agency, directed by Yitzhak Gruenbaum, begins its activities; its first emissaries are sent to Istanbul.
**January–March:** The "Transnistria Plan" to save the Jews of Rumania; the plan did not materialize.
**April:** A plan to transport 20,000 Jewish children from the east to Sweden fails to materialize.
**April 28:** An appeal of the Jews of Warsaw through the Polish government in exile: "The ghetto is in flames... may the heroic battle of those condemned to death awaken the world at last."
**May 2:** The last appeal of the Jews of Warsaw: "The world of freedom and justice is silent and does nothing."
**May 12:** Samuel Zygelbojm, member of the

**The appeal of Warsaw's Jews**

**28 April 1943**

Bund Party, commits suicide in London: "Let my death be a protest against the world's indifference."
**October:** A BBC broadcast in sixteen languages warns the German nation of the atrocities and calls on the non-Jewish population to give assistance to the Jews.
**1944. January 16:** The American Treasury Secretary Henry Morgenthau protests to President Roosevelt about American passivity in view of the extermination of the Jews in Europe.
**January 22:** President Roosevelt sets up the Committee for War Refugees.
**March 14:** Jewish paratroopers from Palestine jump into Yugoslavia, Hungary, and Rumania.
**June 25:** An appeal of Pope Pius XII on behalf of the Jews (his first since the beginning of the genocide) to the Hungarian regent Admiral Horthy.
**June 30–July 6:** The Jewish Agency appeals to Anthony Eden to bomb the camps and the railways from Budapest to

Pius XII, refused to do even that, explaining to President Roosevelt's representative that, although he believed there was some truth in the reports, they were also clearly exaggerated for propaganda purposes.

Auschwitz, symbol of the Holocaust, is also a symbol of the world's silence when facing it. During the summer of 1944, intelligence reports about the camp were accurate and detailed enough to consider bombing it. The Jewish Agency pressed the Allies to bomb the camp and the railways leading to it. Although Winston Churchill, Anthony Eden, and the American Committee for Refugees were in favor of such an operation, they were unable to overcome the opposition of the military establishment in Washington and London. The British explicitly declared themselves unwilling to risk the lives of their pilots in a mission with no clear worthwhile military purpose. Thus, while the synthetic rubber works seven kilometers from Birkenau were bombed in April 1944, the town of Auschwitz in July 1944, and the hospital and S.S. barracks in Birkenau some fifteen yards from the extermination site on December 24, 1944, no action was ever taken against the unguarded camp installations, easily recognizable by the smoking fires of the crematoria.

Admittedly, the two largest Jewish communities in the free world – the American and the *yishuv* in Palestine – were also incapable of fully comprehending the significance of the European horror. American Jews were hesitant to exert their full influence in Washington for fear of evoking antisemitism; and Ben-Gurion, convinced of his inability to change the course of events in Europe, devoted all his energy to planning the post-war order and the possibility of establishing a Jewish state. "The heart is not free at present to contemplate the immensity of the Jewish tragedy, but not out of insensitivity; every Churchill, great or small, has in mind one thing only: to win the war." The work of rescue and relief was delegated to minor officials.

On the other hand, there were, of course, exceptional human beings of all nations who, out of simple human decency, risked their lives to save Jews from the Nazi horror: members of the Danish Resistance who saved all of Denmark's Jews by transferring them clandestinely to neutral Sweden; diplomats, like Raoul Wallenberg in Hungary, who did everything within their power to save as many lives as they possibly could; monasteries across Europe where Jewish children were hidden; peasants who concealed Jews throughout the war; Jewish paratroopers from Palestine who jumped in suicidal operations behind enemy lines to bring a message of hope to their brethren. By their modest efforts these few atoned, to some extent, for the sins of many.

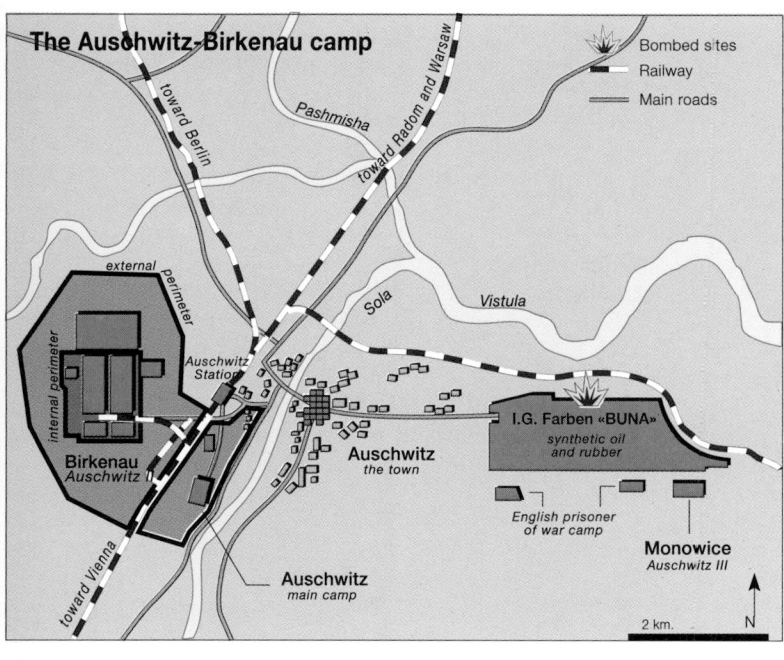

**The Auschwitz-Birkenau camp**

Bombed sites
Railway
Main roads

toward Berlin

Pashmisha

toward Radom and Warsaw

external perimeter

internal perimeter

Auschwitz Station

Sola

Vistula

Birkenau
*Auschwitz II*

Auschwitz
*the town*

I.G. Farben «BUNA»
*synthetic oil and rubber*

English prisoner of war camp

Monowice
*Auschwitz III*

Auschwitz
*main camp*

toward Vienna

2 km.    N

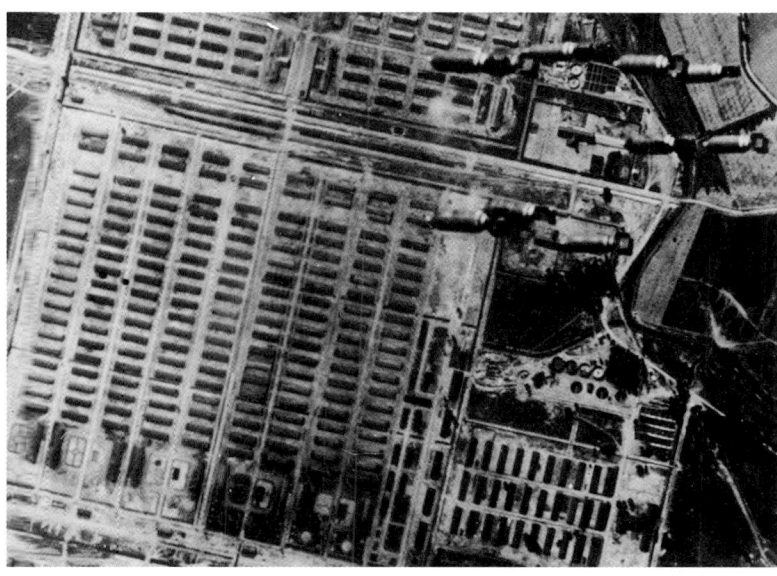

*1 September 13, 1944, several American airplanes bomb the industrial complex I.G. Farben near Auschwitz; several bombs are dropped by mistake on the camp itself, killing fifteen S.S. men and scores of prisoners and workers.*

**The Allies refuse to bomb Auschwitz**

**June–July 1944**

**Wallenberg's rescue operations in Hungary**

**July–October 1944**

*3. Pius XII.*

Auschwitz; the R.A.F. opposes the plan.
**July–October:** The Swedish diplomat Raoul Wallenberg saves thousands of Hungarian Jews by providing them with Swedish documents, food, and shelter. After the war Wallenberg disappeared in Soviet prisons.
**July 4:** The deputy to the American Defense Secretary announces that the bombing of Auschwitz would be "impractical."
**July 11:** Winston Churchill writes to Anthony Eden: "There is no doubt that this is probably the greatest and most horrible single crime ever committed in the whole history of the world."
**September 13:** American airplanes bomb the industrial complex of I.G. Farben near Auschwitz.
**September 20:** Paratroopers from Palestine reach Slovakia. All in all, thirty-two Jewish paratroopers jumped behind enemy lines; seven were killed.
**September 28:** Churchill announces in Parliament the establishment of a Jewish Brigade within the British Army.

*4. Deportation of the Jews of Bielefeld near Hanover, 1942.*

# Resistance

The definition of Jewish resistance to the Nazis during the Holocaust still evokes bitter polemics. Generally, resistance is understood to mean a form of armed struggle, organized by a clandestine movement created for that purpose. However, in the case of a dispersed nation threatened by an industry seeking its total extermination, such a military conception is inadequate.

1. Clandestine study of the Torah in the Warsaw Ghetto, undated photograph.

Jewish existence in the diaspora excluded by definition the basic condition for armed resistance: belonging to a group united by feelings of social and ethnic cohesion. A collective consciousness of this kind was practically non-existent among western Jews, and it had only elementary manifestations in eastern Europe. Therefore, the active participation of Jews in military resistance to the Nazi regime was contingent on the nature of their relations with the local non-Jewish population and on the attitude of that population to the Nazi occupation.

The predominantly middle-class Jews of Germany, who were expectedly individualistic as well, represent the reasons which prevented collective Jewish action in the face of Nazi terror. It was only when they were transported to the east, and confined together in ghettos and camps, that persecution transformed them into a homogeneous group.

Researchers therefore stress other forms of resistance: the zealous preservation of Jewish culture in the ghettos; Jewish contribution to the war effort of the Allies (the Palestinian Jewish brigade in the British army, or those who broke out of the ghettos to join the partisans, thus participating in the general, not specifically Jewish, history of anti-Nazi resistance); and suicide – the ultimate form of refusal.

Yet even this broader definition of resistance does not really take into account the specific circumstances of the persecution of the Jews. The crucial difference between the Jews and all other nations, with the single exception of the Gypsies, was the Nazis' determination to wipe them off the face of the earth. Had the Nazis simply tried to coerce them into one form of behavior or another, the Jews would have found ways to defy them. But there was no tradition of actively resisting total annihilation; even the medieval form of Jewish resistance to enforced conversion, i.e., killing oneself for the "sanctification of God," was inapplicable. In this unprecedented and extreme case of genocide, only by fleeing could the Jews really hope to thwart the enemy's policy. Resisting simply meant saving one's life, surviving.

This definition exposes one of the most painful problems of Jewish experience under Nazism: the conflict between the "underground" – the armed resistance in the ghettos – and the so-called Jewish "autonomy," the *Judenrat*, which was appointed by the German authorities and acted on their behalf. Only in the ghettos was there any chance of organizing resistance; in the labor camps, and all the more so in the death camps where the condemned spent only a short while before being exterminated, collective action was practically impossible. In most cases, the underground movement in the ghettos was organized at the last moment, that is, shortly before the final evacuation, and was in fact the desperate act of those who were prepared to die.

The most important revolt, both militarily and symbolically, took place in the Warsaw Ghetto; this uprising broke out only a short time before

| The "Jewish Fighting Organization" | Uprising of the Warsaw Ghetto | Revolt in Treblinka |
| --- | --- | --- |
| July 1942 | April–May 1943 | August 1943 |

**1941. December:** After a brief period of independent action, the fighting organization in Minsk joins the partisans.
**1942. July 20:** Armed uprising in Nesvizh (Belorussia).
**July 21:** Escape from Ghetto Kletsk.
**July 23:** Adam Czerniakow, president of the *Judenrat* in Warsaw, commits suicide so as not to sign children's deportation orders.
**July 28:** Zionists, Communists, and Bundists form a "Jewish Fighting Organization" in Warsaw; Revisionist Zionists have an organization of their own.
**August 9:** Armed uprising in the Mir Ghetto shortly before its liquidation.
**August 10:** Jewish partisans led by Jechezkiel Atlas wipe out a German garrison in Dereczyn.
**September 2:** Revolt of the Lachva Ghetto; 6000 Jews escape but are recaptured and executed.

3. Captured insurgents in the Warsaw Ghetto. Stereotype plate taken by General Jürgen Stroop.

September 24–26: Uprising in the Totchin Ghetto; most of the insurgents escape but are caught again and put to death.
**September 30:** When the Tarnopol *Judenrat* refuses to take part in the deportations, the Germans take matters into their own hands.
**November 18:** Jews in Przemysl refuse to alight the transport; they are defeated and sent to Belzec.
**Winter 1942–summer 1944:** Uninterrupted partisan activity of the anti-Fascist organization in Kovno until the liquidation of the ghetto.
**1943. January 18:** First uprising in the Warsaw Ghetto.
**February 5:** The Jews of Bialystok resist the first transports.
**April 19:** Beginning of the revolt of the Warsaw Ghetto.
**May 8:** Mordecai Anielewicz and other commanders of the revolt are killed in their bunker in 18 Mila Street. On May 12, Samuel Zygelbojm, the Jewish representative in the Polish government in exile, kills himself

*2. "L'Affiche rouge," Paris, 1944. M.O.I. – a resistance group, composed mostly of Jewish Communists, depicted in this poster as a band of criminals; they were all caught and executed.*

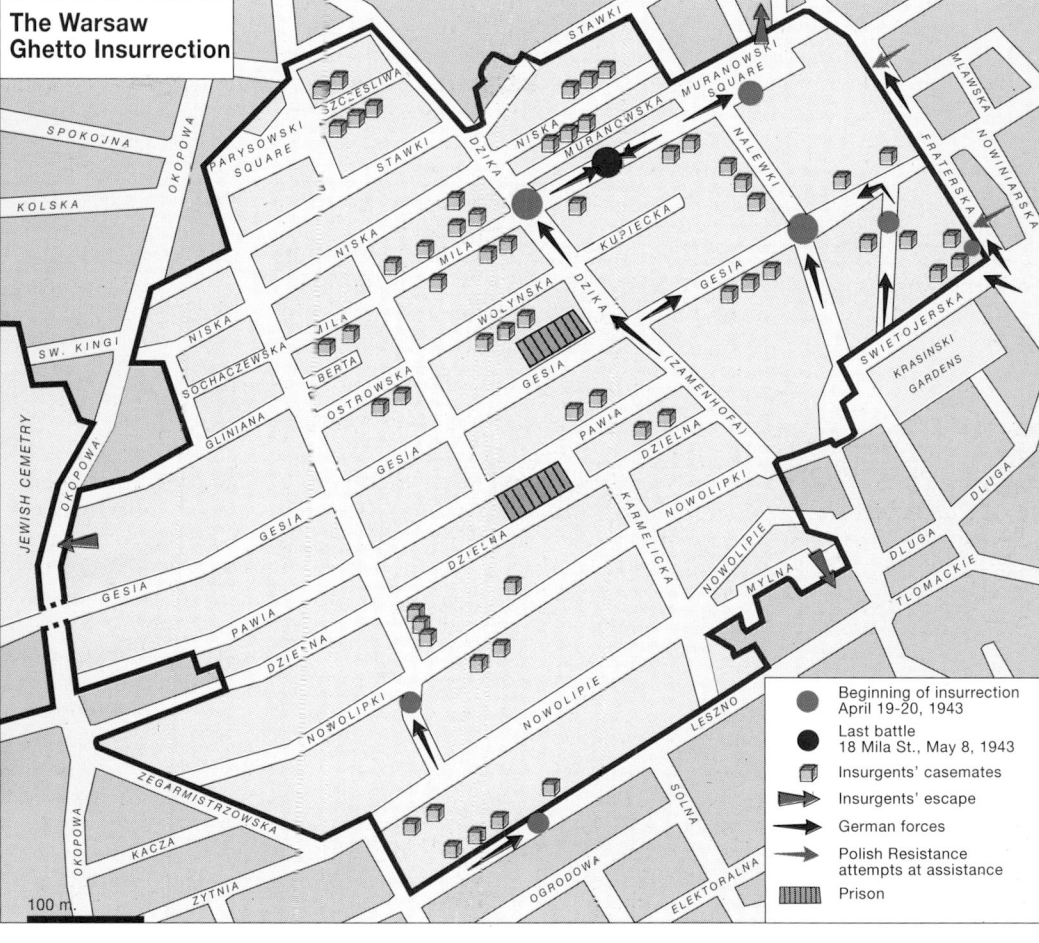

**The Warsaw Ghetto Insurrection**

- ● Beginning of insurrection April 19-20, 1943
- ● Last battle 18 Mila St., May 8, 1943
- Insurgents' casemates
- ➤ Insurgents' escape
- → German forces
- → Polish Resistance attempts at assistance
- ▦ Prison

100 m.

the ghetto was eradicated (the first transports left the ghetto on July 21 and 22, 1942; the first shots of the underground were fired on April 19, 1943). Here as elsewhere, then, the armed uprising represented choosing death over the saving of lives, an heroic gesture for the sake of posterity. The fighters were mostly young people who had no constraining family obligations, and were members of the youth movements which created the social and political cohesion necessary for collective action.

Relations between the armed resistance movement and the *Judenrat* were strained. With few exceptions (the councils in Minsk and Bialystok fully cooperated with the underground; about 40 members of *Judenraete* committed suicide upon realizing that they could do nothing to prevent the transportation to the death camps), these "Jewish councils" represented, against their will, a terrible subversive idea: rescue of a few by the sacrifice of many. Their strategy of saving lives served the interests of the Nazis, and in the end, the fate of members of the *Judenraete* was the same as that of the Jewish population at large.

The collective death sentence pronounced against the Jewish people confronted the leaders of the communities with a tragic alternative: resistance without hope, or compromise without glory. This was one of the most terrible moral dilemmas presented by the Holocaust.

**Abba Kovner's appeal**

**Revolt in Sobibor**

**Revolt of *Sonderkommando* in Auschwitz**

in London in solidarity and protest.
**June 25:** Armed resistance of the Jewish Fighting Organization under the command of Mordecai Zylberberg during the liquidation of the Tchenstochow Ghetto.
**August 1:** Armed resistance in the Bedzin-Sosnowiec Ghetto; most of its inhabitants are sent to Auschwitz.
**August 2:** Revolt in Treblinka; about six hundred prisoners take part in the fighting, armed with only knives and axes; few of them manage to escape.
**August 15–20:** The deportation of the remaining survivors in the Bialystok Ghetto provokes an uprising commanded by Mordecai Tenenbaum.
**September 1:** A desperate attempt to rebel in the Vilna Ghetto; this is where the poet Abba Kovner, one of the commanders of the revolt, issues his famous appeal

*4. Execution of two partisans in Minsk, October 1941. On the left, Masha Bruskina, a 17-year-old Jewish girl.*

urging Jews to fight rather than go like sheep to the slaughter.
**September 2:** Armed resistance at the Tarnow Ghetto.
**September:** The unified fighting organization (FPO) in the Vilna Ghetto does not manage to arrange a full-scale revolt; about two hundred fighters leave the ghetto to join the partisans.
**October 14:** Revolt in Sobibor; the prisoners kill ten S.S. men and take their weapons; only few survive and join the partisans.
**November 19:** Revolt of *Sonderkommando* in the Yanowska camp; tens of prisoners manage to escape, the rest are killed.
**1944. January:** Uprising in the camp of Chelmno.
**October 6–7:** Revolt of *Sonderkommandos* in Auschwitz (Birkenau) made possible by the smuggling of explosives by one of the inmates; the insurgents manage to destroy one of the death installations and kill many S.S. men, but none of the insurgents themselves survive.

# Liberation

Victory Day, on May 8, 1945, arrived too late for the Jewish people. Despite Himmler's order to cease extermination operations (November 1944), the murder industry continued to function until the very last moment. When it became quite clear that Germany was losing the war, the Nazis made frantic attempts to bring the final solution to completion. "Death marches," first organized by Adolf Eichmann in November 1944 in order to lead Hungarian Jews away from the advancing Red Army, claimed tens of thousands of victims.

Executions also continued in some of the camps. The last camp to function was Mauthausen, an extermination camp situated near the Austrian town of Linz. When the Americans liberated the camp on May 5, 1945, three days before Germany's capitulation, they found piles of corpses and thousands of living skeletons who could not be saved from death. A few days earlier, on April 29, an American army unit entered Dachau. This camp, established in March 1933 near Munich, was the first Nazi concentration camp and a model for all the others. Although it did not, strictly speaking, belong to the category of extermination camps, approximately 50,000 men, women and children perished there, mostly through what Nazi terminology defined as "natural causes" – starvation and disease – or as a result of pseudo-scientific experiments. The liberators counted 32,335 survivors; another 20,000, who had been taken by the Germans on a death march to the Alps a few days earlier, were found by American troops shortly afterward. Many thousands of the released camp inmates, however, failed to survive.

On April 15th, British troops liberated Bergen-Belsen. Taken by horrified soldiers, the first photographs to reach the free world revealed the true meaning of the "Final Solution." Towards the end of the war large contingents of human remnants had been transported by way of "death marches" into the camp. Decimated by epidemics, only 60,000 inmates were found, barely alive, on the day of liberation; 14,000 died within a few days. Ben-Gurion, who visited the camp in October 1945, noted that between the liberation of Bergen-Belsen and the time of his visit, 31,000 former inmates had died. Only from the beginning of October did the mortality rate begin to decline.

1. S.S. women captured by the British at Bergen-Belsen. April 1945.

On January 27, 1945, the Red Army liberated Auschwitz; this was the most symbolic liberation because the death factory at Oswiecim represented, more than any other, the Kingdom of Evil created by the Nazis. Soviet soldiers found 648 corpses and 6,700 prisoners still alive – "shadows" rather than human beings, as one of the Polish officers was to describe them. Since the day the first gas chambers had been used, two and a half years earlier, about a million and a half Jews and over one hundred thousand non-Jews – Russian prisoners of war, Polish political prisoners, Gypsies – were exterminated in this huge death factory.

The total number of victims of the Final Solution, by all extermination methods combined, varies between five and six million individuals. We shall probably never know the exact figure. Although the Germans did record the number of deaths in ghettos and in labor and concentration camps, and even the *Einsatzgruppen* recorded their operations of mass murder, their accounts were far from complete. Furthermore, some documentation, for example in Eichmann's office, was methodically destroyed by the Germans on the eve of their defeat in order to erase all evidence of the murder industry. The Korherr Report, (*Korherrbericht*) – a Nazi document on extermination statistics, began in 1942 and updated by its author every three months during 1943–1944 – is an important basis for estimation, but still deficient. Area-by-area, country-by-country statistics, however, comparing the size of the Jewish population on the

2. By order of the American army, the inhabitants of Naumburg bring to burial corpses of concentration-camp inmates who were murdered by the S.S. in a nearby forest.

| Beginning of "Death Marches" | Liberation of Auschwitz | Liberation of Bergen-Belsen |
|---|---|---|
| November 1944 | January 27, 1945 | April 15, 1945 |

**1944. July:** In Auschwitz, the Germans begin burning documents.
**July 13:** Between 4,000 to 5,000 residents of the Kovno Ghetto are transferred to camps in Germany.
**August 29:** Last transport from the Lodz Ghetto to Auschwitz.
**October 7:** Revolt of the Jewish auxiliaries to the *Sonderkommando* ("Special Squad") in Auschwitz.
**October 20:** Extermination by gassing in Auschwitz is terminated.
**November 8:** Beginning of the "death march" ordered by Adolf Eichmann: 20,000 Jews from Budapest are led towards the Austrian border.
**End of November:** Himmler orders the cessation of extermination operations in Auschwitz and the dismantling of the crematoria; but the killing of Jews continues.
**November 28-December 12:** The remaining Jews of Budapest are sent to death camps.
**1945. January 17:** Beginning of the "death march" of prisoners from Auschwitz; liberation of Warsaw.
**January 19:** The Red Army liberates Lodz; according to the Red Cross, only 900 survivors remain in the largest ghetto in Poland.
**January 25:** Beginning of the "death march" of 50,000 prisoners from the Stutthof camp, near Danzig, towards Germany's interior; the camp continued to function till mid-April.
**January 27:** Liberation of Auschwitz by a Red Army unit.
**February:** Transport of the last Slovakian Jews to Theresienstadt in Czechoslovakia.
**February 4–11:** The Yalta Conference.
**February 13:** The Red Army enters Budapest.
**April:** The Germans attempt to evacuate the camp in Dachau: 20,000 prisoners are led to the Alps.
**April 6–10:** "Death march" of about 20,000 prisoners from Buchenwald.
**April 8:** Beginning of the "death march" from the Bavarian camp of Flossenburg.

# 1945

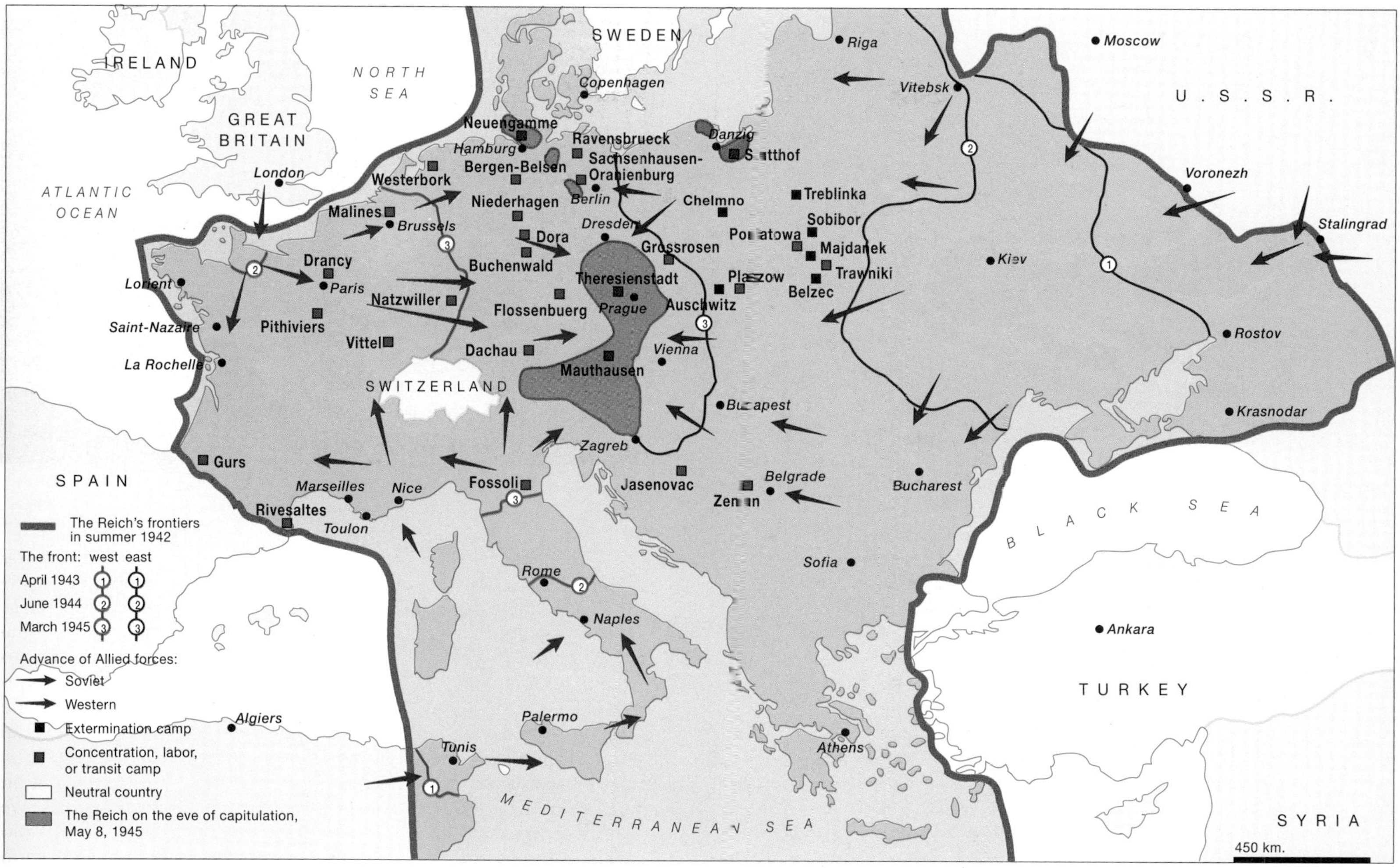

## Map

IRELAND

GREAT BRITAIN

London

ATLANTIC OCEAN

NORTH SEA

SWEDEN

Copenhagen

Riga

Moscow

Vitebsk

U.S.S.R.

Voronezh

Stalingrad

Neuengamme
Hamburg
Westerbork
Malines
Brussels
Niederhagen
Berlin
Dora
Drancy
Paris
Natzwiller
Buchenwald
Flossenbourg
Vittel
Dachau
Mauthausen

Ravensbrueck
Sachsenhausen-Oranienburg
Bergen-Belsen
Danzig
Stutthof
Dresden
Chelmno
Theresienstadt
Prague
Grossrosen
Plaszow
Auschwitz
Vienna

Treblinka
Sobibor
Poniatowa
Majdanek
Trawniki
Belzec

Kiev

Rostov

Krasnodar

SWITZERLAND

Pithiviers

Lorient
Saint-Nazaire
La Rochelle

SPAIN

Gurs

Marseilles
Nice
Rivesaltes
Toulon

Fossoli

Zagreb

Jasenovac

Budapest

Belgrade
Zemun

Bucharest

BLACK SEA

Sofia

Rome

Naples

Ankara

TURKEY

Algiers

Palermo

Tunis

Athens

MEDITERRANEAN SEA

SYRIA

450 km.

**Legend:**
- The Reich's frontiers in summer 1942
- The front: west east
  - April 1943 ① ①
  - June 1944 ② ②
  - March 1945 ③ ③
- Advance of Allied forces:
  - Soviet
  - Western
- ■ Extermination camp
- ■ Concentration, labor, or transit camp
- ☐ Neutral country
- The Reich on the eve of capitulation, May 8, 1945

---

eve of the war with the numbers of the remnants after the war, provide reliable estimates of the magnitude of the mass extermination of European Jewry. A third of the Jewish people, 70% of European Jewry, was destroyed by Hitler's savagery. The demographic structure of the Jewish nation was affected for generations to come. Its largest, oldest, and most flourishing communities were wiped off the face of the earth, and, with them, large parts of Jewish collective memory and culture. The language, customs, manners, humor and ways of life of an entire civilization had come to an end, consumed by the death camps.

| Germany's capitulation | First conference of survivors | The Nuremberg Trials |
|---|---|---|
| May 8, 1945 | July 1945 | November 1945-October 1946 |

**April 11:** Liberation of Buchenwald; the resistance organization takes over the camp before delivering it, two days later, to the Americans.

**April 13:** The Red Army enters Vienna.

**April 15:** A British army unit liberates the camp of Bergen-Belsen; tens of thousands of prisoners die within the first few months following their release.

**April 20:** The American army enters Nuremberg.

**April 29:** Before committing suicide in his Berlin bunker, Hitler signs a testament in which he reaffirms his racist beliefs and his hatred for the Jews. An American army unit liberates Dachau where 32,335 prisoners are found.

**May 2:** The Red Army in Berlin; capitulation of the German forces in the capital.

**May 5:** The Americans liberate the concentration camp of Mauthausen.

**May 7:** The Soviet army liberates the Theresienstadt Ghetto.

**May 8:** Germany's capitulation; the

Thousand Years Reich is dead.

**July:** The first conference of Jewish survivors is held at the St. Ottilien camp near Munich; in their proclamation, delegates of the "surviving remnant" (*She'erit ha-Peletah*) express their demands: the immediate establishment of a Jewish state in Palestine, recognition of the Jewish people as an equal member of the Allied nations, and Jewish participation in the peace negotiations. Similar conferences were held during the following months in several other places, electing the executive bodies of the survivors' organizations.

**August:** The Treaty of London calls for the establishment of an international military court to judge war criminals.

**November 1945-October 1946:** The Nuremberg Trials: Nazi war criminals are judged by an Allies' military tribunal. Twelve defendants were sentenced to death. The charter of the Nuremberg Tribunal served as a basis for other trials of war criminals held during the following years.

3. Dachau survivors, April 1945.

# The Survivors

## An Exodus, 1945-1947

**Occupation zone**
- French
- British
- Soviet
- American

→ Refugees
■ DP Camp
▼ Embarkation port

**EMIGRATIONS**

CANADA — 3,500
UNITED STATES — 40,000
LATIN AMERICA — 7,000
SOUTH AFRICA — 1,000
AUSTRALIA — 1,000
PALESTINE — 83,000

*Map labels:* SWEDEN, DENMARK, Moscow, Riga, Karlskrona, Copenhagen, Trelleborg, Smolensk, Luebeck, Szczecin (Stettin), Vilna (Vilnius), Mogilev, Hamburg, Hanover, POLAND, Minsk, GREAT BRITAIN, NETHER-LANDS, Amsterdam, Berlin, Poznan, Warsaw, Kiev, London, Antwerp, Brussels, BELGIUM, Lodz, Lublin, U.S.S.R., Le Havre, Kielce, Cracow, Paris, Prague, Plzen (Pilsen), Brno, CZECHOSLOVAKIA, Vienna, Bratislava, FRANCE, Basle, Munich, Salzburg, Budapest, SWITZERLAND, Innsbruck, Graz, HUNGARY, Villach, RUMANIA, Venice, Rijeka, Belgrade, Bucharest, Constanta, SPAIN, Sete, Port-de-Bouc, Genoa, La Spezia, Ancona, YUGOSLAVIA, Burgas, Istanbul, Marseilles, ITALY, BULGARIA, Madrid, Barcelona, Civitavecchia, Rome, Bari, ALBANIA, Ankara, Gaeta, Naples, Metaponte, GREECE, TURKEY

---

As the end of the war drew near, the scant remnants of European Jewry – over 1,200,000 emaciated, homeless, uprooted persons – began a mass movement of migration across Europe, which came to be known as "The Flight" (*Berihah*). Of the 400,000 Jews who had found refuge from Nazi persecution in the interior of Russia, those with Polish nationality sought to return to their former homeland. In under a year, encouraged by the Polish government and aided by charity organizations, about 200,000 of these Jews returned, hoping to rebuild their old communities. For a brief moment it seemed as if the nightmare had truly ended. But the pogrom in Kielce, perpetrated in broad daylight in July 1946, destroyed this illusion. 100,000 Jews left the country immediately; some went to the Displaced Persons (DP) Camps set up by the Allies in Germany and Austria, others departed for Palestine through the escape routes of southern Europe.

In Italy about 30,000 Italian Jews and 12,000 refugees survived the war; in Rumania – just over 400,000; in Bulgaria – 50,000; in France, where thousands of children were gathered from their various hiding places in farms and monasteries, about 150,000; the number of Jews who survived the war in Hungary and Czechoslovakia, the last two countries to be liberated, was less than 200,000.

Assembly Centers, set up in Germany and Austria by the Allies and refugee organizations for the purpose of identifying and registering the millions of persons displaced by the war, soon became a permanent home for those who had nowhere else to go. Approximately 250,000 Jews were concentrated in these camps, whose problem could not be simply solved by repatriation. Following a report on conditions in the DP centers, presented to President Truman by jurist Earl G. Harrison, new camps were set up which the Jews themselves administered. Hundreds of volunteers from Palestine, either soldiers in the British Jewish Brigade or special emissaries, together with experts and social workers sent by Jewish

---

| Liberation of Auschwitz | Renewal of clandestine immigration | Ben-Gurion visits the camps |
|---|---|---|
| **January 1945** | **August 1945** | **October 1945** |

**1945. January:** The *Berihah* ("The Flight") organization is founded in Lublin.
**March-September:** The organization transfers thousands of young Jews from Poland to Rumania and Hungary.
**June:** Creation of the Central Committee of Jews liberated in Germany. Soldiers of the British Jewish Brigade make their first contacts with concentration-camp survivors.
**August:** President Truman's representative, Earl G. Harrison, together with "Joint" members, visit the camps in Germany; following this visit, the Jews are separated from other refugees, their food rations are augmented, and the Joint is authorized to carry out assignments in the camps. The ship "Dalin" leaves Italy with 35 immigrants on board, marking the renewal of "illegal" immigration operations of the *Mosad Le-Aliyah Bet*; by December eight vessels reach the shores of Palestine with 1,040 survivors.
**October:** Ben-Gurion visits the camps in Germany: the survivors' plight highlights the urgency of a Zionist solution. The Athlit

*2. Immigrants from the boat "Return to Zion" interned in Cyprus. 1947.*

internment camp is penetrated by *Haganah* units and its internees released.
**November 13:** President Truman and the British Prime Minister Clement Attlee announce the establishment of an Anglo-American Committee of Inquiry into, among other things, the problem of Jewish refugees. The British Foreign Minister, Ernest Bevin, renews the 1939 White Paper policy of restricting Jewish immigration to Palestine.
**December:** The first mission of assistance sent from Palestine to the refugee camps in Germany.
**December 5:** The British prohibit Jews from entering DP camps in their occupation zone; the stream of refugees from the east therefore turns to the American zone and towards Austria and Italy.
**1946. January onwards:** All *Mosad* boats are intercepted by the British and their passengers imprisoned in Athlit, near Haifa.
**April:** The British army prevails on the Italian authorities to prevent the departure from La Spezia harbor of two *Mosad* boats with

# 1945–1948

charity organizations (notably, by the "Joint" – the American Jewish Joint Distribution Committee), became actively involved in rehabilitation work, providing food, medical care, schooling, sports, and workshops for vocational training.

The Zionist movement, in its struggle for the establishment of a Jewish state in Palestine, found in these masses of DPs an effective political weapon, particularly against the policy of the recently-elected Labour Government in Britain which had renewed the restrictions on immigration to Palestine according to the 1939 White Paper. The Anglo-American Committee of Inquiry repeated Harrison's recommendation that the Mandatory government immediately grant 100,000 immigration certificates to Jewish refugees in Europe. But as no immigration certificates were forthcoming, the illegal immigration of Jews to Palestine, organized by the *Mosad Le-Aliyah Bet* before the war, was resumed on an unprecedented scale – a vast clandestine transfer of populations, converging from all over Europe on the shores of the Mediterranean, then transported to Palestine across the sea. In the three years between the end of the war and the establishment of the State of Israel, the *Mosad* navigated 64 vessels out of Europe – small boats carrying under a hundred refugees, as well as ships carrying 7,500 passengers on board – conducting a total of 70,000 men, women, and children to the shores of Palestine; a further 13,000 were brought by other routes.

Aided openly or discreetly by socialist governments formed in post-war Europe by members of the resistance movements, this vast "illegal" immigration totally defeated the White Paper policy, and precipitated the British departure from Palestine.

The affair of the refugee ship "Exodus 1947" symbolized more than any other both the perennial plight of European Jewry and the struggle for the establishment of a Jewish state. Carrying 4,500 extermination-camp survivors, the ship left the French port of Sète on July 11, 1947. It was captured in mid-sea by the Royal Navy and, after a short battle which cost several lives, the refugees were carried by British deportation boats back to the port of departure and from there, a month later, to Germany. The international scandal and the outburst of world public opinion provoked by this affair hastened the resolution of the Middle East problem. Members of the United Nations Special Committee for Palestine (UNSCOP) later admitted that the "Exodus" affair was a major influence on their decision to submit a proposal for the partition of Palestine. Submitted to the U.N. on September 1, 1947, the proposal was adopted by the General Assembly on November 29, 1947. Eventually, the vast majority of Jewish DPs left Europe – the continent where political Zionism was born, and where a third of the Jewish people had perished. Many of them settled in Israel; others emigrated to America. A thousand years of European dominance in Jewish life had come to an end.

1. Paul Georghiau, Deportees to Cyprus. *Oil on wood, 1948.*

| First Zionist Congress after the war | UNSCOP | The "Exodus" affair | The partition resolution |
|---|---|---|---|
| December 1946 | May 1947 | July 1947 | November 1947 |

1,014 clandestine immigrants; the refugees declare a hunger strike which arouses public opinion and compels the British to permit the boats to reach Palestine.
**May 1:** Publication of the conclusions of the Anglo-American Commission recommending, inter alia, the settlement of 100,000 refugees in Palestine.
**June 27:** The S.S. "Wedgewood" with 1257 refugees is intercepted by the British.
**July:** The Czech government decides to open its borders to Jews fleeing from Poland; by September, over 70,000 Polish Jews have fled through Czechoslovakia, their transport paid for by the Czech government.
**July 30:** The Morrison-Grady plan for the cantonization of Palestine under the authority of a British High Commissioner is rejected by all parties.
**August 13:** The British government announces that from now on it will deport all illegal immigrants to internment camps in Cyprus. Over 50,000 people are detained in Cyprus, most of whom reach Israel only after

3. Purim noisemakers are sounded by children when the name of Wicked Haman is read from the Scroll of Esther; this rattle was made in a Palestinian detention camp in Cyprus, 1947.

Independence.
**December:** The first Zionist Congress after the war meets in Basle; it adopts Ben-Gurion's activist position; Weizmann resigns from the presidency.
**1947. March:** A Soviet diplomatic mission visits Palestine.
**April 28:** A special session of the U.N. General Assembly is convened by Britain to discuss the problem of Palestine.
**May 14:** Andrei Gromyko's speech in the U.N. favors the establishment of a Jewish state; a special inquiry commission for Palestine (UNSCOP) is set up.
**July 11:** The "Exodus" affair begins.
**September 1:** UNSCOP presents its conclusions to the U.N.
**November 29:** The partition of Palestine is decided during the U.N. General Assembly by a majority of over two thirds.
**December 26:** In its largest operation, the *Mosad* brings to Palestine two ships with over 15,000 refugees from Rumania and Bulgaria.

# The Struggle for a Jewish State

1. Immigrants from the British internment camps in Cyprus arrive at Haifa port on the boat Atsmaut (Independence), January 1949.

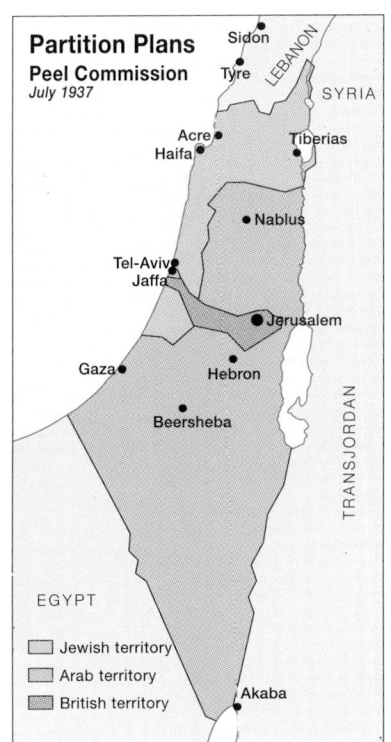

**Partition Plans**
**Peel Commission**
July 1937

Sidon
Tyre
LEBANON
SYRIA
Acre
Haifa
Tiberias
Nablus
Tel-Aviv
Jaffa
Jerusalem
Gaza
Hebron
Beersheba
TRANSJORDAN
EGYPT
Akaba

☐ Jewish territory
☐ Arab territory
☐ British territory

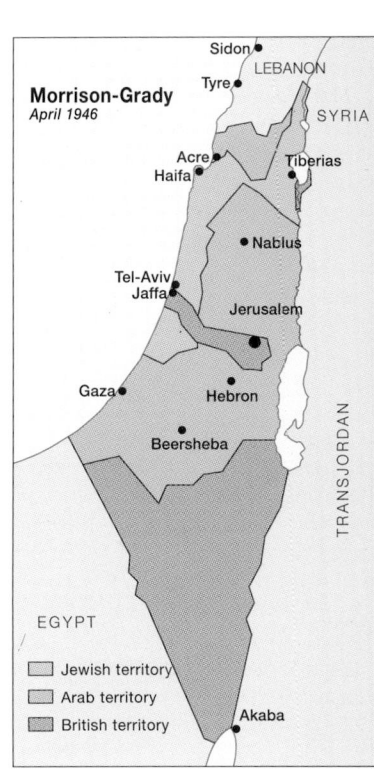

**Morrison-Grady**
April 1946

Sidon
Tyre
LEBANON
SYRIA
Acre
Haifa
Tiberias
Nablus
Tel-Aviv
Jaffa
Jerusalem
Gaza
Hebron
Beersheba
TRANSJORDAN
EGYPT
Akaba

☐ Jewish territory
☐ Arab territory
☐ British territory

The Mandate for Palestine was founded on a Zionist-British collaboration which endorsed the establishment of a Jewish national home. This cooperation ceased in 1939 when the British government decided to end the Mandate and to prepare the country for independence, according to the existing demographic distribution: two-thirds Arab, one-third Jewish. The White Paper of May 1939 stipulated that for a five-year transitional period Jewish immigration and land purchase would be limited in order to maintain existing proportions and that autonomous institutions would be developed within the Jewish and Arab populations. This document signalled the beginning of the struggle for a Jewish state in Palestine. The *yishuv* was willing to accept a solution guaranteeing its sovereignty even if it was to be allocated only a small part of the land, according to the partition plan of the 1937 Peel Commission, but would not comply with policies designed to create a Jewish minority within an Arab state. Divided between "moderates" led by Chaim Weizmann, and "activists" led by David Ben-Gurion, the Zionist leadership finally agreed on a prudent policy of defying the

rules of the White Paper and organizing mass "illegal" immigration, without openly clashing with the British authorities.

World War II deferred the struggle against the White Paper, as the *yishuv* concentrated entirely on the fight against Nazism. With the post-war order in mind, the leadership sought to create a Jewish Brigade within the British armed forces. Defined by Ben-Gurion, the "war objectives" of the Zionist movement were clearly stated in the Biltmore Program (New York, 1942): "That Palestine be established as a Jewish commonwealth integrated in the structure of the new democratic world."

However, when the war ended, the newly elected Labor government in England chose to reinstate the restrictive policy of the 1930s. The *yishuv*, now also facing the urgent task of saving the Holocaust survivors, renewed the struggle with unprecedented vigor. The *Haganah* and the dissenting underground movements, the *Irgun Zeva'i Le'ummi* and *Lohamei Herut Israel (Lehi)*, agreed to form a united front – *Tenu'at ha-Meri ha-Ivri* ("the movement of Hebrew resistance") – which began large-scale attacks on the British to compel them to change their policy. The unified

| White Paper | Creation of the *Palmah* | The Biltmore Program |
|---|---|---|
| **May 1939** | **May 1941** | **May 1942** |

**1939. May 17:** The British colonial secretary, Malcolm MacDonald, publishes a new White Paper: immigration and sale of land to Jews to be severely restricted.
**May–September:** The *yishuv* leadership instructs the Jewish population to ignore the rules of the White Paper. Census of Jewish inhabitants aged 18 to 35. General strike and demonstrations throughout the country. Jewish Agency Executive decides to form special units in the *Haganah* for carrying out attacks on British and Arab targets. Other violent operations are carried out by the *Irgun*. The 21st Zionist Congress debates how to contest the White Paper.
**1941. May:** Close collaboration with the British enables the creation of the *Palmah*, the "strike units" of the *Haganah*. The commander of the *Irgun*, David Raziel, is killed in action in Iraq in an operation mounted by the British; in fact, the *Irgun* too decides to cooperate with the British against the Nazis, and this causes the secession of *Lehi* led by Avraham (Yair) Stern.

3. "The White Paper": a poster condemning the Mandatory policy on immigration. May 1, 1944.

**1943:** As the war front recedes, relations between the British and the *yishuv* deteriorate once again.
**1944:** The *Irgun*, now commanded by Menahem Begin, proclaims "the revolt" against British rule. In response to the assassination of Lord Moyne in Cairo by *Lehi*, the Jewish Agency starts trying to suppress the activities of the dissenting organizations, by, among other things, handing them over to the British ("*la saison*," the "hunting season").
**1945. August:** Renewal of illegal-immigration operations; by 1948 approximately 70,000 immigrants had been brought in 65 vessels; most of them were caught and taken to British internment camps, first in Palestine (Athlit) and then in Cyprus.
**October:** The attack on the internment camp in Athlit marks the beginning of the operations of the unified movement of

resistance: a series of attacks on transportation routes, railways, bridges, police stations, and radar stations, culminating in the "Night of the Bridges" (June 1946) in which *Palmah* units destroy the bridges connecting Palestine with its neighboring countries.
**November:** Ernest Bevin, the British foreign secretary, announces the establishment of an Anglo-American inquiry commission and an additional quota of 1,500 certificates per month for Jewish refugees.
**1946. June 29:** "Black Saturday" – members of the Jewish Agency Executive are arrested; British military forces are sent to settlements suspected of harboring *Palmah* units and arms caches.
**July:** After the unified movement of resistance has ceased all acts of sabotage, the King David Hotel in Jerusalem is blown up by members of the *Irgun* and *Lehi*. The *Haganah* focuses its attention on immigration and settlement operations.
**October:** In a single swift operation, 11 new

**Jewish Agency** 1947

Jewish territory
Arab territory
International territory

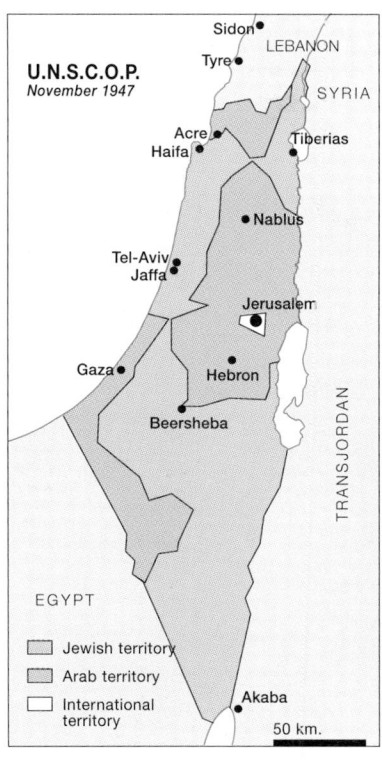

**U.N.S.C.O.P.** November 1947

Jewish territory
Arab territory
International territory

50 km.

2. Ben Gurion speaks at a meeting in Haifa, 1949.

movement operated from October 1945 to June 1946, when insurmountable political and tactical differences within it led to its disintegration. During this period, the British attempted to establish a common policy with the Americans. After visiting Palestine and the displaced persons camps in Europe, an Anglo-American inquiry commission presented conclusions which displeased all parties concerned: the British, who were required to admit 100,000 Jewish immigrants; the Jews, who had to be satisfied now with a bi-national state; and the Arabs, of course, who were dissatisfied with any solution other than an Arab Palestine.

Meanwhile, the British government launched a massive operation to repress the unified movement of resistance and sought out "moderate" Jewish leaders to replace activists who had been interned during the round-up on the "Black Sabbath" (June 29, 1946). But two months later in Paris the Jewish Agency Executive adopted a resolution of momentous importance. Virtually rejecting the Biltmore Program, this highest authority of the Zionist movement declared that it would accept a solution based on partition of the land. It thus ensured the approval of the

Americans, completely frustrating British policy. Bound by the original conditions of the Mandate, Britain had no alternative but to present the question of Palestine to the United Nations for a decision.

At this stage the Zionist leadership ceased its armed struggle against the British forces (with the exception of attacks by the dissenting organizations). This was a time of large-scale illegal immigration operations – the most spectacular being "Exodus 1947" – which secured the support of world public opinion in favor of the Zionist cause, and placed Great Britain in an impossible situation. It was also a time of diplomatic maneuvers: an international inquiry commission set up by the United Nations (UNSCOP) proposed the partition of Palestine into two independent states, and the U.N. General Assembly adopted the proposal by the required two-thirds majority (November 29, 1947). The British government announced that it would not cooperate in the execution of the partition plan and would withdraw British civilian staff and military forces by May 15, 1948. The Mandate was over and the War of Independence had begun.

| The attempt to blow up the King David Hotel | The decision on partition | The Proclamation of the State of Israel |
|---|---|---|
| **July 1946** | **November 1947** | **May 1948** |

settlements are established in the Negev to reinforce Jewish control in the region. President Truman announces his support for the partition plan.
**December:** The 22nd Zionist Congress endorses the policy of the Jewish Agency Executive headed by David Ben-Gurion who takes on the defense portfolio; Weizmann is compelled to resign from the presidency.
**1947. February–November:** The political struggle is transferred to the U.N. arena. In May UNSCOP is set up and Gromyko, the Soviet representative, announces the support of his country for the partition plan. On November 29th the U.N. adopts the fateful resolution favoring the partition and the establishment of a Jewish State.
**November 30:** The first gunshots of the War of Independence: Arabs attack a Jewish bus on its way to Jerusalem.

4. Lord Cunningham, the last British High Commissioner, leaves Palestine.

5. A portrait of the great right-wing poet, Uri Zvi Greenberg, painted by Reuven Rubin. Oil, 1923–1925.

# War of Independence

1. Boris Carmi, A guardpost in Kibbutz Mishmar ha-Emek. On the roof, poet Omer Hillel, a member of the Kibbutz. Passover, 1948.

The war began on November 30, 1947, the day after the U.N. General Assembly adopted the resolution on the partition of Palestine. A week later, the Arab Higher Committee declared a general strike which swiftly deteriorated into outbursts of violence in towns with a mixed Arab-Jewish population, in Jerusalem, and on the outskirts of Tel Aviv. The *yishuv*, conforming to its traditional strategy and in the hope of circumscribing the troubles, restricted its operations to defending isolated settlements and securing their access roads. But in January 1948, Syrian and Egyptian volunteer units of the "Arab Liberation Army" infiltrated into the country. Jerusalem, as well as groups of Jewish settlements south of Bethlehem, in the Negev and in the western Galilee, were completely cut off. The striking force of the *Haganah* (*Palmah*) suffered heavy losses while trying to defend convoys to the besieged settlements.

The political situation was not much better. The British refused to cooperate in implementing the U.N. partition plan, and, preoccupied with their own preparations for the evacuation of Palestine, intervened only by preventing both sides from occupying strategic areas. The United

States withdrew its support of the partition plan, proposing instead a U.N. trusteeship over Palestine. The *yishuv* had therefore no alternative but to venture forth onto the battlefield – thus attempting to gain control over the territories allotted to the Jewish state, and to secure the road to Jerusalem. In April the *Haganah* seized the initiative, deploying and organizing its own forces for a military showdown. The conquest of Arab villages and of towns with a mixed population – Haifa, Tiberias, Safed, and Jaffa – caused panic and a mass exodus of Palestinian Arabs from the areas occupied by the Jewish forces. The Arab entity in Palestine was defeated, and only the intervention of neighboring states saved it from total collapse.

On May 15, the day after the British Mandate officially ended and Ben-Gurion proclaimed the establishment of the State of Israel, the armies of Egypt, Transjordan, Iraq, Syria, and Lebanon invaded Israel. Although modest in size, these forces were well-equipped with tanks, artillery and fighting craft, and thus far superior in fire power to the Israeli forces. Facing them were the Jewish defense units of frontier settlements and the *Haganah* infantry units. Hastily organized into brigades – six regional and three of the *Palmah* – this Jewish army was reinforced during the first few months by artillery units and by two more brigades. Arms purchases in Europe during April and May, and aid from Jewish volunteers from abroad, equipped the Israeli forces with ammunition, artillery, a small airforce and a navy.

During two weeks of bitter fighting the *Haganah* suffered heavy casualties in six abortive counterattacks. Nevertheless, the Arab offensive on all fronts was dying out. Thus, by the time Count Folke Bernadotte, a U.N. mediator, suggested a four-week cease-fire agreement, the Israeli army was in control of almost the entire territory of coterminous Jewish settlement, including West Jerusalem, as well as settlements in the western Galilee which were not supposed to be part of the Jewish state according to the partition plan.

Hostilities were renewed on July 9, lasting ten days. The truce had enabled the Israelis to strengthen and reorganize their troops. The balance now definitely weighed in favor of the Israel Defense Forces (I.D.F., or *Zahal*), officially born during the truce. Concentrating their operations on the central front, against the Transjordanian Arab Legion, the Israeli troops took the towns of Ramleh and Lydda, thus enlarging the "corridor" to Jerusalem and eliminating the threat to Tel Aviv. In the north they occupied the Arab Lower Galilee, including the town of Nazareth. By now only the Egyptians were still resisting in the south and the Negev was still cut off.

A second cease-fire, this time imposed by the Security Council for an indefinite period, was spent on hopeless negotiations. Victorious on the battlefield, the Israelis were no longer satisfied with the territory allotted

---

**End of Mandate, proclamation of the State and Arab invasion**

**May 1948**

**Capture of the Negev and the Galilee**

**October 1948**

**1947. December:** Arab mob attacks in Jerusalem and Tel Aviv; a convoy is attacked on the way to the Ezion bloc (a group of Jewish settlements south of Bethlehem). The British evacuate the Tel Aviv region. Dozens of Jewish workers are killed in the oil refineries in Haifa.
**1948. January:** Attacks by the Arab Liberation Army commanded by Fawzi al-Kaukji on the *kibbutzim* Kefar Szold and Yehi'am in the Upper Galilee, as well as a major offensive against the Ezion bloc, are repulsed.
**February:** Sporadic clashes in the Upper Galilee and near Beth Shean. An explosive charge is set off in Ben-Yehuda Street in Jerusalem: dozens of people are killed and injured.
**March:** An Arab attack on an armored convoy bringing reinforcements to the Ezion bloc; the road to Jerusalem is cut off.
**April:** Israeli efforts to open the road to Jerusalem; conquest of the Arab village of Castel, in the course of which the

commander of the Arab forces in the area, Abd al-Qadir al-Husseini, is killed. The *Irgun* and the *Lehi* attack Deir Yassin, an Arab village on the outskirts of Jerusalem, killing hundreds of civilian inhabitants; the Jewish Agency denounces the attack. In the north, Tiberias and Haifa are captured.
**May:** Conquest of Safed, Beth Shean and Jaffa. The Arab Legion captures the Ezion bloc. The British evacuate Jerusalem.
**May 14–15:** Proclamation of the State of Israel, immediately recognized by the United States and the Soviet Union; departure of the British High Commissioner; invasion of Arab armies. The Syrians take the *kibbutzim* Sha'ar ha-Golan and Massadah, before being repulsed at the gates of Deganyah; in Jerusalem, the Jewish Quarter in the Old City falls to the Legion; two I.D.F. attacks on the Latrun enclave are defeated and many lives are lost; the Egyptians take Yad Mordekhai.
**June:** An Israeli offensive against the Iraqis in the Jenin sector; aerial attack on Amman

3. A Jewish volunteer from abroad in an I.D.F. recruitment office, 1948.

and Damascus; an Egyptian column is blocked near Ashdod; the Syrians take Kibbutz Mishmar ha-Yarden. Truce declared after twenty seven days of fighting. Serious conflict concerning *Altalena*, a ship loaded with a large quantity of arms and 800 volunteers for the *Irgun*: deciding to disband all dissident militias, Ben-Gurion orders the bombardment of the boat which is set on fire off the Tel Aviv shore.
**July:** Important territorial gains on the central front. Failed attempt to conquer the Old City of Jerusalem. Aerial bombings of Cairo and Damascus. A second truce.
**August:** Israel proclaims Jerusalem an "occupied territory" and appoints a military governor there.
**September:** Count Bernadotte, mediator on behalf of the U.N., is assassinated in Jerusalem by *Lehi* members. Units of the *Irgun* join the national army on the orders of the provisional government.
**October:** The I.D.F. begins an offensive to open the road to the Negev. An Egyptian

*2. A mounted unit of the Givati brigade on patrol near Gederah, photo by Boris Carmi, September, 1948.*

to the Jewish state in the partition plan. On October 15, taking advantage of an Egyptian infringement of the cease-fire, the I.D.F. launched a major offensive in the south. Once Beersheba was taken, and the Negev reconnected to the State of Israel, an Egyptian brigade commanded by Gamal Abdul Nasser was encircled in the Faluja "pocket." An attack on the Arab forces in the central and southern Galilee pushed them back beyond the border. The Security Council demanded that Israel return to the cease-fire lines of October 15. Another Israeli offensive on December 22, however, took the troops into the center of the Sinai peninsula. This time Ben-Gurion ceded to American pressure and to British military threats and withdrew the forces back to the international border.

On January 7, 1949, the War of Independence had practically ended. Israel had acquired the state through military prowess, by force of arms gaining a territory greater than the one negotiated by diplomatic efforts. But the price of victory was high: 6,000 Israelis had been killed. the Arab armies lost about 2,000 regular soldiers, and an unknown number of irregular fighters. Finally, approximately 600,000 Palestinians had to leave their homes and the "refugee problem" was born.

| The I.D.F. in Sinai | End of the war and beginning of negotiations |
|---|---|
| **December 1948** | **January 1949** |

*4. Jacky Cohen, a South-African volunteer, in an Israeli airforce uniform.*

navy ship, *Emir Faruq* is sunk off the shore of Gaza. After a week of fighting. the cease-fire is resumed on the southern front. The I.D.F. occupies the central and the Upper Galilee.
**November:** First census in the State of Israel: 712,000 Jewish inhabitants, 69,000 Arabs. The Security Council demands negotiations for a permanent armistice.
**December:** A major offensive to drive the Egyptian army out of Palestine: within a week, the I.D.F. arrive at Abu Aweigila in the Sinai. British threat of military intervention.
**1949. January:** The Egyptian government expresses willingness to enter negotiations for a cease-fire. Five British warplanes are shot down by Israeli planes in the Negev. In Rhodes on January 12, beginning of talks between Israel and Egypt, presided over by Bernadotte's successor, Ralph Bunche. Beginning of mass immigration.

## Map legend

- Jewish location
- Arab location
- Mixed location
- Arab Legion camp
- Jewish territory on the eve of Independence
- Arab forces' advance
- Territory captured by Israel.
  - By July, 18, 1948
  - From October 1948 to January 1949
- Territory acquired by Israel through armistice agreements
- Armistice line, 24 February

*5. The bullet-holed water-tower of Kibbutz Be'erot Yizhak.*

25 km.

# Black Years Under Stalin

1. Stalin, by Evgeny Lvovitch Rotenberg (1899–1966), 1947.

1,000 km.

World war II devastated Soviet Jewry, annihilating more than half of its population. In 1939, this enormous community numbered about three million; following the annexation in 1940–1941 of eastern Poland, the Baltic countries, and Bessarabia, the Jewish population of the Soviet Union totalled over five million people. With the German invasion in June 1941, most of these fell under Nazi occupation – two and a half million perished in the Holocaust. In addition, of the 500,000 Jews who fought in the ranks of the Red Army, about 200,000 men were killed and hundreds of thousands wounded in battle.

To mobilize world Jewish support for the Soviet war effort against Nazi Germany, a Jewish Anti-Fascist Committee was organized on the initiative of the Soviet government. Headed by the actor Solomon Mikhoels, its first appeal, on April 7, 1942, was signed by the most distinguished Jewish writers, actors, doctors, and soldiers. In the absence of any other community organization, it was this body which ensured a modicum of Jewish cohesion in the Soviet Union, renewed ties with world Jewry, and some revival of Yiddish culture. After the war the Committee dealt primarily with assisting Jewish refugees returning to their homes.

Stalin's policy of destroying the religious and cultural identity of the Jewish minority was resumed with a vengeance shortly after the end of the war. A campaign against "Jewish nationalism" was launched in August

| Founding of the Anti-Fascist Committee | Campaign against Jewish "nationalism" |
| --- | --- |
| April 1942 | August 1946 |

3. Andrei Gromyko at the Security Council. Behind him are seated the Zionist leaders Abba Hillel Silver, Moshe Shertok (Sharett) and Golda Meir. New York, February 1948.

**1939. August 23:** The German-Soviet non-aggression pact.
**1941. June 22:** Operation Barbarossa: the Germans invade the Soviet Union.
**December:** Two former Polish Bund (autonomist socialist) leaders, Henryk Erlich and Victor Alter, are arrested, secretly tried and executed.
**1942. April:** Founding of the Jewish Anti-Fascist Committee under the auspices of the Soviet Information Bureau headed by Solomon Lozovski, deputy-minister of foreign affairs.
**June:** Founding of the Yiddish journal Eynikayt ("Unity"); renewed activity of Der Emes ("The Truth") publishing house.
**1943:** A Black Book, containing testimonies and documents concerning the extermination of Jews by the Nazis, is prepared by the Anti-Fascist Committee, but the Soviet authorities prevent its publication.
**1945. July 23:** A play by Z. Okun, based on Jewish folklore, is produced by the Moscow Jewish Theater, receiving a State prize in the

following year.
**1945–1946:** Wave of arrests and trials, mostly for Zionist activities and "illegal" attempts to leave the country.
**1946. August:** Zhdanov's speech to the Central Committee and the resolutions adopted by that body begin the campaign against Jewish "nationalism." The theme is taken up by an article in Eynikayt which attacks Jewish literature and theater. Campaign for the liquidation of Yiddish literature; concealment of the Holocaust and of Jewish contribution to the war against the Nazis.
**1946–1947:** Ilya Ehrenburg, The Storm.
**1947. July-August:** A violent press campaign against writer Itzik Kipnis leads to his expulsion from the Writers' Union and later to his arrest.
**November 29:** The Soviet Union votes in the U.N. in favor of the partition of Palestine.
**1948. January 13:** Solomon Mikhoels is murdered by the Soviet secret police.
**November:** Dissolution of the Jewish Anti-

### Antisemitic articles in the Soviet press

- ■ Total
- ▨ Daily
- □ Periodical

(chart values: 300, 250, 200, 150, 100, 50, 0 across years 1948, 1949, 1950, 1951, 1952, 1953)

Number of Yiddish books published

18 (1946) | 49 (1947) | 47 (1949) | none (1949–1953)

- U.S.S.R. frontiers on the eve of World War II
- Jewish migration
- Annexed territory, 1944–1947
- Frontline, November 1942

Percentage of the Jewish population, 1953:
- □ less than 0.5%
- □ 0.5% – 1%
- ▨ 1% – 1.5%
- ▨ 1.5% – 2%
- ▨ over 2%

(map labels: Tunguska, Angara, oyarsk, Irkutsk, LAKE BAIKAL, Kolyma, Okhotsk, Amur, Khabarovsk, BIROBIDZHAN, Vladivostok)

was thus liquidated. In the following decade the authorities turned against assimilated Jewish intellectuals, and launched a vicious campaign against Israel and the Zionist movement which were portrayed as tools of American capitalist imperialism.

In 1952 the wave of terror culminated in a fresh campaign against "cosmopolitans," "bourgeois nationalists," and Zionists, recalling the great purges of the 1930s. On August 12, 1952, twenty six members of the defunct Anti-Fascist Committee and prominent figures in Jewish Soviet cultural life, were shot after a secret trial. Four months later, on January 13, 1953, *Pravda* and Moscow Radio announced the unmasking of "murderers in white gowns": nine physicians, six of them Jews, were

2. Solomon Mikhoels (on the right) and Zorkin in "Travels of Benjamin the Third" by Mendele Mokher Seforim. Moscow, December 1947.

1946 with a vehement speech by Andrei Zhdanov and a series of resolutions adopted by the Central Committee of the Communist Party. The peak of persecution and antisemitic propaganda was reached in the the years 1948–1953, the last years of Stalin's regime, which came to be known as the "Black Years" of Soviet Jewry. Under the guise of a struggle against "cosmopolitans," the Moscow State Jewish Theater, one of the last vestiges of a once-flourishing culture and among the best troupes in the Soviet Union, was closed down in 1949; writers, poets, and actors were either imprisoned or shot; Mikhoels himself, director of the Jewish Theater, was murdered by the N.K.V.D. on January 13, 1948. Practically the whole communist Jewish intelligentsia with a "nationalist" orientation

accused of murdering two Soviet leaders – Shcherbakov and Zhdanov – and of conspiring to kill a number of high-ranking military figures, including the war minister, the chief of staff, and a popular war hero. The official declaration accused "most of the participants in the terrorist group" of connections with the "international Jewish bourgeois nationalist organization, the Joint, established by American Intelligence."

A wave of panic swept over Soviet Jewry, fearing that the worst was yet to come. Rumors about a plan for a massive deportation of Jews to Eastern Siberia began to circulate. Stalin's death brought some relief. But neither Jewish institutional life, nor their cultural and educational activities could be revived after so many years of systematic crushing.

| The U.S.S.R votes for the partition of Palestine | The "Black Years" | Stalin's Death |
|---|---|---|
| November 1947 | 1948–1953 | March 1953 |

Fascist Committee, arrest of its members, closing of its organ *Eynikayt* and *Der Emes* publishing house.
**1948–1949:** Cessation of Yiddish radio broadcasts; thirteen Yiddish theaters are closed down.
**1952:** Execution of writers Perez Markish, Itzik Fefer, David Bergelson, David Hofshtein, Leib Kvitko, Samuel Persov, and of Benjamin Zuskin, director of the Jewish Theater of Moscow, and literary critic Isaac Nusinov.
**November:** Slansky's trial in Prague: prominent Communist leaders, most of them Jews, are accused of conspiring against the state. Similar show trials were held in Hungary and Bulgaria.
**1953:** Official announcement of the "Doctors' Plot." A plan for a mass deportation of Jews to Siberia.
**March 5:** Stalin's death.

4. Yaacov Shmushkevich (1902–1942), Commander of the Soviet air force, executed in 1942, rehabilitated in 1953.

5. "A band of criminal doctors in the service of American-British espionage discovered in the Soviet Union." The headline in Kol Haam, the daily newspaper of the Israeli Communist Party, on January 14, 1953.

# Hungarian Jewry

1. *Prayer at the Great Synagogue in Dohany Street. Budapest, 1980.*

2. *Members of the Hungarian Revolutionary Ruling Council. At the center, in profile, Bela Kun. Budapest, 1919.*

4. *Hungarian postcard. 1905.*

A fter the collapse of the Austro-Hungarian Monarchy and the dismemberment of Hungary following World War I, the Jewish Hungarian community numbered about 470,000 people. During the interwar years it underwent radical changes. The processes of urbanization, assimilation, and a declining birthrate, characteristic of any society undergoing modernization, were intensified by the fact that the country had lost the provinces with a traditionally higher birthrate, and a more rural and more orthodox Jewish population. After the war, half the Hungarian Jewish population was concentrated in Budapest. Jewish life was affected by these changes in every respect.

Religious congregations in Hungary were composed of three trends: Neolog ("reformed"), Orthodox and the so-called "status quo." Of the three, the Neologs comprised 65% of the community, the Orthodox about 30%. Governed by the strong leadership of the rabbis, the Orthodox current was the most structured. The influence of the Zionist movement was negligible, its weakness reflecting the sociological and mental state of the community, which was caught between assimilationist tendencies and a powerful, fiercely anti-Zionist orthodoxy. Largely middle class, over-represented in the liberal professions, in commerce and in finance, it was particularly vulnerable to economic fluctuations.

| Hungarian Revolution | German invasion |
|---|---|
| **March–July 1919** | **March 1944** |

**1919. March–July:** Bela Kun's revolutionary regime.
**September:** A wave of pogroms, the White Terror, claims about 3,000 victims.
**1920:** The "Awakening Magyars," an extreme right-wing organization comprising about 80,000 members, vows to "extirpate the destructive doctrines propagated by the Jews who had already contaminated the Christian population of Hungary." Introduction of the *numerus clausus* bill: the total percentage of Jews to be admitted to universities is restricted to 5%.
**1921–1931:** Stephen Bethlen's government; the situation of Hungarian Jews is distinctly improved, although antisemitic agitation continues.
**1922:** Rabbi Lajos Venetianer publishes *A History of Hungarian Jewry* which tries to refute the charge that the Jews were responsible for the introduction of Bolshevism to Hungary.
**1925. December:** The Hungarian minister of education, Count Kuno Klebelsberg, defends

in the Council of the League of Nations the *numerus clausus* law introduced in 1920.
**1938:** The "First Jewish Law" restricts to 20% the number of Jews in the liberal professions, in the administration, and in commercial and industrial enterprises.
**1939:** The "Second Jewish Law" extends the definition of "Jew" on a racial basis, now including about 100,000 Christians (converted Jews and their children); it also reduces the percentage of Jews in economic life to 5%. This law, however, exempts from these restrictions all soldiers and prisoners during World War I who were decorated for acts of bravery or wounded, as well as those who took part in anti-revolutionary "national" activities.
**1941:** The "Third Jewish Law," inspired by the Nuremberg Laws in Germany.
**1942. October:** Growing German pressure for the complete elimination of Jews from Hungarian economic and cultural life, the imposition of the "yellow badge," and evacuation to the East; Kallay's government

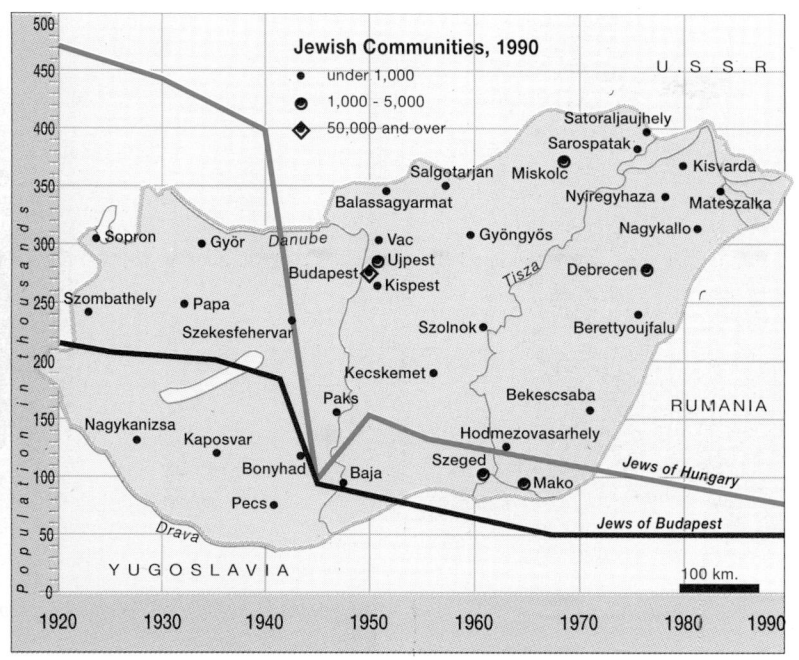

Jewish Communities, 1990
- under 1,000
- 1,000 – 5,000
- 50,000 and over

3. Kosher restaurant of the Orthodox community. Budapest, c. 1980.

Humiliated, amputated, impoverished Hungary, after its defeat in World War I, witnessed several revolutionary upheavals. The government steadily moved left, until Hungary was proclaimed a Soviet republic controlled by Bela Kun. The Communist regime included a large number of Jews in the upper ranks of the government, including Kun himself. When the Rumanian invasion liquidated the Communist experiment, the country shifted abruptly to the right. Antisemitism serves as a partial explanation to the massive Jewish participation in Bela Kun's revolutionary regime. Their role in the revolution, in turn, helps to explain the White Terror unleashed by the conservative regime of regent Nicolas Horthy. Legislation of an increasingly discriminatory nature – first the *numerus clausus* of 1920, then, after a decade of relative stability, racist economic laws in 1938–1939 – were all manifestations of this atmosphere. Ideological antisemitism was not new in Hungary, having risen as a significant force since the 1870s, but it now became an essential element in the political arena.

During World War II Hungarian Jewry, particularly the Jews in the annexed territories and those whose Hungarian nationality was in doubt, was decimated by deportations, massacres, and forced labor. Nevertheless, the community survived till the very last phase of the war. The prime minister Miklos Kallay, supported by Horthy, obstinately refused to obey the injunctions from Berlin. This was one of the reasons for the implementation of Operation Margaret: on March 19, 1944, German troops occupied Hungary, and Adolf Eichmann took charge of the "final solution of the Jewish question" in this country. This was the beginning of the phase of genocide for the Jews of Hungary.

Of the 750,000 Jews in greater Hungary of 1941, approximately 141,000 remained within her postwar borders. A large wave of emigration reduced their number even further. As elsewhere in Eastern Europe, an enfeebled community that was trying to return to normal life, found itself progressively oppressed by the new Communist regime. The tendency to assimilate, which had always been strong, was reinforced by the logic of a system that was equalizing, intolerant and explicitly atheistic, as well as by the enforced isolation of the community from the rest of the Jewish world. From the 1960s onwards, however, the relatively-liberal regime of Jan Kadar allowed a certain measure of freedom of expression and more frequent contacts with foreign countries. The 80,000 Hungarian Jews could thus cultivate their cultural and religious identity even prior to the explosion of liberties which accompanied the downfall of Communism in Hungary as in all countries behind the Iron Curtain.

| The Popular Republic of Hungary | Uprising in Budapest | | First free elections |
|---|---|---|---|
| 1949 | 23 October, 1956 | | 25 March, 8 April, 1990 |

5. Members of the Arrow Cross throwing books into the fire. Budapest, 1944.

resists these demands.

**1943. April:** Meeting between Hitler and Horthy. The Fuehrer denounces the ineffective way in which the Hungarians are handling the "Jewish Question" in their country; in fact, Kallay's government is at that moment secretly negotiating with the Allies for an honorable way to extricate Hungary from the war.

**December:** The perpetrators of the massacre of Serbs and Jews in Bacska in January 1942 are brought to trial in front of a military tribunal – an act which aggravates Hungary's relations with Germany.

**1944. March 19:** Germany occupies Hungary; deportations, pogroms and persecutions have already claimed about 63,000 Jewish victims. On October 15, the Nazi party of Ferenc Szalasi seizes power.

**1945. January 18:** Soviet troops occupy Budapest.

**November:** Founding of the Jewish periodical *Uj Elet* ("New Life").

**1946. May:** Pogrom in Kunmadaras.

**July:** Pogrom in Miskloc: five persons are killed. With the stabilization of the economic situation, the acts of violence abate.

**1948. December:** An agreement between the government and the Jewish community grants freedom of religious practice.

**1949:** Hungary becomes a Popular Republic; Zionist organizations are outlawed.

**1950:** The three currents of Hungarian Judaism found a single community organization.

**1956. October:** The Hungarian anti-Communist uprising; 20,000 Jews flee abroad.

**1959–1968:** The Rabbinical Seminary in Budapest publishes the *Monumenta Hungariae Judaica*.

**1987:** A Wallenberg memorial is erected in Budapest.

**1989. September 17:** Hungary reestablishes diplomatic relations with Israel.

6. Etrog-Box (Etrog, citron, is one of the "four species" of Sukkot) Silver, Hungary 17th century.

# Latin American Communities

1. *Course of preparation for Aliyah. An Israeli-government poster.*

After World War I, when the United States introduced severe immigration quotas, many European Jews tried to circumvent this obstacle by traveling via Cuba and Mexico. But aided by American Jewish organizations, thousands of them settled in these places permanently. Meanwhile, Argentina and Brazil decided to remain open to immigration; in particular they encouraged new settlers in rural regions. Thus, the Jewish agricultural colonies in Argentina and southern Brazil were able to absorb large numbers of new Jewish immigrants, most of whom eventually moved to the larger cities. Later there was also immigration to Chile and Uruguay.

In all these countries, dynamic and well-organized Jewish communities which developed during the 1920s were able to offer to their growing populations a wide variety of social, religious and cultural services. New journals, some of which were in Spanish, began to appear, previously-existing newspapers enlarged their readership, and a local Yiddish literature began to emerge. The congregations were grouped according to country of origin: Ashkenazi, Sephardi, Ladino-speaking, Arabic-speaking, Syrians from Damascus, Syrians from Aleppo, etc. In the Ashkenazi community, further divisions were based on ideological or political adherence. The rise of antisemitism during the 1930s forced all these communities to unite in umbrella institutions. Only the Communists preferred to set up their own organs in the struggle against antisemitism. Loan and mutual assistance funds facilitated the economic integration of new immigrants; some of these funds eventually developed into approved banks.

The 1929 crisis and the rise of nationalism led to a curtailment of immigration. The Latin American countries shut their gates precisely when European Jewry was in the most dire need of finding refuge. When the "Kristallnacht" (November 9–10, 1938) signalled to the world at large the precarious circumstances of the Jews in central Europe, Argentina, Brazil, Mexico, Cuba, Uruguay, and Chile, were inaccessible. The refugees therefore sought other destinations, and it was thus that Colombia, Ecuador, Bolivia, Paraguay and Guatemala, and even countries hostile to immigration, such as Peru and Venezuela, were annexed to the map of the Jewish diaspora. However, by crossing the borders from neighboring countries with or without official permission, approximately 40,000 Jews managed to settle in Argentina between 1933 and 1945. Latin America as a whole absorbed almost 100,000 Jewish refugees, most of them from German-speaking countries.

Remaining neutral until Pearl Harbor, and passive throughout the rest of the war, most Latin American countries enjoyed both during and after the war an economic prosperity which strengthened the middle class. It was during this period that the by now well-established Latin American Jewry, became an integral part of western Jewry. By the time the voice of

| Buenos Aires Congress for Immigration | Committees against Nazi persecutions | "Committee for Jewish Palestine" |
|---|---|---|
| **1928** | **1933–1940** | **1945–1946** |

**1919. January 7–13:** "Tragic Week" in Buenos Aires: a general strike described by the government as a Communist uprising led by a Jewish "Soviet leader," supplies the excuse for a pogrom against Jewish immigrants ("Russians"); the tension affects other Jewish communities in Argentina, as well as the community in Montevideo, Uruguay.
**1921, 1924:** Immigration quotas introduced in the United States.
**1924. August 8:** The president of Mexico, Plutarco Elias Calles, declares that his country will encourage Jewish immigration.
**1928. May 27:** A Jewish Congress for Immigration to Latin America convenes in Buenos Aires.
**1930. July 27:** The first B'nai B'rith Lodge in Latin America is founded.
**1931. May–June:** In Mexico, following an antisemitic provocation instigated by competing merchants supported by the authorities, hundreds of Jewish peddlers are expelled from the central market.

**1933:** A Committee against anti-Jewish persecutions in Germany is founded in Buenos Aires. By 1940, such organizations, which served to fight antisemitism and as representative institutions, were founded in all Latin-American Jewish communities (in Brazil, the *Confederaçao Israelita do Brasil* was founded only in 1951).
**1937. June:** A secret circular from the Brazilian minister of foreign affairs instructs all consuls not to grant visas to Jews.
**1938. July:** The Evian conference: of all the Latin American leaders, only Leonidas Trujillo of the Dominican Republic declares that he is prepared to admit 100,000 refugees from Germany.
**1940:** The *Comité Central Israelita* is established in Uruguay.
**1942. November:** Ceding to the pressure of Jewish organizations, Argentinian president Ramon Castillo agrees to admit 1,000 French Jewish children; but the Argentinian government refuses to implement the President's decision for fear of endangering

3. *The Child. Hebrew reader published in Buenos Aires in 1942 by the Israel publishers. The text praises the Argentinian homeland; on the page on the right – the Argentinian national emblems.*

2. The all-American Maccabiah. The Jewish "olympics," organized by Maccabi, the Zionist sports federation.

**UNITED STATES**

MEXICO **35,000**
- Monterey
- Mazatlan
- Guadalajara
- Mexico City
- Veracruz

BAHAMAS 300
- Havana
- CUBA 700
- PUERTO RICO 1,500
- VIRGIN ISLANDS 300
- HAITI
- DOMINICAN REP. 100
- JAMAICA 300
- Kingston
- THE DUTCH ANTILLES 400
- TRINIDAD AND TOBAGO

BELIZE
GUATEMALA 800
HONDURAS
EL SALVADOR
NICARAGUA
COSTA RICA **2,000**
PANAMA **3,800**

PERU **3,500** — Number of Jews according to 1988 estimate

Rate of Jewish population (per 1,000 inhabitants)
- less than 0.5
- 0.5 - 1
- 1 - 2
- over 2

VENEZUELA **20,000**
- Maracaibo
- Caracas
- Ciudad Guyana
- Medellin
- Georgetown
- Paramaribo
- GUYANA
- SURINAM 200
- Cayenne
- FRENCH GUIANA
- Cali
- Bogota
- COLOMBIA **6,500**
- Quito
- ECUADOR **900**
- Guayaquil
- Manaos
- Santarem
- Belem

PERU **3,500**
- Lima
- BOLIVIA 600
- La Paz
- Santa Cruz

BRAZIL **100,000**
- Fortaleza
- Recife
- Salvador
- Brasilia
- Goiania
- Belo Horizonte
- São Paulo
- Rio de Janeiro
- Curitiba
- Santos

PARAGUAY **900**
- Asuncion

CHILE **15,000**
- Cordoba
- Santa Fe
- Salto
- Porto Alegre
- Rosario
- URUGUAY **24,500**
- Valparaiso
- Mendoza
- Santiago
- Buenos Aires
- Montevideo
- Chillan
- Bahia Blanca
- Concepcion

to Central America

to Israel

ARGENTINA **220,000**

1000 km

···· Immigration from Eastern Europe and North Africa, 1914-1933
······ Immigration from Germany and central Europe, 1933-1947
—→ Emigration, 1947-1991

Latin America was needed to sway the balance in favor of the establishment of a Jewish state, the Jewish communities in these countries were already strong enough to influence their respective governments. On November 29, 1947, it was the thirteen votes of the Latin American bloc which decided the resolution on the partition of Palestine.

Over the past forty years, only small groups of Jewish immigrants have reached Latin America from other continents. It has been mainly internal migration which has changed the map of the Jewish communities. Massive industrialization has drawn many thousands to the cities, thus enlarging the urban communities and depleting the rural Jewish populations. At the same time, the crises accompanying economic transformation have aggravated social tensions and multiplied revolutionary movements. The Castro revolution in Cuba, and later the victory of *Unidad Popular* of Salvador Allende in Chile, both regarded as a threat to the middle classes, caused large numbers of Jews from these countries to depart. The rise of military right-wing dictatorships in Argentina and Chile, which temporarily liquidated the democracy so crucial to the existence of organized Jewish communities, also resulted in the mass departure of Jews. Many Jews now took up residence in other Latin American countries, such as Mexico and Venezuela, or in Spain and, increasingly, in Israel. At present, however, the reestablishment of democracies throughout the continent appears to offer brighter prospects for the remaining Jewish communities in Latin America.

**Latin America votes in favor of the partition of Palestine**

**1947**

**Eichmann captured in Buenos Aires**

**1960**

Argentina's good relations with Nazi Germany (officially, Argentina was neutral).

**1945–1946:** In most Latin American countries, committees for the establishment of a Jewish state in Palestine are founded by intellectuals and public figures.

**1949:** The first kibbutz consisting of Latin American immigrants is founded in Israel.

**1960. May:** Discovered in Argentina, Adolf Eichmann is captured by Israeli *Mosad* agents and brought to trial in Jerusalem; this creates a rift in the relations between the two countries, and sparks off a wave of antisemitism in Argentina which lasts well after the execution of the Nazi criminal (1962). Serious antisemitic disturbances are provoked by the neo-Nazi movement in Uruguay.

**1962:** Founding of a Conservative congregation and its own rabbinical seminary in Buenos Aires modelled on the American Jewish Conservative movement (the liberal trend, strongly opposed by the Orthodox); the movement spreads quickly throughout the continent.

**1967. June:** The Six-Day War; hundreds of young Jews from Latin America volunteer for civil service in Israel.

**1975. October:** The U.N. General Assembly resolution defining Zionism as a form of racism; Brazil and Mexico vote in favor of the resolution, thus provoking an indignant reaction from the Jewish communities in these countries.

**1980. April:** Ten activists from the U.S. *Habad* movement begin operating in Argentina; the influence of this Hasidic movement expands during the 1980s, revealing an increase in ultra-orthodox tendencies in the Latin American communities.

**1986:** Jewish statesman Eric A. Delvalle, is elected president of the Republic of Panama; the following year he is ousted from power by General Manuel Noriega.

**1992. March 17:** The Israeli Embassy in Buenos Aires is destroyed by a terrorist bomb; four Israelis are killed.

4. Jewish gauchos in a Jewish agricultural colony. Argentina,1920s.

# The Jews of Rumania

1. Reuven Rubin, Encounter: Jesus and the Jew. *In the background, a Rumanian village. Oil, 1919.*

Although there is evidence of a Jewish presence in the territory of present-day Rumania even prior to the conquest of Dacia by Emperor Trajan, further settlement in later centuries was very limited. Some merchants arrived there during the Middle Ages, and a number of Sephardi Jews found refuge in the Danubian Principalities of Moldavia and Walachia during the Ottoman period. It was only in the nineteenth century that a large group of Jews, escaping czarist persecutions, settled in the region. At the turn of the century, over a quarter of a million Jews lived in what had become, after the unification of the principalities, the Kingdom of Rumania – the *Regat*, whose sovereignty was internationally recognized by the Congress of Berlin (1878). Prohibited from living in the villages, and practically excluded from the rural economy, the vast majority of Jews lived in the urban

centers. Their massive presence in the cities was augmented after World War I due to the beginning of industrialization.

In defiance of the provisions of the Congress of Berlin, successive governments in Bucharest systematically refused to grant equal rights to the Jews. It was as second-class citizens that thousands of Jews served in the Rumanian army during the Great War. Antisemitism was rife in the *Regat*, and both major political parties, Liberals and Conservatives, made full use of it as a political weapon. However, despite the hostile climate of opinion and the emigration of thousands to the West, Jewish community life was strengthened by the creation of an independent school network and welfare organizations.

With the formation of Greater Rumania after World War I, its Jewish population reached approximately 750,000. This Jewry was composed, in fact, of four distinct communities: the one in the Old Kingdom and those in the annexed provinces of Bukovina, Bessarabia, and Transylvania. Although full legal emancipation had been attained, the actual situation of the Jews was hardly ideal. Violent antisemitism and the rise of extreme right-wing movements affected the entire political scene. Organized on a regional basis, and deprived of a central leadership, Jewish political involvement was centered at first on Rumanian parties. Proper Jewish parties, representing both the national and the assimilationist trends, were formed only at a later stage. Several Zionist movements of different streams made their debut in Rumania in the interwar period, particularly in Bukovina and Transylvania.

Shifting frontiers and displacement of populations during World War II and its aftermath make it difficult to determine the precise number of Rumanian Jews who perished in the Holocaust. Deportation to Transnistria of about 150,000 Jews from the *Regat* proper, from Bessarabia, Bukovina, and the Dorohoi district, began in the spring of 1941. Over 88,000 Jews perished in that huge complex of concentration camps. The Rumanian army actively participated in the conquest of southern Russia. In the occupied regions, Rumanian, Hungarian and German troops

| Union of the Rumanian Principalities | Beginning of the Union of Rumanian Jews | Beginning of the Iron Guard |
|---|---|---|
| 1859 | 1910 | 1927 |

2. The Menorah Orchestra at a Purim party. Bucharest, 1980.

**1859:** Alexanderu Ioan Cuza unites the two Danubian Principalities – Moldavia and Walachia – into one kingdom.
**1867:** Sir Moses Montefiore visits Bucharest and demands that Prince Carol put a stop to the persecution of Jews.
**1885:** Rumanian authorities expel two Jewish leaders who fought for emancipation.
**1893:** Jewish pupils are expelled from public schools.
**1910:** First Jewish political organization, the Union of Native Jews, later named the Union of Rumanian Jews, defends Jewish rights but opposes Zionism.
**1923. March:** The new constitution confirms the naturalization of the Jews in the annexed territories, but the regime does little to implement their full rights.
**1927:** Corneliu Zelea Codreanu founds the Archangel Michael League, which two years later will become the Iron Guard, a paramilitary organization with a radical antisemitic program.
**1928:** Four Jews are elected to the

3. The Great Synagogue in Bucharest, inaugurated in 1850. Postcard.

## Rumanian Jewry Between the Wars

- ▬ ▬ ▬ The *Regat* (until 1918)
- ──── Greater Rumania
- ──── Rumania today
- ▯ Major rabbinical center

Jewish population in 1930

| | Bucharest | Galati | Bacau | Rezina | Dej |
|---|---|---|---|---|---|
| | over 30,000 | 10,000–30,000 | 5,000–10,000 | 2,000–5,000 | 1,000–2,000 |

Jewish population in 1930

- over 10%
- 6 - 10%
- 2 - 6%
- under 2%

| Population in 1930 | |
|---|---|
| total | 18,257,000 |
| Jewish (4.1%) | 756,430 |

**Map labels:** BUKOVINA, Kholin, Viznnitsa, Sadgora, Darabani, Chernovtsy, Gertsa, Soroki, Storozhinets, Siret, Dorohoi, Saveni, Stefanesti, Beltsy, Rezina, Sighet, Valea, Radauti, Suceava, Botosani, Faleshty, Orgeyev, Satu Mare, Baia Mare, Viseul de Sus, Borsa, Sucevita, Harlau, Carei, Tasnad, MARAMURES, Falticeni, Pascani, Jassy, Kishinev, Tighina (Bendery), Marghita, Simleul-Silvaniei, Dej, Bistrita, Piatra Neamt, Roman, Husi, Oradea, Reghin, Buhusi, Vaslui, Leovo, Cluj, Moinesti, Bacau, Barlad, BESSARABIA, Cetatea Alba (Akkerman), CRISANA, TRANSYLVANIA, Tirgu Neamt, Tirgu Frumos, Tirgu Mures, Tirgu Ocna, MOLDAVIA, Cahul (Kagul), Arad, Alba Iulia, Timisoara, Deva, Mures, Sibiu, Olt, Brasov, Focsani, Siret, Galati, Bolgrad, Kiliya, Dniester, Lugoj, Petroseni, BANAT, Rimnicu Sarat, Braila, Tulcea, Buzau, DOBRUJA, Ploesti, WALACHIA, Bucharest, Calarasi, Constanta, Craiova, Giurgiu, BLACK SEA, Danube, Varna, 60 km.

---

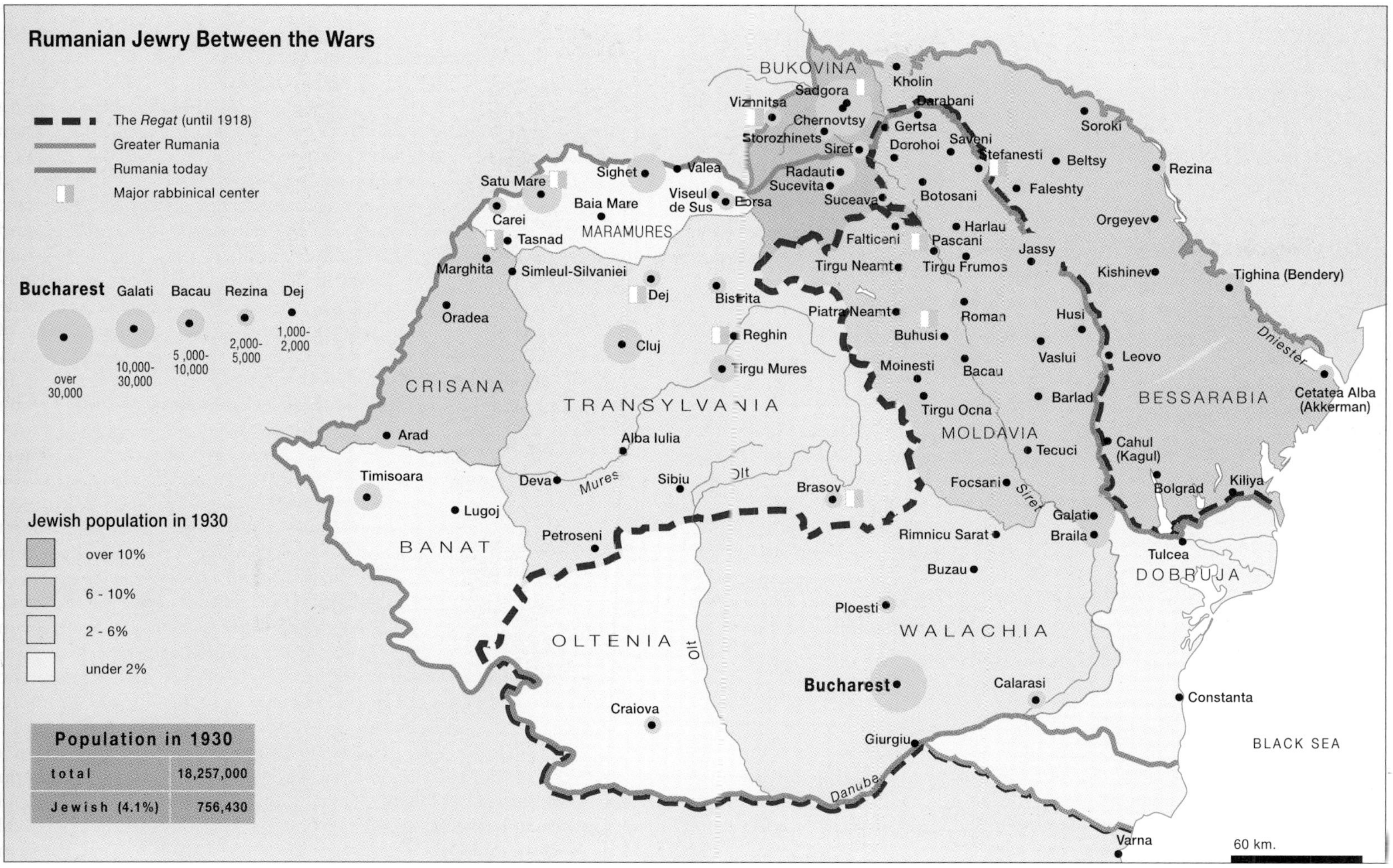

perpetrated systematic massacres. All in all, out of the 608,000 Jews living under Rumanian rule in 1939, a total of 265,000 (43%) perished during World War II.

Jewish life was revived in Rumania after its liberation, only to be suppressed shortly afterwards by the Communist regime. In 1948 Zionist activities were outlawed completely and the network of Jewish education was destroyed when all schools in Rumania were nationalized. In the early 1950s and in the 1960s the vast majority of Rumanian Jews

emigrated, most of them to Israel. By 1967 only about 110,000 remained in Rumania.

The last years of the Ceausescu era were marked by complete freedom of religion and emigration, coupled with a cynical exploitation of antisemitism. The fall of the Rumanian dictatorship and the manifestations of post-communist nationalism and antisemitism hastened the disappearance of the last remnants of the Jewish community from Rumanian soil.

| Pogrom in Jassy | Mass emigration to Israel | Fall of Ceausescu |
|---|---|---|
| 1941 | 1950–1952 | 1990 |

parliament through an agreement with the National Peasants' Party.

**1930:** Founding of the Jewish Party which will win five seats in the 1931 elections.

**1937. December:** The Goga-Cuza cabinet introduces antisemitic laws; King Carol II engineers the removal of the extreme right-wing government, attempts to curb the Iron Guard, and establishes in 1938 the Royal Dictatorship – a single-party regime.

**September 1940-January 1941:** The National Legionary State; Marshal Antonescu cooperates with the Iron Guard, but this organization incites to rebellion against him; during the rebellion, a pogrom in Bucharest is perpetrated by the Iron Guard.

**1941. June:** Pogrom in Jassy, followed by deportations to Transnistria.

**1944. August 23:** Soviet troops liberate Bucharest. Ana Pauker, a Hebrew teacher who became a prominent Communist leader in the 1920s, returns from Moscow to organize the Rumanian Democratic Front.

**1945. June:** Founding of the Jewish

*4. Agricultural training in the Jewish Mother and Child Center. Bucharest, c. 1943.*

Democratic Committee which serves as a courier between the Communist party and the Jewish community.

**1948–1949:** Repression of the Zionist movement which gradually ceases all its activities in Rumania; an antisemitic and anti-Israel campaign.

**1950–1952:** About 100,000 Jews leave Rumania, most of them to Israel.

**1952:** Ana Pauker, secretary of the Communist Party central committee, deputy prime minister and minister of foreign affairs in Petru Groza's government, is deprived of all her posts and put under house arrest.

**1954. April:** Trial of principal Zionist leaders.

**1980, 1984, 1986:** Antisemitic outbreaks libelous poems, acts of vandalism, violence; Ceausescu faces criticism by Chief Rabbi Rosen and Jewish organizations abroad.

**1990–1991:** After the fall of the dictator, there are numerous antisemitic manifestations, Antonescu is rehabilitated and there is nationalist agitation. The Jewish community numbers about 20,000 people.

# The State of Israel: The Formative Years

*1. "Growth versus Siege." A poster of Mapai, the ruling labor party.*

Independence advanced a pressing need for the institutional organization of the sovereign state. David Ben-Gurion, head of the prominent workers' party, laid down principles which were, despite some ambiguity, adopted by the representative bodies with no major upheavals. Israel was to become a western-style parliamentary democracy based on universal suffrage and the separation of powers. It was also proclaimed a secular state, and the Declaration of Independence pledged to "guarantee freedom of religion, conscience, language, education and culture." However, since throughout history religion has always been inexorably linked to nationality in Jewish collective consciousness, and because Israel's religious parties had considerable clout right from the start, certain theocratic elements were admitted, particularly in those aspects of legislation which sanctioned the exclusive jurisdiction of the religious courts in all matters matrimonial. Although no real *kulturkampf* ever evolved, the nonobservant majority resisted religious coercion, while the orthodox persisted in trying to enforce *halakhic* law on modern Israel. This was but one point of contention which agitated political life in Israel, polarizing public opinion and dividing the population into a multitude of parties. Indeed, the ideological fervor sustained from the time of the *yishuv*, coupled with an electoral system of proportional representation established for the Zionist Congresses, created a highly heterogeneous system of political trends, movements, and factions.

Nevertheless, despite the ideological struggles which took place in the political arena and in the domains of Israeli literature, theater, and the media (and, on occasion, in the law courts), the two decades between the War of Independence and the Six-Day War were a time of growth and consolidation for the young state of Israel. First, there was a tremendous influx of immigration which led to huge demographic growth. Thousands of long-suffering Jews flocked to the newborn state from the Displaced Persons' camps, from British detainee camps in Cyprus which held "illegal" immigrants, and, for the first time ever, from all the Islamic countries. This huge wave of new arrivals doubled the Jewish population in Israel within three years.

The absorption of hundreds of thousands of immigrants was a staggering task for such a small state lacking in natural resources. The early years were indeed very difficult: new immigrants were initially set up in tents, then, during the early 1950s they were placed in transit camps (*ma'barot*) which in many cases became a permanent form of housing. The veteran population was burdened with the strain of unemployment, food rationing and other shortages, wage freezes, and compulsory loans. Moreover, the mass *aliyah* from Islamic countries, and the decline in the numbers of immigrants from Europe and the Americas altered the composition of the population. Although the "ingathering of the exiles" had always been part of Zionist ideology and the *raison d'etre* of the Jewish state, the changing proportions among the communities (*edot*) resulted in major social and cultural tensions.

Obviously, immigrant absorption would have been impossible without outside support in the form of American aid, donations from the diaspora, and German reparations ($820,000,000 over twelve years). Thanks to this import of capital, the encouragement of state policy and the availability of highly skilled labor, the early years of the state witnessed spectacular economic growth, with the gross national product increasing by an average of 10% per annum. New "development" townships were swiftly established; the new port of Ashdod, the El Al national airline, and a large merchant fleet facilitated Israel's integration into world economy. An ambitious water project (the National Carrier) conveyed water to arid areas in the center and the south of the country. Agriculture made great strides between 1948 and 1953, when 354 cooperative villages (*moshavim*) and collectives (*kibbutzim*) were established. After the Sinai Campaign, with immigration once more on the rise, the pace of industry development accelerated, doubling its production over ten years.

Only one insurmountable problem remained, namely, Israel's acceptance and recognition by her neighbors. Between 1951 and 1956 roughly 3,000 armed clashes and 6,000 acts of sabotage took place inside Israeli borders, resulting in the deaths of over 400 Israelis, and the injury of 900. The Sinai Campaign, Israel's response to the concentration of Egyptian troops along its borders, and to the closing of the Tiran Straits by Nasser's gunboats, was also an attempt to put a stop to the incessant harassment by regular and irregular Arab troops.

This "second round" in the Arab-Israeli war did not resolve the conflict. Israel was forced to withdraw from the Sinai in return for a precarious security arrangement. Moreover, by aligning herself with imperialist powers in decline Israel came to be regarded by her neighbors as a "tool of western imperialism." Nevertheless, the Sinai Campaign enabled Israel to enjoy ten years of relative tranquillity.

| First government | Law of Return | German reparations | Suez Campaign |
|---|---|---|---|
| **February 1949** | **July 1950** | **January 1952** | **October 1956** |

**1948. June:** The *Altalena* affair: a boat from France, carrying weapons and volunteers to the *Irgun*, is shelled by the newly-established national army. The incident made it clear that no sectional armed force would be tolerated; Ben-Gurion insists on dissolving the *Palmah*, the assault companies of the *Haganah*.
**1949. January 25:** Elections to the Constituent Assembly.
**February 16:** The Assembly adopts the Transition Law as a provisional constitution, outlining the functions and procedures of the legislature, the powers of the president, the formation of the government and its relations with the Assembly which was to be called the Knesset. Chaim Weizmann, elected President of the State of Israel, calls upon David Ben-Gurion to form the first Israeli government.
**May 11:** Israel is admitted to the United Nations.

*2. Men of Unit 101 patrolling the border with Egypt. April 1955.*

**1950. January:** The Arab League initiates an economic boycott on Israel. A tripartite declaration by the U.S., Great Britain and France promises to take action to prevent the violation of borders in the Middle East.
**January 23:** Jerusalem is proclaimed capital of the State of Israel.
**July 5:** The Law of Return is proclaimed; its first clause reads: "Every Jew has the right to come to this country as an *oleh* (immigrant)."
**1952. January:** The Knesset is convened to ratify direct negotiations with Germany for reparations; the resolution provokes stormy street demonstrations, staged by *Herut* opposition party. The Law of Nationality confers Israeli citizenship on non-Jewish inhabitants; the Arabs, however, remain under military administration by virtue of emergency regulations left over from the British Mandatory regime.
**August 18:** Ben-Gurion welcomes the Egyptian "free officers'" revolution and declares that there is no reason for

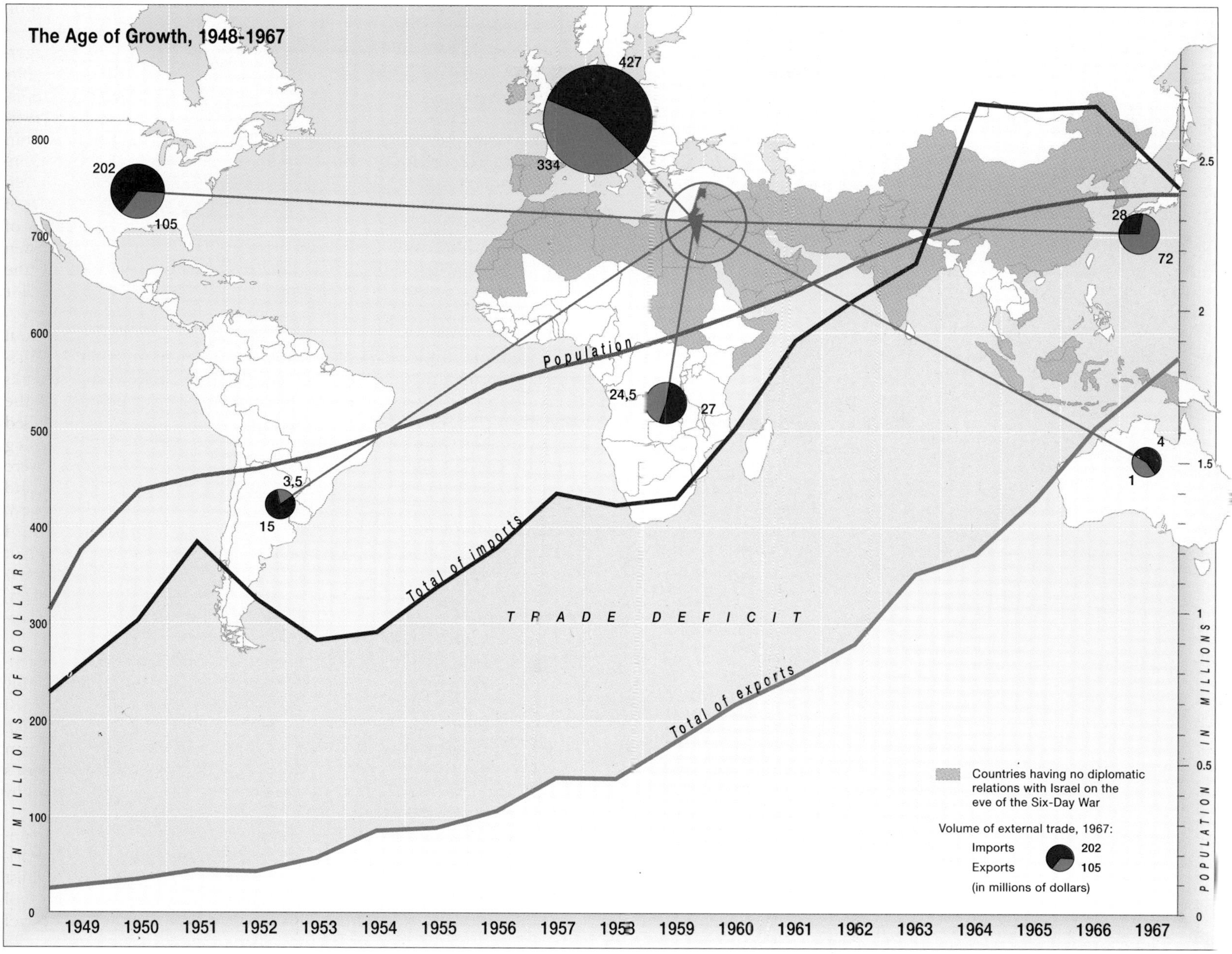

## The Age of Growth, 1948-1967

427
334
202
105
800
700
600
500
400
300
200
100
0

28
72

2.5
2
1.5
1
0.5
0

*I N   M I L L I O N S   O F   D O L L A R S*

*P O P U L A T I O N   I N   M I L L I O N S*

Population

24,5
27

3,5
15

4
1

Total of imports

T R A D E   D E F I C I T

Total of exports

Countries having no diplomatic
relations with Israel on the
eve of the Six-Day War

Volume of external trade, 1967:
Imports          202
Exports          105
(in millions of dollars)

1949 1950 1951 1952 1953 1954 1955 1956 1957 1958 1959 1960 1961 1962 1963 1964 1965 1966 1967

| Riots in Wadi Salib | The Eichmann Trial | Ben-Gurion's retirement | The Six-Day War |
|---|---|---|---|
| **July 1959** | **1961** | **1963** | **June 1967** |

antagonism between the two countries. But when Mohammad Naguib is ousted by Gamal Abdul Nasser (April 1954), who emerges as the leader of the Pan-Arab movement and turns to the Communist bloc for support, prospects for reconciliation are lost.

**October:** In reprisal for the murder of a mother and her two children (October 13), the soldiers of Unit 101 massacre the inhabitants of the Qibya village in Jordan.

**1954. December:** Beginning of large arms purchases from France.

**1955:** The Baghdad Pact signed by Turkey, Iraq, and several other Arab countries renders Israel the only state in the region which does not belong to any military alliance.

**April:** The Bandung Conference of Afro-Asian states; the nonaligned countries refuse to accept Israel; nevertheless, Israel manages to promote technical and economic cooperation with Third World countries.

חסל את השוק השחור
ולא-יחסל הוא אותך

*3. "Destroy the black market or it will destroy you." A government Information Service poster in the 1950s.*

**August:** Nasser signs an arms purchase agreement with Czechoslovakia for the sum of 320 million dollars, a serious threat to the balance of power in the region.

**October 17:** Egypt and Syria sign a military pact.

**1956. January:** Guy Mollet is Prime Minister of France; the French-Israeli accord is established.

**July 26:** Nasser nationalizes the Suez Canal; on October 29, while British and French troops disembark in the Canal zone, Israeli forces enter the Sinai Peninsula; at the end of November, under Soviet-American pressure, Israel begins to withdraw.

**August 19:** In the midst of violent demonstrations, the first ambassador of the German Federal Republic, Rolf Pauls, presents his credentials in Jerusalem.

**1959. July:** Riots in the Haifa slum quarter

of Wadi Salib: its 15,000 "oriental" Jews give vent to bitterness and social malaise that can no longer be held off by ideological promises.

**1960. June:** Ben-Gurion's visit to the Elysée; General de Gaulle speaks of "Israel our friend and ally."

**1961:** Israel is refused associate membership in the European Economic Community, but three years later it obtains a preferential agreement with the Community. Captured in Argentina by the Israeli Secret Service, the Nazi criminal Adolf Eichmann is brought to trial in Jerusalem.

**1962:** Washington renounces the tacit embargo that was imposed on Israel by President Eisenhower.

**1963:** Ben-Gurion resigns and retires to a kibbutz in the Negev; Levi Eshkol is Prime Minister.

**1965:** The *Mittun* (recession) leads to a severe deflation policy, unemployment, social conflicts and emigration. It will end (temporarily) with the Six-Day War.

# The Jews of Yemen

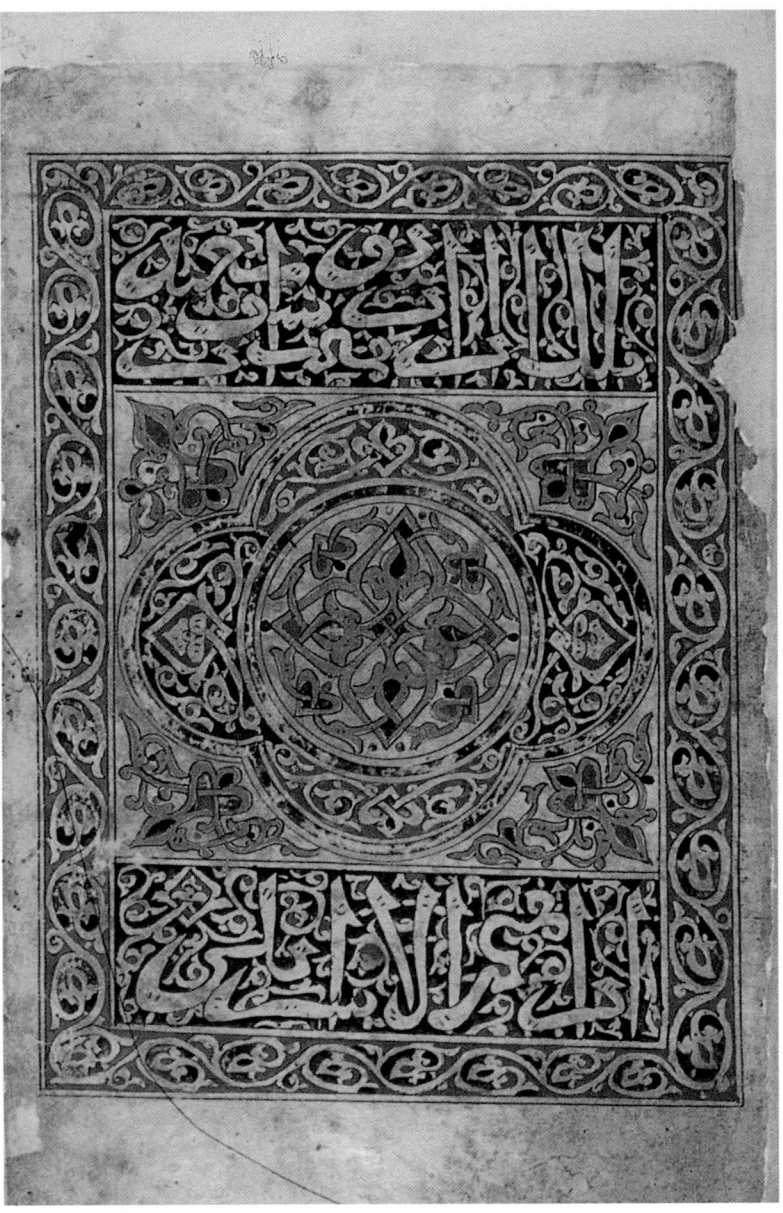

1. *Pentateuch Illumination. The inscriptions in Arabic include the date and the copyist's name. San'a, 1469.*

The origins of Yemenite Jewry are unknown. The myths and legends – about a certain section of the people settling there during the exodus from Egypt, about the Queen of Sheba, or about the ten lost tribes – cannot be substantiated. Most probably, the earliest settlement of Jews in Yemen began between the third century BC and the third century AD when Arab trade in spices and perfumes was at its height. It is also known that in 25 BC King Herod sent an auxiliary force from Judea to assist Roman troops in the conquest of southern Arabia, a force that never returned to its homeland.

The first certain evidence of a Jewish presence in Yemen is, however, derived from inscriptions which mention a Jewish kingdom in Himyar and its last king, Yusuf As'ar Dhu Nuwas (517–525), who embraced Judaism. Information concerning Jewish communities in Yemen is provided in Muslim sources after the conversion of South Arabian tribes to Islam during the seventh century. A ninth-century source reveals that Yemenite Jews could still possess land and that their economic situation was better than might be expected for those relegated to the status of *dhimmi* ("the protected," the legal status of Christians and Jews in Muslim lands). Between the tenth and thirteenth centuries, when the Indian trade flourished, the Jewish community enjoyed economic and cultural prosperity. During this period it gradually broke away from the spiritual centers in Babylon and Palestine and became affiliated to the center in Egypt and the school of Maimonides.

The decline in Indian trade led to the cultural and economic stagnation of Yemenite Jewry. Four centuries of its history, from the beginning of the thirteenth century, are again a blank chapter. Only in 1629, shortly before the expulsion of the Ottomans, are they heard of once more. In that year the country returned to the Shi'ite rule of the Zaydi imams, and the legitimacy of Jewish presence in Yemen came under an attack which culminated in 1680 with the expulsion of the Jews from San'a and central Yemen to Mawza in Tihama, the inhospitable southern shore of the Red Sea. The "expulsion of Mawza" lasted only one year but sufficed to undermine the community, which from then on tended either to assimilate or to emulate the customs and traditions of other Jewish diasporas, ultimately losing much of its vitality.

The second great moment of Yemenite Jewry occurred in the eighteenth century, when the dynasty of the Qasimite imams brought political integrity and economic prosperity to the land. Several Jewish families – first Iraqi, then Halevi Alsheikh – were appointed supervisors of coin minting and tax collection; and their prominence in the imam's court ensured peace for the community. This was also a period of intense intellectual activity and many illustrious spiritual leaders emerged, such as Judah Sa'adi, David Mashreki, and the great scholar Yihya Salih.

In the nineteenth century tribal revolts and invasion caused the

| The Kingdom of Himyar | Maimonides' *Epistle to Yemen* | The "Expulsion of Mawza" | Destruction in the Jewish quarter of San'a |
|---|---|---|---|
| 5th–6th centuries | 1172 | 1679–1680 | 1818 |

3. *Yemenite Jewish merchants: one of them carries the key of his shop on his chest, San'a, c.1930.*

**518–525:** Reign of the Jewish (or proselyte) king, Yusuf As'ar Dhu Nuwas, the last king of the Jewish kingdom in Himyar, killed fighting against Christian Ethiopian invaders.

**7th century:** An inscription containing the 24 shifts of the priests, discovered in the 1970s in the village of Al-Hatzar near the city of San'a.

**11th century:** Letters found in the *Genizah* testify to the existence of relations between the Jewish centers in Iraq and Egypt and the community in Yemen.

**c.1170:** An anonymous pseudo-messiah appears in Yemen; Maimonides writes his famous *Epistle to Yemen*, a fundamental document for the definition of Jewish messianism.

**1198:** Forced conversion of Jews in southern Yemen, particularly in Aden; many leaders, refusing to convert, are put to death.

**1202:** With the death of the "mad" imam the edict of conversion is revoked.

**End of 15th century:** Appearance of a pseudo-messiah in southeast Yemen; an armed conflict between his followers and the forces of the imam practically annihilates the Jewish communities in this region.

**1586:** The Imam al-Mutahhar accuses the Jews of aiding the Turks and persecutes the Jews of San'a.

**1666–1667:** The most important messianic phenomenon in Jewish history – Shabbetai Zevi and his followers – arouses an ecstatic movement in Yemen; it is led by Sliman Alnakash, who is later exiled to an island in the Red Sea, and then by Sliman Aljamal, who is eventually executed.

**1667:** Jews are prohibited from wearing an ornamental head-dress; this may be when Jews were ordered to grow long sidelocks as a distinguishing mark.

**1679–1680:** The "expulsion of Mawza."

**Second half of 17th century:** Life span of Shalom Shabbazi, the greatest poet of Yemenite Jewry.

**18th century:** Under the rule of the Qasimite Dynasty, founded by the Imam al-

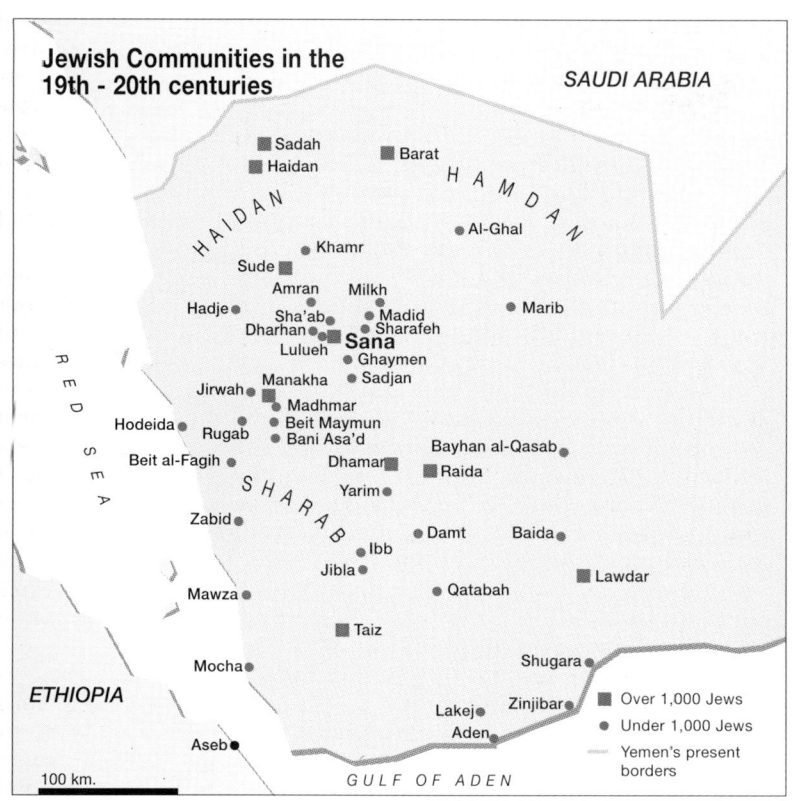

**Jewish Communities in the 19th - 20th centuries**

*SAUDI ARABIA*

- Over 1,000 Jews
- Under 1,000 Jews
- Yemen's present borders

100 km.

*ETHIOPIA*

*GULF OF ADEN*

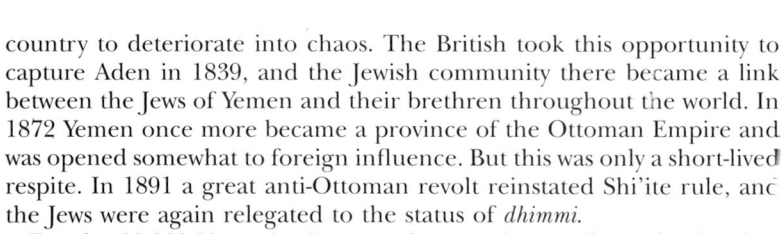

*2. Traditional Yemenite attire.*

country to deteriorate into chaos. The British took this opportunity to capture Aden in 1839, and the Jewish community there became a link between the Jews of Yemen and their brethren throughout the world. In 1872 Yemen once more became a province of the Ottoman Empire and was opened somewhat to foreign influence. But this was only a short-lived respite. In 1891 a great anti-Ottoman revolt reinstated Shi'ite rule, and the Jews were again relegated to the status of *dhimmi*.

For the 80,000 Yemenite Jews to whom emissaries from the Land of Israel brought news of "redemption" in Zion, this was in any case the beginning of the end. In 1881–1882 they began migrating to Palestine, which by 1945 had absorbed almost 30,000 Yemenite Jews. Finally, in September 1950, an operation named "on the wings of eagles" (as in Exodus 19:4), brought to the newly established State of Israel a further 50,000 immigrants. In the reunified Yemen of today there remain about 1200 Jews – a tiny remnant of an extremely ancient community.

**First Yemenite immigration to Palestine**

**1881–1882**

Qasim al-Qabbir, leader of the anti-Ottoman rebellion, the Jewish community prospers. Towards the the end of the century Qasimite rule declines and the southern tribes secede.

**c.1805:** Death of Yahya Salih (Maharis), one of the greatest rabbinic authorities and religious leaders in Yemen, president of the *bet din* (religious court), and author of the book of responsa *Pe'ullat Zaddik*.

**1818:** A revolt of two tribal confederations – Hashed and Bekhil – against the power of the imam, devastates the Jewish quarter in San'a. The incursion of the Wahhabites of Arabia leads to Ottoman intervention. End of the Qasimite Dynasty.

**1839:** Aden becomes a British protectorate; Yemenite Jewry is exposed to the outside world.

**1859:** Rabbi Jacob Saphir of Jerusalem makes an extended visit to Yemen; his book, *Hadrei Teiman* (The interior of Yemen) is a captivating testimony to the life of Yemenite Jewry in that period.

**Second half of 19th century:** Appearance

**Operation "On the Wings of Eagles"**

**1949–1950**

of three successive false messiahs: Shukr Kuhayl the first, pseudo-Shukr, and Joseph ben Abdallah.

**1872:** The Ottoman reconquest.

**1881–1882:** The first large emigration of Jews to Palestine.

**1891:** The beginning of the great anti-Ottoman revolt of Muhamed Yahya Hamid al-din.

**1905:** Imam Yahya besieges San'a; most of the Jews in the city die of starvation.

**c.1930:** Yemenite Jewry is split by a conflict over the Kabbalah. Yihya Kafah, known by the name Darda (from the Hebrew *Dor de'ah*, "generation of wisdom") leads the "modern" school, and the Kabbalists are led by Isaac ha-Levi Yihya.

**1948–1950:** After the assassination of the imam, the Jews of Yemen flee en masse to Aden.

**1949–1950:** Operation "on the wings of eagles" (or the "Magic Carpet"); Israeli planes evacuate the Jews, bringing the Yemenite diaspora to an end.

*4. Jewish children, Yemen. 1990.*

# Mediterranean Zionism

*1. The first committee of the Jewish National Fund in Libya. Tripoli, 1915.*

Zionism made its debut in North Africa and the Middle East immediately after the First Congress in Basle in 1897, and was soon familiar, by means of the press or through occasional visitors, with the general outline of Herzl's program. For communities which were still deeply committed to religious tradition, and residing in countries which were not too distant from the Holy Land, the idea of a "return" to the Land of Israel, did not seem far-fetched. Therefore, young and old, modernists and orthodox, consented to join the earliest Zionist organizations which in fact reached all strata of the Jewish population. Their numbers increased even further following the Balfour Declaration. The Jews of Morocco were so excited that straight after World War I ended, they hurriedly dispatched to Palestine a convoy of immigrants. Unfortunately, as soon as these disembarked in Jaffa they were sent back by the newly-established British authorities. The Zionist leadership made not the slightest gesture to prevent their expulsion.

A similar experience subsequently shared by hundreds of other "illegal" immigrants from Asian and African countries, elucidated the gulf separating Zionism – a modern political ideology – from the traditional attachment to Zion which was always based on religious-messianic beliefs. Therefore, once the initial exhilaration had died down, the Zionist enterprise in all these countries was greatly diminished. First to abandon the Zionist cause were the pious Jews, who came to believe that Zionism was synonymous with atheism. Then there were those who feared that Zionism would antagonize both their Muslim compatriots and the colonial authorities. Finally, there were vast numbers of those whom militant Zionists derisively named "assimilationists" – Jews who were westernized in varying degrees, fearing that Jewish nationalism would destroy the possibility of complete integration in the country their ancestors had lived in for centuries or even millennia. This was the case of the younger generation of Jews in Iraq during the 1920s, as well as in communities under French rule or those influenced by the educational system of the *Alliance Israelite Universelle*. Rifts of this kind seriously impeded the Zionist movement which, until the end of World War II, remained essentially weak and remote from the ideological currents which characterized the movement elsewhere.

A radical turning point took place in the mid-1940s. Nazi genocide and anti-Jewish legislation, in North Africa under Petain and Mussolini and in Iraq under Rashid Ali, disillusioned those who had believed in assimilation, particularly the younger generation. Hundreds of Palestinian Jewish soldiers stationed in Egypt, Syria, Iraq, and Libya during the war, strengthened the ties with the *yishuv*. Zionist emissaries, working in almost all Mediterranean communities, helped to establish active Zionist youth movements, emphasizing the need for "personal fulfillment" (*hagshamah*) of the program, i.e. *aliyah* to the Land of Israel in the spirit of its pioneers. Finally, as the prospects for the establishment of a Jewish state in Palestine became increasingly brighter, relations between Jews and Muslims grew openly hostile and outbursts of violence against the Jewish communities multiplied.

Precarious prior to the creation of the State of Israel, Jewish presence in Islamic countries after 1948 was increasingly endangered by the unrest which accompanied decolonization, nationalist agitation, and militant Islamic movements. The vast majority left in the 1950s, mostly to Israel. Further waves of emigration, precipitated by each Israeli-Arab war or proclamation of independence by one of the Muslim states, gradually eradicated the communities which had existed in these lands from time immemorial. Of the one million Jews who inhabited the oriental diaspora in the mid-twentieth century, only a tiny minority still remains today, impoverished and dispersed in a few urban centers throughout North Africa and the Middle East.

| First Zionist organization in Morocco | The Zionist Union in Algeria | Zionist pioneer organizations in the Maghreb |
|---|---|---|
| **1900** | **1920** | **1943** |

**1896. February:** In Vienna, Theodor Herzl publishes his *Jewish State*.
**1897. February:** *Bar Kokhba*, the first Zionist association in Cairo.
**August 29–31:** A North African delegation participates in the First Zionist Congress in Basle.
**1900:** *Sha'arei Zion*, the first Zionist association in Morocco, is founded in Mogador.
**1901. May:** Herzl is received by Sultan Abd al-Hamid II in Istanbul.
**September:** A "Zionist school" is opened in Cairo.
**1908:** A Zionist Delegation opens in Istanbul.
**1912:** The first Zionist periodical in Egypt, *La Renaissance juive*, appears for the first time.
**1913:** A Zionist federation, uniting all the Zionist associations in the country, is formed in Egypt.
**1916:** The Sykes-Picot Treaty: France and

*4. "Hatikva," a Hebrew primary school in Tripoli, in the 1930s.*

*5. On the way to the synagogue in Hara Kebira ("the large quarter") of Djerba, 1981.*

## The Demise of the Oriental Communities

• Kiev

• Paris
• Frankfort

• Vienna

Venice
• Odessa

Toulouse •
Nice
Marseilles •
• Bucharest

Madrid •
• Sofia

• Istanbul

Tangiers •
Ankara • **T U R K E Y**
**80,000**
**U.S.S.R**
**80,000**

• Oran
Algiers •
• Tunis
**S Y R I A**
**30,000**
• Aleppo
**I R A Q**
**125,000**
1950-1951

Meknes • • Fez
**A L G E R I A**
Constantine •
• Baghdad

**M O R O C C O**
**130,000**
1962
Sfax •
Damascus •
• Basra

**230,000**
1954-1955
**T U N I S I A**
**130,000**
Gabes •

**L I B Y A** • Tripoli
**40,000**
1953-1954

Alexandria •

Cairo •

**E G Y P T**
**66,000**
1956

**Y E M E N**
**52,000**
1948-1950

**M O R O C C O**
**230,000**
Country of origin
Number of Jewish emigrants

954-1955
End of the community
• Sana

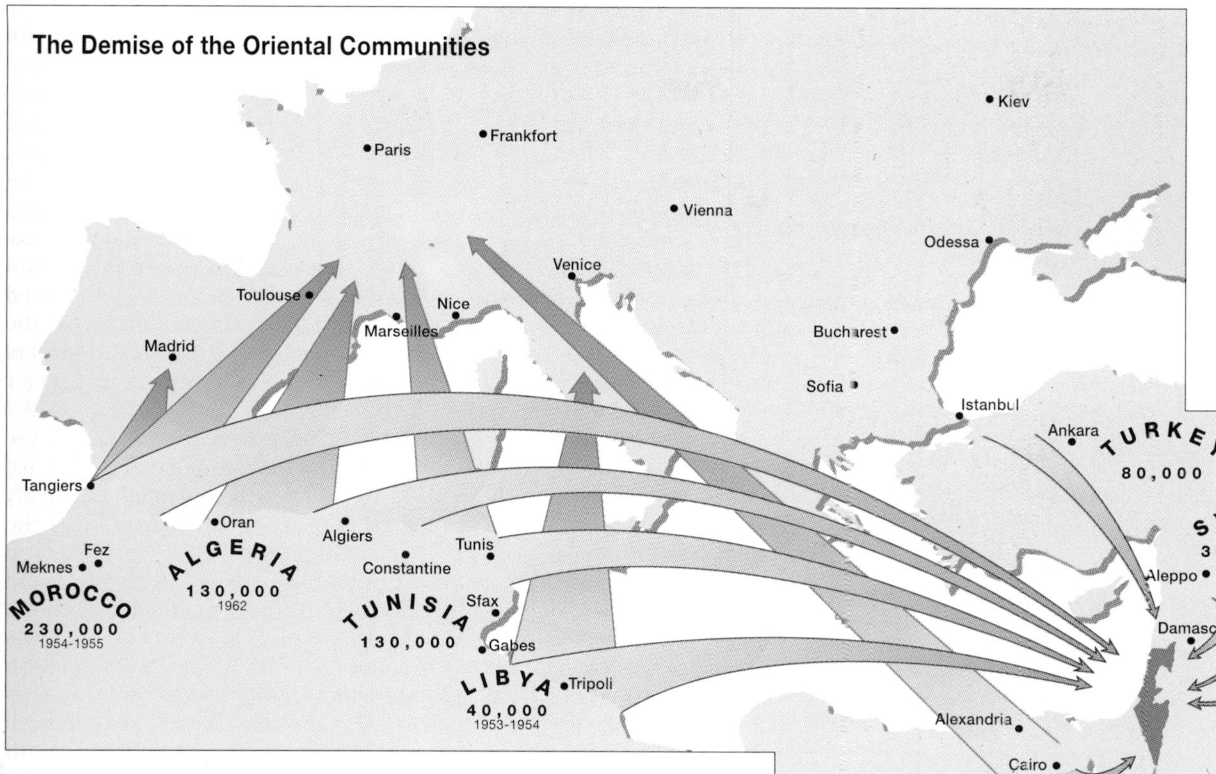

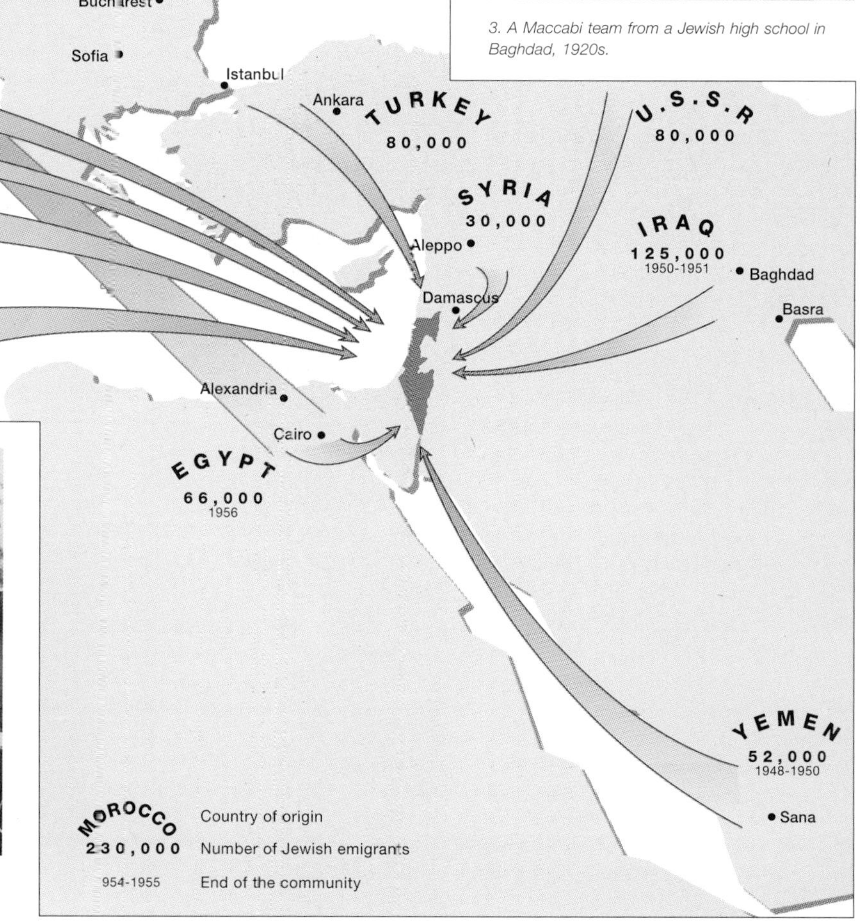

3. A Maccabi team from a Jewish high school in Baghdad, 1920s.

2. On their way to Israel, North African Jews embark on a boat going to Marseille, Algiers, 1949.

| Operation "Magic Carpet" | Operation "Ezra and Nehemiah" | Emigration of Libyan Jews | Beginning of Emigration from the Maghreb | Emigration of Egyptian Jews | Emigration of Algerian Jews |
|---|---|---|---|---|---|
| 1949–1950 | 1950–1951 | 1953–1954 | 1955–1956 | 1956 | 1962 |

Great Britain partition the Levant.
**1917. November:** The Balfour Declaration.
**1918:** The breaking up of the Ottoman Empire.
**1919:** In Teheran, the Central Committee of the Zionist organization of Persia is founded; in Baghdad, the first Zionist association in Iraq is established.
**1920:** The San Remo Conference confers the Palestinian Mandate on Great Britain; founding of the Algerian Zionist Union; a Tunisian Zionist Federation unites all the associations in that country.
**1921:** British authorities authorize the activities of the Zionist association in Baghdad which becomes the Zionist Committee of Mesopotamia.
**1926:** The Moroccan Zionist journal, *L'Avenir illustre* is founded.
**1927:** *Reveil juif*, an organ of the Revisionist (right-wing) faction, appears in Sfax, Tunisia.
**1930:** Attempt to establish a nucleus of *Ha-Shomer ha-Tsa'ir* ("The Young Guard," a left-wing Zionist group) in Tunis.

**1932:** Iraq's independence is accompanied by a prohibition on Zionist activities in that country.
**1934. August:** A pogrom perpetrated by Muslims in Constantine, Algeria, claims 25 victims.
**1940:** Abolition of the Cremieux Decree in Algeria (August 7) and the introduction of the Vichy anti-Jewish legislation in North Africa (October 10).
**1941. June 1–2:** Pogrom in Baghdad.
**1942. April:** Iranian authorities authorize the opening of a Jewish Agency office in Teheran.
**November:** Anglo-American landing in North Africa; Germans and Italians occupy Tunisia.
**December:** The English attack the Axis forces in Libya; end of Italian rule in that country.
**1943. May:** The Germans leave Tunisia; early steps of Zionist pioneer organizations in North Africa.
**October:** The Cremieux Decree is again put into force in Algeria.

**1945. November:** Anti-Jewish violence in Libya and Egypt.
**1947:** Massacre of Jews in Aden.
**1948:** Establishment of the state of Israel.
**1949–1950:** Operation "Magic Carpet": close to 50,000 Yemenite Jews are transferred to Israel.
**1950–1951:** Operation "Ezra and Nehemiah": the entire Iraqi community – about 120,000 people – is brought to Israel.
**1953–1954:** Mass immigration of Libyan Jews to Israel.
**1955–1956:** Independence of Moroccco and Tunisia; mass emigration of Maghreb Jews to Israel and France begins.
**1956:** The Suez Campaign; the Jews leave Egypt.
**1962:** Independence of Algeria; mass exodus of Jews, most of whom go to France.

6. Samarkand Jews in Jerusalem, drawn by poetess Elsa Lasker-Schueler (1869–1945). Colored chalks on paper, 1939.

# The Six-Day War

1. The battle in the Rockefeller Museum in East Jerusalem.

I n the spring of 1957, the Israel Defense Forces withdrew from the Sinai Peninsula and the Gaza Strip occupied since the Suez Campaign of the previous year. The United Nations sent an international Emergency Force (UNEF) to the Egyptian-Israeli border and to Sharm el-Sheikh. The great powers gave Israel assurances concerning the freedom of navigation in the Gulf of Elath, and the government of Israel made it clear that any infringement of that freedom would be regarded as a *casus belli*.

All these arrangements, however, did not secure peace in the region. The terror-reprisal cycle continued on several fronts. The *Fatah* went on sending its men from Jordan to carry out terrorist operations within Israel's borders. Syrian artillery on the Golan Heights frequently shelled settlements in the Upper Galilee and the Jordan Valley, forcing the Israeli air force to retaliate in operations which often turned into mini-wars. Moreover, although the Egyptian border remained relatively quiet, as Egypt was involved since 1962 in a civil war in Yemen, Gamal Abdul Nasser made no secret of his intention to destroy the State of Israel at the first opportune moment.

In the spring of 1967 it seemed as though that moment had come. In three weeks and by five impressive initiatives, Nasser managed to embroil the entire Middle East in a major war. First, Egyptian forces in Sinai were considerably reinforced, under the pretext of coming to Syria's assistance. Then Nasser demanded the evacuation of U.N. forces from Sinai and the Gaza Strip, and U-Thant, the U.N. Secretary General, immediately acceded to his request. On May 20 Egyptian forces occupied Sharm el-Sheikh, closing the Straits of Tiran two days later. While Egyptian propaganda was proclaiming the imminent and inevitable destruction of Israel, the massive rein-

forcement of troops along the borders with Israel brought the numbers of Egyptian soldiers to 100,000 and tanks to 900. Once again, after ten years, Israel was directly confronted by Egyptian forces along the frontier. Finally, Nasser orchestrated a great Arab alliance: in addition to the Egyptian-Syrian military agreement of November 1966, he now signed pacts with Jordan (May 30) and Iraq (June 4). Contingents arrived from other Arab countries, such as Kuwait and Algeria.

As Nasser had foreseen, Israel was forced to respond: the threat of annihilation could not be ignored. Accepting the closure of the Straits would have been interpreted as a sign of weakness and capitulation to Egyptian aggression; the economic strain of prolonged mobilization and the psychological effect of suspense and fear would have been unbearable. After a "waiting period," requested by President Lyndon Johnson who wished to reach a peaceful resolution of the conflict, a "national unity" government was formed in Israel on June 1. Bolstered by the support of world Jewry and the sympathy voiced by western public opinion, Israel attacked on the morning of June 5. Six days later, at the cost of 676 lives and over 3000 wounded, the Arab coalition formed against Israel was routed. The Israeli army occupied Egyptian Sinai, the Syrian Golan, the Jordanian West Bank, and Arab Jerusalem. The Egyptian and the Syrian governments accepted a cease-fire agreement and U.N. observers were posted along the Suez Canal and on the Golan heights. Nasser announced his resignation, but withdrew it in the face of mass demonstrations demanding his return. In his resignation speech he made clear the part the Soviets played in bringing on the war.

In the brief history of the State of Israel, the Six-Day War constitutes a major turning-point. This swift and total victory saved the Zionist entity from destruction, ensured its physical existence, and disillusioned those of her enemies who had hoped that the Jewish State was just a passing phenomenon. On the other hand, these densely-populated territories, regarded as "liberated" by some Israelis and as "occupied" by others, created a whole series of insurmountable problems – political, social, economic, moral and religious – unresolved to this day. The future of the State of Israel, its character and its place among nations, now depends on their solution.

שנה טובה

2. A New Year's greeting card celebrating victory, with two of its architects: Moshe Dayan and Yizhak Rabin; the Old-City walls in the background are formed in the shape of the Hebrew letters for I.D.F.

# 1967

## A Swift Campaign, 5-10 June 1967

### Participant forces

| | Israel | Egypt | Jordan | Syria | Iraq | |
|---|---|---|---|---|---|---|
| | 350 | 450 | 40 | 120 | 200 | |
| | 800 | 1400 | 300 | 550 | 630 | |
| | 264,000 | 270,000 | 55,000 | 65,000 | 75,000 | |

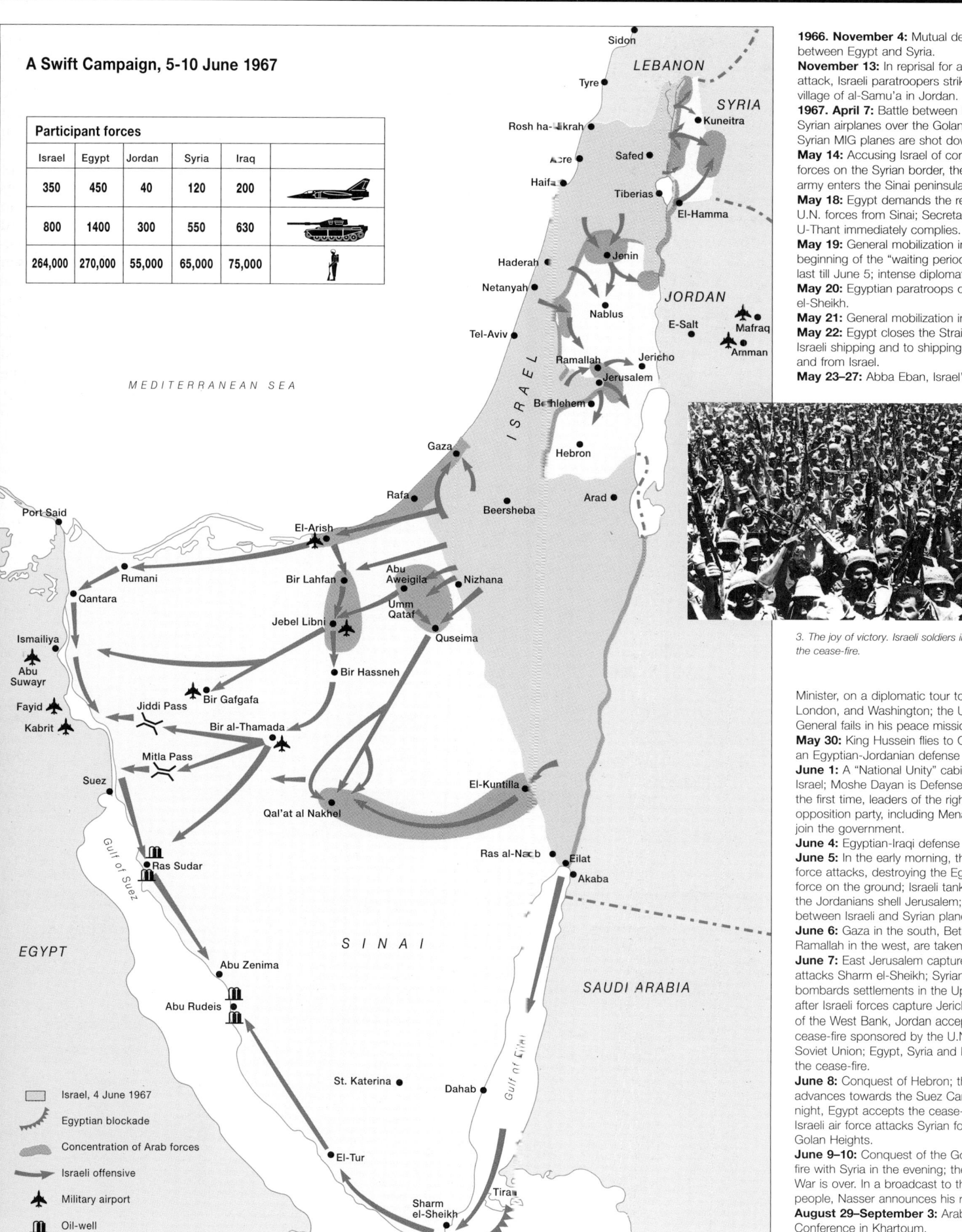

MEDITERRANEAN SEA

SYRIA
LEBANON
Sidon
Tyre
Rosh ha-Nikrah
Kuneitra
Acre
Safed
Haifa
El-Hamma
Tiberias
Jenin
Haderah
Netanyah
Nablus
JORDAN
E-Salt
Tel-Aviv
Mafraq
Ramallah
Jericho
Amman
Jerusalem
ISRAEL
Bethlehem
Gaza
Hebron
Rafa
Arad
Beersheba
El-Arish
Port Said
Rumani
Bir Lahfan
Abu Aweigila
Nizhana
Qantara
Umm Qataf
Ismailiya
Jebel Libni
Abu Suwayr
Bir Hassneh
Quseima
Fayid
Jiddi Pass
Bir Gafgafa
Kabrit
Bir al-Thamada
Mitla Pass
Suez
El-Kuntilla
Qal'at al Nakhel
Ras al-Nacb
Eilat
Ras Sudar
Akaba
EGYPT
SINAI
Abu Zenima
Abu Rudeis
SAUDI ARABIA
Gulf of Suez
St. Katerina
Dahab
Gulf of Eilat
El-Tur
Tiran
Sharm el-Sheikh
RED SEA

Israel, 4 June 1967
Egyptian blockade
Concentration of Arab forces
Israeli offensive
Military airport
Oil-well
Territories captured by Israel, 10 June 1967

50 km.

3. The joy of victory. Israeli soldiers in Sinai learn of the cease-fire.

**1966. November 4:** Mutual defense treaty between Egypt and Syria.

**November 13:** In reprisal for a terrorist attack, Israeli paratroopers strike at the village of al-Samu'a in Jordan.

**1967. April 7:** Battle between Israeli and Syrian airplanes over the Golan Heights, six Syrian MIG planes are shot down.

**May 14:** Accusing Israel of concentrating its forces on the Syrian border, the Egyptian army enters the Sinai peninsula.

**May 18:** Egypt demands the removal of U.N. forces from Sinai; Secretary General U-Thant immediately complies.

**May 19:** General mobilization in Israel; beginning of the "waiting period" which will last till June 5; intense diplomatic activity.

**May 20:** Egyptian paratroops occupy Sharm el-Sheikh.

**May 21:** General mobilization in Egypt.

**May 22:** Egypt closes the Straits of Tiran to Israeli shipping and to shipping bound to and from Israel.

**May 23–27:** Abba Eban, Israel's Foreign Minister, on a diplomatic tour to Paris, London, and Washington; the U.N. Secretary General fails in his peace mission to Cairo.

**May 30:** King Hussein flies to Cairo to sign an Egyptian-Jordanian defense treaty.

**June 1:** A "National Unity" cabinet formed in Israel; Moshe Dayan is Defense Minister; for the first time, leaders of the right-wing opposition party, including Menahem Begin, join the government.

**June 4:** Egyptian-Iraqi defense treaty.

**June 5:** In the early morning, the Israeli air force attacks, destroying the Egyptian air force on the ground; Israeli tanks enter Sinai; the Jordanians shell Jerusalem; air combat between Israeli and Syrian planes.

**June 6:** Gaza in the south, Bethlehem and Ramallah in the west, are taken.

**June 7:** East Jerusalem captured; the navy attacks Sharm el-Sheikh; Syrian artillery bombards settlements in the Upper Galilee; after Israeli forces capture Jericho and most of the West Bank, Jordan accepts the cease-fire sponsored by the U.N. and by the Soviet Union; Egypt, Syria and Iraq refuse the cease-fire.

**June 8:** Conquest of Hebron; the I.D.F. advances towards the Suez Canal; that night, Egypt accepts the cease-fire; the Israeli air force attacks Syrian forces on the Golan Heights.

**June 9–10:** Conquest of the Golan; cease-fire with Syria in the evening; the Six-Day War is over. In a broadcast to the Egyptian people, Nasser announces his resignation

**August 29–September 3:** Arab Summit Conference in Khartoum.

**November 22:** United Nations Resolution 242 calls for Israel's withdrawal from (the) occupied territories.

# Jewish Messianism

The word "messiah" derives from the Hebrew root *m-sh-h*, meaning "to anoint." Throughout history it was applied to a wide spectrum of eschatological expectations of redemption, and in modern times – even to secular utopian or revolutionary ideologies. In biblical Hebrew the word was used in the ordinary secular sense, or in a ritual context: anointing a person for some divine vocation – king, priest, or, metaphorically, patriarch and prophet.

Originally, the term did not have an eschatological ("End of Days") connotation. In the course of time, however, bitter experience taught the Hebrews that reality was far removed from the vision of salvation evoked by the biblical promise. The arrogance of the kings on David's throne and the sinful behavior of the people, they believed, provoked the wrath of God and were punished by disasters. The materialization of divine promises was therefore projected onto an ideal future when, in fulfillment of the covenant between God and his people, a righteous and charismatic scion of the House of David would inaugurate a reign of everlasting peace, justice, and physical and spiritual bliss for Israel (as in Isaiah: "They shall beat their swords into plowshares... [and] the wolf also

century, was apparently regarded by his followers as a messiah, raised up by God to break the yoke of the heathen and to reign over a restored kingdom of Israel. The disastrous debacle of this revolt, however, changed the nature of Jewish messianism in the future: while hopes and expectations remained as high as ever, and were augmented by each new wave of persecutions, Jewish spiritual leaders discouraged any short-term active messianism in order to prevent the tragic consequences of failure. Nevertheless, Jewish history was punctuated by messianic outbursts and by the appearance of harbingers and pretenders. Since all such movements always ended in disaster and bitter disillusionment, their leaders acquired the reputation of "false messiahs."

Rabbinic literature discusses at length the significance of messianic beliefs, their place in Jewish theology, and the features of the messianic age (although desisting from a too-detailed description to avoid the sin of *hubris*). Messianism also became a major component of Jewish mysticism, particularly in the Lurianic Kabbalah (born in Safed in the sixteenth century). Speculations and calculations of the date of the coming of the Messiah, Redeemer of Israel, became a constant feature of Jewish culture in the Middle Ages and early modern times. Nevertheless, despite the mystical dimension added by the Kabbalah, Jewish messianism remained essentially earthy, historical and national.

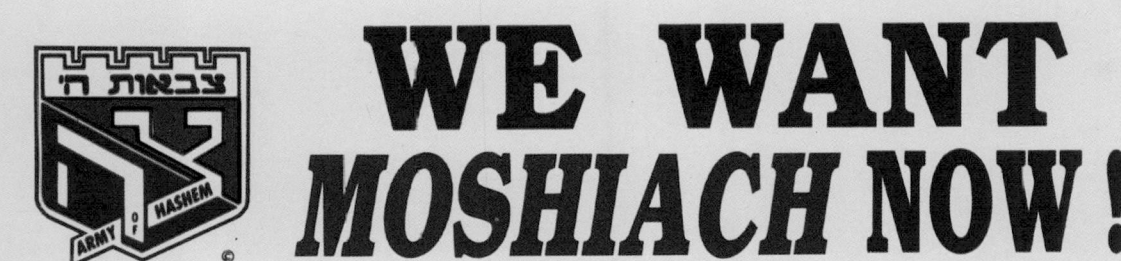

1. The latest manifestation of Jewish messianism: a street poster of the hasidic Habad movement. The emblem carries the initials of "Hosts of the Lord." Israel, 1991.

The Christian transposition of messianic salvation to the spiritual realm, implying that the earthy world was destined to remain the seat of sin and evil, seemed to the Jews a betrayal of true spirituality. Public disputations (usually forced upon the Jews by ecclesiastical or secular authorities), as well as

shall dwell with the lamb," 2:4; 11:6). But, strictly speaking, the term "messiah" representing an eschatological figure, a redeemer or a savior-king, was only inaugurated in post-biblical times.

Messianic expectations and ideologies seem to have developed in the wake of the Babylonian Exile, becoming particularly rife towards the end of the Second Temple period. The fact that the Gospels endowed Jesus with a Davidic lineage to enhance his status as the Redeemer, is an indication of the prevalence and force of the messianic idea among the Jews of that period. In fact, the word *christos* is the Greek equivalent of the Hebrew *mashiah*, "the anointed."

Bar Kokhba, leader of the great revolt against Rome in the second

literary polemics, were mostly based on points of exegesis: since the Church had integrated the Hebrew Bible, calling it the "Old" Testament, into its system, the argument hinged on whether biblical promises and prophecies had been fulfilled in the figure of Christ. The Christians accused the Jews of a materialistic interpretation of their Scriptures, "with eyes of the flesh"; the Jews, on the other hand, regarded the Christian reading of the text "with eyes of the spirit," as a perversion of its true and clear meaning. The great medieval debates, such as the disputation in Barcelona in 1263 and the one in Tortosa in 1413–1414, all revolved around these issues which concerned the nature of the Messiah.

According to rabbinic tradition the messianic age was to be preceded

| Inauguration of the Second Temple | Bar Kokhba's revolt | First Crusade |
|---|---|---|
| 516 BC | 132–135 | 1096–1099 |

**538–516 BC:** The Return to Zion is considered by some to be the earliest manifestation of a messianic movement.
**167–161 BC:** The revolt of the Maccabees is invested with a messianic meaning.
**37–4 BC:** Reign of Herod the Great; the rise of the Herodian dynasty, and then the imposition of direct Roman rule, give birth to new messianic conceptions.
**66–73 AD:** The Great Revolt against Rome is accompanied by a wave of messianic fervor; the birth of Christianity is only one of its many manifestations.
**115–117:** Revolts against Rome in the Jewish communities of Egypt and Cyrenaica; the sources mention a messianic king-figure as leader of the Cyrenaica rebels
**132–135:** The Bar Kokhba revolt ; the "Son of the Star" (the literal meaning of his name) was regarded as the Messiah even by a

4. Samuel anointing David in the presence of his brothers. Detail from a wall painting in the Dura-Europos Synagogue. Syria, c. 245 AD.

5. The cemetery on the Mount of Olives where the resurrection of the dead is to begin with the coming of the Messiah. Jerusalem, 1898.

spiritual leader of Rabbi Akiva's stature.
**448:** A Jew from Crete, claiming to be Moses, promises the Jews to take them to Judea across the sea without a boat; many of his followers drown.

by an apocalyptic stage of great upheavals and terrible suffering: before the birth of the Messiah, the son of Satan will rule over the whole world. This tradition acquired new significance in view of Jewish experience in the twentieth century. Emancipation, liberalism, equal rights, and hopes for the disappearance of antisemitism, endowed with a pseudo-messianic meaning, ended in terrible disillusionment. The two climactic and opposing events of the Holocaust on the one hand, and the establishment of the State of Israel with its vision of the ingathering of the exiles on the other, were seen by some religious Jews as *athalta di-ge'ulla*, signals of imminent redemption (hence the messianic-political ideology of the "Greater Israel" movement, influenced by Rabbi A.I. Kook who taught that the concrete realities of a modern state based on Jewish principles pave the way to the Messiah). Most Orthodox trends, however, strongly oppose the substitution of purely human redemption for the redeemer sent by God, and consider the identification of Zionism with the fulfillment of messianic expectations a dangerous perversion of Jewish teachings. According to this view, messianic hope must retain its eschatological and universal perspective.

2. Yeheskel Kirszenbaum (1900–1953), Jewish villagers greeting the Messiah. *Oil on cardboard, Paris.*

3. Rabbi Shlomo Goren, Chief Rabbi of the Israeli army, blows the shofar on Mount Zion, June 1967.

| Expulsion of the Jews from Spain | Shabbetai Zevi | "Gush Emmunim" |
|---|---|---|
| 1492 | 1665 | 1973 |

**Early 7th century:** The Book of Zerubbabel describes the world-wide kingdom of Armilus, son of Satan, who will reign until the victory of Messiah son of David; a vast literature develops around this vision, elaborating on "the birth pangs of the Messiah."

**8th century:** In Persia, Abu Isa hails himself prophet and herald of the Messiah, leading a Jewish revolt against the Muslims.

**1096–1099:** During the First Crusade, a general movement of repentance is formed among Balkan Jews.

**First half of 12th century:** The remarkable messianic movement of David Alroy spreads from Kurdistan to Baghdad and Persia.

**c. 1170:** A Jew in Yemen comes forth, claiming to be sent by the Messiah and calling for social revolution; this incident causes Maimonides to write his "Epistle to Yemen," warning against false messiahs.

**End of 13th century:** The kabbalist Abraham Abulafia, "the prophet of Avila," proclaims himself the harbinger of the

6. "The wolf also shall dwell with the lamb, and the leopard shall lie down with the kid" (Isaiah, 11:6). *Stained-glass, Bezalel School of Arts, Jerusalem, c. 1925.*

Messiah who would come in 1295.

**1391:** Anti-Jewish riots throughout Spain provoke widespread messianic fermentation.

**1453:** The fall of Constantinople raises messianic hopes among Jews.

**1492:** Expulsion of the Jews from Spain.

**1500–1502:** Asher Lemlein preaches

repentance in north-east Italy and in Germany and proclaims the imminent coming of the Messiah.

**1517:** Luther's revolt against the Church of Rome; many Jews see him as having come to pave the way for the Messiah

**1523:** David Reuveni appears in Italy and is

accepted by Jews and non-Jews as a prince from the legendary kingdom of the lost tribes; his companion, Solomon Molcho, later acquires the reputation of a Messiah.

**1665:** Shabbetai Zevi leads the greatest messianic movement in Jewish history.

**1683:** Following the example of Shabbetai Zevi, 250 families of his followers in Salonika convert to Islam, creating the *doenmeh* sect in the Balkans and Turkey.

**18th century:** The Frankist movement (followers of Jacob Frank), the last great manifestation of Shabbatean messianism.

**1973:** Appearance of *Gush Emmunim* ("Faith Bloc") which regards settlement in Greater Israel as hastening the advent of the Messiah.

**1994:** Repeated proclamations made by some of the Lubavicher's disciples that the *Habad* Rabbi is the Messiah arouse messianic fervor among *Hasidim* in New York and in Israel; many continue to believe in their Rabbi's messianic nature despite his terminal illness.

# Israel between War and Armed Peace

In April 1968 President Nasser proclaimed a three-stage strategy designed to restore to Egypt its honor and lost territories. In practice this policy meant reconstituting the Egyptian army, adopting "preventive defense" measures, and finally, "liquidation of the aggression" – a major war intended to drive Israel out of the occupied territories. Its arsenals replenished with Soviet arms, Egypt declared in March 1969 that the cease-fire was no longer valid, and waged a futile and destructive war of attrition. Lasting many months, with an almost-daily toll of casualties, it drew to an end only after the Egyptian towns along the Canal had been reduced to rubble by the I.D.F. and Israeli planes had wrecked military installations deep inside Egyptian territory.

1. Sadat, Carter, Begin: a peace treaty is signed. Washington, March 1979.

The cease-fire agreement which concluded the war of attrition, although an admission of failure by Egypt, carried grave consequences for Israel. Frustrated in the battlefield, the Arab countries and the Palestinian organizations mounted resistance and terrorist activities in the occupied territories, in Israel itself, and abroad. In the long run, however, they abandoned the policy of attrition, concentrating mainly on preparations for an all-out war. Moreover, within Israel itself, a complacency bred by a history of Arab failure lulled the establishment into a false sense of security. An expression of this smugness was Moshe Dayan's assurance that Israel was awaiting a humble "telephone call" from the

King of Jordan. Arrogance rendered the Meir-Dayan government blind to the political advantages gained by Anwar Sadat, president of Egypt since September 1970. A number of advisers and intelligence reports warning of an impending war went unheeded, thus the attack in October 1973 came as a shocking surprise.

On October 6th, the Jewish Day of Atonement, Egyptian forces crossed the Suez Canal and attacked the reputedly-impregnable "Bar-Lev Line" (a series of fortifications constructed after the Six-Day War along the entire length of the canal). At the same time, the Syrians, in a well-coordinated operation, overran the Golan Heights.

Hard and devastating, conducted under disastrous conditions, the war of 1973 had very little in common with the the war of June 1967. Nevertheless, after bitter fighting and heavy losses, the I.D.F. managed to reverse the situation in a spectacular manner: on the southern front the Egyptian army advance was checked and Israeli troops crossed the Suez Canal; on the northern front the Syrian army was driven back from the Golan Heights to about 30 miles outside Damascus. Militarily, Israel won its most brilliant victory; politically, it was a hard blow.

A confidence crisis of unprecedented proportions overcame the Israelis, breaking out in spontaneous protest movements, demonstrations, and an outcry of public opinion which forced the government to set up an inquiry commission, and led to the resignation of the Prime Minister, Golda Meir. She was replaced by a "new" man – Labor leader, Yizhak Rabin, who had been chief of staff during the Six-Day War. In the long run, however, the Yom Kippur "earthquake," brought about the downfall of the Labor Party and the rise to power, for the first time in Israeli history, of a right-wing coalition headed by Menahem Begin.

Yet the Yom Kippur War dramatically changed the conditions of the Israeli-Arab conflict and provided the first real chance for peace. Final results notwithstanding, the initial blows inflicted on the Israeli army allowed the Arabs to overcome past humiliations and to deal with the Israelis as equals. The courage of their outstanding statesman, President Sadat, and the obstinacy of the President of the United States, Jimmy Carter, did the rest. The process initiated by the Egyptian president as early as 1971 (one which would cost him his life) was completed when the first peace treaty between Israel and an Arab state was signed in Washington on March 26, 1979.

The great expectations roused by the peace with the leading Arab state, however, failed to materialize fully. None of Israel's other neighbors followed Egypt's example, and the activities of the Palestinian organizations escalated, particularly after they established themselves in Lebanon, which was torn by civil war. Operation "Peace for the Galilee" mounted by Israel in June 1982 was the fifth in the series of major Israeli-Arab wars.

| The Six-Day War | The "war of attrition" | Political reversal in Israel | Sadat in Jerusalem |
|---|---|---|---|
| **June 1967** | **March 1969–August 1970** | **May 1977** | **November 1977** |

**1967. August 29-September 3:** After the Six-Day War, the Arab Summit Conference at Khartoum adopts the "four nos" policy: no peace with Israel, no recognition of Israel, no negotiations with Israel, and no compromise at the expense of the rights of the Palestinian people.
**November 22:** Resolution 242 of the United Nations calls for Israel's withdrawal from territories (or *the* territories, according to the French version) conquered in the Six-Day War, termination of the state of belligerency, acknowledgement of the sovereignty of every state in the region and its right to live in peace within recognized and secure borders.
**1969. February 26:** Death of Prime Minister Levi Eshkol; Golda Meir is his successor.
**March 8:** Gamal Abdul Nasser declares a "war of attrition" against Israel.
**December:** The Arab summit in Rabat.
**1970. August 5:** In protest against Israel's acceptance of the American peace initiative, the right-wing parties leave the national-unity government.

**August 7:** A cease-fire between Egypt and Israel achieved through the intervention of the U.S. secretary of state William Rogers.
**September 28:** Death of Nasser; Anwar Sadat is his successor.
**1972. September 4:** Eleven Israeli athletes are murdered by Palestinian terrorists at the Munich Olympics.
**1973. October 6–24:** The Yom Kippur (Day of Atonement) War.
**October 22:** Resolution 338 of the U.N. Security Council calls upon the belligerents to cease fire and to implement resolution 242.
**November 11:** Egyptian-Israeli armistice.
**1974:** A wave of protest movements holds the government responsible for its lack of preparedness for the Yom Kippur War; the Agranat Commission investigates the causes for the initial failures.
**April 10:** Resignation of Golda Meir; Yizhak

2. Ma'alot on May 16, 1974. Young man evacuating his sister wounded in the terrorist attack.

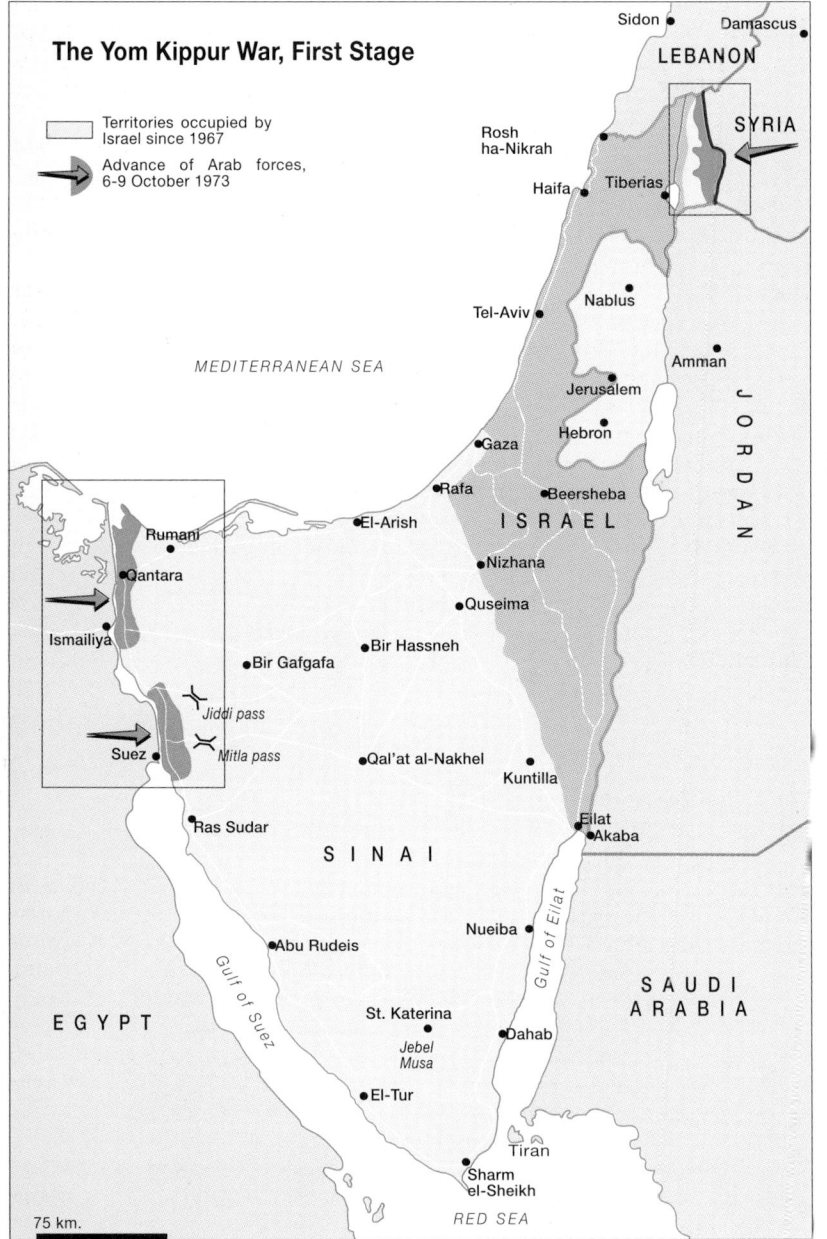

## The Yom Kippur War, First Stage

Territories occupied by Israel since 1967

Advance of Arab forces, 6-9 October 1973

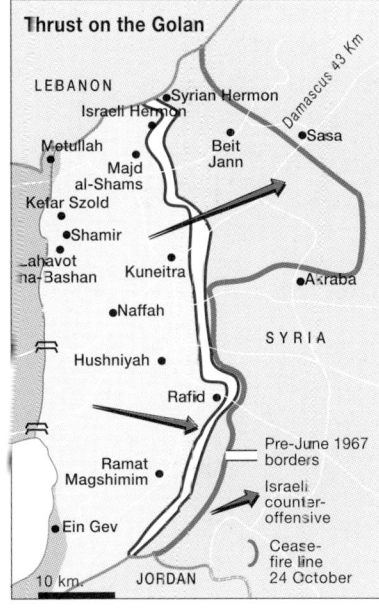

### Thrust on the Golan

Pre-June 1967 borders

Israeli counter-offensive

Cease-fire line 24 October

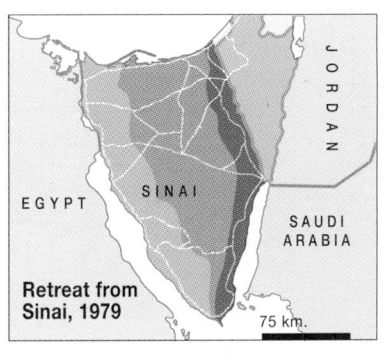

### Retreat from Sinai, 1979

75 km.

### Israel in 1982

Occupied territory

Annexed territory

75 km.

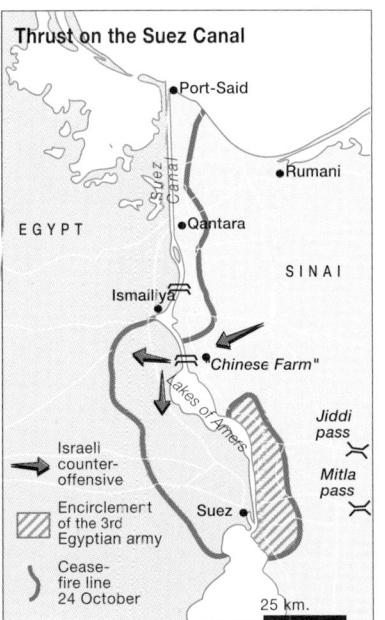

### Thrust on the Suez Canal

Israeli counter-offensive

Encirclement of the 3rd Egyptian army

Cease-fire line 24 October

25 km.

**The Camp David Conference**
September 1978

**Egyptian-Israeli peace treaty**
March 1979

**Assassination of President Sadat**
October 6, 1981

**War in Lebanon**
June 1982

Rabin succeeds her as leader of the Labor Party and as Prime Minister.
**April 11:** A terrorist attack in Kiryat Shemonah, in the Upper Galilee; 18 killed, most of them children.
**May 16:** Ninety school children are taken hostage by terrorists in Ma'alot, in the Upper Galilee; Israeli units attack the terrorists; 16 children are killed.
**May 31:** Israeli-Syrian armistice.
**1975. October 17:** The U.N. General Assembly, by a majority of votes, equates Zionism with racism.
**1977. May 17:** The reversal – for the first time in the history of the *yishuv* and of the State of Israel, the Labor party loses its majority in the general elections.
**November 19:** President Sadat addresses the Knesset in Jerusalem; Israel and Egypt begin peace negotiations under the auspices of the United States.
**1978. September:** The Camp David Conference; President Carter reaches a compromise formula, vague enough on the

Palestinian issue to enable the conclusion of an Egyptian-Israeli peace treaty.
**1979. March 26:** A peace treaty between Israel and Egypt is signed in Washington.
**1980. February:** The two countries exchange ambassadors.
**1981. June 7:** The Israeli air force destroys a nuclear reactor in Iraq.
**July 17:** Israeli bombardment of Beirut; the United States suspends the delivery of F-16 planes to Israel.
**October 6:** Assassination of President Sadat during celebrations of the anniversary of the 1973 war; his successor, President Mubarak, confirms his determination to pursue the peace policy.
**1982. April:** Israeli evacuation of the Sinai Peninsula is completed; strong resistance of extremist Jewish groups.
**June:** Israel invades Lebanon.

*3. Israeli soldiers and Egyptian prisoners under Egyptian fire during the Yom Kippur War. Photo by Mikhah Bar-Am, October 1973.*

# The Black Jews of Ethiopia

1. King Solomon and the Queen of Sheba. Popular Ethiopian art, c. 1950.

The Jews of Ethiopia, who call themselves *Beta Esrael* ("House of Israel"), are better known by the name given to them by the other inhabitants of the land, *Falashas* ("foreigners" or "immigrants"), which seems to confirm their own traditions concerning their origin. These traditions ascribe their ancestry to a Hebrew tribe which wandered off during the exodus from Egypt, or to members of the escort provided by King Solomon for the legendary Queen of Sheba, or to one of the ten tribes lost after the destruction of the First Temple. Most modern scholars, however, believe that the origins of the Jews of Ethiopia lie in Semitic and Jewish cultural influences which penetrated Ethiopia from the Arabian Peninsula, rather than in the actual immigration of

Jews. In any case, it is impossible to reconstruct the history of the Falashas prior to the thirteenth century. All we know is that a group of inhabitants practiced a primitive form of Judaism which was not influenced by any later external factors; that this group of Agau-speaking natives did not belong to the kingdom's elites who used Semitic languages; and that, falling victim to the political turbulence of the Axum dynasty's thousand-year reign, they probably lost their independence when defeated by one of its emperors during the tenth century.

The better-documented chapter in the history of the Jews of Ethiopia, which lasted until the early seventeenth century, began in 1270, with the re-establishment of the Semitic-Christian kingship (the "Solomonid

| Founding of the "Solomonid Dynasty" | Adoption of the Ge'ez language | Adoption of Amharic |
|---|---|---|
| 1270 | 15th century | 17th century |

**7th century BC-4th century AD:** Tribes from the Arabian Peninsula transmit Semitic culture and languages to Ethiopia, including certain Jewish religious elements.

**1st century AD:** Founding of the Axum Kingdom, whose sovereign bears the title "King of Kings" (*negus*).

**330:** Emperor Ezana converts to Christianity; throughout the kingdom, a monastic movement propagates a form of Christianity containing some Jewish elements.

**7th–8th centuries:** The alleged period of autonomy of a Judaizing ethnic group which speaks Agau – a non-written dialect.

**End of 9th century:** Obscure testimony by the traveller Eldad Ha-Dani of a Jewish tribe in Ethiopia.

**12th century:** A similar testimony by Spanish Jew Benjamin of Tudela.

**1270:** For the first time since the fall of the Axum dynasty in the 10th century, the imperial institution is restored by the Semitic-Christian elite; founding of the so-called "Solomonid Dynasty" which reigns

2. Hebrew lesson in Addis Ababa, 1924.

for seven centuries, till 1974.

**1314–1344:** Emperor Amda-Siyon defeats the Falashas and sends missionaries to teach them the rudiments of Christianity.

**1434–1468:** Emperor Zara-Ya'kob defeats the Falashas; monk Abba Sabra and prince Sagga Amlak join the Falashas, establishing monasticism among them; a religious awakening takes place, marked by the adoption of Ge'ez as the sacred written language.

**1529–1542:** Supported by, among others, the Falashas, a Somali Muslim invasion temporarily destroys the Ethiopian state, which is eventually saved by Portuguese intervention.

**1540–1559:** Emperor Galaudeuos refutes Jesuit accusations that Ethiopian observance of the Sabbath and of circumcision are un-Christian.

**1559–1597:** Emperors Minas and Sarsa Dengel defeat the Falashas.

**1607–1632:** Emperor Susenyos converts to Catholicism and finally subjugates the

Dynasty"). Ethiopian chronicles describe the *Beta Esrael* as one of many groups which sought to preserve their autonomy under the centralizing regime of the emperors. Led by their kings or queens (their tradition glorifies the exploits of King Gideon and Queen Judith), and protected by the mountains, they lost many battles, but were able to rise again each time. When the Somali Muslims of Imam Ahmad ibn Ibrahim "Gran" ("the left-handed") invaded and occupied Ethiopia (1521–1542), they were supported for a time by the Falashas.

The restoration of the Christian imperial power in 1542 was accompanied by Portuguese intervention, and religious tension in Ethiopia was intensified. Emperor Susenyos (1607–1632), temporarily converting to Catholicism, eventually managed to liquidate the Falasha kingship by force, thus ending their political role in Ethiopian history.

The original religious and socio-cultural traits of the Jewish community evolved during the fourteenth and fifteenth centuries. The struggle against the Christian power also created the opportunity for contacts with the Jewish elements contained in Ethiopian Christianity, which were more well-developed than Falasha Judaism due to their use of Ge'ez, a Semitic language. The government encouraged missionary activity among the Falashas, and these missionaries provoked a series of reforms and the emergence of a literature in Ge'ez. Thus, the monk Kozmos copied the Scriptures for their benefit, while the monk Abba Sabra instituted Falasha monasticism. But following the prohibition on owning land, imposed on non-Christians ever since the reign of Emperor Ishaq (1414–1430), the Falashas were transformed into an isolated and uprooted mountain community.

Deprived of political organization, the Falashas became one of many confessional, ethnic and linguistic groups living on the margins of Ethiopian society. Banished from the Semyen mountains to the Gondar region, many Falashas converted to Christianity. Their survival as a collective was mainly due to contacts established with the West. Emperor Theodoros II (1855–1868), who was devoted to modernization, welcomed western missionaries, many of whom settled in regions inhabited by Falashas. Some of the Falashas responded by following a pseudo-messiah on a long march to Palestine, a trek which ended tragically in the Tigre Plateau when many Falashas disappeared; the remainder set up a small local community. Their total number, estimated at over 200,000 in the nineteenth century, declined to about 20,000.

Meanwhile, western Jews discovered their lost brethren in the legendary kingdom of Prester John. A visit by orientalist Joseph Halevy in 1867–1868 was followed by several trips made by his student, Jacques Faïtlovitch. It was largely Faïtlovitch's educational and social work which brought the Falashas closer to the mainstream of Jewish history.

Nevertheless, the Jewish religious establishment was ambivalent towards the Falashas. Only in 1973, after bitter disputes, did the Chief Rabbinate of Israel recognize them as proper Jews. The following year, the revolution which brought the imperial rule of Haile Selassie to an end made the Falashas' situation almost intolerable. The State of Israel took radical action: in two spectacular operations, one in the mid-1980s and the other in 1991, practically the whole of the *Beta Esrael* community, approximately 30,000 people, were transferred to Israel.

*3. Amulet. Ink on parchment. Ethiopia, early 20th century.*

| Jacques Faïtlovitch, *Notes d'un voyage chez les Falachas* | | "Operation Moses" | "Operation Solomon" |
|---|---|---|---|
| **1905** | | **1984–1985** | **1991** |

Falashas. His son returns to the Ethiopian Coptic Church recruiting Falashas to his army. Beginning of the assimilation of the Falashas who adopt the Amharic tongue (although Agau will continue to be used till the 19th century). Ge'ez remains, as among the Christians, the language of prayer.
**1790:** Scottish traveller James Bruce publishes in Edinburgh his *Travels to Discover the Sources of the Nile*, from which the West learns for the first time of the Falashas' existence.
**1838–1848:** Two French scholars, the brothers d'Abbadie, sojourn in Ethiopia; Antoine d'Abbadie provides new evidence concerning the Falashas.
**1851–1854:** Filosseno Luzzatto publishes in *Archives israelites* his *Memoire sur les Juifs d'Abyssinie*.
**1855–1868:** Reign of Emperor Theodoros II.

*4. Ethiopian Jews aboard an Israeli plane. May, 1991.*

**1862:** The Falashas set out for the Land of Israel.
**1888–1892:** Famine kills thousands of Falashas.
**1904:** First visit to Ethiopia by Jacques Faïtlovitch on behalf of the *Alliance Israelite Universelle*. The following year he publishes his *Notes d'un voyage chez les Falachas*.
**1913:** The first modern school for Falasha children is inaugurated in Dambiya.
**1973–1975:** The Chief Sephardi Rabbi in Israel, and then his Ashkenazi counterpart, recognize the Falashas as Jews.
**1984–1985:** "Operation Moses": about 15,000 Falashas are brought to Israel via Sudan.
**1991. May 25:** Fall of Mengistu's regime in Ethiopia; "Operation Solomon": between the dictator's flight and Addis Ababa's conquest by the rebels, a 36-hour airlift transfers more than 14,000 Ethiopian Jews to Israel.

*Map labels:*
RED SEA · ARABIA · ERITREA · TIGRE · from Egypt · Asmara · Aksum · SIMEN · Sana · Mocha · Aden · GULF OF ADEN · Gondar · GONDAR · Magdala · Djibouti · SUDAN · Kirin · Dambasha · Harar · Addis Ababa · ETHIOPIA (contemporary borders) · Goba · KENYA · 200 km · Probable origin of Ethiopian Jews · The ancient Himyarite kingdom, up to 525

# Jews and Poles: An Epilogue

In May 1991, Lech Walesa, the newly elected president of post-Communist Poland, made a speech in front of the Knesset building in Jerusalem: in a few simple sentences he summarized the thousand-year history of Jewish-Polish relations, a past which he eloquently portrayed in shades of gray. Walesa skillfully avoided the more disastrous episodes in Jewish-Polish history by elegantly evoking the shared aspects of their culture, pointing out the strong ties linking the two nations. But, as he himself had to admit, this was a history more often tragic than happy; thus, the workers' leader from Gdansk had come to ask forgiveness from the Jewish people.

Independent Poland, which was revived in 1918, was in no position to offer ideal conditions for the harmonious coexistence of the two communities. The Jews constituted a people apart, highly conscious of their singularity, united by their religion, customs and particular culture. Their territorial concentration, their massive presence in occupations lacking in social prestige, the extreme destitution of the *shtetl*, all rendered them at once visible and disliked. The Poles, on the other hand, represented the characteristic traits of the less enlightened Eastern European population: isolationism and xenophobia. In addition, the strong influence of an intolerant Catholicism was combined with fears regarding the continued existence of the newly-formed state and its "pure" Polish character. Indeed, antisemitic outbursts were particularly frequent and violent precisely in those territories whose connection to Poland was still precarious.

The Jewish question was aggravated during the 1930s with the advent of the economic crisis, the penetration of Nazi ideology from neighboring Germany, and the death of Marshal Pilsudski, Poland's strongman who had restrained ethnic strife which he regarded as harmful to the state. In the late 1930s, the Jews were exposed to trade boycotts, "bench ghettos" and a *numerus clausus* in institutes of higher learning, social and professional segregation, and, at times, physical violence.

On the other hand, one should not forget that throughout the interwar period the Jews enjoyed a large measure of autonomy in religious, cultural and educational affairs, and independent political representation in Parliament. Although their legal equality was not fully effected, they conducted a dynamic and enterprising community life and, until Poland's invasion by the Wehrmacht, the existence of the Jewish communities could be described as tolerable. Particularly painful was the situation of those who had cut themselves off from the community and tried to integrate into the Polish society at large. But this was, on the whole, only a small minority.

During Nazi occupation, the Polish population displayed a whole gamut of possible behavior: from the heroic rescue of Jewish lives to willing cooperation with Nazi murders and persecution. There is no way of quantifying these different attitudes. On the whole, however, it is clear that the Jews received no support from their Polish compatriots during the long years of their ghettoization and systematic ruination, nor in their struggle against annihilation. The chasm between the two communities prior to the war was too deep, growing even deeper in the regions occupied by the Soviets following the German-Soviet pact.

Paradoxically perhaps, the end of the war, rather than leading to conciliation between Poles and Jews, only served to reinforce antisemitism.

1. Lech Walesa, President of the Republic of Poland, before the Knesset. Jerusalem, May 20, 1991.

| Independent Poland | Pilsudski's dictatorship | The Holocaust |
|---|---|---|
| 1918 | 1926 | 1939–1945 |

**1918:** Restoration of the Polish state.
**November:** Pogrom in Lvov: 70 killed, hundreds injured.
**1919. April:** Pogrom in Vilnius (Vilna): 80 persons killed.
**1922:** Pilsudski's resignation. The first Sejm (Parliament) includes 45 Jewish deputies. A right-wing antisemitic organization, *Narodowa Demokracja* ("National Democracy") emerges as the dominant group in the Sejm; it proclaims an economic boycott on the Jews and demands the introduction of a *numerus clausus*; opposition of Jewish students leads to violent clashes.
**1924–1928:** Fourth Aliyah: most of the 55,000 immigrants who arrived in Palestine by 1926 are of Polish origin.
**1926:** Pilsudski regains power; great hopes rise among Polish Jews.
**1936. March 9:** Pogrom in Przytyk.
**1939. September 1:** German invasion.
**1944. July 20:** In Lublin, the Polish Committee of National Liberation issues a

solemn declaration promising full equal rights to the survivors of Polish Jewry.
**October:** Founding of the Central Committee of Polish Jews.
**1945. July 6:** The United States and Great Britain recognize the Polish National Union Government. The government and the ruling Polish Workers' Party in power (the Communist F.O.U.P.) are well disposed towards the Jewish Committee, authorizing Zionist activities and displaying a positive attitude to the aspirations of the *yishuv* in Palestine. Many Jews join the army and attain high rank. But at the same time, a wave of antisemitism overflows Poland: 353 Jews are murdered.
**1946. July:** Pogrom in Kielce: 43 dead, 50 injured; public protestations of intellectuals and Polish workers; the government and the party issue declarations designed to placate the Jewish community. 100,00 Jews leave for Palestine, 70,000 of them in the three months following the pogrom. On the other hand, in the same year, about 154,000 Jews

4. Marshal Jozef Pilsudski.

return to Poland from regions occupied by the Soviet Union.
**1946–1947:** Founding of two Yiddish theaters, in Lodz and in Wroclaw.
**1948:** In Poland, the *Haganah*, soon to become the Israeli army, sets up a camp for military training of 1,500 young men who plan to emigrate to Palestine.
**1949:** Beginning of the liquidation of Jewish Zionist and community organizations. 30,000 Jews leave for Israel.
**1950:** The Jewish State Theater is created by combining the previously existing troupes.
**1953:** The Israeli Consul in Warsaw is declared *persona non grata*.
**1956. April:** Gomulka, condemned for Titoism in 1949, is released from prison.
**June:** A workers' uprising in Poznan: 38 are killed. The "October Spring." Wladyslaw Gomulka is head of the Party. Amelioration of relations with Israel. Liberalization of the emigration policy. Renewed activities of Jewish organizations; at the same time, a new wave of rising antisemitism.

*2. Funeral of the victims of the Kielce pogrom, July 1946.*

*3. Solidarity demonstration in commemoration of the Warsaw Ghetto uprising. April 1988.*

Among the reasons one could cite for this are the cruelty which was given free reign during the war, the fear of having to reimburse returning Jews for property which had been confiscated, but above all, the establishment of a Soviet regime. Many Jews had good reason to support a new order which promised them full equality and an end to persecution. Many of the survivors returned with the Red Army, and a large number of Jews participated in the establishment of the new regime. The Polish population, traditionally anti-Communist and anti-Russian, considered these Jews to be collaborators with their archenemy.

A pogrom in Kielce in 1946 claimed dozens of victims. According to some historians this outburst was provoked by unidentified elements wishing to besmear pre-Communist Poland in the eyes of the world. But whoever they were, such appalling events following so soon after the Holocaust drove the Jews to a mass exodus directed mainly towards Palestine, leaving behind a Jewry mostly reduced to an assimilated and left-wing intelligentsia. Naturally, the latter was visible in the administration, in culture and in the ideology of Poland during its darker years of Stalinism. This gave birth to the stereotype of the Communist Jew, who symbolized everything the Polish population found despicable. In the 1950s, a new and particularly virulent wave of antisemitism marked the end of the Stalinist period, effecting the same results: large emigration,

again mostly to Israel. Polish Jewry was now reduced to some forty or fifty thousand individuals, most of whom were assimilated, and had no communal or cultural attachments.

Nevertheless, they too became victims of the next wave of antisemitism, which was the most grotesque of all. In 1968, against a background of economic crisis and bitter conflicts within the Communist Party, the leaders once more exploited the old specter, this time under the guise of a "Zionist plot." Practically the entire remaining "community" now left Poland. Since these were Jews only in the eyes of Gentiles, only very few of this group went to Israel.

Of the few thousand "Poles of Jewish origin," many naturally joined the opposition. In the eyes of most founders of Solidarity, antisemitism appeared to be one of the thorns of the Communist regime. When they won, they made an effort to extirpate the last vestiges of what was regarded by many as a fundamental trait of Polish national culture. This was no mean feat. One of the perverse effects of the newly regained liberty was the reemergence of this peculiar "antisemitism without Jews." Still apprehensive, Polish society reacts nervously to everything foreign, different, or unfamiliar. But all this is not necessarily the final word. Antisemitism was the product of history; and history, in Poland, has now taken a different direction.

| Pogrom in Kielce | Antisemitic campaign | Founding of Solidarity | Walesa in Jerusalem |
|---|---|---|---|
| **1946** | **1968** | **1980** | **1991** |

*5. Death of Jewish officer Bronislaw Mansperl on October 21, 1915. Miniature by Arthur Szyk (1894–1951) from his edition of the Statute of Kalisz.*

**End of 1956–1959:** 70,000 Jews leave Poland.
**1967:** The Six-Day War; following the example of the Soviet Union, Poland severs diplomatic relations with Israel (June 12).
**1968. March:** Gomulka: the Jews, whose loyalty is divided between their homeland and Israel, are "rootless cosmopolitans," unworthy of holding public office. Liquidation of Yiddish publishing.
**1970. December:** Riots in the Baltic ports: six dead; Gomulka resigns and is replaced by Edward Gierek.
**1980. August 14:** A strike in the Gdansk shipyards; the protest movement spreads throughout Poland.
**September:** Founding of "Solidarity"; among its leaders are intellectuals of Jewish origin.
**1981. December 12–13:** General Jaruzelski, First Secretary of the P.O.U.P., proclaims a "state of war": 14,000 arrests.
**1982. October:** "Solidarity" is outlawed.
**1983:** John-Paul II, a Polish pope, pays

homage to the monument commemorating heroes of the Warsaw Ghetto revolt.
**1988. April:** Illegal demonstration of Solidarity on the anniversary of the Warsaw Ghetto revolt.
**1988:** Beginning of the affair concerning the Carmelite monastery in Auschwitz; the erection of this religious house on the site symbolizing the Holocaust raises a wave of protests.
**1990. November–December:** In post-Communist Poland, the presidential campaign is accompanied by some antisemitic manifestations.
**1991:** A pastoral letter by the bishops of the Church of Poland affirms that antisemitism is a sin (January); President Walesa's visit to Israel (May).
**April 1992:** Israeli Chief-of-Staff on an official visit to Poland.

*6. Election poster in Yiddish of the Jewish Popular Party. Lithograph by Solomon Yudovin (1892–1954). Poland, 1921.*

# "America is Different"

In 1954–1955 American Jewry marked its tercentenary, three hundred years of a fairly happy history in the land of opportunity, the modern equivalent of Hellenistic Alexandria. In a society where ethnic pluralism is no longer simply accepted but is even actively encouraged, Jews find it difficult to regard themselves as living in "exile," and the process of their Americanization has assumed some very distinctive traits.

An era of prolonged prosperity during the post-World War II years has transformed this community of nearly six million people into a strong group, overwhelmingly native, extensively college-educated, and heavily concentrated in the mercantile and professional classes. Although a relatively low birth rate and limited immigration have reduced its percentage in the overall population, the self-confidence and the influence of American Jewry in cultural, political, and economic affairs have considerably increased. Antisemitism has all but disappeared from public view; and when John F. Kennedy, the first Catholic President, was elected thanks to the support of most of the minority voters, the prosperous Jewish community also attained political maturity.

As might be expected, most American Jews rally to the liberal camp – a tradition dating from the years of mass immigration, manifested in the enthusiastic support for Roosevelt's New Deal, and still evident today. In all presidential elections about two-thirds of the Jewish votes are cast for liberal candidates.

It was therefore natural for Jews to play a major role in the American Civil Liberties Union and in the National Association for the Advancement of Colored People, and for the whole community to express its satisfaction with the social reforms introduced by the Johnson administration. The battle against antisemitism conducted by Jewish organizations has also always been directed against every other form of religious or racial discrimination. Unfortunately, relations with the black community have been gravely strained since the 1960s. Militant black nationalism, which filled the void created by the assassination of Martin Luther King, was tainted with antisemitism. Some Jewish sectors, on the other hand, feared that the advancement of blacks would be at the expense of Jews.

The tendency of American Jews to fight for liberal causes has also manifested itself in recent decades on the feminist front. The new feminist consciousness is expressed not only in words but in practice as well. More and more women occupy important positions of authority in community organizations; the Reform Movement began to ordain women as rabbis in 1972, and the Conservatives followed suit in 1985. Even within the Orthodox community one hears voices calling for a redefinition of the role of women.

Despite rapid acculturation, the identity problem of the American Jew has grown more complex. In the years following World War II, congregational affiliation was the common solution. The synagogue not only provided religious and educational services but also served as the focus of social and community life. In the last two decades, however, its authority and prestige have declined. Nowadays only one out of two Jews declares affiliation with a synagogue. Yet the transmission of Jewish culture in the United States is carried on through additional channels. In 1948 Brandeis University joined the network of schools in existence from before the war; and, since the 1960s, innumerable programs, departments, and academic chairs of Jewish studies have been opened in many other universities.

A striking feature of American life in the last half century has been the prominence of Jewish intellectuals in various cultural arenas. Jews constitute over 10% of academic faculty members, and their contribution to American science has been remarkable. Furthermore, an outstanding number of Jewish writers, publishers, producers, musicians, artists, and critics have attained distinguished reputations. East European Jewish folk humor has suffused much of American literature, theater, and films. Novels and short stories concerned with specifically Jewish topics have become huge bestsellers. Even Yiddish writers, such as Isaac Bashevis Singer, have become U.S. literary celebrities. An interesting phenomenon evident since the 1950s has been the sense of social and spiritual alienation expressed by so many young creative Jews. It appears that these third-generation Americans wished to satirize as vulgar materialism the ambition of their parents to Americanize at any cost. Oddly perhaps, these feelings of estrangement evoke general identification within the American intelligentsia. In many respects the conflicts of the Jew, despite everything still the perennial outsider, became, particularly during the 1960s, a symbol of American anti-establishment culture.

The fight against assimilation has been on the agenda of the organized Jewish community for a long time. In an open society, however, where explicit discrimination is no longer in evidence, it is an impossible task. The figures of mixed marriages are regarded as alarming: from 7% in the 1950s, they have risen to over 40%. Since less than half the children of these marriages remain in the community, this trend is bound to erode American Judaism.

*3. Jewish Defense League. 1980s.*

*1. Confirmation ceremony in a Reform synagogue. 1980s.*

*2. New Jersey Governor Thomas Kean cleans antisemitic graffiti. 1980s.*

The strong attachment of American Jews to the State of Israel, however, remains firm. It can be explained, no doubt, by the traumatic memory of the Holocaust. The bond was later strengthened by the Six-Day War. The anguish in May and the victory in June 1967 provided a cementing element for the community itself and for its ties with Israel. Admittedly, the exaltation of that summer has cooled down considerably. The war in Lebanon, the Pollard affair, the *Intifada* – to mention but the most painful moments of the last decade – have tempered the unconditional solidarity with Jerusalem. Yet for most American Jews, Zionism still means not only an obligation to sustain the Jewish State with funds, immigrants, and political support, but also to regard it as the center of Jewish culture, religion, and national identity.

5. Hasidim in Brooklyn. 1980s.

4. A Jewish marriage ceremony for a gay couple. 1980s.

world-wide support for Jews in the Soviet Union and in Arab countries.
**Late 1950s–early 1960s:** The "Jewish decade" or "Jewish renaissance" in American literature.
**1957:** Leon Uris publishes *Exodus*.
**1958–1960:** Allen Ginsberg's *Kaddish*.
**1961:** Bernard Malamud's *A New Life*.
**1961–1963:** The Kennedy years. First important arms deal with Israel.
**1964:** Lyndon Johnson is President. Intensification of the war in Vietnam. Saul Bellow's *Herzog*.
**1965:** The *American Jewish Year Book*, appearing since 1899, deletes the section covering antisemitic events.
**1967:** American Jewish volunteers and huge financial contributions are sent to Israel in its hour of greatest danger.
**1968:** A teachers' strike in New York City exacerbates the tensions between Jews and Blacks. In Brooklyn, Meir Kahana founds the Jewish Defense League.
**1969:** Philip Roth's *Portnoy's Complaint*.
**1970s:** Crystallization of the main socio-economic trends of American Jewry. Between the beginning of the decade and its end, the proportion of Jews in the professions and in the business world rises from 40% to 53% (compared with a rise from 21% to 27% in the general population), while their position in manual occupations falls from 21% to 12% (in the general population the percentage remains more or less stable, around 40%). The revenue curve reflects these trends. In the general population the proportion of families earning more than $15,000 per year rises from 15% to 49%; in the Jewish community it rises from 31% to 63%.
**1972:** The Reform Movement ordains the first woman rabbi.
**1973:** Henry Kissinger is Secretary of State. Abraham D. Beame is the first Jewish Mayor of New York City; in 1977 he will be succeeded by another Jew, Edward Koch
**1974–1977:** Presidency of Gerald Ford.
**1977–1981:** Presidency of Jimmy Carter.
**1978:** In an *Open Letter to American Jews*, Anwar Sadat asks them to assume an "historic responsibility" in creating peace between Israel and Egypt.
**1979:** The Camp David Accords (in March). Andrew Young resigns from the State Department because of his unauthorized meeting with the PLO; American black leaders issue an angry statement against American Jews.
**1981–1988:** Presidency of Ronald Reagan.
**1985:** The first woman rabbi in the Conservative Movement.
**1987:** Jonathan Pollard arrested for espionage in the service of Israel.
**End of 1980s:** The proportion of Jews declaring their affiliation to a religious denomination declines from 86% at the beginning of the decade to 75% (34% Conservatives; 29% Reform; only 9% Orthodox).
**1989–1990:** *New York Stories*, Woody Allen supplied in his section of the film a personal Jewish viewpoint.
**1990. October 14:** Death of Leonard Bernstein.
**1991. July 24:** Death of Isaac Bashevis Singer.
**1991. September:** Blacks attack Orthodox Jews in Brooklyn after a Jewish driver kills a black boy in a car accident.

*Habad* Hasidism. The leader of *Habad* (or Lubavich) Hasidism, Joseph Isaac Schneerson, descendant of Shneur Zalman of Lyady, arrived in New York in 1940.
**1948:** President Truman recognizes de facto the State of Israel shortly after its Declaration of Independence. A Displaced Persons Act authorizes the admission of over 200,000 European refugees to the U.S. Brandeis University is founded in Waltham, Massachusetts.
**1949:** Arthur Miller wins the Pulitzer Prize for *Death of a Salesman*.
**1950–1953:** The Korean War. The anti-Communist witch-hunt conducted by Joseph McCarthy.
**1952–1969:** Within seventeen years, fourteen Nobel Prizes are awarded to American Jews in physics, chemistry, medicine, and physiology.
**1954:** Founding of AIPAC (American-Israel Public Affairs Committee), the "official" Israeli lobby in the United States.
**1955:** Nahum Goldmann founds the Conference of Presidents of Major Jewish American Organizations to coordinate activities concerning Middle East affairs, and to organize

**1937–late 1980s:** The proportion of the Jewish community in the general population in the U.S. declines from 3.7% to 2.5%. An internal migration to sunnier regions brings its distribution closer to that of the general population. New York City loses its status as the city where the majority of American Jews reside: the percentage of Jews living there goes from 56% in the 1930s to 38%. The other major Jewish cities are Los Angeles, Miami, Philadelphia, and Chicago.
**1945:** Founding of the monthly *Commentary*, identified for many years with the progressive left.
**1947:** Joel Teitelbaum of Satmar (Satu Mare, in Transylvania) settles in the Williamsburg quarter of Brooklyn, New York, where he establishes an ultra-Orthodox Hasidic congregation. Fiercely opposed to Zionism, he is also a strict opponent of

# From Khrushchev to Gorbachev

1. Commemoration of the Holocaust at Leningrad Jewish cemetery, May 1987.

2. Israeli Independence Day celebrated at the Obrajki railway station. Moscow, May 1978.

Stalin's death in March 1953 brought the period of physical terror to an end, and blackness slowly faded into gray. But this "thaw" did not affect the overall state of affairs in the Soviet Union, for either the population in general, or for the Jews in particular. The victims of the Doctors' Plot were exonerated and released, the campaign against "rootless cosmopolitans" suspended, yet Jewish institutional and cultural life could no longer be restored. Official antisemitism was still prevalent; during the early 1960s, under Khruschev's order, it was masked by the violent campaign against "economic crimes." At the same time, however, new factors began to affect the fate of Soviet Jewry. First of all, renewed communication with the outside world enabled Soviet Jews to resume contact with relatives in the West and in Israel, and Jews from western countries began visiting the Soviet Union. As the plight of the Jewish community was divulged, there were increasing protestations by Jews and non-Jews alike in non-communist countries, demanding the restitution of rights to the Jews both as individuals and as a national and religious minority. Even Communists in the West voiced their disapproval, and the Soviet authorities were compelled to concede to this pressure of world public opinion.

Furthermore, the fight against Nazism, the Holocaust, and above all the creation of the State of Israel, produced amidst Soviet Jews an incredible national reawakening. From the outstanding demonstrations welcoming Golda Meir, Israel's first diplomatic representative to the Soviet Union, to the brave struggle for the right to emigrate conducted during the 1970s and 1980s by "Prisoners of Zion" (the most celebrated among them being Anatoly Shcharansky, Yossef Begun, and Ida Nudel), the solidarity of this community with Israel had become one of its principle hallmarks. The clandestine teaching of Hebrew, Bible and Jewish history classes, *samizdat* publications, Zionist circles, "refuseniks" organizing hunger-strikes and petitions, were all manifestations which the authorities tried to repress but were unable to stifle.

After the Six-Day War, official Soviet propaganda began lashing out at Jews and Zionists indiscriminately, unashamedly equating "Zionist" with "Nazi." Yet at the same time, the emigration policy did not correspond with the attitude to Jews and Israel: in 1968, at the height of the antisemitic campaign, the Soviet authorities allowed some emigration to Israel on the basis of "reunification of families." In the following decade, the gates were opened even wider. Then, after the regressive Brezhnev interim, the policy of *perestroika* removed all remaining barriers. Between 1968 and 1989 approximately 300,000 Jews left the Soviet Union.

| 20th Congress of the C.P.S.U | Yevgeni Yevtushenko, *Babi Yar* | The Helsinki Accords |
|---|---|---|
| **February 1956** | **1961** | **August 1975** |

**1953. April 4:** The Doctors' Plot is officially declared an unfounded "provocation."
**1955:** Surviving Jewish writers are released from prison.
**1956:** Most of the writers who were executed during the "Black Years" after the war are rehabilitated.
**February 14–24:** The 20th Congress of the Communist Party of the Soviet Union; Nikita Khruschev condemns Stalin's "personality cult" and crimes.
**1961:** A new antisemitic campaign, this time in the name of a struggle against "economic crimes" (till 1964). Founding of *Sovietische Heimland* ("Soviet Homeland"), a Yiddish periodical edited by Aaron Vergelis. A Jewish drama ensemble is founded in Moscow, the first since 1953. Yevgeni Yevtushenko, *Babi Yar*; the following year Dmitri Shostakovich dedicates his Thirteenth Symphony to this poem which has received international acclaim.
**1963. February:** Publication of the correspondence between Bertrand Russell

and Khrushchev in which the renowned British philosopher calls for the full restitution of equal rights to Soviet Jews.
**1967. June 10:** Following the Six-Day War, the Soviet Union breaks off diplomatic relations with Israel.
**July:** The campaign against Jews, Zionism, and the State of Israel intensifies.
**1968:** First arrivals of several hundred familes allowed to emigrate to Israel.
**1970. February:** In Riga, first *samizdat* publication in Hebrew.
**June 15:** At the Smolny airport, Leningrad, nine men and women, seven of whom are Jews, are arrested and charged with plotting to hijack a plane.
**December 15–31:** The "Leningrad Trial": the harshness of the sentences raises an outcry throughout the world.
**1972. July 3:** The Supreme Soviet imposes a heavy tax on emigrants with higher education diplomas.

5. A Heder in Georgia in the 1970s.

# 1953–1992

*3. Waiting for an Israeli visa. Moscow, May 1990.*

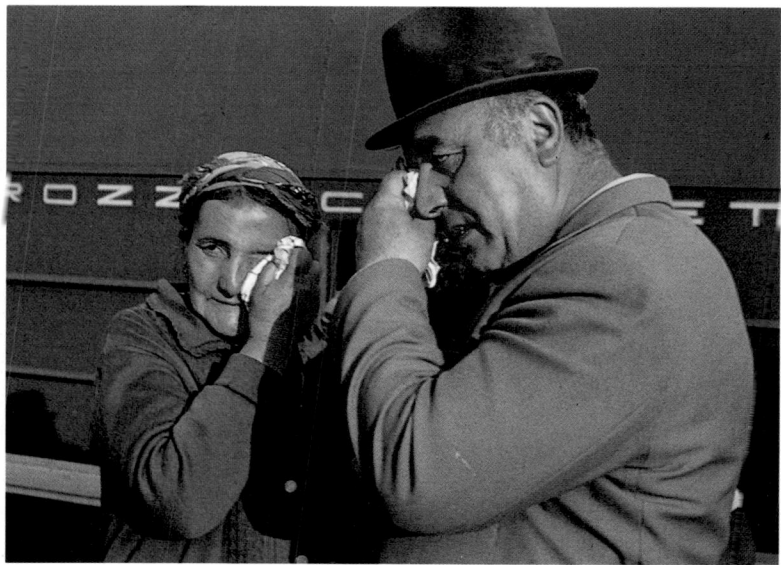

*4. Farewell at a Moscow railway station, May 1990.*

Gorbachev's "reconstruction" also revolutionized the lives of the 1,750,000 Jews still remaining in the Soviet Union. Cultural activities and political organizations, now conducted in broad daylight, reconstituted a dynamic Jewish community, which could at last openly reaffirm its links with world Jewry and with the State of Israel. A Federation of Jewish Communities and Organizations was established in Moscow on December 18–22, 1989. Among its many tasks, it also had to face one of the least attractive facets of Soviet democratization: the resurgence of Russian antisemitism, most viciously expressed by the religious *Pamyat* ("Memory") group.

The major issue on the current agenda of Soviet Jewry is now, more than ever, the question of emigration. Poverty, fear of the unknown in a society undergoing serious upheavals, the old specter of possible pogroms – all these, more than any Zionist ideology, are driving Jews away from the Soviet Union. Since the United States will only allow a trickle of immigrants from the Eastern bloc, the Jews of the former U.S.S.R are flocking to Israel. With the advent of 1990, this recent wave of immigration began to change the face of Israeli society, and is currently approaching colossal proportions: approximately 400,000 people, at the rate of 20,000 a month, have arrived in Israel within two and a half years.

**Gorbachev is First Secretary** — **May 1985**

**Emigration wave to Israel** — **1990...**

**1975. August 1:** Signing of the Helsinki Accords.
**1976. July 8:** Inauguration of a memorial monument in Babi Yar, which fails to mention the 50,000 Jews murdered in this ravine near Kiev in September 1941.
**1977. May 15:** Anatoly Shcharansky, accused of espionage, is arrested.
**1983. April 1:** Founding of the Soviet Anti-Zionist Public Committee.
**1984. June 1:** Birobidzhan celebrates its 50th anniversary; the Jewish population in the "autonomous region" numbers about 13,000 people.
**1985. May 12:** Mikhail Gorbachev is elected First Secretary of the Soviet Union Communist Party; onset of *glasnost* and *perestroika*.
**1987. March:** A group of "Prisoners of Zion" is released.
**July 3:** Over 200 Jews celebrate Israel's Independence Day in a forest near Moscow, and the militia does not intervene.
**From September onwards:** Jewish cultural centers are established in Leningrad, Minsk, and elsewhere.
**September 7:** Several well-known "Prisoners of Zion," and a group of "refuseniks" are allowed to leave for Israel.
**1989. January 27:** A quarter of a century after the fact, the Politburo publicizes the rehabilitation of the Jewish Anti-Fascist Committee by the Supreme Court on November 22, 1955.
**February 2:** Inauguration of the Solomon Mikhoels Jewish Cultural Center in Moscow.
**May 21:** A national assembly of Jewish cultural associations is held in Riga.
**December 18–22:** In Moscow, founding of the Federation of Jewish Communities and Organizations in the Soviet Union.
**1991. August 18–21:** A conservative coup is aborted in Moscow.
**October 18:** Reestablishment of diplomatic relations between Moscow and Jerusalem.
**December 25:** Mikhail Gorbachev resigns; the Union of the Soviet Socialist Republics is dissolved.

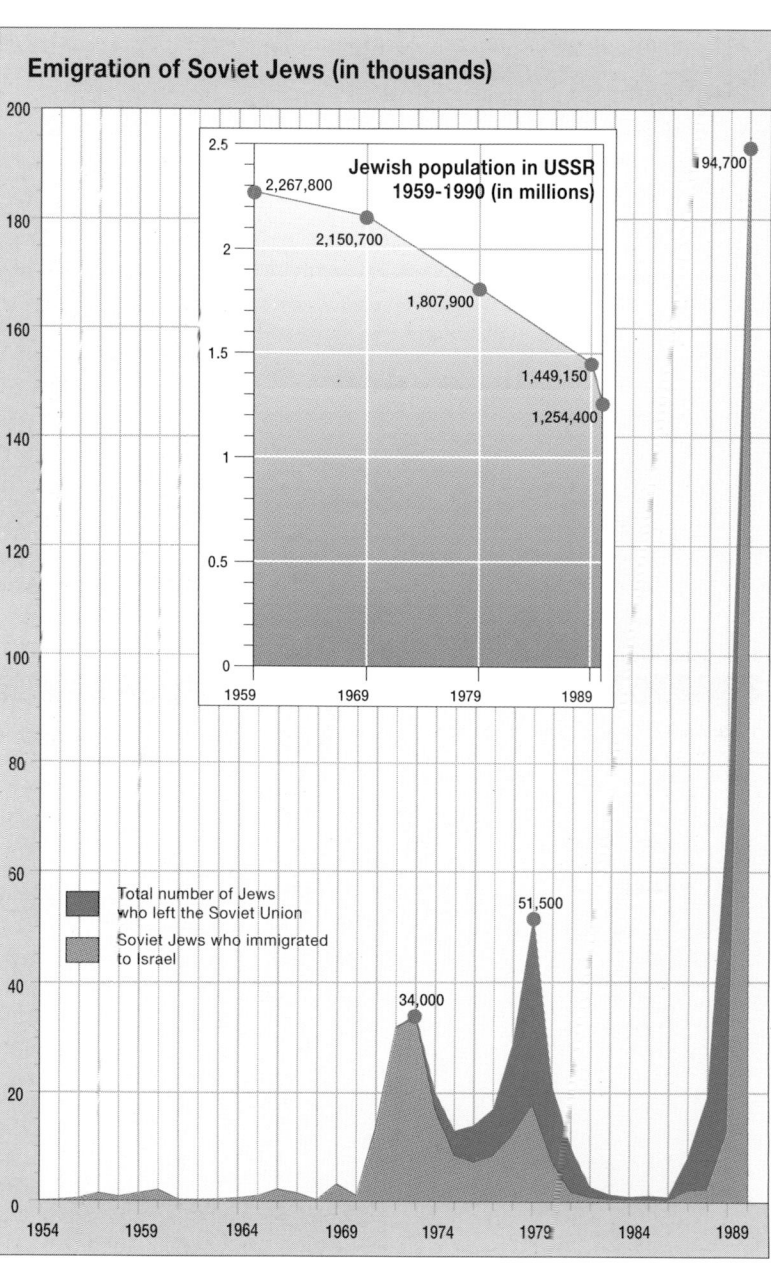

**Emigration of Soviet Jews (in thousands)**

**Jewish population in USSR 1959-1990 (in millions)**
2,267,800
2,150,700
1,807,900
1,449,150
1,254,400

194,700
51,500
34,000

Total number of Jews who left the Soviet Union
Soviet Jews who immigrated to Israel

# State and Religion

The Torah, foundation of historical Judaism, is a religion of the people, not of a state. This has always been its meaning, both from the traditional religious point of view as well as from the perspective of the actual historical reality of the people of Israel.

It is generally assumed that any discussion of religion presupposes a distinction between faith and institutionalized ritual, between belief as the spiritual content and institutions as its material shell. This distinction, however, does not apply to Judaism in which faith and works, or "Torah and *mitsvot*" ("Torah" in the wide sense including both scriptural and oral law), are inseparable.

From its origins until the nineteenth century, for over one hundred generations, the Jewish people has been defined by its adherence to the institutional Torah – not solely to its ideas but precisely to its practice: the *Halakhah* is regarded as the very substance of Jewish nationality. "Our nation is not a nation but by the commandments" – this famous dictum by Saadiah Gaon (10th century) was not a normative rule but an empirical observation. The "commandments" or "teachings" (*torot*) he referred to were the observance of the Law. Judaism and Jewry are one and the same thing; he who abandons Judaism (religious observance), automatically abandons the Jewish nation.

This absolute congruence of religion and people underwent a radical change in the nineteenth century. Jewish nationalism today is no longer defined by a particular set of values, neither intellectual nor practical, which are

1. Secularists protesting against religious interference in archeological digs. The placard shows the Chief Rabbi holding up tablets of the law inscribed "Thou shalt not dig. Thou shall not investigate. Thou shalt not know. For I am the Rabbinate that brought you out of the land of law."

2. Soldiers dancing at the Western Wall. A Rosh ha-Shanah (New Year) greeting-card celebrating the victory in June 1967.

accepted by those conscious of their Jewishness. Hence the problematic character of today's notion of a "Jewish people."

State and political thought – where do they stand in this complex system? In classical Judaism the purpose of the Torah (crystallized in the *Halakhah*) was to provide a framework for the people as a group of individuals, each of whom is aware of his own position in relation to God. In this context, the concept of a "people" does not necessarily imply a society cast in a state, that is, endowed with an established authority with powers of coercion over the inhabitants of a particular territory. Of the three powers governing a state-society, the Torah initially required only a legislative-judicial body (not separating these two functions), whose authority derived from the conviction that the society as a whole fully accepted the rule of the Torah. An executive power – proper government – was not required except in response to a non-essential need.

This fundamental principle explains the intricate relationship between state and religion in classical Judaism during the two periods when the people of Israel attained political independence and set up the mechanism of government (the biblical period and the Hasmonean reign). It also elucidates the nature of the relationship between religion and political thought throughout the era in which the Jews were deprived of political independence (from the destruction of the Second Temple to the emergence of political Zionism). In fact, throughout Jewish history, state and religion have never really met on common intellectual or practical ground. For the religious consciousness, religion is a value – serving God is the purpose of man and of the collective, the

people – while the state is only an instrument, designed to fulfill specific needs of man and nation. This attitude remains valid even when religion regards these needs as legitimate and gives its blessing to their fulfillment. On the other hand, a government must necessarily regard itself as an end in itself, using religion for its own purposes, and when this cannot readily be done, it regards religion as a subversive or disruptive element. Therefore, the encounter between the world of the Torah and the world of political power – even when accepted by religion – has always indicated a confrontation and an ongoing struggle: the kings representing the national-political interest against the trouble-making prophets; the Hasmonean monarchs against the Torah Sages. One of the greatest attributes of the Torah is its independence from political authority and the fact that it had been a shield against the terrible danger of inflating the interest of national-state power to a supreme value in its own right. A religion which identifies with political authority and becomes its handmaid degenerates into idolatry, worshiping the idols of nation, country and state. This is the true meaning of the struggle between Elijah, prophet of God, and the prophets of Baal who served the interests of Ahab and Jezebel (I Kings 18).

The *Halakhah's* attitude towards the state is ambivalent. The realistic approach regards the state as a world apart: while required to conform to halakhic laws, the existing state is not a Torah institution. The utopian approach maintains the vision of a state created by and for the Torah and acting exclusively according to its precepts. This ambivalence is evident also in the political aspects of the expectation for messianic redemption – a dream fostered by

*3. "The State of Israel will be open for Jewish immigration and for the Ingathering of the Exiles; it will foster the development of the country for the benefit of all inhabitants; it will be based on freedom, justice and peace as envisaged by the prophets of Israel; it will ensure complete equality of social and political rights to all its inhabitants irrespective of religion, race and sex; it will guarantee freedom of religion, conscience, language, education and culture; it will safeguard the Holy Places of all religions; and it will be faithful to the principles of the Charter of the United Nations." From the* Declaration of Independence of the State of Israel *(May 1948), on a stamp issued on the 25th anniversary of the State, May 1973.*

*4. The Proclamation of Independence as seen by painter David Tartakover, 1988. At the forefront, above the representatives of the people, the philosopher Yeshayahu Leibowitz, advocate of a radical separation of state and religion and author of this text; on the right, in contrast, promoters of clerical and racist Zionism, Rabbis Lewinger and Kahana (the latter was assassinated in 1989).*

generations deprived of political existence. While awaiting the messiah, one must obey the laws of the powers that be regarding everything that does not pertain to faith itself, while attempting to safeguard the community's internal autonomy.

The State of Israel, which has restored Jewish political independence, is not a "Jewish state" in the sense of "the state of Judaism"; it is simply the state belonging to the Jewish people as it is today. Since this people no longer defines itself

as the people of Judaism (i.e., Judaism as a set of national values acknowledged by all its members), this state is therefore essentially secular, despite the fact that the majority of its citizens perceive themselves as part of the history of the Jewish people, which is also the history of Judaism. As an intellectual idea and as an actual entity, the religion of Israel continues to exist; yet contemporary political reality has obliterated the conflict between religion and the state. A tacit agreement between the

two camps has created a political and social regime which is basically secular yet adorned by symbols borrowed from the religious tradition of the Jewish people. This agreement, based on hypocrisy, is the source of religious, moral, and civil corruption. This can only be remedied by the radical separation of religion and state. Only such separation would enable an open struggle between the two – a struggle of the kind that has maintained the vitality of Jewish nationalism throughout its history.

# Two Peoples, One Land

1. *Issam Abu Shaqra (1961–1990), an Arab-Israeli painter,* The Cactus Fruit, *Oil 1988. Inversion of a symbol: the prickly fruit of the cactus plant, typical of the Palestinian landscape, is used as a nickname (*tsabar *in Hebrew,* sabra *in Arabic) for an Israeli-born Jew.*

On September 13, 1993 an "agreement of principles" between Israel and the P.L.O. was signed on the White House lawn. The process of its implementation is fraught with obstacles: tough negotiations, active resistance on both sides, Arab and Jewish acts of terrorism. Yet all this should not obscure the crucial fact: a veritable revolution, political and above all mental, is taking place, signifying the beginning of the end to a century-long conflict.

The Zionist dream of establishing a modern nation-state in the ancestral homeland was bound to arouse the opposition of the local population in Palestine. The immigration and settlement of Jews from the late nineteenth century on was indeed regarded with suspicion by both the Ottoman administration and the local Arabs. But this hostility towards foreign intruders soon developed into an inevitable clash between two national movements. Arab nationalism – as opposed to ethnic self-awareness – did not appear until the end of the nineteenth century. At the end of World War I, with the disintegration of the Ottoman Empire, Palestine came to be regarded as an entity in its own right by at least some inhabitants of the land. Opposition to Zionism and to the British Mandate completed the process and gave these sentiments a distinctly political character. The first political societies were established toward the end of 1918. In December 1920 the Third Palestinian Conference defined their future policy: absolute rejection of Zionism and the establishment of a local government in Palestine. These goals expressed the rejection of two British policies: the Balfour Declaration which spoke of a Jewish National Home, and the promise to the Hashemites (originating in the Hejaz and regarded as alien by local Arabs) that they would rule over a "Greater Syria" which would include Palestine and Transjordan. The interference of the two European powers – Britain and France – undoubtedly served to aggravate tensions in the region, but even if they had been totally impartial, they could not have prevented the inevitable clash.

Relations between the two communities – Arabs and Jews – soon deteriorated into a violent conflict. Attacks and reprisals followed one another in unending succession, becoming more and more brutal. When the Arab revolt erupted in 1936, the British appointed the Peel Commission which recommended a solution that seemed to provide the only possible answer: partition of the country. A decade later, in November 1947, this solution was adopted by the representatives of all nations.

The Arabs rejected the resolution and announced their determination to prevent its implementation. British evacuation left Arab and Jew facing each other without the problematic yet mediatory presence of a foreign ruling power. The invasion of the regular armies of neighboring Arab states transformed the conflict from a struggle between communities into a war between states. Defeat and exodus turned hundreds of thousands of Palestinian Arabs into refugees: living in camps, caught between

| British Mandate | Arab Revolt | Partition Plan | Creation of the P.L.O. |
|---|---|---|---|
| 1920 | 1936 | 1947 | 1964 |

**British Mandate**

**1917:** The Balfour Declaration. A friendly meeting between Weizmann and Emir Feisal at Akaba.
**1919:** Representing the Arabs at the Peace Conference, Feisal assures the Zionist movement of "the deepest sympathy of his people." But since the English are prevented by the Sykes-Picot agreement (1916) from offering the emir the great kingdom of Syria they had promised him, Arab-Zionist cooperation is cut short.
**1920. April:** Mandate of Great Britain in Palestine.
**1921:** Hajj Amin al-Husseini is appointed mufti of Jerusalem (April). Bloody clashes in Palestine (May). In order to appease the Hashemites, Churchill offers Emir Abdullah the territory of Transjordan, and the emirate is later excluded from the articles relating to the Jewish National Home.
**1922. June:** The first British White Paper inaugurates the policy of restricting Jewish immigration to Palestine.
**1925:** A group of intellectuals in Jerusalem,

including the philosopher Martin Buber, found the "Peace Alliance" (*Berit Shalom*).
**1929. August:** Anti-Jewish riots; the old Jewish community in Hebron is destroyed.
**1930. October:** Lord Passfield's White Paper abrogates the Balfour Declaration.
**1936. April:** The mufti of Jerusalem creates the Arab Higher Committee and proclaims a general strike; beginning of the great Arab revolt in Palestine.
**1937. July:** The Peel Commission proposes for the first time the partition of Palestine.
**1939. May 17:** The last White Paper declares Britain's preference for the creation of a single Palestinian state and closes the gates of Palestine to Jewish immigration.
**1947. November 29:** The United Nations adopts the partition plan.
**1948. May 14–15:** Proclamation of the State of Israel; intervention of the Arab states. The massacre at Deir Yassin (April 9) precipitates the Arab exodus from Palestine.
**1950. April:** The emirate of Transjordan becomes the Hashemite Kingdom of Jordan.

**1951. July 20:** Assassination of King Abdullah of Jordan.
**1964. May:** Founding of the Palestine Liberation Organization (P.L.O.).
**1967. June:** The Six-Day War. The *al-Fatah* joins the P.L.O.
**1969. February:** Yasser Arafat is appointed leader of the P.L.O.
**1970:** "Black September" in Jordan: the Arab Legion crushes the Palestinian organization whose center of activity now shifts to southern Lebanon.
**1972:** Municipal elections in the West Bank: most of the elected mayors sympathize with the P.L.O. Terrorist attack at Lydda airport (May); massacre of Israeli athletes at the Munich Olympics (September).
**1973. October:** The Yom Kippur War. Birth of *Gush Emunim* ("Faith Bloc"), an ultra-nationalist movement.

*3. Hitna'arut (Hebrew for Intifada): a special issue of* Ha'aretz *devoted to the "Territories in the 21st year [of occupation]," Passover, 1988.*

*2. Prefabricated houses in the settlement of Teko'a on the West Bank. 1980.*

Israel's refusal to allow them to return and the cynical way in which Arab governments exploited them for political ends, deprived by Jordan of a territory that should have belonged to them according to the partition plan, they gradually developed a nationalism all of their own.

The Six-Day War was a turning point for both Palestinian and Israeli nationalism. From the Arab point of view, Israel now occupied the entire area which the Arabs perceived as "Palestine." Palestinian organizations now sought freedom of action and attempted to mount a "popular liberation war," resorting to sabotage and terrorism. Meanwhile, among the Israelis, the results of the 1967 war reopened the debate on the rights of Jews and Arabs in the country: linking nation and religion, endowing Zionism with a messianic significance, settlers in "Judea and Samaria" hold Jewish rule over Greater Israel to be more important than the resolution of the Arab-Israeli conflict; others, seeking "normalization" rather than redemption, are willing to negotiate over the "West Bank."

The *Intifada*, which began in December 1987, illustrated with unprecedented strength the existential impasse of two peoples equally convinced of their right to the same stretch of land. Yet, the gradual disillusionment of the Palestinian leadership of the hope of destroying the "Zionist entity," the peace talks inaugurated in October 1991, and the return to power of a Labour government in Israel in June 1992, led to the adoption of a 50-year-old solution: the partition of the land.

| Six-Day War | *Intifada* | Madrid Conference |
|---|---|---|
| 1967 | 1987 | 1991 |

**1974:** Terrorist attacks in Kiryat Shemonah and Ma'alot. Israeli planes bomb Lebanon. Arafat appears before the U.N.
**1977. November 19:** President Sadat in Jerusalem.
**1978:** Birth of the *Shalom Akhshav* ("Peace Now") movement. In March, a terrorist attack on the coastal road north of Tel Aviv provokes the first Israeli invasion of southern Lebanon ("Litani Operation"). The Camp David Accords (September 17) promise autonomy to the inhabitants of the West Bank and Gaza.
**1982. June 6:** War in Lebanon ("Operation Peace for Galilee"). Massacre of Palestinians by Lebanese Christians at the Sabra and Shatilla camps (September); a huge demonstration in Tel Aviv against the war.
**1987. December:** Beginning of the *Intifada*.
**1988. November 15:** The National Palestinian Council, convened in Algiers, issues a proclamation of the establishment of an independent state in Palestine.
**December:** In Geneva, Yasser Arafat

publicly endorses U.N. resolutions 242 (1967) and 338 (1973).
**1990. October 8:** In Jerusalem, eruption of violence on the Temple Mount; the police, overreacting, fire at the Palestinian demonstrators, killing 22 and wounding 140.
**1991. January 16:** The Gulf War. The P.L.O. aligns itself with Baghdad – the political gap between Palestinians and Israelis seems wider than ever; but the war creates new opportunities for negotiations.
**October 30:** In Madrid, opening of an Arab-Israeli peace conference.
**1993. September 13:** The Washington Accord between Israel and the P.L.O.
**1994. February 24:** Massacre of Arabs during prayer in Hebron.
**1994. May 4:** Implementation of the "Gaza and Jericho first" scheme; withdrawal of Israeli forces from these areas.
**1994. July 25:** The Washington Declaration – termination of the state of war between Israel and Jordan. Persistent rumors about an Israeli-Syrian breakthrough

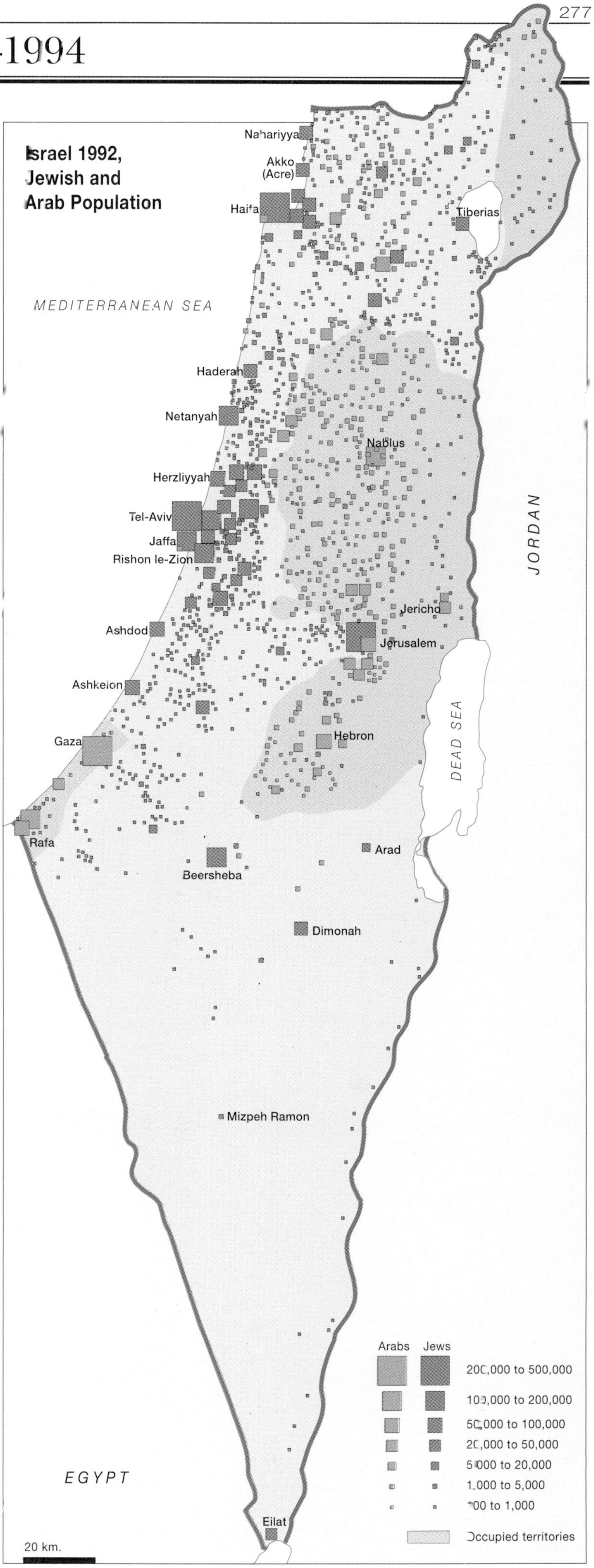

## Israel 1992, Jewish and Arab Population

MEDITERRANEAN SEA

JORDAN

DEAD SEA

EGYPT

Nahariyya
Akko (Acre)
Haifa
Tiberias
Haderah
Netanyah
Nablus
Herzliyyah
Tel-Aviv
Jaffa
Rishon le-Zion
Jericho
Ashdod
Jerusalem
Ashkelon
Hebron
Gaza
Rafa
Arad
Beersheba
Dimonah
Mizpeh Ramon
Eilat

20 km.

| Arabs | Jews | |
|---|---|---|
| | | 200,000 to 500,000 |
| | | 100,000 to 200,000 |
| | | 50,000 to 100,000 |
| | | 20,000 to 50,000 |
| | | 5,000 to 20,000 |
| | | 1,000 to 5,000 |
| | | 100 to 1,000 |

Occupied territories

# Jews in Israel and Elsewhere

## The Jewish World Today

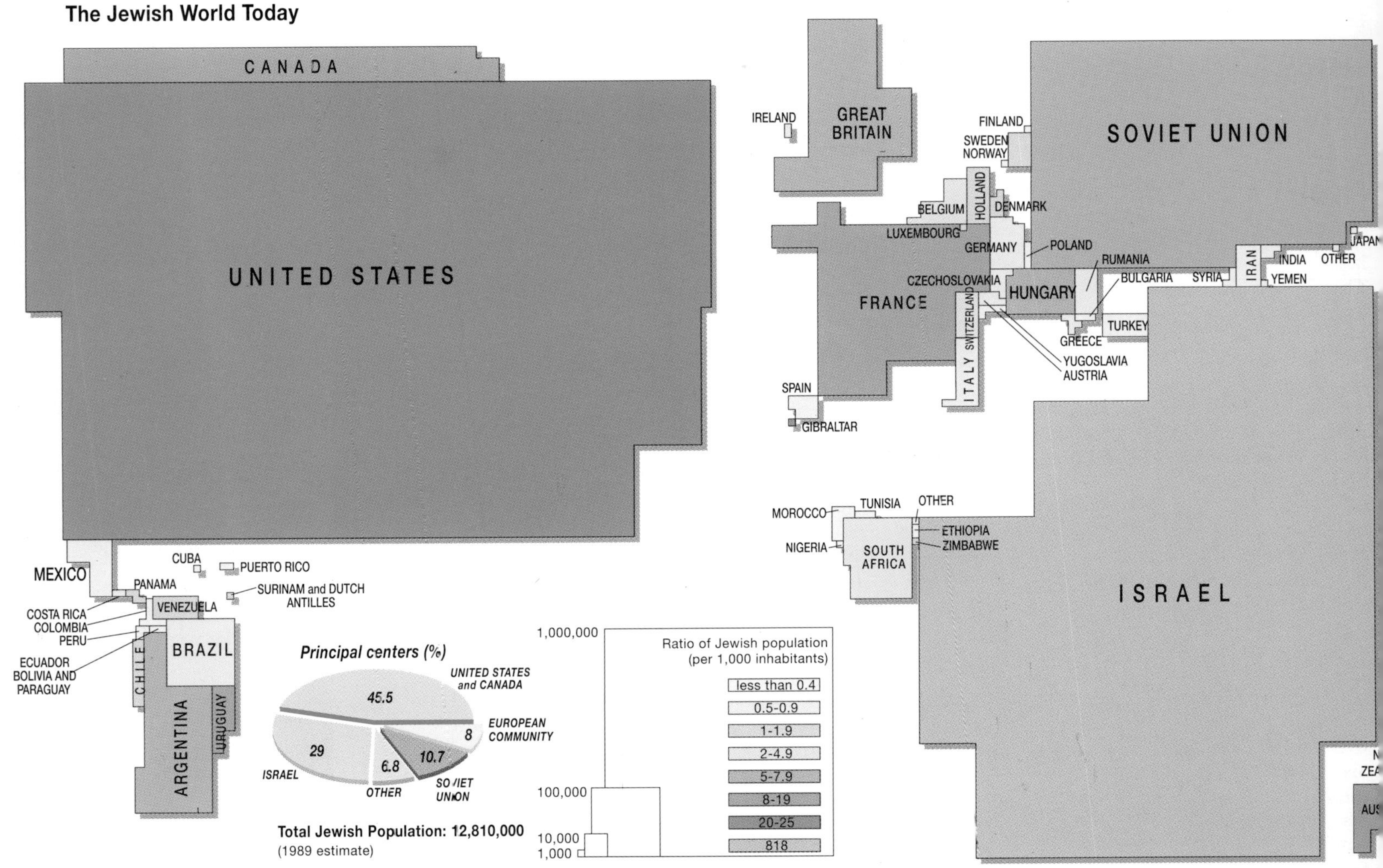

CANADA

IRELAND

GREAT BRITAIN

FINLAND

SWEDEN
NORWAY

SOVIET UNION

UNITED STATES

HOLLAND

BELGIUM

DENMARK

LUXEMBOURG

GERMANY

POLAND

CZECHOSLOVAKIA

RUMANIA

FRANCE

HUNGARY

BULGARIA

SYRIA

IRAN

INDIA

OTHER

JAPAN

YEMEN

SWITZERLAND

ITALY

TURKEY

GREECE

YUGOSLAVIA
AUSTRIA

SPAIN

GIBRALTAR

MEXICO

CUBA

PUERTO RICO

SURINAM and DUTCH ANTILLES

PANAMA

COSTA RICA
COLOMBIA
PERU

VENEZUELA

ECUADOR
BOLIVIA AND
PARAGUAY

CHILE

BRAZIL

ARGENTINA

URUGUAY

MOROCCO

TUNISIA

OTHER

NIGERIA

SOUTH AFRICA

ETHIOPIA
ZIMBABWE

ISRAEL

N
ZEA

AUS

### Principal centers (%)

- 45.5 — UNITED STATES and CANADA
- 8 — EUROPEAN COMMUNITY
- 10.7 — SOVIET UNION
- 6.8 — OTHER
- 29 — ISRAEL

**Total Jewish Population: 12,810,000**
(1989 estimate)

### Ratio of Jewish population (per 1,000 inhabitants)

- less than 0.4
- 0.5-0.9
- 1-1.9
- 2-4.9
- 5-7.9
- 8-19
- 20-25
- 818

1,000,000

100,000

10,000
1,000

According to the founding fathers of political Zionism, from Herzl to Ben-Gurion, the Zionist revolution was to end once and for all the centuries-long dialectic tension between center and diaspora. Zionist dogma implied the "negation of the Diaspora." With the possible exception of pockets of resistance by Ortho-dox or assimilated Jews, all the dispersed communities were to be trans-ferred to the national home in the Land of Israel – a definitive solution to the perennial "Jewish question."

Today, however, less than a third of the 13 million Jews around the world are citizens of the Jewish state. Sovereignty was attained by war, and the state was born into a world very different from the one imagined by the founders of political Zionism. The East-European communities had disappeared in Nazi extermination camps, those in Islamic countries had been liquidated by mass emigration in the wake of decolonization, and the major centers of the diaspora had shifted to the West – a generally democratic, liberal and prosperous West, where, perhaps for the first time

| Birth of the Jewish State | Jerusalem Program | | Six-Day War |
|---|---|---|---|
| 1948 | 1951 | | 1967 |

**1948:** Hundreds of Jewish volunteers flock to Palestine to aid the *yishuv* during the War of Independence.
**1950:** David Ben-Gurion, prime minister of Israel, exchanges letters with Jacob Blaustein, president of the American Council for Judaism (an anti-Zionist group). Ben-Gurion states that Israel can only represent its own citizens.
**1951. August:** The 23rd Zionist Congress, the first to be held in Jerusalem (where all future congresses will be held). The Basle Program is replaced by the Jerusalem Program: "The task of Zionism is the consolidation of the State of Israel, the ingathering of the exiles in Eretz Israel, and the fostering of the unity of the Jewish people."
**1952:** The Knesset votes on the "Law on the Status of the World Zionist Organization – the Jewish Agency," which determines the functions of these two agencies.
**1954:** A "covenant" between the government of Israel and the Executive of the World

Zionist Organization invests the W.Z.O., through the Jewish Agency, with the responsibility for immigration and absorption of immigrants. Founding of A.I.P.A.C. (America-Israel Public Affairs Committee) – the Israeli lobby, later integrated in the Conference of Presidents of Major American Jewish Organizations.
**1965. January:** The 26th Zionist Congress. Debate on the statement by Nahum Goldmann, the controversial president of the World Jewish Congress, that the aim of Zionism is the survival of the Jewish nation in the diaspora and the assistance of the state to the Jewish people. The resolutions of the Congress, however, are phrased along more traditional Zionist lines.
**1967. May-June:** Immense solidarity expressed by the diaspora on the eve of the Six-Day War; volunteers and immigrants flock to the country.
**November 27:** General de Gaulle's statement that the Jews are "an elite people, sure of itself, and domineering."

2. "Our Israel," the Hebrew daily newspaper of the Israeli community in the United States and Canada. June 21, 1991.

**1968:** Raymond Aron, an eminent French sociologist and writer, publishes a series of essays (*De Gaulle, Israel, and the Jews*) in which he accuses de Gaulle of encouraging anti-Jewish elements in French society. Although himself not involved in Jewish affairs, Aron confesses that "a Jew could never maintain absolute objectivity where Israel was concerned."
**June:** The 27th Zionist Congress, the first to be held after the Six-Day War victory. New to this Congress was the participation of youth delegations, students, and members of the *aliyah* movement. New tasks are added to the Jerusalem Program: "The unity of the Jewish people and the centrality of Israel in its life; the ingathering of the Jewish people in its historic homeland in Eretz Israel through *aliyah* from all lands; the strengthening of the State of Israel founded on the prophetic ideals of justice and peace; the preservation of the identity of the Jewish people through the fostering of Jewish education, Hebrew, and of Jewish spiritual

in their history, Jews did not encounter any serious obstacles to assimilation. As the statistics of western immigrants show, the Jews, conforming to an ancient tradition, obviously prefer the comforts of living in exile to the difficult, sometimes harsh, reality of a national sovereign existence. Therefore, unless there are unexpected upheavals in the western world, the only remaining significant reservoir for future *aliyah* is Soviet Jewry.

The State has nonetheless remained fast in its ideology, only slightly mitigating the categorical imperative of Zionism – the Return to Zion – by tacitly accepting substitutes. As Arthur Hertzberg put it, Israel was willing to sell honor and indulgence in exchange for support and consolation. The two sides of this contract, however, are not regarded as equal. The diaspora, with its financial, moral, and political support – achieved mostly through the American Jewish lobby – is indeed the only unconditional ally of Israel. But Israel, on the other hand, provides pride, refuge, and a guarantee for national survival. A source of pride, because only in Israel have the Jews been able to reappropriate for themselves national virtues such as military valor, tilling of the soil, sovereignty and machinery of government. A haven for communities in peril of extinction – where else could the Jews of Ethiopia, Albania, Syria, and, above all, the Soviet Union, find refuge in their direst hour of need? And a reassuring potential haven for Jews everywhere, still living under the trauma of a monstrous genocide perpetrated while all civilized nations kept silent. Finally, Israel is the necessary condition for the survival of diaspora Jewry as a nation: the Jews need Zionism to protect them from total disintegration through assimilation.

Admittedly, the relationship between Israel and the diaspora has undergone several changes. In the 1950s, Ben-Gurion's insistence that Zionism could be realized only by personal presence in the Land of Israel, interpreted as a refusal to acknowledge the right of Diaspora Jews to voice their opinion in matters concerning the State of Israel, aroused tensions and controversy particularly among American Zionists. After the Six-Day War, the furtherance of *aliyah* indeed became a central issue on the Zionist agenda of western Zionist organizations. But the Yom-Kippur War, revealing the shortcomings of Israeli society, as well as Israeli emigration – hundreds of thousands of Israelis, many of them *sabras*, favored joining the diaspora – again alleviated the conscience of those Jews who preferred to express support for the Zionist cause from a distance. Nevertheless, although Israeli "arrogance was turned into effacement," and many diaspora Jews once again stress their right to criticize and question Israel's policies, the notion of Israel as the national and cultural center of the Jewish people still prevails.

Does this mean that the diaspora is condemned to remain but an appendix of the State of Israel? This is certainly the feeling of many in Israel and in the diaspora as well. On the other hand, the distinction

1. Poster of the American Zionist youth movement.

between unconditional support of the very existence of Israel and the democratic criticism of its government, is probably the necessary condition for true dialogue between the Jewish State and the Jews in dispersion. Zionist reality today is closer to Ahad Ha-Am's program than to Herzl's vision: Israel as a focus of emotional identification for the greater part of the people which remains in the diaspora. It is vital that these two branches of the Jewish people continue to inscribe jointly the future chapters of their astonishing four-millennia-long history.

| New Jerusalem Program | | Pollard Affair | Soviet and Ethiopian immigration |
|---|---|---|---|
| 1968 | | 1987 | 1990... |

3. North African Jewry in Paris.

and cultural values; the protection of Jewish rights everywhere."

**1970:** Replacing the American Zionist Council, the Zionist Federation of America is established, offering to affiliate individuals without the mediation of a particular party.

**1972:** The 28th Zionist Congress demands that the leaders of Zionist organizations make a personal commitment to *aliyah*.

**1980:** The Venice resolution (June) marks a further stage in the erosion of Israel's position, and the beginning of a concerted effort on behalf of leaders of European Jewish communities

**1987:** The Pollard affair: accused of divulging information to Israel for reasons of "Jewish patriotism," Pollard's trial affects Israeli-American relations and embarrasses American Jewry.

**Late 1980s on:** Large waves of Ethiopian and Soviet immigration restore Israel's status as the only haven for Jews in distress.

4. American Orthodox Jews demonstrate during an appearance of Prime Minister Menahem Begin at a meeting of the United Nations Assembly. New York, June 1982.

# Note on Transliteration

In a project addressing such a broad range of geographical regions, historical eras, and cultural and linguistic diversity, the transliteration of foreign terms and names – whether geographical, proper, or familial – is bound to pose some problems.

By accepting the norms of transliteration followed by the *Encyclopaedia Judaica* (Vol.1 pp. 7-16, 90-92), the editor of the English version of this atlas has been spared the task of trying to match an assortment of varied transliterations. The usage established by the *Encyclopaedia Judaica* has become standard in publications in English which concern Jewish issues, and which necessitate the use of Hebrew words and names. We have, however, dispensed with the *Judaica's* specialized dotting (for example, "Z" for the Hebrew letter *Zaddik*, or "H" for the Hebrew letter *Het*). Generally speaking, we have also adhered to the rules set by the *Judaica* regarding the transliteration of names and terminology in other languages as well, taking it upon ourselves to replace, for instance, the German *umlaut* with an "e" (i.e. Koenigsberg, rather than Königsberg). In cases where no precedents could be found, we were guided by phonetics and standard usage, occasionally modified for consistency.

As a rule, place names in the Land of Israel are indicated by the phonetically transliterated versions of their modern Hebrew names (Ashdod, Ashkelon, etc.), except when corresponding Anglicized names have become standard (Acre rather than Akko; Jerusalem rather than Yerushalayim; Bethlehem rather than Bet-Lehem). The Land of Israel (*Eretz Yisrael*, in Hebrew) is generally referred to by the name held to be most appropriate for the period under discussion: Canaan for the pre-Israelite era, Judah or Judea for most of the biblical or Hellenistic eras, Palestine (derived from the name of the Philistine people) – for the long era spanning the centuries from the Roman period up to the establishment of the State of Israel.

Proper names usually appear in their Anglicized forms (Solomon for the Hebrew Shlomo, Jacob rather than Yaacov), except in the case of contemporary figures whose Hebrew names are familiar (Moshe Dayan rather than Moses Dayan). Family names are spelt according to their usage by the persons involved, except when available sources do not indicate how they were transcribed into Latin characters.

Finally – biblical quotations. It was not easy to decide which English version of the Bible to use; after considerable deliberation we decided to favor the King James or Authorized Version over more modern translations. In addition to its poetic qualities, preserving the flavor of biblical style, this version seems to have a more universal readership.

# Glossary

It is important to bear in mind three basic elements of Hebrew grammar when reading this glossary. Hebrew has one indefinite article: *ha-*; the suffix *-a* often indicates the feminine; feminine plural is often indicated by the suffix *-ot* and the masculine by *-im*.

**Adar** Sixth month of the Hebrew calendar, corresponding approximately to February-March.

**Aggadah** Sections in the Talmud and the *Midrash* which do not constitute *Halakhah*; stories, popular anecdotes, biblical expositions.

**Agunah** Woman deserted by her husband and prevented by Jewish law from remarrying.

**Aliyah** Literally "ascent"; immigration to the Land of Israel.

**Amora (pl. amoraim)** Title of rabbinical scholars in Palestine and Babylonia in the 3rd to 6th centuries; the *amoraim* were responsible for the composition of the *Gemara*.

**Ark of the Covenant** Chest placed in the Holy of Holies in the Temple where the "Tablets of the Covenant" were kept; by extension, the special place in the synagogue where the Torah scroll is kept (named also Ark of the Law, Torah Ark, Holy Ark).

**Ashkenaz** The medieval Hebrew name for Germany; *Ashkenazim* are Jews originating in Europe, mostly from a Yiddish-speaking environment.

**Av** Eleventh month of the Hebrew calendar, corresponding approximately to July-August; the 9th of *Av (Tishah be-Av)* is a day of fasting commemorating the destruction of the Temple.

**Bar** "Son of..." in Aramaic.

**Bar Mitsvah** Ceremony of initiation celebrated on a boy's 13th birthday, marking his entrance into the adult Jewish community.

**Ben** "Son of..." in Hebrew.

**Berakhah (pl. berakhot)** Benediction; formula of thanksgiving in Jewish prayers.

**Bet din** Rabbinical court or tribunal.

**Bet midrash** School for rabbinical studies, often attached to a synagogue.

**Bilu** Acronym of *Bet Ya'acov Lekhu ve-Nelekhah* ("House of Jacob, let us walk in the light of the Lord"; Isaiah 2:5); first modern movement of pioneering settlement in Palestine, founded in Kharkov, Russia, in 1882.

**Bund** "General Union of Jewish Workers in Lithuania, Poland, and Russia": Socialist party, autonomist and anti-Zionist, founded in Vilna in 1897.

**Coele-Syria** In Seleucid geographical terminology, the area of Palestine and southern Syria, conquered by Antiochus III from the Ptolemies c. 200 BC. The name appears in earlier sources where its precise geographical designation is uncertain.

**Conservative Judaism** Trend in American Judaism, mid-way between Orthodox and Reform.

**Consistory** Governing body of French Jewry at the local or national level, established by imperial decree in March 1808.

**Converso** Jew who converted to Christianity in Spain or Portugal. See also *Marrano*.

**Dayyan** Member of a rabbinical court.

**Dhimmi** "Protected" in Arabic: the legal status, inferior but protected by the ruling power, of the "People of the Book" (Christians and Jews) in Islamic lands.

**Diaspora** Jews living in dispersion outside the Land of Israel, designating either a community in a single specific region or the entire Jewish world outside Palestine.

**Din** A secular or religious law, a legal decision, or lawsuit.

**Einsatzgruppen** Mobile killing units of the Nazis which operated in territories occupied by the Germans during World War II.

**Elul** Twelfth month of the Hebrew calendar, corresponding approximately to August-September.

**Eretz Yisrael** Land of Israel; Palestine.

**Exilarch** "Head of the Exile" (*Rosh ha-Golah* in Hebrew, *Resh Galuta* in Aramaic): lay leader of certain Jewish communities, particularly in Babylonia.

**Final Solution** *Endloesung* in German; the Nazi program for the total annihilation of the Jewish people.

**Galut** "Exile," the condition of the Jewish people in dispersion. See also *Golah*.

**Gaon (pl. Geonim)** Head of a *yeshivah* (academy) in the post-talmudic period, particularly in Babylonia and Palestine.

**Gemara** Commentaries, discussions and rulings concerning the *Mishnah*; the *Mishnah* and *Gemara* together form the Talmud.

**General Government** Polish territory administered from Cracow by a civilian German governor after the German occupation during World War II.

**Genizah** Depository of sacred books, preserved in a room attached to the synagogue or buried in a cemetery. The most important *Genizah* is the one that was found in the synagogue in Cairo.

**Ghetto** A word designating the quarter of the "foundry" (*getto* or *ghetto*) in Venice which in 1516 was walled and reserved for Jews as their obligatory residence. By extension, a quarter where Jews congregated voluntarily or forcibly in certain European towns. The ghettos disappeared in Europe after Emancipation but were reconstituted by the Nazis as centers for assembling the Jews before their deportation to the camps.

**Golah** Hebrew equivalent of Diaspora. See also *Galut*

**Goy (pl. Goyim)** Literally, people or nation; designating non-Jews or Gentiles.

**Habad** Acronym of *Hokhmah, Binah, Da'at* ("Wisdom. intelligence, knowledge"): Hasidic movement founded in Belorussia in the late 18th century and still active today.

**Haganah** Literally, "defense": clandestine military organization of the Jewish community in Palestine during the British Mandate, and the core of the State of Israel's army.

**Haggadah** Ritual recital of the story of the Exodus from Egypt on Passover eve. The *Haggadah* was composed in the 7th century out of biblical passages, *midrashim*, fragments of *Halakhah* and prayers. The *Haggadah* has been published in thousands of editions throughout the ages, often richly illustrated. See also *Pesah* and *Seder*.

**Hakham bashi** Title of the chief rabbi in the Ottoman Empire as well as of principal rabbis in provincial towns. In the Jewish tradition, the word *Hakham*, "sage" designates a scholar of Jewish law.

**Halakhah** Rabbinical legal decision (pl. *halakhot*); more generally, the body of rabbinical literature which constitutes Jewish religious law.

**Halutz** A Jewish pioneer in Palestine.

**Hanukkah** "Inauguration": festival celebrating the victory of the Maccabees over the Syrian Seleucids and the rededication of the Temple in 164 BC.

**Hasid (pl. Hasidim)** "Pious." Member of one of the pietist movements at any stage of Jewish history. *Hasidism* proper designates the pietist movement founded by Israel Ba'al Shem Tov in the first half of the 18th century.

**Haskalah** "Enlightenment": movement for spreading modern European culture among the Jews between the mid-18th century and the late 19th century.

**Hazan** Cantor in the synagogue; in earlier times, a synagogue official.

**Heder** Literally, "room": elementary school for teaching Jewish children the Torah and religious observance.

**Heshvan** (or *Marheshvan*), second month of the Hebrew calendar, corresponding approximately to October-November.

**Hibbat Zion** "Love of Zion," a proto-Zionist movement of *Hovevei Zion* ("Lovers of Zion") founded in Russia in the late–19th century.

**Histadrut** Jewish Labor Federation in the Land of Israel, founded in 1920.

**Holocaust** Genocide perpetrated by the Nazis. The word derives from the sacrifice in the Temple.

**Irgun Zeva'i Le'ummi** "Military National Organization," clandestine right-wing Jewish movement which fought against Arabs and British during the Mandate.

**Iyyar** Eighth month of the Hebrew calendar, corresponding approximately to April-May.

**Jewish Legion** Palestinian Jewish unit in the British Army during World War II.

**Jihad** Arabic word designationg holy war

# Glossary

against the infidels.

**Judenrat (pl. Judenraete)** "Jewish council" in German: a body set up by the Nazis in the Jewish communities and in the ghettos to implement Nazi orders.

**Judenrein** "Clean of Jews" in German; in Nazi vocabulary designates an area from which the Jewish population had been eliminated.

**Kabbalah** "Received tradition" in Hebrew; the sum of Jewish mystical traditions and precepts.

**Kahal (pl. kehalim)** Sephardi Jewish congregation; in Ashkenazi Poland, the term designates the leadership of the community.

**Karaite** Member of a Jewish sect originating in the 8th century which rejected rabbinical Judaism and accepted only the Scriptures (*Mikra*).

**Kasher** (or *Kosher*) Ritually permissible food.

**Kefar** Village (in Arabic, *Kafr*); appears as first part of the name of many settlements in the Land of Israel.

**Ketubbah** Marriage contract.

**Kibbutz (pl. Kibbutzim)** Literally, "gathering"; a commune based essentially on agriculture, first in Mandatory Palestine, then in the State of Israel.

**Kiddush ha-Shem** "Sanctification of the Name," an expression designating martyrdom for the Jewish faith.

**Kislev** Third month of the Hebrew calendar, corresponding approximately to November-December.

**Knesset** "Assembly"; today the word designates the parliament of the State of Israel.

**Kohen (pl. kohanim)** (or: *Cohen, cohanim*); priest in the Temple; by extension, a Jew who according to his family's tradition is of priestly descent.

**Kristallnacht** ("Crystal Night" in German); pogrom in Germany and Austria perpetrated by the Nazis and their sympathizers in November 1938.

**Lag ba-Omer** See *Omer*.

**Lehi** Acronym of *Lohamei Herut Israel* ("Fighters for the Liberty of Israel"): small paramilitary anti-British organization, founded in Palestine in 1940 by dissidents of the *Irgun*.

**Levirate marriage** In accordance with biblical law, marriage of a widow to the brother of her deceased husband.

**Ma'barah** Transit camp for new immigrants during the large waves of immigration to Israel in the 1950s.

**Maggid** "Sayer"; popular preacher.

**Maghreb** "West" in Arabic, designating North Africa, and in the Middle Ages Spain as well

**Mahzor** Book of prayers for the festivals. See also *Siddur*.

**Mandate** The responsibility for the administration and development of Palestine conferred on Great Britain at the end of World War I by the victorious powers, and later ratified by the League of Nations.

**Marrano** In Spain and Portugal, derogatory term for New Christians suspected of "Judaizing," also applied to their descendants in the Sephardi diaspora.

**Mashrek** "East" or "Orient" in Arabic, applied to the Levant.

**Maskil (pl. maskilim)** Adherent of the *Haskalah*.

**Masorah** Body of traditions regarding the correct spelling, writing and pronunciation of the Hebrew Bible.

**Mazzah** Unleavened bread for Passover, "bread of affliction" commemorating the tribulations of the Hebrews in the desert after the Exodus.

**Mellah** Jewish quarter or ghetto in Morocco; the first *mellah* was established in Fez in the first half of the 15th century.

**Menorah** Seven-branched oil candelabra used in the Temple (today, the emblem of the State of Israel); also, the eight-branched candelabra used on Hanukkah.

**Midrash (pl. midrashim)** Method of interpreting the Bible, to elucidate lessons or legal points; a *midrash* comprises elements from the *Aggadah* and the *Halakhah*.

**Mikveh** Ritual bath.

**Minyan** "Number" in Hebrew; a quorum of ten male adults required in order to hold public prayer.

**Mishnah** First codification of Jewish Oral Law. See also *Talmud*.

**Mitnagged (pl. mitnaggedim)** "Opponent" of Hasidism in eastern Europe.

**Mitzvah (pl. mitzvot)** Biblical or rabbinical injuction; also, charitable deed.

**Mosad** Literally "institution"; the Israeli security service for special assignments abroad.

**Mosad Le-Aliyah Bet** Organization responsible for "illegal" immigration during the British Mandate.

**Moshav (pl. moshavim)** Cooperative settlement in Israel.

**Moshavah (pl. moshavot)** Jewish village in Palestine, largely based on privately-owned farms.

**Musar** "Ethics," "morals"; traditional literature concerned with ethical questions; also, a moralist orthodox movement founded in the late 19th century in Lithuania.

**Nagid (pl. negidim)** Title applied in the Middle Ages, mostly in Islamic countries, to a Jewish dignitary recognized by the State as leader of the Jewish community.

**Nasi (pl. nesi'im)** Title of the president of the Sanhedrin during the Talmud period; in the Roman period, applied to the patriarch of the Jews; today, title of the president of the State of Israel.

**Negev** Southern region of Israel, most of which comprises arid desert.

**New Christian** Jew or Muslim who converted to Christianity in Spain or Portugal. See also *converso* and *marrano*.

**Nisan** Seventh month of the Hebrew calendar, approximately corresponding to March-April.

**Nuremberg Laws** Nazi racist legislation, September 1935.

**Omer** Measure of barley offered to the Temple priests; the 49 days of the *Omer* counted between Passover and Shavuot is a period of semi-mourning. The 33rd day (*Lag ba-Omer*), commemorates Bar Kokhba's revolt against the Romans.

**Orthodox** Term applied to the strictly-traditional current in modern Judaism.

**Pale of Settlement** Twenty-five Russian provinces where the czarist authorities permitted the permanent residence of Jews.

**Palmah** Hebrew acronym of *Peluggot Mahaz*, "Shock Companies," the elite units of the *Haganah*.

**Parnas** Elected lay leader of a Jewish community; originally, chief synagogue functionary.

**Parokhet** Richly-embroidered curtain for the Torah Ark in the synagogue.

**Paytan** Composer of *piyyutim*.

**Pesah** Jewish Passover. The word signifies "passage": "For the Lord will pass through to smite the Egyptians and... the Lord will pass over the door [of the Hebrews]."(Exodus 12:23).

**Pilpul** Dialectic method used in discussion of talmudic commentaries, introduced in the Polish *yeshivot* during the 16th century.

**Piyyut (pl. piyyutim)** Liturgical Hebrew hymns.

**Purim** From the word *pur* ("die"): joyous festival celebrating the deliverance of the Jews of Persia thanks to the victory of Queen Esther over evil Haman.

**Rabban** "Our master" in Aramaic; honorific title of the Sanhedrin leaders during the Talmud period.

**Rabbi** "My master": title of the sages in the period of the *Mishnah*; applied to a Torah teacher in general or to a Hasidic leader.

**Reform Judaism** Current of Judaism born in Germany in the 19th century, today constituting the majority of American Jewry, which modified religious orthodoxy adapting it to contemporary life and thought.

**Responsa** Plural of the Latin *responsum* ("answer," "response"): reply by a rabbinical authority to a "question" on Jewish law. A collection of such queries and answers is called in Hebrew *she'elot u-teshuvot* ("Questions and Answers").

**Rosh ha-Golah** See *Exilarch*.

**Rosh ha-Shanah** Literally, "Head of the Year": Jewish New Year, celebrated on the first day of the month of *Tishri* (September-October).

**Rosh Yeshivah** Head of a *yeshivah*.

**Sanhedrin** Assembly of scholars which acted as the supreme religious, judicial, and legislative body of the Jewish community in Palestine during the Roman period. The name was applied to the assembly representing the Jews of France convoked by Napoleon in 1807.

# Glossary

**Savora (pl. savoraim)** Last generation of the Babylonian Sages during the Talmud period, successors of the *amoraim*, active between the late 5th century and the early 7th century.

**Sea Peoples** Tribes from Asia Minor who invaded the shores of the eastern Mediterranean in the 13th century BC. It is generally assumed that the Philistines were one of these "Sea Peoples."

**Seder** The Passover meal at which the *Haggadah* is read.

**Sefirot** Mystical term denoting the ten emanations through which the Divine presence manifests itself to the initiated.

**Sephardi** "Spanish" in Hebrew; descendant of Spanish or Portuguese Jews; extended to apply to Jews of Mediterranean countries in contradistinction to Ashkenazim.

**Shavuot** Literally, "Weeks"; the festival of Pentecost, celebrated seven weeks after Passover, commemorating the receipt of the Torah at Mt. Sinai.

**Shema** "Hear [Israel]", the first word in the Jewish confession of faith proclaiming the unity of God (Deut. 6:4).

**Shemini Azeret** "Assembly on the Eighth (and last day of Sukkot)"; in the Land of Israel it coincides with *Simhat Torah*.

**Shevat** Fifth month of the Hebrew calendar, approximately corresponding to January-February.

**Shin Bet** Hebrew initials of Security Service, a body responsible for internal security in the State of Israel. See also *Mosad*.

**Shoah** Hebrew word for the Holocaust, literally meaning "catastrophe."

**Shofar** Ram's horn sounded in the synagogue on *Rosh ha-Shanah* and *Yom Kippur*.

**Shomer, ha-** "The Guard", organization of Jewish workers in Palestine founded in 1909 to defend agricultural settlements.

**Shtetl** Yiddish word designating a Jewish townlet in Eastern Europe.

**Shulhan Arukh** Literally, "Prepared Table"; name of Joseph Caro's code of Jewish Law, composed in the 16th century and accepted, with minor modifications, throughout the Jewish world.

**Siddur** Volume of the daily prayers in the Ashkenazi community (in distinction to the *Mahzor*).

**Simhat Torah** "Joy of the Torah"; holiday marking the completion of the annual cycle of reading the Pentateuch in the synagogue; in Israel it coincides with the last day of Sukkot (*Shemini Azeret*); in the diaspora it is celebrated on the following day.

**Sivan** Ninth month of the Hebrew year, corresponding approximately to May-June.

**S.S.** Initials of *Schutzstaffel* ("Protection Detachment"): elite corps of the National-Socialist party, and a principal arm in the Nazi machinery of extermination.

**Sukkot** Festival of Tabernacles; beginning on the 15th of *Tishri*, seven days during which religious Jews dwell in a *sukkah* (booth) in commemoration of living in the desert after the Exodus from Egypt.

**Ta'anit Esther** "Fast of Esther" on 13th of *Adar*, the day preceding the festival of Purim.

**Tablets of the Law (of the Covenant)** Text of the Decalogue engraved on stone and given by God to Moses on Mt. Sinai.

**Talmud** "Doctrine," "Teaching," "Study": the fundamental work of *Halakhah* comprising the *Mishnah* and the *Gemara*, as taught in the great *yeshivot* of the first centuries AD (1st–5th centuries). The *Talmud* exists in two versions: the Jerusalem Talmud composed in Palestine, and the Babylonian Talmud.

**Tammuz** Tenth month of the Hebrew year, approximately corresponding to June-July.

**Tanna (pl. tannaim)** Teacher of the Law in Palestine during the period of the *Mishnah*.

**Tell** ("Mound" in Arabic), archeological site, generally composed of several strata of ancient civilizations.

**Tevet** Fourth month of the Hebrew year, approximately corresponding to December-January.

**Tishri** First month of the Hebrew year, approximately corresponding to September-October.

**Torah** "Teaching"; in the strict sense, the Pentateuch; by extension, the entire body of Jewish religious teaching.

**Tosafot** Literally, "additions": glosses added to Rashi's commentary by talmudic scholars in France (the *tosafists*) in the 12th–14th centuries.

**Tosefta** Collection of *tannaim* teachings added to the *Mishnah*.

**Uganda Scheme** Plan proposed by the British government for the establishment of an autonomous Jewish entity in East Africa (1903).

**White Papers** Reports issued by the British government in the 1920s and 1930s concerning their policy in Palestine.

**Yeshivah (pl. yeshivot)** Academy for rabbinical studies. Originally, the *yeshivot* were the institutions for higher religious studies in Palestine and in Babylonia whose work of compilation and clarification produced the two Talmuds; during the time of the *Geonim*, the two great Babylonian *yeshivot* in Sura and Pumbedita, as well as the academy in the Land of Israel, served as spiritual and juridical centers for the entire Jewish world; in medieval and modern Europe, the number of *yeshivot* multiplied until they evolved into their present form: schools for talmudic studies.

**Yishuv** "Settlement": the Jewish community in Palestine in the pre-State period. The "Old *Yishuv*" designates the Jewish community in Palestine prior to the Zionist *aliyot*, and the "New *Yishuv*" – the community which evolved from the 1880s on.

**Yom Kippur, Yom ha-Kippurim** Day of Atonement, a day of fasting and prayers on the 10th of *Tishri*.

**Zaddik** "Pious," "Just": a person of outstanding virtue and piety; ascribed to Hasidic rabbis.

**Zahal** Hebrew acronym for Israel Defense Forces.

**Zion** One of the hills of Jerusalem; by extension, Jerusalem itself or the entire Holy Land.

**Zohar** "Splendor": principal work of the Kabbalah, composed by Moses of Leon in the late 13th century, essentially a mystical commentary on the Pentateuch.

# INDEX

# INDEX

# INDEX

# INDEX

# INDEX

# INDEX

# INDEX

# INDEX

# INDEX

# INDEX

# INDEX

# INDEX

# INDEX

# PICTURE CREDITS

# Table of Contents

# Table of Contents

Printed in Italy by G. Canale & C. S.p.A. - Borgaro T.se - TURIN